HAMMOND

CONCISE

WORLD ATLAS

Mapmakers for the 21st Century

HAMMOND

CONCISE

WORLD ATLAS

Mapmakers for the 21st Century

Contents

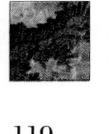

Australia, New Zealand and Pacific

North America

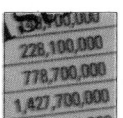

South America and Polar Regions

STATISTICS, TIME ZONES AND INDEX

The section on World Statistics
includes the planets of the solar
system, dimensions of the earth,
oceans and major seas, major
mountain peaks, longest rivers, largest lakes and
major islands. The computer-generated Time
Zones of the World is completely new and reflects
the world's most recent time zone changes. A
Master Index lists 60,000 places and other features
appearing in this atlas, complete with page
numbers and easy-to-use alpha-numeric
references.

Concise World Atlas

ENTIRE CONTENTS
© COPYRIGHT 2004 BY
HAMMOND WORLD ATLAS CORPORATION
All rights reserved. No part of this book may be
reproduced or utilized in any form or by any means,
electronic or mechanical, including photocopying,
recording or by any information storage and retrieval
system, without permission in writing from the Publisher.
Printed in Italy.

PHOTO CREDITS: NASA - National Aeronautics and
Space Administration Earth from Space images: Greece-
Peloponnisos Peninsula-p.26; Pakistan-Indus River
Delta-p.66; Egypt-Sinai Peninsula-p.92; Australia-
Lake Eyre-p.108; United States-Grand Canyon-p.118;
Argentina/Chile-Andes Mountains-p.146.

LIBRARY OF CONGRESS
CATALOGING-IN-PUBLICATION DATA

Hammond World Atlas Corporation.
Hammond concise world atlas.
p. cm.
Includes index.
ISBN 0-8437-1936-2.
1. Atlases. I. Title.
II. Title: Concise world atlas.
G1021. H2668   2000 <G&M>

912--DC21   00-038861
                                        CIP
                                        MAPS

Map Projections

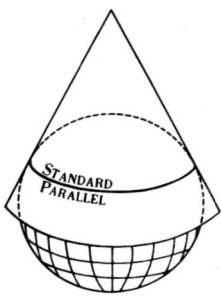

FIGURE 3
Conic Projection
The original idea of a conic projection is to cap the globe with a cone, and then project onto the cone from the planet's center the lines of latitude and longitude (the parallels and meridians). To produce a working map, the cone is simply cut open and laid flat. The conic projection used here is a modification of this idea. A cone can be made tangent to any standard parallel you choose. One popular version of a conic projection, the Lambert Conformal Conic, uses two standard parallels near the top and bottom of the map to further reduce errors of scale.

FIGURE 4
Hammond Optimal Conformal Projection
Like all conformal maps, the Optimal projection preserves angles exactly and minimizes distortion in shapes. This projection is more successful than any previous projection at spreading curvature across the entire map, producing the most distortion-free map possible.

Simply stated, the map-maker's challenge is to project the earth's curved surface onto a flat plane. To achieve this elusive goal, cartographers have developed map projections — equations which govern this conversion of geographic data.

This section explores some of the most widely used projections. It also introduces a new projection, the Hammond Optimal Conformal.

GENERAL PRINCIPLES AND TERMS

The earth rotates around its axis once a day. Its end points are the North and South poles; the line circling the earth midway between the poles is the equator. The arc from the equator to either pole is divided into 90 degrees of latitude. The equator represents 0° latitude. Circles of equal latitude, called parallels, are traditionally shown at every fifth or tenth degree.

The equator is divided into 360 degrees. Lines circling the globe from pole to pole through the degree points on the equator are called meridians, or great circles. All meridians are equal in length, but by international agreement the meridian passing through the Greenwich Observatory near London has been chosen as the prime meridian or 0° longitude. The distance in degrees from the prime meridian to any point east or west is its longitude.

While meridians are all equal in length, parallels become shorter as they approach the poles. Whereas one degree of latitude represents approximately 69 miles (112 km.) anywhere on the globe, a degree of longitude varies from 69 miles (112 km.) at the equator to zero at the poles. Each degree of latitude and longitude is divided into 60 minutes. One minute of latitude equals one nautical mile (1.15 land miles or 1.85 km.).

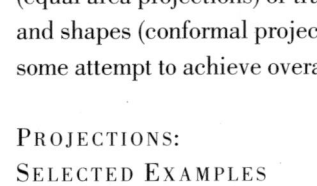

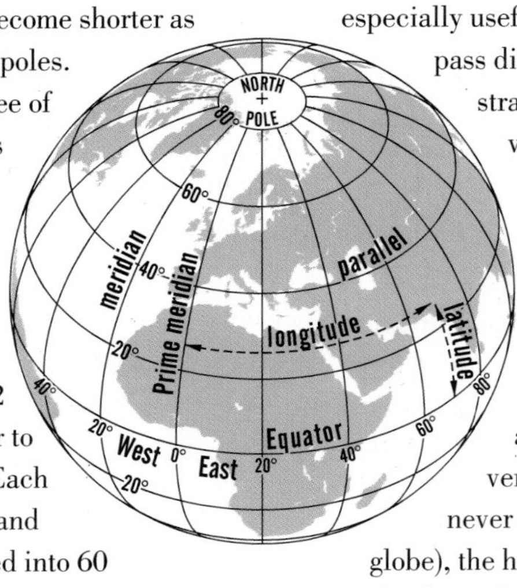

HOW TO FLATTEN A SPHERE: THE ART OF CONTROLLING DISTORTION

There is only one way to represent a sphere with absolute precision: on a globe. All attempts to project our planet's surface onto a plane unevenly stretch or tear the sphere as it flattens, inevitably distorting shapes, distances, area (sizes appear larger or smaller than actual size), angles or direction.

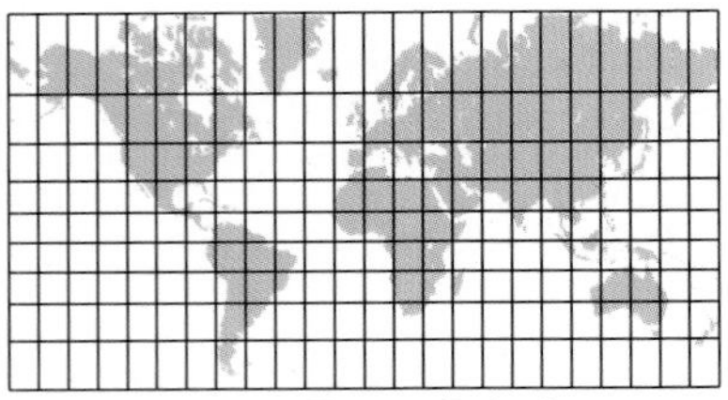

Since representing a sphere on a flat plane always creates distortion, only the parallels or the meridians (or some other set of lines) can maintain the same length as on a globe of corresponding scale. All other lines must be either too long or too short. Accordingly, the scale on a flat map cannot be true everywhere; there will always be different scales in different parts of a map. On world maps or very large areas, variations in scale may be extreme. Most maps seek to preserve either true area relationships (equal area projections) or true angles and shapes (conformal projections); some attempt to achieve overall balance.

FIGURE 1 **Mercator Projection**

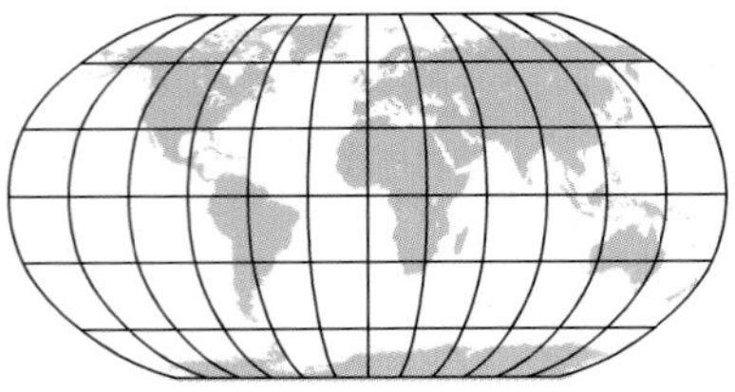

FIGURE 2 **Robinson Projection**

PROJECTIONS: SELECTED EXAMPLES

Mercator (Fig. 1): This projection is especially useful because all compass directions appear as straight lines, making it a valuable navigational tool. Moreover, every small region conforms to its shape on a globe — hence the name conformal. But because its meridians are evenly-spaced vertical lines which never converge (unlike the globe), the horizontal parallels must be drawn farther and farther apart at higher latitudes to maintain a correct relationship.

Only the equator is true to scale, and the size of areas in the higher latitudes is dramatically distorted.

Robinson (Fig. 2): To create the World-Physical and World-Political maps on pages 22-25, the Robinson projection was used. It combines elements of both conformal and equal area projections to show the whole earth with relatively true shapes and reasonably equal areas.

Conic (Fig. 3): This projection has been used frequently for air navigation charts and to create most of the national and regional maps in this atlas. (See text in margin at right).

HAMMOND OPTIMAL CONFORMAL

As its name implies, this new conformal projection (Fig. 4) presents the optimal view of an area by reducing shifts in scale over an entire region to the minimum degree possible. While conformal maps generally preserve all small shapes, large shapes can become very distorted because of varying scales, causing considerable inaccuracy in distance measurements. The concept underlying the Optimal Conformal is that for any region on the globe, there is an ideal projection for which scale variation can be made as small as possible. Consequently, unlike other projections, the Optimal Conformal does not use one standard formula to construct a map. Each map is a unique projection — the optimal projection for that particular area.

After a cartographer defines the subject area, a sophisticated computer program evaluates the size and shape of the region, and projects the most distortion-free conformal map possible.

Using This Atlas

Symbols Used on Maps of the World

First Order (National) Boundary

- Demarcated Land Boundary
- Demarcated Water Boundary
- Disputed Boundary
- Armistice Boundary
- De Facto Boundary
- Undefined

Second Order (Internal) Boundary

- Land Boundary
- Water Boundary

Third Order (Internal) Boundary

- Land Boundary
- Water Boundary

Cities and Towns

- Stockholm — First Order (National) Capital
- Salt Lake City — Second Order (Internal) Capital
- Manchester — Third Order (Internal) Capital
- Towns
- Neighborhood
- City and Urban Area Limits

Transportation

- International Airport
- Other Airport
- Highways/Roads
- Railroads
- Ferries
- Tunnels (Road, Railroad)

Drainage Features

- Shoreline, River
- Intermittent River
- Canal
- Lake, Reservoir
- Intermittent Lake
- Dry Lake
- Salt Pan
- Swamp/Marsh

Other Physical Features

- Elevation
- Pass
- Falls
- Rapids
- Desert/Sand Area
- Lava Flow
- Glacier/Ice Shelf

Cultural Features

- Ruins
- Dam
- Park
- Wildlife Area
- Point of Interest
- Well
- Air Base
- Naval Base
- International Date Line

- Ancient Walls
- Native Reservation/Reserve
- Military/Government Reservation
- State Park/Recreation Area
- National Park/Forest/Recreation/Wildlife Area

Elevation Legend

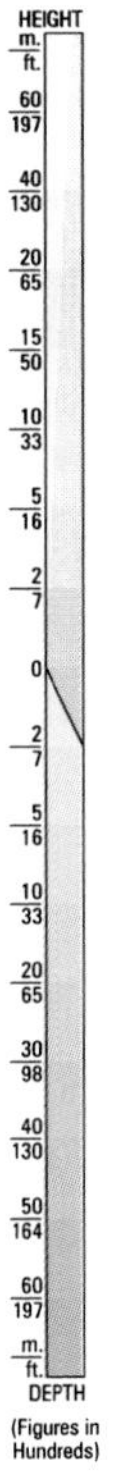

HEIGHT
m.
ft.
60
197
40
130
20
65
15
50
10
33
5
16
2
7
0
2
7
5
16
10
33
20
65
30
98
40
130
50
164
60
197
m.
ft.
DEPTH
(Figures in Hundreds)

The color tints in this bar represent both elevation of land areas and depth of the oceans. The changes between colors are labeled in feet and meters, and are given in hundreds. Selective shading for the land areas highlights those regions with significant relief variations.

Principal Map Abbreviations

Abor. Rsv.	Aboriginal Reserve	Ft.	Fort	NCA	National	Plat.	Plateau
Admin.	Administration	G.	Gulf		Conservation Area	PN	Park National
AFB	Air Force Base	Govt.	Government	NHP	National Historical	Prom.	Promontory
Amm. Dep.	Ammunition Depot	Gd.	Grand		Park	Prsv.	Preserve
Arch.	Archipelago	Gt.	Great	NHS	National Historic	Pt.	Point
Aut.	Autonomous	Har.	Harbor		Site	R.	River
B.	Bay	Hist.	Historic(al)	NL	National Lakeshore	Rec.	Recreation(al)
Bfld.	Battlefield	Hts.	Heights	NM	National Monument	Ref.	Refuge
Bk.	Brook	I., Is.	Island(s)	NMEM	National Memorial	Reg.	Region
Br.	Branch	Ind. Res.	Indian Reservation	NMILP	National Military	Rep.	Republic
C.	Cape	Int'l	International		Park	Res.	Reservoir,
Can.	Canal	IR	Indian Reservation	No.	Northern		Reservation
Cap.	Capital	Isth.	Isthmus	NP	National Park	Sa.	Sierra
C.G.	Coast Guard	Jct.	Junction	NPP	National Park and	Sd.	Sound
Chan.	Channel	L.	Lake		Preserve	So.	Southern
Co.	County	Lag.	Lagoon	NPRSV	National Preserve	SP	State Park
Consv.	Conservation	Mem.	Memorial	NRA	National	Spr., Sprs.	Spring, Springs
Cord.	Cordillera	Mil.	Military		Recreation Area	St.	State
Cr.	Creek	Mon.	Monument	NRIV	National River	Sta.	Station
Ctr.	Center	Mt.	Mount	NRSV	National Reserve	Stm.	Stream
Dep.	Depot	Mtn.	Mountain	NS	National Seashore	Str.	Strait
Depr.	Depression	Mts.	Mountains	NWR	National Wildlife	Terr.	Territory
Des.	Desert	Nat.	Natural		Reserve	Tun.	Tunnel
Dist.	District	Nat'l	National	Obl.	Oblast	Twp.	Township
DMZ	Demilitarized Zone	Nav.	Naval	Occ.	Occupied	UNDOF	United Nations
Est.	Estuary	NB	National	Okr.	Okrug		Disengagement
Fed.	Federal		Battlefield	Passg.	Passage		Observer Force
Fk.	fork	NBP	National	Pen.	Peninsula	Val.	Valley
For.	Forest		Battlefield Park	Pk.	Peak	Vill.	Village

The *Concise World Atlas* has been designed to be easy and enjoyable to use. Only a short time is neededed to familiarize yourself with its organization.

Map Symbols, Colors and Labels

The cartographer selects the natural and cultural features most valuable to the map user. Map legibility requires that small features be represented by symbols that are actually larger than true scale size. Due to the larger symbol sizes and the resulting loss of map space, it is necessary to omit less important features in congested areas.

Most map features are represented by the use of conventional symbols, lines, and patterns printed in appropriate colors. The chart to the left shows the standard symbols used in this atlas. Water features are shown in blue. Lines of various weights, styles, and colors represent the many different linear features in this atlas. Individual point features are represented by a pictorial and/or generic symbol.

Notes may also be added to explain features that cannot be depicted clearly.

Map Scales

A map's scale is the relationship of any length on the map to an identical length on the earth's surface. A scale of 1:3M means that one inch on the map represents 3,000,000 inches (47 miles, 76 km.) on the earth's surface. Thus, a 1:1M scale is larger than 1:3M, just as 1/1 is larger than 1/3.

The most densely populated areas are shown at a scale of 1:1M, while selected metropolitan areas are covered at either 1:500,000 or 1:1M. Other populous areas are presented at 1:3M and 1:6M, allowing you to accurately compare areas and distances of similar regions. Remaining regions, including the continent maps, are presented at 1:9M and smaller scales.

Boundary Policies

This atlas observes the boundary policies of the U.S. Department of State. Disputed, armistice and de facto boundaries are handled with a special symbol treatment. The portrayal of independent nations follows their recognition by the United Nations and/or United States government.

Map Type Styles

Cartographers use a variety of type styles to differentiate between map features. The following styles are used in this Atlas.

Major Political Areas
LUXEMBOURG

Internal Political Divisions
SAXONY-ANHALT

Regions
Polabská Nížina

Cities and Towns
Norfolk Sumter Smyrna

Neighborhoods
BIGGIN HILL

Points of Interest
MISSION SAN BUENAVENTURA

Water Features
L. Elsinore

Capes, Points, Peaks, Passes
Pt. La Jolla *Pacifico Mtn.*

Islands, Peninsulas
Cape Breton I.

Mountains, Uplands
Serra do Norte

Deserts, Plains, Valleys
San Fernando Valley

A Word About Names

Our source for all foreign names is the decision lists of the U.S. Board of Geographic Names and/or official foreign government maps and official gazetteers. This atlas also uses accepted conventional names for certain major foreign place names. The U.S. Board of Geographic Names defines a conventional name as "a name approved for use in addition to, or in lieu of, an approved local official name or names."

In order to make the maps more readily understandable to English-speaking readers, many foreign physical features are translated into more recognizable English forms.

The rendering of city, town and village names for the United States follows the forms and spelling of the U.S. Postal Service.

Population

World's Largest Urban areas

Millions of Inhabitants

Tokyo, Japan 26.5

New York, U.S. 18.0

São Paulo, Brazil 16.9

Osaka, Japan 16.9

Seoul, Korea, 15.8

Mexico, Mexico 15.5

Shanghai, China 14.7

Mumbai, India 14.5

Los Angeles, U.S. 14.5

Moscow, Russia 13.1

Beijing, China 12.0

Calcutta, India 11.4

London, U.K. 11.1

Rio de Janeiro, Brazil 11.0

Jakarta, Indonesia 11.0

Urban & Rural Population Components

Selected Countries

■ Urban ■ Rural

Uruguay 87% / 13%

Australia 85% / 15%

Japan 77% / 23%

United States 74% / 26%

Russia 73% / 27%

Hungary 62% / 38%

Iran 54% / 46%

Egypt 44% / 56%

Philippines 37% / 63%

Portugal 30% / 70%

China 26% / 74%

Maldives 20% / 80%

Bangladesh 15% / 85%

Nepal 6% / 94%

Age Distribution

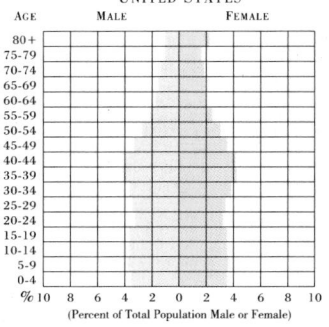
United States

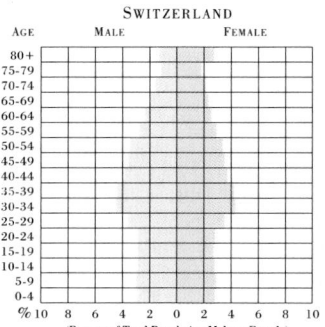
Switzerland

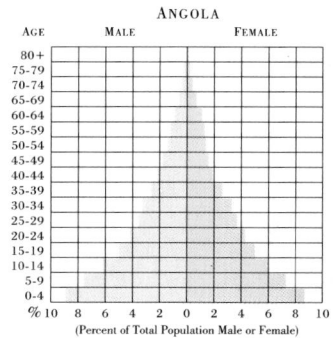
Angola

Source: U.S. Bureau of the Census, International Database

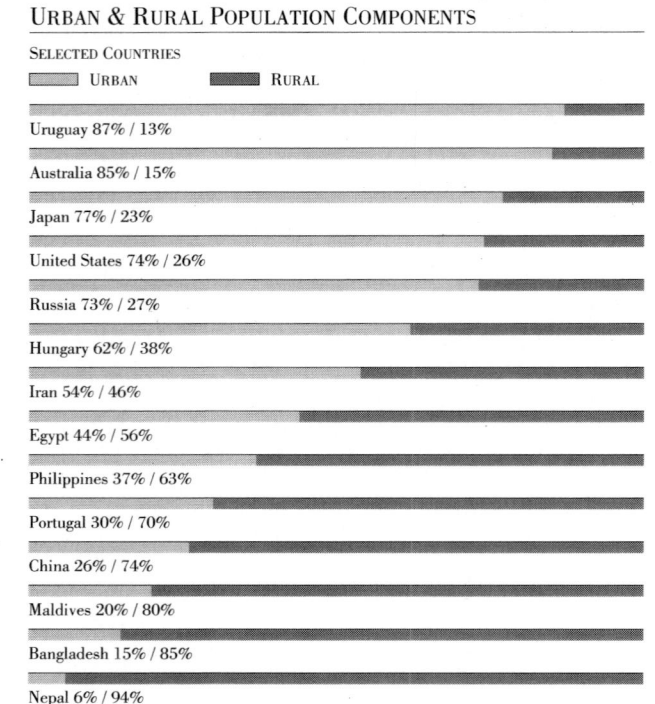

Population Density Per Square Mile (Sq. Km.)

■ 1,000 - 5,000 (390 - 2,000)	■ 500 - 1,000 (195 - 390)
■ 100 - 500 (39 - 195)	■ 30 - 100 (12 - 39)
□ Under 30 (Under 12)	

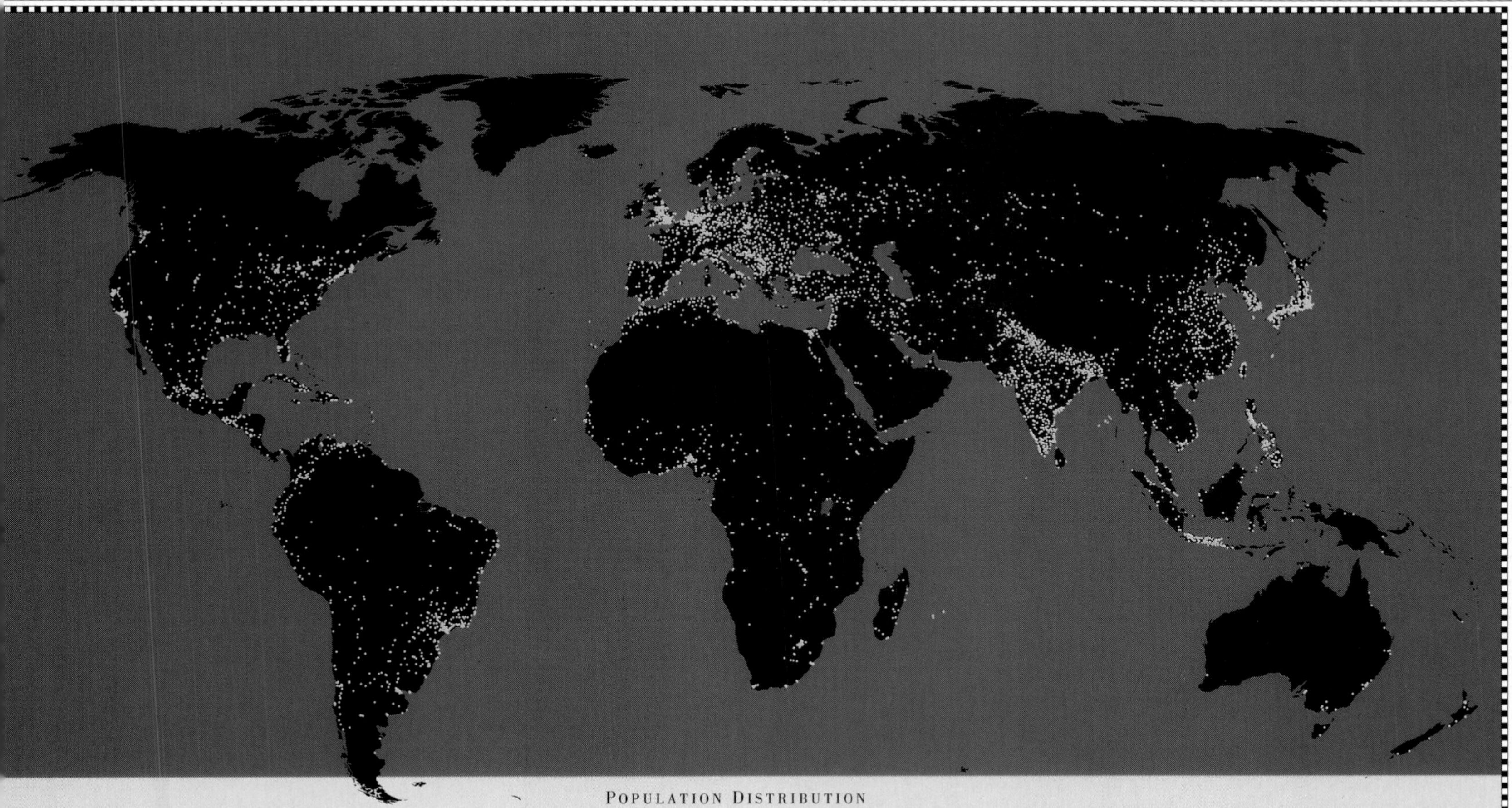

POPULATION DISTRIBUTION

This map provides a dramatic perspective by illuminating populated areas with one point of light for each city over 50,000 residents. Over 675 million people live in cities with populations in excess of 500,000. According to the latest census data, there are 10,000 people per square mile (3,860 per sq km) in London. In New York, there are 11,000 (4,250). Hong Kong has over 16,000 people per square mile (6,200 per sq km), and the Tokyo-Yokohama agglomeration includes over 25,000 (9,650). During the last decade, the movement to the cities has accelerated dramatically, particulary in developing nations. In Lagos, Nigeria, where there are over 24,000 people per square mile (9,290 per sq km), most live in shantytowns. In São Paulo, Brazil, 2,000 buses arrive each day, bringing field hands, farm workers and their families in search of a better life. Tokyo, Mexico and Mumbai are the world's largest urban agglomerations. According to the United Nations, 15 of the 20 largest urban agglomerations are located in less-industrialized nations.

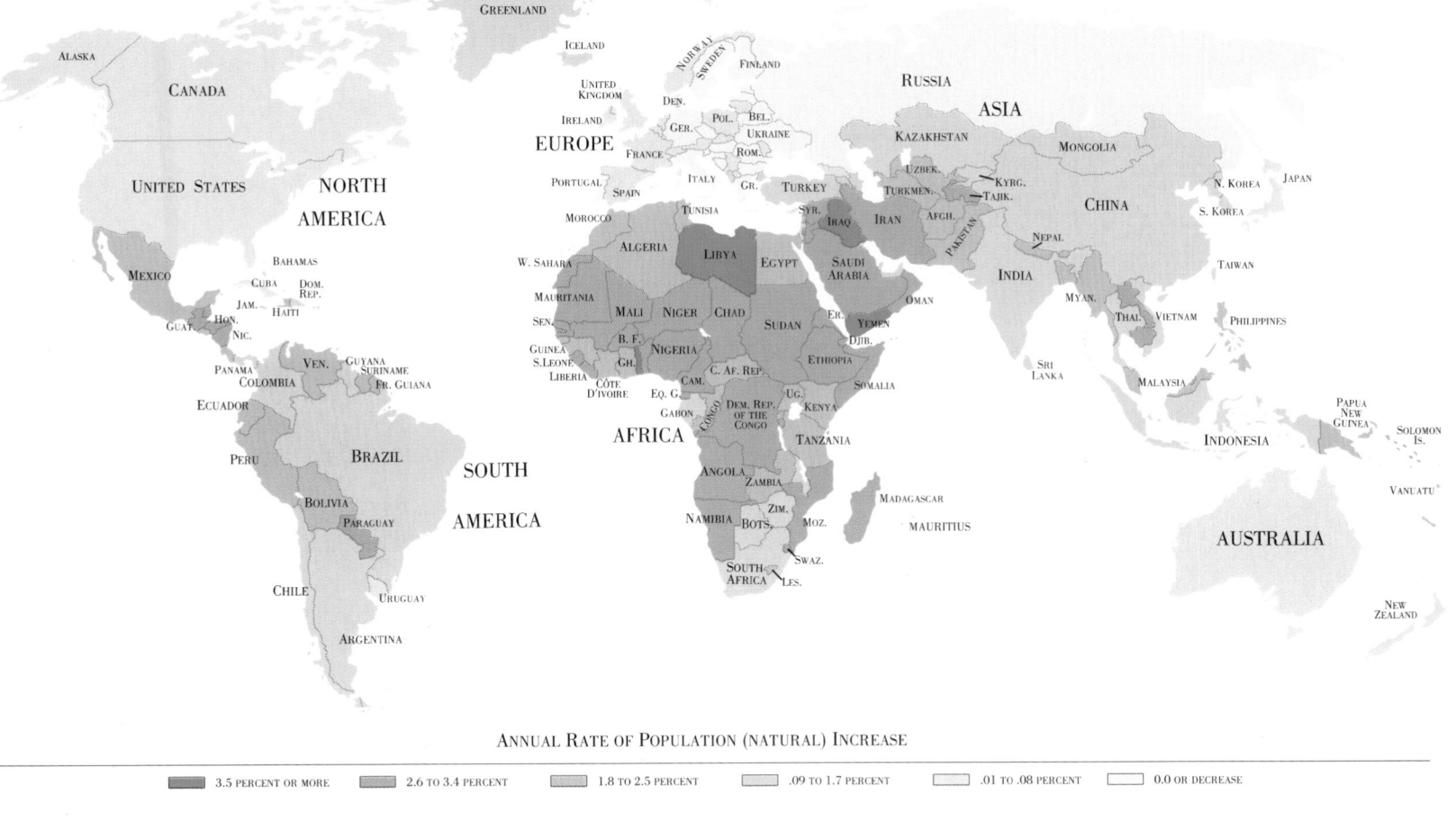

ANNUAL RATE OF POPULATION (NATURAL) INCREASE

3.5 PERCENT OR MORE	2.6 TO 3.4 PERCENT	1.8 TO 2.5 PERCENT	.09 TO 1.7 PERCENT	.01 TO .08 PERCENT	0.0 OR DECREASE

Source: U.S. Bureau of the Census, International Database

Standards of Living

GREENLAND

ALASKA

CANADA

UNITED STATES

EUROPE
The healthy, high-tech economies of many western European nations stand in sharp relief to the obsolete factories, high unemployment and ethnic rivalries of Eastern Europe.

ICELAND · **NORWAY** · **SWEDEN** · **FINLAND**
UNITED KINGDOM · **DEN.** · E.L. · L. · **BEL.**
IRELAND · N. · **POLAND** · **GER.** · CZ. · S. · **UKRAINE**
B. · A. · HUN. · ROM. · M.
FRANCE · S. · C. · A. · **BUL.**
PORTUGAL · **SPAIN** · **ITALY** · GR. · **TURKEY** · G. · A. · A. · TU

UNITED STATES
The United States and other developed countries have committed greater resources to both public and private education. This has helped their populations develop the skills that are necessary in more complex, technical, and competitive societies.

MEXICO
BAHAMAS
CUBA
DOM. REP.
JAM. · **HAITI**
BEL. · HON.
GUAT. · NIC.
EL SAL.
C.R.
PANAMA

VENEZUELA · **GUYANA** · **SURINAME** · FR. GUIANA
COLOMBIA
ECUADOR
PERU
BRAZIL

LATIN AMERICA
The gulf between rich and poor continues to widen, despite efforts to reform oppressive governments, increase literacy, and relieve overburdened cities.

BOLIVIA
PARAGUAY
CHILE
ARGENTINA · **URUGUAY**

TUNISIA
MOROCCO
WESTERN SAHARA
ALGERIA · **LIBYA** · **EGYPT**
SYR. · IRAQ · IRA · K. · Q.
ISR. · **SAUDI U. ARABIA** · **YEMEN**
MAURITANIA · **MALI** · **NIGER** · **CHAD** · **SUDAN** · ER. · DJIB. · ETH.
SEN. · G. · B.F. · **NIGERIA** · C. AF. REP. · SOMA
G.B. · **GUINEA**
S. LEONE · GH.
LIBERIA · CÔTE D'IVOIRE · CAM. · UG.
EQ. G. · **GABON** · CONGO · DEM. REP. OF THE CONGO · **KENYA**
TANZANIA

AFRICA
Disastrous droughts, discriminatory government policies, and ancient tribal rivalries, particularly in South Africa and the Sudan, have resulted in political instability and economic hardship.

ANGOLA · **ZAMBIA** · **MADAGASCAR**
ZIM. · MOZ.
NAMIBIA · BOTS.
SWAZ.
SOUTH AFRICA · LES.

SOUTH AMERICA
Political unrest, rising inflation, and slow economic growth continue to thwart efforts to bring unity and prosperity to the nations of South America.

GROSS DOMESTIC PRODUCT PER CAPITA IN DOLLARS (PER YEAR)

- 10,000 AND MORE
- 5,000-9,999
- 2,500-4,999
- 1,000-2,499
- 700-999
- UNDER 700
- DATA NOT AVAILABLE

Source: CIA World Factbook

WORKER COMPARISONS OF SELECTED COUNTRIES

COUNTRY	AVG. ACTUAL HOURS WORKED PER WEEK	YEARS OF FORMAL SCHOOLING	PERCENT WOMEN OF LABOR FORCE
AUSTRALIA	39	13.6	38
AUSTRIA	34	14.6	39
BELGIUM	33	14.4	33
CANADA	38	17.6	40
FRANCE	39	14.6	41
GERMANY	38	14.6	39
GREECE	41	13.2	27
HUNGARY	37	12.0	44
IRELAND	41	13.1	29
ISRAEL	42	NA	34
JAPAN	38	13.5	40
LUXEMBOURG	41	NA	32
NETHERLANDS	40	15.5	31
NEW ZEALAND	42	15.4	36
NORWAY	37	15.5	41
ROMANIA	38	10.8	45
SOUTH AFRICA	46	12.0	36
SOUTH KOREA	49	13.7	34
SPAIN	37	14.7	25
UNITED KINGDOM	43	14.9	39
UNITED STATES	42	16.0	41

NA=DATA NOT AVAILABLE   SOURCE: UNITED NATIONS

GROSS DOMESTIC PRODUCT GROWTH RATES

BEST GROWTH RATES		WORST GROWTH RATES	
LESOTHO	13.5	AZERBAIJAN	-17
CHINA	10.3	TAJIKISTAN	-12.4
EQUATORIAL GUINEA	10	GEORGIA	-11
ERITREA	10	BELARUS	-10
MALAWI	9.9	TURKMENISTAN	-10
MALAYSIA	9.5	KAZAKHSTAN	-8.9
VIETNAM	9.5	CONGO, DEM. REP. OF THE	-7.4
SOUTH KOREA	9	MEXICO	-6.9
SINGAPORE	8.9	MOROCCO	-6.5
THAILAND	8.6	KYRGYZSTAN	-6
CHILE	8.5	NORTH KOREA	-5
LAOS	8	ARGENTINA	-4.4
SOLOMON ISLANDS	8	RUSSIA	-4
INDONESIA	7.5	SIERRA LEONE	-4
ISRAEL	7.1	UKRAINE	-4
UGANDA	7.1	DJIBOUTI	-3
IRELAND	7	MOLDOVA	-3
MYANMAR	6.8	PAPUA NEW GUINEA	-3
PERU	6.8	RWANDA	-2.7
TURKEY	6.8	MOZAMBIQUE	-2.5

Source: CIA World Factbook

In the United States, the average person earns about $27,500 - the highest per capita Gross Domestic Product in the world. In Rwanda, the same person would earn about $400 in a year.

American workers typically get only 2 or 3 weeks of annual paid vacation, while western Europeans enjoy 4 to 6 weeks off.

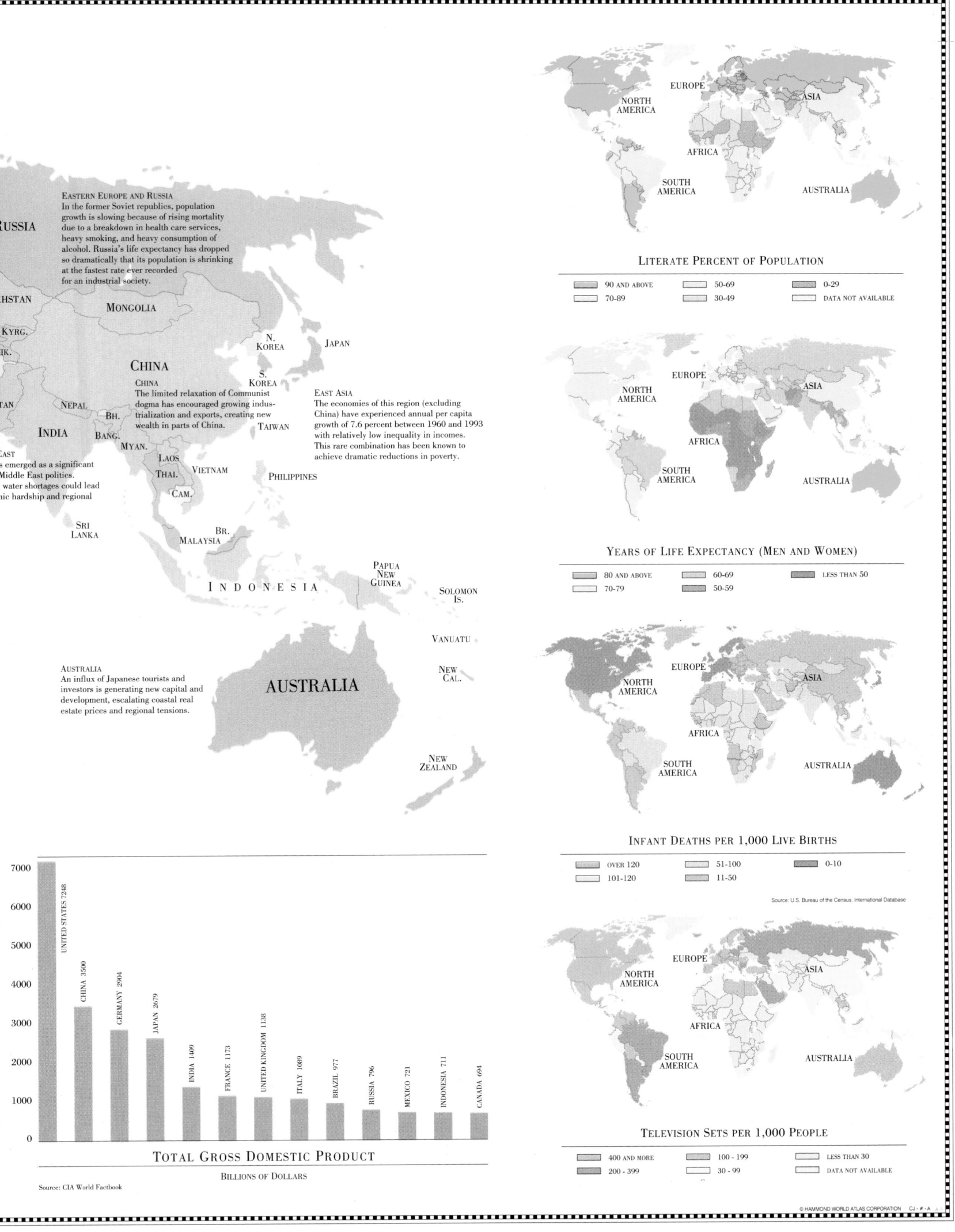

EASTERN EUROPE AND RUSSIA
In the former Soviet republics, population growth is slowing because of rising mortality due to a breakdown in health care services, heavy smoking, and heavy consumption of alcohol. Russia's life expectancy has dropped so dramatically that its population is shrinking at the fastest rate ever recorded for an industrial society.

CHINA
The limited relaxation of Communist dogma has encouraged growing industrialization and exports, creating new wealth in parts of China.

EAST ASIA
The economies of this region (excluding China) have experienced annual per capita growth of 7.6 percent between 1960 and 1993 with relatively low inequality in incomes. This rare combination has been known to achieve dramatic reductions in poverty.

E EAST
has emerged as a significant n Middle East politics. ed water shortages could lead omic hardship and regional .s.

AUSTRALIA
An influx of Japanese tourists and investors is generating new capital and development, escalating coastal real estate prices and regional tensions.

LITERATE PERCENT OF POPULATION

- 90 AND ABOVE
- 70-89
- 50-69
- 30-49
- 0-29
- DATA NOT AVAILABLE

YEARS OF LIFE EXPECTANCY (MEN AND WOMEN)

- 80 AND ABOVE
- 70-79
- 60-69
- 50-59
- LESS THAN 50

INFANT DEATHS PER 1,000 LIVE BIRTHS

- OVER 120
- 101-120
- 51-100
- 11-50
- 0-10

Source: U.S. Bureau of the Census, International Database

TELEVISION SETS PER 1,000 PEOPLE

- 400 AND MORE
- 200 - 399
- 100 - 199
- 30 - 99
- LESS THAN 30
- DATA NOT AVAILABLE

TOTAL GROSS DOMESTIC PRODUCT
BILLIONS OF DOLLARS

- UNITED STATES 7248
- CHINA 3500
- GERMANY 2004
- JAPAN 2679
- INDIA 1409
- FRANCE 1173
- UNITED KINGDOM 1138
- ITALY 1089
- BRAZIL 977
- RUSSIA 796
- MEXICO 721
- INDONESIA 711
- CANADA 694

Source: CIA World Factbook

© HAMMOND WORLD ATLAS CORPORATION   CJ · # · A

Climate

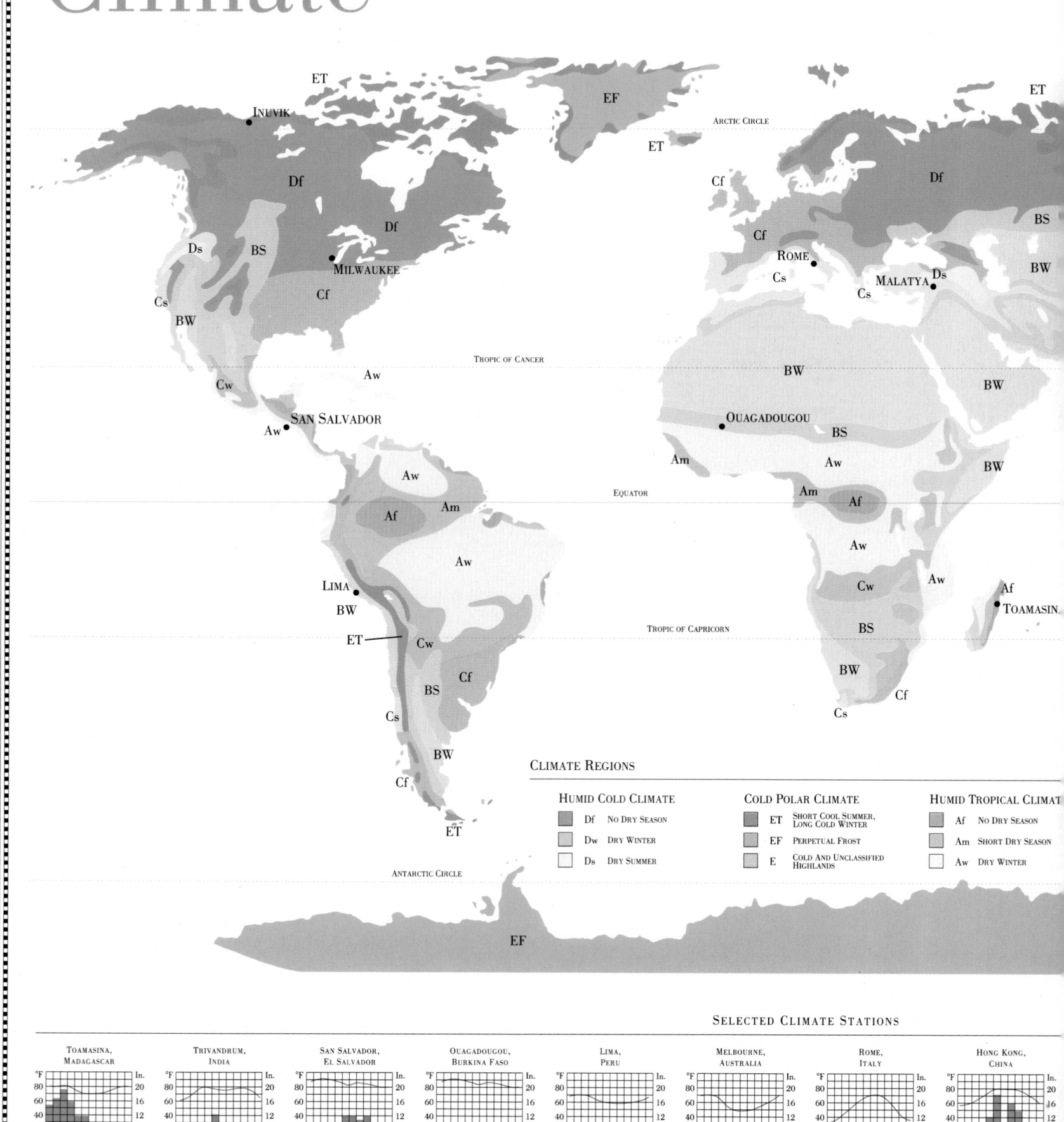

ET

INUVIK

EF

ARCTIC CIRCLE

ET

Df

Cf

Df

ET

Df

BS

Cf

BS

BW

Ds

Cf

BS

ROME

MALATYA

Ds

Milwaukee

Cf

Cs

Cs

Cs

BW

Cw

TROPIC OF CANCER

BW

Aw

SAN SALVADOR

OUAGADOUGOU

BS

BW

Aw

Am

Aw

Aw

Af

BW

Am

Am

EQUATOR

Af

Aw

Af

LIMA

Cw

Aw

TOAMASIN

BW

ET

Cw

TROPIC OF CAPRICORN

BS

BS

Cf

BW

Cs

BW

Cf

Cs

ET

ANTARCTIC CIRCLE

EF

CLIMATE REGIONS

HUMID COLD CLIMATE

Df	NO DRY SEASON
Dw	DRY WINTER
Ds	DRY SUMMER

COLD POLAR CLIMATE

ET	SHORT COOL SUMMER, LONG COLD WINTER
EF	PERPETUAL FROST
E	COLD AND UNCLASSIFIED HIGHLANDS

HUMID TROPICAL CLIMAT

Af	NO DRY SEASON
Am	SHORT DRY SEASON
Aw	DRY WINTER

SELECTED CLIMATE STATIONS

TOAMASINA, MADAGASCAR

TRIVANDRUM, INDIA

SAN SALVADOR, EL SALVADOR

OUAGADOUGOU, BURKINA FASO

LIMA, PERU

MELBOURNE, AUSTRALIA

ROME, ITALY

HONG KONG, CHINA

Temperature in Degrees Fahrenheit (°F)   Annual Rainfall in Inches (In.)

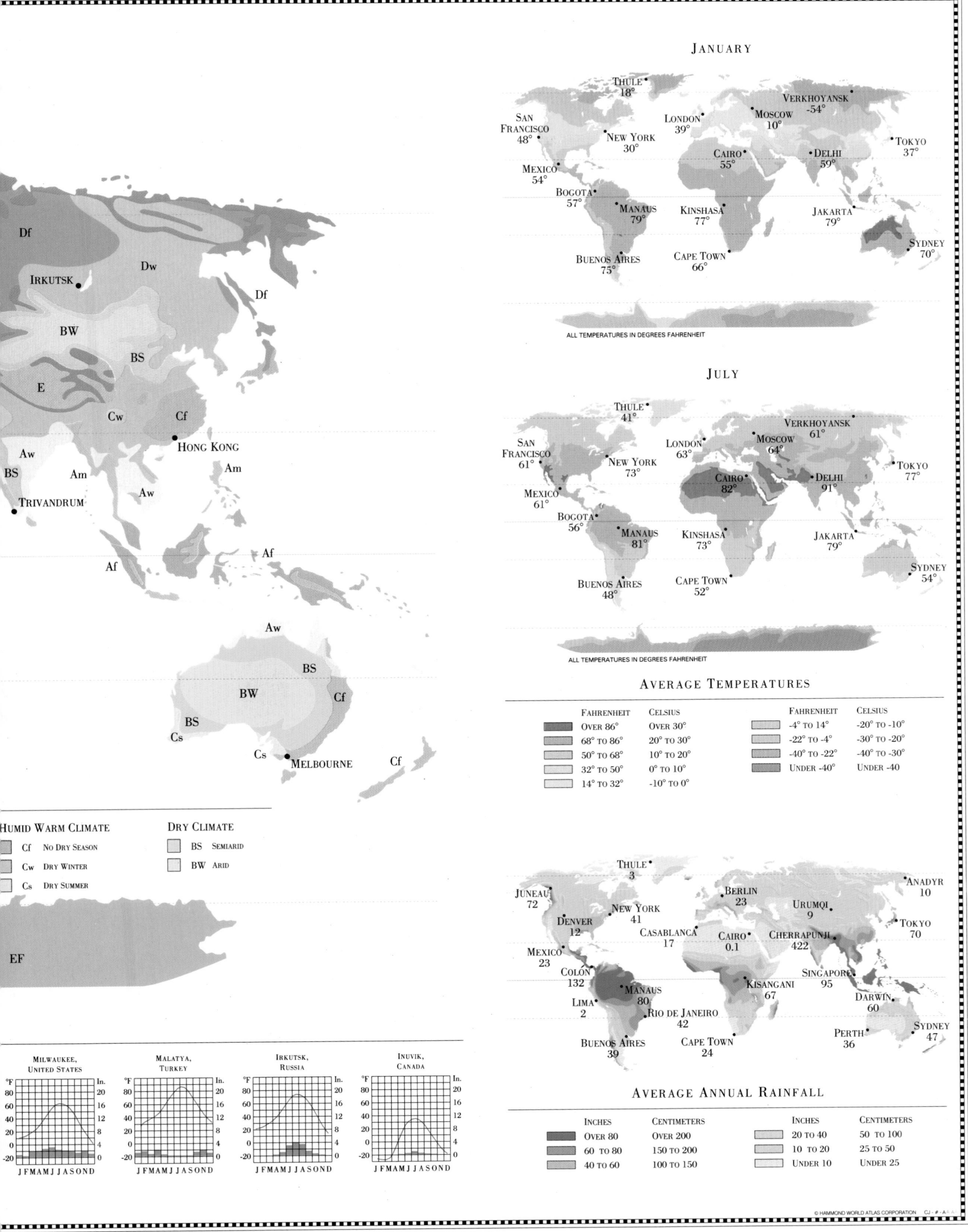

Df

IRKUTSK

Dw

Df

BW

BS

E

Cw

Cf

HONG KONG

Aw

Am

Am

BS

Aw

TRIVANDRUM

Af

Af

Aw

BS

BW

Cf

BS

Cs

Cs

MELBOURNE

Cf

EF

HUMID WARM CLIMATE

Cf NO DRY SEASON

Cw DRY WINTER

Cs DRY SUMMER

DRY CLIMATE

BS SEMIARID

BW ARID

JANUARY

THULE 18°
SAN FRANCISCO 48°
LONDON 39°
MOSCOW 10°
VERKHOYANSK -54°
NEW YORK 30°
CAIRO 55°
DELHI 59°
TOKYO 37°
MEXICO 54°
BOGOTA 57°
MANAUS 79°
KINSHASA 77°
JAKARTA 79°
BUENOS AIRES 75°
CAPE TOWN 66°
SYDNEY 70°

ALL TEMPERATURES IN DEGREES FAHRENHEIT

JULY

THULE 41°
SAN FRANCISCO 61°
LONDON 63°
MOSCOW 64°
VERKHOYANSK 61°
NEW YORK 73°
CAIRO 82°
DELHI 91°
TOKYO 77°
MEXICO 61°
BOGOTA 56°
MANAUS 81°
KINSHASA 73°
JAKARTA 79°
BUENOS AIRES 48°
CAPE TOWN 52°
SYDNEY 54°

ALL TEMPERATURES IN DEGREES FAHRENHEIT

AVERAGE TEMPERATURES

FAHRENHEIT	CELSIUS	FAHRENHEIT	CELSIUS
OVER 86°	OVER 30°	-4° TO 14°	-20° TO -10°
68° TO 86°	20° TO 30°	-22° TO -4°	-30° TO -20°
50° TO 68°	10° TO 20°	-40° TO -22°	-40° TO -30°
32° TO 50°	0° TO 10°	UNDER -40°	UNDER -40
14° TO 32°	-10° TO 0°		

THULE 3
JUNEAU 72
ANADYR 10
BERLIN 23
DENVER 12
NEW YORK 41
URUMQI 9
TOKYO 70
CASABLANCA 17
CAIRO 0.1
CHERRAPUNJI 422
MEXICO 23
COLON 132
MANAUS 80
KISANGANI 67
SINGAPORE 95
LIMA 2
DARWIN 60
RIO DE JANEIRO 42
PERTH 36
SYDNEY 47
BUENOS AIRES 39
CAPE TOWN 24

AVERAGE ANNUAL RAINFALL

INCHES	CENTIMETERS	INCHES	CENTIMETERS
OVER 80	OVER 200	20 TO 40	50 TO 100
60 TO 80	150 TO 200	10 TO 20	25 TO 50
40 TO 60	100 TO 150	UNDER 10	UNDER 25

MILWAUKEE, UNITED STATES

MALATYA, TURKEY

IRKUTSK, RUSSIA

INUVIK, CANADA

Environmental Concerns

GRIZZLY BEAR Much of Pacific temperate rain forest has been clear-cut. Remainder could be gone in 35 years.

WOODLAND CARIBOU

Air pollution and the remains of toxic waste dumping in eastern European nations are hampering recovery.

HUMPBACK WHALE Hydroelectric power projects and development in Quebec are disrupting wildlife habitats.

Pollution in the Black Sea has crea a poisoned habitat for many local species.

SPOTTED OWL

BLACK-FOOTED FERRET

Commercial fishing harvest in the northwest Atlantic has declined over 30 percent since 1970.

SPANISH LYNX

CONDOR

Fragile barrier beaches of the Atlantic coast have been damaged by agricultural runoff, sewage and overdevelopment.

MONK SEAL

MOROCCAN GAZELLE

WHOOPING CRANE

ATLANTIC RIDLEY TURTLE

MANATEE

Ecological balance in coral reefs of the Gulf and Caribbean area is being upset by a booming tourist industry.

ARABIAN GAZELLE

WEST-AFRICAN OSTRICH

It will take decades for marine life to recover from the millions of barrels of oil dumped into the Persian Gulf during the Gulf War.

At the present rate of clearing, half of Central America's rain forest will disappear early in the 21st century.

Erosion, the depletion of water resources for irrigation, and overgrazing have turned range and cropland into desert.

HOWLER MONKEY

One-third of Guinea's tropical forest is expected to disappear in the next decade.

CHEETAH

The Sahara (desert) is expanding; over 150 million acres (60 million hectares) to the south have been added since 1990.

GIANT PANGOLIN

NORTHERN WHITE RHINOCEROS

GALÁPAGOS TORTOISE

BLACK CAIMAN

JAGUAR

Africa's largest forest, in the Congo Basin, is scheduled for massive clearing projects.

GORILLA

VICUÑA

Every year over 5000 square miles (13,000 sq km) of rain forest is destroyed in Brazil's Amazon Basin.

CHINCHILLA

GOLDEN LION TAMARIN

The east coast forests of South America have largely disappeared, and remaining wilderness areas are not being conserved.

BLACK RHINOCEROS

AYE-AY

BROWN HYENA

AFRICAN ELEPHANT

LEMUR

About 80 percent of Madagascar forests have been clear-cut to pr charcoal and farmland.

The Atlantic waters off Patagonia have suffered from over-fishing and oil spills.

GIANT ARMADILLO

Southern Chile's rain forest is threatened by development.

BLUE WHALE

▭ VANISHING WILDERNESS   ✷ ENVIRONMENTAL CRISIS AREA

Acid Rain

Acid rain of nitric and sulfuric acids has killed all life in thousands of lakes, and over 15 million acres (6 million hectares) of virgin forest in Europe and North America are dead or dying.

Deforestation

Each year, 50 million acres (20 million hectares) of tropical rainforests are being felled by loggers. Trees remove carbon dioxide from the atmosphere and are vital to the prevention of soil erosion.

Extinction

Biologists estimate that over 50,000 plant and animal species inhabiting the world's rain forests are disappearing each year due to pollution, unchecked hunting, and the destruction of natural habitats.

Air Pollution

Billions of tons of industrial emissions and toxic pollutants are released into the air each year, depleting our ozone layer, killing our forests and lakes with acid rain, and threatening our health.

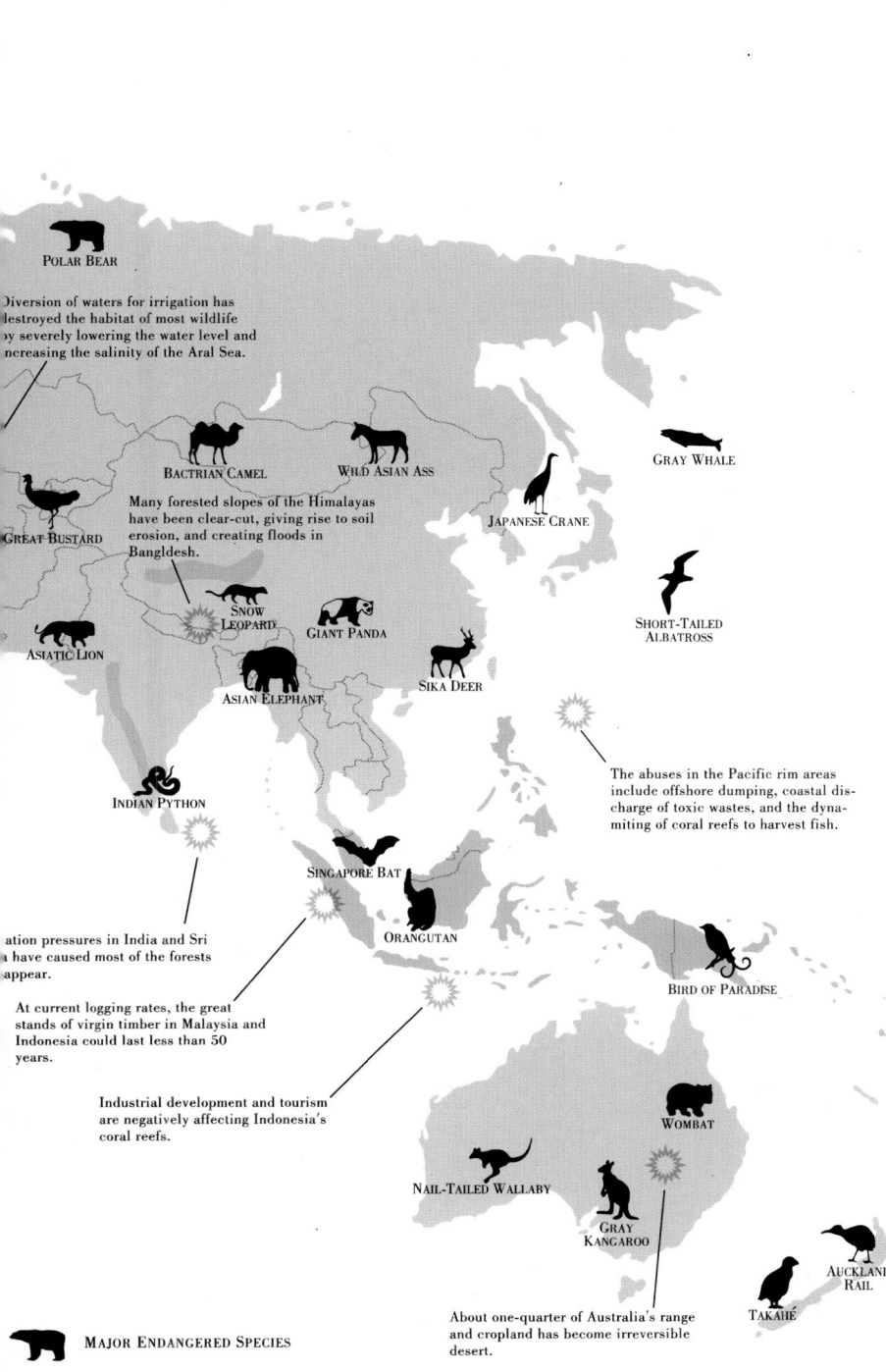

POLAR BEAR

Diversion of waters for irrigation has destroyed the habitat of most wildlife by severely lowering the water level and increasing the salinity of the Aral Sea.

BACTRIAN CAMEL

WILD ASIAN ASS

GRAY WHALE

GREAT BUSTARD

Many forested slopes of the Himalayas have been clear-cut, giving rise to soil erosion, and creating floods in Bangldesh.

JAPANESE CRANE

ASIATIC LION

SNOW LEOPARD

GIANT PANDA

SHORT-TAILED ALBATROSS

ASIAN ELEPHANT

SIKA DEER

INDIAN PYTHON

The abuses in the Pacific rim areas include offshore dumping, coastal discharge of toxic wastes, and the dynamiting of coral reefs to harvest fish.

SINGAPORE BAT

...ation pressures in India and Sri ...a have caused most of the forests ...appear.

ORANGUTAN

BIRD OF PARADISE

At current logging rates, the great stands of virgin timber in Malaysia and Indonesia could last less than 50 years.

Industrial development and tourism are negatively affecting Indonesia's coral reefs.

WOMBAT

NAIL-TAILED WALLABY

GRAY KANGAROO

AUCKLAND RAIL

TAKAHÉ

About one-quarter of Australia's range and cropland has become irreversible desert.

MAJOR ENDANGERED SPECIES

Water Pollution

Only 3 percent of the earth's water is fresh. Pollution from cities, farms, and factories has made much of it unfit to drink. In the developing world, most sewage flows untreated into lakes and rivers.

Ozone Depletion

The layer of ozone in the stratosphere shields earth from harmful ultraviolet radiation. But man-made gases are deystroying this vital barrier, increasing the risk of skin cancer and eye disease.

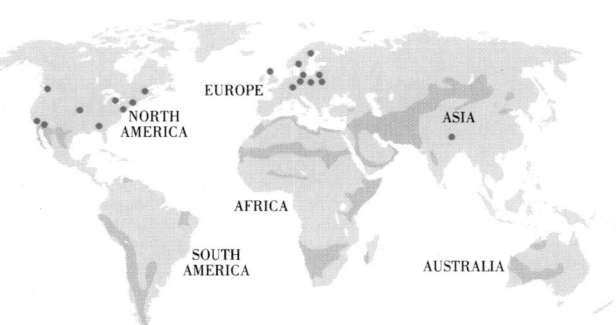

EUROPE

NORTH AMERICA

ASIA

AFRICA

SOUTH AMERICA

AUSTRALIA

DESERTIFICATION AND ACID RAIN DAMAGE

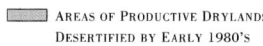
AREAS OF PRODUCTIVE DRYLANDS DESERTIFIED BY EARLY 1980'S

● AREAS OF DAMAGE FROM ACID RAIN AND OTHER AIRBORNE POLLUTANTS

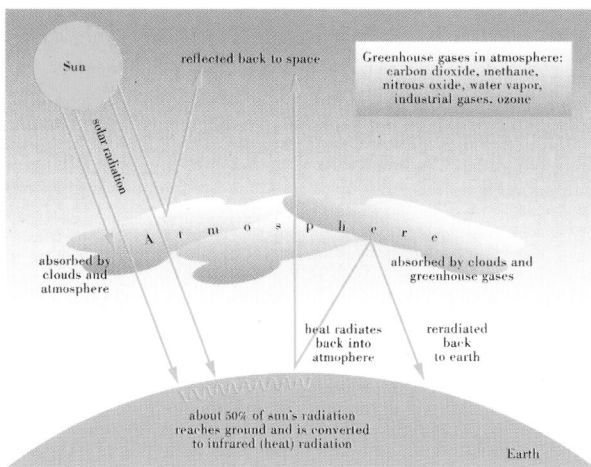

Sun

reflected back to space

Greenhouse gases in atmosphere: carbon dioxide, methane, nitrous oxide, water vapor, industrial gases, ozone

solar radiation

Atmosphere

absorbed by clouds and atmosphere

absorbed by clouds and greenhouse gases

heat radiates back into atmophere

reradiated back to earth

about 50% of sun's radiation reaches ground and is converted to infrared (heat) radiation

Earth

GREENHOUSE EFFECT

Million Tons of Carbon

12	
10	
8	
6	
4	
2	
0	

U.S. China Russia Japan Germany India Ukraine U.K. Canada Italy France Poland

GREENHOUSE EMISSIONS

CARBON DIOXIDE EQUIVALENTS

Source: Handbook of International Economic Statistics

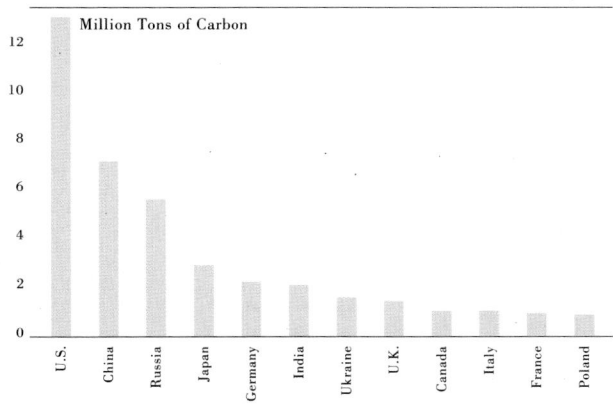

NORTH AMERICA

EUROPE

ASIA

AFRICA

SOUTH AMERICA

AUSTRALIA

MAIN TANKER ROUTES AND MAJOR OIL SPILLS

—— ROUTES OF VERY LARGE CRUDE OIL CARRIERS   ● MAJOR OIL SPILLS

World Flags and Reference Guide

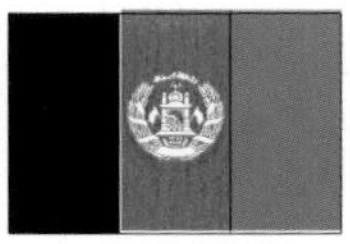

Afghanistan* 89/H2
Capital: Kabul
Area: 250,775 sq. mi.
649,507 sq. km.
Pop.: 28,717,213; growth rate: 3.43%
Govt: transitorial government
Independence: August 19, 1919
U.N. Admission: November 19, 1946
GDP: $21 billion; per capita: $800
Currency: afghani

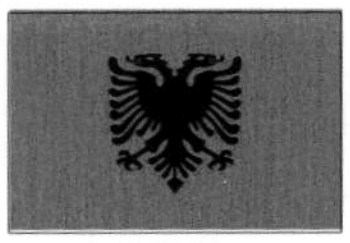

Albania* 75/F2
Capital: Tiranë
Area: 11,100 sq. mi.
28,749 sq. km.
Pop.: 3,582,205; growth rate: 1.06%
Govt: emerging democracy
Independence: November 28, 1912
U.N. Admission: December 14, 1995
GDP: $13.2 billion; per capita: $3,800
Currency: lek

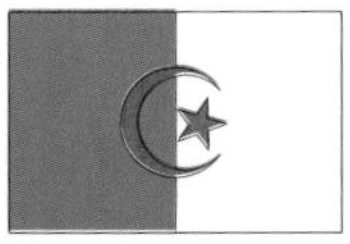

Algeria* 96/F2
Capital: Algiers
Area: 919,591 sq. mi.
2,381,740 sq. km.
Pop.: 32,818,500; growth rate: 1.68%
Govt: republic
Independence: July 5, 1962
U.N. Admission: October 8, 1962
GDP: $177 billion; per capita: $5,600
Currency: Algerian dinar

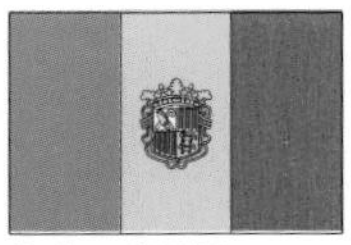

Andorra* 73/F1
Capital: Andorra la Vella
Area: 174 sq. mi.
450 sq. km.
Pop.: 69,150; growth rate: 1.11%
Govt: parliamentary democracy
Independence: 1278
U.N. Admission: July 28, 1993
GDP: $1.3 billion; per capita: $19,000
Currency: euro

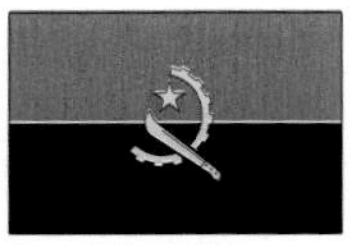

Angola* 105/C3
Capital: Luanda
Area: 481,351 sq. mi.
1,246,700 sq. km.
Pop.: 10,766,471; growth rate: 2.18%
Govt: republic
Independence: November 11, 1975
U.N. Admission: December 1, 1976
GDP: $13.3 billion; per capita: $1,330
Currency: kwanza

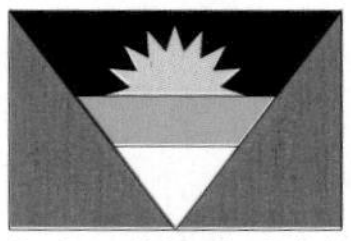

Antigua & Barbuda* 141/N8
Capital: St. John's
Area: 171 sq. mi.
443 sq. km.
Pop.: 67,897; growth rate: 0.69%
Govt: parliamentary democracy
Independence: November 1, 1981
U.N. Admission: November 11, 1981
GDP: $674 million; per capita: $10,000
Currency: EC dollar

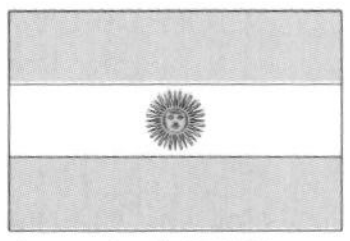

Argentina* 157/C4
Capital: Buenos Aires
Area: 1,068,296 sq. mi.
2,766,890 sq. km.
Pop.: 38,740,807; growth rate: 1.13%
Govt: republic
Independence: July 9, 1816
U.N. Admission: October 24, 1945
GDP: $453 billion; per capita: $12,000
Currency: nuevo peso argentino

Armenia* 63/H5
Capital: Yerevan
Area: 11,506 sq. mi.
29,800 sq. km.
Pop.: 3,326,448; growth rate: -0.15%
Govt: republic
Independence: September 23, 1991
U.N. Admission: March 2, 1992
GDP: $11.2 billion; per capita: $3,350
Currency: dram

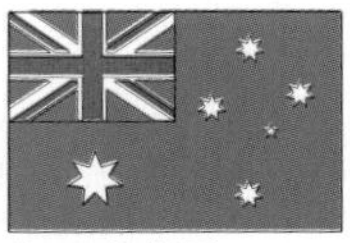

Australia* 109
Capital: Canberra
Area: 2,966,136 sq. mi.
7,682,300 sq. km.
Pop.: 19,731,984 growth rate: 0.96%
Govt: federal parliamentary state
Independence: January 1, 1901
U.N. Admission: November 1, 1945
GDP: $465.9 billion; per capita: $24,000
Currency: Australian dollar

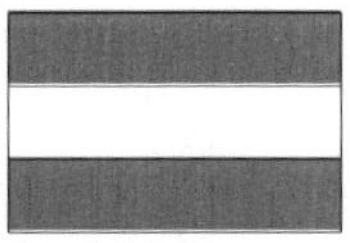

Austria* 43/L3
Capital: Vienna
Area: 32,375 sq. mi.
83,851 sq. km.
Pop.: 8,188,200 growth rate: 0.23%
Govt: federal republic
Independence: 1156
U.N. Admission: December 14, 1955
GDP: $220 billion; per capita: $27,000
Currency: euro

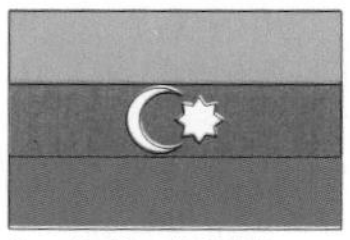

Azerbaijan* 63/H4
Capital: Baku
Area: 33,436 sq. mi.
86,600 sq. km.
Pop.: 7,830,764; growth rate: 0.38%
Govt: republic
Independence: August 30, 1991
U.N. Admission: March 2, 1992
GDP: $24.3 billion; per capita: $3,100
Currency: manat

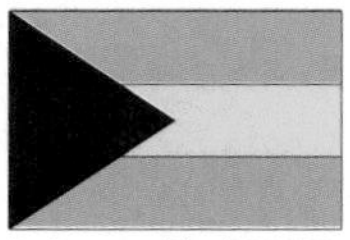

Bahamas, The* 141/F2
Capital: Nassau
Area: 5,382 sq. mi.
13,939 sq. km.
Pop.: 297,477; growth rate: 0.86%
Govt: commonwealth
Independence: July 10, 1973
U.N. Admission: September 18, 1973
GDP: $5 billion; per capita: $16,800
Currency: Bahamian dollar

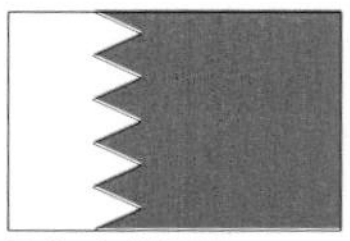

Bahrain* 88/F3
Capital: Manama
Area: 240 sq. mi.
622 sq. km.
Pop.: 667,238; growth rate: 1.67%
Govt: traditional monarchy
Independence: August 15, 1971
U.N. Admission: September 21, 1971
GDP: $8.4 billion; per capita: $13,000
Currency: Bahraini Dinar

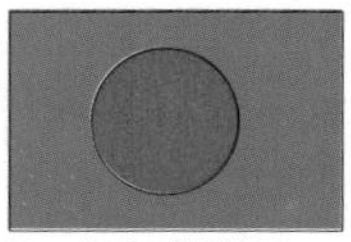

Bangladesh* 82/E3
Capital: Dhākā
Area: 55,598 sq. mi.
144,000 sq. km.
Pop.: 138,448,210; growth rate: 1.59%
Govt: parliamentary democracy
Independence: December 16, 1971
U.N. Admission: September 17, 1974
GDP: $230 billion; per capita: $1,750
Currency: taka

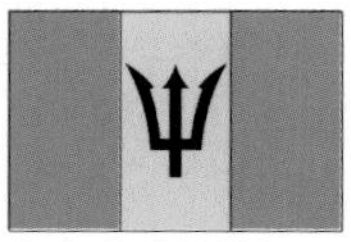

Barbados* 141/P9
Capital: Bridgetown
Area: 166 sq. mi.
430 sq. km.
Pop.: 277,264; growth rate: 0.46%
Govt: parliamentary democracy
Independence: November 30, 1966
U.N. Admission: December 9, 1966
GDP: $4 billion; per capita: $14,500
Currency: Barbadian dollar

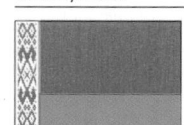

Belarus* 27/G3
Capital: Minsk
Area: 80,154 sq. mi.
207,600 sq. km.
Pop.: 10,322,151; growth rate: -0.14%
Govt: republic
Independence: August 25, 1991
U.N. Admission: October 24, 1945
GDP: $84.8 billion; per capita: $8,200
Currency: Belarusian ruble

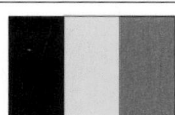

Belgium* 40/C3
Capital: Brussels
Area: 11,781 sq. mi.
30,513 sq. km.
Pop.: 10,289,088; growth rate: 0.15%
Govt: constitutional monarchy
Independence: October 4, 1930
U.N. Admission: December 27, 1945
GDP: $267.7 billion; per capita: $26,100
Currency: euro

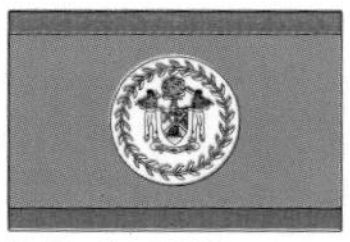

Belize* 144/D2
Capital: Belmopan
Area: 8,867 sq. mi.
22,966 sq. km.
Pop.: 266,440; growth rate: 2.65%
Govt: parliamentary democracy
Independence: September 21, 1981
U.N. Admission: September 25, 1981
GDP: $830 million; per capita: $3,250
Currency: Belizean dollar

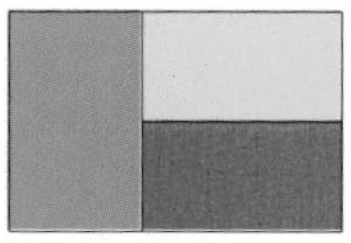

Benin* 103/F4
Capital: Porto-Novo
Area: 43,483 sq. mi.
112,620 sq. km.
Pop.: 7,041,490; growth rate: 2.91%
Govt: republic
Independence: August 1, 1960
U.N. Admission: September 20, 1960
GDP: $6.8 billion; per capita: $1,040
Currency: CFA franc

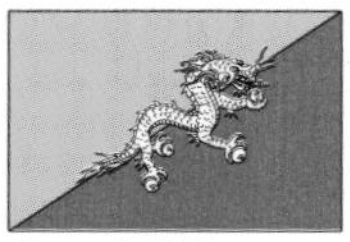

Bhutan* 82/E2
Capital: Thimphu
Area: 18,147 sq. mi.
47,000 sq. km.
Pop.: 2,139,549; growth rate: 2.15%
Govt: monarchy
Independence: August 8, 1949
U.N. Admission: September 21, 1971
GDP: $2.5 billion; per capita: $1,200
Currency: ngultrum

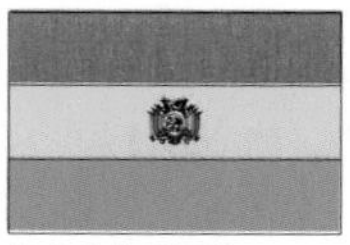

Bolivia* 150/F7
Capital: La Paz; Sucre
Area: 424,163 sq. mi.
1,098,582 sq. km.
Pop.: 8,856,443; growth rate: 1.69%
Govt: republic
Independence: August 6, 1825
U.N. Admission: November 14, 1945
GDP: $2.14 billion; per capita: $2,600
Currency: boliviano

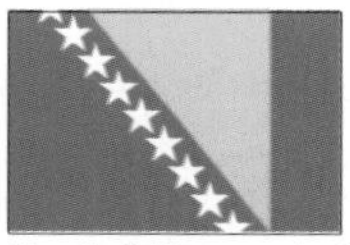

Bosnia & Herzegovina* 48/C3
Capital: Sarajevo
Area: 19,940 sq. mi.
51,645 sq. km.
Pop.: 3,989,018; growth rate: 0.76%
Govt: emerging democracy
Independence: April 1992
U.N. Admission: May 22, 1992
GDP: $7 billion; per capita: $1,800
Currency: marka

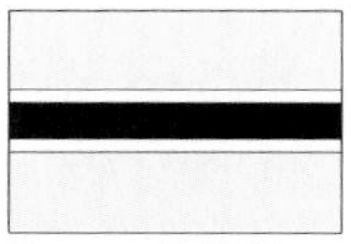

Botswana* 105/D5
Capital: Gaborone
Area: 231,803 sq. mi.
600,370 sq. km.
Pop.: 1,573,267; growth rate: 0.18%
Govt: parliamentary republic
Independence: September 30, 1966
U.N. Admission: October 17, 1966
GDP: $12.4 billion; per capita: $7,800
Currency: pula

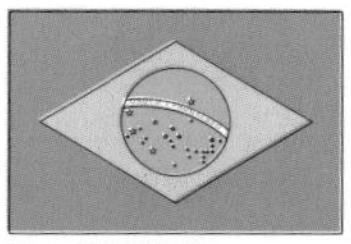

Brazil* 150/F5
Capital: Brasília
Area: 3,286,470; sq. mi.
8,511,965 sq. km.
Pop.: 182,032,604; growth rate: 0.87%
Govt: federal republic
Independence: September 7, 1822
U.N. Admission: October 24, 1945
GDP: $1.34 trillion; per capita: $7,400
Currency: real

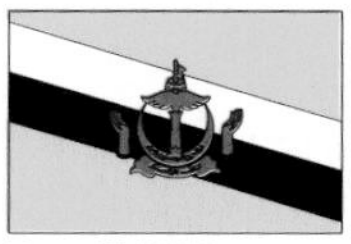

Brunei* 80/D2
Capital: Bandar Seri Begawan
Area: 2,226 sq. mi.
5,765 sq. km.
Pop.: 358,098; growth rate: 2.06%
Govt: constitutional sultanate
Independence: January 1, 1984
U.N. Admission: September 21, 1984
GDP: $6.2 billion; per capita: $18,000
Currency: Bruneian dollar

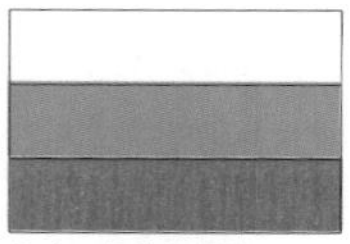

Bulgaria* 62/C4
Capital: Sofia
Area: 42,823 sq. mi.
110,912 sq. km.
Pop.: 7,537,929; growth rate: -1.11%
Govt: emerging democracy
Independence: December 22, 1908
U.N. Admission: December 14, 1955
GDP: $48 billion; per capita: $6,200
Currency: lev

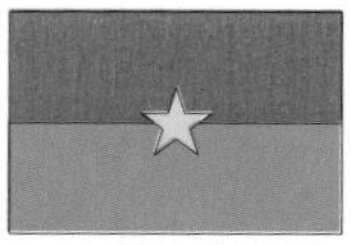

Burkina Faso* 141/E3
Capital: Ouagadougou
Area: 105,869 sq. mi.
274,200 sq. km.
Pop.: 13,228,460; growth rate: 2.64%
Govt: parliamentary
Independence: August 5, 1960
U.N. Admission: September 20, 1960
GDP: $12.8 billion; per capita: $1,040
Currency: CFA franc

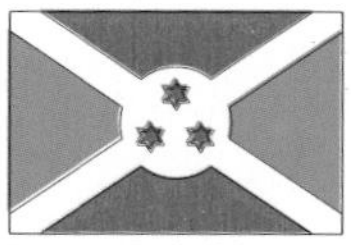

Burundi* 104/A3
Capital: Bujumbura
Area: 10,747 sq. mi.
27,835 sq. km.
Pop.: 6,096,156; growth rate: 2.36%
Govt: republic
Independence: July 1, 1962
U.N. Admission: September 18, 1962
GDP: $3.7 billion; per capita: $600
Currency: Burundi franc

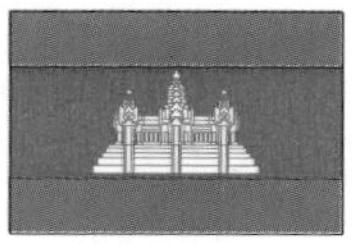

Cambodia* 83/H5
Capital: Phnom Penh
Area: 69,898 sq. mi.
181,036 sq. km.
Pop.: 13,124,764; growth rate: 2.24%
Govt: constitutional monarchy
Independence: November 9, 1949
U.N. Admission: December 14, 1955
GDP: $18.7 billion; per capita: $1,500
Currency: riel

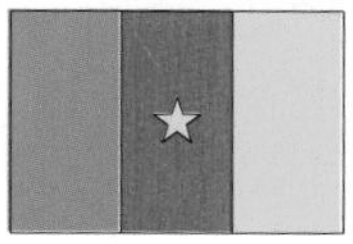

Cameroon* 96/H7
Capital: Yaoundé
Area: 183,568 sq. mi.
475,441 sq. km.
Pop.: 15,746,179; growth rate: 2.36%
Govt: unitary republic
Independence: January 1, 1960
U.N. Admission: September 20, 1960
GDP: $26.4 billion; per capita: $1,700
Currency: CFA franc

* United Nations member
Note - Page and letter-number references in blue type follow the country names. For example: **Bulgaria** 62/C4 refers to page 62, index grid square C4.

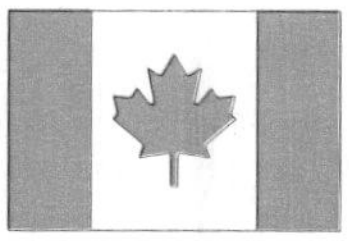

Canada* 122
Capital: Ottawa
Area: 3,851,787 sq. mi.
9,976,139 sq. km.
Pop.: 32,207,113; growth rate: 0.96%
Govt: parliamentary democracy
Independence: July 1, 1867
U.N. Admission: November 9, 1945
GDP: $875 billion; per capita: $27,700
Currency: Canadian dollar

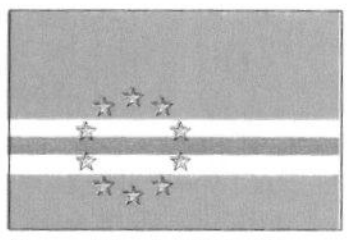

Cape Verde* 93/J9
Capital: Praia
Area: 1,556 sq. mi.
4,030 sq. km.
Pop.: 412,137; growth rate: 0.85%
Govt: republic
Independence: July 5, 1975
U.N. Admission: September 16, 1975
GDP: $600 billion; per capita: $1,500
Currency: Cape Verdean escudo

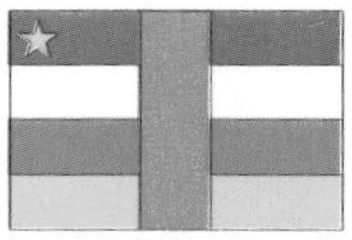

Central African Republic* 97/J6
Capital: Bangui
Area: 240,533 sq. mi.
622,980 sq. km.
Pop.: 3,683,538; growth rate: 1.8%
Govt: republic
Independence: August 13, 1960
U.N. Admission: September 20, 1960
GDP: $4.6 billion; per capita: $1,300
Currency: CFA franc

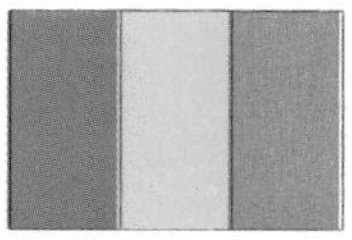

Chad* 97/J4
Capital: N'Djamena
Area: 495,752 sq. mi.
1,283,998 sq. km.
Pop.: 9,253,493; growth rate: 3.27%
Govt: republic
Independence: August 11, 1960
U.N. Admission: September 20, 1960
GDP: $8.9 billion; per capita: $1,030
Currency: CFA franc

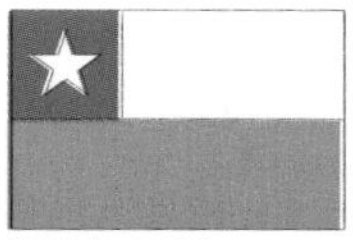

Chile* 157/B3
Capital: Santiago
Area: 292,258 sq. mi.
756,950 sq. km.
Pop.: 15,665,216; growth rate: 1.09%
Govt: republic
Independence: September 18, 1810
U.N. Admission: October 24, 1945
GDP: $153 billion; per capita: $10,000
Currency: Chilean peso

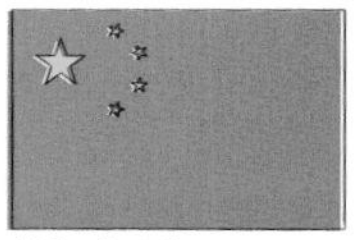

China* 70/G4
Capital: Beijing
Area: 3,705,386 sq. mi.
9,596,960 sq. km.
Pop.: 1,286,975,468; growth rate: 0.87%
Govt: Communist state
Independence: October 1, 1949
U.N. Admission: October 24, 1945
GDP: $5.56 trillion; per capita: $4,300
Currency: yuan

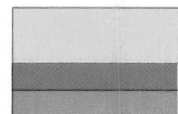

Colombia* 150/D3
Capital: Bogotá
Area: 439,733 sq. mi.
1,138,910 sq. km.
Pop.: 41,662,073; growth rate: 1.6%
Govt: republic
Independence: July 20, 1810
U.N. Admission: November 5, 1945
GDP: $255 billion; per capita: $6,300
Currency: Colombian peso

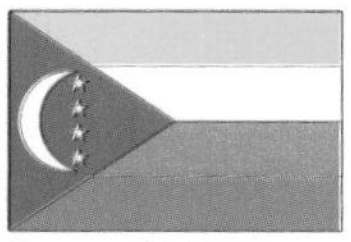

Comoros* 107/G5
Capital: Moroni
Area: 838 sq. mi.
2,170 sq. km.
Pop.: 632,948; growth rate: 2.99%
Govt: independent republic
Independence: July 6, 1975
U.N. Admission: November 12, 1975
GDP: $424 million; per capita: $710
Currency: Comoran franc

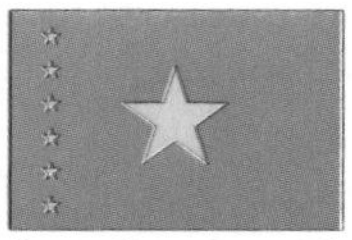

Congo, Dem. Rep. of the* 93/E5
Capital: Kinshasa
Area: 905,563 sq. mi.
2,345,410 sq. km.
Pop.: 56,625,039; growth rate: 2.79%
Govt: dictatorship
Independence: June 30, 1960
U.N. Admission: September 20, 1960
GDP: $32 billion; per capita: $590
Currency: Congolese franc

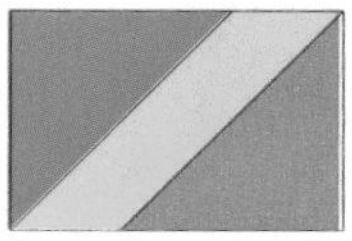

Congo, Rep. of the* 93/D4
Capital: Brazzaville
Area: 132,046 sq. mi.
342,000 sq. km.
Pop.: 2,954,258; growth rate: 2.18%
Govt: republic
Independence: August 15, 1960
U.N. Admission: September 20, 1960
GDP: $2.5 billion; per capita: $900
Currency: CFA franc

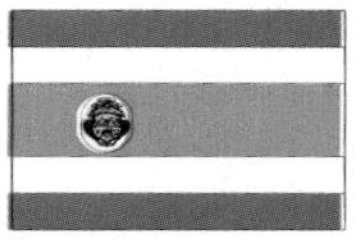

Costa Rica* 145/F4
Capital: San José
Area: 19,730 sq. mi.
51,100 sq. km.
Pop.: 3,896,092; growth rate: 1.61%
Govt: democratic republic
Independence: September 15, 1821
U.N. Admission: November 2, 1945
GDP: $31.9 billion; per capita: $8,500
Currency: Costa Rican colón

Côte d'Ivoire* 102/D5
Capital: Yamoussoukro
Area: 124,502 sq. mi.
322,460 sq. km.
Pop.: 16,962,491; growth rate: 2.45%
Govt: republic
Independence: August 7, 1960
U.N. Admission: September 20, 1960
GDP: $25.5 billion; per capita: $1,550
Currency: CFA franc

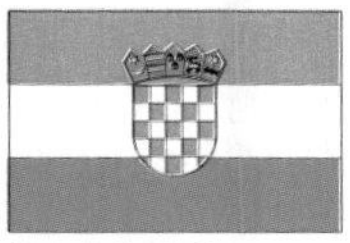

Croatia* 48/B3
Capital: Zagreb
Area: 22,050 sq. mi.
57,110 sq. km.
Pop.: 4,422,248; growth rate: 1.12%
Govt: parliamentary democracy
Independence: June 25, 1991
U.N. Admission: May 22, 1992
GDP: $36.1 billion; per capita: $8,300
Currency: Croatian kuna

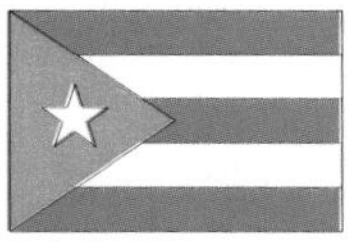

Cuba* 145/F1
Capital: Havana
Area: 42,803 sq. mi.
110,860 sq. km.
Pop.: 11,263,429; growth rate: 0.35%
Govt: Communist state
Independence: May 20, 1902
U.N. Admission: October 24, 1945
GDP: $25.5 billion; per capita: $2,300
Currency: Cuban peso

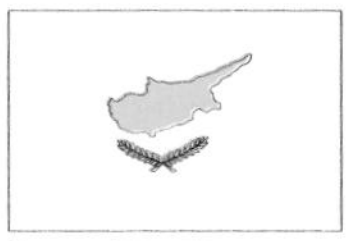

Cyprus* 91/C2
Capital: Nicosia
Area: 3,571 sq. mi.
9,250 sq. km.
Pop.: 771,657; growth rate: 0.57%
Govt: republic
Independence: August 16, 1960
U.N. Admission: September 20, 1960
GDP: $9.1 billion; per capita: $15,000
Currency: Cypriot pound

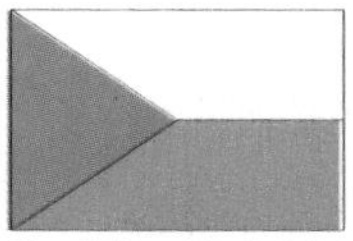

Czech Republic* 41/H4
Capital: Prague
Area: 30,387 sq. mi.
78,703 sq. km.
Pop.: 10,249,216; growth rate: -0.07%
Govt: parliamentary democracy
Independence: January 1, 1993
U.N. Admission: January 19, 1993
GDP: $147.9 billion; per capita: $14,400
Currency: koruna

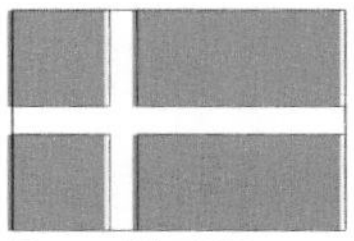

Denmark* 38/C4
Capital: Copenhagen
Area: 16,629 sq. mi.
43,069 sq. km.
Pop.: 5,384,384; growth rate: 0.29%
Govt: constitutional monarchy
Independence: 1849
U.N. Admission: October 24, 1945
GDP: $149.8 billion; per capita: $28,000
Currency: Danish krone

Djibouti* 97/P5
Capital: Djibouti
Area: 8,494 sq. mi.
22,000 sq. km.
Pop.: 457,130; growth rate: 2.59%
Govt: republic
Independence: June 27, 1977
U.N. Admission: September 20, 1977
GDP: $586 million; per capita: $1,400
Currency: Djiboutian franc

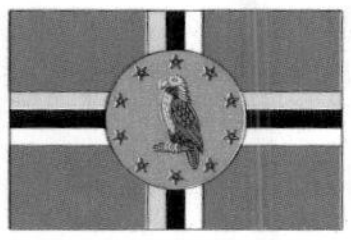

Dominica* 141/N9
Capital: Roseau
Area: 290 sq. mi.
751 sq. km.
Pop.: 69,655; growth rate: -0.81%
Govt: parliamentary democracy
Independence: November 3, 1978
U.N. Admission: December 18, 1978
GDP: $262 million; per capita: $3,700
Currency: EC dollar

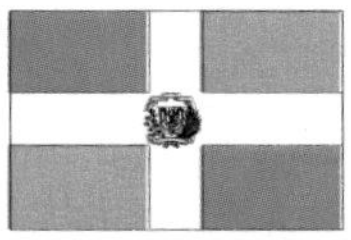

Dominican Republic* 141/H4
Capital: Santo Domingo
Area: 18,815 sq. mi.
48,730 sq. km.
Pop.: 8,715,602; growth rate: 1.61%
Govt: republic
Independence: Febuary 27, 1844
U.N. Admission: October 24, 1945
GDP: $50 billion; per capita: $5,800
Currency: Dominican peso

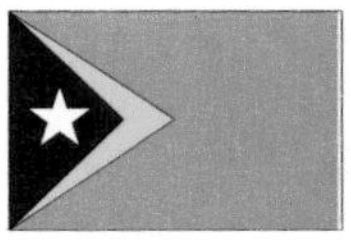

East Timor* 81/G5
Capital: Dili
Area: 5,734 sq. mi.
14,874 sq. km.
Pop.: 997,853; growth rate: 7.26%
Govt: republic
Independence: May 20, 2002
U.N. Admission: September 27, 2002
GDP: $415 million; per capita: $500
Currency: United States dollar

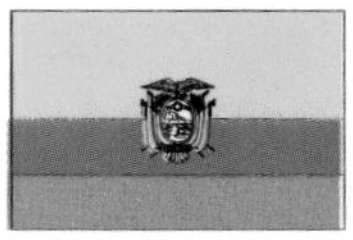

Ecuador* 150/C4
Capital: Quito
Area: 109,483 sq. mi.
283,561 sq. km.
Pop.: 13,710,234; growth rate: 1.96%
Govt: republic
Independence: May 21, 1822
U.N. Admission: December 21, 1945
GDP: $39.6 billion; per capita: $3,000
Currency: United States dollar

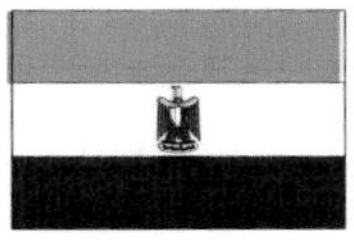

Egypt* 97/L2
Capital: Cairo
Area: 386,659 sq. mi.
1,001,447 sq. km.
Pop.: 74,718,797; growth rate: 1.66%
Govt: republic
Independence: February 28, 1922
U.N. Admission: October 24, 1945
GDP: $258 billion; per capita: $3,700
Currency: Egyptian pound

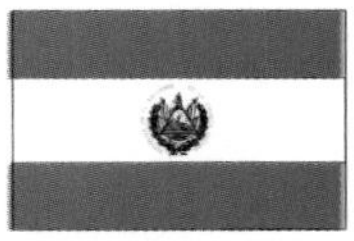

El Salvador* 144/D3
Capital: San Salvador
Area: 8,124 sq. mi.
21,040 sq. km.
Pop.: 6,470,379; growth rate: 1.83%
Govt: republic
Independence: September 15, 1821
U.N. Admission: October 24, 1945
GDP: $28.4 billion; per capita: $4,600
Currency: Salvadoran colón

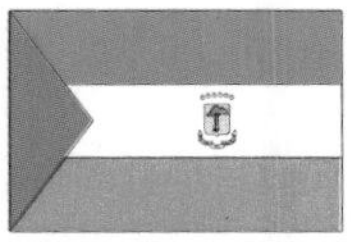

Equatorial Guinea* 96/G7
Capital: Malabo
Area: 10,831 sq. mi.
28,052 sq. km.
Pop.: 510,473; growth rate: 2.45%
Govt: republic in transition
Independence: October 12, 1968
U.N. Admission: November 12, 1968
GDP: $1.04 billion; per capita: $2,100
Currency: CFA franc

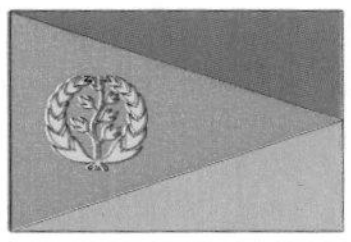

Eritrea* 97/N5
Capital: Asmara
Area: 46,842 sq. mi.
121,320 sq. km.
Pop.: 4,362,254; growth rate: 3.8%
Govt: transitorial government
Independence: May 27, 1993
U.N. Admission: May 28, 1993
GDP: $3.2 billion; per capita: $740
Currency: nafka

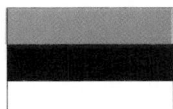

Estonia* 39/L2
Capital: Tallinn
Area: 17,413 sq. mi.
45,100 sq. km.
Pop.: 1,408,556; growth rate: -0.52%
Govt: republic
Independence: September 6, 1991
U.N. Admission: September 17, 1991
GDP: $14.3 billion; per capita: $10,000
Currency: Estonian kroon

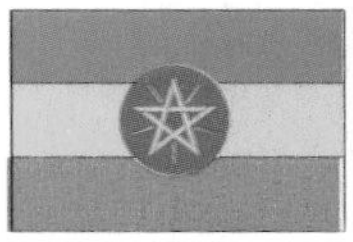

Ethiopia* 97/N5
Capital: Addis Ababa
Area: 435,184 sq. mi.
1,127,127 sq. km.
Pop.: 66,557,553; growth rate: 2.64%
Govt: federal republic
Independence: c. 2nd cent. A.D.
U.N. Admission: November 13, 1945
GDP: $46 billion; per capita: $700
Currency: birr

Fiji* 116/G6
Capital: Suva
Area: 7,055 sq. mi.
18,272 sq. km.
Pop.: 868,531; growth rate: 1.41%
Govt: republic
Independence: October 10, 1970
U.N. Admission: October 13, 1970
GDP: $4.4 billion; per capita: $5,200
Currency: Fijian dollar

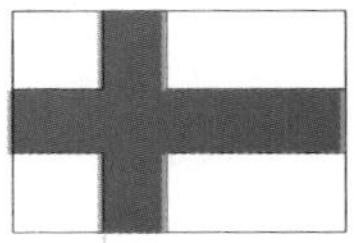

Finland* 37/H2
Capital: Helsinki
Area: 130,128 sq. mi.
337,032 sq. km.
Pop.: 5,190,785; growth rate: 0.14%
Govt: republic
Independence: December 16, 1917
U.N. Admission: December 14, 1955
GDP: $133.5 billion; per capita: $25,800
Currency: euro

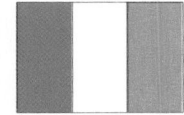

France* 42/D3
Capital: Paris
Area: 211,208 sq. mi.
547,030 sq. km.
Pop.: 60,180,529; growth rate: 0.35%
Govt: republic
Independence: 486
U.N. Admission: October 24, 1945
GDP: $1.51 trillion; per capita: $25,400
Currency: euro

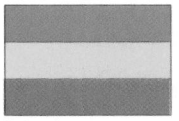

Gabon* 96/H7
Capital: Libreville
Area: 103,347 sq. mi.
267,670 sq. km.
Pop.: 1,321,560; growth rate: 0.97%
Govt: republic
Independence: August 17, 1960
U.N. Admission: September 20, 1960
GDP: $6.7 billion; per capita: $5,500
Currency: CFA franc

Gambia, The* 102/B3
Capital: Banjul
Area: 4,363 sq. mi.
11,300 sq. km.
Pop.: 1,501,050; growth rate: 3.09%
Govt: republic
Independence: February 18, 1965
U.N. Admission: September 21, 1965
GDP: $2.5 billion; per capita: $1,770
Currency: dalasi

Georgia* 63/G4
Capital: T'bilisi
Area: 26,911 sq. mi.
69,700 sq. km.
Pop.: 4,934,413; growth rate: -0.55%
Govt: republic
Independence: April 9, 1991
U.N. Admission: July 13, 1992
GDP: $15.5 billion; per capita: $3,100
Currency: lari

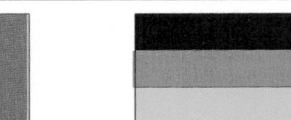

Germany* 40/E3
Capital: Berlin
Area: 137,803 sq. mi.
356,910 sq. km.
Pop.: 83,398,326; growth rate: 0.26%
Govt: federal republic
Independence: January 18, 1871
U.N. Admission: September 18, 1973
GDP: $2.17 trillion; per capita: $26,200
Currency: euro

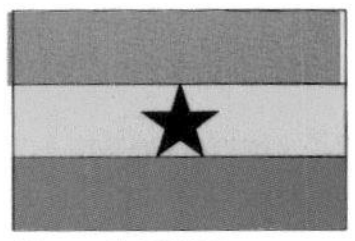

Ghana* 103/E4
Capital: Accra
Area: 92,100 sq. mi.
238,540 sq. km.
Pop.: 20,467,747; growth rate: 1.7%
Govt: constitutional democracy
Independence: March 6, 1957
U.N. Admission: March 8, 1957
GDP: $39.4 billion; per capita: $1,980
Currency: cedi

Sources: The Flag Research Center; U.S. Bureau of the Census, International Data Base; CIA Factbook

World Flags and Reference Guide

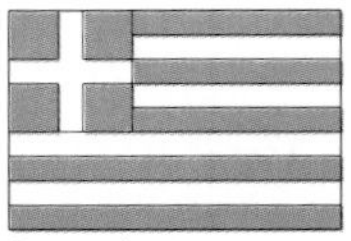

Greece* 42/G3
Capital: Athens
Area: 50,942 sq. mi.
131,940 sq. km.
Pop.: 10,665,989; growth rate: 0.2%
Govt: parliamentary republic
Independence: 1829
U.N. Admission: October 25, 1945
GDP: $189.7 billion; per capita: $17,900
Currency: euro

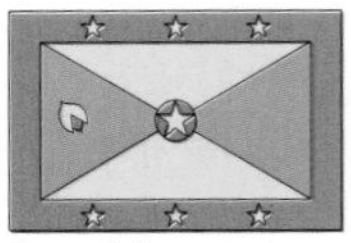

Grenada* 141/N10
Capital: St. George's
Area: 131 sq. mi.
340 sq. km.
Pop.: 89,258; growth rate: 0.02%
Govt: parliamentary democracy
Independence: February 7, 1974
U.N. Admission: September 17, 1974
GDP: $424 million; per capita: $4,750
Currency: EC dollar

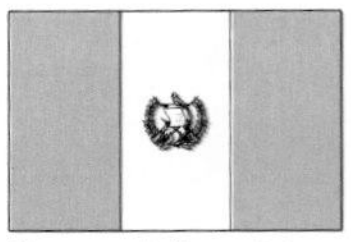

Guatemala* 144/D3
Capital: Guatemala
Area: 42,042 sq. mi.
108,889 sq. km.
Pop.: 13,909,384; growth rate: 2.57%
Govt: republic
Independence: September 15, 1821
U.N. Admission: November 21, 1945
GDP: $48.3 billion; per capita: $3,700
Currency: quetzal

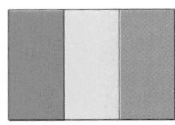

Guinea* 102/C4
Capital: Conakry
Area: 94,927 sq. mi.
245,860 sq. km.
Pop.: 9,030,220; growth rate: 2.23%
Govt: republic
Independence: October 2, 1958
U.N. Admission: December 12, 1958
GDP: $15 billion; per capita: $1,970
Currency: Guinean franc

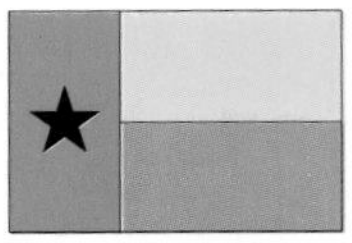

Guinea Bissau* 102/B3
Capital: Bissau
Area: 13,946 sq. mi.
36,120 sq. km.
Pop.: 1,360,827; growth rate: 2.23%
Govt: republic
Independence: September 10, 1974
U.N. Admission: September 17, 1974
GDP: $1.2 billion; per capita: $900
Currency: CFA franc

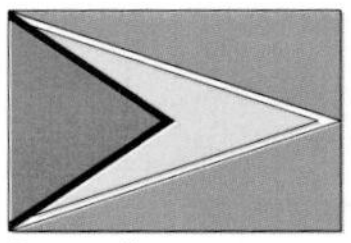

Guyana* 153/G3
Capital: Georgetown
Area: 83,000 sq. mi.
214,970 sq. km.
Pop.: 702,100; growth rate: 0.23%
Govt: republic
Independence: May 28, 1966
U.N. Admission: September 20, 1966
GDP: $2.5 billion; per capita: $3,600
Currency: Guyanese dollar

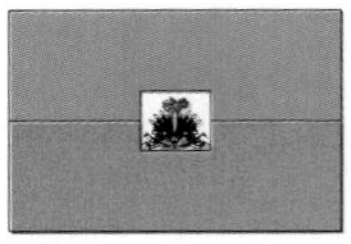

Haiti* 145/H2
Capital: Port-au-Prince
Area: 10,714 sq. mi.
27,750 sq. km.
Pop.: 7,527,817; growth rate: 1.42%
Govt: republic
Independence: January 1, 1804
U.N. Admission: October 24, 1945
GDP: $12 billion; per capita: $1,700
Currency: gourde

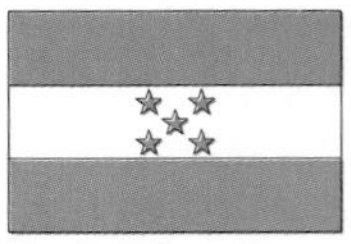

Honduras* 144/E3
Capital: Tegucigalpa
Area: 43,277 sq. mi.
112,087 sq. km.
Pop.: 6,669,789; growth rate: 2.34%
Govt: republic
Independence: September 15, 1921
U.N. Admission: December 17, 1945
GDP: $17 billion; per capita: $2,600
Currency: lempira

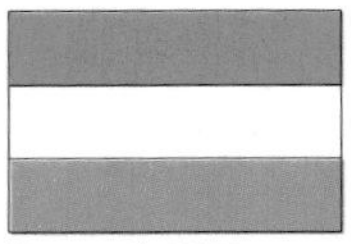

Hungary* 48/D2
Capital: Budapest
Area: 35,919 sq. mi.
93,030 sq. km.
Pop.: 10,045,407; growth rate: -0.3%
Govt: parliamentary democracy
Independence: 1001
U.N. Admission: December 14, 1955
GDP: $120.9 billion; per capita: $12,000
Currency: forint

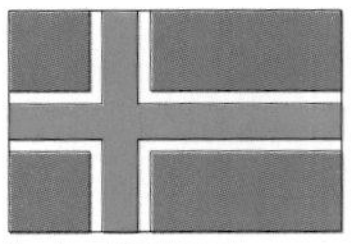

Iceland* 37/N7
Capital: Reykjavík
Area: 39,768 sq. mi.
103,000 sq. km.
Pop.: 280,798; growth rate: 0.52%
Govt: constitutional republic
Independence: June 17, 1944
U.N. Admission: November 19, 1946
GDP: $6.85 billion; per capita: $24,800
Currency: krona

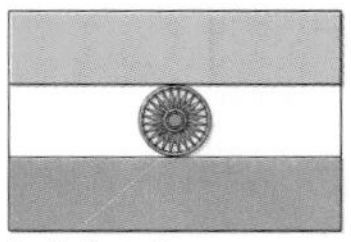

India* 67/G7
Capital: New Delhi
Area: 1,269,339 sq. mi.
3,287,588 sq. km.
Pop.: 1,049,700,118; growth rate: 1.51%
Govt: federal republic
Independence: August 15, 1947
U.N. Admission: October 30, 1947
GDP: $2.5 trillion; per capita: $2,500
Currency: Indian rupee

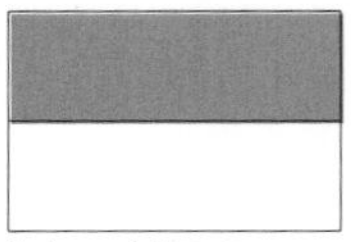

Indonesia* 81/E4
Capital: Jakarta
Area: 741,096 sq. mi.
1,919,440 sq. km.
Pop.: 234,893.453; growth rate: 1.54%
Govt: republic
Independence: August 17, 1945
U.N. Admission: September 28, 1950
GDP: $687 billion; per capita: $3,000
Currency: Indonesian rupiah

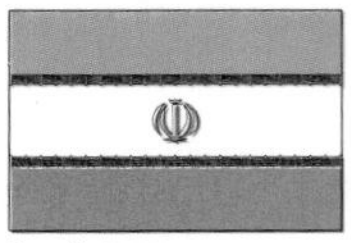

Iran* 67/E6
Capital: Tehrān
Area: 636,293 sq. mi.
1,648,000 sq. km.
Pop.: 68,278,826; growth rate: 0.77%
Govt: teocratic republic
Independence: April 1, 1979
U.N. Admission: October 24, 1945
GDP: $426 billion; per capita: $6,400
Currency: Iranian rial

Iraq* 88/D2
Capital: Baghdad
Area: 168,753 sq. mi.
437,072 sq. km.
Pop.: 24,683,313; growth rate: 2.82%
Govt: republic
Independence: October 3, 1932
U.N. Admission: December 21, 1945
GDP: $59 billion; per capita: $2,500
Currency: Iraqi dinar

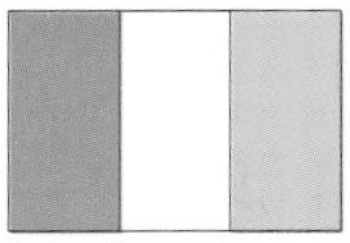

Ireland* 31/P10
Capital: Dublin
Area: 27,136 sq. mi.
70,282 sq. km.
Pop.: 3,924,140; growth rate: 1.07%
Govt: republic
Independence: December 6, 1921
U.N. Admission: December 14, 1955
GDP: $104.7 billion; per capita: $27,300
Currency: euro

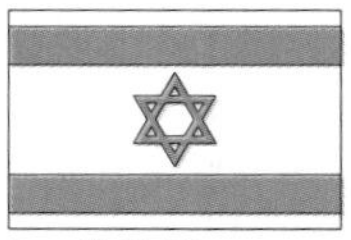

Israel* 91/C3
Capital: Jerusalem
Area: 8,019 sq. mi.
20,770 sq. km.
Pop.: 6,616,533; growth rate: 1.48%
Govt: parliamentary democracy
Independence: May 14, 1948
U.N. Admission: May 11, 1949
GDP: $119 billion; per capita: $20,000
Currency: new Israeli shekel

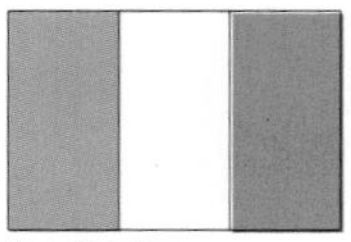

Italy* 27/F4
Capital: Rome
Area: 116,305 sq. mi.
301,230 sq. km.
Pop.: 57,998,353; growth rate: 0.05%
Govt: republic
Independence: March 12, 1861
U.N. Admission: December 14, 1955
GDP: $1.402 trillion; per capita: $24,300
Currency: euro

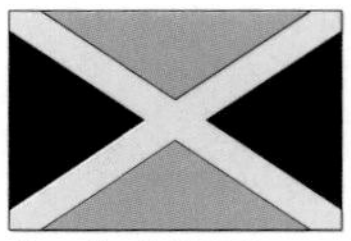

Jamaica* 145/G2
Capital: Kingston
Area: 4,243 sq. mi.
10,990 sq. km.
Pop.: 2,695,867; growth rate: 0.56%
Govt: parliamentary democracy
Independence: August 6, 1962
U.N. Admission: September 18, 1962
GDP: $9.8 billion; per capita: $3,700
Currency: Jamaican dollar

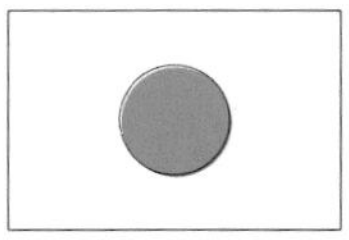

Japan* 71/Q4
Capital: Tōkyō
Area: 145,882 sq. mi.
377,835 sq. km.
Pop.: 127,214,499; growth rate: 0.15%
Govt: constitutional monarchy
Independence: 660 B.C.
U.N. Admission: December 18, 1956
GDP: $3.45 trillion; per capita: $27,200
Currency: yen

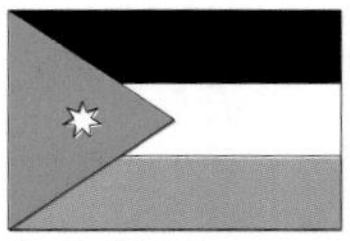

Jordan* 88/C2
Capital: Amman
Area: 34,445 sq. mi.
89,213 sq. km.
Pop.: 5,460,265; growth rate: 2.89%
Govt: constitutional monarchy
Independence: May 25, 1946
U.N. Admission: December 14, 1955
GDP: $21.6 billion; per capita: $4,200
Currency: Jordanian dinar

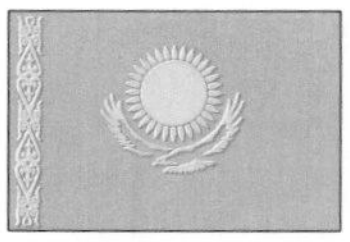

Kazakhstan* 64/G5
Capital: Astana
Area: 1,049,150 sq. mi.
2,717,300 sq. km.
Pop.: 16,763,795; growth rate: 0.1%
Govt: republic
Independence: December 16, 1991
U.N. Admission: March 2, 1992
GDP: $98.1 billion; per capita: $5,900
Currency: tenge

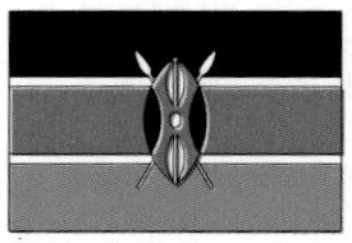

Kenya* 104/C2
Capital: Nairobi
Area: 224, 960 sq. mi.
582,646 sq. km.
Pop.: 31,639,091; growth rate: 1.15%
Govt: republic
Independence: December 12, 1963
U.N. Admission: December 16, 1963
GDP: $31 billion; per capita: $1,000
Currency: Kenyan shilling

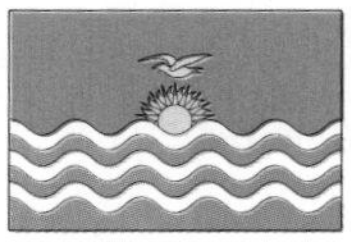

Kiribati* 116/H5
Capital: Tarawa
Area: 277 sq. mi.
717 sq. km.
Pop.: 98,549; growth rate: 2.28%
Govt: republic
Independence: July 12, 1979
U.N. Admission: September 14, 1999
GDP: $79 million; per capita: $840
Currency: Australian dollar

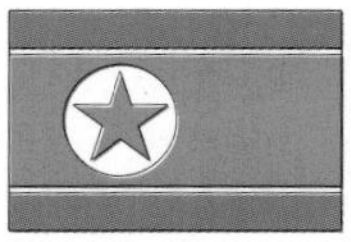

Korea, North* 73/D2
Capital: P'yŏngyang
Area: 46,540 sq. mi.
120,539 sq. km.
Pop.: 22,466,481; growth rate: 1.1%
Govt: Communist state
Independence: September 9, 1948
U.N. Admission: September 17, 1991
GDP: $21.8 billion; per capita: $1,000
Currency: North Korean won

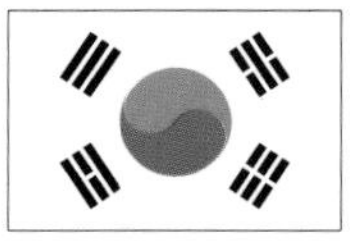

Korea, South* 73/D4
Capital: Seoul
Area: 38,023 sq. mi.
98,480 sq. km.
Pop.: 48,289,037; growth rate: 0.85%
Govt: republic
Independence: August 15, 1948
U.N. Admission: September 17, 1991
GDP: $865 billion; per capita: $18,000
Currency: South Korean won

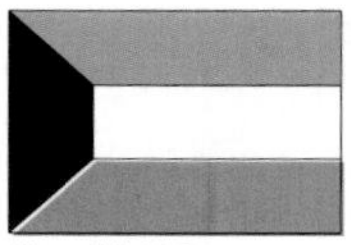

Kuwait* 88/E3
Capital: Kuwait
Area: 6,880 sq. mi.
17,820 sq. km.
Pop.: 2,183,161; growth rate: 3.33%
Govt: constitutional monarchy
Independence: June 19, 1961
U.N. Admission: May 14, 1963
GDP: $30.9 billion; per capita: $15,100
Currency: Kuwaiti dinar

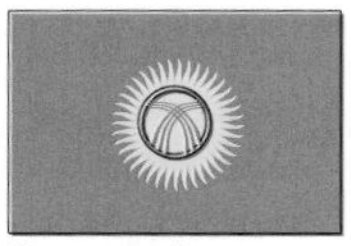

Kyrgyzstan* 87/F4
Capital: Bishkek
Area: 76,641 sq. mi.
198,500 sq. km.
Pop.: 4,892,808; growth rate: 1.45%
Govt: republic
Independence: August 31, 1991
U.N. Admission: March 2, 1992
GDP: $13.5 billion; per capita: $2,800
Currency: Kyrgyzstani som

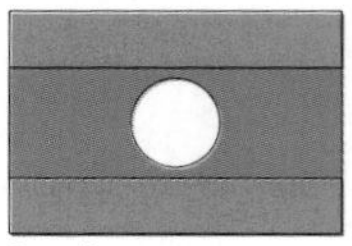

Laos* 78/C2
Capital: Vientiane
Area: 91,428 sq. mi.
236,800 sq. km.
Pop.: 5,921,545; growth rate: 2.47%
Govt: Communist state
Independence: July 19, 1949
U.N. Admission: December 14,1955
GDP: $9.2 billion; per capita: $1,630
Currency: kip

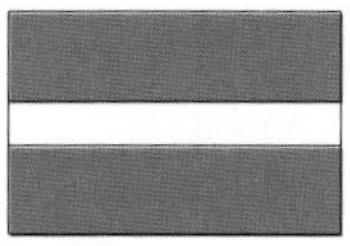

Latvia* 39/L3
Capital: Riga
Area: 24,749 sq. mi.
64,100 sq. km.
Pop.: 2,348,784; growth rate: -0.77%
Govt: parliamentary democracy
Independence: September 6, 1991
U.N. Admission: September 17, 1991
GDP: $18.6 billion; per capita: $7,800
Currency: Latvian lat

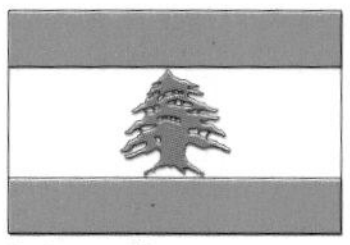

Lebanon* 91/D3
Capital: Beirut
Area: 4,015 sq. mi.
10,339 sq. km.
Pop.: 3,727,703; growth rate: 1.36%
Govt: republic
Independence: November 22, 1943
U.N. Admission: October 24, 1945
GDP: $18.8 billion; per capita: $5,200
Currency: Lebanese pound

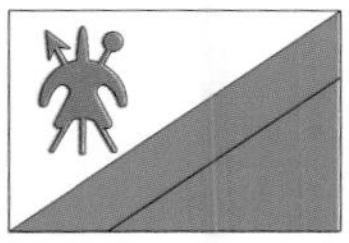

Lesotho* 106/E6
Capital: Maseru
Area: 11,720 sq. mi.
30,355 sq. km.
Pop.: 1,861,959; growth rate: 1.33%
Govt: constitutional monarchy
Independence: October 4, 1966
U.N. Admission: October 17, 1966
GDP: $5.3 billion; per capita: $2,450
Currency: loti; South African rand

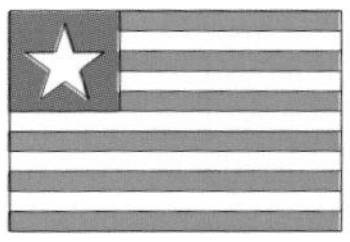

Liberia* 102/C5
Capital: Monrovia
Area: 43,000 sq. mi.
111,370 sq. km.
Pop.: 3,317,176; growth rate: 1.91%
Govt: republic
Independence: July 26, 1847
U.N. Admission: November 2, 1945
GDP: $3.6 billion; per capita: $1,100
Currency: Liberian dollar

Libya* 97/J2
Capital: Tripoli
Area: 679,358 sq. mi.
1,759,537 sq. km.
Pop.: 5,499,074; growth rate: 2.41%
Govt: military dictatorship
Independence: December 24, 1951
U.N. Admission: December 14, 1955
GDP: $40 billion; per capita: $7,600
Currency: Libyan dinar

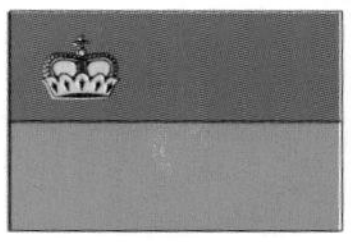

Lietchtenstein* 57/F3
Capital: Vaduz
Area: 61 sq. mi.
158 sq. km.
Pop.: 33,145; growth rate: 0.94%
Govt: constitutional monarchy
Independence: January 23, 1719
U.N. Admission: September 18, 1990
GDP: $730 million; per capita: $23,000
Currency: Swiss franc

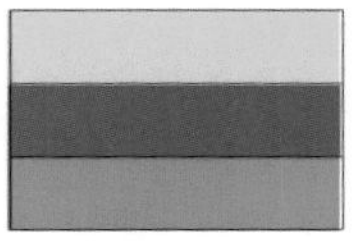

Lithuania* 39/K4
Capital: Vilnius
Area: 25,174 sq. mi.
65,200 sq. km.
Pop.: 3,592,561; growth rate: -0.25%
Govt: parliamentary democracy
Independence: September 6, 1991
U.N. Admission: September 17, 1991
GDP: $27.4 billion; per capita: $7,600
Currency: Lithuanian litas

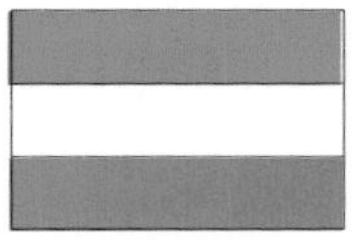

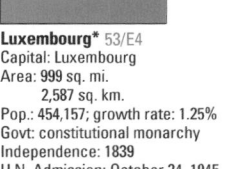

Luxembourg* 53/E4
Capital: Luxembourg
Area: 999 sq. mi.
2,587 sq. km.
Pop.: 454,157; growth rate: 1.25%
Govt: constitutional monarchy
Independence: 1839
U.N. Admission: October 24, 1945
GDP: $19.2 billion; per capita: $43,400
Currency: euro

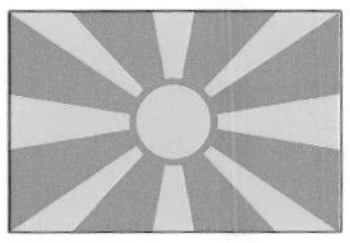

Macedonia (F.Y.R.O.M.)* 47/G2
Capital: Skopje
Area: 9,781 sq. mi.
25,333 sq. km.
Pop.: 2,063,122; growth rate: 0.41%
Govt: emerging democracy
Independence: September 17, 1991
U.N. Admission: April 8, 1993
GDP: $9 billion; per capita: $4,400
Currency: Macedonian denar

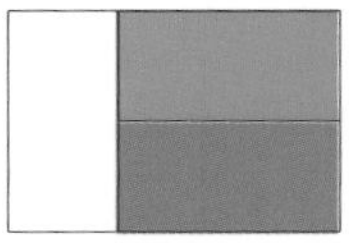

Madagascar* 107/H8
Capital: Antananarivo
Area: 226,657 sq. mi.
587,041 sq. km.
Pop.: 16,979,744; growth rate: 3.03%
Govt: republic
Independence: June 26, 1960
U.N. Admission: September 20, 1960
GDP: $14 billion; per capita: $870
Currency: Malagasy franc

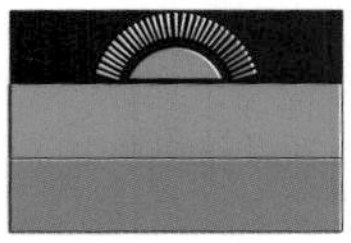

Malawi* 105/F3
Capital: Lilongwe
Area: 45,747 sq. mi.
118,485 sq. km.
Pop.: 11,651,239; growth rate: 1.39%
Govt: multiparty democracy
Independence: July 6, 1964
U.N. Admission: December 1, 1964
GDP: $7 billion; per capita: $660
Currency: Malawian kwacha

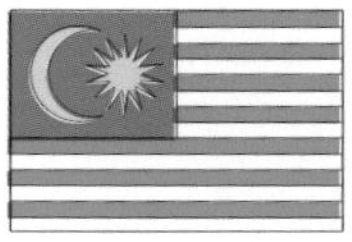

Malaysia* 80/C2
Capital: Kuala Lumpur
Area: 127,316 sq. mi.
329,750 sq. km.
Pop.: 23,092,940; growth rate: 1.91%
Govt: constitutional monarchy
Independence: August 31, 1957
U.N. Admission: September 17, 1957
GDP: $200 billion; per capita: $9,000
Currency: ringgit

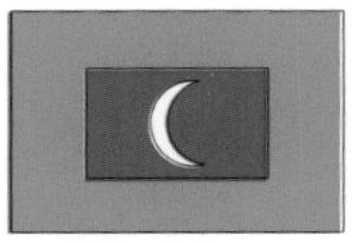

Maldives* 67/G9
Capital: Male
Area: 115 sq. mi.
298 sq. km.
Pop.: 329,684; growth rate: 2.95%
Govt: republic
Independence: July 26, 1965
U.N. Admission: September 21, 1965
GDP: $1.2 billion; per capita: $3,870
Currency: rufiyaa

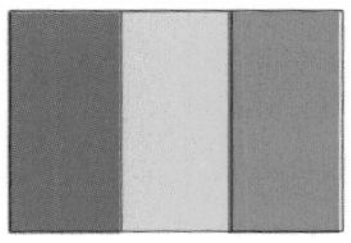

Mali* 96/E4
Capital: Bamako
Area: 478,764 sq. mi.
1,240,000 sq. km.
Pop.: 11,626,219; growth rate: 2.97%
Govt: republic
Independence: September 22, 1960
U.N. Admission: September 28, 1960
GDP: $9.2 billion; per capita: $840
Currency: CFA franc

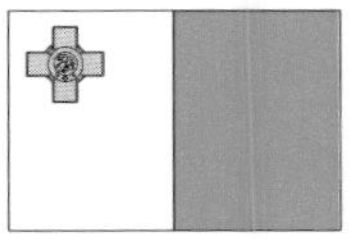

Malta* 46/L7
Capital: Valletta
Area: 122 sq. mi.
316 sq. km.
Pop.: 400,420; growth rate: 0.73%
Govt: republic
Independence: September 21, 1964
U.N. Admission: December 1, 1964
GDP: $5.95 billion; per capita: $15,000
Currency: Maltese lira

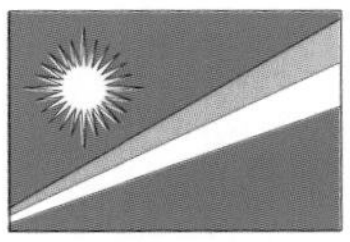

Marshall Islands* 116/G3
Capital: Majuro
Area: 70 sq. mi.
181 sq. km.
Pop.: 56,429; growth rate: 3.89%
Govt: constitutional government
Independence: October 21, 1986
U.N. Admission: September 17, 1991
GDP: $115 million; per capita: $1,600
Currency: US dollar

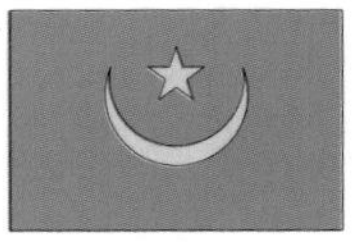

Mauritania* 96/C4
Capital: Nouakchott
Area: 397,953 sq. mi.
1,030,700 sq. km.
Pop.: 2,912,584; growth rate: 2.92%
Govt: republic
Independence: November 28, 1960
U.N. Admission: October 7, 1961
GDP: $5 billion; per capita: $1,800
Currency: ouguiya

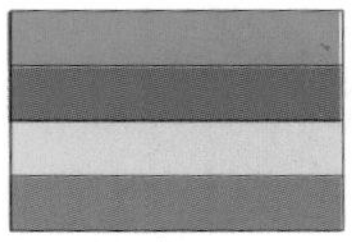

Mauritius* 107/T5
Capital: Port Louis
Area: 718 sq. mi.
1,860 sq. km.
Pop.: 1,210,447; growth rate: 0.86%
Govt: parliamentary democracy
Independence: March 12, 1968
U.N. Admission: April 24, 1964
GDP: $12.9 billion; per capita: $10,800
Currency: Mauritian rupee

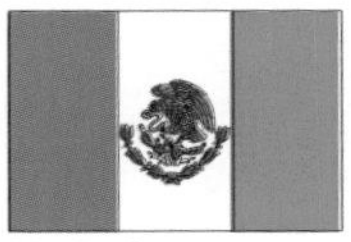

Mexico* 119/G7
Capital: Mexico
Area: 761,601 sq. mi.
1,972,546 sq. km.
Pop.: 104,907,991; growth rate: 1.47%
Govt: federal republic
Independence: September 16, 1810
U.N. Admission: November 7, 1945
GDP: $920 billion; per capita: $9,000
Currency: Mexican peso

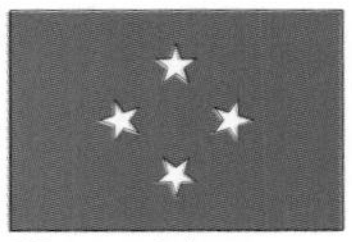

Micronesia* 116/D4
Capital: Palikir
Area: 271 sq. mi.
702 sq. km.
Pop.: 136,973; growth rate: 1.8%
Govt: constitutional government
Independence: November 3, 1986
U.N. Admission: September 17, 1991
GDP: $269 million; per capita: $2,000
Currency: US dollar

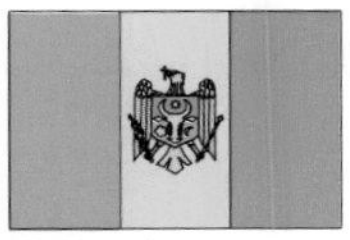

Moldova* 49/H2
Capital: Chişanău
Area: 13,012 sq. mi.
33,700 sq. km.
Pop.: 4,439,502; growth rate: 0.09%
Govt: republic
Independence: August 27, 1991
U.N. Admission: March 2, 1992
GDP: $11.3 billion; per capita: $2,550
Currency: Moldovan leu

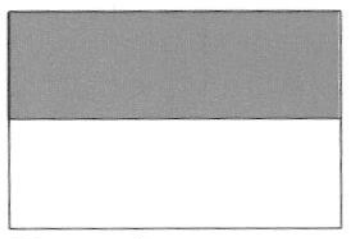

Monaco* 58/J8
Capital: Monaco
Area: 0.7 sq. mi.
1.9 sq. km.
Pop.: 32,130; growth rate: 0.45%
Govt: constitutional monarchy
Independence: 1419
U.N. Admission: May 28, 1993
GDP: $870 million; per capita: $27,000
Currency: euro

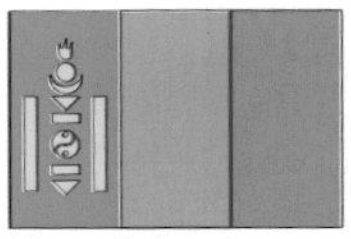

Mongolia* 70/G2
Capital: Ulaanbaatar
Area: 606,163 sq. mi.
1,569,962 sq. km.
Pop.: 2,712,315; growth rate: 1.48%
Govt: republic
Independence: March 13, 1921
U.N. Admission: October 27, 1961
GDP: $4.7 billion; per capita: $1,770
Currency: tugrik

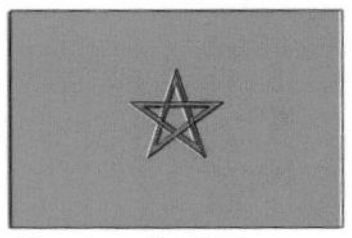

Morocco* 98/D2
Capital: Rabat
Area: 171,414 sq. mi.
446,550 sq. km.
Pop.: 31,689,265; growth rate: 1.68%
Govt: constitutional monarchy
Independence: March 2, 1956
U.N. Admission: November 12, 1956
GDP: $112 billion; per capita: $3,700
Currency: Moroccan dirham

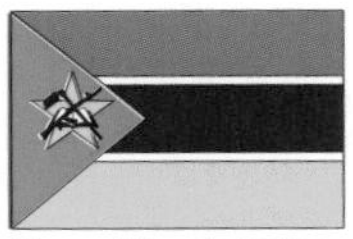

Mozambique* 105/G4
Capital: Maputo
Area: 309,494 sq. mi.
801,590 sq. km.
Pop.: 17,479,266; growth rate: 1.13%
Govt: republic
Independence: June 25, 1975
U.N. Admission: September 16, 1975
GDP: $17.5 billion; per capita: $900
Currency: metical

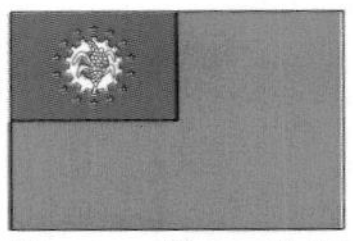

Myanmar (Burma)* 83/G3
Capital: Yangon (Rangoon)
Area: 261,969 sq. mi.
678,500 sq. km.
Pop.: 42,510,537; growth rate: 0.56%
Govt: military regime
Independence: January 4, 1948
U.N. Admission: April 19, 1948
GDP: $63 billion; per capita: $1,500
Currency: kyat

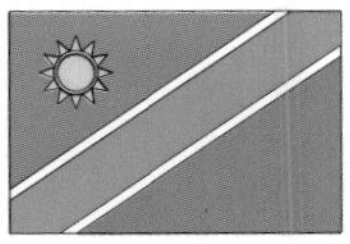

Namibia* 105/G5
Capital: Windhoek
Area: 318,694 sq. mi.
825,418 sq. km.
Pop.: 1,927,447; growth rate: 1.19%
Govt: republic
Independence: March 21, 1990
U.N. Admission: April 23, 1990
GDP: $8.1 billion; per capita: $4,500
Currency: Namibian dollar

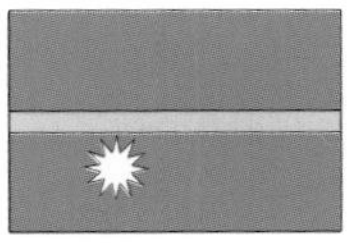

Nauru* 116/F5
Capital: Yaren (district)
Area: 7.7 sq. mi.
20 sq. km.
Pop.: 12,570; growth rate: 1.96%
Govt: republic
Independence: January 31, 1968
U.N. Admission: September 14, 1999
GDP: $60 million; per capita: $5,000
Currency: Australian dollar

Nepal* 84/D1
Capital: Kāthmāndu
Area: 54,663 sq. mi.
141,577 sq. km.
Pop.: 26,469,569; growth rate: 2.29%
Govt: parliamentary democracy
Independence: 1768
U.N. Admission: December 14, 1955
GDP: $35.6 billion; per capita: $1,400
Currency: Nepalese rupee

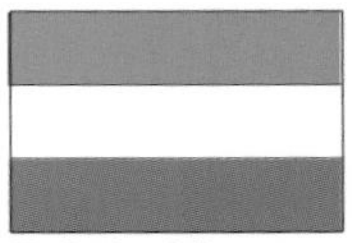

Netherlands* 40/C3
Capital: The Hague; Amsterdam
Area: 14,413 sq. mi.
37,330 sq. km.
Pop.: 16,150,511; growth rate: 0.53%
Govt: constitutional monarchy
Independence: 1579
U.N. Admission: December 10, 1945
GDP: $413 billion; per capita: $25,800
Currency: euro

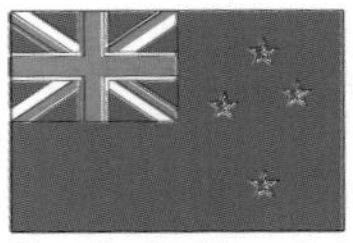

New Zealand* 117/R10
Capital: Wellington
Area: 103,736 sq. mi.
268,676 sq. km.
Pop.: 3,951,307; growth rate: 1.12%
Govt: parliamentary democracy
Independence: September 26, 1907
U.N. Admission: October 24, 1945
GDP: $75.4 billion; per capita: $19,500
Currency: New Zealand dollar

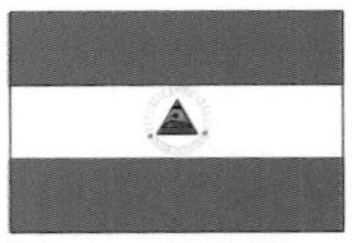

Nicaragua* 145/E3
Capital: Managua
Area: 49,998 sq. mi.
129,494 sq. km.
Pop.: 5,128,517; growth rate: 2.09%
Govt: republic
Independence: September 15, 1821
U.N. Admission: October 24, 1945
GDP: $12.3 billion; per capita: $2,500
Currency: gold cordoba

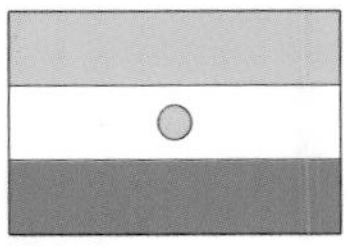

Niger* 96/G4
Capital: Niamey
Area: 489,189 sq. mi.
1,267,000 sq. km.
Pop.: 11,058,590; growth rate: 2.7%
Govt: republic
Independence: August 3, 1960
U.N. Admission: September 20, 1960
GDP: $8.4 billion; per capita: $820
Currency: CFA franc

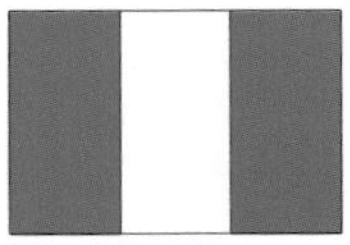

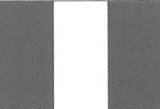

Nigeria* 96/G6
Capital: Abuja
Area: 356,668 sq. mi.
923,770 sq. km.
Pop.: 133,881,703; growth rate: 2.54%
Govt: military government
Independence: October 1, 1960
U.N. Admission: October 7, 1960
GDP: $105.9 billion; per capita: $840
Currency: naira

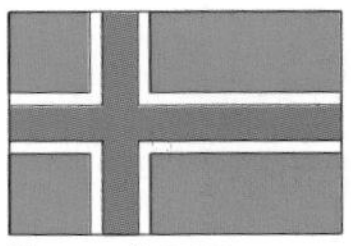

Norway* 37/C3
Capital: Oslo
Area: 125,053 sq. mi.
323,887 sq. km.
Pop.: 4,546,123; growth rate: 0.47%
Govt: constitutional monarchy
Independence: October 26, 1905
U.N. Admission: November 27, 1945
GDP: $138.7 billion; per capita: $30,800
Currency: Norwegian krone

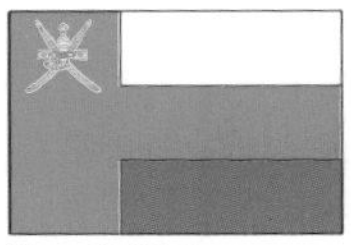

Oman* 89/G4
Capital: Muscat
Area: 82,031 sq. mi.
212,460 sq. km.
Pop.: 2,807,125; growth rate: 3.41%
Govt: monarchy
Independence: 1650
U.N. Admission: October 7, 1971
GDP: $21.5 billion; per capita: $8,200
Currency: Omani rial

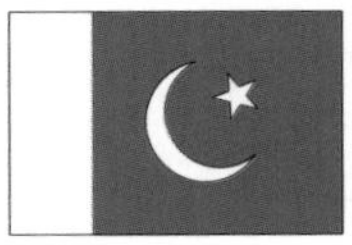

Pakistan* 89/H3
Capital: Islāmābād
Area: 310,403 sq. mi.
803,944 sq. km.
Pop.: 150,694,740; growth rate: 2.06%
Govt: federal republic
Independence: August 14, 1947
U.N. Admission: September 30, 1947
GDP: $299 billion; per capita: $2,100
Currency: Pakistani rupee

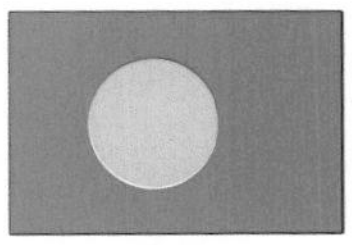

Palau* 116/C4
Capital: Koror
Area: 177 sq. mi.
458 sq. km.
Pop.: 19,717; growth rate: 1.61%
Govt: constitutional government
Independence: October 1, 1994
U.N. Admission: December 15, 1994
GDP: $174 million; per capita: $9,000
Currency: US dollar

World Flags and Reference Guide

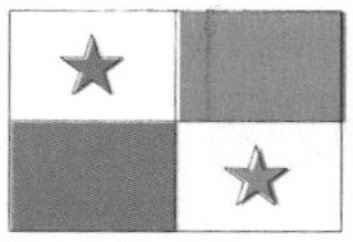

Panamá* 145/F4
Capital: Panamá
Area: 30,193 sq. mi.
78,200 sq. km.
Pop.: 2,960,784; growth rate: 1.26%
Govt: constitutional democracy
Independence: November 3, 1903
U.N. Admission: November 13, 1945
GDP: $16.9 billion; per capita: $5,900
Currency: balboa

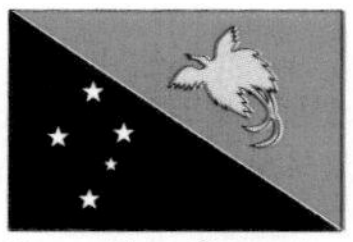

Papua New Guinea* 116/D5
Capital: Port Moresby
Area: 178,259 sq. mi.
461,690 sq. km.
Pop.: 5,295,816; growth rate: 2.39%
Govt: parliamentary democracy
Independence: September 16, 1975
U.N. Admission: October 10, 1975
GDP: $12.2 billion; per capita: $2,400
Currency: kina

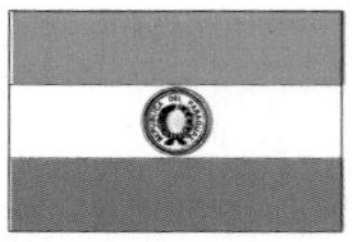

Paraguay* 147/C5
Capital: Asunción
Area: 157,047 sq. mi.
406,752 sq. km.
Pop.: 6,036,900; growth rate: 2.57%
Govt: republic
Independence: May 14, 1811
U.N. Admission: October 24, 1945
GDP: $26.2 billion; per capita: $4,600
Currency: guarani

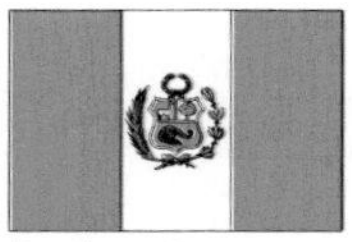

Peru* 156/C3
Capital: Lima
Area: 496,222 sq. mi.
1,285,215 sq. km.
Pop.: 28,409,897; growth rate: 1.66%
Govt: republic
Independence: July 28, 1821
U.N. Admission: October 31, 1945
GDP: $132 billion; per capita: $4,800
Currency: nuevo sol

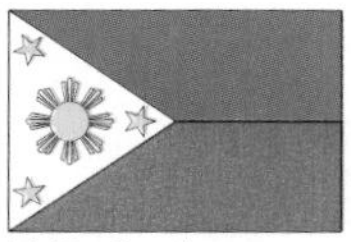

Philippines* 79/D5
Capital: Manila
Area: 115,830 sq. mi.
300,000 sq. km.
Pop.: 84,619,974; growth rate: 1.99%
Govt: republic
Independence: July 4, 1946
U.N. Admission: October 24, 1945
GDP: $335 billion; per capita: $4,000
Currency: Philippine peso

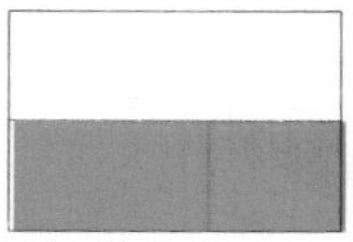

Poland* 41/K2
Capital: Warsaw
Area: 120,725 sq. mi.
312,678 sq. km.
Pop.: 38,622,660; growth rate: -0.02%
Govt: republic
Independence: November 11, 1918
U.N. Admission: October 24, 1945
GDP: $309.6 billion; per capita: $8,800
Currency: zloty

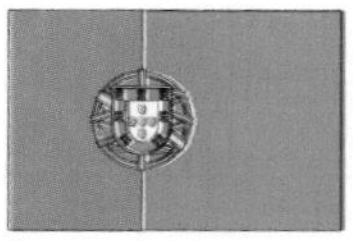

Portugal* 44/A3
Capital: Lisbon
Area: 35,549 sq. mi.
92,072 sq. km.
Pop.: 10,102,022; growth rate: 0.18%
Govt: parliamentary democracy
Independence: October 5, 1910
U.N. Admission: December 14, 1955
GDP: $174.1 billion; per capita: $17,300
Currency: euro

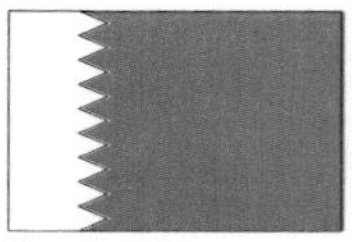

Qatar* 88/F3
Capital: Doha
Area: 4,247 sq. mi.
11,000 sq. km.
Pop.: 817,052; growth rate: 3.02%
Govt: traditional monarchy
Independence: September 3, 1971
U.N. Admission: September 21, 1971
GDP: $16.3 billion; per capita: $21,200
Currency: Qatari rial

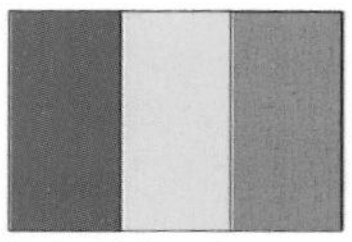

Romania* 49/F3
Capital: Bucharest
Area: 91,690 sq. mi.
237,500 sq. km.
Pop.: 22,271,839; growth rate: -0.21%
Govt: republic
Independence: 1881
U.N. Admission: December 14, 1955
GDP: $152.7 billion; per capita: $6,800
Currency: leu

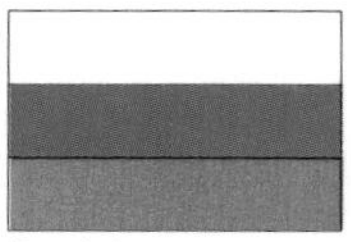

Russia* 64/H3
Capital: Moscow
Area: 6,582,812 sq. mi.
17,075,400 sq. km.
Pop.: 144,526,278; growth rate: -0.33%
Govt: federation
Independence: August 24, 1991
U.N. Admission: October 24, 1945
GDP: $1.2 trillion; per capita: $8,300
Currency: Russian ruble

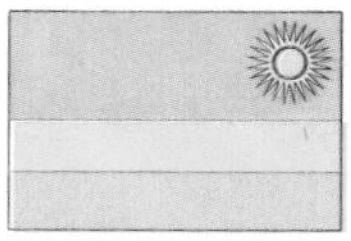

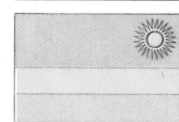

Rwanda* 104/A3
Capital: Kigali
Area: 10,169 sq. mi.
26,337 sq. km.
Pop.: 7,810,056; growth rate: 1.16%
Govt: republic
Independence: July 1, 1962
U.N. Admission: September 18, 1962
GDP: $7.2 billion; per capita: $1,000
Currency: Rwandan franc

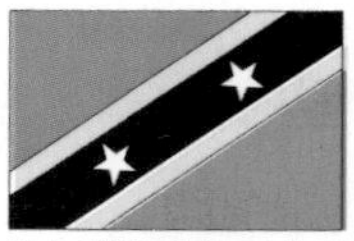

Saint Kitts & Nevis* 141/N8
Capital: Basseterre
Area: 104 sq. mi.
269 sq. km.
Pop.: 38,763; growth rate: 0.01%
Govt: constitutional monarchy
Independence: September 19, 1983
U.N. Admission: September 23, 1983
GDP: $339 million; per capita: $8,700
Currency: EC dollar

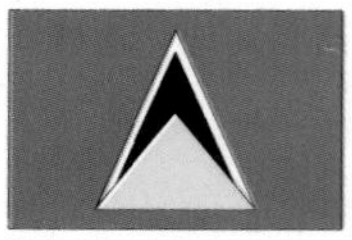

Saint Lucia* 141/N9
Capital: Castries
Area: 238 sq. mi.
616 sq. km.
Pop.: 162,157; growth rate: 1.24%
Govt: parliamentary democracy
Independence: February 22, 1979
U.N. Admission: September 18, 1979
GDP: $700 million; per capita: $4,400
Currency: EC dollar

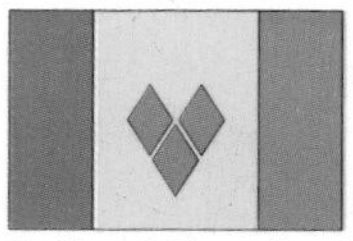

St. Vinc. & Grenadines* 141/N9
Capital: Kingstown
Area: 131 sq. mi.
340 sq. km.
Pop.: 116,812; growth rate: 0.37%
Govt: parliamentary democracy
Independence: October 27, 1979
U.N. Admission: September 16, 1980
GDP: $339 million; per capita: $2,900
Currency: EC dollar

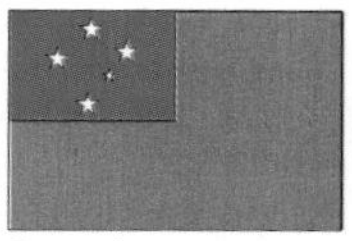

Samoa* 117/H6
Capital: Apia
Area: 1,104 sq. mi.
2,860 sq. km.
Pop.: 178,173; growth rate: -0.25%
Govt: constitutional monarchy
Independence: January 1, 1962
U.N. Admission: December 15, 1976
GDP: $618 million; per capita: $3,500
Currency: tala

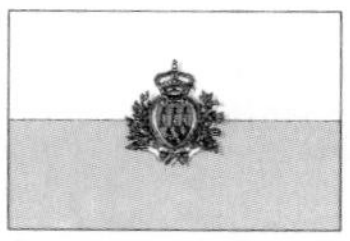

San Marino* 59/F5
Capital: San Marino
Area: 23.4 sq. mi.
60.6 sq. km.
Pop.: 28,119; growth rate: 1.41%
Govt: republic
Independence: 301 A.D.
U.N. Admission: March 2, 1992
GDP: $940 million; per capita: $34,600
Currency: euro

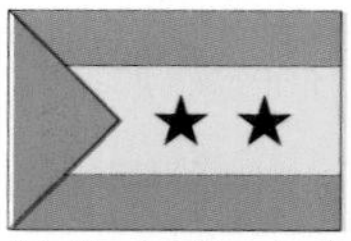

São Tomé & Príncipe* 96/F7
Capital: São Tomé
Area: 371 sq. mi.
960 sq. km.
Pop.: 175,883; growth rate: 3.18%
Govt: republic
Independence: July 12, 1975
U.N. Admission: September 16, 1975
GDP: $189 million; per capita: $1,200
Currency: dobra

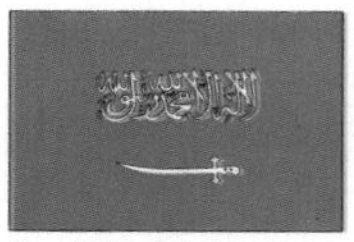

Saudi Arabia* 88/D4
Capital: Riyadh
Area: 756,981 sq. mi.
1,960,582 sq. km.
Pop.: 24,293,844; growth rate: 3.27%
Govt: monarchy
Independence: September 23, 1932
U.N. Admission: October 24, 1945
GDP: $241 billion; per capita: $10,600
Currency: Saudi riyal

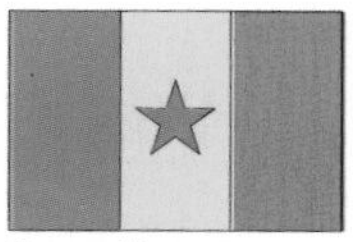

Senegal* 102/B3
Capital: Dakar
Area: 75,954 sq. mi.
196,720 sq. km.
Pop.: 10,580,307; growth rate: 2.91%
Govt: multiparty democracy
Independence: April 4, 1960
U.N. Admission: September 28, 1960
GDP: $16.2 billion; per capita: $1,580
Currency: CFA franc

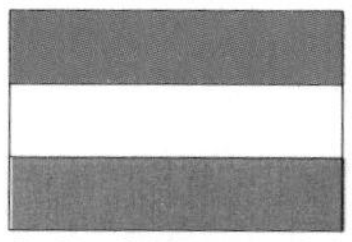

Serbia & Montenegro* 48/D3
Capital: Belgrade
Area: 39,517 sq. mi.
102,350 sq. km.
Pop.: 10,655,774; growth rate: -0.12%
Govt: republic
Independence: April 11, 1992
U.N. Admission: October 24, 1945
GDP: $24 billion; per capita: $2,250
Currency: new Yugoslav dinar

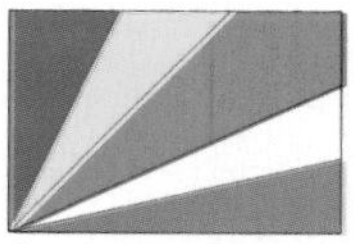

Seychelles* 23/M6
Capital: Victoria
Area: 176 sq. mi.
455 sq. km.
Pop.: 80,469; growth rate: 0.47%
Govt: republic
Independence: June 29, 1976
U.N. Admission: September 1, 1976
GDP: $605 million; per capita: $7,600
Currency: Seychelles rupee

Sierra Leone* 102/B4
Capital: Freetown
Area: 27,699 sq. mi.
71,740 sq. km.
Pop.: 5,732,681; growth rate: 3.21%
Govt: constitutional democracy
Independence: April 27, 1961
U.N. Admission: September 27, 1961
GDP: $2.7 billion; per capita: $500
Currency: leone

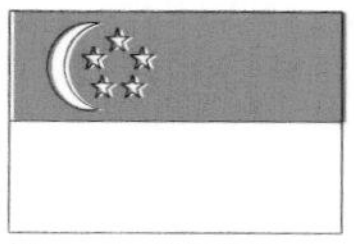

Singapore* 80/B3
Capital: Singapore
Area: 244 sq. mi.
632.6 sq. km.
Pop.: 4,608,595; growth rate: 3.46%
Govt: republic
Independence: August 6, 1965
U.N. Admission: September 21, 1965
GDP: $106.3 billion; per capita: $24,700
Currency: Singapore dollar

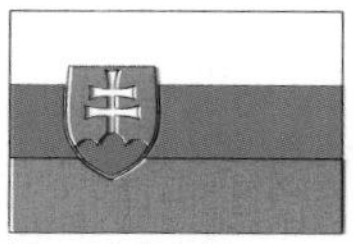

Slovakia* 41/K4
Capital: Bratislava
Area: 18,924 sq. mi.
49,013 sq. km.
Pop.: 5,430,033; growth rate: 0.14%
Govt: parliamentary democracy
Independence: January 1, 1993
U.N. Admission: January 19, 1993
GDP: $62 billion; per capita: $11,500
Currency: Slovak koruna

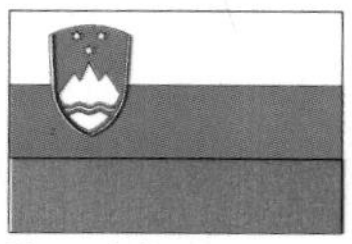

Slovenia* 48/B3
Capital: Ljubljana
Area: 7,898 sq. mi.
20,456 sq. km.
Pop.: 1,935,677; growth rate: 0.14%
Govt: parliamentary republic
Independence: June 25, 1991
U.N. Admission: May 22, 1992
GDP: $31 billion; per capita: $16,000
Currency: tolar

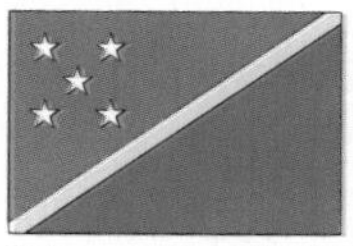

Solomon Islands* 116/E6
Capital: Honiara
Area: 11,500 sq. mi.
29,785 sq. km.
Pop.: 509,190; growth rate: 2.91%
Govt: parliamentary democracy
Independence: July 7, 1978
U.N. Admission: September 19, 1978
GDP: $800 million; per capita: $1,700
Currency: Solomon Islands dollar

Somalia* 97/Q6
Capital: Mogadishu
Area: 246,200 sq. mi.
637,658 sq. km.
Pop.: 8,025,190; growth rate: 3.46%
Govt: transitional
Independence: July 1, 1960
U.N. Admission: September 20, 1960
GDP: $4.1 billion; per capita: $550
Currency: Somali shilling

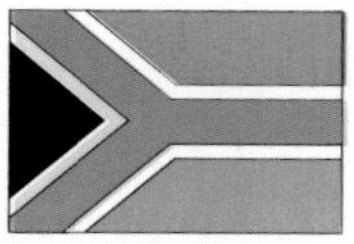

South Africa* 105/D6
Capital: Cape Town; Pretoria
Area: 471,008 sq. mi.
1,219,912 sq. km.
Pop.: 42,768,678; growth rate: 0.02%
Govt: republic
Independence: May 31, 1910
U.N. Admission: November 7, 1945
GDP: $412 billion; per capita: $9,400
Currency: rand

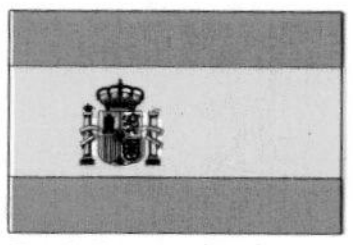

Spain* 44/C2
Capital: Madrid
Area: 194,881 sq. mi.
504,742 sq. km.
Pop.: 40,217,413; growth rate: 0.09%
Govt: parliamentary monarchy
Independence: 1492
U.N. Admission: December 14, 1955
GDP: $757 billion; per capita: $18,900
Currency: euro

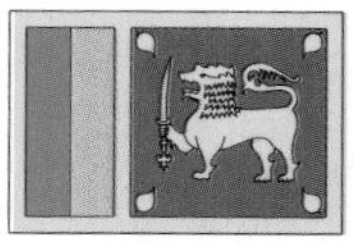

Sri Lanka* 82/D6
Capital: Colombo; Sri Jayewardenepura Kotte
Area: 25,332 sq. mi.
65,610 sq. km.
Pop.: 19,742,439; growth rate: 0.85%
Govt: republic
Independence: February 4, 1948
U.N. Admission: December 14, 1955
GDP: $62.7 billion; per capita: $3,250
Currency: Sri Lankan rupee

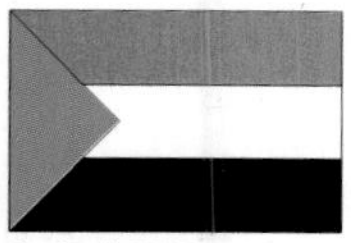

Sudan* 97/L5
Capital: Khartoum
Area: 967,494 sq. mi.
2,505,809 sq. km.
Pop.: 38,114,160; growth rate: 2.73%
Govt: authoritarian regime
Independence: January 1, 1956
U.N. Admission: November 12, 1956
GDP: $49.3 billion; per capita: $1,360
Currency: Sudanese dinar

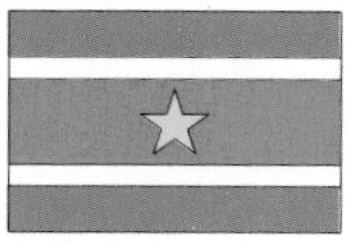

Suriname* 153/G3
Capital: Paramaribo
Area: 63,039 sq. mi.
163,270 sq. km.
Pop.: 435,449; growth rate: 0.55%
Govt: constitutional democracy
Independence: November 25, 1975
U.N. Admission: December 4, 1975
GDP: $1.5 billion; per capita: $3,500
Currency: Surinamese guilder

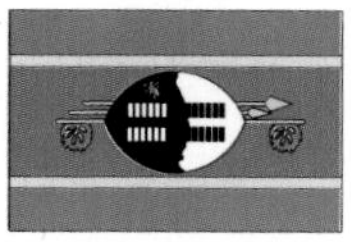

Swaziland* 107/E2
Capital: Mbabane; Lobamba
Area: 6,705 sq. mi.
17,366 sq. km.
Pop.: 1,161,219; growth rate: 1.63%
Govt: monarchy
Independence: September 6, 1968
U.N. Admission: September 24, 1968
GDP: $4.6 billion; per capita: $4,200
Currency: lilangeni

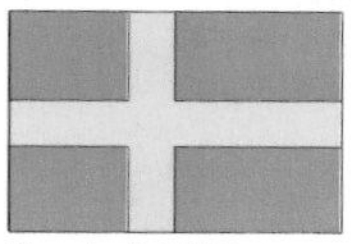

Sweden* 37/E3
Capital: Stockholm
Area: 173,665 sq. mi.
449,792 sq. km.
Pop.: 8,878,085; growth rate: 0.02%
Govt: constitutional monarchy
Independence: June 6, 1523
U.N. Admission: November 19, 1946
GDP: $219 billion; per capita: $24,700
Currency: Swedish krona

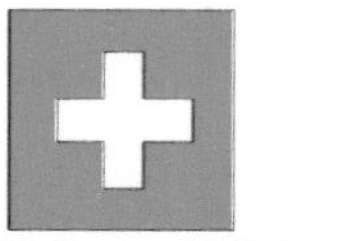

Switzerland* 59/D4
Capital: Bern
Area: 15,493 sq. mi.
41,292 sq. km.
Pop.: 7,318,638; growth rate: 0.24%
Govt: federal republic
Independence: August 1, 1921
U.N. Admission: September 10, 2002
GDP: $226 billion; per capita: $31,100
Currency: Swiss franc

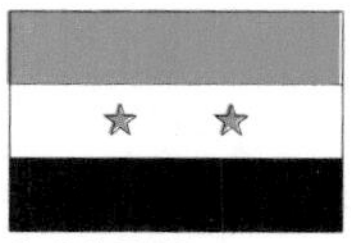

Syria* 90/D3
Capital: Damascus
Area: 71,498 sq. mi.
185,180 sq. km.
Pop.: 17,585,540; growth rate: 2.5%
Govt: military regime
Independence: April 17, 1946
U.N. Admission: October 24, 1945
GDP: $52.4 billion; per capita: $3,200
Currency: Syrian pound

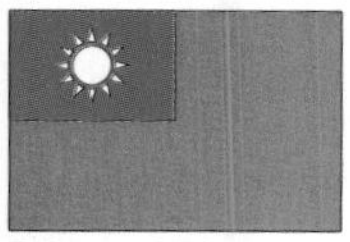

Taiwan 79/D3
Capital: T'aipei
Area: 13,971 sq. mi.
36,185 sq. km.
Pop.: 22,603,000; growth rate: 0.78%
Govt: multiparty democracy
Independence: 1949 (nationalist govt.)
U.N. Admission: non-member
GDP: $386 billion; per capita: $17,200
Currency: New Taiwan dollar

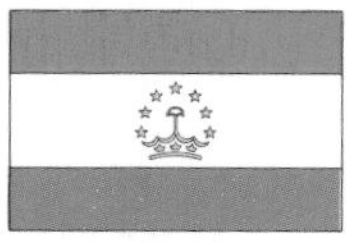

Tajikistan* 87/E5
Capital: Dushande
Area: 55,251 sq. mi.
143,100 sq. km.
Pop.: 6,863,752; growth rate: 2.12%
Govt: republic
Independence: September 9, 1991
U.N. Admission: March 2, 1992
GDP: $7.5 billion; per capita: $1,140
Currency: somoni

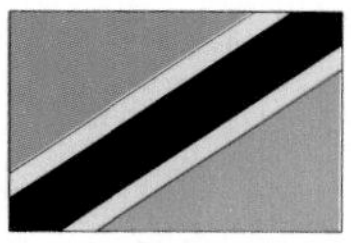

Tanzania* 104/B4
Capital: Dar es Salaam
Area: 364,699 sq. mi.
945.090 sq. km.
Pop.: 35,922,454; growth rate: 2.6%
Govt: republic
Independence: April 26, 1964
U.N. Admission: December 14, 1961
GDP: $22.1 billion; per capita: $610
Currency: Tanzanian shilling

Thailand* 78/C3
Capital: Bangkok
Area: 198,455 sq. mi.
513,998 sq. km.
Pop.: 64,265,276; growth rate: 0.88%
Govt: constitutional monarchy
Independence: 1238 (traditional date)
U.N. Admission: December 16, 1946
GDP: $410 billion; per capita: $6,600
Currency: baht

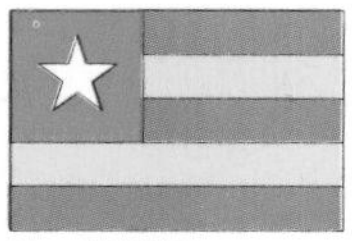

Togo* 103/F4
Capital: Lomé
Area: 21,927 sq. mi.
56,790 sq. km.
Pop.: 5,429,299; growth rate: 2.48%
Govt: republic
Independence: April 27, 1960
U.N. Admission: September 20, 1960
GDP: $7.6 billion; per capita: $1,500
Currency: CFA franc

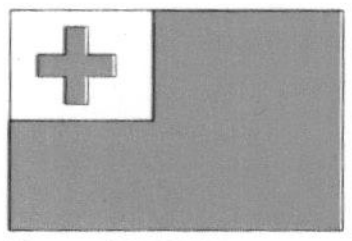

Tonga* 117/H7
Capital: Nuku'alofa
Area: 289 sq. mi.
748 sq. km.
Pop.: 108,141; growth rate: 1.85%
Govt: constitutional monarchy
Independence: June 4, 1970
U.N. Admission: September 14, 1999
GDP: $225 million; per capita: $2,200
Currency: pa'anga

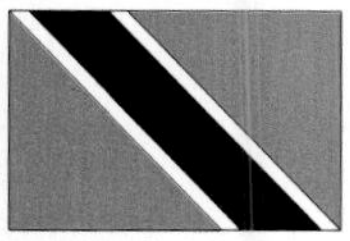

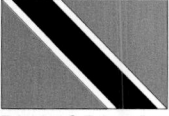

Trinidad & Tobago* 141/N10
Capital: Port-of-Spain
Area: 1,980 sq. mi.
5,128 sq. km.
Pop.: 1,104,209; growth rate: -0.52%
Govt: parliamentary democracy
Independence: August 31, 1962
U.N. Admission: September 18, 1992
GDP: $10.6 billion; per capita: $9,000
Currency: Trinidad & Tobago dollar

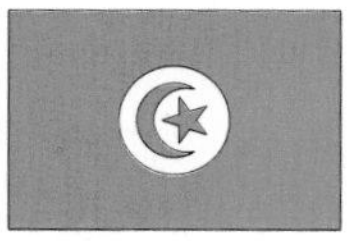

Tunisia* 99/H2
Capital: Tunis
Area: 63,170 sq. mi.
163,610 sq. km.
Pop.: 9,924,742; growth rate: 1.12%
Govt: republic
Independence: March 20, 1956
U.N. Admission: November 12, 1956
GDP: $64.5 billion; per capita: $6,600
Currency: Tunisian dinar

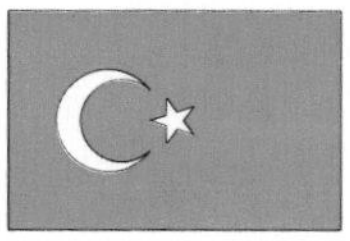

Turkey* 90/C2
Capital: Ankara
Area: 301,382 sq. mi.
780,580 sq. km.
Pop.: 68,109,469; growth rate: 1.2%
Govt: parliamentary democracy
Independence: October 29, 1923
U.N. Admission: December 24, 1945
GDP: $443 billion; per capita: $6,700
Currency: Turkish lira

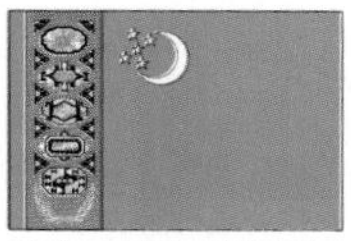

Turkmenistan* 87/C5
Capital: Ashgabat
Area: 188,455 sq. mi.
488,100 sq. km.
Pop.: 4,775,544; growth rate: 1.84%
Govt: republic
Independence: October 27, 1971
U.N. Admission: March 2, 1992
GDP: $21.5 billion; per capita: $4,700
Currency: Turkmen manat

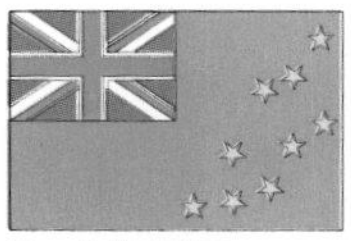

Tuvalu* 116/G5
Capital: Funafuti
Area: 9.78 sq. mi.
25.33 sq. km.
Pop.: 11,305; growth rate: 1.4%
Govt: democracy
Independence: October 1, 1978
U.N. Admission: September 5, 2000
GDP: $12.2 million; per capita: $1,100
Currency: Australian dollar

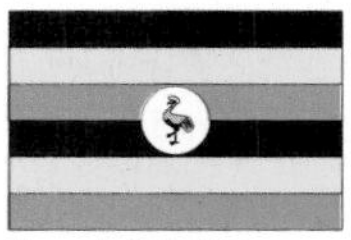

Uganda* 104/B2
Capital: Kampala
Area: 91,076 sq. mi.
235,887 sq. km.
Pop.: 25,632,794; growth rate: 2.94%
Govt: republic
Independence: October 9, 1962
U.N. Admission: October 25, 1992
GDP: $29 billion; per capita: $1,200
Currency: Ugandan shilling

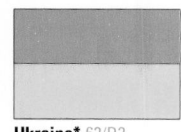

Ukraine* 62/D2
Capital: Kiev
Area: 233,089 sq. mi.
603,700 sq. km.
Pop.: 48,055,439; growth rate: -0.72%
Govt: republic
Independence: December 1, 1991
U.N. Admission: October 24, 1945
GDP: $205 billion; per capita: $4,200
Currency: hryvnia

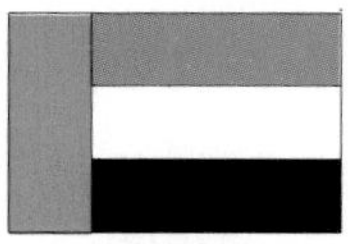

United Arab Emirates* 88/F4
Capital: Abu Dhabi
Area: 29,182 sq. mi.
75,581 sq. km.
Pop.: 2,484,818; growth rate: 1.58%
Govt: federation
Independence: December 2, 1971
U.N. Admission: December 9, 1971
GDP: $51 billion; per capita: $21,100
Currency: Emirati dirham

United Kingdom* 31/R9
Capital: London
Area: 94,399 sq. mi.
244,493 sq. km.
Pop.: 60,094,648; growth rate: 0.21%
Govt: constitutional monarchy
Independence: January 1, 1801
U.N. Admission: October 24, 1945
GDP: $1.47 trillion; per capita: $24,700
Currency: British pound

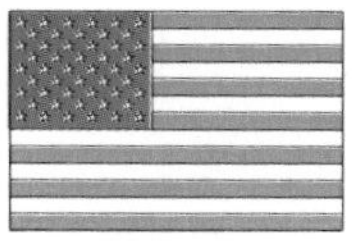

United States* 124
Capital: Washigton, D.C.
Area: 3,618,765 sq. mi.
9,372,610 sq. km.
Pop.: 290,342,554; growth rate: 0.89%
Govt: federal republic
Independence: July 4, 1776
U.N. Admission: October 24, 1945
GDP: $10.08 trillion; per capita: $36,300
Currency: US dollar

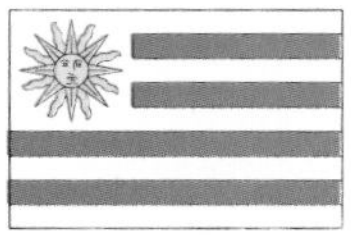

Uruguay* 157/E3
Capital: Montevideo
Area: 68,039 sq. mi.
176,220 sq. km.
Pop.: 3,413,329; growth rate: 0.79%
Govt: republic
Independence: August 25, 1828
U.N. Admission: December 18, 1945
GDP: $31 billion; per capita: $9,200
Currency: Uruguayan peso

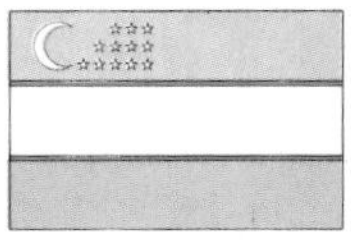

Uzbekistan* 87/D4
Capital: Tashkent
Area: 172,741 sq. mi.
447,400 sq. km.
Pop.: 25,981,647; growth rate: 1.62%
Govt: republic
Independence: August 31, 1991
U.N. Admission: March 2, 1992
GDP: $62 billion; per capita: $2,500
Currency: Uzbekistani sum

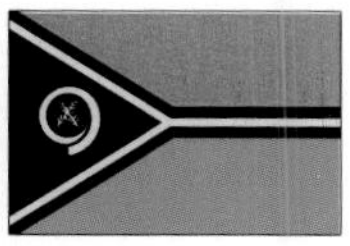

Vanuatu* 116/F6
Capital: Port-Vila
Area: 5,700 sq. mi.
14,763 sq. km.
Pop.: 199,414; growth rate: 1.66%
Govt: republic
Independence: July 30, 1980
U.N. Admission: September 15, 1981
GDP: $257 million; per capita: $1,300
Currency: vatu

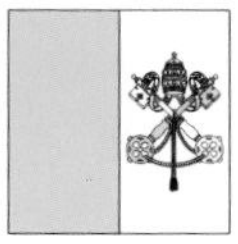

Vatican City 46/C2
Capital: --
Area: 0.17 sq. mi.
0.44 sq. km.
Pop.: 900; growth rate: 1.15%
Govt: ecclesiastical
Independence: February 11, 1929
U.N. Admission: observer status
GDP: N/A; per capita: N/A
Currency: euro

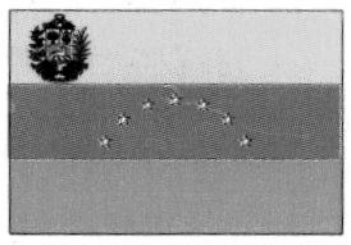

Venezuela* 153/E3
Capital: Caracas
Area: 352,143 sq. mi.
912,050 sq. km.
Pop.: 24,654,694; growth rate: 1.52%
Govt: republic
Independence: July 5, 1811
U.N. Admission: November 15, 1945
GDP: $146.2 billion; per capita: $6,100
Currency: bolivar

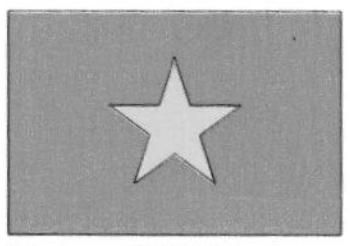

Vietnam* 78/D2
Capital: Hanoi
Area: 127,243 sq. mi.
329,560 sq. km.
Pop.: 81,624,716; growth rate: 1.43%
Govt: communist state
Independence: September 2, 1945
U.N. Admission: September 20, 1977
GDP: $168 billion; per capita: $2,100
Currency: dong

Yemen* 88/E5
Capital: Sanaa
Area: 203,849 sq. mi.
527,970 sq. km.
Pop.: 19,349,881; growth rate: 3.4%
Govt: republic
Independence: May 22, 1990
U.N. Admission: September 7, 1947
GDP: $14.8 billion; per capita: $820
Currency: Yemeni rial

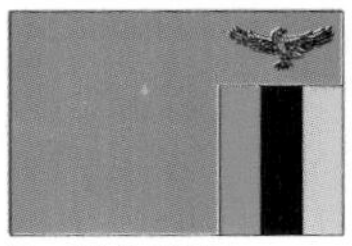

Zambia* 105/E3
Capital: Lusaka
Area: 290.586 sq. mi.
752,618 sq. km.
Pop.: 10,307,333; growth rate: 1.9%
Govt: republic
Independence: October 24, 1964
U.N. Admission: December 1, 1964
GDP: $8.5 billion; per capita: $870
Currency: Zambian kwacha

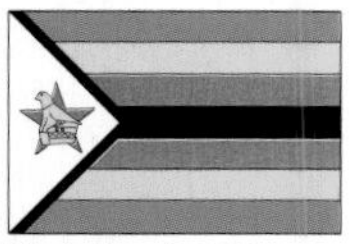

Zimbabwe* 105/E4
Capital: Harare
Area: 150,803 sq. mi.
390,580 sq. km.
Pop.: 12,576,742; growth rate: 0.05%
Govt: parliamentary democracy
Independence: April 18, 1980
U.N. Admission: August 25, 1980
GDP: $28 billion; per capita: $2,450
Currency: Zimbabwean dollar

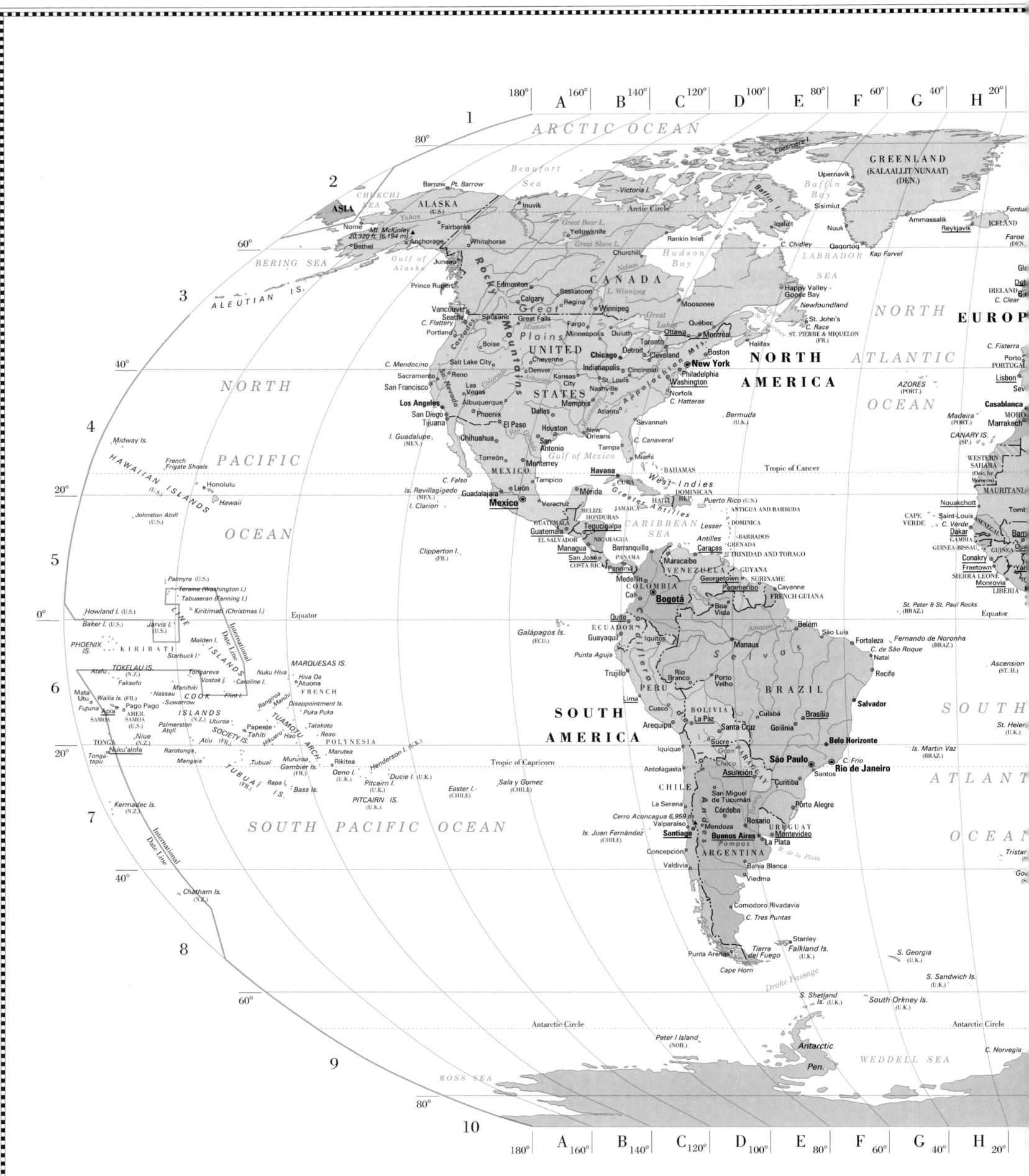

World

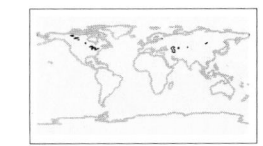

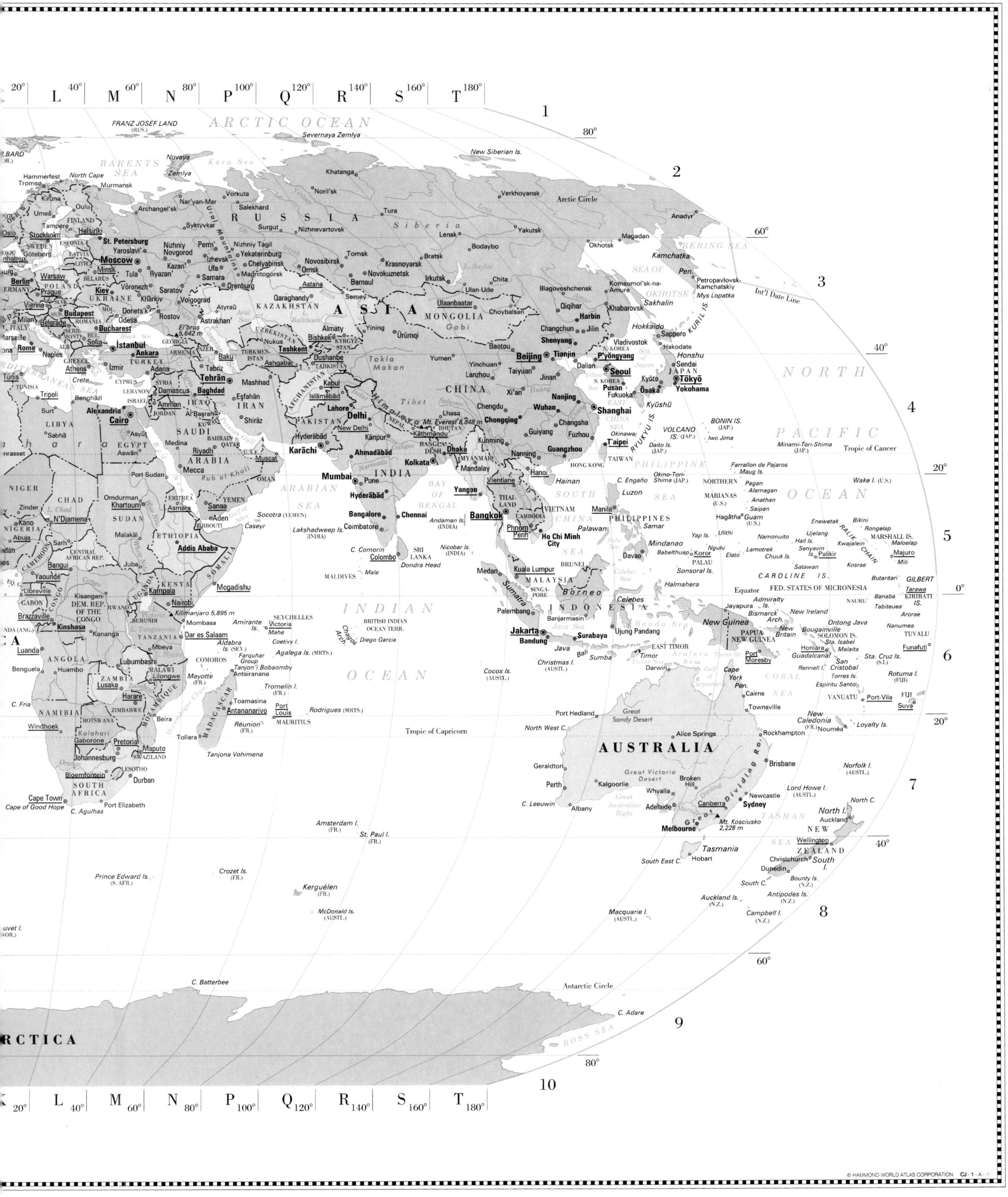

POPULATION OF CITIES AND TOWNS

- ◉ OVER 5,000,000
- ◉ 500,000 - 1,999,999
- ◉ 2,000,000 - 4,999,999
- ○ UNDER 500,000

SCALE 1:79,500,000   ROBINSON PROJECTION   STANDARD PARALLELS 38°N AND 38°S

MILES 0   1000   2000   3000   4000

KILOMETERS 0   1000   2000   3000   4000

© HAMMOND WORLD ATLAS CORPORATION   CJ - 1 - A

Map labels

20° 40° 60° 80° 100° 120° 140° 160° 180°

ARCTIC OCEAN

Svalbard   Franz Josef Land   Severnaya Zemlya   New Siberian Is.   80°

Spbergen   Nordkapp   BARENTS SEA   Novaya Zemlya   Kara Sea   Yamal Pen.   New Siberian Is.   Arctic Circle   60°

EGIAN   Kjølen   Kola Pen.   White Sea   Ob'   West Siberian Plain   Central Siberian Plateau   Lena   Kolyma Ra.   BERING SEA   Kamchatka Pen.

Stockholm   L. Ladoga   Moscow   Yenisey   Lena   Aldan   L. Baikal   SEA OF OKHOTSK   Kuril Is.   NORTHWEST PACIFIC BASIN   40°

EUROPE   Baltic Sea   Dnipro   Volga   Kirgiz Steppe   Irtysh   A S I A   Altai Mts.   Gobi Desert   Hokkaido   NORTH

Alps   Carpathians   Black Sea   Aral Sea   L. Balkhash   Tian Shan   Sea of Japan   Honshu   JAPAN TRENCH   PACIFIC

Rome   Istanbul   Caucasus   El'brus 5,642 m   Caspian Sea   Amu Darya   Takla Makan   Kunlun Mts.   Beijing   Yellow Sea   Tōkyō   East China Sea   20°

MEDITERRANEAN SEA   Sicily   Taurus Mts.   Tehrān   Zagros Mts.   Hindu Kush   Himalaya   Mt. Everest 8,848 m   Huang   RYUKYU TRENCH   OCEAN   Tropic of Cancer

Cyprus   Euphrates   Tigris   Indus   Ganges   Taiwan   PHILIPPINE   MARIANA TRENCH   CENTRAL   20°

Cairo   Hijaz   Arabian Pen.   Persian Gulf   Karāchi   Narmada   Hainan   SOUTH   PHILIPPINE SEA BASIN   Mariana Is.   PACIFIC

FRICA   Red Sea   Rub'al Khali   ARABIAN SEA   Mumbai (Bombay)   BAY OF BENGAL   CHINA   Luzon   Manila   OCEAN   BASIN

Sahara   Sudan   Gulf of Aden   Socotra   C. Comorin   Andaman Is.   Isthmus of Kra   Palawan   Challenger Deep -11,033 m   Marshall Is.   5

L. Chad   Blue Nile   Ethiopian Plateau   CARLSBERG RIDGE   Maldive Is.   Sri Lanka   Malay Pen.   Sulu Sea   Mindanao   Caroline Is.   CENTRAL PACIFIC BASIN

White Nile   SOMALI BASIN   Equator   SEA   Celebes Sea   Halmahera   MELANESIAN BASIN   0°

Congo Basin   Kilimanjaro 5,895 m   INDIAN   CENTRAL INDIAN RIDGE   Chagos Arch.   Sumatra   Borneo   Celebes   Bismarck Arch.   6

Kinshasa   L. Victoria   Seychelles   Jakarta   Java Sea   Banda Sea   New Guinea   New Britain   Solomon Is.

GOLA   L. Tanganyika   OCEAN   NINETYEAST RIDGE   Java   Java Trench -7,450 m   Arafura Sea   CORAL   New Hebrides   Fiji Is.

ASIN   L. Nyasa   Comoros Is.   Cocos Is.   Timor Sea   Gulf of Carpentaria   Cape York   Great Barrier Reef   SEA

Luseka   Zambezi   Madagascar   Réunion   Mauritius   20°   New Caledonia   20°

Namib Desert   Johannesburg   BROKEN PLATEAU   AUSTRALIA   Great Dividing Ra.   7

Orange   Drakesberg   SOUTHWEST INDIAN RIDGE   Great Victoria Desert   Darling   Sydney   North C.

Cape of Good Hope   Kerguélen   C. Leeuwin   Great Australian Bight   Murray   Great Dividing Ra.   Mt. Kosciusko 2,228 m   TASMAN   North   40°

McDonald Is.   SOUTHEAST   Melbourne   SEA   South

KERGUELEN PLATEAU   AUSTRALIAN-ANTARCTIC BASIN   INDIAN   Tasmania   8

ENDERBY ABYSSAL PLAIN   RIDGE   60°

Antarctic Circle   C. Batterbee   C. Adare   9

A N T A R C T I C A   ROSS SEA   80°

10

20° 40° 60° 80° 100° 120° 140° 160° 180°

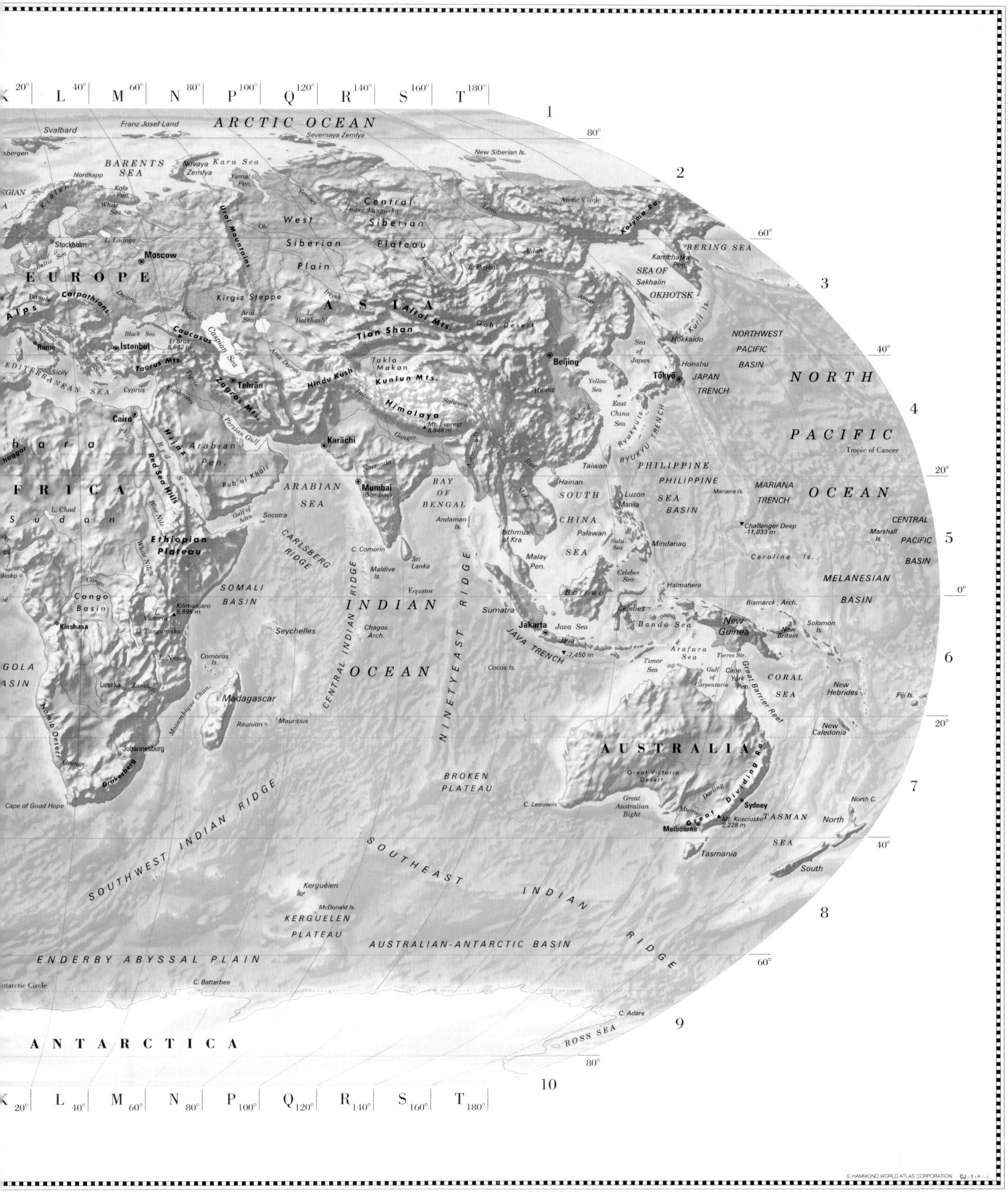

POPULATION OF CITIES AND TOWNS

⊕ OVER 5,000,000   ⊕ 500,000 - 1,999,999
⊕ 2,000,000 - 4,999,999   ⊙ UNDER 500,000

SCALE 1:81,700,000   ROBINSON PROJECTION   STANDARD PARALLELS 38°N AND 38°S

MILES 0 .... 1000 .... 2000 .... 3000 4000

KILOMETERS 0 .... 1000 .... 2000 .... 3000 4000

Europe

The terrain in this high-oblique, northwest-looking image, is indicative of the rugged, mountainous landscape characterizing most of Greece. Two major landform regions are captured in this image: the northwest to southeast-trending Mountains of Pindus in central Greece (north of the Gulf of Corinth), and the Peloponnisos Peninsula (south of the Gulf of Corinth). The Pindus, a massive continuation of the Dinaric Alps of Albania and the former Yugoslavia, make the land inhospitable and travel difficult. This rugged terrain caused the Greeks to become a seafaring people.

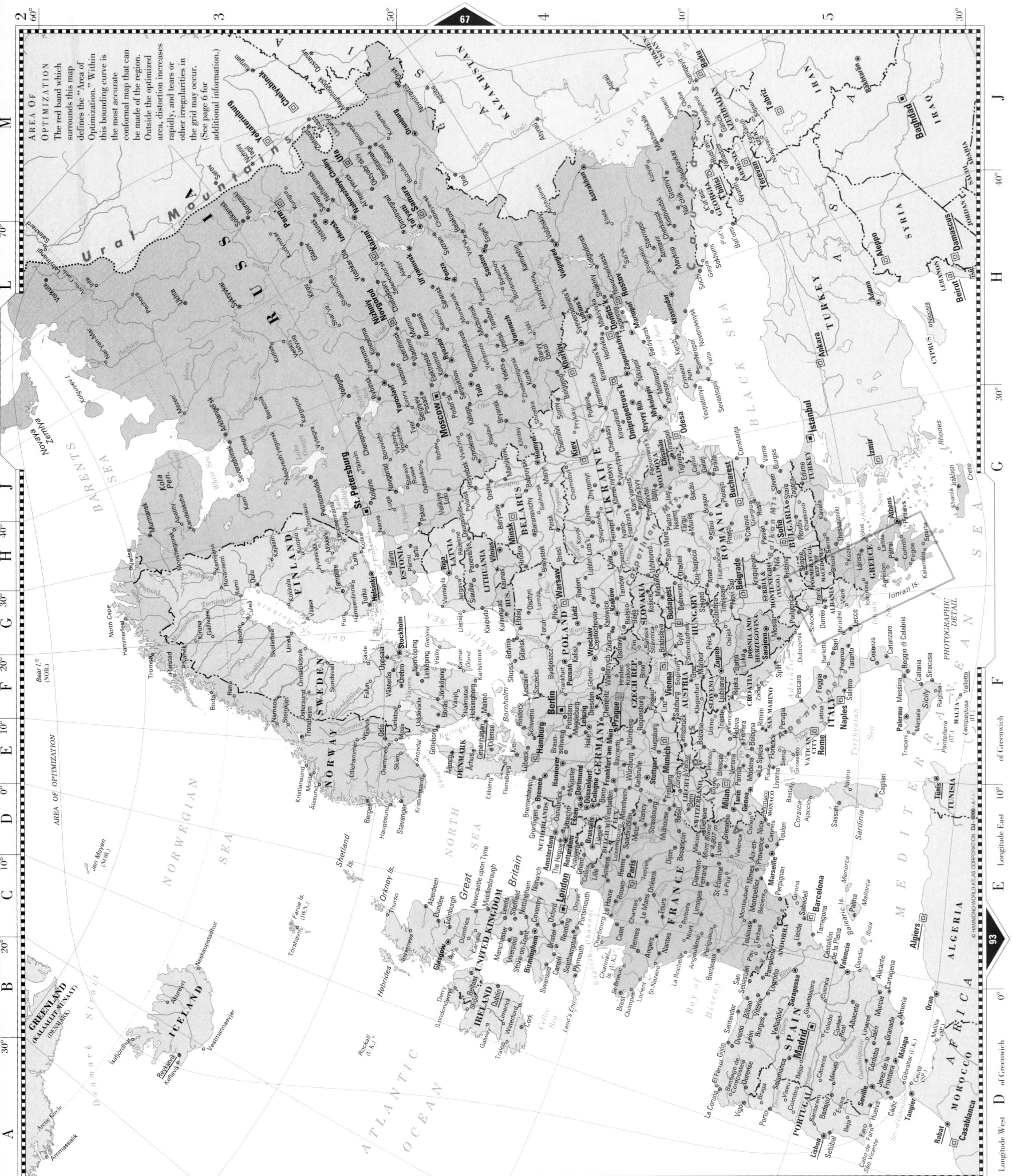

67

93

POPULATION OF CITIES AND TOWNS

◉ OVER 3,000,000   ⊡ 500,000 - 999,999   ● 100,000 - 499,999
⊡ 1,000,000 - 2,999,999   ● 100,000 - 499,999   ○ UNDER 100,000

SCALE 1:20,500,000   OPTIMAL CONFORMAL PROJECTION

MILES   0   300   600   900
KILOMETERS   0   300   600   900

AREA OF OPTIMIZATION The red band which surrounds this map defines the "Area of Optimization." Within this bounding curve is the most accurate conformal map that can be made of the region. Outside the optimized area, distortion increases rapidly, and tears or other irregularities in the grid may occur. (See page 6 for additional information.)

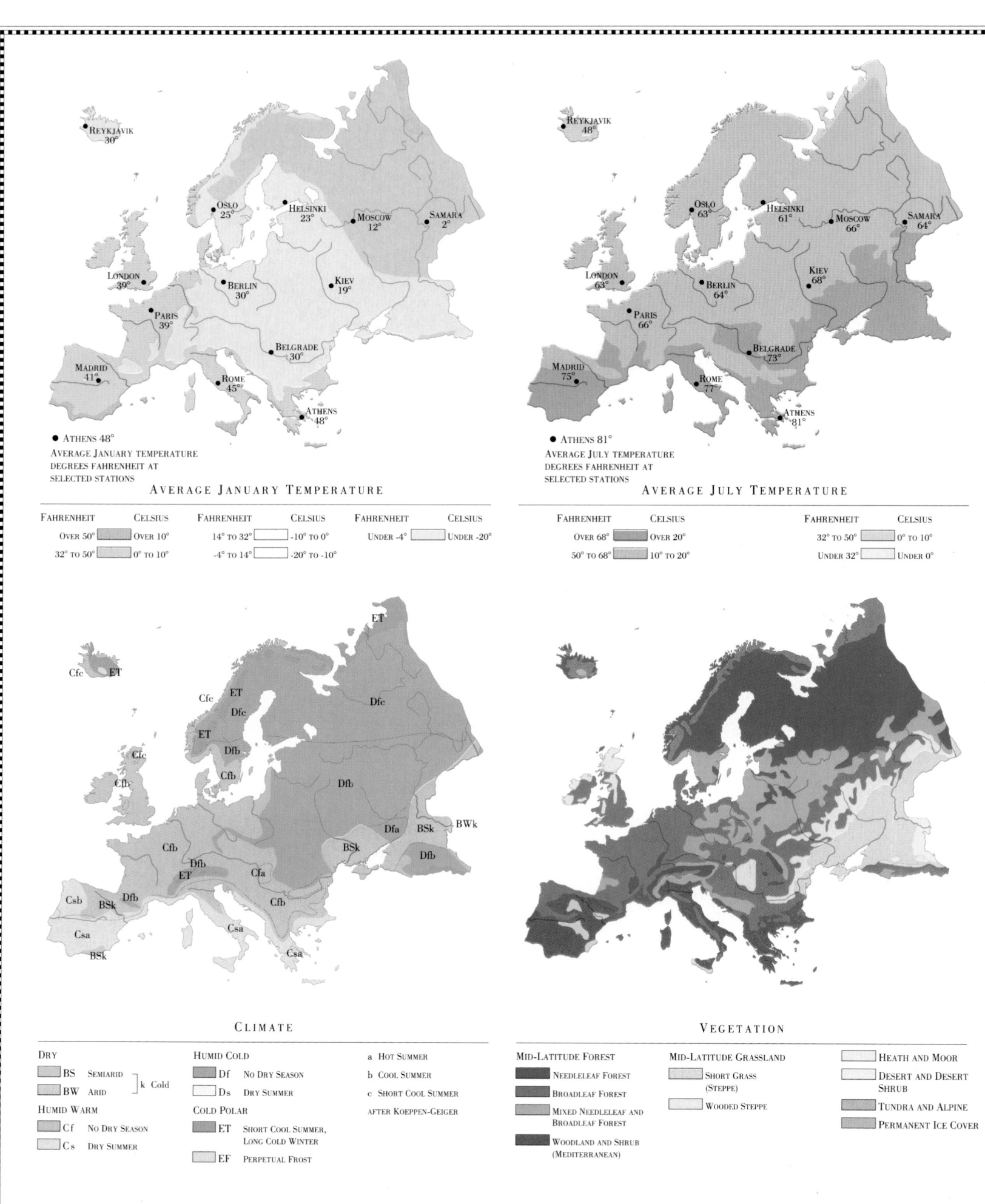

AVERAGE JANUARY TEMPERATURE

● REYKJAVIK 30°
OSLO 25° ● HELSINKI 23° ● MOSCOW 12° ● SAMARA 2°
LONDON 30° ● BERLIN 30° ● KIEV 19°
● PARIS 39°
BELGRADE 30°
MADRID 41° ● ROME 45°
ATHENS 48°

● ATHENS 48°
AVERAGE JANUARY TEMPERATURE
DEGREES FAHRENHEIT AT
SELECTED STATIONS

FAHRENHEIT	CELSIUS	FAHRENHEIT	CELSIUS	FAHRENHEIT	CELSIUS
OVER 50°	OVER 10°	14° TO 32°	-10° TO 0°	UNDER -4°	UNDER -20°
32° TO 50°	0° TO 10°	-4° TO 14°	-20° TO -10°		

AVERAGE JULY TEMPERATURE

● REYKJAVIK 48°
OSLO 63° ● HELSINKI 61° ● MOSCOW 66° ● SAMARA 64°
LONDON 63° ● BERLIN 64° ● KIEV 68°
● PARIS 66°
BELGRADE 73°
MADRID 75° ● ROME 77°
ATHENS 81°

● ATHENS 81°
AVERAGE JULY TEMPERATURE
DEGREES FAHRENHEIT AT
SELECTED STATIONS

FAHRENHEIT	CELSIUS	FAHRENHEIT	CELSIUS
OVER 68°	OVER 20°	32° TO 50°	0° TO 10°
50° TO 68°	10° TO 20°	UNDER 32°	UNDER 0°

CLIMATE

ET
Cfc ET
Cfc ET
Dfc Dfc
ET
Dfb
Cfc Cfb
Cfb
Dfb
Cfb Dfb
Dfb Dfa BSk BWk
BSk
Dfb
Cfb
Dfb Cfa
ET Csa
Csb BSk Dfb Cfb
Csa Csa
BSk

DRY
■ BS SEMIARID ⎱ k Cold
■ BW ARID ⎰

HUMID WARM
■ Cf NO DRY SEASON
□ Cs DRY SUMMER

HUMID COLD
■ Df NO DRY SEASON
□ Ds DRY SUMMER

COLD POLAR
■ ET SHORT COOL SUMMER,
       LONG COLD WINTER
□ EF PERPETUAL FROST

a HOT SUMMER
b COOL SUMMER
c SHORT COOL SUMMER

AFTER KOEPPEN-GEIGER

VEGETATION

MID-LATITUDE FOREST
■ NEEDLELEAF FOREST
■ BROADLEAF FOREST
■ MIXED NEEDLELEAF AND
   BROADLEAF FOREST
■ WOODLAND AND SHRUB
   (MEDITERRANEAN)

MID-LATITUDE GRASSLAND
□ SHORT GRASS
   (STEPPE)
□ WOODED STEPPE

□ HEATH AND MOOR
□ DESERT AND DESERT
   SHRUB
■ TUNDRA AND ALPINE
■ PERMANENT ICE COVER

Europe - Geographical Comparisons

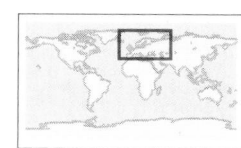

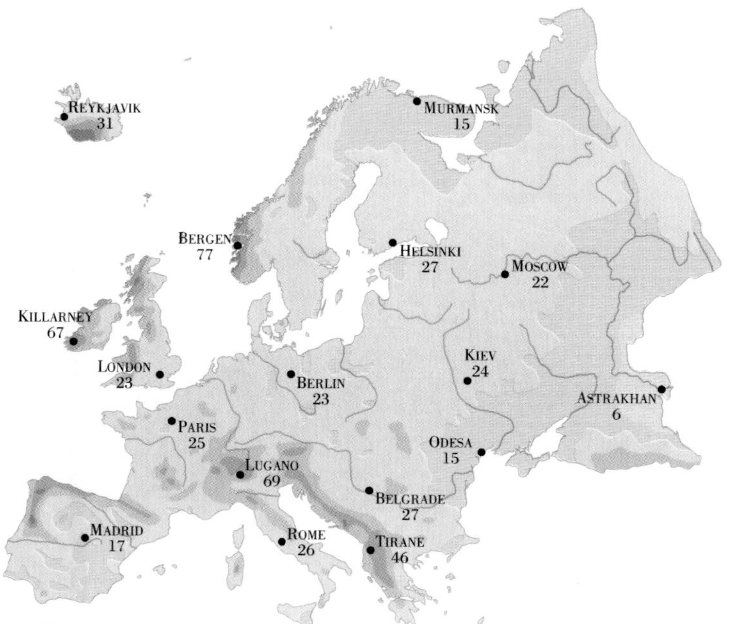

AVERAGE ANNUAL RAINFALL

REYKJAVIK 31
MURMANSK 15
BERGEN 77
HELSINKI 27
MOSCOW 22
KILLARNEY 67
LONDON 23
BERLIN 23
KIEV 24
ASTRAKHAN 6
PARIS 25
ODESA 15
LUGANO 69
BELGRADE 27
MADRID 17
ROME 26
TIRANE 46

● Berlin 23

AVERAGE ANNUAL RAINFALL
IN INCHES AT SELECTED STATIONS

INCHES	CM	INCHES	CM	INCHES	CM
OVER 80	OVER 200	40 TO 60	100 TO 150	10 TO 20	25 TO 50
60 TO 80	150 TO 200	20 TO 40	50 TO 100	UNDER 10	UNDER 25

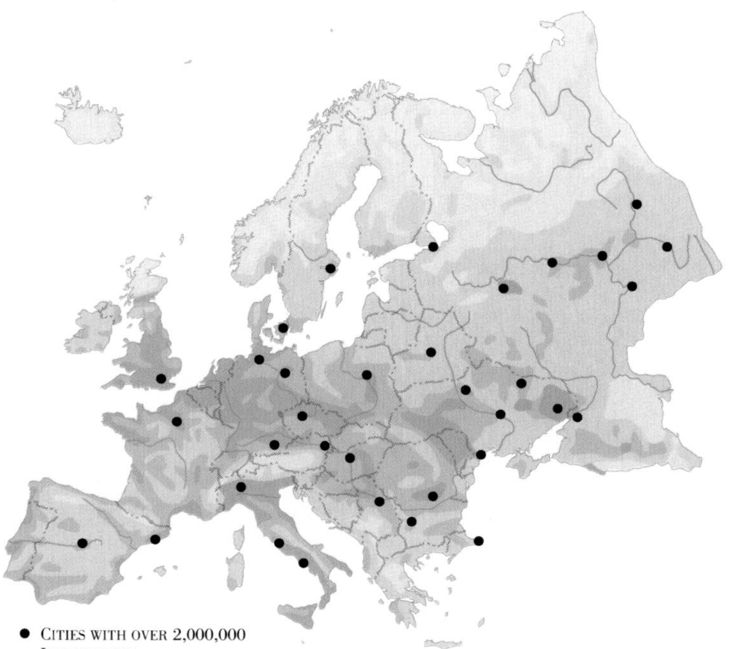

POPULATION DISTRIBUTION

● CITIES WITH OVER 2,000,000 INHABITANTS

DENSITY PER		SQ. MI.	SQ. KM.	SQ. MI.	SQ. KM.
SQ. MI.	SQ. KM.	130 TO 260	50 TO 100	3 TO 25	1 TO 10
OVER 260	OVER 100	25 TO 130	10 TO 50	UNDER 3	UNDER 1

LAND USE

FURS
FURS
OATS
FLAX
RYE
RYE
RYE
HEMP
WHEAT
DAIRY
DAIRY
RYE
POTATOES
WHEAT
SHEEP
DAIRY
DAIRY
RYE
POTATOES
RYE
SUGAR BEETS
CATTLE
WHEAT
OATS
POTATOES
OATS
WHEAT
CORN
HOGS
SHEEP
HOGS
OATS
WHEAT
CORN
BARLEY
CORN
TOBACCO
TEA
DAIRY
WINE
WINE
DAIRY
WHEAT
WINE
CORN
WHEAT
WINE
SHEEP
FRUIT
WHEAT
SHEEP
TOBACCO
OLIVES
WINE
OLIVES

	CEREALS, LIVESTOCK		FRUIT AND TRUCK FARMING		GENERAL FARMING, LIVESTOCK
	DAIRY, LIVESTOCK		PASTURE LIVESTOCK		FORESTS
	LIVESTOCK HERDING		DAIRY, CEREALS		NONPRODUCTIVE
	SPECIAL CROPS				

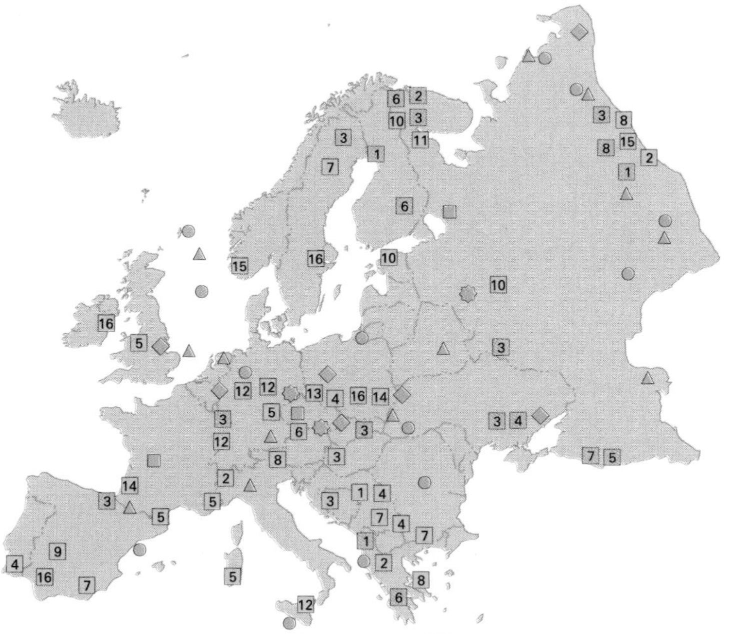

MINERAL RESOURCES

ENERGY & FUELS
◆ COAL
⬡ LIGNITE
△ NATURAL GAS
● PETROLEUM
▢ URANIUM

IRON & FERROALLOYS
1 CHROMIUM
2 COBALT
3 IRON ORE
4 MANGANESE
5 MOLYBDENUM
6 NICKEL
7 TUNGSTEN
8 VANADIUM

OTHER MAJOR RESOURCES
1 ANTIMONY
2 ASBESTOS
3 BAUXITE
4 COPPER
5 FLORSPAR
6 GRAPHITE
7 LEAD
8 MAGNESITE
9 MERCURY
10 PHOSPHATES
11 PLATINUM
12 POTASH
13 SILVER
14 SULFER
15 TITANIUM
16 ZINC

FJ-#-A-A

London, Paris

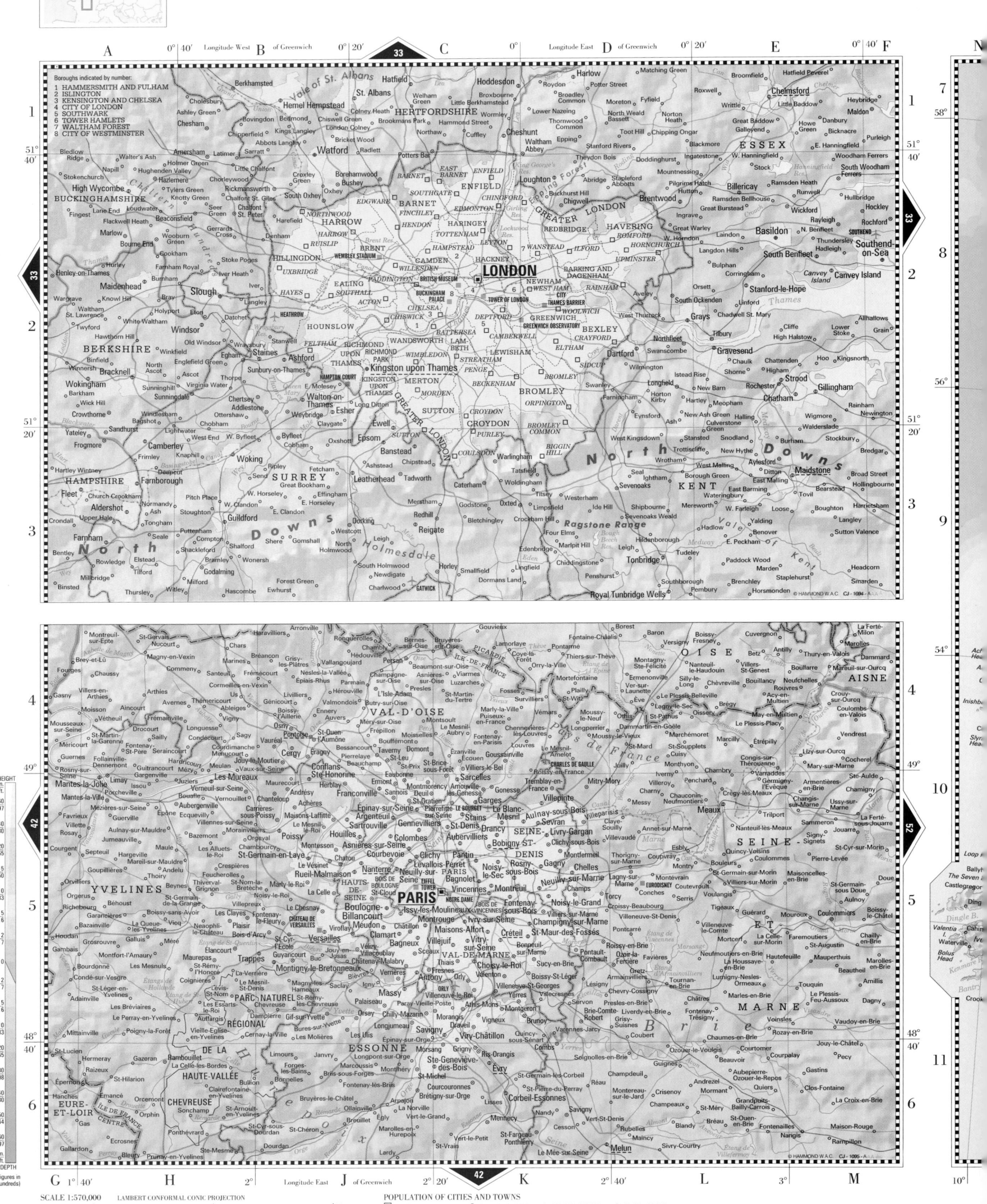

POPULATION OF CITIES AND TOWNS

■ OVER 2,000,000   ● 500,000 - 999,999   ● 100,000 - 249,999   ○ 10,000 - 29,999
■ 1,000,000 - 1,999,999   ● 250,000 - 499,999   ● 30,000 - 99,999   ○ UNDER 10,000

United Kingdom, Ireland

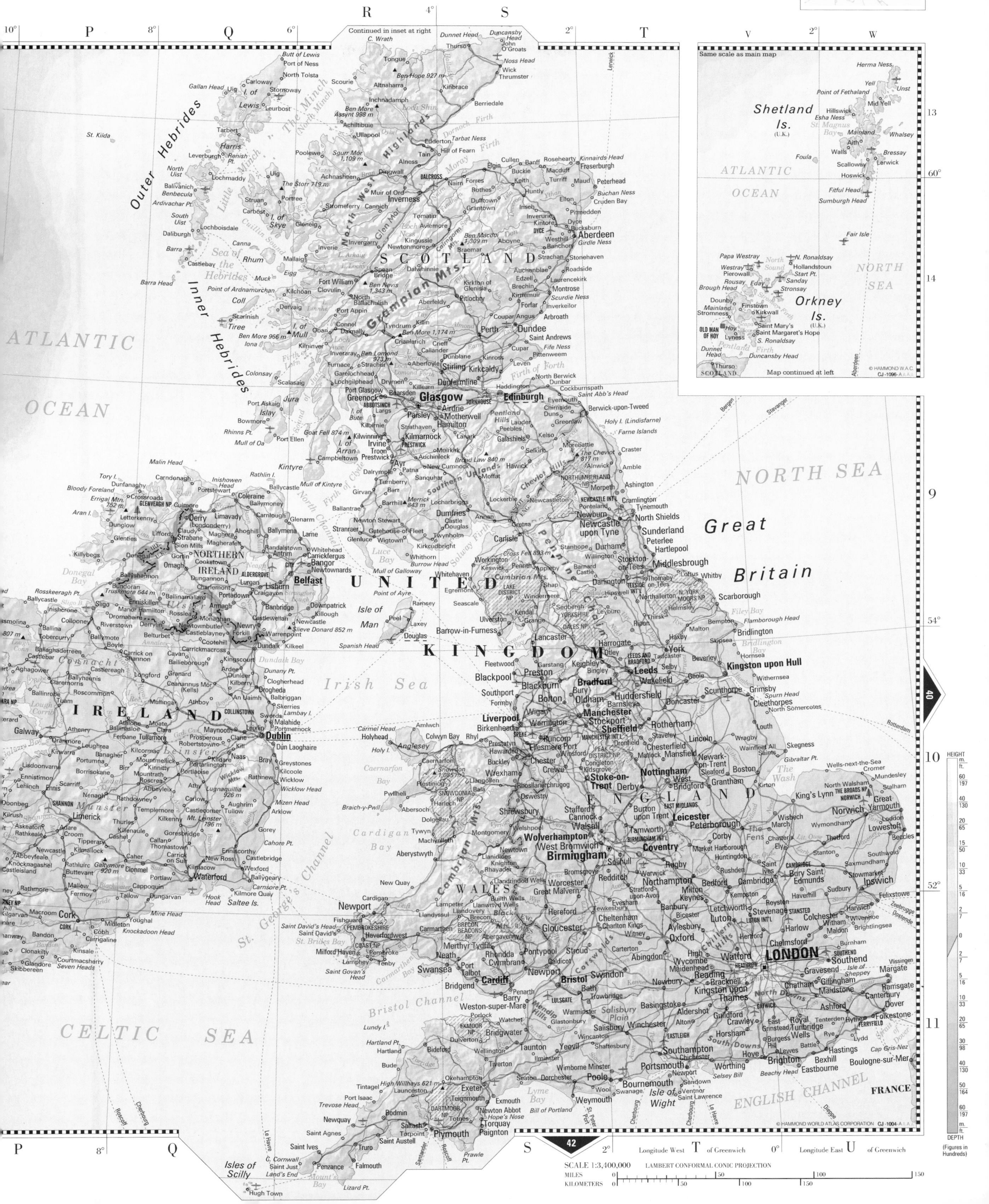

ATLANTIC OCEAN

Outer Hebrides

Inner Hebrides

SCOTLAND

Glasgow Edinburgh

NORTHERN IRELAND

Belfast

IRELAND

Dublin

Isle of Man

Irish Sea

Great Britain

NORTH SEA

UNITED KINGDOM

ENGLAND

WALES

Liverpool Manchester Sheffield

Leeds Bradford

Kingston upon Hull

Birmingham Leicester Coventry

Nottingham Stoke-on-Trent Derby

Cardiff Bristol

LONDON

CELTIC SEA

Cork

St. George's Channel

Bristol Channel

ENGLISH CHANNEL

FRANCE

Isle of Wight

Isles of Scilly

Shetland Is. (U.K.)

Orkney Is. (U.K.)

ATLANTIC OCEAN

NORTH SEA

Same scale as main map

SCALE 1:3,400,000   LAMBERT CONFORMAL CONIC PROJECTION

MILES

KILOMETERS

Longitude West of Greenwich   Longitude East of Greenwich

HEIGHT

DEPTH

(Figures in Hundreds)

© HAMMOND WORLD ATLAS CORPORATION   CJ-1004-A

Southern England and Wales

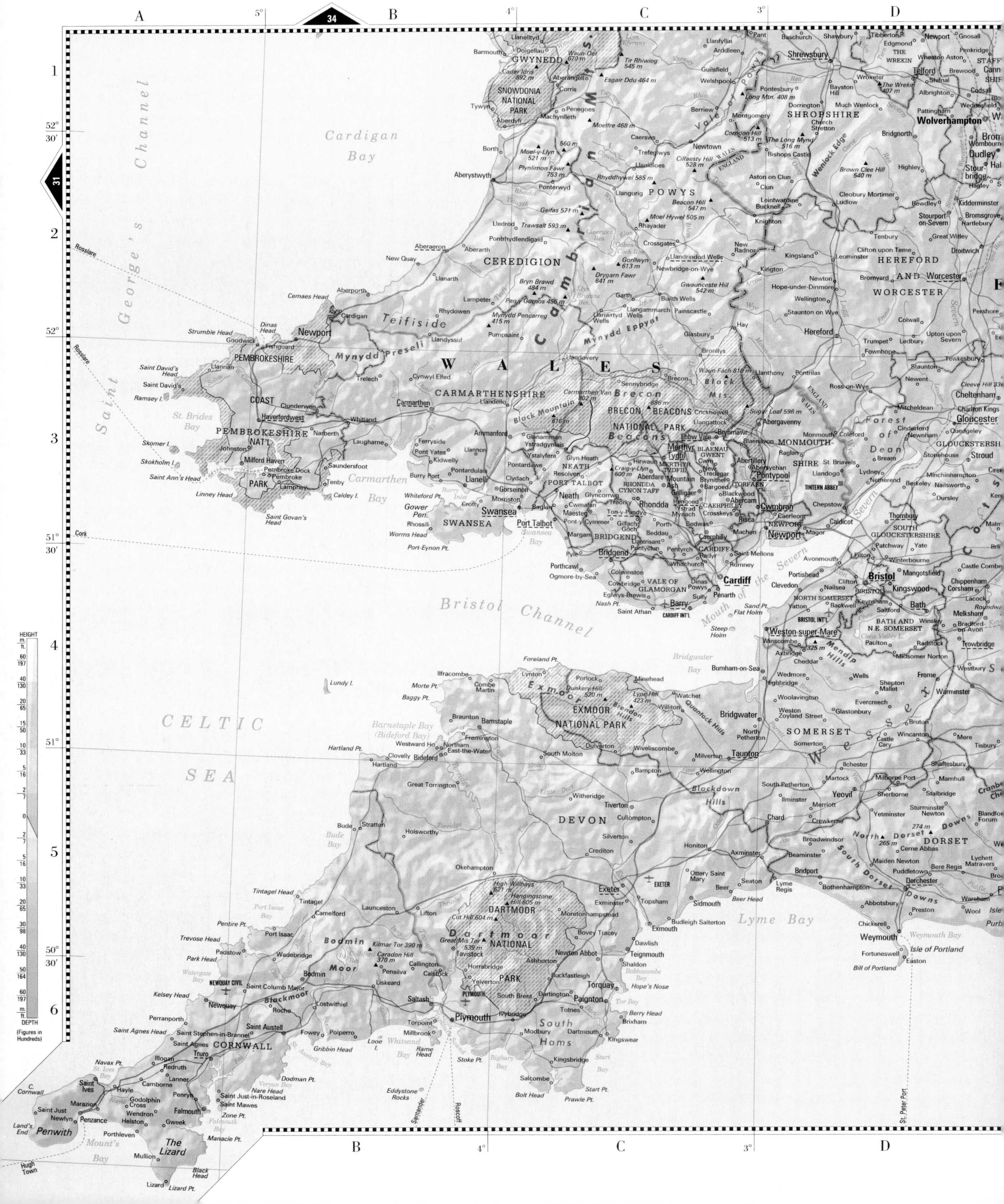

Northeastern Ireland, Northern England and Wales

POPULATION OF CITIES AND TOWNS

SCALE 1:1,140,000   LAMBERT CONFORMAL CONIC PROJECTION

1° Longitude West of Greenwich   0° Longitude East of Greenwich

© HAMMOND WORLD ATLAS CORPORATION

Central Scotland

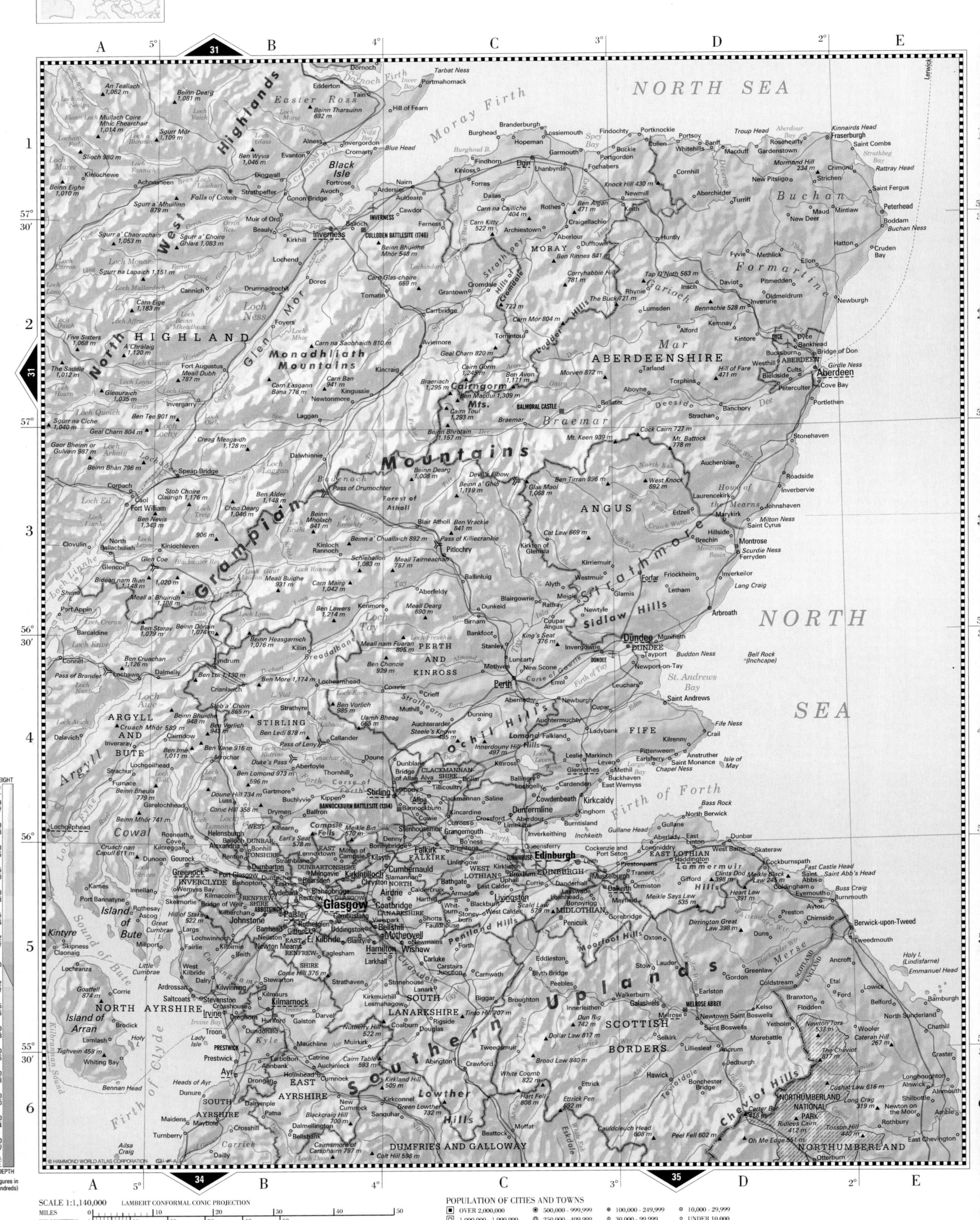

MILES 0   5   10   20   30   40   50

KILOMETERS 0 10   20   30   40   50

POPULATION OF CITIES AND TOWNS

■ OVER 2,000,000   ● 500,000 - 999,999   ◉ 100,000 - 249,999   ● 10,000 - 29,999
▣ 1,000,000 - 1,999,999 ◉ 250,000 - 499,999   ◦ 30,000 - 99,999   ◦ UNDER 10,000

Scandinavia and Finland, Iceland

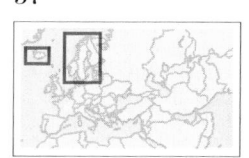

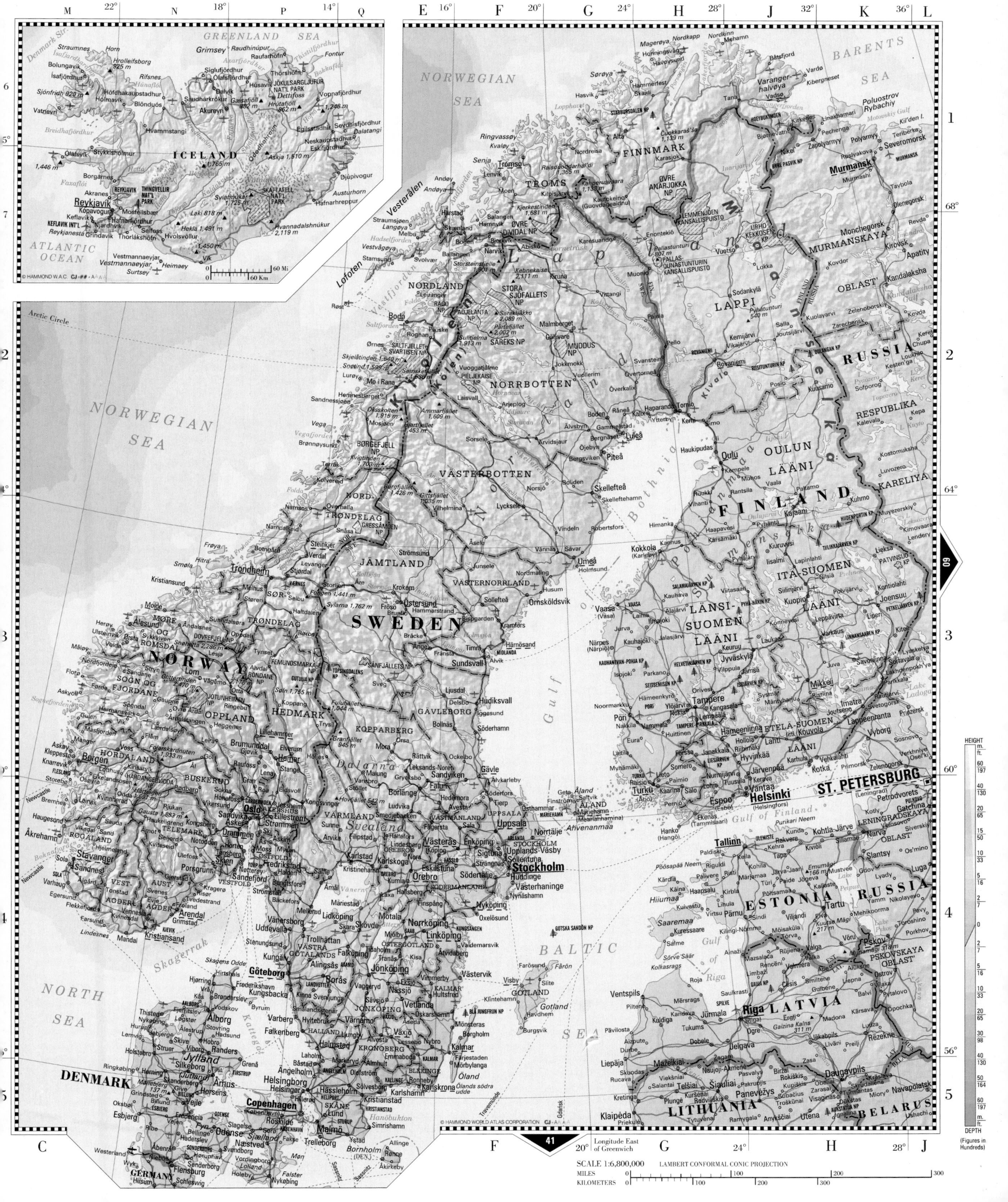

SCALE 1:6,800,000   LAMBERT CONFORMAL CONIC PROJECTION

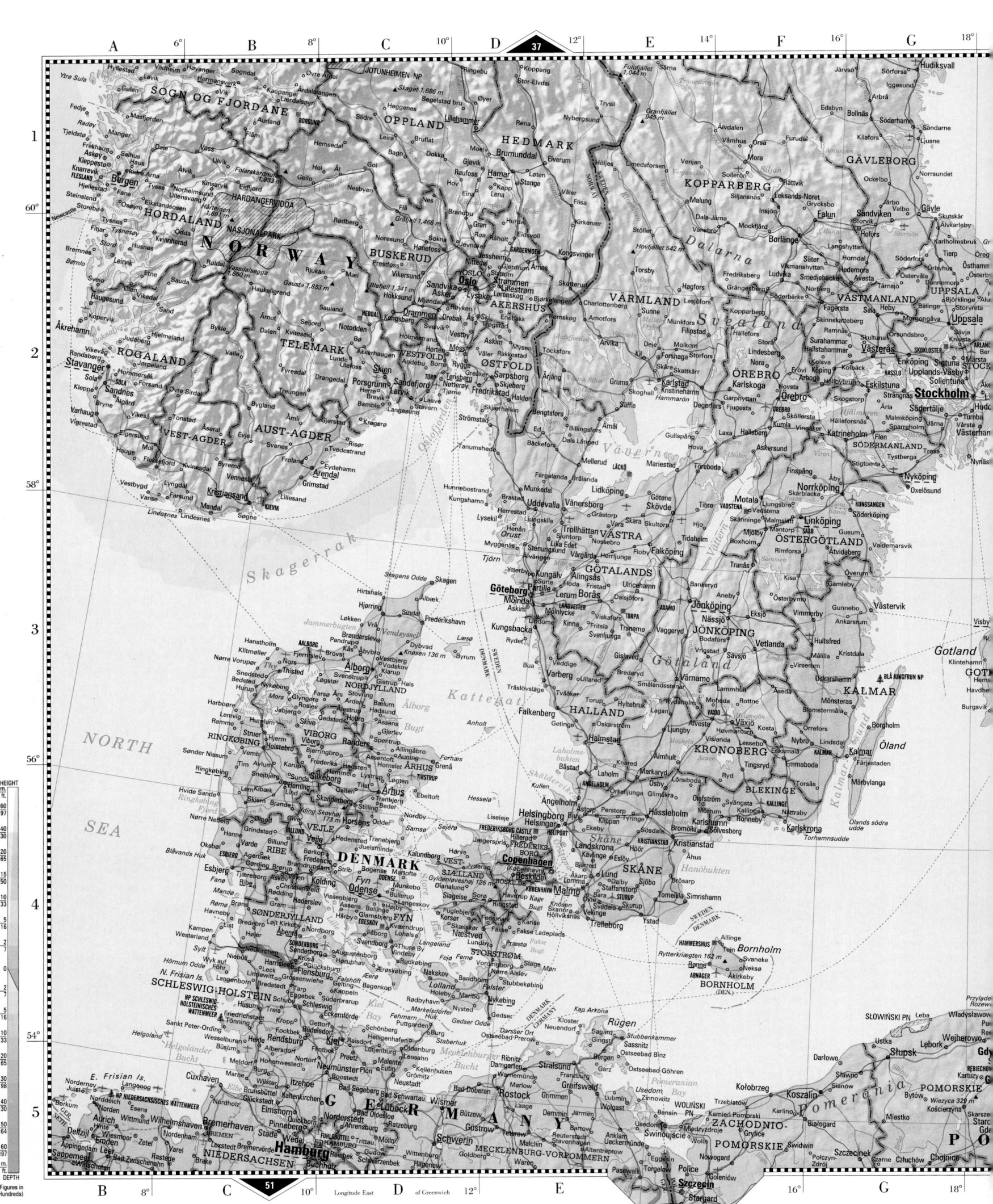

Baltic Region

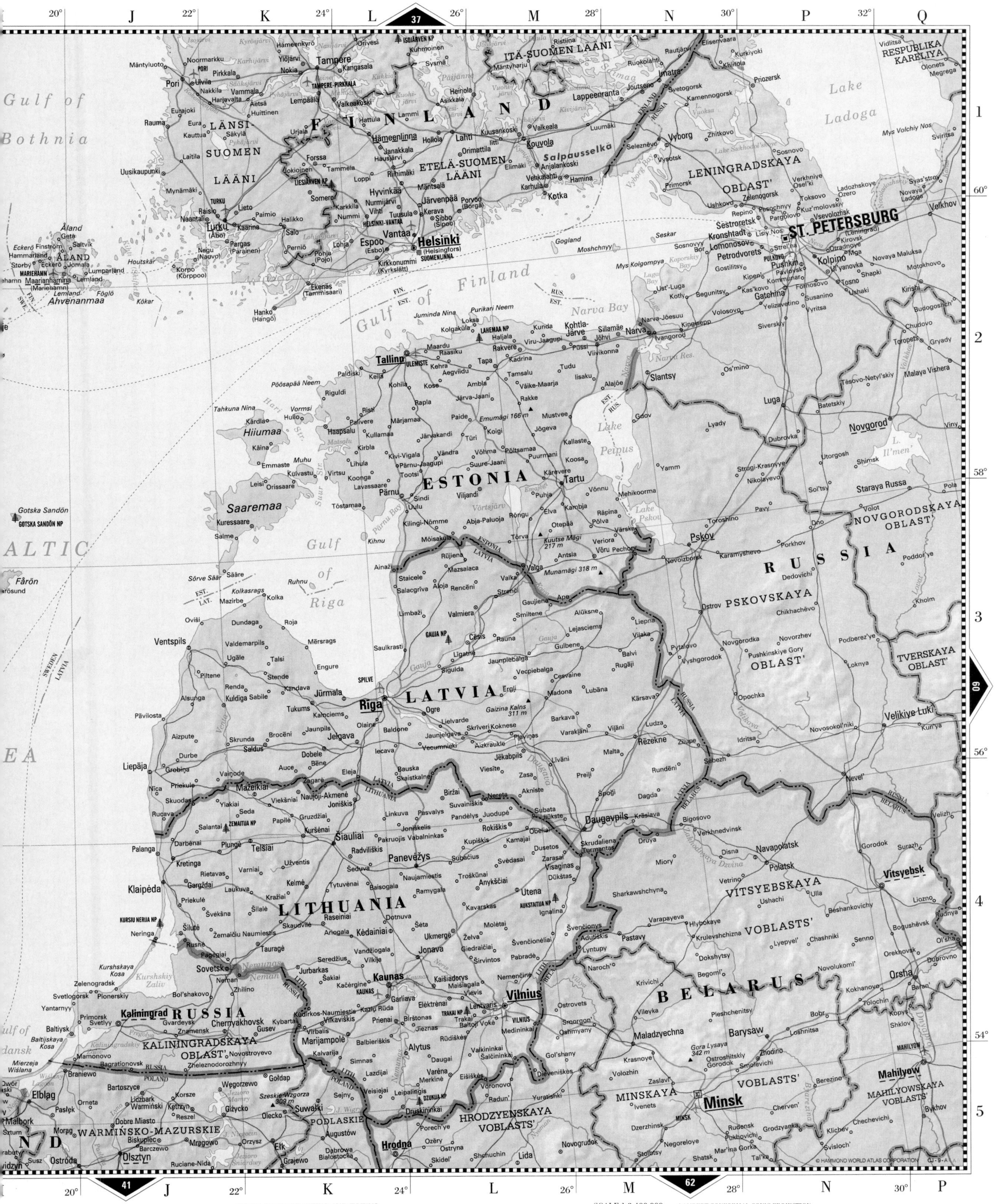

POPULATION OF CITIES AND TOWNS

- OVER 2,000,000
- 1,000,000 - 1,999,999
- 500,000 - 999,999
- 250,000 - 499,999
- 100,000 - 249,999
- 30,000 - 99,999
- 10,000 - 29,999
- UNDER 10,000

SCALE 1:3,400,000   LAMBERT CONFORMAL CONIC PROJECTION

MILES

KILOMETERS

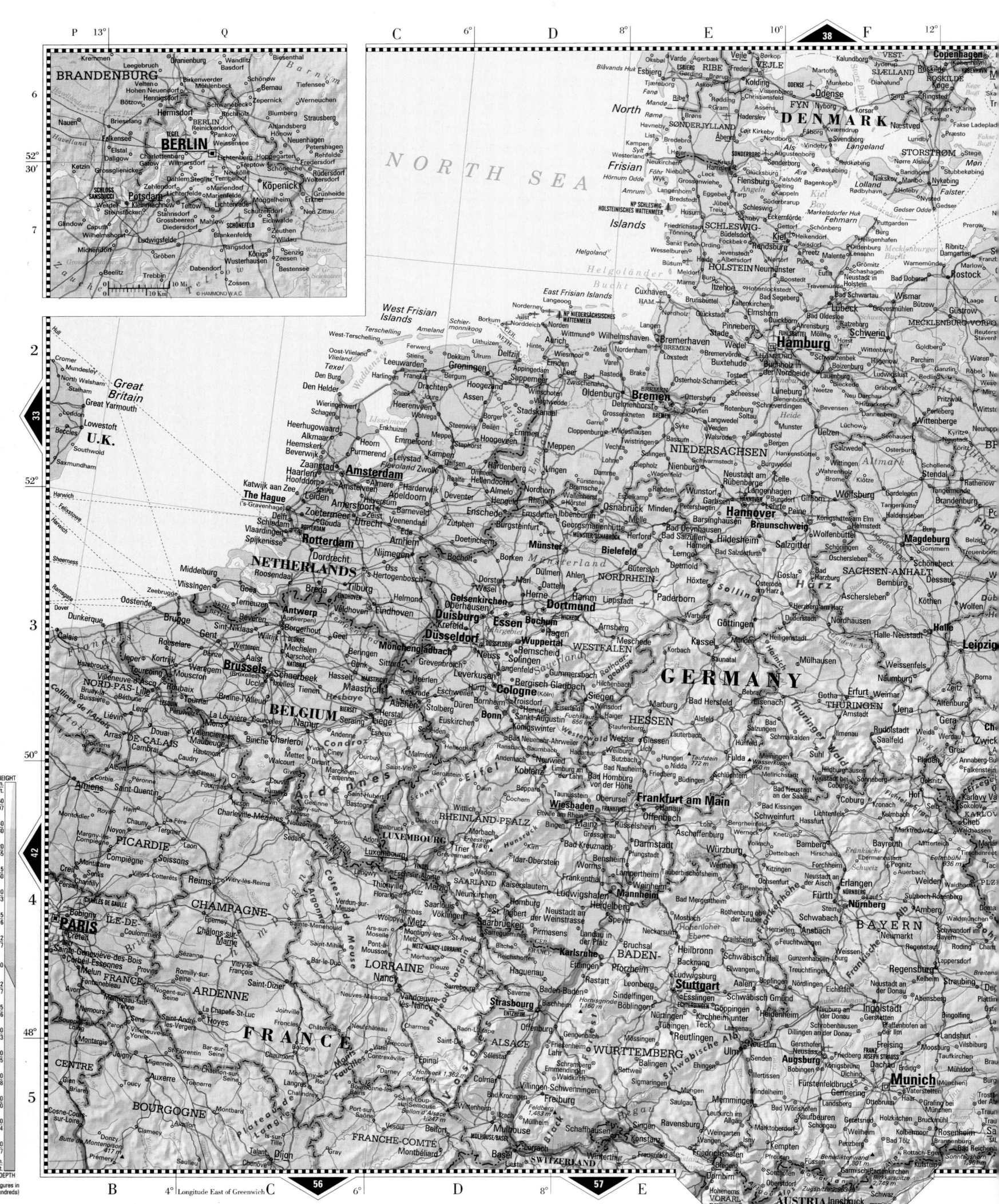

North Central Europe

POPULATION OF CITIES AND TOWNS

| ■ OVER 2,000,000 | □ 500,000 - 999,999 | ● 100,000 - 249,999 | ⊙ 10,000 - 29,999 |
| □ 1,000,000 - 1,999,999 | ⊡ 250,000 - 499,999 | ⊙ 30,000 - 99,999 | ○ UNDER 10,000 |

SCALE 1:3,400,000   LAMBERT CONFORMAL CONIC PROJECTION

West Central Europe

Spain, Portugal

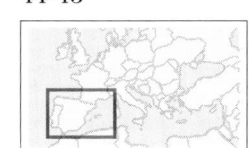

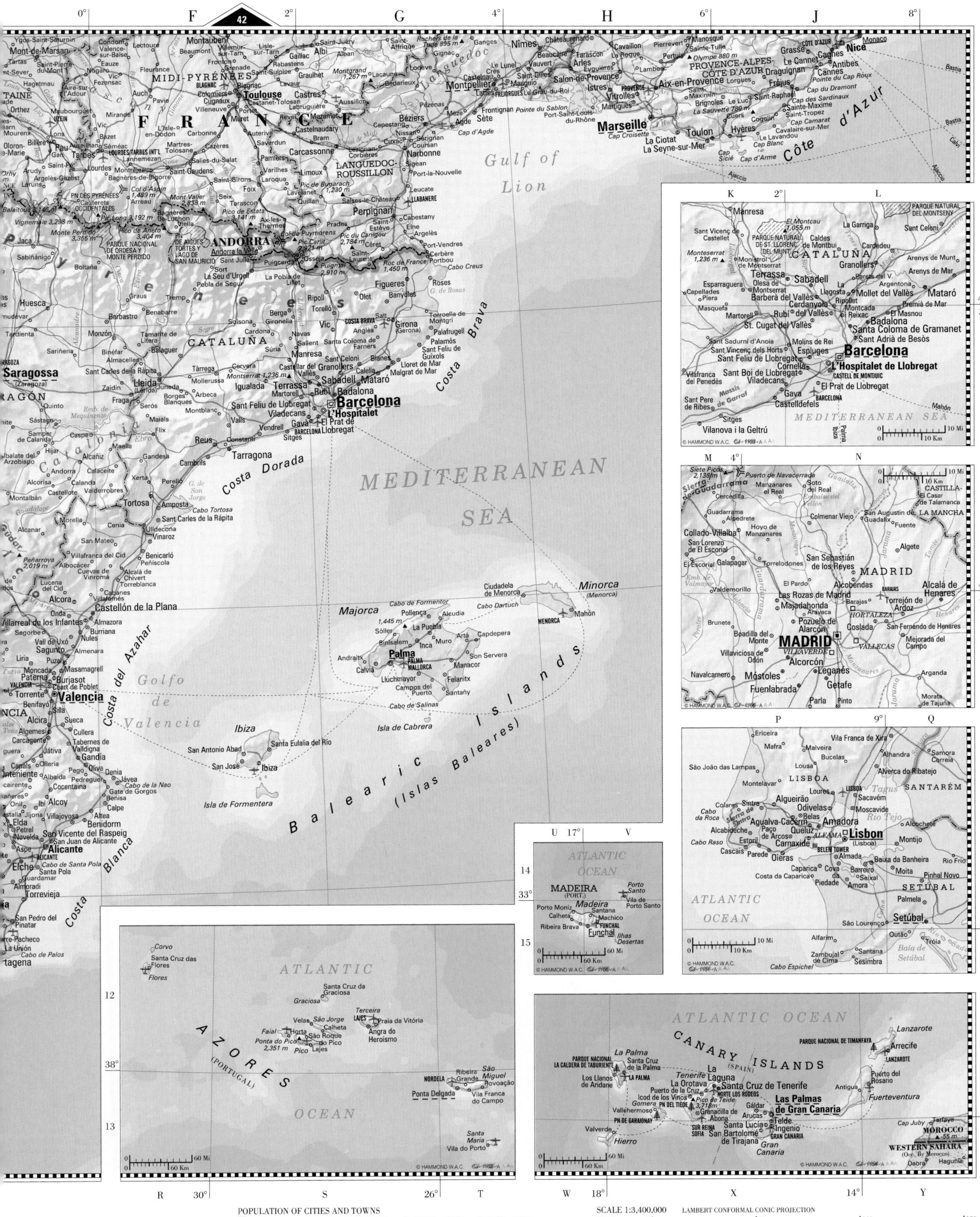

POPULATION OF CITIES AND TOWNS

■ OVER 2,000,000	● 500,000 - 999,999	● 100,000 - 249,999	○ 10,000 - 29,999
□ 1,000,000 - 1,999,999	□ 250,000 - 499,999	● 30,000 - 99,999	○ UNDER 10,000

SCALE 1:3,400,000   LAMBERT CONFORMAL CONIC PROJECTION

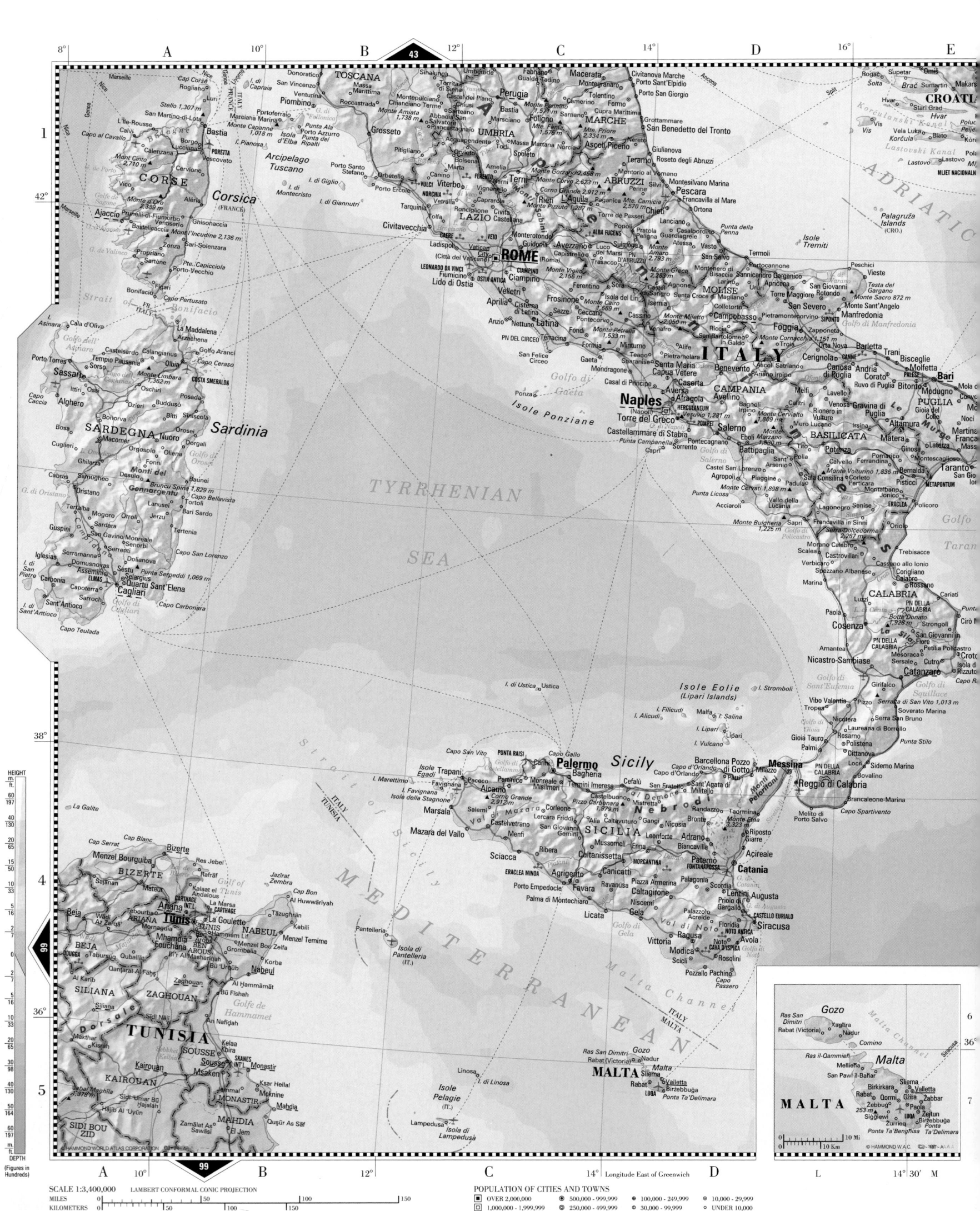

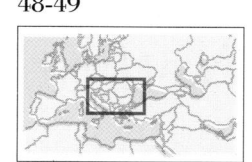

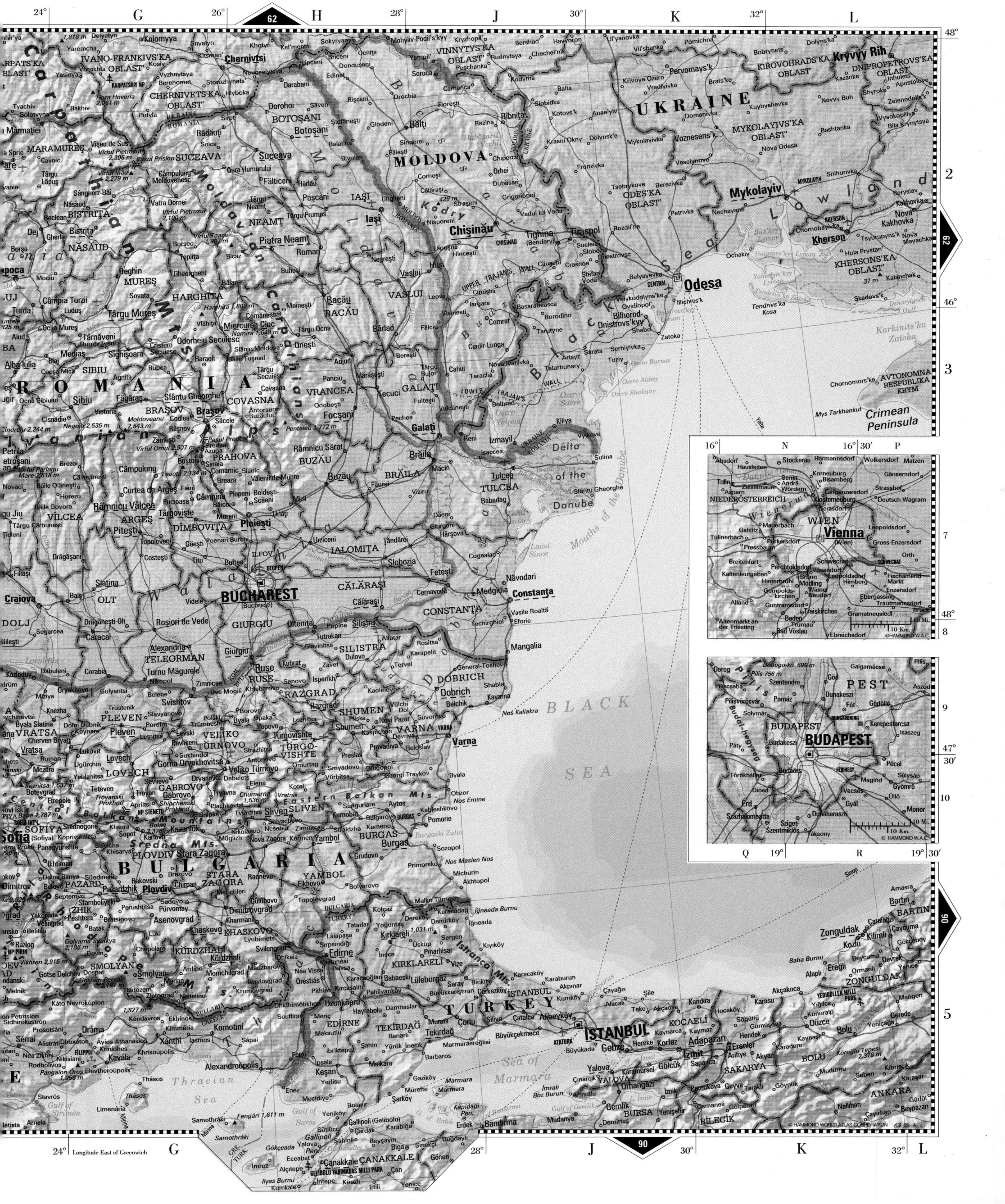

Netherlands, Northwestern Germany

NORTH SEA

West Frisian Islands

Waddenzee

FRIESLAND

GRONINGEN

DRENTHE

NOORD-HOLLAND

IJsselmeer

OVERIJSSEL

FLEVOLAND

Amsterdam

Haarlem

GELDERLAND

UTRECHT

The Hague

Rotterdam

NETHERLANDS

ZUID-HOLLAND

ZEELAND

NOORD-BRABANT

LIMBURG

ANTWERPEN

BELGIUM

Antwerp

OOST-VLAANDEREN

Ghent

Düsseldorf

Mönchengladbach

Duisburg

HEIGHT
m. / ft.
60 / 197
40 / 130
20 / 65
15 / 50
10 / 33
5 / 16
0
2 / 7
5 / 16
10 / 33
20 / 65
30 / 98
40 / 130
50 / 164
60 / 197
m. / ft.
DEPTH
(Figures in Hundreds)

POPULATION OF CITIES AND TOWNS

SCALE 1:1,140,000   LAMBERT CONFORMAL CONIC PROJECTION

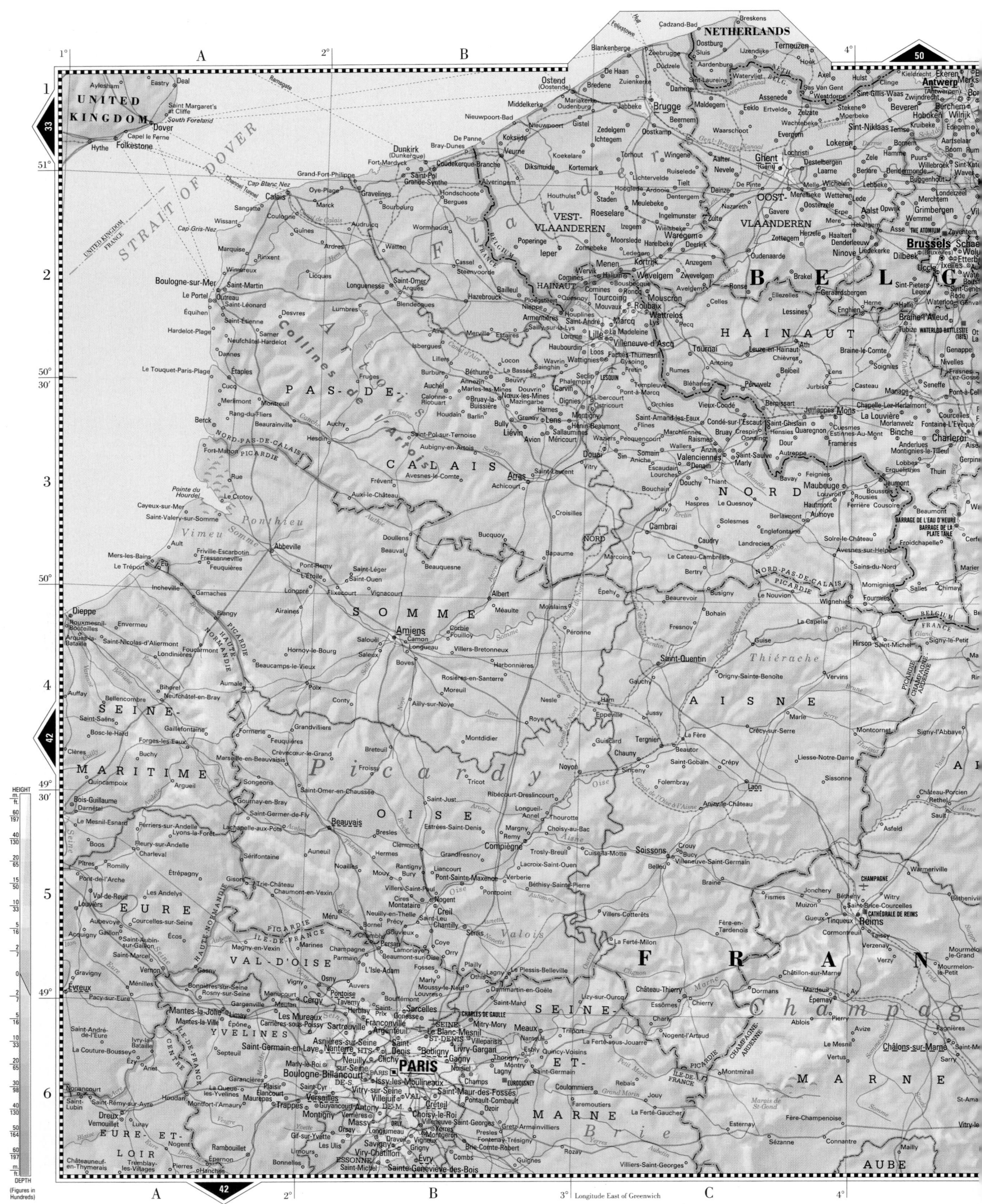

Belgium, Northern France, Western Germany

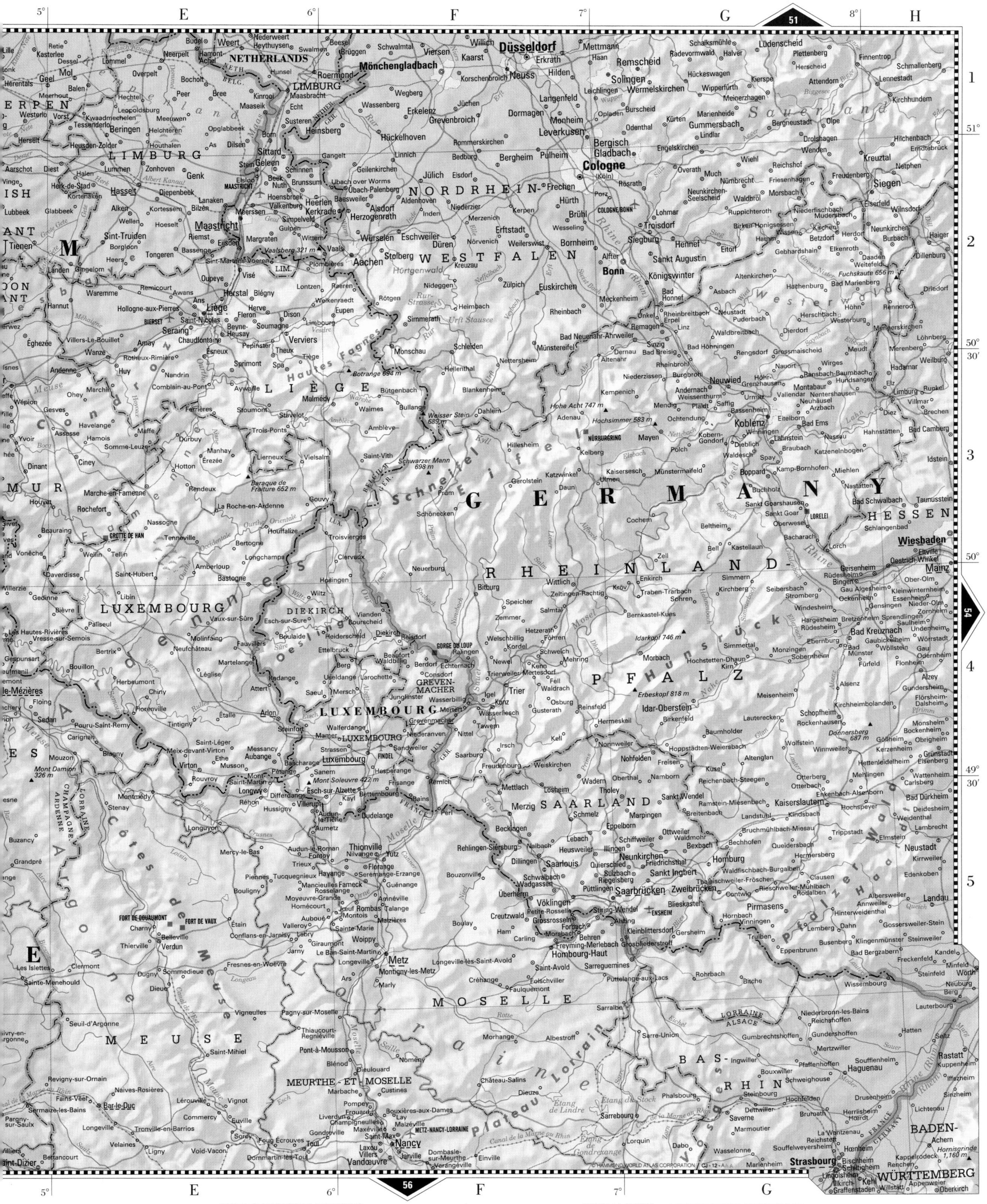

Central Alps Region

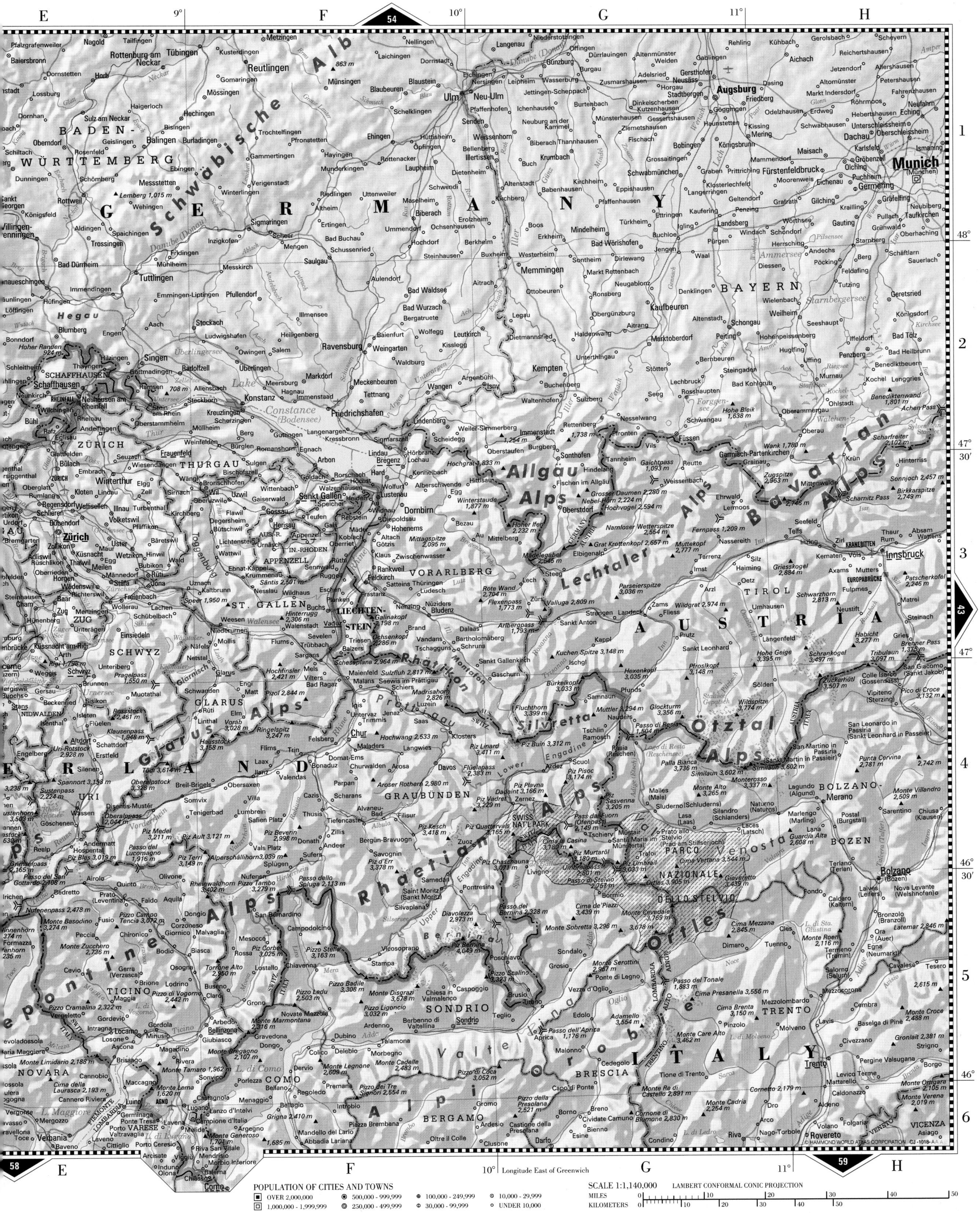

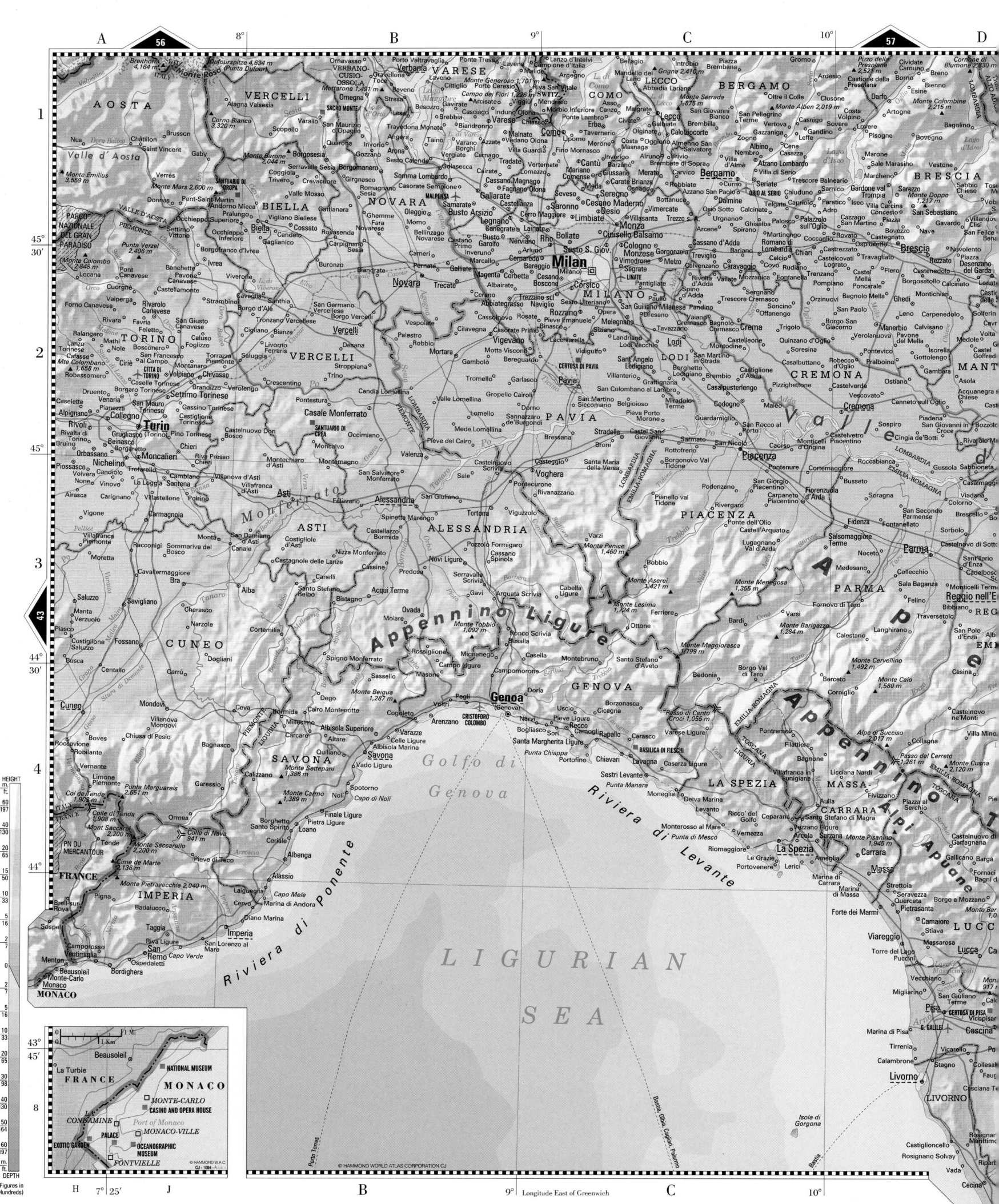

Northern Italy

POPULATION OF CITIES AND TOWNS
- OVER 2,000,000
- 1,000,000 - 1,999,999
- 500,000 - 999,999
- 250,000 - 499,999
- 100,000 - 249,999
- 30,000 - 99,999
- 10,000 - 29,999
- UNDER 10,000

SCALE 1:1,140,000   LAMBERT CONFORMAL CONIC PROJECTION

MILES

KILOMETERS

Major labels: TRENTINO-ALTO-ADIGE, VENETO, BELLUNO, VICENZA, VERONA, TREVISO, PORDENONE, UDINE, GORIZIA, SLOVENIA, FRIULI-VENEZIA GIULIA, PADOVA, VENEZIA, Venice (Venezia), Mestre, Padova, Vicenza, Verona, Trieste, Golfo di Trieste, ISTRIA, CROATIA, Golfo di Venezia, LOMBARDIA, EMILIA-ROMAGNA, Po, ROVIGO, Polesine, FERRARA, Ferrara, Modena, BOLOGNA, Bologna, RAVENNA, Ravenna, Mouths of the Po, ADRIATIC SEA, Valli di Comacchio, Romagna, Forlì, FORLÌ-CESENA, Cesena, Rimini, RIMINI, SAN MARINO, San Marino, Montefeltro, MARCHE, PESARO E URBINO, Pesaro, Fano, Ancona, ANCONA, Jesi, MACERATA, PISTOIA, Prato, PRATO, FIRENZE, Florence (Firenze), AREZZO, Arezzo, SIENA, Siena, PERUGIA, Umbro-Marchigiano, TOSCANA, UMBRIA, Appennino, Monti Palomagno, Monti del Chianti, Chianti, Colline Metallifere

Selected peaks: Corno di Rosazzo, Cima Valdritta 2,218 m, Cima Palon 2,235 m, Cornetto 2,179 m, Monte Verena 2,019 m, Cappella Maggiore, Monte Cesen 1,570 m, Monte Maggiore 916 m, Monte Giovi 992 m, Monte Falterona 1,654 m, Monte Ritorio 1,193 m, Monte Mescolino 969 m, Monte Fumaiolo 1,407 m, Monte Faggiola 1,031 m, Monte Calvi 1,283 m, Monte Carpegna 1,415 m, Simoncello 1,221 m, Monte dei Frati 1,454 m, Monte il Castello 1,415 m, Monte Nerone 1,525 m, Monte Catria 1,702 m, Monte San Vicino 1,479 m, Pian di Serra 1,020 m, Monte Favalto 1,082 m, Alpe di Poti 974 m, Monte Maggio 671 m

Northeastern Europe

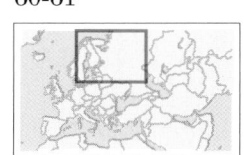

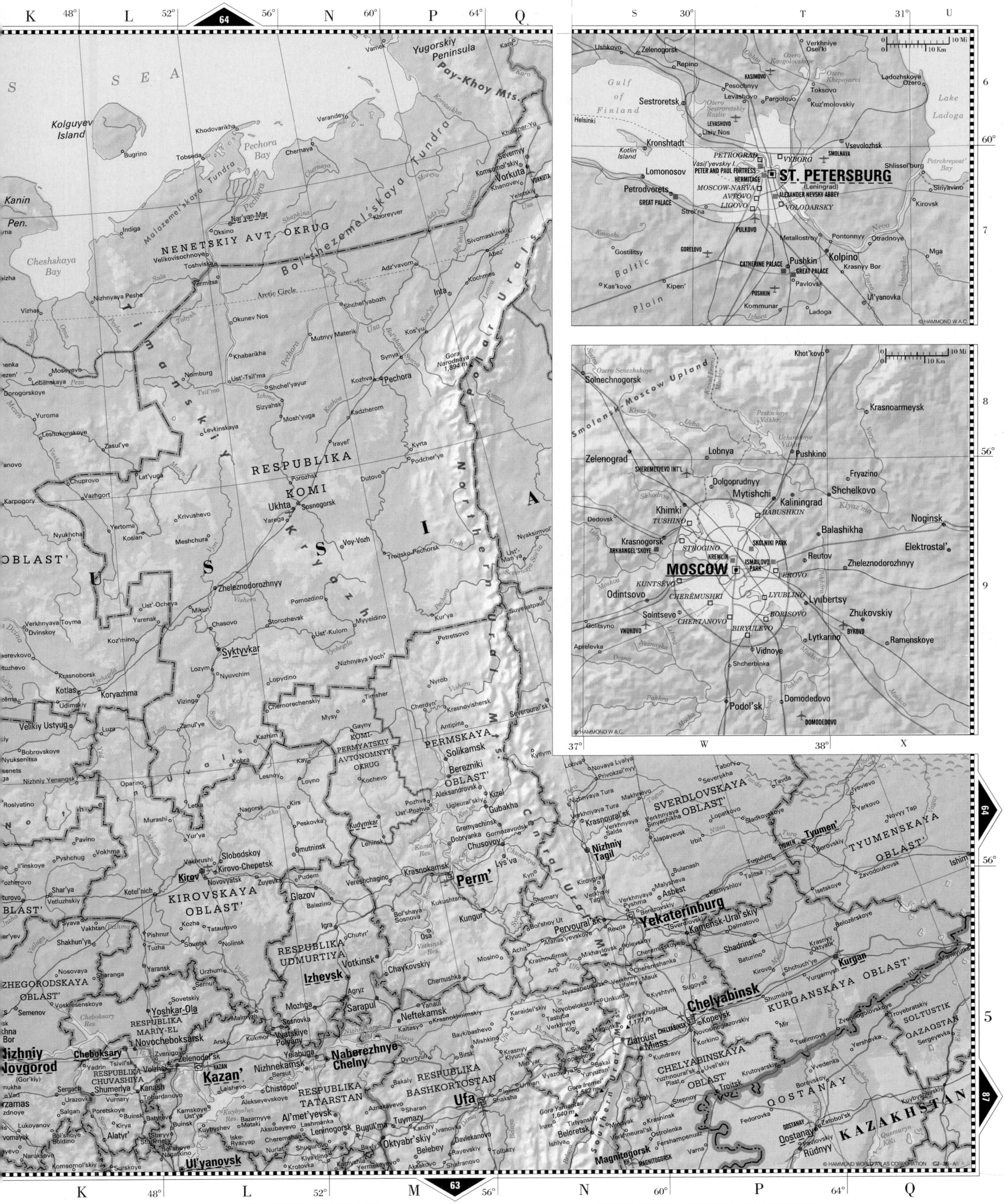

64
63
87

POPULATION OF CITIES AND TOWNS
- OVER 2,000,000
- 1,000,000 - 1,999,999
- 500,000 - 999,999
- 250,000 - 499,999
- 100,000 - 249,999
- 30,000 - 99,999
- 10,000 - 29,999
- UNDER 10,000

SCALE 1:6,800,000 LAMBERT CONFORMAL CONIC PROJECTION

MILES 0 100 200 300

KILOMETERS 0 100 200 300

SCALE 1:6,800,000   LAMBERT CONFORMAL CONIC PROJECTION

MILES

KILOMETERS

POPULATION OF CITIES AND TOWNS

■ OVER 2,000,000
■ 1,000,000 - 1,999,999
● 500,000 - 999,999
● 250,000 - 499,999
● 100,000 - 249,999
● 30,000 - 99,999
○ 10,000 - 29,999
○ UNDER 10,000

HEIGHT
m.
ft.

DEPTH
(Figures in Hundreds)

Southeastern Europe

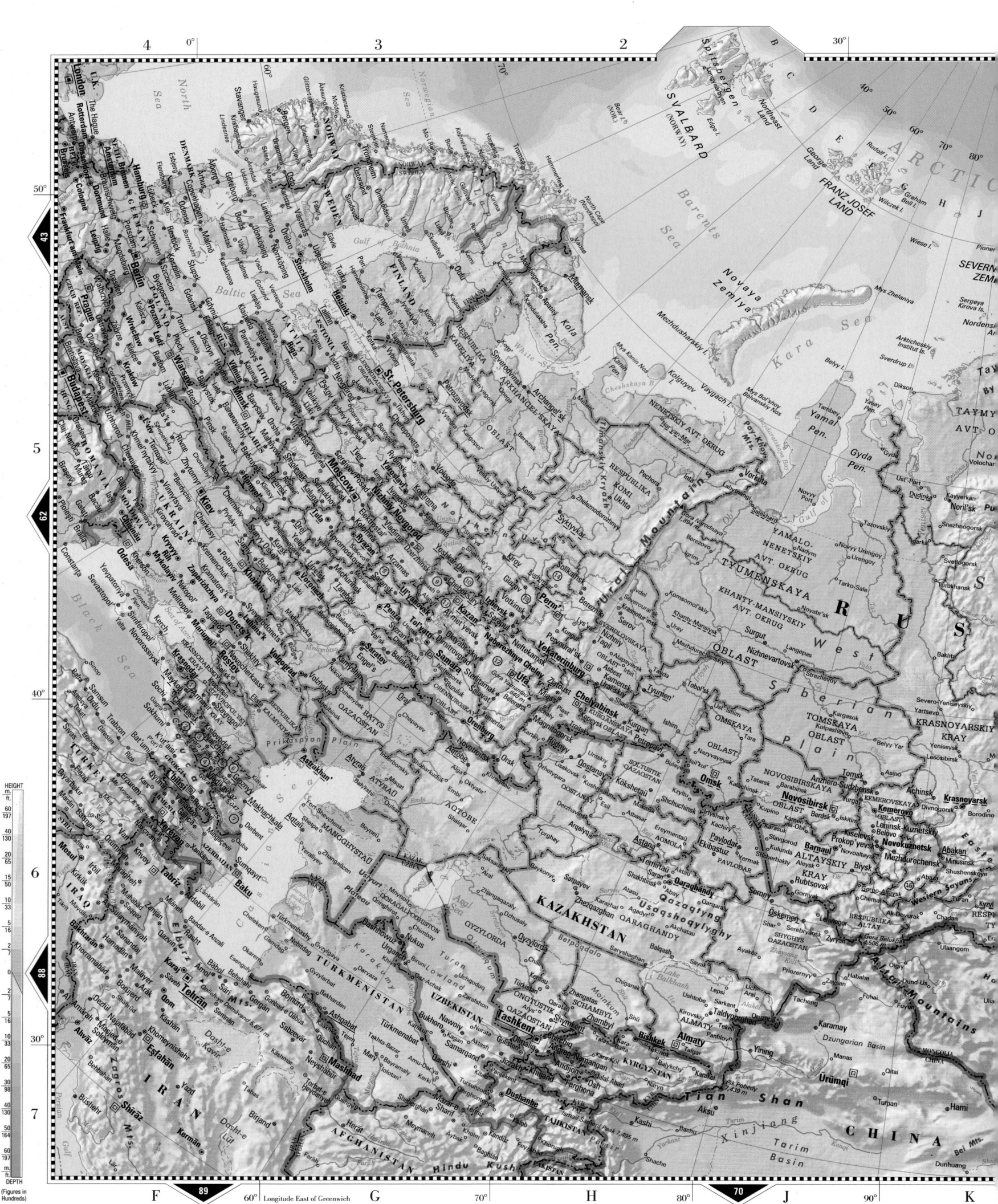

Russia and Neighboring Countries

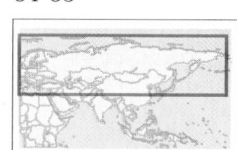

RUSSIA
(Administrative divisions are named only when
they differ from their respective capitals.)

1. RESPUBLIKA ADYGEYA
2. RESPUBLIKA KARACHAYEVO-CHERKESIYA
3. RESPUBLIKA KABARDINO-BALKARIYA
4. RESPUBLIKA SEVERNAYA OSETIYA-ALANIYA
5. RESPUBLIKA INGUSHETIYA
6. RESPUBLIKA CHECHNYA
7. RESPUBLIKA DAGESTAN
8. RESPUBLIKA MORDOVIYA
9. RESPUBLIKA CHUVASHIYA
10. RESPUBLIKA MARIY-EL
11. RESPUBLIKA TATARSTAN
12. RESPUBLIKA BASHKORTOSTAN
13. RESPUBLIKA UDMURTIYA
14. KOMI-PERMYATSKIY AVTONOMNYY OKRUG
15. RESPUBLIKA KHAKASIYA
16. UST'-ORDYNSKIY BURYATSKIY AVT. OKRUG
17. AGINSKIY BURYATSKIY AVT. OKRUG

© HAMMOND WORLD ATLAS CORPORATION   CJ-29-A

POPULATION OF CITIES AND TOWNS
■ OVER 2,000,000   ● 500,000 - 999,999   ◉ 50,000 - 99,999
□ 1,000,000 - 1,999,999   ● 100,000 - 499,999   ○ UNDER 50,000

SCALE 1:20,500,000   LAMBERT CONFORMAL CONIC PROJECTION
MILES   0   300   600   900
KILOMETERS   0   300   600   900

Asia

The delta of the Indus River, the longest river in southwest Asia, is the highlight of this southeast-looking, low-oblique image. Fed by snowmelt and glacial meltwater from the mountains of the Tibet Plateau, the Indus River flows nearly 1800 miles (2897 km.) before emptying into the Arabian Sea. After leaving the Tibet Plateau, the river flows onto the Punjab Plains of western Pakistan and through a vast alluvial lowland where it receives its major tributary, the Panjnad (five streams). In this severely arid landscape the rivers form precarious strips of fertile land.

AREA OF OPTIMIZATION

The red band which surrounds this map defines the "Area of Optimization." Within this bounding curve is the most accurate conformal map that can be made of the region. Outside the optimized area, distortion increases rapidly, and tears or other irregularities in the grid may occur. (See page 6 for additional information.)

POPULATION OF CITIES AND TOWNS
- OVER 3,000,000
- 1,000,000 - 2,999,999
- 500,000 - 999,999
- 100,000 - 499,999
- UNDER 100,000

SCALE 1:47,700,000 OPTIMAL CONFORMAL PROJECTION

© HAMMOND WORLD ATLAS CORPORATION CJ-1000-AM

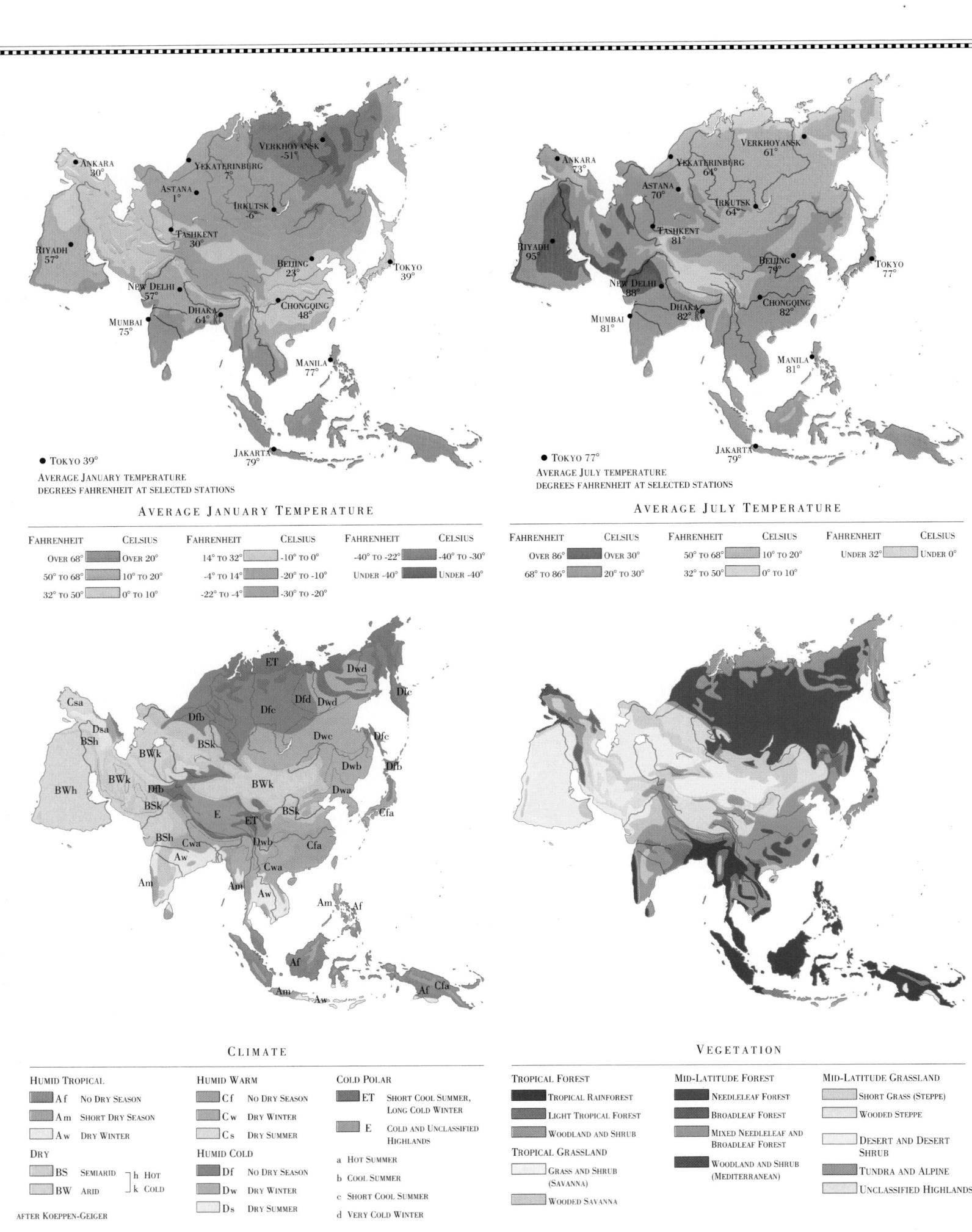

AVERAGE JANUARY TEMPERATURE

• ANKARA 30°
• YEKATERINBURG 7°
• VERKHOYANSK -51°
• ASTANA 1°
• IRKUTSK -6°
• TASHKENT 30°
• RIYADH 57°
• BEIJING 23°
• TOKYO 39°
• NEW DELHI 57°
• CHONGQING 48°
• DHAKA 64°
• MUMBAI 75°
• MANILA 77°
• JAKARTA 79°

• TOKYO 39°
AVERAGE JANUARY TEMPERATURE
DEGREES FAHRENHEIT AT SELECTED STATIONS

FAHRENHEIT	CELSIUS	FAHRENHEIT	CELSIUS	FAHRENHEIT	CELSIUS
OVER 68°	OVER 20°	14° TO 32°	-10° TO 0°	-40° TO -22°	-40° TO -30°
50° TO 68°	10° TO 20°	-4° TO 14°	-20° TO -10°	UNDER -40°	UNDER -40°
32° TO 50°	0° TO 10°	-22° TO -4°	-30° TO -20°		

AVERAGE JULY TEMPERATURE

• ANKARA 73°
• YEKATERINBURG 64°
• VERKHOYANSK 61°
• ASTANA 70°
• IRKUTSK 64°
• TASHKENT 81°
• RIYADH 95°
• BEIJING 79°
• TOKYO 77°
• NEW DELHI 88°
• CHONGQING 82°
• DHAKA 82°
• MUMBAI 81°
• MANILA 81°
• JAKARTA 79°

• TOKYO 77°
AVERAGE JULY TEMPERATURE
DEGREES FAHRENHEIT AT SELECTED STATIONS

FAHRENHEIT	CELSIUS	FAHRENHEIT	CELSIUS	FAHRENHEIT	CELSIUS
OVER 86°	OVER 30°	50° TO 68°	10° TO 20°	UNDER 32°	UNDER 0°
68° TO 86°	20° TO 30°	32° TO 50°	0° TO 10°		

CLIMATE

HUMID TROPICAL
- Af NO DRY SEASON
- Am SHORT DRY SEASON
- Aw DRY WINTER

DRY
- BS SEMIARID ⎤ h HOT
- BW ARID ⎦ k COLD

AFTER KOEPPEN-GEIGER

HUMID WARM
- Cf NO DRY SEASON
- Cw DRY WINTER
- Cs DRY SUMMER

HUMID COLD
- Df NO DRY SEASON
- Dw DRY WINTER
- Ds DRY SUMMER

COLD POLAR
- ET SHORT COOL SUMMER, LONG COLD WINTER
- E COLD AND UNCLASSIFIED HIGHLANDS
- a HOT SUMMER
- b COOL SUMMER
- c SHORT COOL SUMMER
- d VERY COLD WINTER

VEGETATION

TROPICAL FOREST
- TROPICAL RAINFOREST
- LIGHT TROPICAL FOREST
- WOODLAND AND SHRUB

TROPICAL GRASSLAND
- GRASS AND SHRUB (SAVANNA)
- WOODED SAVANNA

MID-LATITUDE FOREST
- NEEDLELEAF FOREST
- BROADLEAF FOREST
- MIXED NEEDLELEAF AND BROADLEAF FOREST
- WOODLAND AND SHRUB (MEDITERRANEAN)

MID-LATITUDE GRASSLAND
- SHORT GRASS (STEPPE)
- WOODED STEPPE
- DESERT AND DESERT SHRUB
- TUNDRA AND ALPINE
- UNCLASSIFIED HIGHLANDS

Asia - Geographical Comparisons

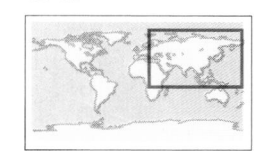

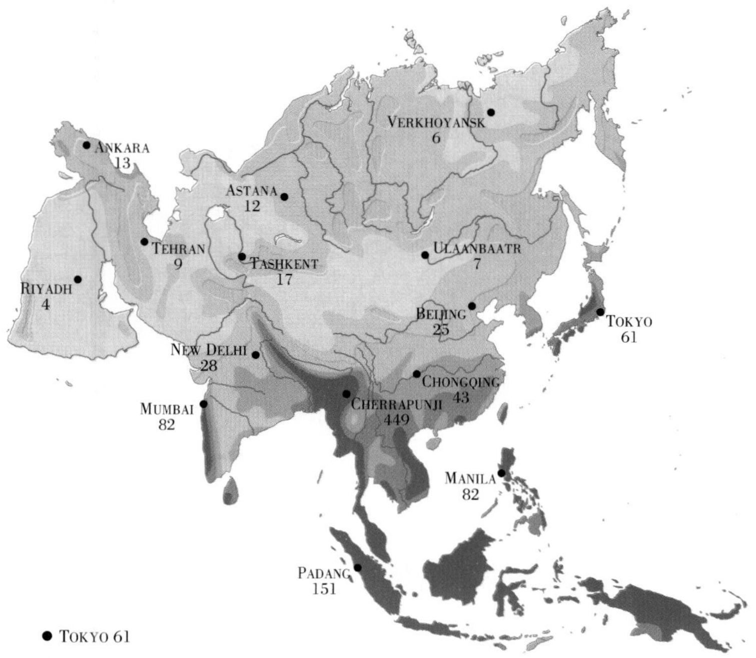

AVERAGE ANNUAL RAINFALL

ANKARA 13
VERKHOYANSK 6
ASTANA 12
TEHRAN 9
TASHKENT 17
ULAANBAATR 7
RIYADH 4
BEIJING 25
TOKYO 61
NEW DELHI 28
CHONGQING 43
CHERRAPUNJI 449
MUMBAI 82
MANILA 82
PADANG 151

● TOKYO 61

AVERAGE ANNUAL RAINFALL
IN INCHES AT SELECTED STATIONS

INCHES	CM	INCHES	CM	INCHES	CM
OVER 80	OVER 200	40 TO 60	100 TO 150	10 TO 20	25 TO 50
60 TO 80	150 TO 200	20 TO 40	50 TO 100	UNDER 10	UNDER 25

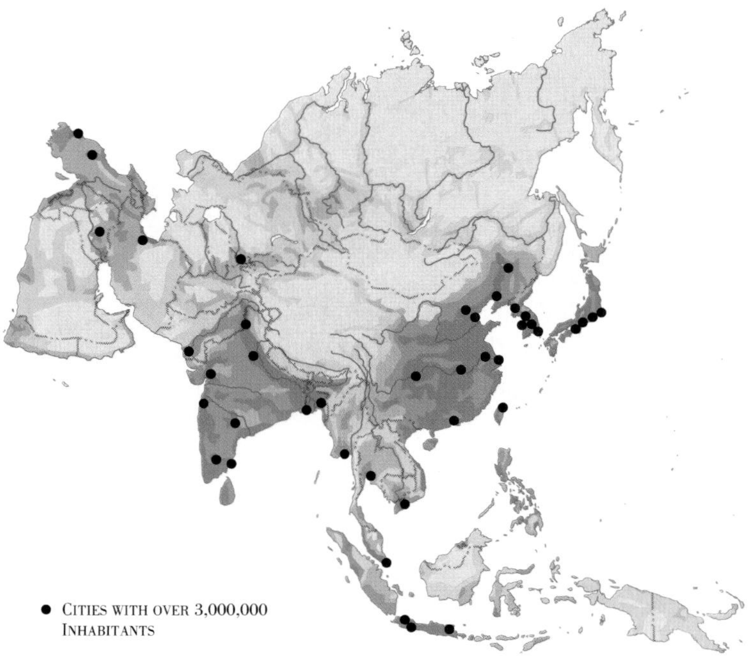

POPULATION DISTRIBUTION

● CITIES WITH OVER 3,000,000 INHABITANTS

DENSITY PER		SQ. MI.	SQ. KM.	SQ. MI.	SQ. KM.
SQ. MI.	SQ. KM.	130 TO 260	50 TO 100	3 TO 25	1 TO 10
OVER 260	OVER 100	25 TO 130	10 TO 50	UNDER 3	UNDER 1

LAND USE

TOBACCO
OLIVES WHEAT
FRUIT
SHEEP
DATES
SHEEP
DATES
FURS
CATTLE POTATOES OATS WHEAT
OATS
WHEAT
OATS
SHEEP
COTTON
SHEEP
WHEAT
SHEEP
POTATOES SOYBEANS
WHEAT
RICE SOYBEANS
CORN COTTON
RICE TEA
HOGS
SUGARCANE
FURS
FRUIT TEA
CATTLE
WHEAT
COTTON RICE TEA
PEANUTS JUTE RICE
RICE
RICE CASSAVA CORN
RICE
RICE TEA
RUBBER
FRUIT
ABACA SUGARCANE
RUBBER
RUBBER
RUBBER
COCONUTS
RICE
COFFEE
SPICES
SPICES
COCONUTS
COCONUTS
COCOA

CEREALS, LIVESTOCK	DIVERSIFIED TROPICAL & SUBTROPICAL CROPS	SPECIAL CROPS
CASH CROPS, MIXED FARMING	LIVESTOCK RANCHING & HERDING	FORESTS
DAIRY, LIVESTOCK		NONPRODUCTIVE

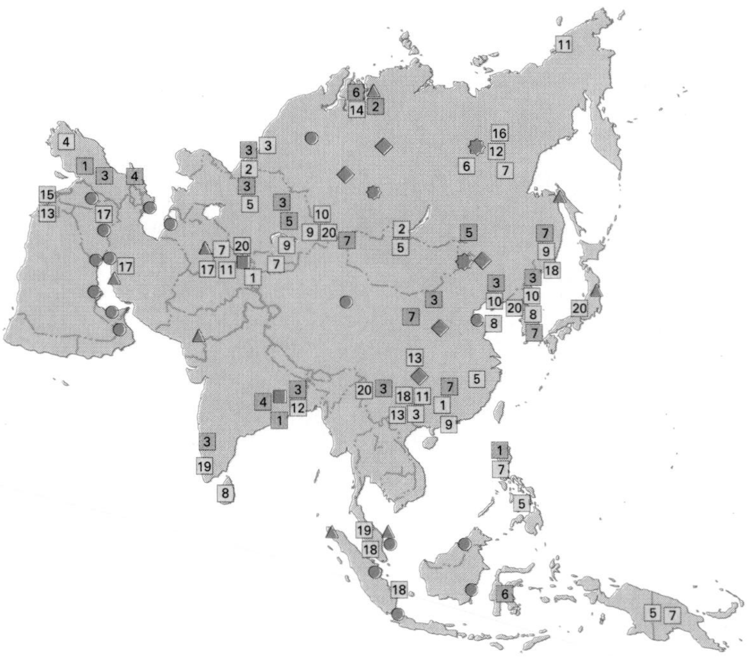

MINERAL RESOURCES

ENERGY & FUELS
◆ COAL
⬡ LIGNITE
▲ NATURAL GAS
● PETROLEUM
■ URANIUM

IRON & FERROALLOYS
1 CHROMIUM
2 COBALT
3 IRON ORE
4 MANGANESE
5 MOLYBDENUM
6 NICKEL
7 TUNGSTEN

OTHER MAJOR RESOURCES
1 ANTIMONY	8 GRAPHITE	15 POTASH
2 ASBESTOS	9 LEAD	16 SILVER
3 BAUXITE	10 MAGNESITE	17 SULFER
4 BORAX	11 MERCURY	18 TIN
5 COPPER	12 MICA	19 TITANIUM
6 DIAMONDS	13 PHOSPHATES	20 ZINC
7 GOLD	14 PLATINUM	

Northeastern China

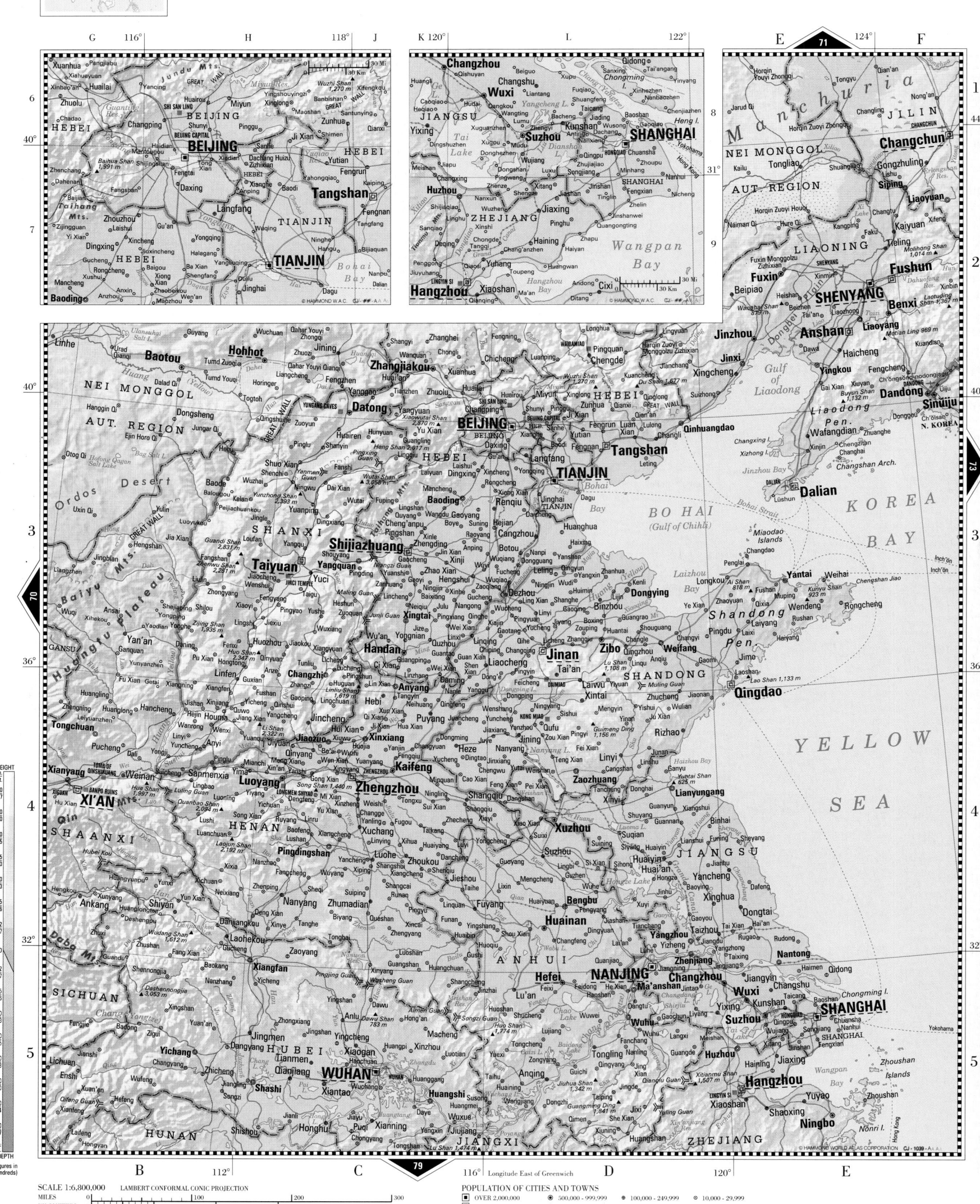

SCALE 1:6,800,000   LAMBERT CONFORMAL CONIC PROJECTION

MILES

KILOMETERS

POPULATION OF CITIES AND TOWNS

- ◉ OVER 2,000,000
- ⬜ 1,000,000 - 1,999,999
- ◉ 500,000 - 999,999
- ◻ 250,000 - 499,999
- ◎ 100,000 - 249,999
- ◉ 30,000 - 99,999
- ⊚ 10,000 - 29,999
- ○ UNDER 10,000

Longitude East of Greenwich

Korea

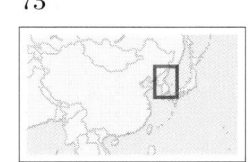

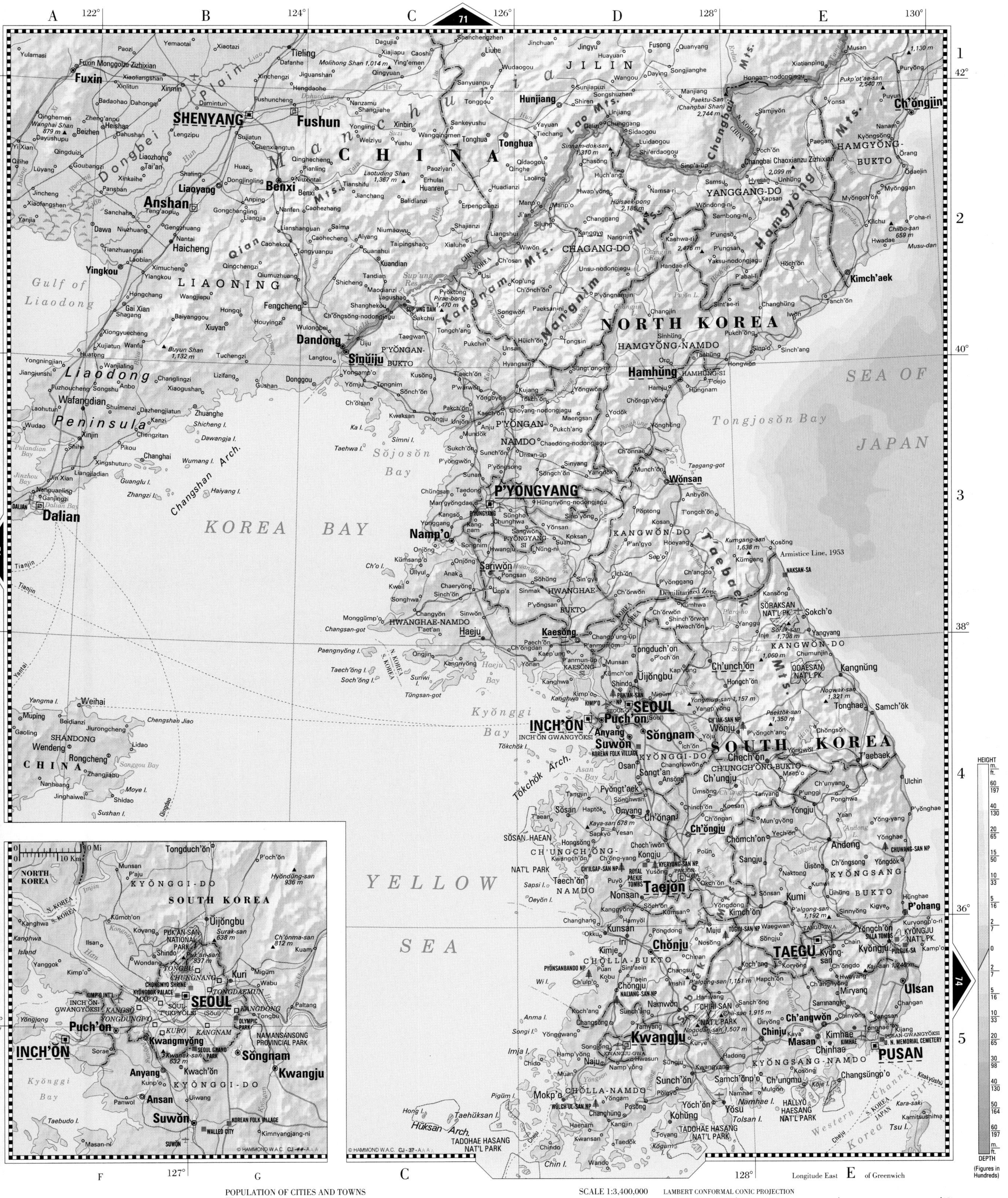

POPULATION OF CITIES AND TOWNS

■ OVER 2,000,000
◻ 1,000,000 - 1,999,999
◼ 500,000 - 999,999
● 250,000 - 499,999
● 100,000 - 249,999
● 30,000 - 99,999
● 10,000 - 29,999
○ UNDER 10,000

SCALE 1:3,400,000   LAMBERT CONFORMAL CONIC PROJECTION

MILES 0   50   100   150

KILOMETERS 0   50   100   150

HEIGHT	
m.	ft.
60	197
40	130
20	65
15	50
10	33
5	16
2	7
0	0
2	7
5	16
10	33
20	65
30	98
50	164
60	197

DEPTH

(Figures in Hundreds)

Longitude East of Greenwich

Central and Southern Japan

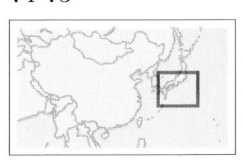

E 138° F 140° 142° H 144° J

Awa-shima
Sagae Higashine MIYAGI Ishinomaki Onagawa
Hajiki-zaki YAMAGATA Tendō Yamoto Matsushima
Murakami Asahi-dake Higashine **Sendai** Shiogama
YAMAGATA **Yamagata** Zaō-san 1,841 m Sendai Bay
Aikawa Ryōtsu BANDAI-ASAHI Nakajo Kaminoyama Iwanuma
NIIGATA NP Nagai Takahata SENDAI Watari
Niigata Niitsu Iide-san 2,105 m **Fukushima** Kakuda
Sado Shibata Gosen Yonezawa Sōma
Sawasaki-bana Ogi Tsubame Shirone Kitakata Hobara Haramachi
Suzu-misaki Sanjō Yamato Aizu- BANDAI-ASAH' Nihonmatsu Namie
Suzu Kamo Mitsuke Wakamatsu NP Motomiya
Toyama Bay Nagaoka Ojiya Bandai-san 1,819 m Miharu Towada
Nanao Tochio **Kōriyama** Ōtakine-yama
WA Itoigawa Joetsu FUKUSHIMA Sukagawa 1,193 m
Himi Nyūzen NIIGATA Tajima Yabuki Ishikawa
Uozu Arai Myōkō-san 2,446 m TŌHOKU Shirakawa **Iwaki**
Namerikawa Iiyama CHŪBU Nasu-san 1,917 m Kuroiso Shioya-saki
Toyama Tate-yama JOSHIN-ETSU Shirane-san 2,578 m Tanagura Kita-Ibaraki
3,015 m Ōmachi NIKKO NAT'L Yaita Daigo Takahagi
TOYAMA Yari-ga-take **Nagano** KOGEN Nantai-san 2,484 m PARK Nikko Otawara Hitachi
wa 3,180 m Hotaka GUMMA Imaichi Ōmiya Hitachi-ōta
Hotaka-dake 3,190 m Toyoshina Azumaya-san 2,333 m Kanuma Mōka Katsuta
JAPANESE Asama-yama 2,542 m Ishibashi Kasama Nakaminato
akayama ALPS NAT'L Maruko Takasaki **Maebashi** TOCHIGI
Norikura-san 3,026 m PARK Saku Isesaki Kiryū Tochigi **Utsunomiya** Mito
Matsumoto Ueda Ōta Oyama Shimodate
NAGANO Okaya Fujioka Sano Yūki Ishioka
Intake-san 3,063 m Suwa Chichibu Kumagaya IBARAKI Tsuchiura
Ina Kobushi-ga-take 2,475 m SAITAMA Sakai Ishige Kashima
GIFU Chino Kasukabe Kuki Mitsukaidō Iwai Kita
Komagane CHICHIBU TAMA Kawagoe Koshigaya Sawara
amigahara MINAMI-ALPS NAT'L PARK Sayama **Kawaguchi** Ryūgasaki
Tajimi Nirasaki **Tokorozawa** Tachikawa NARITA INT'L Chōshi
uyama Akaishi-dake 3,120 m YAMANASHI Enzan **Urawa** Asahi Inubō-zaki
Mizunami Shirane-san 3,192 m Kōfu Tsuru **Hachiōji** Chofu **TŌKYŌ** **Chiba**
Seto Ina Uenohara **Kawasaki** CHIBA
NAGOYA AICHI Fujiyoshida Isehara **Sagamihara** **YOKOHAMA**
Toyota Ena Nakatsugawa KANAGAWA Hadano **Fujisawa** Kisarazu
Okazaki Fujiyama 3,776 m FUJI-Gotemba Kimitsu
Nishio SHIZUOKA HAKONE Chigasaki **Yokosuka** Ōtaki
Toyokawa Susono Odawara Kyonan
Toyohashi Iwata Fukuroi Mishima Futtsu Katsuura
Irago-misaki Tenryū **Shizuoka** Fuji IZU Atami Tomiyama Kamogawa
Hamamatsu Hamakita Shimizu NAT'L PARK Itō Tateyama Nojima-zaki
Kosai Fujieda Yaizu CHŪBU Sagami Sea
Tōi Amagi-san 1,407 m
Suruga Bay Shimoda Ō Island
Omae-zaki IZU Ōshima **Honshū**
iō-zaki FUJI-HAKONE- Peninsula IZU NAT'L PARK
PARK Nii-jima
KANTŌ Kōzu-shima **TŌKYŌ**
Miyake-jima
MIYAKEJIMA

Izu
Mikura-jima

FUJI-HAKONE-
IZU NAT'L
PARK
(JAPAN)
Hachijō-jima
Hachijō
HACHIJŌJIMA
Islands

Aoga-shima

Beyonesu-retsugan

P A C I F I C
O C E A N

Inset map (Kyūshū / Ryūkyū Islands)

Koshiki Sendai Kokubu Miyakonojō
Is. Kushikino Iijin KAGOSHIMA Nichinan
Kushima Tarumizu
Kagoshima Kaseda Kanoya Kōyama Kyūshū
Makurazaki Sata-misaki Nishino'omote
Nishino'omote Tanega- Nakatane
shima
Kamiyaku Ōsumi
Yaku 1,935 m Islands
Shanghai Kuchino-shima
Suwanose-jima
EAST KAGOSHIMA
CHINA Tokara
SEA Islands
Naze Amami-ōshima
Setouchi Kikai
Tokuno Tokunoshima
Amami
Okihoerabu
Iheya Yoron
Ie Motobu Yonaha-dake
Nago 498 m
Gushikawa
Ginowan Gushikawa
Naha Urasoe
Itoman
Kume Kyan-zaki Kitadaitō
Keelung Senkaku-Shotō Minamidaitō
OKINAWA
PACIFIC
OCEAN
Sakishima Islands Hirara
Ishigaki Tamara Miyako
Yonaguni Kitadaitō
Iriomote Miyako Is. Okidaitō
Ishigaki
Yaeyama Is.

R y u k y u Islands
(Nansei - Shotō)
Okinawa Is.
Hedo-misaki

POPULATION OF CITIES AND TOWNS

■ OVER 2,000,000	● 500,000 - 999,999	⊕ 100,000 - 249,999	○ 10,000 - 29,999
□ 1,000,000 - 1,999,999	◉ 250,000 - 499,999	⊙ 30,000 - 99,999	○ UNDER 10,000

SCALE 1:3,400,000 LAMBERT CONFORMAL CONIC PROJECTION

MILES 0 ... 50 ... 100 ... 150
KILOMETERS 0 ... 50 ... 100 ... 150

0 ... 60 Mi
0 ... 60 Km

E 138° F G 124° H 126° J 128° K 130° L

Northern Japan

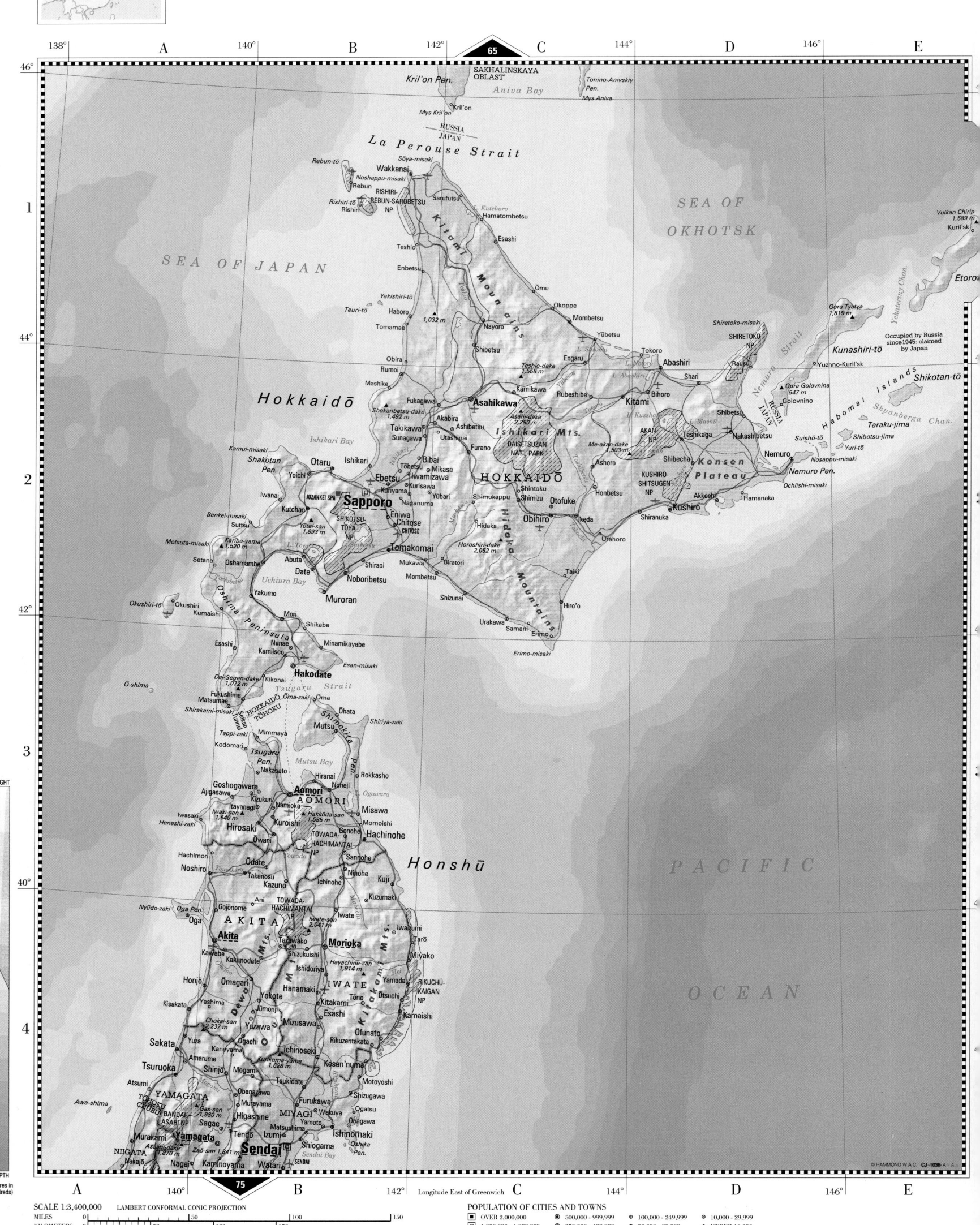

65

75

SCALE 1:3,400,000   LAMBERT CONFORMAL CONIC PROJECTION

MILES 0   50   100   150
KILOMETERS 0   50   100   150

POPULATION OF CITIES AND TOWNS

■ OVER 2,000,000	● 500,000 - 999,999	● 100,000 - 249,999	⊙ 10,000 - 29,999
▣ 1,000,000 - 1,999,999	● 250,000 - 499,999	● 30,000 - 99,999	○ UNDER 10,000

HEIGHT
m. / ft.
60 / 197
40 / 130
20 / 65
15 / 50
10 / 33
5 / 16
0
-2 / -7
-5 / -16
-10 / -33
-20 / -65
-30 / -98
-40 / -130
-50 / -164
-60 / -197
m. / ft.
DEPTH
(Figures in Hundreds)

Tōkyō-Yokohama, Ōsaka-Nagoya

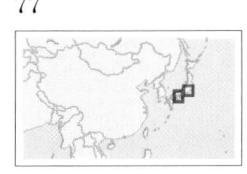

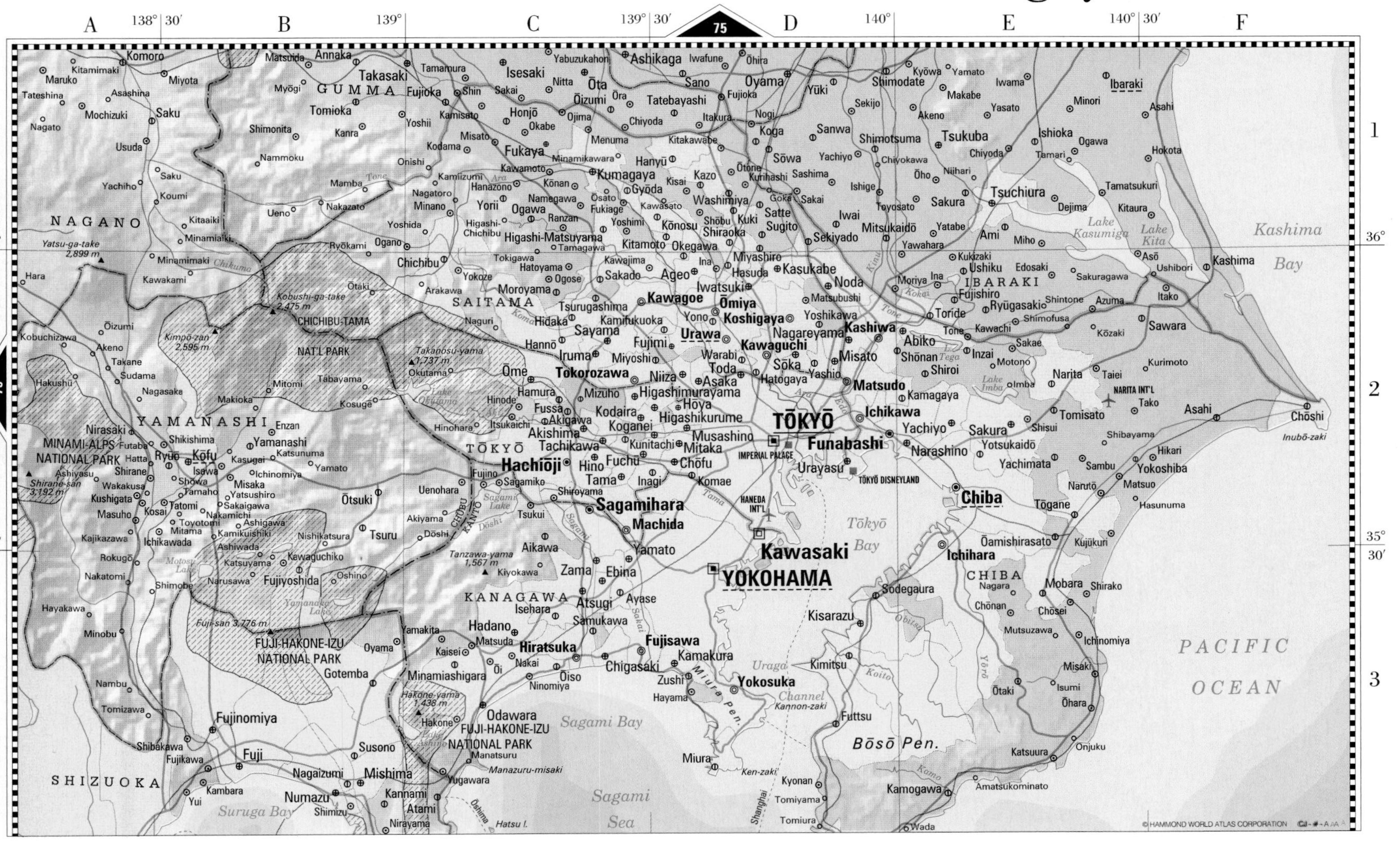

POPULATION OF CITIES AND TOWNS

◉ OVER 2,000,000	◉ 500,000 - 999,999	◎ 100,000 - 249,999	○ 10,000 - 29,999
▣ 1,000,000 - 1,999,999	◉ 250,000 - 499,999	◎ 30,000 - 99,999	○ UNDER 10,000

SCALE 1:1,140,000   LAMBERT CONFORMAL CONIC PROJECTION

MILES

KILOMETERS

HEIGHT
ft.   m
16,400   5,000
13,120   4,000
6,560   2,000
3,280   1,000
1,640   500
820   250
0   0
330   100
660   200
1,640   500
3,280   1,000
6,560   2,000
16,400   5,000
32,800   10,000

DEPTH
(Figures in Hundreds)

© HAMMOND WORLD ATLAS CORPORATION

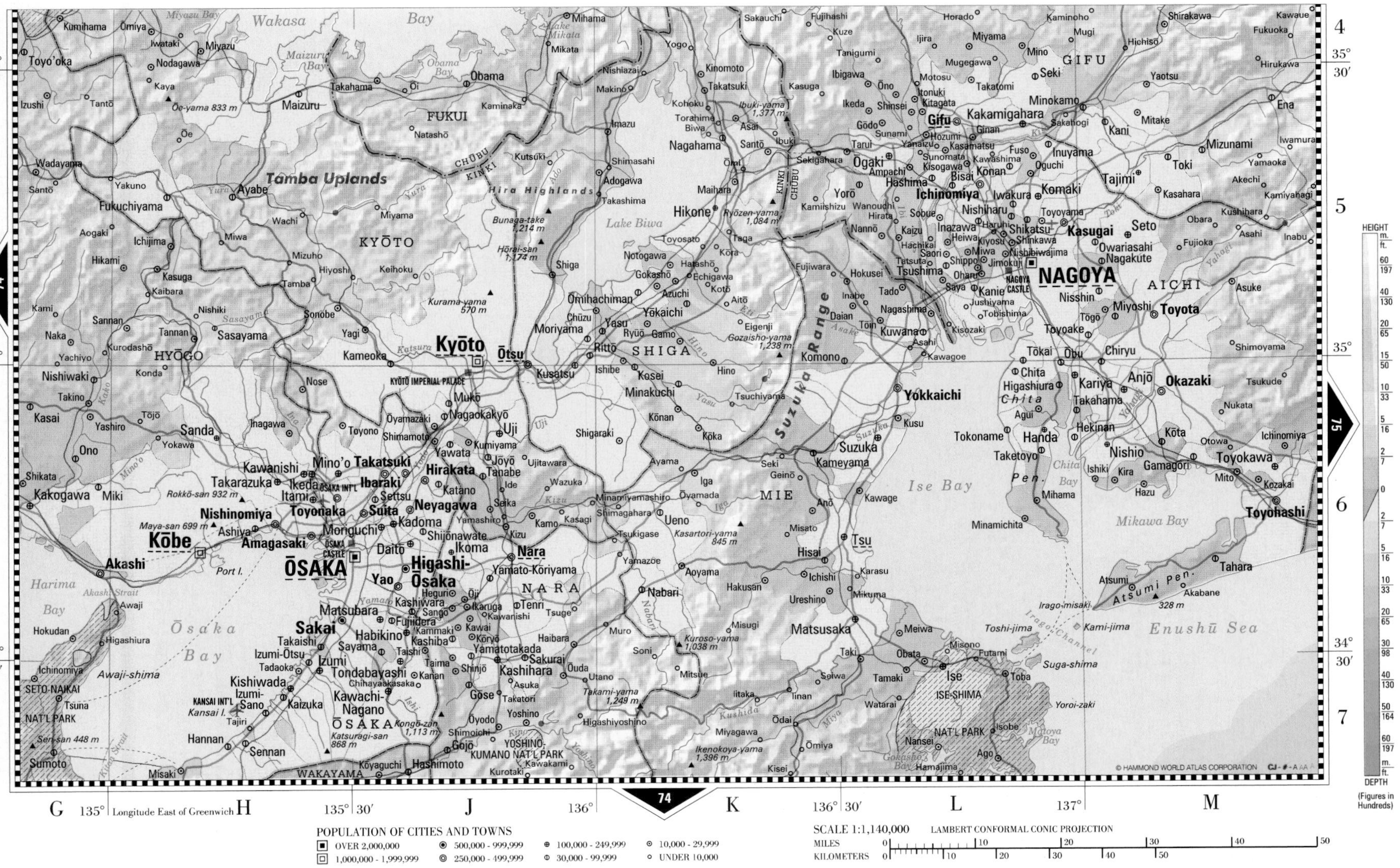

Indochina

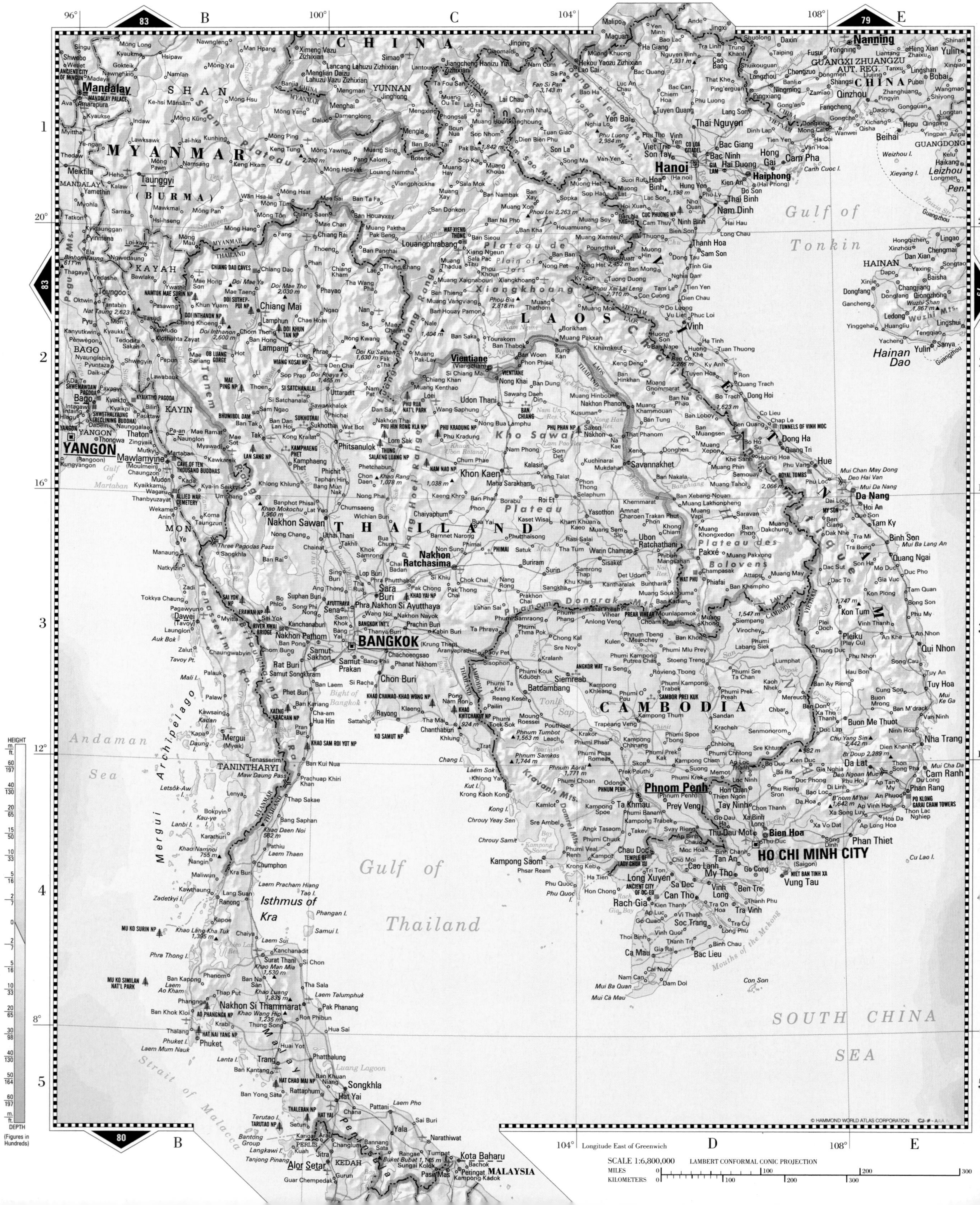

Southeastern China, Taiwan, Philippines

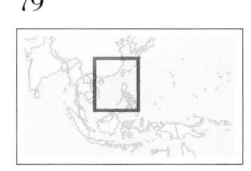

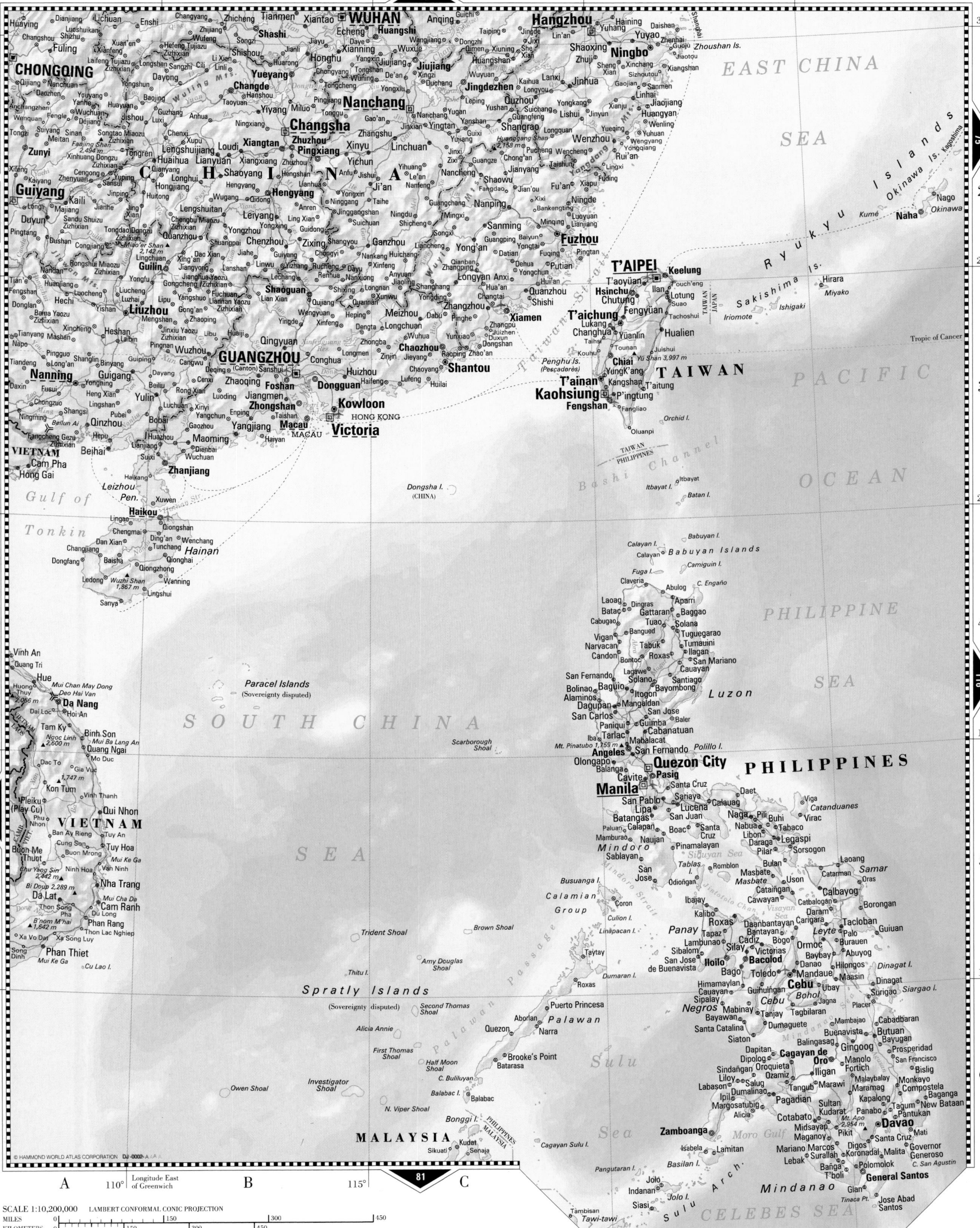

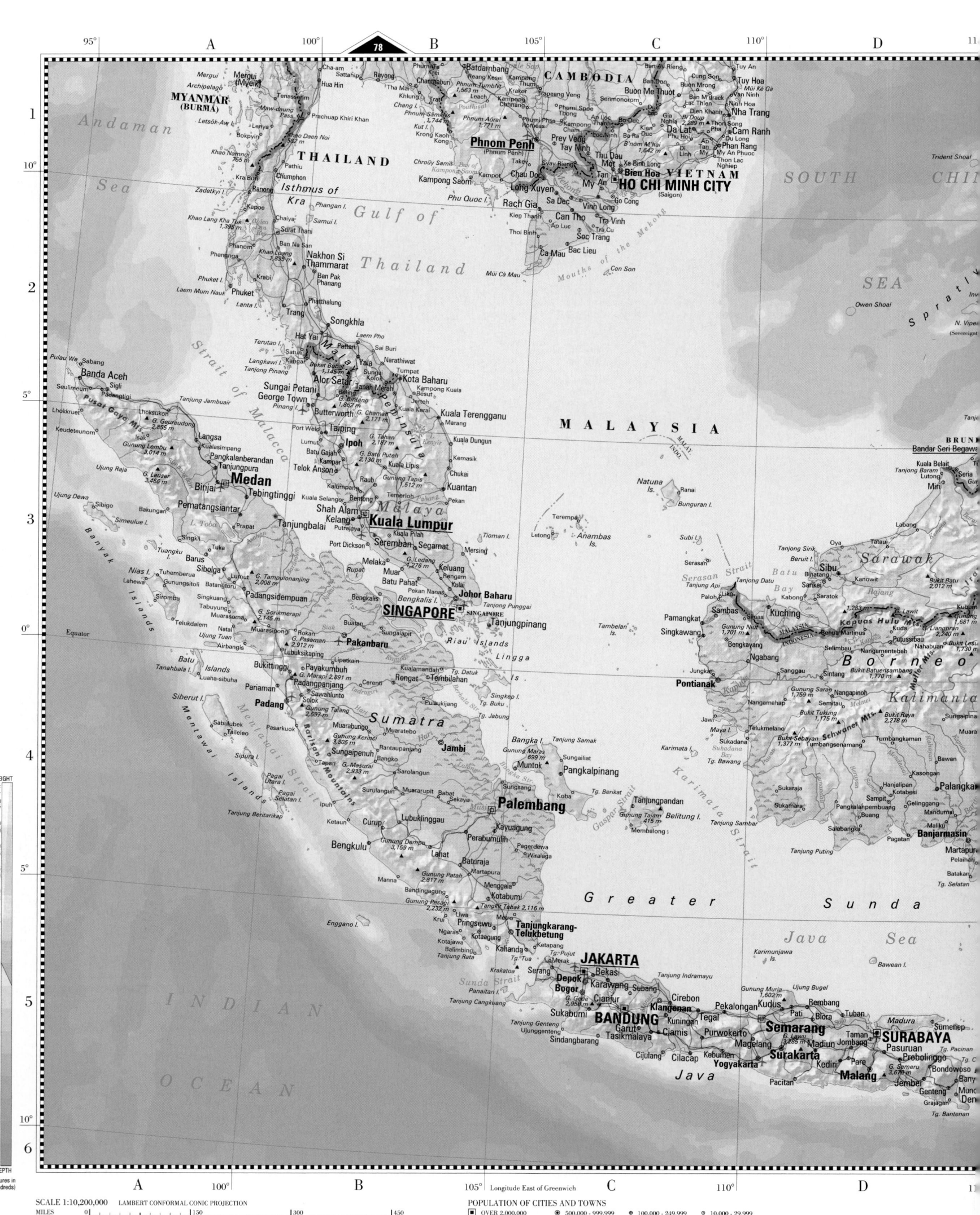

SCALE 1:10,200,000   LAMBERT CONFORMAL CONIC PROJECTION

MILES   0   150   300   450
KILOMETERS 0   150   300   450

POPULATION OF CITIES AND TOWNS

■ OVER 2,000,000   ⊚ 500,000 - 999,999   ● 100,000 - 249,999   ○ 10,000 - 29,999
□ 1,000,000 - 1,999,999   ⊙ 250,000 - 499,999   ● 30,000 - 99,999   ○ UNDER 10,000

Longitude East of Greenwich

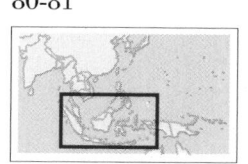

E | 120° | F | H | 135° | J | 140° | K

Main map labels:

PHILIPPINES
Mindoro, Panay, Negros, Cebu, Bohol, Masbate, Luzon
Mamburao, Mt. Halcon 2,582 m, Pinamalayan, Bongabong, Ligao, Daraga, Pilar, Bulan, Uson, Romblon, Sibuyan, Mansalay, Masbate
Calamian Group, Coron, Pulanduta Pt., Kalibo, Roxas, Mt. Nangtud 2,117 m
Cuyo Is., Cuyo, Patnongon, Silay, Sagay, Cadiz, Bacolod, Iloilo
Cleopatra Needle 1,602 m, Roxas, Dumaran I., San Jose, Naso Pt. Canlaon Volcano 2,465 m, Guihulngan, Tagbilaran
Puerto Princesa, Victoria Pk. 1,709 m, Quezon, Narra, Dumaguete, Bayawan, Siaton Pt.
Palawan, Mt. Mantalingajan 2,085 m, Brookes Point, Dipolog, Oroquieta, Pagadian
Zamboanga, Isabela, Lamitan, Basilan Pk. 1,011 m, Basilan I., Jolo, Jolo I.
Cagayan de Oro, Iligan, Marawi, Mt. Ragang 2,815 m, Cotabato, Davao, Tagum, Digos, Mati
Koronadal, General Santos, Jose Abad Santos, Glan
Kudapawan, Mt. Apo 2,954 m, Mt. Matutum 2,293 m, Polomolok, Malita
Sabah, Sandakan, Lahad Datu, Tawau, Semporna, Tawitawi, Bongao, Siasi, South Ubian
Gunung Kinabalu 4,101 m, Kudat, Beluran, Tambisan
Celebes Sea, Sulu Sea, Sulu Arch., Talaud Is., Karakelong I., Rainis, Sangihe I., Tahuna
Tarakan, Nunukan, Malinau, Longbang
Samarinda, Balikpapan, Bontang
Manado, Bitung, Tondano, Gorontalo, Minahasa, Tolitoli, Palu, Poso, Parigi
Celebes (Sulawesi), Gulf of Tomini, Molucca Sea, Banggai Is., Sula Islands, Taliabu, Mangole I.
Kendari, Kolaka, Ujung Pandang, Bonthain, Bulukumba, Parepare, Singkang, Watampone
Gulf of Bone, Buton I., Muna, Selayar
Flores Sea, Lesser Sunda Islands, Sumbawa, Lombok, Bali, Komodo, Flores, Ende, Sumba, Waingapu
Timor, Kupang, EAST TIMOR, Dili, Timor Sea

Halmahera, Ternate, Tidore I., Morotai, Galela, Obi Islands, Bacan, Kayoa I.
Ceram Sea, Buru, Ambon, Ceram, Wahai, Banda Sea, Banda Is.
Tanimbar Islands, Yamdena I., Larat I., Kai Islands, Kai Besar I., Aru Islands, Dobo, Trangan I.
Barat Daya Islands, Babar I., Wetar I., Leti Is., Moa I., Sermata Is.

New Guinea, Doberai Peninsula, Sorong, Misool I., Salawati I., Waigeo I.
Bomberai Pen., Fakfak, Kaimana, Nabire
Irian Jaya, Maoke Mountains, Puncak Jaya 5,030 m, Puncak Tricora 4,730 m, Puncak Mandala 4,700 m
Jayapura, Vanimo, Sentani, Wamena, Enarotali, Mulia
Van Rees Mts. 2,164 m, Tariku-taritatu, Biak I.
Aru Islands, Kobroor I., Wokam I., Banda Elat
Arafura Sea, Yos Sudarso Island, Merauke, Komoran I., Dolok I.

PACIFIC OCEAN
Equator 0°

Scale: 0 — 90 Mi / 0 — 90 Km

© HAMMOND W.A.C. CJ-1127-A-A

I N D O N E S I A

© HAMMOND WORLD ATLAS CORPORATION CJ-1047-A-A

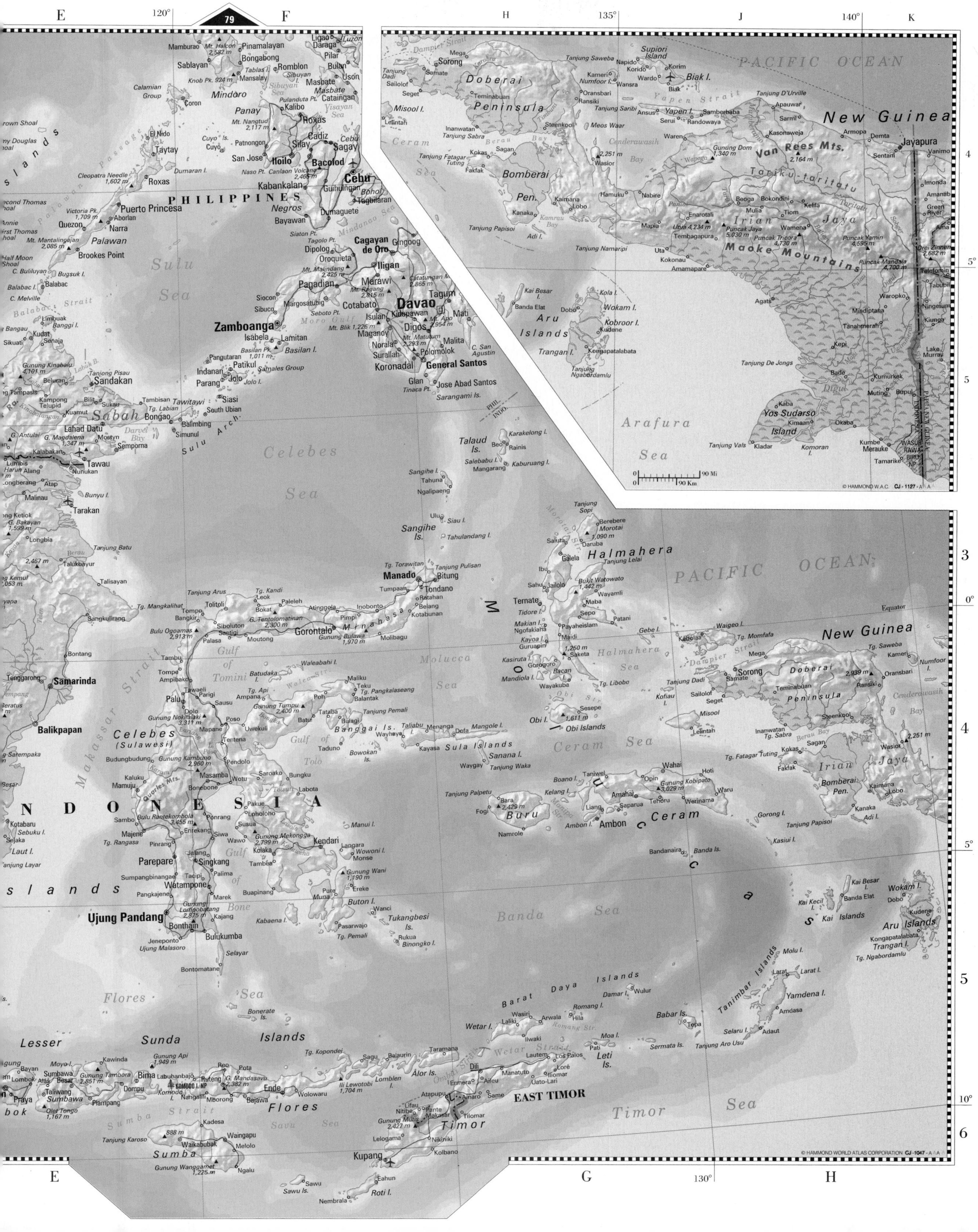

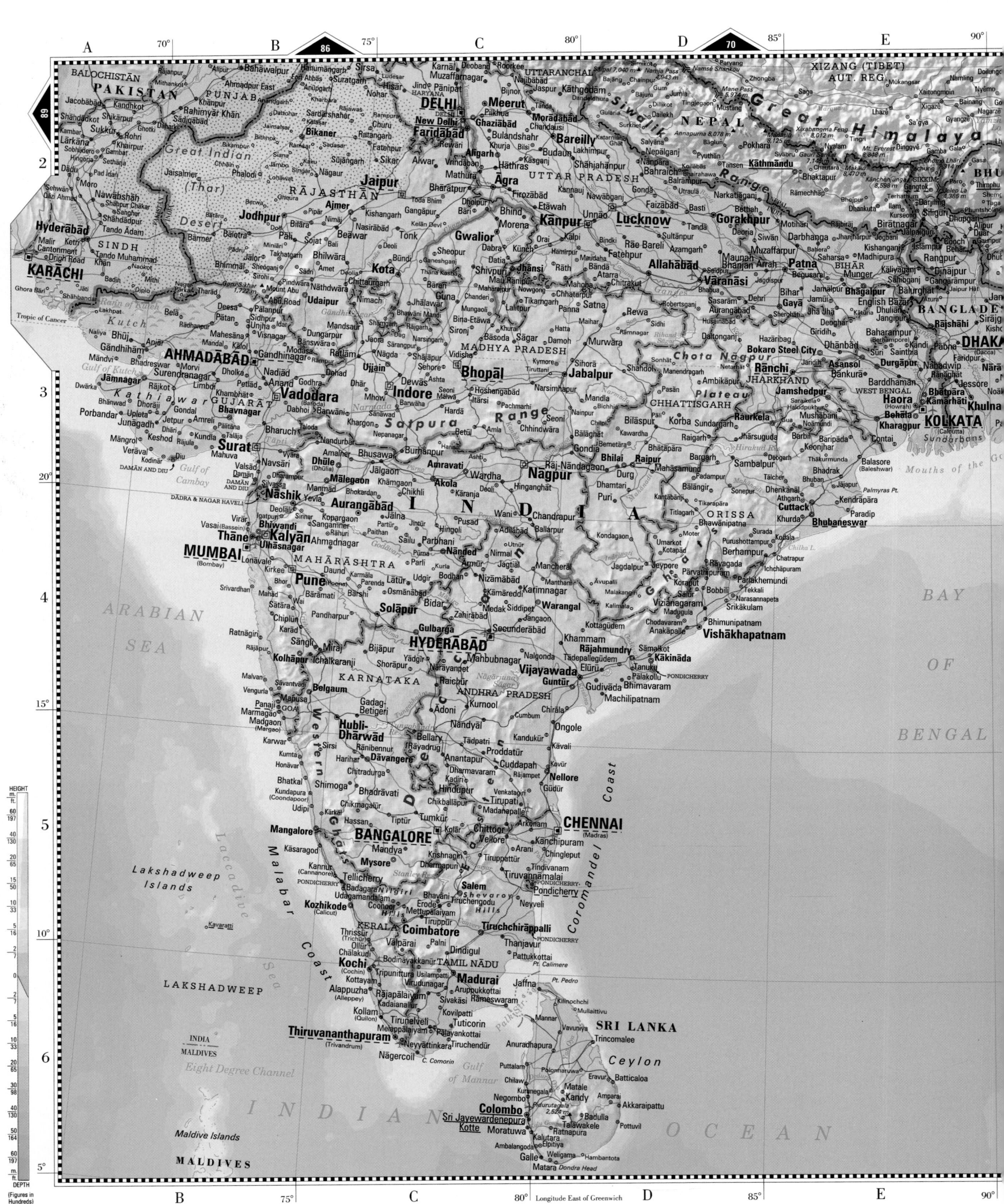

Southern Asia

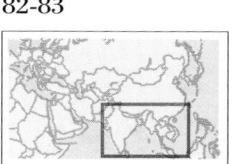

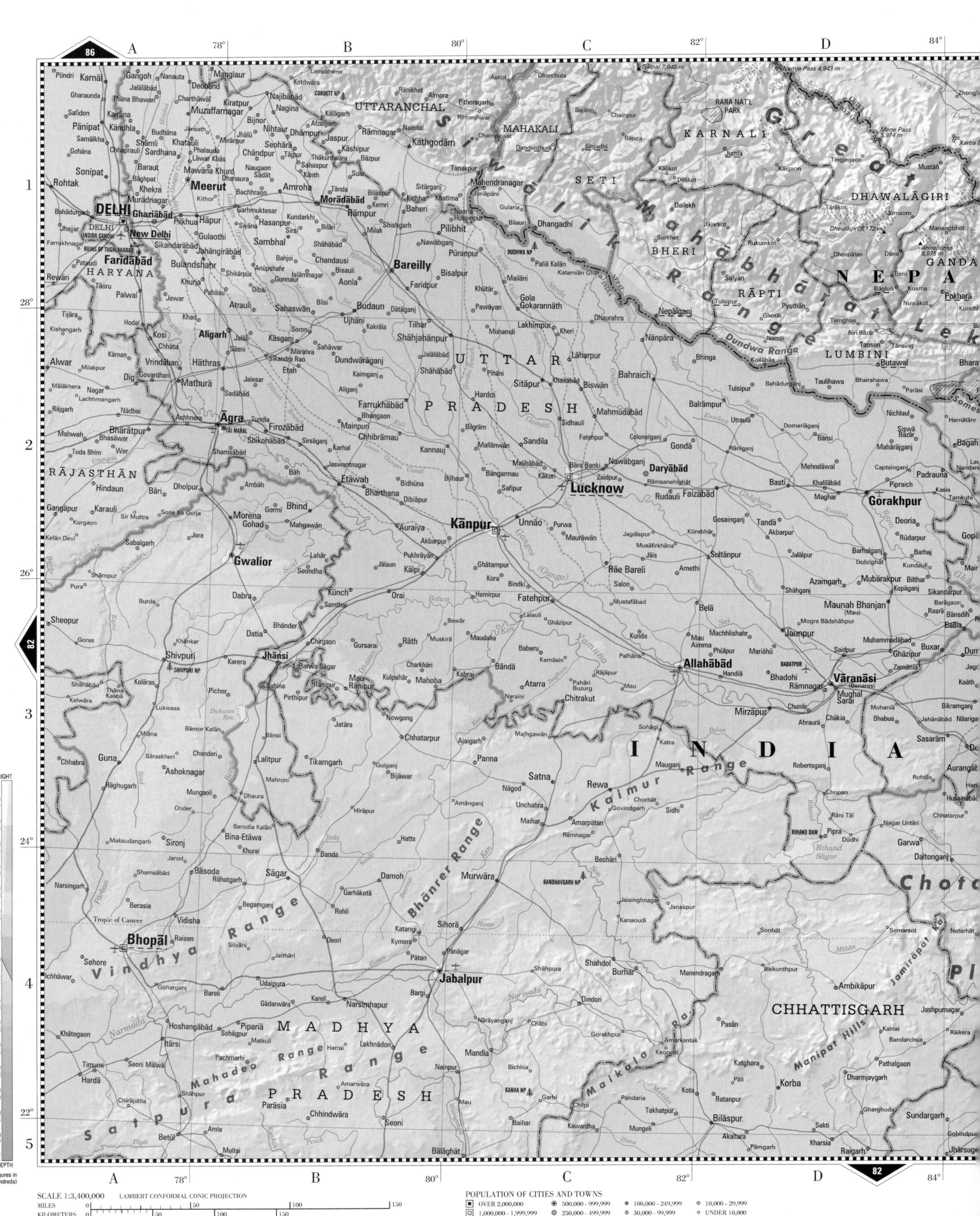

A | 78° | B | 80° | C | 82° | D | 84°

SCALE 1:3,400,000   LAMBERT CONFORMAL CONIC PROJECTION

MILES 0 .... 50 .... 100 150

KILOMETERS 0 .... 50 .... 100 150

POPULATION OF CITIES AND TOWNS

■ OVER 2,000,000
◙ 1,000,000 - 1,999,999
● 500,000 - 999,999
● 250,000 - 499,999
● 100,000 - 249,999
● 30,000 - 99,999
○ 10,000 - 29,999
○ UNDER 10,000

HEIGHT
m.
ft.

6000 / 19700
4000 / 13100
2000 / 6500
1500 / 5000
1000 / 3300
500 / 1600
200 / 700
0

0
200 / 700
2000 / 6500
3000 / 9800
4000 / 13100
5000 / 16400
6000 / 19700
m.
ft.
DEPTH
(Figures in Hundreds)

Ganges Plain

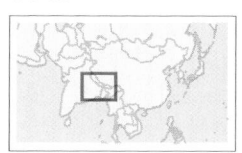

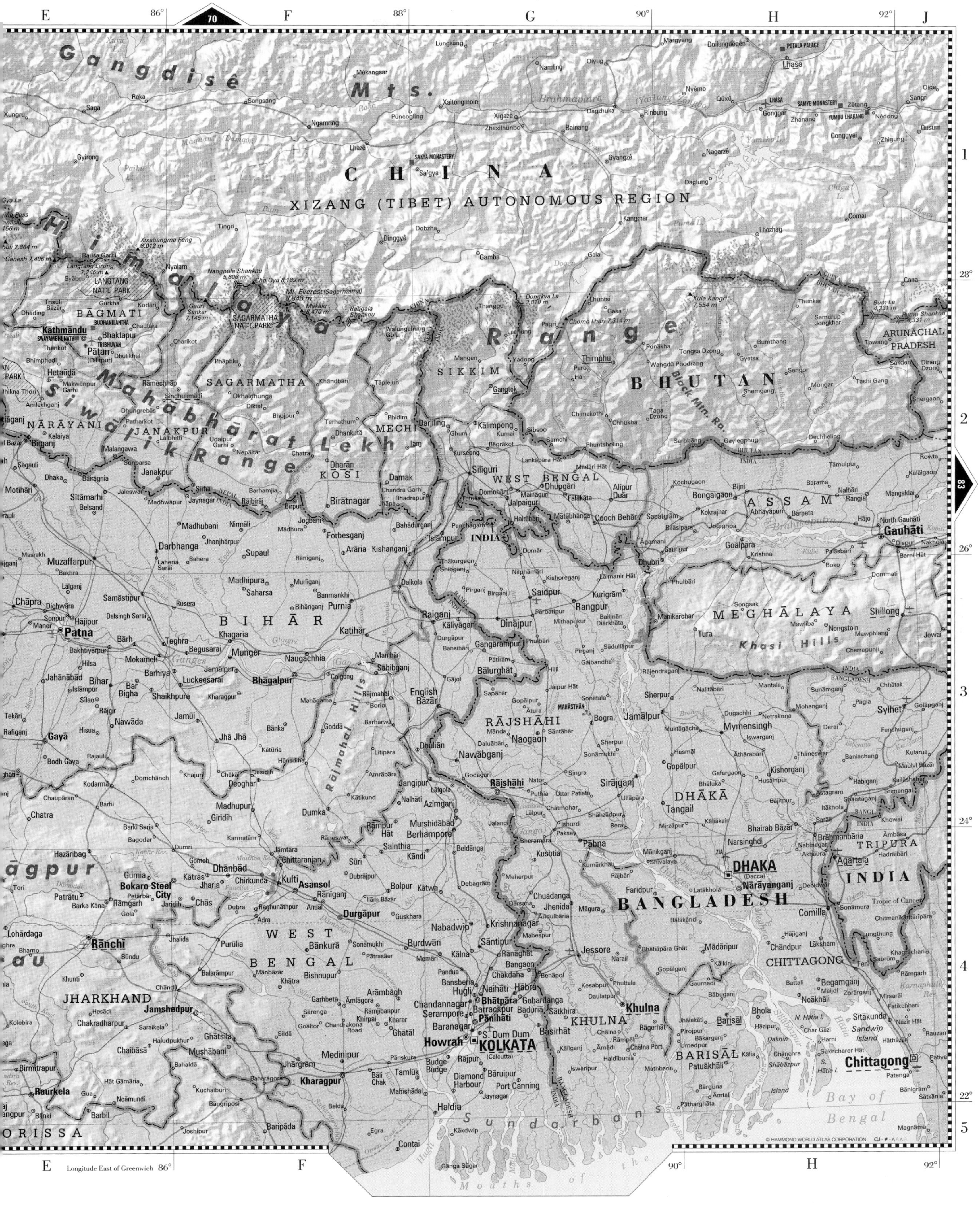

Punjab Plain

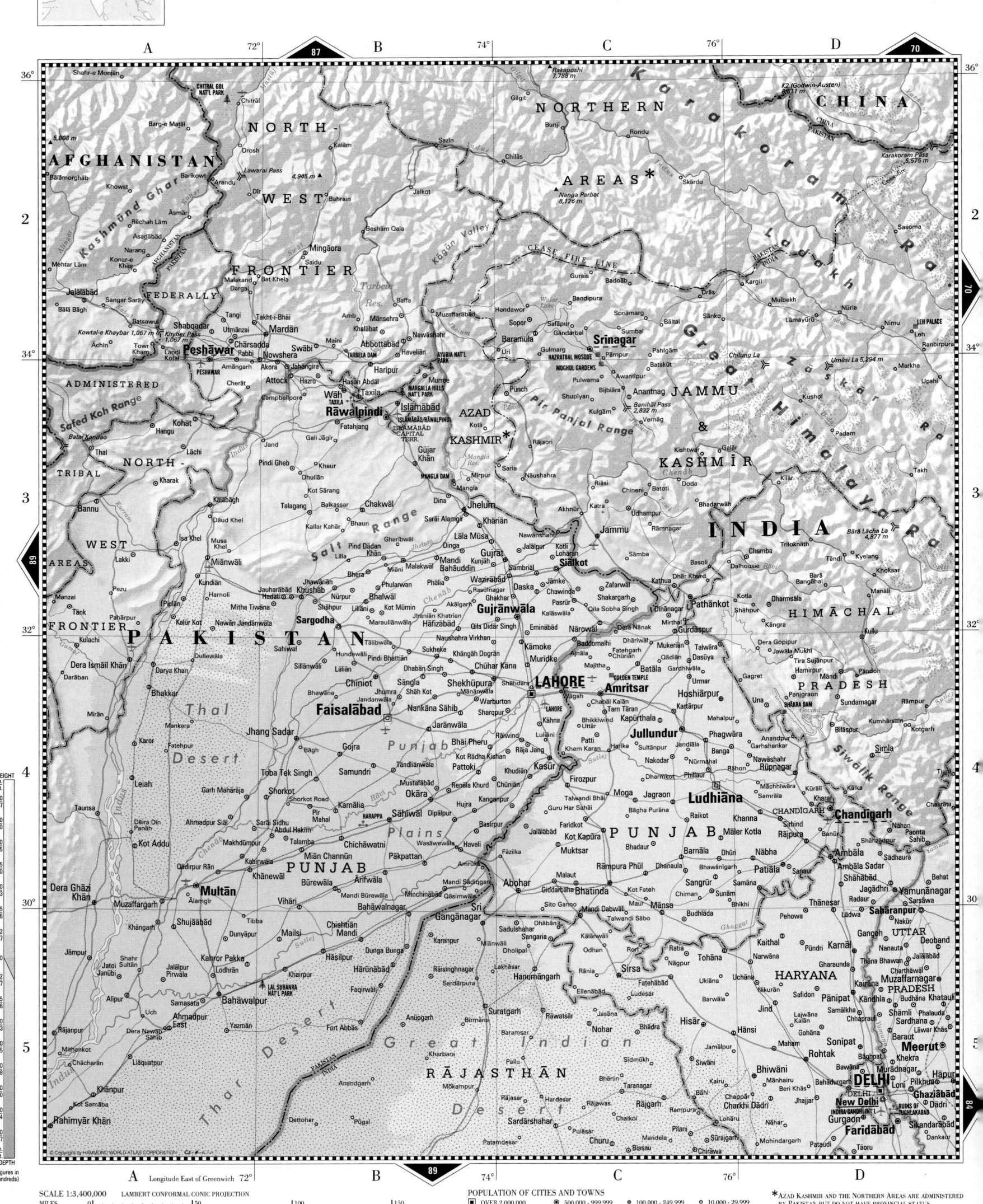

SCALE 1:3,400,000   LAMBERT CONFORMAL CONIC PROJECTION

MILES 0 ⊢⊢⊢⊢ 50 ⊢⊢⊢ 100 ⊢⊢⊢ 150

KILOMETERS 0 ⊢⊢⊢ 50 ⊢⊢⊢ 100 ⊢⊢⊢ 150

POPULATION OF CITIES AND TOWNS

■ OVER 2,000,000   ● 500,000 - 999,999   ● 100,000 - 249,999   ○ 10,000 - 29,999
□ 1,000,000 - 1,999,999   ● 250,000 - 499,999   ● 30,000 - 99,999   ○ UNDER 10,000

*Azad Kashmir and the Northern Areas are administered by Pakistan but do not have provincial status.

Central Asia

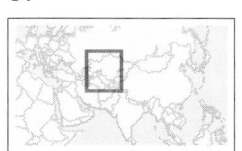

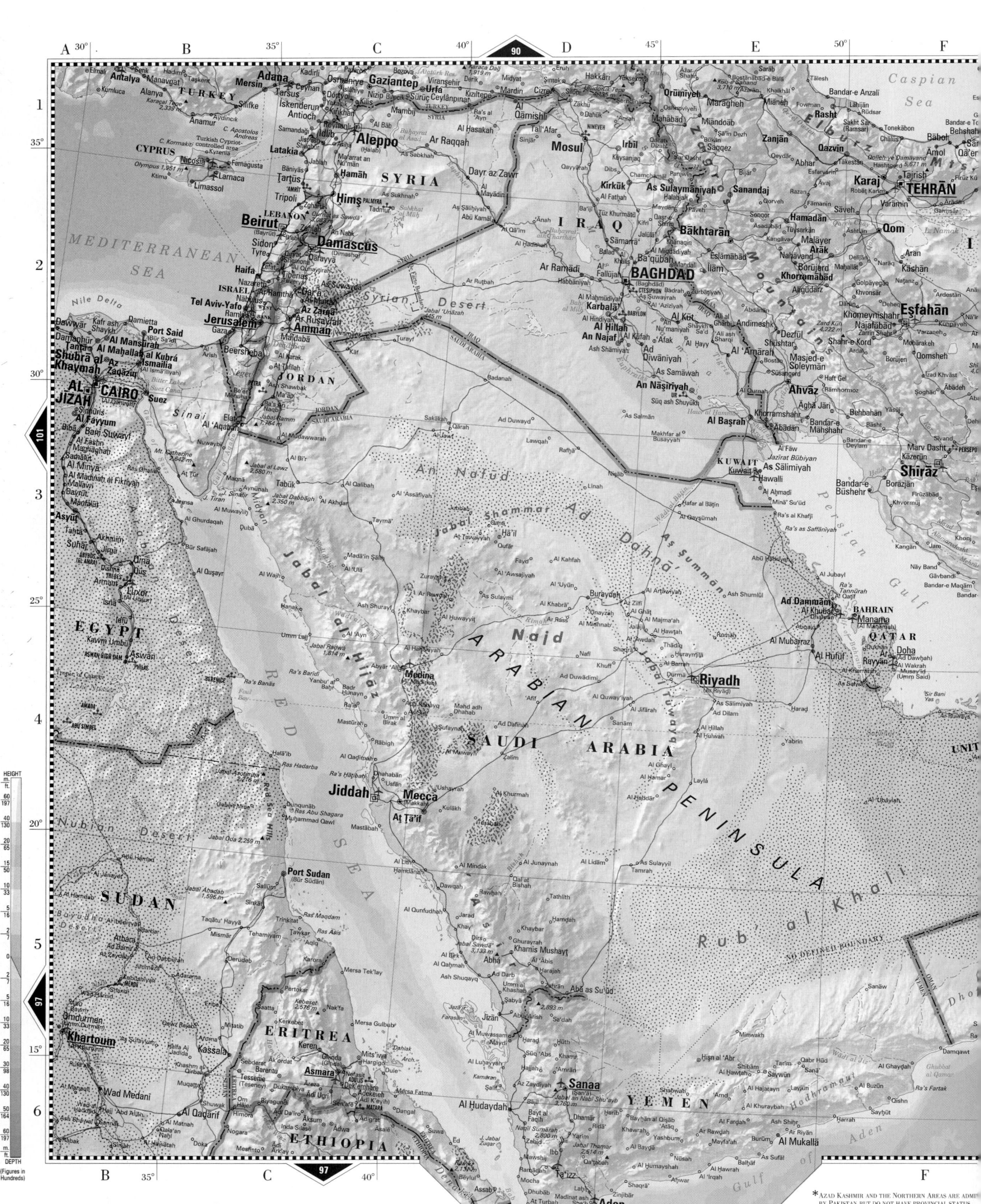

Southwestern Asia

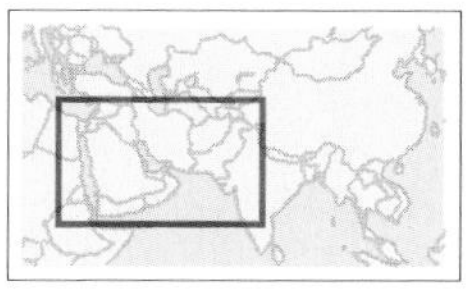

TURKMENISTAN

UZBEKISTAN

TAJIKISTAN

CHINA

AFGHANISTAN

PAKISTAN

INDIA

OMAN

Ashgabat · **Mashhad** · **Kabul** · **Kermān** · **Zāhedān**

Hindu Kush · Karakoram Range · Great Himalaya Range

Peshāwar · **Rāwalpindi** · Islamabad · Srīnagar · **LAHORE** · Ludhiāna · Chandīgarh · **DELHI** · New Delhi

Faisalābad · **Gujrānwāla** · Amritsar · Jullundur

Multān · Bahāwalpur · Bīkaner · Jodhpur · **Jaipur**

BALOCHISTĀN · Quetta · SINDH · PUNJAB · RĀJASTHĀN

Great Indian (Thar) Desert

Hyderābād · **KARACHI** · Mouths of the Indus

AHMADĀBĀD · **Vadodara** (Baroda) · GUJARĀT · MADHYA PRADESH · **Indore**

Jāmnagar · Kathiawar · **Bhāvnagar** · **Surat** · **Nāsik** · **Aurangābād**

Gulf of Kutch · Gulf of Cambay · DĀDRA AND NAGAR HAVELI · DAMĀN AND DIU

MUMBAI (Bombay) · **Kalyān** · Thāna · Pimpri-Chinchwad · **Pune** (Poona)

Sholāpur · MAHĀRĀSHTRA

Kolhāpur · **Belgaum** · KARNĀTAKA · **Hubli-Dhārwār** · GOA

Gulf of Oman · **Muscat** (Masqat) · OMAN · Gulf of Maşīrah

ARABIAN SEA

Tropic of Cancer

Makran Coast

Longitude East of Greenwich

POPULATION OF CITIES AND TOWNS

■ OVER 2,000,000	◉ 500,000 - 999,999	● 100,000 - 249,999	• 10,000 - 29,999	
□ 1,000,000 - 1,999,999	◉ 250,000 - 499,999	● 30,000 - 99,999	∘ UNDER 10,000	

SCALE 1:10,200,000   LAMBERT CONFORMAL CONIC PROJECTION

MILES 0 · · · 150 · · · 300 · · · 450

KILOMETERS 0 · · · 150 · · · 300 · · · 450

© Hammond World Atlas Corporation

Northern Middle East

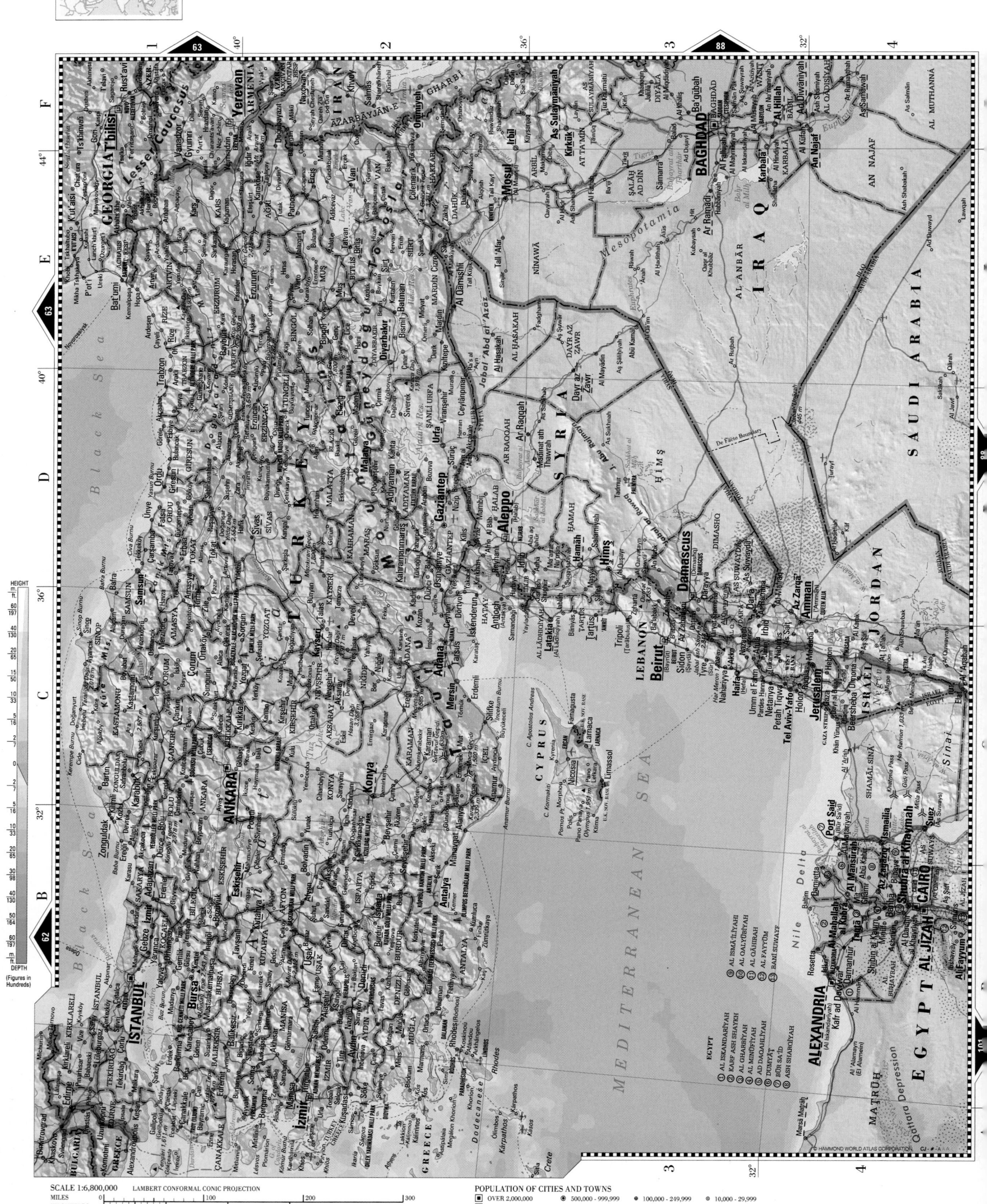

SCALE 1:6,800,000   LAMBERT CONFORMAL CONIC PROJECTION

MILES 0 | 100 | 200 | 300
KILOMETERS 0 | 100 | 200 | 300

POPULATION OF CITIES AND TOWNS

- ■ OVER 2,000,000
- ▣ 1,000,000 - 1,999,999
- ◘ 500,000 - 999,999
- ◉ 250,000 - 499,999
- ⊙ 100,000 - 249,999
- ◎ 30,000 - 99,999
- ⊚ 10,000 - 29,999
- ○ UNDER 10,000

© HAMMOND WORLD ATLAS CORPORATION

Eastern Mediterranean Region

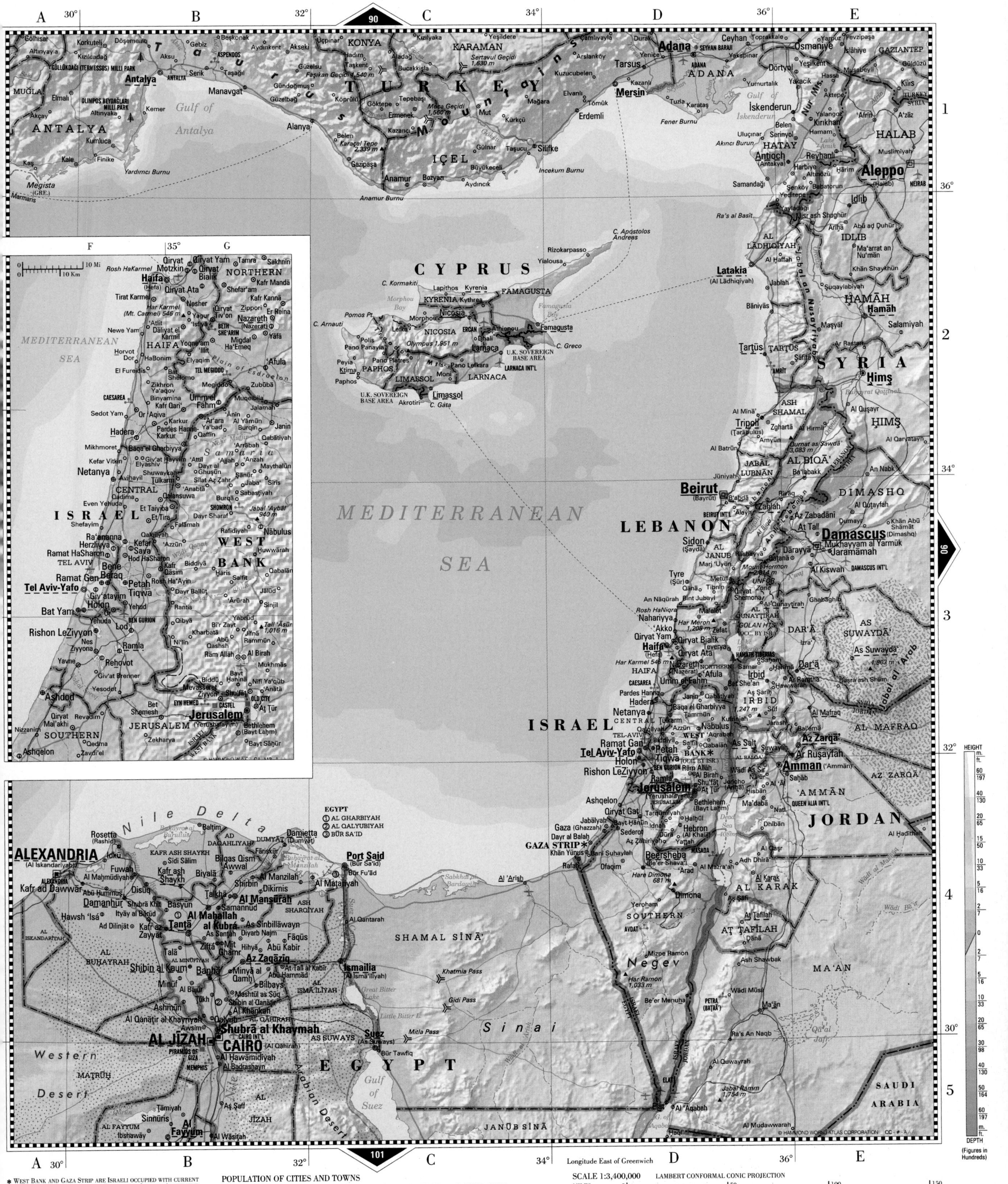

POPULATION OF CITIES AND TOWNS

■ OVER 2,000,000 ● 500,000 - 999,999 ⊙ 100,000 - 249,999 ○ 10,000 - 29,999
□ 1,000,000 - 1,999,999 □ 250,000 - 499,999 ⊙ 30,000 - 99,999 ● UNDER 10,000

★ WEST BANK AND GAZA STRIP ARE ISRAELI OCCUPIED WITH CURRENT
STATUS SUBJECT TO THE ISRAELI-PALESTINIAN INTERIM AGREEMENT
- PERMANENT STATUS TO BE DETERMINED

SCALE 1:3,400,000 LAMBERT CONFORMAL CONIC PROJECTION

MILES
KILOMETERS

Longitude East of Greenwich

Africa

Several physiographic features are captured in this southeast-looking, high-oblique image. The Nile River Delta, the large, dark area at the bottom of the image, extends from the capital city of Cairo at the apex of the delta to the Suez Canal. The entire region is classified as desert (less than 10 inches [25 cm.] of rainfall per year). Desert-like areas are visible southwest of the delta and in the northwestern Sinai. Major rock outcrops (darker areas) are seen encircling the Red Sea. The two bodies of water flanking the southern end of the Sinai Peninsula are the Gulf of Suez and the Gulf of Aqaba.

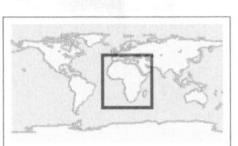

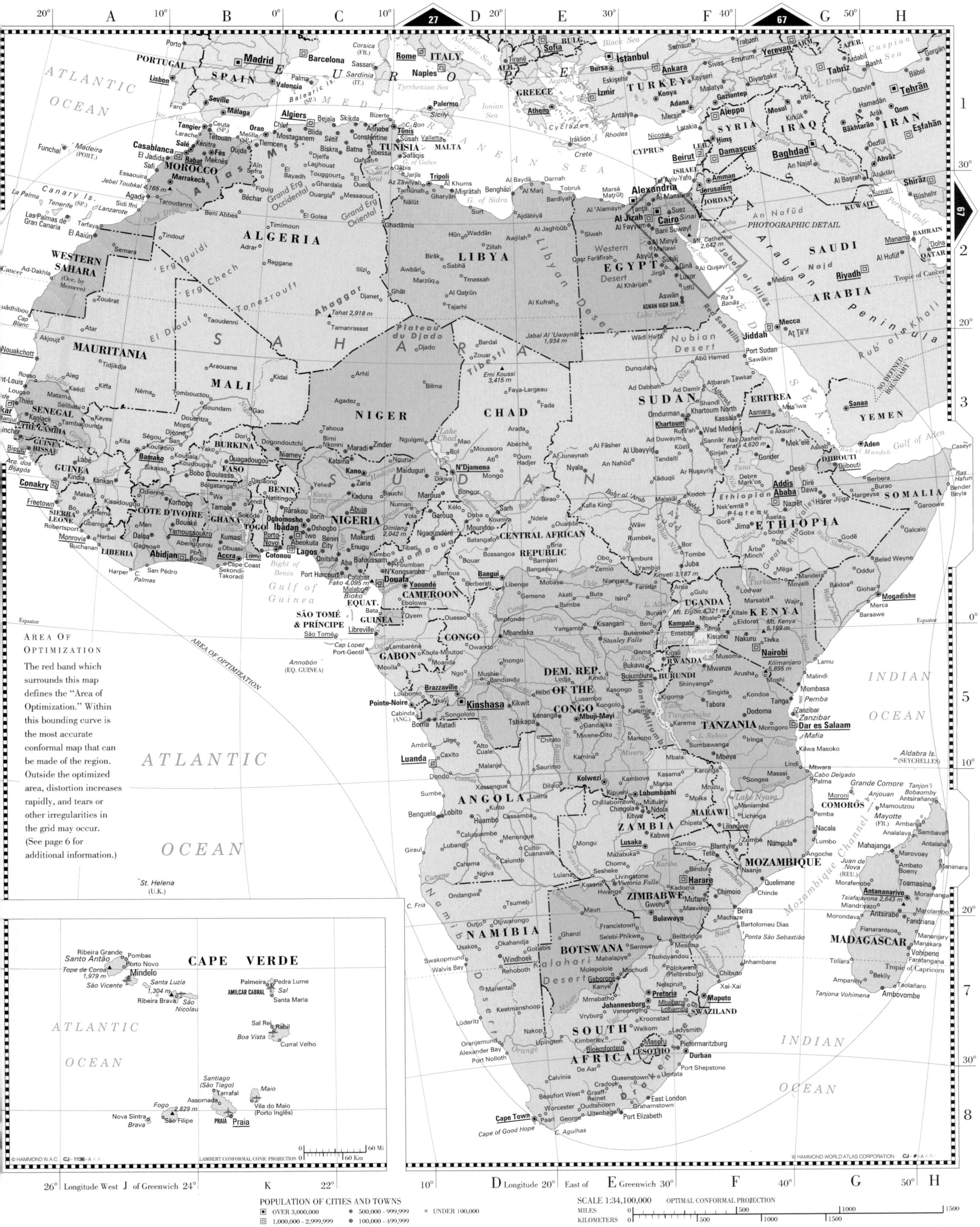

AREA OF
OPTIMIZATION

The red band which surrounds this map defines the "Area of Optimization." Within this bounding curve is the most accurate conformal map that can be made of the region. Outside the optimized area, distortion increases rapidly, and tears or other irregularities in the grid may occur. (See page 6 for additional information.)

CAPE VERDE

POPULATION OF CITIES AND TOWNS
● OVER 3,000,000   ● 500,000 - 999,999   ● UNDER 100,000
▣ 1,000,000 - 2,999,999   ▢ 100,000 - 499,999

SCALE 1:34,100,000   OPTIMAL CONFORMAL PROJECTION

LAMBERT CONFORMAL CONIC PROJECTION

© HAMMOND WORLD ATLAS CORPORATION

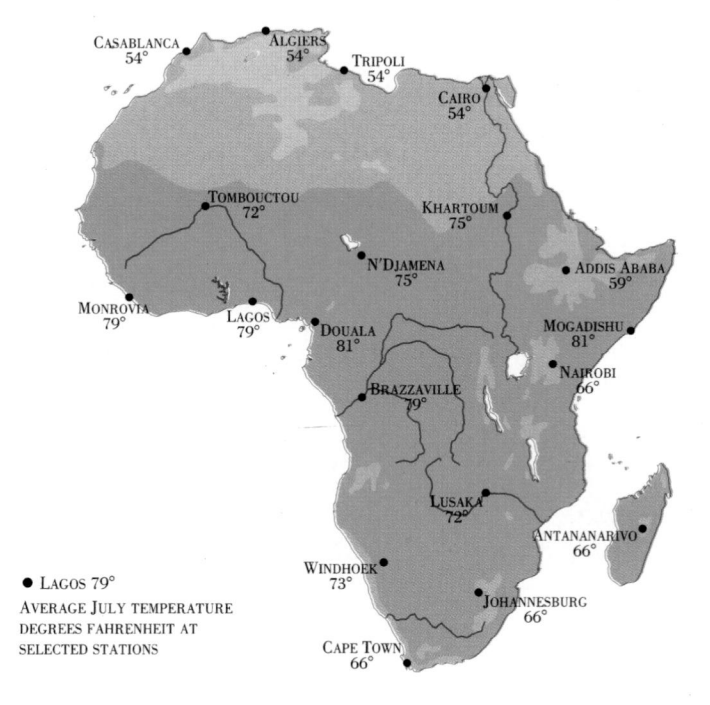

CASABLANCA 54°
ALGIERS 54°
TRIPOLI 54°
CAIRO 54°
TOMBOUCTOU 72°
KHARTOUM 75°
N'DJAMENA 75°
ADDIS ABABA 59°
MONROVIA 79°
LAGOS 79°
DOUALA 81°
MOGADISHU 81°
BRAZZAVILLE 79°
NAIROBI 66°
LUSAKA 72°
ANTANANARIVO 66°
WINDHOEK 73°
JOHANNESBURG 66°
CAPE TOWN 66°

● LAGOS 79°
AVERAGE JULY TEMPERATURE
DEGREES FAHRENHEIT AT
SELECTED STATIONS

AVERAGE JANUARY TEMPERATURE

FAHRENHEIT	CELSIUS		FAHRENHEIT	CELSIUS
OVER 68°	OVER 20°		32° TO 50°	0° TO 10°
50° TO 68°	10° TO 20°		UNDER 32°	UNDER 0°

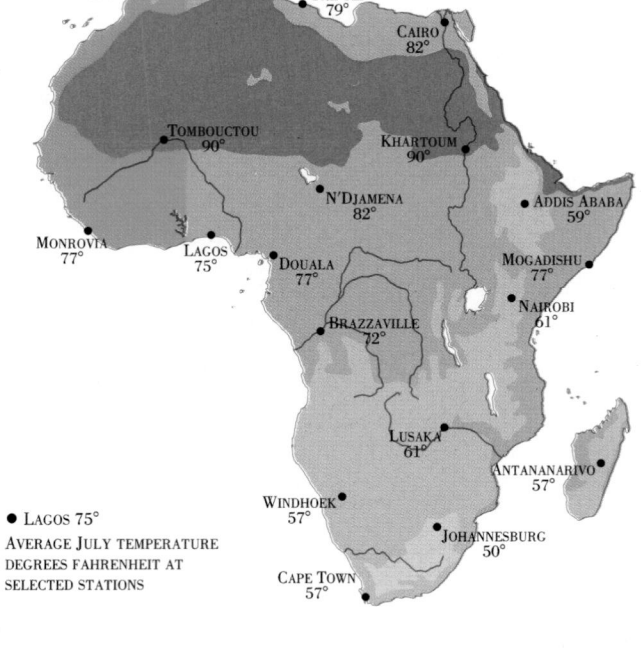

CASABLANCA 72°
ALGIERS 77°
TRIPOLI 79°
CAIRO 82°
TOMBOUCTOU 90°
KHARTOUM 90°
N'DJAMENA 82°
ADDIS ABABA 59°
MONROVIA 77°
LAGOS 75°
DOUALA 77°
MOGADISHU 77°
BRAZZAVILLE 72°
NAIROBI 61°
LUSAKA 61°
ANTANANARIVO 57°
WINDHOEK 57°
JOHANNESBURG 50°
CAPE TOWN 57°

● LAGOS 75°
AVERAGE JULY TEMPERATURE
DEGREES FAHRENHEIT AT
SELECTED STATIONS

AVERAGE JULY TEMPERATURE

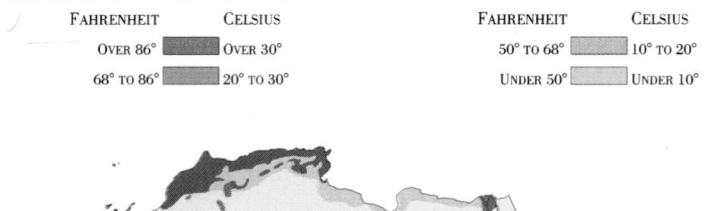

FAHRENHEIT	CELSIUS		FAHRENHEIT	CELSIUS
OVER 86°	OVER 30°		50° TO 68°	10° TO 20°
68° TO 86°	20° TO 30°		UNDER 50°	UNDER 10°

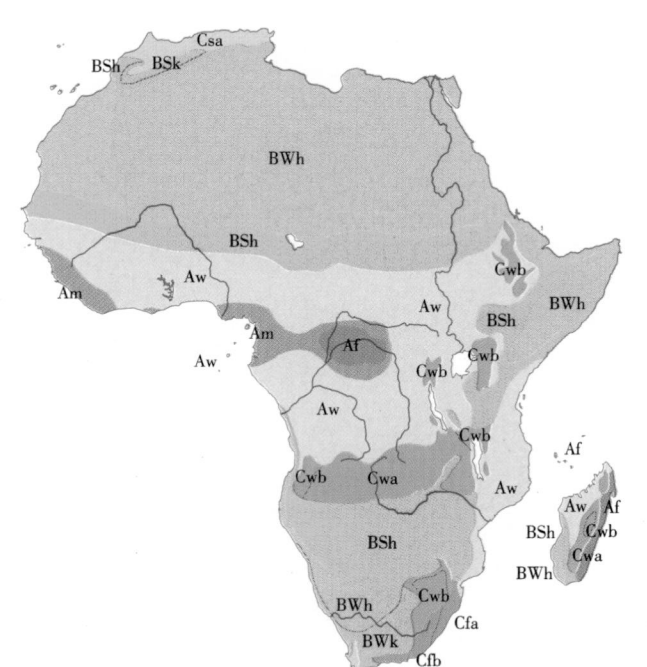

Csa
BSh BSk
BWh
BSh
Am
Aw
Aw
Cwb
Am
Af
Aw
BSh
BWh
Aw
Cwb
Cwb
Cwb
Af
Aw
Cwb
Gwa
Aw
Aw Af
BSh Cwb
Cwb Cwa
BSh
BWh
BWh Cwb
Cfa
BWk
Cfb

CLIMATE

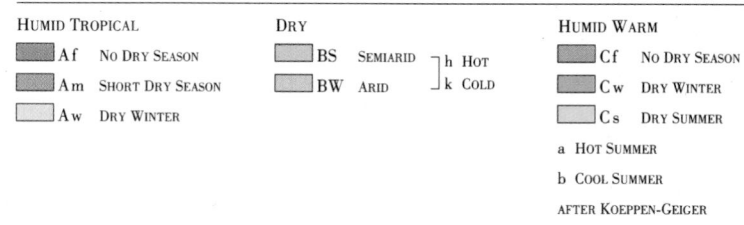

HUMID TROPICAL
- Af NO DRY SEASON
- Am SHORT DRY SEASON
- Aw DRY WINTER

DRY
- BS SEMIARID
- BW ARID
  - h HOT
  - k COLD

HUMID WARM
- Cf NO DRY SEASON
- Cw DRY WINTER
- Cs DRY SUMMER
- a HOT SUMMER
- b COOL SUMMER

AFTER KOEPPEN-GEIGER

VEGETATION

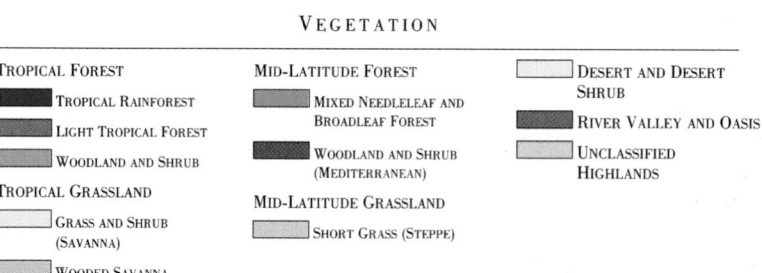

TROPICAL FOREST
- TROPICAL RAINFOREST
- LIGHT TROPICAL FOREST
- WOODLAND AND SHRUB

TROPICAL GRASSLAND
- GRASS AND SHRUB (SAVANNA)
- WOODED SAVANNA

MID-LATITUDE FOREST
- MIXED NEEDLELEAF AND BROADLEAF FOREST
- WOODLAND AND SHRUB (MEDITERRANEAN)

MID-LATITUDE GRASSLAND
- SHORT GRASS (STEPPE)

- DESERT AND DESERT SHRUB
- RIVER VALLEY AND OASIS
- UNCLASSIFIED HIGHLANDS

Africa – Geographical Comparisons

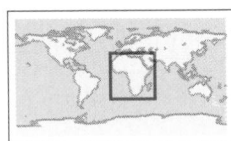

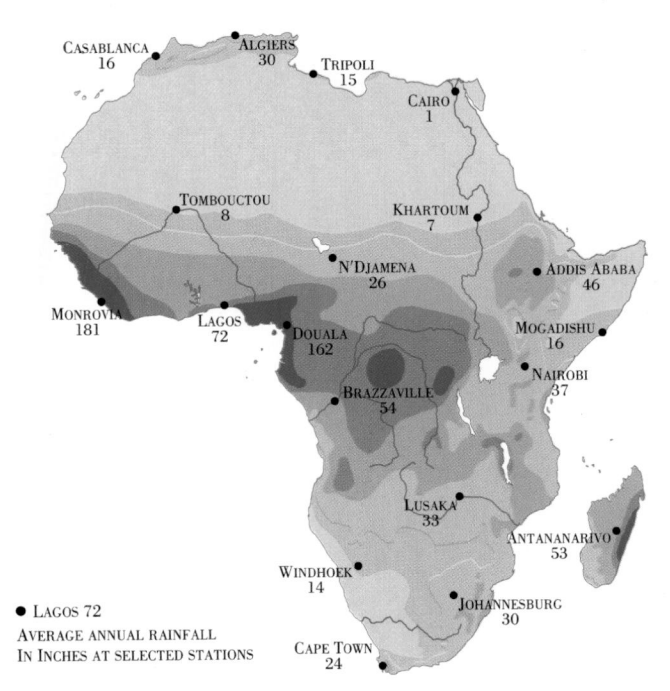

CASABLANCA 16
ALGIERS 30
TRIPOLI 15
CAIRO 1
TOMBOUCTOU 8
KHARTOUM 7
N'DJAMENA 26
ADDIS ABABA 46
MONROVIA 181
LAGOS 72
DOUALA 162
MOGADISHU 16
NAIROBI 37
BRAZZAVILLE 54
LUSAKA 33
ANTANANARIVO 53
WINDHOEK 14
JOHANNESBURG 30
CAPE TOWN 24

● LAGOS 72
AVERAGE ANNUAL RAINFALL
IN INCHES AT SELECTED STATIONS

AVERAGE ANNUAL RAINFALL

INCHES	CM	INCHES	CM	INCHES	CM
OVER 80	OVER 200	40 TO 60	100 TO 150	10 TO 20	25 TO 50
60 TO 80	150 TO 200	20 TO 40	50 TO 100	UNDER 10	UNDER 25

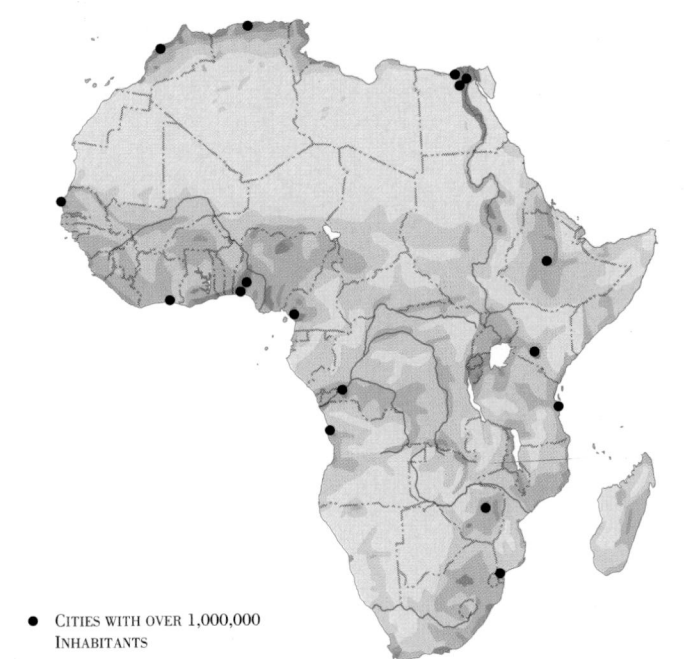

● CITIES WITH OVER 1,000,000 INHABITANTS

POPULATION DISTRIBUTION

DENSITY PER		SQ. MI.	SQ. KM.	SQ. MI.	SQ. KM.
SQ. MI.	SQ. KM.	130 TO 260	50 TO 100	3 TO 25	1 TO 10
OVER 260	OVER 100	25 TO 130	10 TO 50	UNDER 3	UNDER 1

SHEEP
FRUIT WINE
CORN
COTTON
DATES
PEANUTS
CATTLE
CATTLE
COTTON
CATTLE
COFFEE
PEANUTS
HOGS
SHEEP
COFFEE
COCOA
COCOA
PALM OIL
SHEEP
COCOA
BANANAS
COFFEE
CATTLE
SISAL
PALM OIL
COFFEE
CORN
TOBACCO COPRA
SHEEP
CORN
CATTLE
SHEEP SHEEP

LAND USE

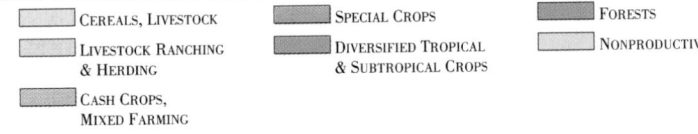

- CEREALS, LIVESTOCK
- LIVESTOCK RANCHING & HERDING
- CASH CROPS, MIXED FARMING
- SPECIAL CROPS
- DIVERSIFIED TROPICAL & SUBTROPICAL CROPS
- FORESTS
- NONPRODUCTIVE

MINERAL RESOURCES

ENERGY & FUELS
- ◆ COAL
- ▲ NATURAL GAS
- ● PETROLEUM
- ■ URANIUM

IRON & FERROALLOYS
- 1 CHROMIUM
- 2 COBALT
- 3 IRON ORE
- 4 MANGANESE
- 5 NICKEL
- 6 VANADIUM

OTHER MAJOR RESOURCES
- 1 ANTIMONY
- 2 ASBESTOS
- 3 BAUXITE
- 4 COPPER
- 5 DIAMONDS
- 6 GOLD
- 7 LEAD
- 8 MICA
- 9 PHOSPHATES
- 10 PLATINUM
- 11 TIN
- 12 ZINC

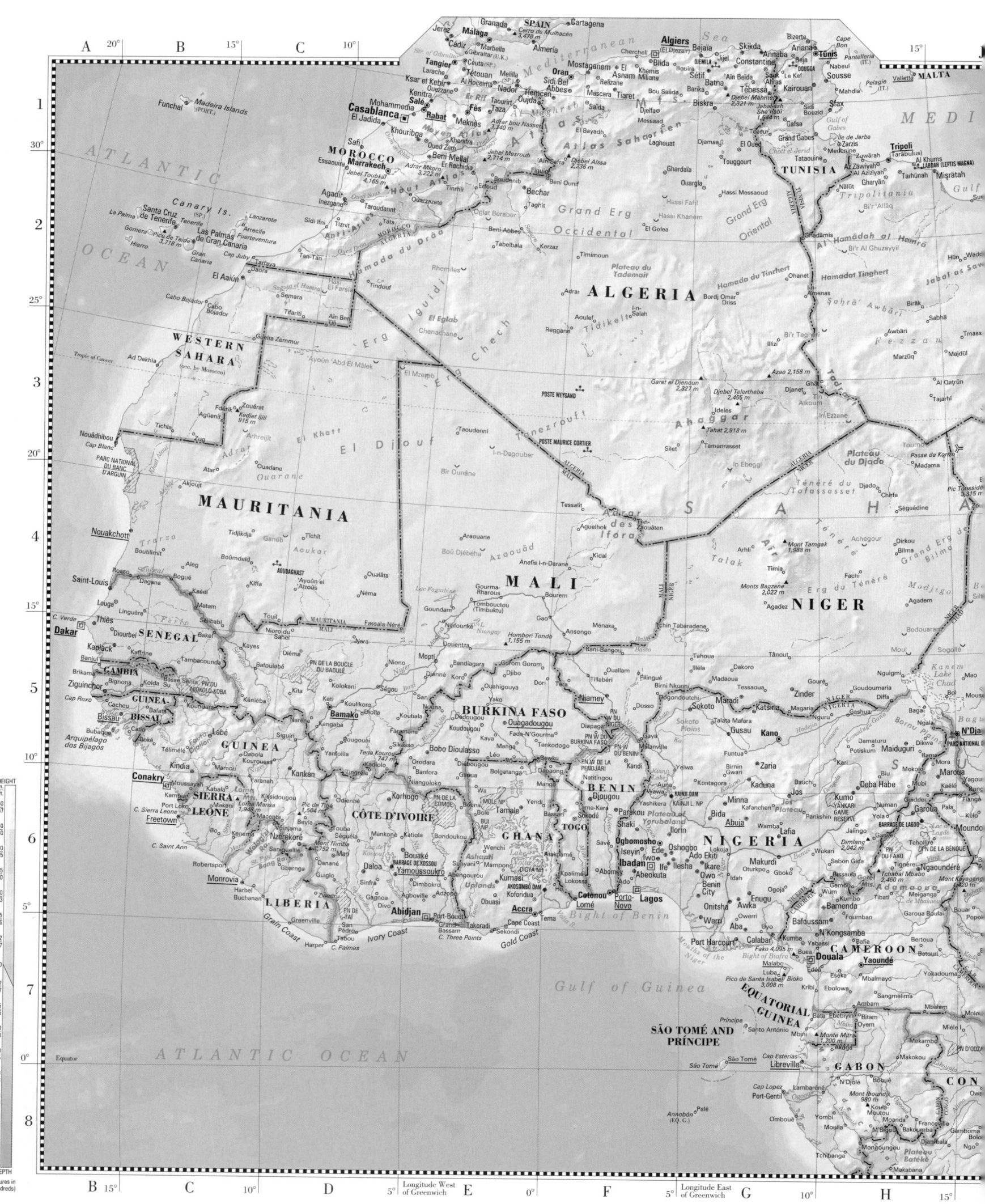

Northern Africa

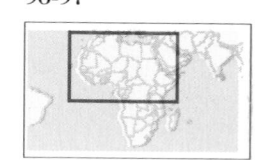

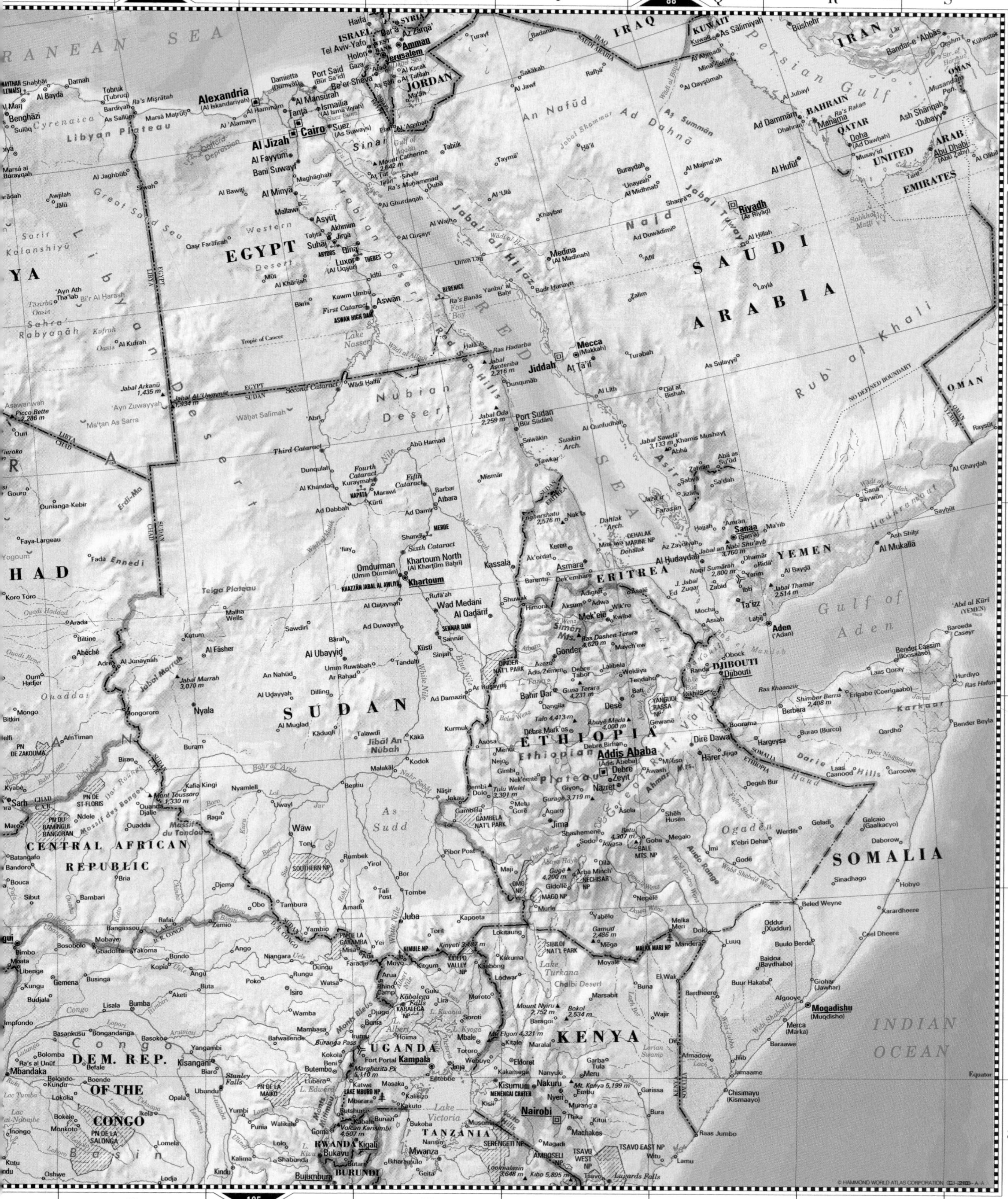

POPULATION OF CITIES AND TOWNS

SCALE 1:17,000,000   POLYCONIC PROJECTION

© Hammond World Atlas Corporation

ATLANTIC

OCEAN

Madeira Is.
(PORT.)

Canary Islands
(SPAIN)

WESTERN

SAHARA
(Occupied by Morocco)

SPAIN

Cádiz
Chiclana de la Frontera
Barbate de France
Algeciras
Gibraltar (U.K.)
La Línea de la Concepción
Ceuta (SP.)

MOROCCO is divided into 7 non-administrative
regions shown here. Scale does not permit
showing the boundaries and names of Morocco's
provinces and prefectures.

Mijas
Marbella

TANGIER (BOUKHALF)
Tangier
(Tanger)
Tétouan
Al Hoceima

Asilah
Larache
Chechaouene
Jebel Bouhalla
2,170 m
AL HOCEIMA
(CÔTE DU RIF)

Ksar el Kebir
Er Rif

Souk el
Arba du Rharb
Ouezzane
Taounate
Taza

NORD
OUEST

Kenitra
Salé
RABAT (SALÉ)
Rabat
Sidi Kacem
Moulay Idriss
Moulay Yakoub
Fès
Meknès
FÈS (SAISS)
Sefrou

CASABLANCA
(Dar-El-Beida)
Mohammedia
Ben Slimane
Khemisset
Ifrane
Azrou
CENTRE-
NORD

CASABLANCA (MOHAMED V)
Berrechid
Mediouna
Settat
Benahmed
Oued Zem
Khenifra

El Jadida
Azemmour
Boulaouane
Khouribga
Boujad
Midelt
Jebel Masker
3,277 m

Cap Safi
El Had
Harrara
Sidi
Bennour
CENTRE
Kasba Tadla
Beni Mellal
Jebel Mesro
2,714 m

Safi
Youssoufia
Benguerir
Azilal
MOROCCO

Essaouira
El Kelaa
des Srarhna
Jebel Azourki
3,690 m
CENTRE-SUD
Er Rachidia

Cap Sim
Chichaoua
Marrakech
MARRAKECH (MENARA)
Aït Ourir
Ihil M'goun
4,071 m
Goulmima
Erfoud

Ounara
Jebel Rhat
3,825 m
Ihil Mkorn
3,222 m

TENSIF
Tahnaout
Jebel Anrhomer
3,609 m
Tinrhir
Boumalne

Tamanar
Imi n'Tanout
Idjel 3,615 m
Jebel Toubkal
4,165 m
Aït Ben
Haddou
OUARZAZATE

Cap Rhir
Djebel Dchka
3,348 m
PN DU
TOUBKAL
Ouarzazate
Jebel Siroua
3,304 m

AGADIR (INEZGANE)
Taroudannt
Jebel Rhart
1,650 m

Agadir
Oulad Teima
Zagora

Inezgane
Irherm
1,730 m
Foum Zguid
Tagounit

Tiznit
Jebel Lkst
2,531 m
SUD

Sidi Ifni
Jebel
2,359 m
Tata
Jebel Bani

Tafraout
Akka

Bou Izakarn
Foum el
Hassane

Goulmine
Assa
Hamada du Drâa
TINDOUF

Cap Drâa
Tindouf
Bou Labar

Tan-Tan
Oued Drâa
BORDJ FLYE SAINT

Tarfaya
Cap Juby
55 m

Daora
Hagunia
Hasi el Farsia
ALGERIA
MAURITANIA

EL AAIUN (HASSAN)
El Aaiún
Saguia el Hamra

Edchera
Semara

Lemsid
El Eglab

Cabo Bojador
Sebjet
Aridol
Bu Craa
Tifariti
'Erg Iguidi

Sebjet
Aarred
Aïn Ben Tili

Bir Aidiat

WESTERN
Aaglet Yeralful
Guelta Zemmur
Bir Moghrein
Bir Bel
Guerdâne
Sebkhet
Iguetti

SAHARA

W. SAHARA
MAURITANIA
Ayoûn 'Abd
el Malek
El Mzereb
El Hank

Sebjet
Agsumal
TIRIS ZEMMOUR
Karêt

Ad Dakhla
Sebkhet Oumm
ed Drôis Telli
Erg el
Ahmar

Tropic of Cancer
Punta Durnford
Sebkhet Oumm
ed Drôis Guebli
Sebkhet de
Rhallamane

El Aargub
Rhallamane
Kreb en Nâga
Hamada Safia

Buir Taiaret
Zemlet Tolfaf
330 m
Erg
Ijoubbane

Fuch
Aaglet Tennuaca
Taoudenni

366 m
El Khatt
Télig

Fdêrik
Zouérat
Guelb er Richat
519 m
MALI

Sebkhet
Ijill

Kediet Ijill
915 m
El Khna

Cabo Barbas
Touâjil
MAURITANIA

Agüenit
MALI

Guerguerat
Golb
Azefal
TOMBOUC

Bou Lanouâr
Tichla
Zug
HODH
El

Nouâdhibou
Ben Amira
Guelb er Richat
ECH
Erg Atouila

Cabo Blanco
Bôir Ahmed
Choûm
CHARGUI
NOUÂDHIBOU
Atâr

DAKHLET
NOUÂDHIBOU
INCHIRI
ADRAR

PARC NATIONAL
DU BANC D'ARGUIN

HEIGHT
m.
ft
60
197
40
130
20
65
15
50
10
33
5
16
0
2
7
5
16
10
33
20
65
30
98
40
130
50
164
60
197
m.
ft
DEPTH
(Figures in
Hundreds)

Longitude West of Greenwich 4°

Northern West Africa

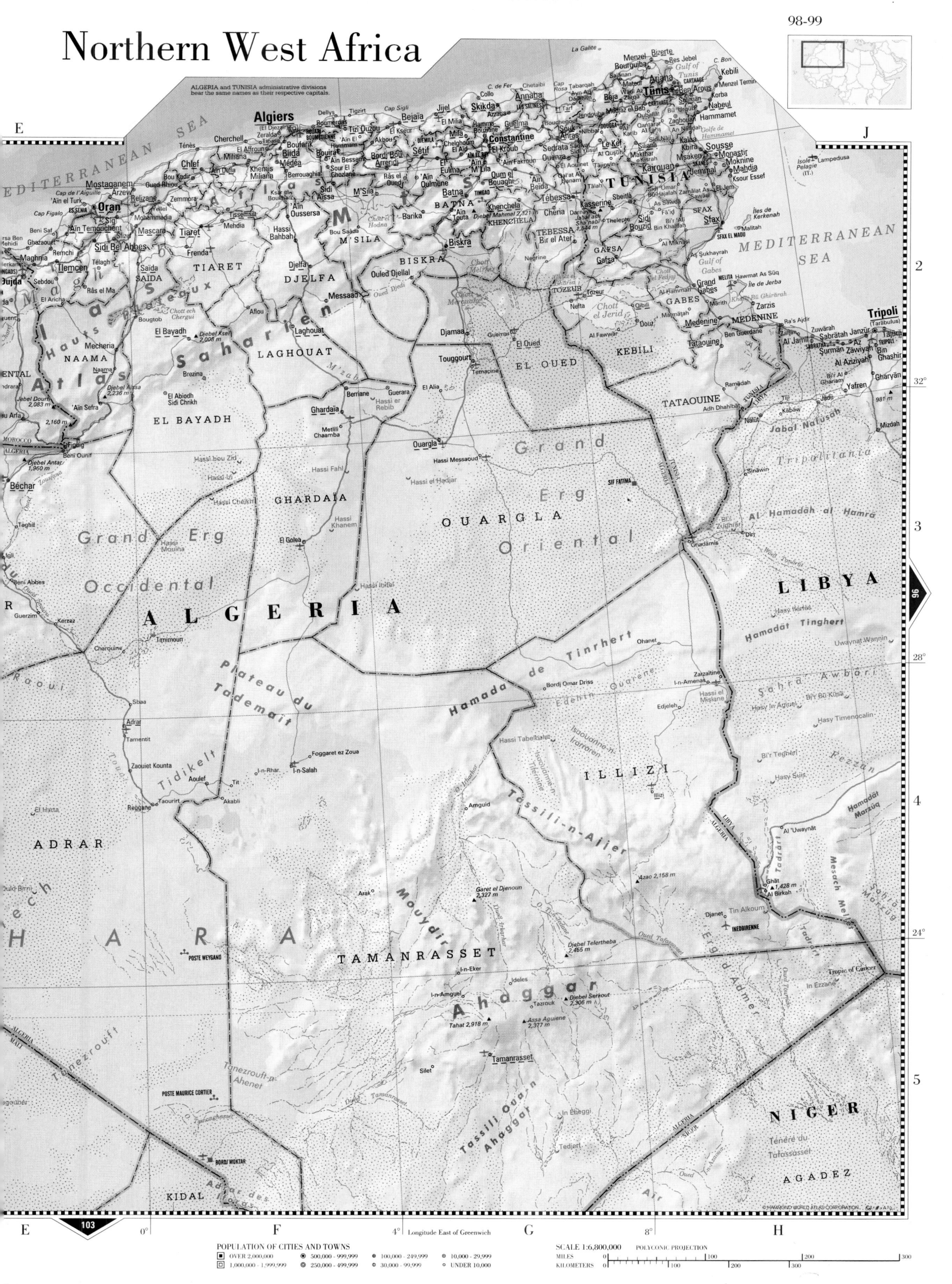

ALGERIA and TUNISIA administrative divisions
bear the same names as their respective capitals.

POPULATION OF CITIES AND TOWNS
■ OVER 2,000,000   ● 500,000 – 999,999   ● 100,000 – 249,999   ● 10,000 – 29,999
□ 1,000,000 – 1,999,999   ◉ 250,000 – 499,999   ● 30,000 – 99,999   ○ UNDER 10,000

SCALE 1:6,800,000   POLYCONIC PROJECTION
MILES   0   100   200   300
KILOMETERS   0   100   200   300

©Hammond World Atlas Corporation

Northern Morocco, Algeria, Tunisia

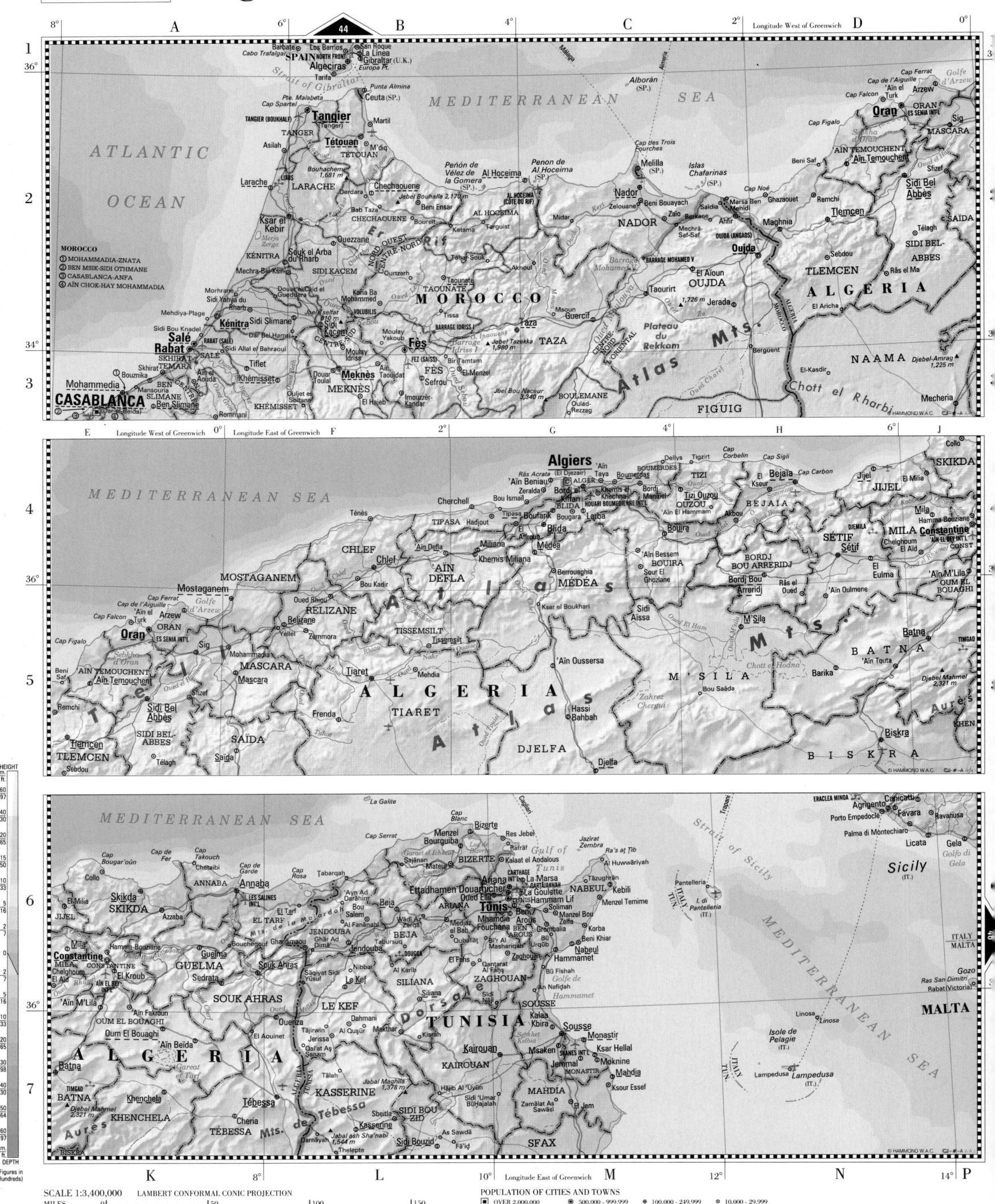

SCALE 1:3,400,000   LAMBERT CONFORMAL CONIC PROJECTION

MILES 0   50   100   150

KILOMETERS 0   50   100   150

POPULATION OF CITIES AND TOWNS

OVER 2,000,000 · 500,000 - 999,999 · 100,000 - 249,999 · 10,000 - 29,999
1,000,000 - 1,999,999 · 250,000 - 499,999 · 30,000 - 99,999 · UNDER 10,000

Northeastern Africa

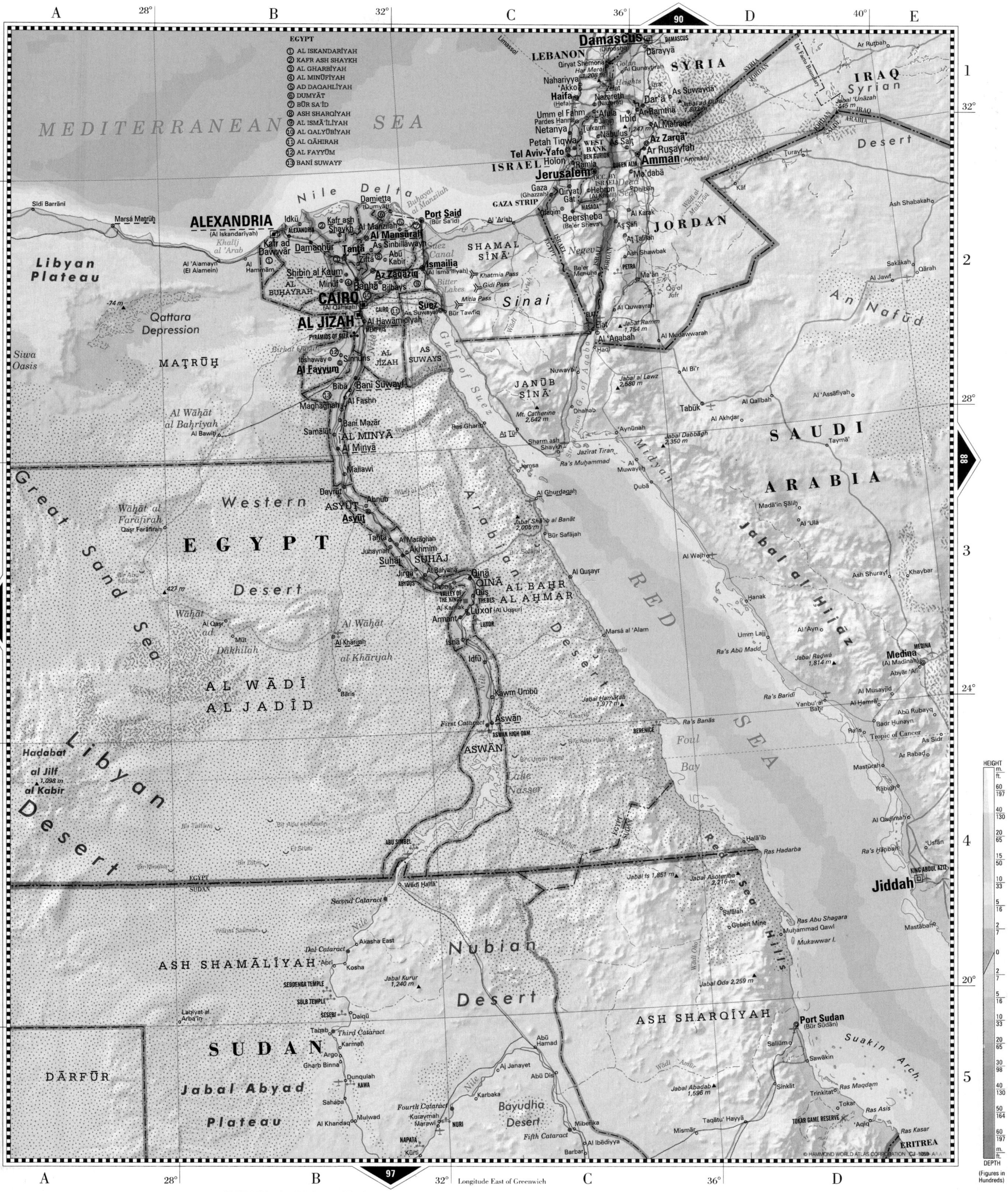

EGYPT
1. AL ISKANDARĪYAH
2. KAFR ASH SHAYKH
3. AL GHARBĪYAH
4. AL MINŪFĪYAH
5. AD DAQAHLĪYAH
6. DUMYĀT
7. BŪR SA'ĪD
8. ASH SHARQĪYAH
9. AL ISMĀ'ĪLĪYAH
10. AL QALYŪBĪYAH
11. AL QĀHIRAH
12. AL FAYYŪM
13. BANĪ SUWAYF

MEDITERRANEAN SEA

Libyan Plateau

Qattara Depression

Siwa Oasis

MAṬRŪḤ

Great Sand Sea

Libyan Desert

EGYPT

Western Desert

Wāḥāt al Farāfirah

AL WĀDĪ AL JADĪD

Hadabat al Jilf al Kabir 1,098 m

Nile Delta

ALEXANDRIA (Al Iskandarīyah)

Damietta (Dumyāt)

Port Said (Būr Sa'īd)

Al Manṣūrah

Tanta

CAIRO (Al Qāhirah)

AL JIZAH

PYRAMIDS OF GIZA

Al Fayyūm

Bani Suwayf

AL MINYĀ

Al Minyā

Mallawi

ASYŪṬ

Asyūṭ

SUHĀJ

Suhāj

QINĀ

Qinā

VALLEY OF THE KINGS

THEBES

Luxor (Al Uqṣur)

AL BAḤR AL AḤMAR

Aswān

ASWĀN HIGH DAM

Lake Nasser

Abu Simbel

SUDAN

Wādī Halfā

Second Cataract

ASH SHAMĀLĪYAH

Nubian Desert

Bayuda Desert

SUDAN

Jabal Abyad Plateau

DĀRFŪR

ASH SHARQĪYAH

Port Sudan (Būr Sūdān)

Suakin Arch

ERITREA

LEBANON

Damascus (Dimashq)

SYRIA

Syrian Desert

IRAQ

Haifa

Tel Aviv-Yafo

ISRAEL

Jerusalem

GAZA STRIP

WEST BANK

Beersheba

Negev

Amman

JORDAN

An Nafūd

Al 'Aqabah

Gulf of Aqaba

Sinai

SHAMAL SĪNĀ'

JANŪB SĪNĀ'

Mt. Catherine 2,642 m

Gulf of Suez

Suez

Ismailia

RED SEA

SAUDI ARABIA

Jabal al Ḥijāz

Medina (Al Madīnah)

Tropic of Cancer

Jiddah

KING ABDUL AZIZ

Foul Bay

Arabian Desert

POPULATION OF CITIES AND TOWNS
- OVER 2,000,000
- 1,000,000 – 1,999,999
- 500,000 – 999,999
- 250,000 – 499,999
- 100,000 – 249,999
- 30,000 – 99,999
- 10,000 – 29,999
- UNDER 10,000

SCALE 1:6,800,000   POLYCONIC PROJECTION
MILES 0 100 200 300
KILOMETERS 0 100 200 300

Longitude East of Greenwich

HEIGHT (ft.)
DEPTH (Figures in Hundreds)

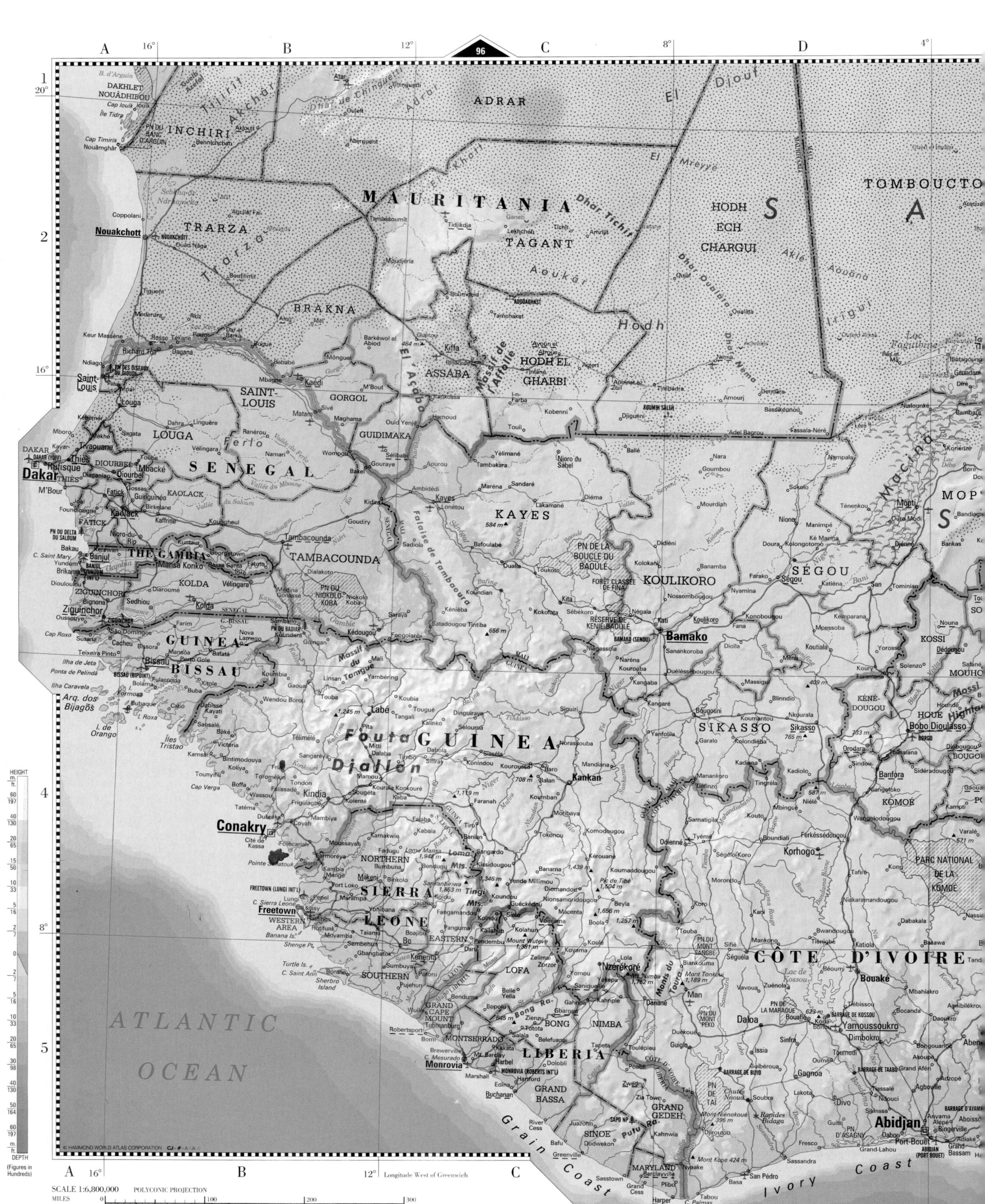

Southern West Africa

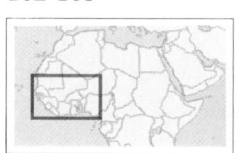

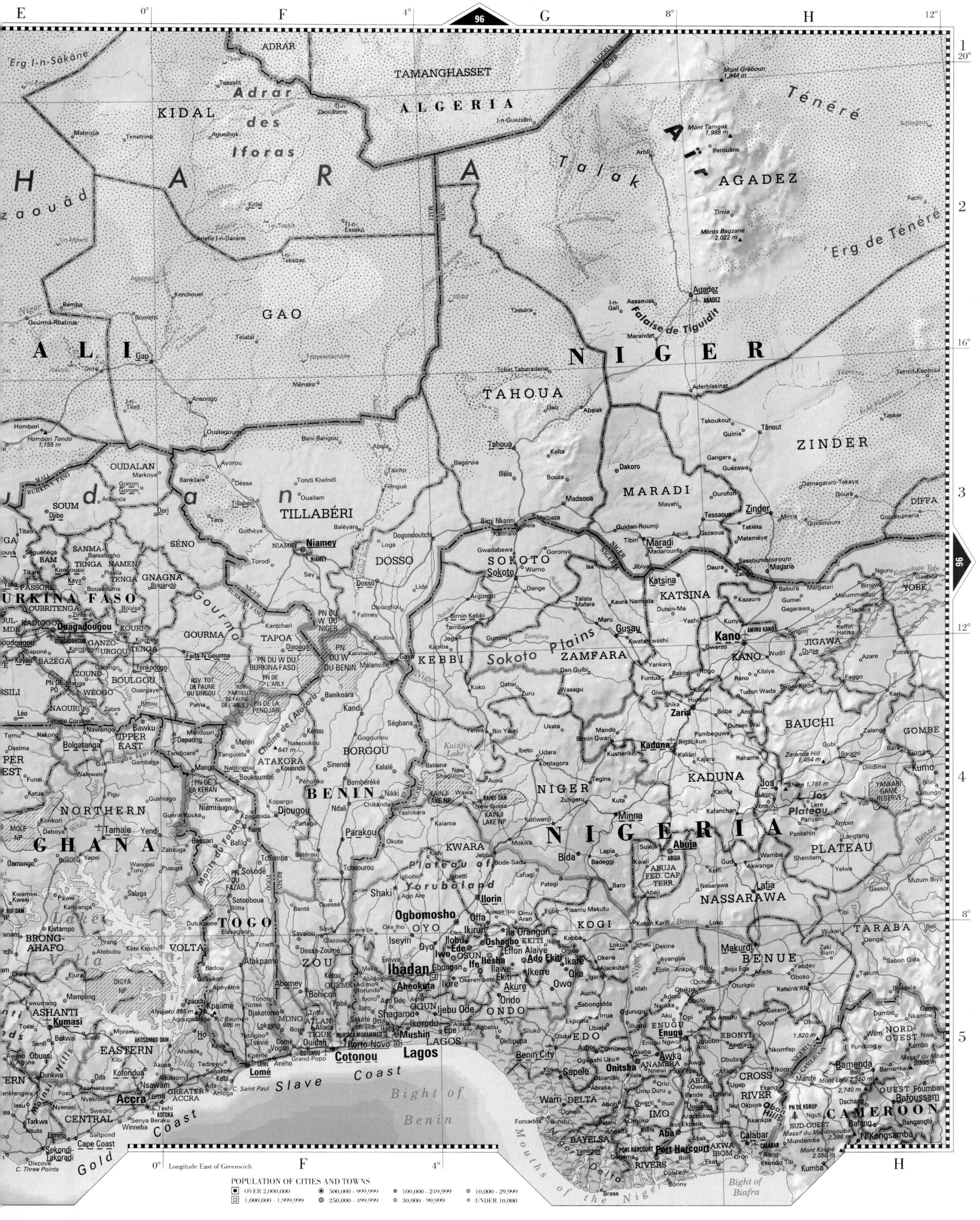

POPULATION OF CITIES AND TOWNS
- OVER 2,000,000
- 1,000,000 - 1,999,999
- 500,000 - 999,999
- 250,000 - 499,999
- 100,000 - 249,999
- 30,000 - 99,999
- 10,000 - 29,999
- UNDER 10,000

East Africa

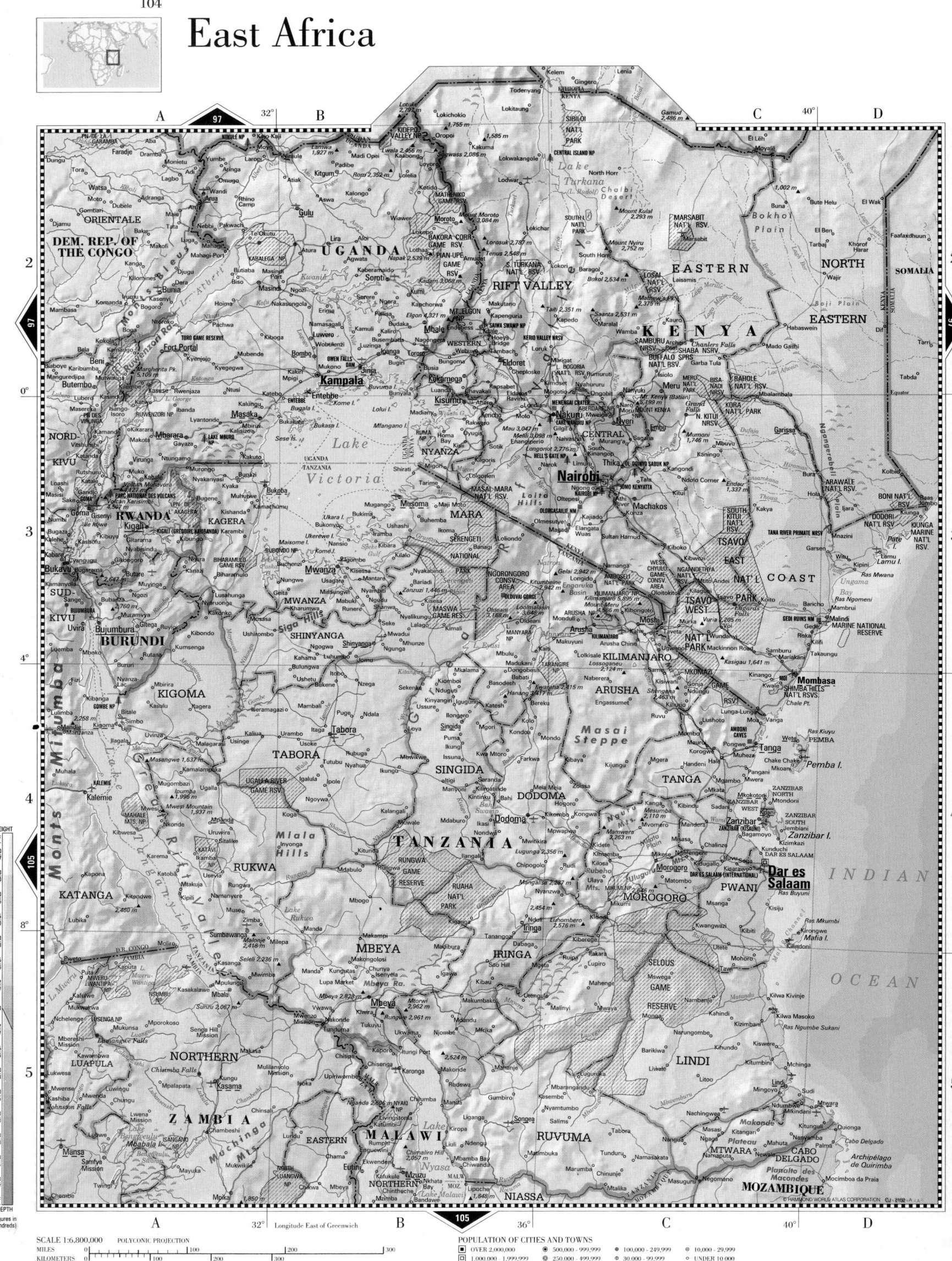

POPULATION OF CITIES AND TOWNS

Southern Africa

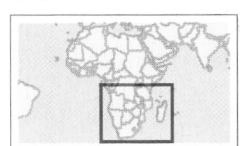

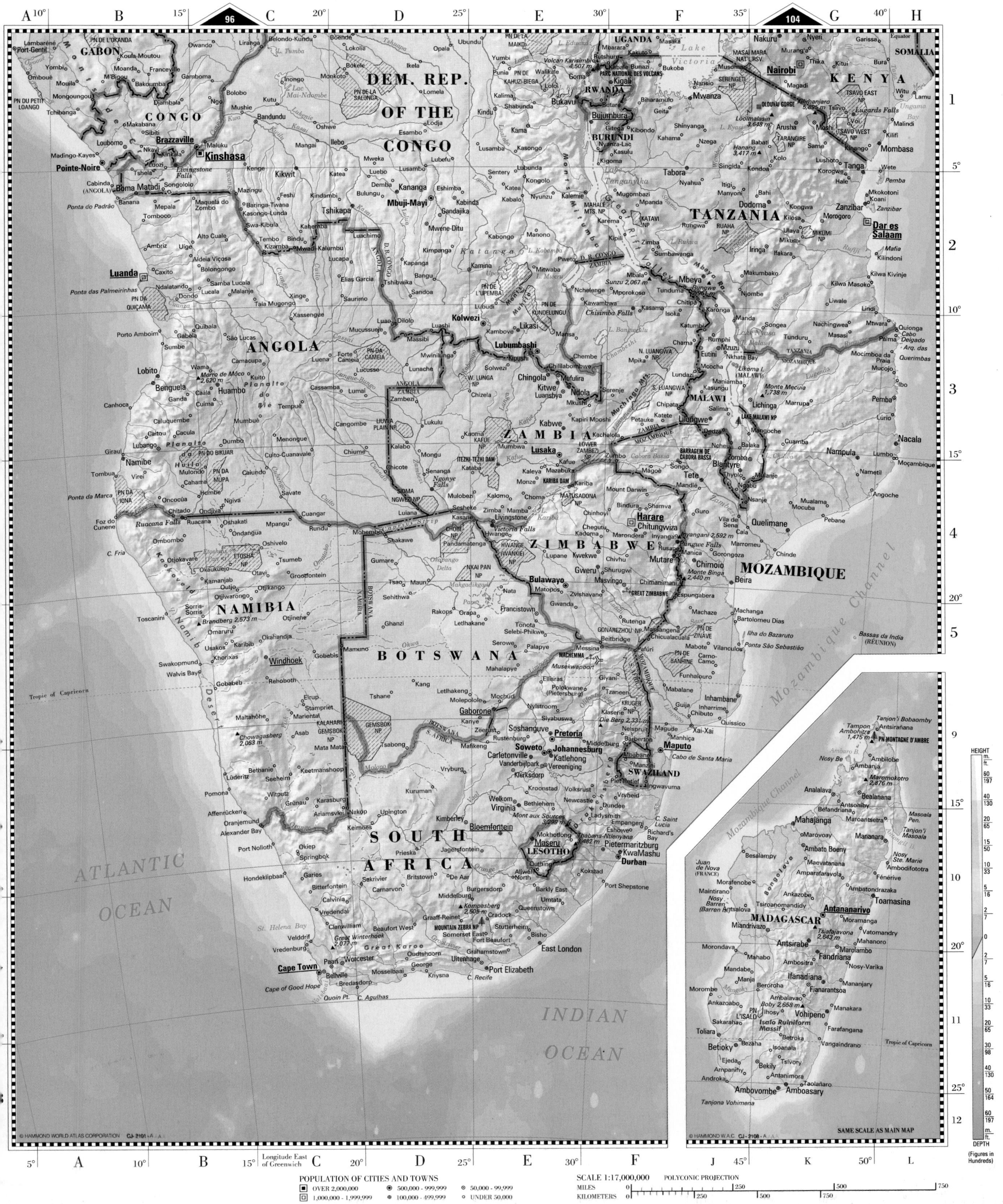

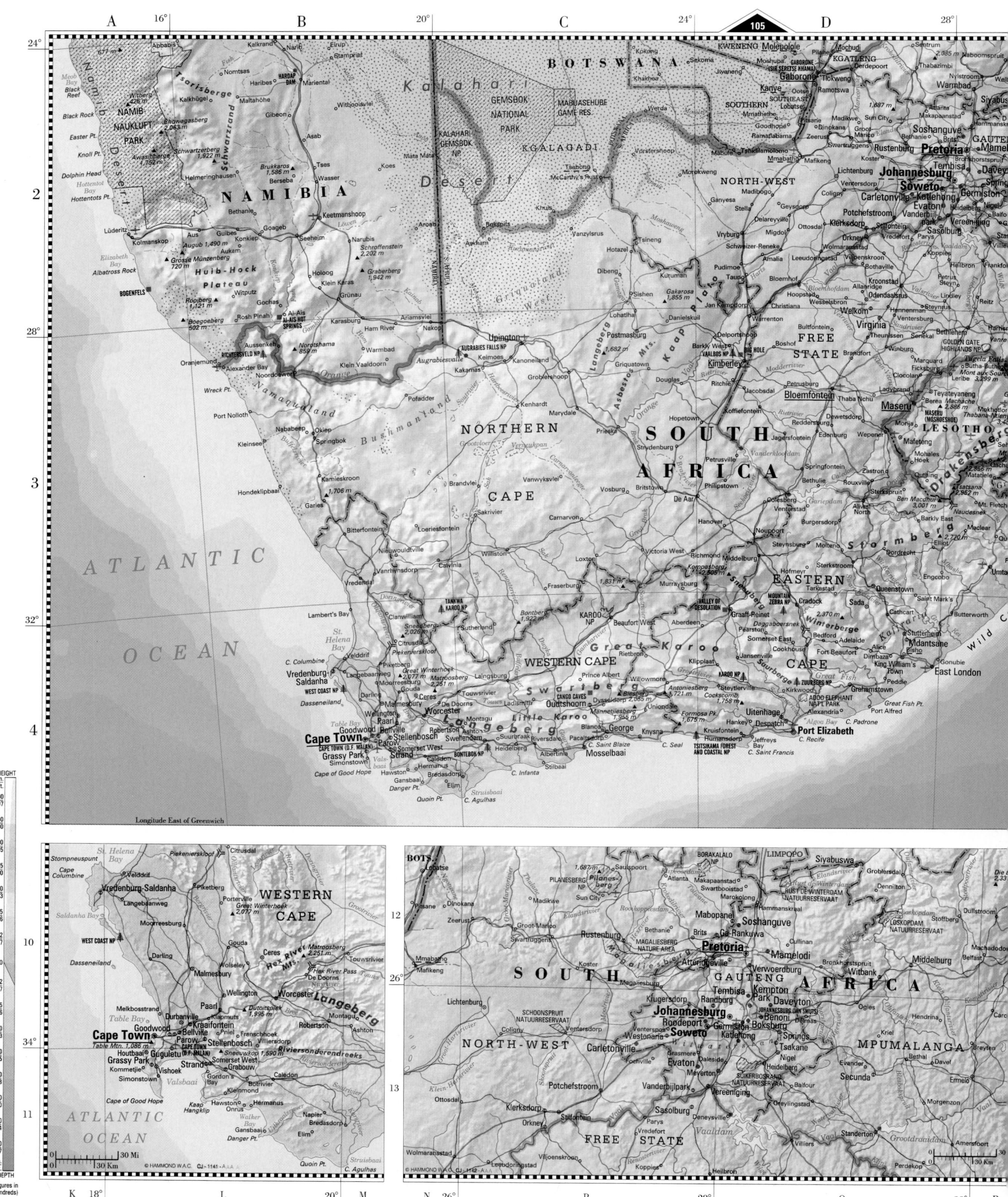

South Africa

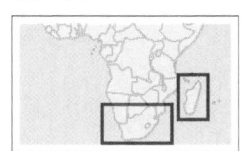

E | 32° | F | G | 44° | H | 48° | J

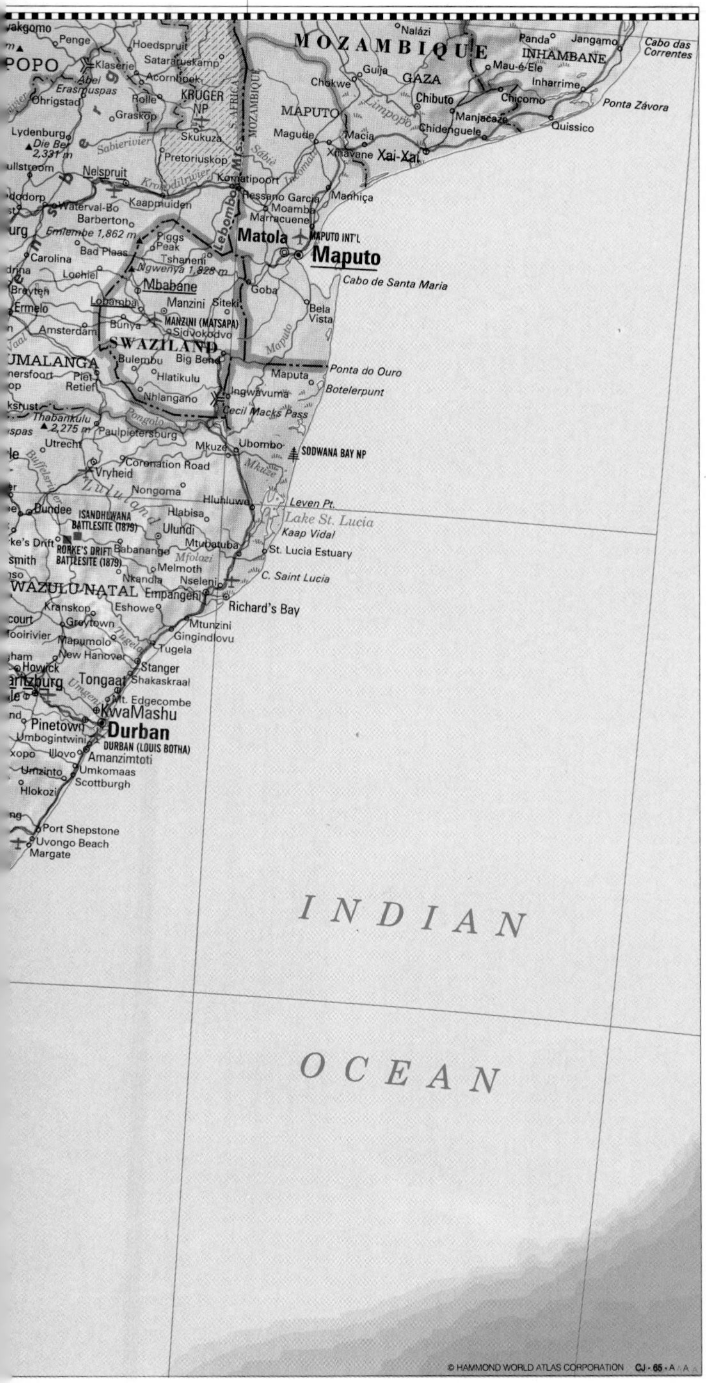

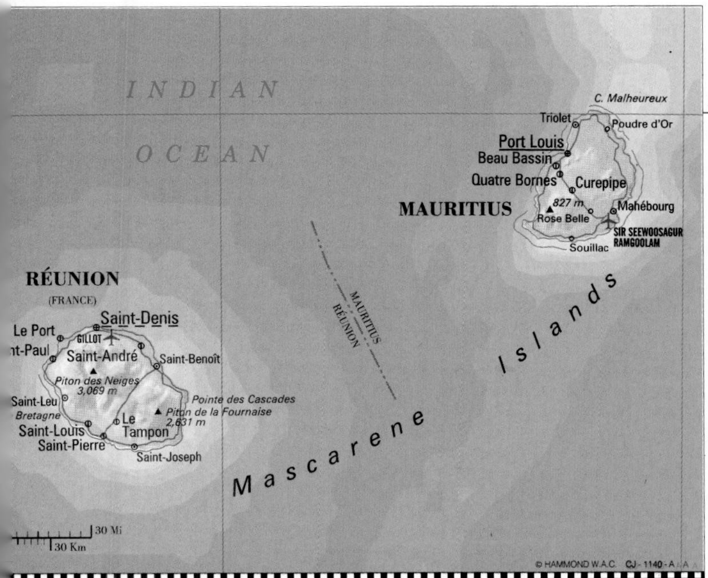

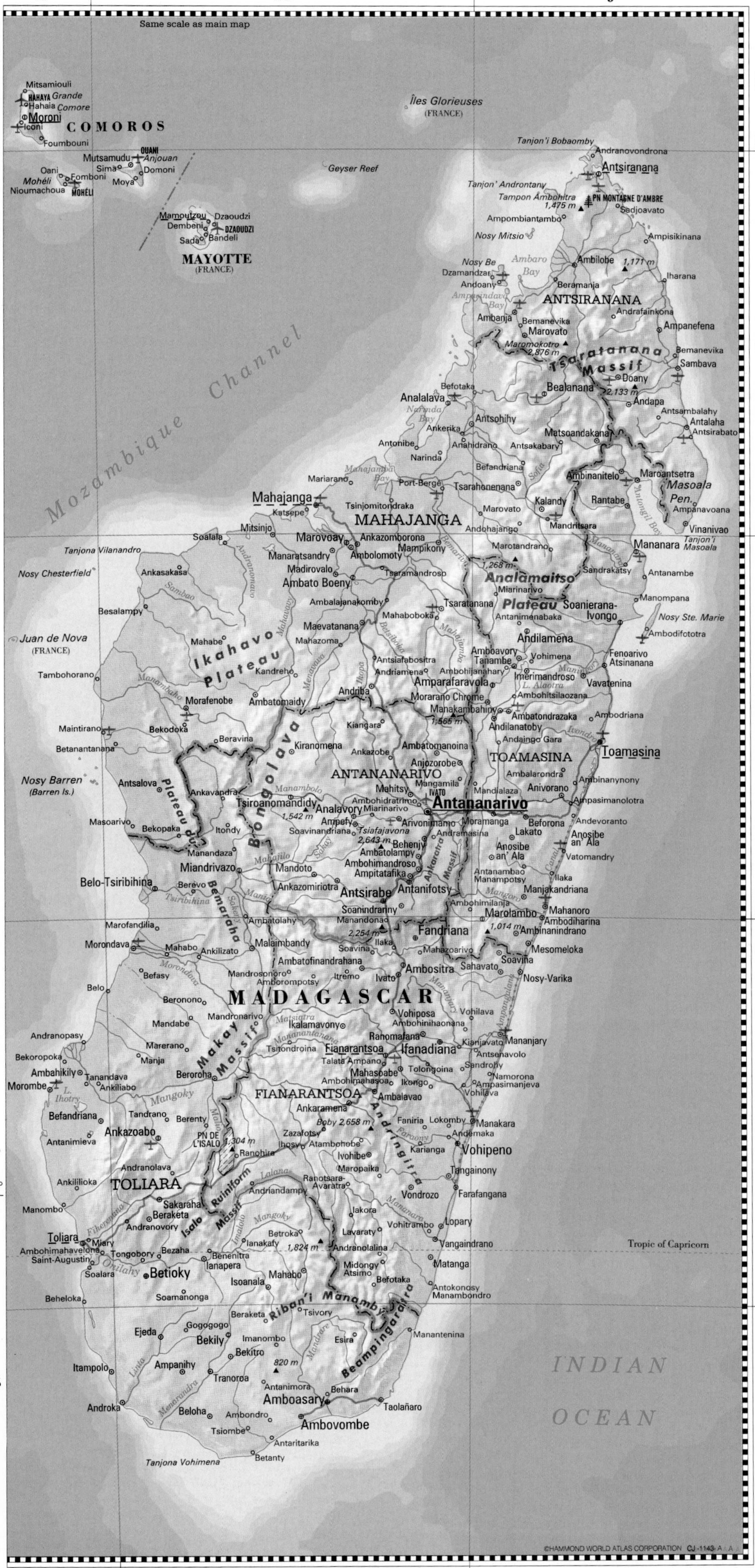

Same scale as main map

MOZAMBIQUE
INHAMBANE
GAZA
KRUGER NP
MAPUTO
SWAZILAND
Maputo
Matola
Mbabane

COMOROS
Moroni
MAYOTTE (FRANCE)
Îles Glorieuses (FRANCE)

ANTSIRANANA
Tsaratanana Massif

KWAZULU-NATAL
Durban (LOUIS BOTHA)

INDIAN OCEAN

Mozambique Channel

MAHAJANGA
Mahajanga

Ikahavo Plateau

Bongolava

ANTANANARIVO
Antananarivo
Antsirabe

TOAMASINA
Toamasina

MADAGASCAR

Makay Massif

FIANARANTSOA
Fianarantsoa

Andringitra

TOLIARA
Toliara

Tropic of Capricorn

Amboasary
Ambovombe

INDIAN OCEAN

14
20°
INDIAN OCEAN

Port Louis
Beau Bassin
Quatre Bornes
Curepipe
Mahébourg
MAURITIUS

RÉUNION (FRANCE)
Saint-Denis
Le Port
Saint-André
Saint-Benoît
Saint-Leu
Saint-Louis
Saint-Pierre
Le Tampon
Saint-Joseph

15

Mascarene Islands

30 Mi
30 Km

5
12°
6
16°
7
20°
8
24°
9

S | 56° | T | 58° | G | 44° | Longitude East of Greenwich | H | 48° | J

POPULATION OF CITIES AND TOWNS
■ OVER 2,000,000
□ 1,000,000 - 1,999,999
● 500,000 - 999,999
◉ 250,000 - 499,999
⊙ 100,000 - 249,999
● 30,000 - 99,999
○ 10,000 - 29,999
○ UNDER 10,000

SCALE 1:6,800,000   LAMBERT CONFORMAL CONIC PROJECTION
MILES 0   100   200   300
KILOMETERS 0   100   200   300

Australia

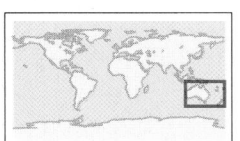

The Lake Eyre Basin is located in the arid interior of south central Australia. This basin is one of the largest areas of internal drainage in the world. It consists of two distinct, but interrelated basins: the north basin and the south basin. The much larger north basin shown here (the highly reflective areas) consists of two very large, normally dry lakebeds. The western lobe (bottom of the image) is Belt Bay, and the eastern lobe is Madigan Bay. The color change, especially in the Madigan Bay lobe, indicates that there was some water in this lobe at the time the image was taken.

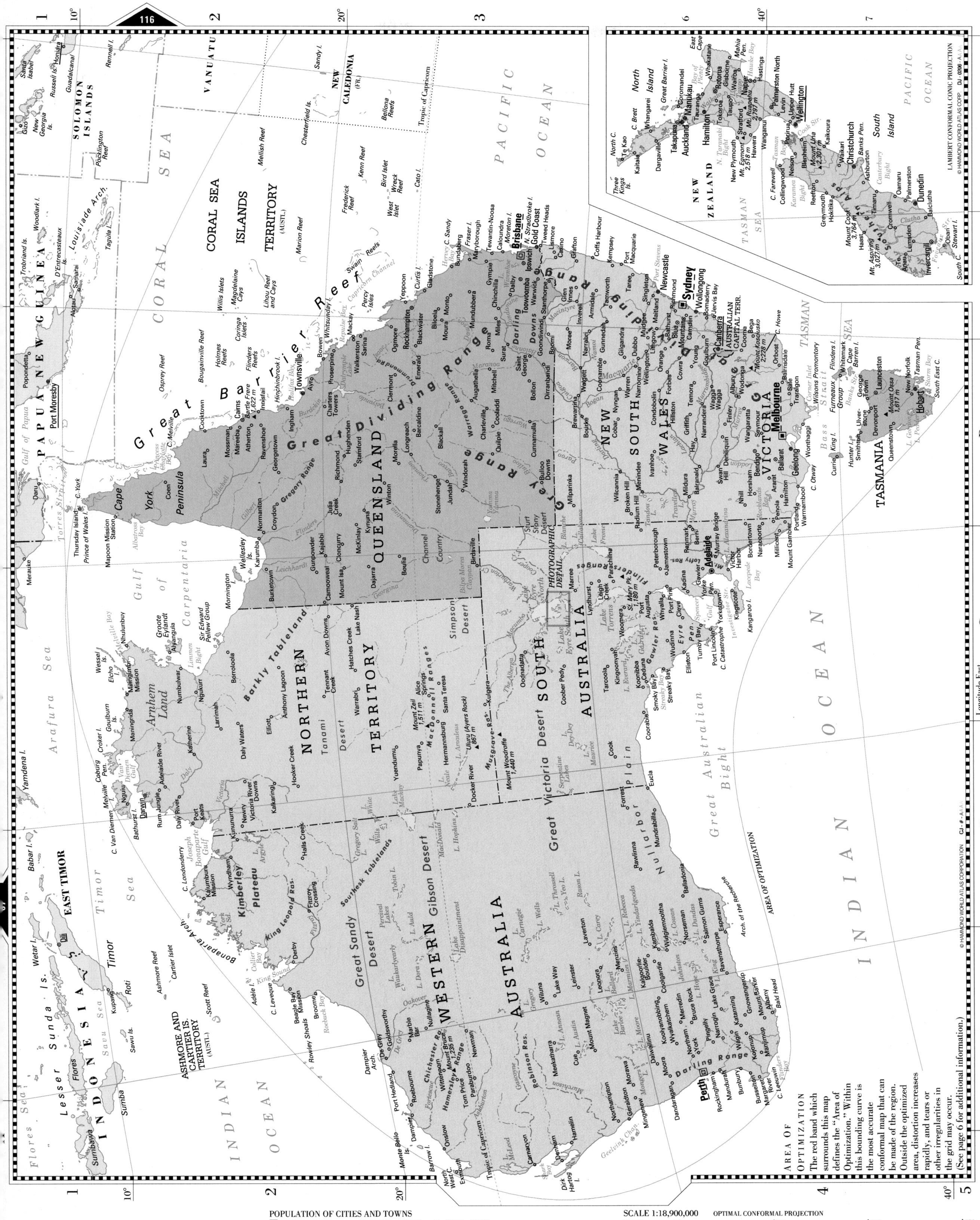

POPULATION OF CITIES AND TOWNS

- ■ OVER 2,000,000
- ☐ 1,000,000 - 1,999,999
- ● 500,000 - 999,999
- ● 100,000 - 499,999
- ● 50,000 - 99,999
- ○ UNDER 50,000

SCALE 1:18,900,000   OPTIMAL CONFORMAL PROJECTION

MILES   0   250   500   750
KILOMETERS   0   250   500   750

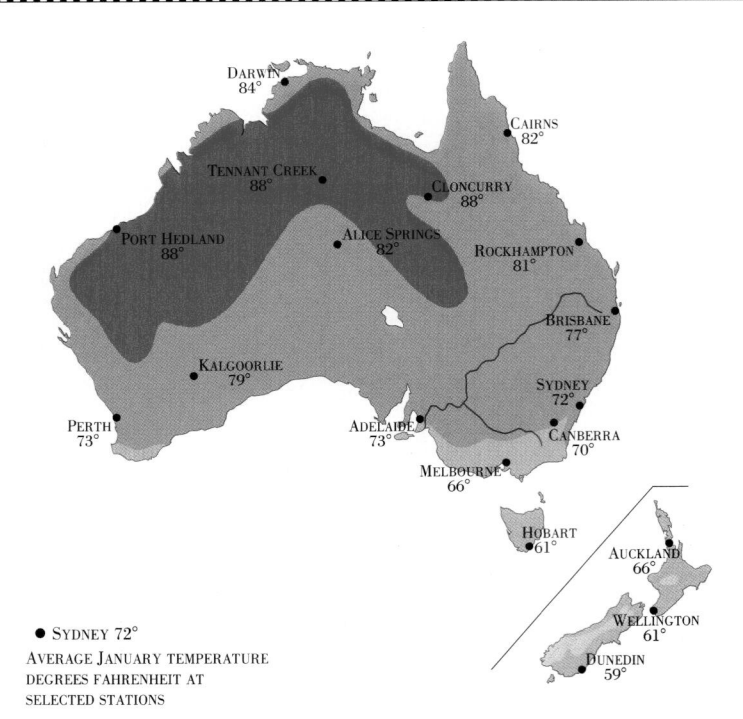

DARWIN
84°

CAIRNS
82°

TENNANT CREEK
88°

CLONCURRY
88°

PORT HEDLAND
88°

ALICE SPRINGS
82°

ROCKHAMPTON
81°

BRISBANE
77°

KALGOORLIE
79°

SYDNEY
72°

PERTH
73°

ADELAIDE
73°

CANBERRA
70°

MELBOURNE
66°

HOBART
61°

AUCKLAND
66°

WELLINGTON
61°

DUNEDIN
59°

● SYDNEY 72°
AVERAGE JANUARY TEMPERATURE
DEGREES FAHRENHEIT AT
SELECTED STATIONS

AVERAGE JANUARY TEMPERATURE

FAHRENHEIT	CELSIUS	FAHRENHEIT	CELSIUS	FAHRENHEIT	CELSIUS
OVER 86°	OVER 30°	50° TO 68°	10° TO 20°	UNDER 32°	UNDER 0°
68° TO 86°	20° TO 30°	32° TO 50°	0° TO 10°		

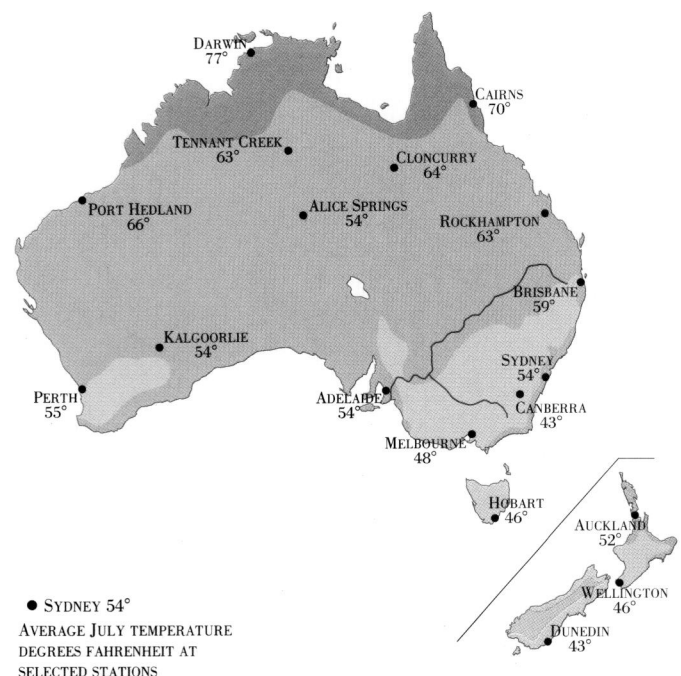

DARWIN
77°

CAIRNS
70°

TENNANT CREEK
63°

CLONCURRY
64°

PORT HEDLAND
66°

ALICE SPRINGS
54°

ROCKHAMPTON
63°

BRISBANE
59°

KALGOORLIE
54°

SYDNEY
54°

PERTH
55°

ADELAIDE
54°

CANBERRA
43°

MELBOURNE
48°

HOBART
46°

AUCKLAND
52°

WELLINGTON
46°

DUNEDIN
43°

● SYDNEY 54°
AVERAGE JULY TEMPERATURE
DEGREES FAHRENHEIT AT
SELECTED STATIONS

AVERAGE JULY TEMPERATURE

FAHRENHEIT	CELSIUS	FAHRENHEIT	CELSIUS
OVER 68°	OVER 20°	32° TO 50°	0° TO 10°
50° TO 68°	10° TO 20°	UNDER 32°	UNDER 0°

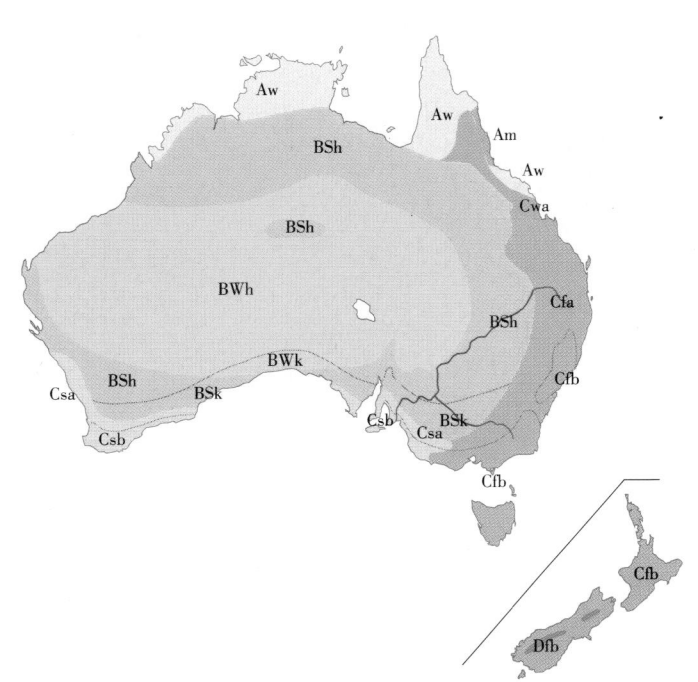

Aw

BSh

Aw

Am

Aw

Cwa

BSh

BWh

BSh

Cfa

BWk

Csa

BSh

BSk

Cfb

Csb

Csb

Csa

BSk

Cfb

Cfb

Dfb

CLIMATE

HUMID TROPICAL
- Am SHORT DRY SEASON
- Aw DRY WINTER

DRY
- BS SEMIARID ⎤ h HOT
- BW ARID ⎦ k COLD

HUMID WARM
- Cf NO DRY SEASON
- Cw DRY WINTER
- Cs DRY SUMMER

HUMID COLD
- Df NO DRY SEASON
- a HOT SUMMER
- b COOL SUMMER

AFTER KOEPPEN-GEIGER

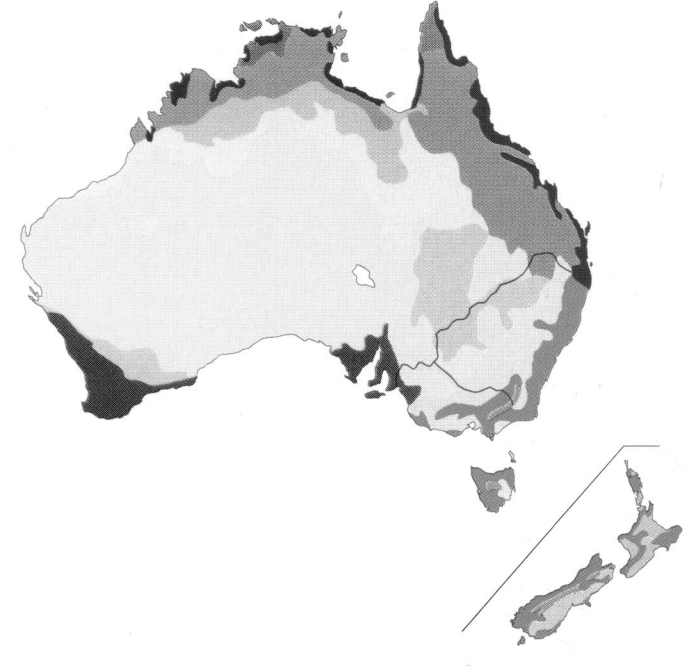

VEGETATION

TROPICAL FOREST
- TROPICAL RAINFOREST
- LIGHT TROPICAL FOREST
- WOODLAND AND SHRUB

TROPICAL GRASSLAND
- GRASS AND SHRUB (SAVANNA)
- WOODED SAVANNA

MID-LATITUDE FOREST
- MIXED NEEDLELEAF AND BROADLEAF FOREST
- MIXED WOODLAND
- WOODLAND AND SHRUB (MEDITERRANEAN)

- MID-LATITUDE GRASSLAND
- SCRUB AND FERNLANDS
- DESERT AND DESERT SHRUB
- ALPINE

Western and Central Australia

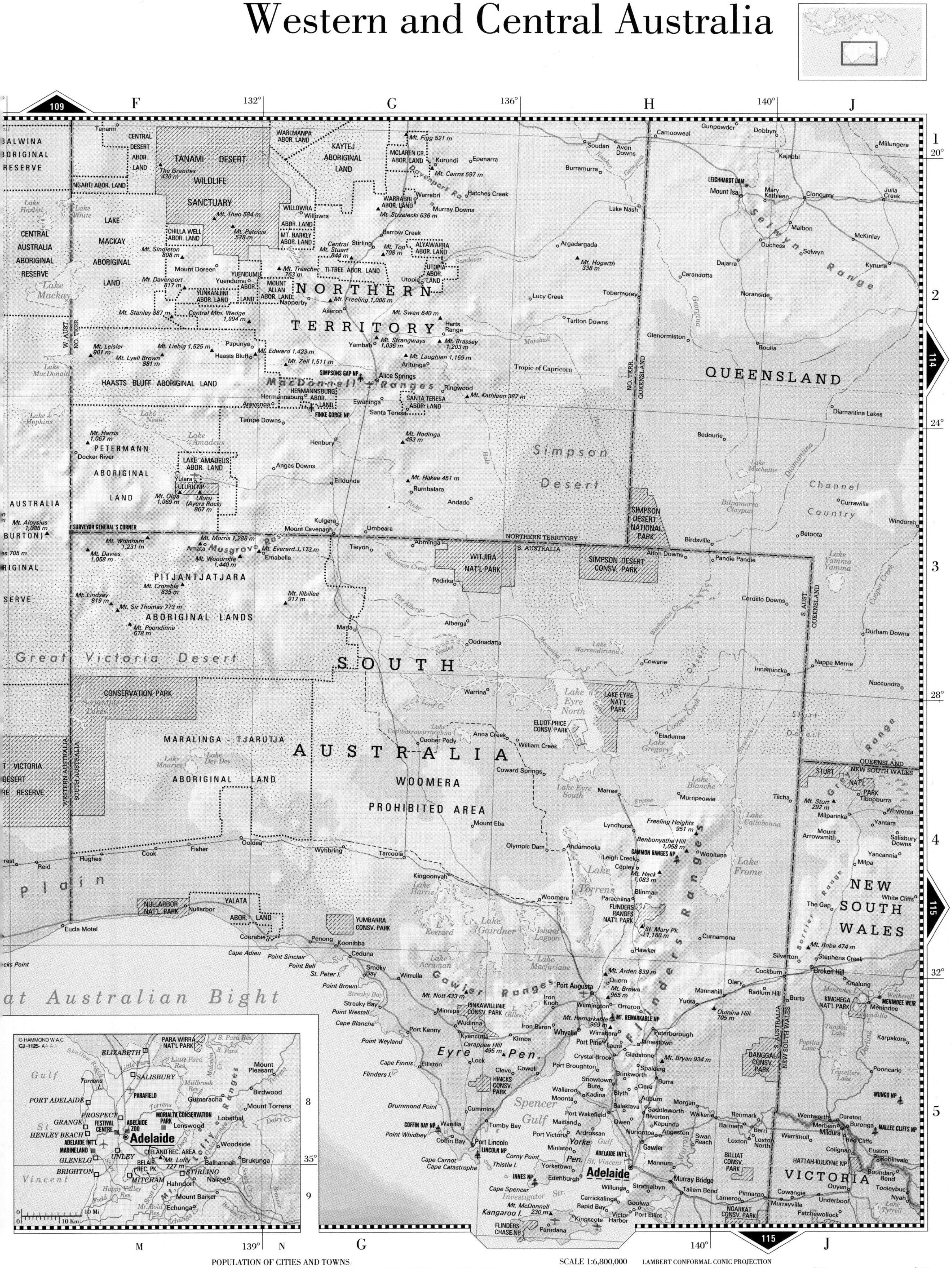

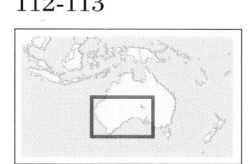

POPULATION OF CITIES AND TOWNS

SCALE 1:6,800,000   LAMBERT CONFORMAL CONIC PROJECTION

MILES

KILOMETERS

Northeastern Australia

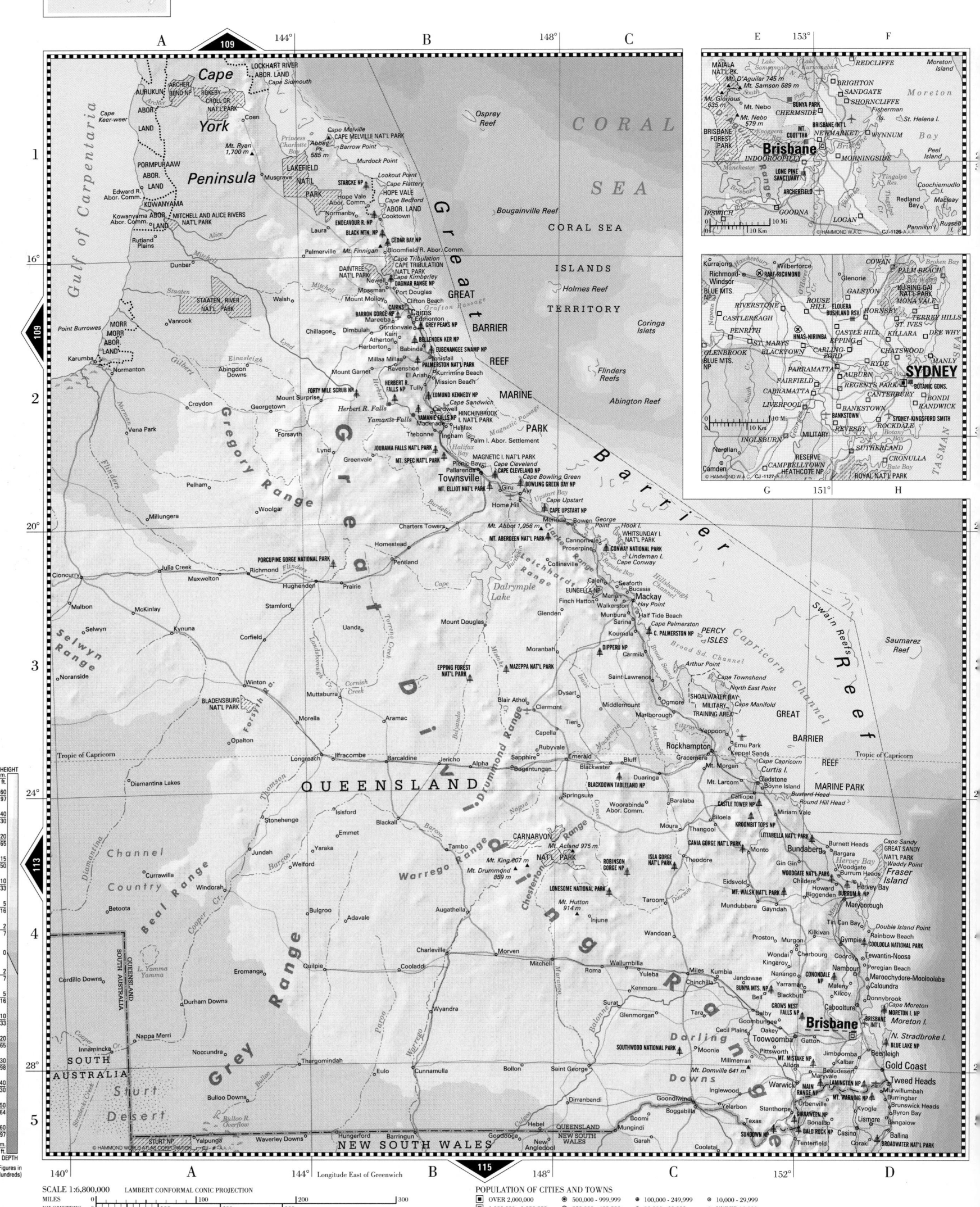

SCALE 1:6,800,000   LAMBERT CONFORMAL CONIC PROJECTION
MILES   0   100   200   300
KILOMETERS   0   100   200   300

POPULATION OF CITIES AND TOWNS
■ OVER 2,000,000
□ 1,000,000 - 1,999,999
● 500,000 - 999,999
□ 250,000 - 499,999
● 100,000 - 249,999
● 30,000 - 99,999
● 10,000 - 29,999
○ UNDER 10,000

Southeastern Australia

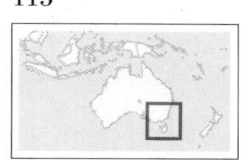

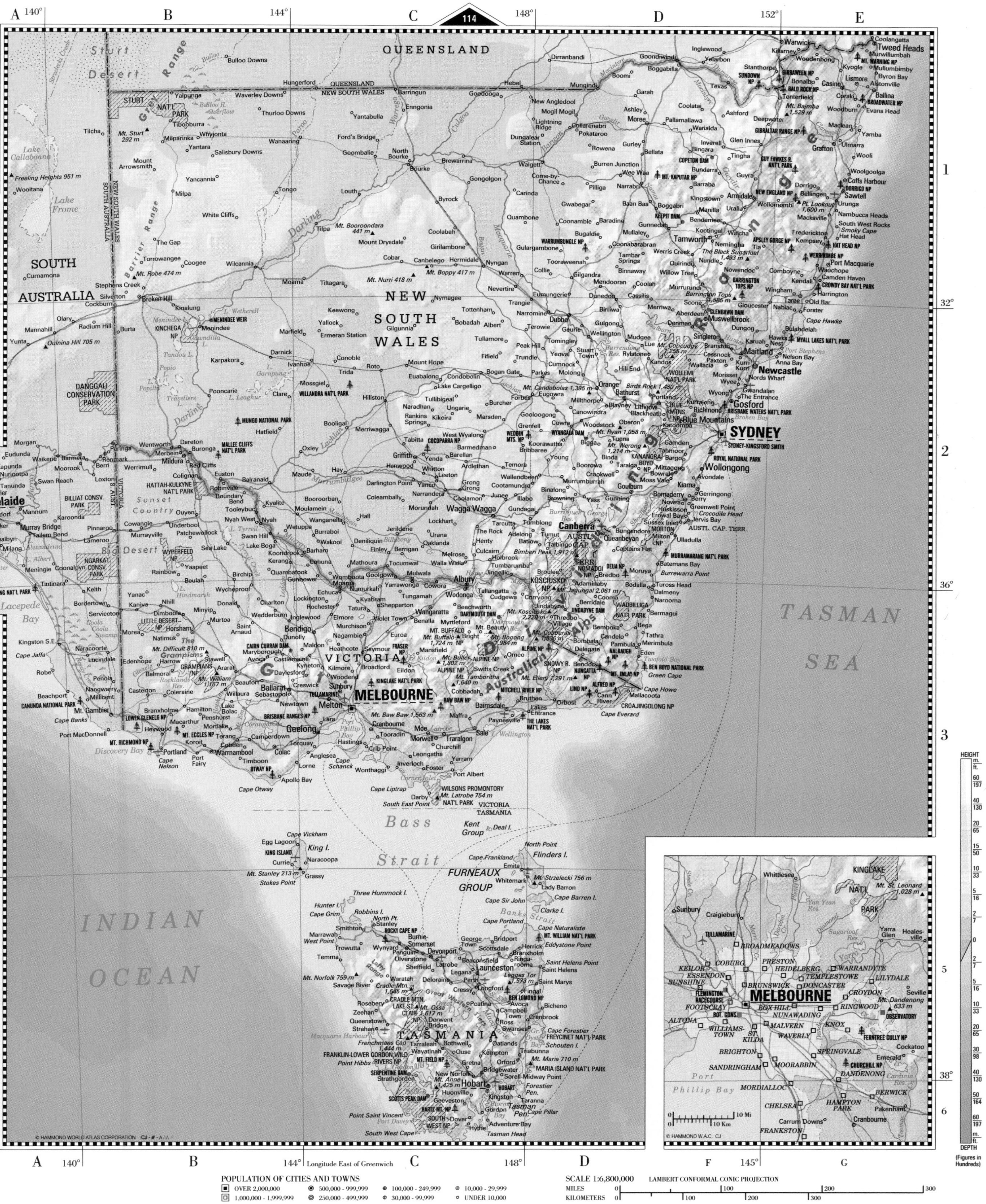

QUEENSLAND

NEW SOUTH WALES

SOUTH AUSTRALIA

VICTORIA

TASMANIA

AUSTL. CAP. TERR.

INDIAN OCEAN

TASMAN SEA

Bass Strait

Great Dividing Range

Australian Alps

Sturt Desert

Barrier Range

Grey Range

Major cities:
- **SYDNEY**
- **MELBOURNE**
- **Canberra** AUSTL. CAP.
- **Newcastle**
- **Wollongong**
- **Geelong**
- **Hobart**
- **Launceston**
- **Gosford**
- **Maitland**
- Wagga Wagga
- Albury
- Ballarat
- Bendigo
- Broken Hill
- Tamworth
- Adelaide

National Parks and mountains (selection):
- Mt. Kosciusko 2,228 m
- Mt. Bogong 1,986 m
- Mt. Ossa 1,617 m
- Bimberi Peak 1,912 m
- Mt. Baw Baw 1,563 m
- Mt. Buller 1,802 m
- Mt. William 1,167 m
- Cradle Mtn. 1,545 m
- Mt. St. Leonard 1,028 m
- Mt. Dandenong 633 m

Melbourne inset
MELBOURNE, with suburbs: TULLAMARINE, BROADMEADOWS, PRESTON, HEIDELBERG, TEMPLESTOWE, WARRANDYTE, LILYDALE, COBURG, BRUNSWICK, ESSENDON, SUNSHINE, KEILOR, DONCASTER, CROYDON, RINGWOOD, BOX HILL, FOOTSCRAY, NUNAWADING, MALVERN, WAVERLY, KNOX, FERNTREE GULLY NP, ALTONA, WILLIAMSTOWN, ST. KILDA, BRIGHTON, SANDRINGHAM, MOORABBIN, SPRINGVALE, DANDENONG, MORDIALLOC, CHELSEA, HAMPTON PARK, FRANKSTON, BERWICK, PAKENHAM, KINGLAKE NAT'L PARK, CHURCHILL NP

Port Phillip Bay

SCALE 1:6,800,000 — LAMBERT CONFORMAL CONIC PROJECTION

POPULATION OF CITIES AND TOWNS
- ■ OVER 2,000,000
- ◻ 1,000,000 – 1,999,999
- ● 500,000 – 999,999
- ◉ 250,000 – 499,999
- ● 100,000 – 249,999
- ● 30,000 – 99,999
- ● 10,000 – 29,999
- ○ UNDER 10,000

MILES 0 100 200 300
KILOMETERS 0 100 200 300

HEIGHT m. / ft.
DEPTH m. / ft. (Figures in Hundreds)

Longitude East of Greenwich

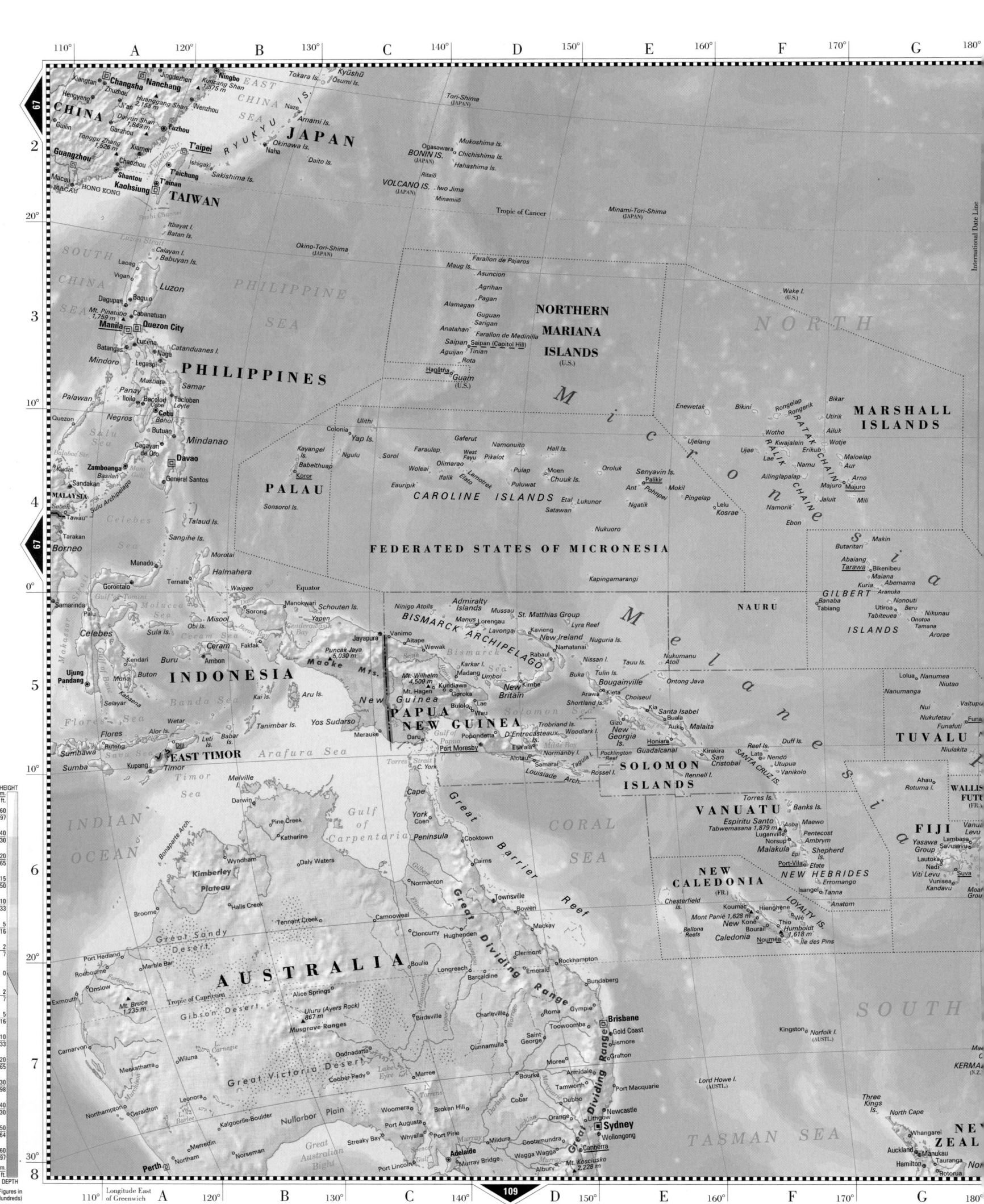

Central Pacific Ocean, New Zealand

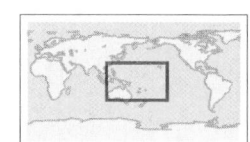

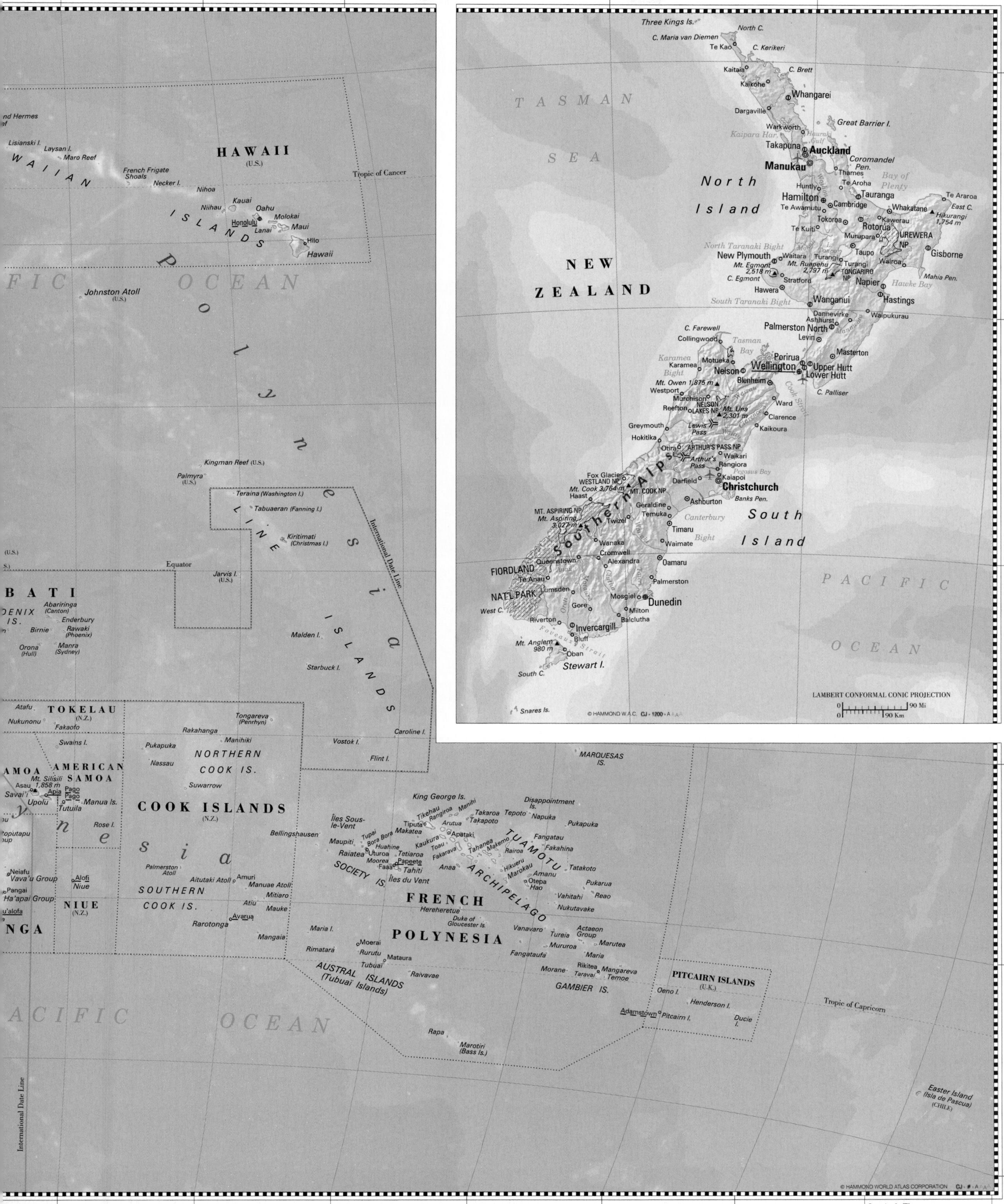

POPULATION OF CITIES AND TOWNS
- OVER 3,000,000
- 1,000,000 - 2,999,999
- 500,000 - 999,999
- 100,000 - 499,999
- UNDER 100,000

SCALE 1:30,700,000 · LAMBERT AZIMUTHAL EQUAL-AREA PROJECTION

MILES 0 · 400 · 800 · 1200
KILOMETERS 0 · 400 · 800 · 1200

© HAMMOND WORLD ATLAS CORPORATION

North America

The Grand Canyon, one of the deepest canyons in the world, with a depth of 1 mile (1.6 km.), can be seen in this spectacular, west-looking, low-oblique image. The Colorado River cut through rocks billions of years old to create this canyon. The Grand Canyon is 277 miles (466 km.) long and averages nearly 10 miles (16 km.) in width. The snow-covered, forested Kaibab Plateau (north of the canyon) and the Coconino Plateau (south of the canyon) are visible. Western portions of the Painted Desert can be seen east of the canyon where the Little Colorado joins the Colorado River.

AREA OF OPTIMIZATION

The red band which surrounds this map defines the "Area of Optimization." Within this bounding curve is the most accurate conformal map that can be made of the region. Outside the optimized area, distortion increases rapidly, and tears or other irregularities in the grid may occur. (See page 6 for additional information.)

POPULATION OF CITIES AND TOWNS

■ OVER 3,000,000   ● 500,000 - 999,999   ○ UNDER 100,000
□ 1,000,000 - 2,999,999   ● 100,000 - 499,999

SCALE 1:34,100,000   OPTIMAL CONFORMAL PROJECTION

MILES   0   500   1000   1500
KILOMETERS   0   500   1000   1500

© HAMMOND WORLD ATLAS CORPORATION

Longitude   West of 100°   Greenwich

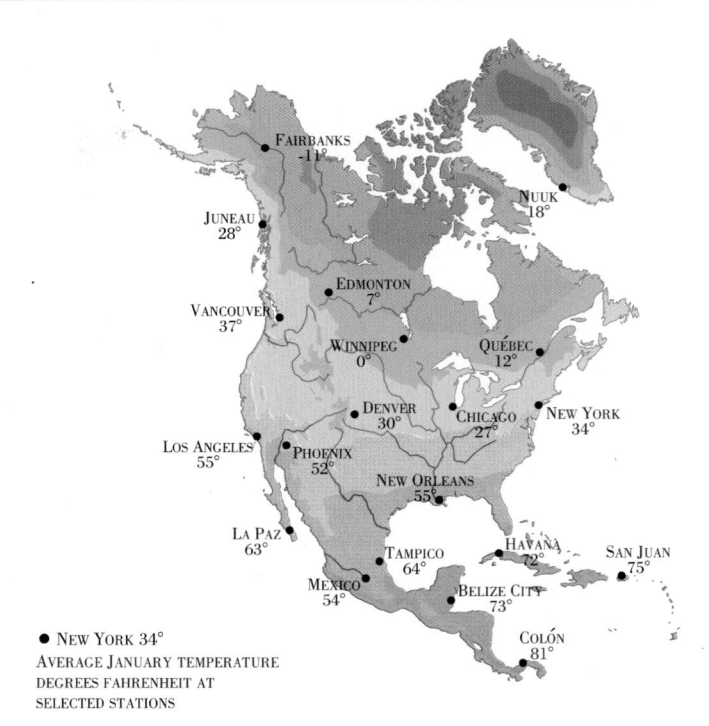

● NEW YORK 34°
AVERAGE JANUARY TEMPERATURE
DEGREES FAHRENHEIT AT
SELECTED STATIONS

AVERAGE JANUARY TEMPERATURE

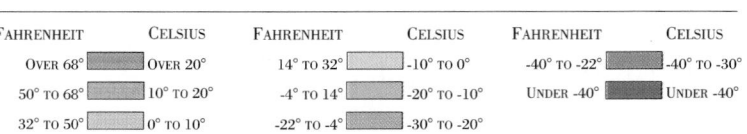

FAHRENHEIT	CELSIUS	FAHRENHEIT	CELSIUS	FAHRENHEIT	CELSIUS
OVER 68°	OVER 20°	14° TO 32°	-10° TO 0°	-40° TO -22°	-40° TO -30°
50° TO 68°	10° TO 20°	-4° TO 14°	-20° TO -10°	UNDER -40°	UNDER -40°
32° TO 50°	0° TO 10°	-22° TO -4°	-30° TO -20°		

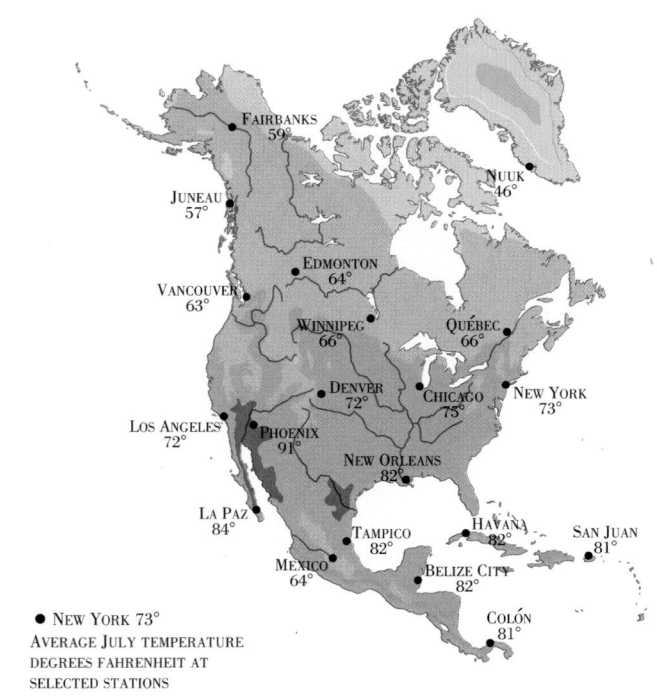

● NEW YORK 73°
AVERAGE JULY TEMPERATURE
DEGREES FAHRENHEIT AT
SELECTED STATIONS

AVERAGE JULY TEMPERATURE

FAHRENHEIT	CELSIUS	FAHRENHEIT	CELSIUS	FAHRENHEIT	CELSIUS
OVER 86°	OVER 30°	50° TO 68°	10° TO 20°	14° 32°	-10° TO 0°
68° TO 86°	20° TO 30°	32° TO 50°	0° TO 10°	UNDER 14°	UNDER -10°

CLIMATE

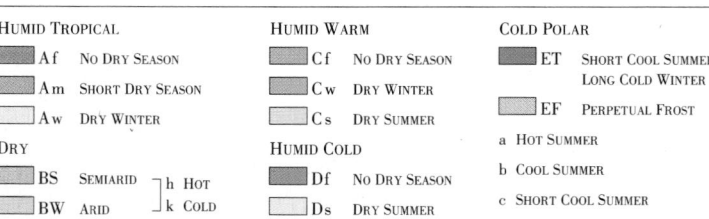

HUMID TROPICAL

Af   NO DRY SEASON

Am   SHORT DRY SEASON

Aw   DRY WINTER

DRY

BS   SEMIARID   ] h HOT

BW   ARID   ] k COLD

HUMID WARM

Cf   NO DRY SEASON

Cw   DRY WINTER

Cs   DRY SUMMER

HUMID COLD

Df   NO DRY SEASON

Ds   DRY SUMMER

COLD POLAR

ET   SHORT COOL SUMMER,
      LONG COLD WINTER

EF   PERPETUAL FROST

a HOT SUMMER

b COOL SUMMER

c SHORT COOL SUMMER

AFTER KOEPPEN-GEIGER

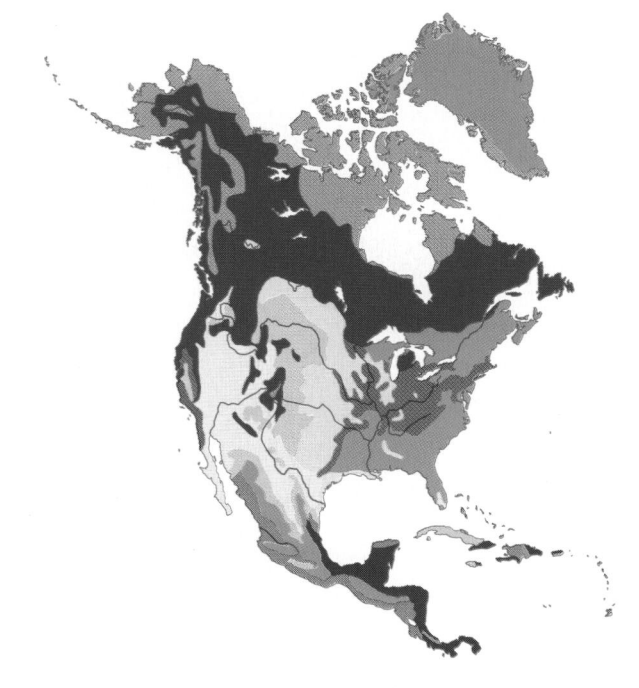

VEGETATION

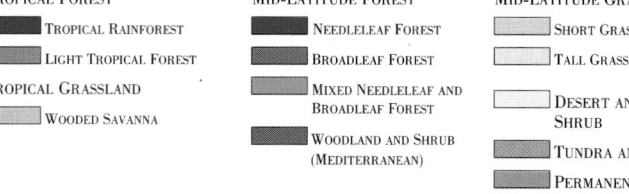

TROPICAL FOREST

TROPICAL RAINFOREST

LIGHT TROPICAL FOREST

TROPICAL GRASSLAND

WOODED SAVANNA

MID-LATITUDE FOREST

NEEDLELEAF FOREST

BROADLEAF FOREST

MIXED NEEDLELEAF AND
BROADLEAF FOREST

WOODLAND AND SHRUB
(MEDITERRANEAN)

MID-LATITUDE GRASSLAND

SHORT GRASS (STEPPE)

TALL GRASS (PRAIRIE)

DESERT AND DESERT
SHRUB

TUNDRA AND ALPINE

PERMANENT ICE COVER

North America - Geographical Comparisons

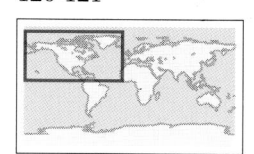

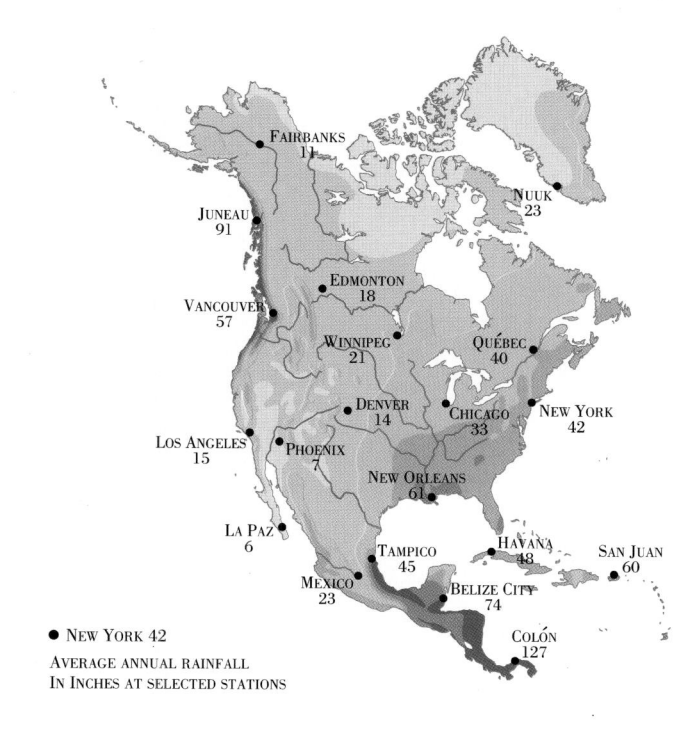

FAIRBANKS 11
NUUK 23
JUNEAU 91
EDMONTON 18
VANCOUVER 57
WINNIPEG 21
QUÉBEC 40
DENVER 14
CHICAGO 33
NEW YORK 42
LOS ANGELES 15
PHOENIX 7
NEW ORLEANS 61
LA PAZ 6
TAMPICO 45
HAVANA 48
SAN JUAN 60
MEXICO 23
BELIZE CITY 74
COLÓN 127

● NEW YORK 42
AVERAGE ANNUAL RAINFALL
IN INCHES AT SELECTED STATIONS

AVERAGE ANNUAL RAINFALL

INCHES	CM	INCHES	CM	INCHES	CM
OVER 80	OVER 200	40 TO 60	100 TO 150	10 TO 20	25 TO 50
60 TO 80	150 TO 200	20 TO 40	50 TO 100	UNDER 10	UNDER 25

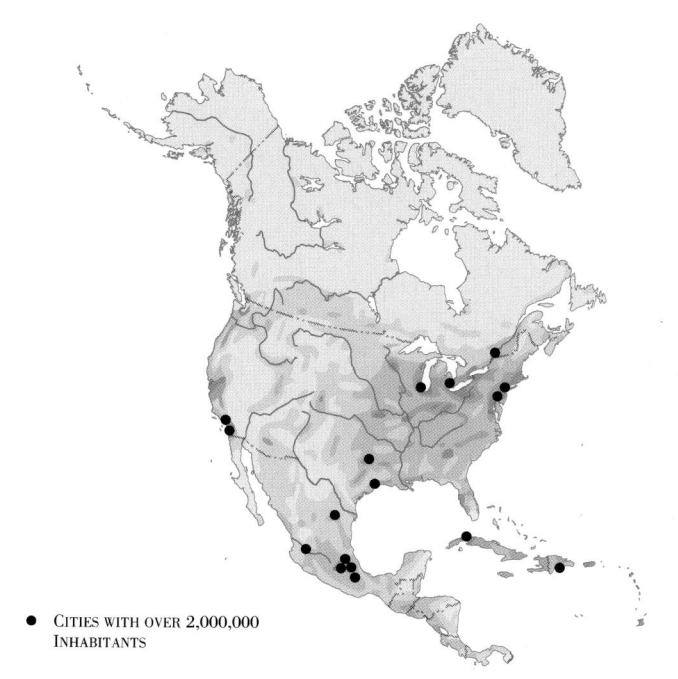

● CITIES WITH OVER 2,000,000 INHABITANTS

POPULATION DISTRIBUTION

DENSITY PER		SQ. MI.	SQ. KM.	SQ. MI.	SQ. KM.
SQ. MI.	SQ. KM.	130 TO 260	50 TO 100	3 TO 25	1 TO 10
OVER 260	OVER 100	25 TO 130	10 TO 50	UNDER 3	UNDER 1

FURS
BARLEY
OATS FLAX
FURS
WHEAT
OATS
WINE
SHEEP
CATTLE CORN CORN
FRUIT
WHEAT
CATTLE SOYBEANS
TOBACCO
COTTON
COTTON
PEANUTS
GOATS
FRUIT
CORN
CATTLE
HOGS
SUGARCANE
COFFEE

LAND USE

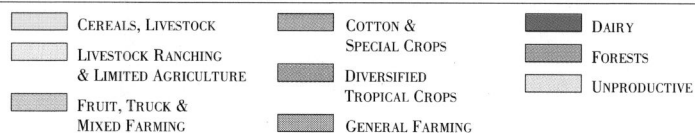

CEREALS, LIVESTOCK
LIVESTOCK RANCHING & LIMITED AGRICULTURE
FRUIT, TRUCK & MIXED FARMING
COTTON & SPECIAL CROPS
DIVERSIFIED TROPICAL CROPS
GENERAL FARMING
DAIRY
FORESTS
UNPRODUCTIVE

MINERAL RESOURCES

ENERGY & FUELS
◆ COAL
▲ NATURAL GAS
● PETROLEUM
■ URANIUM

IRON & FERROALLOYS
1 COBALT
2 IRON ORE
3 MANGANESE
4 MOLYBDENUM
5 NICKEL
6 TUNGSTEN
7 VANADIUM

OTHER MAJOR RESOURCES
1 ANTIMONY
2 ASBESTOS
3 BAUXITE
4 BORAX
5 COPPER
6 FLUORSPAR
7 GOLD
8 GRAPHITE
9 LEAD
10 MERCURY
11 MICA
12 PHOSPHATES
13 PLATINUM
14 POTASH
15 SILVER
16 SULFUR
17 TITANIUM
18 ZINC

Canada

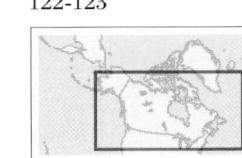

POPULATION OF CITIES AND TOWNS
- ■ OVER 2,000,000
- ▣ 1,000,000 - 1,999,999
- ● 500,000 - 999,999
- ● 100,000 - 499,999
- ○ 50,000 - 99,999
- ○ UNDER 50,000

SCALE 1:13,600,000   LAMBERT CONFORMAL CONIC PROJECTION

MILES 0 — 200 — 400 — 600
KILOMETERS 0 — 200 — 400 — 600

© HAMMOND WORLD ATLAS CORPORATION

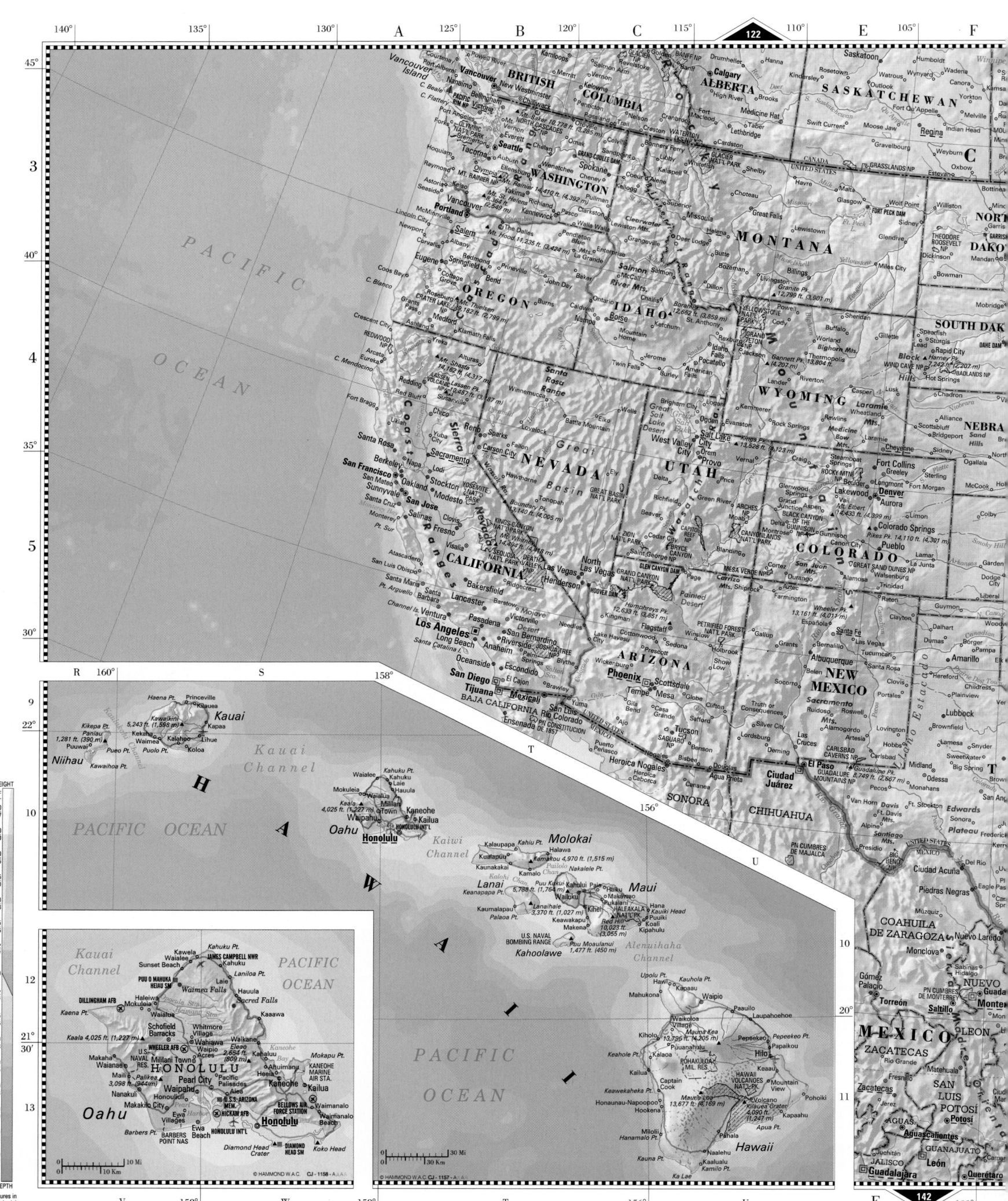

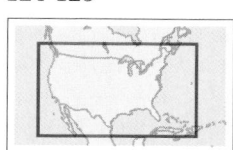

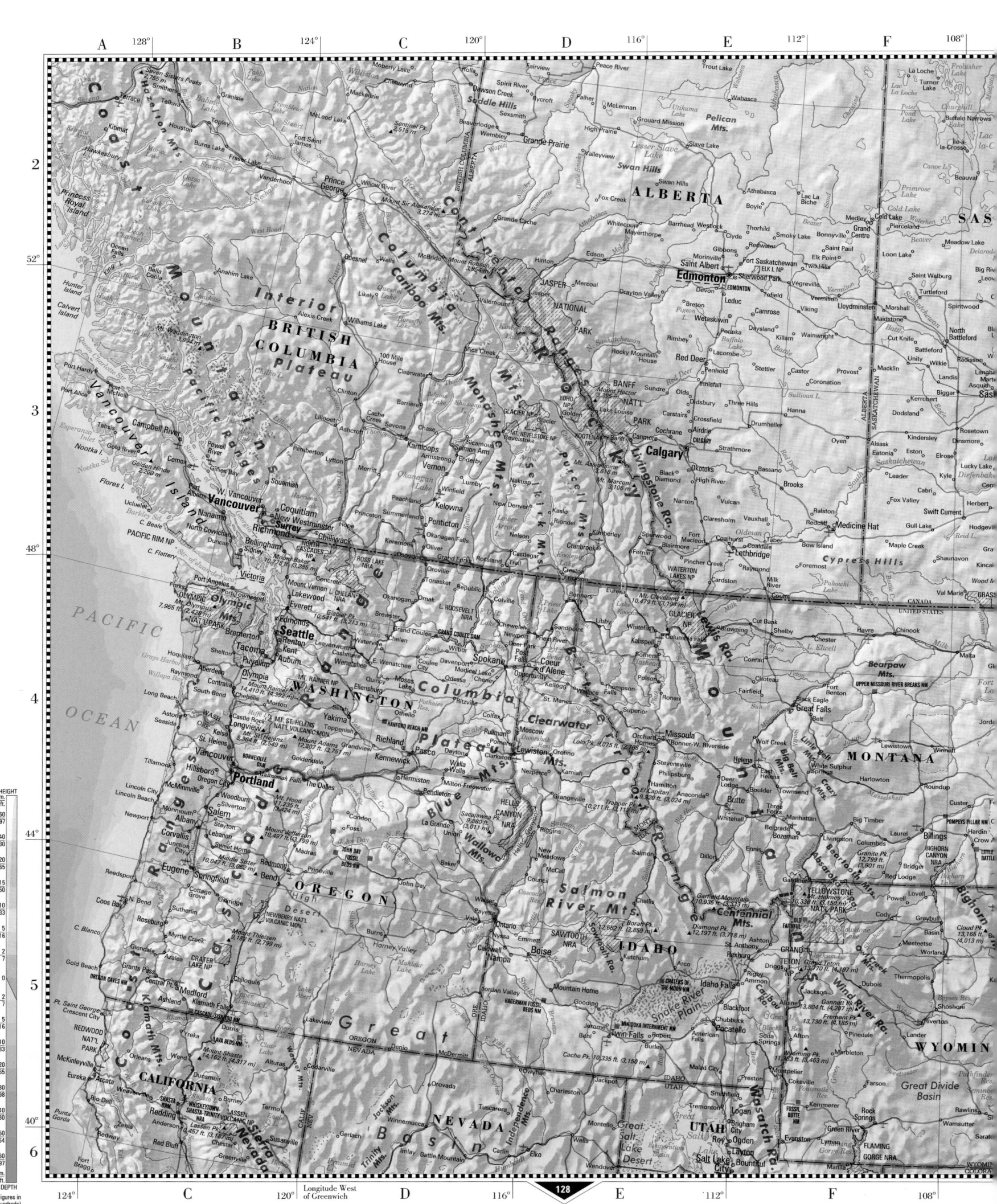

Southwestern United States

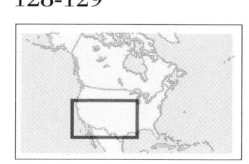

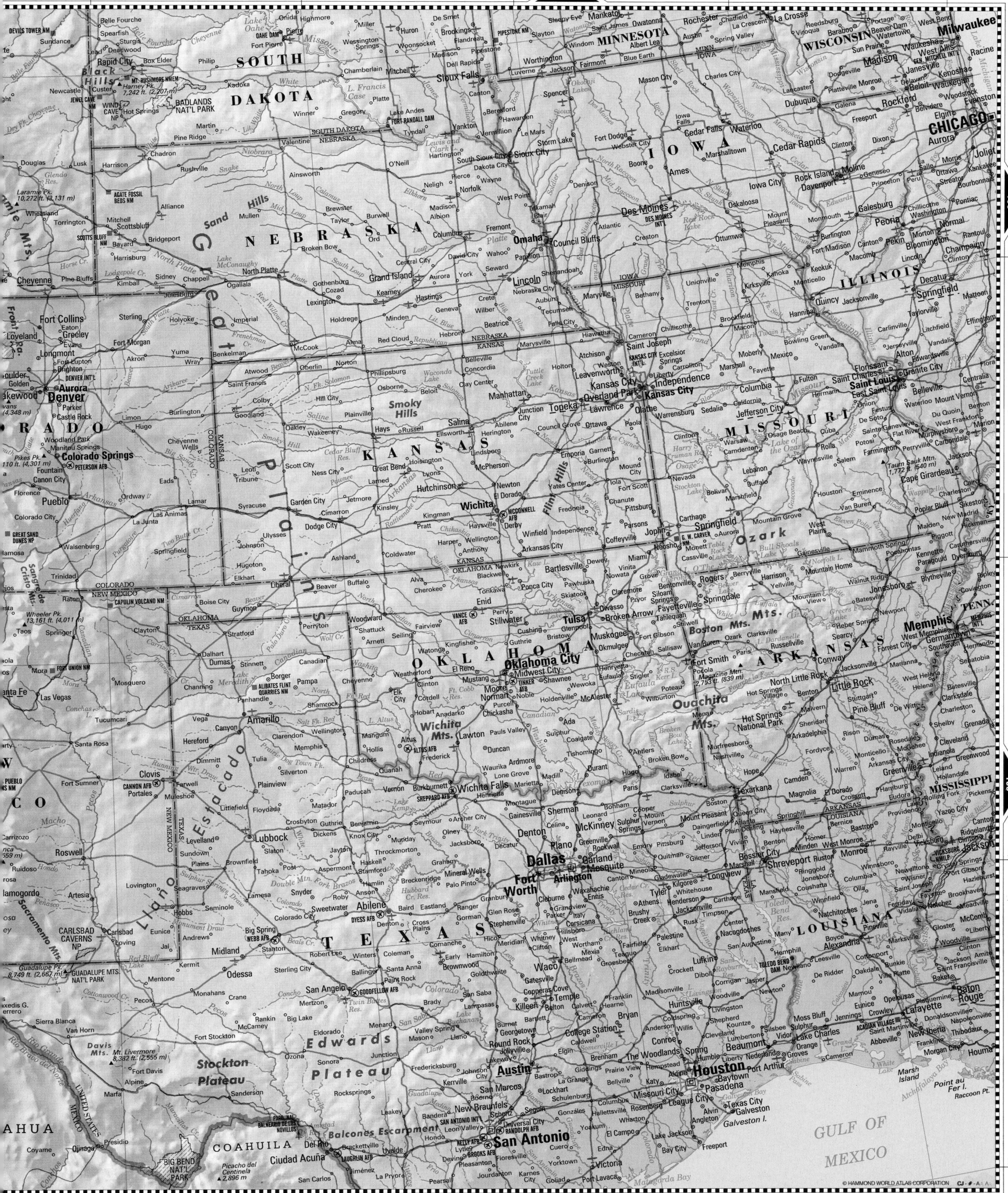

POPULATION OF CITIES AND TOWNS
■ OVER 2,000,000　● 500,000 - 999,999　● 100,000 - 249,999　○ 10,000 - 29,999
□ 1,000,000 - 1,999,999　● 250,000 - 499,999　● 30,000 - 99,999　○ UNDER 10,000

SCALE 1:6,800,000　LAMBERT CONFORMAL CONIC PROJECTION
MILES　0　100　200　300
KILOMETERS　0　100　200　300

© HAMMOND WORLD ATLAS CORPORATION

Southeastern Canada, Northeastern United States

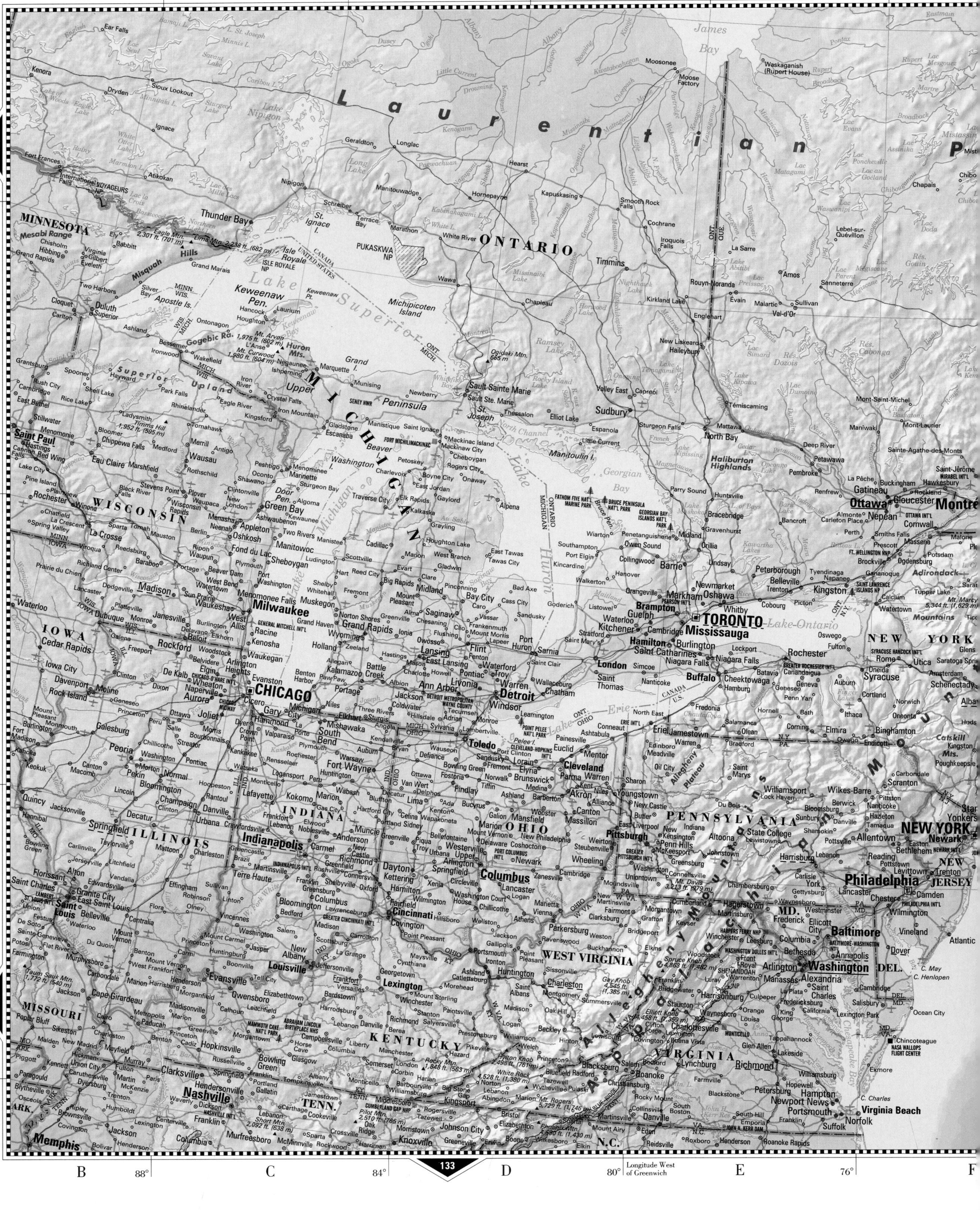

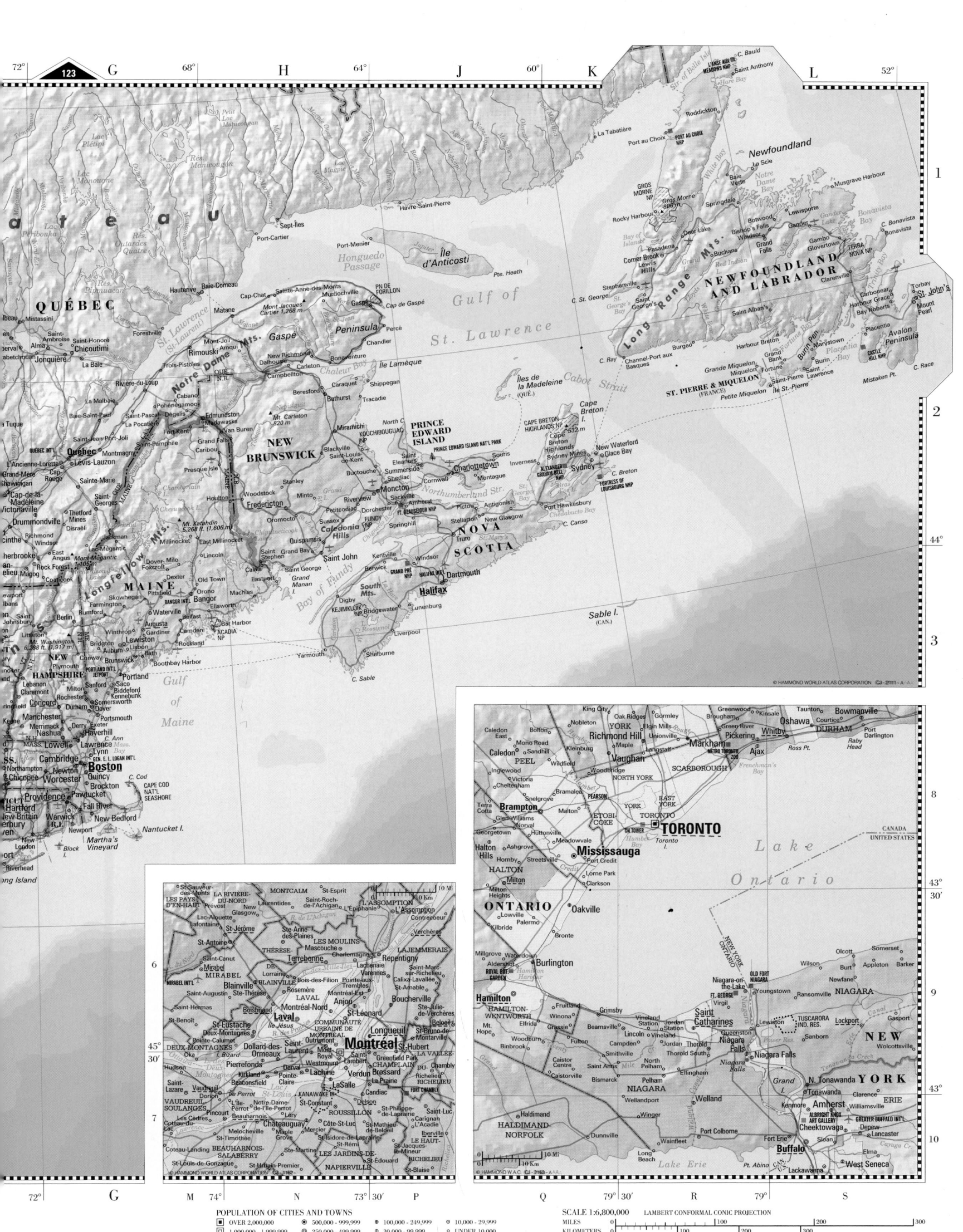

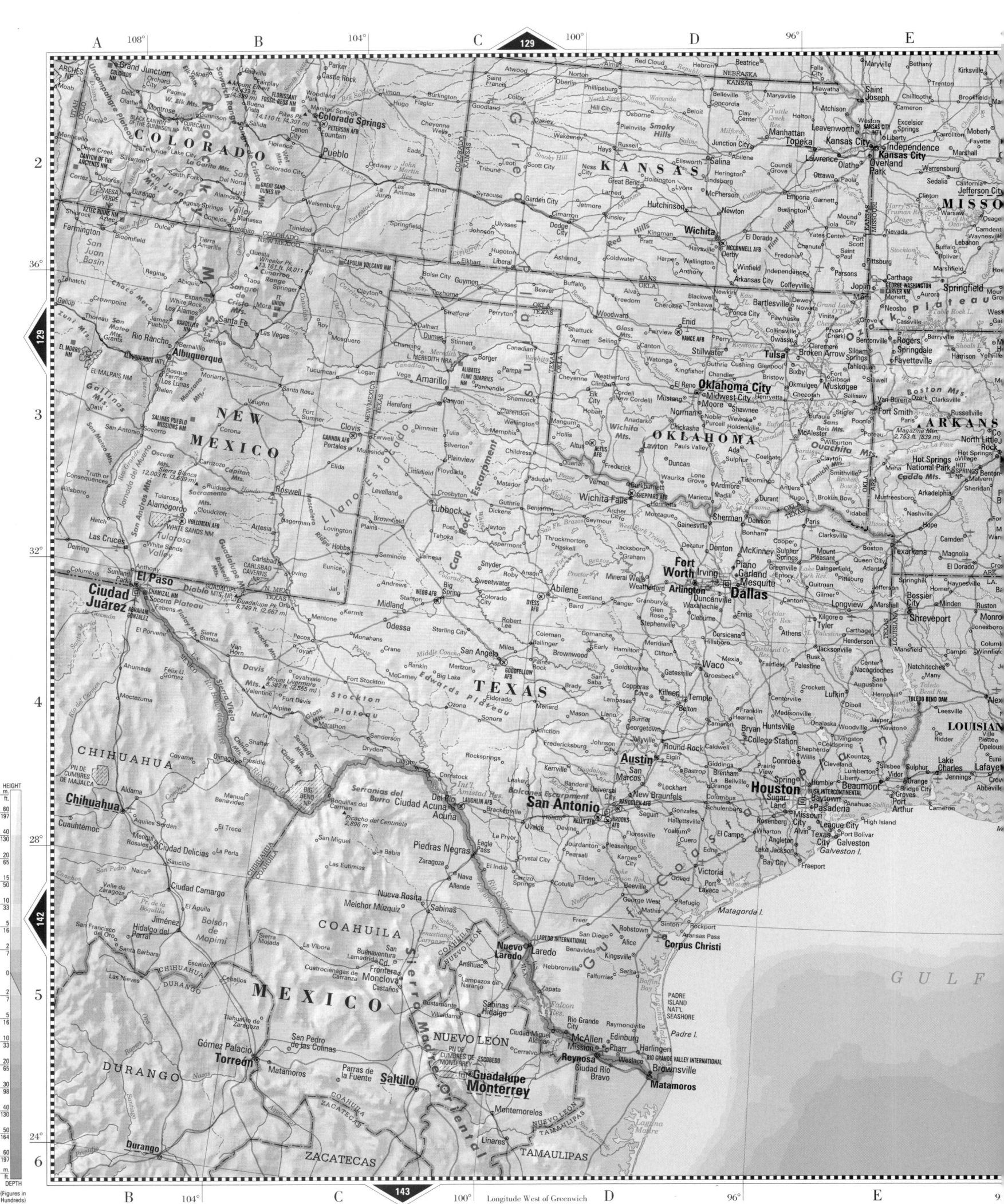

Southeastern United States

POPULATION OF CITIES AND TOWNS

■ OVER 2,000,000   ◉ 500,000 - 999,999   ⊕ 100,000 - 249,999   ⊙ 10,000 - 29,999
◻ 1,000,000 - 1,999,999   ◎ 250,000 - 499,999   ⊙ 30,000 - 99,999   ○ UNDER 10,000

SCALE 1:6,800,000   LAMBERT CONFORMAL CONIC PROJECTION

MILES   0   50   100   200   300
KILOMETERS   0   100   200   300

© HAMMOND WORLD ATLAS CORPORATION

Los Angeles-San Diego

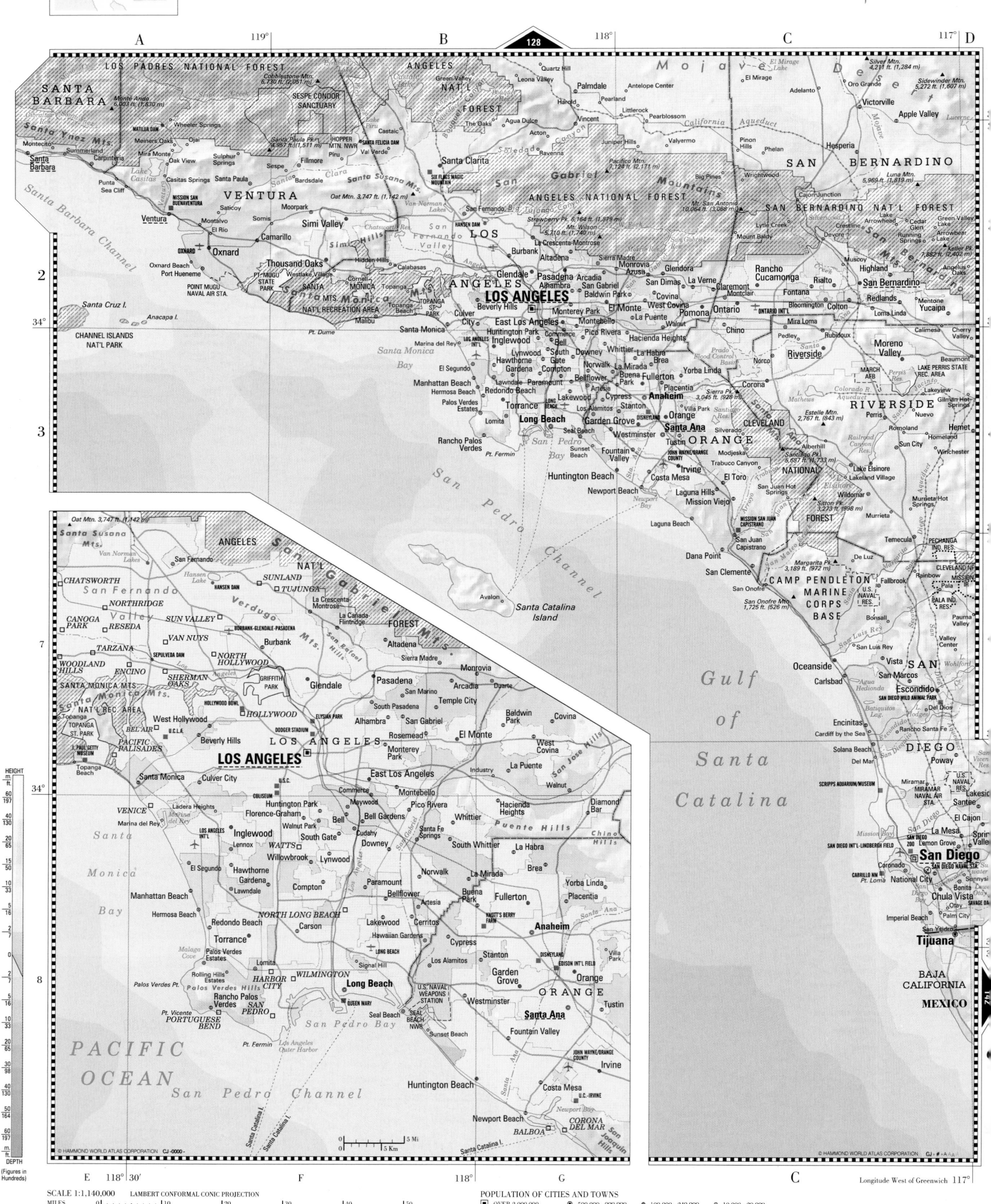

SCALE 1:1,140,000   LAMBERT CONFORMAL CONIC PROJECTION

MILES

KILOMETERS

POPULATION OF CITIES AND TOWNS

▪ OVER 2,000,000   ● 500,000 - 999,999   ● 100,000 - 249,999   ● 10,000 - 29,999
□ 1,000,000 - 1,999,999   ● 250,000 - 499,999   ● 30,000 - 99,999   ○ UNDER 10,000

Longitude West of Greenwich 117°

Phoenix, Salt Lake City, Denver, Oklahoma City, Kansas City, St. Louis, San Antonio, New Orleans

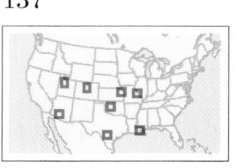

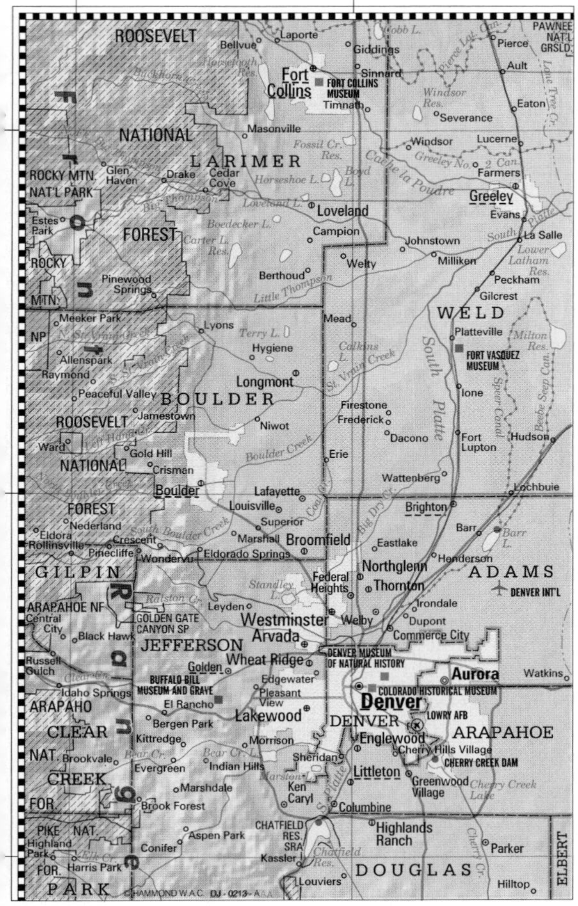

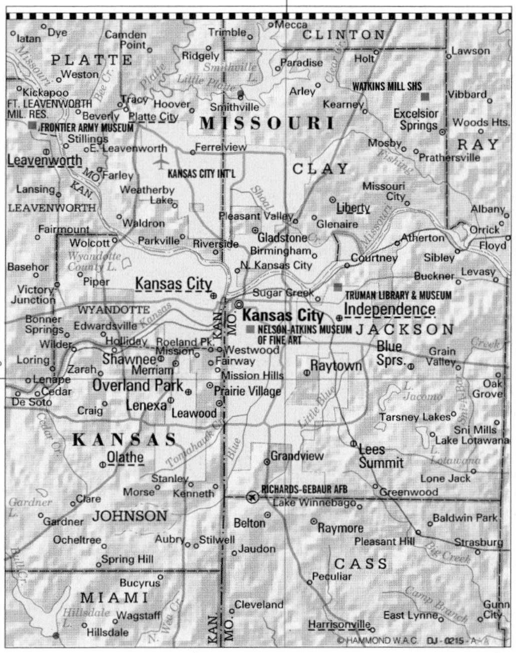

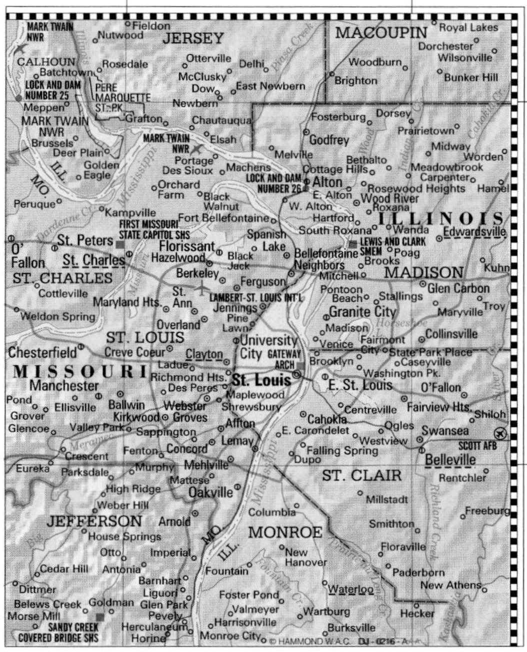

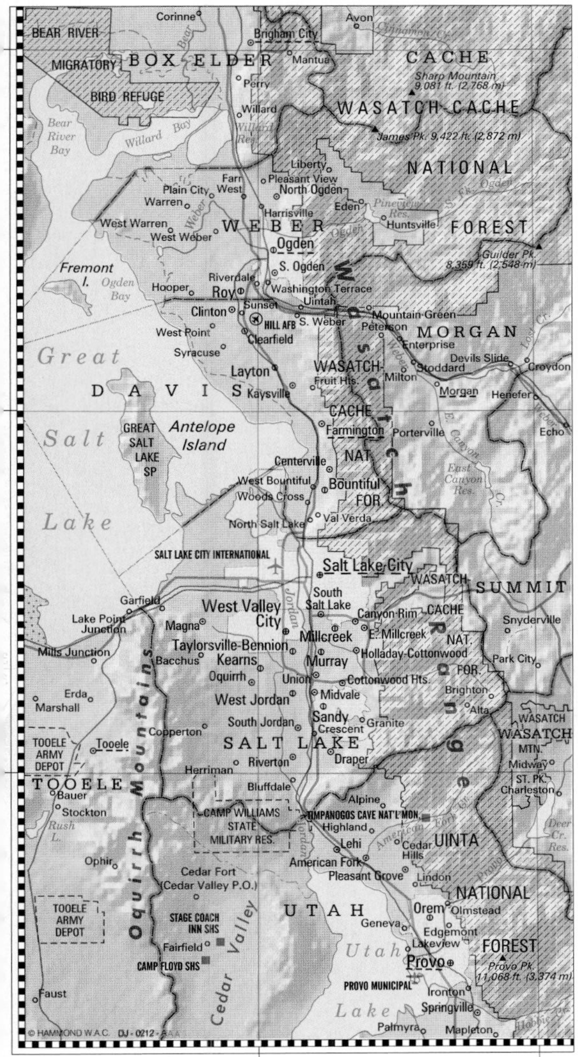

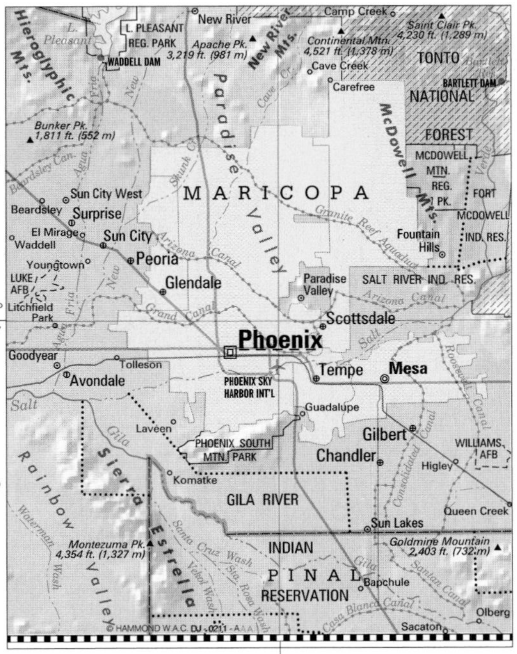

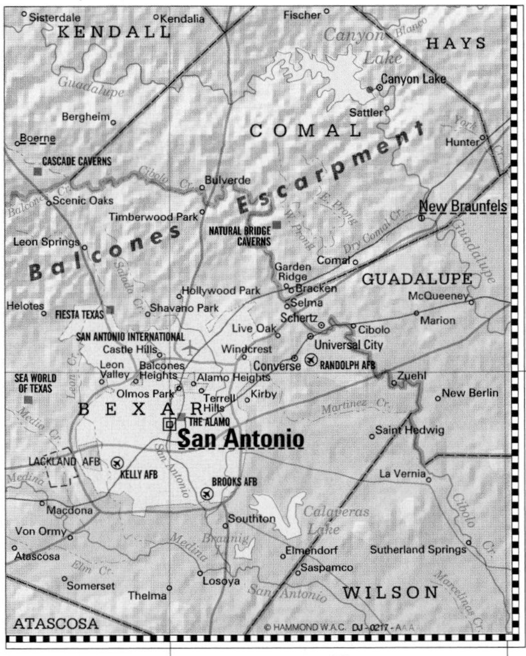

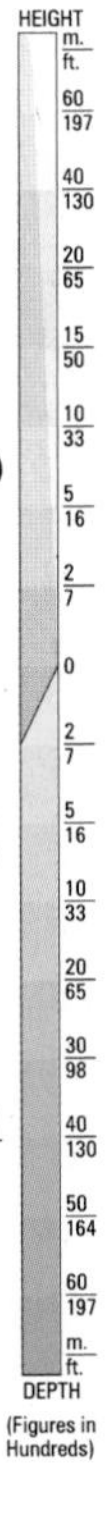

POPULATION OF CITIES AND TOWNS
- ■ OVER 2,000,000
- ⊡ 1,000,000 - 1,999,999
- ⊚ 500,000 - 999,999
- ⊛ 250,000 - 499,999
- ⊕ 100,000 - 249,999
- ◉ 30,000 - 99,999
- ○ 10,000 - 29,999
- ○ UNDER 10,000

SCALE 1:1,140,000   LAMBERT CONFORMAL CONIC PROJECTION

MILES 0 10 20 30 40 50
KILOMETERS 0 10 20 30 40 50

HEIGHT
ft.	m.
6,560	2,000
3,280	1,000
1,640	500
656	200
197	40

DEPTH
(Figures in Hundreds)

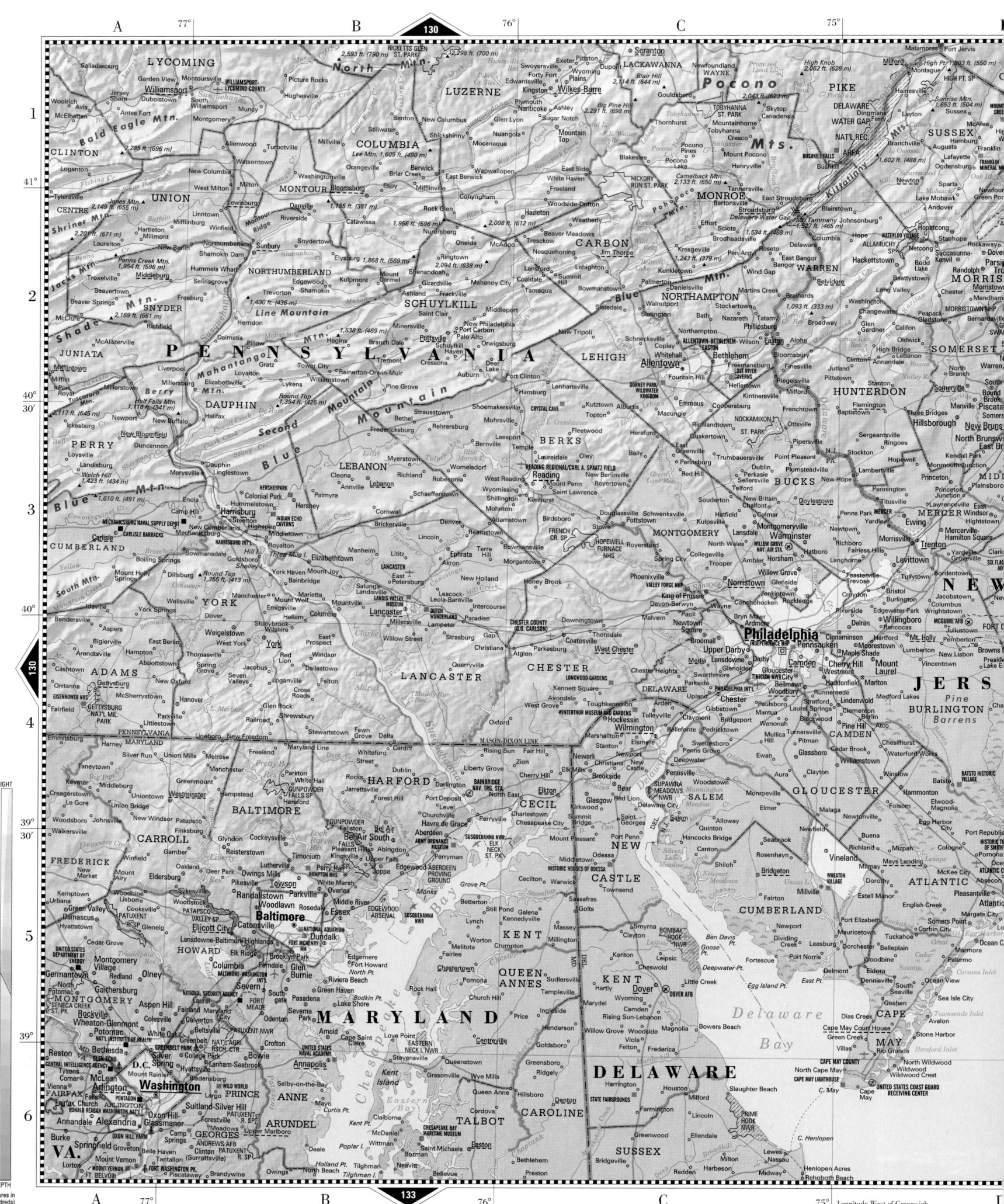

New York-Philadelphia-Washington

Middle America

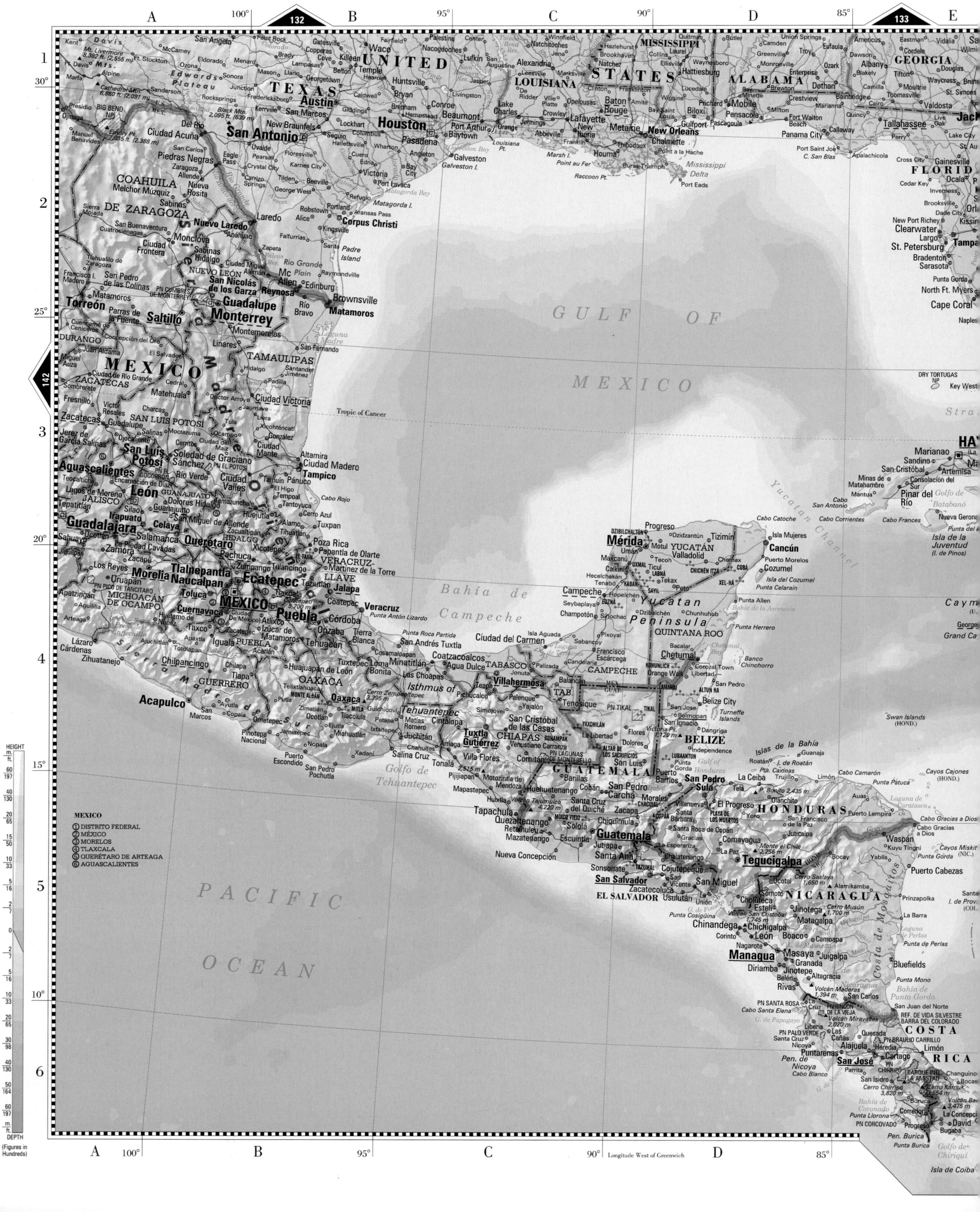

POPULATION OF CITIES AND TOWNS

■ OVER 2,000,000 ● 500,000 - 999,999 ● 100,000 - 249,999 ○ 10,000 - 29,999
□ 1,000,000 - 1,999,999 ● 250,000 - 499,999 ○ 30,000 - 99,999 ○ UNDER 10,000

SCALE 1:10,200,000 LAMBERT CONFORMAL CONIC PROJECTION

MILES 0 — 150 — 300 — 450
KILOMETERS 0 — 150 — 300 — 450

152   153

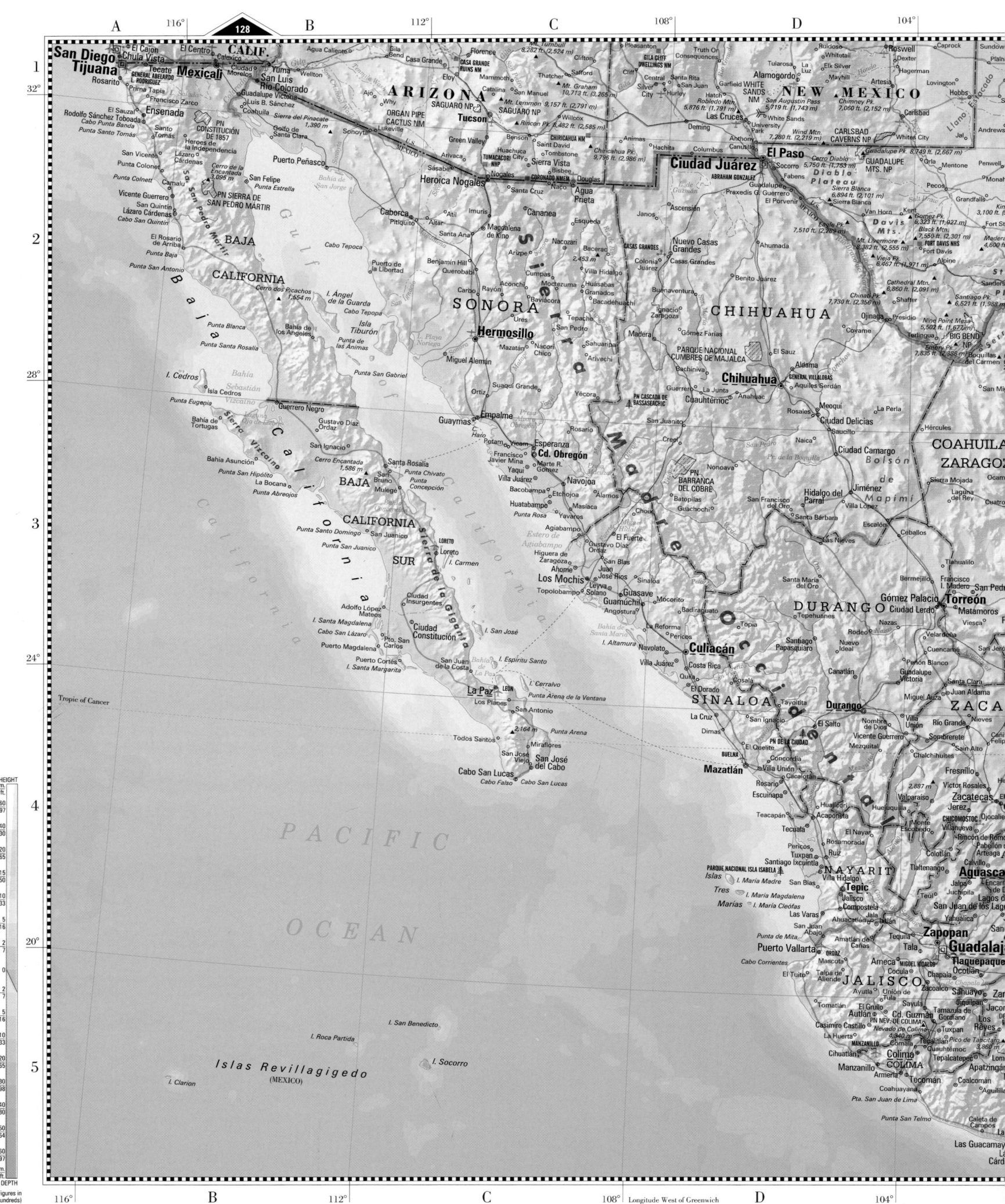

Northern and Central Mexico

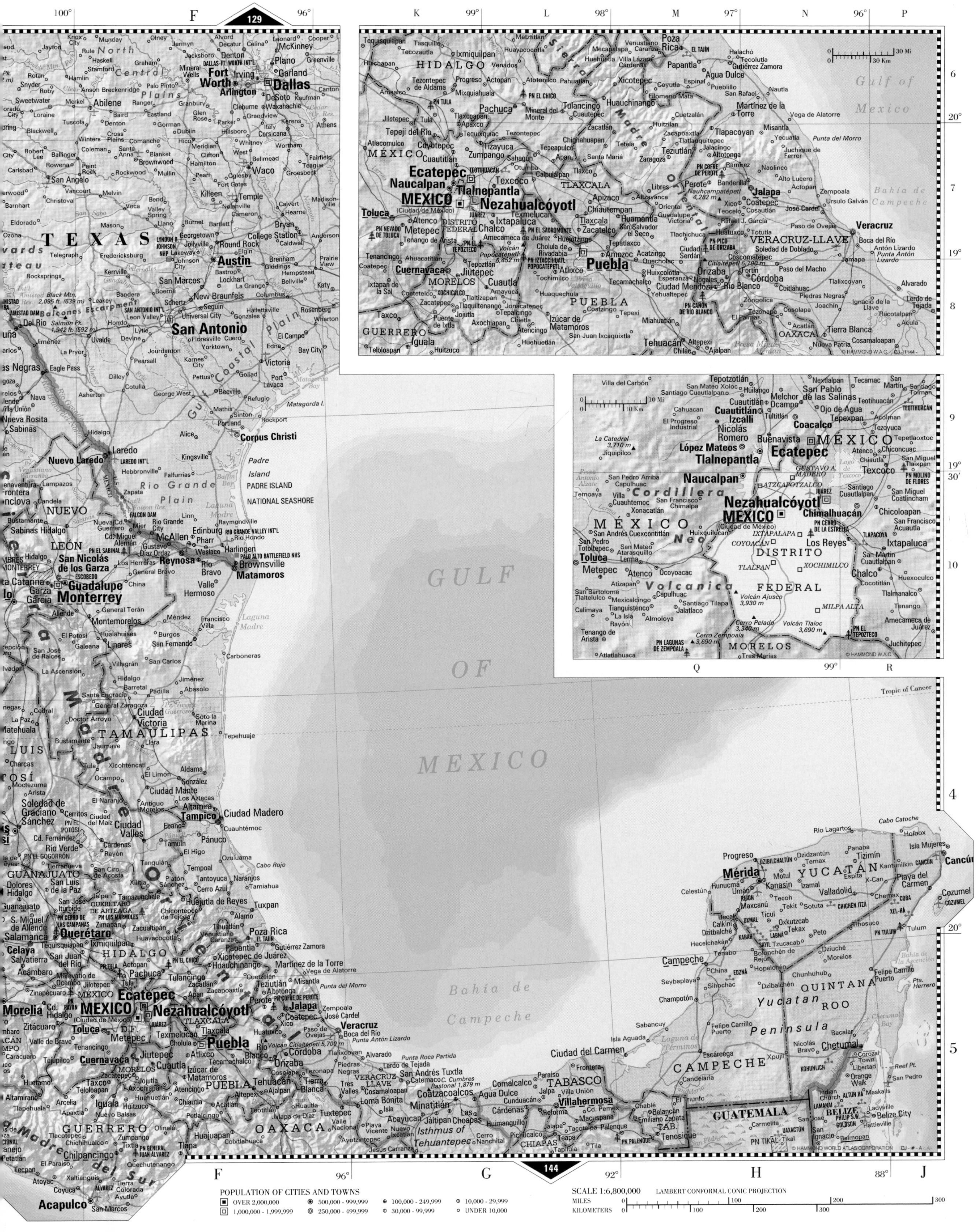

POPULATION OF CITIES AND TOWNS
■ OVER 2,000,000   ● 500,000 - 999,999   ● 100,000 - 249,999   ● 10,000 - 29,999
■ 1,000,000 - 1,999,999   ● 250,000 - 499,999   ● 30,000 - 99,999   ● UNDER 10,000

SCALE 1:6,800,000   LAMBERT CONFORMAL CONIC PROJECTION
MILES
KILOMETERS

GULF - OF - MEXICO

Bahía de Campeche

PACIFIC OCEAN

Golfo de Tehuantepec

Isthmus of Tehuantepec

MEXICO

TAMAULIPAS

SAN LUIS POTOSÍ
Tampico
Ciudad Madero

Querétaro
GUANAJUATO
HIDALGO
MÉXICO
Ecatepec
Nezahualcóyotl
Toluca
Cuernavaca
Puebla
MORELOS
GUERRERO
Acapulco
Chilpancingo

OAXACA
Oaxaca

Veracruz
Jalapa
VERACRUZ
Orizaba
Córdoba

Coatzacoalcos
Minatitlán
TABASCO
Villahermosa
Ciudad del Carmen

CAMPECHE
Peninsula
Yucatán
YUCATÁN
Mérida
Campeche

QUINTANA ROO
Cancún
Cozumel
Chetumal

CHIAPAS
Tuxtla Gutiérrez
San Cristóbal de las Casas

BELIZE
Belize City

GUATEMALA
Guatemala
Quezaltenango

HONDURAS
Tegucigalpa
San Pedro Sula

EL SALVADOR
San Salvador
San Miguel

Managua

SCALE 1:6,800,000   LAMBERT CONFORMAL CONIC PROJECTION
MILES 0   100   200   300
KILOMETERS 0   100   200   300

POPULATION OF CITIES AND TOWNS
■ OVER 2,000,000   ◉ 500,000 - 999,999   ◉ 100,000 - 249,999   ○ 10,000 - 29,999
◻ 1,000,000 - 1,999,999   ◉ 250,000 - 499,999   ◉ 30,000 - 99,999   ○ UNDER 10,000

HEIGHT m. ft.
DEPTH
(Figures in Hundreds)

© HAMMOND WORLD ATLAS CORPORATION

Southern Mexico, Central America, Western Caribbean

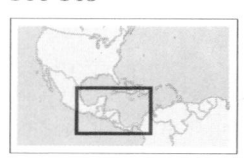

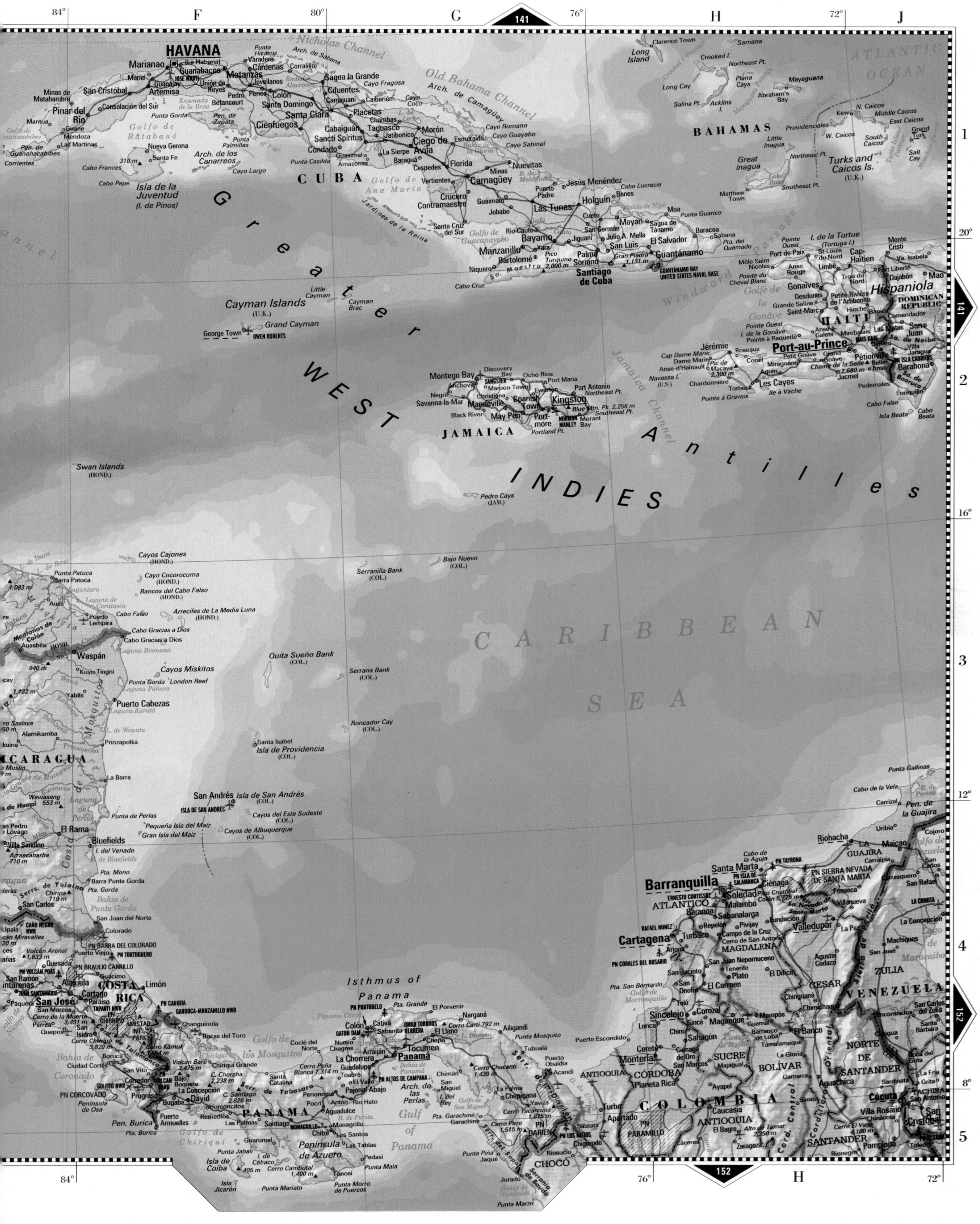

South America

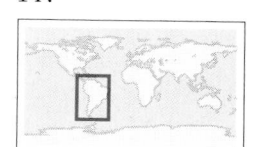

The highest mountain peak in the Americas, Mount Aconcagua, at 22,831 feet (6959 m.) above sea level, is visible in this northeast-looking, low-oblique image. Several major snow-covered peaks with summits exceeding 20,000 feet (6100 m.) rise along the north-south axis of the cohesive and massive structure of the Andes Mountains through this area of Argentina and Chile. The narrow east-west valley immediately south of Mount Aconcagua contains a section of the American Highway that connects Mendoza, Argentina, with Santiago, Chile.

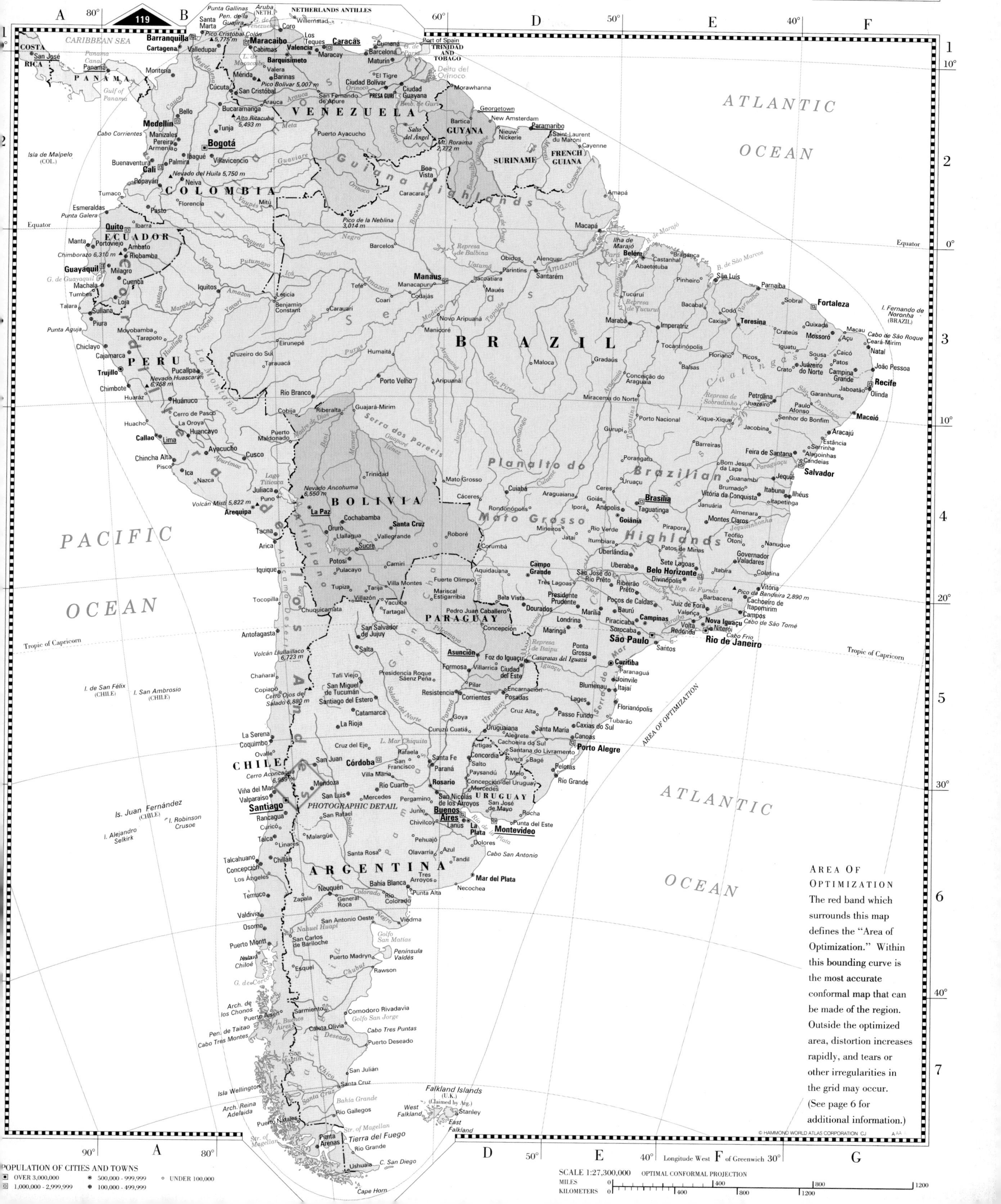

AREA OF OPTIMIZATION

The red band which surrounds this map defines the "Area of Optimization." Within this bounding curve is the most accurate conformal map that can be made of the region. Outside the optimized area, distortion increases rapidly, and tears or other irregularities in the grid may occur.

(See page 6 for additional information.)

POPULATION OF CITIES AND TOWNS
■ OVER 3,000,000   ■ 500,000 - 999,999   ○ UNDER 100,000
■ 1,000,000 - 2,999,999   ■ 100,000 - 499,999

SCALE 1:27,300,000   OPTIMAL CONFORMAL PROJECTION

MILES 0 — 400 — 800 — 1200
KILOMETERS 0 — 400 — 800 — 1200

© HAMMOND WORLD ATLAS CORPORATION CJ

CARACAS 66°
BARRANQUILLA 79°
PARAMARIBO 79°
QUIBDÓ 79°
BOGOTÁ 57°
QUITO 55°
MANAUS 79°
FORTALEZA 81°
LIMA 72°
LA PAZ 52°
BRASILIA 73°
ANTOFAGASTA 68°
RÍO DE JANEIRO 79°
ASUNCIÓN 84°
CURITIBA 68°
SANTIAGO 66°
BUENOS AIRES 73°
COMODORO RIVADAVIA 64°
RÍO GRANDE 48°

● LIMA 72°
AVERAGE JANUARY TEMPERATURE
DEGREES FAHRENHEIT AT
SELECTED STATIONS

CARACAS 70°
BARRANQUILLA 82°
PARAMARIBO 81°
QUIBDÓ 77°
BOGOTÁ 57°
QUITO 55°
MANAUS 81°
FORTALEZA 79°
LIMA 59°
LA PAZ 46°
BRASILIA 64°
ANTOFAGASTA 55°
RÍO DE JANEIRO 66°
ASUNCIÓN 64°
CURITIBA 55°
SANTIAGO 46°
BUENOS AIRES 52°
COMODORO RIVADAVIA 45°
RÍO GRANDE 34°

● LIMA 59°
AVERAGE JULY TEMPERATURE
DEGREES FAHRENHEIT AT
SELECTED STATIONS

AVERAGE JANUARY TEMPERATURE

FAHRENHEIT	CELSIUS	FAHRENHEIT	CELSIUS	FAHRENHEIT	CELSIUS
OVER 86°	OVER 30°	50° TO 68°	10° TO 20°	UNDER 32°	UNDER 0°
68° TO 86°	20° TO 30°	32° TO 50°	0° TO 10°		

AVERAGE JULY TEMPERATURE

FAHRENHEIT	CELSIUS	FAHRENHEIT	CELSIUS	FAHRENHEIT	CELSIUS
OVER 86°	OVER 30°	50° TO 68°	10° TO 20°	UNDER 32°	UNDER 0°
68° TO 86°	20° TO 30°	32° TO 50°	0° TO 10°		

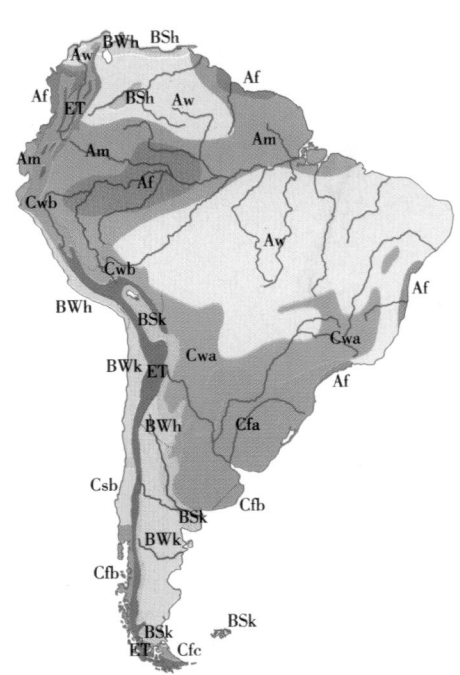

BWh BSh
Aw
Af
BSh Aw
ET
Af
Am
Am Am
Af
Cwb
Aw
Cwb
Af
BWh
BSk
Cwa
BWk ET
Af
BWh
Cfa
Csb
BSk
Cfb
BWk
Cfbs
BSk BSk
ET Cfc

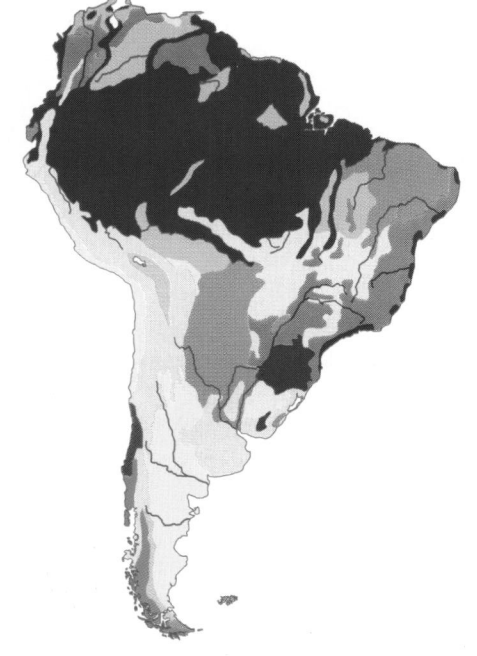

CLIMATE

HUMID TROPICAL
- Af NO DRY SEASON
- Am SHORT DRY SEASON
- Aw DRY WINTER

DRY
- BS SEMIARID
- BW ARID
  - h HOT
  - k COLD

HUMID WARM
- Cf NO DRY SEASON
- Cw DRY WINTER
- Cs DRY SUMMER

COLD POLAR
- ET SHORT COOL SUMMER, LONG COLD WINTER

a HOT SUMMER
b COOL SUMMER
c SHORT COOL SUMMER

AFTER KOEPPEN-GEIGER

VEGETATION

TROPICAL FOREST
- TROPICAL RAINFOREST
- LIGHT TROPICAL FOREST
- WOODLAND AND SHRUB

TROPICAL GRASSLAND
- GRASS AND SHRUB (SAVANNA)
- WOODED SAVANNA

MID-LATITUDE FOREST
- NEEDLELEAF FOREST
- MIXED NEEDLELEAF AND BROADLEAF FOREST
- WOODLAND AND SHRUB (MEDITERRANEAN)

MID-LATITUDE GRASSLAND
- SHORT GRASS (STEPPE)
- TALL GRASS (PRAIRIE) AND WOODED STEPPE

- DESERT AND DESERT SHRUB
- TUNDRA AND ALPINE
- UNCLASSIFIED HIGHLANDS

South America - Geographical Comparisons

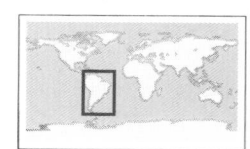

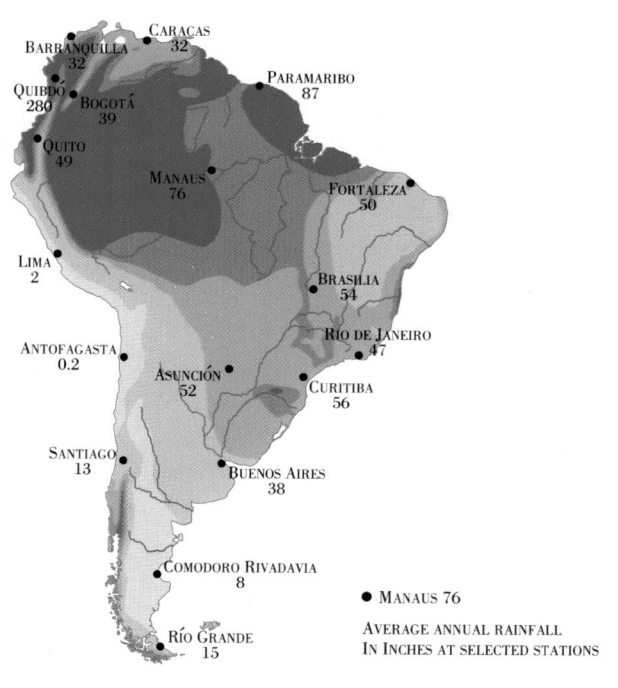

BARRANQUILLA
32
CARACAS
32
QUIBDÓ
280
BOGOTÁ
39
PARAMARIBO
87
QUITO
49
MANAUS
76
FORTALEZA
50
LIMA
2
BRASILIA
54
ANTOFAGASTA
0.2
RÍO DE JANEIRO
47
ASUNCIÓN
52
CURITIBA
56
SANTIAGO
13
BUENOS AIRES
38
COMODORO RIVADAVIA
8
RÍO GRANDE
15

● MANAUS 76
AVERAGE ANNUAL RAINFALL
IN INCHES AT SELECTED STATIONS

AVERAGE ANNUAL RAINFALL

INCHES	CM	INCHES	CM	INCHES	CM
OVER 80	OVER 200	40 TO 60	100 TO 150	10 TO 20	25 TO 50
60 TO 80	150 TO 200	20 TO 40	50 TO 100	UNDER 10	UNDER 25

● CITIES WITH OVER 1,000,000 INHABITANTS

POPULATION DISTRIBUTION

DENSITY PER		SQ. MI.	SQ. KM.	SQ. MI.	SQ. KM.
SQ. MI.	SQ. KM.	130 TO 260	50 TO 100	3 TO 25	1 TO 10
OVER 260	OVER 100	25 TO 130	10 TO 50	UNDER 3	UNDER 1

RICE
HOGS
COFFEE
COCOA
CATTLE
COFFEE
CATTLE
VANILLA
BANANAS
CORN
COTTON
SISAL
BANANAS
SHEEP
WILD RUBBER
BRAZIL
NUTS
CATTLE
TOBACCO
SUGARCANE
SHEEP
CORN
CATTLE
CATTLE
HOGS
COCOA
CITRUS
COTTON
TOBACCO
COTTON
COFFEE
TEA
BANANAS
SUGARCANE
SHEEP
CATTLE
HOGS
TOBACCO
WINE
QUEBRACHO
SOYBEANS
CORN
SHEEP
RICE
CORN
FLAX
CORN
CATTLE
WHEAT
SHEEP
SHEEP

LAND USE

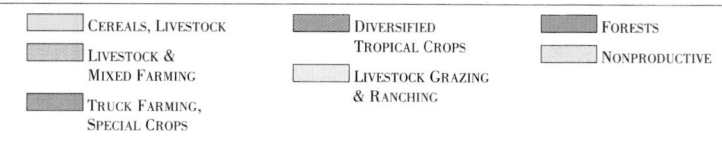

CEREALS, LIVESTOCK
LIVESTOCK & MIXED FARMING
TRUCK FARMING, SPECIAL CROPS
DIVERSIFIED TROPICAL CROPS
LIVESTOCK GRAZING & RANCHING
FORESTS
NONPRODUCTIVE

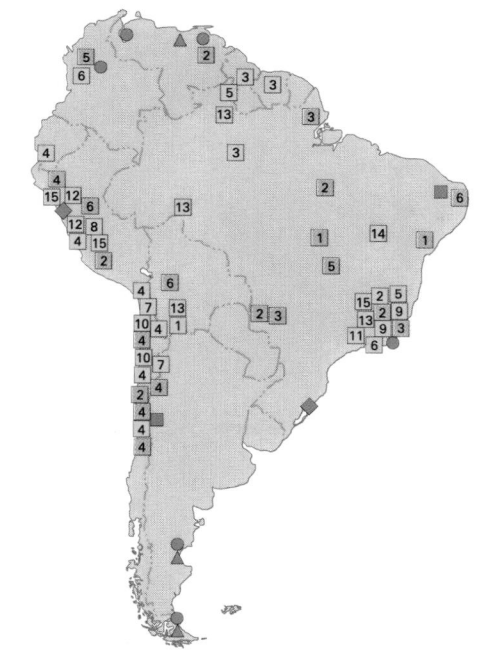

MINERAL RESOURCES

ENERGY & FUELS
◆ COAL
▲ NATURAL GAS
● PETROLEUM
■ URANIUM

IRON & FERROALLOYS
1 CHROMIUM
2 IRON ORE
3 MANGANESE
4 MOLYBDENUM
5 NICKEL
6 TUNGSTEN

OTHER MAJOR RESOURCES
1 ANTIMONY
2 ASBESTOS
3 BAUXITE
4 COPPER
5 DIAMONDS
6 GOLD
7 IODINE
8 LEAD
9 MICA
10 NITRATES
11 PHOSPHATES
12 SILVER
13 TIN
14 TITANIUM
15 ZINC

Northern South America

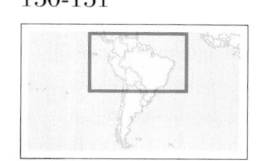

POPULATION OF CITIES AND TOWNS

■ OVER 2,000,000 ● 500,000 - 999,999 ○ 50,000 - 99,999
□ 1,000,000 - 1,999,999 ● 100,000 - 499,999 ○ UNDER 50,000

SCALE 1:14,800,000   LAMBERT CONFORMAL CONIC PROJECTION
MILES 0   200   400   600
KILOMETERS 0   200   400   600

© HAMMOND WORLD ATLAS CORPORATION   CJ - 2107 - A

Colombia, Venezuela, Ecuador

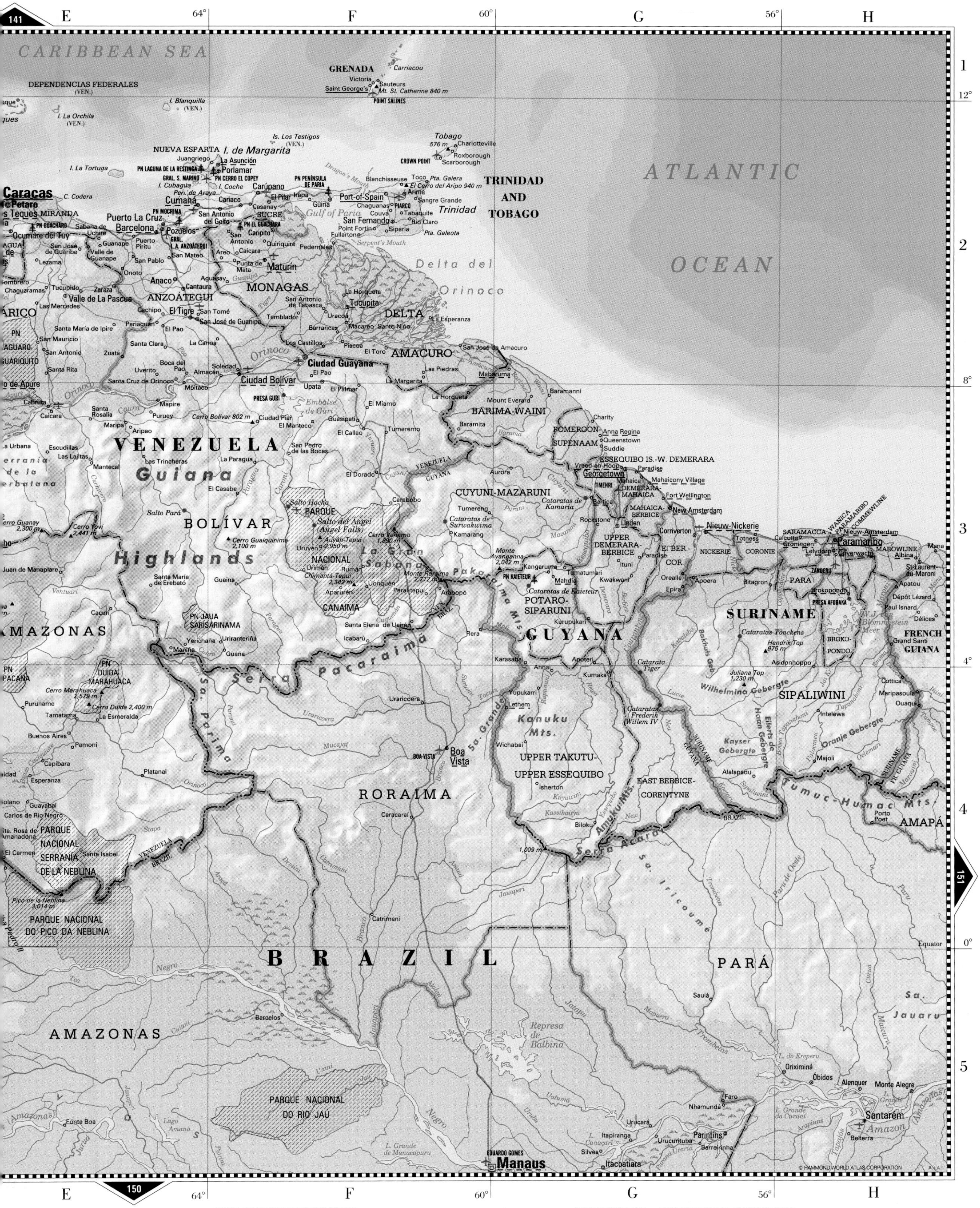

E   64°   F   60°   G   56°   H

CARIBBEAN SEA

ATLANTIC OCEAN

VENEZUELA

GUYANA

SURINAME

FRENCH GUIANA

TRINIDAD AND TOBAGO

BRAZIL

POPULATION OF CITIES AND TOWNS

- ■ OVER 2,000,000
- ▣ 1,000,000 - 1,999,999
- ● 500,000 - 999,999
- ⊙ 250,000 - 499,999
- ● 100,000 - 249,999
- ⊙ 30,000 - 99,999
- ⊙ 10,000 - 29,999
- ○ UNDER 10,000

SCALE 1:6,800,000   LAMBERT CONFORMAL CONIC PROJECTION

MILES 0   100   200   300

KILOMETERS 0   100   200   300

© Hammond World Atlas Corporation

E   64°   F   60°   G   56°   H

Northeastern Brazil

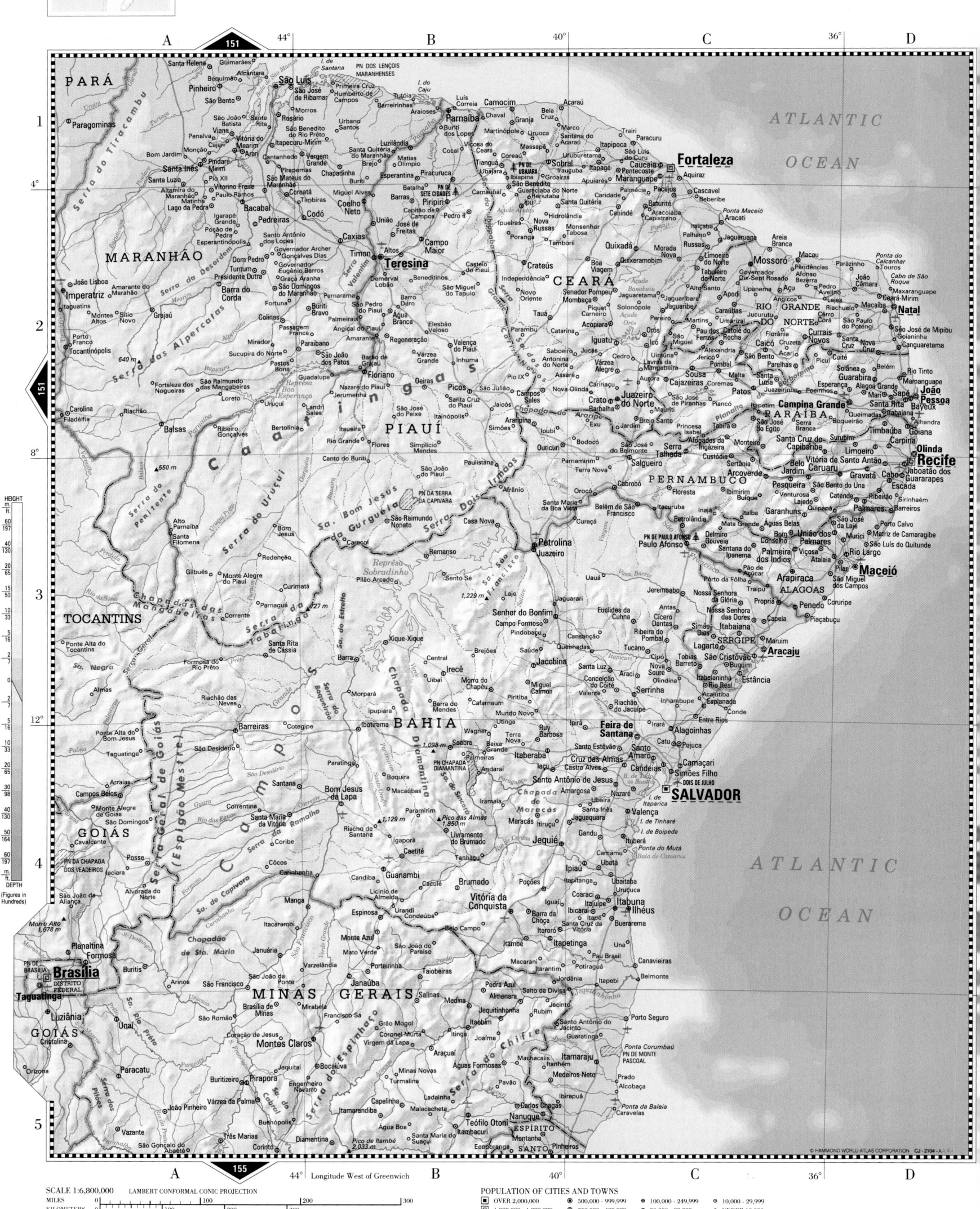

SCALE 1:6,800,000   LAMBERT CONFORMAL CONIC PROJECTION

MILES 0   100   200   300

KILOMETERS 0   100   200   300

44° Longitude West of Greenwich   40°   36°

POPULATION OF CITIES AND TOWNS

■ OVER 2,000,000
□ 1,000,000 - 1,999,999
● 500,000 - 999,999
◉ 250,000 - 499,999
● 100,000 - 249,999
● 30,000 - 99,999
○ 10,000 - 29,999
○ UNDER 10,000

HEIGHT
m. ft.
60 / 197
40 / 130
20 / 65
10 / 33
5 / 16
2 / 7
0
2 / 7
5 / 16
10 / 33
20 / 65
30 / 98
40 / 130
50 / 164
60 / 197
m. ft.
DEPTH
(Figures in Hundreds)

Southeastern Brazil

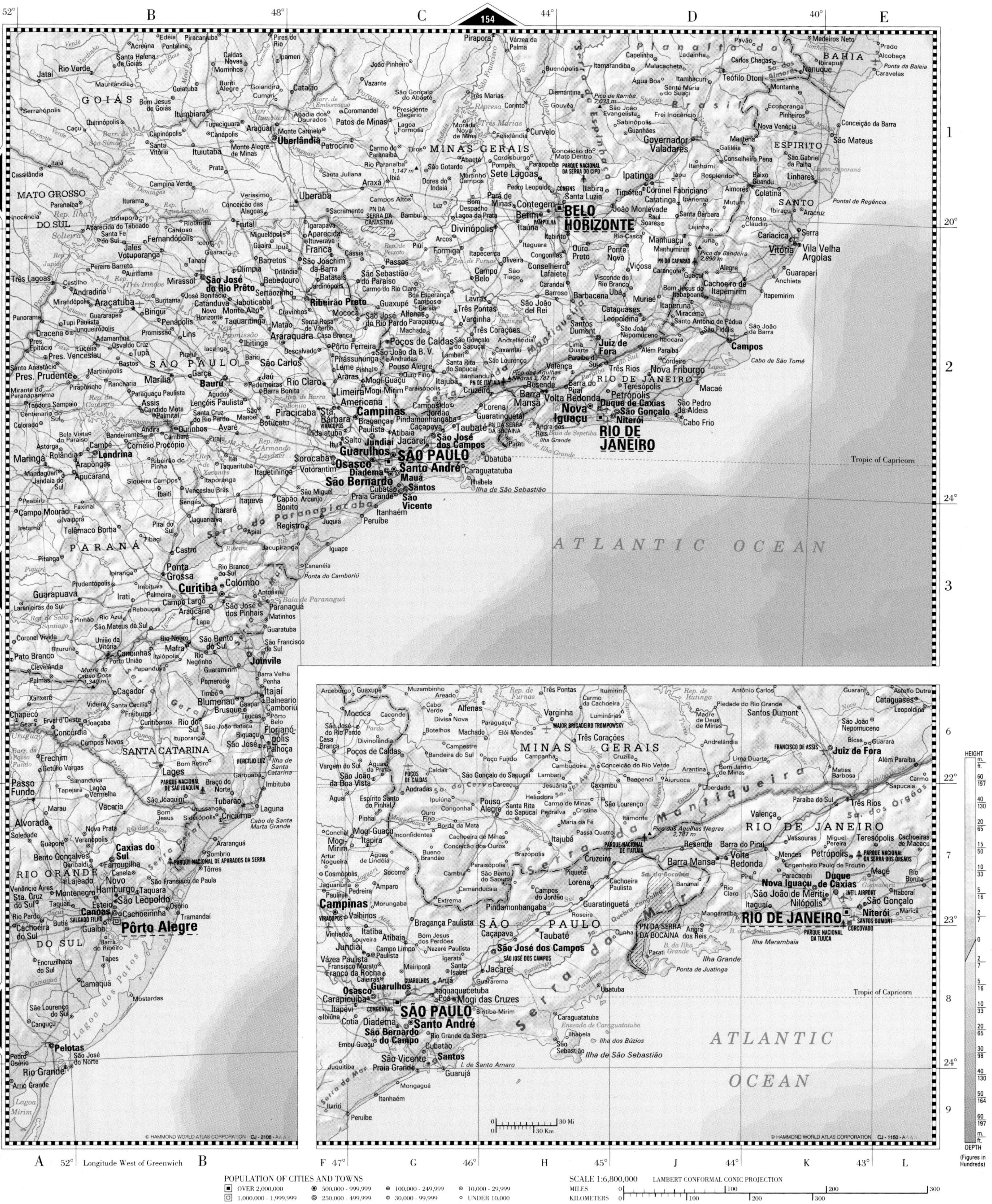

POPULATION OF CITIES AND TOWNS

- ■ OVER 2,000,000
- ◻ 1,000,000 – 1,999,999
- ● 500,000 – 999,999
- ◉ 250,000 – 499,999
- ⊕ 100,000 – 249,999
- ⊙ 30,000 – 99,999
- ○ 10,000 – 29,999
- · UNDER 10,000

SCALE 1:6,800,000   LAMBERT CONFORMAL CONIC PROJECTION

MILES 0   100   200   300
KILOMETERS 0   100   200   300

© HAMMOND WORLD ATLAS CORPORATION

HEIGHT

DEPTH (Figures in Hundreds)

Peru

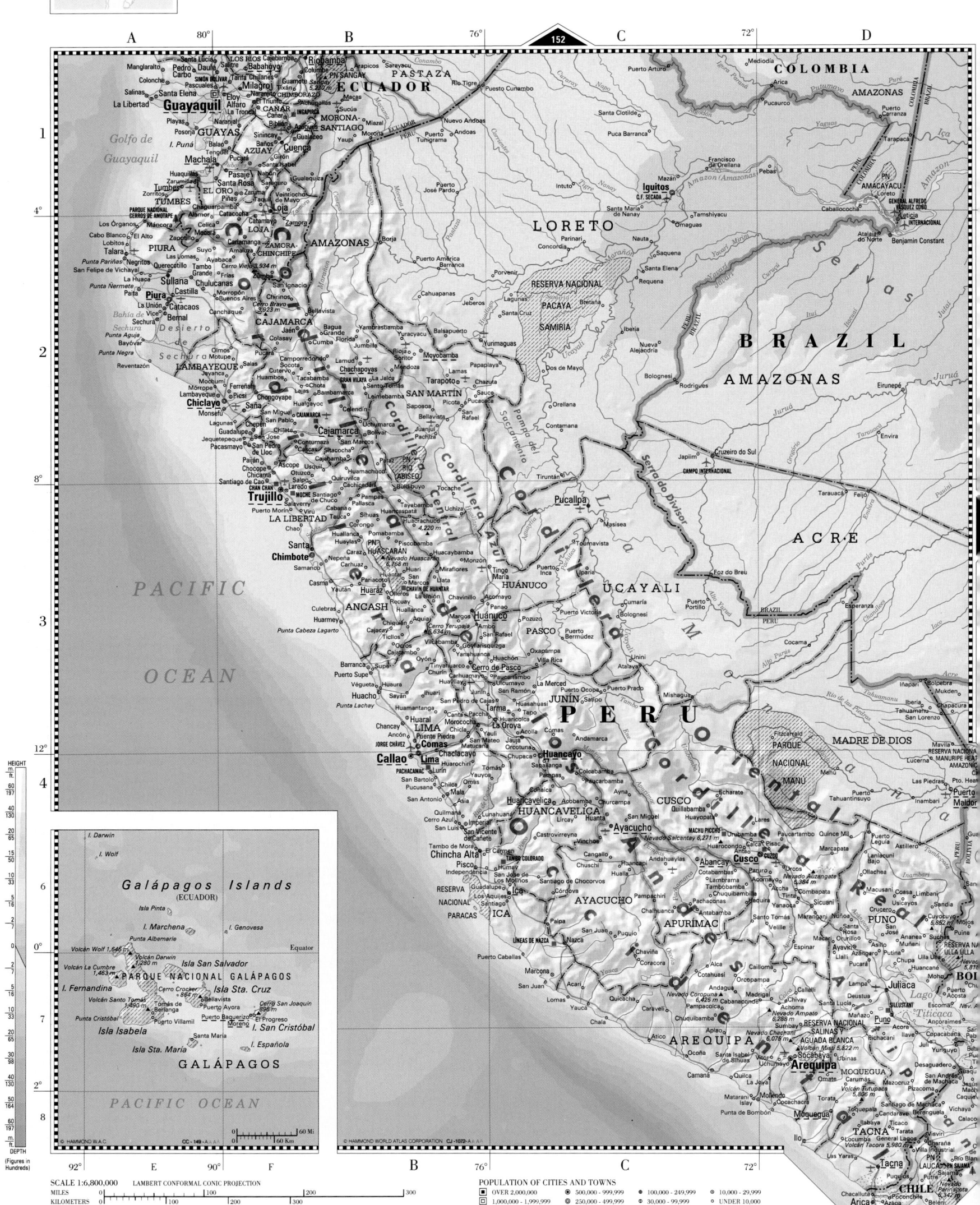

SCALE 1:6,800,000   LAMBERT CONFORMAL CONIC PROJECTION

MILES 0 — 100 — 200 — 300

KILOMETERS 0 — 100 — 200 — 300

POPULATION OF CITIES AND TOWNS

■ OVER 2,000,000	● 500,000 - 999,999	● 100,000 - 249,999	○ 10,000 - 29,999
□ 1,000,000 - 1,999,999	● 250,000 - 499,999	○ 30,000 - 99,999	○ UNDER 10,000

HEIGHT

DEPTH

(Figures in Hundreds)

Southern South America

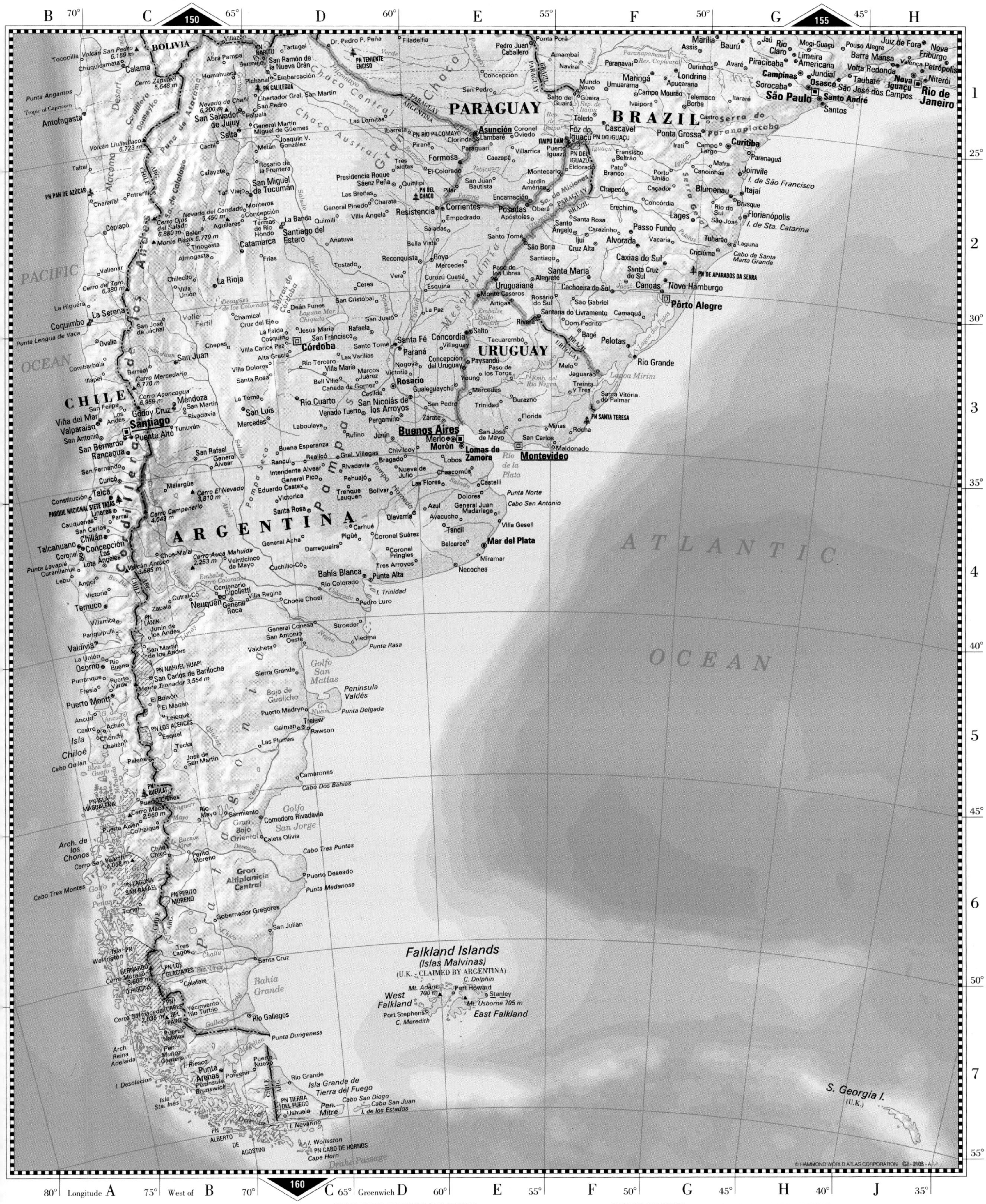

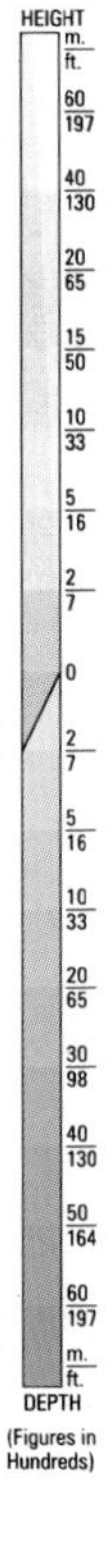

Countries and major regions: BOLIVIA, PARAGUAY, BRAZIL, ARGENTINA, CHILE, URUGUAY

Oceans: PACIFIC OCEAN, ATLANTIC OCEAN, SOUTHERN OCEAN

Major cities: São Paulo, Rio de Janeiro, Buenos Aires, Montevideo, Santiago, Asunción, Córdoba, Rosario, Curitiba, Pôrto Alegre, Mar del Plata

Falkland Islands (Islas Malvinas)
(U.K. - CLAIMED BY ARGENTINA)
West Falkland, East Falkland
Mt. Adam 700 m, Mt. Usborne 705 m
Port Howard, Stanley, Port Stephens, C. Meredith, C. Dolphin, Port Louis

S. Georgia I. (U.K.)

Cape Horn, Drake Passage, Tierra del Fuego, Ushuaia, Río Gallegos, Punta Arenas

Tropic of Capricorn

Longitude West of Greenwich

POPULATION OF CITIES AND TOWNS
- OVER 2,000,000
- 1,000,000 - 1,999,999
- 500,000 - 999,999
- 100,000 - 499,999
- 50,000 - 99,999
- UNDER 50,000

SCALE 1:14,800,000 LAMBERT CONFORMAL CONIC PROJECTION

MILES 0 100 200 400 600
KILOMETERS 0 100 200 400 600

HEIGHT (ft / m) — DEPTH (Figures in Hundreds)

© Hammond World Atlas Corporation   CJ-2105-A

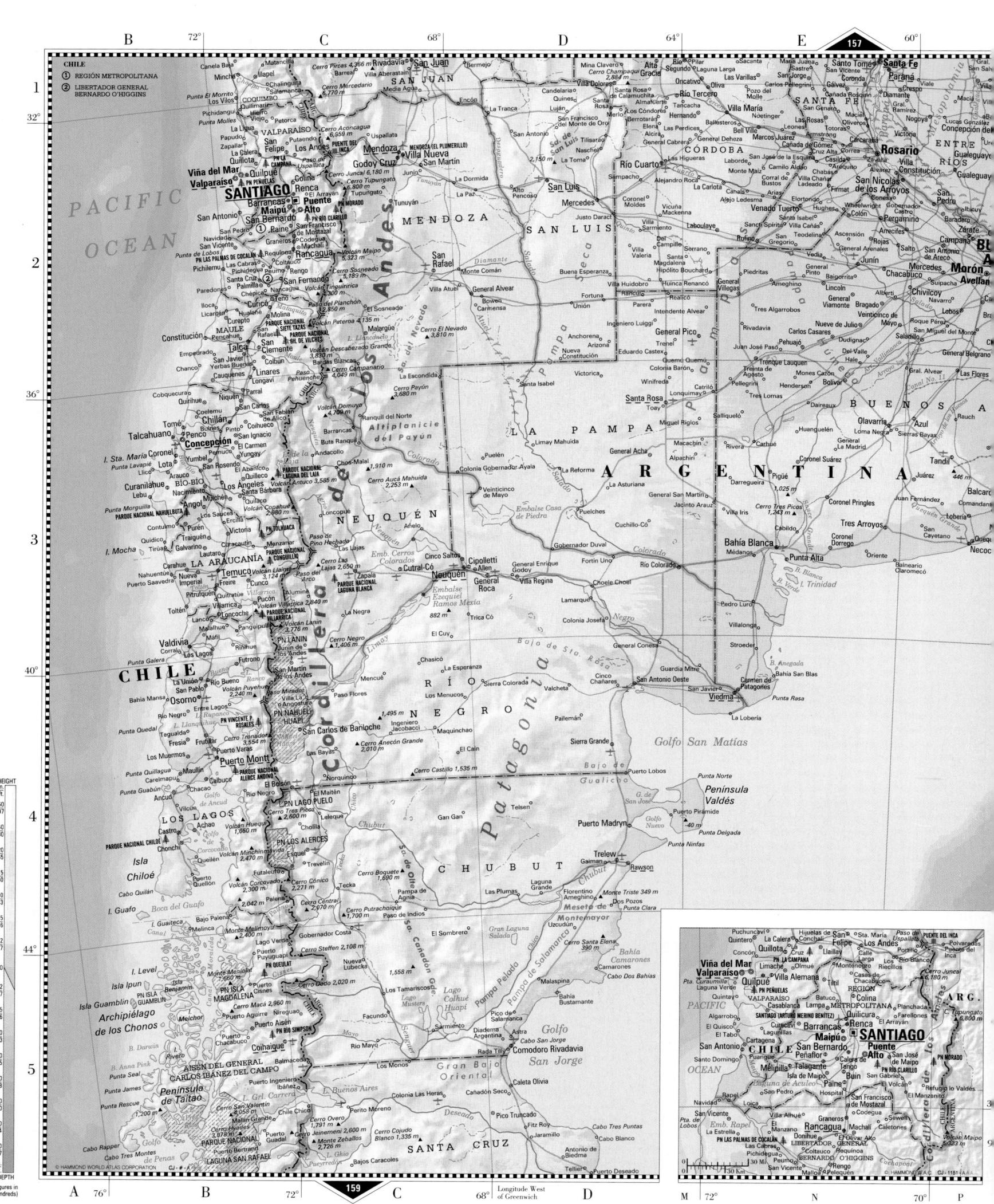

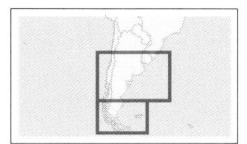

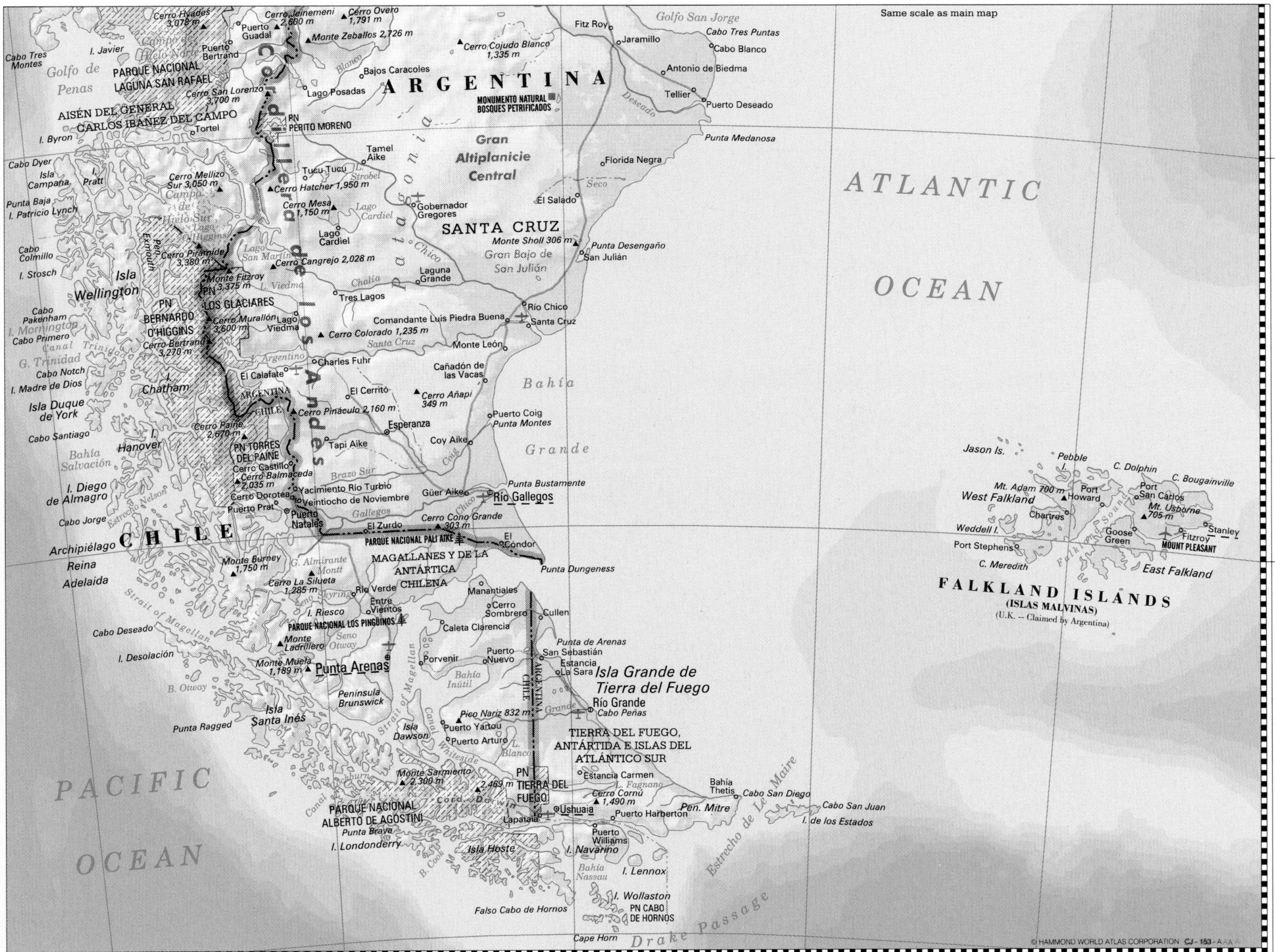

POPULATION OF CITIES AND TOWNS

SCALE 1:6,800,000 LAMBERT CONFORMAL CONIC PROJECTION

© HAMMOND WORLD ATLAS CORPORATION

Arctic Regions, Antarctica

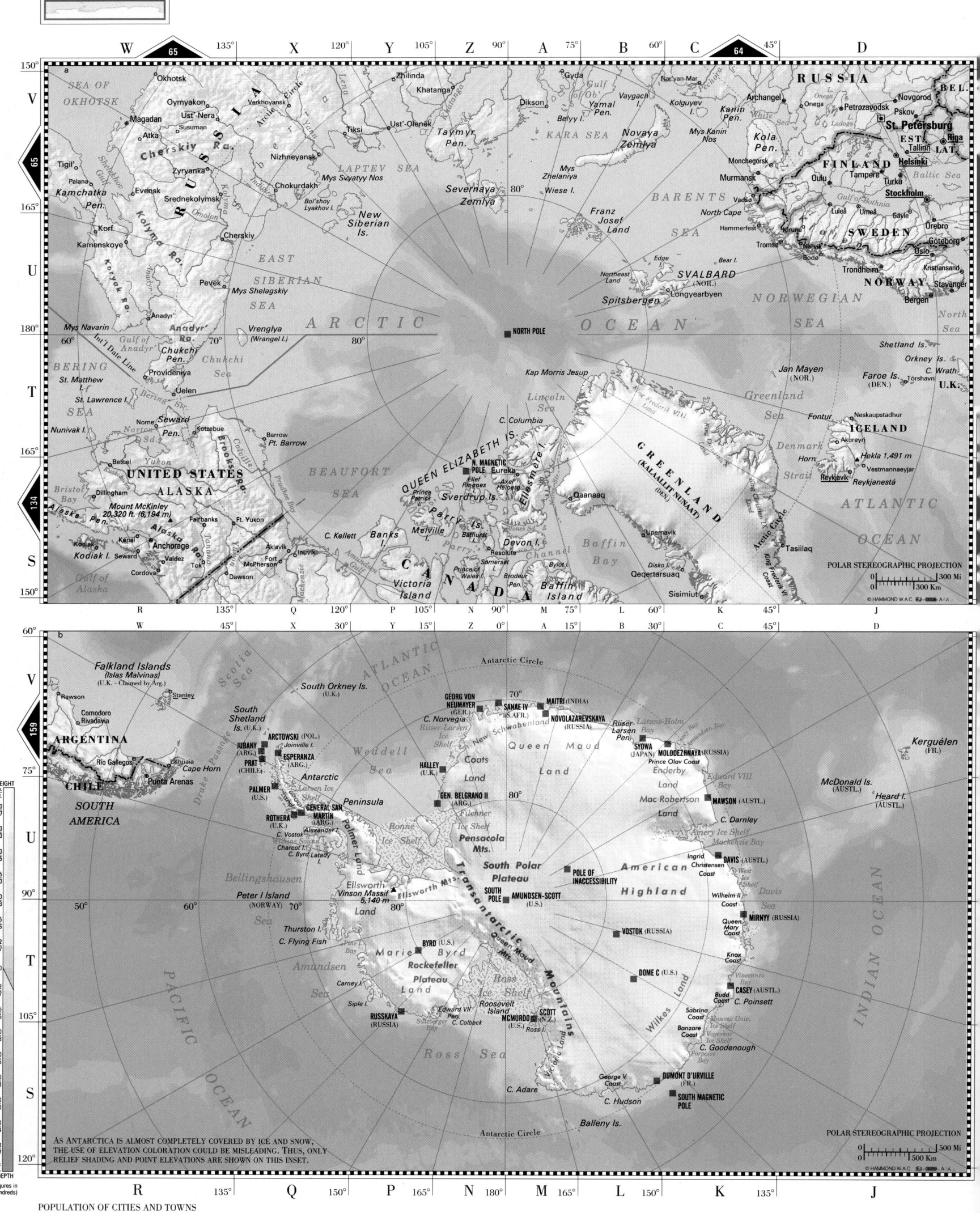

POLAR STEREOGRAPHIC PROJECTION

0   300 Mi
0   300 Km

© HAMMOND W.A.C.

AS ANTARCTICA IS ALMOST COMPLETELY COVERED BY ICE AND SNOW, THE USE OF ELEVATION COLORATION COULD BE MISLEADING. THUS, ONLY RELIEF SHADING AND POINT ELEVATIONS ARE SHOWN ON THIS INSET.

POLAR STEREOGRAPHIC PROJECTION

0   500 Mi
0   500 Km

© HAMMOND W.A.C.

POPULATION OF CITIES AND TOWNS
- ■ OVER 2,000,000
- ◉ 500,000 - 999,999
- ◉ 50,000 - 99,999
- ▣ 1,000,000 - 1,999,999
- ◉ 100,000 - 499,999
- ○ UNDER 50,000

228,100,000

778,700,000

1,427,700,000

2,870,500,000

4,498,800,000 Mean Distance

from S

5,902,800,000 in M

35,9

67

World Statistics

ELEMENTS OF THE SOLAR SYSTEM

	Mean Distance from Sun: in Miles	in Kilometers	Period of Revolution around Sun	Period of Rotation on Axis	Equatorial Diameter in Miles	in Kilometers	Surface Gravity (Earth = 1)	Mass (Earth = 1)	Mean Density (Water = 1)	Number of Satellites
Mercury	35,990,000	57,900,000	87.97 days	58.7 days	3,032	4,880	0.38	0.055	5.4	0
Venus	67,240,000	108,200,000	224.70 days	243.7 days†	7,521	12,104	0.91	0.815	5.2	0
Earth	93,000,000	149,700,000	365.26 days	23h 56m	7,926	12,755	1.00	1.00	5.5	1
Mars	141,610,000	227,900,000	686.98 days	24h 37m	4,221	6,794	0.38	0.107	3.9	2
Jupiter	483,675,000	778,400,000	11.86 years	9h 55m	88,846	142,984	2.36	317.8	1.3	16
Saturn	886,572,000	1,426,800,000	29.46 years	10h 30m	74,898	120,536	0.92	95.2	0.7	18
Uranus	1,783,957,000	2,871,000,000	84.01 years	17h 14m†	31,763	51,118	0.89	14.5	1.3	15
Neptune	2,795,114,000	4,498,300,000	164.79 years	16h 6m	30,778	49,532	1.13	17.1	1.6	8
Pluto	3,670,000,000	5,906,400,000	247.70 years	6.4 days†	1,413	2,274	0.07	0.002	2.1	1

† Retrograde motion

Source: NASA, National Space Science Center

DIMENSIONS OF THE EARTH

	Area in: Sq. Miles	Sq. Kilometers
Superficial area	196,939,000	510,072,000
Land surface	57,506,000	148,940,000
Water surface	139,433,000	361,132,000

	Distance in: Miles	Kilometers
Equatorial circumference	24,902	40,075
Polar circumference	24,860	40,007
Equatorial diameter	7,926.4	12,756.4
Polar diameter	7,899.8	12,713.6
Equatorial radius	3,963.2	6,378.2
Polar radius	3,949.9	6,356.8

Volume of the Earth	2.6×10^{11} cubic miles	10.84×10^{11} cubic kilometers
Mass or weight	6.6×10^{21} short tons	6.0×10^{21} metric tons
Maximum distance from Sun	94,600,000 miles	152,000,000 kilometers
Minimum distance from Sun	91,300,000 miles	147,000,000 kilometers

OCEANS AND MAJOR SEAS

	Area in: Sq. Miles	Sq. Kms.	Greatest Depth in: Feet	Meters
Pacific Ocean	63,855,000	165,384,000	36,198	11,033
Atlantic Ocean	31,744,000	82,217,000	28,374	8,648
Indian Ocean	28,417,000	73,600,000	25,344	7,725
Arctic Ocean	5,427,000	14,056,000	17,880	5,450
Caribbean Sea	970,000	2,512,300	24,720	7,535
Mediterranean Sea	969,000	2,509,700	16,896	5,150
South China Sea	895,000	2,318,000	15,000	4,600
Bering Sea	875,000	2,266,250	15,800	4,800
Gulf of Mexico	600,000	1,554,000	12,300	3,750
Sea of Okhotsk	590,000	1,528,100	11,070	3,370
East China Sea	482,000	1,248,400	9,500	2,900
Yellow Sea	480,000	1,243,200	350	107
Sea of Japan	389,000	1,007,500	12,280	3,740
Hudson Bay	317,500	822,300	846	258
North Sea	222,000	575,000	2,200	670
Black Sea	185,000	479,150	7,365	2,245
Red Sea	169,000	437,700	7,200	2,195
Baltic Sea	163,000	422,170	1,506	459

THE CONTINENTS

	Area in: Sq. Miles	Sq. Kms.	Percent of World's Land
Asia	17,128,500	44,362,815	29.5
Africa	11,707,000	30,321,130	20.2
North America	9,363,000	24,250,170	16.2
South America	6,879,725	17,818,505	11.9
Antarctica	5,405,000	14,000,000	9.4
Europe	4,057,000	10,507,630	7.0
Australia	2,967,893	7,686,850	5.1

MAJOR SHIP CANALS

	Length in: Miles	Kms.	Minimum Depth in: Feet	Meters
Volga-Baltic, Russia	225	362	–	–
Baltic-White Sea, Russia	140	225	16	5
Suez, Egypt	100.76	162	42	13
Albert, Belgium	80	129	16.5	5
Moscow-Volga, Russia	80	129	18	6
Volga-Don, Russia	62	100	–	–
Göta, Sweden	54	87	10	3
Kiel (Nord-Ostsee), Germany	53.2	86	38	12
Panama Canal, Panama	50.72	82	41.6	13
Houston Ship, U.S.A.	50	81	36	11

LARGEST ISLANDS

	Area in: Sq. Miles	Sq. Kms.		Area in: Sq. Miles	Sq. Kms.		Area in: Sq. Miles	Sq. Kms.
Greenland	840,000	2,175,600	Hispaniola, Haiti & Dom. Rep.	29,399	76,143	Somerset, Canada	9,570	24,786
New Guinea	305,000	789,950	Banks, Canada	27,038	70,028	Sardinia, Italy	9,301	24,090
Borneo	286,000	740,740	Tasmania, Australia	26,410	68,402	Shikoku, Japan	6,860	17,767
Madagascar	226,656	587,040	Ceylon, Sri Lanka	25,332	65,610	New Caledonia, France	6,530	16,913
Baffin, Canada	195,928	507,454	Svalbard, Norway	23,957	62,049	Nordaustlandet, Norway	6,409	16,599
Sumatra, Indonesia	164,000	424,760	Devon, Canada	21,331	55,247	Samar, Philippines	5,050	13,080
Honshu, Japan	88,000	227,920	Novaya Zemlya (north isl.), Russia	18,600	48,200	Negros, Philippines	4,906	12,707
Great Britain	84,400	218,896	Tierra del Fuego, Chile & Argentina	18,301	47,400	Palawan, Philippines	4,550	11,785
Victoria, Canada	83,896	217,290	Marajó, Brazil	17,991	46,597	Panay, Philippines	4,446	11,515
Ellesmere, Canada	75,767	196,236	Alexander, Antarctica	16,700	43,250	Jamaica	4,232	10,961
Celebes, Indonesia	72,986	189,034	Axel Heiberg, Canada	16,671	43,178	Hawaii, United States	4,038	10,458
South I., New Zealand	58,393	151,238	Melville, Canada	16,274	42,150	Viti Levu, Fiji	4,010	10,386
Java, Indonesia	48,842	126,501	Southampton, Canada	15,913	41,215	Cape Breton, Canada	3,981	10,311
North I., New Zealand	44,187	114,444	New Britain, Papua New Guinea	14,100	36,519	Mindoro, Philippines	3,759	9,736
Cuba	42,803	110,860	Taiwan	13,836	35,835	Kodiak, Alaska, U.S.A.	3,670	9,505
Newfoundland, Canada	42,031	108,860	Kyushu, Japan	13,770	35,664	Cyprus	3,572	9,251
Luzon, Philippines	40,420	104,688	Hainan, China	13,127	33,999	Puerto Rico, U.S.A.	3,435	8,897
Iceland	39,768	103,000	Prince of Wales, Canada	12,872	33,338	Corsica, France	3,352	8,682
Mindanao, Philippines	36,537	94,631	Spitsbergen, Norway	12,355	31,999	New Ireland, Papua New Guinea	3,340	8,651
Ireland	32,589	84,406	Vancouver, Canada	12,079	31,285	Crete, Greece	3,218	8,335
Hokkaidō, Japan	30,436	78,829	Timor, Indonesia	11,527	29,855	Anticosti, Canada	3,066	7,941
Sakhalin, Russia	29,500	76,405	Sicily, Italy	9,926	25,708	Wrangel, Russia	2,819	7,301

PRINCIPAL MOUNTAINS

Mountain	Height in: Feet	Meters
Everest, Nepal-China	29,028	8,848
K2 (Godwin Austen), Pakistan-China	28,250	8,611
Kánchenjunga, Nepal-India	28,208	8,598
Lhotse, Nepal-China	27,923	8,511
Makalu, Nepal-China	27,789	8,470
Dhaulagiri, Nepal	26,810	8,172
Nanga Parbat, Pakistan	26,660	8,126
Annapurna, Nepal	26,504	8,078
Nanda Devi, India	25,645	7,817
Rakaposhi, Pakistan	25,550	7,788
Kongur Shan, China	25,325	7,719
Tirich Mir, Pakistan	25,230	7,690
Gongga Shan, China	24,790	7,556
Communism Peak, Tajikistan	24,590	7,495
Pobedy Peak, Kyrgyzstan	24,406	7,439
Chomo Lhari, Bhutan-China	23,997	7,314
Muztag, China	23,891	7,282
Cerro Aconcagua, Argentina	22,831	6,959
Ojos del Salado, Chile-Argentina	22,572	6,880
Bonete, Chile-Argentina	22,546	6,872
Tupungato, Chile-Argentina	22,310	6,800
Pissis, Argentina	22,241	6,779
Mercedario, Argentina	22,211	6,770
Huascarán, Peru	22,205	6,768
Llullaillaco, Chile-Argentina	22,057	6,723
Nevada Ancohuma, Bolivia	21,489	6,550
Chimborazo, Ecuador	20,561	6,267
McKinley, Alaska	20,320	6,194
Logan, Yukon, Canada	19,524	5,951
Cotopaxi, Ecuador	19,347	5,897
Kilimanjaro, Tanzania	19,340	5,895
El Misti, Peru	19,101	5,822
Pico Cristóbal Colón, Colombia	18,947	5,775
Huila, Colombia	18,865	5,750
Citlaltépetl (Orizaba), Mexico	18,700	5,700
Damavand, Iran	18,605	5,671
El'brus, Russia	18,510	5,642
St. Elias, Alaska, U.S.A.-Yukon, Canada	18,008	5,489
Dykh-tau, Russia	17,070	5,203
Batian (Kenya), Kenya	17,058	5,199
Ararat, Turkey	16,946	5,165
Vinson Massif, Antarctica	16,864	5,140
Margherita (Ruwenzori), Africa	16,795	5,119
Kazbek, Georgia-Russia	16,558	5,047
Puncak Jaya, Indonesia	16,503	5,030
Blanc, France	15,771	4,807
Klyuchevskaya Sopka, Russia	15,584	4,750
Fairweather, Br. Col., Canada	15,300	4,663
Dufourspitze (Mte. Rosa), Italy-Switzerland	15,203	4,634
Ras Dashen, Ethiopia	15,157	4,620
Matterhorn, Switzerland	14,691	4,478
Whitney, California, U.S.A.	14,494	4,418
Elbert, Colorado, U.S.A.	14,433	4,399
Rainier, Washington, U.S.A.	14,410	4,392
Shasta, California, U.S.A.	14,162	4,317
Pikes Peak, Colorado, U.S.A.	14,110	4,301
Finsteraarhorn, Switzerland	14,022	4,274
Mauna Kea, Hawaii, U.S.A.	13,796	4,205
Mauna Loa, Hawaii, U.S.A.	13,677	4,169
Jungfrau, Switzerland	13,642	4,158
Grossglockner, Austria	12,457	3,797
Fujiyama, Japan	12,389	3,776
Cook, New Zealand	12,349	3,764

LONGEST RIVERS

River	Length in: Miles	Kms.
Nile, Africa	4,145	6,671
Amazon, S. America	4,007	6,448
Mississippi-Missouri-Red Rock, U.S.A.	3,710	5,971
Chang Jiang (Yangtze), China	3,500	5,633
Ob'-Irtysh, Russia-Kazakhstan	3,362	5,411
Yenisey-Angara, Russia	3,100	4,989
Huang He (Yellow), China	2,950	4,747
Congo, Africa	2,780	4,474
Amur-Shilka-Onon, Asia	2,744	4,416
Lena, Russia	2,734	4,400
Mackenzie-Peace-Finlay, Canada	2,635	4,241
Paraná-La Plata, S. America	2,630	4,232
Mekong, Asia	2,610	4,200
Niger, Africa	2,580	4,152
Missouri-Red Rock, U.S.A.	2,564	4,125
Yenisey, Russia	2,500	4,028
Mississippi, U.S.A.	2,348	3,778
Murray-Darling, Australia	2,310	3,718
Volga, Russia	2,290	3,685
Madeira, S. America	2,013	3,240
Purus, S. America	1,995	3,211
Yukon, Alaska-Canada	1,979	3,185
Zambezi, Africa	1,950	3,138
São Francisco, Brazil	1,930	3,106
St. Lawrence, Canada-U.S.A.	1,900	3,058
Rio Grande, Mexico-U.S.A.	1,885	3,034
Syrdarïya-Naryn, Asia	1,859	2,992
Indus, Asia	1,800	2,897
Danube, Europe	1,775	2,857
Brahmaputra, Asia	1,700	2,736
Tocantins, Brazil	1,677	2,699
Salween, Asia	1,675	2,696
Euphrates, Asia	1,650	2,655
Xi (Si), China	1,650	2,655
Amu Darya, Asia	1,616	2,601
Nelson-Saskatchewan, Canada	1,600	2,575
Orinoco, S. America	1,600	2,575
Paraguay, S. America	1,584	2,549
Kolyma, Russia	1,562	2,514
Ganges, Asia	1,550	2,494
Zhayyq (Ural), Kazakhstan-Russia	1,509	2,428
Japurá, S. America	1,500	2,414
Arkansas, U.S.A.	1,450	2,334
Colorado, U.S.A.-Mexico	1.450	2,334
Negro, S. America	1,400	2,253
Dnepr (Dnyapro, Dnipro), Russia-Belarus-Ukraine	1,368	2,202
Orange, Africa	1,350	2,173
Ayeyarwady, Myanmar	1,325	2,132
Brazos, U.S.A.	1,309	2,107
Ohio-Allegheny, U.S.A.	1,306	2,102
Kama, Russia	1,252	2,031
Don, Russia	1,222	1,967
Red, U.S.A.	1,222	1,966
Columbia, U.S.A.-Canada	1,214	1,953
Tigris, Asia	1,181	1,901
Darling, Australia	1,160	1,867
Angara, Russia	1,135	1,827
Sungari, Asia	1,130	1,819
Pechora, Russia	1,124	1,809
Snake, U.S.A.	1,038	1,670
Churchill, Canada	1,000	1,609
Pilcomayo, S. America	1,000	1,609
Uruguay, S. America	994	1.600
Platte-N. Platte, U.S.A.	990	1,593
Ohio, U.S.A.	981	1,578
Magdalena, Colombia	956	1,538
Pecos, U.S.A.	926	1,490
Oka, Russia	918	1,477
Canadian, U.S.A.	906	1,458
Colorado, Texas, U.S.A.	894	1,439
Dnister (Nistru), Ukraine-Moldova	876	1,410
Fraser, Canada	850	1,369
Rhine, Europe	820	1,319
Northern Dvina, Russia	809	1,302
Ottawa, Canada	790	1,271

PRINCIPAL NATURAL LAKES

Lake	Area in: Sq. Miles	Sq. Kms.	Max. Depth in: Feet	Meters
Caspian Sea, Asia	143,243	370,999	3,264	995
Lake Superior, U.S.A.-Canada	31,820	82,414	1,329	405
Lake Victoria, Africa	26,628	69,215	270	82
Lake Huron, U.S.A.-Canada	23,010	59,596	748	228
Lake Michigan, U.S.A.	22,400	58,016	923	281
Aral Sea, Kazakhstan-Uzbekistan	15,830	41,000	213	65
Lake Tanganyika, Africa	12,650	32,764	4,700	1,433
Lake Baykal, Russia	12,162	31,500	5,316	1,620
Great Bear Lake, Canada	12,096	31,328	1,356	413
Lake Nyasa (Malawi), Africa	11,555	29,928	2,320	707
Great Slave Lake, Canada	11,031	28,570	2,015	614
Lake Erie, U.S.A.-Canada	9,940	25,745	210	64
Lake Winnipeg, Canada	9,417	24,390	60	18
Lake Ontario, U.S.A.-Canada	7,540	19,529	775	244
Lake Balkhash, Kazakhstan	7,081	18,340	87	27
Lake Chad, Africa*	7,000	18,130	25	8
Lake Ladoga, Russia	6,900	17,871	738	225
Lake Maracaibo, Venezuela	5,120	13,261	100	31
Lake Onega, Russia	3,761	9,741	377	115
Lake Eyre, Australia*	3,500-0	9,065-0	–	–
Lake Titicaca, Peru-Bolivia	3,200	8,288	1,000	305
Lake Nicaragua, Nicaragua	3,100	8,029	230	70
Lake Athabasca, Canada	3,064	7,936	400	122
Reindeer Lake, Canada*	2,568	6,651	–	–
Lake Turkana (Rudolf), Africa	2,463	6,379	240	73
Ysyk-Köl, Kyrgyzstan	2,425	6,281	2,303	702
Lake Torrens, Australia*	2,230	5,776	–	–
Vänern, Sweden	2,156	5,584	328	100
Nettilling Lake, Canada*	2,140	5,543	–	–
Lake Winnipegosis, Canada	2,075	5,374	38	12
Lake Albert, Africa	2,075	5,374	160	49
Kariba Lake, Zambia-Zimbabwe	2,050	5,310	295	90
Lake Nipigon, Canada	1,872	4,848	540	165
Lake Mweru, Africa	1,800	4,662	60	18
Lake Manitoba, Canada	1,799	4,659	12	4
Lake Taymyr, Russia	1,737	4,499	85	26
Lake Khanka, China-Russia	1,700	4,403	33	10
Lake Kioga, Uganda	1,700	4,403	25	8
Lake of the Woods, U.S.A.-Canada	1,679	4,349	70	21

* Figures subject to great seasonal variations.

Time Zones of the World

165° W	150° W	135° W	120° W	105° W	90° W	75° W	60° W	45° W	30° W	15° W	0°
1 A.M.	2 A.M.	3 A.M.	4 A.M.	5 A.M.	6 A.M.	7 A.M.	8 A.M.	9 A.M.	10 A.M.	11 A.M.	NOON

ARCTIC OCEAN

GREENLAND

NOON

11 A.M.

3 A.M. ALASKA

Anchorage

Whitehorse

CANADA

Edmonton

Winnipeg

Montréal

Nuuk

Reykjavík · ICELAND

NEWFOUNDLAND 8:30 A.M.

ST. PIERRE & MIQUELON 9 A.M.

1 A.M.

Seattle

Boise

Chicago

Detroit

Halifax

UNITED KINGDOM

IRELAND

London

Paris

FRANCE

San Francisco

UNITED STATES

Denver

New York
Washington

Atlanta

PORTUGAL

Madrid

SPAIN

AZORES

Los Angeles

Phoenix

Houston

Miami

BERMUDA

ATLANTIC

MOROCCO

ALGER

Honolulu

HAWAII

MEXICO

Mexico

CUBA

BAHAMAS

HAITI DOM. REP.

PUERTO RICO

CANARY IS.

W. SAHARA

MAURITANIA

MALI

1 A.M.

PACIFIC

GUATEMALA

BELIZE
HONDURAS

JAMAICA

ANTIGUA & BARBUDA
DOMINICA

CAPE VERDE

Dakar

SENEGAL

GAMBIA

BURKINA FASO

EL SALVADOR

NICARAGUA

GRENADA

BARBADOS

TRINIDAD & TOBAGO

GUINEA-BISSAU

GUINEA

BENIN

COSTA RICA

PANAMA

VENEZUELA

GUYANA

SIERRA LEONE

CÔTE D'IVOIRE

GHANA

TOGO

LIBERIA

Honolulu

INTL DATE LINE

KIRIBATI

MIDNIGHT

GÁLAPAGOS IS.

COLOMBIA

Bogotá

ECUADOR

SUR. FR. GUIANA

OCEAN

SÃO TO PRIN

1 A.M.

MARQUESAS IS. 2:30 A.M.

Manaus

ASCENSION

Lima

PERU

BRAZIL

Recife

FRENCH POLYNESIA

La Paz

BOLIVIA

OCEAN

PITCAIRN IS.

EASTER I.

PARAGUAY

Rio de Janeiro

CHILE

Santiago

Buenos Aires

URUGUAY

TRISTAN DA CUNHA

ARGENTINA

FALKLAND IS.

S. GEORGIA

TIME ZONES OF THE WORLD

STANDARD TIME ZONES	3 A.M.	4 A.M.	5 A.M.	6 A.M.
AREAS USING HALF HOUR DEVIATIONS		5:30 P.M.		

© HAMMOND WORLD ATLAS CORPORATION HJ · A

1 A.M.	2 A.M.	3 A.M.	4 A.M.	5 A.M.	6 A.M.	7 A.M.	8 A.M.	9 A.M.	10 A.M.	11 A.M.	NOON

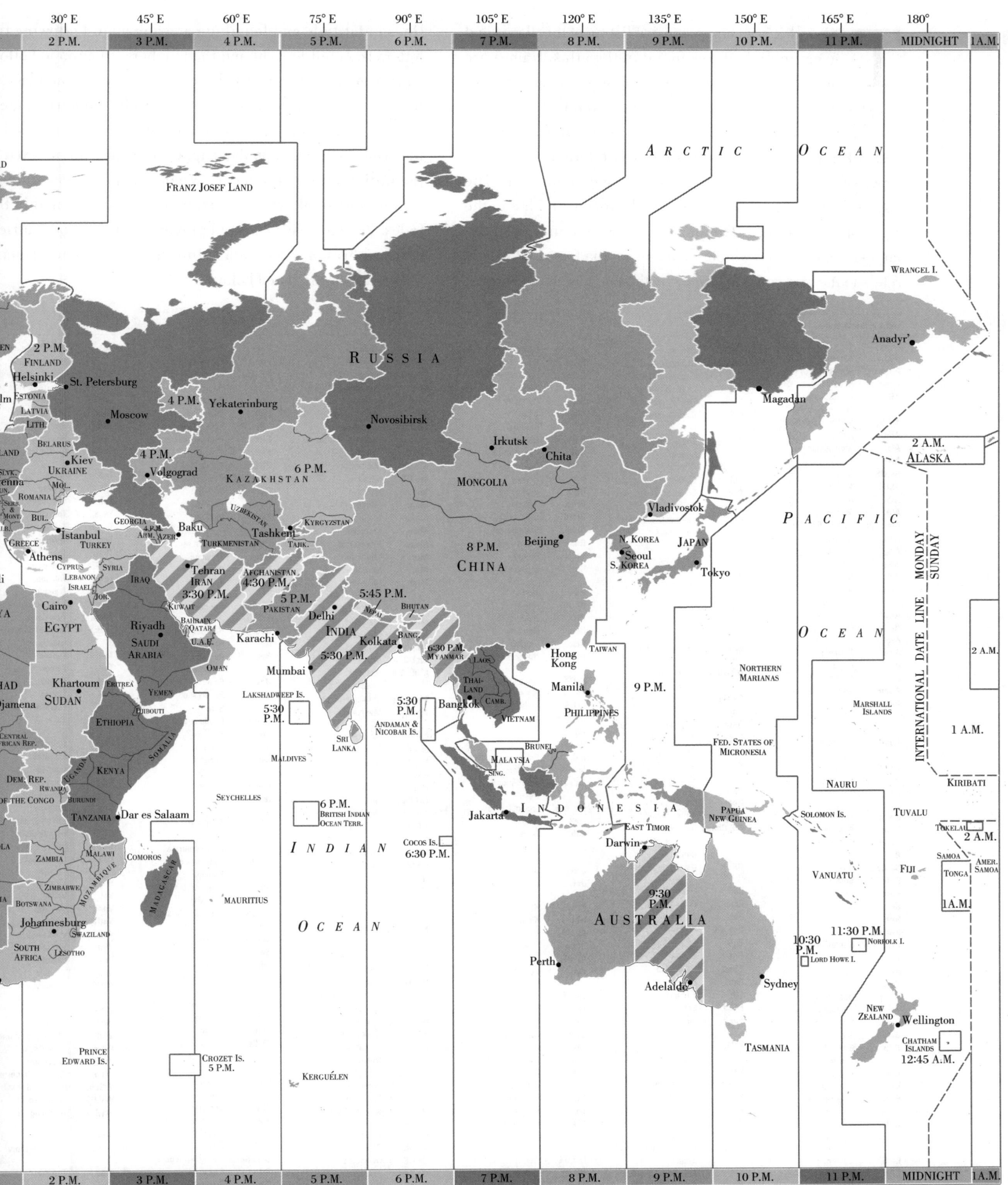

30° E   45° E   60° E   75° E   90° E   105° E   120° E   135° E   150° E   165° E   180°

2 P.M.   3 P.M.   4 P.M.   5 P.M.   6 P.M.   7 P.M.   8 P.M.   9 P.M.   10 P.M.   11 P.M.   MIDNIGHT   1 A.M.

ARCTIC OCEAN

FRANZ JOSEF LAND

WRANGEL I.

R U S S I A

Anadyr'

2 P.M.
FINLAND
Helsinki
St. Petersburg
4 P.M.
Yekaterinburg
Novosibirsk
Irkutsk
Chita
Magadan

Moscow
4 P.M.
Volgograd
KAZAKHSTAN
6 P.M.
MONGOLIA
Vladivostok

2 A.M.
ALASKA

GEORGIA
Baku
Tashkent
KYRGYZSTAN
8 P.M.
Beijing
N. KOREA
Seoul
S. KOREA
JAPAN
Tokyo

Istanbul
TURKEY
Athens
CYPRUS
LEBANON
ISRAEL
SYRIA
JOR.
Tehran
IRAN
3:30 P.M.
AFGHANISTAN
4:30 P.M.
5 P.M.
PAKISTAN
Delhi
NEPAL
BHUTAN
5:45 P.M.
CHINA

PACIFIC OCEAN

Cairo
EGYPT
Riyadh
SAUDI
ARABIA
KUWAIT
BAHRAIN
QATAR
U.A.E.
OMAN
Karachi
INDIA
5:30 P.M.
Kolkata
BANG.
6:30 P.M.
MYANMAR
Hong Kong
TAIWAN
NORTHERN
MARIANAS

MONDAY
SUNDAY
INTERNATIONAL DATE LINE

Khartoum
SUDAN
Djamena
YEMEN
ERITREA
ETHIOPIA
Mumbai
LAKSHADWEEP IS.
5:30
P.M.
LAOS
THAI-
LAND
Bangkok
CAMB.
VIETNAM
Manila
PHILIPPINES
9 P.M.

2 A.M.

CENTRAL
AFRICAN REP.
SOMALIA
MALDIVES
SRI
LANKA
ANDAMAN &
NICOBAR IS.
BRUNEI
MALAYSIA
SING.
FED. STATES OF
MICRONESIA

1 A.M.

DEM. REP.
OF THE CONGO
RWANDA
BURUNDI
UGANDA
KENYA
TANZANIA
Dar es Salaam
SEYCHELLES
6 P.M.
BRITISH INDIAN
OCEAN TERR.
I N D O N E S I A
Jakarta
PAPUA
NEW GUINEA
SOLOMON IS.
NAURU
KIRIBATI
TUVALU

2 A.M.

ZAMBIA
MALAWI
MOZAMBIQUE
COMOROS
MADAGASCAR
MAURITIUS
I N D I A N
O C E A N
COCOS IS.
6:30 P.M.
East Timor
Darwin
9:30
P.M.
A U S T R A L I A
VANUATU
FIJI
TONGA
1 A.M.
SAMOA
AMER.
SAMOA
TOKELAU

Johannesburg
ZIMBABWE
BOTSWANA
SWAZILAND
SOUTH
AFRICA
LESOTHO
Perth
Adelaide
Sydney
10:30
P.M.
LORD HOWE I.
11:30 P.M.
NORFOLK I.

PRINCE
EDWARD IS.
CROZET IS.
5 P.M.
KERGUÉLEN
TASMANIA
NEW
ZEALAND
Wellington
CHATHAM
ISLANDS
12:45 A.M.

2 P.M.   3 P.M.   4 P.M.   5 P.M.   6 P.M.   7 P.M.   8 P.M.   9 P.M.   10 P.M.   11 P.M.   MIDNIGHT   1 A.M.

Index of the World

This index is a comprehensive listing of the places and geographic features found in the atlas. Names are arranged in strict alphabetical order, without regard to hyphens or spaces. Every name is followed by the country or area to which it belongs. Except for cities, towns, countries and cultural areas, all entries include a reference to feature type, such as province, river, island, peak, and so on. The page number and alpha-numeric code appear in blue to the right of each listing. The page number directs you to the largest scale map on which the name can be found. The code refers to the grid squares formed by the horizontal and vertical lines of latitude and longitude on each map. Following th[e] letters from left to right and the numbers from top to botto[m] helps you to locate quickly the square containing the place [or] feature. Inset maps have their own alpha-numeric code[.] Names that are accompanied by a point symbol are indexed [to] the symbol's location on the map. Other names are indexed [to] the initial letter of the name. When a map name contains [a] subordinate or alternate name, both names are listed in th[e] index. To conserve space and provide room for more entrie[s,] many abbreviations are used in this index. The prima[ry] abbreviations are listed below.

Index Abbreviations

A
Ab,Can	Alberta
Abor.	Aboriginal
Acad.	Academy
ACT	Australian Capital Territory
A.F.B.	Air Force Base
Afld.	Airfield
Afg.	Afghanistan
Afr.	Africa
Ak,US	Alaska
Al,US	Alabama
Alb.	Albania
Alg.	Algeria
Amm. Dep.	Ammunition Depot
And.	Andorra
Ang.	Angola
Angu.	Anguilla
Ant.	Antarctica
Anti.	Antigua and Barbuda
Ar,US	Arkansas
Arch.	Archipelago
Arg.	Argentina
Arm.	Armenia
Arpt.	Airport
Aru.	Aruba
ASam.	American Samoa
Ash.	Ashmore and Cartier Islands
Aus.	Austria
Austl.	Australia
Aut.	Autonomous
Az,US	Arizona
Azer.	Azerbaijan
Azor.	Azores

B
Bahm.	Bahamas, The
Bahr.	Bahrain
Bang.	Bangladesh
Bar.	Barbados
BC,Can	British Columbia
Bela.	Belarus
Belg.	Belgium
Belz.	Belize
Ben.	Benin
Berm.	Bermuda
Bfld.	Battlefield
Bhu.	Bhutan
Bol.	Bolivia
Bor.	Borough
Bosn.	Bosnia and Herzegovina
Bots.	Botswana
Braz.	Brazil
Brln.	British Indian Ocean Territory
Bru.	Brunei
Bul.	Bulgaria
Burk.	Burkina Faso
Buru.	Burundi
BVI	British Virgin Islands

C
Ca,US	California
CAfr.	Central African Republic
Camb.	Cambodia
Camr.	Cameroon
Can.	Canada
Can.	Canal
Canl.	Canary Islands
Cap.	Capital
Cap. Dist.	Capital District
Cap. Terr.	Capital Territory
Cay.	Cayman Islands
C.d'Iv.	Côte d'Ivoire
C.G.	Coast Guard
Chan.	Channel
Chl.	Channel Islands
Co.	County
Co,US	Colorado
Col.	Colombia
Com.	Comoros
Cont.	Continent
CpV.	Cape Verde Islands
CR	Costa Rica
Cr.	Creek
Cro.	Croatia
CSea.	Coral Sea Islands Territory
Ct,US	Connecticut
Ctr.	Center
Ctry.	Country
Cyp.	Cyprus
Czh.	Czech Republic

D
DC,US	District of Columbia
De,US	Delaware
Den.	Denmark
Depr.	Depression
Dept.	Department
Des.	Desert
DF	Distrito Federal
Dist.	District
Djib.	Djibouti
Dom.	Dominica
Dpcy.	Dependency
D.R.Congo	Democratic Republic of the Congo
DRep.	Dominican Republic

E
Ecu.	Ecuador
Emb.	Embankment
Eng.	Engineering
Eng,UK	England
EqG.	Equatorial Guinea
Erit.	Eritrea
ESal.	El Salvador
Est.	Estonia
Eth.	Ethiopia
ETim.	East Timor
Eur.	Europe

F
Falk.	Falkland Islands
Far.	Faroe Islands
Fed. Dist.	Federal District
Fin.	Finland
Fl,US	Florida
For.	Forest
Fr.	France
FrAnt.	French Southern and Antarctic Lands
FrG.	French Guiana
FrPol.	French Polynesia
FYROM	Former Yugoslav Rep. of Macedonia

G
Ga,US	Georgia
Galp.	Galapagos Islands
Gam.	Gambia, The
Gaza	Gaza Strip
GBis.	Guinea-Bissau
Geo.	Georgia
Ger.	Germany
Gha.	Ghana
Gib.	Gibraltar
Glac.	Glacier
Gov.	Governorate
Govt.	Government
Gre.	Greece
Grld.	Greenland
Gren.	Grenada
Grsld.	Grassland
Guad.	Guadeloupe
Guat.	Guatemala
Gui.	Guinea
Guy.	Guyana

H
Har.	Harbor
Hi,US	Hawaii
Hist.	Historic(al)
Hon.	Honduras
Hts.	Heights
Hun.	Hungary

I
Ia,US	Iowa
Ice.	Iceland
Id,US	Idaho
Il,US	Illinois
IM	Isle of Man
In,US	Indiana
Ind. Res.	Indian Reservation
Indo.	Indonesia
Int'l	International
Ire.	Ireland
Isl., Isls.	Island, Islands
Isr.	Israel
Isth.	Isthmus
It.	Italy

J
Jam.	Jamaica
Jor.	Jordan

K
Kaz.	Kazakhstan
Kiri.	Kiribati
Ks,US	Kansas
Kuw.	Kuwait
Ky,US	Kentucky
Kyr.	Kyrgyzstan

L
La,US	Louisiana
Lab.	Laboratory
Lag.	Lagoon
Lakesh.	Lakeshore
Lat.	Latvia
Lcht.	Liechtenstein
Ldg.	Landing
Leb.	Lebanon
Les.	Lesotho
Libr.	Liberia
Lith.	Lithuania
Lux.	Luxembourg

M
Ma,US	Massachusetts
Madg.	Madagascar
Madr.	Madeira
Malay.	Malaysia
Mald.	Maldives
Malw.	Malawi
Mart.	Martinique
May.	Mayotte
Mb,Can	Manitoba
Md,US	Maryland
Me,US	Maine
Mem.	Memorial
Mex.	Mexico
Mi,US	Michigan
Micr.	Micronesia, Federated States of
Mil.	Military
Mn,US	Minnesota
Mo,US	Missouri
Mol.	Moldova
Mon.	Monument
Mona.	Monaco
Mong.	Mongolia
Monts.	Montserrat
Mor.	Morocco
Moz.	Mozambique
Mrsh.	Marshall Islands
Mrta.	Mauritania
Mrts.	Mauritius
Ms,US	Mississippi
Mt.	Mount
Mt,US	Montana
Mtn., Mts.	Mountain, Mountains
Mun. Arpt.	Municipal Airport
Myan.	Myanmar

N
NAm.	North America
Namb.	Namibia
NAnt.	Netherlands Antilles
Nat'l	National
Nav.	Naval
NB,Can	New Brunswick
Nbrhd.	Neighborhood
NC,US	North Carolina
NCal.	New Caledonia
ND,US	North Dakota
Ne,US	Nebraska
Neth.	Netherlands
Nf,Can	Newfoundland
Nga.	Nigeria
NH,US	New Hampshire
NI,UK	Northern Ireland
Nic.	Nicaragua
NJ,US	New Jersey
NKor.	North Korea
NM,US	New Mexico
NMar.	Northern Mariana Islands
Nor.	Norway
NS,Can	Nova Scotia
Nv,US	Nevada
Nun.,Can	Nunavut
NW,Can	Northwest Territories
NY,US	New York
NZ	New Zealand

O
Obl.	Oblast
Oh,US	Ohio
Ok,US	Oklahoma
On,Can	Ontario
Or,US	Oregon

P
Pa,US	Pennsylvania
PacUS	Pacific Islands, U.S.
Pak.	Pakistan
Pan.	Panama
Par.	Paraguay
Par.	Parish
PE,Can	Prince Edward Island
Pen.	Peninsula
Phil.	Philippines
Phys. Reg.	Physical Region
Pitc.	Pitcairn Islands
Plat.	Plateau
PNG	Papua New Guinea
Pol.	Poland
Port.	Portugal
Poss.	Possession
Pkwy.	Parkway
PR	Puerto Rico
Pref.	Prefecture
Prov.	Province
Prsv.	Preserve
Pt.	Point

Q
Qu,Can	Quebec

R
Rec.	Recreation(al)
Ref.	Refuge
Reg.	Region
Rep.	Republic
Res.	Reservoir, Reservation
Reun.	Réunion
RI,US	Rhode Island
Riv.	River
Rom.	Romania
Rsv.	Reserve
Rus.	Russia
Rvwy.	Riverway
Rwa.	Rwanda

S
SAfr.	South Africa
Sam.	Samoa
SAm.	South America
SaoT.	São Tomé and Príncipe
SAr.	Saudi Arabia
Sc,UK	Scotland
SC,US	South Carolina
SD,US	South Dakota
Seash.	Seashore
Sen.	Senegal
Serb.	Serbia and Montenegro
Sey.	Seychelles
SGeo.	South Georgia and Sandwich Islands
Sing.	Singapore
Sk,Can	Saskatchewan
SKor.	South Korea
SLeo.	Sierra Leone
Slov.	Slovenia
Slvk.	Slovakia
SMar.	San Marino
Sol.	Solomon Islands
Som.	Somalia
Sp.	Spain
Spr., Sprs.	Spring, Springs
SrL.	Sri Lanka
Sta.	Station
StH.	Saint Helena
Str.	Strait
StK.	Saint Kitts and Nevis
StL.	Saint Lucia
StP.	Saint Pierre and Miquelon
StV.	Saint Vincent and the Grenadines
Sur.	Suriname
Sval.	Svalbard
Swaz.	Swaziland
Swe.	Sweden
Swi.	Switzerland

T
Tah.	Tahiti
Tai.	Taiwan
Taj.	Tajikistan
Tanz.	Tanzania
Ter.	Terrace
Terr.	Territory
Thai.	Thailand
Tn,US	Tennessee
Tok.	Tokelau
Trg.	Training
Trin.	Trinidad and Toba[go]
Trkm.	Turkmenistan
Trks.	Turks and Caicos Islands
Tun.	Tunisia
Tun.	Tunnel
Turk.	Turkey
Tuv.	Tuvalu
Twp.	Township
Tx,US	Texas

U
UAE	United Arab Emirates
Ugan.	Uganda
UK	United Kingdom
Ukr.	Ukraine
Uru.	Uruguay
US	United States
USVI	U.S. Virgin Islands
Ut,US	Utah
Uzb.	Uzbekistan

V
Va,US	Virginia
Val.	Valley
Van.	Vanuatu
VatC.	Vatican City
Ven.	Venezuela
Viet.	Vietnam
Vill.	Village
Vol.	Volcano
Vt,US	Vermont

W
Wa,US	Washington
Wal,UK	Wales
Wall.	Wallis and Futuna
WBnk.	West Bank
Wi,US	Wisconsin
Wild.	Wildlife, Wilderne[ss]
WSah.	Western Sahara
WV,US	West Virginia
Wy,US	Wyoming

Y
Yem.	Yemen
Yk,Can	Yukon Territory

Z
Zam.	Zambia
Zim.	Zimbabwe

A

100 Mile House, BC, Can. 126/C3
Aa (riv.), Ger. 50/D5
Aach (riv.), Ger. 57/F2
Aach, Ger. 57/E2
Aachen, Ger. 53/F2
Aalbach (riv.), Ger. 54/C3
Aalborg (int'l arpt.), Den. 38/C3
Aalburg, Neth. 50/C5
Aalen, Ger. 54/D5
Aalsmeer, Neth. 50/B4
Aalst, Belg. 52/D2
Aalten, Neth. 50/D5
Aalter, Belg. 52/C1
Aar (riv.), Ger. 53/H3
Aarau, Swi. 56/E3
Aarberg, Swi. 56/D3
Aarburg, Swi. 56/D3
Aardenburg, Neth. 52/C1
Aare (riv.), Swi. 43/H3
Aargau (canton), Swi. 57/E3
Aarred (lake), WSah. 98/B4
Aarschot, Belg. 53/D2
Aartselaar, Belg. 53/D1
Aarwangen, Swi. 56/D3
Aba, D.R. Congo 104/A2
Aba, China 70/H5
Aba, Nga. 103/G5
Abā as Su'ūd, SAr. 88/D5
Abacaxis (riv.), Braz. 150/G5
Abadab (peak), Sudan 101/C5
Ābādān, Iran 88/E2
Ābādeh, Iran 88/F2
Abadia dos Dourados, Braz. 155/C1
Abadla, Alg. 99/E3
Abádszalók, Hun. 48/E2
Abaeté, Braz. 155/C1
Abaetetuba, Braz. 151/J4
Abaiang (isl.), Kiri. 116/G4
Abakan, Rus. 64/K4
Abancay, Peru 156/C4
Abano Terme, It. 59/E2
Abar Kūh, Iran 88/F2
Abarán, Sp. 44/E3
Abashiri (lake), Japan 76/C2
Abashiri, Japan 76/D1
Abasolo, Mex. 143/E4
Abasolo, Mex. 143/F3
Abay, Kaz. 87/F3
Ābaya Hayk (lake) 97/N6
Abbadia Lariana, It. 57/F6
Abbadia San Salvatore, It. 43/J5
Abbeville, La, US 129/J5
Abbeville, SC, US 133/H3
Abbeville, Fr. 52/A3
Abbey (peak), Austl. 114/B1
Abbeyfeale, Ire. 31/P10
Abbeyleix, Ire. 31/Q10
Abbiategrasso, It. 58/B2
Abbot (mt.), Austl. 114/B3
Abbotsinch (int'l arpt.), Sc, UK 36/B5
Abbottābād, Pak. 86/B2
Abbottstown, Pa, US 138/B4
Abcoude, Neth. 50/B4
Abdul Hakīm, Pak. 86/B4
Abdulino, Rus. 63/K1
Abéché, Chad 97/K5
Abemama (isl.), Kiri. 116/G4
Abenberg, Ger. 54/D4
Abengourou, C.d'Iv. 102/E5
Åbenrå, Den. 38/C4
Abens (riv.), Ger. 40/F4
Abensberg, Ger. 55/E5
Abeokuta, Nga. 103/F5
Abercarn, Wal, UK 32/C3
Aberchirder, Sc, UK 36/D1
Aberdare, Wal, UK 32/C3
Aberdare NP, Kenya 104/C3
Aberdeen, Austl. 115/D2
Aberdeen (lake), Nun., Can. 122/F2
Aberdeen, SAfr. 106/D4
Aberdeen, Sc, UK 36/D2
Aberdeen (pol. reg.), Sc, UK 36/D2
Aberdeen, SD, US 127/J4
Aberdeen, Ms, US 133/F3
Aberdeen, Md, US 138/B5
Aberdeen, Wa, US 126/C4
Aberdeen Proving Ground, Md, US 138/B5
Aberdeenshire, Sc, UK 36/D2
Aberdeenshire (pol. reg.), Sc, UK 36/D2
Aberdour, Sc, UK 36/C4
Aberdour (bay), Sc, UK 36/D1
Aberfeldy, Sc, UK 36/C3
Aberfoyle, Sc, UK 36/B4
Abergavenny, Wal, UK 32/C3
Abergele, Wal, UK 34/E5
Aberlour, Sc, UK 36/C2
Abernethy, Sc, UK 36/C4
Abert (lake), Or, US 126/C5
Abertillery, Wal, UK 32/C3
Aberystwyth, Wal, UK 32/B2
Abhá, SAr. 88/D5
Abhar, Iran 88/E1
Abhayāpuri, India 85/H2
Abhe Bad (lake), Djib.,Eth 97/P5
Abia (prov.), Nga. 103/G5
Abidjan, C.d'Iv. 102/D5
Abiko, Japan 77/E2
Abilene, Tx, US 129/H4
Abilene, Ks, US 129/H3
Abingdon, Eng, UK 33/E3
Abingdon, Md, US 138/B5
Abington (reef), Austl. 114/C2
Abington, Sc, UK 36/C6
Abino (pt.), On, Can. 131/R10
Abiquiu, NM, US 132/B2
Abitibi (lake), On,Qu, Can. 123/H4
Abitibi (riv.), On, Can. 123/H4
Abkhazia Aut. Rep., Geo. 63/G4
Ableiges, Fr. 30/H4
Abnūb, Egypt 101/B3
Åbo (Turku), Fin. 39/K1
Abohar, India 86/C4
Aboisso, C.d'Iv. 102/E5
Abomey, Ben. 103/F5
Abondance, Fr. 56/C5
Abony, Hun. 48/D2
Aboyne, Sc, UK 36/D2
Abra (riv.), Phil. 79/D4
Abra Pampa, Arg. 157/C1
Abraham Gonzalez (int'l arpt.), Mex. 128/F5
Abrantes, Port. 44/A3
Abreojos (pt.), Mex. 142/B3
Abrud, Rom. 49/F2
Abruzzi (prov.), It. 43/K5
Abruzzo, PN de, It. 46/C2
Absam, Aus. 57/H3
Absaroka (range), Mt,Wy, US 126/F4
Absecon, NJ, US 138/D5
Abtsgmünd, Ger. 54/D5
Abu el-Husein (well), Egypt 101/B4
Abū Ḩammād, Egypt 91/B4
Abu Hashim (well), Egypt 101/C4
Abū Ḩummuş, Egypt 91/B4
Abū Kabīr, Egypt 91/B4
Abū Kamāl, Syria 90/E3
Abū Qashsh, WBnk. 91/G8
Abu Shagara (cape), Sudan 101/D4
Abu Simbel (ruin), Egypt 101/B4
Abū Z̧aby (Abu Dhabi) (cap.), UAE 89/F4
Abuja (cap.), Nga. 103/G4
Abuja (int'l arpt.), Nga. 103/G4
Abuja Capital Territory, Nga. 103/G4
Abukuma (riv.), Japan 75/G2
Abukuma (plat.), Japan 75/G2
Abulog, Phil. 79/D4
Abunã (riv.), Braz. 150/E6
Abuta, Japan 76/B2
Ābuyē Mēda (peak), Eth. 97/N5
Abuyog, Phil. 79/E5
Åby, Swe. 38/G2
Åbybro, Den. 38/C3
Abydos (ruin), Egypt 101/B3
Acacías, Col. 152/C4
Acacoyagua, Mex. 144/C3
Acadia NP, Me, US 131/G2
Acadian Village, La, US 129/J5
Acajutiba, Braz. 154/C3
Acámbaro, Mex. 143/E4
Acampo, Ca, US 135/M10
Acandí, Col. 152/B2
Acaponeta (riv.), Mex. 142/D4
Acaponeta, Mex. 142/D4
Acapulco de Juárez, Mex. 140/B4
Acaraí (mts.), Braz.,Guy. 153/G4
Acaraí, Serra (mts.), Braz. 150/G3
Acaraú (riv.), Braz. 154/B1
Acaraú, Braz. 154/B1
Acari, Braz. 154/C2
Acari (riv.), Braz. 150/G5
Acarí, Peru 156/C4
Acarigua, Ven. 152/D2
Acatlán de Osorio, Mex. 144/B2
Acatlán de Pérez Figueroa, Mex. 143/N8
Acatzingo, Mex. 143/M7
Acayucan, Mex. 144/C2
Accha, Peru 156/D4
Acciaroli, It. 46/D2
Accra (cap.), Gha. 103/E5
Accrington, Eng, UK 35/F4
Aceuchal, Sp. 44/B3
Ach (riv.), Aus. 55/G6
Achacachi, Bol. 150/E7
Achaguas, Ven. 152/D3
Achao, Chile 158/B4
Achar, Uru. 159/K10
Achegour (well), Niger 96/H4
Achen (pass), Ger. 57/H2
Acheng, China 71/N2
Achères, Fr. 30/J5
Achhnera, India 84/A2
Achicourt, Fr. 52/B3
Achill (isl.), Ire. 30/N10
Achill Head (pt.), Ire. 30/N9
Achiltibuie, Sc, UK 31/R7
Achinsk, Rus. 64/K4
Achmîm (well), Mrta. 102/D2
Achnasheen, Sc, UK 36/A1
Achoma, Peru 156/D4
A'chràlaig (peak), Sc, UK 36/A2
Achuapa, Nic. 144/E3
Achupallas, Ecu. 156/B1
Acireale, It. 46/D4
Acklins (isl.), Bahm. 141/G3
Acland (mt.), Austl. 114/C4
Acobamba, Peru 156/C4
Acolla, Peru 156/C3
Acolman, Mex. 143/R9
Acomayo, Peru 156/D4
Acomayo, Peru 156/B3
Aconcagua (peak), Arg. 158/C2
Aconchi, Mex. 142/C2
Acopiara, Braz. 154/C2
Acora, Peru 156/D4
Acqualagna, It. 59/F5
Acquanegra sul Chiese, It. 58/D2
Acquapendente, It. 46/B1
Acqui Terme, It. 58/B3
Acraman (lake), Austl. 113/G5
Acrata (pt.), Alg. 100/G4
Acre (riv.), Braz. 150/E6
Acre (state), Braz. 156/D3
Acreúna, Braz. 155/B1
Acropolis, Gre. 47/N9
Actaeon Group (isls.), FrPol. 117/M7
Acton, Ca, US 136/B2
Actopan, Mex. 143/N7
Actopan, Mex. 143/L6
Açu, Braz. 154/C2
Açude Aratas (res.), Braz. 154/B2
Açude Banabuiu (res.), Braz. 154/C2
Acula, Mex. 143/P8
Aculeo (lag.), Chile 158/N8
Acy-en-Multien, Fr. 30/L4
Ad Dahnā' (des.), SAr. 88/D3
Ad-Dakhla, WSah. 98/B5
Ad Damazin, Sudan 97/M5
Ad Damīr, Sudan 88/B5
Ad Dammām, SAr. 88/F3
Ad Daqahlīyah (gov.), Egypt 101/B1
Ad Dilinjāt, Egypt 91/B4
Ad Dīwānīyah, Iraq 90/F4
Ad Dujayl, Iraq 90/F3
Ad Duwaym, Sudan 97/M5
Ada, Gha. 103/F5
Ada, Serb. 48/E3
Ada, Oh, US 130/D3
Ada, Ok, US 129/H4
Adainville, Fr. 30/G5
Adair (cape), Nun., Can. 123/J1
Adair, Bahia del (bay), Mex. 128/D5
Adaja (riv.), Sp. 44/C2
Adak (isl.), Ak, US 134/C6
Adak (str.), Ak, US 134/C6
Adam (mt.), UK 159/E6
Adamantina, Braz. 155/B2
Adamaoua (plat.), Camr.,Nga. 93/D4
Adamello (peak), It. 57/G5
Adaminaby, Austl. 115/D3
Adams (lake), BC, Can. 126/D3
Adams (co.), Co, US 137/C3
Adams (co.), Pa, US 138/A4
Adams (mt.), Wa, US 126/C4
Adamstown (cap.), Pitc. 117/M7
Adamstown, Pa, US 138/B3
Adamwa (plat.), Nga. 103/H5
'Adan, Yem. 88/D6
Adana (prov.), Turk. 90/C2
Adana, Turk. 91/D1
Adana (int'l arpt.), Turk. 91/D1
Adapazarı, Turk. 49/K5
Adare, Ire. 31/P10
Adare (cape), Ant. 160/M
Adarza (peak), Fr. 44/E1
Add (riv.), Sc, UK 36/A4
Adda (riv.), It. 43/H4
Addison, Il, US 135/P16
Addlestone, Eng, UK 30/B2
Addo Elephant NP, SAfr. 106/D4
Adekeieh (Ādī K'eyih), Erit. 88/C6
Adelaide, SAfr. 106/D4
Adelaide (pen.), Nun., Can. 122/G2
Adelaide (int'l arpt.), Austl. 113/M8
Adelaide, Austl. 113/M8
Adelaide Zoo, Austl. 113/M8
Adelanto, Ca, US 136/C1
Adelebsen, Ger. 51/G5
Adelheidsdorf, Ger. 51/H3
Adelmannsfelden, Ger. 54/D5
Adelong, Austl. 115/D2
Adelschlag, Ger. 54/E5
Adelsheim, Ger. 54/C4
Adelsried, Ger. 54/D6
Aden (gulf), Afr.,Asia 67/D8
Adenau, Ger. 53/F3
Adendorf, Ger. 51/H2
Adh Dhirā', Jor. 91/D4
Adi (isl.), Indo. 81/H4
Ādī Ugrī, Erit. 88/C6
Adieu (cape), Austl. 113/G5
Adige (riv.), It. 43/J4
Adige (Etsch) (riv.), It. 57/G4
Ādīgrat, Eth. 88/C6
Adilābād, India 82/C4
Adilcevaz, Turk. 90/E2
Adiora (well), Mali 103/E2
Adirondack (mts.), NY, US 125/L3
Ādīs Ābeba (Addis Ababa) (cap.), Eth. 97/N6
Adıyaman, Turk. 90/D2
Adıyaman (prov.), Turk. 90/D2
Adjud, Rom. 49/H2
Adjuntas, Presa de la (res.), Mex. 143/F4
Adler/Sochi (int'l arpt.), Rus. 62/F4
Adliswil, Swi. 57/E3
Admiralty (inlet), Nun., Can. 123/H1
Admiralty (isl.), Ak, US 122/C3
Admiralty Island Nat'l Mon., Ak, US 134/M4
Admiralty (isls.), PNG 116/D5
Admiralty (inlet), Wa, US 135/B2
Adnan Menderes (int'l arpt.), Turk. 90/A2
Ado (riv.), Japan 77/J5
Ado Ekiti, Nga. 103/G5
Ado Odo, Nga. 103/F5
Adogawa, Japan 77/K5
Adolfo López Mateos, Mex. 142/B3
Ādoni, India 82/C4
Adour (riv.), Fr. 42/C5
Adra, India 85/F4
Adra, Sp. 44/D4
Adrano, It. 46/D4
Adrar (phys. reg.), Mrta. 96/C3
Adrar, Alg. 99/E4
Adrar (pol. reg.), Mrta. 102/C1
Adrar (prov.), Alg. 99/E4
Adrar (reg.), Mrta. 98/C5
Adrar bou Nasser (peak), Mor. 98/E2
Adrar Sotuf (mts.), WSah. 98/B5
Adria, It. 59/F2
Adrian, Mi, US 130/C3
Adriatic (sea), Eur. 27/F4
Adro, It. 58/C1
Aduana del Sásabe, Mex. 128/E5
Adulis (ruin), Erit. 88/C5
Adur (riv.), Eng, UK 33/F5
Ādwa, Eth. 88/C6
Adwick le Street, Eng, UK 35/G4
Adycha (riv.), Rus. 65/P3
Adygeya, Resp., Rus. 62/F3
Adz'va (riv.), Rus. 61/P2
Aegean (sea), Gre.,Turk 62/C5
Aerø (isl.), Den. 38/D4
Aeron (riv.), Wal, UK 32/B2
Aesch, Swi. 56/D3
Aeschi bei Spiez, Swi. 56/D4
Äetsä, Fin. 39/K1
Afadjoto (peak), Gha. 103/F5
'Afak, Iraq 88/E2
Afándou, Gre. 90/B2
Aff (riv.), Fr. 42/B3
Affoltern im Emmental, Swi. 56/D3
Affric (lake), Sc, UK 36/A2
Affton, Mo, US 137/G8
Afghanistan (ctry.) 89/H2
Afmadow, Som. 97/P7
Afogados da Ingàzeira, Braz. 154/C2
Afognak (mtn.), Ak, US 134/H4
Afognak (isl.), Ak, US 134/H4
Afollé, Massif de (phys. reg.), Mrta. 102/C2
Afonso Bezerra, Braz. 154/C2
Afonso Cláudio, Braz. 155/D2
Afragola, It. 46/D2
Afrânio, Braz. 154/B3
Africa (cont.) 93
Afrin (riv.), Turk. 91/E1
'Afrīn, Syria 91/E1
Afrique (peak), Fr. 56/A3
Afsluitdijk (dam), Neth. 50/C2
Afte (riv.), Ger. 51/F5
Afton, Wy, US 126/F5
Afuidich (lake), WSah. 98/B5
'Afula, Isr. 91/G6
Afyon, Turk. 90/B2
Afyon (prov.), Turk. 90/B2
Afzalgarh, India 84/B1
Agades (int'l arpt.), Niger 103/G2
Agadez, Niger 103/G2
Agadez (dept.), Niger 99/H5
Agadir, Mor. 98/C3
Agago (riv.), Ugan. 104/B2
Agamor (well), Mali 103/F2
Agano (riv.), Japan 75/F2
Agassiz Ice Cap (ice field), Nun., Can. 123/T6
Agattu (isl.), Ak, US 134/A5
Agattu (str.), Ak, US 134/A5
Agbabu, Nga. 103/G5
Agboville, C.d'Iv. 102/D5
Ağdam, Azer. 63/H5
Agde, Fr. 42/E5
Agen, Fr. 42/D4
Ageo, Japan 77/D2
Ager (riv.), Aus. 55/G7
Agerǽk, Den. 38/C4
Agerisee (lake), Swi. 57/E3
Agger (riv.), Ger. 53/G1
Aggteleki NP, Slvk. 48/E1
Āghā Jārī, Iran 88/E2
Aghagallon, NI, UK 34/B3
Aghagower, Ire. 31/P10
Agiabampo, Mex. 142/C3
Ağınskiy Buryatskiy Aut. Okrug, Rus. 65/Q7
Aginskoye, Rus. 71/K1
Agliana, It. 59/D5
Ağlıköy, Turk. 90/C1
Agly (riv.), Fr. 42/E5
Agna, It. 59/E2
Agnanderón, Gre. 47/G3
Agnita, Rom. 49/G3
Agno (riv.), It. 59/E1
Agno (int'l arpt.), Swi. 57/E6
Agnone, It. 46/D2
Ago, Japan 77/L7
Agogna (riv.), It. 43/H4
Agordo, It. 43/K3
Agout (riv.), Fr. 42/D5
Āgra, India 84/B2
Agraciada, Uru. 159/J10
Agrado, Col. 152/C4
Ágreda, Sp. 44/E2
Ağri (prov.), Turk. 90/E2
Agriá, Gre. 47/H3
Agrigento, It. 46/C4
Agrihan (isl.), NMar. 116/D3
Agrínion, Gre. 47/G3
Agrio (riv.), Arg. 158/C3
Agropoli, It. 46/D2
Agryz, Rus. 61/M4
Agsumal (dry lake), WSah. 98/B4
Água Boa, Braz. 154/B5
Água Branca, Braz. 154/B2
Agua Dulce, Ca, US 136/B2
Agua Dulce, Mex. 144/C2
Agua Fria (riv.), Az, US 137/R19
Agua Fria NM, Az, US 128/E4
Agua Hedionda (lake), Ca, US 136/C4
Agua Larga, Ven. 152/D2
Agua Prieta, Mex. 128/E5
Aguachica, Col. 152/C2
Aguadilla, PR 141/M8
Aguadulce, Pan. 152/A2
Aguaí, Braz. 211/G7
Agualva-Cacém, Port. 45/P10
Aguan (riv.), Hon. 140/D4
Aguanus (riv.), Qu, Can. 131/J1
Aguapeí (riv.), Braz. 155/B2
Aguarico (riv.), Peru 152/B5
Águas Belas, Braz. 154/C3
Aguas Corrientes, Uru. 159/K11
Águas da Prata, Braz. 211/G6
Águas de Lindóia, Braz. 211/G7
Águas Formosas, Braz. 154/B5
Águas, Serra das (hills), Braz. 211/H7
Aguasay, Ven. 153/F2
Aguascalientes, Mex. 142/E4
Aguascalientes (state), Mex. 140/A3
Águavermelha, Represa (res.), Braz. 155/B1
Aguaytía (riv.), Peru 156/C3
Agudos, Braz. 155/B2
Agueda (riv.), Sp. 44/B2
Águeda, Port. 44/A2
Aguêraktem (well), Mali 98/D5
Agugliano, It. 59/G5
Agui, Japan 77/L6
Aguijan (isl.), NMar. 116/D3
Aguilar, Sp. 44/C4
Aguilar de Campóo, Sp. 44/C1
Aguilares, Arg. 157/C2
Aguilas, Sp. 44/E4
Aguililla, Mex. 142/E5
Aguja (pt.), Peru 156/A2
Agulhas (cape), SAfr. 106/M11
Agulhas Negras, Pico das (peak), Braz. 211/J7
Agung (vol.), Indo. 81/E5
Agusan (riv.), Phil. 79/E6
Agustín Codazzi, Col. 152/C2
Ahaggar (plat.), Arg. 96/F3
Ahaggar (mts.), Alg. 99/G5
Ahal (pol. reg.), Trkm. 87/C5
Aham, Ger. 55/F5
Ahar, Iran 63/H5
Ahaus, Ger. 50/E4
Ahfir, Mor. 100/C2
Ahırlı, Turk. 90/C2
Ahlat, Turk. 90/E2
Ahlen, Ger. 51/E5
Ahlerstedt, Ger. 51/G2
Ahmadābād, India 89/K4
Ahmadpur East, Pak. 86/A5
Ahmadpur Siāl, Pak. 86/A4
Ahmar (mts.), Eth. 97/P6
Ahmar, 'Erg el (des.), Mali 98/D4
Ahmed (well), WSah. 98/B5
Ahmeyine (well), Mrta. 98/B5
Ahoghill, NI, UK 34/B2
Ahome, Mex. 142/C3
Ahr (riv.), Ger. 43/G1
Ahraurā, India 84/D3
Ahrensburg, Ger. 51/H1
Ahse (riv.), Ger. 51/F5
Ahuacatitlán, Mex. 143/K8
Ahuacatlán, Mex. 142/D4
Ahuachapán, ESal. 144/D3
Ahualulco, Mex. 143/E4
Ahuimanu, Hi, US 124/W13
Ahumada, Mex. 128/F5
Ahun, Fr. 42/E3
Åhus, Swe. 38/F4
Ahvāz, Iran 88/E2
Ahvenanmaa (prov.), Fin. 37/F4
Ai (riv.), China 73/C2
Ai (mtn.), China 72/E3
Ai-Ais Hot Springs, Namb. 106/B2
Ai-shima (isl.), Japan 74/B3
Aibag Gol (riv.), China 72/B2
Aichach, Ger. 54/E6
Aichi (pref.), Japan 75/E3
Aidhausen, Ger. 54/D2
Aidlingen, Ger. 54/B5
Aiea, Hi, US 124/W13
Aiello del Friuli, It. 59/G1
Aiffres, Fr. 42/C3
Aigen im Mühlkreis, Aus. 55/G5
Aigle, Pic de l' (peak), Fr. 56/B4
Aiglemont, Fr. 53/D4
Aigoual (peak), Fr. 42/E4
Aiguá, Uru. 159/G2
Aigues (riv.), Fr. 42/F4
Aigües Tortes y Lago de San Mauricio, PN de, Sp. 45/F1
Aiguille, Cap de l' (cape), Alg. 100/E5
Aiguillon, Fr. 42/D4
Aikawa, Japan 75/F1
Aikawa, Japan 77/C2
Aiken, SC, US 133/H3
Ailigandí, Pan. 152/B2
Ailinglapalap (isl.), Mrsh. 116/F4
Aillevillers-et-Lyaumont, Fr. 56/C2
Ailly-sur-Noye, Fr. 52/B4
Ailsa Craig (isl.), Sc, UK 36/A6
Ailuk (isl.), Mrsh. 116/G3
Aimen (pass), China 72/C5
Aimogasta, Arg. 157/C2
Aimorés, Braz. 155/D1
Aimorés, Serra dos (mts.), Braz. 155/D1
Ain (riv.), Fr. 42/F4
'Aïn Beïda, Alg. 100/K7
'Aïn Beniau, Alg. 100/G4
'Aïn Bessem, Alg. 100/G4
Aïn Chok-Hay Mohammadia (prov.), Mor. 100/A2
'Aïn Defla, Alg. 100/F4
'Aïn Defla (prov.), Alg. 100/F4
Aïn el Aouda, Mor. 100/A3
'Aïn el Bey (int'l arpt.), Alg. 100/K6
'Aïn el Hammam, Alg. 100/H4
'Aïn el Turk, Alg. 100/D2
'Aïn Fakroun, Alg. 100/K6
'Aïn M'lila, Alg. 100/K6
'Aïn Oulmene, Alg. 100/H5
'Aïn Oussersa, Alg. 100/G5
'Aïn Sefra, Alg. 99/E2
Aïn Taoujdat, Mor. 100/B3
'Aïn Taya, Alg. 100/G4
'Aïn Temouchent, Alg. 100/D2
'Aïn Touta, Alg. 100/H5
Aina Haina, Hi, US 124/W13
Aincourt, Fr. 30/H4
Aínos (peak), Gre. 47/G3
Aínos NP, Gre. 47/G3
Aipe, Col. 152/C4
Aïr (plat.), Niger 96/G4
Air Force (isl.), Nun., Can. 123/J2
Airaines, Fr. 52/A4
Airdrie, Ab, Can. 126/E3
Airdrie, Sc, UK 36/C5
Aire (riv.), Fr. 42/F2
Aire, Canal d' (canal), Fr. 52/B2
Aire-sur-la-Lys, Fr. 52/B2
Aire-sur-l'Adour, Fr. 42/C5
Airolo, Swi. 57/E4
Airuno, It. 58/C1
Airvault, Fr. 42/C3
Aisch (riv.), Ger. 43/J2
Aiseau-Presles, Belg. 53/D3
Aisén del General Carlos Ibáñez del Campo (pol. reg.), Chile 158/B5
Aisne (riv.), Fr. 40/B4
Aïssa (peak), Alg. 99/E2
Aist (riv.), Aus. 55/H6
Aït Ourir, Mor. 98/D3
Aitape, PNG 116/D5
Aitō, Japan 77/K5
Aitolikón, Gre. 47/G3
Aitrach, Ger. 57/G2
Aitrang, Ger. 57/G2
Aitutaki Atoll (isl.), Cookls. 117/J6
Aiud, Rom. 49/F2
Aiuruoca, Braz. 211/J6
Aiuruoca (riv.), Braz. 211/J7
Aix-en-Provence, Fr. 42/F5
Aíyina, Gre. 47/H4
Aiyínion, Gre. 47/H2
Aíyion, Gre. 47/H3
Aīzawl, India 83/F3
Aizu-Wakamatsu, Japan 75/F2
Ajaccio, Fr. 46/A2
Ajaccio, Golfe d' (gulf), It. 46/A2
Ajaigarh, India 84/C3
Ajalpan, Mex. 143/M8
Ajaria Aut. Rep., Geo. 63/G4
Ajax, On, Can. 131/R8
Ajay (riv.), India 85/F3
Ajdābiyā, Libya 97/K1
Ajdovščina, Slov. 43/K4
Ajigasawa, Japan 76/B3
'Ajjah, WBnk. 91/G7
Ajka, Hun. 48/C2
Ajo, Az, US 128/D4
Ajo (cape), Sp. 44/D1
Ajuchitlán del Progreso, Mex. 140/A4
Ajusco (vol.), Mex. 143/Q10
Aka (riv.), Japan 75/F1
Akabane, Japan 77/M6
Akabira, Japan 76/C2
Akaishi-dake (peak), Japan 75/F3
Akaltara, India 84/D4
Akan (lake), Japan 76/D2
Akan NP, Japan 76/D2
Åkarp, Swe. 38/E4
Akarsu, Turk. 90/D2
Akashi, Japan 77/G6
Akashi (str.), Japan 77/G6
Akbarpur, India 84/D2
Akbarpur, India 84/B2
Akbaytal (pass), Taj. 87/F5
Akbou, Alg. 100/H4
Akçaabat, Turk. 90/D1
Akçakale, Turk. 90/D2
Akçakoca, Turk. 49/K5
Akçaova, Turk. 49/J5
Akçapınar, Turk. 90/D2
Akçay, Turk. 91/A1
Akchār (riv.), Mrta. 96/B4
Akchâr (phys. reg.), Mrta. 98/B5
Akdağmadeni, Turk. 62/E5
Akechi, Japan 77/M5
Akeno, Japan 77/E1
Akeno, Japan 77/A2
Åkersberga, Swe. 38/H2
Akershus (co.), Nor. 37/D3
Aketi, D.R. Congo 97/K7
Akhalts'ikhe, Geo. 63/G4
Akharnaí, Gre. 47/N8
Akhelóos (riv.), Gre. 47/G3
Akhiok, Ak, US 134/H4
Akhisar, Turk. 90/A2
Akhnūr, India 86/C3
Akhtopol, Bul. 49/H4
Akhtuba (riv.), Rus. 63/H3
Akhtubinsk, Rus. 63/H2
Aki, Japan 74/C4
Aki (riv.), Japan 77/C2
Akiachak, Ak, US 134/F3
Akigawa, Japan 77/C2
Akimiski (isl.), On, Can. 123/H3
Akıncı (pt.), Turk. 91/D1
Akıncılar, Turk. 90/D1
Åkirkeby, Den. 38/F4
Akishima, Japan 77/C2
Akita (pref.), Japan 76/B4
Akita, Japan 76/B4
Akiyama, Japan 77/C2
Akjoujt, Mrta. 102/B2
Akka, Mor. 98/C3
Akkaraipattu, SrL. 82/D6
Akkerhaugen, Nor. 38/C2
Akkeshi, Japan 76/D2
'Akko, Isr. 91/D3
Akkrum, Neth. 50/C2
Aklavik, NW, Can. 134/L2
Akō, Japan 74/D3
Akora, Pak. 86/B2
Āk'ordat, Erit. 88/C5
Akören, Turk. 90/C2
Akosombo (dam), Gha. 103/F5
Akpatok (isl.), Qu, Can. 123/K2
Akpınar, Turk. 49/J5
Akqi, China 87/G4
Akranes, Ice. 37/M7
Åkrathos (cape), Gre. 47/J2
Åkrehamn, Nor. 38/A2
Akrítas (cape), Gre. 47/G4
Akron, Co, US 129/G2
Akron, Oh, US 130/D3
Akron, Pa, US 138/B3
Aksai Chin (reg.), China,India 70/C4
Aksaray, Turk. 90/C2
Aksaray (prov.), Turk. 90/C2
Aksay Kazakzu Zizhixian, China 70/F4
Akşehir, Turk. 90/B2
Akşehir Lake (lake), Turk. 90/B2
Akseki, Turk. 91/B1
Aksoran (peak), Kaz. 87/G3
Aksu, China 70/D3
Aksu, Turk. 91/B1
Aksu (riv.), Turk. 91/B1
Āksum, Eth. 88/C6
Aktepe, Turk. 91/E1
Aktí (pen.), Gre. 62/C4
Akto, China 87/G5
Akune, Japan 74/B4
Akure, Nga. 103/G5
Akureyri, Ice. 37/N6
Akuse, Gha. 103/F5
Akutan (isl.), Ak, US 134/E5
Akutan, Ak, US 134/E5
Akutan Pass (chan.), Ak, US 134/E5
Akwa Ibom (state), Nga. 103/G5
Akyab (Sittwe), Myan. 83/F3
Akyazı, Turk. 49/K5
Ål, Nor. 38/C1
Al 'āl, Jor. 91/D4
Al 'Amārah, Iraq 88/E2
Al Anbār (gov.), Iraq 90/E3
Al 'Aqabah, Jor. 91/D5
Al 'Arīsh, Egypt 91/C4
Al 'Ayn, UAE 89/G4
Al Azīzīyah, Libya 96/H1
Al 'Azīzīyah, Iraq 90/F3
Al Bāb, Syria 90/D2
Al Badrashayn, Egypt 91/B5
Al Baḩr Al Aḩmar (gov.), Egypt 101/C3
Al Bājūr, Egypt 91/B4
Al Balqā' (gov.), Jor. 91/D4
Al Balyanā, Egypt 101/B3
Al Başrah, Iraq 88/E2
Al Batrūn, Leb. 91/D2
Al Baydā, Libya 97/K1
Al Biqā' (gov.), Leb. 91/E2
Al Biqā' (valley), Leb. 91/D3
Al Bīrah, WBnk. 91/G8
Al Birkah, Libya 99/H4
Al Buḩayrah (gov.), Egypt 101/B2
Al Fāsher, Sudan 97/L5
Al Fatḩah, Iraq 90/E3
Al Fāw, Iraq 88/E3
Al Fayyum, Egypt 91/B5
Al Fayyūm (gov.), Egypt 101/B1
Al Ghurdaqah, Egypt 101/C3
Al Ḩadīthah, Iraq 90/E3
Al Ḩaḑr, Iraq 90/E3
Al Ḩaffah, Syria 91/E2
Al Ḩajar ash Sahrqī (mts.), Oman 89/G4
Al Hamādah al Hamrā (upland), Libya 96/H2
Al Ḩammāmāt, Tun. 46/B4
Al Ḩasakah, Syria 90/E2
Al Ḩasakah (prov.), Syria 90/E2
Al Ḩawāmidīyah, Egypt 91/B5
Al Ḩayy, Iraq 88/E2
Al Ḩillah, Iraq 90/F3
Al Hindīyah, Iraq 90/F3
Al Hirmil, Leb. 91/E2
Al Hoceima (prov.), Mor. 100/B2
Al Hoceima, Mor. 100/C2
Al Ḩudaydah, Yem. 88/D6
Al Hufūf, SAr. 88/E3
Al Iskandarīyah, Iraq 90/F3
Al Iskandarīyah, Egypt 91/A4
Al Iskandarīyah (gov.), Egypt 101/B1
Al Ismā'īlīyah, Egypt 91/C4
Al Ismā'īlīyah (gov.), Egypt 91/C4
Al Jabal Akaur (mts.), Oman 89/G4
Al Jaghbūb, Libya 97/K2
Al Jamm, Tun. 46/B5
Al Janub (gov.), Leb. 91/D3
Al Jifārah (plain), Libya 99/H2
Al Jīzah, Egypt 91/B4
Al Junaynah, Sudan 97/K5
Al Kāf, Tun. 100/L6
Al Kāf (gov.), Tun. 100/L6
Al Karak (gov.), Jor. 91/D4
Al Karak, Jor. 91/D4
Al Khābūrah, Oman 89/G4
Al Khalīl (Hebron), WBnk. 91/D4
Al Khāliş, Iraq 90/F3
Al Khānkah, Egypt 91/B4
Al Khārijah, Egypt 101/B3
Al Kharţūm Baḩrī (Khartoum North), Sudan 97/M4
Al Khubar, SAr. 88/F3
Al Khums, Libya 96/H1
Al Kiswah, Syria 91/E3
Al Kūfah, Iraq 90/F3
Al Kufrah, Libya 97/K3
Al Lādhiqīyah (prov.), Syria 90/C3
Al Lādhiqīyah (Latakia), Syria 91/D2
Al Madīnah, SAr. 88/C4
Al Madīnah al Fikrīyah, Egypt 88/B3
Al Mafraq (gov.), Jor. 91/E3
Al Mafraq, Jor. 91/E3
Al Maghrib (reg.), Mor. 96/E1
Al Maḩallah al Kubrá, Egypt 91/B4
Al Mahdīyah, Tun. 46/B5
Al Mahdīyah (prov.), Tun. 100/M7

168

Al Ma – Amist

Al Maḩmūdīyah, Egypt 91/B4
Al Mālikīyah, Syria 90/E2
Al Manşūrah, Egypt 91/B4
Al Manzilah, Egypt 91/B4
Al Marāghah, Egypt 101/B3
Al Marj, Libya 97/K1
Al Marsá, Tun. 46/B4
Al Maţarīyah, Egypt 91/C4
Al Mawşil (Mosul), Iraq 90/E2
Al Mayādīn, Syria 90/E3
Al Mazra'ah, Jor. 91/D4
Al Minyā (gov.), Egypt 101/B2
Al Miqdādīyah, Iraq 90/F3
Al Mubarraz, SAr. 88/E4
Al Mudawwarah, Jor. 91/D5
Al Mukallā, Yem. 88/E6
Al Muknīn, Tun. 46/B5
Al Munastīr, Tun. 46/B5
Al Munastīr (prov.), Alg. 100/M7
Al Murnāqīyah, Tun. 46/B4
Al Musayyib, Iraq 90/F3
Al Muthanná (gov.), Iraq 90/F4
Al Qābil, Oman 89/G4
Al Qaḑārif, Sudan 88/C6
Al Qādisīyah (gov.), Iraq 90/F4
Al Qāhirah (gov.), Egypt 101/B1
Al Qāhirah (Cairo) (cap.), Egypt 91/B5
Al Qā'im, Iraq 90/E3
Al Qāmishlī, Syria 90/E2
Al Qanāţir al Khayrīyah, Egypt 91/B4
Al Qanţarah, Egypt 91/C4
Al Qaşr, Jor. 91/D4
Al Qaşrayn (gov.), Tun. 100/L7
Al Qaşrayn, Tun. 100/L7
Al Qayrawān, Tun. 46/B5
Al Qayrawān (gov.), Tun. 46/A5
Al Qunayţirah (prov.), Syria 91/D3
Al Qunayţirah, Syria 91/D3
Al Qurnah, Iraq 88/E2
Al Quşayr, Syria 91/E2
Al Quţayfah, Syria 91/E3
Al Quwayrah, Jor. 91/D5
Al Ubayyiḑ, Sudan 97/M5
Al 'Uwaynāt (peak), Sudan 97/L3
Al Wādī Al Jadīd (gov.), Egypt 101/B3
Al Wāḩāt al Baḩrīyah (oasis), Egypt 101/B2
Al Wāḩāt al Khārijah (oasis), Egypt 101/B3
Al Wāsiţah, Egypt 91/B5
Al Yāmūn, WBnk. 91/G7
Ala (pt.), It. 46/B1
Ala, It. 59/E1
Alabama (riv.), Al,Ga, US 133/G4
Alabama (state), US 133/G3
Alabaster, Al, US 133/G3
Alaca, Turk. 90/C1
Alacalı, Turk. 49/J5
Alaçam, Turk. 90/C1
Alaçatı, Turk. 47/K3
Alachua, Fl, US 133/H4
Alacrán (reef), Mex. 144/D1
Alacranes (res.), Cuba 145/F1
Aladağ, Turk. 91/C1
Alaejos, Sp. 44/C2
Alagir, Rus. 63/H4
Alagna Valsesia, It. 58/A1
Alagnon (riv.), Fr. 42/E4
Alagoa Grande, Braz. 154/D2
Alagoas (state), Braz. 154/C3
Alagoinhas, Braz. 154/C4
Alagón (riv.), Sp. 44/C2
Alagón, Sp. 45/E2
Alajärvi, Fin. 60/D3
Alajuela, CR 145/E4
Alakanuk, Ak, US 134/F3
Alakol' (lake), Kaz. 70/D2
Alakol (lake), Kaz. 64/J5
Alalaú (riv.), Braz. 153/F5
Alamagan (isl.), NMar. 116/D3
'Alāmarvdasht (riv.), Iran 88/F3
Alameda, Ca, US 135/K11
Alaminos, Phil. 79/C4
Alamo (lake), Az, US 128/D4
Alamo, Mex. 144/B1
Alamo, Ca, US 135/K11
Alamo Heights, Tx, US 137/U21
Alamogordo, NM, US 129/F4
Alamor, Ecu. 156/A2
Álamos, Mex. 142/C3
Åland (isl.), Fin. 37/G3
Aland (riv.), Ger. 40/F2
Alanya, Turk. 91/C1
Alaotra (lake), Madg. 107/J7
Alapaha (riv.), Fl,Ga, US 133/H4
Alaplı, Turk. 49/K5
Alarcón, Embalse de (res.), Sp. 44/D3
Alaşehir, Turk. 90/B2
Alaska (state), US 134/G2
Alaska (range), Ak, US 134/G4
Alaska (pen.), Ak, US 134/G4
Alaska, Gulf of (gulf), Ak, US 134/J4
Alassio, It. 58/B5
Alatyr', Rus. 61/K5
Alaverdi, Arm. 63/H4
Alavus, Fin. 60/D3
Alaw (riv.), Wal, UK 34/D5
Alaw, Llyn (lake), Wal, UK 34/D5
Alayor, Sp. 44/C3
Alayskiy (mts.), Kyr. 87/F5
Alazeya (riv.), Rus. 65/R3
Alb (riv.), Ger. 54/B5
Alba, It. 43/H4
Alba (prov.), Rom. 49/F2
Alba de Tormes, Sp. 44/C2
Alba Fucens (ruin), It. 46/C1
Alba Iulia, Rom. 49/F2
Albacete, Sp. 44/E3
Albaida, Sp. 45/E3
Albairate, It. 58/B2
Albæk, Den. 38/D3
Albalate del Arzobispo, Sp. 45/E2
Alban, Fr. 42/E5
Albanel (lake), Qu, Can. 130/F1
Albania (ctry.) 75/F2
Albany, Austl. 112/C5
Albany (riv.), On, Can. 122/H3
Albany, Ca, US 135/K11
Albany, Ga, US 133/G4
Albany, Ky, US 130/C4
Albany, Mo, US 137/E5
Albany (cap.), NY, US 130/F3
Albany, Or, US 126/C4
Albany County (int'l arpt.), NY, US 130/F3
Albaredo d'Adige, It. 59/E2
Albarine (riv.), Fr. 56/B5
Albarracín, Sp. 44/E2
Albatross (bay), Austl. 109/D2
Albatross Rock (pt.), Namb. 106/A2
Albbruck, Ger. 56/E2
Albemarle (sound), NC, US 133/J2
Albemarle, NC, US 133/H3
Albemarle (pt.), Ecu. 156/E6
Alben (peak), It. 43/H4
Albenga, It. 58/B4
Alberche (riv.), Sp. 44/C2
Alberhill, Ca, US 136/C3
Alberndorf in der Riedmark, Aus. 55/H6
Alberschwende, Aus. 57/F3
Albersdorf, Ger. 38/C4
Albersweiler, Ger. 54/B4
Albert (lake), Austl. 115/A2
Albert (lake), Ugan.,D.R. 93/E4
Albert, Fr. 52/B3
Albert Kanaal (riv.), Belg. 53/E2
Albert Nile (riv.), Ugan. 97/M7
Alberta (prov.), Can. 122/E3
Alberti, Arg. 158/E2
Albertinia, SAfr. 106/C4
Albertirsa, Hun. 48/D2
Alberto de Agostini, PN, Chile 157/B7
Alberton, SAfr. 106/Q13
Albertshofen, Ger. 54/D3
Albertville, Al, US 133/G3
Albertville, Fr. 43/G4
Albestroff, Fr. 53/F6
Albeuve, Swi. 56/D4
Albi, Fr. 42/E5
Albignasego, It. 59/E2
Albina, Sur. 151/H2
Albinea, It. 58/D3
Albino, It. 58/C1
Albion, Mi, US 130/C3
Albisola Marina, It. 58/B4
Albisola Superiore, It. 58/B4
Alblasserdam, Neth. 50/B5
Albocácer, Sp. 45/E2
Alborán (isl.), Mor. 98/E1
Ålborg (bay), Den. 38/D3
Ålborg, Den. 38/C3
Albox, Sp. 44/D4
Albright-Knox Art Gallery, NY, US 131/S10
Albristhorn (peak), Swi. 56/D5
Albufeira, Port. 44/A4
Albula (riv.), Swi. 43/H3
Albuñol, Sp. 44/D4
Albuquerque (int'l arpt.), NM, US 128/F4
Albuquerque, NM, US 128/F4
Albuquerque, Cayos de (isls.), Col. 145/F3
Alburquerque, Sp. 44/B3
Alburtis, Pa, US 138/C3
Albury, Austl. 115/C3
Alby-sur-Chéran, Fr. 56/C6
Alca, Peru 156/C4
Alcabideche, Port. 45/P10
Alcácer do Sal, Port. 44/A3
Alcalá de Chivert, Sp. 45/F2
Alcalá de Guadaira, Sp. 44/C4
Alcalá de Henares, Sp. 45/N9
Alcalá de los Gazules, Sp. 44/C4
Alcalá la Real, Sp. 44/D4
Alcamo, It. 46/C4
Alcanadre (riv.), Sp. 45/E2
Alcanar, Sp. 45/E2
Alcañices, Sp. 44/B2
Alcañiz, Sp. 45/E2
Alcântara, Braz. 154/A1
Alcántara, Sp. 44/B3
Alcántara, Embalse de (res.), Sp. 44/B3
Alcantarilla, Sp. 44/E4
Alcaraz, Sp. 44/D3
Alcaraz, Sierra de (range), Sp. 44/D3
Alcatraz (isl.), Ca, US 135/K11
Alcatrazes, Ilha de (isl.), Braz. 211/H9
Alcaudete, Sp. 44/C4
Alcázar de San Juan, Sp. 44/D3
Alcira, Sp. 45/E3
Alcira, Arg. 158/D2
Alçıtepe, Turk. 47/K2
Alcoa, Tn, US 133/H3
Alcobaça, Braz. 154/C5
Alcobaça, Port. 44/A3
Alcobendas, Sp. 45/N8
Alcochete, Port. 45/Q10
Alcora, Sp. 45/E3
Alcorcón, Sp. 45/N9
Alcorisa, Sp. 45/E2
Alcoutim, Port. 44/B4
Alcoy, Sp. 45/E3
Alcúdia, Sp. 45/G3
Aldabra (isls.), Sey. 93/G5
Aldama, Mex. 132/B4
Aldama, Mex. 143/F4
Aldan (plat.), Rus. 65/N4
Aldan, Rus. 65/N4
Aldan (riv.), Rus. 67/N3
Alde (riv.), Eng, UK 33/H2
Aldeburgh, Eng, UK 33/H2
Aldeia Nova de São Bento, Port. 44/B4
Alden, Il, US 135/N15
Aldenhoven, Ger. 53/F2
Aldeno, It. 57/H6
Aldergrove (int'l arpt.), NI, UK 34/B2
Aldergrove, NI, UK 34/B2
Alderley Edge, Eng, UK 35/F5
Alderney (isl.), Chl, UK 42/B2
Aldershot, Eng, UK 33/F4
Alderwood Manor-Bothell North, Wa, US 135/C2
Aldine, Tx, US 129/J5
Aldingen, Ger. 57/E1
Aldred (lake), Pa, US 138/B4
Aldridge, Eng, UK 33/E1
Ale Water (riv.), Sc, UK 36/D6
Aleg, Mrta. 102/B2
Alegre, Braz. 155/D2
Alegrete, Braz. 157/E2
Alejandro Gallinal, Uru. 159/G2
Alejandro Roca, Arg. 158/E2
Alejandro Selkirk (isl.), Chile 147/A6
Alejo Ledesma, Arg. 158/E2
Aleknagik, Ak, US 134/G4
Aleksandrov, Rus. 60/H4
Aleksandrovac, Serb. 48/E4
Aleksandrovsk, Rus. 61/N4
Aleksandrów Kujawski, Pol. 41/K2
Aleksandrów Łódzki, Pol. 41/K3
Alekseyevka, Kaz. 87/F2
Alekseyevka, Kaz. 87/E2
Alekseyevka, Rus. 62/F2
Aleksin, Rus. 60/H5
Aleksinac, Serb. 48/E4
Além Paraíba, Braz. 211/L6
Alençon, Fr. 42/D2
Alenquer, Braz. 151/H4
Alenuihaha (chan.), US 124/T10
Alerce Andino, PN, Chile 158/B4
Aléria, Fr. 46/A1
Alert (pt.), Nun., Can. 123/S6
Aleşd, Rom. 48/F2
Alessandria (prov.), It. 58/B3
Alessandria, It. 58/B3
Ålestrup, Den. 38/C3
Ålesund, Nor. 37/C3
Aletschhorn (peak), Swi. 56/D5
Aleutian (range), Ak, US 134/G4
Aleutian (isls.), Ak, US 134/B5
Alexander (mt.), Austl. 112/B2
Alexander (arch.), Ak, US 134/L4
Alexander (isl.), Ant. 160/V
Alexander Bay, SAfr. 106/B3
Alexander City, Al, US 133/G3
Alexander Nevsky Abbey, Rus. 61/T7
Alexandria, Braz. 154/C2
Alexandria (int'l arpt.), Egypt 91/A4
Alexándria, Gre. 47/H2
Alexandra, NZ 117/R12
Alexandria, Rom. 49/G4
Alexandria, SAfr. 106/D4
Alexandria, La, US 129/J5
Alexandria, Mn, US 127/K4
Alexandria, Sc, UK 36/B5
Alexandria, Va, US 138/A6
Alexandrina (lake), Austl. 109/C4
Alexandroúpolis, Gre. 47/J2
Alexis Creek, BC, Can. 126/C2
Alfaro, Sp. 44/E1
Alfatar, Bul. 49/H4
Alfbach (riv.), Ger. 53/F3
Alfeld, Ger. 51/G5
Alfenas, Braz. 211/H6
Alfhausen, Ger. 51/E3
Alfiós (riv.), Gre. 47/G4
Alfonsine, It. 59/F3
Alfonso Bonilla Aragón (int'l arpt.), Col. 152/B4
Alfred NP, Austl. 115/D3
Alfreton, Eng, UK 35/G5
Alfter, Ger. 53/G2
Alga, Kaz. 63/L2
Ålgård, Nor. 38/A2
Algarrobo, Chile 158/N8
Algarve (reg.), Port. 44/A4
Algeciras, Sp. 44/C4
Algeciras, Col. 152/C4
Algemesí, Sp. 45/E3
Alger (prov.), Alg. 100/G4
Algeria (ctry.) 96/F2
Algermissen, Ger. 51/G4
Algete, Sp. 45/N8
Alghero, It. 46/A2
Algiers (El Djezair) (cap.), Alg. 100/G4
Algoa (bay), SAfr. 106/D4
Algodón (riv.), Peru 150/D4
Algodonales, Sp. 44/C4
Algoma, Wi, US 127/M4
Algona, Wa, US 135/C3
Algonac, Mi, US 135/G6
Algonquin, Il, US 135/P14
Algorta, Uru. 159/K10
Algueirão, Port. 45/P10
Algund (Lagundo), It. 57/H4
Alhama de Granada, Sp. 44/D4
Alhama de Murcia, Sp. 44/E4
Alhambra, Ca, US 136/F7
Alhandra, Braz. 154/D2
Alhandra, Port. 45/P10
Alhaurín el Grande, Sp. 44/C4
'Alī al Gharbī, Iraq 88/E2
'Alī ash Sharqī, Iraq 88/E2
Āli Bayramlı, Azer. 63/J5
Alia, It. 46/C4
Alía, Sp. 44/C3
Aliağa, Turk. 90/A2
Aliákmon (riv.), Gre. 47/G2
Aliákmonos (lake), Gre. 47/G2
Alíartos, Gre. 47/H3
Alibates Flint Quarries Nat'l Mon., Tx, US 129/G4
Alibey (lake), Ukr. 49/K3
Alibeyköy, Turk. 49/K5
Alicante, Sp. 45/E3
Alicante (int'l arpt.), Sp. 45/E3
Alice, Tx, US 132/D5
Alice (pt.), It. 47/E3
Alice Arm, BC, Can. 134/N4
Alice Springs, Austl. 113/G2
Aliceville, Al, US 133/F3
Alicia, Phil. 79/D6
Alicudi (isl.), It. 46/D3
Alicurá (res.), Arg. 158/C4
Alife, It. 46/D2
Alīganj, India 84/B2
Alijó, Port. 44/B2
Alima (riv.), Congo 96/J8
Alingār (riv.), Afg. 86/A2
Alingsås, Swe. 38/E3
Alīpur, Pak. 86/A5
Alīpur Duār, India 85/G2
Alīrājpur, India 89/K4
Alisos (riv.), Mex. 128/E5
Alistráti, Gre. 47/H2
Alivérion, Gre. 47/J3
Aliwal North, SAfr. 106/D3
Aljezur, Port. 44/A4
Aljustrel, Port. 44/A4
Alken, Belg. 53/E2
Alkmaar, Neth. 50/B3
Alkoum (well), Alg. 99/H4
Alkoven, Aus. 55/H6
Allada, Ben. 103/F5
Allahābād, India 84/C3
Allakaket, Ak, US 134/H2
Allaman, Swi. 56/C5
Allan (hills), Sk, Can. 127/G3
Allan, Sk, Can. 127/G3
Alland, Aus. 55/J6
Allanmyo, Myan. 83/G4
Allanridge, SAfr. 106/D2
Allanson, Austl. 112/C5
'Allāq (well), Libya 96/H1
Allariz, Sp. 44/B1
Alle, Swi. 56/D3
Allegan, Mi, US 130/C3
Allegheny (plat.), US 130/E3
Allegheny (riv.), US 130/D3
Allegheny (mts.), US 125/K4
Allen (riv.), Eng, UK 32/B5
Allen, Arg. 158/D3
Allen Park, Mi, US 135/F7
Allendale, SC, US 133/H3
Allendale, NJ, US 139/J7
Allende, Mex. 132/C4
Allende, Mex. 143/E3
Allendorf, Ger. 51/F6
Allensbach, Ger. 57/F2
Allenspark, Co, US 137/A2
Allentown, Pa, US 138/C2
Allentsteig, Aus. 41/H4
Allenwood, Pa, US 138/B1
Alleppey, India 82/C6
Aller (riv.), Ger. 51/H3
Allerkanal (canal), Ger. 51/H4
Allersberg, Ger. 54/E4
Allershausen, Ger. 55/E6
Allgäu Alps (range), Aus.,Ger. 40/F5
Alliance, Ne, US 127/H5
Alliance, Oh, US 130/D3
Allied War Cemetery, Myan. 78/B2
Allier (riv.), Fr. 42/E3
Alligator (pt.), La, US 137/Q16
Allingåbro, Den. 38/D3
Allinges, Fr. 56/C5
Alloa, Sc, UK 36/C4
Allonnes, Fr. 42/D3
Allora, Austl. 114/C5
Allos, Fr. 43/G4
Alloway, NJ, US 138/C4
Allschwil, Swi. 56/D2
Alm (riv.), Aus. 55/G7
Alma, Mi, US 130/C3
Alma, Qu, Can. 131/G1
Almacelles, Sp. 45/F2
Almada, Port. 45/P10
Almadén, Sp. 44/C3
Almafuerte, Arg. 158/D2
Almagro, Sp. 44/D3
Almanor (lake), Ca, US 128/B2
Almansa, Sp. 45/E3
Almanza, Sp. 44/C1
Almanzor, Pico de (peak), Sp. 44/C2
Almanzora (riv.), Sp. 44/D4
Almas (riv.), Braz. 151/J6
Almas, Braz. 154/A3
Almas, Pico das (peak), Braz. 154/B4
Almaty (int'l arpt.), Kaz. 87/G4
Almaty, Kaz. 87/G4
Almazán, Sp. 44/D2
Almazora, Sp. 45/E3
Almeida, Port. 44/B2
Almeirim, Braz. 151/H4
Almeirim, Port. 44/A3
Almelo, Neth. 50/D4
Almenara, Braz. 154/B5
Almenara (peak), Sp. 44/D3
Almenara, Sp. 45/E3
Almendra, Embalse de (res.), Sp. 44/B2
Almendralejo, Sp. 44/B3
Almenno San Salvatore, It. 58/C1
Almere, Neth. 50/C4
Almería, Sp. 44/D4
Almería, Golfo de (gulf), Sp. 44/D4
Al'met'yevsk, Rus. 61/M5
Älmhult, Swe. 38/F3
Almina (pt.), Sp. 100/B2
Almirós, Gre. 47/H3
Almiroú (gulf), Gre. 47/J5
Almodôvar, Port. 44/A4
Almodóvar del Campo, Sp. 44/C3
Almodóvar del Río, Sp. 44/C4
Almoharín, Sp. 44/B3
Almond (riv.), Sc, UK 36/C4
Almont (riv.), Fr. 30/L6
Almonte, On, Can. 130/E2
Almonte, Sp. 44/B4
Almora, India 84/B1
Almoradí, Sp. 45/E3
Almorox, Sp. 44/C2
Almte. Montt (gulf), Chile 159/B7
Almudévar, Sp. 45/E1
Almuñécar, Sp. 44/D4
Almus, Turk. 90/D1
Alness, Sc, UK 36/B1
Alness (riv.), Sc, UK 36/B1
Alnwick, Eng, UK 36/E6
Alofi (isl.), Wall. 116/H6
Alofi, NZ 117/J6
Along, India 83/G2
Alónnisos (isl.), Gre. 47/H3
Alor (isls.), Indo. 81/F5
Alor Setar, Malay. 83/H6
Álora, Sp. 44/C4
Alotau, PNG 116/E6
Aloysius (mt.), Austl. 113/F3
Alpachiri, Arg. 158/E3
Alpe di Poti (peak), It. 59/E6
Alpedrete, Sp. 45/M8
Alpen, Ger. 50/D5
Alpena, Mi, US 130/D2
Alpercatas (riv.), Braz. 154/A2
Alpercatas, Serra das (mts.), Braz. 151/J5
Alperschällihorn (peak), Swi. 57/F4
Alpes de Provence (range), Fr. 43/G5
Alpha, Austl. 114/B3
Alpha, NJ, US 138/C2
Alphen aan de Rijn, Neth. 50/B4
Alpi Apuane (range), It. 43/J4
Alpi Dolomitiche (range), It. 43/J4
Alpi Orobie (range) It. 43/J3
Alpiarça, Port. 44/A3
Alpine, NJ, US 139/K8
Alpine, Ut, US 137/K13
Alpine, Wy, US 126/F5
Alpirsbach, Ger. 57/E1
Alpnach, Swi. 57/E4
Alps (mts.), Eur. 27/E4
Alqōsh, Iraq 90/E2
Als (isl.), Den. 40/F1
Alsace (pol. reg.), Fr. 40/D4
Alsager, Eng, UK 35/F5
Alsask, Sk, Can. 126/F3
Alsasua, Sp. 44/D1
Alsdorf, Ger. 53/F2
Alsenz (riv.), Ger. 53/G4
Alsenz, Ger. 53/G4
Alsfeld, Ger. 43/H1
Alsheim, Ger. 54/B3
Alsip, Il, US 135/Q16
Alstahaug, Nor. 37/E2
Alster (riv.), Ger. 51/H1
Alsting, Fr. 53/F5
Alstonville, Austl. 115/E1
Alt (riv.), Eng, UK 35/E4
Alta, Ut, US 137/K12
Alta, Nor. 37/G1
Alta Floresta, Braz. 151/G5
Alta Gracia, Arg. 157/D3
Altach, Aus. 57/F3
Altadena, Ca, US 136/F7
Altagracia, Nic. 144/E4
Altai (mts.), Asia 70/E2
Altamaha (riv.), Ga, US 140/E1
Altamira, Braz. 151/H4
Altamira, Mex. 144/B1
Altamira do Maranhão, Braz. 154/A2
Altamonte Springs, Fl, US 133/H4
Altamura, It. 46/E2
Altar, Mex. 142/C2
Altar (vol.), Ecu. 152/B5
Altar de los Sacrificios (ruin), Guat. 144/D2
Altar, Desierto de (des.), Mex. 128/D4
Altare, It. 58/B4
Altavilla Vicentina, It. 59/E1
Altay, China 70/E2
Altay, Mong. 70/E2
Altay, Mong. 70/G2
Altay, Resp., Rus. 64/J4
Altayskiy Kray, Rus. 87/G2
Altdorf, Swi. 57/E4
Altdorf bei Nürnberg, Ger. 55/E4
Altea, Sp. 45/E3
Altedo, It. 59/E3
Altena, Ger. 51/E6
Altenahr, Ger. 53/G2
Altenau, Ger. 51/H5
Altenau (riv.), Ger. 51/F5
Altenbeken, Ger. 51/F5
Altenberg bei Linz, Aus. 55/H6
Altenburg, Ger. 40/G3
Altenfelden, Aus. 55/G6
Altenglan, Ger. 53/G4
Altengottern, Ger. 51/H6
Altenkirchen, Ger. 53/G2
Altenmünster, Ger. 54/D6
Altenstadt, Ger. 57/G1
Altenstadt, Ger. 54/B2
Altensteig, Ger. 54/B5
Altentreptow, Ger. 38/E5
Altepexi, Mex. 143/M8
Alter Rhein (riv.), Ger. 50/D5
Altes Land (phys. reg.), Ger. 51/G1
Altheim, Aus. 55/G6
Althengstett, Ger. 54/B5
Althofen, Aus. 43/L3
Althütte, Ger. 54/C5
Altındere NP, Turk. 90/D1
Altınözü, Turk. 91/E2
Altıntaş, Turk. 90/B2
Altınyaka, Turk. 90/B2
Altınyayla, Turk. 91/A1
Altiplano (plat.), Bol.,Peru 147/C4
Altkirch, Fr. 56/D2
Altlandsberg, Ger. 40/Q6
Altmark (phys. reg.), Ger. 40/F2
Altmühl (riv.), Ger. 43/J2
Altmünster, Aus. 55/G7
Altnaharra, Sc, UK 31/R7
Alto (peak), Braz. 154/A4
Alto (peak), It. 57/G4
Alto Araguaia, Braz. 151/H7
Alto de Tamar (peak), Col. 152/C3
Alto Garças, Braz. 151/H7
Alto Lucero, Mex. 143/N7
Alto Parnaíba, Braz. 154/A3
Alto Purús (riv.), Peru 150/D6
Alto Santo, Braz. 154/C2
Alto Yuruá (riv.), Peru 156/C3
Altomünster, Ger. 54/E6
Alton, La, US 137/Q16
Alton, Il, US 137/G8
Alton, Eng, UK 33/F4
Altona, Mb, Can. 127/J3
Altoona, Pa, US 130/E3
Altopascio, It. 59/D5
Altos, Braz. 154/B2
Altos de Campana NP, Pan. 152/B2
Altotonga, Mex. 143/M7
Altötting, Ger. 55/F6
Altrincham, Eng, UK 35/F5
Altrip, Ger. 54/B4
Altun (mts.), China 67/H6
Altun Ha (ruin), Belz. 144/D2
Alturas, Ca, US 126/C5
Altus (res.), Ok, US 129/H4
Altus, Ok, US 129/H4
Altzayanca, Mex. 143/M7
Alucra, Turk. 90/D1
Aluminé, Arg. 158/C3
Alunda, Swe. 38/H1
Ālūs, Iraq 90/E3
Alushta, Ukr. 62/E3
Alva, Ok, US 129/H3
Alva, Sc, UK 36/C4
Alvalade, Port. 44/A4
Alvängen, Swe. 38/E3
Alvarado, Mex. 143/P8
Álvarez, Arg. 158/E2
Alvaro Obregón, Presa (dam), Mex. 142/C2
Alvdal, Nor. 37/D3
Älvdalen, Swe. 38/F1
Alverca, Port. 45/P10
Alveringem, Belg. 52/B1
Alvesta, Swe. 38/F3
Ålvik, Nor. 38/B1
Alvin, Tx, US 129/J5
Alvito, Port. 44/B3
Älvkarleby, Swe. 38/G1
Alvorada, Braz. 155/A4
Alvorada do Norte, Braz. 154/A4
Älvsborg (co.), Swe. 37/E4
Älvsbyn, Swe. 37/G2
Alwen (riv.), Wal, UK 34/E5
Alxa Youqi, China 70/H4
Alxa Zuoqi, China 70/J4
Alyawarra Abor. Land, Austl. 113/G2
Alyth, Sc, UK 36/C3
Alytus, Lith. 39/L4
Alz (riv.), Ger. 43/K2
Alzano Lombardo, It. 58/C1
Alzenau in Unterfranken, Ger. 54/C2
Alzette (riv.), Lux. 53/F4
Alzey, Ger. 54/B3
Am Timan, Chad 97/K5
Ama, La, US 137/P17
Amacayacú, PN, Col. 150/D4
Amacuro (riv.), Ven. 153/F2
Amacuro (delta), Ven. 153/F2
Amacuzac (riv.), Mex. 143/K8
Amadeus (lake), Austl. 109/C3
Amadjuak (lake), Nun., Can. 123/J2
Amadora, Port. 45/P10
Amagansett, NY, US 139/F2
Amagansett NWR, NY, US 139/F2
Amagasaki, Japan 77/H6
Amagi, Japan 74/B4
Amagi-san (peak), Japan 75/F3
Amaguaña, Ecu. 152/B5
Amajac (riv.), Mex. 143/N7
Åmål, Swe. 38/E2
Amala (riv.), Kenya 104/B3
Amalfi, Col. 152/C3
Amalia, SAfr. 106/D2
Amaliás, Gre. 47/G4
Amaluza, Ecu. 156/B2
Amambaí, Braz. 157/E1
Amambaí (riv.), Braz. 151/H8
Amami (isls.), Japan 67/M7
Amami-O-Shima (isl.), Japan 75/K6
Amanã (lake), Braz. 150/F4
Amance, Fr. 56/C2
Amānganj, India 84/C3
Amāngarh, Pak. 86/A2
Amantea, It. 46/E3
Amanu (isl.), FrPol. 117/L6
Amanzimtoti, SAfr. 107/E3
Amapá, Braz. 151/H3
Amapá (state), Braz. 153/H4
Amarante, Braz. 154/B2
Amarante, Port. 44/A2
Amarante do Marahão, Braz. 154/A2
Amarapura, Myan. 83/G3
Amareleja, Port. 44/B3
Amargosa, Braz. 154/C4
Amargosa (riv.), Ca, US 128/C3
Amarillo, Tx, US 129/G4
Amaro (peak), It. 46/D1
Amarpātan, India 84/C3
Amarume, Japan 76/A4
Amarwāra, India 84/B4
Amasra, Turk. 49/L5
Amasya, Turk. 90/C1
Amasya (prov.), Turk. 90/C1
Amata, Austl. 113/F3
Amatlán de Cañas, Mex. 142/D4
Amatsukominato, Japan 77/E3
Amawalk (res.), NY, US 139/E1
Amay, Belg. 53/E2
Amayuca, Mex. 143/L8
Amazon (Amazonas) (riv.), Braz.,Per 156/C1
Amazonas, Cuba 145/G1
Amazonas (state), Braz. 152/C5
Amazonas (Amazon) (riv.), Braz.,Per 156/C1
Amazônia, PN da (Tapajós), Braz. 151/G4
Ambāh, India 84/B2
Ambahikily, Madg. 107/G8
Ambajogai, India 89/L5
Ambāla Sadar, India 86/D4
Ambalangoda, SrL. 82/D6
Ambalavao, Madg. 107/H8
Ambam, Camr. 96/H7
Ambanja, Madg. 107/J6
Ambaro (bay), Madg. 107/J6
Ambato, Ecu. 152/B5
Ambato Boeny, Madg. 107/H7
Ambatofinandrahana, Madg. 107/H8
Ambatolampy, Madg. 107/H7
Ambatomaidy, Madg. 107/H7
Ambatomanoina, Madg. 107/H7
Ambatondrazaka, Madg. 107/J7
Ambazac, Fr. 42/D4
Ámbelos (cape), Gre. 47/H3
Amberg, Ger. 55/E4
Ambergris Cay (isl.), Belz. 144/E2
Ambérieu-en-Bugey, Fr. 56/B6
Amberloup, Belg. 53/E3
Ambikāpur, India 84/D4
Ambilobe, Madg. 107/J6
Ambinanindrano, Madg. 107/J8
Ambinanitelo, Madg. 107/J6
Ambler, Ak, US 134/G2
Ambler, Pa, US 138/C3
Amblève (riv.), Belg. 40/C3
Amblève, Belg. 53/F3
Ambo, Peru 156/B3
Amboasary, Madg. 107/H9
Amboavory, Madg. 107/J7
Ambodifototra, Madg. 107/J7
Ambodiharina, Madg. 107/J8
Ambohidratrimo, Madg. 107/H7
Ambohijanahary, Madg. 107/J7
Ambohimahasoa, Madg. 107/H8
Ambohimandroso, Madg. 107/H7
Ambohinihaonana, Madg. 107/H8
Ambohitsilaozana, Madg. 107/J7
Ambolomoty, Madg. 107/H7
Ambon (isl.), Indo. 81/G4
Ambon, Indo. 81/G4
Ambondro, Madg. 107/H9
Amboni Caves, Tanz. 104/C4
Amborompotsy, Madg. 107/H8
Amboseli NP, Kenya 104/C3
Ambositra, Madg. 107/H8
Ambovombe, Madg. 107/H9
Ambrym (isl.), Van. 116/F6
Amchitka (isl.), Ak, US 134/B6
Amchitka Pass (chan.), Ak, US 134/B6
Amealco, Mex. 143/K6
Ameca, Mex. 142/D4
Amecameca de Juárez, Mex. 143/R10
Ameghino, Arg. 158/E2
Ameglia, It. 58/C4
Ameisberg (peak), Aus. 55/G5
Ameland (isl.), Neth. 50/C2
Amelia, It. 46/C1
Amelinghausen, Ger. 51/H2
Amer (chan.), Neth. 50/B5
American (lake), Wa, US 135/B3
American (riv.), Ca, US 135/M9
American Falls (mts.), Id, US 128/D2
American Fork, Ut, US 137/K13
American, North Fork (riv.), Ca, US 128/B3
American Samoa (dpcy.), US 117/H6
American, South Fork (riv.), Ca, US 128/B3
Americana, Braz. 155/C2
Americus, Ga, US 133/G3
Ameringkogel (peak), Aus. 43/L3
Amersfoort, SAfr. 107/E2
Amersfoort, Neth. 50/C4
Amersham, Eng, UK 33/F3
Amery Ice Shelf, Ant. 160/E
Amesbury, Eng, UK 33/E4
Amet, India 89/K3
Amethi, India 84/C2
Amfíklia, Gre. 47/H3
Amfilokhía, Gre. 47/G3
Ámfissa, Gre. 47/H3
Amga (riv.), Rus. 65/P3
Amguema (riv.), Rus. 65/T3
Amgun' (riv.), Rus. 65/P4
Amherst, NS, Can. 131/H2
Amherst, NY, US 131/S10
Amherstburg, On, Can. 135/F7
Ami, Japan 77/E1
Amiata (peak), It. 43/J5
Amiens, Fr. 52/B4
Amik (lake), Turk. 90/D2
Amila (isl.), Ak, US 134/D6
Amilcar Cabral (int'l arpt.), CpV. 93/K10
Amillis, Fr. 30/M5
Amindaion, Gre. 47/G2
Aminu Kano (int'l arpt.), Nga. 103/H3
Amisk (lake), Sk, Can. 127/H2
Amistad (res.), Mex.,US 140/A2
Amistad Nat'l Rec. Area, Tx, US 129/G5

169

Amite – Argen

Amite, La, US 129/K5
Amityville, NY, US 139/M9
Amla, India 84/B5
Āmlāgora, India 85/F4
Āmli, Nor. 38/C2
'Ammān (gov.), Jor. 91/E4
Amman (riv.), Wal, UK 32/C3
Amman ('Ammān) (cap.), Jor. 91/D4
Ammanford, Wal, UK 32/C3
Ammarfjället (peak), Swe. 37/E2
Ammassalik, Grld 160/J
Ammer (riv.), Ger. 54/B5
Ammerman (mtn.), Yk, Can. 134/K2
Ammersee (lake), Ger. 43/J3
Amnéville, Fr. 53/F5
Āmol, Iran 88/F1
Amora, Port. 45/P10
Amorbach, Ger. 54/C3
Amorgós, Gre. 47/J4
Amorgós (isl.), Gre. 47/J4
Amory, Ms, US 133/F3
Amos, Qu, Can. 130/E1
Åmot, Nor. 38/B2
Amotfors, Swe. 38/E2
Amozoc, Mex. 143/L7
Ampachi, Japan 77/L5
Ampanefena, Madg. 107/J6
Ampangalana (canal), Madg. 107/J8
Ampanihy, Madg. 107/H9
Amparafaravola, Madg. 107/J7
Amparai, SrL. 82/D6
Amparo, Braz. 211/G7
Ampasindava (bay), Madg. 107/H6
Ampato (peak), Peru 156/D4
Ampefy, Madg. 107/H7
Amper (riv.), Ger. 55/E6
Ampfing, Ger. 55/F6
Ampflwang im Hausruckwald, Aus. 55/G6
Ampitatafika, Madg. 107/H7
Amposta, Sp. 45/F2
Amqui, Qu, Can. 131/H1
Amravati, India 82/C3
Amreli, India 89/K4
'Amrīt (ruin), Syria 91/D2
Amritsar, India 86/C4
Amroha, India 84/B1
Amrum (isl.), Ger. 40/E1
Amstel (riv.), Neth. 50/B4
Amstelveen, Neth. 50/B4
Amsterdam, NY, US 130/F3
Amsterdam, SAfr. 107/E2
Amsterdam (cap.), Neth. 50/B4
Amsterdam (isl.), Fr. 23/N7
Amsterdam Rijnkanaal (riv.), Neth. 50/C4
Amsterdam (Schipol) (int'l arpt.), Neth. 50/B4
Amstetten, Aus. 43/L2
Amu Darya (riv.), Asia 67/F8
Amudat, Ugan. 104/B2
Amukta Pass (chan.), Ak, US 134/D5
Amuku (mts.), Guy. 153/G4
Amund Ringnes (isl.), Nun., Can. 123/S7
Amundsen (gulf), NW, Can. 122/D1
Amundsen (bay), Ant. 160/D
Amundsen (sea), Ant. 160/S
Amundsen-Scott, US, Ant. 160/A
Amunge (lake), Swe. 38/F1
Amur (riv.), Rus. 71/P2
Amurrio, Sp. 44/D1
Amurskaya Oblast, Rus. 65/N4
Amyūn, Leb. 91/D2
An Nabk, Syria 91/E2
An Nahūd, Sudan 97/L5
An Najaf, Iraq 90/F4
An Najaf (gov.),Iraq 90/E4
An Nāşirīyah,Iraq 88/E2
An Nu'manīyah,Iraq 90/F3
An Teallach (peak), Sc, UK 36/A1
An Uaimh, Ire. 31/Q10
Ana María (gulf), Cuba 141/F3
Anaa (isl.), FrPol. 117/L6
Anabar (riv.), Rus. 65/L3
'Anabtā, WBnk. 91/G7
Anachucuna (mtn.), Pan. 152/B2
Anaco, Ven. 153/E2
Anaconda-Deer Lodge County, Mt, US 126/E4
Anadarko, Ok, US 129/H4
Anadyr' (gulf), Rus. 67/T3
Anadyr' (range), Rus. 160/U
Anadyr' (riv.), Rus. 67/S3
Anadyr', Rus. 65/T3
Anáfi (isl.), Gre. 47/J4
Anaheim, Ca, US 136/G8
Anahim Lake, BC, Can. 126/B2
Anáhuac, Mex. 132/C5
Anahuac, Tx, US 132/E4
Anahuac, Mex. 142/D2
Anak, NKor. 73/C3
Anakāpalle, India 82/D4
Anaktuvuk Pass, Ak, US 134/H2
Analalava, Madg. 107/H6
Analamaitso (plat.), Madg. 107/J7
Analavory, Madg. 107/H7
Anambas (isls.), Indo. 80/C3
Anambra (state), Nga. 103/G5
Anamur, Turk. 91/C1
Anamur (pt.), Turk. 91/C1
Anan, Japan 74/D4
Anand, India 89/K4
Ananea, Peru 156/D4
Ananea, Bol. 156/D4
Anantapur, India 82/C5
Anantnag, India 86/C3
Anapa, Rus. 62/F3
Añapi (peak), Arg. 159/C6
Anápolis, Braz. 151/J7
Anapu (riv.), Braz. 151/H4
Anār, Iran 89/G2
Anārak, Iran 88/F2
Anastácio, Braz. 151/G8
'Anātā, WBnk. 91/G8
Anathan (isl.), NMar. 116/D3
Anatolia (reg.), Turk. 90/B2
Añatuya, Arg. 157/D2
Anauá (riv.), Braz. 150/F3
Ancash (dept.), Peru 156/B3
Anchieta, Braz. 155/D2
Anchor (bay), Mi, US 135/G6
Anchor Point, Ak, US 134/H4
Anchorage, Ak, US 134/J3
Anchorville, Mi, US 135/G6
Anchovy, Jam. 145/G2
Ancient City of Oc-Eo, Viet. 78/D4
Ancoeur (riv.), Fr. 30/L6
Ancohuma (peak), Bol. 156/D4
Ancón, Peru 156/B3
Ancón de Sardinas (bay), Col. 152/B4
Ancona (prov.), It. 59/G5
Ancona, It. 59/G5
Ancoraimes, Bol. 156/D4
Ancre (riv.), Fr. 52/B3
Ancrum, Sc, UK 36/D5
Ancud, Chile 158/B4
Ancud, Golfo de (gulf), Chile 157/B5
Anda, China 71/N2
Andacollo, Arg. 158/C3
Andagua, Peru 156/C4
Andahuaylas, Peru 156/C4
Andāl, India 85/F4
Åndalsnes, Nor. 37/C3
Andalucia (aut. comm.), Sp. 44/C4
Andalusia, Al, US 133/G4
Andalusia (reg.), Sp. 44/C4
Andaman (sea), Asia 67/J8
Andaman (isls.), India 67/H8
Andaman and Nicobar (isls.), India 83/F5
Andamarca, Peru 156/C3
Andamooka, Austl. 113/H4
Andapa, Madg. 107/J6
Andaraí, Braz. 154/B4
Andau, Aus. 43/M3
Andebu, Nor. 38/D2
Andechs, Ger. 57/H2
Andeer, Swi. 57/F4
Andelfingen, Swi. 57/E2
Andelle (riv.), Fr. 52/A5
Andelot-Blancheville, Fr. 56/B1
Andelsbach (riv.), Ger. 57/F2
Andelu, Fr. 30/H5
Andemaka, Madg. 107/H8
Andenne, Belg. 53/E3
Anderlues, Belg. 53/D3
Andermatt, Swi. 57/E4
Andernach, Ger. 53/G3
Anderson (riv.), NW, Can. 122/D2
Anderson, Ak, US 134/J3
Anderson, Ca, US 128/B2
Anderson, In, US 130/C3
Anderson, SC, US 133/H3
Anderson, Tx, US 129/J5
Anderson (inlet), Wa, US 135/B3
Anderson (isl.), Wa, US 135/B3
Andes (mts.), SAm. 147/C5
Andes, Cordillera de los (mts.), SAm. 157/B4
Andevoranto, Madg. 107/J7
Andfjorden (chan.), Nor. 37/F1
Andhra Pradesh (state), India 70/D8
Andijk, Neth. 50/C3
Andijon (pol. reg.), Uzb. 87/F4
Andijon, Uzb. 87/F4
Andikíthira (isl.), Gre. 47/H5
Andilamena, Madg. 107/J7
Andilanatoby, Madg. 107/J7
Andīmeshk, Iran 88/E2
Andíparos (isl.), Gre. 47/J4
Andira, Braz. 155/B2
Ándissa, Gre. 47/J3
Andkhvoy, Afg. 87/E5
Andohajango, Madg. 107/J6
Andong, SKor. 74/A2
Andorf, Aus. 55/G6
Andorno Micca, It. 58/B1
Andorra (ctry.) 45/F1
Andorra, Sp. 45/E2
Andorra la Vella (cap.), And. 42/D5
Andover, Eng, UK 33/E4
Andover, NJ, US 138/D2
Andøy, Nor. 37/F1
Andøya (isl.), Nor. 37/E1
Andradas, Braz. 211/G7
Andradina, Braz. 155/B2
Andraitx, Sp. 45/G3
Andramasina, Madg. 107/H7
Andranolava, Madg. 107/H8
Andranomavo (riv.), Madg. 107/H7
Andranopasy, Madg. 107/G8
Andreanof (isls.), Ak, US 134/C6
Andrelândia, Braz. 211/J6
Andrespol, Pol. 41/K3
Andrésy, Fr. 30/J5
Andrezel, Fr. 30/L6
Andria, It. 46/E2
Andriba, Madg. 107/H7
Andringitra (mts.), Madg. 107/H8
Andrítsaina, Gre. 47/G4
Androka, Madg. 107/H9
Androntany (cape), Madg. 107/J6
Ándros, Gre. 47/J4
Ándros (isl.), Gre. 47/J4
Andros (isl.), Bahm. 141/F3
Androscoggin (riv.), US 131/G2
Andújar, Sp. 44/C3
Aneby, Swe. 38/F3
Anecón Grande (peak), Arg. 158/C4
Anegada (isl.), UK 141/J4
Anegada (bay), Arg. 158/E4
Anegada Passage (chan.), NAm. 141/J4
Aného, Togo 103/F5
Aneityum (isl.), Van. 116/F7
Añelo, Arg. 158/C3
Aneto, Pico de (peak), Sp. 45/F1
Anfu, China 83/K2
Ang Nam Ngum (res.), Laos 83/H4
Ang Thong, Thai. 78/C3
Angamos (pt.), Chile 157/B1
Angara (riv.), Rus. 67/J4
Angaston, Austl. 113/H5
Angel (riv.), Ger. 51/E5
Ángel (falls), Ven. 153/F3
Angeles, Phil. 79/D4
Angeles National Forest, Ca, US 136/B1
Ängelholm, Swe. 38/E3
Angelholm (int'l arpt.), Swe. 38/E3
Angelina (riv.), Tx, US 129/J5
Angeln (reg.), Ger. 40/E1
Angelus (lake), Mi, US 135/F6
Angera, It. 58/B1
Ångermanalven (riv.), Swe. 37/E2
Angermünde, Ger. 41/H2
Angers, Fr. 42/C3
Anghiari, It. 59/F5
Angical do Piauí, Braz. 154/B2
Angicos, Braz. 154/C2
Angkor (ruin), Camb. 78/C3
Anglem (mt.), NZ 117/R12
Anglès, Sp. 45/G2
Anglesea, Austl. 115/C3
Anglesey (isl.), Wal, UK 34/D5
Anglet, Fr. 42/C5
Angleton, Tx, US 129/J5
Anglin (riv.), Fr. 42/D3
Angoche, Moz. 105/G4
Angol, Chile 158/B3
Angola (ctry.) 105/C3
Angola, Afr. 105/B2
Angola, In, US 130/C3
Angoon, Ak, US 134/M4
Angostura (res.), Mex. 140/C4
Angostura, Mex. 142/C3
Angoulême, Fr. 42/D4
Angra do Heroísmo, Azor., Port. 45/S12
Angra dos Reis, Braz. 211/J7
Angren, Uzb. 87/F4
Anguilla (isl.), UK 141/N8
Anguillara Veneta, It. 59/E2
Angus (pol. reg.), Sc,UK 36/C3
Angutikada (peak), Ak, US 134/G2
Anhanduí (riv.), Braz. 151/H8
Anhée, Belg. 53/D3
Anholt (isl.), Den. 38/D3
Anhui (prov.), China 71/L5
Ani, Japan 76/B4
Aniak, Ak, US 134/G3
Aniakchak (crater), Ak, US 134/G4
Aniakchak Nat'l Mon. and Prsv., Ak, US 134/F4
Aniche, Fr. 52/C3
Animas (riv.), Co,NM, US 128/F3
Ánimas, Punta De Las (pt.), Mex. 142/B2
'Ānīn, Isr. 91/G6
Anina, Rom. 48/E3
Aniva (cape), Rus. 71/R2
Aniva (bay), Rus. 76/C1
Anivorano, Madg. 107/J7
Anizy-le-Château, Fr. 52/C4
Anjalankoski, Fin. 39/M1
Anjār, India 89/K4
Anjō, Japan 77/M6
Anjou (reg.), Fr. 42/C3
Anjou, Qu, Can. 131/N6
Anjouan (isl.), Com. 107/H6
Anjozorobe, Madg. 107/H7
Anju, NKor. 73/C3
Ankang, China 70/J5
Ankara (cap.), Turk. 90/C2
Ankara (prov.), Turk. 90/C1
Ankaramena, Madg. 107/H8
Ankaratra (mass.), Madg. 107/H7
Ankarsrum, Swe. 38/G3
Ankavandra, Madg. 107/H7
Ankazoabo, Madg. 107/H8
Ankazobe, Madg. 107/H7
Ankazomborona, Madg. 107/H7
Ankazomiriotra, Madg. 107/H7
Ankerika, Madg. 107/H6
Ankililioka, Madg. 107/G8
Ankilizato, Madg. 107/H8
Anklam, Ger. 38/E5
Ankum, Ger. 51/E3
Anlong, China 83/J2
Anloo, Neth. 50/D2
Anlu, China 72/C5
Anma (isl.), SKor. 73/D5
Ann (cape), Ma, US 131/G3
Ann Arbor, Mi, US 130/D3
Anna (lake), Va, US 130/E4
Anna Bay, Austl. 115/E2
Anna Pavlowna, Neth. 50/B3
Anna Pink (bay), Chile 158/B5
Anna Regina, Guy. 153/G3
Annaba, Alg. 100/K6
Annaba (prov.), Alg. 100/K6
Annaberg-Buchholz, Ger. 55/G1
Annaclone, NI, UK 34/B3
Annai, Guy. 153/G4
Annaka, Japan 77/B1
Annalong, NI, UK 34/C3
Annan, Sc, UK 35/E2
Annan (riv.), Sc, UK 36/C6
Annandale, Va, US 138/A6
Annandale, NJ, US 138/D2
Annapolis (cap.), Md, US 138/B6
Annapurna (peak), Nepal 84/D1
Annbank Station, Sc, UK 36/B6
Anne (mt.), Austl. 115/C4
Anne Arundel (co.), Md, US 138/B6
Annean (lake), Austl. 109/A3
Annecy, Fr. 56/C6
Annecy (lake), Fr. 56/C6
Annecy-le-Vieux, Fr. 56/C6
Annemasse, Fr. 56/C5
Annet-sur-Marne, Fr. 30/L5
Annette, Ak, US 134/M4
Annezin, Fr. 52/B2
Anniston, Al, US 133/G3
Annobón (isl.), EqG. 93/C5
Annonay, Fr. 42/F4
Annville, Pa, US 138/B3
Annweiler, Ger. 53/G5
Anō, Japan 77/K6
Áno Viánnos, Gre. 47/J5
Anoia (riv.), Sp. 45/K7
Anoka, Mn, US 127/K4
Anosibe An' Ala, Madg. 107/J7
Ānou-Zeggarene (riv.), Niger 103/G2
Anould, Fr. 56/C1
Anóyia, Gre. 47/J5
Anping, China 72/C3
Anqiu, China 72/D3
Anren, China 83/K2
Anrhomer (peak), Mor. 98/D3
Anröchte, Ger. 51/F5
Ans, Belg. 53/E2
Ansai, China 72/B3
Ansan, SKor. 73/F7
Ansbach, Ger. 54/D4
Anse-à-Galets, Haiti 145/H2
Anse-d'Hainault, Haiti 145/H2
Anse Rouge, Haiti 145/H2
Ansfelden, Aus. 55/H6
Anshan, China 73/B2
Anshun, China 83/J2
Anson, Tx, US 129/H4
Ansŏng, SKor. 73/D4
Ansongo, Mali 103/F3
Ant (riv.), Eng, UK 33/H1
Ant (isl.), Anti. 116/E4
Anta, Peru 156/C4
Antabamba, Peru 156/C4
Antakya, Turk. 91/E1
Antalaha, Madg. 107/J6
Antalya (prov.), Turk. 90/B2
Antalya (int'l arpt.), Turk. 91/B1
Antalya, Turk. 91/B1
Antalya, Gulf of (gulf), Turk. 91/B1
Antanambao Manampotsy, Madg. 107/J7
Antananarivo (prov.), Madg. 107/H7
Antananarivo (cap.), Madg. 107/H7
Antanifotsy, Madg. 107/H7
Antanimieva, Madg. 107/G8
Antanimora, Madg. 107/H9
Antar (peak), Alg. 99/E3
Antarctic (pen.), Ant. 160/W
Antarctic Circle 160/Z
Antarctica (cont.) 160
Antas, Braz. 154/C3
Antas, Rio das (riv.), Braz. 155/B4
Antella, It. 59/E5
Antelope (isl.), Ut, US 137/J12
Antelope Center, Ca, US 136/C1
Antequera, Sp. 44/C4
Antes Fort, Pa, US 138/A1
Anthering, Aus. 55/G7
Anthony, NM, US 128/F4
Anti-Atlas (mts.), Mor. 96/C2
Anti-Lebanon (mts.), Leb. 91/D3
Antibes, Fr. 43/G5
Anticosti, Île d' (isl.), Qu, Can. 123/K4
Antiesen (riv.), Aus. 55/G6
Antifer, Cap d' (cape), Fr. 42/D2
Antigo, Wi, US 127/L4
Antigonish, NS, Can. 131/J2
Antigua, Sp. 98/B3
Antigua (isl.), Anti. 141/N8
Antigua and Barbuda (ctry.) 141/N8
Antigua Guatemala, Guat. 144/D3
Antiguo Morelos, Mex. 143/F4
Antilly, Fr. 30/L4
Antioquia (dept.), Col. 145/H5
Antioquia, Col. 152/C3
Antipodes (isls.), NZ 23/T8
Antisana (vol.), Ecu. 152/B5
Antlers, Ok, US 129/J4
Antofagasta, Chile 157/B1
Antoing, Belg. 52/C2
Antokonosy Manambondro, Madg. 107/H8
Antón, Pan. 152/A2
Antón Lizardo, Mex. 143/P7
Anton Lizardo (pt.), Mex. 143/P7
Antongil (bay), Madg. 105/K10
Antonia, Mo, US 137/G9
Antonibe, Madg. 107/H6
Antoniesberg (peak), SAfr. 106/C4
Antonina, Braz. 155/B3
Antonina do Norte, Braz. 154/C2
Antônio Carlos, Braz. 211/K6
Antonito, Co, US 132/B2
Antonovo, Bul. 49/H4
Antony, Fr. 30/J5
Antrim, NI, UK 34/B2
Antrim (mts.), NI, UK 34/B1
Antrim (dist.), NI, UK 34/B2
Antronapiana, It. 56/E5
Antsalova, Madg. 107/H7
Antsambalahy, Madg. 107/J6
Antsenavolo, Madg. 107/J8
Antsirabe, Madg. 107/H7
Antsiraňana, Madg. 107/J6
Antsiranana (prov.), Madg. 107/J6
Antsohihy, Madg. 107/H6
Antuco (vol.), Chile 158/C3
Antulai (mtn.), Malay. 81/E3
Antwerp (Deurne) (int'l arpt.), Belg. 50/B6
Antwerpen, Belg. 50/B6
Anūpgarh, India 86/B5
Anūpshahr, India 84/B1
Anuradhapura, SrL. 82/D6
Anvik, Ak, US 134/F3
Anvil Peak (vol.), Ak, US 134/B6
Anxi, China 79/C2
Anxi, China 70/G3
Anyang, China 72/C3
Anyang, SKor. 73/F7
A'nyêmaqên (mts.), China 70/G4
Anyi, China 72/B4
Anyuan, China 79/C2
Anza (riv.), It. 56/E6
'Anzah, WBnk. 91/G7
Anze, China 72/C3
Anzegem, Belg. 52/C2
Anzhero-Sudzhensk, Rus. 64/J4
Anzin, Fr. 52/C3
Anzing, Ger. 55/E6
Anzio, It. 46/C2
Anzoátegui, Ven. 152/D2
Anzoátegui (state), Ven. 153/E2
Anzoátegui (int'l arpt.), Ven. 153/E2
Anzola dell'Emilia, It. 59/E3
Ao Kham (pt.), Thai. 78/B4
Ao Phangnga NP, Thai. 78/B4
Aoba (isl.), Van. 116/F6
Aoga (isl.), Japan 75/F4
Aogaki, Japan 77/H5
Aoiz, Sp. 44/E1
Aomori (pref.), Japan 76/B3
Aomori, Japan 76/B3
Aonla, India 84/B1
Aoral (peak), Camb. 78/D3
Āos, Gre. 47/J4
Aosta, It. 43/G4
Aosta, Valle d' (valley), It. 58/A1
Aoudaghast (ruin), Mrta. 102/C2
Aouk, Bahr (riv.), Chad 93/D4
Aoukar (pol. reg.), Mrta. 96/D4
Aoulef, Alg. 99/F4
Aoyama, Japan 77/K6
Apache (mts.), Tx, US 132/B4
Apache (peak), Az, US 137/R18
Apalachicola, Fl, US 133/G4
Apan, Mex. 143/L7
Apaporis (riv.), Col. 150/D3
Aparados da Serra, PN de, Braz. 155/B4
Aparecida, Braz. 155/C2
Aparecida do Taboado, Braz. 155/B2
Aparición, Ven. 152/D2
Aparri, Phil. 79/D4
Apartadó, Col. 152/B3
Apátfalva, Hun. 48/E2
Apatin, Serb. 48/D3
Apatity, Rus. 60/G2
Apatzingán de la Constitución, Mex. 142/E5
Apaxco, Mex. 143/K7
Apaxtla de Castrejon, Mex. 143/F5
Apeldoorn, Neth. 50/C4
Apelern, Ger. 51/G4
Apen, Ger. 51/E2
Apennines (mts.), It. 27/F4
Apensen, Ger. 51/G2
Aphrodisias (ruin), Turk. 90/B2
Api (peak), Indo. 81/E5
Api (cape), Indo. 81/F4
Api (cape), Indo. 80/C3
Apiacás, Serra dos (mts.), Braz. 150/G6
Apiaí, Braz. 155/B3
Apizaco, Mex. 143/L7
Aplao, Peru 156/C5
Apo (mt.), Phil. 79/E6
Apodi, Braz. 154/C2
Apodi (riv.), Braz. 154/C2
Apollo Bay, Austl. 115/B3
Apollonía, Gre. 47/J4
Apolo, Bol. 156/D4
Aporé (riv.), Braz. 151/H7
Apore (riv.), Braz. 155/B1
Apostle (isls.), Wi, US 127/L4
Apostle Islands Nat'l Lakeshore, Wi, US 127/L4
Apóstoles, Arg. 157/E2
Apostolos Andreas (cape), Cyp. 91/D2
Apoteri, Guy. 153/G3
Appalachian (mts.), US 125/K4
Appen, Ger. 51/G1
Appennino Ligure (mts.), It. 43/H4
Appennino Tosco-Emiliano (mts.), It. 43/J4
Appennino Umbro-Marchigiano (mts.), It. 43/K5
Appenweier, Ger. 56/D1
Appenzell, Swi. 57/F3
Appenzell (canton), Swi. 57/F3
Appignano, It. 59/G6
Appingedam, Neth. 50/D2
Apple Valley, Ca, US 136/C1
Appleton, NY, US 131/S9
Aprica, It. 57/G5
Aprica, Passo dell' (pass), It. 57/G5
Aprilia, It. 46/C2
Apriltsi, Bul. 47/J1
Apsheronsk, Rus. 62/F3
Apsley Gorge NP, Austl. 115/E1
Apua (pt.), Hi, US 124/U11
Apucarana, Braz. 155/B2
Apuiarés, Braz. 154/C1
Apure (riv.), Ven. 150/E2
Apure (prov.), Ven. 152/D3
Apurímac (dept.), Peru 156/C4
Apurímac (riv.), Peru 147/B4
Aqaba (gulf), Asia 67/B7
Aqmola (obl.), Kaz. 87/E2
'Aqrabah, WBnk. 91/D3
'Aqrah, Iraq 90/E2
Aqsay, Kaz. 63/K2
Aqtaū, Kaz. 63/J4
Aqtöbe (int'l arpt.), Kaz. 87/C2
Aqtöbe (obl.), Kaz. 87/C3
Aqtöbe, Kaz. 63/L2
Aquanaval (riv.), Mex. 142/E3
Aquaro-Guariquito, PN, Ven. 150/E2
Aquia, Peru 156/B3
Aquidauana, Braz. 151/G8
Aquidauana (riv.), Braz. 151/G8
Aquila, Swi. 57/E5
Aquileia, It. 59/G1
Aquiles Serdán, Mex. 132/B4
Aquin, Haiti 145/H2
Aquiraz, Braz. 154/C1
Aquitaine (pol. reg.), Fr. 42/C4
Ar-Asgat, Mong. 70/J2
Ar Horqin Qi, China 72/E2
Ar Ramādī, Iraq 90/E3
Ar Ramthā, Jor. 91/D3
Ar Raqqah, Syria 90/D3
Ar Raqqah (prov.), Syria 90/D2
Ar Rastan, Syria 91/E2
Ar Rayyān, Qatar 88/F3
Ar Riyāḑ (Riyadh) (cap.), SAr. 88/E4
Ar Rumaythah, Iraq 90/F4
Ar Ruşayfah, Jor. 91/E3
Ar Ruţbah, Iraq 90/E3
Ara (riv.), Japan 75/F2
Arab, Al, US 133/G3
'Arab, Baḩr al (riv.), Sudan 93/E3
Araban, Turk. 90/D2
Arabi, La, US 137/Q17
Arabian (sea), Asia 67/F8
Arabian (des.), Egypt 97/M2
Arabian (pen.), SAr. 88/D3
Araç, Turk. 62/E4
Araç (riv.), Turk. 62/E4
Araca, Bol. 150/E7
Araça (riv.), Braz. 153/F4
Aracaju, Braz. 154/C3
Aracataca, Col. 152/C2
Aracati, Braz. 154/C2
Araçatuba, Braz. 155/B2
Aracena, Sp. 44/B4
Araci, Braz. 154/C3
Aračinovo, FYROM 47/G1
Aracoiaba, Braz. 154/C2
Aracruz, Braz. 155/D1
Araçuai, Braz. 154/B5
Araçuaí (riv.), Braz. 154/B5
Arad, Rom. 48/E2
Arad (prov.), Rom. 48/E2
'Arad, Isr. 91/D4
Ārādān, Iran 88/F1
Arafura (sea), Austl.,Indo. 116/C5
Aragarças, Braz. 151/H7
Aragats (peak), Arm. 63/H4
Aragón (aut. comm.), Sp. 45/E2
Aragón (riv.), Sp. 45/E1
Aragua (state), Ven. 153/E2
Araguaia (riv.), Braz. 147/D3
Araguaia, PN do, Braz. 151/H6
Araguaiana, Braz. 151/H7
Araguaína, Braz. 151/J5
Araguari, Braz. 155/B1
Araguari (riv.), Braz. 151/H3
Araguatins, Braz. 151/J5
Arai, Japan 75/F2
Araioses, Braz. 154/B1
Arāk, Iran 88/E2
Arakamchechan (isl.) 134/D3
Arakan (mts.), Myan. 70/F7
Arakawa, Japan 77/C2
Árakhthos (riv.), Gre. 47/G3
Araklı, Turk. 90/D1
Aral (sea), Asia 87/C3
Aral, Kaz. 87/D3
Aral Mangy Qaraqumy (des.), Kaz. 87/D3
Aralık, Turk. 90/F2
Aralsor (lake), Kaz. 63/H2
Aramac, Austl. 114/B3
Ārāmbāgh, India 85/F4
Aran (isls.), Ire. 31/P10
Aran Fawddwy (peak), Wal, UK 34/E6
Aranda de Duero, Sp. 44/D2
Arandelovac, Serb. 48/E3
Arani, India 82/C5
Aranjuez, Sp. 44/D2
Aransas Pass, Tx, US 132/D5
Arantina, Braz. 211/J6
Aranuka (isl.), Kiri. 116/G5
Arapiraca, Braz. 154/C3
Arapiuns (riv.), Braz. 153/H5
Arapongas, Braz. 155/B2
'Ar'ara, Isr. 91/G7
Araranguá, Braz. 155/B4
Araraquara, Braz. 155/B2
Araras, Braz. 155/C2
Ararat, Austl. 115/B3
Arari, Braz. 154/A1
Arāria, India 85/F2
Araripe, Chapada do (uplands), Braz. 154/B2
Araripina, Braz. 154/B2
Aras (riv.), Iran 63/H5
Aratane (well), Mrta. 102/C2
Aratoca, Col. 152/C3
Arauá (riv.), Braz. 150/F4
Arauca, Col. 152/D3
Arauca (riv.), Col.,Ven. 153/E3
Arauca (dept.), Col. 152/D3
Araucária, Braz. 155/B3
Arauco, Chile 158/B3
Arauquita, Col. 152/D3
Araure, Ven. 152/D2
Aravis, Col des (pass), Fr. 56/C6
Arawa, PNG 116/E5
Arawale Nat'l Rsv., Kenya 104/D3
Araxá, Braz. 155/C1
Araya (pen.), Ven. 153/E2
Ārba Minch', Eth. 97/N6
Arbeca, Sp. 45/F2
Arbīl (gov.), Iraq 90/E3
Arboga, Swe. 38/F2
Arbois, Fr. 56/B4
Arbois, Mont d' (peak), Fr. 56/C6
Arboletes, Col. 152/B2
Arbon, Swi. 57/F2
Arborfield, Sk, Can. 127/H2
Arborg, Mb, Can. 127/J3
Arbrå, Swe. 38/G1
Arbroath, Sc, UK 36/D3
Arc (riv.), Fr. 42/F5
Arc-en-Barrois, Fr. 56/B2
Arc-et-Senans, Fr. 56/B3
Arc-lès-Gray, Fr. 56/B3
Arc-sur-Tille, Fr. 56/B3
Arcachon, Fr. 42/C4
Arcachon, Bassin d' (lag.), Fr. 42/C4
Arcachon, Pointe d' (pt.), Fr. 42/C4
Arcadia, Ca, US 136/F7
Arcadia, Fl, US 133/H5
Arcadia, Ok, US 137/N14
Arcas, Cayos (isl.), Mex. 144/D1
Arcata, Ca, US 126/B5
Arceburgo, Braz. 211/G6
Arcelia, Mex. 143/E5
Arcene, It. 58/C1
Arceto, It. 59/D3
Archena, Sp. 44/E3
Archer City, Tx, US 129/H4
Arches, Fr. 56/C1
Arches NP, Ut, US 128/E3
Archidona, Sp. 44/C4
Archman, Trkm. 63/L5
Arcipelago Toscano (isl.), It. 43/H5
Arcisate, It. 57/E6
Arco, It. 57/G6
Arco, Paso del (pass), Arg. 158/C3
Arcola, It. 58/C4
Arcole, It. 59/E2
Arcos, Braz. 155/C2
Arcos de Jalón, Sp. 44/D2
Arcos de la Frontera, Sp. 44/C4
Arcos de Valdevez, Port. 44/A2
Arcoverde, Braz. 154/C3
Arctic (ocean) 160/U
Arctic (plain), Ak, US 134/F2
Arctic Bay, Nun., Can. 123/H1
Arctic Circle 160/J
Arctic Red (riv.), NW, Can. 134/M2
Arctic Village, Ak, US 134/J2
Arctowski, Pol., Ant. 160/W
Arda (riv.), Bul. 62/C4
Ardabīl, Iran 63/J5
Ardahan, Turk. 90/E1
Ardal, Iran 88/F2
Årdalstangen, Nor. 38/B1
Ardanuç, Turk. 90/E1
Ardèche (riv.), Fr. 42/F4
Ardee, Ire. 34/B4
Arden (mt.), Austl. 113/H5
Arden, De, US 138/C4
Arden, Den. 38/C3
Arden-Arcade, Ca, US 135/M9
Ardennes (for.), Belg. 42/F1
Ardennes (dept.), Fr. 53/D4
Ardennes, Canal des (canal), Fr. 53/D4
Ardenno, It. 57/F5
Ardersier, Sc, UK 36/B1
Ardeşen, Turk. 90/E1
Ardesio, It. 57/F6
Ardestān, Iran 88/F2
Ardez, Swi. 57/G4
Ardila (riv.), Sp. 44/B3
Ardino, Bul. 49/G5
Ardivachar (pt.), Sc, UK 31/Q8
Ardle (riv.), Sc, UK 36/C3
Ardlethan, Austl. 115/C2
Ardmore, Ok, US 129/H4
Ardmore, Pa, US 138/C4
Ardnamurchan (pt.), Sc, UK 31/Q8
Ardon, Swi. 56/D5
Ardooie, Belg. 52/C2
Ardres, Fr. 52/A2
Ardrossan, Austl. 113/H5
Ardrossan, Sc, UK 36/B5
Ards (pen.), Sc, UK 34/C3
Ards (dist.), NI, UK 34/C2
Ardsley, NY, US 139/K7
Åre, Swe. 37/E3
Areado, Braz. 211/G6
Arecibo, PR 141/M8
Areia Branca, Braz. 154/C2
Arena (pt.), Ca, US 128/B3
Arena de la Ventana Punta (pt.), Mex. 142/C3
Arenal (vol.), CR 145/E4
Arenápolis, Braz. 151/G6
Arenas de San Pedro, Sp. 44/C2
Arenas, Punta de (pt.), Arg. 159/C7
Arendal, Nor. 38/C2
Arendonk, Belg. 50/C6
Arendtsville, Pa, US 138/A4
Arenig Fawr (peak), Wal, UK 34/E6
Arenys de Mar, Sp. 45/L6
Arenzano, It. 58/B4
Areo, Ven. 153/F2
Areópolis, Gre. 47/H4
Arequipa (dept.), Peru 156/C5
Arequipa, Peru 156/D5
Arequito, Arg. 158/E2
Aresing, Ger. 54/E5
Arévalo, Sp. 44/C2
Arezzo, It. 59/E6
Arezzo (prov.), It. 59/E5
Arga (riv.), Sp. 44/E1
Argalasti, Gre. 47/H3
Argamasilla de Alba, Sp. 44/D3
Argamasilla de Calatrava, Sp. 44/C3
Arganda, Sp. 45/N9
Argegno, It. 57/F6
Argelès-Gazost, Fr. 42/C5
Argelès-sur-Mer, Fr. 42/E5
Argen (riv.), Ger. 57/F2
Argenbühl, Ger. 57/F2
Argens (riv.), Fr. 43/G5
Argenta, It. 59/E3
Argentan, Fr. 42/C2
Argentat, Fr. 42/D4
Argentera (peak), It. 43/G4
Argenteuil, Fr. 30/J5
Argentière, Aiguille d' (peak), Swi. 56/D6
Argentina (ctry.), Arg. 157/C4
Argentina, It. 58/A5
Argentino (lake), Arg. 159/B6

170
Argen – Ayama

Argenton-sur-Creuse, Fr. 42/D3
Argentona, Sp. 45/L6
Argeş (prov.), Rom. 49/G3
Argeş (riv.), Rom. 62/C3
Arghandab (riv.), Afg. 89/J2
Argıthanı, Turk. 90/B2
Argolis (gulf), Gre. 47/H4
Argonne (for.), Fr. 40/C4
Argonne National Laboratory, Il, US 135/P16
Árgos, Gre. 47/H4
Árgos Orestikón, Gre. 47/G2
Argostólion, Gre. 47/G3
Arguello (pt.), Ca, US 128/B4
Arguin, Cap d' (cape), Mrta. 98/A5
Argun' (riv.), Rus. 65/M4
Arguut, Mong. 70/H2
Argyle (lake), Austl. 109/B2
Argyll and Bute (pol. reg.), Sc, UK 36/A4
Arhangay (prov.), Mong. 70/G2
Arheijît (well), Mrta. 98/B5
Århus, Den. 38/D3
Århus (co.), Den. 38/D3
Ariano Irpino, It. 46/D2
Ariari (riv.), Col. 152/C4
Arias, Arg. 158/E2
Arica, Chile 156/D5
Arıcak, Turk. 90/E2
Arid (cape), Austl. 112/D5
Arida, Japan 74/D3
Aridhaía, Gre. 47/H2
Arido (peak), Ca, US 136/A1
Aridol (lake), WSah. 98/B4
Ariège (riv.), Fr. 42/D5
Arifiye, Turk. 49/K5
Ārifwāla, Pak. 86/B4
Arīḩā, Syria 91/E2
Arikaree (riv.), Co, US 129/G3
Arilje, Serb. 48/E4
Arima, Trin. 153/F2
Arinos (riv.), Braz. 151/G6
Arinos, Braz. 154/A4
Arinthod, Fr. 56/B5
Ario de Rosales, Mex. 143/E5
Aripao, Ven. 153/E3
Aripuanã, Braz. 150/G6
Aripuanã (riv.), Braz. 147/C3
Ariquemes, Braz. 150/F5
Arish, Austl. 114/B2
Arismendi, Ven. 152/D2
Arivechi, Mex. 142/C2
Arivonimamo, Madg. 107/H7
Ariza, Sp. 44/D2
Arizona, Arg. 158/D2
Arizona (canal), Az, US 137/R18
Arizona (state), US 128/D4
Arizpe, Mex. 142/C2
Årjäng, Swe. 38/E2
Arjeplog, Swe. 37/F2
Arjona, Sp. 44/C4
Arjona, Col. 152/C2
Arkadelphia, Ar, US 129/J4
Arkaig (lake), Sc, UK 36/A3
Arkalokhórion, Gre. 47/J5
Arkansas (riv.), US 132/E3
Arkansas (state), US 132/E3
Arkansas City, Ar, US 129/K4
Arkansas City, Ks, US 129/H3
Arkanū (peak), Libya 97/K3
Arkhángelos, Gre. 90/B2
Arkhangel'sk (int'l arpt.), Rus. 60/J2
Arkhangel'sk (Archangel), Rus. 60/J2
Arkhangel'skaya Oblast, Rus. 60/H3
Arkhangel'skoye, Rus. 61/W9
Arklow, Ire. 34/B6
Arkona (cape), Ger. 38/E4
Arkonam, India 82/C5
Arkticheskiy Institut (isls.), Rus. 64/H2
Årla, Swe. 38/G2
Arlan (peak), Trkm. 87/B5
Arlanda (int'l arpt.), Swe. 38/G2
Arlanza (riv.), Sp. 44/C1
Arlazón (riv.), Sp. 44/D1
Arlbergpass (pass), Aus. 57/G3
Arles, Fr. 42/F5
Arlesheim, Swi. 56/D3
Arley, Mo, US 137/E5
Arlington, Mn, US 127/K4
Arlington, Ga, US 133/G4
Arlington, Va, US 138/A6
Arlington Heights, Il, US 130/C3
Arló, Hun. 41/L4
Arlon, Belg. 53/E4
Arluno, It. 58/B1
Arly (riv.), Fr. 56/C6
Arly, PN de l', Burk. 103/F4
Arly, Réserve Totale de Faune de l', Burk. 103/F4
Armada, Mi, US 135/G6
Armadale, Sc, UK 36/C5
Armagh (dist.), NI, UK 34/B3
Armagh, NI, UK 34/B3
Armançon (riv.), Fr. 42/F3
Armando Laydner, Reprêsa de (res.), Braz. 155/B2
Armant, Egypt 101/C3
Armavir, Rus. 63/G3
Arme, Cap d' (cape), Fr. 43/G5
Armenia, Col. 150/C3
Armenia (ctry.) 63/H5
Armentières, Fr. 52/B2
Armentières-en-Brie, Fr. 30/M5
Armería, Mex. 142/E5
Armidale, Austl. 115/D1
Armilla, Sp. 44/D4
Armstrong, Arg. 158/E2
Armstrong, BC, Can. 126/D3
Armthorpe, Eng, UK 35/G4
Ārmūr, India 82/C4
Armutlu, Turk. 49/J5
Army Ordnance Museum, Md, US 138/B5
Arnage, Fr. 42/D3
Arnager (int'l arpt.), Den. 38/F4
Arnaía, Gre. 47/H2
Arnaud (riv.), Qu, Can. 123/J3
Arnauti (cape), Cyp. 91/C2
Arnedo, Sp. 44/D1
Arnett, Ok, US 129/H3
Arnhem, Neth. 50/C5
Arnhem Land (reg.), Austl. 109/C2
Arno (riv.), It. 43/J5
Arno (isl.), Mrsh. 116/G4
Arnold, Eng, UK 35/G6
Arnold, Md, US 138/B5
Arnold, Mo, US 137/G9
Arnoldstein, Aus. 43/K3
Arnon (riv.), Fr. 42/E3
Arnouville-lès-Gonesse, Fr. 30/K5
Arnprior, On, Can. 130/E2
Arnsberg, Ger. 51/F6
Arnstadt, Ger. 43/J1
Arnstein, Ger. 54/C3
Arnstorf, Ger. 55/F5
Aro Usu (cape), Indo. 81/H5
Aroab, Namb. 106/B2
Aroche, Sp. 44/B4
Arolsen, Ger. 51/G6
Aron (riv.), Fr. 42/E3
Arona, Canl. 45/X16
Arona, It. 58/B1
Aronde (riv.), Fr. 52/B5
Arorae (isl.), Kiri. 116/G5
Arosa, Swi. 57/F4
Aroser Rothern (peak), Swi. 57/F4
Ærøskøbing, Den. 38/D4
Arpaçay, Turk. 90/E1
Arpajon, Fr. 30/J6
Arpajon-sur-Cère, Fr. 42/E4
Arqalyq, Kaz. 87/E2
Arquata Scrivia, It. 58/B3
Arques, Fr. 52/B2
'Arrābah, WBnk. 91/G7
Arrah, India 85/E3
Arraias (riv.), Braz. 151/H6
Arraias, Braz. 154/A4
Arraiján, Pan. 152/B2
Arran (isl.), Sc, UK 31/R8
Arrancabarba (peak), Nic. 145/E4
Arras, Fr. 52/B3
Arreau, Fr. 42/D5
Arrecife, Sp. 98/B3
Arrecifes, Arg. 158/E2
Arrée, Monts d' (mts.), Fr. 42/B2
Arriaga, Mex. 144/C2
Arriondas, Sp. 44/C1
Arrochar, Sc, UK 36/B4
Arroio Grande, Braz. 155/A5
Arronville, Fr. 30/J4
Arroscia (riv.), It. 58/B4
Arroux (riv.), Fr. 42/F3
Arrow (riv.), Eng, UK 32/C2
Arrowbear Lake, Ca, US 136/C2
Arroyo de la Luz, Sp. 44/B3
Arroyo Grande, Ca, US 128/B4
Arroyo Hondo (riv.), Ca, US 135/L12
Arroyo Trabuco (riv.), Ca, US 136/C3
Års, Den. 38/C3
Ars-sur-Moselle, Fr. 53/F5
Arsen'yev, Rus. 71/P3
Arsiero, It. 59/E1
Arslanköy, Turk. 91/D1
Arta (gulf), Gre. 47/G3
Árta, Gre. 47/G3
Artá, Sp. 45/G3
Arteaga, Mex. 142/E5
Arteixo, Sp. 44/A1
Artem, Rus. 71/P3
Artemisa, Cuba 145/F1
Artesia, NM, US 129/F4
Artesia, Ca, US 136/F8
Arth, Swi. 57/E3
Arthies, Fr. 30/H4
Arthur (pt.), Austl. 114/C3
Arthur (riv.), Austl. 112/C5
Arthur Kill (riv.), NJ,NY, US 139/J9
Arthur's (pass), NZ 117/S11
Arthur's Pass NP, NZ 117/S11
Artigas, Uru. 157/E3
Artogne, It. 58/D1
Artois (reg.), Fr. 40/A3
Artova, Turk. 90/D1
Artur Nogueira, Braz. 211/F7
Arturo Merino Benitez (Santiago) (int'l arpt.), Chile 158/N8
Artux, China 87/G5
Artvin, Turk. 90/E1
Artvin (prov.), Turk. 90/E1
Aru (isls.), Indo. 81/H5
Arua, Ugan. 104/A2
Aruba (isl.), Aru., Neth. 147/B1
Arucas, Sp. 98/B3
Arudy, Fr. 42/C5
Arujá, Braz. 211/G8
Arun (riv.), China 85/F2
Arunāchal Pradesh (state), India 70/F6
Arundel, Eng, UK 33/F5
Aruppukkottai, India 82/C6
'Arūrah, WBnk. 91/G7
Arus (cape), Indo. 81/F3
Arusha, Tanz. 104/C3
Arusha (pol. reg.), Tanz. 104/C4
Arusha NP, Tanz. 104/C3
Arutua (isl.), FrPol. 117/L6
Aruwimi (riv.), D.R. Congo 93/E4
Arvada, Co, US 137/B3
Arvayheer, Mong. 70/H2
Arve (riv.), Fr. 56/C6
Arviat, Nun., Can. 122/G2
Arvidsjaur, Swe. 37/F2
Arvika, Swe. 38/E2
Arvin, Ca, US 128/C4
Arvon (mt.), Mi, US 127/L4
Aryānah, Tun. 46/B4
Aryānah (gov.), Tun. 46/A4
Arys', Kaz. 87/E4
Arz (riv.), Fr. 42/B3
Arzachena, It. 46/A2
Arzamas, Rus. 61/K5
Arzbach, Ger. 53/G3
Arzberg, Ger. 55/F2
Ärzen, Ger. 51/G4
Arzew, Alg. 100/E5
Arzignano, It. 59/E1
Arzl im Pitztal, Aus. 57/G3
Arzúa, Sp. 44/A1
Ås, Nor. 38/D2
As, Belg. 53/E1
Aš, Czh. 55/F2
As Sabkhah, Syria 90/D3
Aş Şaff, Egypt 91/B5
Aş Şāfī, Jor. 91/D4
As Sālimīyah, Kuw. 88/E3
As Sallūm, Egypt 97/L1
As Salmān, Iraq 90/F4
As Salţ, Jor. 91/D3
As Sanţah, Egypt 91/B4
Aş Şarīḩ, Jor. 91/D3
As Sinbillāwayn, Egypt 91/B4
As Sudd (reg.), Sudan 93/F4
As Sulaymānīyah (gov.), Iraq 90/F3
As Sulaymānīyah, Iraq 90/F3
As Suwaydā' (prov.), Syria 90/D3
As Suwaydā', Syria 91/E3
Aş Şuwayrah, Iraq 90/F3
As Suways (gov.), Egypt 101/C2
As Suways, Egypt 91/C4
Asaba, Nga. 103/G5
Asadābād, Afg. 86/A2
Asadābād, Iran 88/E2
Asagny, PN d', C.d'Iv. 102/D5
Asahan (riv.), Indo. 80/A3
Asahi, Japan 75/G3
Asahi (riv.), Japan 74/C3
Asahi, Japan 77/F1
Asahi, Japan 77/L5
Asahi, Japan 77/M5
Asahi-dake (peak), Japan 76/C2
Asahikawa, Japan 76/C2
Asai, Japan 77/K5
Asaka, Japan 77/D2
Asake (riv.), Japan 77/K5
Asama-yama (peak), Japan 75/F2
Asan (bay), SKor. 73/D4
Asansol, India 85/F4
Asashi-dake (peak), Japan 75/F1
Asashina, Japan 77/A1
Asawanwah (well), Libya 96/J3
Asbach, Ger. 53/G2
Asbach-Bäumenheim, Ger. 54/D5
Asbest, Rus. 61/P4
Asbestos (mts.), SAfr. 106/C3
Asbury Park, NJ, US 138/D3
Ascención, Bol. 150/F7
Ascención (bay), Mex. 140/D4
Ascensión, Mex. 128/F5
Ascensión, Arg. 158/E2
Aschach (riv.), Aus. 55/G6
Aschach an der Donau, Aus. 55/H6
Aschaffenburg, Ger. 54/C3
Aschau am Inn, Ger. 55/F6
Ascheberg, Ger. 51/E5
Aschendorf, Ger. 51/E2
Aschersleben, Ger. 40/F3
Ascoli Piceno, It. 43/K5
Ascoli Satriano, It. 46/D2
Ascona, Swi. 57/E5
Ascope, Peru 156/B2
Åseda, Swe. 38/F3
Åsele, Swe. 37/F2
Asendorf, Ger. 51/G2
Asendorf, Ger. 51/F3
Asenovgrad, Bul. 47/J1
Åseral, Nor. 38/B2
Aserei (peak), It. 58/C3
Asfeld, Fr. 53/D5
Ash, Eng, UK 30/D3
Ash, Eng, UK 30/A3
Ash Shabakah, Iraq 90/E4
Ash Shamal (gov.), Leb. 91/E2
Ash Shāmīyah, Iraq 90/F4
Ash Shāriqah, UAE 89/G3
Ash Sharqāt, Iraq 90/E3
Ash Sharqīyah (state), Sudan 101/C5
Ash Shawbak, Jor. 91/D4
Asha, Nga. 103/F5
Ashanti (uplands), C.d'Iv. 96/E6
Ashanti (pol. reg.), Gha. 103/E5
Asharoken, NY, US 139/M8
Ashbourne, Ire. 34/B4
Ashbourne, Eng, UK 35/G5
Ashburton (riv.), Austl. 109/A3
Ashburton, NZ 117/S11
Ashby (canal), Eng, UK 33/E1
Ashby-de-la-Zouch, Eng, UK 33/E1
Ashcroft, BC, Can. 126/C3
Ashdod, Isr. 91/F8
Asheboro, NC, US 133/J3
Ashern, Mb, Can. 127/J3
Asheville, NC, US 133/H3
Asheweig (riv.), On, Can. 127/M2
Ashford, Austl. 115/D1
Ashford, Eng, UK 33/G4
Ashford, Eng, UK 30/B2
Ashford, Ire. 34/B5
Ashgabat (cap.), Trkm. 89/G1
Ashhurst, NZ 117/T11
Ashibetsu, Japan 76/C2
Ashigawa, Japan 77/B2
Ashikaga, Japan 77/C1
Ashington, Eng, UK 35/G1
Ashino (lake), Japan 77/C3
Ashiwada, Japan 77/B3
Ashiya, Japan 77/H6
Ashiyasu, Japan 77/A2
Ashizuri-misaki (cape), Japan 74/C4
Ashkal (lake), Tun. 100/L6
Ashland, Ks, US 129/H3
Ashland, Ky, US 130/D4
Ashland, Oh, US 130/D3
Ashland, Or, US 126/C5
Ashland, Pa, US 138/B2
Ashley, ND, US 127/J4
Ashley, Pa, US 138/C1
Ashmore (reef), Austl. 109/B2
Ashmore and Cartier Islands Territory (dpcy.), Austl. 109/B2
Ashmūn, Egypt 91/B4
Ashoknagar, India 84/A3
Ashoro, Japan 76/C2
Ashqelon, Isr. 91/F8
Ashta, India 82/C3
Ashtabula, Oh, US 130/D3
Ashton, Id, US 126/F4
Ashton, SAfr. 106/M10
Ashton-in-Makerfield, Eng, UK 35/F5
Ashton-under-Lyne, Eng, UK 35/F5
Asia (cont.) 67
Asia, Peru 156/B4
Asiago, It. 57/H6
Asikkala, Fin. 39/L1
Asilah, Mor. 100/A2
Asillo, Peru 156/D4
Asinara (isl.), It. 46/A2
Asinara, Golfo dell' (gulf), It. 46/A2
Asino, Rus. 64/J4
Asipovichy, Bela. 62/D1
'Asīr (mts.), SAr. 88/D5
Asis (cape), Sudan 101/D5
Aşkale, Turk. 90/E2
Askeaton, Ire. 31/P10
Asker, Nor. 38/D2
Askersund, Swe. 38/F2
Askim, Nor. 38/D2
Askim, Swe. 38/D3
Áskion (peak), Gre. 47/G2
Askja (crater), Ice. 37/P6
Askov, Den. 38/C4
Askvoll, Nor. 37/C3
Asmara (cap.), Erit. 88/C5
Asnen (lake), Swe. 38/F3
Asnières-sur-Oise, Fr. 30/K4
Asnières-sur-Seine, Fr. 30/J5
Asō, Japan 77/E2
Aso NP, Japan 74/B4
Aso-san (peak), Japan 74/B4
Asola, It. 58/D2
Asolo, It. 59/E1
Āsosa, Eth. 97/M5
Asoteriba (peak), Sudan 101/D4
Aspach, Aus. 55/G6
Aspe, Sp. 45/E3
Aspen, Co, US 128/F3
Aspen Hill, Md, US 138/A5
Aspen Park, Co, US 137/B3
Aspendos (ruin), Turk. 91/B1
Asperg, Ger. 54/C5
Aspermont, Tx, US 129/G4
Aspers, Pa, US 138/A4
Aspetuck (riv.), Ct, US 139/E1
Aspiring (mt.), NZ 117/R11
Asprópirgos, Gre. 47/H3
Asquith, Sk, Can. 126/G2
Assa, Mor. 98/C3
Assa Aguiene (peak), Alg. 99/G5
Assab, Erit. 88/D6
Assaba (pol. reg.), Mrta. 102/C2
Assam (state), India 70/F6
Assaré, Braz. 154/C2
Asse, Belg. 53/D2
Assemini, It. 46/A3
Assen, Neth. 50/D3
Assenede, Belg. 52/C1
Assens, Den. 38/C4
Assens, Den. 38/D3
Assentoft, Den. 38/D3
Assesse, Belg. 53/E3
Assiniboia, Sk, Can. 127/G3
Assiniboine (mt.), BC, Can. 126/E3
Assiniboine (riv.), Mb,Sk, Can. 127/H3
Assinika (lake), Qu, Can. 130/F1
Assis, Braz. 155/B2
Assling, Ger. 55/F6
Asso, It. 58/C1
Assomada, CpV. 93/K10
Astakós, Gre. 47/G3
Astana (cap.), Kaz. 87/F2
Asten, Neth. 50/C6
Asten, Aus. 55/H6
Asti (prov.), It. 58/B3
Asti, It. 43/H4
Astico (riv.), It. 59/E1
Astipálaia, Gre. 90/A2
Astolfo Dutra, Braz. 211/L6
Astorga, Braz. 155/B2
Astoria, Or, US 126/C4
Åstorp, Swe. 38/E3
Astrakhan', Rus. 63/J3
Astrakhanskaya Oblast, Rus. 63/H3
Åstros, Gre. 47/H4
Astudillo, Sp. 44/C1
Asturias (aut. comm.), Sp. 44/B1
Asuka, Japan 77/J7
Asuke, Japan 77/M5
Asunción (cap.), Par. 157/E2
Asuncion (isl.), NMar. 116/D3
Asunción Ixtaltepec, Mex. 140/B4
Asunden (lake), Swe. 38/F3
Aswa (riv.), Ugan. 97/M7
Aswān (gov.), Egypt 101/C4
Aswān, Egypt 101/C3
Aswan High (dam), Egypt 101/C4
Asyūţ (gov.), Egypt 101/B3
Asyūţ, Egypt 101/B3
Aszód, Hun. 49/R9
Aţ Ţafīlah, Jor. 91/D4
Aţ Ţafīlah (gov.), Jor. 91/D4
Aţ Ţā'if, SAr. 88/D4
At Tall, Syria 91/E3
At Tall al Kabīr, Egypt 91/B4
At Ta'mīn (gov.), Iraq 90/E3
Aţ Ţūr, WBnk. 91/G8
Atabapo (riv.), Ven. 153/E4
Atacama (des.), Chile 147/B4
Atacames, Ecu. 152/B4
Atafu (isl.), Tok. 117/H5
Atakpamé, Togo 103/F5
Atalaia, Braz. 154/C3
Atalaia do Norte, Braz. 156/D2
Atalándi, Gre. 47/H3
Atalaya, Peru 156/C3
Atami, Japan 75/F3
Atar, Mrta. 96/C3
Atarfe, Sp. 44/D4
Atarra, India 84/C3
Atas Bogd (peak), Mong. 70/G3
Atascadero, Ca, US 128/B4
Atascosa (co.), Tx, US 137/T21
Atascosa, Tx, US 137/T21
Atatürk (dam), Turk. 90/D2
Atatürk (res.), Turk. 90/D2
Ataturk (int'l arpt.), Turk. 49/J5
Atbara (riv.), Eth. 97/N5
Atbara, Sudan 97/M4
Atbasar, Kaz. 87/E2
Atchafalaya (riv.), La, US 129/K5
Atchafalaya (bay), La, US 129/K5
Atchison, Ks, US 129/J3
Atco, NJ, US 138/D4
Atebubu, Gha. 103/E5
Ateca, Sp. 44/E2
Ateelva (riv.), Nor. 37/G1
Atén, Bol. 156/D4
Atencingo, Mex. 143/L8
Atenco, Mex. 143/Q10
Atenco, Mex. 143/R9
Atengo (riv.), Mex. 142/D4
Atessa, It. 46/D1
Atglen, Pa, US 138/C4
Ath, Belg. 52/C2
Athabasca, Ab, Can. 126/E2
Athabasca (riv.), Ab, Can. 122/E3
Athabasca (lake), Ab,Sk, Can. 122/E3
Athapapuskow (lake), Mb, Can. 127/H2
Āthār Ţulmaythah (Ptolemaïs) (ruin), Libya 97/K1
Athboy, Ire. 31/Q10
Athenry, Ire. 31/P10
Athens (Athínai) (cap.), Gre. 47/N9
Athens, Al, US 133/G3
Athens, Ga, US 133/H3
Athens, Tn, US 133/G3
Athens, Tx, US 129/J4
Atherstone, Eng, UK 33/E1
Atherton, Austl. 114/B2
Atherton, Eng, UK 35/F4
Atherton, Mo, US 137/E5
Athgarh, India 82/E3
Athi (riv.), Kenya 104/C3
Athínai (Athens) (cap.), Gre. 47/N9
Athis-Mons, Fr. 30/K5
Athlone, Ire. 31/Q10
Atholl (for.), Sc, UK 36/B3
Áthos (peak), Gre. 47/J2
Athy, Ire. 31/Q10
Ati, Chad 96/J5
Atibaia (riv.), Braz. 211/G7
Atibaia, Braz. 211/G8
Atico, Peru 156/C5
Atienza, Sp. 44/D2
Atikokan, On, Can. 127/L3
Atil, Mex. 142/C2
Atitlán (lake), Guat. 144/D3
Atiu (isl.), Cookls. 117/K7
Atizapan, Mex. 143/Q10
Atka, Ak, US 134/D5
Atka (isl.), Ak, US 134/C5
Atkarsk, Rus. 63/H2
Atkinson (pt.), NW, Can. 134/M2
Atlacomulco de Fabela, Mex. 143/K7
Atlanta (cap.), Ga, US 133/G3
Atlantic (ocean) 22/G3
Atlantic (co.), NJ, US 138/D4
Atlantic Beach, NY, US 139/L9
Atlantic City, NJ, US 138/D5
Atlantic Highlands, NJ, US 139/J10
Atlantico (dept.), Col. 145/H4
Atlántida, Uru. 159/L11
Atlantique (prov.), Ben. 103/F5
Atlas (mts.), Mor. 96/E1
Atlas (peak), Ca, US 135/K10
Atlas Saharien (mts.), Alg. 96/E1
Atlatlahuaca, Mex. 143/Q10
Atlin, BC, Can. 134/M3
'Atlit, Isr. 91/F6
Atlixco, Mex. 143/L8
Atmore, Al, US 133/G4
Atocha, Bol. 150/E8
Atomium, The, Belg. 53/D2
Atotonilco, Mex. 143/L6
Atouila, 'Erg (des.), Mali 98/D5
Atoyac, Mex. 143/E5
Atoyac (riv.), Mex. 144/B2
Atqasuk, Ak, US 134/G1
Atrai (riv.), Bang. 85/G3
Atrak (riv.), Iran 89/G1
Ätran (riv.), Swe. 38/E3
Atrato (riv.), Col. 150/C2
Atrauli, India 84/B1
Atsugi, Japan 77/C3
Atsumi, Japan 77/M6
Atsumi (pen.), Japan 77/M6
Attalens, Swi. 56/C4
Attalla, Al, US 133/G3
Attapu, Laos 78/D3
Attawapiskat (lake), On, Can. 127/L2
Attawapiskat (riv.), On, Can. 123/H3
Attel (riv.), Ger. 55/F7
Attendorn, Ger. 51/E6
Atteridgeville, SAfr. 106/Q12
Attersee (lake), Aus. 43/K3
Attert, Belg. 53/E4
Attica, Mi, US 135/F5
Attigny, Fr. 53/D5
'Attīl, WBnk. 91/G7
Attock, Pak. 86/B3
Attu, Ak, US 134/A5
Attu (isl.), Ak, US 134/A5
Atuel (riv.), Arg. 157/C4
Atuntaqui, Ecu. 152/B4
Åtvidaberg, Swe. 38/G2
Atwater, Ca, US 128/B3
Atyraū (obl.), Kaz. 87/B3
Atyraū, Kaz. 63/J3
Atyraū (int'l arpt.), Kaz. 63/J3
Au, Swi. 57/F3
Au, Aus. 57/F3
Au in der Hallertau, Ger. 55/E5
Au Sable (riv.), Mi, US 130/C2
Auari (riv.), Braz. 153/E3
Aubange, Belg. 53/E4
Aube (dept.), Fr. 53/D6
Aube (riv.), Fr. 40/C4
Aubenas, Fr. 42/F4
Aubepierre-Ozouer-le-Repos, Fr. 30/L6
Aubergenville, Fr. 30/H5
Aubert (peak), Swi. 56/C4
Aubervilliers, Fr. 30/K5
Aubetin (riv.), Fr. 52/C6
Aubette (riv.), Fr. 52/A5
Aubette de Magny (riv.), Fr. 30/H4
Aubigny-en-Artois, Fr. 52/B3
Aubigny-sur-Nère, Fr. 42/E3
Aubin, Fr. 42/E4
Aubonne, Swi. 56/C5
Auboué, Fr. 53/E5
Aubrac, Monts du (mts.), Fr. 42/E4
Aubrives, Fr. 53/D3
Aubry, Ks, US 137/D6
Auburn, Austl. 113/H5
Auburn, Al, US 133/G3
Auburn, Ca, US 128/B3
Auburn, In, US 130/C3
Auburn, Me, US 131/G2
Auburn, Ne, US 129/J2
Auburn, NY, US 130/E3
Auburn, Pa, US 138/B2
Auburn, Wa, US 126/C4
Auburn Hills, Mi, US 135/F6
Aubusson, Fr. 42/E4
Aucá Mahuida (peak), Arg. 158/C3
Auch, Fr. 42/D5
Auchel, Fr. 52/B3
Auchinleck, Sc, UK 36/B6
Auchterarder, Sc, UK 36/C4
Auchtermuchty, Sc, UK 36/C4
Auchy-lès-Hesdin, Fr. 52/B3
Auckland, NZ 117/S10
Auckland (int'l arpt.), NZ 117/S10
Auckland (isls.), NZ 23/T8
Aude (riv.), Fr. 42/E5
Auderghem, Belg. 53/D2
Audeux (riv.), Fr. 56/C3
Audierne (bay), Fr. 42/A3
Audincourt, Fr. 56/C3
Audo (range), Eth. 97/P6
Audruicq, Fr. 52/B2
Audun-le-Roman, Fr. 53/E5
Audun-le-Tiche, Fr. 53/E5
Aue (riv.), Ger. 51/E2
Aue, Ger. 55/F1
Auer (Ora), It. 57/H5
Auerbach, Ger. 55/F1
Auerbach in der Oberpfalz, Ger. 55/E3
Auersberg (peak), Ger. 55/F2
Aufess (riv.), Ger. 54/E3
Auffargis, Fr. 30/H5
Augathella, Austl. 114/B4
Augher, NI, UK 34/A3
Aughnacloy, NI, UK 34/B3
Aughrim, Ire. 34/B6
Augrabies Falls NP, SAfr. 106/C3
Augrabiesvalle (falls), SAfr. 106/C3
Augsburg, Ger. 54/D6
Augub (peak), Namb. 106/A2
Augusta, Ga, US 133/H3
Augusta (cap.), Me, US 131/G2
Augusta, It. 46/D4
Augusta, Austl. 112/B5
Augusta, NJ, US 138/D1
Augusta, Golfo di (gulf), It. 46/D4
Augustdorf, Ger. 51/F5
Augustenborg, Den. 38/C4
Augusto César Sandino (int'l arpt.), Nic. 144/E3
Augustów, Pol. 39/K5
Augustus (mt.), Austl. 112/C3
Auk Bok (isl.), Myan. 78/B3
Auki, Sol. 116/F5
Aukstatija NP, Lith. 39/M4
Auld (lake), Austl. 109/B3
Aulencia (riv.), Sp. 45/M9
Aulendorf, Ger. 57/F2
Aulla, It. 58/C4
Aulnay-sous-Bois, Fr. 30/K5
Aulnay-sur-Mauldre, Fr. 30/H5
Aulne (riv.), Fr. 42/A2
Aulnoy, Fr. 30/M5
Aulnoye-Aymeries, Fr. 52/C3
Aulnut (int'l arpt.), Fr. 42/E4
Ault, Co, US 137/C1
Ault (peak), Swi. 57/F4
Ault, Fr. 52/A3
Aumale, Fr. 52/A4
Aumetz, Fr. 53/E5
Aumühle, Ger. 51/H1
Aunay-sur-Odon, Fr. 42/C2
Aunette (riv.), Fr. 52/B5
Auneuil, Fr. 52/B5
Auning, Den. 38/D3
Aur (isl.), Mrsh. 116/G4
Aura, NJ, US 138/C4
Aurach, Ger. 54/D4
Aurach (riv.), Ger. 54/D3
Auraiya, India 84/B2
Aurangābād, India 85/E3
Aurangābād, India 89/L5
Auray, Fr. 42/B3
Aureilhan, Fr. 42/D5
Aurich, Ger. 51/E2
Auriflama, Braz. 155/B2
Aurillac, Fr. 42/E4
Aurisina, It. 59/G1
Aurland, Nor. 38/B1
Aurolzmünster, Aus. 55/G6
Aurora, Braz. 154/C2
Aurora, Guy. 153/G3
Aurora, Co, US 137/C3
Aurora, Il, US 129/K2
Aurora, Mo, US 129/J3
Aurora Lodge, Ak, US 134/J3
Aus, Namb. 106/B2
Ausa (riv.), It. 59/G1
Aussillon, Fr. 42/E5
Aust-Agder (co.), Nor. 37/C4
Austin, Nv, US 128/C3
Austin (lake), Austl. 109/A3
Austin (isl.), Nun., Can. 122/G2
Austral (Tubuaï Islands) (isls.), FrPol. 117/K7
Australia (cont.) 109
Australia (ctry.) 109
Australian Alps (range), Austl. 115/C3
Australian Capital Territory (cap. terr.), Austl. 109/D4
Australind, Austl. 112/B5
Austria (ctry.) 43/L3
Austurhorn (pt.), Ice. 37/P7
Auterive, Fr. 42/D5
Authie (riv.), Fr. 42/D1
Autlán de Navarro, Mex. 142/D5
Automne (riv.), Fr. 52/B5
Autreppe, Belg. 52/C3
Autun, Fr. 42/F3
Auvergne (pol. reg.), Fr. 42/E4
Auvers-sur-Oise, Fr. 30/J4
Auvézère (riv.), Fr. 42/D4
Aux Sables (riv.), On, Can. 130/D2
Auxerre, Fr. 42/E3
Auxi-le-Château, Fr. 52/B3
Auxonne, Fr. 56/B3
Auyán-Tepuí (peak), Ven. 153/F3
Auyuittuq NP, Nun., Can. 123/K2
Auzangate (peak), Peru 156/D4
Āvaj, Iran 88/E1
Avallon, Fr. 42/E3
Avalon (pen.), Nf, Can. 123/L4
Avalon, Ca, US 136/B4
Avalon, NJ, US 138/D5
Avanne-Aveney, Fr. 56/B3
Avaré, Braz. 155/B2
Avarua, NZ 117/K7
Avdat (ruin), Isr. 91/D4
Avebury Stone Circle, Eng, UK 33/E4
Aveiro, Port. 44/A2
Aveiro (dist.), Port. 44/A2
Aveley, Eng, UK 30/D2
Avelgem, Belg. 52/C2
Avellaneda, Arg. 159/J11
Avellino, It. 46/D2
Avelon (riv.), Fr. 52/A5
Avenal, Ca, US 128/B3
Avenches, Swi. 56/D4
Avenel, NJ, US 139/H9
Avernes, Fr. 30/H4
Aversa, It. 46/D2
Aves (isl.), Ven. 141/J4
Avesnes-le-Comte, Fr. 52/B3
Avesnes-sur-Helpe, Fr. 52/C3
Avesta, Swe. 38/G1
Aveyron (riv.), Fr. 42/D4
Avezzano, It. 46/C1
Avich (lake), Sc, UK 36/A4
Aviemore, Sc, UK 36/C2
Avignon, Fr. 42/F5
Aviḩayil, Isr. 91/F7
Ávila de los Caballeros, Sp. 44/C2
Avilés, Sp. 44/C1
Avio, It. 59/D1
Avion, Fr. 52/B3
Avis, Pa, US 138/A1
Avisio (riv.), It. 57/H5
Avize, Fr. 52/D6
Avlum, Den. 38/C3
Avoca, Austl. 115/C4
Avoca, Austl. 115/B3
Avoca (riv.), Ire. 34/B6
Avoch, Sc, UK 36/B1
Avola, It. 46/D4
Avon (riv.), Eng, UK 32/C6
Avon (riv.), Sc, UK 36/C1
Avon, Fr. 42/E2
Avon (riv.), Fr. 30/L6
Avon Valley NP, Austl. 112/C4
Avon Water (riv.), Sc, UK 36/B5
Avonbeg (riv.), Ire. 34/B6
Avondale, Austl. 115/D2
Avondale, Az, US 137/R19
Avondale, Pa, US 138/C4
Avonlea, Sk, Can. 127/G3
Avonmore (riv.), Ire. 34/B5
Avranches, Fr. 42/C2
Avre (riv.), Fr. 40/B4
Avrillé, Fr. 42/C3
Awa-shima (isl.), Japan 76/A4
A'waj (riv.), Syria 91/E3
Awaji, Japan 77/H6
Awans, Belg. 53/E2
Āwasa, Eth. 97/N6
Āwash, Eth. 97/P6
Āwash Wenz (riv.), Eth. 97/P5
Awaso, Gha. 103/E5
Awat, China 70/D3
Awbārī, Libya 96/H2
Awbārī (des.), Libya 99/H4
Awe (lake), Sc, UK 36/A4
Awjilah, Libya 97/K2
Awka, Nga. 103/G5
Awsīm, Egypt 91/B4
Ax-les-Thermes, Fr. 42/D5
Axamo (int'l arpt.), Swe. 38/F3
Axams, Aus. 57/H3
Axarfjördhur (inlet), Ice. 37/N6
Axel, Neth. 50/A6
Axel Heiberg (isl.), Nun., Can. 123/S7
Axim, Gha. 103/E5
Axios (riv.), Gre. 47/H2
Axis (dam), Wa, US 135/D2
Axminster, Eng, UK 32/D5
Axochiapan, Mex. 143/L8
Ay (riv.), Rus. 61/N5
Ay, Fr. 52/C5
Ayabaca, Peru 156/B2
Ayabe, Japan 77/H5
Ayacucho, Peru 156/C4
Ayacucho (dept.), Peru 156/C4
Ayacucho, Arg. 158/F3
Ayagöz, Kaz. 70/D2
Ayaguz (riv.), Kaz. 70/C2
Ayama, Japan 77/K6

171

Ayamé – Baoto

Ayamé I, Barrage d' (dam), C.d'Iv. 102/E5
Ayamé II, Barrage d' (dam), C.d'Iv. 102/E5
Ayamonte, Sp. 44/B4
Ayancık, Turk. 90/C1
Ayanganna (mtn.), Guy. 153/G3
Ayapel, Col. 152/C2
Ayaş, Turk. 90/C1
Ayase, Japan 77/C3
Ayaviri, Peru 156/D4
Āybak, Afg. 87/E5
'Aybāl, Jabal (peak), WBnk. 91/G7
Aybastı, Turk. 90/D1
Aydar Köli (lake), Trkm. 87/E4
Aydın, Turk. 90/A2
Aydin (prov.), Turk. 90/B2
Aydıncık, Turk. 90/C1
Aydıncık, Turk. 91/C1
Aydınkent, Turk. 91/B1
Ayer, Swi. 56/D5
Ayers Rock (Uluru) (peak), Austl. 113/F3
Ayeyarwady (state), Myan. 83/F4
Ayeyarwady (Irrawaddy), (riv.) Myan. 67/J7
Ayiá, Gre. 47/H3
Ayía Paraskeví, Gre. 47/K3
Ayiásos, Gre. 47/K3
Áyios Ioánnis (cape), Gre. 47/J5
Áyios Kírikos, Gre. 47/K4
Áyios Konstandínos, Gre. 47/H3
Áyios Matthaíos, Gre. 47/F3
Áyios Nikólaos, Gre. 47/J5
Aylesbury, Eng, UK 33/F3
Aylesford, Eng, UK 33/G4
Ayllón, Sp. 44/D2
Aylmer (lake), NW, Can. 122/F2
'Ayn al 'Arab, Syria 90/D2
'Ayn Zuwayyah (well), Libya 97/K3
Ayna, Peru 156/C4
Ayon (isl.), Rus. 65/S3
Ayora, Sp. 45/E3
Ayotzintepec, Mex. 144/B2
'Ayoûn 'Abd el Mâlek (well), Mrta. 98/D4
'Ayoûn el 'Atroûs, Mrta. 102/C2
Ayr, Austl. 114/B2
Ayr, Sc, UK 36/B6
Ayr (riv.), Sc, UK 36/B5
Aytré, Fr. 42/C3
Ayubia NP, Pak. 86/B3
Ayutla, Mex. 142/D4
Ayutla de los Libres, Mex. 140/B4
Ayutthaya (ruin), Thai. 78/C3
Ayvacık, Turk. 47/K3
Ayvalık, Turk. 90/A2
Aywaille, Belg. 53/E3
Az Zabadānī, Syria 91/E3
Az Ẓāhirīyah, WBnk. 91/D4
Az Zaqāzīq, Egypt 91/B4
Az Zarqā' (gov.), Jor. 91/E3
Az Zarqā', Jor. 91/E3
Az Zāwiyah, Libya 96/H1
Az Zaydīyah, Yem. 88/D5
Azad Kashmir (terr.), Pak. 86/B3
Azahar (coast), Sp. 45/F3
Azalea, Or, US 126/C5
Azalia, Mi, US 135/E7
Azamgarh, India 84/D2
Azángaro (riv.), Peru 156/D4
Azángaro, Peru 156/D4
Azao (peak), Alg. 99/H4
Azaouâd (phys. reg.), Mali 96/E4
Āzarān, Iran 88/E1
Āzarbāyjān-e Gharbī (prov.), Iran 90/F2
A'zāz, Syria 91/E1
Azemmour, Mor. 98/C2
Azerbaijan (ctry.) 63/H4
Azilal, Mor. 98/D3
Azīmganj, India 85/G3
Azogues, Ecu. 152/B5
Azores (dpcy.), Port. 45/R12
Azourki (peak), Mor. 98/D3
Azov, Rus. 62/F3
Azov (sea), Ukr.,Rus. 64/D5
Azoyú, Mex. 144/B2
Azpeitia, Sp. 44/D1
Azrou, Mor. 98/D2
Aztec, NM, US 128/F3
Aztec Ruins Nat'l Mon., NM, US 128/E3
Azua de Compostela, DRep. 141/G4
Azuaga, Sp. 44/C3
Azuara, Sp. 45/E2
Azuay (dept.), Ecu. 152/B5
Azuchi, Japan 77/K5
Azuero, Peninsula de (pen.), Pan. 150/B2
Azuga, Rom. 49/G3
Azul (mtn.), CR 144/E4
Azul (riv.), Guat. 144/D2
Azul, Arg. 158/F3
Azul, Cordillera (mts.), Peru 156/B2
Azuma, Japan 77/E2
Azuma-san (peak), Japan 75/G2
Azumaya-san (peak), Japan 75/F2
Azur, Côte d' (coast), Fr. 43/G5
Azusa, Ca, US 136/C2
Azzaba, Alg. 100/K6
Azzano Decimo, It. 59/F1
Azzano San Paolo, It. 58/C1
Azzate, It. 58/B1
'Azzūn, WBnk. 91/G7

B

Ba (riv.), Viet. 79/A5
Bà (riv.), Viet. 83/J5
Ba Lang An (cape), Viet. 78/E3
Ba Quan (cape), Viet. 78/D4
Baar, Swi. 57/E3
Baarle-Hertog, Belg. 50/B6
Baarle-Nassau, Neth. 50/B6
Baarn, Neth. 50/C4
Bab el Mandeb (str.), Asia 88/D6
Baba (mts.), Afg. 89/J2
Baba (peak), Bul. 47/H1
Baba (pt.), Turk. 49/K5
Baba Burnu (pt.), Turk. 47/K3
Babadag, Rom. 49/J3
Babaeski, Turk. 49/H5
Babahoyo, Ecu. 152/B5
Babai Khola (riv.), Nepal 84/C1
Babakale, Turk. 47/K3
Babar (isls.), Indo. 81/G5
Babatorun, Turk. 91/E1
Babatpur (int'l arpt.), India 84/D3
Babbacombe (bay), Eng, UK 32/C6
Babbitt, Mn, US 127/L4
B'abdā, Leb. 91/D3
Babelthuap (isl.), Palau 116/C4
Babenhausen, Ger. 57/G1
Babenhausen, Ger. 54/B3
Babensham, Ger. 55/F6
Baberu, India 84/C3
Babia (peak), Pol. 62/A2
Babian (riv.), China 83/H3
Bābil (gov.), Iraq 90/F3
Bābil (Babylon) (ruin), Iraq 90/F3
Babīna, India 84/B3
Babinda, Austl. 114/B2
Babine (riv.), BC, Can. 122/D3
Bābol, Iran 88/F1
Babruysk, Bela. 62/D1
Babuyan (isl.), Phil. 67/M8
Babylon, NY, US 139/E2
Bac Giang, Viet. 78/D1
Bac Lieu, Viet. 78/D4
Bac Ninh, Viet. 83/J3
Bacabal, Braz. 154/A2
Bacadéhuachi, Mex. 142/C2
Bacajá (riv.), Braz. 151/H4
Bacalar, Mex. 144/D2
Bacalar (lag.), Mex. 144/D2
Bacan (isl.), Indo. 81/G4
Bacău, Rom. 49/H2
Bacău (prov.), Rom. 49/H2
Baccarat, Fr. 56/C1
Bacchiglione (riv.), It. 59/E2
Bacchus, Ut, US 137/J12
Bacerac, Mex. 142/C2
Bacharach, Ger. 53/G3
Bachhraon, India 84/B1
Bachíniva, Mex. 142/D2
Back (riv.), Md, US 138/B5
Back (riv.), Nun., Can. 122/F2
Bačka (reg.), Serb. 48/D3
Bačka Palanka, Serb. 48/D3
Bačka Topola, Serb. 48/D3
Bäckefors, Swe. 38/E2
Backnang, Ger. 54/C5
Bacobampa, Mex. 142/C3
Bacolod, Phil. 81/F1
Bács-Kiskun (prov.), Hun. 48/D2
Bácsalmás, Hun. 48/D2
Bacup, Eng, UK 35/F4
Bad (riv.), SD, US 127/H5
Bad Abbach, Ger. 55/F5
Bad Axe, Mi, US 130/D3
Bad Bellingen, Ger. 56/D2
Bad Bergzabern, Ger. 54/B4
Bad Berneck, Ger. 55/E2
Bad Bocklet, Ger. 54/D2
Bad Brambach, Ger. 55/F2
Bad Breisig, Ger. 53/G3
Bad Brückenau, Ger. 54/C2
Bad Buchau, Ger. 57/F1
Bad Camberg, Ger. 54/B2
Bad Doberan, Ger. 38/D4
Bad Driburg, Ger. 51/G5
Bad Dürkheim, Ger. 54/B4
Bad Dürrheim, Ger. 57/E1
Bad Ems, Ger. 53/G3
Bad Endorf, Ger. 55/F7
Bad Essen, Ger. 51/F4
Bad Freienwalde, Ger. 41/H2
Bad Gandersheim, Ger. 51/H5
Bad Goisern, Aus. 43/K3
Bad Grund, Ger. 51/H5
Bad Hall, Aus. 55/H6
Bad Harzburg, Ger. 51/H5
Bad Heilbrunn, Ger. 57/H2
Bad Herrenalb, Ger. 54/B5
Bad Hersfeld, Ger. 43/H1
Bad Hofgastein, Aus. 43/K3
Bad Homburg vor der Höhe, Ger. 54/B2
Bad Honnef, Ger. 53/G2
Bad Hönningen, Ger. 53/G3
Bad Ischl, Aus. 43/K3
Bad Karlshafen, Ger. 51/G5
Bad Kissingen, Ger. 54/D2
Bad Kohlgrub, Ger. 57/H2
Bad König, Ger. 54/C3
Bad Königshofen, Ger. 54/D2
Bad Kreuznach, Ger. 53/G4
Bad Krozingen, Ger. 56/D2
Bad Langensalza, Ger. 51/H6
Bad Lauterberg, Ger. 51/H5
Bad Leonfelden, Aus. 55/H5
Bad Liebenzell, Ger. 54/B5
Bad Lippspringe, Ger. 51/F3
Bad Marienberg, Ger. 53/G2
Bad Mergentheim, Ger. 54/C4
Bad Munder am Deister, Ger. 51/G4
Bad Nauheim, Ger. 54/B2
Bad Nenndorf, Ger. 51/G4
Bad Neuenahr-Ahrweiler, Ger. 53/G2
Bad Neustadt an der Saale, Ger. 54/D2
Bad Oeynhausen, Ger. 51/F4
Bad Orb, Ger. 54/C2
Bad Peterstal-Griesbach, Ger. 56/E1
Bad Plaas, SAfr. 107/E2
Bad Pyrmont, Ger. 51/G5
Bad Ragaz, Swi. 57/F4
Bad Rappenau, Ger. 54/C4
Bad Reichenhall, Ger. 43/K3
Bad Rothenfelde, Ger. 51/F4
Bad Sachsa, Ger. 51/H5
Bad Salzdetfurth, Ger. 51/G4
Bad Salzschlirf, Ger. 54/C1
Bad Salzuflen, Ger. 51/F4
Bad Salzungen, Ger. 40/F3
Bad Sankt-Leonhard im Lavanttal, Aus. 43/L3
Bad Sassendorf, Ger. 51/F5
Bad Schallerbach, Aus. 55/G6
Bad Schwalbach, Ger. 53/H3
Bad Schwartau, Ger. 38/D5
Bad Segeberg, Ger. 38/D5
Bad Soden-Salmünster, Ger. 54/C2
Bad Sooden-Allendorf, Ger. 51/G6
Bad Tölz, Ger. 57/H2
Bad Vilbel, Ger. 54/B2
Bad Vöslau, Aus. 43/M3
Bad Waldsee, Ger. 57/F2
Bad Wildungen, Ger. 51/G6
Bad Wimpfen, Ger. 54/C4
Bad Wimsbach-Neydharting, Aus. 55/G6
Bad Windsheim, Ger. 54/D3
Bad Wörishofen, Ger. 57/G1
Bad Wurzach, Ger. 57/F2
Bad Zell, Aus. 55/H6
Bad Zwischenahn, Ger. 51/F2
Badagara, India 82/C5
Badain Jaran (des.), China 70/H3
Badajoz, Sp. 44/B3
Badalona, Sp. 45/L7
Badalucco, It. 58/A5
Badbergen, Ger. 51/E3
Baddeckenstedt, Ger. 51/H4
Baddomalhi, Pak. 86/C4
Baden, Aus. 43/M2
Baden, Swi. 57/E3
Baden-Baden, Ger. 54/B5
Baden-Württemberg (state), Ger. 43/H2
Badener (peak), Ger. 54/B5
Badenoch (reg.), Sc, UK 36/B3
Badenweiler, Ger. 56/D2
Badgastein, Aus. 43/K3
Badgingarra NP, Austl. 112/B4
Badia Polesine, It. 59/E2
Badiar, PN du, Gui. 102/B3
Badile (peak), It. 57/F5
Badīn, Pak. 89/J4
Badiraguato, Mex. 142/D3
Badlands (plat.), SD, US 127/H5
Badlands NP, SD, US 127/H5
Badonviller, Fr. 56/C1
Badou, Togo 103/F5
Badovinci, Serb. 48/D3
Badrāh, Pak. 89/J3
Badrah, Iraq 88/E2
Badua (riv.), India 85/F3
Badulla, SrL. 82/D6
Bāduriā, India 85/G4
Baena, Sp. 44/C4
Baependi, Braz. 211/J6
Baerenkopf (peak), Fr. 56/C2
Baesweiler, Ger. 53/F2
Baeza, Sp. 44/D4
Baffa, Pak. 86/B2
Baffin (bay), Can.,Grld. 119/K2
Baffin (isl.), Nun., Can. 123/H1
Baffin (bay), Tx, US 132/D5
Bafia, Camr. 96/H7
Bafilo, Togo 103/F4
Bafing (riv.), Gui. 96/C5
Bafoulabé, Mali 102/C3
Bafoussam, Camr. 96/H6
Bāfq, Iran 89/G2
Bafra, Turk. 90/C1
Bafra (cape), Turk. 90/C1
Bāft, Iran 89/G3
Bag Salt (lake), China 72/B3
Bagaces, CR 144/E4
Bagadó, Col. 152/B3
Bagaha, India 85/E2
Bagamoyo, Tanz. 104/C4
Baganga, Phil. 79/E6
Bagda (mts.), China 70/E3
Bagé, Braz. 157/F3
Bagenkop, Den. 38/D4
Baggao, Phil. 79/D4
Baggy (pt.), Eng, UK 32/B4
Bāgh, Pak. 86/B4
Baghain (riv.), India 84/C3
Baghdād (Baghdad) (cap.), Iraq 90/F3
Bagheria, It. 46/C3
Baghlān, Afg. 89/J1
Bāghpat, India 86/D5
Bağırpaşa (peak), Turk. 90/E2
Bagley, Mn, US 127/K4
Bagluń, Nepal 84/D1
Bāgmati (riv.), India 85/E2
Bāgmati (zone), Nepal 85/E2
Bagn, Nor. 38/C1
Bagnacavallo, It. 59/F4
Bagnasco, It. 58/B4
Bagnères-de-Bigorre, Fr. 42/D5
Bagnères-de-Luchon, Fr. 42/D5
Bagneux, Fr. 30/J5
Bagni di Lucca, It. 58/D4
Bagno a Ripoli, It. 59/E5
Bagnolet, Fr. 30/K5
Bagnoli Irpino, It. 46/D2
Bagnolo Cremasco, It. 58/C2
Bagnolo in Piano, It. 59/D3
Bagnolo Mella, It. 58/D2
Bagnolo San Vito, It. 59/D2
Bagnols-sur-Cèze, Fr. 42/F4
Bagnone, It. 58/C4
Bago, Phil. 79/D5
Bago (div.), Myan. 70/G8
Bago (Pegu), Myan. 83/G4
Bagoe (riv.), Mali 96/D5
Bagolino, It. 58/D1
Bagshot, Eng, UK 30/A3
Bagua Grande, Peru 156/B2
Baguio, Phil. 79/D4
Baguirmi (reg.), Chad 96/J5
Bagzane (peak), Niger 103/H2
Bāh, India 84/B2
Bahādurganj, India 85/F2
Bahādurgarh, India 86/D5
Bahamas, The (ctry.) 141/F2
Bahāwalnagar, Pak. 86/B5
Bahāwalpur, Pak. 86/A5
Bahçe, Turk. 90/D2
Bahçesaray, Turk. 90/E2
Baheri, India 84/B1
Bahi (swamp), Tanz. 104/B4
Bahía (state), Braz. 154/B4
Bahía Asunción, Mex. 142/B3
Bahía Blanca, Arg. 158/E3
Bahía de Caráquez, Ecu. 152/A5
Bahía de los Ángeles, Mex. 142/B2
Bahía de Tortugas, Mex. 142/B3
Bahía, Islas de la (isls.), Hon. 140/D4
Bahía Solano, Col. 152/B3
Bahir Dar, Eth. 97/N5
Bahjoi, India 84/B1
Bahlah, Oman 89/G4
Baḩr al 'Arab (riv.), Sudan 97/L6
Baḩr al Milḩ (lake), Iraq 90/E3
Bahraich, India 84/C2
Bahrain (ctry.) 88/F3
Bahrain, Gulf of (gulf), Asia 88/F3
Baia de Aramă, Rom. 49/F3
Baia Mare, Rom. 49/F2
Baia Sprie, Rom. 49/F2
Baïbokoum, Chad 96/J6
Baicheng, China 70/D3
Baicheng, China 71/M2
Băicoi, Rom. 49/G3
Baidong (lake), China 72/D5
Baie-Comeau, Qu, Can. 131/G1
Baie-Saint-Paul, Qu, Can. 131/G2
Baienfurt, Ger. 57/F2
Baiersbronn, Ger. 54/B5
Baiersdorf, Ger. 54/E3
Baigorrita, Arg. 158/E2
Baigou (riv.), China 72/G7
Baihar, India 84/C4
Baihua (mtn.), China 72/G7
Ba'ījī, Iraq 90/E3
Baikunthpur, India 84/D4
Bailadores, Ven. 152/D2
Baildon, Eng, UK 35/G4
Băile Govora, Rom. 49/G3
Băile Herculane, Rom. 48/F3
Băile Olănești, Rom. 49/G3
Băile Tușnad, Rom. 49/G2
Bailén, Sp. 44/D3
Băilești, Rom. 49/F3
Bailieborough, Ire. 31/Q10
Bailleul, Fr. 52/B2
Bailong (riv.), China 70/H5
Bailu (riv.), China 72/C4
Baima, China 70/H5
Bain (riv.), Eng, UK 35/H5
Bainang, China 85/G1
Bainbridge, Ga, US 133/G4
Bainbridge, Pa, US 138/B3
Bainbridge (isl.), Wa, US 135/B2
Bainbridge Naval Training Sta., Md, US 138/B4
Baingoin, China 70/E5
Bains-les-Bains, Fr. 56/C2
Bairāgnia, India 85/E2
Baird (inlet), Ak, US 134/F3
Baird, Tx, US 129/H4
Bairin Youqi, China 71/L3
Bairnsdale, Austl. 115/C3
Baïse (riv.), Fr. 42/D5
Baixa da Banheira, Port. 45/P10
Baixa Grande, Braz. 154/B4
Baixiang, China 72/C3
Baixo Guandu, Braz. 155/D1
Baiyin, China 70/H4
Baiyu (mts.), China 72/B3
Baiyun (int'l arpt.), China 79/B3
Baja (pt.), Mex. 142/B2
Baja, Hun. 48/D2
Baja (pt.), Chile 159/B6
Baja California (state), Mex. 142/B2
Baja California (pen.), Mex. 142/B2
Baja California Sur (state), Mex. 142/B3
Bājah (gov.), Tun. 46/A4
Bājah, Tun. 100/L6
Bajánsenye, Hun. 43/M3
Bajestān, Iran 89/G2
Bājil, Yem. 88/D5
Bajina Bašta, Serb. 48/D4
Bajmbat (mt.), Austl. 115/E1
Bajmok, Serb. 48/D3
Bajo Boquete, Pan. 145/F4
Bajo de Gualicho (plain), Arg. 157/C5
Bajram Curri, Alb. 47/G1
Bakanas (riv.), Kaz. 87/G3
Bakau, Gam. 102/A3
Bakayan (peak), Indo. 81/E3
Bakel, Sen. 102/B3
Baker (lake), Nun., Can. 122/G2
Baker (riv.), Chile 159/B5
Baker (isl.), Pac., US 117/H4
Baker, La, US 129/K5
Baker, Mt, US 127/G4
Baker (mt.), Wa, US 126/C3
Baker City, Or, US 126/D4
Baker Lake, Nun., Can. 122/G2
Bakersfield, Ca, US 128/C4
Bakhchysaray, Ukr. 62/E3
Bakhmach, Ukr. 62/E2
Bākhtarān, Iran 88/E2
Bakhtiyārpur, India 85/E3
Bakhuis (mts.), Sur. 153/G4
Bakkaflói (bay), Ice. 37/P6
Baklan, Turk. 90/B2
Bakonyszombathely, Hun. 48/C2
Bakora Corridor Game Rsv., Ugan. 104/B2
Bakovský Potok (riv.), Czh. 55/G2
Bakoye (riv.), Gui. 102/C4
Baku (int'l arpt.), Azer. 63/J4
Baku (cap.), Azer. 63/J4
Balâ, Turk. 90/C2
Bala, Wal, UK 34/E6
Balabac, Phil. 81/E2
Balabac (str.), Malay.,Ph 81/E2
Balabac (isl.), Phil. 81/E2
Ba'labakk, Leb. 91/E2
Balāghāt, India 84/C5
Balaguer, Sp. 45/F2
Balaïtous (peak), Fr. 42/C5
Balaka, Malw. 105/F3
Balakhna, Rus. 61/J4
Balaklava, Austl. 113/H5
Balakovo, Rus. 63/H1
Bal'amā, Jor. 91/E3
Bălan, Rom. 49/G2
Balancán, Mex. 144/D2
Balanga, Phil. 79/D5
Bālāngir, India 82/D3
Balao, Ecu. 156/B1
Balarāmpur, India 85/F4
Balashikha, Rus. 61/W9
Balashov, Rus. 63/G2
Balasore (Baleshwar), India 82/E3
Balassagyarmat, Hun. 41/K4
Balaton (lake), Cro. 48/C2
Balatonföldvár, Hun. 48/C2
Balatonfüred, Hun. 48/C2
Balatonszabadi, Hun. 48/D2
Balatonszentgyörgy, Hun. 48/C2
Balbina (res.), Braz. 147/D3
Balbriggan, Ire. 34/B4
Balcarce, Arg. 158/F3
Balcary (pt.), Sc, UK 34/E2
Balchik, Bul. 49/J4
Balclutha, NZ 117/R12
Balcones Escarpment (plat.), Tx, US 137/T20
Balcones Heights, Tx, US 137/T21
Bald (pt.), Austl. 112/C5
Bald Eagle Mtn. (mtn.), Pa, US 138/A1
Bald Rock NP, Austl. 115/E1
Baldock, Eng, UK 33/F3
Baldwin, NY, US 139/L9
Baldwin Harbour, NY, US 139/L9
Baldwin Park, Mo, US 137/E6
Baldwin Park, Ca, US 136/G7
Baldy (mtn.), Mb, Can. 127/H3
Baldy Beacon (peak), Belz. 144/D2
Bale Mountains NP, Eth. 97/N6
Baleares (Balearic) (isls.), Sp. 45/G3
Baleia, Ponta da (pt.), Braz. 154/C5
Baleine, Grand Rivière de la (riv.), Qu, Can. 123/J3
Baleine, Petite Rivière de la (riv.), Qu, Can. 123/J3
Baleine, Rivière à la (riv.), Qu, Can. 123/K3
Balen, Belg. 53/E1
Baler, Phil. 79/D4
Balerna, Swi. 57/E6
Balesa (riv.), Kenya 104/C2
Baleshwar (Balasore), India 82/E3
Balfour, SAfr. 106/E2
Balfron, Sc, UK 36/B4
Balgatay, Mong. 70/G2
Balhannah, Austl. 113/M8
Bali (sea), Indo. 80/D5
Bali (isl.), Indo. 67/L10
Bāli Chak, India 85/F4
Balice (int'l arpt.), Pol. 41/K3
Baliem (riv.), Indo. 81/J4
Balıkesir, Turk. 90/A2
Balıkesir (prov.), Turk. 62/C5
Balikpapan, Indo. 81/E4
Balimbing, Phil. 81/E2
Baling, Malay. 83/H6
Balingasag, Phil. 79/D6
Bälinge, Swe. 38/G2
Balingen, Ger. 57/E1
Balk, Neth. 50/C3
Balkan (pol. reg.), Trkm. 87/B4
Balkan (mts.), Bul.,Serb. 27/F3
Balkhash (lake), Kaz. 67/G5
Ballagan (pt.), Ire. 34/B4
Ballaghaderreen, Ire. 31/P10
Ballangen, Nor. 37/F1
Ballantrae, Sc, UK 34/C1
Ballarat, Austl. 115/B3
Ballard (lake), Austl. 109/B3
Ballarpur, India 82/C4
Ballater, Sc, UK 36/C2
Ballaugh, IM, UK 34/D3
Ballens, Swi. 56/C4
Balleny (isls.), Ant. 160/L
Ballia, India 85/E3
Ballina, Austl. 115/E1
Ballinamallard, NI, UK 31/Q9
Ballinasloe, Ire. 31/P10
Ballinderry (riv.), NI, UK 34/B2
Ballinger, Tx, US 129/H5
Ballingry, Sc, UK 36/C4
Ballinrobe, Ire. 31/P10
Balloch, Sc, UK 36/B2
Ballon, Col du (pass), Fr. 56/C2
Ballon d'Alsace (peak), Fr. 56/C2
Ballon de Sevance (peak), Fr. 56/C2
Ballwin, Mo, US 137/F8
Bally, Pa, US 138/C3
Ballycarry, NI, UK 34/C2
Ballycastle, NI, UK 34/B1
Ballycastle, Ire. 31/P9
Ballyclare, NI, UK 34/B2
Ballyeaston, NI, UK 34/B2
Ballygawley, NI, UK 34/A3
Ballygeary, Ire. 31/Q10
Ballygowan, NI, UK 34/C3
Ballyhaunis, Ire. 31/P10
Ballyheigue, Ire. 30/P10
Ballyliffin, Ire. 34/A1
Ballymena (dist.), NI, UK 34/B2
Ballymena, NI, UK 34/B2
Ballymoney (dist.), NI, UK 34/B1
Ballymoney, NI, UK 34/B1
Ballynahinch, NI, UK 34/C3
Ballynure, NI, UK 34/C2
Ballyquintin (pt.), NI, UK 34/C3
Ballyshannon, Ire. 31/P9
Balmaceda (peak), Chile 159/B6
Balmazújváros, Hun. 41/L5
Balmhorn (peak), Swi. 56/D5
Balmoral, Austl. 115/B3
Balmoral Castle, Sc, UK 36/C2
Balneário Camboriú, Braz. 155/B3
Balneario Claromecó, Arg. 158/E3
Balneario de los Novillos, PN, Mex. 129/G5
Balochistān (reg.), Pak. 89/J3
Balonne (riv.), Austl. 109/D3
Balotra, India 89/K3
Balqash, Kaz. 87/G3
Balrāmpur, India 84/D2
Balranald, Austl. 115/B2
Balş, Rom. 49/G3
Bálsamo (pt.), Ecu. 152/A5
Balsapuerto, Peru 156/B2
Balsas, Braz. 154/A2
Balsas (riv.), Mex. 143/F5
Balsthal, Swi. 56/D3
Baltanás, Sp. 44/C2
Bălți, Mol. 49/H2
Baltic (sea), Swe. 37/F5
Baltic (plain), Rus. 61/S7
Baltic Spit (bar), Pol.,Rus. 39/H4
Balṭīm, Egypt 91/B4
Baltimore, Md, US 138/B5
Baltimore (co.), Md, US 138/B4
Baltimore-Washington (int'l arpt.), Md, US 138/B5
Baltiysk, Rus. 39/H4
Baltray, Ire. 34/B4
Baltrum (isl.), Ger. 51/E1
Bælum, Den. 38/D3
Bālurghāt, India 85/G3
Balve, Ger. 51/E6
Balya, Turk. 62/C5
Balykshi, Kaz. 63/J3
Balzar, Ecu. 152/B5
Balzers, Lcht. 57/F3
Bam (prov.), Burk. 103/E3
Bam, Iran 89/G3
Bama Yaozu Zizhixian, China 83/J3
Bamaji (lake), On, Can. 127/K3
Bamako (cap.), Mali 102/D3
Bamako (Senou) (int'l arpt.), Mali 102/D3
Bambamarca, Peru 156/B2
Bambana (riv.), Nic. 145/E3
Bambari, CAfr. 97/K6
Bamberg, Ger. 54/D3
Bamberg, SC, US 133/H3
Bamble, Nor. 38/C2
Bambuí, Braz. 155/C2
Bamenda, Camr. 103/H5
Bāmīān, Afg. 87/E6
Bamingui-Bangoran, PN du, CAfr. 97/J6
Bammental, Ger. 54/B4
Bampūr (riv.), Iran 89/H3
Ban Boun Tai, Laos 83/H3
Ban Chiang (ruin), Thai. 78/C2
Ban Houayxay, Laos 83/H3
Ban Kantang, Thai. 78/B5
Ban Kengkok, Laos 83/J4
Ban Pak Phanang, Thai. 78/C4
Banaba (isl.), Kiri. 116/F5
Banagher, Ire. 31/Q10
Banamba, Mali 102/D3
Banana (isls.), SLeo. 102/B4
Bananal, Braz. 211/J7
Bananal, Ilha do (isl.), Braz. 151/H6
Banar (riv.), Bang. 85/H3
Banarlı, Turk. 49/H5
Banās (pt.), Egypt 101/C4
Banās (riv.), India 89/L3
Banat (reg.), Serb. 48/E3
Banatsko Novo Selo, Serb. 48/E3
Banaz, Turk. 90/B2
Banbar, China 70/G5
Banbridge, NI, UK 34/B3
Banbridge (dist.), NI, UK 34/B3
Banbury, Eng, UK 33/E2
Banc d'Arguin, Mrta. 98/A5
Banc d'Arguin, PN du, Mrta. 96/B3
Banc d'Arguin, PN du, Mrta. 102/A2
Banchette, It. 58/A2
Banchory, Sc, UK 36/D2
Banco Chinchorro (isls.), Mex. 140/D4
Bancroft, On, Can. 130/E2
Banda (isls.), Indo. 81/H4
Bāndā, India 84/C3
Banda, India 84/B3
Banda (sea), Indo. 67/M10
Banda Aceh, Indo. 80/A2
Bandai-san (peak), Japan 75/G2
Bandama (riv.), C.d'Iv. 96/D6
Bandama Blanc (riv.), C.d'Iv. 102/D4
Bandama Rouge (riv.), C.d'Iv. 102/D4
Bandar Beheshtī, Iran 89/H3
Bandar-e 'Abbās, Iran 89/G3
Bandar-e Anzalī, Iran 88/E1
Bandar-e Deylam, Iran 88/F2
Bandar-e Lengeh, Iran 89/F3
Bandar-e Māhshahr, Iran 88/E2
Bandar-e Torkeman, Iran 88/F1
Bandar Seri Begawan (cap.),Bru. 80/D3
Bande, Sp. 44/B1
Bandeira do Sul, Braz. 211/G6
Bandeira, Pico da (peak), Braz. 155/D2
Bandeirantes, Braz. 155/B2
Bandelier Nat'l Mon., NM, US 129/F4
Bandera, Tx, US 129/H5
Banderilla, Mex. 143/N7
Bandhavgarh NP, India 84/C4
Bandholm, Den. 38/D4
Bandiagara, Mali 102/E3
Bandipura, India 86/C2
Bandırma (gulf), Turk. 49/H5
Bandırma, Turk. 49/H5
Bandon, Ire. 31/P11
Bandon (riv.), Ire. 31/P11
Bandundu, D.R. Congo 105/C1
Bandung, Indo. 80/C5
Bañeres, Sp. 45/E3
Banes, Cuba 145/H1
Banff, Ab, Can. 126/E3
Banff, Sc, UK 36/D1
Banff NP, Ab, Can. 126/E3
Banfora, Burk. 102/D4
Bang Lang (res.), Thai. 78/C5
Bañga, Phil. 79/D6
Banga, India 86/C4
Bangalore, India 82/C5
Bangalow, Austl. 114/D5
Bangaon, India 85/G4
Bāngarmau, India 84/C2
Bangassou, CAfr. 97/K7
Bangau (cape), Malay. 81/E2
Banggai (isls.), Indo. 81/F4
Banghiang (riv.), Laos 78/D2
Bangka (str.), Indo. 80/B4
Bangka (isl.), Indo. 67/K10
Bangkok (int'l arpt.), Thai. 78/C3
Bangkok, Bight of (bay), Thai. 83/H5
Bangkok (Krung Thep) (cap.),Thai. 78/C3
Bangladesh (ctry.) 82/E3
Bangor, NI, UK 34/C2
Bangor (int'l arpt.), Me, US 131/G2
Bangor, Me, US 131/G2
Bangor, Pa, US 138/C2
Bangor, Wal, UK 34/D5
Bangued, Phil. 79/D4
Bangui (cap.), CAfr. 97/J7
Bangweulu (swamp), Zam. 104/A5
Bangweulu (lake), Zam. 105/E3
Banhā, Egypt 91/B4
Banhine, PN de, Moz. 105/F5
Bani (riv.), Mali 96/D5
Baní, DRep. 141/G4
Banī Mazār, Egypt 101/B2
Banī Suhaylah, Gaza 91/D4
Banī Suwayf (gov.), Egypt 101/B1
Banī Suwayf, Egypt 101/B2
Bánica, DRep. 145/J2
Banifing (riv.), Mali 102/D3
Banihāl (pass), India 86/C3
Banikoara, Ben. 103/F4
Banister (riv.), Va, US 133/J2
Bāniyās, Syria 91/D2
Banja Koviljača, Serb. 48/D3
Banja Luka, Bosn. 48/C3
Banjarmasin, Indo. 80/D4
Banjul (cap.), Gam. 102/A3
Bānka, India 85/F3
Bankas, Mali 102/E3
Bankeryd, Swe. 38/F3
Bankfoot, Sc, UK 36/C3
Bankhead, Sc, UK 36/D2
Bānki, India 85/E4
Banks (cape), Austl. 115/B3
Banks (str.), Austl. 109/D5
Banks (isl.), NW, Can. 122/D2
Banks (pen.), NZ 109/H7
Banks (pt.), Ak, US 134/H4
Banks (lake), Wa, US 126/D4
Banks (isls.), Van. 116/F6
Bānkurā, India 85/F4
Bankya, Bul. 47/H1
Banmankhi, India 85/F3
Bann (riv.), Ire. 31/Q10
Bann (riv.), NI, UK 34/B3
Banna (riv.), It. 58/A3
Bannockburn, Sc, UK 36/C4
Bannockburn Battlesite, Sc, UK 36/C4
Bannu, Pak. 86/A3
Baños, Ecu. 156/B1
Banpo Ruins, China 72/B4
Bansberia, India 85/G4
Bānsdīh, India 85/E3
Bānsi, India 84/D2
Bansin, Ger. 38/F5
Banská Bystrica, Slvk. 62/A2
Banská Štiavnica, Slvk. 48/D1
Bansko, Bul. 47/H2
Banskobystrický (pol. reg.), Slvk. 41/K4
Banstead, Eng, UK 30/C3
Bānswāra, India 89/K4
Bantayan, Phil. 79/D5
Banté, Ben. 103/F4
Bantenan (cape), Indo. 80/D5
Bantong Group (isls.), Thai. 78/B5
Bantry, Ire. 31/P11
Bañuelo (peak), Sp. 44/C3
Banyak (isls.), Indo. 80/A3
Banyoles, Sp. 45/G1
Banyuwangi, Indo. 80/D5
Banzare (coast), Ant. 160/J
Banzart (gov.), Tun. 46/A4
Banzart (Bizerte), Tun. 46/A4
Baode, China 72/B3
Baodi, China 72/H7
Baoding, China 72/G7
Baofeng, China 72/C4
Baoji, China 70/J5
Baojing, China 83/J2
Baokang, China 72/B5
Baoruco (mts.), DRep. 145/J2
Baoshan, China 83/G2
Baoshan, China 72/L8
Baotou, China 72/B2

Baoulé (riv.), Mali 96/D5
Baoying, China 72/D4
Bapaume, Fr. 52/B3
Bapchule, Az, US 137/S19
Baptistown, NJ, US 138/C2
Bāqa el Gharbiyya, Isr. 91/G7
Baqên, China 70/F5
Ba'qūbah, Iraq 90/F3
Bar, Serb. 47/F1
Bar (riv.), Fr. 40/C4
Bar Bigha, India 85/E3
Bar el Ksaïb (well), Mali 98/D5
Bar Harbor, Me, US 131/G2
Bar-le-Duc, Fr. 53/E6
Bar-sur-Aube, Fr. 42/F2
Bar-sur-Seine, Fr. 42/F2
Bara, Swe. 38/E4
Bāra Banki, India 84/C2
Bārā Lācha La (pass), India 86/D3
Barabai, Indo. 80/E4
Barabinsk, Rus. 87/G1
Baraboo, Wi, US 127/L5
Baracaldo, Sp. 44/D1
Baracoa, Cuba 145/H1
Barada (riv.), Syria 91/E3
Baradero, Arg. 159/J10
Baradine, Austl. 115/D1
Baragoi, Kenya 104/C2
Baraguá, Cuba 145/G1
Baragua, Ven. 152/D2
Barajas (int'l arpt.), Sp. 45/N9
Barajevo, Serb. 48/E3
Barākar (riv.), India 85/F3
Barakī Barak, Afg. 89/J2
Baralaba, Austl. 114/C4
Baram (cape), Malay. 80/D3
Baram (riv.), Malay. 80/D3
Barama (riv.), Guy. 150/F2
Baramanni, Guy. 153/G3
Baramula, India 86/C2
Bāran, India 89/L3
Baranagar, India 85/G4
Baranavichy, Bela. 62/C1
Barani (well), Alg. 98/E4
Baranoa, Col. 152/C2
Baranof (isl.), Ak, US 122/C3
Baranya (prov.), Hun. 48/C3
Barão de Cocais, Braz. 155/D1
Barão de Grajaú, Braz. 154/B2
Baraolt, Rom. 49/G2
Baraque de Fraiture (hill), Belg. 53/E3
Barat Daya (isls.), Indo. 81/G5
Barataria, La, US 137/P17
Barauli, India 85/E2
Baraut, India 86/D5
Baraya, Col. 152/C4
Barbacena, Braz. 155/D2
Barbacoas, Col. 152/B4
Barbados (ctry.) 141/P9
Barbalha, Braz. 154/C2
Barbaros, Turk. 49/H5
Barbas (cape), Mor. 98/A5
Barbastro, Sp. 45/F1
Barbate de Franco, Sp. 44/C4
Barbeau (peak), Nun., Can. 123/T6
Barberà del Vallès, Sp. 45/L6
Barberino di Mugello, It. 59/E5
Barbers (pt.), Hi, US 124/V13
Barberton, Oh, US 130/D3
Barberton, SAfr. 107/E2
Barbona (peak), It. 58/D5
Barbosa, Col. 152/C3
Barbourville, Ky, US 130/D4
Barbuda (isl.), Anti. 141/N8
Barcaldine, Austl. 114/B3
Barcarrota, Sp. 44/B3
Barcău (riv.), Rom. 48/F2
Barcellona Pozzo di Gotto, It. 46/D3
Barcelona, Ven. 153/E2
Barcelona, Sp. 45/L7
Barcelona (int'l arpt.), Sp. 45/L7
Barcelos, Port. 44/A2
Barcelos, Braz. 153/F5
Barcin, Pol. 41/J2
Barcoo (riv.), Austl. 109/D3
Barcs, Hun. 48/C3
Barczewo, Pol. 39/J5
Bardejov, Slvk. 41/L4
Bardi, It. 58/C3
Bardīyah, Libya 97/L1
Bārdoli, India 89/K4
Bardolino, It. 59/D1
Bardonia, NY, US 139/K7
Bardsdale, Ca, US 136/B2
Bardsey (isl.), Wal, UK 34/D6
Bardstown, Ky, US 130/C4
Bareggio, It. 58/B2
Bareli, India 84/B4
Barellan, Austl. 115/C2
Barendrecht, Neth. 50/B5
Barentin, Fr. 42/D2
Barents (sea), Eur. 27/H1
Barentu, Erit. 88/C5
Bäretswil, Swi. 57/E3
Barfleur, Pointe de (pt.), Fr. 42/C2
Barga, It. 58/D4
Bargara, Austl. 114/D4
Bargarh, India 82/D3
Bargfeld-Stegen, Ger. 51/H1
Bargi, India 84/B4
Bargo, Austl. 115/D2
Bargteheide, Ger. 51/H1
Bārh, India 85/E3
Barhaj, India 84/D2
Barhalganj, India 84/D2
Barham, Austl. 115/C2
Barhiya, India 85/F3
Bāri, India 84/A2
Bari, It. 46/E2
Bari Sardo, It. 46/A3
Bariano, It. 58/C1
Baricella, It. 59/E3
Barichara, Col. 152/C3
Barīdī (pt.), SAr. 88/C4
Barigazzo (peak), It. 58/C3
Barika, Alg. 100/H5
Barillas, Guat. 144/D3
Barima (riv.), Guy. 153/G2
Barima-Waini (pol. reg.), Guy. 153/F3
Barinas (state), Ven. 152/D2
Barinas, Ven. 152/D2
Barinitas, Ven. 152/D2
Bariri, Braz. 155/B2
Barisāl (pol. reg.), Bang. 85/H4
Barisan Mountains (mts.), Indo. 80/B4
Barito (riv.), Indo. 80/D4
Baritu, PN, Arg. 157/D1
Bark (lake), On, Can. 130/E2
Bark (riv.), Wi, US 135/N13
Barka Kāna, India 85/E4
Barker, NY, US 131/S9
Barki Saria, India 85/E3
Barking and Dagenham (bor.), Eng, UK 30/D2
Barkley (sound), BC, Can. 126/B3
Barkley (lake), Ky,Tn, US 133/G2
Barkly East, SAfr. 106/D3
Barkly Tableland (plat.), Austl. 109/C2
Barkly West, SAfr. 106/D3
Barkol Kazak Zizhixian, China 70/F3
Barlee (lake), Austl. 109/A3
Barlee (range), Austl. 112/B2
Barlee Range Nature Rsv., Austl. 112/B2
Barletta, It. 46/E2
Barlin, Fr. 52/B3
Barlinek, Pol. 41/H2
Barmedman, Austl. 115/C2
Barmera, Austl. 113/J5
Barmstedt, Ger. 51/G1
Barnāla, India 86/C4
Bärnbach, Aus. 43/L3
Barnegat (inlet), NJ, US 138/D4
Barnegat (bay), NJ, US 138/D4
Barnegat, NJ, US 138/D4
Barnegat Light, NJ, US 138/D4
Barneveld, Neth. 50/C4
Barnhart, Mo, US 137/G9
Barnoldswick, Eng, UK 35/F4
Barnsley, Eng, UK 35/G4
Barnsley (co.), Eng, UK 35/G5
Barnstaple, Eng, UK 32/B4
Barnstaple (Bideford) (bay), Eng, UK 32/B4
Barnstorf, Ger. 51/F3
Barntrup, Ger. 51/G5
Barnwell, SC, US 133/H3
Baroghil (pass), Pak. 87/F5
Baron, Fr. 30/L4
Barone (peak), It. 58/B1
Barow (riv.), Ire. 34/A5
Barowghīl (pass), Afg. 89/K1
Barquisimeto, Ven. 152/D2
Barquisimeto (int'l arpt.), Ven. 152/D2
Barr (lake), Co, US 137/C3
Barr, Co, US 137/C3
Barr, Fr. 56/D1
Barra, Braz. 154/B3
Barra (isl.), Sc, UK 31/Q8
Barra Bonita, Braz. 155/B2
Barra Bonita, Reprêsa de (res.), Braz. 155/B2
Barra da Choça, Braz. 154/B4
Barra del Colorado, PN, CR 140/E5
Barra do Bugres, Braz. 150/G7
Barra do Corda, Braz. 154/A2
Barra do Garças, Braz. 151/H7
Barra do Mendes, Braz. 154/B3
Barra do Piraí, Braz. 211/K7
Barra do Ribeiro, Braz. 155/B4
Barra Head (pt.), Sc, UK 31/Q8
Barra Mansa, Braz. 211/J7
Barra Velha, Braz. 155/B3
Barraba, Austl. 115/D1
Barrackpur, India 85/G4
Barrage de Lagdo (dam), Camr. 96/H6
Barranca, Peru 156/B3
Barranca, Peru 156/B2
Barranca de Upía, Col. 152/C3
Barranca del Cobre PN, Mex. 142/D3
Barrancabermeja, Col. 152/C3
Barrancas, Ven. 153/F2
Barrancas, Col. 152/C2
Barrancas, Chile 158/N8
Barranco de Loba, Col. 152/C2
Barrancos, Port. 44/B3
Barranquilla, Col. 152/C2
Barras, Braz. 154/B2
Barreal, Arg. 157/C3
Barreiras, Braz. 154/A4
Barreirinhas, Braz. 154/B1
Barreiro, Port. 45/P10
Barreiros, Braz. 154/D3
Barren (isls.), Madg. 105/J10
Barren (isl.), Madg. 107/G7
Barren, Nosy (Barren Islands) (isls.), Madg. 107/G7
Barretal, Mex. 143/F3
Barretos, Braz. 155/B2
Barrhead, Ab, Can. 126/E2
Barrhead, Sc, UK 36/B5
Barrie, On, Can. 130/E2
Barrier (range), Austl. 113/J4
Barrington, Il, US 135/P15
Barrington Hills, Il, US 135/P15
Barrington Tops (peak), Austl. 115/D1
Barrington Tops NP, Austl. 115/D1
Barro Duro, Braz. 154/B2
Barron Gorge NP, Austl. 114/B2
Barroso, Braz. 155/D2
Barrouallie, StV. 141/N9
Barrow, Ak, US 134/G1
Barrow (pt.), Ak, US 134/G1
Barrow (isl.), Austl. 109/A3
Barrow (riv.), Ire. 31/Q10
Barrow (pt.), Austl. 114/B1
Barrow (str.), Nun., Can. 122/G1
Barrow-in-Furness, Eng, UK 35/E3
Barrow Island, Austl. 112/B2
Barrowford, Eng, UK 35/F4
Barruelo de Santullán, Sp. 44/C1
Barry, Wal, UK 32/C4
Barsakel'mes (lake), Uzb. 87/C4
Barsinghausen, Ger. 51/G4
Barssel, Ger. 51/E2
Barstow, Ca, US 128/C4
Bartang (riv.), Taj. 87/F5
Bartenheim, Fr. 56/D2
Barth, Ger. 38/E4
Bartholomä, Ger. 54/C5
Bartholomäberg, Aus. 57/F3
Bartica, Guy. 153/G3
Bartın, Turk. 49/L5
Bartle Frere (peak), Austl. 109/D2
Bartlesville, Ok, US 129/J3
Bartlett, Tx, US 129/H5
Bartlett (dam), Az, US 137/S18
Bartlett (res.), Az, US 137/S18
Bartlett, Il, US 135/P16
Bartolomé Masó, Cuba 145/G1
Bartolomeu Dias, Moz. 105/G5
Bartonsville, Pa, US 138/C2
Bartoszyce, Pol. 39/J4
Bartow, Fl, US 133/H5
Bartow, Ger. 38/E5
Barú (vol.), Pan. 145/F4
Bāruipur, India 85/G4
Barumun (riv.), Indo. 80/B3
Barus, Indo. 80/A3
Baruun-Urt, Mong. 71/K2
Barwa Sāgar, India 84/B3
Barwāha, India 89/L4
Barwāla, India 86/C5
Barwon (riv.), Austl. 109/D3
Barycz (riv.), Pol. 41/J3
Barysaw, Bela. 39/N4
Barysh, Rus. 63/H1
Barzanò, It. 58/C1
Bas-Rhin (dept.), Fr. 56/D1
Basaldella, It. 59/G1
Basauri, Sp. 44/D1
Basavilbaso, Arg. 159/J10
Bascharage, Lux. 53/E4
Basehor, Ks, US 137/D5
Basel, Swi. 56/D2
Basel/Mulhouse (int'l arpt.), Fr. 56/D2
Baselga di Pinè, It. 57/H5
Baselland (canton), Swi. 56/D3
Bashee (riv.), SAfr. 106/E3
Bashi (chan.), Phil.,Tai. 79/C3
Bashkortostan, Resp., Rus. 64/Q6
Bāsht, Iran 88/F2
Basilan (isl.), Phil. 81/F2
Basilan (peak), Phil. 81/F2
Basildon, Eng, UK 33/G3
Basilica di Fieschi, It. 58/C4
Basilicata (reg.), It. 46/D2
Basingstoke, Eng, UK 33/E4
Basingstoke (canal), Eng, UK 30/A3
Basīrhāt, India 85/G4
Basīrpur, Pak. 86/B4
Başkale, Turk. 90/F2
Baskatong (res.), Qu, Can. 130/F2
Baskil, Turk. 90/D2
Başkomutan NP, Turk. 90/B2
Bāsoda, India 84/A4
Basodino (peak), It. 57/E5
Basoko, D.R. Congo 97/K7
Basoli, India 86/C3
Bass (str.), Austl. 109/D4
Bass Rock (isl.), Sc, UK 36/D4
Bassae (Vassés) (ruin), Gre. 47/G4
Bassano, Ab, Can. 126/E3
Bassano del Grappa, It. 59/E1
Bassari, Togo 103/F4
Bassas da India (isl.), Reun. 105/G5
Basse-Normandie (pol. reg.), Fr. 42/C2
Basse Santa Su, Gam. 102/B3
Basse-Terre (isl.), Guad. 141/J4
Basse-Terre, Fr. 141/N8
Bassecourt, Swi. 56/D3
Bassein (riv.), Myan. 83/F4
Bassein (Vasai), India 89/K5
Bassenge, Belg. 53/E2
Bassenheim, Ger. 53/G3
Bassenthwaite (lake), Eng, UK 35/E2
Basseterre (cap.), StK. 141/N8
Bassum, Ger. 51/F3
Basswood (lake), US,Can. 130/B1
Båstad, Swe. 38/E3
Bastak, Iran 89/F3
Basṭām, Iran 89/G1
Bastelicaccia, Fr. 46/A2
Bastheim, Ger. 54/D2
Bastī, India 84/D2
Bastia, Fr. 46/A1
Bastia, It. 43/K5
Bastogne, Belg. 53/E4
Bastos, Braz. 155/B2
Bastrop, Tx, US 129/H5
Basyūn, Egypt 91/B4
Bat Shelomo, Isr. 91/F6
Bat Yam, Isr. 91/F7
Bata, EqG. 96/G7
Batabanó (gulf), Cuba 140/E3
Batac, Phil. 79/D4
Batagay, Rus. 65/P3
Batai (pass), Pak. 86/A3
Batalha, Braz. 154/B2
Batalha, Port. 44/A3
Batan (isls.), Phil. 67/M7
Batang, China 70/G6
Batangafo, CAfr. 96/J6
Batangas, Phil. 79/D5
Batarasa, Phil. 79/C6
Batatais, Braz. 155/C2
Batavia, NY, US 130/E3
Batavia, Il, US 135/P16
Bataysk, Rus. 62/F3
Batchtown, Il, US 137/F7
Bătdâmbang, Camb. 78/C3
Bate (bay), Austl. 114/H9
Batéké (plat.), Congo 96/H8
Batemans Bay, Austl. 115/D2
Batesburg-Leesville, SC, US 133/H3
Batesville, Ms, US 129/K4
Bath, Me, US 131/G3
Bath, NY, US 130/E3
Bath, Eng, UK 32/D4
Bath, Pa, US 138/C2
Bath and Northeast Somerset (co.), Eng, UK 32/D4
Bathgate, Sc, UK 36/C5
Bathmen, Neth. 50/D4
Bathurst, Austl. 115/D2
Bathurst (cape), NW, Can. 134/N1
Bathurst, NB, Can. 131/H2
Bathurst (isl.), Nun., Can. 123/R7
Bathurst (inlet), Nun., Can. 122/F2
Bathurst Inlet, Nun., Can. 122/F2
Batian (Mt. Kenya) (peak), Kenya 104/C3
Batiquitos (lag.), Ca, US 136/C4
Batiscan (riv.), Qu, Can. 131/F2
Batley, Eng, UK 35/G4
Batlow, Austl. 115/D2
Batman, Turk. 90/E2
Batman (dam), Turk. 90/E2
Batna (prov.), Alg. 99/G2
Batna, Alg. 100/J5
Baton Rouge (cap.), La, US 129/K5
Batopilas, Mex. 142/D3
Batoti, India 86/C3
Batouri, Camr. 96/H7
Baṭrā' (Petra) (ruin), Jor. 91/D4
Båtsfjord, Nor. 37/J1
Batsto (riv.), NJ, US 138/D4
Batsto, NJ, US 138/D4
Batsto Historic Village, NJ, US 138/D4
Battaglia Terme, It. 59/E2
Battenberg, Ger. 51/F6
Bätterkinden, Swi. 56/D3
Batticaloa, SrL. 82/D6
Battipaglia, It. 46/D2
Battle, Eng, UK 33/G5
Battle (riv.), Ab,Sk, Can. 122/E3
Battle Creek, Mi, US 130/C3
Battle Mountain, Nv, US 126/D5
Battleford, Sk, Can. 126/F2
Battock (mt.), Sc, UK 36/D3
Batu (peak), Eth. 97/N6
Batu (cape), Indo. 81/E3
Batu (isls.), Indo. 80/A4
Batu (bay), Malay. 80/D3
Batu (peak), Malay. 80/D3
Batu Gajah, Malay. 80/B3
Batu Pahat, Malay. 80/B3
Batu Puteh (peak), Malay. 80/B3
Batudaka (isl.), Indo. 81/F4
Batuensambang (peak), Indo. 80/D3
Bat'umi (int'l arpt.), Geo. 63/G4
Bat'umi, Geo. 63/G4
Baturaja, Indo. 80/B4
Baturité, Braz. 154/C2
Batys Qazaqstan, Kaz. 64/E5
Bauchi (state), Nga. 103/H4
Bauchi, Nga. 103/H4
Baudette, Mn, US 127/K3
Baudó (mts.), Col. 145/G5
Baudó (riv.), Col. 152/B3
Bauer, Ut, US 137/J13
Bauld (cape), Nf, Can. 131/L1
Baulmes, Swi. 56/C4
Bauman (peak), Togo 103/F5
Baume-les-Dames, Fr. 56/C3
Baumholder, Ger. 53/G4
Baunach (riv.), Ger. 54/D2
Baunach, Ger. 54/D3
Baunatal, Ger. 51/G6
Baunei, It. 46/A2
Bauru, Braz. 155/B2
Bautzen, Ger. 41/H3
Bavans, Fr. 56/C3
Bavarian Alps (mts.), Aus.,Ger. 57/G3
Bavay, Fr. 52/C3
Båven (lake), Swe. 38/G2
Baveno, It. 57/E6
Baviácora, Mex. 142/C2
Bavilliers, Fr. 56/C2
Bavispe, Río de (riv.), Mex. 142/C2
Baw Baw (mt.), Austl. 115/C3
Baw Baw NP, Austl. 115/C3
Bawāna, India 86/D5
Bawang (cape), Indo. 80/C4
Bawean (isl.), Indo. 80/D5
Bawku, Gha. 103/E4
Baxoi, China 83/G2
Bay City, Mi, US 130/D3
Bay City, Tx, US 129/J5
Bay Minette, Al, US 133/G4
Bay Roberts, Nf, Can. 131/L2
Bay Saint Louis, Ms, US 133/F4
Bayamo, Cuba 145/G1
Bayamón, PR 141/M8
Bayan, Mong. 70/G2
Bayan Har (mts.), China 70/G5
Bayan-Hongor (prov.), Mong. 70/G2
Bayan-Ölgiy (prov.), Mong. 70/E2
Bayan-Ulaan, Mong. 70/H2
Bayanaul'skiy NP, Kaz. 87/G2
Bayanhongor, Mong. 70/H2
Bayanhushuu, Mong. 70/F2
Bayannuur, Mong. 70/F2
Bayano (lake), Pan. 145/G4
Bayanterem, Mong. 71/K2
Bayantsagaan, Mong. 70/H2
Bayard, Ne, US 127/H5
Bayat, Turk. 90/C1
Bayawan, Phil. 81/F2
Baybach (riv.), Ger. 53/G3
Baybay, Phil. 79/D5
Bayburt, Turk. 90/E1
Bayburt (prov.), Turk. 90/E1
Baydaratskaya (bay), Rus. 64/G2
Baydhabo (Baidoa), Som. 97/P7
Bayel, Fr. 56/A1
Bayerischer Wald (hills), Ger. 55/F4
Bayerischer Wald NP, Ger. 55/G5
Bayern (state), Ger. 40/F4
Bayeux, Braz. 154/D2
Bayeux, Fr. 42/C2
Baygorria (res.), Uru. 159/K10
Baykal (mts.), Rus. 65/L4
Baykal (lake), Rus. 67/L4
Baykan, Turk. 90/E2
Bayombong, Phil. 79/D4
Bayon, Fr. 56/C1
Bayona, Sp. 44/A1
Bayonet Point, Fl, US 133/H4
Bayonne, Fr. 42/C5
Bayonne, NJ, US 139/J9
Bayport, NY, US 139/E2
Bayramaly, Trkm. 89/H1
Bayramıç, Turk. 47/K3
Bayreuth, Ger. 55/E3
Bayrūt (cap.), Leb. 91/D3
Bays, Lake of (lake), On, Can. 130/E2
Bayşehir (lake), Turk. 90/B2
Bayt Ḥanīnā, WBnk. 91/G8
Bayt Ḥānūn, Gaza 91/D4
Bayt Laḥm (Bethlehem), WBnk. 91/G8
Bayt Sāḥūr, WBnk. 91/G8
Baytik Shan (mts.), China,Mon 70/E2
Baytown, Tx, US 129/J5
Bayudha (des.), Sudan 101/C5
Bayugan, Phil. 79/E6
Bayville, NY, US 139/L8
Baza, Sp. 44/D4
Bazainville, Fr. 30/G5
Bazardüzü (peak), Azer. 63/H4
Bazaruto, Ilha do (isl.), Moz. 105/G5
Bazèga (prov.), Burk. 103/E4
Bazemont, Fr. 30/H5
Bazet, Fr. 42/D5
Bazhong, China 70/J5
Bazin (riv.), Qu, Can. 130/F2
Bāzpur, India 84/B1
Bazzano, It. 59/E3
Be, Nosy (isl.), Madg. 107/H6
Beach Haven, NJ, US 138/D4
Beachport, Austl. 115/B3
Beachwood, NJ, US 138/D4
Beachy (head), Eng, UK 33/G5
Beachy Head (pt.), Eng, UK 42/D1
Beacon (peak), Wal, UK 32/C2
Beaconsfield, Austl. 115/C4
Beaconsfield, Eng, UK 33/F3
Beaconsfield, Qu, Can. 131/N7
Beal (range), Austl. 114/A4
Bealanana, Madg. 107/J6
Beale (cape), BC, Can. 126/B3
Beampingaratra (ridge), Madg. 107/H9
Bear (isl.), Nor. 160/E
Bear (riv.), US 128/E2
Bear (mt.), Ak, US 134/K3
Bear (mtn.), Ak, US 134/K2
Bear, De, US 138/C4
Bear (lake), Ut, US 124/D3
Bear Creek (lake), Co, US 137/B3
Bear River (bay), Ut, US 137/J11
Bear River Migratory Bird Refuge (nat'l wild. ref.), Ut, US 137/J10
Beardsley, Az, US 137/R18
Beardsley (canal), Az, US 137/R18
Bearfort (mtn.), NJ, US 139/H7
Bearma (riv.), India 84/B4
Bearpaw (mts.), Mt, US 126/F3
Bearsden, Sc, UK 36/B5
Beartooth (mts.), Mt,Wy, US 126/F4
Beās (riv.), India 84/B3
Beas de Segura, Sp. 44/D3
Beasain, Sp. 44/D1
Beata (isl.), Thai. 145/J2
Beata (cape), DRep. 141/G4
Beata (pt.), DRep. 145/J2
Beatenberg, Swi. 56/D4
Beatty, Nv, US 128/C3
Beattystown, NJ, US 138/D2
Beau Bassin-Rose Hill, Mrts. 107/T15
Beaucaire, Fr. 42/F5
Beaucamps-le-Vieux, Fr. 52/A4
Beauchamp, Fr. 30/J4
Beaucourt, Fr. 56/C3
Beaudesert, Austl. 114/D4
Beaufort, Austl. 115/B3
Beaufort (sea), Can.,US 119/C2
Beaufort, Fr. 56/B4
Beaufort, Lux. 53/F4
Beaufort, SC, US 133/H3
Beaufort West, SAfr. 106/C4
Beaugency, Fr. 42/D3
Beaujolais, Monts du (mts.), Fr. 42/F4
Beauly (riv.), Sc, UK 36/B2
Beauly, Sc, UK 36/B2
Beauly Firth (lake), Sc, UK 36/B2
Beaumaris, Wal, UK 34/D5
Beaume, Fr. 42/F3
Beaumont, Tx, US 129/J5
Beaumont, Ca, US 136/D3
Beaumont, Fr. 42/E4
Beaumont, Belg. 53/D3
Beaumont-de-Lomagne, Fr. 42/D5
Beaumont-sur-Oise, Fr. 30/J4
Beaupréau, Fr. 42/C3
Beauquesne, Fr. 52/B3
Beauraing, Belg. 53/D3
Beaurainville, Fr. 52/A3
Beaurevoir, Fr. 52/C4
Beausejour, Mb, Can. 127/J3
Beautheil, Fr. 30/M5
Beautor, Fr. 52/C4
Beauvais, Fr. 52/B5
Beauval, Sk, Can. 126/G2
Beauval, Fr. 52/B3
Beauvoir, Fr. 30/L6
Beaver (lake), Ar, US 132/E2
Beaver (riv.), Yk, Can. 122/D2
Beaver, Ak, US 134/J2
Beaver (isl.), Mi, US 130/C2
Beaver (riv.), Ok, US 128/G3
Beaver (riv.), On, Can. 127/L2
Beaver, Ut, US 128/D3
Beaver Creek, Yk, Can. 134/K3
Beaver Meadows, Pa, US 138/C2
Beaver Springs, Pa, US 138/A2
Beaverhead (riv.), Mt, US 126/E4
Beaverlodge, Ab, Can. 126/D2
Beavertown, Pa, US 138/A2
Bebedouro, Braz. 155/B2
Beberibe, Braz. 154/C2
Bebington, Eng, UK 35/E5
Bebra, Ger. 51/G7
Becal, Mex. 144/D1
Beccles, Eng, UK 33/H2
Bečej, Serb. 48/E3
Becerreá, Sp. 44/B1
Bechar (prov.), Alg. 98/E3
Bechar, Alg. 99/E3
Becharof (lake), Ak, US 134/G4
Bechhofen, Ger. 53/G5
Bechtheim, Ger. 54/B3
Bechyně, Czh. 55/H4
Beckdorf, Ger. 51/G2
Beckenried, Swi. 57/E4
Beckingen, Ger. 53/F5
Beckley, WV, US 130/D4
Beckum, Ger. 51/F5
Beclean, Rom. 49/G2
Becs de Bosson (peak), Swi. 56/D5
Bédarieux, Fr. 42/E5
Bedburg, Ger. 53/F2
Bedburg-Hau, Ger. 50/D5
Beder, Den. 38/D3
Bedford (cape), Austl. 114/B1
Bedford, Qu, Can. 130/F2
Bedford, Eng, UK 33/F2
Bedford, In, US 130/C4
Bedford, SAfr. 106/D4
Bedford, Va, US 130/E4
Bedford Hills, NY, US 139/E1
Bedford Level (phys. reg.), Eng, UK 33/F2
Bedford Park, Il, US 135/Q16
Bedfordshire (co.), Eng, UK 33/F2
Bedlington, Eng, UK 35/G1
Bedonia, It. 58/C3
Bedouaram (well), Niger 96/H4
Bedretto, Swi. 57/E5
Bedsted, Den. 38/C3
Bedum, Neth. 50/D2
Bedworth, Eng, UK 33/E2
Beebe Seep (canal), Co, US 137/C2
Beechworth, Austl. 115/C3
Beek, Neth. 53/E2
Beelen, Ger. 51/F5
Beelitz, Ger. 40/P7
Beenleigh, Austl. 114/D4
Beer (pt.), Eng, UK 32/C5
Be'er Sheva', Isr. 91/D4
Beerfelden, Ger. 54/B3
Beernem, Belg. 52/C1
Beerzel, Belg. 53/D1
Beesel, Neth. 50/D6
Beeville, Tx, US 132/D4
Befandriana, Madg. 107/J6
Befandriana, Madg. 107/G8
Beforona, Madg. 107/J7
Befotaka, Madg. 107/J6
Beg (lake), NI, UK 34/B2
Bega, Austl. 115/D3
Bega (riv.), Ger. 51/F5
Bega Veche (riv.), Cro. 48/E3
Begamganj, Bang. 85/H4
Begamganj, India 84/B4
Bégard, Fr. 42/B2
Begarslan (peak), Trkm. 63/K4
Begejci, Serb. 48/E3
Begichev (isl.), Rus. 65/M2
Begna (riv.), Nor. 37/D3
Begusarai, India 85/F3
Béhague (pt.), FrG. 151/H3
Behala (str.), Indo. 80/B4
Behāla, India 82/E3
Behamberg, Aus. 55/H6
Behat, India 86/D4
Behbahān, Iran 88/F2
Behenjy-Afovany, Madg. 107/H7
Béhoust, Fr. 30/H5
Behren-lès-Forbach, Fr. 53/F5
Behri (riv.), Nepal 84/C1
Behshahr, Iran 88/F1
Bei (riv.), China 79/A2
Bei (mts.), China 70/F3
Bei'an, China 71/N2
Beierfeld, Ger. 55/F1
Beigua (peak), It. 58/B4
Beijing (mun.), China 71/L3
Beijing (cap.), China 72/H7
Beijing Capital (int'l arpt.), China 72/H6
Beilen, Neth. 50/D3
Beiliu, China 83/K3
Beilngries, Ger. 55/E4
Beilstein, Ger. 54/C4
Beilun (pass), China 79/A3
Bein Tharsuinn (peak), Sc, UK 36/B1
Beindersheim, Ger. 54/B3
Beinn a' Chuallaich (peak), Sc, UK 36/B3
Beinn a' Ghlò (peak), Sc, UK 36/C3
Beinn a' Mheadhoin (lake), Sc, UK 36/B2
Beinn Bhàn (peak), Sc, UK 36/A3
Beinn Bheula (peak), Sc, UK 36/B4
Beinn Bhrotain (peak), Sc, UK 36/C2
Beinn Bhuidhe (peak), Sc, UK 36/B4
Beinn Bhuidhe Mhór (peak),Sc, UK 36/B2
Beinn Dearg (peak), Sc, UK 36/B1
Beinn Dearg (peak), Sc, UK 36/C3
Beinn Dòrain (peak), Sc, UK 36/B4
Beinn Eighe (peak), Sc, UK 36/A1
Beinn Heasgarnich (peak), Sc, UK 36/B3
Beinn Mholach (peak), Sc, UK 36/B3
Beinn Mhór (peak), Sc, UK 36/A4
Beinwil am See, Swi. 56/E3
Beipiao, China 72/E2
Beira, Moz. 105/F4
Beiru (riv.), China 72/C4
Beirut (int'l arpt.), Leb. 91/D3
Beitbridge, Zim. 105/E5
Beith, Sc, UK 36/B5
Beiuş, Rom. 48/F2
Beizhen, China 73/A2
Beja, Port. 44/B3
Beja (dist.), Port. 44/A4
Bejaïa (prov.), Alg. 100/H4
Bejaïa, Alg. 100/H4
Béjar, Sp. 44/C2
Bejhi (riv.), Pak. 89/J3
Bekabad, Uzb. 87/E4
Bekasi, Indo. 80/C5
Békés, Hun. 48/E2
Békés (prov.), Hun. 48/E2
Békéscsaba, Hun. 48/E2
Bekilli, Turk. 90/B2
Bekily, Madg. 107/H9
Bekitro, Madg. 107/H9
Bekwai, Gha. 103/E5
Bel Air, Md, US 138/B4
Bel Air South, Md, US 138/B5
Belā, India 82/D2
Bela, Pak. 89/J3
Belá, Slvk. 41/K4
Bela Crkva, Serb. 48/E3
Bela Cruz, Braz. 154/B1
Bela Palanka, Serb. 47/H1
Bělá pod Bezdězem, Czh. 55/H1
Belā Pratāpgarh, India 84/C3
Bela Vista, Braz. 151/G8
Bela Vista, Moz. 107/F2
Bela Vista do Paraíso, Braz. 155/B2
Belair, La, US 137/Q17
Belair Rec. Pk., Austl. 113/M9
Belan (riv.), India 84/D3
Belarus (ctry.) 27/G3
Belas, Port. 45/P10
Belaya (riv.), Rus. 64/F4
Belbo (riv.), It. 58/B3
Bełchatów, Pol. 41/K3
Belchen (peak), Ger. 56/D2
Belcher (chan.), Nun., Can. 123/S7
Belcher (isls.), On, Can. 123/H3
Belchite, Sp. 45/E2
Belcourt, ND, US 127/J3
Beldānga, India 85/G4
Belebey, Rus. 61/M5
Beled Weyne, Som. 97/Q7
Belém, Braz. 151/J4
Belém, Braz. 154/D2
Belém de São Francisco, Braz. 154/C3
Belem Tower, Port. 45/P10
Belén, Arg. 157/C2
Belen, NM, US 128/F4
Belén, Chile 156/D5
Belén, Nic. 140/D5
Belen, Turk. 91/E1
Belen, Turk. 91/C1
Belén de Escobar, Arg. 159/J11
Belene, Bul. 49/G4
Beles Wenz (riv.), Eth. 97/N5
Belesar, Embalse de (res.), Sp. 44/B1
Belev, Rus. 62/F1
Belews Creek, Mo, US 137/F9
Belfair, Wa, US 135/B3
Belfast (cap.), NI, UK 34/C2
Belfast (dist.), NI, UK 34/B2
Belfast, SAfr. 107/E2
Belfast, Me, US 131/G2
Belfast Lough (bay), NI, UK 34/C2
Belfaux, Swi. 56/D4
Belfield, ND, US 127/H4
Belfort (dept.), Fr. 56/C2
Belfort, Fr. 56/C2
Belgioioso, It. 58/C2
Belgium (ctry.) 40/C3
Belgorod, Rus. 62/F2
Belgorodskaya Oblast, Rus. 62/F2
Belgrade, Mt, US 126/F4
Belgrade (Beograd) (cap.),Serb. 48/E3
Beli Drim (riv.), Serb. 47/G1
Beli Manastir, Cro. 48/D3
Beli Timok (riv.), Serb. 48/F4
Belitsa, Bul. 47/H2
Belitung (isl.), Indo. 80/C4
Belize (riv.), Belz. 144/D2
Belize (ctry.) 144/D2
Belize City, Belz. 144/D2
Beljanica (peak), Serb. 48/E3
Bel'kovskiy (isl.), Rus. 65/N2
Bell, Austl. 114/C4
Bell (pt.), Austl. 113/G5
Bell (pen.), Nun., Can. 123/H2
Bell (riv.), Qu, Can. 123/J4

173
Bell – Bi'r G

Bell, Ca, US 136/F8
Bell, Ger. 53/G3
Bell Gardens, Ca, US 136/F8
Bell Rock (Inchcape) (isl.), Sc, UK 36/D4
Bell Ville, Arg. 157/D3
Bella Coola, BC, Can. 126/B2
Bella Vista, Arg. 157/E2
Bellac, Fr. 42/D3
Bellaghy, NI, UK 34/B2
Bellagio, It. 57/F6
Bellano, It. 57/F5
Bellary, India 82/C4
Bellavista, Peru 156/B2
Bellavista, Peru 156/B2
Bellavista (cape), It. 46/A3
Bellavista, Ecu. 156/E7
Belle (riv.), On, Can. 135/G7
Belle-Anse, Haiti 145/H2
Belle Chasse, La, US 137/Q17
Belle Fourche (riv.), Wy, US 127/G5
Belle Glade, Fl, US 133/H5
Belle Haven, Va, US 138/A6
Belle-Île (isl.), Fr. 42/B3
Belle Isle (str.), NF, Can. 131/K1
Belle Terre, NY, US 139/E2
Belleek, NI, UK 34/B3
Bellefontaine, Oh, US 130/D3
Bellefonte, De, US 138/C4
Bellegarde-sur-Valserine, Fr. 56/B5
Bellenberg, Ger. 57/G1
Bellenden Ker NP, Austl. 114/B2
Belleplain, NJ, US 138/D5
Bellerive-sur-Allier, Fr. 42/E3
Bellerose, NY, US 139/L9
Belleu, Fr. 52/C5
Belleville, On, Can. 130/E2
Belleville, Fr. 56/A5
Belleville, Il, US 137/H8
Belleville, Mi, US 135/E7
Belleville, NJ, US 139/J8
Belleville-sur-Meuse, Fr. 53/E5
Bellevue, Md, US 138/B6
Belley, Fr. 56/B6
Bellflower, Ca, US 136/F8
Bellheim, Ger. 54/B4
Bellignat, Fr. 56/B5
Bellinge, Den. 38/D4
Bellingen, Austl. 115/E1
Bellingham, Wa, US 126/C3
Bellingshausen (isl.), FrPol. 117/K6
Bellingshausen (sea), Ant. 160/U
Bellingwolde, Neth. 51/E2
Bellinzago Novarese, It. 58/B1
Bellinzona, Swi. 57/F5
Bellmawr, NJ, US 138/C4
Bellmead, Tx, US 129/H5
Bellmore, NY, US 139/L9
Bello, Col. 150/C2
Bellona Reefs (reef), NCal. 116/E7
Bellot (str.), Nun., Can. 122/G1
Bellport, NY, US 139/F2
Bellshill, Sc, UK 36/B5
Belluno (prov.), It. 59/E1
Belluno, It. 43/K3
Bellville, Tx, US 129/H5
Bellville, SAfr. 106/L10
Bellvue, Co, US 137/B1
Bellwald, Swi. 56/E5
Belm, Ger. 51/F4
Belmar, NJ, US 138/D3
Bélmez, Sp. 44/C3
Belmont, Ca, US 135/K11
Belmonte, Braz. 154/C4
Belmonte, Sp. 44/D3
Belmonte, Port. 44/B2
Belmopan (cap.), Belz. 144/D2
Belmullet, Ire. 31/P9
Belo Campo, Braz. 154/B4
Belo Horizonte, Braz. 155/D1
Belo Jardim, Braz. 154/C3
Belo-Tsiribihina, Madg. 107/H7
Beloeil, Qu, Can. 131/P6
Beloeil, Belg. 52/C2
Belogorsk, Rus. 71/N1
Beloha, Madg. 107/H9
Beloit, Wi, US 127/L5
Beloit, Ks, US 129/H3
Belomorsk, Rus. 60/G2
Belorado, Sp. 44/D1
Belorechensk, Rus. 62/F3
Belören, Turk. 90/C2
Beloretsk, Rus. 61/N5
Beloslav, Bul. 49/H4
Belovo, Bul. 47/J1
Belovo, Rus. 64/J4
Beloye (lake), Rus. 64/D3
Belper, Eng, UK 35/G5
Belsand, India 85/E2
Belt, Mt, US 126/F4
Belterwijde (lake), Neth. 50/D3
Beltheim, Ger. 53/G3
Belton, Tx, US 129/H5
Belton, Mo, US 137/D6
Beltsville, Md, US 138/B5
Beltzville (lake), Pa, US 138/C2
Belukha (peak), Rus. 70/E2
Belvedere, Ca, US 135/K11
Belvidere, NJ, US 138/C2
Belyando (riv.), Austl. 109/D3
Belyy (isl.), Rus. 160/A
Belzig, Ger. 40/G2
Bełżyce, Pol. 41/M3
Bemaraha (plat.), Madg. 107/H7
Bemarivo (riv.), Madg. 107/H7
Bembéréké, Ben. 103/F4
Bembibre, Sp. 44/B1
Bemboka, Austl. 115/D3
Bemetāra, India 82/D3
Bemidji, Mn, US 127/K4
Bemmel, Neth. 50/C5
Ben Aigan (hill), Sc, UK 36/C1
Ben Alder (peak), Sc, UK 36/B3
Ben Améra (well), Mrta. 98/B5
Ben Avon (peak), Sc, UK 36/C2
Ben Boyd NP, Austl. 115/D3
Ben Chonzie (peak), Sc, UK 36/C4
Ben Cleuch (peak), Sc, UK 36/C4
Ben Cruachan (peak), Sc, UK 36/A4
Ben Davis (pt.), NJ, US 138/C5
Ben Gurion (int'l arpt.), Isr. 91/F7
Ben Hope (peak), Sc, UK 31/R7
Ben Ime (peak), Sc, UK 36/B4
Ben Lawers (peak), Sc, UK 36/B3
Ben Ledi (peak), Sc, UK 36/B4
Ben Lomond (peak), Sc, UK 36/B4
Ben Lomond NP, Austl. 115/C4
Ben Lui (peak), Sc, UK 36/B4
Ben Macdui (peak), Sc, UK 36/C2
Ben More (peak), Sc, UK 31/Q8
Ben More (peak), Sc, UK 36/B4
Ben More Assynt (peak), Sc, UK 31/R7
Ben Msik-Sidi Othmane (prov.), Mor. 100/A2
Ben Nevis (peak), Sc, UK 36/B3
Ben Rinnes (peak), Sc, UK 36/C2
Ben Slimane, Mor. 98/D2
Ben Slimane (prov.), Mor. 100/A3
Ben Starav (peak), Sc, UK 36/A3
Ben Tee (peak), Sc, UK 36/B2
Ben Tirran (peak), Sc, UK 36/C3
Ben Tre, Viet. 78/D4
Ben Vane (peak), Sc, UK 36/B4
Ben Vorlich (peak), Sc, UK 36/B4
Ben Vrackie (peak), Sc, UK 36/C3
Ben Wyvis (peak), Sc, UK 36/B1
Ben Zohra (well), Alg. 98/E3
Benabarre, Sp. 45/F1
Benahmed, Mor. 98/D2
Benalla, Austl. 115/C3
Benalmádena, Sp. 44/C4
Benavente, Sp. 44/C1
Benavides, Tx, US 132/D5
Benbane (pt.), NI, UK 34/B1
Benbecula (isl.), Sc, UK 31/Q8
Benbonyathe (peak), Austl. 113/H4
Benburb, NI, UK 34/B3
Bend, Or, US 126/C4
Bendeleben (mt.), Ak, US 134/F2
Bendemeer, Austl. 115/D1
Bendersville, Pa, US 138/A4
Bendigo, Austl. 115/C3
Bendorf, Ger. 38/C4
Bene Beraq, Isr. 91/F7
Benedict (mt.), Nf, Can. 123/L3
Benediktbeuern, Ger. 57/H2
Benediktenwand (peak), Ger. 57/H2
Beneditinos, Braz. 154/B2
Benenitra, Madg. 107/H8
Benešov, Czh. 55/H3
Benevento, It. 46/D2
Benfeld, Fr. 56/D1
Bengal (bay), Asia 67/H8
Bengal, Bay of (gulf), Asia 70/E7
Bengbu, China 72/D4
Benghāzī, Libya 96/K1
Bengkalis, Indo. 80/B3
Bengkalis (isl.), Indo. 80/B3
Bengkayang, Indo. 80/C3
Bengkulu, Indo. 80/B4
Bengough, Sk, Can. 127/G3
Bengtsfors, Swe. 38/E2
Benguela, Ang. 105/B3
Benguerir, Mor. 98/D2
Beni, D.R. Congo 104/A2
Beni (riv.), Bol. 147/C4
Beni Abbes, Alg. 99/E3
Beni Bouayach, Mor. 100/C2
Beni Ensar, Mor. 100/B2
Beni Khiar, Tun. 100/M6
Beni Mellal, Mor. 98/D2
Beni Ounif, Alg. 99/E2
Benicarló, Sp. 45/F2
Benicia, Ca, US 135/K10
Benidorm, Sp. 45/E3
Benifayó, Sp. 45/E3
Benin (ctry.) 103/F4
Benin, Bight of (bay), Afr. 93/C4
Benin City, Nga. 103/G5
Benisa, Sp. 45/F3
Benito Juárez, Mex. 142/D2
Benjamin, Tx, US 129/H4
Benjamin Constant, Braz. 156/D2
Benjamín Hill, Mex. 142/C2
Benjamin, Isla (isl.), Chile 158/B5
Benkei-misaki (cape), Japan 76/B2
Benkelman, Ne, US 129/G2
Bennachie (hill), Sc, UK 36/D2
Bennan (pt.), Sc, UK 36/A6
Bennett (isl.), Rus. 65/Q2
Bennettsville, SC, US 133/J3
Bennington, Vt, US 130/F3
Bénoue, PN de la, Camr. 96/H6
Bensenville, Il, US 135/Q16
Bensheim, Ger. 54/B3
Benson, Mn, US 127/K4
Benson, Az, US 128/E5
Benta (riv.), Hun. 49/Q10
Bentheim, Ger. 51/E4
Bentley, Eng, UK 35/G4
Bento Gonçalves, Braz. 155/B4
Benton, Ar, US 129/J4
Benton, La, US 129/J4
Benton, Pa, US 138/B1
Benton Harbor, Mi, US 130/C3
Bentong, Malay. 80/B3
Benue (state), Nga. 103/H5
Benue (riv.), Nga. 93/C4
Benxi, China 73/B2
Benxi, China 73/C2
Beočin, Serb. 48/D3
Beograd (int'l arpt.), Serb. 48/E3
Beohāri, India 84/C3
Beppu (bay), Japan 74/B4
Beppu, Japan 74/B4
Bequia (isl.), StV. 141/N9
Bequimão, Braz. 154/A1
Beraber (well), Alg. 96/E1
Beragh, NI, UK 34/A2
Beraketa, Madg. 107/H8
Berasia, India 84/A4
Berat, Alb. 47/F2
Beratus (peak), Indo. 81/E4
Beratzhausen, Ger. 55/E4
Berau (riv.), Indo. 81/E3
Berau (bay), Indo. 81/H4
Berbenno di Valtellina, It. 57/F5
Berbera, Som. 97/Q5
Berbérati, CAfr. 96/J7
Berbice (riv.), Guy. 150/G2
Berceto, It. 58/C3
Berchem, Belg. 50/B6
Bercher, Swi. 56/C4
Berching, Ger. 55/E4
Berchtesgaden, Ger. 43/K3
Berchtesgaden, NP, Ger. 43/K3
Berck, Fr. 52/A3
Berdorf, Lux. 53/F4
Berdsk, Rus. 87/H2
Berdyans'k, Ukr. 62/F3
Berdychiv, Ukr. 62/D2
Berea, Ky, US 130/C4
Bereguardo, It. 58/C2
Berehove, Ukr. 41/M4
Berekum, Gha. 103/E5
Berenguela, Bol. 156/D5
Berenice (ruin), Egypt 101/C4
Beresford, SD, US 127/J5
Beresford, NB, Can. 131/H2
Bereşti, Rom. 49/H2
Berettyóújfalu, Hun. 48/E2
Berevo, Madg. 107/H7
Berezina (riv.), Bela. 62/D1
Berezniki, Rus. 61/N4
Berezovo, Rus. 64/G3
Berg (riv.), SAfr. 106/B4
Berg, Swi. 57/F2
Berg, Lux. 53/F4
Berg, Ger. 54/B5
Berg bei Rohrbach, Aus. 55/G5
Berga, Sp. 45/F1
Bergama, Turk. 90/A2
Bergamo, It. 58/C1
Bergamo (prov.), It. 57/F6
Bergara, Sp. 44/D1
Bergatruete, Ger. 57/F2
Bergen, Ger. 51/G3
Bergen, Ger. 38/E4
Bergen, Neth. 50/B3
Bergen, Nor. 38/A1
Bergen (co.), NJ, US 138/D2
Bergen op Zoom, Neth. 50/B5
Bergen Park, Co, US 137/B3
Bergenfield, NJ, US 139/K8
Bergerac, Fr. 42/D4
Bergeyk, Neth. 50/C6
Bergheim, Tx, US 137/T20
Bergheim, Aus. 55/G7
Bergheim, Ger. 53/F2
Bergisch Gladbach, Ger. 53/G2
Bergkamen, Ger. 51/E5
Bergnäset, Swe. 60/D2
Bergneustadt, Ger. 53/G1
Bergrheinfeld, Ger. 40/F4
Bergse Maas (riv.), Neth. 50/B5
Bergshamra, Swe. 38/H2
Bergsviken, Swe. 37/G2
Bergtheim, Ger. 54/D3
Berguent, Mor. 100/C2
Bergues, Fr. 52/B2
Bergum, Neth. 50/D2
Bergumermeer (lake), Neth. 50/D2
Bergün-Bravuogn, Swi. 57/F4
Bergviken (lake), Swe. 38/G1
Berh, Mong. 71/K2
Berikat (cape), Indo. 80/C4
Bering (isl.), Rus. 65/S4
Bering (sea), Asia,NAm. 65/U4
Bering (str.), Rus.,US 67/U3
Bering Land Bridge Nat'l Prsv., Ak, US 134/E2
Beringen, Belg. 53/E1
Beritarikap (cape), Indo. 80/B4
Berja, Sp. 44/D4
Berkel, Neth. 50/B5
Berkel (riv.), Ger. 40/D2
Berkeley, Ca, US 128/B3
Berkeley, Mo, US 137/G8
Berkeley Heights, NJ, US 139/H9
Berkhamsted, Eng, UK 30/B1
Berkheim, Ger. 57/G1
Berkhout, Neth. 50/B3
Berkley, Mi, US 135/F6
Berkovitsa, Bul. 47/H1
Berks (co.), Pa, US 138/C3
Berkshire (co.), Eng, UK 33/E3
Berkshire Downs (hills), Eng, UK 33/E3
Berlaimont, Fr. 52/C3
Berlanga de Duero, Sp. 44/D2
Berlare, Belg. 52/D1
Berleburg, Ger. 51/F6
Berlicum, Neth. 50/C5
Berlin (cap.), Ger. 40/Q6
Berlin (state), Ger. 40/Q6
Berlin, NH, US 131/G2
Berlin, NJ, US 138/D4
Berlin, Wi, US 127/L5
Bermagui, Austl. 115/D3
Bermejo, Bol. 157/D1
Bermejo (riv.), Arg. 147/D5
Bermeo, Sp. 44/D1
Bermillo de Sayago, Sp. 44/B2
Bermuda (isl.), UK 119/L6
Bern (canton), Swi. 56/D4
Bern (cap.), Swi. 56/D4
Bern-Belp (int'l arpt.), Swi. 56/D4
Bernal, Peru 156/A2
Bernalda, It. 46/E2
Bernalillo, NM, US 128/F4
Bernard (riv.), NW, Can. 122/D1
Bernardo O'Higgins, PN, Chile 157/B6
Bernardsville, NJ, US 138/D2
Bernau, Ger. 56/E2
Bernau, Ger. 40/Q6
Bernay, Fr. 42/D2
Bernbeuren, Ger. 57/G2
Bernburg, Ger. 40/F3
Berne (riv.), Ger. 51/F2
Bernes-sur-Oise, Fr. 30/J4
Bernese Alps (mtn.), Swi. 43/G3
Bernhardswald, Ger. 55/F4
Bernice, La, US 129/J4
Bernier (isl.), Austl. 112/B3
Bernier (bay), Nun., Can. 122/G1
Bernina (peak), Swi. 57/F5
Bernina (mtn.), Swi. 57/F5
Bernina, Passo del (pass), Swi. 57/G5
Bernissart, Belg. 52/C3
Bernkastel-Kues, Ger. 53/G4
Bernsbach, Ger. 55/F1
Bernville, Pa, US 138/B3
Beromünster, Swi. 56/E3
Beroroha, Madg. 107/H8
Beroun, Czh. 55/H3
Berounka (riv.), Czh. 41/G4
Berovo, FYROM 47/H2
Berra, It. 59/E3
Berre, Étang de (lake), Fr. 42/F5
Berrechid, Mor. 98/D2
Berri, Austl. 113/J5
Berriane, Alg. 99/F2
Berridale, Austl. 115/D3
Berriedale, Sc, UK 31/S7
Berrigan, Austl. 115/C2
Berriozábal, Mex. 144/C2
Berrotarán, Arg. 158/D2
Berrouaghia, Alg. 100/G4
Berry, Austl. 115/D2
Berry (isls.), Bahm. 141/F2
Berry (reg.), Fr. 42/D3
Berry (pt.), Eng, UK 32/C6
Berry (mtn.), Pa, US 138/A2
Berryessa (peak), Ca, US 135/K9
Bersenbrück, Ger. 51/E3
Berthoud, Co, US 137/B2
Bertinoro, It. 59/F4
Bertiolo, It. 59/G1
Bertogne, Belg. 53/E3
Bertolínia, Braz. 154/B2
Bertoua, Camr. 96/H7
Bertrand (riv.), Arg. 159/B6
Bertrandville, La, US 137/Q17
Bertrix, Belg. 53/E4
Bertry, Fr. 52/C3
Beru (isl.), Kiri. 116/G5
Beruit (isl.), Malay. 80/D3
Bervie Water (riv.), Sc, UK 36/D3
Berwick, NS, Can. 131/H2
Berwick, Pa, US 138/B1
Berwick-upon-Tweed, Eng, UK 36/D5
Berwyn, Il, US 135/Q16
Berwyn (mts.), Wal, UK 34/E6
Berzence, Hun. 48/C2
Bès (riv.), Fr. 42/E2
Besalampy, Madg. 107/H7
Besançon, Fr. 56/C3
Besar (peak), Indo. 81/E4
Besbre (riv.), Fr. 42/E3
Beşiri, Turk. 90/E2
Beška, Serb. 48/E3
Beskids (mts.), Pol. 41/L4
Beşkonak, Turk. 91/B1
Beslan, Rus. 63/H4
Besna Kobila (peak), Serb. 47/H1
Besozzo, It. 58/B1
Bessacarr, Eng, UK 35/G5
Bessancourt, Fr. 30/J4
Bessarabia (reg.), Mol. 49/J2
Bessbrook, NI, UK 34/B3
Bessemer, Al, US 133/G3
Bessemer (mtn.), Wa, US 135/D2
Bessines-sur-Gartempe, Fr. 42/D3
Best, Neth. 50/C5
Bestensee, Ger. 40/Q7
Bestwig, Ger. 51/F6
Bet She'an, Isr. 91/D3
Bet Shemesh, Isr. 91/F8
Betanantanana, Madg. 107/H7
Betanzos, Sp. 44/A1
Beth She'arim (ruin), Isr. 91/G6
Bethal, SAfr. 106/E2
Bethalto, Il, US 137/G8
Bethanie, Namb. 106/B2
Bethany (res.), Ca, US 135/L11
Bethany, Mo, US 127/K5
Bethany, Ok, US 137/M14
Bethel, Ak, US 134/F3
Bethel, Pa, US 138/B3
Bethel Acres, Ok, US 137/N15
Bethel Island, Ca, US 135/L10
Béthenville, Fr. 53/D5
Bétheny, Fr. 52/D5
Bethesda, Md, US 138/A6
Bethesda, Wal, UK 34/D5
Béthisy-Sainte-Pierre, Fr. 52/B5
Bethlehem, SAfr. 106/E3
Bethlehem, Pa, US 138/C2
Bethlehem, Md, US 138/C6
Bethoncourt, Fr. 56/C2
Bethpage, NY, US 139/M9
Bethulie, SAfr. 106/D3
Bethune, Sk, Can. 127/G3
Béthune (riv.), Fr. 42/D2
Béthune, Fr. 52/B2
Betim, Braz. 155/C1
Betioky, Madg. 107/H8
Betpaqala (plain), Kaz. 70/A2
Betroka, Madg. 107/H8
Betschdorf, Fr. 54/A5
Betsiamites (riv.), Qu, Can. 131/G1
Betsiboka (riv.), Madg. 107/H7
Bettancourt-la-Ferrée, Fr. 53/D6
Bette (peak), Libya 97/J3
Bettembourg, Lux. 53/F4
Betterton, Md, US 138/B5
Bettiah, India 85/E2
Bettlach, Swi. 56/D3
Bettles, Ak, US 134/H2
Betuwe (phys. reg.), Neth. 50/C5
Betwa (riv.), India 84/B3
Betz, Fr. 30/L4
Betzdorf, Ger. 53/G2
Betzenstein, Ger. 55/E3
Beulah, Austl. 115/B2
Beulah, ND, US 127/H4
Beulah (lake), Wi, US 135/P14
Beulakerwijde (lake), Neth. 50/C3
Beuningen, Neth. 50/C5
Beure, Fr. 56/C3
Beuvray (peak), Fr. 42/F3
Beuvron (riv.), Fr. 42/D3
Beuvronne (riv.), Fr. 30/L5
Beuvry, Fr. 52/B2
Bevensen, Ger. 51/H2
Bever (riv.), Ger. 51/E4
Beveren, Belg. 50/B6
Beverin (peak), Swi. 57/F4
Beverley, Austl. 112/C5
Beverley, Eng, UK 35/H4
Beverly, Mo, US 137/D5
Beverly Hills, Ca, US 136/F7
Beverly Hills, Mi, US 135/F6
Beverstedt, Ger. 51/F2
Beverungen, Ger. 51/G5
Beverwijk, Neth. 50/B4
Bewār, India 84/B3
Bewl Bridge (res.), Eng, UK 33/G4
Bex, Swi. 56/D5
Bexar (co.), Tx, US 137/T21
Bexbach, Ger. 53/G5
Bexhill, Eng, UK 33/G5
Bexley (bor.), Eng, UK 30/D2
Beyçayırı, Turk. 49/H5
Beycuma, Turk. 49/K5
Beyne-Heusay, Belg. 53/E2
Beynes, Fr. 30/H5
Beyoneisu-Retsugan (isl.), Japan 75/F5
Beypazarı, Turk. 49/K5
Beyşehir, Turk. 90/B2
Bezaha, Madg. 107/H8
Bezau, Aus. 57/F3
Bezdan, Serb. 48/D3
Bezděz (peak), Czh. 55/H1
Bezdrev (lake), Czh. 55/H4
Bezhetsk, Rus. 60/H4
Béziers, Fr. 42/E5
Bhabua, India 84/D3
Bhadarwāh, India 86/C3
Bhadaur, India 86/C4
Bhadohī, India 84/D3
Bhādra, India 86/C5
Bhadreswar, India 82/A3
Bhāgalpur, India 85/E3
Bhāi Pheru, Pak. 86/B4
Bhairab (riv.), Bang. 85/G4
Bhairab Bāzār, Bang. 85/H3
Bhakkar, Pak. 86/A4
Bhākra (dam), India 86/D4
Bhaktapur, Nepal 85/E2
Bhalwāl, Pak. 86/B3
Bhamo, Myan. 83/G3
Bhānder, India 84/B3
Bhānrer (range), India 84/B4
Bhānwad, India 82/A3
Bharatpur, Nepal 85/E2
Bharātpur, India 84/A2
Bharthana, India 84/B2
Bharuch, India 89/K4
Bhasāwar, India 84/A2
Bhātāpāra, India 82/D3
Bhatinda, India 86/C4
Bhatkal, India 89/K6
Bhātpāra, India 85/G4
Bhavāni, India 82/C5
Bhavnagar, India 89/K4
Bhawāna, Pak. 86/B4
Bhawāni Mandi, India 89/L4
Bhera, Pak. 86/B3
Bheri (zone), Nepal 84/C1
Bhilai, India 82/D3
Bhīlwāra, India 89/K3
Bhīma (riv.), India 89/L5
Bhima (riv.), India 82/C4
Bhīmavaram, India 82/D4
Bhimunipatnam, India 82/D4
Bhinga, India 84/C2
Bhiwandi, India 89/K5
Bhiwāni, India 86/D5
Bhojpur, Nepal 85/F2
Bhokardan, India 82/C3
Bhola, Bang. 85/H4
Bhongaon, India 84/B2
Bhopāl, India 82/C3
Bhor, India 89/K5
Bhraoin (lake), Sc, UK 36/A1
Bhuban, India 82/E3
Bhumibol (dam), Thai. 78/B2
Bhusawal, India 89/L4
Bhutan (ctry.) 82/E2
Bi Doup (peak), Viet. 78/E3
Biá (riv.), Braz. 150/E4
Bia (riv.), C.d'Iv. 102/E5
Biafra, Bight of (bay), Camr. 96/G7
Biak (isl.), Indo. 81/J4
Biak (int'l arpt.), Indo. 81/J4
Biała Podlaska, Pol. 41/M2
Białobrzegi, Pol. 41/L3
Białogard, Pol. 38/G4
Białowieski NP, Pol. 41/K4
Białowieski NP, Pol. 41/M2
Białystok, Pol. 41/M2
Bianca (peak), It. 57/G4
Biancavilla, It. 46/D4
Biandrate, It. 58/B2
Biandronno, It. 58/B1
Bianze, It. 58/B2
Biarritz, Fr. 42/C5
Biasca, Swi. 57/E5
Bibā, Egypt 101/B2
Bibai, Japan 76/B2
Bibbiano, It. 58/D3
Bibbiena, It. 59/E5
Biberach, Ger. 56/E1
Biberach, Ger. 57/G1
Biberach an der Riss, Ger. 57/F1
Biberist, Swi. 56/D3
Bibione, It. 59/G1
Biblián, Ecu. 152/B5
Biblis, Ger. 54/B3
Bicas, Braz. 211/K6
Bicaz, Rom. 49/H2
Bicester, Eng, UK 33/E3
Bicheno, Austl. 115/D4
Bicknacre, Eng, UK 30/E1
Bicske, Hun. 48/D2
Bida, Nga. 103/G4
Bīdar, India 82/C4
Biddeford, Me, US 131/G3
Biddiyā, WBnk. 91/G7
Biddū, WBnk. 91/G8
Biddulph, Eng, UK 35/F5
Bidean nam Bian (peak), Sc, UK 36/A3
Bideford, Eng, UK 32/B4
Bidente (riv.), It. 59/F4
Bidhūna, India 84/B2
Bīdokht, Iran 89/G2
Biebesheim am Rhein, Ger. 54/B3
Biebzra (riv.), Pol. 41/M2
Biel, Swi. 56/D3
Bielawa, Pol. 41/J3
Bieldside, Sc, UK 36/D2
Bielefeld, Ger. 51/F4
Bieler (lake), Nun., Can. 123/J1
Bieler (lake), Swi. 56/D3
Biella, It. 58/B1
Biella (prov.), It. 58/B1
Bielsk Podlaski, Pol. 41/M2
Bielsko-Biała, Pol. 41/K4
Bien Hoa, Viet. 78/D4
Bienenbüttel, Ger. 51/H2
Bienne (riv.), Fr. 56/B5
Bienno, It. 57/G6
Bientina, It. 58/D5
Bienville (lake), Qu, Can. 123/J3
Bière, Swi. 56/C4
Bierset (int'l arpt.), Belg. 53/E2
Bierum, Neth. 50/D2
Bierutów, Pol. 41/J3
Biesbosch (reg.), Neth. 50/B5
Biesenthal, Ger. 40/Q6
Biesles, Fr. 56/B1
Biesme (riv.), Fr. 53/D5
Bieszczadzki NP, Pol. 62/B2
Bieszczadzki NP, Pol. 41/M4
Bietigheim, Ger. 54/C5
Bietschhorn (peak), Swi. 56/D5
Bièvre (riv.), Fr. 30/J5
Bièvre, Belg. 53/E4
Bièvres, Fr. 30/J5
Big (des.), Austl. 115/B2
Big (riv.), Nun., Can. 122/D1
Big (isl.), On, Can. 122/G4
Big (lake), Mi, US 135/E6
Big (riv.), Mo, US 137/F9
Big Belt (mts.), Mt, US 126/F4
Big Bend, Swaz. 107/E2
Big Bend, Wi, US 135/P14
Big Bend NP, Tx, US 140/A2
Big Blue (riv.), Ks,Ne, US 129/H2
Big Diomede (isl.) 134/E2
Big Fork (riv.), Mn, US 127/K4
Big Hole (riv.), Mt, US 126/E4
Big Hole, SAfr. 106/D3
Big Lake, Tx, US 129/G5
Big Lost (riv.), Id, US 128/D2
Big Muskego (lake), Wi, US 135/P14
Big Pine (hill), Pa, US 138/C1
Big Pines, Ca, US 136/C2
Big Rapids, Mi, US 130/C3
Big River, Sk, Can. 126/G2
Big Rock, Il, US 135/N16
Big Sandy (riv.), Wy, US 128/E2
Big Sioux (riv.), Ia,SD, US 127/J5
Big Spring, Tx, US 129/G4
Big Stone (lake), Mn,SD, US 127/J4
Big Thompson (riv.), Co, US 137/B2
Big Thompson, North Fork (riv.), Co, US 137/A2
Big Timber, Mt, US 126/F4
Big Trout (lake), On, Can. 122/H3
Big Tujunga Canyon (canyon), Ca, US 136/B2
Big Wood (riv.), Id, US 128/D2
Biga, Turk. 49/H5
Bigadiç, Turk. 90/B2
Bigbury (bay), Eng, UK 32/C6
Biggar, Sk, Can. 126/G2
Biggar, Sc, UK 36/C5
Bigge (riv.), Ger. 53/G1
Biggenden, Austl. 114/D4
Biggleswade, Eng, UK 33/F2
Bighorn (basin), Wy, US 128/E1
Bighorn (lake), Mt,Wy, US 126/F4
Bighorn (mts.), Wy, US 124/E3
Bighorn (riv.), Wy, US 122/F4
Biglerville, Pa, US 138/A4
Bignona, Sen. 102/A3
Biguaçu, Braz. 155/B3
Bihać, Bosn. 43/L4
Bīhar, India 85/E3
Biharamulo, Tanz. 104/A3
Biharamulo Game Rsv., Tanz. 104/A3
Bihārīganj, India 85/F3
Biharkeresztes, Hun. 48/E2
Bihor (co.), Rom. 41/M5
Bihorel, Fr. 42/D2
Bihoro, Japan 76/D2
Bijagós (arch.), GBis. 93/A3
Bijagós, Arquipélago do (isl.) 96/B5
Bījār, Iran 88/E1
Bijāwar, India 84/B3
Bijbiāra, India 86/C3
Bijeljina, Bosn. 48/D3
Bijelo Polje, Serb. 47/F1
Bijiang, China 83/G2
Bijie, China 83/J2
Bijnor, India 85/H2
Bīkaner, India 89/K3
Bikar (isl.), Mrsh. 116/G3
Bikin, Rus. 71/P2
Bikin (riv.), Rus. 71/Q2
Bikini (isl.), Mrsh. 116/F3
Bikramganj, India 85/E3
Bikuar, PN do, Ang. 105/C4
Bila Tserkva, Ukr. 62/D2
Bilāra, India 82/B2
Bilāri, India 84/B1
Bilāsipāra, India 85/H2
Bilāspur, India 84/D4
Bilāspur, India 84/B1
Bilāspur, India 86/D4
Bilaukraung (range), Myan. 83/G5
Bilauktaung (range), Myan.,Thai 78/B3
Bilba Morea Claypan (lake) ,Austl. 109/C3
Bilbao, Sp. 44/D1
Bilbays, Egypt 91/B4
Bileća, Bosn. 47/F1
Bilecik, Turk. 90/B1
Bilecik (prov.), Turk. 90/B1
Biłgoraj, Pol. 41/M3
Bilgrām, India 84/C2
Bilhaur, India 84/C2
Bilhorod-Dnistrovs'kyy, Ukr. 49/K2
Bilibino, Rus. 65/S3
Bilin, Myan. 83/G4
Bilin (riv.), Myan. 78/B2
Bilina (riv.), Czh. 55/G2
Bilina, Czh. 55/G1
Biliu (riv.), China 73/B3
Bill of Portland (pt.), Eng, UK 32/D5
Bill Williams (riv.), Az, US 128/D4
Bille (riv.), Ger. 51/H1
Billerbeck, Ger. 51/E5
Billère, Fr. 42/C5
Billericay, Eng, UK 30/E2
Billiat Conservation Park, Austl. 115/B2
Billiat Consv. Park, Austl. 113/J5
Billigheim, Ger. 54/C4
Billinge, Eng, UK 35/F4
Billingham, Eng, UK 35/G2
Billings, Mt, US 126/F4
Billingsfors, Swe. 38/E2
Billiton (isl.), Indo. 67/K10
Billund (int'l arpt.), Den. 38/C4
Billund, Den. 38/C4
Bilma, Niger 96/H4
Biloela, Austl. 114/C4
Biloku, Guy. 153/G4
Biloxi, Ms, US 133/F4
Bilpa Morea Claypan (lake), Austl. 113/H3
Bilqas Qism Awwal, Egypt 91/B4
Bilsi, India 84/B1
Bilthar, India 84/D2
Biltine, Chad 97/K5
Bilzen, Belg. 53/E2
Bima, Indo. 81/E5
Bimberi (peak), Austl. 115/D2
Bimbo, CAfr. 97/J7
Bimini (isls.), Bahm. 141/F2
Bin 'Arūs, Tun. 46/B4
Bin 'Arus (gov.), Tun. 46/B4
Bina (riv.), Ger. 55/F6
Bina-Etāwa, India 84/B3
Binalong, Austl. 115/D2
Binasco, It. 58/C2
Binbrook, On, Can. 131/Q9
Binche, Belg. 53/D3
Binchuan, China 83/H2
Bindki, India 84/C2
Bindura, Zim. 105/F4
Binéfar, Sp. 45/F2
Binga (mtn.), Moz. 105/F4
Bingara, Austl. 115/D1
Bingen, Ger. 53/G4
Bingerville, C.d'Iv. 102/E5
Binghamton, NY, US 130/F3
Bingley, Eng, UK 35/G4
Bıngöl, Turk. 90/E2
Bingöl (prov.), Turk. 90/E2
Binh Son, Viet. 78/E3
Binhai, China 72/D4
Binhon (peak), Myan. 83/G4
Binisalem, Sp. 45/G3
Binjai, Indo. 80/A3
Binkılıç, Turk. 49/J5
Binnaway, Austl. 115/D1
Binningen, Swi. 56/D2
Binongko (isl.), Indo. 81/F5
Bintang (peak), Malay. 80/B2
Binyamina, Isr. 91/F6
Bío-Bío (riv.), Chile 157/B4
Bío-Bío (pol. reg.), Chile 158/B3
Biograd, Cro. 48/B4
Biogradska Gora NP, Serb. 47/F1
Biogradska NP, Serb. 48/D4
Bioko (isl.), EqG. 93/C4
Biougra, Mor. 98/C3
Bipoint (Bissau) (int'l arpt.), GBis. 102/B4
Bippen, Ger. 51/E3
Bīr, India 89/L5
Bīr Abu Minqâr (well), Egypt 101/A3
Bir Aïdiat (well), Mrta. 98/C4
Bir Bel Guerdâne (well), Mrta. 98/C4
Bi'r Ghadir (well), Egypt 101/C3

Bîr Ounâne (well), Mali 98/E5
Bi'r Zayt, WBnk. 91/G8
Birāk, Libya 96/H2
Birao, CAfr. 97/K5
Birātnagar, Nepal 85/F2
Biratori, Japan 76/C2
Birch (mts.), Ab, Can. 122/E3
Birch Creek, Ak, US 134/J2
Birch Hills, Sk, Can. 127/G2
Birch River, Mb, Can. 127/H2
Birchip, Austl. 115/B2
Bird Islet (isl.), Austl. 109/E3
Birds Rock (peak), Austl. 115/D2
Birdsboro, Pa, US 138/C3
Birdwood, Austl. 113/M8
Birecik, Turk. 90/D2
Bīrganj, Nepal 85/E2
Biritiba-Mirim, Braz. 211/G8
Bīrjand, Iran 89/G2
Birkat Qārūn (lake), Egypt 90/B4
Birken-Honigsessen, Ger. 53/G2
Birkenau, Ger. 54/B3
Birkenfeld, Ger. 53/G4
Birkenhead, Eng, UK 35/E5
Birkenheide, Ger. 54/B4
Birkenwerder, Ger. 40/Q6
Birkirkara, Malta 46/L7
Birkkarspitze (peak), Aus. 57/H3
Bîrlad, Rom. 49/H2
Birmingham, Eng, UK 33/E2
Birmingham (co.), Eng, UK 33/E2
Birmingham (int'l arpt.), Eng, UK 33/E2
Birmingham, Al, US 133/G3
Birmingham, Mi, US 135/F6
Birmingham, Mo, US 137/E5
Birmitrapur, India 85/E4
Birnam, Sc, UK 36/C3
Birnhorn (peak), Aus. 43/K3
Birni Nkonni, Niger 103/G3
Birnie (isl.), Kiri. 117/H5
Birnin Kebbi, Nga. 103/G3
Birobijan, Rus. 71/P2
Bīrpur, India 85/F2
Birr, Ire. 31/Q10
Birs (riv.), Swi. 43/G3
Birsk, Rus. 61/M5
Birstein, Ger. 54/C2
Biruaca, Ven. 153/E3
Biržai, Lith. 39/L3
Birżebbuġa, Malta 46/M7
Bis (lake), Rom. 49/F4
Bisa-Nadi Nat'l Rsv., Kenya 104/C2
Bisai, Japan 77/L5
Bīsalpur, India 84/B1
Bisamberg, Aus. 49/N7
Bisauli, India 84/B1
Bisbee Douglas (int'l arpt.), Az, US 142/C2
Biscarrosse, Fr. 42/C4
Biscarrosse,Étang de (lake), Fr. 42/C4
Biscay (bay), Fr.,Sp. 27/D4
Biscayne NP, Fl, US 141/E2
Bisceglie, It. 46/E2
Bischberg, Ger. 54/D3
Bischheim, Fr. 53/G6
Bischofsgrün, Ger. 55/E2
Bischofsheim, Ger. 54/B3
Bischofsheim an der Rhön, Ger. 54/D2
Bischofshofen, Aus. 43/K3
Bischofszell, Swi. 57/F3
Bischwiller, Fr. 56/D2
Biscubio (riv.), It. 59/F5
Biscucuy, Ven. 152/D2
Bīshah (riv.), SAr. 88/D4
Bishkek (cap.), Kyr. 87/F4
Bishnupur, India 85/F4
Bishop, Ca, US 128/C3
Bishop Auckland, Eng, UK 35/E2
Bishopbriggs, Sc, UK 36/B5
Bishop's Falls, Nf, Can. 131/L1
Bishop's Stortford, Eng, UK 33/G3
Bishopton, Sc, UK 36/B5
Bisingen, Ger. 54/B6
Biskra, Alg. 100/H5
Biskupiec, Pol. 39/J5
Bislig, Phil. 79/E6
Bismarck (cap.), ND, US 127/H4
Bismarck, On, Can. 131/Q9
Bismarck (arch.), PNG 116/D5
Bismarck (sea), PNG 116/D5
Bismil, Turk. 90/E2
Bismuna (lag.), Nic. 145/F3
Bispgarden, Swe. 37/F3
Bispingen, Ger. 51/G2
Bissau (cap.), GBis. 102/B4
Bissau, India 86/C5
Bissendorf, Ger. 51/F4
Bissett, Mb, Can. 127/K3
Bissingen, Ger. 54/D5
Bistagno, It. 58/B3
Bistrița (riv.), Rom. 49/G2
Bistrița, Rom. 49/G2
Bıstrița-Năsăud (prov.), Rom. 49/G2
Biswān, India 84/C2
Bita (riv.), Col. 150/E2
Bitam, Gabon 96/H7
Bitburg, Ger. 53/F4
Bitche, Fr. 53/G5
Bitkin, Chad 96/J5
Bitlis (prov.), Turk. 90/E2
Bitlis, Turk. 90/E2
Bitola, FYROM 47/G2
Bitonto, It. 46/E2
Bitter (lakes), Egypt 101/C2
Bitterfontein, SAfr. 106/B3
Bitterroot (range), Id,Mt, US 126/E4
Bitti, It. 46/A2
Bitung, Indo. 81/G3
Bituruna, Braz. 155/B3
Biwa, Japan 77/K5
Bixby, Ok, US 132/E3
Biyalā, Egypt 91/B4
Biyang, China 72/C4
Bizard (isl.), Qu, Can. 131/M7
Bjärred, Swe. 38/E4
Bjelovar, Cro. 48/C3
Bjerkvik, Nor. 37/F1
Bjerringbro, Den. 38/C3
Bjørkelangen, Nor. 38/D2
Björklinge, Swe. 38/G1
Bjørnafjorden (estu.), Nor. 38/A1
Bjorne (pen.), Nun., Can. 123/S7
Bjugn, Nor. 37/D3
Bjuv, Swe. 38/E3
Blå Jungfrun NP, Swe. 38/G3
Blace, Serb. 47/G1
Blachownia, Pol. 41/K3
Black (sea), Asia,Eur. 67/C5
Black (bay), On, Can. 127/L3
Black (riv.), On. Can. 127/L2
Black (mt.), Yk, Can. 134/M3
Black (riv.), China,Vie 70/H7
Black (for.), Ger. 40/D5
Black (pt.), Eng, UK 32/A6
Black (pt.), NI, UK 34/C2
Black (isl.), Sc, UK 36/B1
Black (mtn.), Wal, UK 32/C3
Black (mts.), Wal, UK 32/C3
Black (mesa), Az, US 128/E3
Black (mts.), Az, US 129/D4
Black (pt.), Ct, US 139/F1
Black (range), NM, US 128/F4
Black (riv.), NY, US 130/F3
Black (hills), SD, US 124/F3
Black (riv.), Wi, US 127/L4
Black Canyon of the Gunnison Nat'l Park, Co, US 128/F3
Black Diamond, Ab, Can. 126/E3
Black Diamond, Wa, US 135/C3
Black Eagle, Mt, US 126/F4
Black Forest (Schwarzwald) (for.), Ger. 54/B6
Black Hawk, Co, US 137/B3
Black Jack, Mo, US 137/G8
Black Mountain NP, Austl. 114/B1
Black Mtn. (mtn.), Wal, UK 32/C3
Black Point, Ca, US 135/K10
Black River, Jam. 145/G2
Black River Falls, Wi, US 127/L4
Black Rock (des.), Nv, US 128/C2
Black Rock (pt.), RI, US 139/G1
Black Sea Lowland (reg.), Mol.,Ukr. 49/J3
Black Sugarloaf (peak), Austl. 115/D1
Black Volta (riv.), Burk. 93/B4
Black Walnut, Mo, US 137/G8
Black Warrior (riv.), Al, US 133/G3
Blackadder Water (riv.), Sc, UK 36/D5
Blackall, Austl. 114/B4
Blackburn, Eng, UK 35/F4
Blackburn, Sc, UK 36/C5
Blackburn with Darwen, (co.), Eng, UK 35/F4
Blackbutt, Austl. 114/D4
Blackcraig (peak), Sc, UK 36/B6
Blackdown (hills), Eng, UK 32/C5
Blackdown (hill), Eng, UK 33/F4
Blackdown Tableland NP, Austl. 114/C3
Blackfoot (res.), Id, US 126/F5
Blackheath, Austl. 115/D2
Blackmoor (upland), Eng, UK 32/B5
Blackpool, Eng, UK 35/E4
Blackpool (co.), Eng, UK 35/E4
Blackrod, Eng, UK 35/F4
Blackshear (lake), Ga, US 133/H3
Blackstone, Va, US 130/E4
Blackville, NB, Can. 131/H2
Blackwater, Austl. 114/C3
Blackwater (riv.), Ire. 31/P10
Blackwater (riv.), Eng, UK 30/A2
Blackwater (res.), Sc, UK 36/B3
Blackwater (riv.), Mo, US 129/J3
Blackwell, Ok, US 129/H3
Blackwood (riv.), Austl. 112/B5
Blackwood, NJ, US 138/C4
Bladensburg, Md, US 138/B6
Bladensburg NP, Austl. 114/A3
Bladnoch (riv.), Sc, UK 34/D2
Blaenau Gwent (co.), Wal, UK 32/C3
Blagnac, Fr. 42/D5
Blagnac (int'l arpt.), Fr. 42/D5
Blagny, Fr. 53/E4
Blagoevgrad, Bul. 47/H1
Blagoveshchensk, Rus. 71/N1
Blaine Lake, Sk, Can. 126/G2
Blainville, Qu, Can. 131/N6
Blair, Ne, US 127/J5
Blair (hill), Pa, US 138/C1
Blair Atholl, Sc, UK 36/C3
Blairstown, NJ, US 138/D2
Blaise (riv.), Fr. 42/F2
Blaj, Rom. 49/F2
Blakely, Ga, US 133/G4
Blakeslee, Pa, US 138/C1
Blamont, Fr. 56/C3
Blanc (cape), Fr. 43/G5
Blanc (peak), Fr. 56/C6
Blanc (cape), Mrta. 96/B3
Blanc, Cap (cape), Tun. 46/A4
Blanc Nez (cape), Fr. 52/A2
Blanca (peak), NM, US 129/F4
Blanca (pt.), Mex. 142/B2
Blanca (bay), Arg. 147/C6
Blanca, Cordillera (mts.), Peru 150/C5
Blanca, Costa (coast), Sp. 45/E4
Blanchard, Ok, US 137/M15
Blanche (lake), Austl. 109/D3
Blanche (peak), Swi. 56/D5
Blanche (cape), Austl. 113/G5
Blanco (cape), CR 144/E4
Blanco (cape), Mor. 98/A5
Blanco (cape), Peru 150/B4
Blanco (lake), Chile 159/C7
Blanco (riv.), Bol. 150/F6
Blanco (riv.), Tx, US 129/H5
Blanding, Ut, US 128/E3
Blandy, Fr. 30/L6
Blanes, Sp. 45/G2
Blangy-sur-Bresle, Fr. 52/A4
Blankenberge, Belg. 52/C1
Blankenfelde, Ger. 40/Q7
Blankenheim, Ger. 53/F3
Blanquilla (isl.), Ven. 150/F1
Blanquillo, Uru. 159/G2
Blansko, Czh. 41/J4
Blantyre, Malw. 105/G4
Blantyre, Sc, UK 36/B5
Blanzy, Fr. 42/F3
Blaricum, Neth. 50/C4
Blas (peak), Swi. 57/E4
Blatná, Czh. 55/G4
Blato, Cro. 46/E1
Blatten, Swi. 56/D5
Blau (riv.), Ger. 54/C6
Blaubeuren, Ger. 54/C6
Blauen (peak), Ger. 56/D2
Blaustein, Ger. 54/C6
Blauvelt, NY, US 139/K7
Blåvands (pt.), Den. 38/C4
Blavet (riv.), Fr. 42/B3
Blaye, Fr. 42/C4
Blayney, Austl. 115/D2
Bleckede, Ger. 51/H2
Bled, Slov. 43/L3
Blefjell (peak), Nor. 38/C2
Blégny, Belg. 53/E2
Bléharies, Belg. 52/C2
Bleiburg, Aus. 48/B2
Bleicherode, Ger. 51/H6
Bleik (peak), Ger. 57/G2
Bleiswijk, Neth. 50/B4
Blekinge (co.), Swe. 37/E4
Blendecques, Fr. 52/B2
Blender, Ger. 51/G3
Blenheim, NZ 117/S11
Blénod-lès-Pont-à-Mousson, Fr. 53/F6
Bléone (riv.), Fr. 43/G4
Blesberg (peak), SAfr. 106/C4
Blessington, Ire. 34/B5
Bletterans, Fr. 56/B4
Bleury, Fr. 30/H6
Bleus (mts.), D.R. Congo 97/L7
Bleus, Monts (mts.), D.R. Congo 104/A2
Blida (prov.), Alg. 100/G4
Blida, Alg. 100/G4
Blies (riv.), Ger. 53/G5
Blieskastel, Ger. 53/G5
Blik (mt.), Phil. 81/F2
Blinnenhorn (peak), Swi. 57/E5
Blithe (riv.), Eng, UK 35/F6
Blithfield (res.), Eng, UK 35/G6
Block (isl.), RI, US 131/G3
Block Island C. G. Sta., RI, US 139/G1
Block Island (New Shoreham), RI, US 139/G1
Block Island NWR, RI, US 139/G1
Blodelsheim, Fr. 56/D2
Bloemendaal, Neth. 50/B4
Bloemfontein, (cap.), SAfr. 106/D3
Bloemhof, SAfr. 106/D2
Bloemhofdam (res.), SAfr. 106/D2
Blois, Fr. 42/D3
Blomberg, Ger. 51/E1
Blomberg, Ger. 51/G5
Blomstermåla, Swe. 38/G3
Blonay, Swi. 56/C5
Blönduós, Ice. 37/N6
Bloodvein (riv.), Mb,On, Can. 122/G3
Bloody Foreland (pt.), Ire. 31/P9
Bloomfield, NJ, US 139/J8
Bloomfield, NM, US 128/F3
Bloomfield Hills, Mi, US 135/F6
Bloomingdale, NJ, US 139/H7
Bloomingdale, Il, US 135/P16
Bloomington, Mn, US 127/K4
Bloomington, Il, US 127/L5
Bloomington, Ca, US 136/C2
Bloomsburg, Pa, US 138/B2
Bloomsbury, NJ, US 138/C2
Blora, Indo. 80/D5
Blotzheim, Fr. 56/D2
Blountstown, Fl, US 133/G4
Blovice, Czh. 55/G3
Blšanka (riv.), Czh. 43/K1
Bludenz, Aus. 57/F3
Blue (mtn.), India 83/F3
Blue (riv.), Ok, US 132/D3
Blue (mts.), Or,Wa, US 124/C2
Blue Head (pt.), Sc, UK 36/C1
Blue Island, Il, US 135/Q16
Blue Lake NP, Austl. 114/D4
Blue Marsh Lake (res.), Pa, US 138/B3
Blue Mesa (res.), Co, US 128/F3
Blue Mountain (peak), Jam. 145/G2
Blue Mountain (ridge), Pa, US 138/A3
Blue Mountains, Austl. 115/D2
Blue Mountains NP, Austl. 115/D2
Blue Nile (riv.), Sudan, Et 97/M5
Blue Ridge (mts.), US 133/H3
Blue Ridge Parkway, US 130/D4
Blue Springs, Mo, US 137/E5
Bluefield, WV, US 130/D4
Bluefields, Nic. 145/F4
Bluefields (bay), Nic. 145/F4
Bluejoint (lake), Or, US 128/C2
Bluenose (lake), Nun., Can. 122/E2
Bluff, NZ 117/R12
Bluff (pt.), Austl. 112/B3
Bluff, Austl. 114/C3
Bluff (peak), Austl. 112/C5
Bluffdale, Ut, US 137/K13
Bluffton, In, US 130/C3
Blumberg, Ger. 57/E2
Blümlisalp (peak), Swi. 56/D5
Blyn, Wa, US 135/B1
Blyth, Austl. 113/H5
Blyth, Eng, UK 35/G1
Blythe, Ca, US 128/D4
Blytheville, Ar, US 129/K4
Bnom Mhai (peak), Viet. 78/D4
Bo, SLeo. 102/C5
Bø, Nor. 38/C2
Bo Hai (Chihli) (gulf), China 72/D3
Boa Esperança, Braz. 155/C2
Boa Esperança, Represa (res.), Braz. 151/J5
Boa Viagem, Braz. 154/C2
Boa Vista, Braz. 153/F4
Boa Vista (int'l arpt.), Braz. 153/F4
Boa Vista (isl.), CpV. 93/K10
Boac, Phil. 79/D5
Boaco, Nic. 144/E3
Boadilla del Monte, Sp. 45/N9
Bo'ai, China 72/C4
Boano (isl.), Indo. 81/G4
Boas (riv.), Nun., Can. 123/H2
Boavita, Col. 152/C3
Boaz, Al, US 133/G3
Boba, Hun. 48/C2
Bobai, China 83/J3
Bobaomby (cape), Madg. 107/J5
Bobbili, India 82/D4
Bobbio, It. 58/C3
Bobenheim-Roxheim, Ger. 54/B3
Bobigny, Fr. 30/K5
Böblingen, Ger. 54/C5
Bobo Dioulasso, Burk. 102/D4
Boboshevo, Bul. 47/H1
Bobotov Kuk (peak), Serb. 47/F1
Bobovdol, Bul. 47/H1
Bóbr (riv.), Pol. 41/H3
Bobrov, Rus. 62/G2
Bobures, Ven. 152/D2
Boby (peak), Madg. 107/H8
Boca de Aroa, Ven. 152/D2
Boca del Guafo (chan.), Chile 158/B4
Boca del Pao, Ven. 153/E2
Boca del Río, Mex. 143/N7
Bôca do Acre, Braz. 150/E5
Boca Raton, Fl, US 133/H5
Bocaina, Serra da (mts.), Braz. 211/J7
Bocairente, Sp. 45/E3
Bocas del Toro, Pan. 145/F4
Bocay (riv.), Nic. 144/E3
Bochil, Mex. 144/C2
Bochnia, Pol. 41/L4
Bocholt, Ger. 50/D5
Bocholt, Belg. 53/E1
Bochum, Ger. 51/E6
Bockau, Ger. 55/F1
Bockenem, Ger. 51/H4
Bockenheim an der Weinstrasse, Ger. 53/H4
Bockhorn, Ger. 51/F2
Bockhorn, Ger. 55/E6
Boconó, Ven. 152/D2
Bocq (riv.), Belg. 53/D3
Boda, CAfr. 96/J7
Bodafors, Swe. 38/F3
Bodalla, Austl. 115/D3
Bodaybo, Rus. 65/M4
Boddam, Sc, UK 36/E2
Boddington, Austl. 112/C5
Bode (riv.), Ger. 40/F3
Bodega (bay), Ca, US 128/B3
Bodegraven, Neth. 50/B4
Bodélé (reg.), Chad 96/J4
Bodenheim, Ger. 54/B3
Bodenkirchen, Ger. 55/F6
Bodenmais, Ger. 55/G4
Bodensee (Constance) (lake), Swi 43/H3
Bodenteich, Ger. 51/H3
Bodh Gaya, India 85/E3
Bodhan, India 82/C4
Bodināyakkanūr, India 82/C5
Bodio, Swi. 57/E5
Bodkin (pt.), Md, US 138/B5
Bodmin, Eng, UK 32/B6
Bodmin Moor (upland), Eng, UK 32/B6
Bodø, Nor. 37/E2
Bodocó, Braz. 154/C2
Bodrog (riv.), Hun.,Slvk. 41/L4
Bodrum, Turk. 90/A2
Bódvaszilas, Hun. 41/L4
Boedecker (lake), Co, US 137/B2
Boëge, Fr. 56/C5
Boegoeberg (peak), Namb. 106/A2
Boekel, Neth. 50/C5
Boende, D.R. Congo 97/K8
Boerne, Tx, US 137/T20
Boeuf (riv.), La, US 129/K4
Bog of Allen (swamp), Ire. 34/A5
Bogalusa, La, US 133/F4
Bogan (riv.), Austl. 109/D4
Bogan Gate, Austl. 115/C2
Bogandé, Burk. 103/E3
Bogatić, Serb. 48/D3
Bogatynia, Pol. 41/H3
Boğazkale-Alacahöyük NP, Turk. 90/C1
Boğazlıyan, Turk. 90/C2
Bogdanci, FYROM 47/H2
Bogen, Nor. 37/F1
Bogen, Ger. 55/F5
Bogense, Den. 38/D4
Boggabilla, Austl. 114/C5
Boggabri, Austl. 115/D1
Boggy (peak), Anti. 141/N8
Boglárlelle, Hun. 48/C2
Bogliasco, It. 58/C4
Bognor Regis, Eng, UK 33/F5
Bogny-sur-Meuse, Fr. 53/D4
Bogo, Phil. 79/D5
Bogong (mt.), Austl. 115/C3
Bogong NP, Austl. 115/C3
Bogor, Indo. 80/C5
Bogotá (cap.), Col. 150/D3
Bogota, NJ, US 139/J8
Bogovino, FYROM 47/G2
Bogra (pol. reg.), Bang. 85/G3
Bogra, Bang. 85/G3
Bogué, Mrta. 102/B2
Bohain-en-Vermandois, Fr. 52/C4
Bohemia (reg.), Czh. 41/G4
Bohemian (for.), Czh.,Ger. 40/G4
Bohicon, Ben. 103/F5
Böhl-Iggelheim, Ger. 54/B4
Böhme (riv.), Ger. 51/G3
Böhmenkirch, Ger. 54/C5
Bohmte, Ger. 51/F4
Bohners Lake, Wi, US 135/P14
Bohol (isl.), Phil. 79/D6
Böhönye, Hun. 48/C2
Bohu, China 70/E3
Boiling Springs, Pa, US 138/A3
Boipeda, Ilha de (isl.), Braz. 154/C4
Boiro, Sp. 44/A1
Bois-d'Amont, Fr. 56/C4
Bois-d'Arcy, Fr. 30/J5
Bois de Boulogne (dept.), Fr. 30/J5
Bois de Vincennes (dept.), Fr. 30/K5
Bois-des-Filion, Qu, Can. 131/N6
Bois, Rio dos (riv.), Braz. 155/B1
Boisbriand, Qu, Can. 131/N6
Boise (riv.), Id, US 126/E5
Boise City, Ok, US 129/G3
Boissevain, Mb, Can. 127/H3
Boissy-Fresnoy, Fr. 30/L4
Boissy-L'Aillerie, Fr. 30/J4
Boissy-le-Châtel, Fr. 30/M5
Boissy-Saint-Léger, Fr. 30/K5
Boissy-Sans-Avoir, Fr. 30/H5
Boizenburg, Ger. 51/H2
Bojador (cape), Mor. 96/C2
Bojano, It. 48/B5
Boji (plain), Kenya 104/C2
Bojkovice, Czh. 41/J4
Bojnūrd, Iran 89/G1
Bokaro Steel City, India 85/F4
Boké (pol. reg.), Gui. 102/B4
Boké, Gui. 102/B4
Bokhol (plain), Kenya 104/C2
Boknafjorden (estu.), Nor. 37/C4
Bokol (peak), Kenya 104/C2
Bokoro, Chad 96/J5
Bokpyin, Myan. 78/B4
Boksburg, SAfr. 106/Q13
Bokspits, Bots. 106/C2
Bol, Chad 96/H5
Bolama, GBis. 102/B4
Bolān (pass), Pak. 89/J3
Bolaños de Calatrava, Sp. 44/D3
Bolayır, Turk. 47/K2
Bolbec, Fr. 42/D2
Boldeşti-Scăeni, Rom. 49/H3
Boldon, Eng, UK 35/G2
Bole, China 70/D3
Bole, Gha. 103/E4
Bolesławiec, Pol. 41/H3
Bolgatanga, Gha. 103/E4
Boli, China 71/P2
Boliden, Swe. 37/G2
Bolinao, Phil. 79/C4
Bolívar, Arg. 158/E3
Bolívar, Col. 152/B3
Bolívar (dept.), Col. 152/C2
Bolívar, Ecu. 152/A4
Bolívar, Peru 156/B2
Bolivar, Mo, US 129/J3
Bolívar (peak), Ven. 152/D2
Bolívar (peak), Ven. 153/F3
Bolivar (state), Ven. 153/E3
Bolivia (ctry.), Bol. 150/F7
Bollate, It. 58/C1
Bollène, Fr. 42/F4
Bolligen, Swi. 56/D4
Bollin (riv.), Eng, UK 35/F5
Bollnäs, Swe. 38/G1
Bollullos Par del Condado, Sp. 44/B4
Bolmen (lake), Swe. 38/E3
Bolobo, D.R. Congo 96/J8
Bologna, It. 59/E4
Bologna (prov.), It. 59/E3
Bologne, Fr. 56/B1
Bolognesi, Peru 156/C3
Bologoye, Rus. 60/G4
Bolomba, D.R. Congo 97/J7
Bolonchén de Rejón, Mex. 144/D2
Bolovens (plat.), Laos 78/D3
Bolpur, India 85/F4
Bolsena, It. 46/B1
Bolsena (lake), It. 46/B1
Bol'shaya Kinel' (riv.), Rus. 63/K1
Bol'shaya Rogovaya (riv.), Rus. 61/P2
Bol'shaya Synya (riv.), Rus. 61/N2
Bol'shevik (isl.), Rus. 67/H2
Bol'shezemel'skaya (tundra), Rus. 61/M2
Bol'shoy Bolvanskiy Nos (pt.), Rus. 64/F2
Bol'shoy Irgiz (riv.), Rus. 63/J1
Bol'shoy Lyakhov (isl.), Rus. 67/P2
Bol'shoy Lyakhovskiy (isl.), Rus. 65/Q2
Bol'shoy Uzen' (riv.), Rus. 63/J2
Bolsover, Eng, UK 35/G5
Bolsward, Neth. 50/C2
Bolt (pt.), Eng, UK 32/C6
Boltaña, Sp. 45/F1
Boltigen, Swi. 56/D4
Bolton, Eng, UK 35/F4
Bolton (co.), Eng, UK 35/F4
Bolu, Turk. 49/K5
Bolu (prov.), Turk. 49/K5
Bolungavík, Ice. 37/M6
Bolus Head (pt.), Ire. 30/N11
Bolvadin, Turk. 90/B2
Bóly, Hun. 48/D3
Bolzano, It. 57/H5
Bolzano-Bozen (prov.), It. 57/H4
Bom Conselho, Braz. 154/C3
Bom Despacho, Braz. 155/C1
Bom Jardim, Braz. 154/A1
Bom Jardim de Minas, Braz. 211/J6
Bom Jesus, Braz. 155/B4
Bom Jesus, Braz. 154/A3
Bom Jesus da Gurguéia, Serra (mts.), Braz. 151/K5
Bom Jesus de Goiás, Braz. 155/B1
Bom Jesus do Itabapoana, Braz. 155/D2
Bom Jesus dos Perdões, Braz. 211/G8
Bom Retiro, Braz. 155/B3
Boma, D.R. Congo 105/B2
Bomaderry, Austl. 115/D2
Bombala, Austl. 115/D3
Bombay Hook NWR, De, US 138/C5
Bombay (Mumbai), India 89/K5
Bomberai (pen.), Indo. 81/H4
Bombo, Ugan. 104/B2
Bomi, China 83/G2
Bomlitz, Ger. 51/G3
Bømlo (isl.), Nor. 38/A2
Bomu (riv.), D.R. Congo 93/E4
Bon-Encontre, Fr. 42/D4
Bona (mt.), Ak, US 134/K3
Bonaduz, Swi. 57/F4
Bonaire (isl.), NAnt. 141/H5
Bonalbo, Austl. 115/E1
Bonampak (ruin), Mex. 144/D2
Bonao, DRep. 141/G4
Bonaparte (arch.), Austl. 109/B2
Bonaparte (isls.), Austl. 109/B2
Bonasila (mtn.), Ak, US 134/F3
Bonaventure, Qu, Can. 131/H1
Bonaventure (riv.), Qu, Can. 131/H1
Bonavista (bay) Nf, Can. 131/L1
Bonavista, Nf, Can. 131/L1
Bonavista (cape) Nf, Can. 131/L1
Boncourt, Swi. 56/D3
Bondeno, It. 59/E3
Bondo, D.R. Congo 97/K7
Bondoukou, C.d'Iv. 102/E4
Bondowoso, Indo. 80/D5
Bone (gulf), Indo. 67/M10
Bönen, Ger. 51/E5
Bonerate (isls.), Indo. 81/F5
Bonfol, Swi. 56/D3
Bonfouca, La, US 137/Q16
Bong (co.), Libr. 102/C5
Bong (range), Libr. 102/C5
Bongabong, Phil. 81/F1
Bongaigaon, India 85/H2
Bongandanga, D.R. Congo 97/K7
Bongao, Phil. 81/E3
Bonggi (isl.), Malay. 81/E2
Bongka (riv.), Indo. 81/F4
Bongo, Massif des (plat.), CAfr. 97/K6
Bongolava (uplands), Madg. 105/K10
Bongor, Chad 96/J5
Bonham, Tx, US 129/H4
Bonheiden, Belg. 53/D1
Bonhill, Sc, UK 36/B5
Bonhomme, Col du (pass), Fr. 56/D1
Boni Nat'l Rsv., Kenya 104/D3
Bonifacio, Fr. 46/A2
Bonifacio (str.), It. 46/A2
Bonifay, Fl, US 133/G4
Bönigen, Swi. 56/D4
Bonin (isls.), Japan 116/C2
Bonita, Ca, US 136/C5
Bonita Springs, Fl, US 133/H5
Bonito (peak), Hon. 144/E3
Bonn, Ger. 53/G2
Bonndorf im Schwarzwald, Ger. 57/E2
Bonne, Fr. 56/C5
Bonnelles, Fr. 30/J6
Bonner Springs, Ks, US 137/D5
Bonner-West Riverside, Mt, US 126/E4
Bonners Ferry, Id, US 126/D3
Bonnet Carré Spillway, La, US 137/P16
Bonnet, Lac du (lake), Mb, Can. 127/K3
Bonneuil-sur-Marne, Fr. 30/K5
Bonneval, Fr. 42/D2
Bonneville (dam), Wa,Or, US 126/C4
Bonneville, Fr. 56/C5
Bonney Lake, Wa, US 135/C3
Bönnigheim, Ger. 54/C4
Bonnybridge, Sc, UK 36/C5
Bonorva, It. 46/A2
Bons-en-Chablais, Fr. 56/C5
Bonsall, Ca, US 136/C4
Bontberg (peak), SAfr. 106/C4
Bontebok NP, SAfr. 106/C4
Bonthain, Indo. 81/E5
Bonthe, SLeo. 102/B5
Bontoc, Phil. 79/D4
Bonyhád, Hun. 48/D2
Bonzart (lake), Tun. 100/L6
Booker T. Washington Nat'l Mon., Va, US 133/J2
Boom, Belg. 53/D1
Boone, Ia, US 127/K5
Boone, NC, US 130/D4
Booneville, Ms, US 133/F3
Boonton, NJ, US 139/H8
Boorabbin NP, Austl. 112/D4
Boorama, Som. 97/P6
Booroondara (mt.), Austl. 115/C1
Boorowa, Austl. 115/D2
Boos (int'l arpt.), Fr. 42/D2
Boos, Ger. 57/G1
Boosaaso (Bender Cassim), Som. 97/Q5
Boostedt, Ger. 38/D4
Boothbay Harbor, Me, US 131/G3
Boothia (pen.), Nun., Can. 122/G1
Boothia (gulf), Nun., Can. 122/G1
Bootle, Eng, UK 35/E5
Booué, Gabon 96/H8
Bopa, Ben. 103/F5
Bopfingen, Ger. 54/D5
Boppard, Ger. 53/G3
Boppy (mt.), Austl. 115/C1
Boqueirão, Braz. 154/C2
Boqueirão, Serra do (mts.), Braz. 154/B3
Boquete (peak), Arg. 158/C4
Boquilla (res.), Mex. 142/D3
Boquillas del Carmen, Mex. 132/C4
Boquira, Braz. 154/B4
Bor, Czh. 55/F3
Bor, Rus. 61/K4
Bor, Serb. 48/F3
Bor, Turk. 90/C2
Bor Ul (mts.), China 70/G3
Bora Bora (isl.), FrPol. 117/K6
Borah (peak), Id, US 126/E4
Borås, Swe. 38/E3
Borāzjān, Iran 88/F3
Borba, Braz. 150/G4
Borba, Port. 44/B3
Borbera (riv.), It. 58/B3
Borbore (riv.), It. 58/B3
Borborema, Planalto da (plat.), Braz. 151/L5
Borča, Serb. 48/E3
Borcea Branch (riv.), Rom. 49/H3
Borchen, Ger. 51/F5
Borçka, Turk. 63/G4
Borculo, Neth. 50/D4
Borda da Mata, Braz. 211/G7
Bordeaux, Fr. 42/C4
Borden (isl.), NW,Nun., Can. 123/R7
Borden (pen.), Nun., Can. 123/H1
Bordentown, NJ, US 138/D3
Bordertown, Austl. 115/B3
Bordj Bou Arreridj, Alg. 100/H4
Bordj Bou Arreridj (prov.), Alg. 100/H4
Bordj el Kiffan, Alg. 100/G4
Bordj Manaïel, Alg. 100/G4
Bordj Moktar, Alg. 99/F5
Bordj Omar Driss, Alg. 99/G3
Bordj Sainte-Marie, Alg. 98/E4
Borehamwood, Eng, UK 30/C2
Borest, Fr. 30/L4
Boretto, It. 58/D3
Borgå (Porvoo), Fin. 39/L1
Borgaretto, It. 58/A2
Borgarnes, Ice. 37/N7
Borgaro Torinese, It. 58/A2
Børgefjell NP, Nor. 37/E2
Borgentreich, Ger. 51/G5
Borger, Tx, US 129/G4
Börger, Ger. 51/E3
Borger, Neth. 50/D3
Borgerhout, Belg. 50/B6
Borges Blanques, Sp. 45/F2
Borghetto Lodigiano, It. 58/C2
Borghetto Santo Spirito, It. 58/B4
Borgholm, Swe. 38/G3
Borgholzhausen, Ger. 51/F4
Borghorst, Ger. 51/E4
Borgloon, Belg. 53/E2
Borgne (lake), La, US 137/Q17
Borgne (riv.), Swi. 56/D5
Borgo (int'l arpt.), Burk. 102/D4
Borgo, Fr. 46/A1
Borgo, It. 57/H5
Borgo a Mozzano, It. 58/D5
Borgo San Dalmazzo, It. 43/G4
Borgo San Giacomo, It. 58/C2
Borgo San Lorenzo, It. 59/E5
Borgo Tossignano, It. 59/E4
Borgo Val di Taro, It. 58/C4
Borgo Vercelli, It. 58/B2
Borgofranco d'Ivrea, It. 58/A1
Borgomanero, It. 58/B1
Borgonovo Val Tidone, It. 58/C2
Borgosatollo, It. 58/D2
Borgosesia, It. 58/B1
Borgou (prov.), Ben. 103/F4
Borgund, Nor. 38/B1
Borio, India 85/F3
Borisoglebsk, Rus. 63/G2
Borispol (int'l arpt.), Ukr. 62/D2
Borja, Peru 156/B2
Borja, Sp. 44/E2
Borken, Ger. 50/D5
Borken, Ger. 51/G6
Børkop, Den. 38/C4
Borkum, Ger. 50/D1
Borkum (isl.), Ger. 50/D1
Bormida (riv.), It. 43/H4
Bormida, It. 58/B4
Bormida di Millesimo (riv.), It. 58/B4
Bormio, It. 57/G5
Born, Neth. 53/E1
Borna, Ger. 40/G3
Borndiep (chan.), Neth. 50/C2
Borne, Neth. 50/D4
Borne (riv.), Fr. 56/C6
Bornel, Fr. 52/B5
Bornem, Belg. 53/D1
Bornemouth, Eng, UK 33/E5

175

Borne – Bruma

Bornemouth (co.), Eng, UK 33/E5
Borneo (isl.), Indo.,Malay. 67/L9
Bornheim, Ger. 53/G2
Bornholm (co.), Den. 38/F4
Bornholm (isl.), Den., Swe. 27/F3
Bornholmsgat (chan.), Den.,Swi. 41/H1
Borno, It. 57/G6
Bornos, Sp. 44/C4
Börnsen, Ger. 51/H2
Bornu (plain), Nga. 96/H5
Boro (riv.), Sudan 97/L6
Borohoro (mts.), China 70/D3
Borongan, Phil. 79/E5
Borough Green, Eng, UK 30/D3
Borovany, Czh. 55/H5
Borovichi, Rus. 60/G4
Borovo, Bul. 49/G4
Borovo, Cro. 48/D3
Borre, Nor. 38/D2
Borrisokane, Ire. 31/P10
Borrnida (riv.), It. 58/B3
Borşa, Rom. 49/F2
Borsec, Rom. 49/G2
Borso del Grappa, It. 59/E1
Borsod-Abaúj-Zemplén (co.), Hun. 48/E1
Borssele, Neth. 50/A6
Borstel, Ger. 51/F3
Bort-les-Orgues, Fr. 42/E4
Boruca, CR 145/F4
Borūjerd, Iran 88/E2
Boryslav, Ukr. 41/M4
Borzonasca, It. 58/C4
Borzya, Rus. 71/L1
Bosa, It. 46/A2
Bosanska Dubica, Bosn. 48/C3
Bosanska Gradiška, Bosn. 48/C3
Bosanska Kostajnica, Bosn. 48/C3
Bosanska Krupa, Bosn. 48/C3
Bosanski Brod, Bosn. 48/D3
Bosanski Petrovac, Bosn. 48/C3
Bosanski Šamac, Bosn. 48/D3
Bosco Mesola, It. 59/F3
Bosconero, It. 58/A2
Bose, China 83/J3
Boshof, SAfr. 106/D3
Boskoop, Neth. 50/B4
Boskovice, Czh. 41/J4
Bosna (riv.), Bosn. 48/D3
Bosnia and Herzegovina (ctry.) 48/C3
Bošnjaci, Cro. 48/D3
Bōsō (pen.), Japan 75/G3
Bosobolo, D.R. Congo 97/J7
Bosporus (str.), Turk. 49/J5
Bosque Farms, NM, US 128/F4
Bosques Petrificados, Mon. Natural, Arg. 159/C5
Bossangoa, CAfr. 96/J6
Bossier City, La, US 129/J4
Bostān, Iran 88/E2
Bostānābād-e Bālā, Iran 88/E1
Boston (mts.), Ar, US 129/J4
Boston (cap.), Ma, US 131/G3
Boston, Eng, UK 35/H6
Bosut (riv.), Cro. 48/D3
Boswil, Swi. 57/E3
Botād, India 89/K4
Boteler (peak), NC, US 133/H3
Botelerpunt (pt.), SAfr. 107/F2
Botelhos, Braz. 211/G6
Botev (peak), Bul. 47/J1
Botevgrad, Bul. 47/H1
Bothaspas (pass), SAfr. 107/E2
Bothaville, SAfr. 106/D2
Bothel, Ger. 51/G2
Bothell, Wa, US 135/C2
Bothnia (gulf), Swe.,Fin. 160/E
Bothwell, Austl. 115/C4
Botoşani (prov.), Rom. 49/H2
Botoşani, Rom. 49/H2
Botou, China 72/D3
Botrange (peak), Belg. 53/F3
Botrivier, SAfr. 106/L11
Botsford, Ct, US 139/E1
Botswana (ctry.) 105/D5
Bottanuco, It. 58/C1
Botte Donato (peak), It. 46/E3
Botticino, It. 58/D1
Bottineau, ND, US 127/H3
Bottrighe, It. 59/F2
Bottrop, Ger. 50/D5
Botucatu, Braz. 155/B2
Botwood, Nf, Can. 131/L1
Bou (riv.), C.d'Iv. 102/D4
Bou Arfa, Mor. 99/E2
Boû Djébéha (well), Mali 102/E2
Bou Hamdane, Oued (riv.), Alg. 100/K6
Bou Ismaïl, Alg. 100/G4
Bou Izakarn, Mor. 98/C3
Bou Kadir, Alg. 100/F4
Bou Laber (well), Alg. 98/D4
Bou Naceur (peak), Mor. 100/C3
Bou Regreg (riv.), Mor. 100/A3
Bou Salem, Tun. 100/L6
Bou Sellam, Oued (riv.), Alg. 100/H4
Bouaflé, C.d'Iv. 102/D5
Bouafle, Fr. 30/H5
Bouaké, C.d'Iv. 102/D5
Bouar, CAfr. 96/J6
Boubín (peak), Czh. 55/G5
Bouca, CAfr. 96/J6
Bouchain, Fr. 52/C3
Bouchegouf, Alg. 100/K6
Boucherville, Qu, Can. 131/P6
Boucle du Baoulé, PN de la, Mali 96/D5
Boucle Du Baoulé, PN de la, Mali 102/C3
Boudry, Swi. 56/C4
Boufarik, Alg. 100/G4
Bouffémont, Fr. 30/J4
Bougainville (reef), Austl. 109/D2
Bougainville (isl.), PNG 116/E5
Bougainville (cape), UK 159/F6
Bougara, Alg. 100/G4
Bougar'oûn (cape), Alg. 100/K6
Bough Beech (res.), Eng, UK 30/D3
Bougouni, Mali 102/D4
Bougouriba (prov.), Burk. 102/E4
Bouguenais, Fr. 42/C3
Bouhachem (peak), Mor. 100/B2
Bouhalla (peak), Mor. 100/B2
Bouillancy, Fr. 30/L4
Bouillon, Belg. 53/E4
Bouira (prov.), Alg. 100/G4
Bouira, Alg. 100/G4
Boujad, Mor. 98/D2
Boukhalf (Tangier) (int'l arpt.), Mor. 100/B2
Boukoumbé, Ben. 103/F4
Boulaide, Lux. 53/E4
Boulaouane, Mor. 98/C2
Boulay-Moselle, Fr. 53/F5
Boulazac, Fr. 42/D4
Boulder, Co, US 137/B2
Boulder (co.), Co, US 137/B2
Boulder, Mt, US 126/E4
Boulder City, Nv, US 128/D4
Boulder Hill, Il, US 135/P16
Boulemane, Mor. 98/D2
Boulemane (prov.), Mor. 100/C3
Bouleurs, Fr. 30/L5
Boulgo (prov.), Burk. 103/E4
Boulia, Austl. 113/H2
Bouligny, Fr. 53/E5
Boulkiemde (prov.), Burk. 103/E3
Boullarre, Fr. 30/M4
Boulogne (riv.), Fr. 42/C3
Boulogne-Billancourt, Fr. 30/J5
Boulogne-sur-Mer, Fr. 52/A2
Boulsworth (hill), Eng, UK 35/F4
Boumaine, Mor. 98/D3
Boumerdas (prov.), Alg. 100/G4
Boumerdas, Alg. 100/G4
Boun Nua, Laos 83/H3
Bouna, C.d'Iv. 102/E4
Bound Brook, NJ, US 138/D2
Boundary (peak), Nv, US 128/C3
Boundiali, C.d'Iv. 102/D4
Bountiful, Ut, US 137/K12
Bouquet (res.), Ca, US 136/B1
Bouquet (canyon), Ca, US 136/B2
Bourbon l'Archambault, Fr. 42/E3
Bourbonnais (reg.), Fr. 42/D3
Bourbonne-les-Bains, Fr. 56/B2
Bourbourg, Fr. 52/B2
Bourdonné, Fr. 30/G5
Bourem, Mali 103/E2
Bouressa (riv.), Mali 103/F2
Bourg-en-Bresse, Fr. 56/B5
Bourg-lès-Valence, Fr. 42/F4
Bourg-Saint-Andéol, Fr. 42/F4
Bourg-Saint-Maurice, Fr. 43/G4
Bourg-Saint-Pierre, Swi. 56/D6
Bourganeuf, Fr. 42/D4
Bourges, Fr. 42/E3
Bourget (lake), Fr. 56/B6
Bourgneuf (bay), Fr. 42/B3
Bourgogne (pol. reg.), Fr. 42/F3
Bourgogne (canal), Fr. 56/B3
Bourgoin-Jallieu, Fr. 42/F4
Bourke, Austl. 115/C1
Bourmont, Fr. 56/B1
Bourne (riv.), Eng, UK 33/E4
Bourne End, Eng, UK 33/F3
Bourne, The (riv.), Eng, UK 30/B3
Bournemouth, Eng, UK 33/E5
Bourscheid, Lux. 53/F4
Bourtanger Moor (reg.), Ger. 51/E3
Bousbecque, Fr. 52/C2
Bousso, Chad 96/J5
Boussois, Fr. 52/D3
Boutilimit, Mrta. 102/B2
Boutte, La, US 137/P17
Bouvard (cape), Austl. 112/B5
Bouvet (isl.), Nor. 23/K8
Bouxières-aux-Dames, Fr. 53/F6
Bouxwiller, Fr. 53/G6
Bouznika, Mor. 100/A3
Bouzonville, Fr. 53/F5
Bovalino, It. 46/E3
Bovegno, It. 58/D1
Boven Tapanahoni (riv.), Sur. 153/H4
Bovenden, Ger. 51/G5
Bovenwijde (lake), Neth. 50/D3
Boves, Fr. 52/B4
Bovezzo, It. 58/D1
Bovingdon, Eng, UK 30/B1
Bovino, It. 48/B5
Bovolone, It. 59/E2
Bow (riv.), Ab, Can. 122/E3
Bow Island, Ab, Can. 126/F3
Bowdle, SD, US 127/J4
Bowdon, Eng, UK 35/F5
Bowen, Arg. 158/D2
Bowen, Austl. 114/C3
Bowers Beach, De, US 138/C5
Bowie, Az, US 128/E4
Bowie, Md, US 138/B6
Bowling Green (cape), Austl. 114/B2
Bowling Green, Ky, US 130/C4
Bowling Green, Mo, US 129/K3
Bowling Green, Oh, US 130/D3
Bowling Green Bay NP, Austl. 114/B2
Bowman, ND, US 127/H4
Bowman (bay), Nun., Can. 123/J2
Bowmansdale, Pa, US 138/B3
Bowmanstown, Pa, US 138/C2
Bowmansville, Pa, US 138/B3
Bowmore, Sc, UK 31/Q9
Bowokan (isls.), Indo. 81/F4
Bowral, Austl. 115/D2
Bowron (riv.), BC, Can. 126/C2
Box Elder (co.), Ut, US 137/J11
Boxberg, Ger. 54/C4
Boxholm, Swe. 38/F2
Boxing, China 72/D3
Boxmeer, Neth. 50/C5
Boxtel, Neth. 50/C5
Boyabat, Turk. 90/C1
Boyaca (dept.), Col. 152/C3
Boyanup, Austl. 112/B5
Boychinovtsi, Bul. 49/F4
Boyd (lake), Co, US 137/B2
Boye, China 72/C3
Boyer (riv.), Ia, US 127/K5
Boyertown, Pa, US 138/C3
Boyle, Ab, Can. 126/E2
Boyle, Ire. 31/P10
Boyne (riv.), Ire. 31/Q10
Boyne City, Mi, US 130/C2
Boyne Island, Austl. 114/C3
Boynton Beach, Fl, US 133/H5
Boysen (res.), Wy, US 126/F5
Boyup Brook, Austl. 112/C5
Boz (pt.), Turk. 49/J5
Bozashchy Tübegi (pen.), Kaz. 63/J3
Bozcaada (isl.), Gre. 47/J3
Bozcaada, Turk. 47/K3
Bozeman, Mt, US 126/F4
Bozkir, Turk. 90/C2
Bozkurt, Turk. 62/E4
Bozman, Md, US 138/B6
Bozoum, CAfr. 96/J6
Bozova, Turk. 90/D2
Bozüyük, Turk. 90/B2
Bozyazı, Turk. 91/C1
Bozzolo, It. 58/D2
Bra, It. 58/A3
Braan (riv.), Sc, UK 36/C3
Brač (isl.), Cro. 46/E1
Bracciano (lake), It. 46/B1
Bracebridge, On, Can. 130/E2
Brackel, Ger. 51/G2
Bracken, Tx, US 137/U20
Brackenheim, Ger. 54/C4
Brackettville, Tx, US 129/G5
Bracknell, Eng, UK 33/F4
Bracknell Forest (co.), Eng, UK 33/F4
Braço do Norte, Braz. 155/B4
Brad, Rom. 49/F2
Bradano (riv.), It. 48/B5
Bradda (pt.), IM, UK 34/D3
Bradenton, Fl, US 133/H5
Bradford, Eng, UK 35/G4
Bradford (co.), Eng, UK 35/G4
Bradford, Pa, US 130/E3
Bradley (int'l arpt.), Ct, US 131/F3
Bradley Beach, NJ, US 138/D3
Brady, Tx, US 129/H5
Braemar (reg.), Sc, UK 36/C2
Braeriach (peak), Sc, UK 36/C2
Braga (dist.), Port. 44/A2
Braga, Port. 44/A2
Bragado, Arg. 158/E2
Bragança, Braz. 151/J4
Bragança (dist.), Port. 44/B2
Bragança, Port. 44/B2
Brāhmanbāria, Bang. 85/H4
Brahmaputra (riv.), Asia 67/J7
Braich-y-Pwll (pt.), Wal, UK 34/D6
Braid (riv.), NI, UK 34/B2
Brăila (prov.), Rom. 49/H3
Brăila, Rom. 49/H3
Brainards, NJ, US 138/C2
Braine, Fr. 52/C5
Braine-l'Alleud, Belg. 53/D2
Braine-le-Comte, Belg. 53/D2
Brainerd, Mn, US 127/K4
Braintree, Eng, UK 33/G3
Braithwaite, La, US 137/Q17
Brak (riv.), SAfr. 106/C3
Brake, Ger. 51/F2
Brakel, Belg. 52/C2
Brakel, Ger. 51/G5
Brakel, Neth. 50/C5
Brakna (pol. reg.), Mrta. 102/B2
Brålanda, Swe. 38/E2
Bram, Fr. 42/E5
Bramdrupdam, Den. 38/C4
Bramley, Eng, UK 30/B3
Brampton, On, Can. 131/Q8
Bramsche, Ger. 51/F4
Bramstedt, Ger. 51/F2
Bran (riv.), Sc, UK 36/A1
Brancaleone-Marina, It. 46/E4
Branch Dale, Pa, US 138/B2
Branchville, NJ, US 138/D1
Branchville, Ct, US 139/E1
Branco (riv.), Braz. 147/C2
Brand, Aus. 57/F3
Brandberg (peak), Namb. 105/B5
Brandbu, Nor. 38/D1
Brande, Den. 38/C4
Brandenburg (state), Ger. 40/F6
Brandenburg, Ger. 40/G2
Brander, Pass of (pass), Sc, UK 36/A4
Brandfort, SAfr. 106/D3
Brandizzo, It. 58/A2
Brandon, Mb, Can. 127/J3
Brandon, Fl, US 133/H5
Brandon, Ms, US 133/F3
Brandsen, Arg. 159/J11
Brandvlei, SAfr. 106/C3
Brandýs nad Labem, Czh. 55/H2
Brandywine, Md, US 138/B6
Brandywine (riv.), Pa, US 138/C4
Branford, Ct, US 139/F1
Branges, Fr. 56/B4
Braniewo, Pol. 39/H4
Brannenburg, Ger. 43/K3
Brant Beach, NJ, US 138/D4
Branxholm, Austl. 115/C4
Branzoll (Bronzolo), It. 57/H4
Bras d'Or (lake), NS, Can. 131/J2
Brasiléia, Braz. 150/E6
Brasília de Minas, Braz. 154/A5
Brasília, PN de, Braz. 151/J7
Braşov, Rom. 49/G3
Braşov (prov.), Rom. 49/G3
Brasschaat, Belg. 50/B6
Brassey (mt.), Austl. 113/G2
Brasstown Bald (peak), Ga, US 133/H3
Brastad, Swe. 38/D2
Bratislava (cap.), Slvk. 43/M2
Bratislava (Ivanka) (int'l arpt.), Slvk. 48/C1
Bratislavský (pol. reg.), Slvk. 41/J4
Bratsk, Rus. 65/L4
Brattleboro, Vt, US 131/F3
Bratunac, Bosn. 48/D3
Braubach, Ger. 53/G3
Braulio Carrillo, PN, CR 140/E5
Braunau am Inn, Aus. 55/G6
Braunfels, Ger. 54/B1
Braunig (lake), Tx, US 137/U21
Braunlage, Ger. 51/H5
Bräunlingen, Ger. 57/E2
Braunschweig, Ger. 51/H4
Brava (isl.), CpV. 93/J11
Brava (pt.), Chile 159/C7
Brava (pt.), Uru. 159/K11
Brava, Costa (coast), Sp. 45/G2
Bråviken (inlet), Swe. 38/G2
Bravo (peak), Bol. 150/F7
Bravo (peak), Peru 156/B2
Bravo del Norte (riv.), Mex. 140/A2
Brawley, Ca, US 128/D4
Bray (isl.), Nun., Can. 123/J2
Bray, Ire. 34/B5
Bray (pt.), Ire. 34/B5
Bray-Dunes, Fr. 52/B1
Braye (riv.), Fr. 42/D3
Brazey-en-Plaine, Fr. 56/B3
Brazil (ctry.) 150/F5
Brazilian Highlands (uplands), Braz. 147/E4
Brazo Casiquiare (riv.), Ven. 153/E4
Brazo Sur (riv.), Arg. 159/C6
Brazópolis, Braz. 211/H7
Brazos (riv.), Tx, US 132/D3
Brazos, Salt Fork (riv.), Tx, US 132/C3
Brazzaville (cap.), Congo 105/C1
Brčko, Bosn. 48/D3
Brda (riv.), Pol. 38/G5
Brdy (mts.), Czh. 41/G4
Brea, Ca, US 136/G8
Breadalbane (dist.), Sc, UK 36/B4
Breamish (riv.), Eng, UK 36/D6
Bréancon, Fr. 30/J4
Bréau, Fr. 30/L6
Breaza, Rom. 49/G3
Brebbia, It. 58/B1
Brêche (riv.), Fr. 52/B5
Brechen, Ger. 54/B2
Brechin, Sc, UK 36/D3
Brecht, Belg. 50/B6
Breckenridge, Mn, US 127/J4
Breckenridge, Tx, US 129/H4
Breckerfeld, Ger. 51/E6
Breckland (phys. reg.), Eng, UK 33/G2
Brecknock (pen.), Chile 159/C7
Břeclav, Czh. 43/M2
Brecon, Wal, UK 32/C3
Brecon Beacons (mts.), Wal, UK 32/C3
Breda, Neth. 50/B5
Bredaryd, Swe. 38/E3
Bredasdorp, SAfr. 106/M11
Bredebro, Den. 38/C4
Bredene, Belg. 52/B1
Bredstedt, Ger. 38/C4
Breë (riv.), SAfr. 106/B4
Bree, Belg. 53/E1
Breg (riv.), Ger. 40/E5
Bregagno (peak), It. 57/F5
Bregalinca (riv.), FYROM 47/H2
Breganze, It. 59/E1
Bregenz, Aus. 57/F3
Bregenzer Ache (riv.), Aus. 57/F3
Bregovo, Bul. 48/F3
Brégy, Fr. 30/L4
Breidhafjördhur (bay), Ice. 37/M6
Breil-Brigels, Swi. 57/F4
Breisach, Ger. 56/D1
Breitbrunn am Chiemsee, Ger. 55/F7
Breitenauriegel (peak), Ger. 55/G5
Breitenbach, Swi. 56/D3
Breitenbrunn, Ger. 55/E4
Breitenfurt bei Wien, Aus. 49/N7
Breitenworbis, Ger. 51/H6
Breithorn (peak), Swi. 56/D5
Breithorn (peak), Swi. 56/D5
Brejo, Braz. 154/B1
Brejo Santo, Braz. 154/C2
Brejões, Braz. 154/B3
Brembate di Sopra, It. 58/C1
Brembilla, It. 58/C1
Brembio, It. 58/C2
Brembo (riv.), It. 57/F6
Bremen (int'l arpt.), Ger. 51/F2
Bremen, Ger. 51/F2
Bremen (state), Ger. 38/C5
Bremer (riv.), Austl. 114/F7
Bremerhaven, Ger. 51/F1
Bremerton, Wa, US 126/C4
Bremervörde, Ger. 51/G2
Bremgarten, Swi. 57/E3
Bremgarten bei Bern, Swi. 56/D4
Bremnes, Nor. 38/B2
Brend (riv.), Ger. 54/D2
Brendel (lake), Mi, US 135/E7
Brendola, It. 59/E2
Brendon (hills), Eng, UK 32/C4
Brenig, Llyn (lake), Wal, UK 34/E5
Brenne (riv.), Fr. 40/C5
Brenner (pass), Aus. 57/H4
Brenner (riv.), Austl. 113/N9
Brenno (riv.), Swi. 57/E5
Breno, It. 57/G6
Brent (bor.), Eng, UK 30/C2
Brent (res.), Eng, UK 30/C2
Brent (riv.), Eng, UK 30/B2
Brenta (riv.), It. 43/J4
Brenta (peak), It. 57/G5
Brentwood, NY, US 139/E2
Brentwood, Ca, US 135/L11
Brentwood, Eng, UK 30/D2
Brenz (riv.), Ger. 54/D5
Brescello, It. 58/D3
Brescia, It. 58/D1
Brescia (prov.), It. 57/G6
Bresle (riv.), Fr. 42/D1
Bresles, Fr. 52/B5
Bressana, It. 58/C2
Bressanone, It. 43/J3
Bressay (isl.), Sc, UK 31/W13
Bressuire, Fr. 42/C3
Brest, Fr. 42/A2
Brest, Bela. 41/M2
Brest (int'l arpt.), Bela. 41/M2
Brestskaya Voblasts Bela. 62/C1
Bretagne (pol. reg.), Fr. 42/B2
Bretagne, Monts de (mts.), Fr. 42/B2
Bretagne, Pointe de (pt.), Reun. 107/S15
Bretaña, Peru 156/C2
Breteuil, Fr. 52/B4
Brétigny-sur-Orge, Fr. 30/J6
Breton, Ab, Can. 126/E2
Breton (cape), NS, Can. 131/K2
Brett (cape), NZ 117/S10
Brett (riv.), Eng, UK 33/G2
Brettach (riv.), Ger. 54/C4
Bretten, Ger. 54/B4
Bretzenheim, Ger. 53/G4
Breuberg, Ger. 54/C3
Breuillet, Fr. 30/J6
Breukelen, Neth. 50/B4
Breuna, Ger. 51/G6
Breuvannes-en-Bassigny, Fr. 56/B1
Breves, Braz. 151/H4
Brevig Mission, Ak, US 134/E2
Brevik, Nor. 38/C2
Brevoort (isl.), Nun., Can. 123/K2
Brewarrina, Austl. 115/C1
Brewer, Me, US 131/G2
Brewster, Ne, US 127/J5
Brewton, Al, US 133/G4
Brey-et-Lû, Fr. 30/G4
Breyten, SAfr. 107/E2
Brežice, Slov. 43/L4
Brezina, Alg. 99/F2
Březnice, Czh. 55/G3
Breznik, Bul. 47/H1
Brezoi, Rom. 49/G3
Brezovo, Bul. 47/J1
Bria, CAfr. 97/K6
Briançon, Fr. 43/G4
Brianne, Llyn (res.), Wal, UK 32/C2
Briar Creek, Pa, US 138/B1
Briare, Fr. 42/E3
Brickerville, Pa, US 138/B3
Bricktown, NJ, US 138/D3
Bride (riv.), Ire. 31/P10
Bride, IM, UK 34/D3
Bridge City, Tx, US 132/E4
Bridge of Allan, Sc, UK 36/C4
Bridge of Don, Sc, UK 36/D2
Bridge of Weir, Sc, UK 36/B5
Bridgehampton, NY, US 139/F2
Bridgend, Wal, UK 32/C3
Bridgeport, Ca, US 128/C3
Bridgeport, Ct, US 139/E1
Bridgeport, Ne, US 127/H5
Bridgeport, NJ, US 138/C4
Bridger, Mt, US 126/F4
Bridgeton, NJ, US 138/C5
Bridgetown, Austl. 112/C5
Bridgetown (cap.), Bar. 141/P9
Bridgeville, De, US 138/C6
Bridgewater, Austl. 115/C4
Bridgewater, NS, Can. 131/H2
Bridgnorth, Eng, UK 32/D1
Bridgton, Me, US 131/G2
Bridgwater, Eng, UK 32/D4
Bridgwater (bay), Eng, UK 32/C4
Bridlington, Eng, UK 35/H3
Bridlington (bay), Eng, UK 35/H3
Bridport, Austl. 115/C4
Bridport, Eng, UK 32/D5
Brie (reg.), Fr. 40/B4
Brie-Comte-Robert, Fr. 30/K5
Brieg Brzeg, Pol. 41/J3
Brielle, Neth. 50/B5
Brielle, NJ, US 138/D3
Brienz, Swi. 56/E4
Brier, Wa, US 135/C2
Brierfield, Eng, UK 35/F4
Brieselang, Ger. 40/Q6
Brig, Swi. 56/D5
Brigach (riv.), Ger. 54/B7
Brigantine, NJ, US 138/D5
Brigend (co.), Wal, UK 32/C3
Brigham City, Ut, US 137/J10
Brighouse, Eng, UK 35/G4
Bright, Austl. 115/C3
Brightlingsea, Eng, UK 33/H3
Brighton, Eng, UK 33/F5
Brighton and Hove (co.), Eng, UK 33/F5
Brighton, Co, US 137/C3
Brighton, Il, US 137/G7
Brighton, Ut, US 137/K12
Brighton, Wi, US 135/P14
Brignais, Fr. 42/F4
Brignoles, Fr. 42/G5
Brihuega, Sp. 44/D2
Briis-sous-Forges, Fr. 30/J6
Brikama, Gam. 102/A3
Brilhante (riv.), Braz. 151/G8
Brilon, Ger. 51/F6
Brimstone Hill NP, StK. 141/N8
Brindisi, It. 47/E2
Brinkworth, Austl. 113/H5
Brinnon, Wa, US 135/B2
Brión, Sp. 44/A1
Brione, Swi. 57/E5
Briones (res.), Ca, US 135/K11
Brisbane, Austl. 114/F6
Brisbane (int'l arpt.), Austl. 114/F6
Brisbane (riv.), Austl. 114/E7
Brisbane Forest Park, Austl. 114/E6
Brisbane Ranges NP, Austl. 115/C3
Brisbane Water NP, Austl. 115/D2
Brisighella, It. 59/E4
Brissago, Swi. 57/E5
Bristol, Eng, UK 32/D4
Bristol (chan.), Eng,Wal, UK 32/B4
Bristol (co.), Eng, UK 32/D4
Bristol (bay), Ak, US 134/F4
Bristol, Pa, US 138/D3
Bristol, Tn, US 130/D4
Bristow, Ok, US 129/H4
British (mts.), Ak, US 134/K2
British Columbia (prov.), Can. 122/D3
British Empire (range), Nun., Can. 123/S6
British Indian Ocean Territory (dpcy.), UK 67/G10
British Museum, Eng, UK 30/C2
Britstown, SAfr. 106/C3
Brittany (reg.), Fr. 42/B3
Britton, SD, US 127/J4
Brive-la-Gaillarde, Fr. 42/D4
Brives-Charensac, Fr. 42/E4
Briviesca, Sp. 44/D1
Brivio, It. 58/C1
Brněnský (pol. reg.), Slvk. 41/J4
Brnik (int'l arpt.), Slov. 43/L3
Brno, Czh. 41/J4
Broa (bay), Cuba 145/F1
Broad (pass), Ak, US 134/J3
Broad (riv.), NC,SC, US 133/H3
Broad Law (peak), Sc, UK 36/C6
Broad Sound (isls.), Austl. 114/C2
Broadback (riv.), Qu, Can. 130/E1
Broadford, Austl. 115/C3
Broadkill (riv.), De, US 138/C6
Broads NP, The, Eng, UK 33/H1
Broadstairs, Eng, UK 33/H4
Broadus, Mt, US 127/G4
Broadwater NP, Austl. 115/E1
Broadway (hill), Eng, UK 33/E3
Broadway, NJ, US 138/C2
Broc, Swi. 56/D4
Brochet, Mb, Can. 122/F3
Brock (isl.), NW, Can. 123/R7
Brocken (peak), Ger. 51/H5
Brockman (mt.), Austl. 112/C2
Brockton, Ma, US 131/G3
Brockville, On, Can. 130/F2
Brodeur (pen.), Nun., Can. 122/G1
Brodheadsville, Pa, US 138/C2
Brodnica, Pol. 41/K2
Broek in Waterland, Neth. 50/B4
Broek Op Langedijk, Neth. 50/B3
Bröhn (peak), Ger. 51/G4
Broken (bay), Austl. 115/D2
Broken Arrow, Ok, US 129/J3
Broken Bow, Ne, US 127/J5
Broken Bow (lake), Ok, US 129/J4
Broken Bow, Ok, US 129/J4
Broken Hill, Austl. 115/B1
Brokeoff (mts.), NM, US 132/B3
Brokopondo, Sur. 151/G2
Brokopondo (dist.), Sur. 153/H3
Brome, Ger. 40/F2
Bromölla, Swe. 38/F3
Bromsgrove, Eng, UK 32/D2
Bromskirchen, Ger. 51/F6
Bron, Fr. 56/A6
Brønderslev, Den. 38/C3
Brong-Ahafo (pol. reg.), Gha. 103/E5
Broni, It. 58/C2
Bronkhorstspruit, SAfr. 106/E2
Brønnøy, Nor. 37/E2
Brøns, Den. 38/C4
Bronschhofen, Swi. 57/F3
Bronte, It. 46/D4
Bronx (bor.), NY, US 139/E2
Bronx Zoo, NY, US 139/K8
Bronxville, NY, US 139/K8
Brook Forest, Co, US 137/B3
Brooke's Point, Phil. 81/E2
Brookfield, Il, US 135/Q16
Brookhaven, Ms, US 129/K5
Brooklyn (bor.), NY, US 138/D2
Brooklyn, Il, US 137/G8
Brooklyn Park, Md, US 138/B5
Brookmans Park, Eng, UK 30/C1
Brooks (mtn.), Ak, US 134/E2
Brooks, Ab, Can. 126/F3
Brooks, Il, US 137/G8
Brooks (range), Ak, US 134/F2
Brookside, De, US 138/C4
Brooksville, Fl, US 133/H4
Brookton, Austl. 112/C5
Brookvale, Co, US 137/B3
Brookville, NY, US 139/L8
Broomall, Pa, US 138/C4
Broomfield, Co, US 137/B3
Brørup, Den. 38/C4
Brösarp, Swe. 38/F4
Brossard, Qu, Can. 131/P7
Brough (pt.), Sc, UK 31/V14
Broughshane, NI, UK 34/B2
Brousseval, Fr. 56/A1
Brouwersdam (dam), Neth. 50/A5
Brouwershaven, Neth. 50/A5
Brovst, Den. 38/C3
Brown (mt.), Austl. 113/H5
Brown (pt.), Austl. 113/G5
Brown Clee (hill), Eng, UK 32/D2
Brown Shoal (bar) 79/C5
Brownfield, Tx, US 129/G4
Brownhills, Eng, UK 33/E1
Browning, Mt, US 126/E3
Browns Mills, NJ, US 138/D4
Brownsea (isl.), Eng, UK 33/E5
Brownsville, Tn, US 130/B5
Brownsville, Tx, US 132/D5
Brownsville, Wa, US 135/B2
Broxburn, Sc, UK 36/C5
Broye (riv.), Swi. 56/C4
Brozas, Sp. 44/B3
Bruay-la-Buissière, Fr. 52/B3
Bruay-sur-L'Escaut, Fr. 52/C3
Bruce (pen.), On, Can. 130/D2
Bruce (mt.), Austl. 112/C2
Bruce Rock, Austl. 112/C4
Bruchberg (peak), Ger. 51/H5
Bruche (riv.), Fr. 43/G2
Bruchhausen-Vilsen, Ger. 51/G3
Bruchköbel, Ger. 54/B2
Bruchmühlbach-Miesau, Ger. 53/G5
Bruchsal, Ger. 54/B4
Brucht (riv.), Ger. 51/G5
Bruck, Aus. 49/P7
Bruck an der Grossglocknerstrasse, Aus. 43/K3
Bruck an der Mur, Aus. 43/L3
Bruckberg, Ger. 55/F5
Bruckmühl, Ger. 43/J3
Brue (riv.), Eng, UK 32/D4
Bruflat, Nor. 38/C1
Brügg, Swi. 56/D3
Brugg, Swi. 56/E3
Brugge, Belg. 52/C1
Brüggen, Ger. 50/D6
Brugnera, It. 59/F1
Brühl, Ger. 53/F2
Bruinisse, Neth. 50/B5
Brukkaros (peak), Namb. 106/B2
Brukunga, Austl. 113/M8
Brumado, Braz. 154/B4

Calhoun, Ga, US 133/G3
Calhoun, Ky, US 130/C4
Calhoun (co.), WV, US 137/F7
Cali, Col. 152/B4
Calicut (Kozhikode), India 82/C5
Calida, Costa (coast), Sp. 44/E4
Caliente, Nv, US 128/D3
Califon, NJ, US 138/D2
California (gulf), Mex. 142/B2
California (state), US 128/B3
California, Md, US 130/E4
California, Mo, US 129/J3
Calilegua, PN, Arg. 157/D1
Călimăneşti, Rom. 49/G3
Calimaya, Mex. 143/Q10
Calimere (pt.), India 82/C5
Calimesa, Ca, US 136/C2
Calitri, It. 46/D2
Calixa-Lavallée, Qu, Can. 131/P6
Calizzano, It. 58/B4
Calkiní, Mex. 144/D1
Calkins (lake), Co, US 137/B2
Çalköy, Turk. 90/B2
Callabonna (lake), Austl. 115/A1
Callahonna (lake), Austl. 109/D3
Callalli, Peru 156/D4
Callan, Ire. 31/Q10
Callander, Sc, UK 36/B4
Callantsoog, Neth. 50/B3
Callao, Peru 156/B4
Callapa, Bol. 156/D5
Callaway, Fl, US 133/G4
Calle Larga, Chile 158/N8
Calliope, Austl. 114/C4
Callosa de Segura, Sp. 45/E3
Calne, Eng, UK 32/E4
Calolziocorte, It. 58/C1
Calonne-Ricouart, Fr. 52/B3
Calore (riv.), It. 46/D2
Caloundra, Austl. 114/D4
Calpe, Sp. 45/F3
Calpulálpan, Mex. 143/L7
Caltagirone, It. 46/D4
Caltanissetta, It. 46/D4
Caltavuturo, It. 46/C4
Caluire-et-Cuire, Fr. 42/F4
Calumet (riv.), Il, US 135/Q16
Calumet Sag (chan.), Il, US 135/Q16
Caluso, It. 58/A2
Calvello, It. 46/D2
Calvenzano, It. 58/C2
Calvert (isl.), BC, Can. 126/A3
Calvert, Tx, US 129/H5
Calverton, Md, US 138/B5
Calvi (peak), It. 59/E4
Calvi, Fr. 46/A1
Calviá, Sp. 45/G3
Calvillo, Mex. 142/E4
Calvinia, SAfr. 106/B3
Calvisano, It. 58/D2
Calvitero (peak), Sp. 44/C2
Calw, Ger. 54/B5
Calzada de Calatrava, Sp. 44/D3
Cam or Rhee (riv.), Eng, UK 33/F2
Cam Pha, Viet. 79/A3
Cam Ranh, Viet. 78/E4
Camaçari, Braz. 154/C4
Camacho, Mex. 142/E3
Camacupa, Ang. 105/C3
Camaguán, Ven. 153/E2
Camagüey (arch.), Cuba 141/F3
Camagüey, Cuba 145/G1
Camaiore, It. 58/D5
Camajuaní, Cuba 145/G1
Camalu, Mex. 142/A2
Camamu, Braz. 154/C4
Camamu, Baía de (bay), Braz. 154/C4
Camaná, Peru 156/C4
Camanducaia, Braz. 211/G7
Camaquã, Braz. 155/B4
Camaquã (riv.), Braz. 155/A4
Camargo, Sp. 44/D1
Camargos, Represa de (res.), Braz. 211/J6
Camarillo, Ca, US 136/A2
Camariñas, Sp. 44/A1
Camarón (cape), Hon. 145/E3
Camarones (bay), Arg. 158/D5
Camarones, Arg. 158/D5
Camas, Sp. 44/B4
Cambados, Sp. 44/A1
Cambará, Braz. 155/B2
Cambay, Gulf of (gulf), India 82/B3
Cambé, Braz. 155/B2
Camberley, Eng, UK 30/A3
Cambiano, It. 58/A3
Cambodia (ctry.) 83/H5
Camboriú, Ponta do (pt.), Braz. 155/C3
Cambrai, Fr. 52/C3
Cambrian (mts.), Wal, UK 34/E5
Cambridge, Eng, UK 33/G2
Cambridge (int'l arpt.), Eng, UK 33/G2
Cambridge, NZ 117/T10
Cambridge, Ma, US 131/G3
Cambridge, Md, US 130/E4
Cambridge, Oh, US 130/D3
Cambridge, On, Can. 130/D3
Cambridge Bay, Nun., Can. 122/F2
Cambridgeshire (co.), Eng, UK 33/F2
Cambrils, Sp. 45/F2
Cambuí, Braz. 211/G7
Cambuquira, Braz. 211/H6
Cambuslang, Sc, UK 36/B5
Cambutal (mtn.), Pan. 152/A3
Camden, Austl. 114/G9
Camden (co.), Eng, UK 30/C2
Camden, Al, US 133/G4
Camden, De, US 138/C5
Camden, Me, US 131/G2
Camden, NJ, US 138/C4
Camden (co.), NJ, US 138/C4
Camden, SC, US 133/H3
Camden Haven, Austl. 115/E1
Camden Point, Mo, US 137/D5
Cameia, PN da, Ang. 105/D3
Camel (riv.), Eng, UK 32/B6
Camelback (mtn.), Pa, US 138/C1
Camerano, It. 59/G5
Cameri, It. 58/B2
Cameron (isl.), Nun., Can. 123/R7
Cameron, Mo, US 129/J3
Cameron, Tx, US 129/H5
Cameroon (ctry.) 96/H7
Cametá, Braz. 151/J4
Camicia (peak), It. 46/C1
Camiguin (isl.), Phil. 79/D4
Camilla, Ga, US 133/G4
Camilo Aldao, Arg. 158/E2
Caminha, Port. 44/A2
Camiri, Bol. 150/F8
Camisano Vicentino, It. 59/E1
Çamlıdere, Turk. 90/C1
Çamlık NP, Turk. 90/C2
Çamlıyayla, Turk. 91/D1
Camoapa, Nic. 144/E3
Camogli, It. 58/C4
Camon, Fr. 52/B4
Camorta (isl.), India 83/F6
Camp Angelus (Angelus Oaks), Ca, US 136/D2
Camp Creek, Az, US 137/S18
Camp Hill, Pa, US 138/B3
Camp Lake, Wi, US 135/P14
Camp Springs, Md, US 138/B6
Campagna Lupia, It. 59/F2
Campagnola Emilia, It. 59/D3
Campana, Arg. 159/J11
Campana (isl.), Chile 159/B6
Campana, PN de la, Chile 158/N8
Campanario, Sp. 44/C3
Campanario (peak), Arg. 158/C2
Campanella (cape), It. 46/D2
Campanha, Braz. 211/H6
Campania (prov.), It. 46/D2
Campbell, Ca, US 135/L12
Campbell (isl.), NZ 23/T8
Campbell River, BC, Can. 126/B3
Campbell Town, Austl. 115/C4
Campbellsville, Ky, US 130/C4
Campbellton, NB, Can. 131/H1
Campbeltown, Sc, UK 31/R9
Campden, On, Can. 131/R9
Campeche (state), Mex. 140/C4
Campeche, Mex. 144/D2
Campeche (bay), Mex. 143/G5
Camperdown, Austl. 115/B3
Camperville, Mb, Can. 127/H3
Campestre, Braz. 211/G6
Campi Bisenzio, It. 59/E5
Campidano (range), It. 46/A3
Campillo de Altobuey, Sp. 44/E3
Campillos, Sp. 44/C4
Campina Verde, Braz. 155/B1
Campinas, Braz. 211/F7
Campion, Co, US 137/B2
Campione d'Italia, It. 57/E6
Campo (int'l arpt.), Braz. 156/C2
Campo Belo, Braz. 155/C2
Campo de Criptana, Sp. 44/D3
Campo de la Cruz, Col. 152/C2
Campo dei Fiori (peak), It. 58/B1
Campo Grande, Braz. 151/H8
Campo Ligure, It. 58/B3
Campo Limpo Paulista, Braz. 211/G8
Campo Maior, Port. 44/B3
Campo Mourão, Braz. 155/A3
Campo Tencia (peak), Swi. 57/E5
Campo Tizzoro, It. 59/D4
Campoalegre, Col. 152/C4
Campobasso, It. 46/D2
Campodarsego, It. 59/E2
Campodolcino, It. 57/F5
Campogalliano, It. 59/D3
Campomorone, It. 58/B3
Camponogara, It. 59/F2
Camporosso, It. 58/A5
Camporredondo, Peru 156/B2
Camporredondo, Embalse de (res.), Sp. 44/C1
Campos (phys. reg.), Braz. 147/D5
Campos Altos, Braz. 155/C1
Campos Belos, Braz. 154/A4
Campos de Hielo Norte (glacier), Chile 159/B5
Campos de Hielo Sur (glacier), Chile 159/B6
Campos del Puerto, Sp. 45/G3
Campos do Jordão, Braz. 211/H7
Campos Gerais, Braz. 155/C2
Campos Novos, Braz. 155/B3
Campos Sales, Braz. 154/B2
Camposampiero, It. 59/E1
Camposanto, It. 59/E3
Campsie Fells (hills), Sc, UK 36/B4
Campti, La, US 132/E4
Camrose, Ab, Can. 126/E2
Çan, Turk. 49/H5
Can (riv.), Eng, UK 30/E1
Can Tho, Viet. 78/D4
Canaçari (lake), Braz. 153/G5
Canada (ctry.) 122
Cañada de Gómez, Arg. 158/E2
Cañada Nieto, Uru. 159/J10
Cañada Rosquín, Arg. 158/E2
Canadensis, Pa, US 138/C1
Canadian (riv.), US 124/F4
Canadian (co.), Ok, US 137/M15
Canadian, Tx, US 129/G4
Canadian, North (riv.), Ok, US 124/F4
Cañadon Grande (mts.), Arg. 158/C5
Cañadón Seco, Arg. 158/D5
Canaima, PN, Ven. 150/F2
Çanakkale, Turk. 47/K2
Çanakkale (prov.), Turk. 90/A2
Canal de Moraleda (chan.), Chile 157/B6
Canalbianco (riv.), It. 59/E2
Canale, It. 58/A3
Canale Cavour (canal), It. 58/B2
Canals, Sp. 45/E3
Canals, Arg. 158/E2
Canandaigua, NY, US 130/E3
Cananea, Mex. 142/C2
Cananéia, Braz. 155/C3
Canápolis, Braz. 155/B1
Cañar, Ecu. 156/B1
Cañar (dept.), Ecu. 152/B5
Canard (riv.), On, Can. 135/G7
Canary (isls.), Sp. 93/A2
Cañas, CR 144/E4
Cañasgordas, Col. 152/B3
Canatlán de las Manzanas, Mex. 142/D3
Canaveral (cape), Fl, US 133/H4
Canberra, Austl. 115/D2
Canchaque, Peru 156/B2
Canche (riv.), Fr. 42/E1
Cancún, Mex. 144/E1
Cancun (int'l arpt.), Mex. 144/E1
Candado, Nevado del (peak), Arg. 157/C2
Candarave, Peru 156/D5
Çandarli (gulf), Gre.,Turk 62/C5
Candás, Sp. 44/C1
Candeias, Braz. 154/C4
Candelaria, Mex. 144/D2
Candelaria (riv.), Mex. 144/D2
Candelaria, Arg. 158/D2
Candeleda, Sp. 44/C2
Candelo, Austl. 115/D3
Candelo, It. 58/B1
Candia Lomellina, It. 58/B2
Candiac, Qu, Can. 131/N7
Candiba, Braz. 154/B4
Cândido Mota, Braz. 155/B2
Canding (cape), Indo. 80/D5
Çandır, Turk. 90/C2
Candlewood, NJ, US 138/D3
Cando, ND, US 127/J3
Candon, Phil. 79/D4
Canegrate, It. 58/B1
Canela, Braz. 155/B3
Canelli, It. 58/B3
Canelones (dept.), Uru. 159/F2
Canelones, Uru. 159/K11
Canete, Sp. 44/E2
Cañete, Río de (riv.), Peru 156/B4
Caney (riv.), Ks,Ok, US 143/F2
Cangallo, Peru 156/C4
Cangas, Sp. 44/A1
Cangas de Narcea, Sp. 44/B1
Cangas de Onís, Sp. 44/C1
Cangkuang (cape), Indo. 80/C5
Cango Caves, SAfr. 106/C4
Cangrejo (peak), Arg. 159/B6
Cangshan, China 72/D4
Canguaretama, Braz. 154/D2
Canguçu, Braz. 155/A4
Cangwu, China 83/K3
Cangyuan (Cangyuan Vazu Zizhixian), China 83/G3
Cangzhou, China 72/D3
Canh Cuoc (isl.), Viet. 78/D1
Cania Gorge NP, Austl. 114/C4
Caniapiscau (lake), Qu, Can. 123/K3
Caniapiskau (riv.), Qu, Can. 123/J3
Canicatti, It. 46/C4
Canik (mts.), Turk. 90/C1
Caniles, Sp. 44/D4
Canindé (riv.), Braz. 151/K5
Canino, It. 46/B1
Canistear (res.), NJ, US 139/H7
Cañitas de Felipe Pescador, Mex. 142/E4
Canjáyar, Sp. 44/D4
Çankırı, Turk. 90/C1
Çankırı (prov.), Turk. 90/C1
Canlaon (vol.), Phil. 81/F1
Canmore, Ab, Can. 126/E3
Cann River, Austl. 115/D3
Canna (isl.), Sc, UK 31/Q8
Cannanore, India 82/C5
Canne (ruin), It. 46/E2
Canner (riv.), Fr. 53/F5
Cannero Riviera, It. 57/E5
Cannes, Fr. 43/G5
Canneto sull'Oglio, It. 58/D2
Canning (peak), Austl. 112/C4
Canning (dam), Austl. 112/L7
Canning (riv.), Austl. 112/K7
Cannobio, It. 57/E5
Cannock, Eng, UK 32/D1
Cannon Falls, Mn, US 127/K4
Cannonball (riv.), ND, US 127/H4
Cannondale, Ct, US 139/E1
Cannonvale, Austl. 114/C3
Caño Guaritico (riv.), Ven. 152/D3
Caño Negro NWF, CR 145/E4
Canoas, Braz. 155/B4
Canoas (riv.), Braz. 155/B3
Canobolas (mt.), Austl. 115/D2
Canoinhas, Braz. 155/B3
Cañón de Río Blanco, PN, Mex. 143/M8
Cañón del Sumidero, PN, Mex. 144/C2
Canora, Sk, Can. 127/H3
Canosa di Puglia, It. 46/E2
Canouan (isl.), StV. 141/N9
Canowindra, Austl. 115/D2
Cansanção, Braz. 154/C3
Canso (cape), NS, Can. 131/J2
Canta, Peru 156/B3
Cantabria (aut. comm.), Sp. 44/C1
Cantabria, Cordillera (mts.), Sp. 44/B1
Cantal, Massif du (mass.), Fr. 42/E4
Cantalejo, Sp. 44/D2
Cantanhede, Braz. 154/A1
Cantanhede, Port. 44/A2
Cantaura, Ven. 153/E2
Canterbury, Eng, UK 33/H4
Canterbury Bight (bay), NZ 109/H7
Canterbury Cathedral, Eng, UK 33/H4
Cantillana, Sp. 44/C4
Canto do Buriti, Braz. 154/B3
Canton, Mi, US 135/E7
Canton, Ms, US 129/K4
Canton, NJ, US 138/C5
Canton, NY, US 130/F2
Canton, Oh, US 130/D3
Canton, Ok, US 132/D2
Canton (Abariringa) (isl.), Kiri. 117/H5
Cantoria, Sp. 44/D4
Cantù, It. 58/C1
Cantwell, Ak, US 134/J3
Cañuelas, Arg. 159/J11
Canunda NP, Austl. 115/B3
Canvey (isl.), Eng, UK 30/E2
Canvey Island, Eng, UK 33/G3
Canwood, Sk, Can. 126/G2
Canyon, Tx, US 129/G4
Canyon (lake), Tx, US 137/U20
Canyon de Chelly Nat'l Mon., Az, US 128/E3
Canyon Lake, Tx, US 137/U20
Canyonlands Nat'l Park, Ut, US 128/E3
Canyon of the Ancients Nat'l Mon., Co, US 128/E3
Canzo, It. 58/C1
Cao (riv.), China 73/C2
Cao Bang, Viet. 83/J3
Cao Lanh, Viet. 78/D4
Cao Xian, China 72/C4
Caodu (riv.), China 79/A2
Caorle, It. 59/F1
Caorso, It. 58/C2
Cap-Chat, Qu, Can. 131/H1
Cap d'Agde (cape), Fr. 42/E5
Cap-de-la-Madeleine, Qu, Can. 131/F2
Cap-Haïtien, Haiti 145/H2
Cap Rock Escarpment (cliff), Tx, US 132/C3
Cap-Rouge, Qu, Can. 131/G2
Cap Roux, Pointe du (pt.), Fr. 43/G5
Capac, Mi, US 135/G5
Capanaparo (riv.), Ven. 150/E2
Capanema, Braz. 151/J4
Capanne (peak), It. 46/B1
Capannoli, It. 59/D5
Capannori, It. 58/D5
Capão Bonito, Braz. 155/B3
Capão Doce, Morro do (hill), Braz. 155/B3
Caparaó, PN do, Braz. 155/D2
Caparica, Port. 45/P10
Caparo (riv.), Ven. 152/D3
Capay, Ca, US 135/K9
Capbreton, Fr. 42/C5
Capdenac-Gare, Fr. 42/E4
Capdepera, Sp. 45/G3
Cape Arid NP, Austl. 112/D5
Cape Barren (isl.), Austl. 109/D5
Cape Breton (isl.), NS, Can. 131/J2
Cape Breton Highlands (uplands), NS, Can. 131/J2
Cape Breton Highlands NP, NS, Can. 131/J2
Cape Cleveland NP, Austl. 114/B2
Cape Coast, Gha. 103/E5
Cape Cod Nat'l Seashore, Ma, US 131/G3
Cape Coral, Fl, US 133/H5
Cape Dorset, Nun., Can. 123/J2
Cape Fear (riv.), NC, US 133/J3
Cape Hatteras Nat'l Seashore, NC, US 133/K3
Cape Krusenstern Nat'l Mon., Ak, US 134/E2
Cape Le Grand NP, Austl. 112/D5
Cape Lookout Nat'l Seashore, NC, US 133/J3
Cape May, NJ, US 138/D6
Cape May (co.), NJ, US 138/D5
Cape May Court House, NJ, US 138/D5
Cape May Lighthouse, NJ, US 138/D6
Cape Melville NP, Austl. 114/B1
Cape Palmerston NP, Austl. 114/C3
Cape Range NP, Austl. 112/B2
Cape Saint Claire, Md, US 138/B5
Cape Town (cap.), SAfr. 106/L10
Cape Town (D.F. Malan) (int'l arpt.), SAfr. 106/L10
Cape Tribulation NP, Austl. 114/B2
Cape Upstart NP, Austl. 114/B2
Cape Verde (ctry.) 93/J9
Cape Yakataga, Ak, US 134/K3
Cape York (pen.), Austl. 109/D2
Capel, Austl. 112/B5
Capela, Braz. 154/C3
Capelinha, Braz. 154/B5
Capella, Austl. 114/C3
Capellades, Sp. 45/K6
Capestang, Fr. 42/E5
Capicciola (pt.), Fr. 46/A2
Capilla del Señor, Arg. 159/J11
Capim (riv.), Braz. 151/J4
Capinópolis, Braz. 155/B1
Capirara (res.), Braz. 157/F1
Capistrano, Braz. 154/C2
Capistrello, It. 46/C2
Capitan (mts.), NM, US 132/B3
Capitão de Campos, Braz. 154/B2
Capitão Poço, Braz. 151/J4
Capitol Reef NP, Ut, US 128/E3
Capivara, Represa (res.), Braz. 151/H8
Capivara, Serra de (range), Braz. 154/A4
Capivari (riv.), Braz. 211/J6
Čapljina, Bosn. 47/E1
Caplone (peak), It. 58/D1
Capo di Ponte, It. 57/G5
Capo d'Orlando, It. 46/D3
Capodichino (int'l arpt.), It. 46/D2
Capolona, It. 59/E5
Capoterra, It. 46/A3
Cappella Maggiore, It. 59/F1
Cappoquin, Ire. 31/Q10
Capraia (isl.), It. 46/A1
Caprarola, It. 46/C1
Capreol, On, Can. 130/D2
Capricorn (chan.), Austl. 109/E3
Capricorn (cape), Austl. 114/C3
Caprino Veronese, It. 59/D1
Capriolo, It. 58/C1
Caprivi Strip (reg.), Namb. 105/D4
Captain (har.), Ct, US 139/L7
Captain Cook, Hi, US 124/U11
Captainganj, India 84/D2
Captains Flat, Austl. 115/D2
Capua, It. 48/B5
Capulhuac, Mex. 143/Q10
Capulhuac, Mex. 143/Q10
Caputh, Ger. 40/Q7
Caquetá (riv.), Col. 152/D5
Caquetá (dept.), Col. 152/C4
Caquiaviri, Bol. 156/D5
Car Nicobar (isl.), India 83/F6
Carabobo (state), Ven. 152/D2
Caracal, Rom. 49/G3
Caracaraí, Braz. 153/F4
Caracas (cap.), Ven. 150/E1
Carache, Ven. 152/D2
Caracol, Braz. 154/B3
Caracolí, Col. 152/C3
Carácuaro de Morelos, Mex. 143/E5
Caradon (hill), Eng, UK 32/B5
Caraguatatuba, Braz. 211/H8
Caraguatatuba, Enseada de (bay), Braz. 211/H8
Carahue, Chile 158/B3
Carajás, Serra dos (mts.), Braz. 151/H5
Caranavi, Bol. 150/E7
Carandaí, Braz. 155/D2
Carangola, Braz. 155/D2
Caransebeş, Rom. 48/F3
Carapicuíba, Braz. 211/G8
Carappee Hill (peak), Austl. 113/H5
Caraquet, NB, Can. 131/H2
Caraş-Severin (prov.), Rom. 48/E3
Carasco, It. 58/C4
Caratasca (lag.), Hon. 140/E4
Carate Brianza, It. 58/C1
Caratinga, Braz. 155/D1
Carauari, Braz. 150/E4
Caraúbas, Braz. 154/C2
Caravaca de la Cruz, Sp. 44/E3
Caravaggio, It. 58/C2
Caravela, Ilha (isl.), GBis. 102/A4
Caravelas, Braz. 154/C5
Caravelí, Peru 156/C4
Caraz, Peru 156/B3
Carazinho, Braz. 157/F2
Carballino, Sp. 44/A1
Carballo, Sp. 44/A1
Carberry, Mb, Can. 127/J3
Carbo, Mex. 142/C2
Carbon (cape), Alg. 100/H4
Carbon (co.), Pa, US 138/C2
Carbon (riv.), Wa, US 135/C3
Carbonara (cape), It. 46/A3
Carbonara (peak), It. 46/D4
Carbondale, Pa, US 130/F3
Carbonear, Nf, Can. 131/L2
Carbonera, It. 59/F1
Carboneras, Mex. 143/F3
Carbonia, It. 46/A3
Carbonne, Fr. 42/D5
Carbost, Sc, UK 31/Q8
Carcagente, Sp. 45/E3
Carcarañá, Arg. 158/E2
Carcare, It. 58/B4
Carcassonne, Fr. 42/E5
Carche (peak), Sp. 44/E3
Carchi (dept.), Ecu. 152/B4
Carcross, Yk, Can. 134/M3
Çardak, Turk. 49/H5
Cardal, Uru. 159/K11
Cardedeu, Sp. 45/L6
Cárdenas, Mex. 143/F4
Cárdenas, Cuba 145/F1
Cárdenas, Mex. 144/C2
Cardenden, Sc, UK 36/C4
Cardiel (lake), Arg. 159/C6
Cardiff (cap.), Wal, UK 32/C4
Cardiff (co.), Wal, UK 32/C4
Cardiff, Md, US 138/B4
Cardiff by the Sea, Ca, US 136/C4
Cardigan, Wal, UK 32/B2
Cardona, Sp. 45/F2
Cardona, Uru. 159/K10
Cardoso, Braz. 155/B2
Cardozo, Uru. 159/K10
Cardston, Ab, Can. 126/E3
Cardwell, Austl. 114/B2
Care Alto (peak), It. 57/G5
Careaçu, Braz. 211/H7
Carefree, Az, US 137/S18
Carei, Rom. 41/M5
Carentan, Fr. 42/C2
Carev vrh (peak), FYROM 47/H1
Carey (lake), Austl. 109/B3
Carhaix-Plouguer, Fr. 42/B2
Carhuamayo, Peru 156/B3
Carhuaz, Peru 156/B3
Carhué, Arg. 158/E3
Cariacica, Braz. 155/D2
Cariaco, Ven. 153/F2
Cariamanga, Ecu. 156/B2
Cariati, It. 46/E3
Caribbean (sea), NAm,SAm. 119/L8
Cariboo (mts.), BC, Can. 126/C2
Caribou, Me, US 131/G2
Caribou (range), Id, US 126/F5
Caribou (mts.), Ab, Can. 122/E3
Caridade, Braz. 154/C2
Carigara, Phil. 79/D5
Carignan, Qu, Can. 131/P7
Carignan, Fr. 53/E4
Carignano, It. 58/A3
Cariñena, Sp. 44/E2
Carinhanha, Braz. 154/B4
Carinhanha (riv.), Braz. 154/A4
Carini, It. 46/C3
Caripito, Ven. 153/F2
Caririaçu, Braz. 154/C2
Cariris Novos, Serra dos (mts.), Braz. 154/B2
Carleton (mt.), NB, Can. 131/H2
Carleton (riv.), NS, Can. 131/H2
Carleton, Qu, Can. 131/H1
Carleton, Mi, US 135/F7
Carleton Place, On, Can. 130/E2
Carletonville, SAfr. 106/D2
Carlin, Nv, US 126/D5
Carlindie Abor. Land, Austl. 112/C2
Carling, Fr. 53/F5
Carlingford, Ire. 34/B3
Carlingford (lake), Ire. 34/B3
Carlingford (mtn.), Ire. 34/B3
Carlinville, Il, US 129/K3
Carlisle, Pa, US 130/E3
Carlisle, La, US 137/Q17
Carlisle, Eng, UK 35/F2
Carlisle Barracks Mil. Res., Pa, US 138/A3
Carlit (peak), Fr. 42/D5
Carlos Casares, Arg. 158/E2
Carlos Chagas, Braz. 154/B5
Carlos M. de Cespedes, Cuba 145/G1
Carlow, Ire. 31/Q10
Carlow (co.), Ire. 34/B6
Carloway, Sc, UK 31/Q7
Carlsbad, Ca, US 136/C4
Carlsbad, NM, US 129/F4
Carlsbad Caverns NP, NM, US 142/D1
Carlsberg, Ger. 54/B3
Carlsfeld, Ger. 55/F2
Carlton, Eng, UK 35/G6
Carluke, Sc, UK 36/C5
Carlyle (lake), Il, US 129/K3
Carlyle, Sk, Can. 127/H3
Carmacks, Yk, Can. 134/L3
Carmagnola, It. 58/A3
Carman, Mb, Can. 127/J3
Carmarthen, Wal, UK 32/B3
Carmarthen (bay), Wal, UK 32/B3
Carmarthenshire (co.) Wal, UK 32/B3
Carmaux, Fr. 42/E4
Carmel (pt.), Wal, UK 34/D5
Carmelo, Uru. 159/J11
Carmen (isl.), Mex. 144/C2
Carmen (riv.), Mex. 132/B4
Carmen de Patagones, Arg. 158/E4
Carmensa, Arg. 158/D2
Carmo, Braz. 211/L6
Carmo (peak), It. 58/B4
Carmo da Cachoeira, Braz. 211/H6
Carmo de Minas, Braz. 211/H7
Carmo do Paranaíba, Braz. 155/C1
Carmo do Rio Claro, Braz. 155/C2
Carmona, Sp. 44/C4
Carn Ban (peak), Sc, UK 36/B2
Carn Easgann Bàna (peak), Sc, UK 36/B2
Càrn Eige (peak), Sc, UK 36/A2
Carn Glas-choire (peak), Sc, UK 36/C2
Carn Kitty (hill), Sc, UK 36/C2
Carn Mairg (peak), Sc, UK 36/B3
Carn Mór (peak), Sc, UK 36/C2
Carn na Cailliche (hill), Sc, UK 36/C1
Carn na Saobhaidhe (peak), Sc, UK 36/B2
Carnago, It. 58/B1
Carnamah, Austl. 112/B4
Carnarvon, Austl. 109/A3
Carnarvon NP, Austl. 114/B4
Carnarvon, SAfr. 106/C3
Carnarvonleegte (riv.), SAfr. 106/C3
Carnation, Wa, US 135/D2
Carnaubal, Braz. 154/B2
Carnaxide, Port. 45/P10
Carncastle, NI, UK 34/C2
Carndonagh, Ire. 34/A1
Carnduff, Sk, Can. 127/H3
Carnedd Llewelyn (peak), Wal, UK 34/E5
Carnegie (lake), Austl. 109/B3
Carney, Ok, US 137/N14
Carney (isl.), Ant. 160/S
Carnforth, Eng, UK 35/F3
Carnlough, NI, UK 34/B2
Carnot (cape), Austl. 113/G5
Carnot, CAfr. 96/J7
Carnoustie, Sc, UK 36/D4
Carnsore (pt.), Ire. 31/Q10
Carnwath (riv.), NW, Can. 122/D2
Carnwath, Sc, UK 36/C5
Caro, Mi, US 130/D3
Carol Stream, Il, US 135/P16
Carolina, Braz. 154/A2
Carolina, PR 141/M8
Carolina, SAfr. 107/E2
Carolina Beach, NC, US 133/J3
Caroline (isl.), Kiri. 117/K5
Caroline (isls), Micr. 116/D4
Caroní (riv.), Ven. 147/C2
Carora, Ven. 152/D2
Carouge, Swi. 56/C5
Carpaneto Piacentino, It. 58/C3
Carpathian (mts.), Eur. 27/G4
Carpegna (peak), It. 59/F5
Carpegna, It. 59/F5
Carpenedolo, It. 58/D2
Carpentaria, Gulf of (gulf), Austl. 109/C2
Carpenter, Il, US 137/H8
Carpentersville, Il, US 135/P15
Carpentras, Fr. 42/F4
Carpi, It. 59/D3
Carpignano Sesia, It. 58/B1
Carpina, Braz. 154/D2
Carpinteria, Ca, US 136/A2
Carpiquet (int'l arpt.), Fr. 42/C2
Carr (inlet), Wa, US 135/B3
Carrabelle, Fl, US 133/G4
Carrantuohill (peak), Ire. 31/P10
Carrara, It. 58/D4
Carrasco (int'l arpt.), Uru. 159/K11
Carrasquero, Ven. 152/D2
Carreg Ddu (pt.), Wal, UK 34/D6
Carriacou (isl.), Gren. 150/F1
Carrick (reg.), Sc, UK 36/B6
Carrick on Shannon, Ire. 31/P10
Carrick on Suir, Ire. 31/Q10
Carrickalinga, Austl. 113/H5
Carrickfergus, NI, UK 34/C2
Carrickfergus (dist.), NI, UK 34/C2
Carrickmacross, Ire. 31/Q10
Carrickmore, NI, UK 34/A2
Carrières-sous-Poissy, Fr. 30/J5
Carrigaholt, Ire. 31/P10
Carrigaline, Ire. 31/P11
Carrington, ND, US 127/J4
Carrión (riv.), Sp. 44/C1
Carrión de los Condes, Sp. 44/C1
Carrizo (mts.), Az, US 124/D4
Carrizo Plain Nat'l Mon., Ca, US 128/C4
Carrizo Springs, Tx, US 132/D4
Carrizo Wash (riv.), Az,NM, US 128/E4
Carrizozo, NM, US 129/F4
Carroll (co.), Md, US 138/A5
Carrollton, Ky, US 130/C4
Carrollton, Ga, US 133/G3
Carron (lake), Sc, UK 36/A2
Carron (riv.), Sc, UK 36/A2
Carrot (riv.), SK, Can. 127/H2
Carrot River, Sk, Can. 127/H2
Carrowdore, NI, UK 34/C2
Carrowkeel, Ire. 34/A1
Carrù, It. 58/A4
Carrum Downs, Austl. 115/G6
Carryduff, NI, UK 34/C2
Çarşamba, Turk. 90/D1
Carse of Forth (plain), Sc, UK 36/B4
Carse of Gowrie (plain), Sc, UK 36/C4
Carson (riv.), Nv, US 128/C3
Carson, Ca, US 136/F8
Carson City (cap.), Nv, US 128/C3
Carson Sink (dry lake), Nv, US 128/C3
Carstairs, Ab, Can. 126/E3
Cartagena, Chile 158/N8
Cartagena, Col. 152/C2
Cartagena, Sp. 45/E4
Cartago, Col. 150/C3
Cartago, CR 145/F4
Cártama, Sp. 44/C4
Cartaya, Sp. 44/B4
Carter Bar (hill), Eng, UK 36/D6
Carter Lake (res.), Co, US 137/B2
Carteret, NJ, US 139/J9
Cartersville, Ga, US 133/G3
Carterton, Eng, UK 33/E3
Carthage (int'l arpt.), Tun. 46/B4
Carthage, Mo, US 129/J3
Carthage, Ms, US 133/F3
Carthage, Tn, US 130/C4
Carthage, Tx, US 129/J4
Carthage (Qarṭājannah) (ruin), Tun. 46/B4
Cartí (mtn.), Pan. 152/B2
Cartier Islet (isl.), Austl. 109/B2
Cartwright, Nf, Can. 123/L3
Caruaru, Braz. 154/D3
Carumás, Peru 156/D5
Carúpano, Ven. 153/F2
Caruthersville, Mo, US 129/K3
Carvico, It. 58/C1
Carvin, Fr. 52/B3
Carvoeiro (cape), Port. 44/A3
Cary, NC, US 133/J3
Cary, Il, US 135/P15
Casa Blanca (canal), Az, US 137/S19
Casa Branca, Braz. 211/F6

178
Casa – Chape

Casa de Piedra (res.), Arg. 158/D3
Casa Grande, Az, US 128/E4
Casa Grande Nat'l Mon., Az, US 128/E4
Casa Nova, Braz. 154/B3
Casablanca, Chile 158/N8
Casablanca-Anfa (prov.), Mor. 100/A2
Casal di Principe, It. 46/D2
Casalbordino, It. 46/D1
Casalbuttano, It. 58/C2
Casale di Scodosia, It. 59/E2
Casale Monferrato, It. 58/B2
Casale sul Sile, It. 59/F1
Casalecchio di Reno, It. 59/E4
Casaleone, It. 59/E2
Casalmaggiore, It. 58/D3
Casalpusterlengo, It. 58/C2
Casalserugo, It. 59/E2
Casamance (riv.), Sen. 102/A3
Casanare (riv.), Col. 150/D2
Casanare (dept.), Col. 152/D3
Casanay, Ven. 153/F2
Casar de Cáceres, Sp. 44/B3
Casarano, It. 47/F2
Casarsa della Delizia, It. 59/F1
Casarza Ligure, It. 58/C4
Casas Grande (riv.), Mex. 128/E5
Casas Grandes, Mex. 142/D2
Casas Grandes (ruin), Mex. 142/C2
Casas-Ibáñez, Sp. 44/E3
Ca'Savio, It. 59/F2
Casazza, It. 58/C1
Cascada de Bassaseachic, PN, Mex. 142/C2
Cascade (res.), Id, US 126/D4
Cascade (range), Or,Wa, US 122/D4
Cascade Caverns, Tx, US 137/T20
Cascade-Fairwood, Or, US 135/C3
Cascade-Siskiyou Nat'l Mon., Or, US 126/C5
Cascades (pt.), Reun. 107/S15
Cascais, Port. 45/P10
Cascapédia (riv.), Qu, Can. 131/H1
Cascas, Peru 156/B2
Cascavel, Braz. 157/F1
Cascavel, Braz. 154/C2
Casciago, It. 58/B1
Casciana Terme, It. 58/D5
Cascina, It. 58/D5
Case (inlet), Wa, US 135/B3
Casella, It. 58/B3
Caselle, It. 59/E2
Casentino (valley), It. 59/E5
Caserta, It. 46/D2
Casey (bay), Ant. 160/D
Casey, Austl., Ant. 160/H
Caseyr (cape), Som. 97/R5
Caseyville, Il, US 137/G8
Cashel, Ire. 31/Q10
Cashion, Ok, US 137/M14
Cashmere, Wa, US 126/C4
Cashtown, Pa, US 138/A4
Casigua, Ven. 152/C2
Casilda (pt.), Cuba 145/F1
Casilda, Arg. 158/E2
Casimiro Castillo, Mex. 142/D5
Casina, It. 58/D3
Casinalbo, It. 59/D3
Casino, Austl. 115/E1
Casino and Opera House, Mona. 58/J8
Casitas (lake), Ca, US 136/A2
Casitas Springs, Ca, US 136/A2
Casma, Peru 156/B3
Casnigo, It. 58/C1
Casole d'Elsa, It. 59/E6
Casorate Primo, It. 58/C2
Casorate Sempione, It. 58/B1
Caspe, Sp. 45/E2
Casper, Wy, US 127/G5
Caspian (sea), Asia 67/E5
Caspoggio, It. 57/F5
Cass (co.), Mo, US 137/E6
Cass (lake), Mi, US 135/F6
Cass City, Mi, US 130/D3
Cassai (riv.), Ang. 105/D3
Cassano allo Ionio, It. 46/E3
Cassano d'Adda, It. 58/C1
Cassano Magnago, It. 58/B1
Cassano Spinola, It. 58/B3
Cassel, Fr. 52/B2
Cássia, Braz. 155/C2
Cassiar, BC, Can. 134/N3
Cassiar (mts.), BC, Can. 122/C3
Cassilândia, Braz. 155/B1
Cassine, It. 58/B3
Cassino, It. 46/C2
Cassolnovo, It. 58/B2
Castagnaro, It. 59/E2
Castagneto Carducci, It. 43/J5
Castagnole delle Lanze, It. 58/B3
Castaic, Ca, US 136/B2
Castalla, Sp. 45/E3
Castanet-Tolosan, Fr. 42/D5
Castanhal, Braz. 151/J4
Castaños, Mex. 132/C5
Casteggio, It. 58/C3
Castegnato, It. 58/D1
Castel, Isr. 91/G8
Castel Bolognese, It. 59/E4
Castel d'Ario, It. 59/D2
Castel di Sangro, It. 46/D2
Castel Goffredo, It. 58/D2
Castel Mella, It. 58/D2
Castel San Giovanni, It. 58/C2
Castel San Lorenzo, It. 46/D2
Castel San Pietro Terme, It. 59/E4
Castelbuono, It. 46/D4
Castelcovati, It. 58/C2
Castelfidardo, It. 59/G6
Castelfiorentino, It. 59/D5
Castelfranco di Sopra, It. 59/E5
Castelfranco Emilia, It. 59/E3
Castelfranco Veneto, It. 59/E1
Castelgomberto, It. 59/E1
Casteljaloux, Fr. 42/D4
Castell de Montjuic, Sp. 45/L7
Castellammare di Stabia, It. 46/D2
Castellammare, Golfo di (gulf), It. 46/C3
Castellamonte, It. 58/A2
Castellanza, It. 58/B1
Castellar del Vallès, Sp. 45/G2
Castellarano, It. 59/D3
Castell'Arquato, It. 58/C3
Castellazzo Bormida, It. 58/B3
Castelldefels, Sp. 45/K7
Castelleone, It. 58/C2
Castelli, Arg. 159/K12
Castellina in Chianti, It. 59/E6
Castello di Godego, It. 59/E1
Castello di Miramare, It. 59/G1
Castello Eurialo (ruin), It. 46/D4
Castello, Monte il (peak), It. 59/E5
Castellón de la Plana, Sp. 45/E3
Castellote, Sp. 45/E2
Castellucchio, It. 58/D2
Castelmassa, It. 59/E2
Castelnau-le-Lez, Fr. 42/E5
Castelnaudary, Fr. 42/D5
Castelnovo di Sotto, It. 58/D3
Castelnovo ne'Monti, It. 58/D4
Castelnuovo Berardenga, It. 59/E6
Castelnuovo di Garfagnana, It. 58/D4
Castelnuovo Don Bosco, It. 58/A2
Castelnuovo Scrivia, It. 58/B3
Castelo Branco, Port. 44/B3
Castelo Branco (dist.), Port. 44/B2
Castelo de Vide, Port. 44/B3
Castelo do Piauí, Braz. 154/B2
Castelsardo, It. 46/A2
Castelsarrasin, Fr. 42/D4
Castelverde, It. 58/C2
Castelvetrano, It. 46/C4
Castelvetro di Modena, It. 59/D3
Castelvetro Piacentino, It. 58/C2
Castenaso, It. 59/E3
Castenedolo, It. 58/D2
Casterton, Austl. 115/B3
Castiglion Fiorentino, It. 43/J5
Castiglione, It. 59/F4
Castiglione d'Adda, It. 58/C2
Castiglione dei Pepoli, It. 59/E4
Castiglione delle Stiviere, It. 58/D2
Castiglione Torinese, It. 58/A2
Castilho, Braz. 155/B2
Castilla, Peru 156/A2
Castilla-La Mancha (aut. comm.), Sp. 44/C3
Castilla y León (aut. comm.), Sp. 44/D2
Castilla y Léon Treviño, Sp. 44/D1
Castillo (peak), Arg. 158/C4
Castillo de San Marcos Nat'l Mon., Fl, US 133/H4
Castillos, Uru. 159/G2
Castione della Presolana, It. 57/G6
Castions, It. 59/F1
Castions di Strada, It. 59/G1
Castle Dale, Ut, US 128/E3
Castle Douglas, Sc, UK 34/E2
Castle Hills, Tx, US 137/T20
Castle Rock, Co, US 129/F3
Castle Rock, Wa, US 126/C4
Castle Rock (lake), Wi, US 127/L5
Castle Tower NP, Austl. 114/C4
Castlebar, Ire. 31/P10
Castlebay, Sc, UK 31/Q8
Castlebellingham, Ire. 34/B4
Castlebridge, Ire. 31/Q10
Castlecaufield, NI, UK 34/B3
Castlecomer, Ire. 31/Q10
Castledawson, NI, UK 34/B2
Castleford, Eng, UK 35/G4
Castlegar, BC, Can. 126/D3
Castlegregory, Ire. 30/N10
Castleisland, Ire. 31/P10
Castlemaine, Austl. 115/C3
Castlereagh, Ire. 31/P10
Castletown, IM, UK 34/D3
Castlewellan, NI, UK 34/C3
Castor, Ab, Can. 126/F2
Castos (riv.), Libr. 96/D6
Castres, Fr. 42/E5
Castrezzato, It. 58/C1
Castricum, Neth. 50/B3
Castries (cap.), StL. 141/N9
Castro, Braz. 155/B3
Castro, Chile 158/B4
Castro Alves, Braz. 154/C4
Castro Daire, Port. 44/B2
Castro de Rey, Sp. 44/B1
Castro del Río, Sp. 44/C4
Castro-Urdiales, Sp. 44/D1
Castro Verde, Port. 44/A4
Castrojeriz, Sp. 44/C1
Castrop-Rauxel, Ger. 51/E5
Castropol, Sp. 44/B1
Castrovillari, It. 46/E3
Castrovirreyna, Peru 156/C4
Castuera, Sp. 44/C3
Casupá, Uru. 159/G2
Cat (isl.), Bahm. 141/F3
Cat (lake), On, Can. 127/K3
Cat Law (peak), Sc, UK 36/C3
Catacamas, Hon. 144/E3
Catacaos, Peru 156/A2
Catacocha, Ecu. 156/B2
Cataduanes (isl.), Phil. 79/D5
Cataguases, Braz. 211/L6
Çatak, Turk. 90/E2
Çatalağzı, Turk. 49/K5
Çatalca, Turk. 49/J5
Çatalçam, Turk. 90/D2
Catalina, Az, US 128/E4
Catalonia (reg.), Sp. 45/E2
Cataluña (aut. comm.), Sp. 45/F2
Catamarca, Arg. 157/C2
Catamayo, Ecu. 156/B1
Catanduanes (isl.), Phil. 79/D5
Catanduva, Braz. 155/B2
Catania, It. 46/D4
Catania, Golfo di (gulf), It. 46/D4
Catanzaro, It. 46/E3
Cataouatche (lake), La, US 137/P17
Catarina, Braz. 154/C2
Catarman, Phil. 81/F1
Catastrophe (cape), Austl. 113/G5
Catatumbo (riv.), Col. 141/G6
Catatungan (mtn.), Phil. 81/F2
Catawba (riv.), NC,SC, US 133/H3
Catawissa, Pa, US 138/B2
Catbalogan, Phil. 79/D5
Catedral (peak), Uru. 159/G2
Catemaco (lake), Mex. 144/C2
Catemaco, Mex. 144/C2
Catende, Braz. 154/D3
Cateran (hill), Eng, UK 36/E5
Caterham, Eng, UK 30/C3
Caterham and Warlingham, Eng, UK 33/F4
Cathcart, SAfr. 106/D4
Cathédrale de Reims, Fr. 52/D5
Catherine (Kātrīnā) (peak), Egypt 101/C2
Catherine Palace, Rus. 61/T7
Ca'Tiepolo, It. 59/F3
Cativá, Pan. 145/G4
Çatköyü, Turk. 90/E2
Catlettsburg, Ky, US 130/D4
Cato (isl.), Austl. 109/E3
Catoche, Cabo (cape), Mex. 144/E1
Catolé do Rocha, Braz. 154/C2
Catonsville, Md, US 138/B5
Catria (peak), It. 59/F6
Catriló, Arg. 158/E3
Catrimani (riv.), Braz. 150/F3
Catrine, Sc, UK 36/B6
Catskill (mts.), NY, US 130/F3
Cattolica, It. 59/F5
Catu, Braz. 154/C4
Cauayan, Phil. 79/D4
Cauayan, Phil. 79/D6
Cauca (dept.), Col. 152/B4
Cauca (riv.), Col. 152/C3
Cauca (riv.), Col. 147/B2
Caucaia, Braz. 154/C1
Caucasia, Col. 152/C3
Caucasus (mts.), Geo. 63/G4
Caudete, Sp. 45/E3
Caudry, Fr. 52/C3
Cauldcleuch Head (peak), Sc, UK 36/D6
Cauquenes, Chile 158/B2
Caura (riv.), Ven. 150/F2
Caussade, Fr. 42/D4
Cauterets, Fr. 42/C5
Cauto (riv.), Cuba 145/G1
Cauvery (riv.), India 82/C5
Cava d'Ispica (ruin), It. 46/D4
Cávado (riv.), Port. 44/A2
Cavaglià, It. 58/B2
Cavaillon, Fr. 42/F5
Cavalaire-sur-Mer, Fr. 43/G5
Cavalcante, Braz. 154/A4
Cavalese, It. 57/H5
Cavalier, ND, US 127/J3
Cavalla (riv.), Libr. 96/D6
Cavallermaggiore, It. 58/A3
Cavallino, It. 59/F2
Cavallo, Capo al (cape), Fr. 46/A1
Cavally (riv.), C.d'Iv. 102/C5
Cavan, Ire. 31/Q10
Cavarzere, It. 59/F2
Cave Creek, Az, US 137/S18
Cave of Ten Thousand Buddhas, Myan. 78/B2
Cavezzo, It. 59/E3
Caviana (isl.), Braz. 151/J3
Cavite, Phil. 79/D5
Cavriana, It. 58/D2
Cawayan, Phil. 79/D5
Cawdor, Sc, UK 36/C1
Cawndilla (lake), Austl. 115/B2
Caxias do Sul, Braz. 155/B4
Caxinas (pt.), Hon. 144/E2
Caxito, Ang. 105/B2
Çay, Turk. 90/B2
Çayağzı, Turk. 49/J5
Cayambe, Ecu. 152/B4
Cayambe (vol.), Ecu. 152/B4
Cayce, SC, US 133/H3
Çaycuma, Turk. 49/L5
Çayeli, Turk. 90/E1
Cayenne (cap.), FrG. 151/H3
Cayeux-sur-Mer, Fr. 52/A3
Çayırhan, Turk. 49/K5
Çaylar, Turk. 90/E2
Cayman (isls.), UK 140/E4
Cayman Brac (isl.), UK 141/F4
Cazalla de la Sierra, Sp. 44/C4
Cazères, Fr. 42/D5
Cazin, Bosn. 43/L4
Cazis, Swi. 57/F4
Cazones (riv.), Mex. 144/B1
Cazorla, Sp. 44/D4
Cazzago San Martino, It. 58/D1
Cea (riv.), Sp. 44/C1
Ceanannus Mór (kells), Ire. 31/Q10
Ceará (state), Braz. 154/B2
Cébaco (isl.), Pan. 145/F5
Ceballos, Mex. 142/D3
Cebollati (riv.), Uru. 159/G2
Cebollatí, Uru. 159/G2
Cebreros, Sp. 44/C2
Cebu, Phil. 79/D5
Cebu (int'l arpt.), Phil. 79/D5
Cebu (isl.), Phil. 79/D6
Ceccano, It. 46/C2
Cecil (co.), Md, US 138/C4
Cecil Macks (pass), Swaz. 107/E2
Cecil Plains, Austl. 114/C4
Cecil Rhodes (mt.), Austl. 112/D3
Cecilton, Md, US 138/C5
Cecina, It. 43/J5
Cecina (riv.), It. 59/D6
Cecita (lake), It. 46/E3
Ceclavín, Sp. 44/B3
Cedar (riv.), Ia, US 127/L5
Cedar, Ks, US 137/D6
Cedar (valley), Ut, US 137/J13
Cedar (lake), Sk,Mb, Can. 122/F3
Cedar (mtn.), Ca, US 135/L11
Cedar Bay NP, Austl. 114/B1
Cedar Bluff (res.), Ks, US 129/G3
Cedar Breaks Nat'l Mon., Ut, US 128/D3
Cedar Brook, NJ, US 138/D4
Cedar City, Ut, US 128/D3
Cedar Cove, Co, US 137/B2
Cedar Creek (res.), Tx, US 143/F1
Cedar Falls (dam), Wa, US 135/D3
Cedar Falls, Wa, US 135/D3
Cedar Fort (Cedar Valley), Ut, US 137/J13
Cedar Glen, Ca, US 136/C2
Cedar Grove, Md, US 138/A5
Cedar Grove, NJ, US 139/J8
Cedar Hill, Mo, US 137/F9
Cedar Hills, Ut, US 137/K13
Cedar Key, Fl, US 133/H4
Cedarhurst, NY, US 139/L9
Cedartown, Ga, US 133/G3
Cedarville, Ca, US 126/C5
Cedegolo, It. 57/G5
Cedeira, Sp. 44/A1
Cedral, Mex. 143/E4
Cedro, Braz. 154/C2
Cedros (isl.), Mex. 142/B2
Ceduna, Austl. 113/G5
Cee, Sp. 44/A1
Cefalù, It. 46/D3
Cefni (riv.), Wal, UK 34/D5
Cega (riv.), Sp. 44/C2
Ceggia, It. 59/F1
Cegléd, Hun. 48/D2
Čegrane, FYROM 47/G2
Cehegín, Sp. 44/E3
Ceheng Bouyeizu Zizhixian, China 83/J3
Cehu Silvaniei, Rom. 49/F2
Ceiriog (riv.), Wal, UK 35/E6
Çekerek (riv.), Turk. 62/F4
Celákovice, Czh. 55/H2
Celanova, Sp. 44/B1
Celaya, Mex. 143/E4
Celebes (isl.), Indo. 67/L10
Celebes (sea), Asia 67/M9
Celendín, Peru 156/B2
Celestún, Mex. 144/D1
Celica, Ecu. 156/B2
Céligny, Swi. 56/C5
Celina, Tx, US 129/H4
Celina, Oh, US 130/C3
Celje, Slov. 43/L3
Cella, Sp. 44/E2
Celldömölk, Hun. 48/C2
Celle, Ger. 51/H3
Celle (riv.), Fr. 40/B4
Celle Ligure, It. 58/B4
Celles, Belg. 52/C2
Čelopek, FYROM 48/E5
Celorico da Beira, Port. 44/B2
Celtic (sea), Eur. 31/P11
Cemaes (pt.), Wal, UK 32/B2
Cemaru (peak), Indo. 80/D3
Cembra, It. 57/H5
Cenajo, Embalse del (res.), Sp. 44/E3
Cenderawasih (bay), Indo. 81/H4
Cene, It. 58/C1
Cenepa (riv.), Peru 156/B1
Cengong, China 83/J2
Cenia, Sp. 45/F2
Ceno (riv.), It. 58/C3
Centenario, Arg. 157/C4
Centenario do Sul, Braz. 155/B2
Centennial (mts.), Id, US 126/E4
Center, ND, US 127/H4
Center Moriches, NY, US 139/F2
Center Point, Al, US 133/G3
Centerbrook, Ct, US 139/F1
Centereach, NY, US 139/E2
Centerville, Tn, US 130/C5
Centerville, Tx, US 132/E4
Centerville, Ut, US 137/K12
Cento, It. 59/E3
Cento Croci, Passo di (pass), It. 58/C4
Central (peak), Arg. 158/C4
Central, Braz. 154/B3
Central (pol. reg.), Gha. 103/E5
Central (prov.), Kenya 104/C3
Central (int'l arpt.), Ukr. 49/K2
Central, Ak, US 134/K2
Central, NM, US 128/E4
Central African Republic (ctry.) 97/J6
Central Australia Abor. Land, Austl. 113/F2
Central Australia (Warburton) Abor. Rsv., Austl. 113/E3
Central Butte, Sk, Can. 126/G3
Central City, Ne, US 127/J5
Central City, Co, US 137/A3
Central, Cordillera (mts.), SAm. 150/C5
Central Desert Abor. Rsv., Austl. 113/F2
Central Intelligence Agency Fed. Govt. Res., Va, US 138/A6
Central Island NP, Kenya 104/C2
Central Islip, NY, US 139/E2
Central Makrān (range), Pak. 89/H3
Central, Massif (mass.), Fr. 42/E4
Central Mount Stuart (peak), Austl. 113/G2
Central Mount Wedge (peak), Austl. 113/F2
Central Park, NY, US 139/K8
Central, Planalto (plat.), Braz. 151/J7
Central Point, Or, US 126/C5
Central Siberian (plat.), Rus. 65/L3
Central Ural (mts.), Rus. 61/N4
Central Valley, NY, US 138/D1
Centralia, Wa, US 126/C4
Centralia, Il, US 129/K3
Centre (pol. reg.), Fr. 42/D3
Centre (pol. reg.), Mor. 98/D2
Centre (co.), Pa, US 138/A2
Centre Island, NY, US 139/L8
Centre-Nord (pol. reg.), Mor. 100/B2
Centre-Sud (pol. reg.), Mor. 100/B2
Centreville, Al, US 133/G3
Centreville, Il, US 137/G8
Centreville, Md, US 138/B5
Cenxi, China 83/K3
Čepin, Cro. 48/D3
Ceram (isl.), Indo. 67/N10
Ceram (sea), Indo. 81/G4
Cerano, It. 58/B2
Ceraso (cape), It. 46/A2
Cerbère, Fr. 42/E5
Cercal, Port. 44/A4
Cercedilla, Sp. 45/M8
Čerchov (peak), Czh. 55/F4
Cerdanyola del Vallès, Sp. 45/L7
Cère (riv.), Fr. 42/E4
Cerea, It. 59/E2
Ceredigion (co.), Wal, UK 32/B2
Ceres, Arg. 157/D2
Ceres, Braz. 151/J7
Ceres, SAfr. 106/L10
Cerese, It. 59/D2
Céret, Fr. 42/E5
Cereté, Col. 152/C2
Cerfone (riv.), It. 59/E6
Cerfontaine, Belg. 53/D3
Cergy, Fr. 30/J4
Ceriale, It. 58/B4
Cerignola, It. 46/D2
Çerkeş, Turk. 62/E4
Çerkezköy, Turk. 49/J5
Çermik, Turk. 90/D2
Černá (riv.), Czh. 55/H5
Černá (peak), Czh. 55/G5
Cernavodă, Rom. 49/J3
Cernay, Fr. 56/D2
Cernay-la-Ville, Fr. 30/H5
Cernier, Swi. 56/C3
Cérou (riv.), Fr. 42/D4
Cerralvo, Mex. 132/D5
Cerralvo (isl.), Mex. 142/C3
Cerreto Guidi, It. 59/D5
Cerreto, Passo del (pass), It. 58/D4
Cërrik, Alb. 47/F2
Cerritos, Mex. 143/E4
Cerritos, Ca, US 136/F8
Cerro Azul, Peru 156/B4
Cerro Azul, Mex. 144/B1
Cerro Castillo, Chile 159/B6
Cerro Chato, Uru. 159/G2
Cêrro Corá, Braz. 154/C2
Cerro de la Estrella, PN, Mex. 143/Q10
Cerro de las Campanas, PN, Mex. 143/E4
Cerro de Pasco, Peru 156/B3
Cerro de San Antonio, Col. 152/C2
Cerro El Copey, PN, Ven. 153/F2
Cerro Maggiore, It. 58/B1
Cerro Nanchital, Mex. 144/C2
Cerro Pinacate (peak), Mex. 128/D5
Cerros Colorados (res.), Arg. 157/C4
Cerros de Amotape, PN, Peru 156/A2
Certaldo, It. 59/E5
Certosa di Pavia, It. 58/C2
Certosa di Pisa, It. 58/D5
Cervantes, Austl. 112/B4
Cervaro (riv.), It. 48/B5
Cervati (peak), It. 46/D2
Cervellino (peak), It. 58/D3
Cervera, Sp. 45/F2
Cervera de Pisuerga, Sp. 44/C1
Cervera del Río Alhama, Sp. 44/E1
Cervia, It. 59/F4
Cervialto (peak), It. 46/D2
Cervignano del Friuli, It. 59/G1
Cervina (peak), It. 57/H4
Cervione, Fr. 46/A1
Cervo (riv.), It. 58/B2
Cervo, Sp. 44/B1
Cervo, It. 58/B5
Cervo, Serra do (hills), Braz. 211/G7
Cesano (riv.), It. 59/F6
Cesano Boscone, It. 58/C2
Cesano Maderno, It. 58/C1
César (riv.), Col. 141/G5
Cesar (prov.), Col. 145/H4
César (dept.), Col. 152/C2
Cesen (peak), It. 59/F1
Cesena, It. 59/F4
Cesenatico, It. 59/F4
Cēsis, Lat. 39/L3
České Budějovice, Czh. 55/H5
České Středohoří (mts.), Czh. 55/G2
Českomoravská Vysočina (mts.), Czh. 41/H4
Český Brod, Czh. 55/H2
Český Krumlov, Czh. 55/H5
Český Les Sumava (mts.), Czh. 55/F3
Česma (riv.), Cro. 48/C3
Çeşme, Turk. 47/K3
Cesson, Fr. 30/K6
Cesson-Sévigné, Fr. 42/C2
Cestos (riv.), Libr. 102/C5
Cetinje, Serb. 47/F1
Çetinkaya, Turk. 90/D2
Ceurda del Pozo, Embalse de la (res.), Sp. 44/D2
Ceuta, Sp. 100/B2
Ceva, It. 58/B4
Cevedale (peak), It. 57/G5
Cévennes (mts.), Fr. 42/E4
Cevio, Swi. 57/E5
Ceyhan, Turk. 91/D1
Ceylânpınar, Turk. 90/E2
Ceylon (isl.), SrL. 67/H9
Ceyzériat, Fr. 56/B5
Cèze (riv.), Fr. 42/F4
Cha Da (cape), Viet. 78/E4
Chabás, Arg. 158/E2
Chabjuwardoo (bay), Austl. 112/B2
Chablé, Mex. 144/D2
Chacabuco, Arg. 158/E2
Chachani (peak), Peru 156/D5
Chachapoyas, Peru 156/B2
Chachoengsao, Thai. 78/C3
Chaclacayo, Peru 156/B3
Chaco (riv.), NM, US 128/F3
Chaco (mesa), NM, US 132/B3
Chaco Austral (plain), Arg. 157/D1
Chaco Boreal (plain), Par. 150/F8
Chaco Central (plain), Arg. 157/D1
Chaco, PN, Arg. 157/E2
Chacujal (ruin), Guat. 144/D3
Chad (lake), Niger 96/H5
Chad (ctry.) 97/J4
Chafarinas (isl.), Sp. 100/C2
Chagang-do (prov.), NKor. 73/D2
Chagda, Rus. 65/P4
Chaghcharān, Afg. 87/E6
Chagny, Fr. 42/F3
Chagos (arch.), BIOT, UK 67/G10
Chaguanas, Trin. 153/F2
Chaguarpamba, Ecu. 156/B1
Chahuites, Mex. 144/C2
Chaibāsā, India 85/E4
Chailly-en-Brie, Fr. 30/M5
Chain, SKor. 73/E5
Chainat, Thai. 78/C3
Chaîne Annamitique (mts.), Laos 83/H4
Chaine de la Selle (peak), Haiti 145/J2
Chaîne de l'Atacora (mts.), Ben. 103/F4
Chaitén, Chile 157/B5
Chaiyaphum, Thai. 78/C3
Chākdaha, India 85/G4
Chake Chake, Tanz. 104/C4
Chākia, India 84/D3
Chakradharpur, India 85/E4
Chakrāta, India 86/D4
Chakwāl, Pak. 86/B3
Chala, Peru 156/C4
Chalain (lake), Fr. 56/B4
Chalais, Swi. 56/D5
Chālakudi, India 82/C5
Chalaronne (riv.), Fr. 56/A5
Chalatenango, ESal. 144/D3
Chalbi (des.), Kenya 97/N7
Chalchihuites, Mex. 142/E4
Chalco, Mex. 143/R10
Chale (pt.), Kenya 104/C4
Chaleur (bay), NB,Qu, Can. 131/H2
Chalfont, Pa, US 138/C3
Chalfont Saint Giles, Eng, UK 30/B2
Chalfont Saint Peter, Eng, UK 30/B2
Chalhuanca, Peru 156/C4
Chalifert (canal), Fr. 30/L5
Chalindrey, Fr. 56/B2
Chalk (mts.), Tx, US 132/C4
Chalkyitsik, Ak, US 134/K2
Challans, Fr. 42/C3
Challapata, Bol. 150/E7
Challenger (mts.), Nun., Can. 123/T6
Chalmette, La, US 137/Q17
Chālna Port, Bang. 85/G4
Chalon-sur-Saône, Fr. 56/A4
Châlons-sur-Marne, Fr. 53/D6
Châlonvillars, Fr. 56/C2
Chālūs, Iran 88/F1
Cham, Ger. 55/F4
Cham (riv.), Ger. 55/F4
Cham, Swi. 57/E3
Chama, Zam. 104/B5
Chama (riv.), NM, US 128/F3
Chamah (peak), Malay. 80/B2
Chaman, Pak. 89/J2
Chamba, India 86/D3
Chambal (riv.), India 89/L3
Chambaran, Plateau de (plat.), Fr. 42/F4
Chambas, Cuba 145/G1
Chamberlain (lake), Me, US 131/G2
Chamberlin (mt.),]Ak, US 134/K2
Chambersburg, Pa, US 130/E4
Chambéry, Fr. 42/F4
Chambeshi (riv.), Zam. 105/F3
Chambly, Qu, Can. 131/P7
Chambly, Fr. 30/J4
Chambourcy, Fr. 30/J5
Chambry, Fr. 30/L5
Chamchamāl, Iraq 88/D1
Chamechaude (peak), Fr. 42/F4
Chamical, Arg. 157/C3
Chamigny, Fr. 30/M5
Chamizal Nat'l Mem., Tx, US 132/B4
Chamizo, Uru. 159/L11
Chamonix-Mont-Blanc, Fr. 56/C6
Champagne, Yk, Can. 134/L3
Champagne (reg.), Fr. 40/C4
Champagne-Ardenne (pol. reg), Fr. 42/F2
Champagne-sur-Oise, Fr. 30/J4
Champagney, Fr. 56/C2
Champagnole, Fr. 56/B4
Champasak, Laos 78/D3
Champawat, India 84/C1
Champdeuil, Fr. 30/L6
Champeaux, Fr. 30/L6
Champéry, Swi. 56/C5
Champigneulles, Fr. 53/F6
Champigny-sur-Marne, Fr. 30/K5
Champlain (lake), NY,Vt, US 125/M3
Champlitte, Fr. 56/B2
Champotón, Mex. 144/D2
Champotón (riv.), Mex. 144/D2
Champs-sur-Marne, Fr. 30/K5
Champsevraine, Fr. 56/B2
Champvans, Fr. 56/B3
Chamusca, Port. 44/A3
Chan Chan (ruin), Peru 156/B3
Chan May Dong (cape), Viet. 78/E2
Chañaral, Chile 157/B2
Chança (riv.), Port. 44/B4
Chancay, Peru 156/B3
Chanco, Chile 158/B2
Chancy, Swi. 56/B5
Chandalar, Ak, US 134/J2
Chandalar (riv.), Ak, US 134/J2
Chandalar, East Fork (riv.), Ak, US 134/J2
Chandannagar, India 85/G4
Chandausi, India 84/B1
Chanderi, India 84/B3
Chandīgarh, India 86/D4
Chandīgarh (state), India 86/D4
Chandlees (riv.), Braz. 150/D6
Chandler (riv.), Ak, US 134/H2
Chandler, Ok, US 132/D3
Chandler, Qu, Can. 131/H1
Chandler, Az, US 137/S19
Chandolin, Swi. 56/D5
Chāndpur, Bang. 85/H4
Chāndpur, India 84/B1
Chandrapur, India 82/C4
Chanduy, Ecu. 152/A5
Chang (riv.), China 67/L6
Chang (lake), China 72/C5
Changan, SKor. 73/E5
Changbai (peak), China 73/E2
Changbai Chaoxianzu Zizhixian, China 73/E2
Changchun, China 71/N3
Changdang (lake), China 72/D5
Changdao, China 72/E3
Changde, China 79/B2
Changé, Fr. 42/D3
Changewater, NJ, US 138/D2
Changfeng, China 72/D4
Changge, China 72/C4
Changgi-ap (cape), SKor. 74/A2
Changhai, China 73/B3
Changhang, SKor. 73/D4
Changhowŏn, SKor. 73/D4
Changhua, Tai. 79/D3
Changhŭng, SKor. 73/D5
Changis-sur-Marne, Fr. 30/M5
Changji, China 70/E3
Changjiang, China 83/J4
Changjin (res.), NKor. 73/D2
Changjin (lake), NKor. 73/D2
Changle, China 72/D3
Changli, China 72/D3
Changling, China 72/E1
Changning, China 83/H2
Changning, China 83/G3
Ch'angnyŏng, SKor. 73/E5
Changping, China 72/H6
Changqing, China 72/D3
Changsan-got (cape), NKor. 73/C3
Changsha, China 83/K2
Changshou, China 79/A2
Changshu, China 72/L8
Changshun, China 83/J2
Changsŏng, SKor. 73/D5
Changsu, SKor. 73/D5
Changsŭngp'o, SKor. 73/E5
Changtai, China 79/C3
Changtu, China 72/F2
Changuinola, Pan. 145/F4
Ch'angwŏn, SKor. 73/E5
Changxing, China 72/K8
Changyang, China 79/B1
Changyi, China 72/D3
Changyŏn, NKor. 73/C3
Changyuan, China 72/C4
Changzhi, China 72/C3
Changzhou, China 72/K8
Chañi, Nevado de (peak), Arg. 157/C1
Chanlers (falls), Kenya 104/C2
Channel (isls.), UK 27/D4
Channel Country (phys. reg.), Austl. 109/C3
Channel Islands NP, Ca, US 128/C4
Channel-Port aux Basques, Nf, Can. 131/K2
Channel Tunnel, Eng, Fr.,UK 33/H5
Channing, Tx, US 129/G4
Chantada, Sp. 44/B1
Chanteloup-les-Vignes, Fr. 30/J5
Chanthaburi, Thai. 78/C3
Chantilly, Fr. 52/B5
Chantraine, Fr. 56/C1
Chantrey (inlet), Nun., Can. 122/G2
Chao (lake), China 72/D5
Chao Phraya (riv.), Thai. 78/C3
Chaoyang, China 79/C3
Chaoyang, China 72/E2
Chapacura, Bol. 156/D3
Chapada Diamantina, PN, Braz. 151/K6
Chapada dos Veadeiros, PN da, Braz. 151/J6
Chapadinha, Braz. 154/B1
Chapais, Qu, Can. 130/F1
Chapala (lake), Mex. 142/E4
Chapala, Mex. 142/E4
Chaparral, Col. 152/C4
Chaparrosa, Mex. 142/E4
Chapayevsk, Rus. 63/J1
Chapel Hill, NC, US 133/J3

179
Chape – Chüy

Chapel Ness (pt.), Sc, UK 36/D4
Chapelfell Top (peak), Eng, UK 35/F2
Chapelle-lez-Herlaimont, Belg. 53/D3
Chapeltown, Eng, UK 35/G5
Chaplain (lake), Wa, US 135/D2
Chapleau, On, Can. 130/D2
Chaplin, Sk, Can. 126/G3
Chāpra, India 85/E3
Char (well), Mrta. 98/B5
Chara (riv.), Rus. 65/M4
Charambirá (pt.), Col. 152/B3
Charaña, Bol. 156/D5
Charandra (riv.), Gre. 47/N8
Charata, Arg. 157/D2
Charcas, Mex. 143/E4
Charcot (isl.), Ant. 160/U
Chardonnière, Haiti 145/H2
Charente (riv.), Fr. 42/C4
Chari (riv.), Chad 93/D3
Chārīkār, Afg. 89/J1
Chariton (riv.), Ia,Mo, US 129/J2
Charity, Guy. 153/G3
Chärjew, Trkm. 87/D5
Charkhāri, India 84/B3
Charkhi Dādri, India 86/D5
Charlemagne, Qu, Can. 131/P6
Charlemont, NI, UK 34/B3
Charleroi, Belg. 53/D3
Charleroi à Bruxelles, Canal de (canal), Belg. 53/D2
Charles (peak), Austl. 112/D5
Charles (mt.), Austl. 112/C3
Charles (isl.), Nu, Can. 123/J2
Charles City, Ia, US 127/K5
Charles de Gaulle (int'l arpt.), Fr. 30/K4
Charleston, Ms, US 129/K4
Charleston, Wv, US 126/E5
Charleston, SC, US 133/J3
Charleston, Ut, US 137/L13
Charleston (cap.), WV, US 130/D4
Charlestown, StK. 141/N8
Charlestown, Md, US 138/C4
Charleville, Austl. 114/B4
Charleville-Mézières, Fr. 53/D4
Charlevoix, Mi, US 130/C2
Charlotte (lake), BC, Can. 126/B2
Charlotte, Mi, US 130/C3
Charlotte, NC, US 133/H3
Charlotte Amalie, USVI 141/M8
Charlotte/Douglas (int'l arpt.), NC, US 133/H3
Charlottenberg, Swe. 38/E2
Charlottenburg, Ger. 40/Q6
Charlottetown (cap.), PE, Can. 131/J2
Charlton, Austl. 115/B3
Charlton (isl.), Nu, Can. 123/H3
Charlton Kings, Eng, UK 32/D3
Charly, Fr. 52/C6
Charmes (res.), Fr. 56/B2
Charmes, Fr. 56/C1
Charmey, Swi. 56/D4
Charnay-lès-Mâcon, Fr. 42/F3
Charny, Fr. 30/L5
Charny-sur-Meuse, Fr. 53/E5
Charolais, Monts du (mts.), Fr. 42/F3
Charouine, Alg. 99/E3
Charquemont, Fr. 56/C3
Chars, Fr. 30/H4
Chārsadda, Pak. 86/A2
Charters Towers, Austl. 114/B3
Charthawāl, India 86/D5
Chartres, Fr. 42/D2
Chās, India 85/F4
Chaschauna (peak), Swi. 57/G4
Chascomús, Arg. 158/F2
Chase, BC, Can. 126/D3
Chasŏng, NKor. 73/D2
Chassezac (riv.), Fr. 42/F4
Chastre-Villeroux-Blanmont, Belg. 53/D2
Chatanika, Ak, US 134/J2
Château Bougon (int'l arpt.), Fr. 42/C3
Chateau de Versailles, Fr. 30/J5
Château-d'Olonne, Fr. 42/C3
Château-du-Loir, Fr. 42/D3
Château-Porcien, Fr. 53/D4
Château-Renault, Fr. 42/D3
Château-Salins, Fr. 53/F6
Château-Thierry, Fr. 52/C5
Châteaubriant, Fr. 42/C3
Châteaudun, Fr. 42/D2
Châteauguay, Qu, Can. 131/N7
Châteauneuf-sur-Charente, Fr. 42/C4
Châteaurenard, Fr. 42/F5
Châteauroux, Fr. 42/D3
Châteauvillain, Fr. 56/A1
Châtel-Saint-Denis, Swi. 56/C4
Châtelaillon-Plage, Fr. 42/C3
Châtelet, Belg. 53/D3
Châtellerault, Fr. 42/D3
Châtenay-Malabry, Fr. 30/J5
Châtenois, Fr. 56/B1
Châtenois-les-Forges, Fr. 56/C2
Chatfield (res.), Co, US 137/B3
Chatham (isls.), Chile 159/B6
Chatham, On, Can. 130/D3
Chatham, Eng, UK 33/G4
Chatham, NJ, US 139/H9
Châtillon, It. 43/G4
Châtillon, Fr. 30/J5
Châtillon-sur-Chalaronne, Fr. 56/A5
Châtillon-sur-Marne, Fr. 52/C5
Châtillon-sur-Seine, Fr. 42/F3
Chatkal (riv.), Kyr. 87/F4
Chatou, Fr. 30/J5
Chatra, India 85/E3
Chatrapur, India 82/E4
Châtres, Fr. 30/L5
Chatsworth (res.), Ca, US 136/B2
Chatsworth, NJ, US 138/D4
Chattahoochee (riv.),US 133/G4
Chattahoochee, Fl, US 133/G4
Chattanooga, Tn, US 133/G3
Chatteris, Eng, UK 33/G2
Chau Doc, Viet. 78/D4
Chaucey, Îles (isls.), Fr. 42/C2
Chauconin-Neufmontiers, Fr. 30/L5
Chaudfontaine, Belg. 53/E2
Chaudière (riv.), Qu, Can. 131/G2
Chauk, Myan. 83/F3
Chaukan (pass), India 83/G2
Chaumes-en-Brie, Fr. 30/L5
Chaumont, Fr. 56/B1
Chaumont-en-Vexin, Fr. 52/A5
Chaunskaya (bay), Rus. 65/T3
Chauny, Fr. 52/C4
Chaussin, Fr. 56/B4
Chaussy, Fr. 30/H4
Chautauqua (lake), NY, US 130/E3
Chautauqua, Il, US 137/G8
Chauvigny, Fr. 42/D3
Chaval, Braz. 154/B1
Chavanoz, Fr. 56/B6
Chaves, Port. 44/B2
Chavín de Huantar (ruin), Peru 156/B3
Chaviña, Peru 156/C4
Chavinillo, Peru 156/B3
Chavornay, Swi. 56/C4
Chawinda, Pak. 86/C3
Chay (riv.), Viet. 78/D1
Chayana (riv.), Bol. 150/E7
Chaykovskiy, Rus. 61/M4
Chazuta, Peru 156/B2
Cheadle, Eng, UK 35/G6
Cheaha (mtn.), Al, US 133/G3
Cheb, Czh. 55/F2
Cheboksary, Rus. 61/K4
Cheboksary (res.), Rus. 61/K4
Cheboygan, Mi, US 130/C2
Chechaouene, Mor. 100/B2
Chechaouene (prov.), Mor. 100/B2
Chechen' (isl.), Rus. 63/H3
Chechnya, Resp., Rus. 64/Q6
Chech'ŏn, SKor. 73/E4
Checotah, Ok, US 129/J4
Chedabucto (bay), NS, Can. 131/J2
Cheduba (isl.), Myan. 83/F4
Cheektowaga, NY, US 131/S10
Cheepash (riv.), On, Can. 130/D1
Cheepay (riv.), On, Can. 130/D1
Chefornak, Ak, US 134/F3
Chegutu, Zim. 105/F4
Chehalis, Wa, US 126/C4
Cheïkh (well), Alg. 99/F3
Cheju, SKor. 71/N5
Cheju (str.), SKor. 71/N5
Cheju (isl.), SKor. 71/N5
Cheka (peak), Rus. 87/C2
Chelan, Wa, US 126/C4
Chelan (lake), Wa, US 126/C4
Chelghoum El Aïd, Alg. 100/J4
Chelles, Fr. 30/K5
Chełm, Pol. 41/M3
Chełmno, Pol. 41/K2
Chelmsford, Eng, UK 33/G3
Chełmża, Pol. 41/K2
Cheltenham, Eng, UK 32/D3
Chelva, Sp. 45/E3
Chelyabinsk (int'l arpt.), Rus. 61/P5
Chelyabinsk, Rus. 61/P5
Chelyabinskaya Oblast, Rus. 87/D2
Chelyuskina (cape), Rus. 65/L2
Chemaïa, Mor. 98/C2
Chemax, Mex. 144/E1
Chemnitz, Ger. 40/G3
Chen (riv.), China 79/A2
Chena Hot Springs, Ak, US 134/J2
Chenāb (riv.), Pak. 89/K2
Chenachane (well), Alg. 98/D4
Cheney, Wa, US 126/D4
Cheng'anpu, China 72/C3
Chengbu Miaozu Zizhixian, China 83/K2
Chengde, China 72/D2
Chengdu, China 70/H5
Chengkou, China 70/J5
Chengmai, China 83/J4
Chengshan Jiao (cape), China 73/B4
Chengwu, China 72/C4
Cheniménil, Fr. 56/C1
Chennai (Madras), India 82/D5
Chennevières-lès-Louvres, Fr. 30/K4
Chenòve, Fr. 56/A3
Chenxi, China 83/K2
Chenzhou, China 83/K2
Chep Lak Kok (int'l arpt.), China 71/T10
Chepelare, Bul. 47/J2
Chepén, Peru 156/B2
Chepes, Arg. 157/C3
Chépica, Chile 158/C2
Chepigana, Pan. 152/B2
Chepo, Pan. 152/B2
Chepstow, Wal, UK 32/D3
Cheptsa (riv.), Rus. 61/M4
Cher (riv.), Fr. 42/E3
Chéran (riv.), Fr. 56/C6
Cherasco, It. 58/A3
Cherāt, Pak. 86/A3
Cherbourg, Fr. 42/C2
Cherbourg, Austl. 114/C4
Cherchell, Alg. 100/G4
Cherepovets, Rus. 60/H4
Cherf, Oued (riv.), Alg. 100/K6
Cheria, Alg. 100/K7
Cherkas'ka Oblasti, Ukr. 62/D2
Cherkasy, Ukr. 62/E2
Cherkessk, Rus. 63/G3
Chermignon, Swi. 56/D5
Chernaya (riv.), Rus. 61/N1
Cherni Lom (riv.), Bul. 49/H4
Cherni Vrŭkh (peak), Bul. 47/H1
Chernihiv, Ukr. 62/D2
Chernihivs'ka Oblasti, Ukr. 62/D2
Chernivets'ka Oblasti, Ukr. 62/C2
Chernivtsi, Ukr. 49/G1
Chernushka, Rus. 61/N4
Cherokee, Ok, US 129/H3
Cherry Creek (dam), Co, US 137/C3
Cherry Creek (lake), Co, US 137/C3
Cherry Hill, Md, US 138/C4
Cherry Hill, NJ, US 138/C4
Cherry Valley, Ca, US 136/D3
Cherski (range), Rus. 67/P3
Chertsey, Eng, UK 30/B2
Cherven Bryag, Bul. 49/G4
Chervonohrad, Ukr. 62/C2
Cherwell (riv.), Eng, UK 33/E3
Chesaning, Mi, US 130/C3
Chesapeake (bay), US 130/E4
Chesapeake and Delaware (canal), De,Md, US 138/C4
Chesapeake Bay Maritime Museum, Md, US 138/B6
Chesapeake City, Md, US 138/C4
Chesham, Eng, UK 33/F3
Cheshire (co.), Eng, UK 35/F5
Cheshire (plain), Eng, UK 35/F5
Cheshskaya (bay), Rus. 64/E3
Cheshunt, Eng, UK 30/C1
Chesilhurst, NJ, US 138/D4
Chester, Eng, UK 35/F5
Chester, Ca, US 126/C5
Chester (riv.), Md, US 138/B5
Chester, Mt, US 126/F3
Chester, NJ, US 138/D2
Chester, Pa, US 138/C4
Chester (co.), Pa, US 138/C4
Chester, SC, US 133/H3
Chester Heights, Pa, US 138/C4
Chester-le-Street, Eng, UK 35/G2
Chester Morse (lake), Wa, US 135/D3
Chesterfield, Eng, UK 35/G5
Chesterfield, Mo, US 137/F8
Chesterfield (isls.), NCal. 116/E6
Chesterfield (inlet), Nun., Can. 122/G2
Chesterfield Inlet, Nun., Can. 122/G2
Chesterfield, Nosy (isl.), Madg. 107/G7
Chesterton (range), Austl. 114/B4
Chestertown, Md, US 138/B5
Chesuncook (lake), Me, US 131/G2
Cheswold, De, US 138/C5
Chetumal (bay), Mex. 140/D4
Chetumal, Mex. 144/D2
Chetwynd, BC, Can. 126/C2
Cheung Chau (isl.), China 71/T11
Chevak, Ak, US 134/E3
Cheval Blanc (pt.), Haiti 145/H2
Chevigny-Saint-Sauveur, Fr. 56/B3
Cheviot (hills), Sc, UK 36/D6
Cheviot, The (peak), Eng, UK 36/D6
Chevreuse, Fr. 30/J5
Chevry-Cossigny, Fr. 30/K5
Chew (riv.), Eng, UK 32/D4
Chew Valley (lake), Eng, UK 32/D4
Chewelah, Wa, US 126/D3
Chexbres, Swi. 56/C5
Cheyenne (riv.), SD,Wy, US 127/H5
Cheyenne (cap.), Wy, US 127/G5
Cheyenne, Ok, US 129/H4
Cheyenne Wells, Co, US 129/G3
Cheyres, Swi. 56/C4
Chhabra, India 84/A3
Chhaprauli, India 86/D5
Chhāta, India 84/A2
Chhatarpur, India 84/B3
Chhattisgarh (state), India 82/D3
Chhibrāmau, India 84/B2
Chhindwāra, India 84/B4
Chi (riv.), Thai. 83/H4
Chiai, Tai. 79/D3
Ch'iak-san NP, SKor. 73/E4
Chiampo, It. 59/E1
Chianciano Terme, It. 43/J5
Chiang Kai Shek (int'l arpt.), Tai. 79/D2
Chiang Mai, Thai. 83/G4
Chiang Rai, Thai. 83/G4
Chianti (reg.), It. 59/E5
Chianti, Monti del (mts.), It. 59/E5
Chiapa de Corzo, Mex. 144/C2
Chiapas (state), Mex. 140/C4
Chiappa (pt.), It. 58/C4
Chiaravalle, It. 59/G5
Chiari, It. 58/C1
Chiasso, Swi. 57/F6
Chiat'ura, Geo. 63/G4
Chiautempan, Mex. 143/L7
Chiautla, Mex. 143/R9
Chiautla de Tapia, Mex. 144/B2
Chiavari, It. 58/C4
Chiavenna, It. 57/F5
Chiba, Japan 75/G3
Chibougamau, Qu, Can. 130/F1
Chibougamau (riv.), Qu, Can. 130/F1
Chibougamau (lake), Qu, Can. 130/F1
Chibukak (pt.), Ak, US 134/D3
Chibuto, Moz. 105/F5
Chicago, Il, US 127/M5
Chicago Heights, Il, US 135/Q16
Chicago Midway (int'l arpt.), Il, US 129/L2
Chicago, North Branch (riv.), Il, US 135/Q15
Chicago-O'Hare (int'l arpt.), Il, US 127/M5
Chicago Ridge, Il, US 135/Q16
Chicago Sanitary and Ship Canal, Il, US 135/P16
Chicama, Peru 156/B2
Chichagof (isl.), Ak, US 122/C3
Chichaoua, Mor. 98/C3
Chīchāwatni, Pak. 86/B4
Chichén Itzá (ruin), Mex. 144/D1
Chicheng, China 71/L3
Chichester (range), Austl. 109/A3
Chichester, Eng, UK 33/F5
Chichibu, Japan 75/F3
Chichicastenango, Guat. 144/D3
Chichigalpa, Nic. 144/E3
Chichihualco, Mex. 143/F5
Chichiriviche, Ven. 152/D2
Chichishima (isls.), Japan 116/D2
Chickaloon, Ak, US 134/J3
Chickamauga (lake), Tn, US 133/G3
Chickasaw Nat'l Rec. Area, Ok, US 129/H4
Chickasha, Ok, US 129/H4
Chicla, Peru 156/B3
Chiclana de la Frontera, Sp. 44/B4
Chiclayo, Peru 156/B2
Chico, Ca, US 128/B3
Chico (riv.), Arg. 147/B7
Chicoloapan, Mex. 143/R10
Chicomostoc (ruin), Mex. 142/E4
Chicomuselo, Mex. 144/C3
Chiconcuac, Mex. 143/R9
Chicontepec de Tejeda, Mex. 144/B1
Chicopee, Ma, US 131/F3
Chicoutimi, Qu, Can. 131/G1
Chicualacuala, Moz. 105/F5
Chidley (cape), Nf, Can. 123/K2
Chido, SKor. 73/D5
Chiefland, Fl, US 133/H4
Chiemsee (lake), Ger. 43/K3
Chieo Lan (res.), Thai. 83/G6
Chieri, It. 58/A2
Chierry, Fr. 52/C5
Chiers (riv.), Fr. 53/E5
Chiesa in Valmalenco, It. 57/F5
Chiese (riv.), It. 43/J3
Chieti, It. 46/D1
Chietla, Mex. 143/L8
Chièvres, Belg. 52/C2
Chifeng, China 71/L3
Chifre, Serra do (mts.), Braz. 151/K7
Chigasaki, Japan 75/F3
Chiginagak (mt.), Ak, US 134/G4
Chignahuapan, Mex. 143/L7
Chignecto (bay), NB,NS, Can. 131/H2
Chignik, Ak, US 134/G4
Chignik Lake, Ak, US 134/G4
Chigorodó, Col. 152/B3
Chigu (lake), China 85/H1
Chigwell, Eng, UK 30/D2
Chihayaakasaka, Japan 77/J7
Chihli (Bo Hai) (gulf), China 72/D3
Chihuahua, Mex. 132/B4
Chihuahua (state), Mex. 142/D2
Chikaskia (riv.), Ks,Ok, US 129/H3
Chikballāpur, India 82/C5
Chikhli, India 89/L4
Chikmagalūr, India 89/L6
Chikoy (riv.), Rus. 65/L5
Chikugo (riv.), Japan 74/B4
Chikuma (riv.), Japan 75/F2
Chilac, Mex. 143/M8
Chilaw, SrL. 82/C6
Chilbo-san (peak), NKor. 73/E2
Chilca, Peru 156/B4
Chilcotin (riv.), BC, Can. 122/D3
Childers, Austl. 114/D4
Childersburg, Al, US 133/G3
Childress, Tx, US 129/G4
Chile (ctry.) 157/B3
Chile Chico, Chile 158/C5
Chile, Monte el (peak), Hon. 144/E3
Chilecito, Arg. 157/C2
Chilete, Peru 156/B2
Ch'ilgap-san NP, SKor. 73/D4
Chililabombwe, Zam. 105/E3
Chilka (lake), India 82/E4
Chilko (lake), BC, Can. 122/D3
Chilkoot (pass), Can.,US 134/L4
Chilkoot (pass), Ak, US 134/L3
Chilla Well Abor. Land, Austl. 113/F2
Chillán, Chile 158/B3
Chillanes, Ecu. 156/B1
Chillicothe, Il, US 127/L5
Chilliwack, BC, Can. 126/C3
Chillon, Swi. 56/C5
Chilly-Mazarin, Fr. 30/J5
Chiloé (isl.), Chile 147/B7
Chiloé, PN, Chile 158/B4
Chiloquin, Or, US 126/C5
Chilpancingo de los Bravos, Mex. 143/F5
Chiltern (hills), Eng, UK 33/E3
Chiltern Hundreds (reg.), Eng, UK 30/A2
Chilung La (pass), India 86/D3
Chilwa (lake), Malw. 105/G4
Chimacum, Wa, US 135/B1
Chimalhuacán, Mex. 143/R10
Chimaliro (hill), Malw. 104/B5
Chimaltenango, Guat. 144/D3
Chimán, Pan. 152/B2
Chimanimani, Zim. 105/F4
Chimantá-Tepuí (peak), Ven. 153/F3
Chimay, Belg. 53/D3
Chimbay, Uzb. 87/C4
Chimborazo (dept.), Ecu. 152/B5
Chimborazo (vol.), Ecu. 152/B5
Chimbote, Peru 156/B3
Chimichaqua, Col. 152/C2
Chimoio, Moz. 105/F4
Chimtarga (peak), Taj. 87/E5
Chin (state), Myan. 70/F7
China, Mex. 143/F3
China, Mex. 144/D2
China (ctry.) 70/G4
Chinácota, Col. 152/C3
Chinan, SKor. 73/D5
Chinandega, Nic. 144/E3
Chinati (mts.), Tx, US 132/B4
Chincha Alta, Peru 156/B4
Chinchaga (riv.), Ab,BC, Can. 122/E3
Chinchilla, Sp. 44/E3
Chinchilla, Austl. 114/C4
Chinch'ŏn, SKor. 73/D4
Chinchón, Sp. 44/D2
Chincoteague, Va, US 130/F4
Chinde, Moz. 105/G4
Chindo, SKor. 73/D5
Chindrieux, Fr. 56/B6
Chindu, China 70/G4
Chindwin (riv.), Myan. 70/F7
Chingaza, PN, Col. 152/C3
Chingleput, India 82/C5
Chingola, Zam. 105/E3
Chinguetti, Dhar de (cliff), Mrta. 98/B5
Chinhae, SKor. 73/E5
Chinhoyi, Zim. 105/F4
Chiniak (cape), Ak, US 134/H4
Chiniot, Pak. 86/B4
Chinit (riv.), Camb. 78/D3
Chinju, SKor. 73/E5
Chinko (riv.), CAfr. 97/K6
Chinle, Az, US 128/E3
Chinnor, Eng, UK 33/F3
Chino, Japan 75/F3
Chino, Ca, US 136/C2
Chino (hills), Ca, US 136/G8
Chinook, Mt, US 126/F3
Chinsali, Zam. 104/B5
Chinú, Col. 152/C2
Chiny, Belg. 53/E4
Chinyŏng, SKor. 73/E5
Chioggia, It. 59/F2
Chipatá, Col. 152/C3
Chipata, Zam. 105/F3
Chiping, China 72/D3
Chipiona, Sp. 44/B4
Chipley, Fl, US 133/G4
Chiplūn, India 89/K5
Chippenham, Eng, UK 32/D4
Chippewa (co.), Wi, US 127/L4
Chippewa (riv.), Wi, US 127/L4
Chipping Ongar, Eng, UK 30/D1
Chiprovtsi, Bul. 48/F4
Chiputneticook (lakes), US,Can. 131/H2
Chiquián, Peru 156/B3
Chiquimula, Guat. 144/D3
Chiquimulilla, Guat. 144/D3
Chiquinquirá, Col. 150/D2
Chiquita (sea), Arg. 147/C6
Chirāla, India 82/D4
Chirāwa, India 86/C5
Chirchiq, Uzb. 87/E4
Chīrgaon, India 84/B3
Chiri-san (peak), SKor. 73/D5
Chiri-san NP, SKor. 73/D5
Chiricahua Nat'l Mon., Az, US 142/C1
Chiriguaná, Col. 152/C2
Chirikof (isl.), Ak, US 134/G4
Chirinos, Peru 156/B2
Chirip (peak), Rus. 76/E1
Chiripa (peak), Nic. 145/E4
Chiriquí (lag.), Pan. 145/F4
Chiriquí, Golfo de (gulf), Pan. 150/B2
Chirkunda, India 85/F4
Chirnside, Sc, UK 36/D5
Chironico, Swi. 57/E5
Chirpan, Bul. 47/J1
Chirripó (mtn.), CR 145/F4
Chirripó, PN, CR 140/E6
Chiryu, Japan 77/M6
Chisana, Ak, US 134/K3
Chisasibi (Fort-George), Qu, Can. 123/J3
Chisholm, Mn, US 130/A2
Chishtiān Mandi, Pak. 86/B5
Chisimba (falls), Zam. 104/A5
Chişinău (cap.), Mol. 49/J2
Chişinău (int'l arpt.), Mol. 49/J2
Chişineu Criş, Rom. 48/E2
Chistochina, Ak, US 134/K3
Chistopol', Rus. 61/L5
Chita, Col. 152/C3
Chita (bay), Japan 77/L6
Chita, Japan 77/L6
Chita (pen.), Japan 77/L6
Chitina, Ak, US 134/K3
Chitinskaya Oblast, Rus. 65/M4
Chitipa, Malw. 104/B5
Chitose (int'l arpt.), Japan 76/B2
Chitose, Japan 76/B2
Chitradurga, India 82/C5
Chitrakut, India 84/C3
Chitral Gol NP, Pak. 86/A2
Chitré, Pan. 152/A3
Chittagong (pol. div.), Bang. 85/H4
Chittagong, Bang. 83/F3
Chittaranjan, India 85/F4
Chittoor, India 82/C5
Chitungwiza, Zim. 105/F4
Chiuduno, It. 58/C1
Chiuppano, It. 59/E1
Chiusa di Pesio, It. 58/A4
Chiusella (riv.), It. 58/A1
Chiusi, It. 43/J5
Chivacoa, Ven. 152/D2
Chivasso, It. 58/A2
Chivato (pt.), Mex. 142/C3
Chivay, Peru 156/D4
Chivé, Bol. 156/D4
Chivhu, Zim. 105/F4
Chivilcoy, Arg. 158/E2
Chixoy (riv.), Guat. 144/D3
Chiyoda, Japan 77/C1
Chiyoda, Japan 77/E1
Chiyokawa, Japan 77/D1
Chizela, Zam. 105/E3
Chlef (riv.), Alg. 100/F4
Chlef (prov.), Alg. 100/F4
Chlef, Alg. 100/F4
Chlum (peak), Czh. 55/H5
Chno Dearg (peak), Sc, UK 36/B3
Ch'o (isl.), NKor. 73/C3
Cho Oyu (peak), Nepal 85/F1
Chobe NP, Bots. 105/D4
Chobham, Eng, UK 30/B3
Choceň, Czh. 41/J4
Choch'iwŏn, SKor. 73/D4
Chocianów, Pol. 41/H3
Chocó (dept.), Col. 145/G5
Chocolate (mts.), Ca, US 128/D4
Chocontá, Col. 152/C3
Chocope, Peru 156/B2
Choctaw, Ok, US 137/N15
Chodavaram, India 82/D4
Chodov, Czh. 55/F2
Chodzież, Pol. 41/J2
Choele Choel, Arg. 158/D3
Chōfu, Japan 75/F3
Choiseul (isl.), Sol. 116/E5
Choisy-au-Bac, Fr. 52/B5
Choisy-le-Roi, Fr. 30/K5
Choix, Mex. 142/C3
Chojna, Pol. 41/H2
Chojnice, Pol. 38/G5
Chojnów, Pol. 41/H3
Chokai-san (peak), Japan 76/B4
Choke Canyon (res.), Tx, US 132/D4
Chola (mts.), China 70/G5
Cholet, Fr. 42/C3
Cholila, Arg. 158/C4
Chŏlla-bukto (prov.), SKor. 73/D5
Ch'ŏlla-namdo (prov.), SKor. 73/D5
Cholula de Rivadabia, Mex. 143/L7
Choluteca (riv.), Hon. 140/D5
Choluteca, Hon. 144/E3
Choma, Zam. 105/E4
Chŏmch'on, SKor. 73/E4
Chomo Lhāri (peak), Bhu. 85/G2
Chomutov, Czh. 55/G2
Chomutovka (riv.), Czh. 55/G2
Chon Buri, Thai. 78/C3
Ch'ŏnan, SKor. 73/D4
Chōnan, Japan 77/E3
Chonchi, Chile 158/B4
Ch'ŏnch'ŏn, NKor. 73/D2
Chone, Ecu. 152/A5
Ch'ŏng-yang, SKor. 73/D4
Chong'an, China 79/C2
Ch'ŏngch'ŏn (riv.), NKor. 73/D2
Ch'ŏngdo, SKor. 73/E5
Ch'ŏngjin, NKor. 73/E2
Ch'ŏngjin -si (prov.), NKor. 73/E2
Chŏngju, SKor. 73/D5
Ch'ŏngju, SKor. 73/D4
Chŏngju, NKor. 73/C3
Chongli, China 72/C2
Chongmyo Shrine, SKor. 73/G6
Chongoyape, Peru 156/B2
Chŏngsŏn, SKor. 73/E4
Ch'ŏngsong, SKor. 74/A2
Chongyi, China 83/K2
Chongzuo, China 83/J3
Chŏnju, SKor. 73/D5
Ch'ŏnma-san (peak), SKor. 73/G6
Chonos, Archipiélago de los (arch.), Chile 158/B5
Chopan, India 84/D3
Chorcha (mtn.), Pan. 145/F4
Chorley, Eng, UK 35/F4
Chorleywood, Eng, UK 30/B2
Choroszcz, Pol. 41/M2
Chortkiv, Ukr. 62/C2
Ch'ŏrwŏn, SKor. 73/D4
Chorzele, Pol. 41/L2
Chorzów, Pol. 41/K3
Chos-Malal, Arg. 158/C3
Ch'osan, NKor. 73/C2
Chōsei, Japan 77/E3
Chōshi, Japan 75/G3
Choszczno, Pol. 41/H2
Chota, Peru 156/B2
Chota Nāgpur (plat.), India 82/D3
Choteau, Mt, US 126/E4
Chott el Rharbi (depr.), Alg. 100/D3
Chotýšanka (riv.), Czh. 55/H3
Chowagasberg (peak), Namb. 105/C6
Chowan (riv.), NC, US 133/J2
Choybalsan, Mong. 71/K2
Choyr, Mong. 70/J2
Chreïrik (well), Mrta. 98/B5
Christchurch (int'l arpt.), NZ 117/S11
Christchurch, NZ 117/S11
Christchurch (bay), Eng, UK 33/E5
Christchurch, Eng, UK 33/E5
Christian (sound), Ak, US 134/M4
Christiana, Jam. 145/G2
Christiana, SAfr. 106/D2
Christiana, De, US 138/C4
Christiana, Pa, US 138/C4
Christiansfeld, Den. 38/C4
Christiansted, USVI 141/M8
Christina (riv.), De, US 138/C5
Christmas (isl.), Austl. 67/K11
Chrudim, Czh. 41/H4
Chryston, Sc, UK 36/B5
Chrzanów, Pol. 41/K3
Chu Yang Sin (peak), Viet. 78/E3
Chuādanga, Bang. 85/G4
Chuansha, China 72/L8
Chuathbaluk, Ak, US 134/G3
Chubut (riv.), Arg. 147/C7
Chubut (prov.), Arg. 158/C4
Chucanti (peak), Pan. 152/B2
Chūgoku (mts.), Japan 74/C3
Chūgoku (prov.), Japan 74/B4
Chūhar Kāna, Pak. 86/B4
Chukai, Malay. 80/B3
Chukchi (sea), Rus. 67/T3
Chukchi (pen.), Rus. 67/T3
Chukotskiy Aut. Okrug, Rus. 65/S3
Chukotskiy (cape), Rus. 134/D3
Chula Vista, Ca, US 136/C5
Ch'ulp'o, SKor. 73/D5
Chulucanas, Peru 156/A2
Chulym (riv.), Rus. 64/J4
Chuma, Bol. 156/D4
Chumerna (peak), Bul. 47/J1
Chumphon, Thai. 78/B4
Chuna (riv.), Rus. 64/K4
Chunār, India 84/D3
Ch'unch'ŏn, SKor. 73/D4
Ch'ungch'ŏng-bukto (prov.), SKor. 73/D4
Ch'ungch'ŏng-namdo (prov.), SKor. 73/D4
Ch'ungju (lake), SKor. 74/A2
Ch'ungju, SKor. 73/D4
Ch'ungman (riv.), NKor. 73/C2
Ch'ungmu, SKor. 73/E5
Chŭngsan, NKor. 73/C3
Chunhuhub, Mex. 144/D2
Chūniān, Pak. 86/B4
Chunya, Tanz. 104/B5
Chunya (riv.), Rus. 65/L3
Ch'unyang, SKor. 73/E4
Chupa, Peru 156/D4
Chupaca, Peru 156/C4
Chuquibamba, Peru 156/C4
Chuquibambilla, Peru 156/C4
Chuquicamata, Chile 157/C1
Chur, Swi. 57/F4
Churachandpur, India 83/F3
Churcampa, Peru 156/C4
Church, Eng, UK 35/F4
Church Hill, Md, US 138/C5
Churchill, Austl. 115/C3
Churchill (peak), BC, Can. 122/D3
Churchill, Mb, Can. 122/G3
Churchill (cape), Mb, Can. 122/G3
Churchill (riv.), Mb,Sk, Can. 122/F3
Churchill (lake), Sk, Can. 122/F3
Churchill Falls, Nf, Can. 123/K3
Churchill NP, Austl. 115/G5
Churchville, Md, US 138/B4
Churia Ghats (mts.), Nepal 85/E2
Churín, Peru 156/B3
Churnet (riv.), Eng, UK 35/G5
Churu, India 86/C5
Churuguara, Ven. 152/D2
Churumuco de Morelos, Mex. 143/E5
Churwalden, Swi. 57/F4
Chuschi, Peru 156/C4
Chuska (mts.), Az,NM, US 128/E3
Chusovaya (riv.), Rus. 61/N4
Chusovoy, Rus. 61/N4
Chutung, Tai. 79/D3
Chuvashiya, Resp., Rus. 64/Q6
Chuwang-san NP, SKor. 74/A2
Chuxiong, China 83/H2
Chüy (obl.), Kyr. 87/F4

180
Chuzh – Congu

Chuzhou, China 71/L5
Chūzu, Japan 77/K5
Ci Xian, China 72/C3
Ciadîr-Lunga, Mol. 49/J2
Ciamis, Indo. 80/C5
Ciampino (int'l arpt.), It. 46/C2
Ciampino, It. 46/C2
Cianjur, Indo. 80/C5
Cibolo, Tx, US 137/U20
Cicagna, It. 58/C4
Cicero, Il, US 130/C3
Cícero Dantas, Braz. 154/C3
Ćićevac, Serb. 48/E4
Cide, Turk. 90/C1
Ciechanów, Pol. 41/L2
Ciechocinek, Pol. 41/K2
Ciego de Ávila, Cuba 145/G1
Ciénaga, Col. 152/C2
Ciénaga de Oro, Col. 152/C2
Cienfuegos, Cuba 145/F1
Cieplice Śląskie Zdrój, Pol. 41/H3
Cieszyn, Pol. 41/K4
Cieza, Sp. 44/E3
Çifteler, Turk. 90/B2
Cifuentes, Sp. 44/D2
Cifuentes, Cuba 145/F1
Cigánd, Hun. 41/L4
Cigliano, It. 58/B2
Cigüela (riv.), Sp. 44/D3
Cihanbeyli, Turk. 90/C2
Cihuatlán, Mex. 142/D5
Cijara, Embalse de (res.), Sp. 44/C3
Cijulang, Indo. 80/C5
Cilacap, Indo. 80/C5
Cilavegna, It. 58/B2
Çıldır (lake), Turk. 90/E1
Cilfaesty (peak), Wal, UK 32/C2
Cili, China 79/B2
Cilleros, Sp. 44/B2
Cima della Laurasca (peak), It. 57/E5
Cima de'Piazzi (peak), It. 57/G5
Cima la Casina (peak), It. 57/G4
Cimarron (range), NM, US 132/B2
Cimarron (riv.), Ks,Ok, US 124/G4
Cime du Cheiron (peak), Fr. 43/G5
Cime du Diable (peak), Fr. 43/G4
Cimone (peak), It. 59/D4
Cîmpeni, Rom. 49/F2
Cîmpia Turzii, Rom. 49/F2
Cîmpina, Rom. 49/G3
Cîmpulung, Rom. 49/G3
Cîmpulung Moldovenesc, Rom. 49/G2
Çınar, Turk. 90/E2
Çınarcık, Turk. 49/J5
Cinaruco (riv.), Ven. 152/D3
Cinca (riv.), Sp. 45/F1
Cincar (peak), Bosn. 48/C4
Cincinnati, Oh, US 130/C4
Cinco Saltos, Arg. 158/C3
Cîndrelu (peak), Rom. 49/F3
Çine, Turk. 90/B2
Ciney, Belg. 53/E3
Cingia de'Botti, It. 58/D2
Cingoli, It. 59/G6
Cinisello Balsamo, It. 58/C1
Cinnaminson, NJ, US 138/D4
Cintalapa de Figueroa, Mex. 144/C2
Cinto (peak), Fr. 46/A1
Cinto Caomaggiore, It. 59/F1
Cintruénigo, Sp. 44/E1
Čiovo (isl.), Cro. 48/C4
Cipó, Braz. 154/C3
Cipolletti, Arg. 158/D3
Circeo, PN del, It. 46/C2
Circle, Ak, US 134/K2
Circle, Mt, US 127/G4
Circle Hot Springs, Ak, US 134/K2
Cirebon, Indo. 80/C5
Cirencester, Eng, UK 32/E3
Cires-lès-Mello, Fr. 52/B5
Cirò Marina, It. 47/E3
Ciron (riv.), Fr. 42/C4
Ciserano, It. 58/C1
Cisnădie, Rom. 49/G3
Cisneros, Col. 152/C3
Cisnes (riv.), Chile 158/B5
Cisse (riv.), Fr. 42/D3
Cisterna di Latina, It. 46/C2
Cistierna, Sp. 44/C1
Citlaltépetl (vol.),Mex. 143/M7
Citrus Heights, Ca, US 128/B3
Citrusdal, SAfr. 106/L10
Città del Vaticano (Vatican City) (cap.), VatC. 46/C2
Città di Castello, It. 59/F6
Citta di Torino (int'l arpt.), It. 43/G4
Cittadella, It. 59/E1
Cittanova, It. 46/E3
Cittiglio, It. 57/E6
City (isl.), NY, US 139/K8
City (int'l arpt.), NI, UK 34/C2
Ciudad Acuña, Mex. 129/G5
Ciudad Altamirano, Mex. 143/E5
Ciudad Bolívar, Ven. 153/F2
Ciudad Bolivia, Ven. 152/D2
Ciudad Camargo, Mex. 142/D3
Ciudad Constitución, Mex. 142/C3
Ciudad Cortés, CR 145/F4
Ciudad Cuauhtémoc, Mex. 144/B1
Ciudad de Dolores Hidalgo, Mex. 143/E4
Ciudad de México (Mexico) (cap.), Mex. 143/Q10
Ciudad de Nutrias, Ven. 152/D2
Ciudad de Río Grande, Mex. 142/E4
Ciudad del Carmen, Mex. 144/D2
Ciudad del Maíz, Mex. 143/F4
Ciudad Delicias, Mex. 132/B4
Ciudad Fernández, Mex. 143/E4
Ciudad Frontera, Mex. 132/C5
Ciudad Guayana, Ven. 153/F2
Ciudad Guzmán, Mex. 142/E5
Ciudad Hidalgo, Mex. 143/E5
Ciudad Hidalgo, Mex. 144/C3
Ciudad Insurgentes, Mex. 142/C3
Ciudad Ixtepec, Mex. 144/C2
Ciudad Juárez, Mex. 128/F5
Ciudad Lerdo, Mex. 142/E3
Ciudad Madero, Mex. 144/B1
Ciudad Mante, Mex. 143/F4
Ciudad Mendoza, Mex. 143/M8
Ciudad Miguel Alemán, Mex. 132/D5
Ciudad Obregón, Mex. 142/C3
Ciudad Ojeda, Ven. 152/D2
Ciudad Pemex, Mex. 144/C2
Ciudad Piar, Ven. 153/F3
Ciudad, PN de la, Mex. 142/D4
Ciudad Real, Sp. 44/D3
Ciudad Rodrigo, Sp. 44/B2
Ciudad Serdán, Mex. 143/M8
Ciudad Valles, Mex. 144/B1
Ciudad Victoria, Mex. 143/F4
Ciutadella de Menorca, Sp. 45/G3
Civa Burnu (pt.), Turk. 90/D1
Civate, It. 58/C1
Civezzano, It. 57/H5
Cividale del Friuli, It. 43/K3
Cividate Camuno, It. 57/G6
Civita Castellana, It. 46/C1
Civitavecchia, It. 46/B1
Civray, Fr. 42/D3
Çivril, Turk. 90/B2
Cixi, China 72/L9
Cize, Fr. 56/B4
Cizre, Turk. 90/E2
Cizre (dam), Turk. 90/E2
Cizur, Sp. 44/E1
Clackmannan, Sc, UK 36/C4
Clackmannanshire (pol. reg.), Sc, UK 36/C4
Clarewen (res.), Wal, UK 32/C2
Claiborne, Md, US 138/B6
Clain (riv.), Fr. 42/D3
Clair Engle (lake), Ca, US 128/B2
Claire (lake), Ab, Can. 122/E3
Clairefontaine-en-Yvelines, Fr. 30/H6
Clairvaux-les-Lacs, Fr. 56/B4
Claise (riv.), Fr. 42/D3
Clallam (co.), Wa, US 135/A2
Clamart, Fr. 30/J5
Clamecy, Fr. 42/E3
Clane, Ire. 31/Q10
Clanton, Al, US 133/G3
Clanwilliam, SAfr. 106/B4
Clara (pt.), Arg. 158/D4
Clara, Ire. 31/Q10
Clare, Austl. 113/H5
Clare (isl.), Ire. 30/N10
Clare (riv.), Ire. 31/P10
Clare, Ks, US 137/D6
Clare, Mi, US 130/C3
Claremont, NH, US 131/F3
Claremont, Ca, US 136/C2
Claremore, Ok, US 129/J3
Claremorris, Ire. 31/P10
Clarence (pt.), Nun., Can. 123/T7
Clarence, NZ 117/S11
Clarence (riv.), NZ 117/S11
Clarence, NY, US 131/S9
Clarence Town, Bahm. 141/G3
Clarendon, Tx, US 129/G4
Clarenville, Nf, Can. 131/L1
Claresholm, Ab, Can. 126/E3
Clarion (isl.), Mex. 142/B5
Clark, SD, US 127/J4
Clark, NJ, US 139/H9
Clark Fork (riv.), Mt, US 126/E3
Clark Fork (riv.), Id, US 122/E4
Clarke (isl.), Austl. 115/D4
Clarke (lake), Pa, US 138/B4
Clarks Point, Ak, US 134/G4
Clarksburg, WV, US 130/D4
Clarksburg, NJ, US 138/D3
Clarksburg, Ca, US 135/L10
Clarksdale, Ms, US 129/K4
Clarkston, Wa, US 126/D4
Clarkston, Mi, US 135/F6
Clarksville, Ar, US 129/J4
Clarksville, Tn, US 130/C4
Clarksville, Tx, US 129/J4
Claro (riv.), Braz. 151/H7
Claro, Swi. 57/F5
Clatteringshaws Loch (lake), Sc, UK 34/D1
Claudy, NI, UK 34/A2
Clausen, Ger. 53/G5
Clausthal-Zellerfeld, Ger. 51/H5
Claveria, Phil. 79/D4
Clawson, Mi, US 135/F6
Clay (pt.), IM, UK 34/D3
Clay (co.), Mo, US 137/E5
Clay Center, Ks, US 129/H3
Clay Cross-North Wingfield, Eng, UK 35/G5
Claye-Souilly, Fr. 30/L5
Claymont, De, US 138/C4
Clayton, Ca, US 135/L11
Clayton, De, US 138/C5
Clayton, Ga, US 133/H3
Clayton, Mo, US 137/G8
Clayton, NJ, US 138/C4
Clayton, NM, US 129/G3
Clayton, Ok, US 132/E3
Clayton-le-Moors, Eng, UK 35/F4
Clear (lake), Ca, US 128/B3
Clear (hills), Ab, Can. 122/E3
Clear (cape), Ire. 31/P11
Clear Fork (riv.), Tx, US 143/E1
Clear Fork Brazos (riv.), Tx, US 129/H4
Clear Lake, SD, US 127/J4
Cleare (cape), Ak, US 134/J4
Clearfield, Ut, US 137/J11
Clearwater, BC, Can. 126/C3
Clearwater, Fl, US 133/H5
Clearwater (mts.), Id, US 124/C2
Clearwater (riv.), Mn, US 127/K4
Cleburne, Tx, US 129/H4
Cleethorpes, Eng, UK 35/H4
Cleeve (hill), Eng, UK 32/D3
Cleland Rec. Area, Austl. 113/M8
Clementon, NJ, US 138/D4
Clemson, SC, US 133/H3
Cleona, Pa, US 138/B3
Cleopatra Needle (peak), Phil. 81/E1
Clermont, Austl. 114/B3
Clermont, Fr. 52/B5
Clermont-en-Argonne, Fr. 53/E5
Clermont-Ferrand, Fr. 42/E4
Clerval, Fr. 56/C3
Clervaux, Lux. 53/F3
Cles, It. 57/H5
Cleve, Austl. 113/H5
Clevedon, Eng, UK 32/D4
Cleveland (cape), Austl. 114/B2
Cleveland (hills), Eng, UK 35/G3
Cleveland, Mo, US 137/D6
Cleveland, Ms, US 129/K4
Cleveland (mt.), Mt, US 126/E3
Cleveland, Oh, US 130/D3
Cleveland (co.), Ok, US 137/N15
Cleveland, Tn, US 133/G3
Cleveland, Tx, US 129/J5
Cleveland-Hopkins (int'l arpt.), Oh, US 130/D3
Cleveland National Forest, Ca, US 136/C3
Clevelândia, Braz. 155/A3
Clew (bay), Ire. 31/P10
Clewiston, Fl, US 133/H5
Clichy, Fr. 30/J5
Clichy-sous-Bois, Fr. 30/K5
Clifden, Ire. 30/F10
Cliffside Park, NJ, US 139/K8
Cliffwood, NJ, US 139/J10
Clifton, Az, US 128/E4
Clifton, NJ, US 139/J8
Clifton Beach, Austl. 114/B2
Clifton Forge, Va, US 133/J2
Clignon (riv.), Fr. 52/C5
Clingmans (peak), NC,Tn, US 133/H3
Clinton, BC, Can. 126/C3
Clinton, Ct, US 139/F1
Clinton, Ia, US 127/L5
Clinton, La, US 129/K5
Clinton, Mi, US 135/G6
Clinton (riv.), Mi, US 135/F6
Clinton, Mo, US 129/J3
Clinton (co.), Mo, US 137/E5
Clinton, Ms, US 129/K4
Clinton, NC, US 133/J3
Clinton, NJ, US 138/D2
Clinton (res.), NJ, US 138/D1
Clinton, Ok, US 129/H4
Clinton (co.), Pa, US 138/A1
Clinton, SC, US 133/H3
Clinton, Ut, US 137/J11
Clinton, Wa, US 135/C2
Clinton-Colden (lake), NW, Can. 122/F2
Clinton, Middle Branch (riv.), Mi, US 135/G6
Clinton, North Branch (riv.), Mi, US 135/G6
Clintonville, Wi, US 130/B2
Clints Dod (hill), Sc, UK 36/D5
Clio, Mi, US 130/D3
Clitheroe, Eng, UK 35/F4
Cloates (pt.), Austl. 112/B2
Clocolan, SAfr. 106/D3
Clogherhead, Ire. 34/B4
Clonakilty, Ire. 31/P11
Cloncurry, Austl. 114/A3
Clondalkin, Ire. 34/B5
Clonmany, Ire. 34/A1
Clonmel, Ire. 31/Q10
Cloppenburg, Ger. 51/F3
Clorinda, Arg. 157/E2
Clos-Fontaine, Fr. 30/M6
Closter, NJ, US 139/K8
Cloudcroft, NM, US 132/B3
Cloudy (mtn.), Ak, US 134/G3
Cloughmills, NI, UK 34/B2
Cloverdale, Ca, US 128/B3
Clovis, Ca, US 128/C3
Clovis, NM, US 129/G4
Cluanie (lake), Sc, UK 36/A2
Cluj (co.), Rom. 49/F2
Cluj-Napoca, Rom. 49/F2
Cluses, Fr. 56/C5
Clusone, It. 57/F6
Clutha (riv.), NZ 109/G7
Clwyd (co.), Wal, UK 35/E5
Clwyd (riv.), Wal, UK 35/E5
Clwydian (range), Wal, UK 35/E5
Clyde (riv.), NS, Can. 131/H2
Clyde (riv.), Sc, UK 36/B5
Clyde, Firth of (inlet), Sc, UK 31/R8
Clyde Hill, Wa, US 135/C2
Clydesdale (valley), Sc, UK 36/C5
Clywedog (riv.), Wal, UK 32/C2
CN Tower, On, Can. 131/R8
Co Loa Citadel, Viet. 78/D1
Côa (riv.), Port. 44/B2
Coacalco, Mex. 143/Q9
Coachella, Ca, US 128/C4
Coagh, NI, UK 34/B2
Coahuayana de Hidalgo, Mex. 142/E5
Coahuila (state), Mex. 132/C5
Coahuila, Mex. 142/B1
Coalburn, Sc, UK 36/C5
Coalcomán de Matamoros, Mex. 142/E5
Coaldale, Ab, Can. 126/E3
Coaldale, Pa, US 138/C2
Coalgate, Ok, US 129/H3
Coalhurst, Ab, Can. 126/E3
Coalisland, NI, UK 34/B2
Coalville, Ut, US 128/E2
Coalville, Eng, UK 33/E1
Coaraci, Braz. 154/C4
Coari, Braz. 150/F4
Coari (riv.), Braz. 150/F5
Coasa, Peru 156/D4
Coast (mts.), Can.,US 122/C2
Coast (prov.), Kenya 104/C3
Coast (ranges), Ca, US 126/C5
Coatbridge, Sc, UK 36/B5
Coatepec, Mex. 143/N7
Coatepec Harinas, Mex. 143/K8
Coatesville, Pa, US 138/C4
Coatetelco, Mex. 143/K8
Coaticook, Qu, Can. 131/G2
Coats (isl.), Nun., Can. 123/H2
Coats Land (pol. reg.), Ant. 160/Y
Coatzacoalcos, Mex. 144/C2
Coatzingo, Mex. 143/L8
Coba (ruin), Mex. 144/E1
Coba de Serpe, Sierra de (peak), Sp. 44/B1
Cobán, Guat. 144/D3
Cobar, Austl. 115/C1
Cobb (lake), Co, US 137/C1
Cobberas (mt.), Austl. 115/D3
Cobblestone (mtn.), Ca, US 136/B1
Cobden, Austl. 115/B3
Cóbh, Ire. 31/P11
Cobham (riv.), Mb,On, Can. 127/K2
Cobija, Bol. 150/E6
Cobourg, On, Can. 130/E3
Cobquecura, Chile 158/B3
Cobourg (pen.), Austl. 109/C2
Coburg (isl.), Nun., Can. 123/T7
Coburg, Ger. 54/D2
Coca, Ecu. 152/B5
Coca (riv.), Ecu. 152/B5
Cocachacra, Peru 156/D5
Cocal, Braz. 154/B1
Coccaglio, It. 58/C1
Cocentaina, Sp. 45/E3
Cochabamba, Bol. 150/E7
Coche (isl.), Ven. 153/F2
Cochem, Ger. 53/G3
Cocherel, Fr. 30/M4
Cochin, India 82/C6
Cochran, Ga, US 133/H3
Cochrane, Ab, Can. 126/E3
Cochrane, On, Can. 130/D1
Cock Cairn (peak), Sc, UK 36/D3
Cockatoo, Austl. 115/G5
Cockburn (sound), Austl. 112/K7
Cockburn (chan.), Chile 159/B7
Cockeysville, Md, US 138/B5
Cockscomb (peak), SAfr. 106/D4
Coclé del Norte, Pan. 145/F4
Coco (riv.), Hon. 140/E5
Coco, Cayo (isl.), Cuba 145/G1
Coco, Isla del (isl.), CR 150/A2
Cocoa, Fl, US 133/H4
Coconino (plat.), Az, US 128/D4
Cocoparra NP, Austl. 115/C2
Cocorocuma, Cayo (isl.), Hon. 145/F3
Cocos (isls.), Austl. 67/J11
Côcos, Braz. 154/A4
Cocotitlán, Mex. 143/R10
Cod (isl.), Nf, Can. 123/K3
Codajás, Braz. 150/F4
Codegua, Chile 158/N9
Codigoro, It. 59/F3
Codlea, Rom. 49/G3
Codogno, It. 58/C2
Codsall, Eng, UK 32/D1
Coelemu, Chile 158/B3
Coelho Neto, Braz. 154/B2
Coesfeld, Ger. 51/E5
Coeur d'Alene (lake), Id, US 126/D4
Coeur d'Alene, Id, US 126/D4
Coevorden, Neth. 50/D3
Coffin Bay, Austl. 113/G5
Coffin Bay NP, Austl. 113/G5
Coffs Harbour, Austl. 115/E1
Cofre de Perote, PN, Mex. 143/M7
Coggiola, It. 58/B1
Coghinas (lake), It. 46/A2
Cognac, Fr. 42/C4
Cogoleto, It. 58/B4
Cogolin, Fr. 43/G5
Cogollo del Cengio, It. 59/E1
Cogolludo, Sp. 44/D2
Cohansey (riv.), NJ, US 138/C5
Cohuna, Austl. 115/C2
Cohunu NP, Austl. 112/L7
Coiba, Isla de (isl.), Pan. 150/B2
Coig (riv.), Arg. 157/C7
Coignières, Fr. 30/H5
Coihaique, Chile 158/B5
Coihueco, Chile 158/C3
Coimbatore, India 82/C5
Coimbra (dist.), Port. 44/A2
Coimbra, Port. 44/A2
Coín, Sp. 44/C4
Coina (riv.), Port. 45/P10
Coise (riv.), Fr. 42/F4
Cojedes (riv.), Ven. 150/E2
Cojedes (state), Ven. 152/D2
Cojimíes, Ecu. 152/A4
Cojudo Blanco (peak), Arg. 159/C5
Cojutepeque, ESal. 144/D3
Čoka, Serb. 48/E3
Cokeville, Wy, US 126/F5
Col d'Ispéguy (pass), Fr. 42/C5
Col San Martino, It. 59/F1
Colac, Austl. 115/B3
Colares, Port. 45/P10
Colasay, Peru 156/B2
Colatina, Braz. 155/D1
Colbeck (cape), Ant. 160/P
Colbún, Chile 158/C2
Colby, Wa, US 135/B2
Colca (riv.), Peru 156/D4
Colcabamba, Peru 156/C4
Colchester, Eng, UK 33/G3
Cold Bay, Ak, US 134/F4
Cold Fell (peak), Eng, UK 35/F2
Cold Lake, Ab, Can. 126/F2
Cold Spring, Mn, US 127/K4
Cold Spring Harbor, NY, US 139/M8
Coldstream, Sc, UK 36/D5
Coldwater, Ks, US 129/H3
Coldwater, Mi, US 130/C3
Cole, Ok, US 137/M15
Cole (riv.), Eng, UK 33/E3
Coleambally, Austl. 115/C2
Coleman, Tx, US 129/H5
Çölemerik, Turk. 90/E2
Colenso, SAfr. 107/E3
Coleraine, Austl. 115/B3
Coleraine (dist.), NI, UK 34/B1
Coleraine, NI, UK 34/B1
Colesberg, SAfr. 106/D3
Colesville, Md, US 138/A5
Colfax, Wa, US 126/D4
Colgate (cape), Nun., Can. 123/S6
Colgong, India 85/F3
Colhué Huapí (lake), Arg. 158/C5
Colico, It. 57/F5
Coligny, SAfr. 106/D2
Coligny, Fr. 56/B5
Colima, Mex. 142/E5
Colima (state), Mex. 142/D5
Colima, Nevado de (peak), Mex. 142/E5
Colina, Chile 158/N8
Coliseum, Ca, US 136/F8
Coll (isl.), Sc, UK 31/Q8
Collado-Villalba, Sp. 45/N8
Collagna, It. 58/D4
Collarenebri, Austl. 115/D1
Colle di Val d'Elsa, It. 59/E6
Collecchio, It. 58/D3
College, Ak, US 134/J3
College Park, Md, US 138/B6
College Station, Tx, US 129/H5
Collegeville, Pa, US 138/C3
Collegno, It. 43/G4
Collesalvetti, It. 58/D5
Colletorto, It. 46/D2
Collie, Austl. 112/C5
Collier (bay), Austl. 109/B2
Collier (range), Austl. 112/C3
Collier Range NP, Austl. 112/C3
Collierville, Tn, US 129/K4
Colliford (res.), Eng, UK 32/B5
Collingwood, On, Can. 130/D2
Collins, Ms, US 133/F4
Collinstown (int'l arpt.), Ire. 34/B5
Collinsville, Austl. 114/B3
Collinsville, Ca, US 135/L10
Collinsville, Il, US 137/H8
Collinsville, Ok, US 132/E2
Collo, Alg. 100/K6
Collombey, Swi. 56/C5
Collon, Ire. 34/B4
Collonges, Fr. 56/B5
Colma, Ca, US 135/K11
Colmar, Fr. 56/D1
Colmar, Pa, US 138/C3
Colmberg, Ger. 54/D4
Colmenar, Sp. 44/C4
Colmenar de Oreja, Sp. 44/D2
Colmenar Viejo, Sp. 45/N8
Colmillo (cape), Chile 159/B6
Colne (riv.), Eng, UK 35/G4
Colne, Eng, UK 35/F4
Cologna Veneta, It. 59/E2
Cologne, It. 58/C1
Cologne, NJ, US 138/D5
Cologne/Bonn (int'l arpt.), Ger. 53/G2
Cologno Monzese, It. 58/C1
Colombes, Fr. 30/J5
Colombey-les-Belles, Fr. 56/B1
Colombia (ctry.) 150/D3
Colombia, Col. 152/C4
Colombier, Swi. 56/C4
Colombine (peak), It. 58/D1
Colombo, Braz. 155/B3
Colombo (cap.), SrL. 82/C6
Colomiers, Fr. 42/D5
Colomoncagua, Hon. 144/D3
Colón, Arg. 158/E2
Colón, Cuba 145/F1
Colón (mts.), Hon. 145/E3
Colón, Pan. 145/G4
Colón, Uru. 159/G2
Colonche, Ecu. 156/A1
Colonelganj, India 84/C2
Colonia, Micr. 116/C4
Colonia (dept.), Uru. 158/F2
Colonia, NJ, US 139/H9
Colonia Barón, Arg. 158/E3
Colonia del Sacramento, Uru. 159/K11
Colonia Juárez, Mex. 142/C2
Colonia Las Heras, Arg. 158/C5
Colonial Park, Pa, US 138/B3
Colonsay (isl.), Sc, UK 31/Q8
Colorado (peak), Arg. 159/C6
Colorado (riv.), Arg. 157/C4
Colorado, Braz. 155/B2
Colorado (plat.), US 128/E3
Colorado (riv.), US 128/D4
Colorado (state), US 128/F3
Colorado City, Tx, US 129/G4
Colorado Historical Museum, Co, US 137/C3
Colorado Springs, Co, US 129/F3
Colorno, It. 58/D3
Colotlán, Mex. 142/E4
Colquiri, Bol. 150/E7
Colson (pt.), Belz. 144/D2
Colstrip, Mt, US 126/G4
Colt (hill), Sc, UK 36/B6
Coltauco, Chile 158/N9
Colton, Ca, US 136/C2
Colts Neck, NJ, US 138/D3
Coluene (riv.), Braz. 147/D4
Columbe, Ecu. 156/B1
Columbia (riv.), Can.,US 126/C4
Columbia (plat.), US 126/C4
Columbia, Il, US 137/G9
Columbia, Ky, US 130/C4
Columbia, La, US 129/J4
Columbia, Md, US 138/B5
Columbia, Ms, US 133/F4
Columbia, NJ, US 138/C2
Columbia, Pa, US 138/B3
Columbia (co.), Pa, US 138/B1
Columbia (cap.), SC, US 133/H3
Columbia, Tn, US 130/C5
Columbia Falls, Mt, US 126/E3
Columbine (cape), SAfr. 106/K10
Columbus, Ga, US 133/G3
Columbus, In, US 130/C4
Columbus, Ms, US 133/F3
Columbus, Mt, US 126/F4
Columbus, Ne, US 127/J5
Columbus, NJ, US 138/D3
Columbus, NM, US 132/B4
Columbus (cap.), Oh, US 130/D4
Columbus, Tx, US 129/H5
Colunga, Sp. 44/C1
Colusa, Ca, US 128/B3
Colville (riv.), Ak, US 134/G2
Colville, Wa, US 126/D3
Colville (lake), NW, Can. 122/D2
Colvos (passg.), Wa, US 135/B3
Colwyn Bay, Wal, UK 34/E5
Comacchio, It. 59/F3
Comacchio, Valli di (lag.), It. 43/K4
Comai, China 85/H1
Comal, Tx, US 137/U20
Comal (co.), Tx, US 137/U20
Comala, Mex. 142/E5
Comalcalco, Mex. 144/C2
Comanche, Tx, US 129/H5
Comandante Luis Piedra Buena, Arg. 159/C6
Comandante Nicanor Otamendi, Arg. 158/F3
Comănești, Rom. 49/H2
Comarnic, Rom. 49/G3
Comas, Peru 156/C3
Comas, Peru 156/B3
Comayagua, Hon. 144/E3
Comayagua (mts.), Hon. 144/D3
Combapata, Peru 156/D4
Combarbalá, Chile 157/B3
Combeaufontaine, Fr. 56/B2
Comber, On, Can. 135/G7
Comber, NI, UK 34/C2
Comblain-au-Pont, Belg. 53/E3
Combloux, Fr. 56/C6
Combs-la-Ville, Fr. 30/K6
Comé, Ben. 103/F5
Comendador, DRep. 145/J2
Comilla (pol. reg.), Bang. 85/H4
Comines, Fr. 52/C2
Comines, Belg. 52/B2
Comino (isl.), Malta 46/L6
Comitán de Domínguez, Mex. 144/C2
Commack, NY, US 139/E2
Commentry, Fr. 42/E3
Commeny, Fr. 30/H4
Commerce, Ca, US 136/F7
Commerce City, Co, US 137/C3
Commercy, Fr. 53/E6
Commewijne (dist.), Sur. 153/H3
Committee (bay), Nun., Can. 123/H2
Como (lake), It. 43/H3
Como, It. 57/F6
Como, Wi, US 135/P14
Comodoro Rivadavia, Arg. 158/D5
Comoé (prov.), Burk. 102/D4
Comoe, PN de la, C.d'Iv. 96/E6
Comoé, PN de la, C.d'Iv. 102/D4
Comorin (cape), India 82/C6
Comoros (ctry.) 107/G5
Comox, BC, Can. 126/B3
Compiègne, Fr. 52/B5
Compostela, Phil. 79/E6
Compostela, Mex. 142/D4
Compton, Ca, US 136/F8
Comrat, Mol. 49/J2
Comrie, Sc, UK 36/C4
Comstock, Tx, US 132/C4
Con Son (isl.), Viet. 83/J6
Cona, China 83/F2
Conaica, Peru 156/C4
Conakry (pol. reg.), Gui. 102/B4
Conakry (cap.), Gui. 102/B4
Conakry (int'l arpt.), Gui. 102/B4
Conambo (riv.), Ecu. 152/B5
Conca (riv.), It. 59/F5
Concarneau, Fr. 42/B3
Conceição da Barra, Braz. 155/E1
Conceição das Alagoas, Braz. 155/B1
Conceição do Araguaia, Braz. 151/J5
Conceição do Coité, Braz. 154/C3
Conceição do Mato Dentro, Braz. 155/D1
Conceição do Rio Verde, Braz. 211/H6
Conceição dos Ouros, Braz. 211/H7
Concepción (lake), Bol. 150/F7
Concepción, Arg. 157/C2
Concepción, Bol. 150/E6
Concepción, Chile 158/B3
Concepción (pt.), Mex. 142/C3
Concepción, Par. 157/E1
Concepción, Peru 150/C6
Concepción (bay), Mex. 142/B3
Concepción de La Vega, DRep. 141/G4
Concepción del Oro, Mex. 143/E3
Concepción del Uruguay, Arg. 159/J10
Conception (pt.), Ca, US 128/B4
Concesio, It. 58/D1
Conchal, Braz. 211/F7
Conchas (lake), NM, US 129/F4
Conches, Fr. 30/L5
Conchillas, Uru. 159/J11
Concho (riv.), Tx, US 129/G5
Conchos (riv.), Mex. 142/D2
Concord, Ca, US 128/B3
Concord, NC, US 133/H3
Concord (cap.), NH, US 131/G3
Concord, Wi, US 135/N13
Concordia, Arg. 157/E3
Concórdia, Braz. 155/A3
Concordia, Mex. 142/D4
Concordia, Peru 156/C2
Concordia Sagittaria, It. 59/F1
Concordia sulla Secchia, It. 59/D3
Concrete, Wa, US 126/C3
Condado, Cuba 145/G1
Condamine (riv.), Austl. 109/E3
Condamine, Austl. 114/C3
Conde, Braz. 154/C3
Condé-sur-L'Escaut, Fr. 52/C3
Condé-sur-Noireau, Fr. 42/C2
Condé-sur-Vesgre, Fr. 30/G5
Condé-sur-Vire, Fr. 42/C2
Condécourt, Fr. 30/H4
Condeúba, Braz. 154/B4
Condino, It. 57/G6
Condobolin, Austl. 115/C2
Condom, Fr. 42/D5
Condon, Or, US 126/C4
Condroz (plat.), Belg. 40/C3
Conecuh (riv.), Al, US 133/G4
Conegliano, It. 59/F1
Conejos, Co, US 129/F3
Conesa, Arg. 158/E2
Conestoga (riv.), Pa, US 138/B3
Conewago (lake), Pa, US 138/A3
Confins (int'l arpt.), Braz. 155/D1
Conflans-en-Jarnisy, Fr. 53/E5
Conflans-Sainte-Honorine, Fr. 30/J5
Congaree Swamp Nat'l Mon., SC, US 133/H3
Congers, NY, US 139/K7
Congis-sur-Thérouanne, Fr. 30/L4
Congjiang, China 83/J2
Congleton, Eng, UK 35/F5
Congo (basin), D.R. Congo 97/K7
Congo, Rep. of the (ctry.) 93/D4
Congo (riv.), Afr. 93/D4
Congo, Democratic Republic of the (ctry.) 93/E5
Congonhal, Braz. 211/G7
Congonhas, Braz. 155/D2
Congonhas (int'l arpt.), Braz. 211/G8
Conguillío, PN, Chile 158/C3

182
Cuckm – Delni

Cuckmere (riv.), Eng, UK 33/G5
Cucq, Fr. 42/D1
Cúcuta, Col. 152/C3
Cucuyagua, Hon. 144/D3
Cudahy, Ca, US 136/F8
Cuddapah, India 82/C5
Cudgewa, Austl. 115/C3
Cudillero, Sp. 44/B1
Cudrefin, Swi. 56/D4
Cudworth, Eng, UK 35/G4
Cue, Austl. 112/C3
Cuéllar, Sp. 44/C2
Cuéllar-Baza, Sp. 44/D4
Cuenca, Sp. 44/D2
Cuenca, Ecu. 152/B5
Cuenca, Sierra de (range), Sp. 44/E2
Cuencamé de Ceniceros, Mex. 142/E3
Cuernavaca, Mex. 143/K8
Cuero, Tx, US 129/H5
Cuers, Fr. 42/G5
Cueto, Cuba 145/H1
Cuetzalán, Mex. 143/M6
Cueva de los Guácharos, PN, Col. 150/C3
Cuevas de Vinromá, Sp. 45/F2
Cuevas del Almanzora, Sp. 44/E4
Cuffley, Eng, UK 30/C1
Cufré, Uru. 159/K11
Cugir, Rom. 49/F3
Cuglieri, It. 46/A2
Cugnaux, Fr. 42/D5
Cuiabá (riv.), Braz. 151/G7
Cuiabá, Braz. 151/G7
Cuicas, Ven. 152/D2
Cuijk, Neth. 50/C5
Cuilapa, Guat. 144/D3
Cuilco (riv.), Guat. 144/C3
Cuillin (sound), Sc, UK 31/Q8
Cuilo (riv.), Ang. 105/C2
Cuisance (riv.), Fr. 56/B4
Cuise-la-Motte, Fr. 52/C5
Cuiseaux, Fr. 56/B5
Cuisery, Fr. 56/A4
Cuisy, Fr. 30/L4
Cuité, Braz. 154/C2
Cuitláhuac, Mex. 143/N8
Cuito (riv.), Ang. 105/C4
Cuiuni (riv.), Braz. 150/F4
Culcairn, Austl. 115/C2
Culdaff (riv.), Ire. 34/A1
Culemborg, Neth. 50/C5
Culgoa (riv.), Austl. 109/D3
Culiacán Rosales, Mex. 142/D3
Culion (isl.), Phil. 79/D5
Cullen, Sc, UK 36/D1
Cullera, Sp. 45/E3
Culleredo, Sp. 44/A1
Cullman, Al, US 133/G3
Culloden Battlesite, Sc, UK 36/B2
Cully, Swi. 56/C5
Cullybackey, NI, UK 34/B2
Culmback (dam), Wa, US 135/D2
Culmore, NI, UK 34/A1
Culoz, Fr. 56/B6
Culpeper, Va, US 130/E4
Culross, Sc, UK 36/C4
Cults, Sc, UK 36/D2
Culver (pt.), Austl. 112/E5
Culver City, Ca, US 136/F7
Culvers (lake), NJ, US 138/D1
Cumaná, Ven. 153/E2
Cumari, Braz. 155/B1
Cumba, Peru 156/B2
Cumbal, Col. 152/B4
Cumbal, Nevado de (peak), Col. 152/B4
Cumberland (pen.), Nun., Can. 123/K2
Cumberland (sound), Nun., Can. 123/K2
Cumberland (lake), Sk, Can. 127/H2
Cumberland (plat.), US 133/G3
Cumberland (isl.), Ga, US 133/H4
Cumberland (falls), Ky, US 133/G2
Cumberland (lake), Ky, US 130/C4
Cumberland (riv.), Ky,Tn, US 125/J4
Cumberland, Md, US 130/E4
Cumberland (co.), NJ, US 138/A3
Cumberland, Wa, US 135/D3
Cumberland House, Sk, Can. 127/H2
Cumbernauld, Sc, UK 36/C5
Cumbres Bastonal, Cerro (peak), Mex. 144/C2
Cumbres de Majalca, PN, Mex. 142/D2
Cumbres de Monterrey, PN de, Mex. 143/E3
Cumbria (co.), Eng, UK 35/E2
Cumbrian (mts.), Eng, UK 35/E2
Cumbum, India 82/C4
Cummins, Austl. 113/G5
Cumnock, Austl. 115/D2
Cumpas, Mex. 142/C2
Çumra, Turk. 90/C2
Cumshewa (pt.), BC, Can. 134/M5
Cunaviche, Ven. 153/E3
Cunco, Chile 158/B3
Cundeelee Abor. Rsv., Austl. 112/D4
Cunderdin, Austl. 112/C4
Cundinamarca (dept.), Col. 152/C3
Cunduacán, Mex. 144/C2
Cunene (riv.), Ang. 93/D6
Cuneo (prov.), It. 58/A3
Cuneo, It. 43/G4
Cunha, Braz. 211/J8
Cunnamulla, Austl. 114/B5
Cunninghame (reg.), Sc, UK 36/B5
Čuokkaraš'ša (peak), Nor. 37/H1
Cuorgnè, It. 43/G4
Cupar, Sc, UK 36/C4
Cupertino, Ca, US 135/K12
Cupra Marittima, It. 43/K5
Cupramontana, It. 59/G6
Cuprija, Serb. 48/E4
Ćuprija, Serb. 48/E4
Cuquenán (riv.), Ven. 153/F3
Curaçá, Braz. 154/C3
Curaçao (isl.), NAnt. 150/E1
Curacautín, Chile 158/C3
Curacaví, Chile 158/N8
Curahuara de Carangas, Bol. 156/D5
Curanilahue, Chile 158/B3
Curaray (riv.), Ecu. 150/C4
Curaray (riv.), Ecu.,Peru 152/C5
Curarén, Hon. 144/E3
Curaumilla (pt.), Chile 158/N8
Curcubăta (peak), Rom. 49/F2
Cure (riv.), Fr. 40/B5
Curecanti Nat'l Rec. Area, Co, US 132/B2
Curepipe, Mrts. 107/T15
Curepto, Chile 158/B2
Curicó, Chile 158/C2
Curimatá, Braz. 154/A3
Curitibanos, Braz. 155/B3
Curno, It. 58/C1
Curone (riv.), It. 58/B3
Curral Velho, CpV. 93/K10
Current (riv.), Ar,Mo, US 129/K3
Currie, Austl. 115/B3
Currie, Sc, UK 36/C5
Curry, Ak, US 134/H3
Curtea de Argeş, Rom. 49/G3
Curtici, Rom. 48/E2
Curtis (riv.), Austl. 114/D4
Curtis (isl.), NZ 116/G8
Curtis, Sp. 44/A1
Curtis (pt.), Md, US 138/B6
Curú NWR, CR 145/E4
Curuá (riv.), Braz. 151/G4
Curuá Una (riv.), Braz. 153/H5
Curuçú (riv.), Braz. 150/D5
Curup, Indo. 80/B4
Cururupu, Braz. 151/K4
Curuzú Cuatiá, Arg. 157/E2
Curvelo, Braz. 155/C1
Cusco (dept.), Peru 156/C4
Cusco, Peru 156/D4
Cusher (riv.), NI, UK 34/B3
Cushet Law (peak), Eng, UK 36/D6
Cushing, Ok, US 129/H4
Cusna (peak), It. 58/D4
Cusset, Fr. 42/E3
Cusseta, Ga, US 133/G3
Custer, Mt, US 126/G4
Custer, SD, US 127/H5
Custines, Fr. 53/F6
Custódia, Braz. 154/C3
Cut (hill), Eng, UK 32/C5
Cut Bank, Mt, US 126/E3
Cut Knife, Sk, Can. 126/F2
Cutchogue, NY, US 139/F2
Cutervo, Peru 156/B2
Cuthbert, Ga, US 133/G4
Cutral-Có, Arg. 158/C3
Cutro, It. 47/E3
Cuttack, India 82/E3
Cuvergnon, Fr. 30/L4
Cuvier (cape), Austl. 112/B3
Cuxhaven, Ger. 51/F1
Cuyabeno, Ecu. 152/C5
Cuyama (riv.), Ca, US 128/C4
Cuyo (isls.), Phil. 81/F1
Cuyo, Phil. 81/F1
Cuyocuyo, Peru 156/D4
Cuyuni (riv.), Ven. 150/F2
Cuyuni (riv.), Guy., Ven. 153/G3
Cuyuni-Mazaruni (pol. reg.), Guy. 153/F3
Cuzco (ruin), Peru 156/D4
Cwmbran, Wal, UK 32/C3
Cyangugu, Rwa. 104/A3
Cyclades (isls.), Gre. 47/J4
Cypress (hills), Ab,Sk, Can. 126/F3
Cypress, Ca, US 136/F8
Cyprus (ctry.) 91/C2
Cyrenaica (reg.), Libya 97/K1
Cysoing, Fr. 52/C2
Cywyn (riv.), Wal, UK 32/B3
Czaplinek, Pol. 41/J2
Czarna Białostocka, Pol. 41/M2
Czarnków, Pol. 41/J2
Czech Republic (ctry.) 41/H4
Częstochowa, Pol. 41/K3
Człuchów, Pol. 38/G5

D

Da (riv.), China 79/D2
Da Hinggan (mts.), China 67/M5
Da Lat, Viet. 78/E4
Da Nang (cape), Viet. 78/E2
Da Nang, Viet. 78/E2
Da Xian, China 70/J5
Daaden, Ger. 53/G2
Da'an, China 71/M2
Daanbantayan, Phil. 79/D5
Daba (mts.), China 70/J5
Dabajuro, Ven. 152/D2
Dabakala, C.d'Iv. 102/D4
Dabas, Hun. 48/D2
Dabbāgh, Jabal (peak), SAr. 98/D3
Dabeiba, Col. 152/B3
Dabo, Fr. 53/G6
Dabob (bay), Wa, US 135/B2
Dabou, C.d'Iv. 102/D5
Daboya, Gha. 103/E4
Dabra, India 84/B3
Dąbrowa Białostocka, Pol. 39/K5
Dąbrowa Górnicza, Pol. 41/K3
Dabu, China 79/C3
Dachang Huizu Zizhixian, China 72/H7
Dachau, Ger. 55/E6
Dacono, Co, US 137/C2
Dade City, Fl, US 133/H4
Dades, Oued (riv.), Mor. 98/D3
Dadi (cape), Indo. 81/H4
Dādra and Nagar Haveli (state), India 82/B4
Dādri, India 86/D5
Dādu, Pak. 89/J3
Daduru (riv.), SrL. 82/C6
Daen Noi (peak), Thai. 78/B4
Daet, Phil. 79/D5
Dafang, China 83/J2
Dafeng, China 72/E4
Dagana, Sen. 102/B2
Dağardı, Turk. 90/B2
Dağbaşı, Turk. 90/D2
Dagestan, Resp., Rus. 63/H4
Daggaboersnek (pass), SAfr. 106/D4
Dagmar Range NP, Austl. 114/B2
Dagneux, Fr. 56/B6
Dagny, Fr. 30/M5
Dagu, China 72/H7
Daguan, China 83/H2
D'Aguilar (range), Austl. 114/E6
D'Aguilar (mt.), Austl. 114/E6
Dagupan, Phil. 79/D4
Dahana (des.), SAr. 67/D7
Daharki, Pak. 82/A2
Dahei (riv.), China 72/B2
Dahlak (arch.), Erit. 97/N4
Dahlem, Ger. 53/F3
Dahlenburg, Ger. 51/H2
Dahlonega, Ga, US 133/H3
Dahmani, Tun. 100/L7
Dahme (riv.), Ger. 41/G3
Dahn, Ger. 53/G5
Dahūk, Iraq 90/E2
Dahūk (gov.), Iraq 90/E2
Dahuofang (res.), China 72/D2
Dai (lake), China 72/C2
Dai-Segen-dake (peak), Japan 76/B3
Dai-sen (peak), Japan 74/C3
Dai Xian, China 72/C3
Daian, Japan 77/L5
Daicheng, China 72/D3
Daigo, Japan 75/G2
Dailekh, Nepal 84/C1
Dailly, Sc, UK 36/B6
Daimiao, China 72/D3
Daimiel, Sp. 44/D3
Daingerfield, Tx, US 129/J4
Daiō-zaki (pt.), Japan 75/E3
Dāira Dīn Panāh, Pak. 86/A4
Daireaux, Arg. 158/E3
Daisen-Oki NP, Japan 74/C3
Daisetsuzan NP, Japan 76/C2
Daishan, China 79/D1
Daito (isl.), Japan 67/N7
Daitō, Japan 77/J6
Daiyun (peak), China 71/L6
Dajabón, DRep. 145/J2
Dakar (cap.), Sen. 102/A3
Dakar (pol. reg.), Sen. 102/A3
Dākhilah, Wāḩāt ad (oasis), Egypt 101/B3
Dakhin Shābāzpur (isl.), Bang. 85/H4
Dakhlet Nouadhibou (pol. reg.), Mrta. 98/A5
Dakoro, Niger 103/G3
Dakota City, Ne, US 127/J5
Dakovica, Serb. 47/G1
Dakovo, Cro. 48/D3
Dal (falls), Sudan 101/B4
Dal (riv.), Swe. 64/B3
Dala-Järna, Swe. 38/F1
Dalaas, Aus. 57/F3
Dalad Qi, China 72/B2
Dalaman, Turk. 90/B2
Dalaman (int'l arpt.), Turk. 90/B2
Dalandzadgad, Mong. 70/H3
Dalarna (reg.), Swe. 37/E3
Dalatangi (pt.), Ice. 37/Q6
Dalbeattie, Sc, UK 34/E2
Dalby, Austl. 114/C4
Dalby, Swe. 38/E4
Dalcour, La, US 137/Q17
Dalcross (int'l arpt.), Sc, UK 36/B1
Dale, Ok, US 137/N15
Dale, Nor. 38/A1
Dalen, Neth. 50/D3
Dalen, Nor. 38/C2
Dalfsen, Neth. 50/D3
Dalgaranger (mt.), Austl. 112/C3
Dalhart, Tx, US 129/G3
Dalhousie (cape), NW, Can. 134/N1
Dalhousie, NB, Can. 131/H1
Dalhousie, India 86/C3
Dali, China 83/H2
Dali, China 72/B4
Dalian (bay), China 73/A3
Dalian, China 73/A3
Dalian (int'l arpt.), China 72/E3
Dalías, Sp. 44/D4
Dalidag (peak), Azer. 63/H5
Dāliyat el Karmil, Isr. 91/G6
Dalj, Cro. 48/D3
Dalkeith, Sc, UK 36/C5
Dalkola, India 85/F3
Dall (lake), Ak, US 134/F3
Dall (isl.), Ak, US 122/C3
Dallas, Tx, US 129/H4
Dallas-Fort Worth (int'l arpt.), Tx, US 129/H4
Dallastown, Pa, US 138/B4
Dallgow, Ger. 40/Q6
Dallol Bosso (riv.), Niger,Mali 103/F3
Dalmatia (reg.), Cro. 48/B3
Dalmatia, Pa, US 138/B2
Dalmellington, Sc, UK 36/B6
Dalmeny, Austl. 115/D3
Dalmine, It. 58/C1
Dal'negorsk, Rus. 71/Q3
Dal'nerechensk, Rus. 71/P2
Daloa, C.d'Iv. 102/D5
Dalry, Sc, UK 36/B5
Dalrymple (lake), Austl. 109/D3
Dalrymple, Sc, UK 36/B6
Dals Långed, Swe. 38/E2
Dalsingh Sarai, India 85/E3
Dalsjöfors, Swe. 38/E3
Dalton, Ga, US 133/G3
Daltonganj, India 85/E3
Dalvik, Ice. 37/N6
Dalwallinu, Austl. 112/C4
Daly (riv.), Austl. 109/C2
Daly (bay), Nun., Can. 122/G2
Damak, Nepal 85/F2
Damān, India 82/B3
Damān and Diu (state), India 82/B3
Damanhūr, Egypt 91/B4
Damar (isl.), Indo. 81/G5
Damascus (int'l arpt.), Syria 91/E3
Damascus, Md, US 138/A5
Damascus (Dimashq) (cap.), Syria 91/E3
Damaturu, Nga. 96/H5
Damavānd (mt.), Iran 88/F1
Dambach-la-Ville, Fr. 56/D1
Dambaslar, Turk. 49/H5
Dame Marie (cape), Haiti 145/H2
Dame Marie, Haiti 145/H2
Dāmghān, Iran 89/F1
Damietta (riv.), Egypt 91/B4
Damietta (Dumyāţ), Egypt 91/B4
Daming, China 72/C3
Damion (peak), Fr. 53/D4
Dammard, Fr. 30/M4
Dammartin-en-Goële, Fr. 30/L4
Dammastock (peak), Swi. 57/E4
Damme, Ger. 51/F3
Damme, Belg. 52/C1
Dāmodar (riv.), India 82/E3
Damoh, India 84/B4
Damongo, Gha. 103/E4
Damparis, Fr. 56/B3
Dampier (str.), Indo. 81/H4
Dampier (arch.), Austl. 109/A2
Dampier, Austl. 112/C2
Dampierre, Fr. 30/H5
Dampierre-sur-Salon, Fr. 56/B2
Damprichard, Fr. 56/C3
Damrei (mts.), Camb. 78/C4
Damsterdiep (riv.), Neth. 50/D2
Damvant, Swi. 56/C3
Damxung, China 70/F5
Dan (riv.), NC,Va, US 133/H2
Dan Xian, China 83/J4
Ḑānā, Jor. 91/D4
Dana Point, Ca, US 136/C4
Danané, C.d'Iv. 102/C5
Danao, Phil. 79/D5
Danba, China 70/H5
Danbury, Eng, UK 33/G3
Dancheng, China 72/C4
Dandaragan, Austl. 112/B4
Dandeldhurā, Nepal 84/C1
Dandenong (mt.), Austl. 115/G5
Danderhall, Sc, UK 36/C5
Dandong, China 73/C2
Dane (riv.), Eng, UK 35/F5
Danger (pt.), SAfr. 106/L11
Danggali Conservation Park, Austl. 115/B2
Dangriga, Belz. 144/D2
Dangshan, China 72/D4
Dangtu, China 72/D5
Dangyang, China 71/K5
Danielskuil, SAfr. 106/C3
Danielsville, Pa, US 138/C2
Danilov, Rus. 60/J4
Daning, China 72/B3
Danjoutin, Fr. 56/C2
Dankaur, India 86/D5
Dankov, Rus. 62/F1
Dankova (peak), Kyr. 87/G4
Danlí, Hon. 144/E3
Dannelly (res.), Al, US 133/G3
Dannemora, Swe. 38/G1
Dannenberg, Ger. 40/F2
Dannes, Fr. 52/A2
Dannevirke, NZ 117/T11
Dannhauser, SAfr. 107/E3
Danube (riv.), Eur. 27/F4
Danube, Delta of the (delta), Rom. 49/J3
Danube (Donau) (riv.), Ger. 43/H2
Danube, Mouths of the (delta), Rom.,Ukr. 62/D3
Danville, Il, US 130/C3
Danville, Ky, US 130/C4
Danville, Pa, US 138/B2
Dao Xian, China 83/K2
Daoura, Oued ed (riv.), Alg. 98/D3
Daozhen, China 83/J2
Dapaong, Togo 103/F4
Daphne, Al, US 133/G4
Dapitan, Phil. 79/D6
Daqing, China 71/N2
Daqing (riv.), China 72/H7
Dar-el-Beida (Casablanca), Mor. 98/D2
Dar es Salaam (int'l arpt.), Tanz. 104/C4
Dar es Salaam (pol. reg.), Tanz. 104/C4
Dar es Salaam (cap.), Tanz. 104/C4
Dar Rounga (reg.), CAfr. 97/K6
Dar'ā (prov.), Syria 90/C3
Dar'ā (prov.), Syria 91/E3
Dar'ā, Syria 91/E3
Dārāb, Iran 89/F3
Darabani, Rom. 49/H1
Daraga, Phil. 81/F1
Daram, Phil. 79/D5
Dārān, Iran 88/F2
Đaravica (peak), Serb. 47/G1
Dārayyā, Syria 91/E3
Darbhanga, India 85/E2
Darby (cape), Ak, US 134/F3
Darby, Pa, US 138/C4
Darda, Cro. 48/D3
Dardanelle (lake), Ar, US 129/J4
Dardanelles (str.), Turk. 90/A2
Darent (riv.), Eng, UK 30/D3
Dareton, Austl. 115/B2
Darfield, NZ 117/S11
Darfo, It. 57/G6
Dārfūr (state), Sudan 101/A5
Dargaville, NZ 117/S10
Dargle (riv.), Ire. 34/B5
D'Arguin (bay), Mrta. 102/A1
Darhan, Mong. 70/J2
Darie (hills), Som. 97/Q6
Darien, Ga, US 133/H4
Darien, Ct, US 139/M7
Darien, Il, US 135/P16
Darién, PN, Pan. 150/C2
Darién, Serranía del (mts.), Pan. 150/C2
Darkan, Austl. 112/C5
Darlag, China 70/G5
Darling (range), Austl. 109/A4
Darling (riv.), Austl. 109/D4
Darling, SAfr. 106/L10
Darling Downs (reg.), Austl. 109/D3
Darling Downs (range), Austl. 114/C3
Darlington, Eng, UK 35/G2
Darlington (co.), Eng, UK 35/G2
Darlington, Md, US 138/B4
Darlington, SC, US 133/J3
Darlington Point, Austl. 115/C2
Darłowo, Pol. 38/G4
Darmstadt, Ger. 54/B3
Darnah, Libya 97/K1
Darney, Fr. 56/C1
Darnley (bay), NW, Can. 122/D2
Darnley (cape), Ant. 160/E
Daroca, Sp. 44/E2
Darregueira, Arg. 158/E3
Darsser (cape), Ger. 38/E4
Dart (riv.), Eng, UK 32/C6
Dart, West (riv.), Eng, UK 32/C6
Dartford, Eng, UK 30/D2
Dartmoor (upland), Eng, UK 32/B5
Dartmoor NP, Eng, UK 42/A1
Dartmouth (dam), Austl. 115/C3
Dartmouth (res.), Austl. 115/C3
Dartmouth, NS, Can. 131/J2
Dartmouth, Eng, UK 32/C6
Darton, Eng, UK 35/G4
Dartuch (cape), Sp. 45/G3
Daruvar, Cro. 48/C3
Darvel (bay), Malay. 81/E3
Darvel, Sc, UK 36/B5
Darwen, Eng, UK 35/F4
Darwin (bay), Chile 158/B5
Darwin (isl.), Ecu. 156/E6
Darwin (vol.), Ecu. 156/E7
Darwin, Cordillera (mts.), Chile 157/B7
Darya Khan, Pak. 86/A4
Daryābād, India 84/C2
Dashennongjia (peak), China 72/B5
Dashhowuz, Trkm. 87/C4
Dashhowuz (pol. reg.), Trkm. 87/C4
Dashhowuz (int'l arpt.), Trkm. 87/C4
Dasht-e Kavīr (des.), Iran 89/F2
Dasht-e Lūt (des.), Iran 89/G2
Dasht-e Mārgow (des.), Afg. 89/H2
Dasht Kaur (riv.), Pak. 89/H3
Dasing, Ger. 54/E6
Daska, Pak. 86/C3
Dassa-Zoumé, Ben. 103/F5
Dassel, Ger. 51/G5
Dassendorf, Ger. 51/H1
Dasseneiland (isl.), SAfr. 106/B4
Dasūya, India 86/C4
Dātāganj, India 84/B1
Datchet, Eng, UK 30/B2
Date, Japan 76/B2
Datia, India 84/B3
Datian, China 79/C2
Datil, NM, US 132/B3
Datong (mts.), China 70/G4
Datong, China 70/H4
Datong, China 72/C2
Datteln, Ger. 51/E5
Datu (cape), Indo. 80/C3
Datuk (cape), Indo. 80/B3
Daugava (riv.), Lat. 39/L3
Daugavpils, Lat. 39/M4
Daule, Ecu. 152/B5
Daule (riv.), Ecu. 152/B5
Daun, Ger. 53/F3
Daund, India 89/K5
Daung (isl.), Myan. 78/B3
Dauphin, Mb, Can. 127/H3
Dauphin (lake), Mb, Can. 127/J3
Dauphin, Pa, US 138/B3
Dauphin (co.), Pa, US 138/B3
Dauphiné (reg.), Fr. 42/F4
Dauphiné, Alpes du (range), Fr. 42/F4
Dāvangere, India 89/L6
Davao, Phil. 79/E6
Davel, SAfr. 107/E2
Davenport, Wa, US 126/D4
Davenport, Ia, US 127/L5
Davenport (mt.), Austl. 113/F2
Daventry, Eng, UK 33/E2
Daverdisse, Belg. 53/E3
Daveyton, SAfr. 106/E2
Davgaard-Jensen Land (phys. reg.), Grld. 123/T6
David, Pan. 145/F4
David City, Ne, US 127/J5
Davidson, Sk, Can. 127/G3
Davidson (mt.), Ca, US 135/J11
Davies (mt.), Austl. 113/F3
Davis (sea), Ant. 160/F
Davis, Austl., Ant. 160/F
Davis, Ca, US 128/B3
Davis (mt.), Pa, US 130/E4
Davis (mts.), Tx, US 132/B4
Davis (str.), Can.,Grld. 123/L2
Davlekanovo, Rus. 61/M5
Davo (riv.), C.d'Iv. 102/D5
Davos, Swi. 57/F4
Dawa, China 73/B2
Dawa Wenz (riv.), Eth. 97/N7
Dawangja (isl.), China 73/B3
Dawson, Yk, Can. 134/L3
Dawson, Ga, US 133/G4
Dawson (riv.), Austl. 109/D3
Dawson (isl.), Chile 159/C7
Dawson Creek, BC, Can. 126/C2
Dawu, China 70/H5
Dawu (mtn.), China 72/C5
Dawu, China 72/C5
Dax, Fr. 42/C5
Daxing, China 72/H7
Daxue (mts.), China 70/H5
Dayang (riv.), China 73/B2
Dayao, China 83/H2
Daye, China 79/B1
Daying (riv.), China 83/G3
Daylesford, Austl. 115/C3
Dayong, China 79/B2
Dayr al Balaḩ, Gaza 91/D4
Dayr al Ghuşūn, WBnk. 91/G7
Dayr Az Zawr (prov.), Syria 90/E3
Dayr Ballūţ, WBnk. 91/G7
Dayr Sharaf, WBnk. 91/G7
Dayrūt, Egypt 101/B3
Daysland, Ab, Can. 126/E2
Dayton, Wa, US 126/D4
Dayton, Tn, US 133/G3
Dayton, NJ, US 138/D3
Daytona Beach, Fl, US 133/H4
Dayu, China 83/K2
Dazhizhu Dau (isl.), China 71/T11
D.C. (fed. dist.), US 138/A6
De Aar, SAfr. 106/D3
De Bilt, Neth. 50/C4
De Doorns, SAfr. 106/L10
De Funiak Springs, Fl, US 133/G4
De Grey (riv.), Austl. 109/A3
De Haan, Belg. 52/C1
De Hart (res.), Pa, US 138/B3
De Hoge Veluwe, NP, Neth. 50/C4
De Kalb (co.), Il, US 135/N16
De Land, Fl, US 133/H4
De Leijen (lake), Neth. 50/D2
De Lier, Neth. 50/B5
De Luz, Ca, US 136/C4
De Panne, Belg. 52/B1
De Peel (phys. reg.), Neth. 50/C6
De Pinte, Belg. 52/C2
De Ridder, La, US 129/J5
De Soto, Ks, US 137/D6
De Soto, Mo, US 129/K3
De Wijk, Neth. 50/D3
Dead Sea (sea), Jor.,Isr. 90/C4
Deadhorse, Ak, US 134/J1
Deadman (peak), Austl. 112/C2
Deadwood, SD, US 127/H4
Deal (isl.), Austl. 115/C3
Deal, NJ, US 138/D3
Deale, Md, US 138/B6
Dean (riv.), BC, Can. 126/B2
Dean (chan.), BC, Can. 126/B2
De'an, China 79/C2
Dean (for.), Eng, UK 32/D3
Deán Funes, Arg. 157/D3
Deanmill, Austl. 112/C5
Dearborn Heights, Mi, US 135/F7
Dearne, Eng, UK 35/G4
Dease (str.), Nun., Can. 122/F2
Dease (riv.), BC, Can. 122/D3
Dease Lake, BC, Can. 134/M4
Death Valley NP, Ca, US 128/C3
Debar, FYROM 47/G2
Debauch (mtn.), Ak, US 134/G3
Debe Habe, Nga. 96/H5
Debelets, Bul. 47/J1
Deben (riv.), Eng, UK 33/H2
Dębica, Pol. 41/L3
Dęblin, Pol. 41/L3
Dębno, Pol. 41/H2
Débo (lake), Mali 102/E3
Deborah (mt.), Ak, US 134/J3
Debre Birhan, Eth. 97/N6
Debre Mark'os, Eth. 97/N5
Debre Tabor, Eth. 97/N5
Debre Zeyit, Eth. 97/N6
Debrecen, Hun. 41/L5
Decatur, Al, US 133/G3
Decatur, Il, US 127/L6
Decatur, In, US 130/C3
Decatur, Ga, US 133/G3
Decatur, Tx, US 129/H4
Decazeville, Fr. 42/E4
Deccan (plat.), India 82/C5
Decima, It. 59/E3
Děčín, Czh. 41/H3
Décines-Charpieu, Fr. 56/A6
Decize, Fr. 42/E3
Dedemsvaart, Neth. 50/D3
Dedo (peak), Arg. 158/C5
Dédougou, Burk. 102/E3
Dedza, Malw. 105/F3
Dee (riv.), Sc, UK 36/C3
Deel (riv.), Ire. 34/A4
Deep Fork (riv.), Ok, US 137/N14
Deep River, On, Can. 130/E2
Deepcut, Eng, UK 30/F3
Deepwater, Austl. 115/D1
Deepwater, NJ, US 138/C4
Deer (pt.), De, US 138/C5
Deer (isl.), Ak, US 134/F5
Deer Creek (res.), Ut, US 137/L13
Deer Lake, Nf, Can. 131/K1
Deer Lake, Pa, US 138/B2
Deer Lodge, Mt, US 126/E4
Deer Park, Il, US 135/P15
Deer Park, Md, US 138/B5
Deer Park, NY, US 139/E2
Deer Park, Wa, US 126/D4
Deer Plain, Il, US 137/F8
Deerfield, Il, US 135/P15
Deering, Ak, US 134/F2
Deerlijk, Belg. 52/C2
Deeside (valley), Sc, UK 36/D2
Deex Nugaaleed (riv.), Som. 97/Q6
Defensores del Chaco, PN, Par. 150/F8
Defiance, Oh, US 130/C3
Dégelis, Qu, Can. 131/G2
Degerfors, Swe. 38/F2
Degersheim, Swi. 57/F3
Deggendorf, Ger. 55/F5
Deggingen, Ger. 54/C5
Dego, It. 58/B4
DeGrey (riv.), Austl. 112/C2
Deh Bīd, Iran 88/F2
Dehalak (isl.), Erit. 97/P4
Dehalak Marine NP, Erit. 97/P4
Deheq, Iran 88/F2
Dehra Dūn, India 89/L2
Dehri, India 85/E3
Dehua, China 79/C2
Deidesheim, Ger. 54/B4
Deinste, Ger. 51/G1
Deinze, Belg. 52/C2
Deister (mts.), Ger. 51/G4
Deiva Marina, It. 58/C4
Dej, Rom. 49/F2
Deje, Swe. 38/E2
Dejiang, China 83/J2
Dejima, Japan 77/E1
Dekemhare (Dek'emhāre), Erit. 88/C5
Del Campillo, Arg. 158/D2
Del Carril, Arg. 158/J11
Del City, Ok, US 137/N15
Del Dios, Ca, US 136/C4
Del Gran Paradiso, It. 58/A2
Del Mar, Ca, US 136/C5
Del Norte, Co, US 129/F3
Del Rio, Tx, US 129/G5
Del Valle, Arg. 158/E2
Del Valle (lake), Ca, US 135/L11
Delacroix, La, US 137/Q17
Delafield, Wi, US 135/P13
Delano, Ca, US 128/C4
Delareyville, SAfr. 106/D2
Delarode (lake), Sk, Can. 126/G2
Delavan, Wi, US 129/K2
Delavan (lake), Wi, US 135/P14
Delavan Lake, Wi, US 135/N14
Delaware (riv.), US 130/F3
Delaware (state), US 130/F4
Delaware, NJ, US 138/C2
Delaware (bay), NJ, US 130/F4
Delaware, Oh, US 130/D3
Delaware (co.), Pa, US 138/C4
Delaware (pass), Pa, US 138/C2
Delaware City, De, US 138/C4
Delaware Water Gap Nat'l Rec. Area, Pa, US 130/F3
Delbrück, Ger. 51/F5
Delčevo, FYROM 47/H2
Delden, Neth. 50/D4
Delebio, It. 57/F5
Delegate, Austl. 115/D3
Delémont, Swi. 56/D3
Delft, Neth. 50/B4
Delfzijl, Neth. 50/D2
Delgada (pt.), Arg. 158/E4
Delgado (cape), Moz. 104/D5
Delhi, India 86/D5
Delhi (state), India 82/C2
Delhi, Il, US 137/G7
Delhi, La, US 129/K4
Delice, Turk. 90/C2
Delice (riv.), Turk. 62/E5
Delījān, Iran 88/F2
Déline, NW, Can. 122/D2
Delisle, Sk, Can. 126/G3
Dell Rapids, SD, US 127/J5
Delligsen, Ger. 51/G5
Delmas, SAfr. 106/Q13
Delme (riv.), Ger. 51/F3
Delmenhorst, Ger. 51/F2
Delmiro Gouveia, Braz. 154/C3
Delmont, NJ, US 138/D5
Delnice, Cro. 48/B3

183
Delor – Dörve

Deloraine, Austl. 115/C4
Deloraine, Mb, Can. 127/H3
Delphi (Dhelfoi) (ruin), Gre. 47/H3
Delphos, Oh, US 130/C3
Delportshoop, SAfr. 106/D3
Delran, NJ, US 138/D4
Delray Beach, Fl, US 133/H5
Delson, Qu, Can. 131/N7
Delta, Ut, US 128/D3
Delta (state), Nga. 103/G5
Delta, Pa, US 138/B4
Delta del Tigre, Uru. 159/K11
Delta du Saloum, PN du, Sen. 102/A3
Delta Junction, Ak, US 134/J3
Delta-Mendota (canal), Ca, US 135/M11
Deltona, Fl, US 133/H4
Delvinë, Alb. 47/G3
Dëma (riv.), Rus. 87/C2
Demanda, Sierra de la (range), Sp. 44/D1
Demarcation (pt.), Ak, US 134/K2
Demarest, NJ, US 139/K8
Demba, D.R. Congo 105/D2
Dembī Dolo, Eth. 97/M6
Demer (riv.), Belg. 40/C3
Demerara (riv.), Guy. 153/G3
Demerara-Mahaica (pol. reg.), Guy. 153/G3
Demerval Lobão, Braz. 154/B2
Deming, NM, US 132/B3
Demini (riv.), Braz. 150/F3
Demirci, Turk. 90/B2
Demirkent, Turk. 90/C2
Demirköprü (dam), Turk. 90/B2
Demirköy, Turk. 49/H5
Demirtaş, Turk. 49/J5
Demmin, Ger. 38/E5
Democratic Republic of the Congo (ctry.) 93/E5
Demone (valley), It. 46/D4
Demopolis, Al, US 133/G3
Dempo (peak), Indo. 80/B4
Dempster (pt.), Austl. 112/D5
Den Burg, Neth. 50/B2
Den Ham, Neth. 50/D4
Den Helder, Neth. 50/B3
Den Oever, Neth. 50/C3
Denain, Fr. 52/C3
Denakil (reg.), Djib.,Eth 97/P5
Denali NP and Prsv., Ak, US 134/H3
Denare Beach, Sk, Can. 127/H2
Denbigh, Wal, UK 35/E5
Denbighshire (co.), Wal, UK 35/E5
Dender (riv.), Belg. 40/B3
Denderleeuw, Belg. 53/D2
Dendermonde, Belg. 53/D1
Denekamp, Neth. 50/E4
Deng Xian, China 72/C4
Dengfeng, China 72/C4
Dengkou, China 70/J3
Dengta, China 79/B3
Denham (sound), Austl. 112/B3
Denham, Austl. 112/B3
Denholme, Eng, UK 35/G4
Denia, Sp. 45/F3
Deniliquin, Austl. 115/C2
Denio, Nv, US 126/D5
Denison (mt.), Ak, US 134/H4
Denison, Ia, US 127/K5
Denison, Tx, US 129/H4
Denizli, Turk. 90/B2
Denizli (prov.), Turk. 90/B2
Denkendorf, Ger. 55/E5
Denklingen, Ger. 57/G2
Denman, Austl. 115/D2
Denmark, Austl. 112/C5
Denmark (str.), Grld.,Ice. 119/R3
Denmark (ctry.) 38/C4
Dennisville, NJ, US 138/D5
Denpasar, Indo. 80/E5
Dent de Lys (peak), Swi. 56/C4
Dent d'Hérens (peak), It. 56/D6
Dentergem, Belg. 52/C2
Dentlein am Forst, Ger. 54/D4
Denton, Eng, UK 35/F5
Denton, Md, US 138/C6
Denton, Tx, US 132/D3
Denton, Tx, US 129/H4
D'Entrecasteaux (isls.), PNG 116/D5
D'Entrecasteaux (pt.), Austl. 112/B5
Dents du Midi (peak), Swi. 56/C5
Denver (cap.), Co, US 137/C3
Denver (co.), Co, US 137/B3
Denver, Pa, US 138/B3
Denver International (int'l arpt.), Co, US 137/C3
Denver Museum of Natural History, Co, US 137/C3
Denville, NJ, US 138/D2
Denzlingen, Ger. 56/D1
Deoband, India 86/D5
Deogarh, India 82/D3
Deoghar, India 85/F3
Deohā (riv.), India 84/B1
Deolāli, India 89/K5
Deoli, India 82/C3
Déols, Fr. 42/D3
Deorī, India 84/B4
Deoria, India 84/D2
Dependencias Federales (state), Ven. 153/E1
Depew, NY, US 131/S10
Depok, Indo. 80/C5
Deqing, China 79/B3
Deqing, China 72/L9
Dera Ghāzi Khān, Pak. 86/A4
Dera Gopipur, India 86/D4
Dera Ismāīl Khān, Pak. 86/A4
Derbent, Rus. 63/J4
Derby, Eng, UK 35/G6
Derby (co.), Eng, UK 35/G6
Derby, Ct, US 139/E1
Derbyshire (co.), Eng, UK 35/G6
Derdap NP, Serb. 62/B3
Derecske, Hun. 48/E2
Dereköy, Turk. 49/H5
Derendingen, Swi. 56/D3
Derg, Lough (lake), Ire. 31/P10
Derik, Turk. 90/E2
Derinkuyu, Turk. 90/C2
Dernau, Ger. 53/G2
Déroute, Passage de la (chan.), Fr. 42/B2
Derravaragh (lake), Ire. 34/A4
Derry, NH, US 131/G3
Derryboy, NI, UK 34/C3
Dervaig, Sc, UK 31/Q8
Derventa, Bosn. 48/C3
Dervio, It. 57/F5
Derwent (riv.), Austl. 115/C4
Derwent (riv.), Eng, UK 35/E2
Derwent (res.), Eng, UK 35/F2
Derwent Water (lake), Eng, UK 35/E2
Des Allemands, La, US 137/P17
Des Moines (cap.), Ia, US 127/K5
Des Moines (riv.), Ia,Mn, US 125/H3
Des Peres, Mo, US 137/G8
Desaguadero (riv.), Bol. 150/E7
Desaguadero, Peru 156/D5
Desagües de los Colorados (dry lake), Arg. 157/C2
Desana, It. 58/D2
Descabezado Grande (vol.), Chile 158/C2
Descalvado, Braz. 155/C2
Descartes, Fr. 42/D3
Deschambault (lake), Sk, Can. 127/H2
Deschambault Lake, Sk, Can. 127/H2
Deschutes (riv.), Or, US 126/C4
Desdunes, Haiti 145/H2
Desē, Eth. 97/N5
Dese (riv.), It. 59/F2
Deseado (riv.), Arg. 147/C7
Deseado (cape), Chile 159/B7
Desengaño (pt.), Arg. 159/D6
Desenzano del Garda, It. 58/D2
Désertines, Fr. 42/E3
Desio, It. 58/C1
Desna (riv.), Ukr. 62/D2
Desolación (isl.), Chile 157/A7
Desordem, Serra da (range), Braz. 154/A2
Despatch, SAfr. 106/D4
Dessau, Ger. 40/E3
Dessel, Belg. 50/C6
Dessoubre (riv.), Fr. 56/C3
Destelbergen, Belg. 52/C1
Destrehan, La, US 137/P17
Destruction Bay, Yk, Can. 134/L3
Desulo, It. 46/A2
Desvres, Fr. 52/A2
Deta, Rom. 48/E3
Detern, Ger. 51/E2
Detmold, Ger. 51/F5
Detroit (riv.), Can.,US 135/F7
Detroit Lakes, Mn, US 127/K4
Detroit Metropolitan Wayne County (int'l arpt.), Mi, US 130/D3
Dettelbach, Ger. 54/D3
Dettifoss (falls), Ice. 37/P6
Dettwiller, Fr. 53/G6
Deua NP, Austl. 115/D2
Deuil-la-Barre, Fr. 30/J5
Deûle (riv.), Fr. 52/B2
Deurne, Belg. 50/B6
Deurne, Neth. 50/C6
Deustua, Peru 156/D4
Deutsch Evern, Ger. 51/H2
Deutsch Wagram, Aus. 49/P7
Deutschkreutz, Aus. 43/M3
Deutschlandsberg, Aus. 43/L3
Deux-Montagnes, Qu, Can. 131/N6
Deux-Montagnes (co.), Qu, Can. 131/M6
Deux-Montagnes, Lac des (lake), Qu, Can. 131/M7
Deva, Rom. 48/F3
Dévaványa, Hun. 48/E2
Develi, Turk. 90/C2
Deventer, Neth. 50/D4
Deveron (riv.), Sc, UK 36/D2
Deville, Fr. 53/D4
Devil's (isl.), FrG. 151/H2
Devils (riv.), Mex. 143/E2
Devil's Elbow (pass), Sc, UK 36/C3
Devils Lake, ND, US 127/J3
Devils Paw (peak), Ak, US 134/M4
Devils Postpile Nat'l Mon., Ca, US 128/C3
Devils Slide, Ut, US 137/K11
Devine, Tx, US 129/H5
Devizes, Eng, UK 32/E4
Devnya, Bul. 49/H4
Devoll (riv.), Alb.,Gre. 48/E5
Devon, Ab, Can. 126/E2
Devon (isl.), Nun., Can. 123/S7
Devon (co.), Eng, UK 32/C5
Devon (riv.), Sc, UK 36/C4
Devon-Berwyn, Pa, US 138/C3
Devonport, Austl. 115/C4
Devore, Ca, US 136/C2
Devrek, Turk. 49/K5
Devrek (riv.), Turk. 49/K5
Devrez (riv.), Turk. 62/E4
Dewa (pt.), Indo. 80/A3
Dewa (mts.), Japan 76/B4
Dewās, India 89/L4
Dewetsdorp, SAfr. 106/D3
Dewsbury, Eng, UK 35/G4
Dexter, Me, US 131/G2
Dey-Dey (lake), Austl. 109/C3
Deyang, China 70/H5
Dez (riv.), Iran 64/E6
Dezfūl, Iran 88/E2
Dezhneva (cape), Rus. 134/E2
Dezhou, China 72/D3
Dhaban Singh, Pak. 86/B4
Dhākā (div.), Bang. 85/H4
Dhāka, India 85/E2
Dhaleswari (riv.), Bang. 85/H4
Dhali, Cyp. 91/C2
Dhāmpur, India 84/B1
Dhamtari, India 82/D3
Dhanaula, India 86/C4
Dhanaura, India 84/B1
Dhānbād, India 85/E4
Dhangadhī, Nepal 84/C1
Dhankutā, Nepal 85/F2
Dhār, India 89/L4
Dharampur, India 89/K4
Dharān, Nepal 85/F2
Dhāri, India 89/K4
Dhārīwāl, India 86/C4
Dharmapuri, India 82/C5
Dharmavaram, India 82/C5
Dharmjaygarh, India 84/D4
Dharmsāla, India 86/D3
Dhasan (riv.), India 84/B3
Dhaulāgiri (peak), Nepal 84/D1
Dhaulāgiri (zone), Nepal 84/D1
Dhaurahra, India 84/C1
Dhelfoí, Gre. 47/G3
Dhelvinákion, Gre. 47/G3
Dheskáti, Gre. 47/G3
Dheune (riv.), Fr. 56/A4
Dhībān, Jor. 91/D4
Dhidhimótikhon, Gre. 47/K2
Dhikaia, Gre. 47/K2
Dhilos (ruin), Gre. 47/J4
Dhimitsána, Gre. 47/H4
Dhírfis (peak), Gre. 47/H3
Dhistomon, Gre. 47/H3
Dhofar (reg.), Oman 88/F5
Dhokímion, Gre. 47/G3
Dholka, India 89/K4
Dhomokós, Gre. 47/H3
Dhonoúsa (isl.), Gre. 47/J4
Dhorāji, India 89/K4
Dhronbach (riv.), Ger. 53/F4
Dhūlia, India 89/K4
Dhuliān, India 85/F3
Dhulikhel, Nepal 85/E2
Dhupgāri, India 85/G2
Dhūri, India 86/C4
Di Linh, Viet. 78/E4
Dia (isl.), Gre. 47/J5
Diablo (mt.), Ak, US 134/H4
Diablo (range), Ca, US 128/B3
Diablo (plat.), Tx, US 132/B4
Diablo, Punta del (pt.), Uru. 159/G2
Diablotin (peak), Dom. 141/N9
Diadema, Braz. 211/G8
Diadema Argentina, Arg. 158/D5
Diamante (riv.), Arg. 158/D2
Diamantina, Braz. 154/B5
Diamantina (riv.), Austl. 109/D3
Diamantina, Chapada (hills), Braz. 151/K6
Diamantino, Braz. 151/G6
Diamond Bar, Ca, US 136/G8
Diamond Harbour, India 85/G4
Diamond Head (pt.), Hi, US 124/W13
Dianalund, Den. 38/D4
Dianbai, China 83/K3
Dianjiang, China 79/A1
Diano Marina, It. 58/B5
Dianshan (lake), China 72/L8
Diapaga, Burk. 103/F3
Dias Creek, NJ, US 138/D5
Diavolezza (peak), Swi. 57/F5
Dibai, India 84/B1
Dibeng, SAfr. 106/C2
Dibiāpur, India 84/B2
Dibis (well), Egypt 101/B4
Dibs, Iraq 90/F3
Dickens, Tx, US 129/G4
Dickens (pt.), RI, US 139/G1
Dickinson, ND, US 127/H4
Dickson, Tn, US 130/C4
Dicle (dam), Turk. 90/E2
Dicomano, It. 59/E5
Didam, Neth. 50/D5
Didcot, Eng, UK 33/E3
Didsbury, Ab, Can. 126/E3
Dīdwāna, India 89/K3
Didyma (ruin), Turk. 90/A2
Die Berg (peak), SAfr. 105/F6
Dieblich, Ger. 53/G3
Diébougou, Burk. 102/E4
Dieburg, Ger. 54/B3
Diedersdorf, Ger. 40/Q7
Diefenbaker (lake), Sk, Can. 126/G3
Diego de Almagro (isl.), Chile 159/B6
Diego Garcia (isl.), UK 67/G10
Diekirch (dist.), Lux. 53/E4
Diekirch, Lux. 53/F4
Diemen, Neth. 50/B4
Diemtigen, Swi. 56/D4
Diepenbeek, Belg. 53/E2
Diepenveen, Neth. 50/D4
Diepholz, Ger. 51/F3
Diepoldsau, Swi. 57/F3
Dieppe, Fr. 42/D2
Dierdorf, Ger. 53/G2
Diespeck, Ger. 54/D3
Diessen am Ammersee, Ger. 57/H2
Diest, Belg. 53/E2
Dietenheim, Ger. 57/G1
Dietenhofen, Ger. 54/D4
Dietersheim, Ger. 54/D3
Dietfurt an der Altmühl, Ger. 55/E4
Dietikon, Swi. 57/E3
Dietmannsried, Ger. 57/G2
Dietzenbach, Ger. 54/B2
Dieue-sur-Meuse, Fr. 53/E5
Dieulouard, Fr. 53/F6
Dieuze, Fr. 53/F6
Diever, Neth. 50/D3
Diez, Ger. 54/B2
Diffa, Niger 96/H5
Diffa (dept.), Niger 103/H3
Differdange, Lux. 53/E4
Difficult (mt.), Austl. 115/B3
Dīg, India 84/A2
Digboi, India 83/G2
Digby, NS, Can. 131/H2
Dighwāra, India 85/E3
Digne-les-Bains, Fr. 43/G4
Digoin, Fr. 42/E3
Digor, Turk. 90/E1
Digul (riv.), Indo. 81/K4
Digya NP, Gha. 103/E5
Dijon, Fr. 56/A3
Dikirnis, Egypt 91/B4
Diklosmta (peak), Geo. 63/H4
Diksmuide, Belg. 52/B1
Dīla, Eth. 97/N6
Dilbeek, Belg. 53/D2
Dilek Yarımadası NP, Turk. 90/A2
Dili (cap.), ETim. 81/G5
Dillenburg, Ger. 53/H2
Dillingen, Ger. 53/F5
Dillingen an der Donau, Ger. 54/D5
Dillingham, Ak, US 134/G4
Dillon, Mt, US 126/E4
Dillon, SC, US 133/J3
Dillsburg, Pa, US 138/A3
Dilolo, D.R. Congo 105/D3
Dilsen, Belg. 53/E1
Dimāpur, India 83/F2
Dimaro, It. 57/G5
Dimas, Mex. 142/D4
Dimashq (prov.), Syria 90/D3
Dimbokro, C.d'Iv. 102/D5
Dimboola, Austl. 115/B3
Dîmbovița (prov.), Rom. 49/G3
Dimbulah, Austl. 114/B2
Dimitriya Lapteva (str.), Rus. 65/P2
Dimitrovgrad, Bul. 47/J1
Dimitrovgrad, Serb. 47/H1
Dimitrovgrad, Rus. 63/J1
Dimlang (peak), Nga. 96/H6
Dimmitt, Tx, US 129/G4
Dimona, Isr. 91/D4
Dimovo, Bul. 49/F4
Dina, Pak. 86/B3
Dinagat (isl.), Phil. 79/E5
Dinagat, Phil. 79/E6
Dinājpur (pol. reg.), Bang. 85/G3
Dinan, Fr. 42/B2
Dīnānagar, India 86/C3
Dinant, Belg. 53/D3
Dinar, Turk. 90/B2
Dinard, Fr. 42/B2
Dinaric Alps (mts.), Cro. 48/C3
Dinas (pt.), Wal, UK 32/B2
Dinder NP, Sudan 97/N5
Dindigul, India 82/C5
Dindori, India 84/C4
Dinga, Pak. 86/B3
Ding'an, China 83/K4
Dingbian, China 70/J4
Dingelstädt, Ger. 51/H6
Dinggyê, China 85/F1
Dingle, Ire. 30/F10
Dingle (bay), Ire. 30/N10
Dingmans Ferry, Pa, US 138/D1
Dingnan, China 79/C3
Dingolfing, Ger. 55/F5
Dingras, Phil. 79/D4
Dingtao, China 72/C4
Dingwall, Sc, UK 36/B1
Dingxi, China 70/H4
Dingxiang, China 72/C3
Dingxing, China 72/G7
Dingyuan, China 72/D4
Dinkel (riv.), Ger. 40/M4
Dinkelsbühl, Ger. 54/D4
Dinkelscherben, Ger. 54/D6
Dinklage, Ger. 51/F3
Dinosaur Nat'l Mon., US 128/E2
Dinslaken, Ger. 50/D5
Dinsmore, Sk, Can. 126/G3
Dintel Mark (riv.), Neth. 50/B5
Dinuba, Ca, US 128/C3
Dinxperlo, Neth. 50/D5
Dioïla, Mali 102/D3
Dion (riv.), Gui. 102/C4
Diósd, Hun. 49/Q10
Diourbel (pol. reg.), Sen. 102/A3
Diourbel, Sen. 102/A3
Dīpālpur, Pak. 86/B4
Diphu, India 83/F2
Diplo, Pak. 89/J4
Dipni (dam), Turk. 90/E2
Dipperu NP, Austl. 114/C3
Dipperz, Ger. 54/C1
Dique (canal), Col. 145/H4
Diré, Mali 102/E2
Dirē Dawa, Eth. 97/P6
Diriamba, Nic. 144/E4
Dirj, Libya 99/H3
Dirk Hartog (isl.), Austl. 109/A3
Dirksland, Neth. 50/B5
Dirlewang, Ger. 57/G2
Dirranbandi, Austl. 114/C5
Dirrington Great Law (hill), Sc, UK 36/D5
Dirty Devil (riv.), Ut, US 128/E3
Disappointment (lake), Austl. 109/B3
Disappointment (isls.), FrPol. 117/L6
Discovery (bay), Austl. 115/B3
Discovery Bay, Jam. 145/G2
Disentis-Mustér, Swi. 57/E4
Disgrazi (peak), It. 57/F5
Disko (isl.), Grld. 119/M3
Disko (Qeqertarsuaq) (isl.), Grld. 123/L2
Disneyland, Ca, US 136/G8
Dison, Belg. 53/E2
Dispur, India 83/F2
Disraëli, Qu, Can. 131/G2
Dissen am Teutoburger Wald, Ger. 51/F4
District of Columbia (fed. dist.), US 138/A6
Distrito Féderal (fed. dist.), Braz. 154/A4
Distrito Federal (fed. dist.), Mex. 140/A5
Distrito Federal (fed. dist.), Ven. 153/E2
Distrito Federal (fed. dist.), Col. 152/C3
Disūq, Egypt 91/B4
Ditchling Beacon (hill), Eng, UK 33/F5
Dittaino (riv.), It. 46/D4
Dittelbrunn, Ger. 54/D2
Ditzingen, Ger. 54/C5
Diu, India 82/B3
Diva (riv.), Serb. 48/D4
Dive (riv.), Fr. 42/D3
Dividing Creek, NJ, US 138/C5
Divinolândia, Braz. 211/G6
Divinópolis, Braz. 155/C2
Divisa Nova, Braz. 211/G6
Divisor, Serra do (mts.), Braz. 150/D5
Divo, C.d'Iv. 102/D5
Divonne-les-Bains, Fr. 56/C5
Divriği, Turk. 90/D2
Dix (lake), Swi. 56/D5
Dixmoor, Il, US 135/Q16
Dixon, Il, US 127/L5
Dixon Entrance (chan.), Can.,US 134/M4
Diyadin, Turk. 90/E2
Diyāla (gov.), Iraq 90/F3
Diyarb Najm, Egypt 91/B4
Diyarbakır (prov.), Turk. 90/E2
Diyarbakır, Turk. 90/E2
Djado (plat.), Niger 93/D2
Djakotomé, Ben. 103/F5
Djamaa, Alg. 99/G2
Djambala, Congo 96/H8
Djanet, Alg. 99/H4
Djebel-Amrag (mtn.), Alg. 100/D3
Djebel Tichka (peak), Mor. 98/C3
Djedi, Oued (riv.), Alg. 99/G2
Djelfa, Alg. 96/F1
Djema, CAfr. 97/L6
Djemila (ruin), Alg. 100/H4
Djénné, Mali 102/D3
Djibo, Burk. 103/E3
Djibouti (ctry.) 97/P5
Djibouti (cap.), Djib. 97/P5
Djougou, Ben. 103/F4
Djúpivogur, Ice. 37/P7
Dnepr (riv.), Rus. 62/D1
Dnipro (riv.), Ukr. 27/H3
Dniprodzerzhyns'k, Ukr. 62/E2
Dnipropetrovs'k, Ukr. 62/E2
Dnipropetrovs'ka Oblasti, Ukr. 62/E2
Dniprovs'kyy Lyman (estu.), Ukr. 49/K2
Dnister (riv.), Ukr. 40/M4
Dnistrovs'kyy Lyman (estu.), Ukr. 49/K2
Dnyapro (riv.), Bela. 39/P4
Do (lake), Mali 103/E3
Do Rāh (pass), Afg. 89/K1
Do Son, Viet. 78/D1
Doany, Madg. 107/J6
Doba, Chad 96/J6
Dobbs Ferry, NY, US 139/K7
Dobele, Lat. 39/K3
Döbeln, Ger. 40/G3
Doberai (pen.), Indo. 81/H4
Dobiegniew, Pol. 41/H2
Dobogó-kó (peak), Hun. 49/Q9
Doboj, Bosn. 48/D3
Dobřany, Czh. 55/G3
Dobre Miasto, Pol. 39/J5
Dobrich, Bul. 49/H4
Dobříš, Czh. 55/H3
Dobruja (reg.), Bul. 49/H4
Dobrush, Bela. 62/D1
Dobryanka, Rus. 61/N4
Doce (riv.), Braz. 151/K7
Dochart (riv.), Sc, UK 36/B4
Dock Junction, Ga, US 133/H4
Docker River, Austl. 113/F3
Doctor Arroyo, Mex. 143/E4
Doctor Pedro P. Peña, Par. 157/D1
Doctor Petru Groza, Rom. 48/F2
Doda (lake), Qu, Can. 130/F1
Doda, India 86/C3
Doda (riv.), India 86/D3
Dodder (riv.), Ire. 34/B5
Doddinghurst, Eng, UK 30/D2
Dodecanese (isl.), Gre. 90/A2
Dodge City, Ks, US 129/G3
Dodger Stadium, Ca, US 136/F7
Dodgeville, Wi, US 127/L5
Dodman (pt.), Eng, UK 32/B6
Dodoma, Tanz. 104/B4
Dodoma (pol. reg.), Tanz. 104/B4
Dodori Nat'l Rsv., Kenya 104/D3
Dodsland, Sk, Can. 126/F3
Dodworth, Eng, UK 35/G4
Doesburg, Neth. 50/D4
Doetinchem, Neth. 50/D5
Doğanhisar, Turk. 90/B2
Doğankent (riv.), Turk. 90/D1
Doğanşar, Turk. 90/D1
Doğanşehir, Turk. 90/D2
Doğanyurt, Turk. 90/C1
Döğer, Turk. 90/B2
Dogliani, It. 58/A3
Dogondoutchi, Niger 103/G3
Doğubayazıt, Turk. 90/F2
Doğukaradeniz (mts.), Turk. 90/D1
Dohad, India 89/K4
Dohrīghāt, India 84/D2
Doi Khun Tan NP, Thai. 78/B2
Doilungdêqên, China 82/F2
Doiras, Embalse de (res.), Sp. 44/B1
Dois de Julho (int'l arpt.), Braz. 154/C4
Dois Irmãos, Serra (mts.), Braz. 151/K5
Doische, Belg. 53/D3
Dokka, Nor. 38/D1
Dokkum, Neth. 50/D2
Dokkumer Ee (riv.), Neth. 50/C2
Doksy, Czh. 55/H1
Dolbeau, Qu, Can. 131/F1
Dolcedorme (peak), It. 46/E3
Dole, Fr. 56/B3
Dolent (peak), Swi. 56/D6
Dolgellau, Wal, UK 32/C1
Dolgoprudnyy, Rus. 61/W9
Dolianova, It. 46/A3
Dolinsk, Rus. 71/R2
Dolj (prov.), Rom. 49/F3
Dollar, Sc, UK 36/C4
Dollar Law (peak), Sc, UK 36/C5
Dollard-des-Ormeaux, Qu, Can. 131/N7
Dollard (Dollart) (bay), Neth.,Ger. 51/E2
Doller (riv.), Fr. 40/D5
Dollnstein, Ger. 54/E5
Dollmar (peak), Ger. 54/D1
Dolmen (ruin), It. 46/E2
Dolna Banya, Bul. 47/H1
Dolni Dŭbnik, Bul. 49/G4
Dolnośląskie (prov.), Pol. 41/J2
Dolo, Eth. 97/P7
Dolo, It. 59/F2
Dolo (riv.), It. 58/D4
Doloon, Mong. 70/J3
Dolores, Arg. 158/F3
Dolores, Guat. 144/D2
Dolores (riv.), Co, US 128/E3
Dolores, Co, US 132/A2
Dolores, Uru. 159/J10
Dolores, Ven. 152/D2
Dolphin (cape), UK 159/F6
Dolphin and Union (str.), Nun., Can. 122/E2
Dölsach, Aus. 43/K3
Dolton, Il, US 135/Q16
Dom (peak), Swi. 56/D5
Dom (peak), Indo. 81/J4
Dom Noi (res.), Thai. 78/D3
Dom Pedrito, Braz. 157/F3
Dom Pedro, Braz. 154/A2
Domat-Ems, Swi. 57/F4
Domažlice, Czh. 55/F4
Dombasle-sur-Meurthe, Fr. 53/F6
Dombay-Ul'gen (peak), Geo. 63/G4
Dombes (lake), Fr. 56/B5
Dombóvár, Hun. 48/D2
Dombrád, Hun. 48/E1
Domburg, Neth. 50/A5
Dome C, US, Ant. 160/J
Domérat, Fr. 42/E3
Domeyko, Cordillera (mts.), Chile 157/C1
Dominica (ctry.) 141/N9
Dominica Passage (chan.), Dom.,Guad. 141/N9
Dominican Republic (ctry.) 141/H4
Dommartin-lès-Remiremont, Fr. 56/C2
Dommartin-lès-Toul, Fr. 53/E6
Dommel (riv.), Belg. 53/E1
Domodedovo (int'l arpt.), Rus. 61/W9
Domodossola, It. 57/E5
Domohāni, India 85/G2
Domont, Fr. 30/J4
Dompu, Indo. 81/E5
Domrémy-la-Pucelle, Fr. 56/B1
Dömsöd, Hun. 48/D2
Domusnovas, It. 46/A3
Domuyo (vol.), Arg. 158/C3
Domvilk (mt.), Austl. 114/C5
Domžale, Slov. 43/L3
Don (riv.), Eng, UK 35/G5
Don (ridge), Rus. 64/E5
Don (riv.), Rus. 27/J4
Don Benito, Sp. 44/C3
Donabate, Ire. 34/B5
Donada, It. 59/F2
Donaghadee, NI, UK 34/C2
Donaghmore, NI, UK 34/B2
Donald, Austl. 115/B3
Donaldsonville, La, US 129/K5
Doñana NP, Sp. 44/B4
Donath, Swi. 57/F4
Donau (Danube) (riv.), Ger. 43/H2
Donaueschingen, Ger. 57/E2
Donauwörth, Ger. 54/D5
Doncaster, Eng, UK 35/G4
Doncaster (co.), Eng, UK 35/G4
Donchery, Fr. 53/D4
Dondra Head (pt.), SrL. 82/D6
Donegal, Ire. 31/P9
Donegal (dist.), Ire. 34/A1
Donegal (bay), Ire. 31/P9
Donets (riv.), Rus., Ukr. 63/G2
Donets'k, Ukr. 62/F2
Donets'k (int'l arpt.), Ukr. 62/F2
Donets'ka Oblasti, Ukr. 62/F3
Dong (riv.), Viet. 78/D2
Dong Ha, Viet. 78/D2
Dong Hoi, Viet. 78/D2
Dong Noi (riv.), Viet. 79/A5
Donga (riv.), Nga. 103/H4
Dongar Parāsia, India 84/B4
Dongara, Austl. 112/B4
Dongbei (plain), China 72/E2
Dongchuan, China 83/H2
Dong'e, China 72/D3
Dongen, Neth. 50/B5
Dongfang, China 83/J4
Donggou, China 73/C3
Dongguan, China 83/K3
Dongguang, China 72/D3
Donghai, China 72/D4
Dongio, Swi. 57/E5
Dongkya (pass), China 85/G2
Donglan, China 79/A3
Dongliao (riv.), China 72/F2
Dongming, China 72/C4
Dongo, It. 57/F5
Dongping, China 72/D4
Dongsha (isl.), China 79/C3
Dongshan, China 79/C3
Dongtai, China 72/E4
Dongtiao (riv.), China 72/L9
Dongting (lake), China 79/B2
Dongzhi, China 79/C1
Donihue, Chile 158/N9
Donjek (riv.), Yk, Can. 122/C2
Donji Komren, Serb. 47/G1
Donji Vakuf, Bosn. 48/C3
Donnas, It. 58/A1
Donnersberg (peak), Ger. 53/G4
Donnybrook, Austl. 114/D4
Donnybrook, Austl. 112/B5
Donon (peak), Fr. 56/D1
Donoratico, It. 43/J5
Donzdorf, Ger. 54/C5
Donzy, Fr. 42/E3
Dooleena (peak), Austl. 112/C2
Doon (riv.), Sc, UK 36/B6
Doon (lake), Sc, UK 36/B6
Doonbeg, Ire. 31/P10
Doonerak (mt.), Ak, US 134/H2
Door (pen.), Wi, US 127/M4
Doorn (riv.), SAfr. 106/B3
Doorn, Neth. 50/C4
Doppo (peak), It. 58/D1
Doqên (lake), China 85/G1
Dora (lake), Austl. 109/B3
Dora Riparia (riv.), It. 43/G4
Dorada (coast), Sp. 45/F2
Dorchester, NB, Can. 131/H2
Dorchester, Il, US 137/H7
Dorchester, Eng, UK 32/D5
Dorchester (cape), Nun., Can. 123/J2
Dorchester, NJ, US 138/D5
Dordogne (riv.), Fr. 42/D4
Dordrecht, SAfr. 106/D3
Dordrecht, Neth. 50/B5
Dore (lake), Sk, Can. 126/G2
Dore, Monts (mts.), Fr. 42/E4
Dores do Indaiá, Braz. 155/C1
Dorfen, Ger. 55/F6
Dorfen (riv.), Ger. 55/E6
Dorgali, It. 46/A2
Dori, Burk. 103/E3
Dorion, Qu, Can. 131/M7
Dorking, Eng, UK 30/C3
Dorlisheim, Fr. 56/D1
Dormagen, Ger. 53/F1
Dormans, Fr. 52/C5
Dornach, Swi. 56/D3
Dornbirn, Aus. 57/F3
Dorney Park/ Wildwater Kingdom, Pa, US 138/C2
Dornhan, Ger. 57/E1
Dorno, It. 58/B2
Dornoch Firth (inlet), Sc, UK 36/B1
Dornod (prov.), Mong. 71/K2
Dornogovĭ (prov.), Mong. 71/J3
Dornstadt, Ger. 54/C6
Dornstetten, Ger. 54/B6
Dorog, Hun. 49/Q9
Dorothy, NJ, US 138/D5
Dörpen, Ger. 51/E3
Dorre (isl.), Austl. 112/B3
Dorrigo, Austl. 115/E1
Dorrigo NP, Austl. 115/E1
Dorsale (mts.), Tun. 46/A5
Dorsbach (riv.), Ger. 54/B2
Dorset (co.), Eng, UK 32/D5
Dorsey, Il, US 137/G8
Dorsten, Ger. 50/D5
Dortan, Fr. 56/B5
Dortmund, Ger. 51/E5
Dortmund-Ems (canal), Ger. 51/E4
Dortmund (Wickede) (int'l arpt.), Ger. 51/E5
Dörtyol, Turk. 91/E1
Dorum, Ger. 51/F1
Dorval, Qu, Can. 131/N7
Dörverden, Ger. 51/G3

Dos B – Edwar

Dos Bahias (cape), Arg. 158/D5
Dos de Mayo, Peru 156/C2
Dos Hermanas, Sp. 44/C4
Döşemealtı, Turk. 91/B1
Dosewallips (riv.), Wa, US 135/A2
Dōshi, Japan 77/C2
Dōshi (riv.), Japan 77/C2
Dosse (riv.), Ger. 40/G2
Dosso, Niger 103/F3
Dosso (dept.), Niger 103/F3
Dosson, It. 59/F1
Dossor, Kaz. 63/K3
Dot Lake, Ak, US 134/K3
Dothan, Al, US 133/G4
Dötlingen, Ger. 51/F3
Döttingen, Swi. 57/E2
Douai, Fr. 52/C3
Douala, Camr. 96/G7
Douar el Caïd el Gueddara, Mor. 100/A2
Douar Toulal, Mor. 100/B3
Douarnenez, Fr. 42/A2
Douarnenez, Baie de (bay), Fr. 42/A2
Double Island (pt.), Austl. 114/D4
Double Mountain Fork Brazos (riv.), Tx, US 129/G4
Double Mtn. Fork (riv.), Tx, US 143/E1
Doubs (riv.), Fr. 42/F3
Doubs (dept.), Fr. 56/C3
Doubs, Fr. 56/C4
Doubtful Island (bay), Austl. 112/C5
Douchy-les-Mines, Fr. 52/C3
Doue, Fr. 30/M5
Doué-la-Fontaine, Fr. 42/C3
Douentza, Mali 102/E3
Dougga (ruin), Tun. 100/L6
Douglas, SAfr. 106/C3
Douglas (cap.), IM, UK 34/D3
Douglas, Sc, UK 36/C5
Douglas (mt.), Ak, US 134/H4
Douglas (co.), Co, US 137/C4
Douglas, Ga, US 133/H4
Douglas, Wy, US 127/G5
Douglassville, Pa, US 138/C3
Doulaincourt-Saucourt, Fr. 56/B1
Doullens, Fr. 52/B3
Doune, Sc, UK 36/B4
Doune (peak), Sc, UK 36/B4
Doupovské Hory (mts.), Czh. 43/K1
Dour, Belg. 52/C3
Dourados, Braz. 151/H8
Dourdan, Fr. 30/J6
Dourdou (riv.), Fr. 42/E4
Dourh (peak), Mor. 99/E2
Douro (riv.), Port. 44/B2
Dousman, Wi, US 135/P13
Doussard, Fr. 56/C6
Douvaine, Fr. 56/C5
Douvrin, Fr. 52/B2
Doux (riv.), Fr. 42/F4
Douze (riv.), Fr. 42/C4
Dove Creek, Co, US 128/E3
Dover, Austl. 115/C4
Dover (pt.), Austl. 112/E5
Dover, Eng, UK 33/H4
Dover (cap.), De, US 138/C5
Dover, NJ, US 138/D2
Dover, Pa, US 138/B4
Dover-Foxcroft, Me, US 131/G2
Dover, Strait of (str.), Fr.,UK 42/D1
Dovrefjell NP, Nor. 37/D3
Dow, Il, US 137/G7
Dowerin, Austl. 112/C4
Dowlatābād, Iran 89/G3
Down (dist.), NI, UK 34/C3
Downers Grove, Il, US 135/P16
Downey, Ca, US 136/F8
Downieville, Ca, US 128/B3
Downingtown, Pa, US 138/C4
Downpatrick, NI, UK 34/C3
Doylestown, Pa, US 138/C3
Dōzen (isl.), Japan 74/C3
Dozois (res.), Qu, Can. 130/E2
Drâa (cape), Mor. 98/C3
Drâa, Oued (riv.), Mor. 93/B2
Drac (riv.), Fr. 42/F4
Dracena, Braz. 155/B2
Drachten, Neth. 50/D2
Drăgăneşti-Olt, Rom. 49/G3
Dragoman, Bul. 47/H1
Dragon's Mouth (str.), Trin.,Ven. 153/F2
Draguignan, Fr. 43/G5
Drake (passg.) 157/C8
Drake, Co, US 137/B2
Drake (passg.), SAm. 159/D8
Drakensberg (mts.), SAfr. 93/E8
Dráma, Gre. 47/J2
Drammen, Nor. 38/D2
Drance (riv.), Swi. 56/D5
Drancy, Fr. 30/K5
Drangedal, Nor. 38/C2
Dranse (riv.), Fr. 56/C5
Dransfeld, Ger. 51/G5
Draper, Ut, US 137/K12
Drau (riv.), Aus. 43/K3
Dráva (riv.), Aus. 48/C3
Drava (riv.), Slov. 43/L3
Draveil, Fr. 30/K5
Drawa (riv.), Pol. 41/H2
Drawienski NP, Pol. 41/H2
Drawsko Pomorskie, Pol. 41/H2
Drayton, ND, US 127/J3
Drayton Valley, Ab, Can. 126/E2
Dreghorn, Sc, UK 36/B5
Drei Zinnen (peak), PNG 81/K4
Dreiesselberg (peak), Ger. 55/G5
Dreisam (riv.), Ger. 56/D2
Drensteinfurt, Ger. 51/E5
Drenthe (prov.), Neth. 50/D3
Drentse Hoofdvaart (riv.), Neth. 50/D3
Drentwede, Ger. 51/F3
Dresano, It. 58/C2
Dresden, Ger. 41/G3
Drezdenko, Pol. 41/H2
Driebergen, Neth. 50/C4
Driedorf, Ger. 53/H2
Drigh Road, Pak. 89/J4
Drimoleague, Ire. 31/P11
Drin (gulf), Alb. 47/F2
Drin (riv.), Alb. 47/F1
Drina (riv.), Bosn. 48/D4
Drniš, Cro. 48/C4
Dro, It. 57/G6
Drøbak, Nor. 38/D2
Drobeta-Turnu Severin, Rom. 48/F3
Drochtersen, Ger. 51/G1
Drocourt, Fr. 30/H4
Drogheda, Ire. 34/B4
Drohobych, Ukr. 62/B2
Droitwich, Eng, UK 32/D2
Drolshagen, Ger. 53/G1
Dromiskin, Ire. 34/B4
Dromore (riv.), Ire. 34/A3
Dromore, NI, UK 34/B3
Dronero, It. 43/G4
Dronfield, Eng, UK 35/G5
Drongan, Sc, UK 36/B6
Dronne (riv.), Fr. 42/D4
Dronten, Neth. 50/C3
Dropt (riv.), Fr. 42/D4
Drouette (riv.), Fr. 52/A6
Drowning (riv.), On, Can. 130/C1
Drumbeg, NI, UK 34/C2
Drumcar, Ire. 34/B4
Drumheller, Ab, Can. 126/E3
Drumleck (pt.), Ire. 34/B5
Drummond (range), Austl. 109/D3
Drummond (pt.), Austl. 113/G5
Drummond (mt.), Austl. 114/B4
Drummondville, Qu, Can. 131/F2
Drumochter, Pass of (pass), Sc, UK 36/B3
Drunen, Neth. 50/C5
Druridge (bay), Eng, UK 35/G1
Drusenheim, Fr. 53/G6
Druskininkai, Lith. 39/K4
Druten, Neth. 50/C5
Drvar, Bosn. 48/C3
Drwęca (riv.), Pol. 41/K2
Dry Fork Cheyenne (riv.), Wy, US 129/F2
Dry Tortugas (isl.), Fl, US 133/H5
Dry Tortugas NP, Fl, US 133/H5
Dryanovo, Bul. 47/J1
Dryden, On, Can. 127/K3
Dryden, Tx, US 132/C4
Dryden, Mi, US 135/F6
Drygarn Fawr (peak), Wal, UK 32/C2
Du Bois, Pa, US 130/E3
Du Page (co.), Il, US 135/P16
Du Page (riv.), Il, US 135/P16
Du Page, East Br. (riv.), Il, US 135/P16
Du Quoin, Il, US 129/K3
Duaringa, Austl. 114/C3
Duarte (peak), DRep. 141/G4
Duarte, Ca, US 136/G7
Dubawnt (riv.), NW, Can. 122/F2
Dubawnt (lake), Nun., Can. 122/F2
Dubayy, UAE 89/G3
Dubbo, Austl. 115/D2
Dübendorf, Swi. 57/E3
Dübener Heide (phys. reg.), Ger. 40/G3
Dubino, It. 57/F5
Dublin (cap.), Ire. 34/B5
Dublin (co.), Ire. 34/B5
Dublin, Ca, US 135/L11
Dublin, Ga, US 133/H3
Dublin, Md, US 138/B4
Dublin, Pa, US 138/C3
Dubna, Rus. 60/H4
Dubnica nad Váhom, Slvk. 41/K4
Dubno, Ukr. 62/C2
Dubois, Wy, US 126/F5
Duboistown, Pa, US 138/A1
Dubossary (res.), Mol. 49/J2
Dubrājpur, India 85/F4
Dubrovnik, Cro. 47/F1
Dubrovnik (int'l arpt.), Cro. 47/F1
Dubuque, Ia, US 127/L5
Duchang, China 79/C2
Duchcov, Czh. 55/G1
Duchesne (riv.), Ut, US 128/E2
Duchesne, Ut, US 128/E2
Ducie (isl.), Pitc. 117/N7
Duck (riv.), Tn, US 130/C5
Duck (lake), Mi, US 135/E7
Duckabush (riv.), Wa, US 135/A2
Duda (riv.), Col. 152/C4
Duddon (riv.), Eng, UK 35/E3
Dudelange, Lux. 53/F5
Dudenhofen, Ger. 54/B4
Duderstadt, Ger. 51/H5
Dudh Kosi (riv.), Nepal 85/F2
Dūdhi, India 84/D3
Dudhwa NP, India 84/C1
Düdingen, Swi. 56/D4
Dudinka, Rus. 64/J3
Dudley, Eng, UK 32/D1
Dudley (co.), Eng, UK 32/D2
Dueñas, Sp. 44/C2
Duero (riv.), Sp. 44/C2
Dueville, It. 59/E1
Dufaja (riv.), Kenya 104/C3
Duff (isls.), Sol. 116/F5
Duffel, Belg. 53/D1
Dufftown, Sc, UK 36/C2
Dufour (Dufourspitze) (peak), Swi. 58/A1
Dufourspitze (peak), Swi. 43/G4
Dugi Otok (isl.), Cro. 48/B3
Dugny-sur-Meuse, Fr. 53/E5
Dugo Selo, Cro. 48/C3
Dugway, Ut, US 128/D2
Duich (lake), Sc, UK 36/A2
Duida (peak), Ven. 153/E4
Duida Marahuaca, PN, Ven. 150/E3
Duingen, Ger. 51/G4
Duisburg, Ger. 50/D6
Duitama, Col. 152/C3
Duiven, Neth. 50/D5
Duke of Gloucester (isls.), FrPol. 117/L7
Duke's (pass), Sc, UK 36/B4
Dukielska (Dukla Pass) (pass), Pol. 41/L4
Dulan, China 70/G4
Dulce (riv.), Arg. 157/D2
Dulce, NM, US 128/F3
Dulce (gulf), Pan. 145/F4
Dulce Nombre de Culmí, Hon. 144/E3
Duleek, Ire. 34/B4
Dŭlgopol, Bul. 49/H4
Duliu (riv.), China 83/J2
Dullewāla, Pak. 86/A4
Dülmen, Ger. 51/E5
Dulnain (riv.), Sc, UK 36/C2
Dulovo, Bul. 49/H4
Dumalinao, Phil. 79/D6
Dumaran (isl.), Phil. 81/E1
Dumaresq (riv.), Austl. 115/D1
Dumas, Ar, US 129/K4
Dumas, Tx, US 129/G4
Dumbarton, Sc, UK 36/B5
Ďumbier (peak), Slvk. 41/K4
Dumbleyung, Austl. 112/C5
Dumbrăveni, Rom. 49/G2
Dume (pt.), Ca, US 136/B2
Dumfries, Sc, UK 34/E1
Dumfries and Galloway (pol. reg.), Sc, UK 36/C6
Dumka, India 85/F3
Dumlu, Turk. 63/G4
Dümmer (lake), Ger. 51/F3
Dumoine (riv.), Qu, Can. 130/E2
Dumoine (lake), Qu, Can. 123/J4
Dumont, NJ, US 139/K8
Dumont d'Urville, Fr., Ant. 160/K
Dumraon, India 85/E3
Dumyāţ (gov.), Egypt 101/B1
Dún Laoghaire, Ire. 34/B5
Dun Rig (peak), Sc, UK 36/C5
Dunaföldvár, Hun. 48/D2
Dunaharaszti, Hun. 49/R10
Dunajec (riv.), Pol. 41/L4
Dunakeszi, Hun. 49/R9
Dunany (pt.), Ire. 34/B4
Dunaszekcso, Hun. 48/D2
Dunaújváros, Hun. 48/D2
Dunavecse, Hun. 48/D2
Dunavtsi, Bul. 48/F4
Dunbar, Sc, UK 36/D5
Dunblane, Sc, UK 36/C4
Dunboyne, Ire. 34/B5
Duncan, BC, Can. 126/C3
Duncan, Ok, US 129/H4
Duncannon, Pa, US 138/A3
Duncansby Head (pt.), Sc, UK 31/V14
Duncanville, Tx, US 132/D3
Dund-Us, Mong. 70/F2
Dundalk (bay), Ire. 31/Q10
Dundalk, Md, US 138/B5
Dundalk, Ire. 34/B4
Dundas (lake), Austl. 109/B4
Dundas, On, Can. 131/Q9
Dundas (pen.), NW, Can. 123/R7
Dundee, SAfr. 107/E3
Dundee, Sc, UK 36/D4
Dundee (pol. reg.), Sc, UK 36/D4
Dundgovĭ (prov.), Mong. 70/J2
Dundonald, Sc, UK 36/B5
Dundrum, NI, UK 34/C3
Dundrum (bay), NI, UK 34/C3
Dundurn, Sk, Can. 126/G3
Dundwa (range), Nepal 84/D2
Dundwārāganj, India 84/B2
Dunedin, Fl, US 133/H4
Dunedin, NZ 117/S12
Dunedoo, Austl. 115/D2
Dunellen, NJ, US 139/H9
Dunfanaghy, Ire. 31/Q9
Dunfermline, Sc, UK 36/C4
Dunga Bunga, Pak. 86/B5
Dungannon, NI, UK 34/B3
Dungannon (co.), NI, UK 34/B3
Dungarpur, India 89/K4
Dungarvan, Ire. 31/Q10
Dungau (reg.), Ger. 55/F5
Dungeness (pt.), Eng, UK 33/G5
Dungeness (pt.), Arg. 159/C7
Dungiven, NI, UK 34/B2
Dunglow, Ire. 31/P9
Dungog, Austl. 115/D2
Dungu, D.R. Congo 104/A2
Dungu (riv.), D.R. Congo 104/A2
Dunhua, China 71/N3
Dunhuang, China 70/F3
Dunkeld, Sc, UK 36/C3
Dunkerque (Dunkirk), Fr. 42/E1
Dunkery (hill), Eng, UK 32/C4
Dunkirk (Dunkerque), Fr. 42/E1
Dunkwa, Gha. 103/E5
Dunleer, Ire. 34/B4
Dunloy, NI, UK 34/B2
Dunmanway, Ire. 31/P11
Dunmurry, NI, UK 34/B2
Dunn, NC, US 133/J3
Dunnamanagh, NI, UK 34/A2
Dünnern (riv.), Swi. 56/D3
Dunnet Head (pt.), Sc, UK 31/V14
Dunningen, Ger. 57/E1
Dunnville, On, Can. 131/Q10
Dunolly, Austl. 115/B3
Dunoon, Sc, UK 36/B5
Dunqulah, Sudan 101/B5
Duns, Sc, UK 36/D5
Dunsborough, Austl. 112/B5
Dunseith, ND, US 127/H3
Dunshaughlin, Ire. 34/B4
Dunsmuir, Ca, US 128/B2
Dunstable, Eng, UK 33/F3
Dunyāpur, Pak. 86/A5
Duolun, China 71/L3
Dupo, Il, US 137/G8
Dupont, Pa, US 138/C1
Dupree, SD, US 127/H4
Dupuy (cape), Austl. 112/B2
Duque de Caxias, Braz. 211/K7
Duque de York (isl.), Chile 159/A6
Dūrā, WBnk. 91/D4
Durağan, Turk. 90/C1
Durak, Turk. 91/D1
Durance (riv.), Fr. 42/F5
Durango (state), Mex. 140/A3
Durango, Sp. 44/D1
Durango de Victoria, Mex. 142/D3
Durant, Ok, US 129/H4
Durazno (dept.), Uru. 159/F2
Durazno, Uru. 159/K10
Durban, SAfr. 107/E3
Durbanville, SAfr. 106/L10
Durbion (riv.), Fr. 56/C1
Durbuy, Belg. 53/E3
Dúrcal, Sp. 44/D4
Durdevac, Cro. 48/C2
Durdevo, Serb. 48/E3
Düren, Ger. 53/F2
Durg, India 82/D3
Durgāpur, India 85/F4
Durham, NH, US 131/G3
Durham, NC, US 133/J3
Durham, Eng, UK 35/G2
Durham (co.), Eng, UK 35/F2
Durlston (pt.), Eng, UK 32/E5
Durmitor NP, Serb. 47/F1
Durnford (pt.), WSah. 98/B5
Dürrenroth, Swi. 56/D3
Durrës, Alb. 47/F2
Dürrlauingen, Ger. 54/D6
Dürrwangen, Ger. 54/D4
Dursunbey, Turk. 90/B2
Durūz (peak), Syria 91/E3
D'Urville (cape), Indo. 81/J4
Dusanovo, Serb. 47/G1
Dusey (riv.), On, Can. 127/M3
Dushan, China 83/J2
Dushanbe (cap.), Taj. 87/E5
Dushanbe (int'l arpt.), Taj. 87/E5
Düsseldorf (int'l arpt.), Ger. 50/D6
Düsseldorf, Ger. 50/D6
Duszniki-Zdrój, Pol. 41/J3
Dutch (riv.), Eng, UK 35/H4
Dutch Harbor, Ak, US 134/E5
Dutch Wonderland, Pa, US 138/B3
Dutoitspiek (peak), SAfr. 106/L10
Dutse, Nga. 103/H4
Duvall, Wa, US 135/D2
Duvno, Bosn. 48/C4
Duyun, China 83/J2
Düzce, Turk. 49/K5
Düzici, Turk. 90/D2
Dve Mogili, Bul. 49/G4
Dvina (bay), Rus. 60/H2
Dvořiště (lake), Czh. 55/H4
Dwārka, India 89/J4
Dwārkeswar (riv.), India 85/F4
Dworshak (res.), Id, US 126/D4
Dwyfor (riv.), Wal, UK 34/D6
Dwyka (riv.), SAfr. 106/C4
Dyat'kovo, Rus. 62/E1
Dybvad, Den. 38/D3
Dyce (int'l arpt.), Sc, UK 36/D2
Dyce, Sc, UK 36/D2
Dye, Mo, US 137/D5
Dyer (cape), Nun., Can. 123/K2
Dyer (cape), Chile 159/B6
Dyer, In, US 130/C3
Dyfi (riv.), Wal, UK 32/C1
Dyje (riv.), Czh. 41/J4
Dykh-tau (peak), Rus. 63/G4
Dyle (riv.), Belg. 40/C3
Dyleň (peak), Czh. 55/F3
Dylewska (peak), Pol. 41/K2
Dysart, Austl. 114/C3
Dysselsdorp, SAfr. 106/C4
Dyul'tydag (peak), Rus. 63/H4
Dzaoudzi (cap.), May. 107/H6
Dzaoudzi (int'l arpt.), May. 107/H6
Dzavhan (prov.), Mong. 70/G2
Dzavhan (riv.), Mong. 70/F2
Dzenzik (pt.), Ukr. 62/F3
Dzerzhinsk, Rus. 60/J4
Dzhankoy, Ukr. 62/E3
Dzharylgach (gulf), Ukr. 49/L2
Dzhebel, Bul. 47/J2
Dzhugdzhur (range), Rus. 67/N4
Działdowo, Pol. 41/L2
Dzibalchén, Mex. 144/D2
Dzibilchaltún (ruin), Mex. 144/D1
Dzidzantún, Mex. 144/D1
Dzierżoniów, Pol. 41/J3
Dzitbalché, Mex. 144/D1
Dziuché, Mex. 144/D2
Dzukija NP, Lith. 39/L4
Dzungarian (basin), China 70/E3
Dzur, Mong. 70/G2
Dzüünbayan, Mong. 71/K3
Dzüünbulag, Mong. 71/K2
Dzüünharaa, Mong. 70/J2
Dzuunmod, Mong. 70/J2

E

Eads, Co, US 129/G3
Eagle (riv.), Nf, Can. 123/L3
Eagle (lake), On, Can. 130/A1
Eagle, Ak, US 134/K3
Eagle (lake), Ca, US 126/C5
Eagle, Co, US 128/F3
Eagle (mtn.), Mn, US 127/L4
Eagle, Wi, US 135/P14
Eagle (lake), Wi, US 127/K3
Eagle Butte, SD, US 127/H4
Eagle Pass, Tx, US 132/C4
Eagle River, Wi, US 127/L4
Eaglesham, Sc, UK 36/B5
Ealing (bor.), Eng, UK 30/B2
Ear Falls, On, Can. 127/K3
Earle Naval Weapons Center, NJ, US 138/D3
Earlimart, Ca, US 128/C4
Earl's Seat (peak), Sc, UK 36/B4
Earlston, Sc, UK 36/D5
Earn (riv.), Sc, UK 36/C4
Earn (lake), Sc, UK 36/B4
Easley, SC, US 133/H3
East (mt.), Austl. 112/D4
East (cape), NZ 117/T10
East (cape), Ak, US 134/B6
East (pt.), NJ, US 138/C5
East (riv.), NY, US 139/K8
East (passg.), Wa, US 135/C3
East Alton, Il, US 137/G8
East Anglia (reg.), Eng, UK 33/H2
East Angus, Qu, Can. 131/G2
East Ayrshire (pol. reg.), Sc, UK 36/B6
East Bangor, Pa, US 138/C2
East Berbice-Corentyne (pol. reg.), Guy. 153/G3
East Berlin, Pa, US 138/B4
East Berwick, Pa, US 138/B1
East Brunswick, NJ, US 139/H10
East Caicos (isl.), UK 145/J1
East Canyon (res.), Ut, US 137/K12
East Carondelet, Il, US 137/G8
East China (sea), Asia 67/M6
East Dart (riv.), Eng, UK 32/C5
East Dereham, Eng, UK 33/G1
East Dunbartonshire (pol. reg.), Sc, UK 36/B5
East Falkland (isl.), UK 147/D8
East Farmingdale, NY, US 139/M9
East Frisian (isls.), Ger. 40/D2
East Glen (riv.), Eng, UK 35/H6
East Greenville, Pa, US 138/C3
East Grinstead, Eng, UK 33/F4
East Hampton, NY, US 139/F2
East Haven, Ct, US 139/F1
East Helena, Mt, US 126/F4
East Hill-Meridian, Wa, US 135/C3
East Hills, NY, US 139/L8
East Jordan, Mi, US 130/C2
East Kilbride, Sc, UK 36/B5
East Korea (bay), NKor. 71/N4
East Lamma (chan.), China 71/U11
East Lansing, Mi, US 130/C3
East Leavenworth, Mo, US 137/D5
East Linton, Sc, UK 36/D5
East Liverpool, Oh, US 130/D3
East London, SAfr. 106/D4
East Los Angeles, Ca, US 136/F7
East Lothian (pol. reg.), Sc, UK 36/D5
East Lynne, Mo, US 137/E6
East Meadow, NY, US 139/L9
East Midlands (int'l arpt.), Eng, UK 35/G6
East Millcreek, Ut, US 137/K12
East Millinocket, Me, US 131/G2
East Newark, NJ, US 139/J9
East Newbern, Il, US 137/G7
East Nishnabotna (riv.), Ia, US 129/J2
East Northport, NY, US 139/E2
East Orange, NJ, US 139/J8
East Peckham, Eng, UK 30/E3
East Petersburg, Pa, US 138/B3
East Point, Ga, US 133/G3
East Pointe (East Detroit), Mi, US 135/G7
East Port Orchard, Wa, US 135/B2
East Prospect, Pa, US 138/B4
East Quogue, NY, US 139/F2
East Renfrewshire (pol. reg.), Sc, UK 36/B5
East Retford, Eng, UK 35/H5
East Riding of Yorkshire (co.), Eng, UK 35/H4
East Rockaway, NY, US 139/L9
East Rutherford, NJ, US 139/J8
East Saint Louis, Il, US 137/G8
East Siberian (sea), Rus. 65/S2
East Side, Pa, US 138/C1
East Stroudsburg, Pa, US 138/C2
East Sussex (co.), Eng, UK 33/G5
East Tawas, Mi, US 130/D2
East Timor (ctry.) 81/G5
East Troy, Wi, US 135/P14
East Wemyss, Sc, UK 36/C4
East Wenatchee, Wa, US 126/C4
East Windsor, NJ, US 138/D3
East York, Can. 131/R8
Eastbourne, Eng, UK 33/G5
Eastern (plain), Eng, UK 35/H4
Eastern (pol. reg.), Gha. 103/E5
Eastern (chan.), Japan 74/A4
Eastern (prov.), SLeo. 102/C4
Eastern (bay), Md, US 138/B6
Eastern (prov.), Zam. 104/B5
Eastern Ghats (mts.), India 82/C5
Eastern Neck Island NWR, Md, US 138/B5
Eastern Sayans (mts.), Rus. 64/K4
Easterville, Mb, Can. 127/J2
Eastlake, Co, US 137/C3
Eastleigh (int'l arpt.), Eng, UK 33/E5
Eastleigh, Eng, UK 33/E5
Eastmain (riv.), Qu, Can. 123/J3
Eastman, Ga, US 133/H3
Easton, Ct, US 139/E1
Easton (res.), Ct, US 139/E1
Easton, Pa, US 138/C2
Eastport, Me, US 131/H2
Eastport, NY, US 139/F2
Eastriggs, Sc, UK 35/E2
Eastwood, Eng, UK 35/G6
Eaton, Co, US 137/C1
Eatonia, Sk, Can. 126/F3
Eatons Neck (pt.), NY, US 139/M8
Eatontown, NJ, US 138/D3
Eau (riv.), Eng, UK 35/H5
Eau Claire (lake), Qu, Can. 123/J3
Eau d'Heure (riv.), Belg. 53/D3
Eau d'Heure, Barrage de l' (dam), Belg. 53/D3
Eaubonne, Fr. 30/J5
Eaulne (riv.), Fr. 52/A4
Eauripik (isl.), Micr. 116/D4
Eauze, Fr. 42/D5
Ebano, Mex. 144/B1
Ebble (riv.), Eng, UK 33/E4
Ebbw Vale, Wal, UK 32/C3
Ebebiyín, EqG. 96/H7
Ebeggi (well), Alg. 99/G5
Ebeleben, Ger. 51/H6
Ebeltoft, Den. 38/D3
Ebensee, Aus. 43/K3
Eberbach, Ger. 54/B4
Ebergassing, Aus. 49/P7
Ebergötzen, Ger. 51/H5
Ebermannstadt, Ger. 54/E3
Ebern, Ger. 54/D2
Ebersbach an der Fils, Ger. 54/C5
Ebersberg, Ger. 55/E6
Eberschwang, Aus. 55/G6
Ebersheim, Fr. 56/D1
Eberswalde-Finow, Ger. 41/G2
Ebetsu, Japan 76/B2
Ebian, China 83/H2
Ebina, Japan 77/C3
Ebnat-Kappel, Swi. 57/F3
Eboli, It. 46/D2
Ebolowa, Camr. 96/H7
Ebon (isl.), Mrsh. 116/F4
Ebonyi (state), Nga. 103/H5
Ebrach, Ger. 54/D3
Ebreichsdorf, Aus. 49/N8
Ebro (riv.), Sp. 27/D4
Ebstorf, Ger. 51/H2
Ecatepec, Mex. 143/Q9
Ecclefechan, Sc, UK 35/E1
Eccles, Eng, UK 35/F5
Eceabat, Turk. 49/H5
Echallens, Swi. 56/C4
Echarate, Peru 156/C4
Echaz (riv.), Ger. 54/C6
Éché Fadadinga (riv.), Niger 103/H3
Echigawa, Japan 77/K5
Eching, Ger. 55/E6
Échirolles, Fr. 42/F4
Echo (lake), NJ, US 138/D1
Echo, Ut, US 137/L12
Echoing (riv.), Mb,On, Can. 127/L2
Echt, Neth. 53/E1
Echterdingen (int'l arpt.), Ger. 54/C5
Echternach, Lux. 53/F4
Echuca, Austl. 115/C3
Echunga, Austl. 113/M9
Echzell, Ger. 54/B2
Écija, Sp. 44/C4
Ečka, Serb. 48/E3
Eckernförde, Ger. 38/C4
Eckerö (isl.), Fin. 39/H1
Eckerö, Fin. 39/H1
Eclipse Sound (bay), Nun., Can. 123/H1
Écommoy, Fr. 42/D3
Ecoporanga, Braz. 154/B5
Ecorse (riv.), Mi, US 135/F7
Ecorse, Mi, US 135/F7
Écouen, Fr. 30/K4
Ecquevilly, Fr. 30/H5
Ecrins, PN des, Fr. 43/G4
Écrosnes, Fr. 30/H6
Écrouves, Fr. 53/E6
Ecuador (ctry.) 150/C4
Ecublens, Swi. 56/C4
Ed, Swe. 38/D2
Eday (isl.), Sc, UK 31/V14
Eddystone (pt.), Austl. 115/D4
Eddystone Rocks (isls.), Eng, UK 32/B6
Ede, Nga. 103/G5
Ede, Neth. 50/C4
Edéa, Camr. 96/H7
Edegem, Belg. 53/D1
Edehin Ouarene (des.), Alg. 99/G4
Edéia, Braz. 155/B1
Edelény, Hun. 41/L4
Edemissen, Ger. 51/H4
Eden, Austl. 115/D3
Eden (riv.), Sc, UK 36/D4
Eden, NC, US 130/E4
Eden, Ut, US 137/K11
Edenbridge, Eng, UK 30/D3
Edenburg, SAfr. 106/D3
Edendale, SAfr. 107/E3
Edenhope, Austl. 115/B3
Edenkoben, Ger. 54/B4
Edenside (valley), Eng, UK 35/F2
Edenton, NC, US 133/J2
Eder (riv.), Ger. 40/E3
Eder-Stausee (lake), Ger. 51/F6
Edewecht, Ger. 51/E2
Edgar (mt.), Austl. 112/D2
Edge (isl.), Sval. 160/E
Edgecumbe (cape), Ak, US 134/L4
Edgell (isl.), Nun., Can. 123/K2
Edgemere, Md, US 138/B5
Edgemont, Ut, US 137/K13
Edgerton, Wy, US 127/G5
Edgewater, Co, US 137/B3
Edgewater Park, NJ, US 138/D3
Edgewood, Pa, US 138/B2
Edgewood, Md, US 138/B5
Edgewood Arsenal, Md, US 138/B5
Edgewood-North Hill, Wa, US 135/C3
Édhessa, Gre. 47/H2
Edinboro, Pa, US 130/D3
Edinburg, Tx, US 132/D5
Edinburgh (cap.), Sc, UK 36/C5
Edinburgh (pol. reg.), Sc, UK 36/C5
Edirne (prov.), Turk. 49/H5
Edirne, Turk. 49/H5
Edison, NJ, US 139/H9
Edison International Field, Ca, US 136/G8
Edison Nat'l Hist. Site, NJ, US 139/J8
Edisto Island, SC, US 133/H3
Edisto, South Fork (riv.), SC, US 133/H3
Edithburgh, Austl. 113/H5
Édjérir (riv.), Mali 103/F2
Edmond, Ok, US 137/N14
Edmonds, Wa, US 126/C4
Edmonton (int'l arpt.), Ab, Can. 126/E2
Edmonton (cap.), Ab, Can. 126/E2
Edmund Kennedy NP, Austl. 114/B2
Edmundston, NB, Can. 131/G2
Edna, Tx, US 129/H5
Edna Bay, Ak, US 134/M4
Edo (state), Nga. 103/G5
Edo (riv.), Japan 77/D2
Edolo, It. 57/G5
Edosaki, Japan 77/E2
Edremit, Turk. 90/A2
Edremit (gulf), Gre.,Turk. 90/A2
Edsbyn, Swe. 38/F1
Edson, Ab, Can. 126/D2
Eduardo Castex, Arg. 158/D2
Edward (mt.), Austl. 113/F2
Edward (lake), D.R. Congo 93/E5
Edward River Aboriginal Community, Austl. 114/A1
Edward VII (pen.), Ant. 160/P
Edward VIII (bay), Ant. 160/D

185
Edwar – Erlen

Edwards (riv.), Il, US 129/K2
Edwards (plat.), Tx, US 124/F5
Edwardsville, Il, US 137/H8
Edwardsville, Ks, US 137/D5
Edwardsville, Pa, US 138/C1
Edzell, Sc, UK 36/D3
Edzná (ruin), Mex. 144/D2
Eek, Ak, US 134/F3
Eeklo, Belg. 52/C1
Eel (riv.), Ca, US 128/B3
Eelde-Paterswolde, Neth. 50/D2
Eem (riv.), Neth. 50/C4
Eemenes, Neth. 50/C4
Eems (Ems) (riv.), Ger., Neth 50/D2
Eemshaven (har.), Neth. 50/D2
Eemskanaal (riv.), Neth. 50/D2
Eersel, Neth. 50/C6
Efate (isl.), Van. 116/F6
Eferding, Aus. 55/H6
Effigy Mounds Nat'l Mon., Ia, US 127/L5
Effingham, Il, US 129/K3
Effingham, On, Can. 131/R9
Effon Alaiye, Nga. 103/G5
Effort, Pa, US 138/C2
Eforie, Rom. 49/J3
Efringen-Kirchen, Ger. 56/D2
Efyrnwy, Llyn (lake), Wal, UK 34/E6
Egadi (isls.), It. 46/B3
Egan (range), Nv, US 128/D3
Egan (riv.), Ger. 54/D5
Egaña, Uru. 159/K10
Egegik, Ak, US 134/G4
Eger (riv.), Ger. 40/G3
Eger, Hun. 41/L5
Egeskov, Den. 38/D4
Egestorf, Ger. 51/H2
Egg, Aus. 57/F3
Egg, Swi. 57/E3
Egg Harbor City, NJ, US 138/D4
Egg Island (pt.), NJ, US 138/C5
Eggebek, Ger. 38/C4
Eggegebirge (ridge), Ger. 51/F5
Eggelsberg, Aus. 55/F6
Eggenburg, Aus. 43/L2
Eggenfelden, Ger. 55/F6
Eggenstein-Leopoldshafen, Ger. 54/B4
Eggesin, Ger. 38/F5
Eggiwil, Swi. 56/D4
Egglescliffe, Eng, UK 35/G3
Eggstätt, Ger. 55/F7
Egham, Eng, UK 30/B2
Éghezée, Belg. 53/D2
Egilsstadhir, Ice. 37/P6
Égletons, Fr. 42/E4
Eglinton (isl.), NW, Can. 123/R7
Eglinton, NI, UK 34/A1
Eglisau, Swi. 57/E2
Égly, Fr. 30/J6
Egmond aan Zee, Neth. 50/B3
Egmont (cape), NZ 117/S10
Egmont (mt.), NZ 117/S10
Egna (Neumarkt), It. 57/H5
Egnach, Swi. 57/F2
Eğridir, Turk. 90/B2
Eğridir (lake), Turk. 90/B2
Éguas, Rio das (riv.), Braz. 154/A4
Egypt (ctry.) 97/L2
Ehebach (riv.), Ger. 54/D3
Ehekirchen, Ger. 54/D5
Ehime (pref.), Japan 74/C4
Ehingen, Ger. 57/F1
Ehingen, Ger. 54/D4
Ehringshausen, Ger. 54/B1
Ehrwald, Aus. 57/G3
Eibar, Sp. 44/D1
Eibelstadt, Ger. 54/C3
Eibenstock, Ger. 55/F1
Eibergen, Neth. 50/D4
Eich, Ger. 54/B3
Eichel (riv.), Fr. 53/G6
Eichenau, Ger. 54/E6
Eichenbühl, Ger. 54/C3
Eichendorf, Ger. 55/F5
Eichenzell, Ger. 54/C2
Eichstätt, Ger. 54/E5
Eichwalde, Ger. 40/Q7
Eicklingen, Ger. 51/H3
Eid, Nor. 37/C3
Eidfjord, Nor. 38/B1
Eidsvold, Austl. 114/C4
Eidsvoll, Nor. 38/D1
Eifel (plat.), Ger. 40/D3
Eiffel Tower, Fr. 30/J5
Eigenji, Japan 77/K5
Eiger (peak), Swi. 56/D4
Eigersund, Nor. 38/A2
Eigg (isl.), Sc, UK 31/Q8
Eight Degree (chan.), India,Mal 82/B6
Eijerlandse Gat (chan.), Neth. 50/B2
Eijsden, Neth. 53/E2
Eikelandsosen, Nor. 38/A1
Eil, Loch (inlet), Sc, UK 36/A3
Eildon (lake), Austl. 115/C3
Eildon, Austl. 115/C3
Eilerts de Haan (mts.), Sur. 153/G4
Einbeck, Ger. 51/G5
Eindhoven (int'l arpt.), Neth. 50/C6
Eindhoven, Neth. 50/C6
Einsiedeln, Swi. 57/E3
Einville-au-Jard, Fr. 53/F6
Eirunepé, Braz. 156/D2
Eisch (riv.), Lux. 53/E4
Eisenach, Ger. 51/H7
Eisenberg, Ger. 54/B3
Eisenhower Nat'l Hist. Site, Pa, US 138/A4
Eisenhüttenstadt, Ger. 41/H2
Eiserfeld, Ger. 53/G2
Eisfeld, Ger. 54/D2
Eisingen, Ger. 54/C3
Eislingen, Ger. 54/C5
Eitelborn, Ger. 53/G3
Eiter (riv.), Ger. 51/F3
Eitorf, Ger. 53/G2
Eitting, Ger. 55/E6
Ejea de los Caballeros, Sp. 45/E1
Ejeda, Madg. 107/H9
Ejido, Ven. 152/D2
Ejin Horo Qi, China 72/B3
Ejin Qi, China 70/H3
Ejutla de Crespo, Mex. 144/B2
Ekeby, Swe. 38/E3
Ekenäs (Tammisaari), Fin. 39/K2
Ekeren, Belg. 50/B6
Ekhínos, Gre. 47/J2
Ekibastuz, Kaz. 87/G2
Eksjö, Swe. 38/F3
Ekuk, Ak, US 134/G4
Ekwan (riv.), On, Can. 123/H3
Ekwok, Ak, US 134/G4
El Aaiún, WSah. 98/B4
El Aatf (reg.), WSah. 98/B5
El Abiodh Sidi Chrikh, Alg. 99/F2
El 'Açâba (mass.), Mrta. 102/C2
El Affroun, Alg. 100/G4
El Águila, Mex. 132/B5
El Aïoun, Mor. 100/C2
El Alto, Peru 156/A2
El Amparo de Apure, Ven. 152/D3
El Anegado, Ecu. 152/A5
El Aouinet, Alg. 100/K7
El Arahal, Sp. 44/C4
El Arhlaf (well), Mrta. 102/D2
El Astillero, Sp. 44/D1
El Bagre, Col. 152/C3
El Banco, Col. 152/C2
El Barco, Sp. 44/B1
El Barco de Ávila, Sp. 44/C2
El Baúl, Ven. 152/D2
El Bayadh (prov.), Alg. 99/F2
El Bayadh, Alg. 99/F2
El Bolsón, Arg. 158/C4
El Bonillo, Sp. 44/D3
El Borouj, Mor. 98/D2
El Burgo de Osma, Sp. 44/D2
El Cajon, Ca, US 136/D5
El Cajón (res.), Hon. 144/E3
El Calafate, Arg. 159/B6
El Callao, Ven. 153/F3
El Capitan (peak), Mt, US 126/E4
El Carmen, Chile 158/B3
El Carmen, Col. 152/B3
El Carmen, Peru 156/B4
El Carmen de Bolívar, Col. 152/C2
El Casar de Talamanca, Sp. 45/N8
El Centro, Ca, US 128/D4
El Cerrito, Col. 152/B4
El Cerrito, Ca, US 135/K11
El Cerro del Aripo (peak), Trin. 153/F2
El Cerrón (peak), Ven. 152/D2
El Chico, PN, Mex. 143/L6
El Cocuy, Col. 152/C3
El Cocuy, PN, Col. 150/D2
El Colorado, Arg. 157/E2
El Difícil, Col. 152/C2
El Djouf (des.), Mrta. 96/D3
El Dorado, Mex. 142/D3
El Dorado, Ar, US 129/J4
El Dorado, Ks, US 129/H3
El Dorado, Ven. 153/F3
El Eglab (plat.), Alg. 96/D2
El Empedrado, Ven. 152/D2
El Escorial, Sp. 45/M8
El Espinar, Sp. 44/C2
El Eulma, Alg. 100/H4
El Fahs, Tun. 100/L6
El Ferrol, Sp. 44/A1
El Fuerte, Mex. 142/C3
El Fureidīs, Isr. 91/F6
El Gogorrón, PN, Mex. 140/A3
El Golea, Alg. 99/F3
El Golfete (lake), Guat. 144/D3
El Granada, Ca, US 135/K11
El Grullo, Mex. 142/D5
El Guachara, PN, Ven. 153/F2
El Hajeb, Mor. 100/B3
El Hank (cliff), Mali 98/D4
El Harino, Pan. 152/A2
El Harta (well), Alg. 99/E4
El Higo, Mex. 144/B1
El Indio, Tx, US 132/C4
El Jadida, Mor. 98/C2
El Kelaâ des Srarhna, Mor. 98/D2
El Khatt (cliff), Mrta. 96/C3
El Khatt (depr.), Mrta. 102/C2
El Khnâchîch (cliff), Mali 98/E5
El Kroub, Alg. 100/K6
El Kseur, Alg. 100/H4
El Libertador General Bernardo O'Higgins (pol. reg.), Chile 158/N8
El Limón, Mex. 143/F4
El Mahia (phys. reg.), Mali 99/E5
El Maitén, Arg. 158/C4
El Malpais Nat'l Mon., NM, US 128/F4
El Manteco, Ven. 153/F3
El-Menzel, Mor. 100/B3
El Miamo, Ven. 153/F3
El Milia, Alg. 100/J4
El Mirage, Az, US 137/R18
El Mirage, Ca, US 136/C1
El Montcau (peak), Sp. 45/K6
El Monte, Ca, US 136/F7
El Morrito (pt.), Chile 158/C1
El Mrâyer (well), Mrta. 98/C5
El Mreyyé (phys. reg.), Mrta. 102/C2
El Mzereb (well), Mali 98/D4
El Naranjo de Carlos Sarabia, Mex. 143/F4
El Nayar, Mex. 142/D4
El Nevado (peak), Arg. 158/C2
El Nido, Phil. 81/E1
El Olivar Alto, Chile 158/N9
El Oro (prov.), Ecu. 156/A1
El Oued (prov.), Alg. 99/G2
El Oued, Alg. 99/G2
El Palmar, Ven. 153/F3
El Pao, Ven. 153/F2
El Pao, Ven. 153/E2
El Paraíso, Mex. 143/E5
El Paraíso, Hon. 144/E3
El Paso, Tx, US 128/F5
El Paso International (int'l arpt.), Tx, US 129/F5
El Pilar, Ven. 153/F2
El Porvenir, Mex. 129/F5
El Porvenir, Pan. 152/B2
El Potosí, Mex. 143/E3
El Potosí, PN, Mex. 140/B3
El Prat de Llobregat, Sp. 45/L7
El Progreso, Hon. 144/E3
El Progreso, Guat. 144/D3
El Progreso, Ecu. 156/F7
El Progreso Industrial, Mex. 143/Q9
El Puerto de Santa María, Sp. 44/B4
El Quelite, Mex. 142/D4
El Quisco, Chile 158/N8
El Rama, Nic. 145/E3
El Rancho, Co, US 137/B3
El Reno, Ok, US 129/H4
El Rio, Ca, US 136/A2
El Roble, Pan. 152/A2
El Rosario de Arriba, Mex. 142/B2
El Sacromonte, PN, Mex. 143/L7
El Salto, Mex. 142/D4
El Salvador (ctry.) 144/D3
El Salvador, Mex. 143/E3
El Salvador, Cuba 145/H1
El Salvador (int'l arpt.), ESal. 144/D3
El Samán de Apure, Ven. 152/D3
El Sauz, Mex. 129/F5
El Sauzal, Mex. 142/A2
El Segundo, Ca, US 136/F8
El Shab (well), Egypt 101/B4
El Tabo, Chile 158/N8
El Tajín (ruin), Mex. 143/M6
El Tama, PN, Ven. 152/C3
El Tambo, Ecu. 152/B5
El Tarf (prov.), Alg. 100/K6
El Tarf, Alg. 100/L6
El Teleno (peak), Sp. 44/B1
El Tepozteco, PN, Mex. 143/R10
El Tiemblo, Sp. 44/C2
El Tigre, Ven. 153/E2
El Tocuyo, Ven. 152/D2
El Toro, Ca, US 136/C3
El Triunfo, Ecu. 152/B5
El Triunfo, Mex. 144/D2
El Tucuche (peak), Trin. 153/F2
El Tuito, Mex. 142/D4
El Tuparro, PN, Col. 150/E3
El Valle, Pan. 152/A2
El Venado (isl.), Nic. 145/F4
El Viejo, Nic. 144/E3
El Viejo (peak), Col. 152/C3
El Vigía, Ven. 152/D2
El Yagual, Ven. 152/D3
El Yunque (peak), PR 141/M8
El Zacatón, Mex. 142/E4
Elan (riv.), Wal, UK 32/C2
Élancourt, Fr. 30/H5
Elandsrivier (riv.), SAfr. 106/Q12
Elassón, Gre. 47/H3
Elat (int'l arpt.), Isr. 91/D5
Elat, Isr. 91/D5
Elátia, Gre. 47/H3
Elato (isl.), Micr. 116/D4
Elazığ, Turk. 90/D2
Elazig (prov.), Turk. 90/D2
Elba, Al, US 133/G4
Elba (isl.), It. 43/H5
Elbasan, Alb. 47/G2
Elbbach (riv.), Ger. 53/G2
Elbe (riv.), Ger. 27/F3
Elbe (Labe) (riv.), Czh.,Ger. 41/H2
Elbe-Seitenkanaal (canal), Ger. 51/H2
Elbert (co.), Co, US 137/C4
Elberton, Ga, US 133/H3
Elbeuf, Fr. 42/D2
Elbigenalp, Aus. 57/G3
Elbląg, Pol. 39/H4
Elbow, Sk, Can. 126/G3
El'brus (peak), Rus. 63/G4
Elburg, Neth. 50/C4
Elburn, Il, US 135/N16
Elburz (mts.), Iran 88/E1
Elche, Sp. 45/E3
Elche de la Sierra, Sp. 44/D3
Elchingen, Ger. 54/D6
Elcho (isl.), Austl. 109/C2
Eld (inlet), Wa, US 135/A3
Elda, Sp. 45/E3
Elde (riv.), Ger. 40/G2
Eldersburg, Md, US 138/B5
Eldivan, Turk. 90/C1
Eldon, Wa, US 135/A2
Eldora, Co, US 137/A3
Eldora, NJ, US 138/D5
Eldorado, Arg. 157/F2
Eldorado, Tx, US 129/G5
Eldorado Springs, Co, US 137/B3
Eldoret, Kenya 104/B2
Eleao (peak), Hi, US 124/W13
Elefsís, Gre. 47/H3
Elek, Hun. 48/E2
Elektrostal', Rus. 61/X9
Elena, Arg. 158/D2
Elesbão Veloso, Braz. 154/B2
Eleşkirt, Turk. 90/E2
Eleuthera (isl.), Bahm. 141/F2
Eleven Point (riv.), Mo, US 129/K3
Elevsís (ruin), Gre. 47/N8
Elevtheroúpolis, Gre. 47/J2
Elfershausen, Ger. 54/C2
Elgg, Swi. 57/E3
Elgin, ND, US 127/H4
Elgin, Il, US 127/L5
Elgin, Tx, US 129/H5
Elgin, Sc, UK 36/C1
Elgóibar, Sp. 44/D1
Elgon (Wagagai) (peak), Ugan. 104/B2
Elida, NM, US 132/C3
Elim, Ak, US 134/F3
Elimäki, Fin. 39/M1
Elista, Rus. 63/H3
Elixhausen, Aus. 55/G7
Elizabeth (bay), Namb. 106/A2
Elizabeth, NJ, US 139/J9
Elizabeth City, NC, US 133/J2
Elizabethan Village Hist. Site, Austl. 112/L7
Elizabethton, Tn, US 130/D4
Elizabethtown, Pa, US 138/B3
Elizabethville, Pa, US 138/B2
Elk (mts.), Co, US 132/B2
Elk (riv.), WV, US 133/H2
Elk, Pol. 39/K5
Elk City, Ok, US 129/H4
Elk Grove, Ca, US 135/M10
Elk Grove Village, Il, US 135/P16
Elk Island NP, Ab, Can. 126/E2
Elk Mills, Md, US 138/C4
Elk Point, Ab, Can. 126/F2
Elk Rapids, Mi, US 130/C2
Elk Ridge, Md, US 138/B5
Elk River, Mn, US 127/K4
Elk Slough (riv.), Ca, US 135/L10
Elkenroth, Ger. 53/G2
Elkhart, In, US 130/C3
Elkhart, Ks, US 129/G3
Elkhart, Tx, US 129/J5
Elkhorn, Mb, Can. 127/H3
Elkhorn, Wi, US 130/B3
Elkhorn (riv.), Ne, US 125/G3
Elkhovo, Bul. 47/K1
Elkin, NC, US 130/D4
Elko, Nv, US 126/E5
Elkton, Md, US 138/C4
Ellamar, Ak, US 134/J3
Elland, Eng, UK 35/G4
Elle (riv.), Ger. 53/F2
Ellef Ringnes (isl.), Nun., Can. 123/R7
Ellefeld, Ger. 55/F2
Ellen (riv.), Eng, UK 35/E2
Ellenberg, Ger. 54/D4
Ellendale, ND, US 127/J4
Ellendale, De, US 138/C6
Ellensburg, Wa, US 126/C4
Eller (riv.), Ger. 51/H5
Ellerbach (riv.), Ger. 53/G4
Ellero (riv.), It. 58/A4
Ellery (mt.), Austl. 115/D3
Ellesmere (isl.), Nun., Can. 123/S6
Ellesmere Port, Eng, UK 35/F5
Ellezelles, Belg. 52/C2
Ellice (riv.), Nun., Can. 122/F2
Ellicott City, Md, US 138/B5
Ellinikón (int'l arpt.), Gre. 47/N9
Elliot, SAfr. 106/D3
Elliot Lake, On, Can. 130/D2
Elliot Price Consv. Park, Austl. 113/H4
Elliott (peak), Va, US 133/J2
Ellis Island, NJ,NY, US 139/J9
Ellisras, SAfr. 105/E5
Elliston, Austl. 113/G5
Ellisville, Mo, US 137/F8
Ellon, Sc, UK 36/D2
Ellrich, Ger. 51/H5
Ellsworth (mts.), Ant. 160/U
Ellsworth, Ks, US 129/H3
Ellsworth, Me, US 131/G2
Ellsworth, Wi, US 130/A2
Ellsworth Land (phys. reg.), Ant. 160/U
Ellwangen, Ger. 54/D5
Elm, Swi. 57/F4
Elm Grove, Wi, US 135/P13
Elma, NY, US 131/S10
Elmadağ, Turk. 62/E5
Elmalı, Turk. 91/A1
Elmas (int'l arpt.), It. 46/A3
Elmendorf, Tx, US 137/U21
Elmer, NJ, US 138/C4
Elmhurst, Il, US 135/Q16
Elmina, Gha. 103/E5
Elmira, NY, US 130/E3
Elmont, NY, US 139/L9
Elmore, Austl. 115/C3
Elmsford, NY, US 139/K7
Elmshorn, Ger. 51/G1
Elmstein, Ger. 53/G5
Elmwood Park, Wi, US 135/Q14
Elmwood Park, NJ, US 139/J8
Elmwood Park, Il, US 135/Q16
Elne, Fr. 42/E5
Elói Mendes, Braz. 211/H6
Élorn (riv.), Fr. 42/A2
Elortondo, Arg. 158/E2
Elorza, Ven. 152/D3
Elouera Nat'l Rsv., Austl. 114/H8
Eloy, Az, US 128/E4
Eloy Alfaro, Ecu. 152/B5
Éloyes, Fr. 56/C1
Elpitiya, SrL. 82/D6
Elrose, Sk, Can. 126/F3
Elsa, Yk, Can. 134/L3
Elsa (riv.), It. 43/J5
Elsa, Embalse de (res.), Sp. 44/B2
Elsah, Il, US 137/G8
Elsdorf, Ger. 51/G2
Elsdorf, Ger. 53/F2
Else (riv.), Ger. 51/F4
Elsenfeld, Ger. 54/C3
Elsenz (riv.), Ger. 54/B4
Elsfleth, Ger. 51/F2
Elsinore (lake), Ca, US 136/C3
Elsmere, De, US 138/C4
Elst, Neth. 50/C5
Elstal, Ger. 40/Q6
Elstead, Eng, UK 33/F4
Elsterberg, Ger. 55/F1
Eltmann, Ger. 54/D3
El'ton (lake), Rus. 63/H2
Eltville am Rhein, Ger. 54/B2
Elūrū, India 82/D4
Elvanlı, Turk. 91/D1
Elvas, Port. 44/B3
Elverum, Nor. 38/D1
Elvire (mt.), Austl. 112/C2
Elvo (riv.), It. 58/B2
Elwell (lake), Mt, US 126/F3
Elwood, In, US 130/C3
Elwood-Magnolia, NJ, US 138/D4
Elwy (riv.), Wal, UK 34/E5
Ely, Nv, US 128/D3
Ely, Eng, UK 33/G2
Elyaqim, Isr. 91/G6
Elyashiv, Isr. 91/F7
Elyria, Oh, US 130/D3
Elysburg, Pa, US 138/B2
Elysian Park, Ca, US 136/F7
Elz (riv.), Ger. 54/B6
Elz, Ger. 54/B2
Elzach, Ger. 56/E1
Elzbach (riv.), Ger. 53/G3
Elze, Ger. 51/G4
Emajõgi (riv.), Est. 39/M2
Emāmshahr (Shāhrūd), Iran 89/F1
Emån (riv.), Swe. 38/F3
Emancé, Fr. 30/H6
Emas, PN das, Braz. 151/H7
Emba (riv.), Kaz. 62/K3
Embarcación, Arg. 157/D1
Embarras (riv.), Il, US 133/F2
Embi, Kaz. 63/L2
Embi (riv.), Kaz. 64/F5
Embira (riv.), Braz. 150/D5
Emborcação, Barragem de (res.), Braz. 155/C1
Embrach, Swi. 57/E3
Embrun, Fr. 43/G4
Embsen, Ger. 51/H2
Embu, Kenya 104/C3
Emden, Ger. 51/E2
Emeishan, China 83/H2
Emerald, Austl. 114/C3
Emerald, Austl. 115/G5
Emerson, Mb, Can. 127/J3
Emerson, NJ, US 139/J8
Emeryville, Ca, US 135/K11
Emet, Turk. 90/B2
Emigsville, Pa, US 138/B3
Emilia-Romagna (pol. reg.), It. 43/J4
Emiliano Zapata, Mex. 144/D2
Emin, China 70/D2
Eminābād, Pak. 86/C3
Eminence, Mo, US 129/K3
Emir Pasha (gulf), Tanz. 104/A3
Emirdağ, Turk. 90/B2
Emirgazi, Turk. 90/C2
Emlembe (peak), Swaz. 107/E2
Emlichheim, Ger. 50/D3
Emma (riv.), Sur. 153/H4
Emmaboda, Swe. 38/F3
Emmanuel Head (pt.), Eng, UK 36/E5
Emmaus, Pa, US 138/C2
Emme (riv.), Swi. 56/D4
Emmeloord, Neth. 50/C3
Emmen, Neth. 50/D3
Emmendingen, Ger. 56/D1
Emmental (valley), Swi. 56/D3
Emmer (riv.), Ger. 51/G4
Emmerbach (riv.), Ger. 51/E5
Emmerich, Ger. 50/D5
Emmett, Mi, US 135/G6
Emmingen-Liptingen, Ger. 57/E2
Emmitsburg, Md, US 138/A4
Emmonak, Ak, US 134/F3
Emneth, Eng, UK 33/G1
Emőd, Hun. 48/E2
Emory, Tx, US 129/J4
Emosson (lake), Swi. 56/C5
Empalme, Mex. 142/C3
Empangeni, SAfr. 107/E3
Empedrado, Arg. 157/E2
Empedrado, Chile 158/B2
Empoli, It. 59/D5
Emporia, Ks, US 129/H3
'Emrānī, Iran 89/G2
Ems (Eems) (riv.), Ger.,Neth. 50/D2
Ems-Jade (canal), Ger. 51/E2
Emsbüren, Ger. 51/E4
Emsdetten, Ger. 51/E4
Emskirchen, Ger. 54/D3
Emsland (reg.), Ger. 40/D2
Emstek, Ger. 51/F3
Emu Park, Austl. 114/C3
Emumägi (hill), Est. 39/M2
Emyvale, Ire. 34/B3
Ena, Japan 75/E3
Enbetsu, Japan 76/B1
Encantada, Cerro (peak), Mex. 142/B3
Encantada, Cerro de la (peak), Mex. 142/B2
Encarnación, Par. 157/E2
Encarnación de Díaz, Mex. 142/E4
Enchi, Gha. 102/E5
Encinitas, Ca, US 136/C4
Enciso, Col. 152/C3
Encontrados, Ven. 152/C2
Encounter (bay), Austl. 115/A2
Encruzilhada do Sul, Braz. 155/A4
Encs, Hun. 41/L4
Endau (peak), Kenya 104/C3
Endeavour River NP, Austl. 114/B1
Enderbury (isl.), Kiri. 117/H5
Enderby, BC, Can. 126/D3
Enderby Land (phys. reg.), Ant. 160/D
Enderlin, ND, US 127/J4
Endicott, NY, US 130/E3
Endingen, Ger. 56/D1
Ene (riv.), Peru 150/D6
Eneabba, Austl. 112/B4
Enebakk, Nor. 38/D2
Enewetak (isl.), Mrsh. 116/F3
Enez, Turk. 47/K2
Enfield (bor.), Eng, UK 30/C2
Engaño (cape), Phil. 79/D4
Engaru, Japan 76/C1
Engaruka (basin), Tanz. 104/B3
Engelberg, Swi. 57/E4
Engelhartszell, Aus. 55/G5
Engel's, Rus. 63/H2
Engelskirchen, Ger. 53/G2
Engelsmanplaat (isl.), Neth. 50/D2
Engen, Ger. 57/E2
Engenheiro Navarro, Braz. 154/B5
Engenheiro Paulo de Frontin, Braz. 211/K7
Enger, Ger. 51/F4
Engerwitzdorf, Aus. 55/H6
Enggano (isl.), Indo. 80/B5
Enghershatu (peak), Erit. 88/C5
Enghien, Belg. 52/D2
Engi, Swi. 57/F4
England, UK 32/D2
Englefontaine, Fr. 52/C3
Englehart, On, Can. 130/E2
Englewood, Co, US 137/C3
Englewood, NJ, US 139/K8
Englewood Cliffs, NJ, US 139/K8
English (riv.), On, Can. 127/K3
English (chan.), UK,Fr. 27/D4
English Bay, Ak, US 134/H4
English Bāzār, India 85/G3
English Creek, NJ, US 138/D5
Englishtown, NJ, US 138/D3
Énguera, Sp. 45/E3
Enguri (riv.), Geo. 63/G4
Enhtal, Mong. 70/J2
Enid, Ok, US 129/H3
Eniwa, Japan 76/B2
Enkenbach-Alsenborn, Ger. 53/G5
Enkhuizen, Neth. 50/C3
Enkirch, Ger. 53/G4
Enköping, Swe. 38/G2
Enna, It. 46/D4
Ennedi (plat.), Chad 97/K4
Ennepe (riv.), Ger. 51/E6
Ennepetal, Ger. 51/E6
Ennery, Fr. 30/J4
Enningerloh, Ger. 51/F5
Ennis, Mt, US 126/F4
Ennis, Tx, US 129/H4
Ennis, Ire. 31/P10
Enniscorthy, Ire. 31/Q10
Enniskerry, Ire. 34/B5
Enniskillen, NI, UK 31/Q9
Ennistimon, Ire. 31/P10
Enns, Aus. 55/H6
Enns (riv.), Aus. 41/H5
Enogger (res.), Austl. 114/E6
Enola, Pa, US 138/B3
Enontekiö, Fin. 37/G1
Enoree (riv.), SC, US 133/H3
Enping, China 83/K3
Enrick (riv.), Sc, UK 36/B2
Enrique Carbó, Arg. 159/J10
Enriquillo, DRep. 145/J2
Enschede, Neth. 50/D4
Ensdorf, Ger. 55/E4
Ense, Ger. 51/E5
Enseleni, SAfr. 107/F3
Ensenada, Mex. 142/A2
Ensenada, Arg. 159/K11
Enshi, China 79/A1
Ensisheim, Fr. 56/D2
Entebbe (int'l arpt.), Ugan. 104/B2
Entebbe, Ugan. 104/B2
Entenbühl (peak), Ger. 55/F3
Enterprise, Al, US 133/G4
Enterprise, Ut, US 137/K11
Entlebuch, Swi. 56/E4
Entre Rios, Braz. 154/C3
Entre Rios (mts.), Hon. 144/E3
Entroncamento, Port. 44/A3
Entzheim, Fr. 56/D1
Enugu, Nga. 103/G5
Enugu (state), Nga. 103/G5
Enumclaw, Wa, US 135/D3
Enushū (sea), Japan 77/M6
Envira, Braz. 156/D2
Enz (riv.), Ger. 43/H2
Enza (riv.), It. 58/D4
Enzan, Japan 75/F3
Enzbach (riv.), Ger. 53/F4
Enzersdorf an der Fischa, Aus. 49/P7
Enzklösterle, Ger. 54/B5
Epalinges, Swi. 56/C4
Epáno Arkhánai, Gre. 47/J5
Epanomí, Gre. 47/H2
Epe, Nga. 103/F5
Epe, Neth. 50/C4
Épehy, Fr. 52/C3
Épernay, Fr. 52/C5
Epfig, Fr. 56/D1
Ephrata, Pa, US 138/B3
Epi (isl.), Van. 116/F6
Épiais-Rhus, Fr. 30/J4
Epídhavros (Epidaurus) (ruin), Gre. 47/H4
Épinal, Fr. 56/C1
Épinay-sur-Orge, Fr. 30/J6
Épinay-sur-Seine, Fr. 30/J5
Epira, Guy. 153/G3
Epirus (reg.), Gre. 47/G3
Épône, Fr. 52/A6
Eppelborn, Ger. 53/F5
Eppelheim, Ger. 54/B4
Eppenbrunn, Ger. 53/G5
Eppeville, Fr. 52/C4
Epping (for.), Eng, UK 30/D2
Epping, Eng, UK 30/D1
Epping Forest NP, Austl. 114/B3
Eppingen, Ger. 54/B4
Eppishausen, Ger. 57/G1
Epsom, Eng, UK 30/C3
Epsom and Ewell, Eng, UK 33/F4
Epte (riv.), Fr. 52/A4
Equator (fall), Ecu. 152/A4
Equatorial Guinea (ctry.) 96/G7
Équihen-Plage, Fr. 52/A2
Er (lake), China 83/H2
Er Rachidia, Mor. 98/D3
Er Reina, Isr. 91/G6
Er Rif (mts.), Mor. 96/D1
Era (riv.), It. 59/D6
Eraclea, It. 59/F1
Eraclea (ruin), It. 46/E2
Eraclea Minoa (ruin), It. 46/C4
Éragny, Fr. 30/J4
Erandique, Hon. 144/D3
Eravur, SrL. 82/D6
Erawan NP, Thai. 78/B3
Erba, It. 58/C1
Erbaa, Turk. 90/D1
Erbach, Ger. 54/B3
Erbendorf, Ger. 55/F3
Erbeskopf (peak), Ger. 53/G4
Ercan (int'l arpt.), Cyp. 91/C2
Erçek, Turk. 90/E2
Erçek (lake), Turk. 90/E2
Ercilla, Chile 158/B3
Erciş, Turk. 90/E2
Erciyes (peak), Turk. 90/C2
Erclin (riv.), Fr. 52/C3
Érd, Hun. 49/Q10
Erda, Ut, US 137/J12
Erdek (gulf), Turk. 49/H5
Erdek, Turk. 49/H5
Erdemli, Turk. 91/D1
Erdenet, Mong. 70/H2
Erdi-Ma (plat.), Chad 97/K4
Erding, Ger. 55/E6
Erdre (riv.), Fr. 42/C3
Erdweg, Ger. 54/E6
Erechim, Braz. 155/A3
Ereen Davaanī (mts.), Mong. 71/K2
Ereğli, Turk. 90/C2
Ereğli, Turk. 49/K5
Eremo di Camaldoli, It. 59/E5
Erenhaberga (mts.), China 70/D3
Erenhot, China 71/K3
Erenler, Turk. 49/K5
Erentepe, Turk. 90/E2
Erepecu, Lago do (lake), Braz. 151/G4
Eresma (riv.), Sp. 44/C2
Erétria, Gre. 47/H3
Ereymentaū, Kaz. 87/F2
Érezée, Belg. 53/E3
Erfa (riv.), Ger. 54/C3
Erfoud, Mor. 98/D3
Erft (riv.), Ger. 40/D3
Erftstadt, Ger. 53/F2
Erfurt, Ger. 40/F3
'Erg Chech (des.), Mali,Alg. 93/B2
'Erg Iguidi (des.), Alg.,Mrta. 98/D4
Ergene Nehri (riv.), Turk. 49/H5
Erguig (riv.), Chad 96/J5
Ergun Youqi, China 71/M1
Ergun Zuoqi, China 71/M1
Ericeira, Port. 45/P10
Ericht (lake), Sc, UK 36/B3
Ericht (riv.), Sc, UK 36/B3
Erickson, Mb, Can. 127/J3
Erickson, BC, Can. 126/D3
Erie (lake), Can.,US 130/D3
Erie, Co, US 137/B2
Erie (canal), NY, US 131/S9
Erie (co.), NY, US 131/S10
Erie, Pa, US 130/D3
Erie (int'l arpt.), Pa, US 130/D3
Eriksdale, Mb, Can. 127/J3
Eriksmalå, Swe. 38/F3
Erikub (isl.), Mrsh. 116/F4
Erímanthos (peak), Gre. 47/G4
Erimo, Japan 76/C2
Erimo-misaki (cape), Japan 76/C3
Erithraí, Gre. 47/H3
Eritrea (ctry.) 97/N5
Erkelenz, Ger. 53/F1
Erken (lake), Swe. 39/H1
Erkheim, Ger. 57/G1
Erkner, Ger. 40/Q7
Erkrath, Ger. 50/D6
Erlach, Swi. 56/D3
Erlands Point-Kitsap Lake, Wa, US 135/B2
Erlangen, Ger. 54/D3
Erlau (riv.), Ger. 55/G5
Erlenbach (riv.), Ger. 54/B4
Erlenbach am Main, Ger. 54/C3

186

Erlen – Ferri

Erlenbach bei Marktheidenfeld, Ger. 54/C3
Erlenbach im Simmental, Swi. 56/D4
Erlinsbach, Swi. 56/E3
Erlongshan (res.), China 72/F2
Erme (riv.), Eng, UK 32/C6
Ermelo, SAfr. 107/E2
Ermelo, Neth. 50/C4
Ermenek (riv.), Turk. 91/C1
Ermenek, Turk. 91/C1
Ermenonville, Fr. 30/L4
Ermióni, Gre. 47/H4
Ermont, Fr. 30/J5
Ermoúpolis, Gre. 47/J4
Erms (riv.), Ger. 54/C6
Erndtebrück, Ger. 53/H2
Ernée (riv.), Fr. 42/C2
Ernée, Fr. 42/C2
Ernesto Cortissoz (int'l arpt.), Col. 152/C2
Ernsthofen, Aus. 55/H6
Erode, India 82/C5
Erolzheim, Ger. 57/G1
Erowal Bay, Austl. 115/D2
Erpel, Ger. 53/G2
Erquelinnes, Belg. 53/D3
Errigal (mtn.), Ire. 31/P9
Erris Head (pt.), Ire. 31/P9
Erro (riv.), It. 58/B4
Errochty (lake), Sc, UK 36/B3
Erromango (isl.), Van. 116/F6
Erse (riv.), Ger. 51/H4
Ersekë, Alb. 47/G2
Erstein, Fr. 56/D1
Erstfeld, Swi. 57/E4
Ertingen, Ger. 57/F1
Ertis (riv.), Kaz. 64/H4
Ertix (riv.), China 70/E2
Eruh, Turk. 90/E2
Eruwa, Nga. 103/F5
Erwin, Tn, US 130/D4
Erwitte, Ger. 51/F5
Eryuan, China 83/G2
Erzegebirge (Krušné Hory) (mts.), Czh.,Ger. 43/K1
Erzen (riv.), Alb. 47/F2
Erzhausen, Ger. 54/B3
Erzincan, Turk. 90/D2
Erzurum, Turk. 90/E2
Erzurum (prov.), Turk. 90/E1
Es Senia (int'l arpt.), Alg. 100/E5
Esan-misaki (cape), Japan 76/B3
Esashi, Japan 76/C1
Esashi, Japan 76/B3
Esashi, Japan 76/B4
Esbiye, Turk. 90/D1
Esbjerg, Den. 38/C4
Esbjerg (int'l arpt.), Den. 38/C4
Esbly, Fr. 30/L5
Esbo (Espoo), Fin. 39/L1
Escada, Braz. 154/D3
Escalante (riv.), Ut, US 128/E3
Escalón, Mex. 142/D3
Escalona, Sp. 44/C2
Escambia (riv.), Fl, US 133/G4
Escaudain, Fr. 52/C3
Escaut (riv.), Fr. 40/B3
Esch (riv.), Fr. 53/E6
Esch-sur-Alzette, Lux. 53/E4
Esch-sur-Sure, Lux. 53/E4
Eschach (riv.), Ger. 57/E1
Eschau, Fr. 56/D1
Eschborn, Ger. 54/B2
Eschede, Ger. 51/H3
Eschen, Lcht. 57/F3
Eschenbach, Ger. 54/C5
Eschenbach in der Oberpfalz, Ger. 55/E3
Eschershausen, Ger. 51/G5
Esches (riv.), Fr. 52/B5
Escholzmatt, Swi. 56/D4
Eschwege, Ger. 51/H6
Eschweiler, Ger. 53/F2
Escobedo (int'l arpt.), Mex. 132/C5
Escoma, Bol. 156/D4
Escondido, Ca, US 136/C4
Escuinapa de Hidalgo, Mex. 142/D4
Escuintla, Guat. 144/D3
Esdraelon, Plain of (plain), Isr. 91/G6
Eséka, Camr. 96/H7
Esenboga (int'l arpt.), Turk. 90/C1
Esence (peak), Turk. 90/D2
Esens, Ger. 51/E1
Esera (riv.), Sp. 45/F1
Eşfahān, Iran 88/F2
Esfandak, Iran 89/H3
Esgair Ddu (peak), Wal, UK 32/C1
Esha Ness (cape), Sc, UK 31/W13
Esher, Eng, UK 30/B2
Eshowe, SAfr. 107/E3
Esil, Kaz. 87/E2
Esil (riv.), Kaz. 67/F4
Esine, It. 57/G6
Esino (riv.), It. 59/G6
Esk (riv.), Eng, UK 35/E2
Eskdale (valley), Sc, UK 36/C6
Eskifjördhur, Ice. 37/Q6
Eskil, Turk. 90/C2
Eskilstuna, Swe. 38/G2
Eskimalatya, Turk. 90/D2
Eskimo (lakes), NW, Can. 122/C2
Eskipazar, Turk. 90/C1
Eskişehir, Turk. 90/B2
Eskişehir (prov.), Turk. 90/B2
Esla (riv.), Sp. 44/C1
Eslāmābād, Iran 88/E2
Eslohe, Ger. 51/F6
Eslöv, Swe. 38/E4
Eşme, Turk. 90/B2
Esmeralda, Cuba 145/G1
Esmeraldas, Ecu. 152/B4
Esmeraldas (dept.), Ecu. 152/B4
Esneux, Belg. 53/E2
Espada (pt.), Col. 152/D1
Espalion, Fr. 42/E4
Española, NM, US 129/F4
Espanola, On, Can. 130/D2
Española (isl.), Ecu. 156/F7
Esparraguera, Sp. 45/K6
Esparta, Hon. 144/E3
Esparto, Ca, US 135/K9
Espejo, Sp. 44/C4
Espelkamp, Ger. 51/F4
Esperança, Braz. 154/D2
Esperance (bay), Austl. 112/D5
Esperance, Austl. 112/D5
Esperantina, Braz. 154/B1
Esperantinópolis, Braz. 154/A2
Esperanza, Arg., Ant. 160/W
Esperanza (inlet), BC, Can. 126/B3
Esperanza (mts.), Hon. 144/E3
Esperanza, Mex. 142/C3
Esperanza, Mex. 143/M8
Esperanza, Peru 156/D3
Espichel (cape), Port. 45/P11
Espinal, Mex. 143/M6
Espinal, Col. 152/C3
Espinar, Peru 156/D4
Espinhaço, Serra do (mts.), Braz. 151/K7
Espinho, Port. 44/A2
Espinillo (pt.), Uru. 159/F2
Espinosa, Braz. 154/B4
Espírito Santo (state), Braz. 155/D2
Espiritu Santo (isl.), Van. 116/F6
Espíritu Santo (bay), Cuba 144/E2
Espita, Mex. 144/D1
Esplanada, Braz. 154/C3
Espluga de Francolí, Sp. 45/E2
Espluges, Sp. 45/L7
Esposende, Port. 44/A2
Espungabera, Moz. 105/F5
Espy, Pa, US 138/B1
Esqueda, Mex. 142/C2
Esquel, Arg. 158/C4
Esquina, Arg. 157/E3
Essaouira, Mor. 98/C3
Esse (riv.), Ger. 51/G5
Essen, Belg. 50/B6
Essen, Ger. 50/E6
Essen, Ger. 51/E3
Essenbach, Ger. 55/F5
Essendon (mt.), Austl. 112/D3
Essenheim, Ger. 53/H4
Essequibo (riv.), Guy. 147/D2
Essequibo Island-West Demerara (pol. reg.), Guy. 153/G3
Essex, On, Can. 135/G7
Essex (co.), On, Can. 135/G7
Essex (co.), Eng, UK 30/E1
Essex, Md, US 138/B5
Essex (co.), NJ, US 138/D2
Essex Fells, NJ, US 139/H8
Esslingen, Ger. 54/C5
Essômes-sur-Marne, Fr. 52/C5
Essonne (riv.), Fr. 42/E2
Est, Canal de l' (canal), Fr. 53/E5
Estaca de Bares, Punta de la (cape), Sp. 44/B1
Estación Santa Engracia, Mex. 143/F3
Estados, Isla de los (isl.), Arg. 157/D7
Eşţahbān, Iran 88/F3
Estaires, Fr. 52/B2
Estância, Braz. 154/C3
Estats, Pico de (peak), Sp. 45/F1
Estavayer-le-Lac, Swi. 56/C4
Estcourt, SAfr. 107/E3
Este, It. 59/E2
Este, Punta del (pt.), Cuba 140/E3
Este Sudeste, Cayos del (isls.), Col. 145/F3
Esteio, Braz. 155/B4
Estelí, Nic. 144/E3
Estell Manor (Risley), NJ, US 138/D5
Estella, Sp. 44/D1
Estelle (mtn.), Ca, US 136/C3
Estelle, La, US 137/P17
Estepa, Sp. 44/C4
Estepona, Sp. 44/C4
Ester, Ak, US 134/J3
Esterhazy, Sk, Can. 127/H3
Esterias (cape), Gabon 96/G7
Esternay, Fr. 52/C6
Estero de Agiabampo (lag.), Mex. 142/C3
Estéron (riv.), Fr. 43/G5
Esterwegen, Ger. 51/E3
Estes Park, Co, US 137/A2
Estevan, Sk, Can. 127/H3
Estinnes-au-Mont, Belg. 53/D3
Eston, Sk, Can. 126/F3
Eston and South Bank, Eng, UK 35/G2
Estonia (ctry.) 39/L2
Estoril, Port. 45/P10
Estral Beach, Mi, US 135/F8
Estrées-Saint-Denis, Fr. 52/B5
Estrela, Serra da (mts.), Port. 44/A3
Estrela, Serra da (peak), Port. 44/B2
Estrella (pt.), Mex. 142/B2
Estrelto, Serra do (range), Braz. 154/B3
Estremoz, Port. 44/B3
Estrondo, Serra do (mts.), Braz. 151/J5
Esztergom, Hun. 48/D2
Eţ Taiyiba, Isr. 91/G7
Eţ Tīra, Isr. 91/F7
Etah, India 84/B2
Étain, Fr. 53/E5
Etal (isl.), Micr. 116/E4
Étalle, Belg. 53/E4
Étaples, Fr. 52/A2
Etāwah, India 84/B2
Etāwah Branch (riv.), India 84/B2
Etchojoa, Mex. 142/C3
Ethelbert, Mb, Can. 127/H3
Ethiopia (ctry.) 97/N5
Ethiopian (plat.), Eth. 97/N6
Eti (riv.), Japan 77/K5
Etili, Turk. 49/H6
Étival-Clairefontaine, Fr. 56/C1
Etive, Loch (inlet), Sc, UK 36/A4
Etna (peak), It. 46/D4
Etna, Monte (Mount Etna) (vol.), It. 46/D4
Etne, Nor. 38/A2
Etobicoke, Can. 131/Q8
Etolin (str.), Ak, US 134/E3
Eton, Eng, UK 30/B2
Etorofu (isl.), Japan 71/S2
Etorofu (isl.), Rus. 67/P5
Etosha (salt pan), Namb. 105/C4
Etosha NP, Namb. 105/C4
Etowah, Ok, US 137/N15
Étrépilly, Fr. 30/L4
Etropole, Bul. 47/J1
Etroubles, It. 56/D6
Ettadhamen Douarhicher, Tun. 100/M6
Ettelbruck, Lux. 53/F4
Etten-Leur, Neth. 50/B5
Ettenheim, Ger. 56/D1
Etterbeek, Belg. 53/D2
Etters (Goldsboro), Pa, US 138/B3
Ettlingen, Ger. 54/B5
Ettrick Pen (peak), Sc, UK 36/C6
Ettrick Water (riv.), Sc, UK 36/C5
Ettringen, Ger. 57/G1
Eu, Fr. 52/A3
'Eua (isl.), Tonga 117/H7
Eubenangee Swamp NP, Austl. 114/B2
Euclid, Oh, US 130/D3
Euclides da Cuhna, Braz. 154/C3
Eudora, Ar, US 129/K4
Eudunda, Austl. 115/A2
Euerbach, Ger. 54/D2
Eufaula, Al, US 133/G4
Eufaula (lake), Ok, US 125/G4
Eugendorf, Aus. 55/G7
Eugene, Or, US 126/C4
Eugene O'Neill NHS, Ca, US 135/L11
Eugenia (pt.), Mex. 142/B3
Eugowra, Austl. 115/D2
Eume, Embalse de (res.), Sp. 44/B1
Eungella NP, Austl. 114/C3
Eunice, La, US 129/J5
Eunice, NM, US 129/G4
Eupen, Belg. 53/F2
Euphrates (riv.), Iraq,Syria 67/D6
Eura, Fin. 39/K1
Eurajoki, Fin. 39/J1
Eure (riv.), Fr. 42/D2
Eure (dept.), Fr. 52/A5
Eure-et-Loir (dept.), Fr. 52/A6
Eureka (sound), Nun., Can. 123/S7
Eureka, Ca, US 126/B5
Eureka, Mo, US 137/F9
Eureka, Mt, US 126/E3
Eureka, Nv, US 128/D3
Eureka, SD, US 127/J4
Euroa, Austl. 115/C3
Eurodisney, Fr. 30/L5
Euron (riv.), Fr. 56/C1
Europa (pt.), Gib. 44/C4
Europabrücke, Aus. 57/H3
Europe (cont.) 27
Europoort, Neth. 50/B5
Euskirchen, Ger. 53/F2
Eussenheim, Ger. 54/C3
Eustis, Fl, US 133/H4
Euston, Austl. 115/B2
Eutin, Ger. 38/D4
Eutini, Malw. 104/B5
Eutsuk (lake), BC, Can. 126/B2
Euville, Fr. 53/E6
Évain, Qu, Can. 130/E1
Evander, SAfr. 106/E2
Evans (mt.), Co, US 129/F3
Evans (lake), Qu, Can. 130/E1
Evans, Co, US 137/C2
Evans (str.), Nun., Can. 123/H2
Evans Head, Austl. 115/E1
Evanston, Wy, US 126/F5
Evansville, In, US 130/C4
Evansville, Wy, US 129/F2
Evaporation (basin), Ut, US 126/E5
Evart, Mi, US 130/C3
Evaton, SAfr. 106/D2
Evaz, Iran 88/F3
Ève, Fr. 30/L4
Even Yehuda, Isr. 91/F7
Evenlode (riv.), Eng, UK 33/E3
Evenkiyskiy Aut. Okrug, Rus. 64/K3
Everard (cape), Austl. 115/D3
Everard (lake), Austl. 109/C4
Everard (mt.), Austl. 113/G3
Everest (peak), China, Nepal 82/E2
Everest (Sagarmatha) (mtn.), China,Nepal 85/F2
Everett, Wa, US 126/C4
Evergem, Belg. 52/C1
Everglades (swamp), Fl, US 133/H5
Everglades NP, Fl, US 133/H5
Evergreen, Al, US 133/G4
Evergreen, Co, US 137/B3
Evergreen Park, Il, US 135/Q16
Everswinkel, Ger. 51/E5
Evesham, Eng, UK 33/E2
Evesham, Vale of (valley), Eng, UK 32/D2
Évian-les-Bains, Fr. 56/C5
Évinos (riv.), Gre. 47/G3
Evje, Nor. 38/B2
Evolène, Swi. 56/D5
Évora, Port. 44/B3
Évora (dist.), Port. 44/A3
Évreux, Fr. 42/D2
Évron, Fr. 42/C2
Evrótas (riv.), Gre. 47/H4
Évry, Fr. 30/K6
Évvoia (gulf), Gre. 47/H3
Évvoia (gulf), Gre. 62/B5
Évvoia (isl.), Gre. 47/H3
Evvoia (isl.), Gre. 62/B5
Evxinoúpolis, Gre. 47/H3
Ewa Beach, Hi, US 124/V13
Ewa Villages, Hi, US 124/V13
Ewan, NJ, US 138/C4
Ewarton, Jam. 145/G2
Ewaso Ng'iro (riv.), Kenya 104/C2
Ewell, Eng, UK 30/C3
Ewing, NJ, US 138/D3
Exaplátanos, Gre. 47/H2
Excelsior Springs, Mo, US 137/E5
Excursion Inlet, Ak, US 134/L4
Exe (riv.), Eng, UK 32/C4
Exeter, NH, US 131/G3
Exmoor (upland), Eng, UK 32/C4
Exmoor NP, Eng, UK 32/C4
Exmore, Va, US 133/K2
Exmouth, Austl. 112/B2
Exmouth (gulf), Austl. 112/B2
Exmouth (pen.), Chile 159/B6
Extrema, Braz. 211/G7
Extremadura (reg.), Sp. 44/B3
Exu, Braz. 154/C2
Exuma (sound), Bahm. 141/F3
Eyach (riv.), Ger. 54/B6
Eyak, Ak, US 134/J3
Eyasi (lake), Tanz. 105/F1
Eyb (riv.), Ger. 54/C5
Eydehamn, Nor. 38/C2
Eyemouth, Sc, UK 36/D5
Eyguières, Fr. 42/F5
Eyn Hemed (ruin), Isr. 91/G8
Eyre (pen.), Austl. 109/C4
Eyre North (lake), Austl. 109/C3
Eyre South (lake), Austl. 109/C3
Ézanville, Fr. 30/K4
Ezequiel Ramos Mexía (res.), Arg. 158/C3
Ezhou, China 79/B1
Ezine, Turk. 47/K3
Ezzane (well), Alg. 96/H3

F

F.E. Walter (res.), Pa, US 138/C1
Fabbrico, It. 59/D3
Fabens, Tx, US 132/B4
Fabero, Sp. 44/B1
Fåborg, Den. 38/D4
Fabriano, It. 43/K5
Facatativá, Col. 150/D3
Faches-Thumesnil, Fr. 52/C2
Fada (lake), Sc, UK 36/A1
Fada-N'Gourma, Burk. 103/F3
Faenza, It. 59/E4
Fafa (riv.), CAfr. 97/J6
Fafe, Port. 44/A2
Fafen Shet' (riv.), Eth. 97/P6
Făgăraş, Rom. 49/G3
Fagersta, Swe. 38/F2
Faggiola (peak), It. 59/E4
Fagnano (lake), Arg. 159/D7
Fagnano Olona, It. 58/B1
Fagnières, Fr. 53/D6
Faguibine (lake), Mali 96/D4
Fahl (well), Alg. 99/F3
Fahrenzhausen, Ger. 55/E6
Faial (isl.), Azor., Port. 45/S12
Faido, Swi. 57/E5
Failsworth, Eng, UK 35/F4
Fains-Véel, Fr. 53/E6
Fair Haven, Mi, US 135/G6
Fair Haven, Vt, US 130/F3
Fair Hill, Md, US 138/C4
Fair Isle (isl.), Sc, UK 31/W14
Fair Lawn, NJ, US 139/J8
Fair Oaks, Ca, US 135/M9
Fairbanks, Ak, US 134/J3
Fairfax, Ca, US 135/J11
Fairfax, Va, US 138/A6
Fairfax (co.), Va, US 138/A6
Fairfield, Ca, US 128/B3
Fairfield, Ct, US 139/E1
Fairfield (co.), Ct, US 139/L7
Fairfield, Mt, US 126/F4
Fairfield, NJ, US 139/H8
Fairfield, Pa, US 138/A4
Fairfield, Tx, US 129/H5
Fairfield, Ut, US 137/J13
Fairland, Md, US 138/B5
Fairlee, Md, US 138/B5
Fairless Hills, Pa, US 138/D3
Fairlie, Sc, UK 36/B5
Fairmont, WV, US 130/D4
Fairmont City, Il, US 137/G8
Fairmount, Ks, US 137/D5
Fairplay, Co, US 132/B2
Fairton, NJ, US 138/C5
Fairview, NJ, US 139/K8
Fairview, Ok, US 129/H3
Fairview Heights, Il, US 137/G8
Fairway, Ks, US 137/D5
Fairweather (mt.), Ak, US 134/L4
Fairweather (cape), Ak, US 134/L4
Fairweather (mt.), BC, Can. 122/C3
Faisalābad, Pak. 86/B4
Faistós (ruin), Gre. 47/J5
Faizābād, India 84/D2
Fajardo, PR 141/M8
Fakahina (isl.), FrPol. 117/M6
Fakaofo (isl.), Tok. 117/H5
Fakarava (isl.), FrPol. 117/L6
Fako (peak), Camr. 96/G7
Fakse, Den. 38/E4
Fakse Ladeplads, Den. 38/E4
Faku, China 72/E2
Fal (riv.), Eng, UK 32/B6
Fālākāta, India 85/G2
Falāmah, WBnk. 91/G7
Fálanna, Gre. 47/H3
Falcon (res.), Mex.,US 140/B2
Falcon (cape), Alg. 100/D2
Falcón (state), Ven. 152/D2
Falconara Marittima, It. 59/G5
Falémé (riv.), Mali 96/C5
Falfurrias, Tx, US 132/D5
Falher, Ab, Can. 126/D2
Falkenberg, Swe. 38/E3
Falkensee, Ger. 40/Q6
Falkenstein, Ger. 55/F4
Falkenstein, Ger. 55/F2
Falkirk, Sc, UK 36/C5
Falkirk (pol. reg.), Sc, UK 36/C5
Falkland (isls.), UK 147/C8
Falkland, Sc, UK 36/C4
Falkland Sound (str.), UK 159/E7
Falköping, Swe. 38/E2
Fall City, Wa, US 135/D2
Fall River, Ma, US 131/G3
Fallbrook, Ca, US 136/C4
Fallere (peak), It. 56/D6
Falling Spring, Il, US 137/G8
Fallingbostel, Ger. 51/G3
Fallis, Ok, US 137/N14
Fallon, Nv, US 128/C3
Falls Church, Va, US 138/A6
Fallston, Md, US 138/B4
Falmouth, Anti. 141/N8
Falmouth, Eng, UK 32/A6
Falmouth (bay), Eng, UK 32/A6
False Pass, Ak, US 134/F5
Falshöft (pt.), Ger. 38/C4
Falso (cape), Hon. 145/F3
Falso, Cabo (cape), Mex. 142/C4
Falso Cabo de Hornos (cape), Chile 159/C7
Falster (isl.), Den. 37/E5
Falterona (peak), It. 59/E5
Fălticeni, Rom. 49/H2
Falun, Swe. 38/F1
Famagusta (bay), Cyp. 91/C2
Famagusta (dist.), Cyp. 91/C2
Famagusta, Cyp. 91/C2
Fameck, Fr. 53/F5
Famenne (reg.), Belg. 53/E3
Fammau, Moel (peak), Wal, UK 35/E5
Fan Si Pan (peak), Viet. 83/H3
Fana, Nor. 38/A1
Fanchang, China 72/D5
Fandriana, Madg. 107/H8
Fang Xian, China 72/B4
Fangatau (isl.), FrPol. 117/L6
Fangataufa (isl.), FrPol. 117/L7
Fangcheng, China 72/C4
Fangcheng Gezu Zizhixian, China 83/J3
Fangshan, China 72/B3
Fanjing (peak), China 83/J2
Fannich (lake), Sc, UK 36/A1
Fanning (Tabuaeran) (isl.), Kiri. 117/K4
Fano, It. 59/G5
Fanø (isl.), Den. 38/C4
Fanshi, China 72/C3
Fanwood, NJ, US 139/H9
Faqīrwāli, Pak. 86/B5
Fāqūs, Egypt 91/B4
Fara Novarese, It. 58/B1
Faradje, D.R. Congo 104/A2
Farafangana, Madg. 107/H8
Farāfirah, Wāḩāt al (oasis), Egypt 101/A3
Farāh, Afg. 89/H2
Farāh (riv.), Afg. 89/H2
Farallon (isls.), Ca, US 128/B3
Farallon de Medinilla (isl.), NMar. 116/D3
Farallon de Pajaros (isl.), NMar. 116/D2
Farallones de Cali, PN, Col. 150/C3
Faranah (pol. reg.), Gui. 102/C4
Faranah, Gui. 102/C4
Farángi Samariás NP, Gre. 47/H5
Faraony (riv.), Madg. 107/H8
Faraulep (isl.), Micr. 116/D4
Farciennes, Belg. 53/D3
Fareham, Eng, UK 33/E5
Faremoutiers, Fr. 52/C6
Farewell, Ak, US 134/H3
Farewell (cape), NZ 117/S11
Färgelanda, Swe. 38/D2
Farghona (pol. reg.), Uzb. 87/F4
Farghona, Uzb. 87/F4
Fargo, ND, US 127/J4
Faribault, Mn, US 127/K4
Farīdābād, India 86/D5
Farīdkot, India 86/C4
Farīdpur, Bang. 85/G4
Farīdpur (pol. reg.), Bang. 85/G4
Farīdpur, India 84/B1
Fāriskūr, Egypt 91/B4
Färjestaden, Swe. 38/G3
Farkadhón, Gre. 47/H3
Farkasgyepú, Hun. 48/C2
Farley, Mo, US 137/D5
Farmers, Co, US 137/C2
Farmingdale, NJ, US 138/D3
Farmingdale, NY, US 139/M9
Farmington, De, US 138/C6
Farmington, Me, US 131/G2
Farmington, Mi, US 135/F7
Farmington, Mo, US 129/K3
Farmington, NM, US 128/E3
Farmington, Ut, US 137/K12
Farmington Hills, Mi, US 135/E6
Farnborough, Eng, UK 33/F4
Farnham, Eng, UK 33/F4
Farnham Royal, Eng, UK 30/B2
Farnworth, Eng, UK 35/F4
Faro, Yk, Can. 134/M3
Faro (dist.), Port. 44/A4
Faro, Port. 44/B4
Faro (int'l arpt.), Port. 44/B4
Faro, PN du, Camr. 96/H6
Faroe (isls.), Den. 160/G
Fåron (isl.), Swe. 39/H3
Farösund, Swe. 39/H3
Farquhar (cape), Austl. 112/B2
Farr West, Ut, US 137/J11
Farroupilha, Braz. 155/B4
Farrukhābād, India 84/B2
Fársala, Gre. 47/H3
Farsø, Den. 38/C3
Farson, Wy, US 126/F5
Farsund, Nor. 38/B2
Fartak, Ras (pt.), Yem. 88/F5
Farwell, Tx, US 129/G4
Fasā, Iran 88/F3
Fasano, It. 47/E2
Faşıkan (pass), Turk. 91/C1
Fassberg, Ger. 51/H3
Fast Castle (pt.), Sc, UK 36/D5
Fastiv, Ukr. 62/D2
Fatagar Tuting (cape), Indo. 81/H4
Fatahjang, Pak. 86/B3
Fatehābād, India 86/C5
Fatehpur, India 84/C3
Fatehpur, India 84/C2
Fatehpur, India 89/K3
Fatick (pol. reg.), Sen. 102/A3
Fatick, Sen. 102/A3
Fátima, Port. 44/A3
Fatsa, Turk. 90/D1
Fatu Hiva (isl.), FrPol. 117/M6
Faucille, Col de la (pass), Fr. 56/C5
Faucilles (mts.), Fr. 40/C4
Faughan (riv.), NI, UK 34/A2
Fauglia, It. 58/D5
Fauldhouse, Sc, UK 36/C5
Faulkton, SD, US 127/J4
Faulquemont, Fr. 53/F5
Faure (isl.), Austl. 112/B3
Făurei, Rom. 49/H3
Fauske, Nor. 37/E2
Faust, Ut, US 137/J13
Fauvillers, Belg. 53/E4
Faux, Tête de (peak), Fr. 56/D1
Favalto (peak), It. 59/F6
Favara, It. 46/C4
Fave (riv.), Fr. 56/C1
Faverges, Fr. 56/C6
Faverney, Fr. 56/C2
Faversham, Eng, UK 33/G4
Favières, Fr. 30/L5
Favignana, It. 46/C4
Favria, It. 58/A2
Favrieux, Fr. 30/G5
Fawn (riv.), On, Can. 127/L2
Fawn Grove, Pa, US 138/B4
Faxaflói (bay), Ice. 37/M7
Faxinal, Braz. 155/B2
Faya-Largeau, Chad 97/J4
Fayette, Al, US 133/G3
Fayette, Ms, US 129/K5
Fayetteville, Tn, US 133/G3
Fayetteville, Ga, US 133/G3
Fayetteville, NC, US 133/J3
Fayl-la-Forêt, Fr. 56/B2
Fazao, Monts du (mts.), Togo 103/F4
Fazao, PN du, Togo 103/F4
Fdérik, Mrta. 98/B5
Feale (riv.), Ire. 31/P10
Fear (cape), NC, US 133/J3
Feasterville-Trevose, Pa, US 138/D3
Feather (riv.), Ca, US 128/B3
Featherstone, Eng, UK 35/G4
Fécamp, Fr. 42/D2
Fecht (riv.), Fr. 56/D1
Federal Hall Nat'l Mem., NY, US 139/K9
Federal Heights, Co, US 137/B3
Federally Admin. Tribal Areas, Pak. 86/A2
Federsee (lake), Ger. 54/C6
Fedje, Nor. 38/A1
Feeny, NI, UK 34/A2
Fegersheim, Fr. 54/A6
Fehérgyarmat, Hun. 48/F2
Fehmarn (isl.), Den. 38/D4
Fehmarn Belt (str.), Den. 40/F1
Fei Huang (riv.), China 72/D4
Fei Xian, China 72/D4
Feia, Lagoa (lake), Braz. 155/D2
Feicheng, China 72/D3
Feidong, China 72/D5
Feignies, Fr. 52/C3
Feijó, Braz. 156/D3
Feillans, Fr. 56/A5
Feira, Port. 44/A2
Feira de Santana, Braz. 154/C4
Feistritz (riv.), Aus. 43/L3
Feixi, China 72/D5
Fejér (co.), Hun. 48/D2
Fejø (isl.), Ger. 38/D4
Feke, Turk. 90/C2
Feketić, Serb. 48/D3
Felanitx, Sp. 45/G3
Feldafing, Ger. 57/H2
Feldaist (riv.), Aus. 55/H6
Feldberg (peak), Ger. 56/E2
Feldkirch, Aus. 57/F3
Feldkirchen an der Donau, Aus. 55/H6
Feldkirchen bei Graz, Aus. 48/B2
Feldkirchen in Kärnten, Aus. 43/L3
Feletto, It. 58/A2
Feletto Umberto, It. 59/G1
Felino, It. 58/D3
Felipe Carillo Puerto, Mex. 144/D2
Felixdorf, Aus. 48/C2
Felixlândia, Braz. 155/C1
Felixstowe, Eng, UK 33/H3
Felizzano, It. 58/B3
Fell, Ger. 53/F4
Fellbach, Ger. 54/C5
Felling, Eng, UK 35/G2
Felsberg, Ger. 51/G6
Felsberg, Swi. 57/F4
Felton, Pa, US 138/B4
Felton, De, US 138/C5
Fema (peak), It. 43/K5
Femø (isl.), Den. 38/D4
Femundsmarka NP, Nor. 37/D3
Fénay, Fr. 56/B3
Fene, Sp. 44/A1
Fener (pt.), Turk. 91/D1
Fénérive, Madg. 105/K10
Feng Xian, China 72/D4
Fengári (peak), Gre. 47/J2
Fengcheng, China 71/L6
Fengcheng, China 73/C2
Fenghuang, China 83/J2
Fengle (riv.), China 72/D5
Fengnan, China 72/J7
Fengning, China 72/D2
Fengqing, China 83/G3
Fengqiu, China 72/C4
Fengrun, China 72/J7
Fengshan, Tai. 79/D3
Fengtai, China 72/H7
Fengxian, China 72/L9
Fengyang, China 72/D4
Fengyüan, Tai. 79/D3
Fengzhen, China 72/C2
Fenimore Pass (chan.), Ak, US 134/C5
Fenoarivo Atsinanana, Madg. 107/J7
Fens (phys. reg.), Eng, UK 33/G1
Fensmark, Den. 38/D4
Fensterbach (riv.), Ger. 55/F4
Fenton, Mi, US 130/D3
Fenton, Mo, US 137/G8
Fenton (lake), Mi, US 135/E7
Fenxi, China 72/B3
Feodosiya, Ukr. 62/E3
Fer, Cap de (cape), Alg. 100/K6
Ferbane, Ire. 31/Q10
Ferdinandshof, Ger. 41/G2
Fère-Champenoise, Fr. 52/C6
Fère-en-Tardenois, Fr. 52/C5
Ferentino, It. 46/C2
Ferento (ruin), It. 46/C1
Fergus Falls, Mn, US 127/J4
Ferguson, Mo, US 137/G8
Ferguson (lake), Nun., Can. 122/F2
Ferihegy (int'l arpt.), Hun. 48/D2
Ferkéssédougou, C.d'Iv. 102/D4
Ferlach, Aus. 43/L3
Fermanagh (dist.), NI, UK 34/A3
Fermi National Accelerator Laboratory, Il, US 135/P16
Fermignano, It. 59/F5
Fermin (pt.), Ca, US 136/F8
Fermo, It. 43/K5
Fermoselle, Sp. 44/B2
Fermoy, Ire. 31/P10
Fernán-Núñez, Sp. 44/C4
Fernandina (isl.), Ecu. 156/E7
Fernandina Beach, Fl, US 133/H4
Fernando de Noronha (isl.), Braz. 147/F3
Fernandópolis, Braz. 155/B2
Ferndale, Md, US 138/B5
Ferndale, Mi, US 135/F7
Ferney-Voltaire, Fr. 56/C5
Fernie, BC, Can. 126/E3
Fernpass (pass), Aus. 57/G3
Ferntree Gully NP, Austl. 115/G5
Ferrandina, It. 46/E2
Ferrara (prov.), It. 59/E3
Ferrara, It. 59/E3
Ferrat (cape), Alg. 100/E5
Ferreira do Alentejo, Port. 44/A3
Ferrelview, Mo, US 137/D5
Ferreñafe, Peru 156/B2
Ferret (cape), Fr. 42/C4
Ferrette, Fr. 56/D3
Ferriday, La, US 129/K5

187
Ferri – Freel

Ferriere, It. 58/C2
Ferrière-la-Grande, Fr. 52/D3
Ferrières, Belg. 53/E3
Ferryden, Sc, UK 36/D3
Ferryfield (int'l arpt.), Eng, UK 33/G5
Ferryhill, Eng, UK 35/G2
Fertő (Neusiedler See) (lake), Aus. 43/M3
Ferté-Bernard, Fr. 42/D2
Fértil (valley), Arg. 157/C3
Ferwerd, Neth. 50/C2
Fès, Mor. 100/B2
Fès (prov.), Mor. 100/B3
Fesches-le-Châtel, Fr. 56/C2
Feshie (riv.), Sc, UK 36/C2
Fessenheim, Fr. 56/D2
Festival Centre, Austl. 113/M8
Fetești, Rom. 49/H3
Fethaland (pt.), Sc, UK 31/W13
Fethiye, Turk. 90/B2
Feucherolles, Fr. 30/H5
Feucht, Ger. 54/E4
Feuchtwangen, Ger. 54/D4
Feuilles (lake), Qu, Can. 123/J3
Feuilles, Rivière aux (riv.), Qu, Can. 123/J3
Feuquières, Fr. 52/A4
Feuquières-en-Vimeu, Fr. 52/A3
Feurs, Fr. 42/F4
Fevzipaşa, Turk. 91/E1
Feyzābād, Afg. 89/K1
Fez (Saiss) (int'l arpt.), Mor. 100/B3
Fezzan (reg.), Libya 96/H2
Fferna, Moel (peak), Wal, UK 35/E6
Ffestiniog, Wal, UK 34/E6
Fianarantsoa (prov.), Madg. 107/H8
Fianarantsoa, Madg. 107/H8
Fianga, Chad 96/J6
Ficarolo, It. 59/E3
Fichtelberg (peak), Ger. 55/F2
Fichtelgebirge (mts.), Ger. 40/F3
Fichtelnaab (riv.), Ger. 55/E3
Ficksburg, SAfr. 106/D3
Fidenza, It. 58/D3
Fié (riv.), Gui. 102/C4
Field (riv.), Austl. 113/M9
Fieldon, Il, US 137/G7
Fieni, Rom. 49/G3
Fier (riv.), Fr. 56/B6
Fierzë (lake), Alb. 47/G1
Fiesch, Swi. 56/E5
Fiesole, It. 59/E5
Fiesso, It. 59/F2
Fiesso Umbertiano, It. 59/E3
Fiesta Texas, Tx, US 137/T20
Fife, Wa, US 135/C3
Fife (pol. reg.), Sc, UK 36/D4
Fife Ness (pt.), Sc, UK 36/D4
Fifth Cataract (falls), Sudan 101/C5
Figalo (cape), Alg. 100/D2
Figari, Fr. 46/A2
Figeac, Fr. 42/E4
Figline Valdarno, It. 59/E5
Figueira da Foz, Port. 44/A2
Figueres, Sp. 45/G1
Figuig, Mor. 99/E2
Figuig (prov.), Mor. 100/C3
Fiherenana (riv.), Madg. 107/G8
Fiji (ctry.) 116/G6
Filadelfia, Par. 157/D1
Filadélfia, Braz. 154/A2
Filattiera, It. 58/C4
Filchner Ice Shelf, Ant. 160/Y
Filey (bay), Eng, UK 35/H3
Filí, Gre. 47/N8
Filiași, Rom. 49/F3
Filiatai, Gre. 47/G3
Filiatrá, Gre. 47/G4
Filicudi (isl.), It. 46/D3
Filingué, Niger 103/F3
Filippiás, Gre. 47/G3
Filippoi (ruin), Gre. 47/J2
Filipstad, Swe. 38/F2
Filisur, Swi. 57/F4
Fillière (riv.), Fr. 56/C6
Fillmore, Ut, US 128/D3
Fillmore, Ca, US 136/B2
Filomeno Mata, Mex. 143/M6
Filótion, Gre. 47/J4
Filottrano, It. 59/G6
Fils (riv.), Ger. 54/C5
Filsum, Ger. 51/E2
Fimi (riv.), D.R. Congo 96/J8
Fina, Forêt Classée de, Mali 102/C3
Finale Emilia, It. 59/E3
Finale Ligure, It. 58/B4
Fiñana, Sp. 44/D4
Finch Hatton, Austl. 114/C3
Findel (int'l arpt.), Lux. 53/F4
Findhorn (riv.), Sc, UK 36/B2
Findhorn, Sc, UK 36/C1
Findlay, Oh, US 130/D3
Findochty, Sc, UK 36/D1
Finesville, NJ, US 138/C2
Fingal, Austl. 115/C4
Finger (lake), On, Can. 127/K2
Finhaut, Swi. 56/C5
Finike, Turk. 91/B1
Finisterre, Sp. 44/A1
Finisterre (cape), Sp. 44/A1
Finke (riv.), Austl. 113/G3
Finke Gorge NP, Austl. 113/G3
Finkenstein, Aus. 43/K3
Finksburg, Md, US 138/B5
Finland (ctry.) 37/H2
Finland (gulf), Eur. 37/H2
Finlay (mts.), Tx, US 132/B4
Finlay (riv.), BC, Can. 122/D3
Finley, Austl. 115/C2
Finn (riv.), Ire. 31/Q9
Finnentrop, Ger. 51/E6
Finnigan (mt.), Austl. 114/B1
Finnis (cape), Austl. 113/G5
Finnmark (co.), Nor. 37/G1
Fino Mornasco, It. 58/C1
Finsing, Ger. 55/E6
Finspång, Swe. 38/F2
Finsteraarhorn (peak), Swi. 56/E4
Finström, Fin. 39/H1
Fintel, Ger. 51/G2
Fintona, NI, UK 34/A3
Fionn Loch (lake), Sc, UK 36/A1
Fiora (riv.), It. 43/J5
Fiorano, It. 59/D3
Fiordland NP, NZ 117/R12
Fiorenzuola d'Arda, It. 58/C3
Fircrest, Wa, US 135/C3
Fire Island Nat'l Seashore, NY, US 139/E2
Firenze (prov.), It. 59/E5
Firenze (Florence), It. 59/E5
Firenzuola, It. 59/E4
Firestone, Co, US 137/C2
Firmat, Arg. 158/E2
Firmi, Fr. 42/E4
Firminy, Fr. 42/F4
Firozābād, India 84/B2
Firozpur, India 86/C4
First Cataract (falls), Egypt 101/C3
Fīrūz Kūh, Iran 88/F1
Firūzābād, Iran 88/F3
Fischa (riv.), Aus. 49/P7
Fischach, Ger. 57/G1
Fischamend Markt, Aus. 49/P7
Fischbacher Alpen (mts.), Aus. 43/L3
Fischen im Allgäu, Ger. 57/G3
Fischer, Tx, US 137/U20
Fish (riv.), Namb. 105/C5
Fisher (bay), Mb, Can. 127/J3
Fisher (str.), Nun., Can. 123/H2
Fisher Branch, Mb, Can. 127/J3
Fisherman (isl.), Austl. 114/F6
Fishers (isl.), NY, US 139/G1
Fishguard, Wal, UK 32/B3
Fisht (peak), Rus. 62/F4
Fismes, Fr. 52/C5
Fitful Head (pt.), Sc, UK 31/W14
Fitjar, Nor. 38/A2
Fitton (mt.), Yk, Can. 134/L2
Fitzgerald, Ga, US 133/H4
Fitzgerald River NP, Austl. 112/C5
Fitzroy (riv.), Austl. 109/B2
Fitzroy (peak), Arg. 159/B6
Fitzwilliam (str.), NW, Can. 123/R7
Fiume Veneto, It. 59/F1
Fiumicino, It. 46/C2
Five Sisters (peak), Sc, UK 36/A2
Fivemiletown, NI, UK 34/A3
Fivizzano, It. 58/D4
Fjell, Nor. 38/A1
Fjerritslev, Den. 38/C3
Fjugesta, Swe. 38/E2
Flå, Nor. 38/C1
Flachslanden, Ger. 54/D4
Fladungen, Ger. 54/D1
Flagler, Co, US 132/C2
Flagler Beach, Fl, US 133/H4
Flagstaff, Az, US 128/E4
Flambeau (riv.), Wi, US 127/L4
Flamborough, On, Can. 131/J4
Flamborough Head (pt.), Eng, UK 35/H3
Fläming (hills), Ger. 40/G2
Flaming Gorge (res.), Ut,Wy, US 126/F5
Flaming Gorge Nat'l Rec. Area, Ut,Wy, US 128/E2
Flamingo Field (int'l arpt.), NAnt. 152/D1
Flanagan (riv.), On, Can. 127/K2
Flanders (reg.), Fr. 42/E1
Flanders, NY, US 139/F2
Flat Holm (isl.), Eng, UK 32/C4
Flat River, Mo, US 129/K3
Flathead (riv.), Mt, US 126/E4
Flathead (lake), Mt, US 126/E4
Flathead, South Fork (riv.), Mt, US 126/E3
Flattery (cape), Austl. 114/B1
Flattery (cape), Wa, US 126/B3
Flavio Alfaro, Ecu. 152/B5
Flawil, Swi. 57/F3
Flaxlanden, Fr. 56/D2
Fleet, Eng, UK 33/F4
Fleetwood, Pa, US 138/C3
Fleetwood, Eng, UK 35/E4
Flekkefjord, Nor. 38/B2
Flemington, NJ, US 138/D2
Flemington Racecourse, Austl. 115/F5
Flemish Brabant (prov.), Belg. 53/D2
Flen, Swe. 38/G2
Flensburg, Ger. 38/C4
Flero, It. 58/D2
Fleron, Belg. 53/E2
Flers, Fr. 42/C2
Flesland (int'l arpt.), Nor. 38/A1
Fletschhorn (peak), Swi. 56/D5
Fleurance, Fr. 42/D5
Fleurier, Swi. 56/C4
Fleurus, Belg. 53/D3
Fleury-les-Aubrais, Fr. 42/D3
Flevoland (prov.), Neth. 50/C4
Flevoland (isl.), Neth. 40/C2
Flexenpass (pass), Aus. 57/G3
Flieden, Ger. 54/C2
Flieden (riv.), Ger. 54/C2
Fliess, Aus. 57/G3
Flims, Swi. 57/F4
Flin Flon, Mb, Can. 127/H2
Flinders (ranges), Austl. 109/C4
Flinders (bay), Austl. 109/A4
Flinders (reef), Austl. 109/D2
Flinders (riv.), Austl. 109/D2
Flinders (reefs), Austl. 109/D4
Flinders (range), Austl. 113/H5
Flinders Chase NP, Austl. 113/H5
Flinders Ranges NP, Austl. 113/H4
Flinders Reefs (isls.), Austl. 114/C2
Flines-lez-Raches, Fr. 52/C3
Flint (hills), Ks, US 129/H3
Flint (riv.), Ga, US 133/G4
Flint, Mi, US 130/D3
Flint (isl.), Kiri. 117/K6
Flint (lake), Nun., Can. 123/J2
Flint, Wal, UK 35/E5
Flint, South Branch (riv.), Mi, US 135/F5
Flintbek, Ger. 38/D4
Flintshire (co.), Wal, UK 35/E5
Flisa, Nor. 38/E1
Flix, Sp. 45/F2
Flixecourt, Fr. 52/B3
Flize, Fr. 53/D4
Floby, Swe. 38/E2
Floda, Swe. 38/E3
Flögelner See (riv.), Ger. 51/F1
Flöha (riv.), Ger. 41/G3
Floing, Fr. 53/D4
Flonheim, Ger. 54/B3
Flora, Il, US 129/K3
Flora (mt.), Austl. 112/C2
Flora, Nor. 37/C3
Floral Park, NY, US 139/L9
Florange, Fr. 53/F5
Florânia, Braz. 154/C2
Floraville, Il, US 137/G9
Floreffe, Belg. 53/D3
Florence, SC, US 133/J3
Florence, Al, US 133/G3
Florence, Az, US 128/E4
Florence (Firenze), It. 43/J5
Florence-Graham, Ca, US 136/F8
Florencia, Col. 152/C4
Florennes, Belg. 53/D3
Florenville, Belg. 53/E4
Flores (sea), Indo. 67/L10
Flores (isl.), Indo. 67/M10
Flores, Guat. 144/D2
Flores (dept.), Uru. 159/F2
Flores do Piauí, Braz. 154/B2
Floresta, Braz. 154/C3
Florham Park, NJ, US 139/H8
Floriano, Braz. 154/B2
Florianópolis, Braz. 155/B3
Florida, Peru 156/B2
Florida (bay), Fl, US 133/H5
Florida, Hon. 144/D3
Florida, Cuba 145/G1
Florida, Col. 152/B4
Florida (dept.), Uru. 159/F2
Florida, Uru. 159/K11
Florida (state), US 133/H4
Florida, NY, US 138/D1
Florida (str.), Cuba,US 125/K7
Florida Keys (isls.), Fl, US 133/H5
Floridablanca, Col. 152/C3
Floridia, It. 46/D4
Florin, Ca, US 135/M10
Flórina, Gre. 47/G2
Florissant, Mo, US 137/G8
Florissant Fossil Beds Nat'l Mon., Co, US 132/B2
Flörsbachtal, Ger. 54/C2
Flörsheim am Main, Ger. 54/B2
Flörsheim-Dalsheim, Ger. 54/B3
Florstadt, Ger. 54/B2
Flossenbürg, Ger. 55/F3
Floyd, Mo, US 137/E5
Floydada, Tx, US 129/G4
Fluchthorn (peak), Aus. 57/G4
Flüelapass (pass), Swi. 57/F4
Flüelen, Swi. 57/E4
Fluessen (lake), Neth. 50/C3
Flums, Swi. 57/F3
Flushing, Mi, US 130/D3
Fly (riv.), PNG 116/D5
Flying Fish (cape), Ant. 160/T
Fnjóská (riv.), Ice. 37/P6
Foam Lake, Sk, Can. 127/H3
Foča, Bosn. 48/D4
Fochabers, Sc, UK 36/C1
Fochville, SAfr. 106/P13
Fockbek, Ger. 38/C4
Focșani, Rom. 49/H3
Fogang, China 83/K3
Foggia, It. 46/D2
Foglia (riv.), It. 59/F5
Foglizzo, It. 58/A2
Föglö (isl.), Fin. 39/J3
Fogo (isl.), CpV. 93/J10
Fohnsdorf, Aus. 43/L3
Föhren, Ger. 53/F4
Foix, Fr. 42/D5
Folarskardnuten (peak), Nor. 38/B1
Folda (inlet), Nor. 37/E2
Földeák, Hun. 48/E2
Folégandros (isl.), Gre. 47/J4
Folembray, Fr. 52/C4
Foley (isl.), Nun., Can. 123/J2
Folgaria, It. 57/H6
Foligno, It. 43/K5
Folkestone, Eng, UK 33/H4
Folkston, Ga, US 133/H4
Follainville-Dennemont, Fr. 30/H4
Follonica, Golfo di (gulf), It. 43/J5
Folschviller, Fr. 53/F5
Folsom, NJ, US 138/D4
Fomboni, Com. 107/G6
Fond du Lac, Wi, US 127/L5
Fond du Lac, Sk, Can. 122/F3
Fond du Lac (riv.), Sk, Can. 122/F3
Fondi, It. 46/C2
Fondo, It. 57/H5
Fongen (peak), Nor. 37/D3
Fonni, It. 46/A2
Fonsagrada, Sp. 44/B1
Fonseca (gulf), Nic. 140/D5
Fonseca, Col. 152/C2
Font Sancte, Pic de la (peak), Fr. 43/G4
Fontaine, Fr. 42/F4
Fontaine-Châalis, Fr. 30/L4
Fontaine-lès-Dijon, Fr. 56/A3
Fontaine-lès-Luxeuil, Fr. 56/C2
Fontaine-L'Evêque, Belg. 53/D3
Fontainebleau, Fr. 42/E2
Fontana, Ca, US 136/C2
Fontanarossa (int'l arpt.), It. 46/D4
Fontanella, It. 58/C2
Fontanellato, It. 58/D3
Fontaniva, It. 59/E1
Fonte Boa, Braz. 153/E5
Fontenailles, Fr. 30/L6
Fontenais, Swi. 56/D3
Fontenay-en-Parisis, Fr. 30/K4
Fontenay-le-Comte, Fr. 42/C3
Fontenay-le-Fleury, Fr. 30/J5
Fontenay-lès-Briis, Fr. 30/J6
Fontenay-Saint-Père, Fr. 30/H4
Fontenay-sous-Bois, Fr. 30/K5
Fontenay-Trésigny, Fr. 30/L5
Fontenelle (res.), Wy, US 126/F5
Fontoy, Fr. 53/F5
Fontur (pt.), Ice. 37/P6
Foping, China 70/J5
Foraker (mt.), Ak, US 134/H3
Forbach, Fr. 53/F5
Forbach, Ger. 54/B5
Forbes, Austl. 115/D2
Forbesganj, India 85/F2
Forcarey, Sp. 44/A1
Forchheim, Ger. 54/E3
Forclaz, Col de la (pass), Swi. 56/D5
Førde, Nor. 37/C3
Fords, NJ, US 139/H9
Foreland (pt.), Eng, UK 32/C4
Foreland, The (pt.), Eng, UK 33/E5
Foremost, Ab, Can. 126/F3
Foreness (pt.), Eng, UK 33/H4
Forest, Ms, US 133/F3
Forest Hill, Md, US 138/B4
Forest Park, Ok, US 137/N14
Forestier (pen.), Austl. 115/D4
Forestier (cape), Austl. 115/D4
Forestville, Qu, Can. 131/G1
Forestville, Md, US 138/B6
Forez, Monts du (mts.), Fr. 42/E4
Forfar, Sc, UK 36/D3
Forges-les-Bains, Fr. 30/J6
Forggensee (lake), Ger. 57/G2
Forillon NP, Qu, Can. 131/H1
Forked River, NJ, US 138/D4
Forkill, NI, UK 34/B3
Forks, Wa, US 126/B4
Forlì, It. 59/F4
Forlì-Cesena (prov.), It. 59/F4
Forlimpopoli, It. 59/F4
Formartine (reg.), Sc, UK 36/D2
Formby, Eng, UK 35/E4
Formby (pt.), Eng, UK 35/E4
Formentera, Isla de (isl.), Sp. 45/F3
Formentor (cape), Sp. 45/G3
Formerie, Fr. 52/A4
Formia, It. 46/C2
Formiga, Braz. 155/C2
Formigine, It. 59/D3
Formignana, It. 59/E3
Formosa, Arg. 157/E2
Formosa, Braz. 154/A4
Formosa (peak), SAfr. 106/C4
Formosa (isl.), GBis. 102/B4
Formosa do Rio Prêto, Braz. 154/A3
Formosa, Serra (mts.), Braz. 151/G6
Formoso (riv.), Braz. 151/J6
Fornacelle, It. 59/E5
Fornaci di Barga, It. 58/D4
Fornæs (cape), Den. 38/D3
Fornebu (int'l arpt.), Nor. 38/D2
Fornovo di Taro, It. 58/D3
Forres, Sc, UK 36/C1
Forrest City, Ar, US 129/K4
Forsand, Nor. 38/B2
Forshaga, Swe. 38/E2
Forssa, Fin. 39/K1
Forstern, Ger. 55/E6
Forstinning, Ger. 55/E6
Forsyth, Mt, US 126/G4
Forsyth, Ga, US 133/H3
Forsyth (range), Austl. 114/A3
Forsythe NWR, NJ, US 138/D5
Fort Abbās, Pak. 86/B5
Fort Augustus, Sc, UK 36/B2
Fort Beaufort, SAfr. 106/D4
Fort Belvoir, Va, US 138/A6
Fort Benton, Mt, US 126/F4
Fort Bragg, Ca, US 126/C6
Fort Chambly Nat'l Hist. Park, Qu, Can. 131/P7
Fort Chipewyan, Ab, Can. 122/E3
Fort Cobb (res.), Ok, US 129/H4
Fort Collins, Co, US 137/B1
Fort Collins Museum, Co, US 137/B1
Fort Davis, Tx, US 129/G5
Fort de Douaumont, Fr. 53/E5
Fort-de-France, Guad. 141/N9
Fort de Vaux, Fr. 53/E5
Fort Desaix Mil. Res., Fr. 141/N9
Fort Dodge, Ia, US 127/K5
Fort Erie, On, Can. 131/S10
Fort Frances, On, Can. 127/K3
Fort Frederica Nat'l Mon., Ga, US 133/H4
Fort George Nat'l Hist. Park, On, Can. 131/R9
Fort Gibson (lake), Ok, US 132/E3
Fort Good Hope, NW, Can. 122/D2
Fort Hancock, NJ, US 139/J10
Fort Howard, Md, US 138/B5
Fort Kent, Me, US 131/G2
Fort Lauderdale, Fl, US 133/H5
Fort Lauderdale-Hollywood (int'l arpt.), Fl, US 133/H5
Fort Lee, NJ, US 139/K8
Fort Lewis, Wa, US 135/B3
Fort Liard, NW, Can. 122/D2
Fort Liberté, Haiti 145/J2
Fort Lupton, Co, US 137/C2
Fort Macleod, Ab, Can. 126/E3
Fort Madison, Ia, US 127/L5
Fort-Mahon-Plage, Fr. 52/A3
Fort Malden Nat'l Hist. Park, On, Can. 135/F7
Fort-Mardyck, Fr. 52/B1
Fort Matanzas Nat'l Mon., Fl, US 133/H4
Fort McDowell Ind. Res., Az, US 137/S18
Fort McHenry Nat'l Mon., Md, US 138/B5
Fort McMurray, Ab, Can. 122/E3
Fort McPherson, NW, Can. 134/M2
Fort Meade, Md, US 138/B5
Fort Morgan, Co, US 129/G2
Fort Myers, Fl, US 133/H5
Fort Nelson, BC, Can. 122/D3
Fort Nelson (riv.), BC, Can. 122/D3
Fort Nottingham, SAfr. 107/E3
Fort Payne, Al, US 133/G3
Fort Peck (dam), Mt, US 127/G4
Fort Peck (lake), Mt, US 126/G4
Fort Pierce, Fl, US 133/H5
Fort Portal, Ugan. 104/A2
Fort Providence, NW, Can. 122/E2
Fort Qu'Appelle, Sk, Can. 127/H3
Fort Randall (dam), SD, US 127/J5
Fort Resolution, NW, Can. 122/E2
Fort Saint James, BC, Can. 126/B2
Fort Saint John, BC, Can. 122/D3
Fort Saskatchewan, Ab, Can. 126/E2
Fort Scott, Ks, US 129/J3
Fort-Shevchenko, Kaz. 63/J3
Fort Simpson, NW, Can. 122/D2
Fort Smith, Ar, US 129/J4
Fort Smith, NW, Can. 122/E2
Fort Stanwix Nat'l Mon., NY, US 130/F3
Fort Stockton, Tx, US 129/G5
Fort Sumner, NM, US 129/F4
Fort Sumter, SC, US 133/J3
Fort Tilden, NY, US 139/K9
Fort Totten, ND, US 127/J4
Fort Vasquez Museum, Co, US 137/C2
Fort Vermilion, Ab, Can. 122/E3
Fort Wadsworth, NY, US 139/J9
Fort Walton Beach, Fl, US 133/G4
Fort Wayne, In, US 130/C3
Fort Wellington Nat'l Hist. Park, Can. 130/F2
Fort William, Sc, UK 36/A3
Fort Yates, ND, US 127/H4
Fort Yukon, Ak, US 134/J2
Fortaleza, Braz. 154/C1
Fortaleza dos Nogueiras, Braz. 154/A2
Fortaleza Santa Teresa, Uru. 159/G2
Forte dei Marmi, It. 58/D5
Fortescue (riv.), Austl. 112/C2
Fortescue, NJ, US 138/C5
Forth, Sc, UK 36/C5
Forth (riv.), Sc, UK 36/B4
Forth, Firth of (inlet), Sc, UK 36/C4
Fortín, Mex. 143/N8
Fortore (riv.), It. 46/D2
Fortrose, Sc, UK 36/B1
Fortuna, Braz. 154/A2
Fortuna, Arg. 158/D2
Fortuna Ledge, Ak, US 134/F3
Fortune (bay), Nf, Can. 131/L2
Fortune, Nf, Can. 131/L2
Forty Fort, Pa, US 138/C1
Forty Mile Scrub NP, Austl. 114/B2
Foshan, China 83/K3
Fosheim (pen.), Nun., Can. 123/S7
Foss (riv.), Eng, UK 35/G3
Fossalta di Piave, It. 59/F1
Fossalta di Portogruaro, It. 59/F1
Fossano, It. 58/A3
Fosses, Fr. 30/K4
Fosses-la-Ville, Belg. 53/D3
Fossil, Or, US 126/C4
Fossil Creek (res.), Co, US 137/B2
Fossò, It. 59/F2
Fossombrone, It. 59/F5
Foster, Austl. 115/C3
Foster Pond, Il, US 137/G9
Fosterburg, Il, US 137/G8
Fostoria, Oh, US 130/D3
Fót, Hun. 49/R9
Foucarmont, Fr. 52/A4
Foucherans, Fr. 56/B3
Foug, Fr. 53/E6
Fougères, Fr. 42/C2
Fougerolles, Fr. 56/C2
Fouilloy, Fr. 52/B4
Foul (bay), Egypt, Su 97/N3
Foula (isl.), Sc, UK 31/V13
Foulness (pt.), Eng, UK 33/G3
Foulness (isl.), Eng, UK 33/G3
Foulness (riv.), Eng, UK 35/H4
Foum Zguid, Mor. 98/D3
Foumban, Camr. 96/H6
Foundiougne, Sen. 102/A3
Fountain, Il, US 137/G9
Fountain Hill, Pa, US 138/C2
Fountain Hills, Az, US 137/S18
Fountain Valley, Ca, US 136/G8
Fountains Abbey, Eng, UK 35/G3
Fourchambault, Fr. 42/E3
Fourche La Fave (riv.), Ar, US 129/J4
Fourges, Fr. 30/G4
Fourmies, Fr. 52/D4
Fourth Cataract (falls), Sudan 101/C5
Fouta Djallon (phys. reg.), Gui. 96/C5
Foveaux (str.), NZ 109/G7
Fowey (riv.), Eng, UK 32/B6
Fowman, Iran 88/E1
Fox (isls.), Ak, US 134/E5
Fox (mtn.), Yk, Can. 134/M3
Fox (riv.), Il,Wi, US 127/L5
Fox (isl.), Wa, US 135/B3
Fox Creek, Ab, Can. 126/D2
Fox Glacier, NZ 117/S11
Fox Lake, Il, US 135/P15
Fox River Grove, Il, US 135/P15
Fox Valley, Sk, Can. 126/F3
Foxe (pen.), Nun., Can. 123/J2
Foxe (chan.), Nun., Can. 123/H2
Foxe Basin (chan.), Nun., Can. 123/J2
Foxen (lake), Swe. 38/D2
Foyle (riv.), NI, UK 34/A2
Foz, Sp. 44/B1
Foz do Iguaçu, Braz. 157/F2
Frackville, Pa, US 138/B2
Fraga, Sp. 45/F2
Fragosa, Cayo (isl.), Cuba 145/G1
Fraiburgo, Braz. 155/B3
Frailes, Cordillera de los (mts.), Ven. 150/E7
Fraisans, Fr. 56/B3
Fraize, Fr. 56/D1
Frameries, Belg. 52/C3
Framlingham, Eng, UK 33/H2
Frammersbach, Ger. 54/C2
Franca, Braz. 155/C2
Francavilla al Mare, It. 46/D1
Francavilla Fontana, It. 47/E2
Francavilla in Sinni, It. 46/E2
France (ctry.) 42/D3
Frances (cape), Cuba 145/F1
Frances (lake), Yk, Can. 122/C2
Francés Viejo (cape), DRep. 141/H4
Franceville, Gabon 96/H8
Franche-Comté (pol. reg.), Fr. 56/B5
Franche-Comteé (pol. reg.), Fr. 43/G3
Francis Case (lake), SD, US 127/J5
Francisco de Orellana, Peru 156/C1
Francisco Escárcega, Mex. 144/D2
Francisco Javier Mina, Mex. 142/C3
Francisco Sá, Braz. 154/B5
Francisco Zarco, Mex. 142/A1
Francistown, Bots. 105/E5
Franco da Rocha, Braz. 211/G8
Francolino, It. 59/E3
Franconville, Fr. 30/J5
Franeker, Neth. 50/C2
Frangy, Fr. 56/B5
Frank Hahn NP, Austl. 112/C5
Franken Wald (for.), Ger. 55/E2
Frankenau, Ger. 51/F6
Frankenberg-Eder, Ger. 51/F6
Frankenburg am Hausruck, Aus. 55/G6
Frankenhöhe (mts.), Ger. 40/F4
Frankenmarkt, Aus. 55/G7
Frankenmuth, Mi, US 130/D3
Frankenthal, Ger. 54/B3
Frankfort (cap.), Ky, US 130/C4
Frankfort, SAfr. 106/E2
Frankfurt, Ger. 41/H2
Frankfurt (int'l arpt.), Ger. 54/B2
Frankfurt am Main, Ger. 54/B2
Fränkische Alb (mts.), Ger. 40/F4
Fränkische Rezat (riv.), Ger. 54/D4
Fränkische Saale (riv.), Ger. 40/E3
Fränkische Schweiz (reg.), Ger. 43/J2
Fränkische Schweiz (reg.), Ger. 40/F4
Frankland (cape), Austl. 115/C3
Franklin (pt.), Ak, US 134/G1
Franklin, NC, US 133/H3
Franklin, La, US 129/K5
Franklin, Ky, US 130/C4
Franklin, In, US 130/C4
Franklin, Tn, US 130/C5
Franklin, WV, US 130/E4
Franklin, NJ, US 138/D1
Franklin (mts.), NW, Can. 122/D2
Franklin (bay), NW, Can. 122/D2
Franklin, Mi, US 135/F6
Franklin D. Roosevelt (lake), Wa, US 126/D3
Franklin Lakes, NJ, US 139/J7
Franklin-Lower Gordon Wild Rivers NP, Austl. 115/C4
Franklin Mineral Museum, NJ, US 138/D1
Franklin Park, Il, US 135/Q16
Franklin Square, NY, US 139/L9
Franksville, Wi, US 135/Q14
Franois, Fr. 56/B3
Franschhoek, SAfr. 106/L10
Fransisco Beltrão, Braz. 157/F2
Fransisco Morato, Braz. 211/G8
Františkovy Lázně, Czh. 55/F2
Franz Josef Land (isls.), Rus. 160/C
Franz Joseph Strauss (int'l arpt.), Ger. 55/E6
Franzburg, Ger. 38/E4
Fraser (riv.), BC, Can. 126/C2
Fraser (isl.), Austl. 109/E3
Fraser (mt.), Austl. 112/C3
Fraser, Mi, US 135/G6
Fraser Lake, BC, Can. 126/B2
Fraser NP, Austl. 115/C3
Fraserburg, SAfr. 106/C3
Fraserburgh, Sc, UK 36/D1
Frasne, Fr. 56/C4
Frassine (riv.), It. 59/E2
Frassino, It. 59/D2
Frastanz, Aus. 57/F3
Frati, Monte dei (peak), It. 59/F5
Frauenfeld, Swi. 57/E2
Fraunberg, Ger. 55/F6
Fray Bentos, Uru. 159/J10
Fray Marcos, Uru. 159/L11
Frazier Park, Ca, US 128/C4
Frechen, Ger. 53/F2
Freckenfeld, Ger. 54/B4
Fred (mt.), Les. 106/E3
Frederica, De, US 138/C6
Fredericia, Den. 38/C4
Frederick (reef), Austl. 109/E3
Frederick, Co, US 137/C2
Frederick, Md, US 130/E4
Frederick (co.), Md, US 138/A5
Frederick, Ok, US 129/H4
Fredericksburg, Pa, US 138/B3
Fredericksburg, Tx, US 129/H5
Fredericton, Austl. 115/E1
Fredericton (cap.), NB, Can. 131/H2
Frederik Willem IV (falls), Sur. 153/G4
Frederiks, Den. 38/C3
Frederiksborg (co.), Den. 38/E4
Frederiksborg Slot (Frederiksborg Castle), Den. 38/E4
Frederikshavn, Den. 38/D3
Frederiksted, USVI 141/M8
Fredersdorf bei Berlin, Ger. 40/Q7
Fredonia, Az, US 128/D3
Fredonia, NY, US 130/E3
Fredriksberg, Swe. 38/F1
Fredrikstad, Nor. 38/D2
Free State (prov.), SAfr. 106/P13
Freeburg, Il, US 137/H9
Freeburg, Pa, US 138/B2
Freedom, Ok, US 132/D2
Freehold, NJ, US 138/D3
Freeland, Pa, US 138/C1
Freeland, Md, US 138/B4
Freeland, Wa, US 135/B1
Freeling (mt.), Austl. 113/G2

188
Freel – Gener

Freeling Heights (peak), Austl. 113/H4
Freemansburg, Pa, US 138/C2
Freeport, Il, US 127/L5
Freeport, Tx, US 129/J5
Freeport, Bahm. 141/F2
Freeport, NY, US 139/L9
Freer, Tx, US 132/D5
Freetown (cap.), SLeo. 102/B4
Fregenal de la Sierra, Sp. 44/B3
Fréhel (cape), Fr. 42/B2
Frei Inocêncio, Braz. 155/D1
Freib Mulde (riv.), Ger. 40/G3
Freiberg, Ger. 41/G3
Freiburg, Ger. 51/G1
Freiburg, Ger. 56/D2
Freienbach, Swi. 57/E3
Freihung, Ger. 55/E3
Freilassing, Ger. 55/F7
Freinsheim, Ger. 54/B3
Freire, Chile 158/B3
Freisen, Ger. 53/G4
Freising, Ger. 55/E6
Freistadt, Aus. 55/H5
Freital, Ger. 41/G3
Freixo de Espada à Cinta, Port. 44/B2
Frejorgues (int'l arpt.), Fr. 42/E5
Fréjus, Fr. 43/G5
Frekhaug, Nor. 38/A1
Frémainfille, Fr. 30/H4
Fremdingen, Ger. 54/D5
Frémécourt, Fr. 30/J4
Fremont (riv.), Ut, US 128/E3
Fremont, Oh, US 130/D3
Fremont, Mi, US 130/C3
Fremont, Ca, US 128/B3
Fremont (isl.), Ut, US 137/J11
French (riv.), On, Can. 130/D2
French Creek State Park, Pa, US 138/C3
French Frigate Shoals (bar), Hi, US 117/J2
French Guiana (dpcy.), Fr. 151/H3
French Polynesia (terr.), Fr. 117/L6
Frenchman (riv.), Can.,US 122/F4
Frenchman's (bay), On, Can. 131/R8
Frenchmans Cap (peak), Austl. 115/C4
Frenchtown, NJ, US 138/C2
Frenda, Alg. 100/F5
Frépillon, Fr. 30/J4
Freren, Ger. 51/E4
Fresco (riv.), Braz. 151/H5
Fresco, C.d'Iv. 102/D5
Fresia, Chile 158/B4
Fresnes, Fr. 30/J5
Fresnes-en-Woëvre, Fr. 53/E5
Fresnillo, Mex. 142/E4
Fresno, Ca, US 128/C3
Fresnoy-le-Grand, Fr. 52/C4
Fresse-sur-Moselle, Fr. 56/C2
Fressenneville, Fr. 52/A3
Fretin, Fr. 52/C2
Freuchie (lake), Sc, UK 36/C3
Freudenberg, Ger. 55/E4
Freudenberg, Ger. 53/G2
Freudenburg, Ger. 53/F4
Freudenstadt, Ger. 57/E1
Frévent, Fr. 52/B3
Freycinet (har.), Austl. 112/B3
Freycinet NP, Austl. 115/D4
Freyming-Merlebach, Fr. 53/F5
Freystadt, Ger. 55/E4
Freyung, Ger. 55/G5
Fria (cape), Namb. 105/B4
Frías, Arg. 157/C2
Frías, Peru 156/B2
Fribourg, Swi. 56/D4
Fribourg (canton), Swi. 56/D4
Frick, Swi. 56/E3
Frickenhausen am Main, Ger. 54/D3
Fridingen an der Donau, Ger. 57/E1
Fridolfing, Ger. 55/F6
Friedberg, Ger. 54/B2
Friedberg, Ger. 54/D6
Friedeburg, Ger. 51/E2
Friedrichsdorf, Ger. 54/B2
Friedrichshafen, Ger. 57/F2
Friedrichstadt, Ger. 38/C4
Friedrichsthal, Ger. 53/G5
Frielendorf, Ger. 51/G7
Friesenhagen, Ger. 53/G2
Friesenheim, Ger. 56/D1
Friesland (prov.), Neth. 50/C2
Friesoythe, Ger. 51/E2
Frignicourt, Fr. 53/D6
Frio (riv.), Tx, US 143/F2
Friockheim, Sc, UK 36/D3
Friol, Sp. 44/B1
Frisange, Lux. 53/F4
Fristad, Swe. 38/E3
Fritsla, Swe. 38/E3
Fritzlar, Ger. 51/G6
Friuli-Venezia Giula (prov.), It. 43/K3
Friville-Escarbotin, Fr. 52/A3
Frobisher (bay), Nun., Can. 123/K2
Frogmore, Eng, UK 30/A3
Frohavel (inlet), Nor. 37/D3
Frohnleiten, Aus. 43/L3
Froid-Chapelle, Belg. 53/D3
Froideconche, Fr. 56/C2
Froissy, Fr. 52/B4
Froland, Nor. 38/C2
Frolovo, Rus. 63/G2
Frome (lake), Austl. 109/D4
Frome (riv.), Eng, UK 32/D5
Frome, Eng, UK 32/D4
Frome (riv.), Austl. 113/H4
Froncles, Fr. 56/B1
Front (range), Co, US 129/F2
Fronteira, Port. 44/B3
Frontenhausen, Ger. 55/F5
Frontera, Mex. 144/C2
Frontera Comalapa, Mex. 144/C3
Frontier Army Museum, Ks, US 137/D5
Frontignan, Fr. 42/E5
Fronton, Fr. 42/D5
Frosinone, It. 46/C2
Frösö, Swe. 37/E3
Frotey-lès-Vesoul, Fr. 56/C2
Frouard, Fr. 53/F6
Frövi, Swe. 38/F2
Frøya (isl.), Nor. 37/D3
Frozen (str.), Nun., Can. 123/H2
Fruges, Fr. 52/B2
Fruit Heights, Ut, US 137/K11
Fruška Gora NP, Cro. 48/D3
Frutal, Braz. 155/B1
Frutigen, Swi. 56/D4
Frutillar, Chile 158/B4
Fryazino, Rus. 61/X9
Frýdek-Místek, Czh. 41/K4
Fu Xian, China 72/B4
Fu'an, China 79/C2
Fucecchio, It. 59/D5
Fucheng, China 72/D3
Fuchskaute (peak), Ger. 43/H1
Fuchū, Japan 74/C3
Fuchū, Japan 77/C2
Fuchuan, China 79/B3
Fuchun (riv.), China 72/D5
Fuding, China 79/D2
Fuengirola, Sp. 44/C4
Fuenlabrada, Sp. 45/N9
Fuensalida, Sp. 44/C2
Fuente, Sp. 45/N8
Fuente de Cantos, Sp. 44/B3
Fuente del Maestre, Sp. 44/B3
Fuente Obejuna, Sp. 44/C3
Fuentelapeña, Sp. 44/C2
Fuentes de Oñoro, Sp. 44/B2
Fuentesaúco, Sp. 44/C2
Fuerte (riv.), Mex. 142/C3
Fuerte Olimpo, Par. 150/G8
Fuerteventura (isl.) 96/C2
Fuga (isl.), Phil. 79/D4
Fuglebjerg, Den. 38/D4
Fugong, China 83/G2
Fugou, China 72/C4
Fuhai, China 70/E2
Fuhne (riv.), Ger. 40/F3
Fuhse (riv.), Ger. 51/H4
Fuji (riv.), Japan 75/F3
Fuji, Japan 75/F3
Fuji-Hakone-Izu NP, Japan 75/F3
Fuji-san (peak), Japan 75/F3
Fujian (prov.), China 71/L6
Fujieda, Japan 75/F3
Fujihashi, Japan 77/K4
Fujiidera, Japan 77/J6
Fujikawa, Japan 77/B3
Fujimi, Japan 77/D2
Fujino, Japan 77/C2
Fujinomiya, Japan 77/B3
Fujioka, Japan 75/F2
Fujioka, Japan 77/D1
Fujioka, Japan 77/M5
Fujisawa, Japan 75/F3
Fujishiro, Japan 77/E2
Fujiwara, Japan 77/K5
Fujiyoshida, Japan 75/F3
Fukagawa, Japan 76/C2
Fukang, China 70/E3
Fukaya, Japan 77/C1
Fukiage, Japan 77/C1
Fukuchiyama, Japan 77/H5
Fukue, Japan 74/A4
Fukui (pref.), Japan 74/E3
Fukui, Japan 74/E2
Fukuoka, Japan 74/B4
Fukuoka (int'l arpt.), Japan 74/B4
Fukuoka (pref.), Japan 74/B4
Fukuoka, Japan 77/M4
Fukuroi, Japan 75/E3
Fukushima, Japan 75/G2
Fukushima (pref.), Japan 75/F2
Fukushima, Japan 76/B3
Fukuyama, Japan 74/C3
Fūlādī (mtn.), Afg. 89/J2
Fulda (riv.), Ger. 40/E3
Fulda, Ger. 54/C1
Fullerton, Ca, US 136/G8
Fullerton (Whitehall), Pa, US 138/C2
Fully, Swi. 56/D5
Fulpmes, Aus. 57/H3
Fulton, Mo, US 129/K3
Fulton, NY, US 130/E3
Fulton, Ky, US 130/B4
Fulufjället (peak), Swe. 38/E1
Fumaiolo (peak), It. 59/F5
Fumay, Fr. 53/D4
Fumel, Fr. 42/D4
Fumin, China 83/H2
Funabashi, Japan 77/D2
Funafuti (cap.), Tuv. 116/G5
Funafuti (isl.), Tuv. 116/G5
Funan, China 72/C4
Funchal, Port. 98/A2
Funchal (int'l arpt.), Port. 98/A2
Fundación, Col. 152/C2
Fundão, Port. 44/B2
Fundy (bay), US,Can. 131/H2
Fundy NP, NB, Can. 131/H2
Funhalouro, Moz. 105/F5
Funing, China 83/J3
Funing, China 72/D4
Fuorn, Pass dal (Ofenpass) (pass), Swi. 57/G4
Fuping, China 72/C3
Fuqing, China 79/C2
Fuquan, China 83/J2
Fur (riv.), China 73/C2
Furan (riv.), Fr. 56/B6
Furano, Japan 76/C2
Fürfeld, Ger. 53/G4
Furmanov, Rus. 60/J4
Furnas (res.), Braz. 147/E5
Furneaux Group (isls.), Austl. 109/D4
Fürstenau, Ger. 51/E3
Fürstenfeld, Aus. 43/M3
Fürstenfeldbruck, Ger. 54/E6
Fürstenwalde, Ger. 41/H2
Fürth, Ger. 54/B3
Fürth, Ger. 54/D4
Furth, Ger. 55/F5
Furth im Wald, Ger. 55/F4
Furtwangen im Schwarzwald, Ger. 56/E1
Furudal, Swe. 38/F1
Furukawa, Japan 76/B4
Fury and Hecla (str.), Nun., Can. 123/H2
Fushan, China 72/B4
Fushan, China 72/E3
Fushun, China 73/B2
Fushun, China 83/J2
Fusignano, It. 59/E4
Fusio, Swi. 57/E5
Fuso, Japan 77/L5
Fussa, Japan 77/C2
Füssen, Ger. 57/G2
Fusui, China 78/D1
Futaba, Japan 77/A2
Futaleufú, Chile 158/C4
Futami, Japan 77/L7
Futog, Serb. 48/D3
Futrono, Chile 158/B4
Futtsu, Japan 75/F3
Futuna (isl.), Wall. 116/H6
Fuwah, Egypt 91/B4
Fuxian (lake), China 83/H3
Fuxin, China 72/E2
Fuxin Monggolzu Zizhixian, China 72/E2
Fuyang, China 72/C4
Fuyi (riv.), China 79/B2
Fuyu, China 71/M2
Fuyu, China 71/M2
Fuyuan, China 83/H2
Fuyun, China 70/E2
Füzesabony, Hun. 48/E2
Fuzhou, China 79/C2
Fyn (co.), Den. 38/D4
Fyn (isl.), Den. 37/D5
Fyne, Loch (inlet), Sc, UK 36/A5
Fyresdal, Nor. 38/C2

G

Ga Vache (isl.), Haiti 145/H2
Gaast, Neth. 50/C2
Gabas (riv.), Fr. 42/C5
Gabela, Ang. 105/B3
Gabes (gulf), Tun. 93/D1
Gabicce Mare, It. 59/F5
Gablingen, Ger. 54/D6
Gablitz, Aus. 49/N7
Gabon (ctry.) 96/H7
Gaborone (cap.), Bots. 105/E5
Gabriel Leyva Solano, Mex. 142/C3
Gabrovo, Bul. 47/J1
Gaby, It. 58/A1
Gacko, Bosn. 47/F1
Gādarwāra, India 84/B4
Gaddy, Ok, US 137/N15
Gadmen, Swi. 57/E4
Gadsden, Al, US 133/G3
Găeşti, Rom. 49/G3
Gaeta, It. 46/C2
Gaeta, Golfo di (gulf), It. 46/C2
Gaferut (isl.), Micr. 116/D4
Gaffney, SC, US 133/H3
Gagarin, Rus. 60/G5
Gaggenau, Ger. 54/B5
Gaggio Montano, It. 59/D4
Gaglianico, It. 58/B1
Gagnoa, C.d'Iv. 102/D5
Gagny, Fr. 30/K5
Gagra, Geo. 62/G4
Gagret, India 86/D4
Gai Xian, China 73/B2
Gaichtpass (pass), Aus. 57/G3
Gail (riv.), Aus. 43/K3
Gaildorf, Ger. 54/C5
Gaillac, Fr. 42/D5
Gailtaler (mts.), Aus. 43/K3
Gaiman, Arg. 158/D4
Gaimersheim, Ger. 55/E5
Gainesville, Tx, US 129/H4
Gainesville, Ga, US 133/H3
Gainesville, Fl, US 133/H4
Gainsborough, Eng, UK 35/H5
Gairdner (lake), Austl. 109/C4
Gairn (riv.), Sc, UK 36/C2
Gais, Swi. 57/F3
Gaiserwald, Swi. 57/F3
Gaizina (peak), Lat. 39/L3
Gakarosa (peak), SAfr. 106/C2
Gakona, Ak, US 134/J3
Galana (riv.), Kenya 104/C3
Galand, Iran 89/G1
Galapagar, Sp. 45/M8
Galápagos (isls.), Ecu. 156/E6
Galápagos (dept.), Ecu. 156/E7
Galápagos, PN, Ecu. 156/E7
Galashiels, Sc, UK 36/D5
Galaţi (prov.), Rom. 49/H3
Galaţi, Rom. 49/J3
Galatina, It. 47/F2
Galatiní, Gre. 47/G2
Galátista, Gre. 47/H2
Galatone, It. 47/F2
Galb Azefal (hill), WSah. 98/B5
Galbiate, It. 58/C1
Galdácano, Sp. 44/D1
Gáldar, Sp. 98/B3
Galeana, Mex. 143/E3
Galela, Indo. 81/G3
Galena, Ak, US 134/G3
Galena, Md, US 138/C5
Galeota (pt.), Trin. 153/F2
Galera (pt.), Ecu. 152/A4
Galera (pt.), Trin. 153/F2
Galera (pt.), Chile 158/B3
Galesburg, Il, US 127/L5
Galey (riv.), Ire. 31/P10
Galga (riv.), Hun. 49/R9
Galgamácsa, Hun. 49/R9
Galgorm, NI, UK 34/B2
Galich, Rus. 60/J4
Galicia (aut. comm.), Sp. 44/A1
Galičica NP, FYROM 47/G2
Galiléia, Braz. 155/D1
Galileo Galilei (int'l arpt.), It. 58/D5
Galinakopf (peak), Aus. 57/F3
Galion, Oh, US 130/D3
Gallan Head (pt.), Sc, UK 31/Q7
Gallarate, It. 58/B1
Gallatin, Tn, US 130/C4
Galle, SrL. 82/D6
Gallegos (riv.), Arg. 157/B7
Galliate, It. 58/B2
Gallicano, It. 58/D4
Galliera Veneta, It. 59/E1
Gallinas (mts.), NM, US 132/B3
Gallinas (pt.), Col. 152/D1
Gallipoli, It. 47/E2
Gallipoli (pen.), Turk. 49/H5
Gällivare, Swe. 37/G2
Gallneukirchen, Aus. 55/H6
Gallo (cape), It. 46/C3
Gallo (lake), It. 57/G4
Gallspach, Aus. 55/G6
Galluis, Fr. 30/H5
Gallup, NM, US 128/E4
Gallur, Sp. 44/E2
Gally (riv.), Fr. 30/H5
Galston, Sc, UK 36/B5
Galten, Den. 38/C3
Galtymore (peak), Ire. 31/P10
Galva, La, US 137/P16
Galvarino, Chile 158/B3
Galveston, Tx, US 129/J5
Galveston (bay), Tx, US 140/C2
Galveston (isl.), Tx, US 140/C2
Gálvez, Sp. 44/C3
Galway, Ire. 31/P10
Galway (bay), Ire. 31/P10
Galzignano, It. 59/E2
Gam (riv.), Viet. 83/J3
Gamaches, Fr. 52/A4
Gamagara (riv.), SAfr. 106/C2
Gamagōri, Japan 77/M6
Gamarra, Col. 152/C2
Gamba, China 85/G1
Gambaga, Gha. 103/E4
Gambaga Scarp (cliff), Gha. 103/E4
Gambais, Fr. 30/H5
Gambara, It. 58/D2
Gambat, Pak. 82/A2
Gambela NP, Eth. 97/M6
Gambell, Ak, US 134/D3
Gambellara, It. 59/E2
Gamber, Md, US 138/B5
Gambettola, It. 59/F4
Gambia, The (ctry.) 102/B3
Gambia (riv.), Gam. 102/A3
Gambier (isls.), FrPol. 117/M7
Gámbita, Col. 152/C3
Gambo, Nf, Can. 131/L1
Gambolò, It. 58/B2
Gambsheim, Fr. 54/A5
Gaming, Aus. 43/L3
Gamka (riv.), SAfr. 106/C4
Gamkab (riv.), Namb. 106/B3
Gamleby, Swe. 38/G3
Gammelstad, Swe. 60/D2
Gammertingen, Ger. 57/F1
Gammon Ranges NP, Austl. 113/H4
Gamo, Japan 77/K5
Gampern, Aus. 55/G7
Gamud (peak), Eth. 104/C1
Gan (riv.), China 71/L6
Gan, Fr. 42/C5
Gananoque, On, Can. 130/E2
Gäncä, Azer. 63/H4
Ganda, Ang. 105/B3
Gandajika, D.R. Congo 105/D2
Gandak (riv.), India 85/E2
Gandaki (zone), Nepal 84/D1
Gander (lake), Nf, Can. 131/L1
Gander, Nf, Can. 131/L1
Ganderkesee, Ger. 51/F2
Gandesa, Sp. 45/F2
Gāndhi Sāgar (res.), India 82/B3
Gāndhīdhām, India 89/K4
Gandhinagar, India 89/K4
Gandía, Sp. 45/E3
Gandino, It. 58/C1
Gandoca-Manzanillo NWR, CR 145/F4
Gandu, Braz. 154/C4
Ganeb (well), Mrta. 102/C2
Ganesh (mtn.), China 85/E1
Gangāpur, India 89/L3
Gangārāmpur, India 85/G3
Gangaw, Myan. 83/F3
Gangca, China 70/H4
Gangdisê (mts.), China 70/D5
Gangelt, Ger. 53/F2
Ganges, Fr. 42/E5
Ganges (riv.), Asia 67/A5
Ganges (Ganga) (riv.), India 84/B1
Ganges, Mouths of the (delta), Bang. 70/E7
Gangi, It. 46/D4
Gangkofen, Ger. 55/F6
Gangoh, India 86/D5
Gangtok, India 85/G2
Ganluo, China 83/H2
Gannat, Fr. 42/E3
Ganquan, China 72/B3
Gansbaai, SAfr. 106/L11
Gänserndorf, Aus. 49/P7
Gansu (prov.), China 70/H4
Gantrisch (peak), Swi. 56/D4
Ganyu, China 72/D4
Ganzhou, China 79/B2
Ganzlin, Ger. 40/G2
Ganzourgou (prov.), Burk. 103/E3
Gao (pol. reg.), Mali 103/F2
Gao, Mali 103/E2
Gao'an, China 79/C2
Gaocheng, China 72/C3
Gaochun, China 72/D5
Gaomi, China 72/D3
Gaoping, China 72/C4
Gaoqing, China 72/D3
Gaor Bheinn (Gulvain) (peak), Sc, UK 36/A3
Gaotai, China 70/G4
Gaotang, China 72/D3
Gaoua, Burk. 102/E4
Gaoyang, China 72/C3
Gaoyi, China 72/C3
Gaoyou, China 72/D4
Gaozhou, China 83/K3
Gap, Fr. 43/G4
Gap, Pa, US 138/B4
Gar, China 70/C5
Garabogazköl Aylagy (gulf), Trrkm. 63/K4
Garachiné, Pan. 152/B2
Garachiné (pt.), Pan. 145/G4
Garai (riv.), Bang. 82/E3
Garajonay, PN de, Sp. 98/A3
Garamba, PN de la, D.R. Congo 97/L7
Garancières, Fr. 52/A6
Garanhuns, Braz. 154/C3
Garbsen, Ger. 51/G4
Garça, Braz. 155/B2
Garças (riv.), Braz. 151/H7
Garching an der Alz, Ger. 55/F6
Garcia de Sota, Embalse de (res.), Sp. 44/C3
Gard (riv.), Fr. 42/F4
Garda (lake), It. 43/J4
Garda, It. 59/D1
Garde, Cap de (cape), Alg. 100/K6
Gardelegen, Ger. 40/F2
Garden (isl.), Austl. 112/K7
Garden City, Ga, US 133/H3
Garden City, NY, US 139/L9
Garden City, Mi, US 135/F7
Garden City Park, NY, US 139/L9
Garden Grove, Ca, US 136/G8
Garden Ridge, Tx, US 137/U20
Garden View, Pa, US 138/A1
Gardena, Ca, US 136/F8
Gardenstown, Sc, UK 36/D1
Gardēz, Afg. 89/J2
Gardiner, Mt, US 126/F4
Gardiner, Me, US 131/G2
Gardiner, Wa, US 135/B1
Gardiners (isl.), NY, US 139/F1
Gardiners (bay), NY, US 139/F1
Gardner (lake), Ks, US 137/D6
Gardner, Ks, US 137/D6
Gardone val Trompia, It. 58/D1
Gare Loch (inlet), Sc, UK 36/B4
Gareat el Tarf (salt pan), Alg. 100/K7
Garelochhead, Sc, UK 36/B4
Garessio, It. 58/B4
Garet el Djenoun (peak), Alg. 99/G4
Garfield (mtn.), Mt, US 126/E4
Garfield, Ut, US 137/J12
Garfield, NJ, US 139/J8
Garforth, Eng, UK 35/G4
Gargaliánoi, Gre. 47/G4
Gargan (peak), Fr. 42/D4
Gargenville, Fr. 52/A6
Garges-lès-Gonesse, Fr. 30/K5
Gargnano, It. 59/D1
Garh Mahārāja, Pak. 86/A4
Garhākotā, India 84/B4
Garhbeta, India 85/F4
Garhmuktesar, India 84/B1
Garibaldi, Braz. 155/B4
Garies, SAfr. 106/B3
Garioch (reg.), Sc, UK 36/D2
Garissa, Kenya 104/C3
Garland, Tx, US 129/H4
Garlasco, It. 58/B2
Garmisch-Partenkirchen, Ger. 57/H3
Garmsār, Iran 88/F1
Garnpung (lake), Austl. 115/B2
Garonne (riv.), Fr. 42/D4
Garopaba, Braz. 155/B4
Garou (lake), Mali 103/E2
Garoua, Camr. 96/H6
Garphyttan, Swe. 38/F2
Garraf (mts.), Sp. 45/K7
Garrel, Ger. 51/F3
Garrison (dam), ND, US 127/H4
Garrison, ND, US 127/H4
Garron (pt.), NI, UK 34/C1
Garrovillas, Sp. 44/B3
Garry (bay), Nun., Can. 123/H2
Garry (lake), Nun., Can. 122/F2
Garry (lake), Sc, UK 36/B2
Garry (riv.), Sc, UK 36/A2
Gars am Inn, Ger. 55/F6
Garsten, Aus. 55/H6
Garte (riv.), Ger. 51/H6
Gartempe (riv.), Fr. 42/D3
Gärtringen, Ger. 54/B5
Garut, Indo. 80/C5
Garvagh, NI, UK 34/B2
Garwa, India 84/D3
Garwolin, Pol. 41/L3
Garwood, NJ, US 139/H9
Gary, In, US 130/C3
Garza García, Mex. 143/E3
Garzê, China 70/H5
Garzón, Col. 152/C4
Gas, Fr. 30/G6
Gas City, In, US 130/C3
Gas-san (peak), Japan 76/B4
Gæsafjöll (peak), Ice. 37/P6
Gaschurn, Aus. 57/G4
Gasconade (riv.), Mo, US 129/J3
Gascony (reg.), Fr. 42/C5
Gascoyne (riv.), Austl. 109/A3
Gascoyne (mt.), Austl. 112/C3
Gaspar (str.), Indo. 80/C4
Gaspar, Braz. 155/B3
Gaspé, Qu, Can. 131/H1
Gaspé (pen.), Qu, Can. 131/H1
Gaspé, Cap de (cape), Qu, Can. 131/H1
Gaspoltshofen, Aus. 55/G6
Gasport, NY, US 131/S9
Gassino Torinese, It. 58/A2
Gastins, Fr. 30/M6
Gaston (lake), NC, US 133/J2
Gastonia, NC, US 133/H3
Gastoúni, Gre. 47/G4
Gata (cape), Sp. 44/D4
Gata (cape), Cyp. 91/C2
Gata de Gorgos, Sp. 45/F3
Gata, Sierra de (mts.), Sp. 44/B2
Gatchina, Rus. 39/P2
Gatehouse-of-Fleet, Sc, UK 34/D2
Gates of the Arctic NP and Prsv., Ak, US 134/G2
Gateshead (isl.), Nun., Can. 122/F1
Gateshead, Eng, UK 35/G2
Gateshead (co.), Eng, UK 35/G2
Gatesville, Tx, US 132/D4
Gateway Arch (arch), Mo, US 137/G8
Gateway NRA, NJ,NY, US 139/K9
Gatineau, Qu, Can. 130/F2
Gatineau (riv.), Qu, Can. 123/J4
Gatow, Ger. 40/Q7
Gattaran, Phil. 79/D4
Gattendorf, Aus. 43/M2
Gattianara, It. 58/B1
Gatton, Austl. 114/D4
Gatún (dam), Pan. 145/G4
Gatún (lake), Pan. 145/G4
Gatwick (int'l arpt.), Eng, UK 30/C3
Gau Algesheim, Ger. 54/B3
Gau Bischofsheim, Ger. 54/B3
Gau Odernheim, Ger. 54/B3
Gaubickelheim, Ger. 53/H4
Gauchy, Fr. 52/C4
Gaucín, Sp. 44/C4
Gauja (riv.), Est.,Lat. 39/L3
Gauja NP, Lat. 39/L3
Gaukönigshofen, Ger. 54/C3
Gaunless (riv.), Eng, UK 35/G2
Gaupne, Nor. 37/C3
Gaur (riv.), Sc, UK 36/B3
Gauri Sankar (peak), Nepal 85/F2
Gauripur, India 85/G2
Gausta (peak), Nor. 38/C2
Gauting, Ger. 55/E6
Gavà, Sp. 45/L7
Gávdhos (isl.), Gre. 47/J5
Gavere, Belg. 52/C2
Gavi, It. 58/B3
Gavião, Port. 44/B3
Gavirate, It. 58/B1
Gävle, Swe. 38/G1
Gävleborg (co.), Swe. 37/E3
Gawler (ranges), Austl. 109/C4
Gawler, Austl. 113/H5
Gay (peak), WV, US 130/D4
Gay, Rus. 63/L2
Gaya, Niger 103/F4
Gayaza, Ugan. 104/A3
Gaylord, Mi, US 130/C2
Gayndah, Austl. 114/C4
Gaza Strip, Isr. 90/C4
Gazeran, Fr. 30/H6
Gaziantep (prov.), Turk. 90/D2
Gaziantep, Turk. 90/D2
Gaziköy, Turk. 49/H5
Gazipaşa, Turk. 91/C1
Gazon de Faing (peak), Fr. 56/D1
Gazzaniga, It. 58/C1
Gbadolite, D.R. Congo 97/K7
Gbarnga, Libr. 102/C5
Gbongan, Nga. 103/G5
Gdańsk (gulf), Pol. 41/K1
Gdańsk, Pol. 38/H4
Gdynia, Pol. 38/H4
Ge (lake), China 72/D5
Geal Charn (peak), Sc, UK 36/C2
Geal Charn (peak), Sc, UK 36/A3
Gebaberg (peak), Ger. 54/D1
Gebe (isl.), Indo. 81/G3
Gebhardshain, Ger. 53/G2
Gebiz, Turk. 91/B1
Gebze, Turk. 49/J5
Gede (peak), Indo. 80/C5
Gedern, Ger. 54/C2
Gedi Ruins Nat'l Mon., Kenya 104/D3
Gedikbulak, Turk. 90/E2
Gedinne, Belg. 53/D4
Gediz, Turk. 90/B2
Gediz (riv.), Turk. 90/A2
Gedser (cape), Den. 38/D4
Gedser, Den. 38/D4
Gedsted, Den. 38/C3
Geel, Belg. 53/E1
Geelong, Austl. 115/C3
Geelvink (chan.), Austl. 109/A3
Geertruidenberg, Neth. 50/B5
Geeste (riv.), Ger. 51/F1
Geeste, Ger. 51/E3
Geesthacht, Ger. 51/H2
Geeveston, Austl. 115/C4
Gefrees, Ger. 55/E2
Gê'gyai, China 70/D5
Gehrde, Ger. 51/F3
Gehrden, Ger. 51/G4
Geifas (peak), Wal, UK 32/C2
Geikie (riv.), Sk, Can. 122/F3
Geilenkirchen, Ger. 53/F2
Geilo, Nor. 38/C1
Geinō, Japan 77/K6
Geiselhöring, Ger. 55/F5
Geiselwind, Ger. 54/D3
Geisenfeld, Ger. 55/E5
Geisenhausen, Ger. 55/F6
Geisenheim, Ger. 53/G4
Geislingen, Ger. 57/E1
Geislingen an der Steige, Ger. 54/C5
Geita, Tanz. 104/B3
Gejiu, China 83/H3
Gela, It. 46/D4
Gela, Golfo di (gulf), It. 46/D4
Gelai (peak), Tanz. 104/C3
Gelderland (prov.), Neth. 50/C4
Geldermalsen, Neth. 50/C5
Geldern, Ger. 50/D5
Geldersheim, Ger. 54/D2
Geldrop, Neth. 50/C6
Geleen, Neth. 53/E2
Gelendost, Turk. 90/B2
Gelendzhik, Rus. 62/F3
Gelibolu (Gallipoli), Turk. 47/K2
Gelibolu Yarımadas NP, Turk. 47/K2
Gelincik (peak), Turk. 90/E2
Gelligaer, Wal, UK 32/C3
Gelnhausen, Ger. 54/C2
Gelsenkirchen, Ger. 50/E5
Geltendorf, Ger. 57/H1
Gelterkinden, Swi. 56/D3
Gelting, Ger. 38/C4
Gemas, Malay. 80/B3
Gembloux, Belg. 53/D2
Gemena, D.R. Congo 97/J7
Gemert, Neth. 50/C5
Gemlik (gulf), Turk. 49/J5
Gemlik, Turk. 49/J5
Gemona del Friuli, It. 43/K3
Gemsbok NP, Bots. 105/D6
Gemuk (mtn.), Ak, US 134/G3
Gemünden am Main, Ger. 54/C2
Genalē Wenz (riv.), Eth. 97/N6
Genappe, Belg. 53/D2
Genay, Fr. 56/A6
Genç, Turk. 90/E2
Gendringen, Neth. 50/D5
Gendt, Neth. 50/C5
Genemuiden, Neth. 50/D3
General Abelardo L. Rodriguez (int'l arpt.), Mex. 128/C4
General Acha, Arg. 158/D3
General Alfredo Vasquez Cobo (int'l arpt.), Col. 156/D2
General Alvear, Arg. 158/D2
General Alvear, Arg. 158/E3
General Arenales, Arg. 158/E2
General Belgrano, Arg. 158/F2
General Belgrano II, Arg., Ant. 160/X
General Cabrera, Arg. 158/E2
General Carrera (lake), Chile 157/B6
General Cepeda, Mex. 143/E3
General Conesa, Arg. 158/D4
General Deheza, Arg. 158/E2
General Edward Lawrence Logan (Logan Int'l) (int'l arpt.), Ma, US 131/G3
General Enrique Godoy, Arg. 158/D3
General Francisco Villa, Mex. 143/F3
General Galarza, Arg. 159/J10
General Grant Nat'l Mem., NY, US 139/K8
General Juan Álvarez, PN, Mex. 143/F5
General Juan José Ríos, Mex. 142/C3
General Juan Madariaga, Arg. 159/F3
General La Madrid, Arg. 158/E3
General Lagos, Chile 156/D5
General Las Heras, Arg. 159/J11
General Lavalle, Arg. 159/K12
General Martín Miguel de Güemes, Arg. 157/C1
General Pico, Arg. 158/E2
General Pinedo, Arg. 157/D2
General Pinto, Arg. 158/E2
General Roca, Arg. 158/D3
General San Martín, Arg. 158/E3
General San Martín, Arg. 159/J11
General San Martín, Arg., Ant. 160/V
General Santiago Marino (int'l arpt.),Ven. 153/F2
General Terán, Mex. 143/F3
General-Toshevo, Bul. 49/J4
General Viamonte, Arg. 158/E2
General Villalobas (int'l arpt.), Mex. 132/B4
General Villegas, Arg. 158/E2
General Zaragoza, Mex. 143/F4
Generoso (peak), Swi. 57/F6

189
Genes – Govar

Genesee (co.), Mi, US 135/E6
Genesee (riv.), NY, US 130/E3
Genesee, Wi, US 135/P14
Genesee Depot, Wi, US 135/P14
Geneseo, Il, US 127/L5
Geneseo, NY, US 130/E3
Geneva (Léman) (lake), Fr. 43/G3
Geneva (Genève), Swi. 43/G3
Geneva (int'l arpt.), Swi. 56/C5
Geneva, Al, US 133/G4
Geneva, Ne, US 129/H2
Geneva, NY, US 130/E3
Geneva, Ut, US 137/K13
Genève (canton), Swi. 56/C5
Genève, Swi. 56/C5
Gengenbach, Ger. 56/E1
Génicourt, Fr. 30/J4
Genk, Belg. 53/E2
Genlis, Fr. 56/B3
Gennach (riv.), Ger. 57/G2
Gennargentu (mts.), It. 46/A2
Gennep, Neth. 50/C5
Gennevilliers, Fr. 30/J5
Genoa (Genova), It. 43/H4
Genoa City, Wi, US 135/P14
Genova (prov.), It. 58/C4
Genova (Genoa), It. 58/B4
Genova, Golfo di (gulf), It. 43/H4
Genovesa (isl.), Ecu. 156/F6
Gensingen, Ger. 53/G4
Gent-Brugge Kanaal (canal), Belg. 52/C1
Gent (Ghent), Belg. 52/C1
Genteng (cape), Indo. 80/C5
Genteng, Indo. 80/D5
Geographe (bay), Austl. 112/B5
Geographe (chan.), Austl. 112/B3
Georg von Neumayer, Ger., Ant. 160/Z
George (lake), Austl. 113/D2
George (pt.), Austl. 114/C3
George (riv.), Qu, Can. 123/K3
George, SAfr. 106/C4
George (lake), Ugan. 104/A3
George (lake), Fl, US 133/H4
George Land (isl.), Rus. 64/E2
George Town, Austl. 115/C4
George Town (cap.), Cay. 145/F2
George Town, Malay. 80/B2
George V (coast), Ant. 160/L
George Washington Birthplace Nat'l Mon., Va, US 133/J2
George West, Tx, US 132/D4
Georgensmünd, Ger. 54/E4
Georges (riv.), Austl. 114/G9
Georgetown, Austl. 114/A2
Georgetown, Gam. 102/B3
Georgetown (cap.), Guy. 153/G3
Georgetown, StV. 141/N9
Georgetown, Ct, US 139/E1
Georgetown, Ga, US 133/H4
Georgetown, Ky, US 130/C4
Georgetown, SC, US 133/J3
Georgetown, Tx, US 129/H5
Georgi Traykov, Bul. 49/H4
Georgia (ctry.) 63/G4
Georgia, Strait of (str.), BC, Can. 126/B3
Georgia (state), US 133/G3
Georgian (bay), On, Can. 123/H4
Georgian Bay Islands NP, On, Can. 130/D2
Georgina (riv.), Austl. 109/C3
Georgsmarienhütte, Ger. 51/F4
Gepatsch (lake), Aus. 57/G4
Gera, Ger. 40/G3
Geraardsbergen, Belg. 52/C2
Geral de Goiás, Serra (mts.), Braz. 151/J6
Geral, Serra (mts.), Braz. 157/F2
Geraldine, NZ 117/S11
Geraldton, Austl. 112/B4
Gérardmer, Fr. 56/C1
Gerasdorf bei Wien, Aus. 49/N7
Gerbéviller, Fr. 56/C1
Gerbier de Jonc (peak), Fr. 42/F4
Gerbrunn, Ger. 54/C3
Gerdau (riv.), Ger. 51/H3
Gerdine (mt.), Ak, US 134/H3
Gerede, Turk. 49/L5
Geretsried, Ger. 57/H2
Gérgal, Sp. 44/D4
Gerger, Turk. 90/D2
Gerlach, Nv, US 126/D5
Gerlachovský Štít (peak), Slvk. 41/L4
Gerlafingen, Swi. 56/D3
Germantown, Tn, US 129/K4
Germantown, Md, US 138/A5
Germany (ctry.) 40/E3
Germering, Ger. 55/E6
Germersheim, Ger. 54/B4
Germigny-l'Evêque, Fr. 30/L5
Germinaga, It. 57/E6
Germiston, SAfr. 106/E2
Gernsbach, Ger. 54/B5
Geroldsgrün, Ger. 55/E2
Gerolsbach, Ger. 55/E5
Gerolstein, Ger. 53/F3
Gerolzhofen, Ger. 54/D3
Gerpinnes, Belg. 53/D3
Gerra (Verzasca), Swi. 57/E5
Gerringong, Austl. 115/D2
Gers (riv.), Fr. 42/D5
Gersau, Swi. 57/E4
Gersfeld, Ger. 54/C2
Gersheim, Ger. 53/G5
Gerspenz (riv.), Ger. 54/B3
Gerstetten, Ger. 54/E5
Gerstheim, Fr. 56/D1
Gersthofen, Ger. 54/D6
Gerstungen, Ger. 51/H7
Gêrzê, China 70/D5
Gerze, Turk. 62/E4
Gescher, Ger. 50/E5
Geseke, Ger. 51/F5
Gespunsart, Fr. 53/D4
Gessertshausen, Ger. 54/D6
Gestro Wenz (riv.), Eth. 97/P6
Gesves, Belg. 53/E3
Geta, Fin. 39/H1
Getafe, Sp. 45/N9
Gete (riv.), Belg. 53/E2
Getinge, Swe. 38/E3
Gettorf, Ger. 38/C4
Gettysburg, SD, US 127/J4
Gettysburg, Pa, US 130/E4
Gettysburg Nat'l Mil. Park, Pa, US 138/A4
Getúlio Vargas, Braz. 155/A3
Geul (riv.), Neth. 53/E2
Geureudong (peak), Indo. 80/A3
Geurie, Austl. 115/D2
Gevaş, Turk. 90/E2
Gevelsberg, Ger. 51/E6
Gevgelija, FYROM 47/H2
Gex, Fr. 56/C5
Geyer, Ger. 55/F1
Geyersberg (peak), Ger. 54/C3
Geyikli, Turk. 47/K3
Geyser (reef), Madg. 107/H6
Geyve, Turk. 49/K5
Gez (riv.), China 87/F5
Ghadāmis, Libya 99/H3
Ghaggar (riv.), India 86/C5
Ghaghara (riv.), India 84/C2
Ghakhar, Pak. 86/C3
Ghana (ctry.) 103/E4
Ghanzi, Bots. 105/D5
Gharaunda, India 86/D5
Ghardaïa, Alg. 99/F2
Ghardaïa (prov.), Alg. 99/F3
Ghardimaou, Tun. 100/L6
Gharghoda, India 84/D4
Gharyān, Libya 96/H1
Ghāt, Libya 99/H4
Ghātāl, India 85/F4
Ghātampur, India 84/C2
Ghātsīla, India 85/F4
Ghazal, Bahr el (riv.), Chad 96/J5
Ghazaouet, Alg. 100/D2
Ghāzīpur, India 84/D3
Ghaznī, Afg. 89/J2
Ghedi, It. 58/D2
Gheens, La, US 137/P17
Ghemme, It. 58/B1
Ghenghis Khan, Wall of, Mong. 71/K2
Gheorghe Gheorghiu-Dej, Rom. 49/H2
Gheorgheni, Rom. 49/G2
Gherla, Rom. 49/F2
Ghilarza, It. 46/A2
Ghinda (Gīnda), Erit. 88/C5
Ghio (lake), Arg. 158/C5
Ghirārah (gulf), Gabon 99/H2
Ghisalba, It. 58/C1
Ghisonaccia, Fr. 46/A1
Ghotki, Pak. 87/A2
Ghugri (riv.), India 85/F3
Ghūrīān, Afg. 89/H2
Ghuzayyil, Bi'r al (well), Libya 96/H2
Giannutri (isl.), It. 46/B1
Giant's Castle (peak), SAfr. 106/E3
Giant's Causeway, NI, UK 34/B1
Giant Sequoia Nat'l Mon., Ca, US 128/C4
Giarre, It. 46/D4
Gibbons, Ab, Can. 126/E2
Gibbstown, NJ, US 138/C4
Gibloux (peak), Swi. 56/D4
Gibraleón, Sp. 44/B4
Gibraltar (pt.), Eng, UK 35/J5
Gibraltar (cap.), Gib. 44/C4
Gibraltar (str.), Mor.,Sp. 27/D5
Gibraltar (res.), Ca, US 136/A1
Gibraltar, Mi, US 135/F7
Gibraltar, Ven. 141/G6
Gibraltar Range NP, Austl. 115/E1
Gibson (des.), Austl. 109/B3
Gibson Desert Nature Reserve, Austl. 112/E3
Giddarbāha, India 86/C4
Giddings, Tx, US 129/H5
Giddings, Co, US 137/B1
Gidi (pass), Egypt 91/C4
Giebelstadt, Ger. 54/C3
Gieboldehausen, Ger. 51/H5
Gien, Fr. 42/E3
Giengen an der Brenz, Ger. 54/D5
Gier (riv.), Fr. 42/F4
Giessbachfälle (falls), Swi. 56/E4
Giessen (riv.), Fr.,Ger. 56/D1
Giessen, Ger. 54/B1
Giessendam, Neth. 50/B5
Gieten, Neth. 50/D2
Gif-sur-Yvette, Fr. 30/J5
Gīfān, Iran 63/L5
Gifford, Fl, US 133/H5
Gifford (riv.), Nun., Can. 123/H1
Giffre (riv.), Fr. 56/C5
Gifhorn, Ger. 51/H4
Gifu, Japan 77/L5
Giganta, Sierra de la (mts.), Mex. 142/C3
Gigante, Col. 152/C4
Giglio (isl.), It. 46/B1
Gijón, Sp. 44/C1
Gil de Vilches, PN, Chile 158/C2
Gila (riv.), Az, US 128/D4
Gila Bend, Az, US 128/D4
Gila Cliff Dwellings Nat'l Mon., NM, US 128/E4
Gila River Ind. Res., Az, US 137/R19
Gilbert, Mn, US 130/A2
Gilbert (riv.), Austl. 109/D2
Gilbert, Az, US 137/S19
Gilbert (isls.), Kiri. 116/G5
Gilberts, Il, US 135/P15
Gilbués, Braz. 154/A3
Gilching, Ger. 54/E6
Gilcrest, Co, US 137/C2
Gilford, NI, UK 34/B3
Gilford Park, NJ, US 138/D4
Gilgandra, Austl. 115/D1
Gilgil, Kenya 104/C3
Gilgit (riv.), Pak. 87/F5
Gilles (lake), Austl. 113/H5
Gillette, Wy, US 127/G4
Gillies Bay, BC, Can. 126/B3
Gillingham, Eng, UK 33/G4
Gillot (int'l arpt.), Reun. 107/S15
Gilly, Swi. 56/C5
Gilman Hot Springs, Ca, US 136/D3
Gilmer, Tx, US 129/J4
Gilpin, Co, US 137/A3
Gilgit (riv.), Pak. 89/K1
Gilze, Neth. 50/B5
Gīmbī, Eth. 97/N6
Gimbsheim, Ger. 54/B3
Gimel, Swi. 56/C4
Gimie (mt.), StL. 141/N9
Gimli, Mb, Can. 127/J3
Gimo, Swe. 38/H1
Gin Gin, Austl. 114/C4
Ginan, Japan 77/L5
Gingelom, Belg. 53/E2
Gingin, Austl. 112/B4
Gingindlovu, SAfr. 107/E3
Gingoog, Phil. 79/E6
Gingst, Ger. 38/E4
Ginosa, It. 46/E2
Ginowan, Japan 75/J7
Gioia (gulf), It. 46/D3
Gioia del Colle, It. 46/E2
Gioia Tauro, It. 46/D3
Giornico, Swi. 57/E5
Gioūra (isl.), Gre. 47/J3
Giovenetto (peak), It. 57/G5
Giovi (peak), It. 59/E5
Gipping (riv.), Eng, UK 33/G2
Girardot, Col. 150/D3
Girardville, Pa, US 138/B2
Giraumont, Fr. 53/E5
Girdle Ness (pt.), Sc, UK 36/D2
Giresun (prov.), Turk. 90/D1
Giresun, Turk. 90/D1
Girgnasco, It. 58/B1
Girīdīh, India 85/F3
Girifalco, It. 46/E3
Girling (res.), Eng, UK 30/C2
Giromagny, Fr. 56/C2
Girón, Ecu. 152/B5
Girón, Col. 152/C3
Girona, Sp. 45/G2
Gironcourt-sur-Vraine, Fr. 56/B1
Gironde (riv.), Fr. 42/C4
Gironella, Sp. 45/F1
Girraween NP, Austl. 115/D1
Giru, Austl. 114/B2
Girvan, Sc, UK 34/D1
Gisborne, NZ 117/T10
Gisenyi, Rwa. 104/A3
Gislaved, Swe. 38/E3
Gisors, Fr. 52/A5
Gistel, Belg. 52/B1
Gistrup, Den. 38/D3
Gitega, Buru. 104/A3
Gittsfjället (peak), Swe. 37/E2
Giubiasco, Swi. 57/F5
Giugliano in Campania, It. 48/B5
Giulianova, It. 43/K5
Giurgiu (prov.), Rom. 49/G3
Giurgiu, Rom. 49/G4
Giussano, It. 58/C1
Giv'at Brenner, Isr. 91/F8
Giv'at Ḥayyim, Isr. 91/F7
Giv'atayim, Isr. 91/F7
Give, Den. 38/C4
Givet, Fr. 53/D3
Givors, Fr. 42/F4
Givrine, Col de la (pass), Swi. 56/C5
Giyani, SAfr. 105/F5
Gizhiga (bay), Rus. 65/R3
Gizo, Sol. 116/E5
Giżycko, Pol. 39/J4
Gjerdrum, Nor. 38/D1
Gjerlev, Den. 38/D3
Gjerstad, Nor. 38/C2
Gjirokastër, Alb. 47/G2
Gjoa Haven, Nun., Can. 122/G2
Gjøvik, Nor. 38/D1
Glabbeek, Belg. 53/E2
Glace Bay, NS, Can. 131/K2
Glacier (peak), Wa, US 126/C3
Glacier Bay NP and Prsv., Ak, US 134/L4
Glacier NP, BC, Can. 126/D3
Gladbeck, Ger. 50/D5
Gladewater, Tx, US 129/J4
Gladstone, Mo, US 137/D5
Gladstone, Austl. 114/C3
Gladstone, Austl. 113/H5
Gladwin, Mi, US 130/C3
Glafsfjorden (lake), Swe. 38/D2
Glåma (riv.), Nor. 37/D3
Glamis, Sc, UK 36/D3
Glamsbjerg, Den. 38/D4
Glan, Phil. 79/E6
Glan (riv.), Ger. 40/D4
Glanamman, Wal, UK 32/C3
Gland, Swi. 56/C5
Gland (riv.), Fr. 53/D4
Glandorf, Ger. 51/F4
Glärnisch (range), Swi. 57/E3
Glarus, Swi. 57/F3
Glarus (canton), Swi. 57/E4
Glarus Alps (range), Swi. 43/H3
Glas Maol (peak), Sc, UK 36/C3
Glasgow, Mt, US 126/G3
Glasgow, Ky, US 130/C4
Glasgow, De, US 138/C4
Glasgow, Sc, UK 36/B5
Glashütten, Ger. 54/B2
Glaslyn (riv.), Wal, UK 34/D6
Glass (mts.), Ok, US 132/D2
Glass (lake), Sc, UK 36/B1
Glass (riv.), Sc, UK 36/B2
Glassboro, NJ, US 138/C4
Glastonbury, Eng, UK 32/D4
Glatt (riv.), Ger. 54/B6
Glattbach, Ger. 54/C3
Glattfelden, Swi. 57/E2
Glavinitsa, Bul. 49/H4
Glazoué, Ben. 103/F5
Glazov, Rus. 61/M4
Glems (riv.), Ger. 54/C5
Glen (riv.), Eng, UK 35/H6
Glen Burnie, Md, US 138/B5
Glen Canyon (dam), Az, US 128/E3
Glen Canyon Nat'l Rec. Area, US 128/E3
Glen Carbon, Il, US 137/H8
Glen Coe (pass), Sc, UK 36/B3
Glen Cove, NY, US 139/L8
Glen Gardner, NJ, US 138/D2
Glen Haven, Co, US 137/B2
Glen Innes, Austl. 115/D1
Glen Lyon, Pa, US 138/B1
Glen Mòr (valley), Sc, UK 36/B2
Glen Park, Mo, US 137/G9
Glen Ridge, NJ, US 139/J8
Glen Rock, Pa, US 138/B4
Glen Rock, NJ, US 139/J8
Glen Ullin, ND, US 127/H4
Glenaire, Mo, US 137/E5
Glénan, Îles de (isls.), Fr. 42/A3
Glenarm, NI, UK 34/C2
Glenarm (riv.), NI, UK 34/C2
Glenavy, NI, UK 34/B2
Glenbawn (dam), Austl. 115/D2
Glenboro, Mb, Can. 127/J3
Glencoe, SAfr. 107/E3
Glencoe, Mo, US 137/F8
Glencoe, Il, US 135/Q15
Glencoe, Sc, UK 36/A3
Glendale, Or, US 126/C5
Glendale, Az, US 137/R18
Glendale, Ca, US 136/F7
Glendale Heights, Il, US 135/P16
Glenden, Austl. 114/C3
Glendive, Mt, US 127/G4
Glendo (res.), Wy, US 127/G5
Glendora, Ca, US 136/C2
Glendun (riv.), NI, UK 34/B1
Glenealy, Ire. 34/B6
Glenelg (riv.), Austl. 115/B3
Glenelg, Md, US 138/B5
Glenelg, Sc, UK 31/R8
Glenelly (riv.), NI, UK 34/A2
Glengarry (range), Austl. 112/C3
Glenluce, Sc, UK 34/D2
Glenmere (lake), NY, US 138/D1
Glennallen, Ak, US 134/J3
Glenolden, Pa, US 138/C4
Glenorie, Austl. 114/H8
Glenpool, Ok, US 129/H4
Glenrothes, Sc, UK 36/C4
Glens Falls, NY, US 130/F3
Glenshane (pass), NI, UK 34/B2
Glenside, Pa, US 138/C3
Glenties, Ire. 31/P9
Glenveagh NP, Ire. 31/Q9
Glenview, Il, US 135/Q15
Glenwood, NJ, US 138/D1
Glenwood Springs, Co, US 128/F3
Gleouraich (peak), Sc, UK 36/A2
Glifádha, Gre. 47/N9
Glimåkra, Swe. 38/F3
Glina, Cro. 48/C3
Glinde, Ger. 51/H1
Glindow, Ger. 40/P7
Gliwice, Pol. 41/K3
Globe, Az, US 128/E4
Glockturm (peak), Aus. 57/G4
Gloggnitz, Aus. 41/H5
Głogów, Pol. 41/J3
Głogówek, Pol. 41/J3
Glonn (riv.), Ger. 54/E6
Gloria (bay), Cuba 145/G1
Glorieuses, Îles (isls.), Reun. 107/H5
Glorious (mt.), Austl. 114/E6
Glory of Russia (cape), Ak, US 134/D3
Glossop, Eng, UK 35/G5
Gloster, Ms, US 129/K5
Gloucester, Austl. 115/D1
Gloucester, On, Can. 130/F2
Gloucester, Eng, UK 32/D3
Gloucester (co.), NJ, US 138/C4
Gloucester City, NJ, US 138/C4
Gloucestershire (co.), Eng, UK 32/D3
Glovers (reef), Belz. 144/E2
Glovertown, Nf, Can. 131/L1
Głowno, Pol. 41/K3
Głubczyce, Pol. 41/J3
Głuchołazy, Pol. 41/J3
Glücksburg, Ger. 38/C4
Glückstadt, Ger. 51/G1
Glyndon, Md, US 138/B5
Glyngøre, Den. 38/C3
Glynn, NI, UK 34/C2
Gmünd, Aus. 41/H4
Gmunden, Aus. 55/G7
Gnagna (prov.), Burk. 103/E3
Gnarrenburg, Ger. 51/G2
Gniew, Pol. 39/H5
Gniezno, Pol. 41/J2
Gnjilane, Serb. 47/G1
Gnowangerup, Austl. 112/C5
Gō (riv.), Japan 74/C3
Go Cong, Viet. 78/D4
Goa (state), India 82/B4
Goālpāra, India 85/H2
Goat Fell (peak), Sc, UK 36/A5
Goba, Eth. 97/N6
Gobabis, Namb. 105/C5
Gobardānga, India 85/G4
Gobernador Castro, Arg. 158/F2
Gobernador Costa, Arg. 158/C5
Gobernador Gregores, Arg. 159/C6
Gobernador Mansilla, Arg. 159/J10
Gobi (des.), China,Mon 67/K5
Göblberg (peak), Aus. 55/G6
Gobō, Japan 74/D4
Goch, Ger. 50/D5
Gochsheim, Ger. 54/D2
Godalming, Eng, UK 33/F4
Godāvari (riv.), India 67/G8
Goddā, India 85/F3
Godeanu (peak), Rom. 48/F3
Godech, Bul. 47/H1
Goderich, On, Can. 130/D3
Godfrey, Il, US 137/G8
Gōdo, Japan 77/L5
Gödöllő, Hun. 41/K5
Godoy Cruz, Arg. 158/C2
Gods (riv.), Mb, Can. 122/G3
Gods (lake), Mb, Can. 122/G3
Gods Mercy (bay), Nun., Can. 123/H2
Godthåb (Nuuk), Grld. 119/M3
Godwin Austen (K2) (peak), Pak. 86/D2
Goéland (lake), Qu, Can. 130/E1
Goeree (isl.), Neth. 50/A5
Goes, Neth. 50/A5
Gogebic (range), Mi, US 127/L4
Göggingen, Ger. 54/D6
Gogland (isl.), Rus. 39/M1
Gogōme, Japan 76/B4
Gogounou, Ben. 103/F4
Gogra (riv.), India 82/D2
Gohad, India 84/B2
Gohāna, India 86/D5
Gohbach (riv.), Ger. 51/G3
Goiana, Braz. 154/D2
Goiandira, Braz. 155/B1
Goiânia, Braz. 151/J7
Goianinha, Braz. 154/D2
Goiás, Braz. 151/H7
Goiás (state), Braz. 154/A5
Goiatuba, Braz. 155/B1
Goil (lake), Sc, UK 36/B4
Goirle, Neth. 50/C5
Góis, Port. 44/A2
Goito, It. 59/D2
Gojō, Japan 74/D3
Gojra, Pak. 86/B4
Gok (riv.), Turk. 62/E4
Goka, Japan 77/D1
Gokase (riv.), Japan 74/B4
Gokashō, Japan 77/K5
Gokasho (bay), Japan 77/L7
Gökçeada (isl.), Turk. 90/A1
Gökçebey, Turk. 49/L5
Gökçekaya (dam), Turk. 90/B1
Göksu (riv.), Turk. 90/D2
Göksun, Turk. 90/D2
Göktepe, Turk. 91/C1
Gol, Nor. 38/C1
Gola Gokarannāth, India 84/C1
Golan Hts. (reg.), Syria 91/D3
Golasecca, It. 58/B1
Gölbaşı, Turk. 90/D2
Golbey, Fr. 56/C1
Golborne, Eng, UK 35/F5
Gölcük, Turk. 49/J5
Gold (coast), Gha. 96/E7
Gold (mtn.), Wa, US 135/B2
Gold Bar, Wa, US 135/D2
Gold Beach, Or, US 126/B5
Gold Coast, Austl. 114/D5
Gold Hill, Co, US 137/B2
Gold River, BC, Can. 126/B3
Goldach, Swi. 57/F3
Gołdap, Pol. 39/K4
Goldbach, Ger. 54/C3
Goldberg, Ger. 38/E5
Golden, BC, Can. 126/D3
Golden, Co, US 137/B3
Golden Eagle, Il, US 137/F8
Golden Gate (chan.), Ca, US 135/J11
Golden Gate Highlands NP, SAfr. 106/D3
Golden Hinde (peak), BC, Can. 126/B3
Golden Temple, India 86/C4
Goldendale, Wa, US 126/C4
Goldene Aue (reg.), Ger. 40/F3
Goldenstedt, Ger. 51/F3
Goldkronach, Ger. 55/E2
Goldman, Mo, US 137/F9
Goldmine (mtn.), Az, US 137/S19
Goldsboro, NC, US 133/J3
Goldsboro, Md, US 138/C5
Goldsby, Ok, US 137/N15
Goldsworthy, Austl. 112/C2
Goldthwaite, Tx, US 132/D4
Göle, Turk. 90/E1
Goleniów, Pol. 38/F5
Golfito NWR, CR 145/F4
Golfo Aranci, It. 46/A2
Golfo de Santa Clara, Mex. 142/B2
Gölhisar, Turk. 91/A1
Goliad, Tx, US 132/D4
Gölköy, Turk. 90/D1
Gollach (riv.), Ger. 54/D3
Göllheim, Ger. 54/B3
Gölmarmara, Turk. 90/A2
Golmud, China 70/F4
Golovin, Ak, US 134/F3
Golovnina (peak), Rus. 76/D2
Golpāyegān, Iran 88/F2
Gölpazarı, Turk. 49/K5
Gols, Aus. 43/M3
Golts, Md, US 138/C5
Golub-Dobrzyń, Pol. 41/K2
Golubovci (int'l arpt.), Serb. 47/F1
Golyam Perelik (peak), Bul. 47/J2
Golyama Kamchiya (riv.), Bul. 49/H4
Golyama Syutkya (peak), Bul. 47/J2
Goma, D.R. Congo 104/A3
Goma (int'l arpt.), D.R. Congo 104/A3
Gomaringen, Ger. 54/C6
Gomati (riv.), India 84/C2
Gombe (state), Nga. 103/H4
Gombe (riv.), Tanz. 104/A4
Gombe NP, Tanz. 104/A4
Gomera (isl.) 96/B2
Gómez Farías, Mex. 142/D2
Gómez Palacio, Mex. 142/E3
Gomīshān, Iran 88/F1
Gommern, Ger. 40/F2
Gomoh, India 85/F4
Goms (valley), Swi. 56/E5
Gonābād, Iran 89/G2
Gonaïves, Haiti 145/H2
Gonarezhou NP, Zim. 105/F5
Gonâve (gulf), Haiti 141/G4
Gonâve (isl.), Haiti 145/H2
Gonbad-e Qābūs, Iran 89/G1
Gonbadī, Iran 87/D5
Gönc, Hun. 41/L4
Gonçalves Dias, Braz. 154/A2
Gondelsheim, Ger. 54/B4
Gonder, Eth. 97/N5
Gondia, India 82/D3
Gondomar, Sp. 44/A1
Gondomar, Port. 44/A2
Gondrecourt-le-Château, Fr. 56/B1
Gondreville, Fr. 53/E6
Gondrexange (lake), Fr. 53/F6
Gönen, Turk. 49/H5
Gonesse, Fr. 30/K5
Gong Xian, China 83/H2
Gong Xian, China 72/C4
Gong'an, China 83/K3
Gongbo'gyamda, China 83/F2
Gongcheng, China 79/B3
Gongga (peak), China 83/H2
Gonggar, China 85/H1
Gonghe, China 70/H4
Gongliu, China 70/D3
Gongola (riv.), Nga. 96/H5
Gongshan Drungzu Nuzu Zizhixian, China 83/G2
Gongzhuling, China 72/F2
Goñi, Uru. 159/K10
Gonjo, China 70/G5
Gónnoi, Gre. 47/H3
Gonohe, Japan 76/B3
Gonubie, SAfr. 106/D4
Gonyű, Hun. 48/C2
Gonzaga, It. 59/D3
Gonzales, Tx, US 129/H5
González, Mex. 143/F4
Good Hope, La, US 137/P17
Good Hope, Cape of (cape), SAfr. 106/L11
Goodenough (cape), Ant. 160/J
Goodnews Bay, Ak, US 134/F4
Goodooga, Austl. 115/C1
Goodrich, Mi, US 135/F6
Goodwick, Wal, UK 32/B2
Goodwood, SAfr. 106/L10
Goodyear, Az, US 137/R19
Gooimeer (lake), Neth. 50/C4
Goole, Eng, UK 35/H4
Goolgowi, Austl. 115/C2
Gooloogong, Austl. 115/D2
Goolwa, Austl. 113/H5
Goomalling, Austl. 112/C4
Goombungee, Austl. 114/C4
Goondiwindi, Austl. 114/C5
Goongarrie NP, Austl. 112/D4
Goor, Neth. 50/D4
Goose (lake), Mb, Can. 127/H2
Goose (pt.), La, US 137/Q16
Goose (lake), Ca, US 124/B3
Goose (pt.), De, US 138/C5
Gopālganj, India 85/E2
Gopālpur, Bang. 85/G3
Gopat (riv.), India 84/D3
Göppingen, Ger. 54/C5
Góra, Pol. 41/J3
Góra Kalwaria, Pol. 41/L3
Goražde, Bosn. 48/D4
Gorczański NP, Pol. 41/L4
Gorda (pt.), Nic. 145/F3
Gorda (pt.), Cuba 145/F1
Gorda (pt.), Nic. 145/F4
Gordevio, Swi. 57/E5
Gørding, Den. 38/C4
Gordola, Swi. 57/E5
Gordon, Austl. 115/C4
Gordon (lake), Austl. 109/D5
Gordonsbaai, SAfr. 106/L11
Gordonvale, Austl. 114/B2
Gore (pt.), Ak, US 134/H4
Goré, Chad 96/J6
Gorē, Eth. 97/N6
Gore, NZ 117/R12
Gorebridge, Sc, UK 36/C5
Görele, Turk. 90/D1
Goresbridge, Ire. 31/Q10
Gorey, Chl, UK 42/B2
Gorey, Ire. 31/Q10
Gorgān, Iran 89/F1
Gorge du Loup, Lux. 53/F4
Gorges du Ziz, Mor. 98/D2
Gorgol (pol. reg.), Mrta. 102/B3
Gorgol (riv.), Mrta. 102/B2
Gorgona, Isola di (isl.), It. 58/C6
Gorgonzola, It. 58/C1
Gori, Geo. 63/H4
Gorinchem, Neth. 50/B5
Gorizia, It. 59/G1
Gorizia (prov.), It. 59/G1
Gorj (prov.), Rom. 49/F3
Gorki, Bela. 62/D1
Gor'kiy (res.), Rus. 60/J4
Gorlice, Pol. 41/L4
Görlitz, Ger. 41/H3
Gorllwyn (peak), Wal, UK 32/C2
Gorman, Tx, US 129/H4
Gormanstown, Ire. 34/B4
Gormī, India 84/B2
Gorner (glacier), Swi. 56/D6
Gornji Milanovac, Serb. 48/E3
Gornji Vakuf, Bosn. 48/C4
Gorno-Altay Aut. Rep., Rus. 64/J4
Goro, It. 59/F3
Gorodets, Rus. 61/J4
Gorom Gorom, Burk. 103/E3
Gorong (isl.), Indo. 81/H4
Gorongosa, Moz. 105/F4
Gorontalo, Indo. 81/F3
Gorssel, Neth. 50/D4
Gorst, Wa, US 135/B2
Gortin, NI, UK 34/A2
Görwihl, Ger. 56/E2
Goryn' (riv.), Ukr. 62/C2
Gorzano (peak), It. 43/K5
Gorzów Wielkopolski, Pol. 41/H2
Gosainganj, India 84/D2
Göschenen, Swi. 57/E4
Gōse, Japan 77/J7
Gosen, Japan 75/F2
Gosford, Austl. 115/D2
Gosforth, Eng, UK 35/G2
Goshen, NJ, US 138/D5
Goshogawara, Japan 76/B3
Goslar, Ger. 51/H5
Gospić, Cro. 48/B3
Gosport, Eng, UK 33/E5
Gossas, Sen. 102/A3
Gossau, Swi. 57/F3
Gossersweiler-Stein, Ger. 53/G5
Gostivar, FYROM 47/G2
Gostyń, Pol. 41/J3
Gostynin, Pol. 41/K2
Göta (riv.), Swe. 38/E2
Götaland (reg.), Swe. 38/E3
Göteborg, Swe. 38/D3
Göteborg Och Bohus (co.), Swe. 37/D4
Gotel (mts.), Nga. 96/H6
Gotemba, Japan 75/F3
Götene, Swe. 38/E2
Gotha, Ger. 51/H7
Gotland (co.), Swe. 37/F4
Gotland (isl.), Swe. 37/F4
Gotse Delchev, Bul. 47/H2
Gotska Sandön (isl.), Swe. 39/H2
Gotska Sandön NP, Swe. 39/H2
Gōtsu, Japan 74/C3
Gottenheim, Ger. 56/D1
Göttingen, Ger. 51/G5
Gottmadingen, Ger. 57/E2
Gottolengo, It. 58/D2
Götzis, Aus. 57/F3
Gouda, Neth. 50/B4
Gouda, SAfr. 106/L10
Gough (isl.), StH 22/J7
Gouin (res.), Qu, Can. 123/J4
Goulais (riv.), On, Can. 130/C2
Goulburn (riv.), Austl. 115/D2
Goulburn, Austl. 115/D2
Goulburn (isls.), Austl. 109/C2
Gould, Ar, US 132/F3
Gould (mt.), Austl. 112/C3
Gouldsboro, Pa, US 138/C1
Goulimine, Mor. 98/C3
Goulmima, Mor. 98/D3
Goundam, Mali 102/E2
Goupillières, Fr. 30/H5
Gourdon, Fr. 42/D4
Gouré, Niger 103/H3
Gourin, Fr. 42/B2
Gourits (riv.), SAfr. 106/C4
Gourma (phys. reg.), Burk. 103/F3
Gourma (prov.), Burk. 103/F3
Gourma Rharous, Mali 103/E2
Gournay-en-Bray, Fr. 52/A5
Gourock, Sc, UK 36/B5
Goussainville, Fr. 30/K4
Gouvêa, Braz. 155/D1
Gouveia, Port. 44/B2
Gouvieux, Fr. 30/K4
Gouvy, Belg. 53/E3
Gouyave, Gren. 141/N9
Govardhan, India 84/A2

Gover – Guama

Goverla (peak), Ukr. 49/G1
Governador Archer, Braz. 154/A2
Governador Dix-Sept Rosado, Braz. 154/C2
Governador Eugênio Barros, Braz. 154/A2
Governador Valadares, Braz. 155/D1
Governor Generoso, Phil. 79/E6
Governors (isl.), NY, US 139/J9
Govi-Altay (prov.), Mong. 70/F2
Govĭ Altayn (mts.), Mong. 70/G3
Govind Sāgar (res.), India 86/D4
Govindgarh, India 84/C3
Gower (pen.), Wal, UK 32/B3
Goya, Arg. 157/E2
Goyllarisquizga, Peru 156/B3
Göynük, Turk. 49/K5
Goyt (riv.), Eng, UK 35/F5
Gozaisho-yama (peak), Japan 77/K5
Gözeli, Turk. 90/D2
Gozo (isl.), Malta 46/D4
Gozzano, It. 58/B1
Graaff-Reinet, SAfr. 106/D4
Graafschap (phys. reg.), Neth. 50/D4
Graben, Ger. 57/G1
Graberberg (peak), Namb. 106/B2
Grabouw, SAfr. 106/L11
Grabow, Ger. 40/F2
Graça Aranha, Braz. 154/A2
Gračac, Cro. 48/B3
Gračanica, Bosn. 48/D3
Gracemere, Austl. 114/C3
Graceville, Fl, US 133/G4
Grächen, Swi. 56/D5
Gracias, Hon. 144/D3
Gracias a Dios (cape), Hon. 145/F3
Graciosa (isl.), Azor., Port. 45/S12
Grad Sofiya (prov.), Bul. 47/H1
Gradačac, Bosn. 48/D3
Gradisca d'Isonzo, It. 59/G1
Grado, It. 59/G1
Grado, Sp. 44/B1
Grady (co.), Ok, US 137/M15
Gräfelfing, Ger. 55/E6
Grafenau, Ger. 55/G5
Gräfenberg, Ger. 54/E3
Grafenrheinfeld, Ger. 54/D3
Gräfentonna, Ger. 51/H6
Grafenwöhr, Ger. 55/E3
Graffignana, It. 58/C2
Grafing bei München, Ger. 55/E6
Gråfjell (peak), Nor. 38/C1
Grafrath, Ger. 57/H1
Grafton, Austl. 115/E1
Grafton, ND, US 127/J3
Grafton, WV, US 130/D4
Grafton, Il, US 137/G8
Grafton Passage, Austl. 114/B2
Graham, Tx, US 129/H4
Graham (isl.), Nun., Can. 123/S7
Graham (isl.), BC, Can. 122/C3
Graham Bell (isl.), Rus. 64/G1
Graham Land (phys. reg.), Ant. 160/V
Grahamstown, SAfr. 106/D4
Graian Alps (range), It. 43/G4
Grain (coast), Libr. 96/D6
Grain Valley, Mo, US 137/E5
Grainau, Ger. 57/H3
Grajaú (riv.), Braz. 151/J5
Grajaú, Braz. 154/A2
Grajewo, Pol. 39/K5
Gram, Den. 38/C4
Gramada, Bul. 48/F4
Gramastetten, Aus. 55/H6
Gramat, Fr. 42/D4
Gramat, Causse de (plat.), Fr. 42/D4
Gramatneusiedl, Aus. 49/N7
Grampian (pol. reg.), Sc, UK 36/C2
Grampian (mts.), Sc, UK 36/B3
Grampians NP, Austl. 115/B3
Grampians, The (phys. reg.), Austl. 115/B3
Gramsbergen, Neth. 50/D3
Gramsh, Alb. 47/G2
Gran, Nor. 38/D1
Gran Altiplanicie Central (plat.), Arg. 157/C6
Gran Bajo de San Julián (plain),Arg. 159/C6
Gran Bajo Oriental (plain), Arg. 157/C6
Gran Canaria (isl.) 96/B2
Gran Canaria (int'l arpt.), Sp. 98/B4
Gran Chaco (plain), SAm. 147/C5
Gran Isla del Maíz (isl.), Nic. 145/F3
Gran Laguna Salada (lag.), Arg. 158/D5
Gran Paradiso, PN del, It. 43/G4
Gran Piedra (hill), Cuba 145/H2
Gran Pilastro (peak), It. 43/J3
Gran Vilaya (ruin), Peru 156/B2
Granada, Sp. 44/D4
Granada, Nic. 144/E4
Granada, Col. 152/C4
Granadilla de Abona, Sp. 98/A3
Granados, Mex. 142/C2
Granard, Ire. 31/Q10
Granarolo dell'Emilia, It. 59/E3
Granbury, Tx, US 129/H4
Grand (lake), Nf, Can. 123/L4
Grand (canal), China 72/D4
Grand (falls), Kenya 104/C3
Grand (canal), Az, US 137/R18
Grand (isl.), NY, US 127/M4
Grand (isl.), Mi, US 130/C2
Grand (riv.), Mo, US 132/E2
Grand (riv.), SD, US 127/H4
Grand Bahama (isl.), Bahm. 141/F2
Grand Bank, Nf, Can. 131/L2
Grand Bassa (co.), Libr. 102/C5
Grand-Bassam, C.d'Iv. 102/E5
Grand Bay, NB, Can. 131/H2
Grand Canal d'Alsace (canal), Fr. 56/D2
Grand Canyon, Az, US 128/D3
Grand Canyon Nat'l Park, Az, US 128/D3
Grand Canyon-Parashant Nat'l Mon., Az, US 128/D3
Grand Cape Mount (co.), Libr. 102/C5
Grand Cayman (isl.), Cay. 140/E4
Grand Centre, Ab, Can. 126/F2
Grand-Charmont, Fr. 56/C2
Grand Colombier (peak), Fr. 56/B6
Grand Combine (peak), Swi. 56/D6
Grand Coulee, Wa, US 126/D4
Grand Coulee (dam), Wa, US 126/D4
Grand Drumont (peak), Fr. 56/C2
Grand Erg de Bilma (des.), Niger 96/H4
Grand Erg Occidental (des.), Alg. 93/C1
Grand Erg Oriental (des.), Alg. 93/C1
Grand Falls, NB, Can. 131/H2
Grand Falls, Nf, Can. 131/L1
Grand Forks, ND, US 127/J4
Grand Forks, BC, Can. 126/D3
Grand-Fort-Philippe, Fr. 52/B2
Grand Goâve, Haiti 145/H2
Grand Haven, Mi, US 130/C3
Grand Isle, La, US 133/F4
Grand Jide (co.), Libr. 102/D5
Grand Junction, Co, US 128/E3
Grand-lahou, C.d'Iv. 102/D5
Grand Lake o' the Cherokees (lake), Ok, US 129/J3
Grand Manan (isl.), NB, Can. 131/H2
Grand-Mère, Qu, Can. 131/F2
Grand Mont Ruan (peak), Fr. 56/C5
Grand Muveran (peak), Swi. 56/D5
Grand-Popo, Ben. 103/F5
Grand Portage Nat'l Mon., Mn, US 127/L4
Grand Rapids, Mb, Can. 127/J2
Grand Rapids, Mi, US 130/C3
Grand Rhône (riv.), Fr. 42/F5
Grand Saint-Bernard, Col du (pass), Swi. 56/D6
Grand Staircase-Escalante Nat'l Mon., Ut, US 128/E3
Grand Taureau (peak), Fr. 56/C4
Grand Teton NP, Wy, US 128/E2
Grandcour, Swi. 56/C4
Grande (riv.), Braz. 150/J7
Grande (isl.), Braz. 155/C2
Grande (peak), It. 46/C1
Grande (peak), It. 46/C4
Grande (pt.), Pan. 145/G4
Grande (bay), Arg. 147/C8
Grande (lake), Braz. 153/H5
Grande Cache, Ab, Can. 126/D2
Grande Comore (isl.), Com. 93/G6
Grande de Gurupá, Ilha (isl.), Braz. 151/H4
Grande de Manacapuru, Lago (lake), Braz. 150/F4
Grande de Matagalpa (riv.), Nic. 140/D5
Grande de Santiago (riv.), Mex. 142/D4
Grande de Tierra del Fuego (isl.), Arg.,Chil 157/C7
Grande Dixence, Barrage de la (dam), Swi. 56/D5
Grande do Curuaí (lake), Braz. 153/H5
Grande Miquelon (isl.), StP. 131/K2
Grande Prairie, Ab, Can. 126/D2
Grande Saline, Haiti 145/H2
Grande, Serra (mts.), Braz. 153/F4
Grande-Synthe, Fr. 52/B1
Grande-Terre (isl.), Guad. 141/J4
Grandes Jorasses (peak), It. 56/D6
Grandfresnoy, Fr. 52/B5
Grândola, Port. 44/A3
Grandpuits-Bailly-Carrois, Fr. 30/L6
Grandson, Swi. 56/C4
Grandview, Wa, US 126/D4
Grandview, Mb, Can. 127/H3
Grandview, Tx, US 129/H4
Grandview, Mo, US 137/D6
Grandvillars, Fr. 56/C2
Grandvilliers, Fr. 52/A4
Graneros, Chile 158/N9
Granfjället (peak), Swe. 38/E1
Grange, Mont de (peak), Fr. 56/C5
Grangemouth, Sc, UK 36/C4
Granger (mt.), Yk, Can. 134/L3
Granges-sur-Vologne, Fr. 56/C1
Grängesberg, Swe. 38/F1
Grangeville, Id, US 126/D4
Granisle, BC, Can. 126/B2
Granite (peak), Mt, US 126/F4
Granite, Ut, US 137/K12
Granite City, Il, US 137/G8
Granite Reef Aqueduct, Az, US 137/S18
Granites, The (peak), Austl. 113/F2
Granja, Braz. 154/B1
Granollers, Sp. 45/L6
Grantham, Eng, UK 35/H6
Grantown-on-Spey, Sc, UK 36/C2
Grants, NM, US 128/F4
Grants Pass, Or, US 126/C5
Granville, Fr. 42/C2
Granville (lake), Mb, Can. 122/F3
Grão Mogol, Braz. 154/B5
Grapeview, Wa, US 135/B3
Gras-Ellenbach, Ger. 54/B3
Grasberg, Ger. 51/F2
Grasbrunn, Ger. 55/E6
Grasø (isl.), Swe. 38/H1
Grasonville, Md, US 138/B6
Grass (lake), Il, US 135/P15
Grasse, Fr. 43/G5
Grassie, On, Can. 131/Q9
Grasslands NP, Sk, Can. 126/G3
Grassy, Austl. 115/C4
Grassy Park, SAfr. 106/L11
Grästorp, Swe. 38/E2
Gratkorn, Aus. 43/L3
Gratz, Pa, US 138/B2
Graubünden (canton), Swi. 57/F4
Graulhet, Fr. 42/E5
Graus, Sp. 45/F1
Gravatá, Braz. 154/D3
Grave, Neth. 50/C5
Gravedona, It. 57/F5
Gravelbourg, Sk, Can. 126/G3
Gravelines, Fr. 52/B2
Gravellona Toce, It. 57/E6
Gravenhurst, On, Can. 130/E2
Grävenwiesbach, Ger. 54/B2
Gravesend, Eng, UK 30/E2
Gravina di Puglia, It. 46/E2
Gravois (pt.), Haiti 145/H2
Gray, Fr. 56/B3
Grayling, Ak, US 134/F3
Grayling, Mi, US 130/C2
Grays (har.), Wa, US 126/B4
Grays (lake), Id, US 126/F5
Grays, Eng, UK 30/E2
Grayslake, Il, US 135/P15
Grayson, Sk, Can. 127/H3
Graz, Aus. 43/L3
Grazalema, Sp. 44/C4
Great (lake), Austl. 115/C4
Great (falls), Can.,US 127/G3
Great (basin), Nv, US 124/C4
Great (falls), NJ, US 139/J8
Great Abaco (isl.), Bahm. 141/F2
Great Alfold (plain), Serb. 48/D2
Great America, Ca, US 135/L12
Great Australian Bight (bay), Austl. 109/B4
Great Barrier (reef), Austl. 109/D2
Great Barrier (isl.), NZ 109/H6
Great Basin NP, Nv, US 128/D3
Great Bear (lake), NW, Can. 122/D2
Great Bend, Ks, US 129/H3
Great Bitter (lake), Egypt 91/C4
Great Brak (riv.), SAfr. 106/C3
Great Britain (isl.), UK 27/D3
Great Cedar (swamp), NJ, US 138/D5
Great Coco (isl.), Myan. 83/F5
Great Cumbrae (isl.), Sc, UK 36/B5
Great Divide (basin), Wy, US 126/F5
Great Dividing (range), Austl. 109/D2
Great Egg (har.), NJ, US 138/D5
Great Egg Harbor (riv.), NJ, US 138/D4
Great Exuma (isl.), Bahm. 141/F3
Great Falls, Mt, US 126/F4
Great Fish (riv.), SAfr. 106/D4
Great Fish (pt.), SAfr. 106/D4
Great Guana Cay (isl.), Bahm. 141/F3
Great Harwood, Eng, UK 35/F4
Great Himalaya (range), Asia 70/D6
Great Inagua (isl.), Bahm. 141/G3
Great Indian (des.), India, Pak. 82/B2
Great Karoo (plat.), SAfr. 105/D7
Great Kei (riv.), SAfr. 106/D4
Great Mis Tor (hill), Eng, UK 32/B5
Great Missenden, Eng, UK 33/F3
Great Neck, NY, US 139/L8
Great Nicobar (isl.), India 83/F6
Great Ouse (riv.), Eng, UK 33/E2
Great Oyster (bay), Austl. 115/D4
Great Palace, Rus. 61/T7
Great Palace, Rus. 61/S7
Great Peconic (bay), NY, US 139/F2
Great Pee Dee (riv.), SC, US 133/J3
Great Piece Meadows (swamp), NJ, US 139/H8
Great Rift (valley), Afr. 105/F1
Great Ruaha (riv.), Tanz. 105/F2
Great Salt (lake), Ut, US 128/D2
Great Salt Lake (lake), Ut, US 137/J11
Great Salt Lake (des.), Ut, US 124/D3
Great Sand Dunes Nat'l Park, Co, US 129/F3
Great Sand Sea (des.), Egypt, Li 97/K2
Great Sandy (des.), Austl. 109/B2
Great Scarcies (riv.), SLeo. 102/B4
Great Shunner Fell (peak), Eng, UK 35/F3
Great Slave (lake), NW, Can. 122/E2
Great Smoky Mountains NP, NC,Tn, US 133/H3
Great South (bay), NY, US 139/E2
Great Stour (riv.), Eng, UK 33/G4
Great. Tenasserim (riv.), Myan. 78/B3
Great Victoria (des.), Austl. 109/B3
Great Victoria Desert Nature Rsv., Austl. 113/E4
Great Wall, China 70/J4
Great Western Tiers (mts.),Austl. 115/C4
Great Winterhoek (peak), SAfr. 106/L10
Great Yarmouth, Eng, UK 33/H1
Great Zab (riv.), Iraq 90/E2
Great Zimbabwe (ruin), Zim. 105/F5
Greater Accra (pol. reg.), Gha. 103/F5
Greater Antilles (isls.), NAm. 141/F3
Greater Buffalo (int'l arpt.), NY, US 131/S10
Greater Cincinnati (int'l arpt.), Ky, US 130/C4
Greater London (co.), Eng, UK 30/D2
Greater Manchester (co.), Eng, UK 35/F4
Greater Pittsburgh (int'l arpt.), Pa, US 130/D3
Greater Rochester (int'l arpt.), NY, US 130/E3
Greater Sunda (isls.), Indo. 80/C4
Grebenhain, Ger. 54/C2
Grebenstein, Ger. 51/G6
Grébon (peak), Niger 103/H2
Grecco, Uru. 159/K10
Greco (peak), It. 46/C2
Greco (cape), Cyp. 91/D2
Greding, Ger. 55/E4
Gredos, Sierra de (mts.), Sp. 44/C2
Greece (ctry.) 47/G3
Greeley, Co, US 137/C2
Greeley Number 2 (canal), Co, US 137/C2
Greely (fjord), Nun., Can. 123/S6
Green (cape), Austl. 115/D3
Green (bay), Mi,Wi, US 127/M4
Green (riv.), Ky, US 130/C4
Green (mts.), Vt, US 130/F3
Green (riv.), Ut,Wy, US 124/E4
Green Cove Springs, Fl, US 133/H4
Green Creek, NJ, US 138/D5
Green Haven, Md, US 138/B5
Green Lane (res.), Pa, US 138/C3
Green Lowther (peak), Sc, UK 36/C6
Green Pond, NJ, US 138/D1
Green River, Wy, US 126/F5
Green Valley, Az, US 128/E5
Green Valley, Ca, US 136/B1
Green Valley Lake, Ca, US 136/C2
Green Village, NJ, US 139/H9
Greenbelt, Md, US 138/B6
Greenbushes, Austl. 112/C5
Greencastle, In, US 130/C4
Greencastle, Ire. 34/B1
Greendale, Wi, US 135/Q14
Greeneville, Tn, US 130/D4
Greenfield, Ma, US 131/F3
Greenfield, In, US 130/C4
Greenfield, Wi, US 135/P14
Greenfield Park, Qu, Can. 131/P7
Greenisland, NI, UK 34/C2
Greenland (sea) 119/R2
Greenmount, Md, US 138/B4
Greenock, Sc, UK 36/B5
Greenough (mt.), Ak, US 134/K2
Greenough (riv.), Austl. 112/B4
Greenport, NY, US 139/F1
Greensboro, NC, US 133/J2
Greensboro, Al, US 133/G3
Greensboro, Md, US 138/C6
Greensburg, In, US 130/C4
Greensburg, Pa, US 130/E3
Greenvale, Austl. 114/B2
Greenville, Ca, US 126/C5
Greenville, SC, US 133/H3
Greenville, Al, US 133/G4
Greenville, Mi, US 130/C3
Greenville, NC, US 133/J3
Greenville, Tx, US 129/H4
Greenville, Ms, US 129/K4
Greenville, Oh, US 130/C3
Greenville, Libr. 102/C5
Greenwater (riv.), Wa, US 135/D3
Greenwell Point, Austl. 115/D2
Greenwich, Ct, US 139/L7
Greenwich (bor.), Eng, UK 30/D2
Greenwich (pt.), Ct, US 139/L8
Greenwich Observatory, Eng, UK 30/D2
Greenwood (lake), SC, US 133/H3
Greenwood, SC, US 133/H3
Greenwood, Ms, US 129/K4
Greenwood, Mo, US 137/E6
Greenwood, De, US 138/C6
Greenwood Lake, NY, US 138/D1
Greers Ferry (lake), Ar, US 129/J4
Grefrath, Ger. 50/D6
Gregório (riv.), Braz. 150/D5
Gregory, SD, US 127/J5
Gregory (range), Austl. 109/D2
Gregory (lake), Austl. 109/B3
Greifswald, Ger. 38/E4
Greifswalder Bodden (bay), Ger. 41/G1
Greimberg (peak), Aus. 43/L3
Greiz, Ger. 43/K1
Gremyachinsk, Rus. 61/N4
Grenå, Den. 38/D3
Grenada, Ms, US 129/K4
Grenada (ctry.) 141/N10
Grenade, Fr. 42/D5
Grenay, Fr. 52/B3
Grenchen, Swi. 56/D3
Grenfell, Austl. 115/D2
Grenfell, Sk, Can. 127/H3
Grennach (riv.), Ger. 54/D6
Grenoble, Fr. 42/F4
Grenzach-Wyhlen, Ger. 56/D2
Gressåmoen NP, Nor. 37/E2
Greta (riv.), Eng, UK 35/E2
Gretna, Mb, Can. 127/J3
Gretna, La, US 137/P17
Gretna, Sc, UK 35/E2
Grettstadt, Ger. 54/D3
Gretz-Armainvilliers, Fr. 30/L5
Greve (riv.), It. 59/E5
Greve in Chianti, It. 59/E5
Grevelingendam (dam), Neth. 50/B5
Greven, Ger. 51/E4
Grevená, Gre. 47/G2
Grevenbroich, Ger. 53/F1
Grevenmacher (dist.), Lux. 53/F4
Grevenmacher, Lux. 53/F4
Grevesmühlen, Ger. 40/F2
Grevlingen (chan.), Neth. 50/A5
Grey (range), Austl. 109/D3
Grey (riv.), Nf, Can. 131/K2
Grey (pt.), NI, UK 34/C2
Grey Abbey, NI, UK 34/C2
Grey Hunter (peak), Yk, Can. 134/L3
Grey Peaks NP, Austl. 114/B2
Greybull, Wy, US 126/F4
Greylingstad, SAfr. 106/E2
Greymouth, NZ 117/S11
Greystones, Ire. 34/B5
Greytown, SAfr. 107/E3
Grez-Doiceau, Belg. 53/D2
Grezzana, It. 59/E1
Gribbin (pt.), Eng, UK 32/B6
Griefensee (lake), Swi. 57/E3
Griekwastad, SAfr. 106/C3
Griend (isl.), Neth. 50/C2
Gries am Brenner, Aus. 57/H3
Griesheim, Ger. 54/B3
Grieskirchen, Aus. 55/G6
Griesskogel (peak), Aus. 57/H3
Griesstätt, Ger. 55/F7
Griffin, Ga, US 133/G3
Griffith, Austl. 115/C2
Griffith, In, US 135/R16
Griffith Park, Ca, US 136/F7
Grigna (peak), It. 57/F6
Grignano Polesine, It. 59/E2
Grigny, Fr. 30/K6
Grijalva (riv.), Mex. 144/C2
Grijpskerk, Neth. 50/D2
Grim (cape), Austl. 115/C4
Grimbergen, Belg. 53/D2
Grimisuat, Swi. 56/D5
Grimmen, Ger. 38/E4
Grimsby, On, Can. 131/Q9
Grimsby, Eng, UK 35/H4
Grimselpass (pass), Swi. 57/E4
Grimsey (isl.), Ice. 37/N6
Grimstad, Nor. 38/C2
Grindavík, Ice. 37/M7
Grindelwald, Swi. 56/E4
Grindsted, Den. 38/C4
Grinnell (pen.), Nun., Can. 123/S7
Grintavec (peak), Slov. 43/L3
Griqualand East (reg.), SAfr. 106/E3
Griqualand West (reg.), SAfr. 106/C2
Gris-Nez (cape), Fr. 52/A2
Grise Fiord, Nun., Can. 123/S7
Grisslehamn, Swe. 39/H1
Grisy-les-Plâtres, Fr. 30/J4
Grisy-Suisnes, Fr. 30/L5
Grivette (riv.), Fr. 30/L4
Grizzly (bay), Ca, US 135/K10
Grmeč (mts.), Bosn. 48/C3
Groaíras, Braz. 154/B1
Grobbendonk, Belg. 50/B6
Gröbenzell, Ger. 55/E6
Groblershoop, SAfr. 106/C3
Grodków, Pol. 41/J3
Grodzisk Wielkopolski, Pol. 41/J2
Groenlo, Neth. 50/D4
Groesbeck, Tx, US 132/D4
Groesbeek, Neth. 50/C5
Groix (isl.), Fr. 42/B3
Grójec, Pol. 41/L3
Grömitz, Ger. 38/D4
Gromo, It. 57/F6
Gronau, Ger. 50/E4
Gronau, Ger. 51/G4
Groningen, Neth. 50/D2
Groningen (prov.), Neth. 50/D2
Gronlait (peak), It. 57/H5
Grono, Swi. 57/F5
Groot (riv.), SAfr. 105/D7
Groot-Marico (riv.), SAfr. 106/D2
Grootdraaidam (res.), SAfr. 106/Q13
Groote Eylandt (isl.), Austl. 109/C2
Grootegast, Neth. 50/D2
Grootfontein, Namb. 105/C4
Grootvloer (salt pan), SAfr. 106/C3
Gropello Cairoli, It. 58/B2
Gros Islet, StL. 141/N9
Gros Morne (peak), Nf, Can. 131/K1
Gros Morne NP, Nf, Can. 131/K1
Grossbliederstroff, Fr. 53/G5
Grosio, It. 57/G5
Grosne (riv.), Fr. 42/F3
Grosrouvre, Fr. 30/H5
Gross Bieberau, Ger. 54/B3
Gross-Enzersdorf, Aus. 49/P7
Gross-Gerungs, Aus. 41/H4
Gross Oesingen, Ger. 51/H3
Gross Unstadt, Ger. 54/B3
Gross-Zimmern, Ger. 54/B3
Grossaitingen, Ger. 57/G1
Grossalmerode, Ger. 51/G6
Grossbeeren, Ger. 40/Q7
Grossbottwar, Ger. 54/C5
Grossbreitenbach, Ger. 54/D1
Grosse (isl.), Mi, US 135/F7
Grosse Aue (riv.), Ger. 51/F4
Grosse Ile, Mi, US 135/F7
Grosse Laber (riv.), Ger. 55/F5
Grosse Mühl (riv.), Aus. 55/G6
Grosse Münzenberg (peak), Namb. 106/A2
Grosse Nister (riv.), Ger. 53/G2
Grosse Pointe, Mi, US 135/G7
Grosse Pointe Farms, Mi, US 135/G7
Grosse Pointe Park, Mi, US 135/G7
Grosse Pointe Shores, Mi, US 135/G7
Grosse Pointe Woods, Mi, US 135/G7
Grosse Rodl (riv.), Aus. 55/H6
Grossengottern, Ger. 51/H6
Grossenkneten, Ger. 51/F3
Grossenlüder, Ger. 54/C1
Grossenwiehe, Ger. 38/C4
Grosser Ahrensberg (peak), Ger. 51/G5
Grosser Aletsch (glacier), Swi. 56/D5
Grosser Arber (peak), Ger. 55/G4
Grosser Beer-Berg (peak), Ger. 43/J1
Grosser Bösenstein (peak), Aus. 43/L3
Grosser Daumen (peak), Ger. 57/G3
Grosser Feldberg (peak), Ger. 54/B2
Grosser Gleichberg (peak), Ger. 54/D2
Grosser Heuberg (mts.), Ger. 54/B6
Grosser Knechtsand (isl.), Ger. 51/F1
Grosser Peilstein (peak), Aus. 41/H4
Grosser Plessower (lake), Ger. 40/P7
Grosser Priel (peak), Aus. 43/L3
Grosser Rachel (peak), Ger. 55/G5
Grosser Seddiner (lake), Ger. 40/P7
Grosser Selchower (lake), Ger. 40/Q7
Grosses Meer (lake), Ger. 51/E2
Grosses Moor (swamp), Ger. 51/H3
Grosseto, It. 43/J5
Grossgerau, Ger. 54/B3
Grossglienicke, Ger. 40/Q7
Grossglockner (peak), Aus. 43/K3
Grosshansdorf, Ger. 51/H1
Grossheubach, Ger. 54/C3
Grosskrotzenburg, Ger. 54/B2
Grossmaischeid, Ger. 53/G3
Grosso (cape), Fr. 43/H5
Grossrosseln, Ger. 53/F5
Grosssiegharts, Aus. 41/H4
Grosswallstadt, Ger. 54/C3
Grosswangen, Swi. 56/E3
Grosuplje, Slov. 43/L4
Grote Gete (riv.), Belg. 53/D2
Groton, SD, US 127/J4
Grotta Gigante, It. 59/G1
Grottaglie, It. 47/E2
Grottammare, It. 43/K5
Grotte de Han, Belg. 53/E3
Grouard Mission, Ab, Can. 126/D2
Groundhog (riv.), On, Can. 130/D1
Grouw, Neth. 50/C2
Grovdageaidnu-Kautokeino, Nor. 37/G1
Grove, Ok, US 129/J3
Grove (pt.), Md, US 138/B5
Grover, Mo, US 137/F8
Grover City, Ca, US 128/B4
Groves, Tx, US 129/J5
Groveton, Va, US 138/A6
Groznyy, Rus. 63/H4
Grudovo, Bul. 49/H4
Grudziądz, Pol. 41/K2
Grumeti (riv.), Tanz. 104/B3
Grums, Swe. 38/E2
Grünau im Almtal, Aus. 55/G7
Grünburg, Aus. 55/H7
Gründau, Ger. 54/C2
Grune (pt.), Eng, UK 35/E2
Grünsfeld, Ger. 54/C3
Grünstadt, Ger. 54/B3
Grünwald, Ger. 55/E6
Gruyères, Swi. 56/D4
Gryazi, Rus. 62/F1
Grycksbo, Swe. 38/F1
Gryfice, Pol. 38/F5
Gryfino, Pol. 41/H2
Gryon, Swi. 56/D5
Gschwandt, Aus. 55/G7
Gschwend, Ger. 54/C5
Gsteig, Swi. 56/D5
Gua, India 85/E4
Guabún (pt.), Chile 158/B4
Guaca, Col. 152/C3
Guacanayabo (gulf), Cuba 141/F3
Guacarí, Col. 152/B4
Guachochi, Mex. 142/D3
Guácimo, CR 145/F4
Guaçuí, Braz. 155/D2
Guadalajara, Mex. 142/E4
Guadalajara, Sp. 44/D2
Guadalcanal, Sp. 44/C3
Guadalcanal (isl.), Sol. 116/E6
Guadalentín (riv.), Sp. 44/D4
Guadalimar (riv.), Sp. 44/D3
Guadalix (riv.), Sp. 45/N8
Guadalope (riv.), Sp. 45/E2
Guadalquivir (riv.), Sp. 44/D4
Guadalupe, Braz. 154/B2
Guadalupe, Col. 152/C4
Guadalupe, Mex. 142/E4
Guadalupe, Mex. 143/E3
Guadalupe (isl.), Mex. 119/E7
Guadalupe, Pan. 152/B2
Guadalupe, Peru 156/C4
Guadalupe, Peru 156/B2
Guadalupe, Sp. 44/C3
Guadalupe (mts.), NM,Tx, US 132/B3
Guadalupe (co.), Tx, US 137/U20
Guadalupe (peak), Tx, US 129/F5
Guadalupe (riv.), Tx, US 140/B2
Guadalupe Mountains NP, Tx, US 129/F5
Guadalupe, Sierra de (mts.), Sp. 44/C3
Guadalupe Victoria, Mex. 142/B1
Guadalupe Victoria, Mex. 142/D3
Guadalupe Victoria, Mex. 143/M7
Guadarrama (riv.), Sp. 44/C3
Guadarrama, Ven. 152/D2
Guadarrama, Sp. 45/M8
Guadarrama, Sierra de (mts.), Sp. 44/C2
Guadeloupe (isl.), Fr. 141/N8
Guadeloupe NP, Fr. 141/N8
Guadeloupe Passage (chan.), Fr. 141/J4
Guadiana (riv.), Port.,Sp. 44/B3
Guadiana Menor (riv.), Sp. 44/D4
Guadix, Sp. 44/D4
Guafo (isl.), Chile 158/B4
Guafo, Boca del (mouth) 157/B5
Guagua Pichincha (peak), Ecu. 152/B5
Guaíba, Braz. 155/B4
Guaíba (riv.), Braz. 155/B4
Guáimaro, Cuba 145/G1
Guainía (riv.), Col. 150/E3
Guainía (dept.), Col. 152/D4
Guaiquinima (peak), Ven. 153/F3
Guaira, Braz. 157/F1
Guaíra, Braz. 155/B2
Guaiteca (isl.), Chile 158/B4
Guajará-Mirim, Braz. 150/E6
Guajira (pen.), Col. 147/B1
Gualaceo, Ecu. 152/B5
Gualaco, Hon. 144/E3
Gualán, Guat. 144/D3
Gualaquiza, Ecu. 156/B1
Gualeguay, Arg. 159/J10
Gualeguaychú, Arg. 159/J10
Gualtieri, It. 58/D3
Guam (isl.), Pac., US 116/D3
Guamal, Col. 152/C2

191

Guamb – Har R

Guamblin, Isla (isl.), Chile 158/A5
Guamote, Ecu. 156/B1
Guamúchil, Mex. 142/C3
Gu'an, China 72/H7
Guan Xian, China 70/H5
Guan Xian, China 72/C3
Guanabacoa, Cuba 145/F1
Guanabara (bay), Braz. 211/K7
Guanahacabibes (gulf), Cuba 144/E1
Guanahacabibes (pen.), Cuba 145/E1
Guanaja (isl.), Hon. 144/E2
Guanaja, Hon. 144/E2
Guanajay, Cuba 145/F1
Guanajuato, Mex. 143/E4
Guanajuato (state), Mex. 140/A3
Guanambi, Braz. 154/B4
Guanape, Ven. 153/E2
Guanare (riv.), Ven. 150/E2
Guanare, Ven. 152/D2
Guanarito, Ven. 152/D2
Guanay (peak), Ven. 153/E3
Guandi (mtn.), China 72/B3
Guane, Cuba 145/E1
Guangchang, China 79/C2
Guangde, China 72/D5
Guangdong (prov.), China 71/K7
Guangfeng, China 79/C2
Guangling, China 72/C3
Guanglu (isl.), China 73/B3
Guangnan, China 83/J3
Guangping, China 79/C2
Guangping, China 72/C3
Guangrao, China 72/D3
Guangshan, China 72/C4
Guangxi Zhuangzu (aut. reg.), China 70/J7
Guangyuan, China 70/J5
Guangze, China 79/C2
Guangzhou, China 83/K3
Guanhães, Braz. 155/D1
Guanipa (riv.), Ven. 150/F2
Guannan, China 72/D4
Guantánamo, Cuba 145/H1
Guantánamo Bay U.S. Naval Base, Cuba 145/H2
Guantao, China 72/C3
Guanting (res.), China 72/G6
Guanujo, Ecu. 152/B5
Guanyun, China 72/D4
Guapí, Col. 152/B4
Guaporé, Braz. 155/B4
Guaporé (riv.), Braz. 147/C4
Guaqui, Bol. 156/D5
Guarabira, Braz. 154/D2
Guaraci, Braz. 155/B2
Guaraciaba do Norte, Braz. 154/B2
Guaraí, Braz. 151/J5
Guaramirim, Braz. 155/B3
Guaranda, Ecu. 152/B5
Guarani, Braz. 211/K6
Guarapari, Braz. 155/D2
Guarapuava, Braz. 155/B3
Guarará, Braz. 211/K6
Guararapes (int'l arpt.), Braz. 154/D3
Guararapes, Braz. 155/B2
Guararema, Braz. 211/G8
Guaratinga, Braz. 154/C5
Guaratinguetá, Braz. 211/H7
Guaratuba, Braz. 155/B3
Guarda (dist.), Port. 44/B2
Guarda, Port. 44/B2
Guardamar, Sp. 45/E3
Guardamiglio, It. 58/C2
Guardarrama (riv.), Sp. 45/N8
Guardia Alta (peak), It. 57/H4
Guardia Mitre, Arg. 158/E4
Guardia Sanframondi, It. 48/B5
Guardiagrele, It. 46/D1
Guareña, Sp. 44/B3
Guarico (pt.), Cuba 145/H1
Guárico (riv.), Ven. 141/H6
Guárico (state), Ven. 153/E2
Guárico, Embalse de (res.), Ven. 150/E2
Guarujá, Braz. 211/G9
Guarulhos (int'l arpt.), Braz. 211/G8
Guarulhos, Braz. 211/G8
Guarumal, Pan. 152/A3
Guasave, Mex. 142/C3
Guasdualito, Ven. 152/D3
Guasimal, Cuba 145/G1
Guasipati, Ven. 153/F3
Guastalla, It. 58/D3
Guatemala (ctry.) 144/D3
Guatemala (cap.), Guat. 144/D3
Guateque, Col. 152/C3
Guaviare (dept.), Col. 152/C4
Guaviare (riv.), Col. 147/C2
Guaxupé, Braz. 211/G6
Guayabero (riv.), Col. 152/C4
Guayabo, Cayo (isl.), Cuba 145/G1
Guayalejo (riv.), Mex. 143/F4
Guayama, PR 141/M8
Guayape (riv.), Hon. 144/E3
Guayaquil (gulf), Ecu.,Peru 147/A3
Guayaquil, Ecu. 152/B5
Guayaquil, Gulf of (gulf), Ecu.,Peru 156/A1
Guayaramerín, Bol. 150/E6
Guayas, Ecu. 152/B5
Guayas (prov.), Ecu. 152/A5
Guayas (riv.), Col. 152/C4
Guaymas, Mex. 142/C3
Gubakha, Rus. 61/N4
Gubbio, It. 59/F6
Guben, Ger. 41/H3
Gubin, Pol. 41/H3
Gubkin, Rus. 62/F2
Gucheng, China 72/B4
Gucheng, China 72/C3
Gúdar, Sierra de (range), Sp. 45/E2
Gudenå (riv.), Den. 38/D3
Gudensberg, Ger. 51/G6
Gudermes, Rus. 63/H4
Gudivāda, India 82/D4
Gudow, Ger. 51/H1
Güdül, Turk. 49/L5
Güdür, India 82/C5
Guebli (lake), Mrta. 98/B5
Guebwiller, Fr. 56/D2
Guecho, Sp. 44/D1
Guelb Azefal (hill), Mrta. 98/B5
Guelb er Rîchât (peak), Mrta. 98/C5
Guelma, Alg. 100/K6
Guelma (prov.), Alg. 100/K6
Guelph, On, Can. 130/D3
Guémené-Penfao, Fr. 42/C3
Guénange, Fr. 53/F5
Guérande, Fr. 42/B3
Guerara, Alg. 99/G2
Guérard, Fr. 30/L5
Guercif, Mor. 100/C2
Guéret, Fr. 42/D3
Guernes, Fr. 30/G4
Guernsey (int'l arpt.), Chl, UK 42/B2
Guernsey (isl.), Chl, UK 42/B2
Guerrero (state), Mex. 140/B4
Guerrero, Mex. 142/D2
Guerrero Negro, Mex. 142/B3
Guerville, Fr. 30/H5
Guesle (riv.), Fr. 30/H6
Gueugnon, Fr. 42/F3
Gueux, Fr. 52/C5
Gugē (peak), Eth. 97/N6
Guggisberg, Swi. 56/D4
Guglielmo Marconi (int'l arpt.), It. 59/E3
Güglingen, Ger. 54/B4
Guguan (isl.), NMar. 116/D3
Guguletu, SAfr. 106/L11
Gui (riv.), China 79/B3
Guiana Highlands (uplands), SAm. 147/C2
Guichen, Fr. 42/C3
Guichón, Uru. 159/K10
Guidder, Camr. 96/H6
Guidimaka (pol. reg.), Mrta. 102/B3
Guiding, China 83/J2
Guidizzolo, It. 58/D2
Guidong, China 83/K2
Guidonia, It. 46/C2
Guiglo, C.d'Iv. 102/D5
Guignes-Rabutin, Fr. 30/L6
Guihulngan, Phil. 81/F1
Guija, Moz. 105/F5
Guijuelo, Sp. 44/C2
Guilder (peak), Ut, US 137/L11
Guilderton, Austl. 112/B4
Guildford, Eng, UK 30/B3
Guilherand, Fr. 42/F4
Guilin (int'l arpt.), China 79/B2
Guilin, China 83/K2
Guillaume-Delisle (lake), Qu, Can. 123/J2
Guillena, Sp. 44/B4
Guimarães, Braz. 154/A1
Guimarães, Port. 44/A2
Guimba, Phil. 79/D4
Guimeng (mtn.), China 72/D4
Guinan, China 70/H4
Guinard (riv.), Sc, UK 36/A1
Guinea (ctry.) 102/C4
Guinea (gulf), Afr. 93/C4
Guinea-Bissau (ctry.) 102/B3
Guînes, Fr. 52/A2
Guingamp, Fr. 42/B2
Guinguinéo, Sen. 102/B3
Guiones (pt.), CR 144/E4
Güipavas, Fr. 42/A2
Guipavas (int'l arpt.), Fr. 42/A2
Guir, Oued (riv.), Alg. 98/E2
Guiratinga, Braz. 151/H7
Güiria, Ven. 153/F2
Guisborough, Eng, UK 35/G2
Guiscard, Fr. 52/C4
Guise, Fr. 52/C4
Guitiriz, Sp. 44/B1
Guitrancourt, Fr. 30/H4
Guiuan, Phil. 79/E5
Güiza (riv.), Col. 152/B4
Guizhou (prov.), China 70/J6
Gujan-Mestras, Fr. 42/C4
Gujar Khān, Pak. 86/B3
Gujarāt (state), India 82/B3
Gujrānwāla, Pak. 86/C3
Gujrāt, Pak. 86/C3
Gukovo, Rus. 62/F2
Gulaothi, India 84/A1
Gulargambone, Austl. 115/D1
Gulbarga, India 82/C4
Guldenbach (riv.), Ger. 53/G3
Güldüzü, Turk. 91/E1
Gulen, Nor. 38/A1
Gulf Coastal (plain), Tx, US 132/D5
Gulf Islands Nat'l Seashore, US 133/F4
Gulf Shores, Al, US 133/G4
Gulfport, Ms, US 133/F4
Gulgong, Austl. 115/D2
Guliston, Uzb. 87/E4
Gulkana, Ak, US 134/J3
Gull Lake, Sk, Can. 126/F3
Gulladuff, NI, UK 34/B2
Gullane, Sc, UK 36/D4
Gullane (pt.), Sc, UK 36/D4
Gullspång, Swe. 38/F2
Güllükdağı (Termessos) NP, Turk. 91/B1
Gulmarg, India 86/C2
Gülnar, Turk. 91/C1
Gulpen, Neth. 53/E2
Gülpınar, Turk. 47/K3
Gulu, Ugan. 104/B2
Gulyantsi, Bul. 49/G4
Gumal (riv.), Pak. 86/A4
Gumare, Bots. 105/D4
Gumbrechtshoffen, Fr. 53/G6
Gumdag, Trkm. 63/K5
Gumeracha, Austl. 113/M8
Gumia, India 85/E4
Gumla, India 85/E4
Gumma (pref.), Japan 75/F2
Gummersbach, Ger. 53/G1
Gumpoldskirchen, Aus. 49/N7
Gumti (riv.), India 85/H4
Gümüşhacıköy, Turk. 62/E4
Gümüşhane, Turk. 90/D1
Gümüşhane (prov.), Turk. 90/D1
Guna (peak), Eth. 97/N5
Gunbower, Austl. 115/C2
Gundagai, Austl. 115/D2
Gundelfingen, Ger. 56/D1
Gundelfingen an der Donau, Ger. 54/D5
Gundelsheim, Ger. 54/C4
Gundersheim, Ger. 54/B3
Gundershoffen, Fr. 53/G6
Gündoğmuş, Turk. 91/C1
Güneydogu Toroslar (mts.), Turk. 90/D2
Gunisao (riv.), Mb, Can. 127/J2
Gunisao (lake), Mb, Can. 127/J2
Gunja, Cro. 48/D3
Gunn City, Mo, US 137/E6
Gunnar, India 84/B1
Gunnebo, Swe. 38/G3
Gunnedah, Austl. 115/D1
Gunning, Austl. 115/D2
Gunnison (riv.), Co, US 128/F3
Gunnison, Ut, US 128/E3
Gunpowder (riv.), Md, US 138/B5
Gunpowder Falls State Park, Md, US 138/B4
Gunskirchen, Aus. 55/G6
Guntersblum, Ger. 54/B3
Guntersville, Al, US 133/G3
Guntersville (lake), Al, US 133/G3
Guntramsdorf, Aus. 49/N7
Guntūr, India 82/D4
Günz (riv.), Ger. 40/F4
Günzburg, Ger. 54/D6
Gunzenhausen, Ger. 54/D4
Guoyang, China 72/D4
Gura Humorului, Rom. 49/G2
Guragē (peak), Eth. 97/N6
Gurbantünggut (des.), China 70/E2
Gurdāspur, India 86/C3
Gurgaon, India 86/D5
Gürgentepe, Turk. 90/D1
Gurguéia (riv.), Braz. 151/K6
Guri (res.), Ven. 147/C2
Guri (dam), Ven. 153/F3
Gurk (riv.), Aus. 43/L3
Gurkthaler Alpen (mts.), Aus. 43/K3
Gurnee, Il, US 135/Q15
Guro, Moz. 105/F4
Gürpınar, Turk. 90/E3
Gursarai, India 84/B3
Gürsu, Turk. 90/B1
Guru Sikhar (peak), India 89/K4
Gürün, Turk. 90/D2
Gurupi, Braz. 151/J6
Gurupi (riv.), Braz. 151/J4
Gurupi, Serra do (mts.), Braz. 151/J4
Gus'-Khrustal'nyy, Rus. 60/J5
Gusau, Nga. 103/G3
Gushi, China 72/C4
Gushikawa, Japan 75/J7
Gusinje, Serb. 47/F1
Guskhara, India 85/F4
Guspini, It. 46/A3
Gussola, It. 58/D3
Gustavo Díaz Ordaz, Mex. 142/C3
Gustavo Díaz Ordaz, Mex. 142/B3
Gusterath, Ger. 53/F4
Güstrow, Ger. 38/E5
Gusum, Swe. 38/G2
Gutau, Aus. 55/H6
Gütersloh, Ger. 51/F5
Guthrie, Tx, US 129/G4
Guthrie, Ok, US 137/N14
Gutiérrez Zamora, Mex. 143/M6
Guttannen, Swi. 57/E4
Guttenberg, NJ, US 139/K8
Guttingen, Swi. 57/F2
Gutulia NP, Nor. 37/E3
Guwāhati, India 83/F2
Guxhagen, Ger. 51/G6
Guxian, China 72/B3
Guy Fawkes River NP, Austl. 115/E1
Guyana (ctry.) 153/G3
Guyancourt, Fr. 30/J5
Guyandotte (riv.), WV, US 133/H2
Guyang, China 72/B2
Guyenne (reg.), Fr. 42/C4
Guymon, Ok, US 129/G3
Guyra, Austl. 115/D1
Guyuan, China 70/J4
Güzelbağ, Turk. 91/B1
Güzelsu, Turk. 91/B1
Guzhang, China 83/J2
Guzhen, China 72/D4
Guzmán (lake), Mex. 142/D2
Gwādar, Pak. 89/H3
Gwaii Haanas NP, BC, Can. 122/C3
Gwalior, India 84/B2
Gwanda, Zim. 105/E5
Gwandalan, Austl. 115/D2
Gwash (riv.), Eng, UK 33/F1
Gwaunceste (peak), Wal, UK 32/C2
Gwda (riv.), Pol. 41/J2
Gwersyllt, Wal, UK 35/E5
Gweru, Zim. 105/E4
Gwydir (riv.), Austl. 115/D1
Gwynedd (co.), Wal, UK 34/D5
Gwyrfai (riv.), Wal, UK 34/D5
Gy, Fr. 56/B3
Gya (pass), China 85/E1
Gyaca, China 85/F1
Gyál, Hun. 49/R10
Gyasikan, Gha. 103/F5
Gyda (pen.), Rus. 67/G2
Gyhum, Ger. 51/G2
Gyirong, China 85/E1
Gyldenløveshøj (peak), Den. 38/D4
Gympie, Austl. 114/D4
Gyōda, Japan 77/C1
Gyoma, Hun. 48/E2
Gyömrő, Hun. 49/R10
Győr, Hun. 48/C2
Győr-Moson-Sopron (co.), Hun. 41/J5
Győrújbarát, Hun. 48/C2
Gyumri, Arm. 63/G4
Gyzylarbat, Trkm. 63/L5
Gżira, Malta 46/L7

H

Hå, Nor. 38/A2
Ha Giang, Viet. 83/H3
Ha Noi (Hanoi) (cap.), Viet. 83/J3
Haacht, Belg. 53/D2
Haag, Aus. 55/H6
Haag am Hausruck, Aus. 55/G6
Haag an der Amper, Ger. 55/E6
Haag in Oberbayern, Ger. 55/F6
Haaksbergen, Neth. 50/D4
Haaltert, Belg. 52/D2
Haamstede, Neth. 50/A5
Haan, Ger. 50/E6
Ha'apai Group (isl.), Tonga 117/H7
Haapavesi, Fin. 60/E2
Haapsalu, Est. 39/K2
Haar, Ger. 55/E6
Haardt (mts.), Ger. 43/G2
Haarlem, Neth. 50/B4
Haast, NZ 117/R11
Haasts Bluff Abor. Land, Austl. 113/F2
Hab (riv.), Pak. 89/J3
Habahe, China 70/E2
Habartov, Czh. 55/F2
Habbānīyah, Iraq 90/E3
Habicht (peak), Aus. 57/H3
Habiganj, Bang. 85/H3
Habikino, Japan 77/J6
Habomai (isls.), Rus. 76/D2
HaBonim, Isr. 91/F6
Haboro, Japan 76/B1
Hābra, India 85/G4
Habsheim, Fr. 56/D2
Hacha (falls), Ven. 153/F3
Hache (riv.), Ger. 51/F3
Hachenburg, Ger. 53/G2
Hachijō, Japan 75/F4
Hachikai, Japan 71/L5
Hachimori, Japan 76/B3
Hachinohe, Japan 76/B3
Hachiōji, Japan 75/F3
Hacıbektaş, Turk. 90/C2
Hacienda Heights, Ca, US 136/G8
Hacılar, Turk. 90/C2
Hack (mt.), Austl. 113/H4
Hackensack, NJ, US 139/J8
Hackensack (riv.), NJ, US 139/J9
Hackettstown, NJ, US 138/D2
Hackney (bor.), Eng, UK 30/C2
Ḩadabat al Jilf al Kabīr (plat.), Egypt 101/A4
Hadāli, Pak. 86/B3
Hadamar, Ger. 54/B2
Hadano, Japan 75/F3
Hadarba (cape), Sudan 101/D4
Ḩadd, Ra's al (pt.), Oman 89/G4
Haddenham, Eng, UK 33/F3
Haddington, Sc, UK 36/D5
Haddonfield, NJ, US 138/C4
Hadejia (riv.), Nga. 93/C3
Hadelner (canal), Ger. 51/F1
Ḩadera, Isr. 91/F7
Haderslev, Den. 38/C4
Hadhramaut (reg.), Yem. 88/E6
Hadım, Turk. 91/C1
Hadjout, Alg. 100/G4
Hadleigh, Eng, UK 30/E2
Hadley (bay), Nun., Can. 122/F1
Hadlow, Eng, UK 30/E3
Hadrian's Wall, Eng, UK 35/F1
Hadselfjorden (inlet), Nor. 37/E1
Hadsten, Den. 38/D3
Hadsund, Den. 38/D3
Haeju (bay), NKor. 73/C4
Haeju, NKor. 73/C3
Haena (pt.), Hi, US 124/S9
Haenam, SKor. 73/D5
Hafik, Turk. 90/D2
Ḩāfizābād, Pak. 86/B3
Hāflong, India 83/F2
Hafnarfjördhur, Ice. 37/N7
Hafnarhreppur, Ice. 37/M7
Haft Gel, Iran 88/E2
Hafun (pt.), Som. 97/R5
Hagåtña (cap.), Guam 116/D3
Hagelstadt, Ger. 55/F5
Hagemeister (isl.), Ak, US 134/F4
Hagen, Ger. 51/E6
Hagen am Teutoburger Wald, Ger. 51/E4
Hagen im Bremischen, Ger. 51/F2
Hagenow, Ger. 38/D5
Hagerman, NM, US 132/B3
Hagerstown, Md, US 130/E4
Hagetmau, Fr. 42/C5
Hagfors, Swe. 38/E1
Hagi, Japan 74/B3
Hagnau am Bodensee, Ger. 57/F2
Hags (pt.), Ire. 31/P10
Hague, Sk, Can. 127/G2
Hague, Cap de la (cape), Fr. 42/C2
Haguenau, Fr. 53/G6
Hahashima (isls.), Japan 116/D2
Hahaya (int'l arpt.), Com. 107/G5
Hahle (riv.), Ger. 51/H5
Hahndorf, Austl. 113/M9
Hahnenbach (riv.), Ger. 53/G4
Hahnstätten, Ger. 54/B2
Hahnville, La, US 137/P17
Ḩahrā Awbārī (des.), Libya 96/H2
Hai (riv.), China 72/D3
Hai Duong, Viet. 78/D1
Hai Phong, Viet. 83/J3
Hai Van (pass), Viet. 78/E2
Hai'an, China 72/E4
Haibach, Ger. 54/C3
Haibara, Japan 77/J6
Haicheng, China 73/B2
Haidenaab (riv.), Ger. 55/E3
Haidershofen, Aus. 55/H6
Haifa (dist.), Isr. 91/D3
Haifeng, China 79/C3
Haiger, Ger. 43/H1
Haigerloch, Ger. 54/B6
Haikou (int'l arpt.), China 79/B3
Haikou, China 83/K3
Haiku-Pauwela, Hi, US 124/T10
Ḩā'il, SAr. 88/D3
Hailākāndi, India 83/F3
Hailar (riv.), China 71/M2
Haileybury, On, Can. 130/E2
Hailsham, Eng, UK 33/G5
Hailun, China 71/N2
Haimen, China 72/E5
Haimhausen, Ger. 55/E6
Haiming, Aus. 57/G3
Haiming, Ger. 55/F6
Hainan, Ger. 51/F6
Hainan (prov.), China 70/J8
Hainan (str.), China 83/K3
Hainan (isl.), China 67/L8
Hainaut (prov.), Belg. 52/B2
Hainburg, Ger. 54/C1
Haines, Ak, US 134/L3
Haines City, Fl, US 133/H4
Haines Junction, Yk, Can. 134/L3
Hainesville, NJ, US 138/D1
Hainesville, Il, US 135/P15
Hainich (mts.), Ger. 40/F3
Haining, China 72/L9
Haiti (ctry.) 145/H2
Haixia (str.), China 71/K7
Haixing, China 72/D3
Haiyan, China 79/B3
Haiyan, China 70/H4
Haiyang (isl.), China 73/B3
Haiyang, China 72/E3
Haiyuan, China 70/J4
Haizhou (bay), China 72/D4
Háj (peak), Czh. 55/F2
Hajdú-Bihár (co.), Hun. 40/E7
Hajdúboszormény, Hun. 41/L5
Hajdúdorog, Hun. 41/L5
Hajdúhadház, Hun. 48/E2
Hajdúnánás, Hun. 41/L5
Hajdúszoboszló, Hun. 41/L5
Hajiki-zaki (pt.), Japan 75/F1
Hājīpur, India 85/E3
Ḩajjah, Yem. 88/D5
Hajnówka, Pol. 41/M2
Hājo, India 85/H2
Hajós, Hun. 48/D2
Haka, Myan. 83/F3
Hakee (mt.), Austl. 113/G3
Hakkari (prov.), Turk. 90/E2
Hakken-san (peak), Japan 74/D3
Hakkōda-san (peak), Japan 76/B3
Hakodate, Japan 76/B3
Hakone, Japan 77/C3
Hakone-yama (peak), Japan 77/C3
Haku-san (peak), Japan 75/E2
Hakui, Japan 75/E2
Hakusan, Japan 77/K6
Hakusan NP, Japan 75/E2
Hakushū, Japan 77/A2
Hāla, Pak. 89/J3
Ḩalab (prov.), Syria 90/D2
Ḩalab (Aleppo), Syria 91/E1
Ḩalabjah, Iraq 88/E1
Halachó, Mex. 143/M6
Halawa, Hi, US 124/T10
Halcon (mt.), Phil. 81/F1
Halden, Nor. 38/D2
Haldensleben, Ger. 40/F2
Haldenwang, Ger. 57/G2
Haldīa, India 85/G4
Haldībāri, India 85/G2
Haldimand, On, Can. 131/Q10
Haldimand-Norfolk (co.), On, Can. 131/Q10
Hale (riv.), Austl. 113/G3
Hale (mt.), Austl. 112/C3
Hale, Eng, UK 35/F5
Haleakala NP, Hi, US 124/T10
Haledon, NJ, US 139/J8
Haleiwa, Hi, US 124/V12
Halen, Belg. 53/E2
Hales Corners, Wi, US 135/P14
Halesowen, Eng, UK 32/D2
Haleyville, Al, US 133/G3
Half Assini, Gha. 102/E5
Half Falls (mtn.), Pa, US 138/A3
Half Moon Bay, Ca, US 135/K12
Half Tide Beach, Austl. 114/C3
Halfing, Ger. 55/F7
Halfweg, Neth. 50/B4
Ḩalḩūl, WBnk. 91/D4
Haliburton Highlands (uplands), On, Can. 130/E2
Halifax (cap.), NS, Can. 131/J2
Halifax (int'l arpt.), NS, Can. 131/J2
Halifax (bay), Austl. 109/D2
Halifax, Austl. 114/B2
Halifax, Pa, US 138/B3
Halifax, Eng, UK 35/G4
Halikko, Fin. 39/K1
Halīl (riv.), Iran 89/G3
Haliun, Mong. 70/G2
Halkett (cape), Ak, US 134/H1
Hall, Austl. 115/C2
Hall (isl.), Ak, US 134/D3
Hall (isls.), Micr. 116/E4
Hall (pen.), Nun., Can. 123/K2
Hall Beach, Nun., Can. 123/H2
Hall Park, Ok, US 137/N15
Halladale (riv.), Sc, UK 31/S7
Hallam (Hellam), Pa, US 138/B4
Halland (co.), Swe. 37/E4
Hällbybrunn, Swe. 38/G2
Halle, Ger. 51/F4
Halle, Ger. 41/G3
Halle, Belg. 53/D2
Halle-Neustadt, Ger. 40/F3
Hällefors, Swe. 38/F2
Hälleforsnäs, Swe. 38/G2
Hallein, Aus. 43/K3
Hallenberg, Ger. 51/F6
Hallertau (reg.), Ger. 55/E5
Hallettsville, Tx, US 129/H5
Halley, UK, Ant. 160/Y
Hallingdalselvi (riv.), Nor. 38/C1
Hallock, Mn, US 127/J3
Hallsberg, Swe. 38/F2
Hallstahammar, Swe. 38/G2
Hallstavik, Swe. 38/H1
Hallu (riv.), Fr. 40/B4
Halluin, Fr. 52/C2
Hallwang, Aus. 55/G7
Hallwilersee (lake), Swi. 56/E3
Hallyŏ Haesang NP, SKor. 74/A3
Halmahera (sea), Indo. 81/G4
Halmahera (isl.), Indo. 67/M9
Halmstad, Swe. 38/E3
Ḩalq al Wādī, Tun. 46/B4
Hals, Den. 38/D3
Hälsingborg (Helsingborg), Swe. 38/E3
Halsteren, Neth. 50/B5
Haltern, Ger. 51/E5
Halton (co.), On, Can. 131/Q8
Halton (co.), Eng, UK 35/F5
Halton Hills, On, Can. 131/Q8
Halver, Ger. 51/E6
Halverder Aa (riv.), Ger. 51/E4
Ham, Fr. 52/C4
Ham, Oued el (riv.), Alg. 100/G5
Ham-sous-Varsberg, Fr. 53/F5
Hamada, Japan 74/C3
Hamada de Tinrhert (plat.), Alg. 99/G4
Hamada du Drâa (plat.), Alg. 96/D2
Hamada du Tinrhert (plat.), Arg. 96/G2
Hamada Safia (plat.), Mali 98/D5
Hamadān, Iran 88/E2
Hamādat Marzūq (plat.), Libya 99/H4
Hamadat Tinghert (uplands),Libya 96/H2
Ḩamādat Tinghert (uplands),Libya 99/H3
Ḩamāh (prov.), Syria 91/E2
Hamajima, Japan 77/L7
Hamakita, Japan 75/E3
Hamam, Turk. 91/E1
Hamamatsu, Japan 75/E3
Hamami (reg.), Mrta. 98/C5
Hamanaka, Japan 76/D2
Hamar, Nor. 38/D1
Ḩamāṭah (peak), Egypt 101/C3
Hamath Tiberias NP, Isr. 91/D3
Hamatombetsu, Japan 76/C1
Hambantota, SrL. 82/D6
Hambergen, Ger. 51/F2
Hambleton (hills), Eng, UK 35/G3
Hambühren, Ger. 51/G3
Hamburg, NY, US 130/E3
Hamburg, Ger. 51/G1
Hamburg, NJ, US 138/D1
Hamburg, Pa, US 138/C2
Hamburg (state), Ger. 38/D5
Hamburg (Fuhlsbüttel) (int'l arpt.), Ger. 51/G1
Häme (prov.), Fin. 37/G3
Hämeenkyrö, Fin. 39/K1
Hämeenlinna, Fin. 39/L1
Hamel, Il, US 137/H8
Hamelin Pool (bay), Austl. 112/B3
Hameln, Ger. 51/G4
Hamersley (range), Austl. 109/A3
Hamersley Range NP, Austl. 112/C2
Hamford Water (inlet), Eng, UK 33/H3
Hamgyŏng-bukto (prov.), NKor. 73/E2
Hamgyŏng-namdo (prov.), NKor. 73/D2
Ḩamh, Syria 90/D3
Hamhŭng, NKor. 73/D3
Hamhŭng-si (prov.), NKor. 73/D3
Hami, China 70/F3
Hamilton, Austl. 115/B3
Hamilton, Mt, US 126/E4
Hamilton, Tx, US 129/H5
Hamilton, Al, US 133/G3
Hamilton (har.), On, Can. 131/Q9
Hamilton, NZ 117/T10
Hamilton, On, Can. 131/Q9
Hamilton (inlet), Nf, Can. 123/L3
Hamilton (mt.), Ca, US 135/L12
Hamilton, Sc, UK 36/B5
Hamilton Mil. Res., NY, US 139/J9
Hamilton-Wentworth (co.), On, Can. 131/Q9
Hamina, Fin. 39/M1
Hamīrpur, India 84/C3
Hamīrpur, India 86/D4
Hamlin, Tx, US 129/G4
Hamm, Ger. 51/E5
Hamm, Ger. 54/B3
Hamm, Ger. 53/G2
Hamma-Bouziane, Alg. 100/K6
Ḩammām Al Anf, Tun. 46/B4
Ḩammāmāt (gulf), Gabon 99/H1
Hammarland, Fin. 39/H1
Hammarön (isl.), Swe. 38/E2
Hammarstrand, Swe. 37/F3
Hamme (riv.), Ger. 51/F2
Hamme, Belg. 53/D1
Hammel, Den. 38/C3
Hammelburg, Ger. 54/C2
Hammerfest, Nor. 37/G1
Hammershus, Den. 38/F4
Hammersmith and Fulham (bor.), Eng, UK 30/A1
Hamminkeln, Ger. 50/D5
Hammonasset (pt.), Ct, US 139/F1
Hammond, In, US 130/C3
Hammond, La, US 133/F4
Hammonton, NJ, US 138/D4
Hamnvik, Nor. 37/F1
Hamois, Belg. 53/E3
Hamont-Achel, Belg. 50/C6
Hampshire Downs (hills), Eng, UK 33/E4
Hampstead, Md, US 138/B4
Hampton, Pa, US 138/A4
Hampton Bays, NY, US 139/F2
Hampton Court, Eng, UK 30/C2
Hampton Nat'l Hist. Site, Md, US 138/B5
Hamp'yŏng, SKor. 73/D5
Hamtramck, Mi, US 135/F7
Hamura, Japan 77/C2
Hamyang, SKor. 73/D5
Hamyŏl, SKor. 73/D4
Han (riv.), China 67/M6
Hana (riv.), India 84/C5
Hana, Hi, US 124/U10
Hanak, Turk. 90/E1
Hanamaki, Japan 76/B4
Hanamalo (pt.), Hi, US 124/U11
Hanang (peak), Tanz. 104/B4
Hanau, Ger. 54/B2
Hanazono, Japan 77/C1
Hancocks Bridge, NJ, US 138/C5
Handa, Japan 77/L6
Handawor, India 86/C2
Handeloh, Ger. 51/G2
Handīa, India 84/D3
Hanford, Ca, US 128/C3
Hanford Reach Nat'l Mon., Wa, US 126/D4
Hangayn (mts.), Mong. 70/G2
Hangingstone (hill), Eng, UK 32/C5
Hangklip (cape), SAfr. 106/L11
Hangu, Pak. 86/A3
Hangzhou (bay), China 72/L9
Hanhofen, Ger. 54/B4
Hanhöhiy (mts.), Mong. 70/F2
Hani, Turk. 90/E2
Haninge, Swe. 38/H2
Hankensbüttel, Ger. 51/H3
Hankey, SAfr. 106/D4
Hankinson, ND, US 127/J4
Hanko (Hangö), Fin. 39/K2
Hanley, Sk, Can. 127/G3
Hanna, Ab, Can. 126/F3
Hannan, Japan 77/H7
Hanningfield (res.), Eng, UK 30/E2
Hannō, Japan 77/C2
Hannover (int'l arpt.), Ger. 51/G4
Hannover, Ger. 51/G4
Hannut, Belg. 53/E2
Hanöbukten (bay), Swe. 37/E5
Hanover, NH, US 131/F3
Hanover, On, Can. 130/D2
Hanover, SAfr. 106/D3
Hanover, Pa, US 138/B4
Hanover (isl.), Chile 159/B6
Hanover Park, Il, US 135/P16
Hansen (dam), Ca, US 136/F7
Hanshan, China 72/D5
Hanshou, China 79/B2
Hānsi, India 86/C5
Hanstedt, Ger. 51/H2
Hanstholm, Den. 38/C3
Hansville, Wa, US 135/B2
Hantzsch (riv.), Nun., Can. 123/J2
Hanumāngarh, India 86/C5
Hanwood, Austl. 115/C2
Hanyū, Japan 77/D1
Hanyuan, China 83/H2
Hanzhong, China 70/J5
Hao (isl.), FrPol. 117/L6
Haparanda, Swe. 60/E2
Hapch'ŏn, SKor. 73/E5
Happy Valley (res.), Austl. 113/M9
Happy Valley-Goose Bay, Nf, Can. 123/K3
Haptŏk, SKor. 73/D4
Hāpur, India 84/A1
Haquira, Peru 156/C4
Har-Ayrag, Mong. 71/J2
Har Karmel (Mount Carmel) (peak), Isr. 91/G6
Har Meron (peak), Isr. 91/D3
Har Ramon (peak), Isr. 91/D4

192
Hara – Highl

Hara, Japan 77/A2
Harahan, La, US 137/P17
Haramachi, Japan 75/G2
Harappa (ruin), Pak. 86/B4
Harare (cap.), Zim. 105/F4
Ḩarash, Bi'r al (well), Libya 97/K2
Haravilliers, Fr. 30/J4
Harbel, Libr. 102/C5
Harbeson, De, US 138/C6
Harbin, China 71/N2
Harbiye, Turk. 91/E1
Harbonnières, Fr. 52/B4
Harbour Breton, Nf, Can. 131/L2
Harbour Grace, Nf, Can. 131/L2
Hårby, Den. 38/D4
Hard, Aus. 57/F3
Hardā, India 89/L4
Hardangervidda NP, Nor. 38/B1
Hardau (riv.), Ger. 51/H3
Hardegsen, Ger. 51/G5
Hardenberg, Neth. 50/D3
Harderwijk, Neth. 50/C4
Hardheim, Ger. 54/C3
Hardin, Mt, US 126/G4
Harding, SAfr. 107/E3
Hardoi, India 84/C2
Hardoi Branch (riv.), India 84/C2
Hardricourt, Fr. 30/H4
Hardy (pen.), Chile 159/C7
Hare (bay), Nf, Can. 131/L1
Hare Dimona (peak), Isr. 91/D4
Harefield, Eng, UK 30/B2
Harelbeke, Belg. 52/C2
Haren, Ger. 51/E3
Haren, Neth. 50/D2
Hārer, Eth. 97/P6
Harford (co.), Md, US 138/B4
Hargesheim, Ger. 53/G4
Hargeville, Fr. 30/H5
Hargeysa, Som. 97/P6
Harghita (prov.), Rom. 49/G2
Harghita (peak), Rom. 49/G2
Hari (riv.), Indo. 80/B4
Hari (str.), Est. 39/K2
Harihar, India 89/L6
Ḩārim, Syria 91/E1
Harima (sea), Japan 74/D3
Ḩarīmā, Jor. 91/D3
Harima, Japan 77/G6
Harima (bay), Japan 77/G6
Haringey (bor.), Eng, UK 30/C2
Haringhāta (riv.), Bang. 85/G4
Haringvliet (chan.), Neth. 50/B5
Haringvlietdam (dam), Neth. 50/B5
Harīpur, Pak. 86/B3
Harīrūd (riv.), Afg. 67/F6
Ḩāris, WBnk. 91/G7
Harjavalta, Fin. 39/K1
Harlan, Ky, US 130/D4
Harlech, Wal, UK 34/D6
Harlingen, Tx, US 132/D5
Harlingen, Neth. 50/C2
Harlow, Eng, UK 30/D1
Harlowton, Mt, US 126/F4
Harmannsdorf, Aus. 49/N7
Harmelen, Neth. 50/B4
Harnes, Fr. 52/B3
Harney (basin), Or, US 128/C2
Harney (lake), Or, US 126/D5
Harney (peak), SD, US 127/H5
Harney (valley), Or, US 126/D5
Harney, Md, US 138/A4
Harnoli, Pak. 86/A3
Haro (cape), Mex. 142/C3
Haro, Sp. 44/D1
Harold, Ca, US 136/B1
Harpenden, Eng, UK 33/F3
Harper (mt.), Yk, Can. 134/L3
Harper (mt.), Ak, US 134/K3
Harper, Ks, US 129/H3
Harper, Libr. 102/D5
Harper, Wa, US 135/B2
Harper Woods, Mi, US 135/F7
Harpstedt, Ger. 51/F3
Harqin Zuoyi Monggolzu Zizhixian, China 72/D2
Harrah, Ok, US 137/N15
Harrai, India 84/B4
Harran, Turk. 90/D2
Harricana (riv.), Qu, Can. 123/J4
Harriman, Tn, US 130/C5
Harriman, NY, US 138/D1
Harrington, Austl. 115/E1
Harrington, De, US 138/C6
Harrington Park, NJ, US 139/K8
Harris (mt.), Austl. 113/F3
Harris (lake), Austl. 113/G4
Harris (isl.), Sc, UK 31/Q8
Harris Park, Co, US 137/B4
Harrisburg, Ne, US 127/H5
Harrisburg, Il, US 130/B4
Harrisburg (cap.), Pa, US 138/B3
Harrislee, Ger. 38/C4
Harrismith, SAfr. 106/E3
Harrison (bay), Ak, US 134/H1
Harrison, Ar, US 129/J3
Harrison, Mi, US 130/C2
Harrison, NY, US 139/L8
Harrison, NJ, US 139/J9
Harrison (cape), Nf, Can. 123/L3
Harrison (lake), BC, Can. 126/C3
Harrisonville, Il, US 137/G9
Harrisonville, Mo, US 137/E6
Harrisville, Ut, US 137/K11
Harrodsburg, Ky, US 130/C4
Harrogate, Eng, UK 35/G4
Harrow (bor.), Eng, UK 30/B2
Harry S Truman (res.), Mo, US 129/J3
Harsefeld, Ger. 51/G2
Harsewinkel, Ger. 51/F5
Harson's Island, Mi, US 135/G6
Hart (lake), Or, US 128/C2
Hart, Mi, US 130/C3
Hart (riv.), Yk, Can. 122/C2
Hart (riv.), Eng, UK 30/A3
Hart (isl.), NY, US 139/K8
Hart Fell (peak), Sc, UK 36/C6
Hartbeesrivier (riv.), SAfr. 106/C3
Hårteigen (peak), Nor. 38/B1
Hartelkanaal (riv.), Neth. 50/B5
Hartford (cap.), Ct, US 131/F3
Hartford, Il, US 137/G8
Hartford, NJ, US 138/D4
Hartford City, In, US 130/C3
Hartheim, Ger. 56/D2
Hartington, Ne, US 129/H2
Hartkirchen, Aus. 55/H6
Hartland (pt.), Eng, UK 32/B4
Hartland, Mi, US 135/E6
Hartlepool, Eng, UK 35/G2
Hartlepool (co.), Eng, UK 35/G2
Hartleton, Pa, US 138/A2
Hartley Wintney, Eng, UK 30/A3
Hartly, De, US 138/C5
Hartney, Mb, Can. 127/H3
Hartsdale, NY, US 139/K7
Hartselle, Al, US 133/G3
Hartshill, Eng, UK 33/E1
Hartstene (isl.), Wa, US 135/B3
Hartwell, Ga, US 133/H3
Hartwell (lake), Ga,SC, US 133/H3
Hartz Mountain NP, Austl. 115/C4
Haruhi, Japan 77/L5
Harun (peak), Indo. 81/E3
Hārūnābād, Pak. 86/B5
Hārūt (riv.), Afg. 89/H2
Harvey, ND, US 127/J4
Harvey, La, US 137/P17
Harvey, Austl. 112/B5
Harvey, Il, US 135/Q16
Harveys (lake), Pa, US 138/B1
Harwich, Eng, UK 33/H3
Haryana (state), India 82/C2
Harz (mts.), Ger. 40/F3
Hasan (peak), Turk. 90/C2
Hasan Abdāl, Pak. 86/B3
Hasanpur, India 84/B1
Hasbrouck Heights, NJ, US 139/J8
Hasdo (riv.), India 84/D4
Hase (riv.), Ger. 40/D2
Hasel (riv.), Ger. 54/D1
Haselünne, Ger. 51/E3
Hasenmatt (peak), Swi. 56/D3
Hashima, Japan 77/L5
Hashimoto, Japan 74/D3
Hasi el Farsía (well), WSah. 98/C4
Hāsilpur, Pak. 86/B5
Haskell, Tx, US 129/H4
Haslach an der Mühl, Aus. 55/H5
Haslach im Kinzigtal, Ger. 56/E1
Hasle bei Burgdorf, Swi. 56/D3
Haslemere, Eng, UK 33/F4
Haslingden, Eng, UK 35/F4
Hasloh, Ger. 51/G1
Haspres, Fr. 52/C3
Hassa, Turk. 91/E1
Hassan, India 82/C5
Hassan (El Aaiún) (int'l arpt.), WSah. 98/B4
Hassberge (hills), Ger. 54/D2
Hassel, Ger. 51/G3
Hassel Sound (str.), Nun., Can. 123/S7
Hasselt, Neth. 50/D3
Hasselt, Belg. 53/E2
Hassfurt, Ger. 54/D2
Hassi Bahbah, Alg. 100/G5
Hassi bou Zid (well), Alg. 99/F3
Hassi el Hadjar (well), Alg. 99/G3
Hassi el Mislane (well), Alg. 99/H4
Hassi er Rebib (well), Alg. 99/G2
Hässleholm, Swe. 38/E3
Hasslo (int'l arpt.), Swe. 38/G2
Hassloch, Ger. 54/B4
Haste, Ger. 51/G4
Hastings, Austl. 115/C3
Hastings, Ne, US 129/H2
Hastings, Mi, US 130/C3
Hastings, NZ 117/T10
Hastings, Eng, UK 33/G5
Hastings Battlesite, Eng, UK 33/G5
Hastings-On-Hudson, NY, US 139/K7
Hasuda, Japan 77/D2
Hasunuma, Japan 77/E2
Hasvik, Nor. 37/G1
Hat Chao Mai NP, Thai. 78/B5
Hat Head, Austl. 115/E1
Hat Head NP, Austl. 115/E1
Hat Nai Yang NP, Thai. 78/B5
Hat Yai, Thai. 78/C5
Hat Yai (int'l arpt.), Thai. 78/C5
Hatashō, Japan 77/K5
Hatavch, Mong. 71/K2
Hatay (prov.), Turk. 90/C2
Hatboro, Pa, US 138/C3
Hatch, NM, US 128/F4
Hatcher (peak), Arg. 159/B6
Haţeg, Rom. 48/F3
Hatfield, Pa, US 138/C3
Hatfield, Eng, UK 30/C1
Hatfield Peverel, Eng, UK 30/E1
Hatgal, Mong. 70/H1
Hāthras, India 84/B2
Hātia (riv.), Bang. 85/H4
Hātia, North (isl.), Bang. 85/H4
Hātia, South (isl.), Bang. 85/H4
Ḩaţībah, Ras (pt.), SAr. 88/C4
Hato (int'l arpt.), NAnt. 152/D1
Hato Corozal, Col. 152/D3
Hato Mayor, DRep. 141/H4
Hatogaya, Japan 77/D2
Hatoyama, Japan 77/C2
Hatsu (isl.), Japan 77/C3
Hatta, India 84/B3
Hatta, Japan 77/A2
Hattah-Kulkyne NP, Austl. 113/J5
Hattem, Neth. 50/D4
Hatten, Ger. 51/F2
Hatten, Fr. 53/G6
Hatteras, NC, US 133/K3
Hatteras (cape), NC, US 133/K3
Hattersheim am Mein, Ger. 54/B2
Hattiesburg, Ms, US 133/F4
Hattieville, Belz. 144/D2
Hattingen, Ger. 51/E6
Hattula, Fin. 39/L1
Hatvan, Hun. 48/D2
Hatzenbühl, Ger. 54/B4
Hatzfeld, Ger. 51/F6
Hau Giang (riv.), Viet. 78/D4
Haubourdin, Fr. 52/B2
Haud (reg.), Eth. 97/Q6
Hauge, Nor. 38/B2
Haugesund, Nor. 38/A2
Haukipudas, Fin. 60/E2
Haune (riv.), Ger. 40/E3
Haunsberg (peak), Aus. 55/F7
Hauppauge, NY, US 139/E2
Hauraki (gulf), NZ 117/S10
Haus, Nor. 38/A1
Hausach, Ger. 56/E1
Hausjärvi, Fin. 39/L1
Hausleiten, Aus. 49/N7
Hausstock (peak), Swi. 57/F4
Haut Atlas (mts.), Mor. 96/D1
Haut-Rhin (dept.), Fr. 56/D2
Haute-Normandie (pol. reg.), Fr. 42/D2
Haute-Saône (dept.), Fr. 56/B2
Haute-Savoie (dept.), Fr. 56/C5
Hautefeuille, Fr. 30/L5
Hautes Fagnes (uplands), Belg. 53/E3
Hauteurs de Gâtine (uplands), Fr. 42/C3
Hauteville-Lompnes, Fr. 56/B6
Hautmont, Fr. 52/C3
Hauts (plat.), Alg.,Mor. 99/E2
Hauula, Hi, US 124/W12
Havant, Eng, UK 33/F5
Havasu (lake), Az,Ca, US 128/D4
Havdhem, Swe. 38/H3
Havel (canal), Ger. 40/P6
Havel (riv.), Ger. 41/G2
Havelange, Belg. 53/E3
Haveli, Pak. 86/B4
Haveliān, Pak. 86/B2
Havelländischer Grosser Hauptkanal (canal), Ger. 40/P6
Havelock, NC, US 133/J3
Havelte, Neth. 50/D3
Havencore (isl.), Eng, UK 33/G3
Haverfordwest, Wal, UK 32/B3
Haverhill, Ma, US 131/G3
Haverhill, Eng, UK 33/G2
Havering (bor.), Eng, UK 30/D2
Havířov, Czh. 41/K4
Havixbeck, Ger. 51/E5
Havlíčkuv Brod, Czh. 41/H4
Havneby, Den. 38/C4
Havre, Mt, US 126/F3
Havre de Grace, Md, US 138/B4
Havre-Saint-Pierre, Qu, Can. 131/J1
Havsa, Turk. 47/K2
Havza, Turk. 90/C1
Haw (riv.), NC, US 133/J3
Hawaii (state), US 124/S10
Hawaii (isl.), Hi, US 124/U11
Hawaiian (isls.), Hi, US 117/H2
Hawaii Kai, Hi, US 124/W13
Hawaii Volcanoes NP, Hi, US 124/U11
Hawaiian Gardens, Ca, US 136/F8
Ḩawallī, Kuw. 88/E3
Hawarden, Wal, UK 35/E5
Hawera, NZ 117/S10
Haweswater (res.), Eng/UK 35/F2
Hawi, Hi, US 124/U10
Hawick, Sc, UK 36/D6
Hawke (cape), Austl. 115/E2
Hawke (bay), NZ 109/H6
Hawker, Austl. 113/H4
Hawkesbury (isl.), BC, Can. 126/A2
Hawkesbury, On, Can. 130/F2
Hawkesbury (riv.), Austl. 114/G8
Hawks Nest, Austl. 115/E2
Haworth, NJ, US 139/K8
Ḩawsh 'Īsá, Egypt 91/B4
Hawston, SAfr. 106/L11
Hawthorn Woods, Il, US 135/P15
Hawthorne, Nv, US 128/C3
Hawthorne, Ca, US 136/F8
Hawthorne, NJ, US 139/J8
Hawthorne, NY, US 139/K8
Ḩawwārah, Jor. 91/D3
Haxby, Eng, UK 35/G3
Hay, Austl. 115/C2
Hay (pt.), Austl. 114/C3
Hay (riv.), Ab,BC, Can. 122/E3
Hay River, NW, Can. 122/E2
Hayachine-san (peak), Japan 76/B4
Hayakawa, Japan 77/A3
Hayama, Japan 77/D3
Hayange, Fr. 53/F5
Haybes, Fr. 53/D4
Haycock, Ak, US 134/F2
Haydock, Eng, UK 35/F5
Hayes (mt.), Ak, US 134/J3
Hayes (pen.), Grld. 123/T7
Hayes (riv.), Mb, Can. 122/G3
Hayingen, Ger. 57/F1
Haylaastay, Mong. 71/K2
Hayle (riv.), Eng, UK 32/A6
Hayling (isl.), Eng, UK 33/F5
Haymana, Turk. 90/C2
Haynesville, La, US 129/J4
Hayrabolu, Turk. 49/H5
Hays, Ks, US 129/H3
Hays (co.), Tx, US 137/U20
Haysyn, Ukr. 62/D2
Hayward, Wi, US 127/L4
Hazār (mtn.), Iran 89/G3
Hazard, Ky, US 130/D4
Hazāribag, India 85/E4
Hazebrouck, Fr. 52/B2
Hazel Park, Mi, US 135/F7
Hazelwood, Mo, US 137/G8
Hazen (bay), Ak, US 134/E3
Hazen (str.), NW,Nun., Can. 123/R7
Hazlehurst, Ms, US 129/K5
Hazlemere, Eng, UK 30/A2
Hazlet, NJ, US 139/J10
Hazleton (mts.), BC, Can. 126/A2
Hazleton, Pa, US 138/C2
Hazlett (lake), Austl. 113/F2
Hazratbal Mosque, India 86/C2
Hazro, Pak. 86/B3
Hazu, Japan 77/M6
He (riv.), China 79/B3
He Xian, China 72/D5
Headcorn, Eng, UK 33/G4
Heads of Ayr (pt.), Sc, UK 36/B6
Healdsburg, Ca, US 128/B3
Healesville, Austl. 115/G5
Healy, Ak, US 134/J3
Heanor, Eng, UK 35/G6
Heard (isl.), Austl. 160/E
Hearst, On, Can. 130/D1
Heart (riv.), ND, US 127/H4
Heart Law (hill), Sc, UK 36/D5
Heath (pt.), Qu, Can. 131/J1
Heathcote, Austl. 115/C3
Heathcote NP, Austl. 114/G9
Heathrow (int'l arpt.), Eng, UK 30/B2
Hebbronville, Tx, US 132/D5
Hebei (prov.), China 71/K4
Hebertshausen, Ger. 55/E6
Hebrides (isls.), UK 27/D3
Hebrides (sea), Sc, UK 31/Q8
Hebron, Ne, US 129/H2
Hebron, Il, US 135/P15
Heby, Swe. 38/G2
Hecate (str.), BC, Can. 122/C3
Hecelchakán, Mex. 144/D1
Hechi, China 83/J3
Hechingen, Ger. 54/B6
Hechtel, Belg. 53/E1
Hechthausen, Ger. 51/G1
Hecker, Il, US 137/H9
Hecla, SD, US 127/J4
Hecla and Griper (bay), NW,Nun., Can. 123/R7
Hector (mt.), Ab, Can. 126/D3
Heddal, Nor. 38/C2
Hedel, Neth. 50/C5
Hedemora, Swe. 38/F1
Hedensted, Den. 38/C4
Hedmark (co.), Nor. 37/D3
Hedo-misaki (cape), Japan 75/K7
Hédouville, Fr. 30/J4
Heede, Ger. 51/E3
Heeia, Hi, US 124/W13
Heek, Ger. 51/E4
Heemskerk, Neth. 50/B3
Heemstede, Neth. 50/B4
Heerde, Neth. 50/D4
Heerenveen, Neth. 50/C3
Heerhugowaard, Neth. 50/B3
Heerlen, Neth. 53/E2
Heers, Belg. 53/E2
Heesch, Neth. 50/C5
Heeslingen, Ger. 51/G2
Heeze, Neth. 50/C6
Ḩefa (Haifa), Isr. 91/F6
Hefei, China 72/D5
Hefeng Tujiazu Zizhixian, China 79/B2
Hefner (lake), Ok, US 137/M14
Hegang, China 71/P2
Hegau (mts.), Ger. 43/H3
Hegau (reg.), Ger. 40/E5
Heggenes, Nor. 38/C1
Hegins, Pa, US 138/B2
Heguri, Japan 77/J6
Hei (riv.), Japan 76/B4
Heide, Ger. 38/C4
Heideck, Ger. 54/E4
Heidelberg, Ms, US 133/F4
Heidelberg, SAfr. 106/C4
Heidelberg, SAfr. 106/E2
Heidelberg, Ger. 54/B4
Heiden, Ger. 50/D5
Heiden, Swi. 57/F3
Heidenheim, Ger. 54/D4
Heidenheim, Ger. 54/D5
Heidenreichstein, Aus. 41/H4
Heiderscheid, Lux. 53/E4
Heigenbrücken, Ger. 54/C2
Heihe, China 71/N1
Heikendorf, Ger. 38/D4
Heilbron, SAfr. 106/D2
Heilbronn, Ger. 54/C4
Heilbronn, Ger. 54/D4
Heiligenberg, Ger. 57/F2
Heiligenblut, Aus. 43/K3
Heiligenhafen, Ger. 38/D4
Heiligenhaus, Ger. 50/D6
Heiligenstadt, Ger. 51/H6
Heilong (Amur) (riv.), China, Rus 65/N5
Heilongjiang (prov.), China 71/N2
Heiloo, Neth. 50/B3
Heimaey (isl.), Ice. 37/N7
Heimbach, Ger. 53/F2
Heimberg, Swi. 56/D4
Heimsheim, Ger. 54/B5
Heino, Neth. 50/D4
Heinola, Fin. 39/M1
Heinsberg, Ger. 53/F1
Heishan, China 73/B2
Heist-op-den-Berg, Belg. 53/D1
Heitersheim, Ger. 56/D2
Heiwa, Japan 77/L5
Hejian, China 72/D3
Hejin, China 72/B4
Hejing, China 70/E3
Hekimhan, Turk. 90/D2
Hekinan, Japan 77/L6
Hekla (vol.), Ice. 37/N7
Hekou, China 83/H3
Hel, Pol. 39/H4
Helan (mts.), China 70/J4
Helbe (riv.), Ger. 51/H6
Helden, Neth. 50/D6
Helena (cap.), Mt, US 126/E4
Helena (riv.), Austl. 112/L6
Helensburgh, Sc, UK 36/B4
Helgasjön (lake), Swe. 38/F3
Helgoland (isl.), Ger. 38/B4
Helgoländer (bay), Wa, US 135/B3
Helgoländer (bay), Ger. 38/C5
Heliodora, Braz. 211/H7
Heliport (int'l arpt.), Swe. 38/E3
Hellas (see Greece) 27/G5
Ḩelleh (riv.), Iran 88/F3
Hellendoorn, Neth. 50/D4
Hellenthal, Ger. 53/F3
Hellertown, Pa, US 138/C2
Hellevoetsluis, Neth. 50/B5
Hellín, Sp. 44/E3
Hells (canyon), Id, US 126/D4
Hells Canyon Nat'l Rec. Area, US 126/D4
Hell's Gate NP, Kenya 104/C3
Helmand (riv.), Afg. 67/F6
Helmbrechts, Ger. 55/E2
Helmet (mtn.), Ak, US 134/K2
Helmetta, NJ, US 139/H10
Helmond, Neth. 50/C6
Helmstadt, Ger. 54/C3
Helmstedt, Ger. 40/F2
Helong, China 71/N3
Helotes, Tx, US 137/T20
Helper, Ut, US 128/E3
Helsenhorn (peak), Swi. 56/E5
Helsingør, Den. 38/E3
Helsinki (Helsingfors) (cap.), Fin. 37/H3
Helsinki-Vantaa (int'l arpt.), Fin. 39/L1
Hem (riv.), Fr. 52/B2
Hemau, Ger. 55/E4
Hemel Hempstead, Eng, UK 30/B1
Hemer, Ger. 51/E6
Hemet, Ca, US 136/D3
Hemmingen, Ger. 51/G4
Hemmoor, Ger. 51/G1
Hemphill, Tx, US 132/E4
Hempstead, Tx, US 129/H5
Hempstead (har.), NY, US 139/L8
Hempstead, NY, US 139/L9
Hemse, Swe. 38/H3
Hemsedal, Nor. 38/C1
Hemsworth, Eng, UK 35/G4
Henan (prov.), China 71/K5
Henån, Swe. 38/D2
Henares (riv.), Sp. 44/D2
Henashi-zaki (pt.), Japan 76/A3
Hendaye, Fr. 42/C5
Hendek, Turk. 49/K5
Henderson, NC, US 130/E4
Henderson, Nv, US 128/D3
Henderson, Tn, US 130/B5
Henderson, Ky, US 130/C4
Henderson, Co, US 137/C3
Henderson (isl.), Pitc. 117/N7
Henderson, Arg. 158/E3
Henderson, Md, US 138/C5
Hendersonville, Tn, US 130/C4
Hendersonville, NC, US 133/H3
Hendrik-Ido-Ambacht, Neth. 50/B5
Hendrik Verwoerdam (res.), SAfr. 106/D3
Hendrina, SAfr. 107/E2
Henefer, Ut, US 137/L11
Heng (mtn.), China 72/C3
Heng (isl.), China 72/L8
Heng Xian, China 83/J3
Hengduan (mts.), China 70/G6
Hengelo, Neth. 50/D4
Hengersberg, Ger. 55/G5
Hengoed, Wal, UK 32/C3
Hengshan, China 79/B2
Hengshan, China 72/B3
Hengshui, China 72/C3
Hengyang, China 79/B2
Heniches'k, Ukr. 62/E3
Hénin-Beaumont, Fr. 52/B3
Henley-on-Thames, Eng, UK 33/F3
Henlopen (cape), De, US 138/C6
Henlopen Acres, De, US 138/C6
Henndorf am Wallersee, Aus. 55/G7
Henne, Den. 38/C4
Hennebont, Fr. 42/B3
Hennef, Ger. 53/G2
Hennenman, SAfr. 106/D2
Hennigsdorf, Ger. 40/Q6
Henrietta, Tx, US 129/H4
Henrietta Maria (cape), On, Can. 123/H3
Henry (cape), BC, Can. 134/M5
Henry (mts.), Ut, US 128/E3
Henry Ford Museum and Greenfield Village Historical Site, Mi, US 135/E7
Henryetta, Ok, US 129/J4
Henryville, Pa, US 138/C1
Hensies, Belg. 52/C3
Hentiy (prov.), Mong. 71/J2
Hentiyn (mts.), Mong. 70/J2
Henty, Austl. 115/C2
Henzada, Myan. 83/G4
Heping, China 79/B3
Heppenheim an der Bergstrasse, Ger. 54/B3
Hepu, China 83/J3
Heqing, China 83/H2
Hequ, China 72/B3
Heradhsvötn (riv.), Ice. 37/N6
Herāt, Afg. 89/H2
Herbert, Sk, Can. 126/G3
Herbert River (falls), Austl. 114/B2
Herbert River Falls NP, Austl. 114/B2
Herberton, Austl. 114/B2
Herbeumont, Belg. 53/E4
Herblay, Fr. 30/J5
Herbolzheim, Ger. 56/D1
Herbrechtingen, Ger. 54/D5
Herbstein, Ger. 54/C1
Hercegnovi, Serb. 47/F1
Hercílio Luz (int'l arpt.), Braz. 155/B3
Herculaneum, Mo, US 137/G9
Herculaneum (ruin), It. 46/D2
Hercules, Ca, US 135/K10
Herdecke, Ger. 51/E6
Herdorf, Ger. 53/G2
Heredia, CR 145/E4
Hereford, Eng, UK 32/D2
Hereford, Md, US 138/B4
Hereford (inlet), NJ, US 138/D5
Hereford, Pa, US 138/C3
Hereford, Tx, US 129/G4
Herefordshire (co.), Eng, UK 32/D2
Hereheretue (isl.), FrPol. 117/L7
Hereke, Turk. 49/J5
Herencia, Sp. 44/C3
Herentals, Belg. 50/B6
Herford, Ger. 51/F4
Hergiswil, Swi. 57/E4
Héricourt, Fr. 56/C2
Hérimoncourt, Fr. 56/C3
Herington, Ks, US 129/H3
Herisau, Swi. 57/F3
Herk (riv.), Belg. 53/E2
Herk-de-Stad, Belg. 53/E2
Hèrlèn Gol (Kerulen) (riv.), Mong. 71/K2
Herleshausen, Ger. 51/H6
Herma Ness (cape), Sc, UK 31/W13
Hermann, Mo, US 129/K3
Hermannsburg, Ger. 51/H3
Hermannsburg, Austl. 113/G2
Hermannsburg Abor. Land, Austl. 113/G2
Hermansverk, Nor. 38/B1
Hermanus, SAfr. 106/L11
Hermeray, Fr. 30/G6
Hermersberg, Ger. 53/G5
Hermes, Fr. 52/B5
Hermeskeil, Ger. 53/F4
Hermiston, Or, US 126/D4
Hermitage, Rus. 61/T7
Hermosa Beach, Ca, US 136/F8
Hermosillo, Mex. 142/C2
Hermsdorf, Ger. 40/Q6
Hernández, Mex. 142/E4
Hernando, Ms, US 129/K4
Hernani, Sp. 44/E1
Herndon, Pa, US 138/B2
Herne, Ger. 51/E5
Herne, Belg. 52/D2
Herne Bay, Eng, UK 33/H4
Herning, Den. 38/C3
Heroes de la Independencia, Mex. 142/B2
Heroica Caborca, Mex. 142/B2
Heroica Ciudad de Tlaxiaco, Mex. 144/B2
Heroica Matamoros, Mex. 132/D5
Heroica Nogales, Mex. 128/E5
Heroldsberg, Ger. 54/E3
Hérouville, Fr. 30/J4
Hérouville-Saint-Clair, Fr. 42/C2
Herøy, Nor. 37/C3
Herpf (riv.), Ger. 54/D1
Herre, Nor. 38/C2
Herrenberg, Ger. 54/B5
Herrera, Sp. 44/C4
Herrera de Pisuerga, Sp. 44/C1
Herrera del Duque, Sp. 44/C3
Herrero (pt.), Mex. 144/E2
Herrestad, Swe. 38/D2
Herrieden, Ger. 54/D4
Herriman, Ut, US 137/J12
Herrlisheim, Fr. 53/G6
Herrljunga, Swe. 38/E2
Herrsching am Ammersee, Ger. 57/H2
Hers (riv.), Fr. 42/D5
Hersbruck, Ger. 55/E3
Herschbach, Ger. 53/G2
Herscheid, Ger. 51/E6
Herselt, Belg. 53/D1
Hershey, Pa, US 138/B3
Hersheypark, Pa, US 138/B3
Herstal, Belg. 53/E2
Herten, Ger. 51/E5
Hertford, NC, US 133/J2
Hertford, Eng, UK 33/F3
Herval d'Oeste, Braz. 155/B3
Hervás, Sp. 44/C2
Herve, Belg. 53/E2
Hervey (bay), Austl. 109/E3
Hervey Bay, Austl. 114/D4
Hervey Bay (reef), Austl. 114/D3
Herxheim bei Landau, Ger. 54/B4
Herzberg am Harz, Ger. 51/H5
Herzebrock-Clarholz, Ger. 51/F5
Herzele, Belg. 52/C2
Herzliyya, Isr. 91/F7
Herzogenaurach, Ger. 54/D3
Herzogenbuchsee, Swi. 56/D3
Herzogenburg, Aus. 48/B1
Herzogenrath, Ger. 53/F2
Hesbaye (plat.), Belg. 40/C3
Hesdin, Fr. 52/B3
Hesel, Ger. 51/E2
Heshui, China 70/J4
Heshun, China 72/C3
Hésingue, Fr. 56/D2
Hesperange, Lux. 53/F4
Hesperia, Ca, US 136/C2
Hess (riv.), Yk, Can. 122/C2
Hessel (riv.), Ger. 51/F5
Hesselø (isl.), Den. 38/D3
Hessen (state), Ger. 43/H1
Hessen, Ger. 51/H4
Hessisch Lichtenau, Ger. 51/G6
Hessisch Oldendorf, Ger. 51/G4
Heṭauḍā, Nepal 85/E2
Heteren, Neth. 50/C5
Hettenleidelheim, Ger. 54/B3
Hettinger, ND, US 127/H4
Hetton-le-Hole, Eng, UK 35/G2
Hettstadt, Ger. 54/C3
Hetzerath, Ger. 53/F4
Heubach (riv.), Ger. 51/E5
Heubach, Ger. 54/C5
Heuchelheim, Ger. 54/B1
Heukuppe (peak), Aus. 41/H5
Heusden, Neth. 50/C5
Heusden-Zolder, Belg. 53/E1
Heusenstamm, Ger. 54/B2
Heusweiler, Ger. 53/F5
Hève, Cap de la (cape), Fr. 42/D2
Heves, Hun. 48/E2
Heves (co.), Hun. 41/L5
Hewitt, NJ, US 139/H7
Hewlett (pt.), NY, US 139/L8
Hewlett, NY, US 139/L9
Hex River (mts.), SAfr. 106/L10
Hex River (pass), SAfr. 106/L10
Hexenkopf (peak), Aus. 57/G3
Heyerode, Ger. 51/H6
Heythuysen, Neth. 50/C6
Heywood, Austl. 115/B3
Heywood, Eng, UK 35/F4
Heze, China 72/C4
Hialeah, Fl, US 133/H5
Hiawatha, Ks, US 129/J3
Hibbing, Mn, US 127/K4
Hibbs (pt.), Austl. 115/C4
Hicacos (pt.), Cuba 145/F1
Hichisō, Japan 77/M4
Hickman (mt.), BC, Can. 134/M4
Hickory, NC, US 133/H3
Hickory, La, US 137/Q16
Hickory Run State Park, Pa, US 138/C1
Hicksville, NY, US 139/L8
Hico, Tx, US 129/H5
Hida (riv.), Japan 75/E3
Hidaka (riv.), Japan 74/D4
Hidaka, Japan 76/C2
Hidaka (mts.), Japan 76/C2
Hidaka, Japan 77/C2
Hidalgo, Mex. 143/F3
Hidalgo (state), Mex. 140/B3
Hidalgo del Parral, Mex. 142/D3
Hidden Hills, Ca, US 136/B2
Hiddenhausen, Ger. 51/F4
Hidrolândia, Braz. 154/B2
Hierapolis (ruin), Turk. 90/B2
Hieroglyphic (mts.), Az, US 137/R18
Hierro (isl.) 96/B2
Hieve (lake), Ger. 51/E2
Higashi-Chichibu, Japan 77/C1
Higashi-Matsuyama, Japan 77/C1
Higashi-Ōsaka, Japan 77/J6
Higashikurume, Japan 77/D2
Higashimurayama, Japan 77/C2
Higashine, Japan 76/B4
Higashiura, Japan 77/G6
Higashiura, Japan 77/L6
Higashiyoshino, Japan 77/J7
High (des.), Or, US 126/C5
High (hill), Pa, US 138/C1
High (isl.), China 71/V10
High Bridge, NJ, US 138/D2
High Island, Tx, US 132/E4
High Level, Ab, Can. 122/E3
High Point, NC, US 133/H3
High Ridge, Mo, US 137/F9
High River, Ab, Can. 126/E3
High Street (peak), Eng, UK 35/F3
High Willhays (hill), Eng, UK 32/B5
High Wycombe, Eng, UK 33/F3
Higham, Eng, UK 30/E2
Higham Ferrers, Eng, UK 33/F2
Highland, Ca, US 136/C2
Highland, Ut, US 137/K13
Highland, In, US 135/R16
Highland (pol. reg.), Sc, US 36/A2
Highland Lakes, NJ, US 138/D1
Highland Park, Co, US 137/A4
Highland Park, Mi, US 135/F7

193
Highl – Humid

Highland Park, NJ, US 139/H10
Highlands, NJ, US 139/K10
Highrock (lake), Mb, Can. 127/H2
Highspire, Pa, US 138/B3
Hightstown, NJ, US 138/D3
Highwood, Il, US 135/Q15
Higley, Az, US 137/S19
Higuera de Zaragoza, Mex. 142/C3
Hihyā, Egypt 91/B4
Hiidenportin NP, Fin. 60/F3
Hiiumaa (isl.), Est. 60/D4
Híjar, Sp. 45/E2
Hijāz, Jabal al (mts.), SAr. 88/C3
Hiji, Japan 74/B4
Hijuelas de Conchali, Chile 158/N8
Hikami, Japan 77/H5
Hikari, Japan 77/F2
Hikone, Japan 77/K5
Hikueru (isl.), FrPol. 117/L6
Hikurangi (peak), NZ 117/T10
Hildburghausen, Ger. 54/D2
Hilden, Ger. 53/F1
Hilders, Ger. 54/C1
Hildesheim, Ger. 51/G4
Hilgermissen, Ger. 51/G3
Hill (isl.), Pa, US 138/B3
Hill City, Ks, US 129/H3
Hill of Fare (hill), Sc, UK 36/D2
Hill of Stake (hill), Sc, UK 36/B5
Hillaby (mt.), Bar. 141/P9
Hillburn, NY, US 139/J7
Hillcrest, NY, US 139/J7
Hille, Ger. 51/F4
Hillegom, Neth. 50/B4
Hillerød, Den. 38/E4
Hillesheim, Ger. 53/F3
Hillingdon (bor.), Eng, UK 30/B2
Hillsboro, Md, US 138/C6
Hillsboro, ND, US 127/J4
Hillsboro, Oh, US 130/D4
Hillsboro, Or, US 126/C4
Hillsboro, Tx, US 129/H4
Hillsborough (chan.), Austl. 114/C3
Hillsborough, Ca, US 135/K11
Hillsborough, NJ, US 138/D3
Hillsdale, Mi, US 130/C3
Hillsdale, Ks, US 137/D6
Hillsdale (lake), Ks, US 137/D6
Hillsdale, NJ, US 139/J7
Hillside, NJ, US 139/J9
Hillside, Sc, UK 36/D3
Hillston, Austl. 115/C2
Hillswick, Sc, UK 31/W13
Hilltop, Co, US 137/C4
Hilltown, NI, UK 34/B3
Hilo, Hi, US 124/U11
Hilongos, Phil. 79/D5
Hilpoltstein, Ger. 54/E4
Hilpsford (pt.), Eng, UK 35/E3
Hilsa, India 85/E3
Hilterfingen, Swi. 56/D4
Hilton Head (isl.), SC, US 133/H3
Hilton Head Island, SC, US 133/H3
Hilvarenbeek, Neth. 50/C6
Hilversum, Neth. 50/C4
Hilzingen, Ger. 57/E2
Himāchal Pradesh (state), India 70/C5
Himalaya (range), Asia 67/G6
Himālchuli (peak), Nepal 85/E1
Himamaylan, Phil. 79/D5
Himanka, Fin. 60/D2
Himberg, Aus. 49/N7
Himeji, Japan 74/D3
Himeji Castle, Japan 74/D3
Himi, Japan 75/E2
Himmelpforten, Ger. 51/G1
Himş (prov.), Syria 90/D3
Himş, Syria 91/E2
Hinche, Haiti 145/H2
Hinchinbrook (isl.), Austl. 109/D2
Hinchinbrook Entrance (chan.) 134/J3
Hinchinbrook Island, Austl. 114/B2
Hinckley, Eng, UK 33/E1
Hincks Conservation Park, Austl. 113/H5
Hindan (riv.), India 84/A1
Hindaun, India 84/A2
Hindelang, Ger. 57/G3
Hindeloopen, Neth. 50/C3
Hindley, Eng, UK 35/F4
Hindmarsh (lake), Austl. 115/B3
Hindu Kush (mts.), Asia 67/F6
Hindupur, India 82/C5
Hinesville, Ga, US 133/H4
Hinganghāt, India 82/C3
Hingol (riv.), Pak. 89/J3
Hingoli, India 82/C4
Hingorja, Pak. 89/J3
Hinis, Turk. 90/E2
Hino, Japan 77/K5
Hino, Japan 77/C2
Hino (riv.), Japan 77/K5
Hino-misaki (cape), Japan 74/C3
Hinode, Japan 77/C2
Hinohara, Japan 77/C2
Hinojosa del Duque, Sp. 44/C3
Hinsdale, Il, US 135/Q16
Hinte, Ger. 51/E2
Hinterbrühl, Aus. 49/N7
Hinterrhein (riv.), Swi. 57/F4
Hinterrugg (peak), Swi. 57/F3
Hinterweidenthal, Ger. 53/G5
Hinton, Ab, Can. 126/D2
Hinton, WV, US 130/D4
Hinwil, Swi. 57/E3
Hipólito Bouchard, Arg. 158/E2
Hippolytushoef, Neth. 50/B3
Hipswell, Eng, UK 35/G3
Hira Highlands (uplands), Japan 77/J5
Hirado, Japan 74/A4
Hirakata, Japan 77/J6
Hirakud (res.), India 82/D3
Hiraman (riv.), Kenya 104/C3
Hiran (riv.), India 84/B4
Hiranai, Japan 76/B3
Hirara, Japan 75/H8
Hirata, Japan 74/C3
Hirata, Japan 77/L5
Hiratsuka, Japan 77/C3
Hirfanlı (dam), Turk. 90/C2
Hîrlău, Rom. 49/H2
Hiro'o, Japan 76/C2
Hirosaki, Japan 76/B3
Hiroshima, Japan 74/C3
Hiroshima (pref.), Japan 74/C3
Hirschaid, Ger. 54/D3
Hirschau, Ger. 55/E3
Hirschhorn, Ger. 54/B4
Hirson, Fr. 53/D4
Hîrşova, Rom. 49/H3
Hirtshals, Den. 38/C3
Hirukawa, Japan 77/M4
Hisai, Japan 77/K6
Hisarcık, Turk. 90/B2
Ḩisbān, Jor. 91/D4
Ḩişn al 'Abr, Yem. 88/E5
Hispaniola (isl.), DRep.,Haiti 141/G4
Historic Houses of Odessa, De, US 138/C5
Historic Towne of Smithville, NJ, US 138/D5
Hisua, India 85/E3
Hīt, Iraq 90/E3
Hitachi, Japan 75/G2
Hitachi-Ōta, Japan 75/G2
Hitchin, Eng, UK 33/F3
Hitoyoshi, Japan 74/B4
Hitra (isl.), Nor. 37/C3
Hittisau, Aus. 57/F3
Hitzacker, Ger. 40/F2
Hitzkirch, Swi. 57/E3
Hiyoshi, Japan 77/J5
Hizan, Turk. 90/E2
Hjälmaren (lake), Swe. 38/G2
Hjartfjellet (peak), Nor. 37/E2
Hjelmeland, Nor. 38/B2
Hjerm, Den. 38/C3
Hjo, Swe. 38/F2
Hjørring, Den. 38/C3
Hka (riv.), Myan. 78/B1
Hkakabo (peak), Myan. 83/G2
Hlabisa, SAfr. 107/E3
Hlohovec, Slvk. 48/C1
Hluboká nad Vltava, Czh. 55/H4
Hluhluwe, SAfr. 107/F3
Hlukhiv, Ukr. 62/E2
Hmawbi, Myan. 83/G4
Ho, Gha. 103/F5
Hoa Binh, Viet. 78/D1
Hoare (bay), Nun., Can. 123/K2
Hobara, Japan 75/G2
Hobart, Austl. 115/C4
Hobart (int'l arpt.), Austl. 115/C4
Hobart, Wa, US 135/D3
Hobbs, NM, US 129/G4
Hoboken, Belg. 50/B6
Hoboken, NJ, US 139/J8
Hoboksar Monggol Zizhixian, China 70/E2
Hobro, Den. 38/C3
Hochalmspitze (peak), Aus. 43/K3
Höchberg, Ger. 54/C3
Hochdorf, Ger. 57/F1
Hochfelden, Fr. 53/G6
Hochfinsler (peak), Swi. 57/F3
Hochgrat (peak), Ger. 57/G3
Hochheim am Main, Ger. 54/B2
Hochkönig (peak), Aus. 43/K3
Hŏch'ŏn (riv.), NKor. 73/D2
Hochschwab (peak), Aus. 43/L3
Hochsimmer (peak), Ger. 53/G3
Hochspeyer, Ger. 53/G5
Höchst, Aus. 57/F3
Höchst im Odenwald, Ger. 54/B3
Hochstadt am Main, Ger. 54/E2
Höchstadt an der Aisch, Ger. 54/D3
Höchstädt an der Donau, Ger. 54/D5
Hochstetten-Dhaun, Ger. 53/G4
Hochvogel (peak), Aus. 57/G3
Hochwang (peak), Swi. 57/F4
Hockenheim, Ger. 54/B4
Hockessin, De, US 138/C4
Hockley, Eng, UK 30/F2
Hod Hasharon, Isr. 91/F7
Hodal, India 84/A2
Hodder (riv.), Eng, UK 35/F4
Hoddesdon, Eng, UK 30/D1
Hodenhagen, Ger. 51/G3
Hodges (lake), Ca, US 136/C4
Hodgeville, Sk, Can. 126/G3
Hodh (phys. reg.), Mrta. 102/C2
Hodh El Gharbi (pol. reg.), Mrta. 102/C2
Hódmezővásárhely, Hun. 48/E2
Hodonín, Czh. 41/J4
Hoekse Waard (isl.), Neth. 50/B5
Hoensbroek, Neth. 53/E2
Hoeselt, Belg. 53/E2
Hoevelaken, Neth. 50/C4
Hoeven, Neth. 50/B5
Hoeybuktmoen (int'l arpt.), Nor. 37/J1
Hof, Ger. 55/E2
Hofbieber, Ger. 54/C1
Höfdhakaupstadhur, Ice. 37/N6
Hoffman Estates, Il, US 135/P15
Hofgeismar, Ger. 51/G6
Hofheim am Taunus, Ger. 54/B2
Hofheim in Unterfranken, Ger. 54/D2
Hofmeyr, SAfr. 106/D3
Hofrong Qagan Salt (lake), China 72/B3
Hofors, Swe. 38/G1
Hofsá (riv.), Ice. 37/P6
Hofsjökull (glacier), Ice. 37/N7
Hōfu, Japan 74/B3
Hogarth (mt.), Austl. 113/H2
Hogyész, Hun. 48/D2
Hoh Xil (mts.), China 70/E4
Höhbürd, Mong. 70/H2
Hohe Acht (peak), Ger. 53/G3
Hohe Geige (peak), Aus. 57/G4
Hohe Tauern (mts.), Aus. 43/K3
Hohe Tauern NP, Aus. 43/K3
Hohegrass (peak), Ger. 51/G6
Hohen Neuendorf, Ger. 40/Q6
Hohenbrunn, Ger. 55/E6
Hohenems, Aus. 57/F3
Hohenhameln, Ger. 51/H4
Hohenlinden, Ger. 55/F6
Hohenlockstedt, Ger. 40/E2
Hohenloher Ebene (plain), Ger. 40/E4
Hohenpeissenberg, Ger. 57/G2
Hohenroth, Ger. 54/D2
Hoher Dachstein (peak), Aus. 43/K3
Hoher Ifen (peak), Ger. 57/G3
Hoher Randen (peak), Ger. 57/E2
Hohgant (peak), Swi. 56/D4
Hohhot, China 71/K3
Höhn, Ger. 53/G2
Hohneck (peak), Fr. 56/D1
Hohnstorf, Ger. 51/H2
Hohokam Pima Nat'l Mon., Az, US 128/E4
Höhr-Grenzhausen, Ger. 53/G3
Hoi An, Viet. 78/E3
Hoima, Ugan. 104/A2
Hoisington, Ks, US 129/H3
Højby, Den. 38/D4
Højer, Den. 38/C4
Hōjō, Japan 74/C3
Hokitika, NZ 117/S11
Hokkaidō (isl.), Japan 67/P5
Hokksund, Nor. 38/C2
Hokota, Japan 75/G2
Hokudan, Japan 77/G6
Hokusei, Japan 77/L5
Hol, Nor. 38/C1
Holbox, Mex. 144/E1
Holbrook, Austl. 115/C2
Holbrook, Az, US 128/E4
Holbrook, NY, US 139/E2
Holderness (pen.), Eng, UK 35/H4
Holdorf, Ger. 51/F3
Holdrege, Ne, US 129/H2
Holeby, Den. 38/D4
Holguín, Cuba 145/G1
Holiday Hills, Il, US 135/P15
Holitna (riv.), Ak, US 134/G3
Höljes, Swe. 38/E1
Holladay-Cottonwood, Ut, US 137/K12
Holland, Mi, US 130/C3
Holland (pt.), Md, US 138/B6
Hollandale, Ms, US 129/K4
Hollandse IJssel (riv.), Neth. 50/B5
Hollandstoun, Sc, UK 31/V14
Hollenstedt, Ger. 51/G2
Hollfeld, Ger. 54/E3
Holliday, Ks, US 137/D5
Hollis, Ok, US 129/H4
Hollis, Ak, US 134/M4
Hollister, Ca, US 128/B3
Hollister (mt.), Austl. 112/B2
Hollogne-aux-Pierres, Belg. 53/E2
Hollola, Fin. 39/L1
Höllviksnäs, Swe. 38/E4
Holly, Wa, US 135/B2
Holly Springs, Ms, US 133/F3
Hollywood, Fl, US 133/H5
Hollywood Bowl, Ca, US 136/F7
Hollywood Park, Tx, US 137/U20
Holm, Ger. 51/G1
Holman, NW, Can. 122/E1
Hólmavík, Ice. 37/N6
Holmdel, NJ, US 138/D3
Holmes (reefs), Austl. 109/D2
Holmesdale (valley), Eng, UK 30/C3
Holmestrand, Nor. 38/D2
Holmfirth, Eng, UK 35/G4
Holmsjön (lake), Swe. 37/F3
Holmsund, Swe. 37/G3
Holon, Isr. 91/F7
Holstebro, Den. 38/C3
Holston (riv.), Tn, US 133/H2
Holt, Mo, US 137/E5
Holt, Ca, US 135/M11
Holtålen, Nor. 37/D3
Holten, Neth. 50/D4
Holtland, Ger. 51/E2
Holton, Ks, US 129/J3
Holtsville, NY, US 139/E2
Holy (isl.), Sc, UK 36/A5
Holy Cross, Ak, US 134/G3
Holyhead, Wal, UK 34/D5
Holyoke, Co, US 129/G2
Holyoke, Ma, US 131/F3
Holywell, Wal, UK 35/E5
Holywood, NI, UK 34/C2
Holzkirchen, Ger. 43/J3
Holzminden, Ger. 51/G5
Holzwickede, Ger. 51/E5
Hom (riv.), Namb. 106/B3
Homberg, Ger. 51/G6
Homberg, Ger. 50/D6
Hombori Tondo (peak), Mali 103/E3
Hombourg-Haut, Fr. 53/F5
Homburg, Ger. 53/G5
Home (bay), Nun., Can. 123/K2
Home Hill, Austl. 114/B2
Homécourt, Fr. 53/E5
Homeland, Ca, US 136/C3
Homer, Ak, US 134/H4
Homer, La, US 129/J4
Homestead, Fl, US 133/H5
Homestead Nat'l Mon. of America, Ne, US 129/H2
Homewood, Al, US 133/G3
Homewood, Il, US 135/Q16
Homib (riv.), Erit. 88/C5
Hommersåk, Nor. 38/A2
Homochitto (riv.), Ms, US 132/F4
Homyel', Bela. 62/D1
Homyel'skaya Voblasts, Bela. 62/D1
Hon Quan, Viet. 78/D4
Honaunau-Napoopoo, Hi, US 124/U11
Honbetsu, Japan 76/C2
Honddu (riv.), Wal, UK 32/C3
Hondeklipbaai, SAfr. 106/B3
Hondo (riv.), Belz. 144/D2
Hondo, Japan 74/B4
Hondo, Tx, US 129/H5
Hondschoote, Fr. 52/B2
Hondsrug (reg.), Neth. 50/D3
Hondsrug (hills), Neth. 40/D2
Honduras (gulf), NAm. 144/E2
Honduras (ctry.) 144/E3
Honey (lake), Ca, US 126/C5
Honey Brook, Pa, US 138/C3
Honey Creek, Wi, US 135/P14
Hong (isl.), SKor. 73/C5
Hong (lake), China 72/C5
Hong (riv.), China 72/C4
Hong Gai, Viet. 83/J3
Hong Kong (dpcy.), China 67/L7
Hong Kong (isl.), China 71/U10
Hong'an, China 72/C5
Hongch'ŏn, SKor. 73/D4
Hongdu (riv.), China 83/J2
Honghu, China 79/B2
Hongjiang, China 83/J2
Hongqiao (int'l arpt.), China 72/L8
Hongshui (riv.), China 70/J6
Hongsŏng, SKor. 73/D4
Hongtong, China 72/B3
Honguedo (passg.), Qu, Can. 131/H1
Hongwŏn, NKor. 73/D3
Hongze, China 72/D4
Hoenheim, Fr. 53/G6
Honiara (cap.), Sol. 116/E5
Honjō, Japan 76/B4
Honjō, Japan 77/C1
Honolulu (cap.), Hi, US 124/T10
Honolulu (co.), Hi, US 124/V13
Honolulu (int'l arpt.), Hi, US 124/W13
Honouliuli, Hi, US 124/V13
Hönow, Ger. 40/Q6
Honshū (isl.), Japan 71/Q5
Hood (pt.), Austl. 112/C5
Hood, Ca, US 135/L10
Hood (mt.), Ca, US 135/J10
Hood (mt.), Or, US 126/C4
Hood Canal (str.), Wa, US 126/C4
Hoofddorp, Neth. 50/B4
Hoogeloon, Neth. 50/C6
Hoogeveen, Neth. 50/D3
Hoogeveense Vaart (canal), Neth. 50/D3
Hoogezand, Neth. 50/D2
Hooghly (riv.), India 85/F5
Hooghly-Chinsura, India 85/G4
Hoogkarspel, Neth. 50/C3
Hooglede, Belg. 52/C2
Hoogstraten, Belg. 50/B6
Hook (pt.), Ire. 31/Q10
Hook (sound), Austl. 114/C3
Hookena, Hi, US 124/U11
Hoonah, Ak, US 134/L4
Hooper, Ut, US 137/J11
Hooper Bay, Ak, US 134/E3
Hoopeston, Il, US 130/C3
Hoopstad, SAfr. 106/D2
Höör, Swe. 38/E4
Hoorn, Neth. 50/C3
Hoornse Hop (bay), Neth. 50/C3
Hoover (dam), Az, US 128/D3
Hoover, Mo, US 137/D5
Hopa, Turk. 90/E1
Hopatcong, NJ, US 138/D2
Hopatcong (lake), NJ, US 138/D2
Hope (lake), Austl. 109/A4
Hope, BC, Can. 126/C3
Hope, Ak, US 134/J3
Hope, NJ, US 138/D2
Hope Vale Aboriginal Community, Austl. 114/B1
Hopedale, Nf, Can. 123/K3
Hopelchén, Mex. 144/D2
Hopeman, Sc, UK 36/C1
Hopes Advance (cape), Qu, Can. 123/K2
Hope's Nose (pt.), Eng, UK 32/C6
Hopetown, SAfr. 106/D3
Hopewell, NJ, US 138/D3
Hopewell Furnace NHS, Pa, US 138/C3
Hopkins (riv.), Austl. 115/B3
Hopkins (lake), Austl. 109/B3
Hopkinsville, Ky, US 130/C4
Hoppecke (riv.), Ger. 51/F6
Hoppegarten, Ger. 40/Q6
Hoppstädten-Weiersbach, Ger. 53/G4
Hopsten, Ger. 51/E4
Hoquiam, Wa, US 126/C4
Horace (mtn.), Ak, US 134/J2
Horado, Japan 77/L4
Hōrai-san (peak), Japan 77/J5
Horasan, Turk. 90/E1
Horažďovice, Czh. 55/G4
Horb am Neckar, Ger. 54/B6
Horbourg-Wihr, Fr. 56/D1
Hörbranz, Aus. 57/F2
Horche, Sp. 44/D2
Horconcitos, Pan. 145/F4
Hordaland (co.), Nor. 37/C3
Hördt, Ger. 54/B4
Hœrdt, Fr. 53/G6
Horezu, Rom. 49/G3
Horgau, Ger. 54/D6
Horgen, Swi. 57/E3
Horine, Mo, US 137/G9
Horinger, China 72/B2
Horley, Eng, UK 30/C3
Horlivka, Ukr. 62/F2
Hormigüeros, PR 141/M8
Hormuz (str.), Oman 89/G3
Horn, Aus. 43/L2
Horn (pt.), Ice. 160/H
Horn-Bad Meinberg, Ger. 51/F5
Hornachuelos, Sp. 44/C4
Hornád (riv.), Slvk. 41/L4
Hornavan (lake), Swe. 37/F2
Hornbach, Ger. 53/G5
Hornberg, Ger. 57/E1
Horndal, Swe. 38/G1
Horneburg, Ger. 51/G1
Hornell, NY, US 130/E3
Horní Bříza, Czh. 55/G3
Horní Slavkov, Czh. 55/F2
Hornisgrinde (peak), Ger. 54/B5
Hornos (cape), Chile 159/D7
Hornoy-le-Bourg, Fr. 52/A4
Hornslet, Den. 38/D3
Hörnum (cape), Ger. 38/C4
Horoshiri-dake (peak), Japan 76/C2
Hořovice, Czh. 55/G3
Horqin Zuoyi Houqi, China 72/E2
Horqin Zuoyi Zhongqi, China 72/E1
Hörsching, Aus. 55/H6
Horse Cave, Ky, US 130/C4
Horsefly (lake), BC, Can. 126/C2
Horsens, Den. 38/C4
Horseshoe (lake), Il, US 137/G8
Horseshoe (lake), Co, US 137/B2
Horsetooth (res.), Co, US 137/B1
Horsey (isl.), Eng, UK 33/H3
Horsforth, Eng, UK 35/G4
Horsham, Austl. 115/B3
Horsham, Eng, UK 33/F4
Horsham, Pa, US 138/C3
Horšovský Týn, Czh. 55/F3
Horst, Neth. 50/D6
Hörstel, Ger. 51/E4
Horstmar, Ger. 51/E4
Horta, Azor., Port. 45/S12
Horten, Nor. 38/D2
Hortes, Fr. 56/B2
Hortobágyi NP, Hun. 62/B3
Horton (pt.), NY, US 139/F1
Horton (riv.), NW, Can. 122/D2
Høruphav, Den. 38/C4
Horusický Rybník (lake), Czh. 55/H4
Hørve, Den. 38/D4
Ḩorvot Dor, Isr. 91/F6
Horw, Swi. 57/E3
Horwich, Eng, UK 35/F4
Horwood (lake), On, Can. 130/D2
Hösbach, Ger. 54/C2
Hosenfeld, Ger. 54/C1
Hoshiārpur, India 86/C4
Hosingen, Lux. 53/F3
Hospental, Swi. 57/E4
Hosszúpereszteg, Hun. 48/C2
Hoste (isl.), Chile 159/C7
Hot Springs, SD, US 127/H5
Hot Springs NP, Ar, US 129/J4
Hotaka, Japan 75/E2
Hotaka-dake (peak), Japan 75/E2
Hotan, China 70/C4
Hotan (riv.), China 70/D4
Hotazel, SAfr. 106/C2
Hotont, Mong. 70/H2
Hottah (lake), NW, Can. 122/E2
Hottentot (bay), Namb. 106/A2
Hotton, Belg. 53/E3
Houari Boumedienne (int'l arpt.), Alg. 100/G4
Houdain, Fr. 52/B3
Houdan, Fr. 30/G5
Houet (prov.), Burk. 102/D4
Houffalize, Belg. 53/E3
Houghton Lake, Mi, US 130/C2
Houghton-le-Spring, Eng, UK 35/G2
Houilles, Fr. 30/J5
Houlton, Me, US 131/H2
Houma, China 72/B4
Houplines, Fr. 52/B2
Hourdel (pt.), Fr. 52/A3
Hourn, Loch (inlet), Sc, UK 36/A2
Hourtin, Fr. 42/C4
Housatonic (riv.), Ct, US 139/E1
House (range), Ut, US 128/D3
House Springs, Mo, US 137/F9
Housesteads Roman Fort, Eng, UK 35/F1
Houssen, Fr. 56/D1
Houston, BC, Can. 126/B2
Houston, Ak, US 134/J3
Houston, De, US 138/C6
Houston, Mo, US 129/K3
Houston, Ms, US 133/F3
Houston, Tx, US 129/J5
Houtbaai, SAfr. 106/L11
Houten, Neth. 50/C4
Houthulst, Belg. 52/B2
Houtman Abrolhos (isl.), Austl. 112/B4
Houtribdijk (dam), Neth. 50/C3
Houtskär (isl.), Fin. 39/J1
Houyet, Belg. 53/E3
Hov, Nor. 38/D1
Hova, Swe. 38/F2
Hovd (prov.), Mong. 70/F2
Hovd, Mong. 70/F2
Hövelhof, Ger. 51/F5
Hovenweep Nat'l Mon., Ut, US 128/E3
Hovfjället (peak), Swe. 38/E1
Hovmantorp, Swe. 38/F3
Hövsgöl (prov.), Mong. 70/G1
Hovsta, Swe. 38/F2
Howard, Austl. 114/D4
Howard (hill), Ak, US 134/H2
Howard (pass), Ak, US 134/G2
Howard (co.), Md, US 138/B5
Howard Hanson (res.), Wa, US 135/D3
Howard Hanson (dam), Wa, US 135/D3
Howe (cape), Austl. 115/D3
Howe of the Mearns (reg.), Sc, UK 36/D3
Howell, Mi, US 130/D3
Howell, NJ, US 138/D3
Howick, SAfr. 107/E3
Howland (isl.), Pac., US 117/H4
Höxter, Ger. 51/G5
Hoxud, China 70/E3
Hoy (isl.), Sc, UK 31/V14
Hoya, Ger. 51/G3
Hōya, Japan 77/D2
Høyanger, Nor. 38/B1
Hoyerswerda, Ger. 41/H3
Hoylake, Eng, UK 35/E5
Hoyland Nether, Eng, UK 35/G4
Hoyo de Manzanares, Sp. 45/N8
Hoyos, Sp. 44/B2
Hoyoux (riv.), Belg. 53/E3
Hozumi, Japan 77/L5
Hracholusky (res.), Czh. 55/F3
Hradec Králové, Czh. 41/H3
Hradiště (peak), Czh. 55/G2
Hrasnica, Bosn. 48/D4
Hrastnik, Slov. 43/L3
Hrazdan, Arm. 63/H4
Hrodna, Bela. 39/K5
Hrodzyenskaya Voblasts, Bela. 60/E5
Hrolleifsborg (peak), Ice. 37/M6
Hron (riv.), Slvk. 62/A2
Hronov, Czh. 41/J3
Hrubieszów, Pol. 41/M3
Hrubý Jeseník (mts.), Czh.,Pol. 41/J3
Hrútafjöll (peak), Ice. 37/P6
Hsinchu, Tai. 79/D3
Hua (peak), China 72/B4
Hua Hin, Thai. 78/B3
Hua Xian, China 72/C4
Hua'an, China 79/C2
Huacaybamba, Peru 156/B3
Huachi, China 70/J4
Huacho, Peru 156/B3
Huachón, Peru 156/C3
Huachuca City, Az, US 128/E5
Huacrachuco, Peru 156/B3
Huade, China 71/K3
Huahine (isl.), FrPol. 117/K6
Huai (riv.), China 72/C4
Huai'an, China 72/C2
Huai'an, China 72/D4
Huaibei, China 71/L5
Huaibin, China 72/C4
Huaiji, China 83/K3
Huailai, China 72/G6
Huainan, China 72/D4
Huairen, China 72/C3
Huairou, China 72/H6
Huaiyang, China 72/C4
Huaiyin, China 72/D4
Huaiyin, China 72/D4
Huaiyuan, China 72/D4
Huajicori, Mex. 142/D4
Huajuapan de León, Mex. 144/B2
Hualahuises, Mex. 143/F3
Hualañé, Chile 158/C2
Hualgayoc, Peru 156/B2
Hualien, Tai. 79/D3
Hualla, Peru 156/C4
Huallaga (riv.), Peru 147/B3
Huallanca, Peru 156/B3
Huallanca, Peru 156/B3
Huamachuco, Peru 156/B2
Huamantanga, Peru 156/B3
Huamantla, Mex. 143/M7
Huambo, Ang. 105/C3
Huambos, Peru 156/B2
Huan (riv.), China 72/C5
Huan Xian, China 70/J4
Huancané, Peru 156/D4
Huancapi, Peru 156/C4
Huancaspata, Peru 156/B3
Huancavelica (dept.), Peru 156/C4
Huancavelica, Peru 156/C4
Huancayo, Peru 156/C4
Huanchaca (peak), Bol. 150/E8
Huang (riv.), China 67/L6
Huangchuan, China 72/C4
Huanggang (peak), China 79/C2
Huanghua, China 72/D3
Huangling, China 72/B4
Huanglong, China 72/B4
Huangping, China 83/J2
Huangqi (lake), China 72/C2
Huangshan, China 79/C2
Huangtang (lake), China 72/C5
Huangtu (plat.), China 72/B4
Huanguelén, Arg. 158/E3
Huangyan, China 79/D2
Huangzhong, China 70/H4
Huanren, China 73/C2
Huanta, Peru 156/C4
Huantai, China 72/D3
Huántar, Peru 156/B3
Huánuco (dept.), Peru 156/B3
Huánuco, Peru 156/B3
Huanuni, Bol. 150/E7
Huapi (mts.), Nic. 144/E3
Huaquechula, Mex. 143/L8
Huaquillas, Ecu. 156/A1
Huaral, Peru 156/B3
Huaraz, Peru 156/B3
Huari, Peru 156/B3
Huaricolca, Peru 156/C3
Huarina, Bol. 156/D5
Huarmey, Peru 156/B3
Huarochirí, Peru 156/B4
Huarocondo, Peru 156/C4
Huarong, China 79/B2
Huásabas, Mex. 142/C2
Huasahuasi, Peru 156/C3
Huascarán (peak), Peru 156/B3
Huatabampo, Mex. 142/C3
Huatunas (lake), Bol. 150/E6
Huatuxco, Mex. 143/N7
Huauchinango, Mex. 143/L6
Huaura, Peru 156/B3
Huautla de Jiménez, Mex. 144/B2
Huayacocotla, Mex. 143/L6
Huaying, China 79/A1
Huaylas, Peru 156/B3
Huayllay, Peru 156/B3
Huayopata, Peru 156/C4
Huayuan, China 83/J2
Huazhou, China 83/K3
Hubbard (mt.), Ak, US 134/L3
Hubbard Creek (res.), Tx, US 129/H4
Hubei (prov.), China 71/K5
Hubei (pass), China 72/B4
Hubli-Dhārwār, India 89/L5
Huch'ang, NKor. 73/D2
Hückelhoven, Ger. 53/F1
Hückeswagen, Ger. 53/G1
Hucknall, Eng, UK 35/G5
Huddersfield, Eng, UK 35/G4
Huddinge, Swe. 38/G2
Hude, Ger. 51/F2
Hudiksvall, Swe. 38/G1
Hudson (cape), Ant. 160/L
Hudson (bay), Can. 123/H2
Hudson (str.), Nun.,Qu, Can. 123/J2
Hudson, Qu, Can. 131/M7
Hudson, Co, US 137/C2
Hudson (co.), NJ, US 139/J9
Hudson (riv.), NJ,NY, US 130/F3
Hudson, NY, US 130/F3
Hudson Bay, Sk, Can. 127/H2
Hudson's Hope, BC, Can. 122/D3
Hue, Viet. 78/D2
Huedin, Rom. 49/F2
Huehuetenango, Guat. 144/D3
Huehuetla, Mex. 143/L6
Huehuetlán, Mex. 143/L8
Huejotzingo, Mex. 143/L7
Huejuquilla el Alto, Mex. 142/E4
Huejutla de Reyes, Mex. 144/B1
Huelma, Sp. 44/D4
Huelva, Sp. 44/B4
Huelva (riv.), Sp. 44/B4
Huequi (vol.), Chile 158/B4
Huercal-Overa, Sp. 44/E4
Huerfano (riv.), Co, US 129/F3
Huesca, Sp. 45/E1
Huéscar, Sp. 44/D4
Huetamo de Nuñez, Mex. 143/E5
Huete, Sp. 44/D2
Huexoculco, Mex. 143/R10
Hüfingen, Ger. 57/E2
Hugh Town, Eng, UK 31/Q12
Hughenden, Austl. 114/B3
Hughenden Valley, Eng, UK 30/A2
Hughes, Ak, US 134/H2
Hughes, Arg. 158/E2
Hughesville, Pa, US 138/B1
Huglfing, Ger. 57/H2
Hugli (riv.), India 82/E3
Hugo, Ok, US 129/J4
Huguan, China 72/C3
Hui Xian, China 72/C4
Hui'an, China 79/C2
Huib-Hock (plat.), Namb. 106/B2
Huichang, China 79/C2
Huichapan, Mex. 143/K6
Hŭich'ŏn, NKor. 73/D2
Huila (dept.), Col. 152/C4
Huila, Nevado del (peak), Col. 152/C4
Huilai, China 79/C3
Huilango, Mex. 143/Q9
Huili, China 83/H2
Huimanguillo, Mex. 144/C2
Huimin, China 72/D3
Huinca Renancó, Arg. 158/D2
Huining, China 70/J4
Hŭisaek-pong (peak), NKor. 73/D2
Huishui, China 83/J2
Huisne (riv.), Fr. 42/D2
Huissen, Neth. 50/C5
Huitong, China 83/J2
Huittinen, Fin. 39/K1
Huitzilan, Mex. 143/M7
Huitzuco, Mex. 143/K8
Huixcolotla, Mex. 143/M8
Huixquilucan, Mex. 143/Q10
Huixtla, Mex. 144/C3
Huize, China 83/H2
Huizen, Neth. 50/C4
Hujra, Pak. 86/B4
Hulan, China 71/N2
Hulett, Wy, US 127/G4
Hull (riv.), Eng, UK 35/H4
Hullbridge, Eng, UK 30/E2
Hüllhorst, Ger. 51/F4
Hulst, Neth. 50/B6
Hultsfred, Swe. 38/F3
Huma, China 71/N1
Huma (riv.), China 71/M1
Humahuaca, Arg. 157/C1
Humaitá, Braz. 150/F5
Humansdorp, SAfr. 106/D4
Humay, Peru 156/C4
Humber (riv.), Nf, Can. 131/K1
Humber (bay), On, Can. 131/R8
Humber (riv.), Eng, UK 35/H4
Humberto de Campos, Braz. 154/B1
Humble, Tx, US 129/J5
Humboldt, Sk, Can. 127/G2
Humboldt (range), Nv, US 128/C2
Humboldt, Tn, US 130/B5
Humboldt (bay), Col. 145/G5
Humboldt (riv.), Nv, US 124/C3
Hume (lake), Austl. 115/C2
Húmeda, Pampa (plain), Arg. 158/E2
Humenné, Slvk. 41/L4
Humida, Pampa (plain), Arg. 157/D4

Humlu – Ishik

Humlum, Den. 38/C3
Hummels Wharf, Pa, US 138/B2
Hummelstown, Pa, US 138/B3
Humphrey (pt.), Ak, US 134/K2
Humphreys (peak), Az, US 128/E4
Hūn, Libya 96/J2
Húnaflói (bay), Ice. 37/N6
Hunan (prov.), China 71/K6
Hundsangen, Ger. 53/G3
Hunedoara, Rom. 48/F3
Hunedoara (prov.), Rom. 48/F3
Hünenberg, Swi. 57/E3
Hünfeld, Ger. 43/H1
Hung Yen, Viet. 78/D1
Hungaroring, Hun. 49/R9
Hungary (ctry.) 48/D2
Hungen, Ger. 54/B2
Hŭngnam, NKor. 73/D3
Hunjiang, China 73/D2
Hunnebostrand, Swe. 38/D2
Hunsel, Neth. 50/C6
Hunsrück (mts.), Ger. 40/D4
Hunte (riv.), Ger. 40/E2
Hunter (isl.), Austl. 109/D5
Hunter (riv.), Austl. 115/D2
Hunter (mt.), Ak, US 134/H3
Hunter, Tx, US 137/U20
Hunterdon (co.), NJ, US 138/C2
Huntingburg, In, US 130/C4
Huntingdon, Eng, UK 33/F2
Huntington, In, US 130/C3
Huntington, NY, US 139/M8
Huntington (bay), NY, US 139/M8
Huntington, WV, US 130/D4
Huntington Bay, NY, US 139/M8
Huntington Beach, Ca, US 136/G8
Huntington Park, Ca, US 136/F8
Huntington Station, NY, US 139/M8
Huntington Woods, Mi, US 135/F7
Huntley, Il, US 135/P15
Huntly, NZ 117/T10
Huntly, Sc, UK 36/D2
Hunts Inlet, BC, Can. 134/M4
Hunts Point, Wa, US 135/C2
Huntsville, Al, US 133/G3
Huntsville, On, Can. 130/E2
Huntsville, Ut, US 137/K11
Huntsville (res.), Pa, US 138/B1
Hunucmá, Mex. 144/D1
Hünxe, Ger. 50/D5
Hunyuan, China 72/C3
Huo (mtn.), China 72/B3
Huo (mtn.), China 72/D5
Huocheng, China 70/D3
Huojia, China 72/C4
Huolin Gol, China 71/L2
Huoqiu, China 72/D4
Huoshan, China 72/D5
Huozhou, China 72/B3
Hurdal, Nor. 38/D1
Hure Qi, China 72/E2
Hurepoix (reg.), Fr. 30/H6
Hurley, NM, US 128/E4
Hurley, Eng, UK 30/A2
Hurley (riv.), Ire. 34/B4
Hurlford, Sc, UK 36/B5
Huron (lake), Can.,US 130/D2
Huron (mts.), Mi, US 130/B2
Huron (pt.), Mi, US 135/G6
Huron (riv.), Mi, US 135/E7
Hurricane, WV, US 130/D4
Hurtaut (riv.), Fr. 52/D4
Hürtgenwald (reg.), Ger. 53/F2
Hürth, Ger. 53/F2
Hurup, Den. 38/C3
Husainābād, India 85/E3
Húsavík, Ice. 37/P6
Huscarán, PN, Peru 150/C5
Husher, Wi, US 135/Q14
Huşi, Rom. 49/J2
Huskisson, Austl. 115/D2
Huslia, Ak, US 134/G2
Husnes, Nor. 38/A2
Hussigny-Godbrange, Fr. 53/E5
Husum, Ger. 38/C4
Husum, Swe. 37/F3
Hutag, Mong. 70/H2
Hutchinson, Mn, US 127/K4
Hutchinson, Ks, US 129/H3
Hüttisheim, Ger. 57/F1
Hüttlingen, Ger. 54/D5
Hutton (mt.), Austl. 114/C4
Hutton, Eng, UK 30/E2
Huttwil, Swi. 56/D3
Hutuo (riv.), China 72/C3
Ḩuwwārah, WBnk. 91/G7
Huy, Belg. 53/E2
Huyton-with-Roby, Eng, UK 35/F5
Huzhou, China 72/L9
Hvammstangi, Ice. 37/N6
Hvannadalshnúkur (peak), Ice. 37/P7
Hvar (isl.), Cro. 46/E1
Hvide Sande, Den. 38/C4
Hvítá (riv.), Ice. 37/N7
Hvolsvöllur, Ice. 37/N7
Hwange, Zim. 105/E4
Hwange (Wankie) NP, Zim. 105/E4
Hwanghae-bukto (prov.), NKor. 73/D3
Hwanghae-namdo (prov.), NKor. 73/C3
Hwangju, NKor. 73/C3
Hwangju (riv.), NKor. 73/C3
Hwasun, SKor. 73/D5
Hyades (peak), Chile 158/B5
Hyattstown, Md, US 138/A5
Hyattsville, Md, US 138/B6
Hydaburg, Ak, US 134/M4
Hyde, Eng, UK 35/F5
Hyder, Ak, US 134/M4
Hyderābād, India 82/C4
Hyderābād, Pak. 89/J3
Hyères, Fr. 43/G5
Hyères, Îles d' (isls.), Fr 43/G5
Hyesan, NKor. 73/E2
Hygiene, Co, US 137/B2
Hyland (riv.), Yk, Can. 122/D2
Hyllestad, Nor. 38/A1
Hyltebruk, Swe. 38/E3
Hylton (hill), Ky, US 130/D4
Hyō-no-sen (peak), Japan 74/D3
Hyōgo (pref.), Japan 74/D3
Hyŏndŭng-san (peak), SKor. 73/G6
Hyrum, Ut, US 128/E2
Hythe, Eng, UK 33/H4
Hyūga, Japan 74/B4
Hyvinkää, Fin. 39/L1
Hywel, Moel (peak), Wal, UK 32/C2

I

I-n-Amenas, Alg. 99/H3
I-n-Azaoua, Oued (riv.), Niger 99/H5
I-n-Dagouber (well), Mali 99/E5
I-n-Échaï (well), Mali 103/E1
I-n-Gall, Niger 103/G2
I-n-Guezzâm, Alg. 103/G2
I-n-Milach (well), Mali 103/E2
I-n-Sâkâne, 'Erg (des.), Mali 103/E1
I-n-Salah, Alg. 99/F4
I-n-Tassik (well), Mali 103/F2
Iacanga, Braz. 155/B2
Iaciara, Braz. 154/A4
Iaco (riv.), Braz. 150/E6
Iaçu, Braz. 154/B4
Iâf di Montasio (peak), It. 43/K3
Iakora, Madg. 107/H8
Ialomiţa (riv.), Rom. 62/C3
Ialomiţa (prov.), Rom. 49/H3
Ianapera, Madg. 107/H8
Iapu, Braz. 155/D1
Iaşi (prov.), Rom. 49/H2
Iaşi, Rom. 49/H2
Íasmos, Gre. 47/J2
Iatan, Mo, US 137/D5
Iba, Phil. 79/C4
Ibadan, Nga. 103/F5
Ibagué, Col. 150/C3
Ibaiti, Braz. 155/B2
Ibajay, Phil. 79/D5
Ibanda, Ugan. 104/A3
Ibans (lake), Nic. 145/E3
Ibapaba, Serra da (range), Braz. 154/B1
Ibar (riv.), Serb. 48/E4
Ibara, Japan 74/C3
Ibaraki (pref.), Japan 75/F2
Ibaraki, Japan 77/J6
Ibaraki, Japan 77/E1
Ibarra, Ecu. 152/B4
Ibarreta, Arg. 157/E2
Ibb, Yem. 88/D6
Ibba (riv.), Sudan 97/L6
Ibbenbüren, Ger. 51/E4
Ibdekkene (riv.), Mali 103/F2
Iberia, Peru 156/D3
Iberia, Peru 156/C2
Ibérico, Sistema (range), Sp. 44/D2
Iberville, Qu, Can. 131/P7
Ibi, Sp. 45/E3
Ibiá, Braz. 155/C1
Ibiapina, Braz. 154/B1
Ibicaraí, Braz. 154/C4
Ibicuy, Arg. 159/J10
Ibigawa, Japan 77/L5
Ibimirim, Braz. 154/C3
Ibiraçu, Braz. 155/D1
Ibirapuã, Braz. 154/B5
Ibitinga, Braz. 155/B2
Ibiúna, Braz. 211/F8
Ibiza (isl.) 45/F3
Ibiza, Sp. 45/F3
Ibo, Moz. 105/H3
Ibo (riv.), Japan 74/D3
Iboro, Nga. 103/F5
Ibotirama, Braz. 154/B4
Iboundji (peak), Gabon 96/H8
Ibrány, Hun. 41/L4
Ibshawāy, Egypt 91/B5
Ibuki, Japan 77/K5
Ibuki-yama (peak), Japan 77/K5
Ica (dept.), Peru 156/C4
Ica, Peru 156/C4
Içá (riv.), SAm. 147/D3
Içana (riv.), Braz. 150/E3
Icel (prov.), Turk. 90/C2
Iceland (ctry.) 37/N7
Icém, Braz. 155/B2
Ichalkaranji, India 89/K5
Ichāmati (riv.), Bang. 85/G3
Ichchāpuram, India 82/D4
Ichenhausen, Ger. 54/D6
Ichhāwar, India 84/A4
Ichihara, Japan 77/E3
Ichijima, Japan 77/H5
Ichikawa, Japan 77/D2
Ichikawada, Japan 77/B2
Ichinohe, Japan 76/B3
Ichinomiya, Japan 77/B2
Ichinomiya, Japan 77/E3
Ichinomiya, Japan 77/G7
Ichinomiya, Japan 77/M6
Ichinomiya, Japan 77/L5
Ichinoseki, Japan 76/B4
Ichishi, Japan 77/K6
Ich'ŏn, SKor. 73/D4
Ichtegem, Belg. 52/C1
Ickesburg, Pa, US 138/A3
Icó, Braz. 154/C2
Icod de los Vinos, Sp. 98/A3
Icy (cape), Ak, US 134/F1
Icy (pt.), Ak, US 134/L4
Icy (str.), Ak, US 134/L4
Icy (bay), Ak, US 122/B3
Idabel, Ok, US 129/J4
Idaho (state), US 126/E5
Idaho Springs, Co, US 137/A3
Idanha-a-Nova, Port. 44/B3
Idar, India 82/B3
Idar-Oberstein, Ger. 53/G4
Idarkopf (peak), Ger. 53/G4
Idaville, Pa, US 138/A3
Ide, Japan 77/J6
Ideles, Alg. 99/G5
Idfū, Egypt 101/C3
Ídhi (peak), Gre. 47/J5
Ídhra, Gre. 47/H4
Idice (riv.), It. 59/E4
Idjwe, Île (isl.), D.R. Congo 104/A3
Idkū, Egypt 91/B4
Idle (riv.), Eng, UK 35/H5
Idlib (prov.), Syria 90/D3
Idlib, Syria 91/E2
Idnah, WBnk. 91/D4
Idrija, Slov. 43/L4
Idriss I (dam), Mor. 100/B2
Idriss I, Barrage (res.), Mor. 100/B2
Idro, Lago d' (lake), It. 58/D1
Idstein, Ger. 54/B2
Ie (isl.), Japan 75/J7
Ieper, Belg. 52/B2
Ierápetra, Gre. 47/J5
Ierissós, Gre. 47/H2
Iesolo, It. 59/F1
Ifalik (isl.), Micr. 116/D4
Ifanadiana, Madg. 107/H8
Ife, Nga. 103/G5
Iferfes (well), Libya 99/H3
Iffeldorf, Ger. 57/H2
Iffezheim, Ger. 54/B5
Iforas, Adrar des (upland), Alg.,Mali 96/F4
Ifrane, Mor. 98/D2
Iga (riv.), Japan 77/K6
Iga, Japan 77/K6
Igal, Hun. 48/C2
Iganga, Ugan. 104/B2
Igaporã, Braz. 154/B4
Igara Paraná (riv.), Col. 152/C5
Igarapava, Braz. 155/C2
Igarapé Grande, Braz. 154/A2
Igarapé-Miri, Braz. 151/J4
Igaratá, Braz. 211/G8
Igarka, Rus. 64/J3
Igatpuri, India 82/B4
Igdet (peak), Mor. 98/C3
Iğdır, Turk. 90/F2
Igel, Ger. 53/F4
Iggesund, Swe. 38/G1
Ightham, Eng, UK 30/D3
Igikpak (mt.), Ak, US 134/H2
Igis, Swi. 57/F4
Igiugig, Ak, US 134/G4
Iglesias, It. 46/A3
Igli, Alg. 99/E3
Igling, Ger. 57/G1
Igloolik, Nun., Can. 123/H2
Ignace, On, Can. 127/L3
Ignacio, Ca, US 135/J10
Ignacio de la Llave, Mex. 143/P8
Ignacio Zaragoza, Mex. 142/D2
İğneada Burnu (cape), Turk. 49/J5
Igney, Fr. 56/C1
Ignon (riv.), Fr. 56/A2
Igny, Fr. 30/J5
Igombe (riv.), Tanz. 104/B4
Igora Paraná (riv.), Col. 156/C1
Igoumenítsa, Gre. 47/G3
Igra, Rus. 61/M4
Igreja, Morro da (peak), Braz. 155/B4
Iguaçu (riv.), Braz. 147/D5
Iguaçu, PN do, Braz. 157/F2
Iguaí, Braz. 154/B4
Iguala, Mex. 143/K8
Igualada, Sp. 45/F2
Iguape, Braz. 155/C3
Iguape (riv.), Braz. 155/B3
Iguatu, Braz. 154/C2
Iguazú, PN del, Arg. 157/F2
Iguetti (lake), Mrta. 98/C4
Iheya (isl.), Japan 75/J7
Ihhayrhan, Mong. 70/J2
Ihosy, Madg. 107/H8
Ihotry (lake), Madg. 107/G8
Ihuari, Peru 156/B3
Ii, Fin. 60/E2
Ii (riv.), Fin. 64/C3
Iida, Japan 75/E3
Iide-san (peak), Japan 75/F2
Iijoki (riv.), Fin. 60/F2
Iinan, Japan 77/K7
Iisalmi, Fin. 60/E3
Iitaka, Japan 77/K7
Iitti, Fin. 39/M1
Iiyama, Japan 75/F2
Iizuka, Japan 74/B4
Ijebu Ode, Nga. 103/F5
Ijill (peak), Mrta. 98/B5
Ijill (lake), Mrta. 98/B5
Ijira, Japan 77/L4
IJmeer (bay), Neth. 50/C4
Ijmuiden, Neth. 50/B4
Ijnaoun (well), Mrta. 102/B2
Ijoki (riv.), Fin. 37/H2
Ijoubbane, 'Erg (des.), Mali 98/D5
IJssel (riv.), Neth. 50/C3
Ijsselmeer (lake), Neth. 40/C2
Ijsselmuiden, Neth. 50/C3
Ijsselstein, Neth. 50/C4
Ijuí, Braz. 157/F2
Ijūin, Japan 74/B5
Ijzer (riv.), Belg. 40/B3
Ik (riv.), Rus. 61/M5
Ikahavo (plat.), Madg. 107/H7
Ikalamavony, Madg. 107/H8
Ikare, Nga. 103/G5
Ikaría, Gre. 90/A2
Ikaría (isl.), Gre. 47/J4
Ikaruga, Japan 77/J6
Ikeda, Japan 74/C3
Ikeda, Japan 76/C2
Ikeda, Japan 77/H6
Ikeda, Japan 77/L5
Ikeja, Nga. 103/F5
Ikenokoya-yama (peak), Japan 77/K7
Ikerre, Nga. 103/G5
Ikhtiman, Bul. 47/H1
Iki (isl.), Japan 74/A4
Iki (chan.), Japan 74/A4
Ikire, Nga. 103/G5
Ikirun, Nga. 103/G5
İkizce, Turk. 90/C2
İkizdere, Turk. 90/E1
Ikoma, Japan 77/J6
Ikongo, Madg. 107/H8
Ikopa (riv.), Madg. 107/H7
Ikorodu, Nga. 103/F5
Ikuno, Japan 74/D3
Ila Orangun, Nga. 103/G4
Ilabaya, Peru 156/D5
Ilagan, Phil. 79/D4
Ilam, Nepal 85/F2
Īlām, Iran 88/E2
Ilan, Tai. 79/D3
Ilanz, Swi. 57/F4
Ilaro, Nga. 103/F5
Ilave, Peru 156/D5
Iława, Pol. 41/K2
Ilawe-Ekiti, Nga. 103/G5
Ile (riv.), China.,Ka 70/C3
Île-à-la-Crosse, Sk, Can. 126/G2
Ile-a-la-Crosse (lake), Sk, Can. 126/G2
Île-de-France (pol. reg.), Fr. 52/A6
Ilebo, D.R. Congo 105/D1
Ilek (riv.), Rus. 63/K2
Îles Ehotilés, PN des, C.d'Iv. 102/E5
Iles Tristao, Îles (isls.), Gui. 102/B4
Ilesha, Nga. 103/G5
Ilfis (riv.), Swi. 56/D4
Ilgaz, Turk. 62/E4
Ilgın, Turk. 90/B2
Ilha Grande (bay), Braz. 211/J8
Ilha Grande, Baía de (bay), Braz. 155/C2
Ilha Solteira, Represa (res.), Braz. 151/H7
Ilhabela, Braz. 211/H8
Ílhavo, Port. 44/A2
Ilhéus, Braz. 154/C4
Iliamna, Ak, US 134/H4
Iliamna (lake), Ak, US 134/G4
Iliamna (vol.), Ak, US 134/H3
İliç, Turk. 90/D2
Ilıca, Turk. 63/G5
Ilijaš, Bosn. 48/D4
Iliniza (peak), Ecu. 152/B5
Ilirska Bistrica, Slov. 43/L4
Ilısu (dam), Turk. 90/E2
Ilısu (res.), Turk. 90/E2
Ilium (Troy) (ruin), Turk. 47/K3
Ilkeston, Eng, UK 35/G6
Ilkley, Eng, UK 35/G4
Ill (riv.), Aus. 43/H3
Ill (riv.), Fr. 43/G3
Illana, Sp. 44/D2
Illapel, Chile 157/B3
Illasi (riv.), It. 59/E1
Illbillee (mt.), Austl. 113/G3
Illéla, Niger 103/G3
Iller (riv.), Ger. 43/J2
Illertissen, Ger. 57/G1
Illescas, Sp. 44/D2
Illiers-Combray, Fr. 42/D2
Illimani (peak), Bol. 150/E7
Illingen, Ger. 53/G5
Illinois (riv.), Il, US 130/B3
Illinois (state), US 130/B4
Illizi, Alg. 99/H4
Illizi (prov.), Alg. 99/G4
Illkirch-Graffenstaden, Fr. 56/D1
Illmensee, Ger. 57/F2
Illnau, Swi. 57/E3
Illora, Sp. 44/D4
Illovo, SAfr. 107/E3
Illzach, Fr. 56/D2
Ilm (riv.), Ger. 40/F4
Ilmajoki, Fin. 37/G3
Ilme (riv.), Ger. 51/G5
Il'men (lake), Rus. 64/D4
Ilmenau, Ger. 43/J1
Ilmenau (riv.), Ger. 51/H2
Ilo, Peru 156/D5
Ilobu, Nga. 103/G5
Ilorin, Nga. 103/G4
Ilovlya (riv.), Rus. 63/H2
Ilpendam, Neth. 50/B4
Ilse (riv.), Ger. 51/H5
Ilsede, Ger. 51/H4
Ilsenburg, Ger. 51/H5
Ilsfeld, Ger. 54/C4
Ilshofen, Ger. 54/C4
Ilyas Burnu (pt.), Turk. 49/H5
Ilych (riv.), Rus. 61/N3
Ilz (riv.), Ger. 41/G4
Imabari, Japan 74/C3
Imaichi, Japan 75/F2
Imaloto (riv.), Madg. 107/H8
İmamoğlu, Turk. 90/C2
Imandra (lake), Rus. 37/J2
Imari, Japan 74/A4
Imatra, Fin. 39/N1
Imazu, Japan 77/K5
Imba (lake), Japan 77/E2
Imba, Japan 77/E2
Imbabura (prov.), Ecu. 152/B4
Imbituba, Braz. 155/B4
Imbituva, Braz. 155/B3
Imeni Moskvy (canal), Rus. 61/W9
Imerimandroso, Madg. 107/J7
Imi n'tanout, Mor. 98/C3
İmişli, Azer. 63/J5
Imittós (peak), Gre. 47/N9
Imja (isl.), SKor. 73/C5
Imlay, Nv, US 126/D5
Immendingen, Ger. 57/E2
Immenhausen, Ger. 51/G6
Immenstaad am Bodensee, Ger. 57/F2
Immenstadt im Allgäu, Ger. 57/G2
Immingham, Eng, UK 35/H4
Immokalee, Fl, US 133/H5
Imnavait (mtn.), Ak, US 134/J2
Imo (state), Nga. 103/G5
Imola, It. 59/E4
Imouzzèr-Kandar, Mor. 100/B3
Imperatriz, Braz. 154/A2
Imperia, It. 58/B5
Imperial, Sk, Can. 127/G3
Imperial, Peru 156/B4
Imperial, Ne, US 129/G2
Imperial, Mo, US 137/G9
Imperial Beach, Ca, US 136/C5
Imperial Palace, Japan 77/D2
Impero (riv.), It. 58/B5
Impfondo, Congo 96/J7
Imphāl, India 83/F3
Imphy, Fr. 42/E3
Impruneta, It. 59/E5
İmrali (isl.), Turk. 49/J5
İmranlı, Turk. 90/D2
İmroz, Gre. 47/J2
Imshil, SKor. 73/D5
Imst, Aus. 57/G3
Imuris, Mex. 142/C2
Ina, Japan 75/E3
Ina, Japan 77/E2
Ina, Japan 77/D2
Ina (riv.), Pol. 38/F5
Inabe, Japan 77/L5
Inabu, Japan 77/M5
Inagawa, Japan 77/H6
Inagi, Japan 77/D2
Inajá, Braz. 154/C3
Inambari (riv.), Peru 156/D4
Inami, Japan 77/G6
Inaouene (riv.), Mor. 100/B2
Iñapari, Peru 156/D3
Inarjärvi (lake), Fin. 37/H1
Inău (peak), Rom. 49/G2
Inawashiro (lake), Japan 75/F2
Inazawa, Japan 77/L5
Inca, Sp. 45/G3
Incekum (pt.), Turk. 91/C1
Incheville, Fr. 52/A3
Inchinnan, Sc, UK 36/B5
Inchkeith (isl.), Sc, UK 36/C4
Inchnadamph, Sc, UK 31/R7
Inch'ŏn, SKor. 73/F7
Inch'on-Gwangyŏksi (prov.), SKor. 73/D4
İncirliova, Turk. 90/A2
Incisa in Val d'Arno, It. 59/E5
Inconfidentes, Braz. 211/G7
Incudine, Mont l' (peak), Fr. 46/A2
Indaiá (riv.), Braz. 155/C1
Indaiatuba, Braz. 155/C2
Indalsälven (riv.), Swe. 37/E3
Indanan, Phil. 81/F2
Inde (riv.), Ger. 53/F2
Inden, Ger. 53/F2
Independence (mts.), Nv, US 126/E5
Independence, Ks, US 129/J3
Independence, Ca, US 128/C3
Independence, Mo, US 137/E5
Independence, Belz. 144/D2
Independence Nat'l Hist. Park, Pa, US 138/C4
Independência, Braz. 154/B2
Independencia, Peru 156/B4
Index, Wa, US 135/D2
India (ctry.) 67/G7
Indian (ocean) 23/N6
Indian Echo Caverns, Pa, US 138/B3
Indian Head, Sk, Can. 127/H3
Indian Hills, Co, US 137/B3
Indian Peaks Wilderness Area, Co, US 137/A2
Indiana (state), US 130/C3
Indiana, Pa, US 130/E3
Indianapolis (int'l arpt.), In, US 130/C4
Indianapolis (cap.), In, US 130/C4
Indianola, Ms, US 129/K4
Indianola, Wa, US 135/B2
Indiantown, Fl, US 133/H5
Indiaporã, Braz. 155/B1
Indigirka (riv.), Rus. 67/P3
Ind ija, Serb. 48/E3
Indio, Ca, US 128/C4
Indira Gandhi (int'l arpt.), India 86/D5
Indochina (reg.), Laos 83/H4
Indonesia (ctry.) 81/E4
Indore, India 89/L4
Indragiri (riv.), Indo. 80/B4
Indramayu (cape), Indo. 80/C5
Indrāvati (riv.), India 70/D8
Indre (riv.), Fr. 42/D3
Indre Arna, Nor. 38/A1
Indrois (riv.), Fr. 42/D3
Induno Olona, It. 57/E6
Indus (riv.), Asia 67/G6
Industry, Ca, US 136/G7
İnebolu, Turk. 90/C1
İnece, Turk. 49/H5
İnecik, Turk. 49/H5
Inedbirenne (int'l arpt.), Alg. 99/H4
İnegöl, Turk. 90/B1
Iner (riv.), Ger. 54/C3
Ineu, Rom. 48/E2
Inezgane, Mor. 98/C3
Inezgane (Agadir) (int'l arpt.), Mor. 98/C3
Infanta (cape), SAfr. 106/C4
Infiernillo (res.), Mex. 140/A4
Infiernillo, Presa del (dam), Mex. 142/E5
Infiesto, Sp. 44/C1
Ingapirca (ruin), Ecu. 152/B5
Ingatestone, Eng, UK 30/E2
Ingelmunster, Belg. 52/C2
Ingeniero Jacobacci, Arg. 158/C4
Ingeniero Luiggi, Arg. 158/D2
Ingenio, Sp. 98/B4
Ingersheim, Fr. 56/D1
Ingettolgoy, Mong. 70/H2
Ingham, Austl. 114/B2
Ingleside, Md, US 138/C5
Inglewood, Austl. 115/B3
Inglewood, Austl. 114/C5
Inglewood, Ca, US 136/F8
Inglewood-Finn Hill, Wa, US 135/C2
Inglis, Fl, US 133/H4
Ingoda (riv.), Rus. 65/M4
Ingolstadt, Ger. 55/E5
Ingrid Christianson (coast), Ant. 160/F
Ingushetia, Resp., Rus. 63/H4
Ingwavuma, SAfr. 107/E2
Ingwiller, Fr. 53/G6
Inhambane, Moz. 105/G5
Inhambupe, Braz. 154/C3
Inharrime, Moz. 105/G5
Inhuma, Braz. 154/B2
Inhumas, Braz. 151/J7
Iniesta, Sp. 44/E3
Inifel (well), Alg. 99/F3
Inini (riv.), FrG. 153/H4
Inírida (riv.), Col. 150/E3
Inishbofin (isl.), Ire. 30/N10
Inishowen (pen.), Ire. 34/A1
Inishowen (pt.), Ire. 34/B1
Inje, SKor. 73/E3
Injune, Austl. 114/C4
Inkster, Mi, US 135/F7
Inland (sea), Japan 74/C4
Inle (lake), Myan. 83/G3
Inn (riv.), Aus. 43/J3
Inn (riv.), Ger. 43/K2
Inn (riv.), Swi. 43/J3
Innbach (riv.), Aus. 55/H6
Innellan, Sc, UK 36/B5
Inner (chan.), Belz. 144/D2
Inner (sound), Sc, UK 31/R8
Inner Hebrides (isls.), Sc, UK 31/Q8
Inner Mongolia (reg.), China 67/L5
Innerdouny (hill), Sc, UK 36/C4
Innerleithen, Sc, UK 36/C5
Innerste (riv.), Ger. 51/G4
Innertkirchen, Swi. 57/E4
Innes NP, Austl. 113/H5
Innichen (San Candito), It. 43/K3
Innisfail, Ab, Can. 126/E2
Innisfail, Austl. 114/B2
Innoko (riv.), Ak, US 134/G3
Innsbruck, Aus. 57/H3
Innviertel (reg.), Aus. 55/G6
Inny (riv.), Eng, UK 32/B5
Ino, Japan 74/C4
Inocência, Braz. 155/B1
Inongo, D.R. Congo 97/J8
İnönü, Turk. 90/B2
Inowrocław, Pol. 41/K2
Insch, Sc, UK 36/D2
Inscription (cape), Austl. 112/B3
Insein, Myan. 83/G4
Inside (passg.), BC, Can. 126/A2
Insjön, Swe. 38/F1
Inta, Rus. 61/N2
Intendente Alvear, Arg. 158/E2
İntepe, Turk. 47/K2
Intercourse, Pa, US 138/B3
Interior (plat.), BC, Can. 126/B2
Interlaken, Swi. 56/D4
Internacional (int'l arpt.), Braz. 156/D2
Internacional (int'l arpt.), Mex. 143/E5
International Peace Garden, ND, US 127/H3
Inthanon (peak), Thai. 83/G4
Întorsura Buzăului, Rom. 49/H3
Intracoastal Waterway, La, US 137/P17
Intragna, Swi. 57/E5
Introbio, It. 57/F6
Inubō-zaki (pt.), Japan 75/G3
Inukjuak, Qu, Can. 123/J3
Inutil (bay), Chile 159/C7
Inuvik, NW, Can. 134/M2
Inuyama, Japan 77/L5
Inver (bay), Sc, UK 36/C1
Inveraray, Sc, UK 36/A4
Inverbervie, Sc, UK 36/D3
Invercargill, NZ 117/R12
Inverclyde (pol. reg.), Sc, UK 36/B5
Inverell, Austl. 115/D1
Invergordon, Sc, UK 36/B1
Inverie, Sc, UK 31/R8
Inverigo, It. 58/C1
Inverkeithing, Sc, UK 36/C4
Inverloch, Austl. 115/C3
Invermay, Sk, Can. 127/H3
Inverness, Sc, UK 36/B2
Inverness, Al, US 133/G3
Inverness, Fl, US 133/H4
Inveruno, It. 58/B1
Inverurie, Sc, UK 36/D2
Investigator (str.), Austl. 109/C4
Invorio, It. 58/B1
Inwood, NY, US 139/L9
Inyanga, Zim. 105/F4
Inyangani (peak), Zim. 105/F4
Inymney (peak), Rus. 134/D2
Inyo (mts.), Ca, US 128/C3
Inza, Rus. 63/H1
Inzai, Japan 77/E2
Inzigkofen, Ger. 57/F1
Inzing, Aus. 57/H3
Iō-shima (isl.), Japan 74/B5
Ioánnina (int'l arpt.), Gre. 47/G3
Ioánnina, Gre. 47/G3
Iolotan', Trkm. 89/H1
Iona (isl.), Sc, UK 31/Q8
Iona, PN da, Ang. 105/B4
Ione, Co, US 137/C2
Ionia, Mi, US 130/C3
Ionian (sea), Gre. 47/F3
Ionian (isls.), Gre. 27/F5
Íos (isl.), Gre. 47/J4
Iouîk (cape), Mrta. 102/A2
Iowa (state), US 129/J2
Iowa (riv.), Ia, US 127/K5
Iowa Falls, Ia, US 127/K5
Ipameri, Braz. 155/B1
Ipanema, Braz. 155/D1
Iparia, Peru 156/C3
Ipatinga, Braz. 155/D1
Ipel' (riv.), Slvk. 41/K4
Iphofen, Ger. 54/D3
Ipiales, Col. 152/B4
Ipiaú, Braz. 154/C4
Ipil, Phil. 79/D6
Ipirá, Braz. 154/C4
Ipiranga, Braz. 155/B3
Ipoh, Malay. 80/B3
Ipoly (riv.), Hun. 41/K4
Iporá, Braz. 151/H7
Ipsala, Turk. 47/K2
Ipsheim, Ger. 54/D3
Ipswich, SD, US 127/J4
Ipswich, Eng, UK 33/H2
Ipu, Braz. 154/B2
Ipuã, Braz. 155/B2
Ipubi, Braz. 154/B2
Ipueiras, Braz. 154/B2
Ipuiúna, Braz. 211/G7
Ipumba (hill), Tanz. 104/A4
Ipun, Isla (isl.), Chile 158/B5
Ipupiara, Braz. 154/B3
Iqaluit (cap.), Nun, Can. 123/K2
Iquique, Chile 150/D8
Iquitos, Peru 156/C1
Irago (chan.), Japan 77/L6
Irago-misaki (cape), Japan 77/M6
Iráklia, Gre. 47/H2
Iráklia (isl.), Gre. 47/J4
Iráklion, Gre. 47/J5
Iráklion (int'l arpt.), Gre. 47/J5
Iramaia, Braz. 154/B4
Iran (mts.), Indo.,Mal 80/D3
Iran (ctry.) 67/E6
Irapa, Ven. 153/F2
Irapuato, Mex. 143/E4
Iraq (ctry.) 88/D2
Irará, Braz. 154/C4
Irati, Braz. 155/B3
Irauçuba, Braz. 154/C1
Irbid (gov.), Jor. 91/D3
Irbid, Jor. 91/D3
Irbīl, Iraq 90/F2
Irecê, Braz. 154/B3
Ireland (ctry.) 31/P10
Ireland's Eye (isl.), Ire. 34/B5
Iremel' (peak), Rus. 61/N5
Iretama, Braz. 155/A3
Irfon (riv.), Wal, UK 32/C2
Irharhar, Oued (riv.), Alg. 99/G4
Irhazer Oua-n-Agadez (riv.), Niger 103/G2
Iri, SKor. 73/D5
Irian Jaya (reg.), Indo. 81/H4
Iricoume (mts.), Braz. 153/G4
Irig, Serb. 48/D3
Irîgui (phys. reg.), Mali 102/D2
Iriklinskiy (res.), Rus. 63/L2
Iringa (prov.), Tanz. 104/B5
Iringa, Tanz. 104/B4
Iriomote (isl.), Japan 79/D3
Iriri (riv.), Braz. 151/H4
Irish (sea), Ire.,UK 34/C4
Irlam, Eng, UK 35/F5
Irō-zaki (pt.), Japan 75/F3
Iroise (bay), Fr. 42/A2
Iron Baron, Austl. 113/H5
Iron Knob, Austl. 113/H5
Iron Mountain, Mi, US 127/L4
Irondale, Co, US 137/C3
Ironton, Oh, US 130/D4
Ironton, Ut, US 137/K13
Ironwood, Mi, US 127/L4
Ironwood Forest Nat'l Mon., Az, US 128/E4
Irput' (riv.), Rus. 62/E1
Irrawaddy (Ayeyarwady) (riv.), Myan. 67/J7
Irrawaddy, Mouths of the (delta), Myan. 83/F4
Irsch, Ger. 53/F4
Irsen (riv.), Ger. 53/F3
Irsina, It. 46/E2
Irt (riv.), Eng, UK 35/E3
Irthing (riv.), Eng, UK 35/F1
Irthlingborough, Eng, UK 33/F2
Irtysh (riv.), Rus. 67/G4
Iruma, Japan 77/C2
Irumu, D.R. Congo 104/A2
Irún, Sp. 44/E1
Irvine, Ca, US 136/G8
Irvine, Sc, UK 36/B5
Irvine (bay), Sc, UK 36/B5
Irvine (riv.), Sc, UK 36/B5
Irving, Tx, US 132/D3
Irvington, NJ, US 139/J9
Irvington, NY, US 139/K7
Is (peak), Sudan 101/C4
Is-sur-Tille, Fr. 56/B2
Īsa Khel, Pak. 86/A3
Isaac (riv.), Austl. 109/D3
Isabela, Phil. 81/F2
Isabela, PR 141/M8
Isabela (isl.), Ecu. 156/E7
Isabelia (mts.), Nic. 144/E3
Isabella (bay), Nun., Can. 123/K2
Isaccea, Rom. 49/J3
Isachsen (cape), Nun., Can. 123/R7
Ísafjardhardjúp (inlet), Ice. 37/M6
Ísafjördhur, Ice. 37/M6
Isahaya, Japan 74/B4
Isalo, PN de l', Madg. 107/H8
Isalo Ruiniform (mass.), Madg. 107/H8
Isana (riv.), Col. 152/D4
Isandhlwana Battlesite, SAfr. 107/E3
Isangano NP, Zam. 104/A5
Isaouanne-n-Irarraren (des.), Alg. 99/G4
Isaouanne-n-Tifernine (des.), Alg. 99/G4
Isarco (riv.), It. 43/J3
Isarco (Eisack) (riv.), It. 57/H4
Isaszeg, Hun. 49/R9
Isawa, Japan 77/B2
Isbergues, Fr. 52/B2
Iscar, Sp. 44/C2
Ischgl, Aus. 57/G3
Ischia, It. 48/A5
Ise (bay), Japan 75/E3
Ise (riv.), Eng, UK 33/F2
Ise, Japan 77/L7
Ise-Shima NP, Japan 75/E3
Isehara, Japan 75/F3
Iselin, NJ, US 139/H9
Isen, Ger. 55/F6
Isen (riv.), Ger. 40/G4
Isenthal, Swi. 57/E4
Iseo (lake), It. 43/J4
Iseo, It. 58/D1
Iseo, Lago d' (lake), It. 58/C1
Isère (riv.), Fr. 42/F4
Isère (dept.), Fr. 56/B6
Iserlohn, Ger. 51/E6
Isernia, It. 46/D2
Isesaki, Japan 75/F2
Iset' (riv.), Rus. 87/D1
Iseyin, Nga. 103/F5
'Isfiyā, Isr. 91/G6
Ishi (riv.), Japan 77/J7
Ishibashi, Japan 75/F2
Ishibe, Japan 77/K5
Ishidoriya, Japan 76/B4
Ishigaki (isl.), Japan 79/D3
Ishige, Japan 75/F2
Ishikari, Japan 76/B2

Jing Xian, China 83/J2
Jingbian, China 72/B3
Jingde, China 79/C1
Jingdezhen, China 79/C2
Jingdong, China 83/H3
Jinggangshan, China 83/K2
Jinghai, China 72/H7
Jinghe, China 70/D3
Jinghong, China 83/H3
Jingjiang, China 72/E4
Jingle, China 72/B3
Jingmen, China 72/C5
Jingshan, China 72/C5
Jingxi, China 83/J3
Jingyuan, China 70/H4
Jinhu, China 72/D4
Jinhua, China 79/C2
Jining, China 72/C2
Jining, China 72/D4
Jinja, Ugan. 104/B2
Jinkouhe, China 83/H2
Jinotega, Nic. 144/E3
Jinotepe, Nic. 144/E4
Jinping, China 83/J2
Jinsha, China 83/J2
Jinsha (riv.), China 67/J7
Jinshan, China 72/L9
Jinshi, China 83/K2
Jintan, China 72/D5
Jintotolo (chan.), Phil. 79/D5
Jintūr, India 89/L5
Jinxi, China 79/C2
Jinxi, China 72/E2
Jinxian, China 79/C2
Jinxiang, China 72/D4
Jinyun, China 79/D2
Jinzhai, China 72/C5
Jinzhou (bay), China 73/A3
Jinzhou, China 72/E2
Jiparana (riv.), Braz. 150/F5
Jipijapa, Ecu. 152/A5
Jiquilpan de Juárez, Mex. 142/E5
Jiquipilco, Mex. 143/Q9
Jiřkov, Czh. 55/G1
Jishan, China 72/B4
Jishou, China 83/J2
Jishui, China 79/C2
Jisr ash Shughūr, Syria 91/E2
Jiu (riv.), Rom. 62/B3
Jiujiang, China 79/C2
Jiujiang, China 79/C2
Jiulong, China 83/H2
Jiutai, China 71/N3
Jiutepec, Mex. 143/K8
Jiuwan (mts.), China 70/J6
Jixi, China 71/P2
Jixi, China 79/C1
Jiyang, China 72/D3
Jiyuan, China 72/C4
Jīzān, SAr. 88/D5
Jize, China 72/C3
Jizera (riv.), Czh. 41/H3
Jizō-zaki (pt.), Japan 74/C3
Jizzakh, Uzb. 87/E4
Jizzakh (pol. reg.), Uzb. 87/E4
Joaçaba, Braz. 155/B3
Joachín, Mex. 143/N8
Joaíma, Braz. 154/B5
João Câmara, Braz. 154/D2
João Lisboa, Braz. 154/A2
João Monlevade, Braz. 155/D1
João Pessoa, Braz. 154/D2
João Pinheiro, Braz. 154/A5
Joaquín V. González, Arg. 157/D2
Jobabo, Cuba 145/G1
Jockgrim, Ger. 54/B4
Jocón, Hon. 144/E3
Jódar, Sp. 44/D4
Jodhpur, India 89/K3
Jodoigne, Belg. 53/D2
Joensuu, Fin. 60/F3
Jōetsu, Japan 75/F2
Jogbani, India 85/F2
Johannesberg, Ger. 54/C2
Johannesburg, SAfr. 106/E2
Johanngeorgenstadt, Ger. 55/F2
Johilla (riv.), India 84/C4
John Day, Or, US 126/D4
John Day (riv.), Or, US 124/B2
John Day Fossil Beds Nat'l Mon., Or, US 126/C4
John Day, Middle Fork (riv.), Or, US 126/D4
John Day, North Fork (riv.), Or, US 126/D4
John F. Kennedy (int'l arpt.), NY, US 139/K9
John Forrest NP, Austl. 112/L6
John H. Kerr (res.), NC,Va, US 133/J2
John Martin (res.), Co, US 132/C2
John Wayne/Orange County (int'l arpt.), Ca, US 136/G8
Johnson (co.), Ks, US 137/D6
Johnson City, Tn, US 130/D4
Johnsonburg, NJ, US 138/D2
Johnsons Crossing, Yk, Can. 134/M3
Johnston (falls), Zam. 104/A5
Johnston (lake), Austl. 109/B4
Johnston Atoll (isl.), Pac., US 117/J3
Johnstone, Sc, UK 36/B5
Johnstown, Pa, US 130/E3
Johnstown, Co, US 137/C2
Johnsville, Md, US 138/A4
Johor Baharu, Malay. 80/B3
Jöhstadt, Ger. 55/G1
Joigny, Fr. 42/E3
Joinvile, Braz. 155/B3
Joinville, Fr. 56/B1
Jojutla, Mex. 143/K8
Jokioinen, Fin. 39/K1
Jokkmokk, Swe. 37/F2
Jökulsargljufur NP, Ice. 37/P6
Jolanda di Savoia, It. 59/E3
Joliette, Qu, Can. 130/F2
Jollyville, Tx, US 129/H5
Jolo (isl.), Phil. 81/F2
Jolo, Phil. 81/F2
Jomala, Fin. 39/H1
Jombang, Indo. 80/D5
Jomda, China 70/G5
Jomo Kenyatta (int'l arpt.), Kenya 104/C3
Jona, Swi. 57/E3
Jonacatepec, Mex. 143/L8
Jonava, Lith. 39/L4
Jonchery-sur-Vesle, Fr. 52/C5
Jones, Ok, US 137/N14
Jones (inlet), NY, US 139/L9
Jones (mtn.), Pa, US 138/A2
Jones (sound), Nun., Can. 123/S7
Jones Beach State Park, NY, US 139/L9
Jonesboro, Ar, US 129/K4
Jonesboro, La, US 129/J4
Jönköping, Swe. 38/F3
Jönköping (co.), Swe. 37/E4
Jonquière, Qu, Can. 131/G1
Jonuta, Mex. 140/C4
Joondalup (lake), Austl. 112/K6
Joplin, Mo, US 129/J3
Joppatowne (Joppa), Md, US 138/B5
Jora, India 84/A2
Jordan, Mt, US 126/G4
Jordan, On, Can. 131/R9
Jordan (riv.), Isr.,Jor. 91/D4
Jordan (ctry.) 88/C2
Jordan Valley, Or, US 126/D5
Jordânia, Braz. 154/B4
Jorge (cape), Chile 159/B6
Jorge Chavez (int'l arpt.), Peru 156/B4
Jork, Ger. 51/G1
Jornada del Muerto (valley), NM, US 132/B3
Jørpeland, Nor. 38/B2
Jos (plat.), Nga. 96/G6
Jos, Nga. 103/H4
Jose Abad Santos, Phil. 81/G2
José Batlle y Ordóñez, Uru. 159/G2
José Bonifácio, Braz. 155/B2
José Cardel, Mex. 143/N7
José de Freitas, Braz. 154/B2
José de San Martín, Arg. 157/B5
José Enrique Rodó, Uru. 159/K10
José María Morelos, Mex. 144/D2
Jose Marti (int'l arpt.), Cuba 145/F1
José Pedro Varela, Uru. 159/G2
José, South (dept.), Uru. 159/F2
Josefa Camejo (int'l arpt.), Ven. 152/D2
Joseph Bonaparte (gulf), Austl. 109/B2
Joshin-Etsu Kogen NP, Japan 75/F2
Joshua (pt.), Ct, US 139/F1
Joshua Tree NP, Ca, US 128/D4
Jossa (riv.), Ger. 54/C2
Jotunheimen NP, Nor. 38/C1
Jouanne (riv.), Fr. 42/C2
Jouarre, Fr. 30/M5
Joué-lès-Tours, Fr. 42/D3
Jœuf, Fr. 53/F5
Jourama Falls NP, Austl. 114/B2
Jourdanton, Tx, US 129/H5
Joure, Neth. 50/C3
Joutseno, Fin. 39/N1
Joux (lake), Swi. 56/C4
Jouy-en-Josas, Fr. 30/J5
Jouy-le-Châtel, Fr. 30/M6
Jouy-le-Moutier, Fr. 30/J4
Jouy-sur-Morin, Fr. 52/C6
Jovellanos, Cuba 145/F1
Joveyn (riv.), Iran 89/G1
Jowai, India 83/F2
Joy (mt.), Yk, Can. 134/M3
Jōyō, Japan 77/J6
Jozankei Spa, Japan 76/B2
Ju Xian, China 72/D4
Juan Aldama, Mex. 142/E3
Juan de Fuca (str.), BC, Can.,US 122/D4
Juan de Fuca, Strait of (str.), US,Can. 126/B3
Juan de Nova (isl.), Fr. 93/G6
Juan Fernández (isls.), Chile 147/A6
Juan Fernández, Arg. 158/F3
Juan José Paso, Arg. 158/E2
Juan L. Lacaze, Uru. 159/K11
Juan Santamaria (int'l arpt.), CR 145/E4
Juancheng, China 72/C4
Juangriego, Ven. 153/F2
Juanjuí, Peru 156/B2
Juárez, Arg. 158/F3
Juarez, Sierra de (mts.), Mex. 128/D4
Juatinga, Ponta de (pt.), Braz. 211/J8
Juazeirinho, Braz. 154/C2
Juazeiro, Braz. 154/B3
Juazeiro do Norte, Braz. 154/C2
Juba, Sudan 97/M7
Jubany, Arg., Ant. 160/W
Jubba (riv.), Som. 97/P7
Jübek, Ger. 40/E1
Jubones (riv.), Ecu. 156/B1
Juby (cape), Mor. 98/B4
Júcar (riv.), Sp. 44/D3
Jucás, Braz. 154/C2
Jüchen, Ger. 53/F1
Juchipila, Mex. 142/E4
Juchique de Ferrer, Mex. 143/N7
Juchitán de Zaragoza, Mex. 144/C2
Juchitepec, Mex. 143/R10
Jucurutu, Braz. 154/C2
Judaberg, Nor. 38/A2
Judenburg, Aus. 43/L3
Judith (riv.), Mt, US 126/F4
Juelsminde, Den. 38/D4
Juhaynah, Egypt 101/B3
Juigalpa, Nic. 144/E3
Juilly, Fr. 30/L4
Juine (riv.), Fr. 42/E2
Juist (isl.), Ger. 50/D1
Juist, Ger. 50/E1
Juiz de Fora, Braz. 211/K6
Jujurieux, Fr. 56/B5
Julbach, Ger. 55/F6
Julesburg, Co, US 127/H5
Juli, Peru 156/D5
Julia Creek, Austl. 114/A3
Juliaca, Peru 156/D4
Julian Alps (mts.), It. 43/K3
Juliana Top (peak), Sur. 151/G3
Jülich, Ger. 53/F2
Julio A. Mella, Cuba 145/H1
Juliustown, NJ, US 138/D3
Jullundur, India 86/C4
Julu, China 72/C3
Jumbilla, Peru 156/B2
Jumeauville, Fr. 30/H5
Jumilla, Sp. 44/E3
Juminda (pt.), Est. 39/L2
Jumla, Nepal 84/D1
Jümme (riv.), Ger. 51/E2
Jūmonji, Japan 76/B4
Junāgadh, India 89/K4
Junan, China 72/D4
Juncal (peak), Chile 158/N8
Junction, Ut, US 128/D3
Junction, Tx, US 129/H5
Junction City, Or, US 126/C4
Jundiaí, Braz. 211/G8
Jundu (mts.), China 72/H6
Juneda, Sp. 45/F2
Junee, Austl. 115/C2
Jungar Qi, China 72/B3
Jungfrau (peak), Swi. 56/D4
Jungfraujoch, Swi. 56/D4
Junglinster, Lux. 53/F4
Juniata (co.), Pa, US 138/A2
Juniata (riv.), Pa, US 130/E3
Junik, Serb. 47/G1
Junín, Peru 156/B3
Junín (dept.), Peru 156/C3
Junín, Ecu. 152/A5
Junín, Arg. 158/C2
Junín, Arg. 158/E2
Junín de los Andes, Arg. 158/C3
Juniper Hills, Ca, US 136/C2
Junji (pass), China 72/C3
Juno Beach, Fl, US 133/H5
Junqueirópolis, Braz. 155/B2
Junsele, Swe. 37/F3
Juparanã, Lagoa (lake), Braz. 155/D1
Jupiter (riv.), Qu, Can. 131/J1
Jupiter, Fl, US 133/H5
Jupiter (mt.), Wa, US 135/A2
Juquiá, Braz. 155/C3
Juquitiba, Braz. 211/F8
Jur (riv.), Sudan 97/L6
Jur pri Bratislave, Slvk. 48/C1
Jura (mts.), Fr. 42/F3
Jura (dept.), Fr. 56/B4
Jura (pen.), Sc, UK 31/R8
Jura (isl.), Sc, UK 31/Q9
Juradó, Col. 152/B3
Jurançon, Fr. 42/C5
Jurbise, Belg. 52/C2
Jurien, Austl. 112/B4
Jūrmala, Lat. 39/K3
Juruá (riv.), Braz. 147/C3
Juruena (riv.), Braz. 147/D4
Juruti, Braz. 151/G4
Jushiyama, Japan 77/L5
Juskatla, BC, Can. 134/M5
Jussey, Fr. 56/B2
Jussy, Swi. 56/C5
Jussy, Fr. 52/C4
Justo Daract, Arg. 158/D2
Jutaí, Braz. 150/E5
Jutaí (riv.), Braz. 150/E4
Jutiapa, Guat. 144/D3
Juticalpa, Hon. 144/E3
Jutland, NJ, US 138/D2
Jutland (pen.), Den. 37/D4
Juventud, La (isl.), Cuba 145/F1
Juye, China 72/D4
Juzhang (riv.), China 72/C5
Juziers, Fr. 30/H4
Južna Morava (riv.), Serb. 48/E4
Juzur Qarqannah (isl.), Congo 99/H2
Jyderup, Den. 38/D4

K

Ka (riv.), Nga. 96/F5
Ka (isl.), NKor. 73/C3
Ka Lae (cape), Hi, US 124/U11
Kaaawa, Hi, US 124/W12
Kaabong, Ugan. 104/B2
Kaala (peak), Hi, US 124/V12
Kaalualu, Hi, US 124/U11
Kaap Plato (plat.), SAfr. 106/C3
Kaarina, Fin. 39/K1
Kaarst, Ger. 50/D6
Kaba, Hun. 48/E2
Kabadak (riv.), Bang. 85/G4
Kabaena (isl.), Indo. 81/F5
Kabah (ruin), Mex. 144/D1
Kabala, SLeo. 102/C4
Kabale, Ugan. 104/A3
Kabalega (falls), Ugan. 104/A2
Kabalega NP, Ugan. 97/M7
Kabalo, D.R. Congo 105/E2
Kabamba, Lac (lake), D.R. Congo 105/E2
Kabankalan, Phil. 81/F2
Kabardino-Balkaria, Resp., Rus. 63/G4
Kabare, D.R. Congo 104/A3
Kaberamaido, Ugan. 104/B2
Kabinakagani (lake), On, Can. 130/C1
Kabinda, D.R. Congo 105/D2
Kabîr, Oued el (riv.), Alg. 100/H4
Kabīrwāla, Pak. 86/A4
Kabīyah, Sabkhat al (swamp), Tun. 46/A5
Kableshkovo, Bul. 49/H4
Kābol (Kabul) (cap.), Afg. 89/J2
Kabompo (riv.), Zam. 105/D3
Kabongo, D.R. Congo 105/E2
Kabrai, India 84/C3
Kābul (riv.), Afg. 89/J2
Kabul (Kābol) (cap.), Afg. 89/J2
Kaburuang (isl.), Indo. 81/G3
Kabwe, Zam. 105/E3
Kačanik, Serb. 47/G1
Kachalola, Zam. 105/F3
Kachemak (bay) 134/H4
Kachemak, Ak, US 134/H4
Kachin (div), Myan. 70/G6
Kaçkar Daì (peak), Turk. 90/E1
Kadaianallur, India 82/C6
Kadam (peak), Ugan. 104/B2
Kadam (isl.), Myan. 83/G5
Kadan (isl.), Myan. 78/B3
Kadaň, Czh. 55/G2
Kadavu (isl.), Fiji 116/G6
Kadéï (riv.), CAfr.,Cam 96/J7
Kadina, Austl. 113/H5
Kadınhanı, Turk. 90/C2
Kadiogo (prov.), Burk. 103/E3
Kadiolo, Mali 102/D4
Kadiri, India 82/C5
Kadirli, Turk. 90/D2
Kadışehri, Turk. 90/C1
Kadoka, SD, US 127/H5
Kadoma, Zim. 105/E4
Kadoma, Japan 77/J6
Kaduna (state), Nga. 103/G4
Kaduna, Nga. 103/G4
Kaduna (riv.), Nga. 93/C4
Kāduqli, Sudan 97/L5
Kaech'ŏn, NKor. 73/C3
Kaédi, Mrta. 102/B2
Kaélé, Camr. 96/H5
Kaena (pt.), Hi, US 124/V12
Kaeng Krachan NP, Thai. 78/B3
Kaesŏng, NKor. 73/D3
Kaesŏng-si (prov.), NKor. 73/D4
Kafar Jar Ghar (mts.), Afg. 89/J2
Kaffraria (reg.), SAfr. 106/D4
Kaffrine, Sen. 102/B3
Kafirévs (cape), Gre. 47/J3
Kafr Ash Shaykh (gov.), Egypt 101/B1
Kafr ash Shaykh, Egypt 91/B4
Kafr az Zayyāt, Egypt 91/B4
Kafr Kannā, Isr. 91/G6
Kafr Mandā, Isr. 91/G6
Kafr Qari', Isr. 91/G6
Kafr Qāsim, Isr. 91/F7
Kafu (riv.), Ugan. 104/A2
Kafue (riv.), Zam. 105/E4
Kafue, Zam. 105/E4
Kafue NP, Zam. 105/E3
Kaga, Japan 74/E2
Kaga Bandoro, CAfr. 97/J6
Kagan, Uzb. 87/D5
Kāgān (valley), Pak. 86/B2
Kagawa (pref.), Japan 74/D3
Kagera (riv.), Tanz. 104/A3
Kağızman, Turk. 90/E1
Kagoshima (int'l arpt.), Japan 74/B5
Kagoshima, Japan 74/B5
Kagoshima (bay), Japan 74/B5
Kagoshima (dept.), Japan 75/L5
Kahaluu, Hi, US 124/W13
Kahama, Tanz. 104/B3
Kahayan (riv.), Indo. 80/D4
Kahiu (pt.), Hi, US 124/T10
Kahl am Main, Ger. 54/C2
Kāhna, Pak. 86/C4
Kahoka, Mo, US 127/L5
Kahoolawe (isl.), Hi, US 124/T10
Kahperusvaara (peak), Fin. 37/G1
Kahraman Maraş (prov.), Turk. 90/D2
Kahramanmaraş, Turk. 90/D2
Kahror Pakka, Pak. 86/A5
Kâhta, Turk. 90/D2
Kahuku, Hi, US 124/W12
Kahuku (pt.), Hi, US 124/W12
Kahului, Hi, US 124/T10
Kahuzi-Biega, PN de, D.R. Congo 105/E1
Kai (isls.), Indo. 81/H5
Kai Besar (isl.), Indo. 81/H5
Kai Kecil (isl.), Indo. 81/H5
Kaiapoi, NZ 117/S11
Kaibab (plat.), Az, US 128/D3
Kaibara, Japan 77/H5
Kaieteur (falls), Guy. 153/G3
Kaieteur NP, Guy. 153/G3
Kaifeng, China 71/K5
Kaifeng, China 72/C4
Kaihua, China 79/C2
Kaikohe, NZ 117/S10
Kaikoura, NZ 117/S11
Kaili, China 83/J2
Kailu, China 72/E2
Kailua, Hi, US 124/U11
Kailua, Hi, US 124/W13
Kaimganj, India 84/B2
Kaimur (range), India 84/C3
Kainab (riv.), Namb. 106/B2
Kainach (riv.), Aus. 48/B2
Kainan, Japan 74/D3
Kainji (dam), Nga. 103/G4
Kainji (lake), Nga. 93/C3
Kainji Lake NP, Nga. 103/F4
Kainoúryion, Gre. 47/G3
Kaipara (har.), NZ 117/S10
Kairāna, India 86/D5
Kairi, Austl. 114/B2
Kaisei, Japan 77/C3
Kaiseregg (peak), Swi. 56/D4
Kaisersesch, Ger. 53/G3
Kaiserslautern, Ger. 53/G5
Kaisheim, Ger. 54/D5
Kaitaia, NZ 117/S10
Kaithal, India 86/D5
Kaiwi (chan.), Hi, US 124/T10
Kaiyang, China 83/J2
Kaiyuan, China 83/H3
Kaiyuan, China 72/F2
Kaizu, Japan 77/L5
Kaizuka, Japan 77/H7
Kajaani, Fin. 37/H2
Kaji-san (peak), SKor. 74/A3
Kajiado, Kenya 104/C3
Kajikazawa, Japan 77/A2
Kakamas, SAfr. 106/C3
Kakamega, Kenya 104/B2
Kakamigahara, Japan 77/L5
Kakanj, Bosn. 48/D3
Kake, Ak, US 134/M4
Kaketsa (mtn.), BC, Can. 134/M4
Kakhovka, Ukr. 49/L2
Kakhovs'ke Vodoskhovyshche (res.), Ukr. 62/E3
Kākināda, India 82/D4
Kakiri, Ugan. 104/B2
Kako (riv.), Japan 77/G6
Kakogawa, Japan 77/G6
Kākori, India 84/C2
Kakrāla, India 84/B2
Kakrima (riv.), Gui. 102/B4
Kaktovik, Ak, US 134/K1
Kakuda, Japan 75/G2
Kakunodate, Japan 76/B4
Kalaa Kebira, Tun. 46/B5
Kālābāgh, Pak. 86/A3
Kalabo, Zam. 105/D3
Kalach, Rus. 63/G2
Kalach-na-Donu, Rus. 63/G2
Kalachinsk, Rus. 87/F1
Kaladan (riv.), Myan. 83/F3
Kālāgarh, India 84/B1
Kalahari (des.), Namb. 93/D7
Kalahari-Gemsbok NP, SAfr. 105/C6
Kalaheo, Hi, US 124/S10
Kalaiya, Nepal 85/E2
Kalalé, Ben. 103/F4
Kalamákion, Gre. 47/N8
Kalamaloué, PN de, Camr. 96/H5
Kalamariá, Gre. 47/H2
Kalamáta, Gre. 47/H4
Kalamazoo, Mi, US 130/C3
Kalampáka, Gre. 47/G3
Kalandy, Madg. 107/J6
Kalaoa, Hi, US 124/U11
Kalasin, Thai. 78/C2
Kalāswāla, Pak. 86/C3
Kalāt, Pak. 89/J3
Kalaupapa, Hi, US 124/T10
Kalávrita, Gre. 47/H3
Kalbach, Ger. 54/B2
Kalbar, Austl. 114/D4
Kalbarri, Austl. 112/B3
Kalbarri NP, Austl. 112/B3
Kaldakvísl (riv.), Ice. 37/N7
Kale, Turk. 62/F4
Kale, Turk. 91/A1
Kalecik, Turk. 90/C1
Kalefeld, Ger. 51/H5
Kalemie (int'l arpt.), D.R. Congo 104/A4
Kalemie, D.R. Congo 104/A4
Kalemyo, Myan. 83/F3
Kalety, Pol. 41/K3
Kalewa, Myan. 83/F3
Kaleya, Zam. 105/E4
Kalgoorlie-Boulder, Austl. 112/D4
Kāli (riv.), India 84/B1
Kali (riv.), India 84/B2
Kāli (riv.), Nepal 84/D2
Kalianda, Indo. 80/C5
Kalima, D.R. Congo 97/L8
Kalimantan (reg.), Indo. 80/D4
Kálimnos, Gre. 90/A2
Kálimnos (isl.), Gre. 90/A2
Kālimpong, India 85/G2
Kaliningrad, Rus. 61/W9
Kaliningrad, Rus. 39/J4
Kaliningradskaya Oblast, Rus. 60/D5
Kalininsk, Rus. 63/H2
Kalinkavichy, Bela. 62/D1
Kaliro, Ugan. 104/B2
Kalisizo, Ugan. 104/A3
Kalispell, Mt, US 126/E3
Kalisz, Pol. 41/K3
Kalix, Swe. 60/D2
Kalixälven (riv.), Swe. 37/G2
Kāliyāganj, India 85/G3
Kalkaska, Mi, US 130/C2
Kallham, Aus. 55/G6
Kallinge, Swe. 38/F3
Kallinge (int'l arpt.), Swe. 38/F3
Kallithéa, Gre. 47/N9
Kallsjön (lake), Swe. 37/E3
Kalmar, Swe. 38/G3
Kalmar (co.), Swe. 37/F4
Kalmar (int'l arpt.), Swe. 38/G3
Kalmarsund (sound), Swe. 38/G3
Kalmthout, Belg. 50/B6
Kalmykia, Resp., Rus. 64/E5
Kālna, India 85/G4
Kalni (riv.), Bang. 85/H3
Kalocsa, Hun. 48/D2
Kalofer, Bul. 47/J1
Kalohi (chan.), Hi, US 124/T10
Kalokhórion, Gre. 47/H2
Kālol, India 89/K4
Kalomo, Zam. 105/E4
Kalongo, Ugan. 104/B2
Kālpi, India 84/B2
Kalpin, China 70/C3
Kalsdorf bei Graz, Aus. 43/L3
Kaltag, Ak, US 134/G3
Kaltbrunn, Swi. 57/F3
Kaltenleutgeben, Aus. 49/N7
Kaltennordheim, Ger. 54/D1
Kaltern (Caldaro), It. 43/J3
Kalu (riv.), SrL. 82/D6
Kaluga, Rus. 60/H5
Kalundborg, Den. 38/D4
Kalungu, Ugan. 104/A3
Kalungwishi (riv.), Zam. 104/A5
Kalūr Kot, Pak. 86/A3
Kalush, Ukr. 62/C2
Kalutara, SrL. 82/C6
Kaluzhskaya Oblast, Rus. 60/G5
Kalyān, India 89/K5
Kama, D.R. Congo 105/E1
Kama (res.), Rus. 61/M4
Kama (riv.), Rus. 27/K3
Kamagaya, Japan 77/E2
Kamaishi, Japan 76/B4
Kamakou (peak), Hi, US 124/T10
Kamakura, Japan 77/D3
Kamālia, Pak. 86/B4
Kamalo, Hi, US 124/T10
Kāman, India 84/A2
Kaman, Turk. 90/C2
Kamango (lake), Mali 102/E2
Kamanjab, Namb. 105/B4
Kamarang, Guy. 153/F3
Kāmāreddi, India 82/C4
Kāmārhāti, India 82/E3
Kamaria (falls), Guy. 153/G3
Kambalda, Austl. 112/D4
Kambar, Pak. 82/A2
Kambara, Japan 77/B3
Kambia, SLeo. 102/B4
Kambove, D.R. Congo 105/E3
Kambuno (peak), Indo. 81/F4
Kamchatka (pen.), Rus. 67/Q4
Kamchatskaya Oblast, Rus. 65/R4
Kamchiya (riv.), Bul. 62/C4
Kamen, Ger. 51/E5
Kamen'-na-Obi, Rus. 87/H2
Kamenka, Rus. 63/H1
Kameno, Bul. 49/H4
Kamensk-Shakhtinskiy, Rus. 62/G2
Kamensk-Ural'skiy, Rus. 61/P4
Kameoka, Japan 77/J5
Kameyama, Japan 77/K6
Kami, Japan 77/G5
Kami (isl.), Japan 77/M6
Kami-koshiki (isl.), Japan 74/A5
Kamiah, Id, US 126/D4
Kamień Pomorski, Pol. 38/F5
Kamieskroon, SAfr. 106/B3
Kamifukuoka, Japan 77/D2
Kamiisco, Japan 76/B3
Kamiishizu, Japan 77/K5
Kamiizumi, Japan 77/C1
Kamikawa, Japan 76/C2
Kamikuishiki, Japan 77/B2
Kamilo (pt.), Hi, US 124/U11
Kamina, D.R. Congo 105/E2
Kaminaka, Japan 77/J5
Kaminoho, Japan 77/M4
Kaminoyama, Japan 75/G1
Kamisato, Japan 77/C1
Kamishak (bay), Ak, US 134/H4
Kamiyahagi, Japan 77/M5
Kamiyaku, Japan 75/L5
Kamla (riv.), India 85/F3
Kamloops, BC, Can. 126/C3
Kammaki, Japan 77/J6
Kamnik, Slov. 43/L3
Kamo, Japan 75/F2
Kamo, Japan 77/J6
Kamo (riv.), Japan 77/E3
Kamogawa, Japan 75/G3
Kamojima, Japan 74/D3
Kāmoke, Pak. 86/C4
Kamp (riv.), Aus. 41/H4
Kamp-Bornhofen, Ger. 53/G3
Kamp-Lintfort, Ger. 50/D5
Kampala (cap.), Ugan. 104/B2
Kampar, Malay. 80/B3
Kampar (riv.), Indo. 80/B3
Kampen, Neth. 50/C3
Kampen, Ger. 38/C4
Kamphaeng Phet, Thai. 78/C5
Kamphaeng Phet (ruin), Thai. 78/B2
Kampinoski NP, Pol. 62/B1
Kamp'o, SKor. 73/E5
Kampong Kuala Besut, Malay. 80/B2
Kampong Saom (bay), Camb. 80/B1
Kampong Saom, Camb. 78/C4
Kampville, Mo, US 137/F8
Kamsack, Sk, Can. 127/H3
Kamsdorf, Ger. 55/E1
Kamuchawie (lake), Mb,Sk, Can. 127/H1
Kamui-misaki (cape), Japan 76/B2
Kámuk (mtn.), CR 145/F4
Kamuli, Ugan. 104/B2
Kam'yanets'-Podil's'kyy, Ukr. 62/C2
Kamyshin, Rus. 63/H2
Kanaaupscow (riv.), Qu, Can. 123/J3
Kanab, Ut, US 128/D3
Kanaga (vol.), Ak, US 134/C6
Kanairiktok (riv.), Nf, Can. 123/K3
Kanan, Japan 77/J7
Kananga, D.R. Congo 105/D2
Kanangra-Boyd NP, Austl. 115/D2
Kanash, Rus. 61/K5
Kanasin, Mex. 144/D1
Kanawake Ind. Res., Qu, Can. 131/N7
Kanawha (riv.), WV, US 133/H2
Kanazawa, Japan 75/E2
Kanchanaburi, Thai. 78/B3
Kānchenjunga (peak), Nepal 82/E2
Kānchīpuram, India 82/C5
Kandahār, Afg. 89/J2
Kandalaksha, Rus. 60/G2
Kandalaksha (gulf), Rus. 37/K2
Kándanos, Gre. 47/H5
Kandé, Togo 103/F4
Kandel (peak), Ger. 56/E1
Kandel, Ger. 54/B4
Kander (riv.), Swi. 56/D4
Kandern, Ger. 56/D2
Kandersteg, Swi. 56/D5
Kandhkot, Pak. 89/J3
Kāndhla, India 86/D5
Kandi (cape), Indo. 81/F3
Kandi, Ben. 103/F4
Kāndi, India 85/G4
Kandıra, Turk. 49/K5
Kandos, Austl. 115/D2
Kandukūr, India 82/C4
Kandy, SrL. 82/D6
Kane (basin), Grld. 123/T7
Kane (co.), Il, US 135/P16
Kanem (reg.), Chad 96/H5
Kaneohe, Hi, US 124/W13
Kaneohe (bay), Hi, US 124/W13
Kaneohe Marine Air Corps Station, Hi, US 124/W13
Kaneville, Il, US 135/N16
Kaneyama, Japan 76/B4
Kang, Bots. 105/D5
Kanga (riv.), Bang. 85/G5
Kangaba, Mali 102/C4
Kangal, Turk. 90/D2
Kangān, Iran 88/F3
Kangan Abor. Land, Austl. 112/C2
Kanganpur, Pak. 86/C4
Kangar, Malay. 78/C5
Kangaroo (isl.), Austl. 109/C4
Kangasala, Fin. 39/L1
Kangāvar, Iran 88/E2
Kangbao, China 71/K3
Kangding, China 70/H5
Kangean (isls.), Indo. 81/E5
Kanggye, NKor. 73/D2
Kanggyŏng, SKor. 73/D4
Kanghwa, SKor. 73/F6
Kangiqsualujjuaq, Qu, Can. 123/K3
Kangiqsujuaq, Qu, Can. 123/J2
Kangirsuk, Qu, Can. 123/J2
Kangjin, SKor. 73/D5
Kangmar, China 85/G1
Kangnam (mts.), NKor. 73/C2
Kangnŭng, SKor. 74/A2
Kangping, China 72/E2
Kāngra, India 86/D3
Kangrinboqê (peak), China 70/D5
Kangšhan, Tai. 79/D3
Kangto (peak), China 83/F2
Kangwŏn-do (prov.), SKor. 74/A2
Kanha NP, India 84/C4
Kanhān (riv.), India 82/C3
Kani, Japan 77/M5
Kanie, Japan 77/L5
Kanin (pen.), Rus. 160/C
Kanin Nos (pt.), Rus. 64/E3
Kaniva, Austl. 115/B3
Kanjiža, Serb. 48/E2
Kankakee (riv.), Il,In, US 130/C3
Kankan (pol. reg.), Gui. 102/C4
Kankan, Gui. 102/C4
Kanmuri-yama (peak), Japan 74/C3
Kannami, Japan 77/B3
Kannapolis, NC, US 133/H3
Kannauj, India 84/B2
Kannon-zaki (pt.), Japan 77/D3
Kannus, Fin. 60/D3
Kano, Nga. 103/H4
Kano (state), Nga. 103/H4
Kan'onji, Japan 74/C3
Kanouse (mtn.), NJ, US 139/H7
Kanoya, Japan 74/B5
Kanra, Japan 77/B1
Kansai (int'l arpt.), Japan 77/H7
Kansai (isl.), Japan 77/H7
Kansas (state), US 129/H3
Kansas (riv.), Ks, US 129/H3
Kansas City (int'l arpt.), Mo, US 129/J3
Kansas City, Ks, US 137/D5
Kansas City, Mo, US 137/D5
Kansasville, Wi, US 135/P14
Kansk, Rus. 64/K4
Kansŏng, SKor. 73/E3
Kantābānji, India 82/D3
Kānth, India 84/B1
Kantō (prov.), Japan 75/F2
Kantunilkin, Mex. 144/E1
Kanuku (mts.), Guy. 150/G3
Kanuma, Japan 75/F2
Kanye, Bots. 105/E5
Kaohsiung, Tai. 79/D3
Kaohsiung (int'l arpt.), Tai. 79/D3
Kaokoveld (mts.), Namb. 105/B4
Kaolack, Sen. 102/A3
Kaolack (pol. reg.), Sen. 102/B3
Kaolinovo, Bul. 49/H4
Kaoma, Zam. 105/D3
Kapaa, Hi, US 124/S9
Kapaahu, Hi, US 124/U11
Kapaau, Hi, US 124/U10
Kapalong, Phil. 79/E6
Kapan, Arm. 63/H5
Kapchorwa, Ugan. 104/B2
Kapellen, Belg. 50/B6
Kapenguria, Kenya 104/B2
Kapidaği (pen.), Turk. 49/H5
Kapingamarangi (isl.), Micr. 116/E4
Kapiri Mposhi, Zam. 105/E3
Kapiskau (riv.), On, Can. 123/H3
Kaplice, Czh. 55/H5
Kapos (riv.), Hun. 48/C2
Kaposvár, Hun. 48/C2
Kappl, Aus. 57/G3
Kapsan, NKor. 73/E2
Kapuas (riv.), Indo. 80/C4
Kapuas Hulu (mts.), Indo.,Mal 80/D3
Kapunda, Austl. 113/H5
Kapūrthala, India 86/C4
Kapuskasing, On, Can. 130/D1
Kapuskasing (riv.), On, Can. 130/D1
Kapuvár, Hun. 43/M3
Kapydzhik (peak), Azer. 63/H5

Kap'yŏng, SKor. 73/D4
Kara, Togo 103/F4
Kara (sea), Rus. 160/A
Kara (riv.), Rus. 61/Q1
Kara-saki (pt.), Japan 74/A3
Karaali, Turk. 90/C2
Karabiğa, Turk. 49/H5
Karabük, Turk. 90/C1
Karaburun, Turk. 49/J5
Karaca (peak), Turk. 90/D2
Karacabey, Turk. 90/B1
Karacaköy, Turk. 49/J5
Karaçal (peak), Turk. 91/C1
Karacaoğlan, Turk. 49/H5
Karachayevo-Cherkesiya, Resp., Rus. 63/G4
Karachev, Rus. 62/E1
Karāchi, Pak. 89/J4
Karadere, Turk. 49/K5
Karaginskiy (isl.), Rus. 67/R4
Karaj, Iran 88/F1
Karakax (riv.), China 89/L1
Karakaya (dam), Turk. 90/D2
Karakelong (isl.), Indo. 81/G3
Karakhoto (ruin), China 70/H3
Karakol, Kyr. 87/G4
Karakoram (range), India 70/C4
Karakoram (pass), India 86/D2
Karakoro (riv.), Mali 102/C3
Karakorum (ruin), Mong. 70/H2
Karakorum (ruin), Mong. 87/G5
Karakorum (pass), China 89/L1
Karaköse, Turk. 90/E2
Karaköy, Turk. 90/E2
Karakul' (lake), Taj. 87/F5
Karakumy (des.), Trkm. 64/F5
Karakyon (peak), Trkm. 87/B4
Karakyr (peak), Trkm. 89/H1
Karam (riv.), Indo. 81/E4
Karaman (prov.), Turk. 90/C2
Karaman, Turk. 90/C2
Karamay, China 70/D2
Karamea Bight (bay), NZ 109/H7
Karamoja (prov.), Ugan. 104/B2
Karamürsel, Turk. 49/J5
Karangasem, Indo. 81/E5
Karanginskiy (isl.), Rus. 65/S4
Karanginskiy (bay), Rus. 65/S4
Kāranja, India 82/C3
Karanpur, India 86/B5
Karapınar, Turk. 90/C2
Karasabai, Guy. 153/G3
Karaşar, Turk. 49/L5
Karasburg, Namb. 106/B3
Karasjohka-Karasjok, Nor. 37/H1
Karasu, Turk. 49/K5
Karasu, Japan 77/L6
Karasuk, Rus. 87/G2
Karatá (lag.), Nic. 145/F3
Karataş, Turk. 91/D1
Karatoya (riv.), Bang. 85/G3
Karatsu, Japan 74/A4
Karauli, India 84/A2
Karaurgan, Turk. 90/E1
Karáva (peak), Gre. 47/G3
Karawang, Indo. 80/C5
Karayaka, Turk. 62/F4
Karayazı, Turk. 90/E2
Karazhal, Kaz. 87/F3
Karbalā' (gov.), Iraq 90/E3
Karbalā', Iraq 90/F3
Karben, Ger. 54/B2
Karcag, Hun. 48/E2
Kardhámila, Gre. 47/K3
Kardhítsa, Gre. 47/G3
Kardhitsomagoúla, Gre. 47/G3
Kareha (riv.), India 85/E3
Karelī, India 84/B4
Karelia (reg.), Rus. 37/J2
Karelia, Resp., Rus. 64/D3
Karera, India 84/B3
Karesuando, Swe. 37/G1
Karêt (reg.), Mrta. 98/D4
Karf Ash Shaykh (gov.) 90/B4
Kargı, Turk. 90/C1
Kargil, India 86/D2
Karhal, India 84/B2
Karhijärvi (lake), Fin. 39/K1
Karhula, Fin. 39/M1
Kariá, Gre. 47/G3
Karia Ba Mohammed, Mor. 100/B2
Kariaí, Gre. 47/J2
Karianga, Madg. 107/H8
Kariba (dam), Zam. 105/E4
Kariba, Zim. 105/E4
Kariba (lake), Zim. 93/E6
Kariba-yama (peak), Japan 76/A2
Karibib, Namb. 105/C5
Karimama, Ben. 103/F3
Karimata (isl.), Indo. 80/D4
Karimata (str.), Indo. 80/C4
Karīmnagar, India 82/C4
Karimunjawa (isls.), Indo. 80/D5
Kariótissa, Gre. 47/H2
Karise, Den. 38/E4
Karisimbi (vol.), D.R. Congo 104/A3
Karisimbi (vol.), Rwa. 105/E1
Káristos, Gre. 47/J3
Kariya, Japan 77/L6
Karkaar (mts.), Som. 97/Q6
Kārkāl, India 82/B5
Karkar (isl.), PNG 116/D5
Karkinits'ka Zatoka (gulf), Ukr. 62/D3
Karkkila, Fin. 39/L1
Karkonski NP, Pol. 41/H3
Karla Marksa (peak), Taj. 89/K1
Karlholmsbruk, Swe. 38/G1
Karlino, Pol. 38/F4
Karlovac, Cro. 48/B3
Karlovarský (pol. reg.), Czh. 55/F2
Karlovo, Bul. 47/J1
Karlovy Vary, Czh. 55/F2
Karlsdorf-Neuthard, Ger. 54/B4
Karlsfeld, Ger. 55/E6
Karlshamn, Swe. 38/F3
Karlshuld, Ger. 54/E5
Karlskoga, Swe. 38/F2
Karlskron, Ger. 55/E5
Karlskrona, Swe. 38/F3
Karlsruhe, Ger. 54/B4
Karlstad, Swe. 38/E2
Karlstadt, Ger. 54/C3
Karlstein am Main, Ger. 54/C2
Karluk, Ak, US 134/H4
Karmāla, India 89/L5
Karnali (riv.), Nepal 70/D6
Karnali (zone), Nepal 84/C1
Karnaphuli (res.), Bang. 85/H4
Karnataka (state), India 82/C4
Karnes City, Tx, US 129/H5
Karnobat, Bul. 47/K1
Kärnten (prov.), Aus. 43/K3
Karonga, Malw. 104/B5
Karoo NP, SAfr. 106/D4
Karoo NP, SAfr. 106/C4
Karoonda, Austl. 115/A2
Karor, Pak. 86/A4
Karoso (cape), Indo. 81/E5
Kárpathos, Gre. 90/A3
Kárpathos (isl.), Gre. 90/A3
Karpatskiy NP, Ukr. 49/G1
Karpenísion, Gre. 47/G3
Karratha, Austl. 112/C2
Kars, Turk. 90/E1
Kars (prov.), Turk. 90/E1
Kars (riv.), Turk. 63/G4
Kärsämäki, Fin. 60/E3
Karsantı, Turk. 90/C2
Karshi (int'l arpt.), Uzb. 87/E5
Kartaly, Rus. 63/M1
Kartārpur, India 86/C4
Kartuzy, Pol. 38/H4
Karuah, Austl. 115/D2
Karuma (falls), Ugan. 104/B2
Karumba, Austl. 114/A2
Karūn (riv.), Iran 88/E2
Karup, Den. 38/C3
Karviná, Czh. 41/K4
Kaş, Turk. 91/A1
Kås, Den. 38/C3
Kasaan, Ak, US 134/M4
Kasabonika (lake), On, Can. 127/L2
Kasagi, Japan 77/J6
Kasahara, Japan 77/M5
Kāsai (riv.), India 85/F4
Kasai, Japan 74/D3
Kasai (riv.), D.R. Congo 93/D5
Kasama, Zam. 104/A5
Kasama, Japan 75/G2
Kasamatsu, Japan 77/L5
Kasane, Bots. 105/E4
Kasaoka, Japan 74/C3
Kasar (cape), Sudan 101/D5
Kāsaragod, India 82/C5
Kasartori-yama (peak), Japan 77/K6
Kasba (lake), NW,Nun., Can. 122/F2
Kasba Tadla, Mor. 98/D2
Kaseda, Japan 74/B5
Kasese, Ugan. 104/A2
Kashaf (riv.), Iran 89/H1
Kāshān, Iran 88/F2
Kashi, China 87/G5
Kashiba, Japan 77/J6
Kashihara, Japan 77/J6
Kashima, Japan 74/B4
Kashima, Japan 75/G3
Kashima (bay), Japan 77/F1
Kashin, Rus. 60/H4
Kāshīpur, India 84/B1
Kashiwa, Japan 77/D2
Kashiwara, Japan 77/J6
Kashiwazaki, Japan 75/F2
Kāshmar, Iran 89/G1
Kashmir (reg.), India,Pak 87/G5
Kashmūnd Ghar (range), Afg. 86/A2
Kasigau (peak), Kenya 104/C3
Kasigluk, Ak, US 134/F3
Kasilof, Ak, US 134/H3
Kasimov, Rus. 60/J5
Kasiruta (isl.), Indo. 81/G4
Kasiui (isl.), Indo. 81/H4
Kaskaskia (riv.), Il, US 129/K3
Kaslo, BC, Can. 126/D3
Kasongo, D.R. Congo 105/E1
Kásos (isl.), Gre. 90/A3
Kaspichan, Bul. 49/H4
Kaspiysk, Rus. 63/H4
Kassala, Sudan 88/C5
Kassándra (pen.), Gre. 62/B5
Kassándria, Gre. 47/H2
Kassel, Ger. 51/G6
Kassikaityu (riv.), Guy. 153/G4
Kassler, Co, US 137/B4
Kasson, Mn, US 127/K4
Kastamonu, Turk. 90/C1
Kastamonu (prov.), Turk. 90/C1
Kastanéai, Gre. 47/K2
Kaštel Stari, Cro. 48/C4
Kaštel Sućurac, Cro. 48/C4
Kastellaun, Ger. 53/G3
Kastéllion, Gre. 47/J5
Kasterlee, Belg. 50/B6
Kastl, Ger. 55/E4
Kastoría, Gre. 47/G2
Kastrakíou (lake), Gre. 47/G3
Kasuga, Japan 77/H5
Kasuga, Japan 77/K5
Kasugai, Japan 77/B2
Kasugai, Japan 77/L5
Kasukabe, Japan 75/F3
Kasumiga (lake), Japan 75/G2
Kasungu, Malw. 105/F3
Kasūr, Pak. 86/C4
Kat O Chau (isl.), China 71/V9
Katahdin (mt.), Me, US 131/G2
Katákolon, Gre. 47/G4
Katanga (reg.), D.R. Congo 105/D2
Katanga (pol. reg.), D.R. Congo 104/A5
Katangi, India 84/B4
Katanning, Austl. 112/C5
Katano, Japan 77/J6
Katastárion, Gre. 47/G4
Katavi NP, Tanz. 105/F2
Katchall (isl.), India 83/F6
Kateríni, Gre. 47/H2
Kates Needle (peak), Ak, US 134/M4
Katete, Zam. 105/F3
Katghora, India 84/D4
Kāthgodām, India 84/B1
Kathiawar (pen.), India 89/K4
Kathleen (mt.), Austl. 113/G2
Kāthmāndu (cap.), Nepal 85/E2
Kathua, India 86/C3
Kati, Mali 102/C3
Katiola, C.d'Iv. 102/D4
Katlehong, SAfr. 106/E2
Katlenburg-Lindau, Ger. 51/H5
Katmai (vol.), Ak, US 134/H4
Katmai NP, Ak, US 134/G4
Káto Akhaía, Gre. 47/G3
Katokhí, Gre. 47/G3
Katonah, NY, US 139/E1
Katonga (riv.), Ugan. 104/A2
Katoúna, Gre. 47/G3
Katowice, Pol. 41/K3
Katra, India 86/C3
Kātrās, India 85/F4
Katrine (lake), Sc, UK 36/B4
Katrineholm, Swe. 38/G2
Katsikás, Gre. 47/G3
Katsina (state), Nga. 103/G3
Katsina, Nga. 103/G3
Katsina Ala (riv.), Nga. 103/H5
Katsunuma, Japan 77/B2
Katsura (riv.), Japan 77/J5
Katsuragi, Japan 74/D3
Katsuragi-san (peak), Japan 77/H7
Katsuta, Japan 75/G2
Katsuura, Japan 75/G3
Katsuyama, Japan 74/E2
Katsuyama, Japan 77/B3
Kattakurgan, Uzb. 87/E5
Kattegat (str.), Den. 27/F3
Katumbi, Malw. 104/B5
Kātwa, India 85/G4
Katwe-Kabatooro, Ugan. 104/A3
Katwijk aan Zee, Neth. 50/B4
Katy, Tx, US 129/J5
Katzenbach (riv.), Ger. 54/B4
Katzenbuckel (peak), Ger. 54/C4
Katzenelnbogen, Ger. 53/G3
Katzhütte, Ger. 54/D1
Katzwinkel, Ger. 53/F3
Kau-ye (isl.), Myan. 78/B4
Kauai (chan.), Hi, US 124/S10
Kauai (isl.), Hi, US 124/S9
Kaufbeuren, Ger. 57/G2
Kaufering, Ger. 57/G1
Kaufungen, Ger. 51/G6
Kauhava, Fin. 60/D3
Kauhola (pt.), Hi, US 124/U10
Kauiki (pt.), Hi, US 124/U10
Kaukaveld (uplands), Namb. 105/C5
Kaukura (isl.), FrPol. 117/L6
Kaulakahi (chan.), Hi, US 124/R9
Kaulsdorf, Ger. 55/E1
Kaumalapau, Hi, US 124/T10
Kauna (pt.), Hi, US 124/U11
Kaunakakai, Hi, US 124/T10
Kaunas (int'l arpt.), Lith. 39/K4
Kaunas (res.), Lith. 39/L4
Kaunas, Lith. 39/K4
Kaupanger, Nor. 38/B1
Kauttua, Fin. 39/K1
Kavadarci, FYROM 47/H2
Kavajë, Alb. 47/F2
Kavála, Gre. 47/J2
Kavalerovo, Rus. 71/Q3
Kāvali, India 82/C5
Kavangel (isls.), Palau 116/C4
Kavaratti, India 82/B5
Kavarna, Bul. 49/J4
Kavgolovskoye (lake), Rus. 61/T6
Kavieng, PNG 116/E5
Kavīr-e Namak (dry lake), Iran 87/C6
Kävlinge, Swe. 38/E4
Kaw (lake), Ok, US 129/H3
Kawa (ruin), Sudan 101/B5
Kawabe, Japan 76/B4
Kawachi, Japan 77/E2
Kawachi-Nagano, Japan 77/J7
Kawage, Japan 77/L6
Kawagoe, Japan 75/F3
Kawagoe, Japan 77/L5
Kawaguchi, Japan 75/F3
Kawaguchiko, Japan 77/B3
Kawai, Japan 77/J6
Kawaihoa (pt.), Hi, US 124/R10
Kawaikini (peak), Hi, US 124/S9
Kawajima, Japan 77/C2
Kawakami, Japan 77/B2
Kawakami, Japan 77/J7
Kawamata, Japan 75/G2
Kawambwa, Zam. 104/A5
Kawamoto, Japan 77/C1
Kawanishi, Japan 77/H6
Kawanishi, Japan 77/J6
Kawardha, India 84/C4
Kawartha (lakes), On, Can. 130/E2
Kawasaki, Japan 75/F3
Kawasato, Japan 77/D1
Kawashima, Japan 77/L5
Kawaue, Japan 77/M4
Kawela (Kawela Bay), Hi, US 124/V12
Kawerau, NZ 117/T10
Kawlin, Myan. 83/G3
Kawthaung, Myan. 78/B4
Kax (riv.), China 70/D3
Kay (pt.), Yk, Can. 134/L2
Kaya, SKor. 73/E5
Kaya, Japan 77/H5
Kaya-san (peak), SKor. 73/D4
Kayadibi, Turk. 90/C2
Kayagangiri (peak), CAfr. 96/J6
Kayah (div.), Myan. 70/G8
Kayah (state), Myan. 83/G4
Kayan (riv.), Indo. 67/L9
Kayanga (riv.), Sen. 102/B3
Kaycee, Wy, US 126/G5
Kayenta, Az, US 128/E3
Kayes, Mali 102/C3
Kayes (pol. reg.), Mali 102/C3
Kayin (state), Myan. 83/G4
Kayl, Lux. 53/F5
Kaymaz, Turk. 49/K5
Kaynarca, Turk. 49/J5
Kaynaşlı, Turk. 49/K5
Kayoa (isl.), Indo. 81/G3
Kayser (mts.), Sur. 153/G4
Kayseri, Turk. 90/C2
Kayseri (prov.), Turk. 90/C2
Kaysersberg, Fr. 56/D1
Kaysville, Ut, US 137/K11
Kayuagung, Indo. 80/B4
Kazakhstan (ctry.) 64/G5
Kazan', Rus. 61/L5
Kazan (int'l arpt.), Rus. 61/L5
Kazan (riv.), Nun., Can. 122/F2
Kazancı, Turk. 91/C1
Kazanlı, Turk. 91/D1
Kazanlŭk, Bul. 47/J1
Kazbek (peak), Geo. 63/H4
Kāzerūn, Iran 88/F3
Kazgar (riv.), China 70/C4
Kazimierza Wielka, Pol. 41/L3
Kâzımkarabekir, Turk. 90/C2
Kazincbarcika, Hun. 41/L4
Kazo, Japan 77/D1
Kazuno, Japan 76/B3
Ke Ga (cape), Viet. 78/E3
Ké Macina, Mali 102/D3
Kéa (isl.), Gre. 47/J4
Kéa, Gre. 47/J4
Keaau, Hi, US 124/U11
Keady, NI, UK 34/B3
Keahole (pt.), Hi, US 124/T11
Keanapapa (pt.), Hi, US 124/T10
Keansburg, NJ, US 139/J10
Kearney, Ne, US 129/H2
Kearney, Mo, US 137/E5
Kearns, Ut, US 137/K12
Kearny, NJ, US 139/J8
Kearny (pt.), NI, UK 34/C3
Keawakapu, Hi, US 124/T10
Keawekaheka (pt.), Hi, US 124/U11
Keban (dam), Turk. 90/D2
Kebbi (state), Nga. 103/G4
Kébémer, Sen. 102/A3
Kebnekaise (peak), Swe. 37/F2
Kebumen, Indo. 80/C5
Kecel, Hun. 48/D2
Keçiborlu, Turk. 90/B2
Kecskemét, Hun. 48/D2
Kedah (state), Malay. 78/C5
Kėdainiai, Lith. 39/K4
Kediri, Indo. 80/D5
Kédougou, Sen. 102/B3
Kędzierzyn-Koźle, Pol. 41/K3
Keego Harbor, Mi, US 135/F6
Keele (riv.), NW, Can. 122/D2
Keele (peak), Yk, Can. 122/C2
Keelung, Tai. 79/D2
Keelung, Japan 75/G8
Keen (mt.), Sc, UK 36/D3
Keene, NH, US 131/F3
Keepit (dam), Austl. 115/D1
Keer-Weer (cape), Austl. 114/A1
Keetmanshoop, Namb. 106/B2
Kefallinía (isl.), Gre. 47/G3
Kefar Sava, Isr. 91/F7
Kefar Vitkin, Isr. 91/F7
Keflavik (int'l arpt.), Ice. 37/M7
Keflavík, Ice. 37/M7
Kehl, Ger. 56/D1
Kehrsatz, Swi. 56/D4
Keighley, Eng, UK 35/G4
Keihoku, Japan 77/J5
Keimoes, SAfr. 106/C3
Kéita (riv.), Chad 97/J6
Keith, Austl. 115/B3
Keith, Sc, UK 36/D1
Kejimkujik NP, NS, Can. 131/H2
Kekaha, Hi, US 124/S10
Kékes (peak), Hun. 41/K5
Kelan, China 72/B3
Kelang (isl.), Indo. 81/G4
Kelang, Malay. 80/B3
Kelberg, Ger. 53/F3
Keles, Turk. 62/D5
Kelheim, Ger. 55/E5
Kelkheim, Ger. 54/B2
Kelkıt, Turk. 62/F4
Kelkıt (riv.), Turk. 90/D1
Kell, Ger. 53/F4
Kellenhusen, Ger. 38/D4
Keller (peak), Ca, US 136/C2
Keller (lake), NW, Can. 122/D2
Kellerberrin, Austl. 112/C4
Kellogg, Id, US 126/D4
Kells, NI, UK 34/B2
Kélo, Chad 96/J6
Kelowna, BC, Can. 126/D3
Kelsey (pt.), Eng, UK 32/A6
Kelso, Wa, US 126/C4
Kelso, Sc, UK 36/D5
Kelsterbach, Ger. 54/B2
Keluang, Malay. 80/B3
Kelvington, Sk, Can. 127/H2
Kem' (riv.), Rus. 64/D3
Kem', Rus. 60/G2
Kemah, Turk. 62/F5
Kemaliye, Turk. 90/D2
Kemalpaşa, Turk. 90/E1
Kemasik, Malay. 80/B3
Kematen an der Ybbs, Aus. 55/H6
Kematen in Tirol, Aus. 57/H3
Kembs, Fr. 56/D2
Kemecse, Hun. 41/L4
Kemena (riv.), Malay. 80/D3
Kemence, Hun. 41/K4
Kemer (dam), Turk. 90/B2
Kemer, Turk. 91/B1
Kemerhisar, Turk. 90/C2
Kemerovo, Rus. 64/J4
Kemerovskaya Oblast, Rus. 64/J4
Kemi, Fin. 37/H2
Kemijärvi, Fin. 60/E2
Kemijoki (riv.), Fin. 37/H2
Kemmerer, Wy, US 126/F5
Kemnath, Ger. 55/E3
Kemnay, Sc, UK 36/D2
Kemp (lake), Tx, US 129/H4
Kempele, Fin. 60/E2
Kempen, Ger. 50/D6
Kempenich, Ger. 53/G3
Kempenland (phys. reg.), Belg. 50/C6
Kempisch Kanaal (canal), Belg. 53/E1
Kempsey, Austl. 115/E1
Kempston, Eng, UK 33/F2
Kempt (res.), Qu, Can. 130/F2
Kempten, Ger. 57/G2
Kempton, Austl. 115/C4
Kempton Park, SAfr. 106/Q13
Kemptown, Md, US 138/A5
Kemri, India 84/B1
Kemul (peak), Indo. 81/E3
Ken (riv.), India 84/C3
Ken (lake), Sc, UK 34/D1
Ken-zaki (pt.), Japan 77/D3
Kenadsa, Alg. 99/E3
Kenai, Ak, US 134/H3
Kenai Fjords NP, Ak, US 134/H4
Kendal, Eng, UK 35/F3
Kendalia, Tx, US 137/T20
Kendall, Austl. 115/E1
Kendall, Fl, US 133/H5
Kendall (co.), Il, US 135/P16
Kendall (co.), Tx, US 137/T20
Kendall Park, NJ, US 138/D3
Kendallville, In, US 130/C3
Kendari, Indo. 81/F4
Kéndavros, Gre. 47/J2
Kendel (riv.), Ger. 50/D5
Kendrāpāra, India 82/E3
Kénédougou (prov.), Burk. 102/D4
Kenema, SLeo. 102/C5
Kenge, D.R. Congo 105/C1
Kenhardt, SAfr. 106/C3
Kenhorst, Pa, US 138/C3
Kenié-Baoulé, Réserve de, Mali 102/C3
Kenilworth, Eng, UK 33/E2
Kenilworth, NJ, US 139/H9
Kénitra (prov.), Mor. 100/A2
Kénitra, Mor. 100/A2
Kenli, China 72/D3
Kenmare, ND, US 127/H3
Kenmare, Ire. 31/P11
Kenmore, NY, US 131/S10
Kenmore, Wa, US 135/C2
Kenn (reef), Austl. 109/E3
Kenn, Ger. 53/F4
Kennebec (riv.), Me, US 131/G2
Kennebunk, Me, US 131/G3
Kennedy (chan.), Grld.,Nun., Can. 123/T6
Kennedy (range), Austl. 112/B3
Kennedy Entrance (chan.) 134/H4
Kennedyville, Md, US 138/C5
Kennelbach, Aus. 57/F3
Kennemerduinen, NP de, Neth. 50/B4
Kenner, La, US 137/P17
Kennet (riv.), Eng, UK 33/E4
Kennet and Avon (canal), Eng, UK 32/D4
Kenneth, Ks, US 137/D6
Kennett, Mo, US 129/K3
Kennett Square, Pa, US 138/C4
Kennewick, Wa, US 126/D4
Keno Hill, Yk, Can. 134/L3
Kenogami (riv.), On, Can. 123/H3
Kenora, On, Can. 127/K3
Kenosha, Wi, US 135/Q14
Kenosha (co.), Wi, US 135/P14
Kensico (res.), NY, US 139/K7
Kensington and Chelsea (bor.), Eng, UK 30/A1
Kent (pen.), Nun., Can. 122/F2
Kent (co.), On, Can. 135/G6
Kent (riv.), Eng, UK 35/F3
Kent (isl.), Md, US 138/B6
Kent (pt.), Md, US 138/B6
Kent (lake), Mi, US 135/E7
Kent, Oh, US 130/D3
Kent, Wa, US 126/C4
Kent County (int'l arpt.), Mi, US 130/C3
Kent Group (isls.), Austl. 115/C3
Kentaū, Kaz. 87/E4
Kenton, De, US 138/C5
Kenton, Oh, US 130/D3
Kentucky (state), US 133/G2
Kentucky (riv.), Ky, US 130/C4
Kentucky (lake), Ky, US 133/F2
Kentville, NS, Can. 131/H2
Kenya (ctry.) 104/C2
Kenzingen, Ger. 56/D1
Keonjhar, India 82/E3
Kep i Gjuhëzës (cape), Alb. 47/F2
Kep i Rodonit (cape), Alb. 47/F2
Kępno, Pol. 41/J3
Keppel Sands, Austl. 114/C3
Kerala (state), India 82/C5
Kéran, PN de la, Togo 103/F4
Kerang, Austl. 115/B2
Keratéa, Gre. 47/N9
Kerava, Fin. 39/L1
Kerch' (str.), Rus.,Ukr. 62/F3
Kerch, Ukr. 62/F3
Keremeos, BC, Can. 126/D3
Kerempe Burnu (cape), Turk. 90/C1
Keren, Erit. 88/C5
Kerepestarcsa, Hun. 49/R9
Keret' (lake), Rus. 37/K2
Kerguélen (isl.), Fr. 23/N8
Kericho, Kenya 104/B3
Kerikeri (cape), NZ 117/S9
Kerinci (peak), Indo. 80/B4
Kerio (riv.), Kenya 104/C2
Kerio Valley Nat'l Rsv., Kenya 104/B2
Kerkdriel, Neth. 50/C5
Kerken, Ger. 50/D6
Kerki, Trkm. 87/E5
Kerkínis (lake), Gre. 47/H2
Kérkira, Gre. 47/F3
Kerkrade, Neth. 53/F2
Kerkwijk, Neth. 50/C5
Kermadec (isls.), NZ 116/G8
Kermān, Iran 89/G2
Kern (riv.), Ca, US 128/C4
Kern, South Kern (riv.), Ca, US 128/C4
Kerns, Swi. 57/E4
Kéros (isl.), Gre. 47/J4
Kérou, Ben. 103/F4
Kerr (lake), Ok, US 129/J4
Kerr (res.), NC,Va, US 133/J2
Kerrobert, Sk, Can. 126/F3
Kerrville, Tx, US 129/H5
Kert (riv.), Mor. 100/C2
Kerulen (riv.), Mong. 67/L5
Kerzaz, Alg. 99/E3
Kerzenheim, Ger. 53/H4
Kerzers, Swi. 56/D4
Kesagami (riv.), On, Can. 130/D1
Keşan, Turk. 47/K2
Kesch (peak), Swi. 57/F4
Kesen'numa, Japan 76/B4
Keshan, China 71/N2
Keshod, India 82/B3
Keski-Suomi (prov.), Fin. 37/H3
Keskin, Turk. 90/C2
Kesselbach (riv.), Ger. 54/D5
Kestel, Turk. 90/B1
Kesteren, Neth. 50/C5
Keszthely, Hun. 48/C2
Ket' (riv.), Rus. 64/J4
Keta, Gha. 103/F5
Keta (riv.), Rus. 64/K3
Ketchikan, Ak, US 134/M4
Kete Krachi, Gha. 103/E5
Ketelmeer (lake), Neth. 50/C3
Kétou, Ben. 103/F5
Kętrzyn, Pol. 39/J4
Ketsch, Ger. 54/B4
Kettering, Eng, UK 33/F2
Kettle (riv.), Mn, US 126/D3
Kettle Moraine State Forest, Wi, US 135/P14
Ketzin, Ger. 40/P7
Keukenhof, Neth. 50/B4
Kevelaer, Ger. 50/D5
Kewaunee, Wi, US 130/C2
Keweenaw (pen.), Mi, US 127/L4
Keweenaw (pt.), Mi, US 127/M4
Keweenaw (bay), Mi, US 127/L4
Key Largo, Fl, US 133/H5
Key West, Fl, US 133/H5
Keymar, Md, US 138/A4
Keyport, NJ, US 139/J10
Keyport, Wa, US 135/B2
Keystone (lake), Ok, US 129/H3
Kežmarok, Slvk. 41/L4
Khaanziir (cape), Som. 97/Q5
Khabarovsk, Rus. 71/Q2
Khabarovskiy Kray, Rus. 65/P4
Khagaria, India 85/F3
Khair, India 84/A2
Khairābād, India 84/C2
Khairpur, Pak. 86/B5
Khairpur, Pak. 89/J3
Khakasiya, Resp., Rus. 65/P6
Khalándrion, Gre. 47/N8
Khalīj al Hammāmāt (gulf), Tun. 46/B4
Khalīlābād, India 84/D2
Khalkhāl, Iran 88/E1
Khalkhidhikhi (pen.), Gre. 47/H2
Khalkidhón, Gre. 47/H2
Khalkís, Gre. 47/H3
Khamar-Daban (mts.), Rus. 70/H1
Khambhāliya, India 89/J4
Khambhat, India 89/K4
Khamīs Mushayţ, SAr. 88/D5
Khammam, India 82/D4
Khamr, Yem. 88/D5
Khān Yūnus, Gaza 91/D4
Khānābād, Afg. 89/J1
Khānaqīn, Iraq 90/F3
Khandwa, India 89/L4
Khanem (well), Alg. 99/F3
Khānewāl, Pak. 86/A4
Khāngāh Dogrān, Pak. 86/B4
Khāngarh, Pak. 86/A5
Khaniá, Gre. 47/J5
Khanka (lake), China,Rus 67/N5
Khanna, India 86/D4
Khānpur, Pak. 86/A5
Khanty-Mansiysk, Rus. 64/G3
Khanty-Mansiyskiy Aut. Okrug, Rus. 64/G3
Khao Chamao-Khao Wong NP, Thai. 78/C3
Khao Khitchakut NP, Thai. 78/C3
Khao Laem (res.), Thai. 83/G4
Khao Sam Roi Yot NP, Thai. 78/B3
Khao Yai NP, Thai. 78/C3
Kharagpur, India 85/F4
Kharagpur, India 85/F3
Kharak, Pak. 86/A3
Khārān, Pak. 89/J3
Kharar, India 85/F4
Kharar, India 86/D4
Kharbatā, Isr. 91/G8
Khargon, India 89/L4
Khāriān, Pak. 86/B3
Kharkiv (int'l arpt.), Ukr. 62/F2
Kharkiv, Ukr. 62/F2
Kharkivs'ka Oblasti, Ukr. 62/F2
Kharmanli, Bul. 47/J2
Kharovsk, Rus. 60/J4
Kharrour (riv.), Mor. 100/B2
Kharsia, India 84/D5
Khartoum (Kharţūm) (cap.), Sudan 88/B5
Khasavyurt, Rus. 63/H4
Khāsh (riv.), Afg. 89/H2
Khashuri, Geo. 63/G4
Khasi (hills), India 85/H3
Khaskovo (pol. reg.), Bul. 47/J2
Khaskovo (prov.), Bul. 49/G5
Khatanga (riv.), Rus. 160/Z
Khatanga (gulf), Rus. 65/L2
Khatauli, India 86/D5
Khātegaon, India 84/A4
Khatīma, India 84/B1
Khatlon (obl.), Taj. 87/E5
Khatmia (pass), Egypt 91/C4
Khātra, India 85/F4
Khatt Atoui (riv.), Mrta. 96/B3
Khaur, Pak. 86/B3
Khaybar (pass), Afg. 86/A2
Khazzān Dūkān (res.), Iraq 90/F3
Khazzān Jabal Al Awliyā (dam), Sudan 97/M4
Khekra, India 86/D5
Khemis el Khechna, Alg. 100/G4
Khemis Miliana, Alg. 100/G4
Khémisset (prov.), Mor. 100/A3
Khémisset, Mor. 100/A3
Khenchela (prov.), Alg. 99/G2
Khenchela, Alg. 100/K7
Khénifra, Mor. 98/D2
Khepoyarvi (lake), Rus. 61/T6
Kheri, India 84/C2
Khersān (riv.), Iran 88/F2
Kherson, Ukr. 49/L2
Kherson (int'l arpt.), Ukr. 49/L2
Khersons'ka Oblasti, Ukr. 62/E3
Khilok, Rus. 71/K1
Khimki, Rus. 61/W9
Khíos, Gre. 47/K3
Khíos (isl.), Gre. 62/C5
Khirpai, India 85/F4
Khisarya, Bul. 47/J1
Khiva, Uzb. 87/D4
Khlebarovo, Bul. 49/H4
Khmel'nyts'ka Oblasti, Ukr. 62/C2
Khmel'nytskyy, Ukr. 62/C2
Kho Sawai (plat.), Thai. 83/H4
Khodzheyli, Uzb. 87/C4
Khojak (pass), Pak. 89/J2
Kholm, Afg. 89/J1
Kholmsk, Rus. 71/R2
Khomeynīshahr, Iran 88/F2

198

Khon – Konji

Khon Kaen, Thai. 78/C2
Khopër (riv.), Rus. 64/E4
Khor (riv.), Rus. 65/P5
Khóra Sfakíon, Gre. 47/J5
Khorazm (pol. reg.), Uzb. 87/D4
Khoríon, Gre. 90/A2
Khorramābād, Iran 88/E2
Khorramshahr, Iran 88/E2
Khorugh, Taj. 89/K1
Khotol (mtn.), Ak, US 134/G3
Khouribga, Mor. 98/D2
Khowai, India 83/F3
Khrisoúpolis, Gre. 47/J2
Khromtaū, Kaz. 63/L2
Khrysí (isl.), Gre. 47/J5
Khuan Ubon Ratana (lake), Thai. 78/C2
Khudiān, Pak. 86/C4
Khuis, Bots. 106/C2
Khujand, Taj. 87/E4
Khulna (pol. div.), Bang. 85/G4
Khūnjerāb (pass), Pak. 89/L1
Khunjerab NP, Pak. 87/G5
Khunti, India 85/E4
Khurai, India 84/B3
Khurda, India 82/E3
Khurja, India 84/A1
Khushāb, Pak. 86/B3
Khust, Ukr. 41/M4
Khūtār, India 84/C1
Khuzdār, Pak. 89/J3
Khvalynka, Rus. 71/P3
Khvonsār, Iran 88/F2
Khvor, Iran 89/G2
Khvoy, Iran 63/H5
Khwaja Rawash (int'l arpt.), Afg. 87/E6
Khyber (pass), Pak. 86/A2
Kia, Sol. 116/E5
Kiama, Austl. 115/D2
Kiamichi (mts.), Ok, US 132/E3
Kiana, Ak, US 134/F2
Kibæk, Den. 38/C3
Kibali (riv.), D.R. Congo 104/A2
Kibergneset (pt.), Nor. 37/J1
Kibo (Kilimanjaro) (peak), Tanz. 104/C3
Kiboga, Ugan. 104/A2
Kıbrısçık, Turk. 49/K5
Kibwezi, Kenya 104/C3
Kičevo, FYROM 47/G2
Kichha, India 84/B1
Kickapoo, Ks, US 137/D5
Kidal, Mali 103/F2
Kidal (pol. reg.), Mali 103/F2
Kidapawan, Phil. 81/G2
Kidderminster, Eng, UK 32/D2
Kidepo Valley NP, Ugan. 97/M7
Kidsgrove, Eng, UK 35/F5
Kiel (bay), Den. 37/D5
Kiel, Ger. 38/D4
Kielce, Pol. 41/L3
Kielder (res.), Eng, UK 35/F1
Kien An, Viet. 78/D1
Kierspe, Ger. 53/G1
Kiev (Kyyiv) (cap.), Ukr. 62/D2
Kiffa, Mrta. 102/C2
Kifisiá, Gre. 47/N8
Kigali (cap.), Rwa. 104/A3
Kigali (Gregoire Kayibanda) (int'l arpt.), Rwa. 104/A3
Kiği, Turk. 90/E2
Kigoma (pol. reg.), Tanz. 104/A4
Kigoma, Tanz. 104/A4
Kigye, SKor. 73/E4
Kihei, Hi, US 124/T10
Kihnu (isl.), Est. 39/L2
Kiholo, Hi, US 124/U11
Kihti (str.), Fin. 39/J1
Kii (chan.), Japan 74/D4
Kii (mts.), Japan 74/D4
Kijang, SKor. 73/E5
Kikai (isl.), Japan 75/L6
Kikepa (pt.), Hi, US 124/R9
Kikiktat (mtn.), Ak, US 134/H2
Kikinda, Serb. 48/E3
Kikonai, Japan 76/B3
Kikwit, D.R. Congo 105/C2
Kil, Swe. 38/E2
Kilafors, Swe. 38/G1
Kilauea, Hi, US 124/S9
Kilbarchan, Sc, UK 36/B5
Kilberry, Ire. 31/Q10
Kilbirnie, Sc, UK 36/B5
Kilbrannan (sound), Sc, UK 36/A5
Kilchoan, Sc, UK 31/Q8
Kilchu, NKor. 73/E2
Kilcoole, Ire. 34/B5
Kilcormac, Ire. 31/Q10
Kilcoy, Austl. 114/D4
Kildare, Ire. 31/Q10
Kildeer, Il, US 135/P15
Kil'den (isl.), Rus. 60/G1
Kilembe Estates, Ugan. 104/A2
Kilgarvan, Ire. 31/P11
Kilgore, Tx, US 129/J4
Kilian (isl.), Nun., Can. 122/E1
Kilifi, Kenya 104/C3
Kilimanjaro (pol. reg.), Tanz. 104/C3
Kilimanjaro (int'l arpt.), Tanz. 104/C3
Kilimanjaro NP, Tanz. 104/C3
Kilimli, Turk. 49/K5
Kilinochchi, SrL. 82/D6
Kilis, Turk. 91/E1
Kiliya, Ukr. 49/J3
Kilkee, Ire. 31/P10
Kilkeel, NI, UK 34/B3
Kilkenny, Ire. 31/Q10
Kilkenny (co.), Ire. 34/A6
Kilkís, Gre. 47/H2
Kilkivan, Austl. 114/D4
Kill, Ire. 31/Q10
Kill Van Kull (riv.), NJ,NY, US 139/J9
Killam, Ab, Can. 126/F2
Killarney, Austl. 115/E1
Killarney, Mb, Can. 127/J3
Killarney, Ire. 31/P10
Killarney NP, Ire. 31/P10
Killdeer, ND, US 127/H4
Killearn, Sc, UK 36/B4
Killeen, Tx, US 129/H5
Killenaule, Ire. 31/Q10
Killiecrankie, Pass of (pass), Sc, UK 36/C3
Killin, Sc, UK 36/B4
Killinchy, NI, UK 34/C3
Killinek (isl.), Nun., Can. 123/K2
Killíni (peak), Gre. 47/H4
Killíni, Gre. 47/G4
Killough, NI, UK 34/C3
Killybegs, Ire. 31/P9
Killyclogher, NI, UK 34/A2
Killyleagh, NI, UK 34/C3
Kilmacanogue, Ire. 34/B5
Kilmacolm, Sc, UK 36/B5
Kilmacow, Ire. 31/Q10
Kilmallock, Ire. 31/P10
Kilmar Tor (hill), Eng, UK 32/B5
Kilmarnock, Sc, UK 36/B5
Kilmaurs, Sc, UK 36/B5
Kilmichael (pt.), Ire. 34/B6
Kilmore, Austl. 115/C3
Kilmore Quay, Ire. 31/Q10
Kilombero (riv.), Tanz. 104/C5
Kilosa, Tanz. 104/C4
Kilraghts, NI, UK 34/B1
Kilrea, NI, UK 34/B2
Kilrush, Ire. 31/P10
Kilsyth, Sc, UK 36/B5
Kilwa Kivinje, Tanz. 104/C5
Kilwinning, Sc, UK 36/B5
Kimba, Austl. 113/H5
Kimball, SD, US 127/J5
Kimbe, PNG 116/E5
Kimberley, BC, Can. 126/E3
Kimberley (plat.), Austl. 109/B2
Kimberley, SAfr. 106/D3
Kimberley (cape), Austl. 114/B2
Kimch'aek, NKor. 73/E2
Kimch'ŏn, SKor. 73/E4
Kimhae, SKor. 74/A3
Kimhae (int'l arpt.), SKor. 74/A3
Kími, Gre. 47/J3
Kímina, Gre. 47/H2
Kimitsu, Japan 75/F3
Kimje, SKor. 73/D5
Kimméria, Gre. 47/J2
Kimmirut, Nun., Can. 123/K2
Kímolos (isl.), Gre. 47/J4
Kimovsk, Rus. 62/F1
Kimp'o, SKor. 73/F6
Kimp'o (int'l arpt.), SKor. 73/F6
Kimpō-zan (peak), Japan 77/B2
Kimry, Rus. 60/H4
Kinabalu (peak), Malay. 81/E2
Kinabatangan (riv.), Malay. 81/E2
Kinango, Kenya 104/C4
Kinbasket (lake), BC, Can. 126/D2
Kinbrace, Sc, UK 31/S7
Kincaid, Sk, Can. 126/G3
Kincardine, On, Can. 130/D2
Kincardine, Sc, UK 36/C4
Kinchega NP, Austl. 115/B2
Kinder Scout (peak), Eng, UK 35/G5
Kindersley, Sk, Can. 126/F3
Kindia, Gui. 102/B4
Kindia (pol. reg.), Gui. 102/B4
Kinding, Ger. 55/E5
Kindsbach, Ger. 53/G5
Kindu, D.R. Congo 105/E1
Kinel', Rus. 63/J1
Kineshma, Rus. 60/J4
King (lake), Austl. 109/A4
King (mt.), Austl. 114/B4
King (sound), Austl. 109/B2
King (isl.), BC, Can. 126/B2
King (mt.), BC, Can. 134/N4
King (peak), Yk, Can. 134/K3
King (isl.), NZ 109/H6
King (co.), Wa, US 135/D2
King Christian (isl.), Nun., Can. 123/R7
King Christian IX Land (reg.), Grld. 119/P3
King Christian X Land (reg.),Grld. 119/Q2
King City, Ca, US 128/B3
King Cove, Ak, US 134/F4
King Frederik VI Coast (reg.), Grld. 119/N3
King Frederik VIII Land (reg.), Grld. 119/Q2
King George (isls.), FrPol. 117/L6
King George Is. (isls.), Qu, Can. 123/J3
King George's (res.), Eng, UK 30/C2
King Leopold (ranges), Austl. 109/B2
King of Prussia, Pa, US 138/C3
King Salmon, Ak, US 134/G4
King William (isl.), Nun., Can. 122/G2
King William's Town, SAfr. 106/D4
Kingaroy, Austl. 114/C4
Kingfisher, Ok, US 129/H4
Kingfisher (co.), Ok, US 137/M14
Kinghorn, Sc, UK 36/C4
Kinglake NP, Austl. 115/C3
Kinglake NP, Austl. 115/G5
Kingman, Ks, US 129/H3
Kingman, Az, US 128/D4
Kingman (reef), Pac., US 117/J4
Kings (riv.), Ca, US 128/C3
Kings (co.), NY, US 139/K9
Kings (peak), Ut, US 128/E2
Kings Canyon NP, Ca, US 128/C3
Kings Langley, Eng, UK 30/B1
King's Lynn, Eng, UK 33/G1
Kings Park, Austl. 112/K6
Kings Point, NY, US 139/L8
King's Seat (hill), Sc, UK 36/C4
Kingsbridge, Eng, UK 32/C6
Kingscote, Austl. 113/H5
Kingscourt, Ire. 31/Q10
Kingsford, Mi, US 130/B2
Kingsport, Tn, US 130/D4
Kingston, Austl. 115/C4
Kingston, Austl. 116/F7
Kingston, On, Can. 130/E2
Kingston, NY, US 130/F3
Kingston (cap.), Jam. 145/G2
Kingston, Pa, US 138/C1
Kingston, Wa, US 135/B2
Kingston S.E., Austl. 115/A3
Kingston upon Hull, Eng, UK 35/H4
Kingston upon Hull (co.), Eng, UK 35/H4
Kingston upon Thames, Eng, UK 30/C2
Kingston upon Thames (bor.), Eng, UK 30/C2
Kingstown (cap.), StV. 141/N9
Kingstree, SC, US 133/J3
Kingsville, Tx, US 132/D5
Kingsville, Md, US 138/B5
Kingswood, Eng, UK 32/D4
Kingussie, Sc, UK 36/B2
Kınık, Turk. 90/A2
Kinkaid (mt.), Ak, US 134/L4
Kinkala, Congo 105/B1
Kinki (prov.), Japan 74/D3
Kinlochewe, Sc, UK 36/A1
Kinlochleven, Sc, UK 36/B3
Kinloss, Sc, UK 36/C1
Kinna, Swe. 38/E3
Kinnairds (pt.), Sc, UK 36/D1
Kinnelon, NJ, US 139/H8
Kinnelon (lake), NJ, US 139/H8
Kinnitty, Ire. 31/Q10
Kino (riv.), Japan 74/D3
Kinoje (riv.), On, Can. 130/D1
Kinomoto, Japan 77/K5
Kinrooi, Belg. 53/E1
Kinross, Sc, UK 36/C4
Kinsach (riv.), Ger. 55/F4
Kinsale, Ire. 31/P11
Kinsarvik, Nor. 38/B1
Kinshasa (cap.), D.R. Congo 105/C1
Kinston, NC, US 133/J3
Kintampo, Gha. 103/E4
Kintnersville, Pa, US 138/C2
Kintore, Sc, UK 36/D2
Kintyre (isl.), Sc, UK 31/R8
Kintzheim, Fr. 56/D1
Kinu (riv.), Japan 75/F2
Kinvarra, Ire. 31/P10
Kinyeti (peak), Sudan 97/M7
Kinzig (riv.), Ger. 40/E4
Kipahulu, Hi, US 124/T10
Kiparissía (gulf), Gre. 47/G4
Kiparissía, Gre. 47/G4
Kipawa (lake), Qu, Can. 130/E2
Kipkarren (riv.), Kenya 104/B2
Kipling, Sk, Can. 127/H3
Kipnuk, Ak, US 134/F4
Kippel, Swi. 56/D5
Kippen, Sc, UK 36/B4
Kippure (peak), Ire. 34/B5
Kipushi, D.R. Congo 105/E3
Kira, Japan 77/M6
Kira Panayía (isl.), Gre. 47/H3
Kirakira, Sol. 116/F6
Kiranomena, Madg. 107/H7
Kīratpur, India 84/B1
Kirazlı, Turk. 47/K2
Kirby, Tx, US 137/U21
Kırcasalih, Turk. 47/K2
Kirchberg, Swi. 56/D3
Kirchberg, Swi. 57/F3
Kirchberg, Ger. 53/G4
Kirchberg, Ger. 55/F1
Kirchberg an der Iller, Ger. 57/G1
Kirchberg an der Jagst, Ger. 54/C4
Kirchdorf, Ger. 51/F3
Kirchdorf an der Krems, Aus. 55/H7
Kirchenlamitz, Ger. 55/E2
Kirchenthumbach, Ger. 55/E3
Kirchheim, Ger. 57/G1
Kirchheim bei München, Ger. 55/E6
Kirchheim unter Teck, Ger. 54/C5
Kirchheimbolanden, Ger. 54/B3
Kirchhundem, Ger. 51/F6
Kirchlengern, Ger. 51/F4
Kirchlinteln, Ger. 51/G3
Kirchsee (lake), Ger. 57/H2
Kirchseeon, Ger. 55/E6
Kirchweidach, Ger. 55/F6
Kirchzarten, Ger. 56/D2
Kirchzell, Ger. 54/C3
Kircudbright (bay), Sc, UK 34/D2
Kirensk, Rus. 65/L4
Kirgiz Steppe (upland), Kaz. 64/F5
Kirgizskiy (mts.), Kyr. 70/B3
Kiriákion, Gre. 47/H3
Kiribati (ctry.) 116/H5
Kırık, Turk. 90/E1
Kırıkhan, Turk. 91/E1
Kırıkkale, Turk. 90/C2
Kirikkale (prov.), Turk. 90/C2
Kirishi, Rus. 39/Q2
Kirishima-Yaku NP, Japan 74/B5
Kirishima-yama (peak), Japan 74/B5
Kiritimati (Christmas) (isl.), Kiri. 117/K4
Kırkağaç, Turk. 90/A2
Kirkby, Eng, UK 35/F5
Kirkby in Ashfield, Eng, UK 35/G5
Kirkcaldy, Sc, UK 36/C4
Kirkconnel, Sc, UK 36/C6
Kirkcudbright, Sc, UK 34/D2
Kirkee, India 89/K5
Kirkenær, Nor. 38/E1
Kirkintilloch, Sc, UK 36/B5
Kirklees (co.), Eng, UK 35/G4
Kirkkonummi (Kyrkslätt), Fin. 39/L1
Kirkland, Qu, Can. 131/N7
Kirkland (hill), Sc, UK 36/C6
Kirkland Lake, On, Can. 130/D1
Kırklar (peak), Turk. 90/A2
Kırklareli, Turk. 49/H5
Kirklareli (prov.), Turk. 49/H5
Kirkliston, Sc, UK 36/C5
Kirkstone (pass), Eng, UK 35/F3
Kirkūk, Iraq 90/F3
Kirkwall, Sc, UK 31/V14
Kirkwood, SAfr. 106/D4
Kirkwood, De, US 138/C4
Kirn, Ger. 53/G4
Kirov, Rus. 62/E1
Kirov, Rus. 61/L4
Kirovskaya Oblast, Rus. 61/L4
Kirovo-Chepetsk, Rus. 61/L4
Kirovohrad, Ukr. 62/E2
Kirovohrads'ka Oblasti, Ukr. 62/D2
Kirovsk, Rus. 60/G2
Kirriemuir, Sc, UK 36/D3
Kirrweiler, Ger. 54/B4
Kirsanov, Rus. 63/G1
Kirşehir (prov.), Turk. 90/C2
Kırşehir, Turk. 90/C2
Kiruna, Swe. 37/G2
Kiryū, Japan 75/F2
Kisa, Swe. 38/F3
Kisai, Japan 77/D1
Kisakata, Japan 76/A4
Kisangani, D.R. Congo 97/L7
Kisarazu, Japan 75/F3
Kisber, Hun. 41/K5
Kisei, Japan 77/K7
Kiselevsk, Rus. 64/J4
Kishanganj, India 85/F2
Kishangarh, India 89/K3
Kishiwada, Japan 77/H7
Kishorganj, Bang. 85/H3
Kishtwar, India 86/C3
Kishwaukee (riv.), Il, US 135/N15
Kisigo (riv.), Tanz. 104/B4
Kisii, Kenya 104/B3
Kiska (vol.), Ak, US 134/B5
Kiska (isl.), Ak, US 134/B6
Kiskatinnaw (riv.), BC, Can. 126/C2
Kiskitto (lake), Mb, Can. 127/J2
Kiskőrös, Hun. 48/D2
Kiskunfélegyháza, Hun. 48/D2
Kiskunhalas, Hun. 48/D2
Kiskunmajsa, Hun. 48/D2
Kiskunsági Nemzeti NP, Hun. 48/D2
Kislovodsk, Rus. 63/G4
Kismaayo (Chisimayu), Som. 97/P8
Kiso (riv.), Japan 75/E3
Kisogawa, Japan 77/L5
Kisozaki, Japan 77/L5
Kíssamos, Gre. 47/H5
Kissimmee (lake), Fl, US 133/H4
Kissimmee, Fl, US 133/H4
Kissing, Ger. 54/D6
Kississing (lake), Mb, Can. 127/H2
Kisslegg, Ger. 57/F2
Kist, Ger. 54/C3
Kisújszállás, Hun. 48/E2
Kisumu, Kenya 104/B3
Kisvárda, Hun. 41/M4
Kita, Mali 102/C3
Kita (lake), Japan 75/G2
Kita-Ibaraki, Japan 75/G2
Kitaaiki, Japan 77/B1
Kitadaitō (isl.), Japan 75/L8
Kitagata, Japan 77/L5
Kitakami (mts.), Japan 76/B4
Kitakami (riv.), Japan 76/B4
Kitakami, Japan 76/B4
Kitakata, Japan 75/F2
Kitakawabe, Japan 77/D1
Kitakyūshū, Japan 74/B4
Kitale, Kenya 104/B2
Kitami, Japan 76/C2
Kitamimaki, Japan 77/A1
Kitamoto, Japan 77/D1
Kitan (str.), Japan 77/G7
Kitangiri (lake), Tanz. 104/B4
Kitaura, Japan 77/F1
Kitchener, On, Can. 130/D3
Kitgum, Ugan. 104/B2
Kíthira, Gre. 47/H4
Kíthira (isl.), Gre. 47/H4
Kíthnos, Gre. 47/J4
Kíthnos (isl.), Gre. 47/J4
Kitimat Arm (lake), BC, Can. 126/A2
Kitsap (co.), Wa, US 135/B3
Kittatinny (mts.), NJ, US 138/C1
Kittery, Me, US 131/G3
Kittredge, Co, US 137/B3
Kitui, Kenya 104/C3
Kitumbeine (peak), Tanz. 104/C3
Kitwe, Zam. 105/E3
Kitzbühel, Aus. 43/K3
Kitzingen, Ger. 54/D3
Kiunga Marine Nat'l Rsv., Kenya 104/D3
Kiuruvesi, Fin. 60/E3
Kiuyu (pt.), Tanz. 104/C4
Kivalina, Ak, US 134/F2
Kivalo (mts.), Fin. 37/H2
Kivijärvi (lake), Fin. 39/M1
Kiviõli, Est. 39/M2
Kivu (lake), D.R. Congo 93/E5
Kıyıköy, Turk. 49/J5
Kiyokawa, Japan 77/C3
Kiyosu, Japan 77/L5
Kizel, Rus. 61/N4
Kizil (riv.), China 64/H6
Kızılcadağ, Turk. 91/A1
Kızılcahamam, Turk. 90/C1
Kızıldag NP, Turk. 90/B2
Kızılhisar, Turk. 90/B2
Kızılırmak (riv.), Turk. 90/C1
Kızıltepe, Turk. 90/E2
Kızılyaka, Turk. 91/C1
Kizlyar, Rus. 63/H4
Kizu (riv.), Japan 74/E3
Kizu, Japan 77/J6
Kizukuri, Japan 76/B3
Kjerkestinden (peak), Nor. 37/F1
Kjevik (int'l arpt.), Nor. 38/C2
Kjølen (mts.), Nor. 37/E2
Klabava (riv.), Czh. 55/G3
Kladanj, Bosn. 48/D3
Kladno, Czh. 55/H2
Kladovo, Serb. 48/F3
Klagenfurt, Aus. 40/G5
Klaipėda, Lith. 39/J4
Klamath (mts.), Ca,Or, US 126/C5
Klamath (riv.), Ca, US 124/B3
Klamath Falls, Or, US 126/C5
Klangenan, Indo. 80/C5
Klarälven (riv.), Swe. 37/E3
Klarup, Den. 38/D3
Klášterec nad Ohří, Czh. 55/G2
Klatovy, Czh. 55/G4
Klaus, Aus. 57/F3
Klausen (Chiusa), It. 57/H4
Klausenpass (pass), Swi. 57/E4
Klawock, Ak, US 134/M4
Klaza (mtn.), Yk, Can. 134/L3
Klazienaveen, Neth. 50/E3
Kleinblittersdorf, Ger. 53/G5
Kleine Elster (riv.), Ger. 41/G3
Kleine Emme (riv.), Swi. 56/E4
Kleine Gete (riv.), Belg. 53/D2
Kleine Laber (riv.), Ger. 55/F5
Kleine Nete (riv.), Belg. 53/D1
Kleinheubach, Ger. 54/C3
Kleinlützel, Swi. 56/D3
Kleinmachnow, Ger. 40/Q7
Kleinmond, SAfr. 106/L11
Kleinolifants (riv.), SAfr. 106/Q12
Kleinrinderfeld, Ger. 54/C3
Kleinsee, SAfr. 106/B3
Kleinwallstadt, Ger. 54/C3
Kleinwinternheim, Ger. 54/B3
Kleppe, Nor. 38/A2
Kleppestø, Nor. 38/A1
Klerksdorp, SAfr. 106/D2
Klet' (peak), Czh. 55/H5
Kleve, Ger. 50/D5
Klina, Serb. 47/G1
Klingenberg am Main, Ger. 54/C3
Klingenmünster, Ger. 54/B4
Klingenthal, Ger. 55/F2
Klínovec (peak), Czh. 55/F2
Klintehamn, Swe. 38/H3
Klintsy, Rus. 62/E1
Klip (riv.), SAfr. 106/E2
Klippan, Swe. 38/E3
Klipplaat, SAfr. 106/D4
Klisura, Bul. 47/J1
Klitmøller, Den. 38/C3
Kljajićevo, Serb. 48/D3
Ključ, Bosn. 48/C3
Kłodawa, Pol. 41/K2
Kłodzko, Pol. 41/J3
Klöntaler-See (lake), Swi. 57/E3
Klosterbach (riv.), Ger. 51/F3
Klosterlechfeld, Ger. 57/G1
Klosterneuburg, Aus. 49/N7
Klosters, Swi. 57/F4
Klosterwappen (peak), Aus. 41/H5
Kloten, Swi. 57/E3
Klötze, Ger. 40/F2
Kluane NP, Yk, Can. 134/K3
Kluczbork, Pol. 41/K3
Klukwan, Ak, US 134/L3
Klundert, Neth. 50/B5
Klyaz'ma (riv.), Rus. 60/J4
Klyuchevskaya (peak), Rus. 65/S4
Knäred, Swe. 38/E3
Knaresborough, Eng, UK 35/G3
Knee (lake), Mb, Can. 127/K2
Knetzgau, Ger. 54/D3
Knezha, Bul. 49/G4
Knight (inlet), BC, Can. 126/B3
Knighton, Wal, UK 32/C2
Knightsen, Ca, US 135/L11
Knin, Cro. 48/C3
Knittelfeld, Aus. 43/L3
Knittlingen, Ger. 54/B4
Knivsta, Swe. 38/G2
Knížecí Stolec (peak), Czh. 55/H5
Knížecí Strom (peak), Czh. 55/G3
Knjaževac, Serb. 48/F4
Knob (peak), Phil. 81/F1
Knob (cape), Austl. 112/C5
Knobby (pt.), Austl. 112/B4
Knoch (hill), Sc, UK 36/D1
Knockcloghrim, NI, UK 34/B2
Knösen (pt.), Swe. 38/E4
Knøsen (peak), Den. 38/D3
Knosós (Knossos) (ruin), Gre. 47/J5
Knottingley, Eng, UK 35/G4
Knott's Berry Farm, Ca, US 136/G8
Knowsley (co.), Eng, UK 35/F5
Knox (coast), Ant. 160/G
Knox (cape), BC, Can. 134/M4
Knox City, Tx, US 129/H4
Knoxville, Tn, US 130/D5
Knutsford, Eng, UK 35/F5
Knysna, SAfr. 106/C4
Ko (riv.), Sen. 102/B3
Ko-saki (pt.), Japan 74/A3
Ko Samut NP, Thai. 78/C3
Koali, Hi, US 124/T10
Koani, Tanz. 104/C4
Koāth, India 85/E3
Kobayashi, Japan 74/B5
Kōbe, Japan 77/H6
København (int'l arpt.), Den. 38/E4
Kobern-Gondorf, Ger. 53/G3
Kobipato (peak), Indo. 81/G4
Koblach, Aus. 57/F3
Koblenz, Swi. 57/E2
Koblenz, Ger. 53/G3
Kobryn, Bela. 41/N2
Kobuchizawa, Japan 77/A2
Kobuk (riv.), Ak, US 134/G2
Kobuk, Ak, US 134/G2
Kobuk Valley NP, Ak, US 134/G2
Kobushi-ga-take (peak), Japan 75/F3
Kocába (riv.), Czh. 55/H3
Kocaeli (prov.), Turk. 49/J5
Koçalı, Turk. 90/D2
Kočani, FYROM 47/H2
Kocapınar, Turk. 90/E2
Kočevje, Slov. 43/L4
Koch (isl.), Nun., Can. 123/J2
Koch'ang, SKor. 73/D5
Koch'ang, SKor. 73/D5
Kochel am See, Ger. 57/H2
Kochelsee (lake), Ger. 57/H2
Kocher (riv.), Ger. 43/H2
Kocherinovo, Bul. 47/H1
Kōchi, Japan 74/C4
Kōchi (pref.), Japan 74/C4
Kodaira, Japan 77/C2
Kodala, India 82/E4
Kodama, Japan 77/C1
Kodarmā, India 85/E3
Kodiak, Ak, US 134/H4
Kodiak (isl.), Ak, US 134/H4
Kodinār, India 89/K4
Kodomari, Japan 76/B3
Kodry (hills), Mol. 49/H2
Koekelare, Belg. 52/B1
Koel (riv.), India 82/D3
Koes, Namb. 106/B2
Koesan, SKor. 73/D4
Koetari (riv.), Sur. 153/G4
Kofa (mts.), Az, US 128/D4
Kofarnihon (riv.), Taj. 87/E5
Kofçaz, Turk. 49/H5
Koffiefontein, SAfr. 106/D3
Kofiau (isl.), Indo. 81/G4
Koforidua, Gha. 103/E5
Kōfu, Japan 75/F3
Koga, Japan 75/F2
Koganei, Japan 77/D2
Køge (bay), Den. 38/E4
Kogi, Nga. 103/G4
Kogon (riv.), Gui. 96/C5
Kŏgum (isl.), SKor. 73/D5
Kohāt, Pak. 86/A3
Kohīma, India 83/F2
Kohoku, Japan 77/K5
Kohout (peak), Czh. 55/H5
Kohtla-Järve, Est. 39/M2
Kohŭng, SKor. 73/D5
Kohunlich (ruin), Mex. 144/D2
Koímisis, Gre. 47/H2
Koito (riv.), Japan 77/D3
Koiva (riv.), Lat. 39/M3
Kŏje (isl.), SKor. 74/A3
Kojonup, Austl. 112/C5
Kojšovská (peak), Slvk. 41/L4
Kok (riv.), Myan. 78/B1
Kōka, Japan 77/K6
Kokai (riv.), Japan 77/E2
Kökar (isl.), Fin. 39/J3
Kokemäenjoki (riv.), Fin. 39/J1
Kokhonak, Ak, US 134/H4
Kokkola (Karleby), Fin. 60/D3
Koko Head (pt.), Hi, US 124/W13
Kokomo, In, US 130/C3
Kokrajhar, India 85/H2
Kokrines, Ak, US 134/H3
Koksan, NKor. 73/D3
Kökshetaū, Kaz. 87/E2
Kökshetaū (obl.), Kaz. 87/E2
Koksijde, Belg. 52/B1
Koksoak (riv.), Qu, Can. 123/K3
Kokstad, SAfr. 106/E3
Kokubu, Japan 74/B5
Kola (pen.), Rus. 160/D
Kola (riv.), Rus. 60/G1
Kolaka, Indo. 81/F4
Kolār, India 82/C5
Kolāras, India 84/A3
Kolašin, Serb. 47/F1
Kolbäck, Swe. 38/G2
Kol'bay (peak), Kaz. 87/B4
Kolbermoor, Ger. 43/K3
Kolbuszowa, Pol. 41/L3
Kolda, Sen. 102/B3
Kolda (pol. reg.), Sen. 102/B3
Kolding, Den. 38/C4
Kölen (mts.), Swe. 37/E2
Kolgompya (cape), Rus. 39/N2
Kolguyev (isl.), Rus. 160/C
Kolhāpur, India 89/K5
Koliba (riv.), Gui. 102/B3
Koliganek, Ak, US 134/G4
Kolín, Czh. 41/H3
Kolkasrags (pt.), Lat. 39/K3
Kolkata (Calcutta), India 85/G4
Kolkata (Calcutta) (int'l arpt.), India 85/G4
Kollbach (riv.), Ger. 55/F5
Kollnburg, Ger. 55/F4
Kollum, Neth. 50/D2
Köln (Cologne), Ger. 53/F2
Kolno, Pol. 41/L2
Koło, Pol. 62/A1
Koloa, Hi, US 124/S10
Kołobrzeg, Pol. 38/F4
Kolokani, Mali 102/C3
Kolomna, Rus. 60/H5
Kolomyya, Ukr. 49/G1
Kolondiéba, Mali 102/D4
Kolossa (riv.), Mali 102/D3
Kolpashevo, Rus. 64/J4
Kolpino, Rus. 61/T7
Kolsva, Swe. 38/F2
Kolubara (riv.), Serb. 48/D3
Koluszki, Pol. 41/K3
Kolva (riv.), Rus. 61/N2
Kolwezi, D.R. Congo 105/E3
Kolyma (riv.), Rus. 67/Q3
Kolyma (range), Rus. 67/Q3
Kolyma Lowland (plain), Rus. 65/R2
Kom (peak), Bul. 47/H1
Koma (riv.), Japan 77/C2
Komádi, Hun. 48/E2
Komadugu Gana (riv.), Niger.,Ng 96/H5
Komadugu Yobe (riv.), Nga. 103/H3
Komae, Japan 77/D2
Komagane, Japan 75/E3
Komaki, Japan 77/L5
Komandorskiye (isls.), Rus. 67/R4
Komárno, Slvk. 48/D2
Komárom, Hun. 48/D2
Komárom-Esztergom (prov.), Hun. 48/D2
Komatirivier (riv.), SAfr. 106/Q13
Komatke, Az, US 137/R19
Komatsu, Japan 74/E2
Komatsu (int'l arpt.), Japan 74/E2
Komatsushima, Japan 74/D3
Kombissiri, Burk. 103/E3
Kome (isl.), Tanz. 104/B3
Komi, Resp., Rus. 61/M2
Komi-Permyatskiy Aut. Okrug, Rus. 61/M2
Komló, Hun. 48/D2
Kommetjie, SAfr. 106/L11
Kommunizma (peak), Taj. 87/F5
Komodo (isl.), Indo. 81/E5
Komodo Island NP, Indo. 81/E5
Komoé (riv.), C.d'Iv. 96/E6
Komono, Japan 77/L5
Komoran (isl.), Indo. 81/J5
Komoro, Japan 77/A1
Komotiní, Gre. 47/J2
Kompasberg (peak), SAfr. 106/D3
Komsomolets (isl.), Rus. 67/J1
Komsomol'skiy, Rus. 61/P2
Kömür (pt.), Turk. 47/K3
Kon Tum, Viet. 78/D3
Konakovo, Rus. 60/H4
Kōnan, Japan 77/C1
Kōnan, Japan 77/L5
Kōnan, Japan 77/K6
Konār (riv.), India 85/E4
Konār (res.), India 85/E4
Konar (riv.), Afg. 86/A2
Konaweha (riv.), Indo. 81/F4
Konda, Japan 77/H6
Kondagaon, India 82/D4
Kondinin, Austl. 112/C5
Kondoa, Tanz. 104/B4
Kondopoga, Rus. 60/G3
Kondūz, Afg. 87/E5
Kong, C.d'Iv. 102/D4
Kong (riv.), Laos 78/D3
Kong (isl.), Camb. 78/C4
Kong Miao, China 72/D4
Kongiganak, Ak, US 134/F4
Kongju, SKor. 73/D4
Kongō-zan (peak), Japan 77/J7
Kongolo, D.R. Congo 105/E2
Kongoussi, Burk. 103/E3
Kongsberg, Nor. 38/C2
Kongsvinger, Nor. 38/E1
Kongur (peak), China 87/G5
Koniecpol, Pol. 41/K3
Königs Wusterhausen, Ger. 40/Q7
Königsberg in Bayern, Ger. 54/D2
Königsberg-Stein, Ger. 54/B5
Königsbronn, Ger. 54/D5
Königsbrunn, Ger. 57/G1
Königsdorf, Ger. 57/H2
Königsfeld im Schwarzwald, Ger. 57/E1
Königslutter am Elm, Ger. 51/H4
Königstein im Taunus, Ger. 54/B2
Königswinter, Ger. 53/G2
Konin, Pol. 41/K2
Kónitsa, Gre. 47/G2
Köniz, Swi. 56/D4
Konjic, Bosn. 48/C4

önkämäeno (riv.), n. 60/D1
onkouré (riv.), Gui. 102/B4
onnevesi, Fin. 60/E3
onolfingen, Swi. 56/D4
önosu, Japan 77/D1
onotop, Ukr. 62/E2
onqi (riv.), China 64/J5
onsen (plat.), apan 76/D2
onskie, Pol. 41/L3
onstancin-Jeziorna, ol. 41/L2
onstantynów Łódzki, ol. 41/K3
onstanz, Ger. 57/F2
ontich, Belg. 53/D1
ontiolahti, Fin. 60/F3
onuralp, Turk. 49/K5
öny, Hun. 48/C2
onya, Turk. 90/C2
onya (prov.), Turk. 90/C2
onz, Ger. 53/F4
oondrook, Austl. 115/C2
oorawatha, Austl. 115/D2
oorda, Austl. 112/C4
ootenai (riv.), , US 126/D3
ootenay (lake), C, Can. 122/E3
ootenay NP, BC, Can. 126/D3
ootingal, Austl. 115/D1
op-Gejdi (pass), urk. 90/E2
opäganj, India 84/D2
opargaon, India 89/K5
opavogur, Ice. 37/N7
ope (peak), C.d'Iv. 102/D5
öpenick, Ger. 40/Q7
oper, Slov. 43/K4
opervik, Nor. 38/A2
opeysk, Rus. 61/P5
opfing im Innkreis, us. 55/G6
öping, Swe. 38/G2
opondei (cape), do. 81/F5
oporskiy (bay), Rus. 39/N2
oppang, Nor. 38/D1
opparberg, Swe. 38/F2
opparberg (co.), we. 37/E3
oppies, SAfr. 106/D2
oprivnica, Cro. 48/C2
oprivshtitsa, Bul. 47/J1
öprü (riv.), Turk. 91/B1
öprülü, Turk. 91/C1
öprülü Kanyon NP, urk. 90/B2
or (riv.), Iran 88/F2
ora, India 84/C2
öra, Japan 77/K5
ora NP, Kenya 104/C3
orab (peak), Alb. 47/G2
oráb (peak), Czh. 55/G4
orakuen Garden, apan 74/C3
oraluk (riv.), Nf, Can. 123/K3
orana (riv.), Cro. 43/L4
oraput, India 82/D4
orba, India 84/D4
orbach, Ger. 51/F6
orçë, Alb. 47/G2
orčula (isl.), Cro. 46/E1
orčulanski Kanal chan.), Cro. 46/E1
ord Küy, Iran 88/F1
ordel, Ger. 53/F4
orea (bay), hina,NKor. 73/B3
orea (str.), apan,SKor. 74/A4
orea, North (ctry.) 73/D2
orea, South (ctry.) 73/D4
orean Folk Village, Kor. 73/G7
orenovsk, Rus. 62/F3
orhogo, C.d'Iv. 102/D4
orinós, Gre. 47/H2
orinthos (Corinth), re. 47/H4
öris-hegy (peak), un. 48/C2
öriyama, Japan 75/G2
orizo, Passe de (pass), had 96/J3
orkodon (riv.), Rus. 65/R3
orkuteli, Turk. 91/B1
orla, China 70/E3
ormakiti (cape), Cyp. 91/C2
örmend, Hun. 43/M3
ornat (isl.), Cro. 48/B4
örner, Ger. 51/H6
orneuburg, Aus. 49/N7
orntal-Münchingen, er. 54/C5
ornwestheim, Ger. 54/C5
oro (sea), Fiji 116/G6
öroğlu (peak), Turk. 49/K5
orogwe, Tanz. 104/C4
oroit, Austl. 115/B3
oronadal, Phil. 81/F2
orónia (lake), Gre. 47/H2
oronowo, Pol. 41/J2
oropion, Gre. 47/N9
oror (cap.), Palau 116/C4
örös (riv.), Hun. 48/E2
orosten', Ukr. 62/D2
orostyshiv, Ukr. 62/D2
orotaikha (riv.), us. 61/P1
orovin (vol.), k, US 134/D5
orpo (Korppoo), Fin. 39/J1
orsakov, Rus. 71/R2
orschenbroich, er. 50/D6
Korsør, Den. 38/D4
Korsze, Pol. 39/J4
Kortemark, Belg. 52/C1
Kortenaken, Belg. 53/E2
Kortenberg, Belg. 53/D2
Kortessem, Belg. 53/E2
Kortrijk, Belg. 52/C2
Korup, PN de, Camr. 103/H5
Koryak (range), Rus. 67/R3
Koryakskiy Aut. Okrug, Rus. 65/S3
Koryazhma, Rus. 61/K3
Kōryō, Japan 77/J6
Koryŏng, SKor. 73/E5
Kós (isl.), Gre. 90/A2
Kós, Gre. 90/A2
Kosai, Japan 75/E3
Kosai, Japan 77/A2
Kösching, Ger. 55/E5
Kościan, Pol. 41/J2
Kościerzyna, Pol. 38/G4
Kosciusko (mt.), Austl. 115/D3
Kosciusko, Ms, US 133/F3
Kosciusko NP, Austl. 115/D3
Köse, Turk. 90/D1
Kosei, Japan 77/K6
Koshigaya, Japan 75/F3
Kōshim (riv.), Kaz. 87/B3
Koshiki (isls.), Japan 75/K5
Kosi, India 84/A2
Kosi (zone), Nepal 85/F2
Kosi (riv.), India 82/F2
Košice, Slvk. 41/L4
Košický (pol. reg.), Slvk. 41/L4
Koskinoú, Gre. 90/B2
Kosoba (peak), Kaz. 87/G3
Kosŏng, SKor. 73/E5
Kosŏng, NKor. 73/E3
Kosovo (reg.), Serb. 47/G1
Kosovo (prov.), Serb. 48/E4
Kosovo Polje, Serb. 47/G1
Kosovska Kamenica, Serb. 47/G1
Kosovska Mitrovica, Serb. 47/G1
Kosový (riv.), Czh. 55/F3
Kosrae (isl.), Micr. 116/F4
Kossi (prov.), Burk. 102/D3
Kossou, Barrage de (dam), C.d'Iv. 102/D5
Kossou, Lac de (lake), C.d'Iv. 96/D6
Kosta, Swe. 38/F3
Kostelec nad Černými Lesy, Czh. 55/H3
Koster, SAfr. 106/D2
Kostinbrod, Bul. 47/H1
Kostopil', Ukr. 62/C2
Kostroma (riv.), Rus. 60/J4
Kostroma, Rus. 60/J4
Kostromskaya Oblast, Rus. 60/J4
Kostrzyn, Pol. 41/H2
Kostrzyn, Pol. 41/J2
Kostyantynivka, Ukr. 62/F2
Kosuge, Japan 77/B2
Kos'va (riv.), Rus. 61/N4
Kos'yu (riv.), Rus. 61/N2
Koszalin, Pol. 38/G4
Kőszeg, Hun. 43/M3
Kot Addu, Pak. 86/A4
Kot Kapūra, India 86/C4
Kot Mūmin, Pak. 86/B3
Kot Rādha Kishan, Pak. 86/C4
Kot Samāba, Pak. 86/A5
Kota, India 84/D4
Kota, India 89/L3
Kōta, Japan 77/M6
Kota Baharu, Malay. 83/H6
Kota Kinabalu, Malay. 81/E2
Kotaagung, Indo. 80/B5
Kotabaru, Indo. 81/E4
Kotabumi, Indo. 80/B4
Kotapād, India 82/D4
Kotdwāra, India 84/B1
Kotel, Bul. 47/K1
Kotel'nich, Rus. 61/L4
Kotel'nikovo, Rus. 63/G3
Kotel'nyy (isl.), Rus. 65/P2
Kothagūdem, India 82/D4
Köthen, Ger. 40/F3
Kotido, Ugan. 104/B2
Kotka, Fin. 39/M1
Kotlas, Rus. 61/K3
Kotli Lohārān, Pak. 86/C3
Kotlik, Ak, US 134/F3
Kotlin (isl.), Rus. 61/S7
Kotō, Japan 77/K5
Kotoka (int'l arpt.), Gha. 103/E5
Kotor, Serb. 47/F1
Kotor Varoš, Bosn. 48/C3
Kotovo, Rus. 63/H2
Kotovsk, Rus. 63/G1
Kotri, Pak. 89/J3
Kottayam, India 82/C6
Kotto (riv.), CAfr. 97/K6
Kotuy (riv.), Rus. 67/K3
Kotzebue, Ak, US 134/F2
Kotzebue (sound), Ak, US 134/E2
Kötzting, Ger. 55/F4
Kouandé, Ben. 103/F4
Kouchibouguac NP, NB, Can. 131/H2
Koudougou, Burk. 103/E3
Koufonision (isl.), Gre. 47/J5
Kougarok (mtn.), Ak, US 134/E2
Koukdjuak (riv.), Nun., Can. 123/J2
Koula-Moutou, Gabon 96/H8
Koulikoro, Mali 102/D3
Koulikoro (pol. reg.), Mali 102/C3
Koulountou (riv.), Sen. 102/B3
Koumbi Saleh (ruin), Mrta. 102/D3
Koumi, Japan 77/A1
Koumra, Chad 96/J6
Koundara, Gui. 102/B3
Kounradskiy, Kaz. 87/G3
Kountze, Tx, US 129/J5
Koupela, Burk. 103/E3
Kouritenga (prov.), Burk. 103/E3
Kourou, FrG. 151/H2
Koussi (peak), Chad 96/J4
Koutiala, Mali 102/D3
Kouvola, Fin. 39/M1
Kovačica, Serb. 48/E3
Kovada Gölü NP, Turk. 90/B2
Kovashi (riv.), Rus. 61/S7
Kovdozero (lake), Rus. 37/J2
Kovel', Ukr. 62/C2
Kovilj, Serb. 48/E3
Kovilpatti, India 82/C6
Kovrov, Rus. 60/J4
Kovūr, India 82/C5
Kovylkino, Rus. 63/G1
Kowanyama Aboriginal Community, Austl. 114/A1
Kowkcheh (riv.), Afg. 89/J1
Kowl-e Namaksār (lake), Afg. 87/D6
Kowloon, China 79/B3
Kowt-e 'Ashrow, Afg. 89/J2
Kōyaguchi, Japan 77/J7
Kōyama, Japan 74/B5
Koynare, Bul. 47/G4
Koyuk, Ak, US 134/F3
Koyukuk (riv.), Ak, US 134/H2
Koyukuk, Ak, US 134/G3
Koyukuk, South Fork (riv.), Ak, US 134/H2
Kozakai, Japan 77/M6
Kōzaki, Japan 77/E2
Kozaklı, Turk. 90/C2
Kozan, Turk. 90/C2
Kozáni, Gre. 47/G2
Kozara NP, Bosn. 48/C3
Kozhikode (Calicut), India 82/C5
Kozhozero (lake), Rus. 60/H3
Kozhva (riv.), Rus. 61/M2
Kozienice, Pol. 41/L3
Kozloduy, Bul. 49/F4
Kozlu, Turk. 49/K5
Kozluk, Turk. 90/E2
Koźmin, Pol. 41/J3
Koznitsa (peak), Bul. 47/H1
Kōzu (isl.), Japan 75/F3
Kożuchów, Pol. 41/H3
Kozyatyn, Ukr. 62/D2
Kpalimé, Togo 103/F5
Kpandu, Gha. 103/E5
Kpémé, Togo 103/F5
Kra (isth.), Myan. 83/G6
Kraai (riv.), SAfr. 106/D3
Kraaifontein, SAfr. 106/L10
Krabi, Thai. 78/B4
Kragerø, Nor. 38/C2
Kragujevac, Serb. 48/E3
Kraiburg am Inn, Ger. 55/F6
Kraichbach (riv.), Ger. 54/B4
Kraichgau (reg.), Ger. 43/H2
Krailling, Ger. 55/E6
Krakatau (vol.), Indo. 80/C5
Kraków, Pol. 41/K3
Kralendijk, NAnt. 152/D1
Kraljevo, Serb. 48/E4
Kralkızı (dam), Turk. 90/E2
Královéhradecký (pol. reg.), Czh. 41/H3
Kralovice, Czh. 55/G3
Kralupy nad Vltavou, Czh. 55/H2
Kramators'k, Ukr. 62/F2
Kramfors, Swe. 37/F3
Krammer (chan.), Neth. 50/B5
Kranéa Elassónos, Gre. 47/G3
Kranebitten (int'l arpt.), Aus. 57/H3
Kranenburg, Ger. 50/D5
Kranidhion, Gre. 47/H4
Kranj, Slov. 43/L3
Kranskop, SAfr. 107/E3
Kraslice, Czh. 55/F2
Kraśnik, Pol. 41/M3
Kraśnik Fabryczny, Pol. 41/M3
Krasnoarmeysk, Rus. 63/H2
Krasnodar, Rus. 62/F3
Krasnodar (int'l arpt.), Rus. 62/F3
Krasnodarskiy Kray, Rus. 64/D5
Krasnogorsk, Rus. 61/W9
Krasnohrad, Ukr. 62/E2
Krasnokamensk, Rus. 71/L1
Krasnokamsk, Rus. 61/M4
Krasnoslobodsk, Rus. 63/H2
Krasnotur'insk, Rus. 64/G4
Krasnoural'sk, Rus. 61/P4
Krasnowodsk (int'l arpt.), Trkm. 63/K4
Krasnowodsk (Tĭrkmenbashi), Trkm. 63/K5
Krasnoyarsk, Rus. 64/K4
Krasnoyarskiy Kray, Rus. 64/J4
Krasnyy Kut, Rus. 63/H2
Krasnyy Luch, Ukr. 62/F2
Krasnyy Sulin, Rus. 62/G3
Kratovo, FYROM 47/H1
Krautheim, Ger. 54/C4
Kravanh (mts.), Camb. 83/H5
Kreb en Nâga (cliff), Mali 98/D5
Kreck (riv.), Ger. 54/D2
Krefeld, Ger. 50/D6
Kreiensen, Ger. 51/G5
Kremastón (lake), Gre. 47/G3
Křemelna (riv.), Czh. 55/G4
Kremenchuk, Ukr. 62/E2
Kremenchuts'ke Vodoskhovyshche (res.), Ukr. 62/E2
Kremlin, Rus. 61/W9
Kremmen, Ger. 40/G6
Kremmling, Co, US 128/F2
Krempe, Ger. 51/G1
Krems an der Donau, Aus. 41/H4
Kremsmünster, Aus. 55/H6
Krenglbach, Aus. 55/G6
Kresgeville, Pa, US 138/C2
Kresna, Bul. 47/H2
Kressbronn am Bodensee, Ger. 57/F2
Kresta (gulf), Rus. 65/T3
Kréstena, Gre. 47/G4
Kretinga, Lith. 39/J4
Kreuzau, Ger. 53/F2
Kreuzberg (peak), Ger. 54/C2
Kreuzlingen, Swi. 57/F2
Kreuztal, Ger. 53/G2
Kreuzwertheim, Ger. 54/C3
Kría Vrísi, Gre. 47/H2
Kribi, Camr. 96/G7
Krieglach, Aus. 43/L3
Kriens, Swi. 57/E3
Kriftel, Ger. 54/B2
Kril'on (pen.), Rus. 76/B1
Kril'on (cape), Rus. 76/C1
Krimpen aan de IJssel, Neth. 50/B5
Krinidhes, Gre. 47/J2
Kriós (cape), Gre. 47/H5
Krishna (riv.), India 67/G8
Krishnagiri, India 82/C5
Krishnanagar, India 85/G4
Kristdala, Swe. 38/G3
Kristiansand, Nor. 38/B2
Kristianstad, Swe. 38/F3
Kristianstad (co.), Swe. 37/E4
Kristianstad (int'l arpt.), Swe. 38/F4
Kristiansund, Nor. 37/C3
Kristinehamn, Swe. 38/F2
Kriva Palanka, FYROM 47/H1
Krk (isl.), Cro. 48/B3
Krk, Cro. 48/B3
Krnov, Czh. 41/J3
Krokom, Swe. 37/E3
Krókos, Gre. 47/G2
Krolevets', Ukr. 62/E2
Krombach, Ger. 54/C2
Kroměříž, Czh. 41/J4
Kronach, Ger. 55/E2
Kronberg im Taunus, Ger. 54/B2
Kronoberg (co.), Swe. 37/E4
Kronshtadt, Rus. 61/S6
Kronstorf, Aus. 55/H6
Kroombit Tops NP, Austl. 114/C4
Kroonstad, SAfr. 106/D2
Kropotkin, Rus. 63/G3
Kropp, Ger. 38/C4
Krosno, Pol. 41/L4
Krosno Odrzańskie, Pol. 41/H2
Krotoszyn, Pol. 41/J3
Krottenkopf (peak), Aus. 57/G3
Krousón, Gre. 47/J5
Kröv, Ger. 53/G4
Krško, Slov. 43/L4
Kruckau (riv.), Ger. 51/G1
Kruger NP, SAfr. 105/F5
Krugersdorp, SAfr. 106/P13
Kruglitsa (peak), Rus. 61/N5
Kruibeke, Belg. 50/B6
Kruisfontein, SAfr. 106/D4
Krujë, Alb. 47/F2
Krumbach, Ger. 57/G1
Krummenau, Swi. 57/F3
Krumovgrad, Bul. 47/J2
Krün, Ger. 57/H3
Krupina, Slvk. 48/D1
Kruså, Den. 38/C4
Krusenstern (cape), Ak, US 134/F2
Kruševac, Serb. 48/E4
Kruševo, FYROM 47/G2
Krušné Hory (Erzgebirge) (mts.), Czh.,Ger. 43/K1
Kruszwica, Pol. 41/K2
Kruzof (isl.), Ak, US 134/L4
Krychaw, Bela. 62/D1
Krym, Aut. Rep., Ukr. 62/E3
Krymsk, Rus. 62/F3
Krynica, Pol. 41/L4
Kryvyy Rih, Ukr. 49/L2
Krzna (riv.), Pol. 41/M3
Krzyż, Pol. 41/J2
Ksar el Kebir, Mor. 100/B2
Ksel (peak), Alg. 99/F2
Ktima, Cyp. 91/C2
Ku-Ring-Gai NP, Austl. 114/H8
Ku Sathan (peak), Thai. 78/C2
Kuah, Malay. 78/B5
Kuala Belait, Bru. 80/D3
Kuala Dungun, Malay. 80/B3
Kuala Kerai, Malay. 83/H6
Kuala Lipis, Malay. 80/B3
Kuala Lumpur (cap.), Malay. 80/B3
Kuala Pilah, Malay. 80/B3
Kuala Selangor, Malay. 80/B3
Kuala Terengganu, Malay. 83/H6
Kualapuu, Hi, US 124/T10
Kuancheng, China 72/D2
Kuandian, China 73/C2
Kuantan, Malay. 80/B3
Kuban' (riv.), Rus. 64/D5
Kubaysah, Iraq 90/E3
Kubenskoye (lake), Rus. 60/H4
Kubokawa, Japan 74/C4
Kubrat, Bul. 49/H4
Kučevo, Serb. 48/E3
Kuchen (peak), Aus. 57/G3
Kuchen, Ger. 54/C5
Kuching, Malay. 80/D3
Kuchino (isl.), Japan 75/K6
Kuchinoerabu (isl.), Japan 74/A5
Kuchl, Aus. 43/K3
Küçükbahçe, Turk. 47/K3
Küçükkuyu, Turk. 47/K3
Kudamatsu, Japan 74/B3
Kudat, Malay. 81/E2
Kudus, Indo. 80/D5
Kudymkar, Rus. 61/M4
Kufrah (oasis), Libya 97/K3
Kufrinjah, Jor. 91/D3
Kufstein, Aus. 43/K3
Kugluktuk, Nun., Can. 122/E2
Kuhardt, Ger. 54/B4
Kühbach, Ger. 54/E6
Kuhmo, Fin. 60/G2
Kuhmoinen, Fin. 39/L1
Kuhn, Il, US 137/H8
Kūhpāyeh, Iran 88/F2
Kuinder of Tjonger (riv.), Neth. 50/C3
Kuito, Ang. 105/C3
Kuiu (isl.), Ak, US 122/C3
Kujawsko-Pomorskie (prov.), Pol. 41/K2
Kujawy (reg.), Pol. 41/K2
Kuji, Japan 76/B3
Kujū-san (peak), Japan 74/B4
Kujūkuri, Japan 77/E2
Kukalaya (riv.), Nic. 145/E3
Kuki, Japan 77/E2
Kukizaki, Japan 77/E2
Kukkia (lake), Fin. 39/L1
Kūl (riv.), Iran 88/C3
Kula, Serb. 48/D3
Kula, Bul. 48/F4
Kula Kangri (peak), Bhu. 85/H1
Kulachi, Pak. 86/A4
Kulai, Malay. 80/B3
Kulal (mt.), Kenya 104/C2
Kulaly (isl.), Kaz. 63/J3
Kulandag (mts.), Kaz. 87/B4
Kuldīga, Lat. 39/J3
Kulebaki, Rus. 60/J5
Kulgām, India 86/C3
Kulin, Austl. 112/C5
Kullen (cape), Swe. 38/E3
Kullu, India 86/D4
Kulmbach, Ger. 55/E2
Kŭlob, Taj. 89/J1
Kuloy (riv.), Rus. 61/J2
Kulpahār, India 84/B3
Kulpmont, Pa, US 138/B2
Kulpsville, Pa, US 138/C3
Kul'sary, Kaz. 63/K3
Külsheim, Ger. 54/C3
Kulsi (riv.), India 85/H3
Kulti, India 85/F4
Kulunda (lake), Rus. 87/G2
Kulunda, Rus. 87/G2
Kŭm (riv.), SKor. 73/D4
Kuma (riv.), Rus. 64/E5
Kumagaya, Japan 75/F2
Kumaishi, Japan 76/A2
Kumamoto, Japan 74/B4
Kumamoto (int'l arpt.), Japan 74/B4
Kumamoto (pref.), Japan 74/B4
Kumano (riv.), Japan 74/D4
Kumano, Japan 74/E4
Kumanovo, FYROM 47/G1
Kumār (riv.), Bang. 85/G4
Kumasi, Gha. 103/E5
Kumatori, Japan 77/H7
Kumba, Camr. 96/G7
Kumbia, Austl. 114/C4
Kumbo, Camr. 96/H6
Kŭmch'on, SKor. 73/E6
Kumé (isl.), Japan 79/E2
Kumertau, Rus. 63/K1
Kumgang-san (peak), NKor. 73/E3
Kŭmho (riv.), SKor. 73/E5
Kumi, Ugan. 104/B2
Kumi, SKor. 73/E4
Kumihama, Japan 77/G4
Kumiyama, Japan 77/J6
Kumkale, Turk. 49/H6
Kumköy, Turk. 49/J5
Kumla, Swe. 38/F2
Kumluca, Turk. 91/B1
Kümmersbruck, Ger. 55/E4
Kumo, Nga. 96/H5
Kumon (range), Myan. 70/G6
Kŭmsan, SKor. 73/D4
Kumta, India 89/K6
Kunashiri (isl.), Rus. 65/Q5
Künch, India 84/B3
Kunda, India 84/C3
Kundapura (Coondapoor), India 89/K6
Kundarkhi, India 84/B1
Kundelungu, PN de, D.R. Congo 105/E3
Kundiān, Pak. 86/A3
Kundla, India 89/K4
Kungälv, Swe. 38/D3
Kungsangen (int'l arpt.), Swe. 38/G2
Kungsbacka, Swe. 38/E3
Kungshamn, Swe. 38/D2
Kungur, Rus. 61/N4
Kunhegyes, Hun. 48/E2
Kunimi-dake (peak), Japan 74/B4
Kuningan, Indo. 80/C5
Kunishiri (isl.), Rus. 67/P5
Kunitachi, Japan 77/C2
Kunjāh, Pak. 86/B3
Kunjirap (pass), China 89/L1
Kunkletown, Pa, US 138/C2
Kunlun (mts.), China 67/H6
Kunmadaras, Hun. 41/L5
Kunming, China 67/K6
Kunsan, SKor. 73/D5
Kunshan, China 72/L8
Kunszentmárton, Hun. 48/E2
Kunu (riv.), India 89/L3
Kunwāri (riv.), India 84/A2
Kunwi, SKor. 73/E4
Kunyu (mtn.), China 72/E3
Künzell, Ger. 54/C1
Kunžvartské (pass), Czh. 55/G5
Kuocang (peak), China 71/M6
Kuohijärvi (lake), Fin. 39/L1
Kuolimo (lake), Fin. 39/M1
Kuopio, Fin. 60/E3
Kuopio (prov.), Fin. 37/H3
Kupa (riv.), Cro. 48/B3
Kupang, Indo. 81/F6
Kupino, Rus. 87/G2
Kuppenheim, Ger. 54/B5
Kupreanof (isl.), Ak, US 122/C3
Kup'yans'k, Ukr. 62/F2
Kuqa, China 71/L3
Kür (riv.), Azer. 63/J5
Kūrālī, India 86/D4
Kurama-yama (peak), Japan 77/J5
Kurashiki, Japan 74/C3
Kurayoshi, Japan 74/C3
Kurdistan (reg.), Asia 64/E6
Kŭrdzhali, Bul. 47/J2
Kŭrdzhali (res.), Bul. 47/J2
Küre (mts.), Turk. 90/C1
Kure, Japan 74/C3
Küre, Turk. 90/C1
Kure (isl.), Hi, US 116/H2
Kuressaare, Est. 39/K2
Kureyka (riv.), Rus. 64/K3
Kurgan, Rus. 61/Q5
Kurganskaya Oblast, Rus. 87/D1
Kuri, SKor. 73/G6
Kuria (isl.), Kiri. 116/G4
Kuria Muria (isls.), Oman 67/F5
Kurīgrām, Bang. 85/G3
Kurihashi, Japan 77/D1
Kurikoma-yama (peak), Japan 76/B4
Kuril (isls.), Rus. 67/Q5
Kurimoto, Japan 77/F2
Kurinwas (riv.), Nic. 145/E3
Kurisawa, Japan 76/B2
Kuriyama, Japan 76/B2
Kürkçü, Turk. 91/C1
Kurla, India 87/K5
Kurnool, India 82/C4
Kuro-shima (isl.), Japan 74/A5
Kurodashō, Japan 77/G5
Kuroishi, Japan 76/A2
Kuroiso, Japan 76/B3
Kuroso-yama (peak), Japan 77/K6
Kurotaki, Japan 77/J7
Kurrajong, Austl. 114/G8
Kurram (riv.), Afg.,Pak. 89/K2
Kurrimine Beach, Austl. 114/B2
Kuršėnai, Lith. 39/K3
Kurseong, India 85/G2
Kursiu Nerija NP, Lith. 39/J4
Kursk, Rus. 62/F2
Kurskskaya Oblast, Rus. 62/E2
Kurskaya Spit (bar), Lith.,Rus. 39/J4
Kurskiy (lag.), Lith.,Rus. 39/J4
Kuršumlija, Serb. 47/G1
Kurşunlu, Turk. 90/C1
Kurtalan, Turk. 90/E2
Kürten, Ger. 53/G1
Kuru (riv.), Sudan 97/L6
Kuruca (pass), Turk. 90/E2
Kuruçay, Turk. 90/D2
Kuruçay (riv.), Turk. 63/G4
Kuruktag (mts.), China 70/E3
Kuruman, SAfr. 106/C2
Kurumansrivier (riv.), SAfr. 106/C2
Kurume, Japan 74/B4
Kurunegala, SrL. 82/D6
Kurupukari, Guy. 153/G3
Kurur (peak), Sudan 101/B4
Kurwongbah (lake), Austl. 114/E6
Kurye, SKor. 73/D5
Kuryong (riv.), NKor. 73/C3
Kuş Cenneti NP, Turk. 90/B1
Kuşadası, Turk. 90/A2
Kusatsu, Japan 77/J5
Kusel, Ger. 53/G4
Kushālgarh, India 89/K4
Kushida (riv.), Japan 77/K7
Kushigata, Japan 77/A2
Kushihara, Japan 77/M5
Kushikino, Japan 74/B5
Kushima, Japan 74/B5
Kushimoto, Japan 74/D4
Kushiro, Japan 76/D2
Kushiro (riv.), Japan 76/D2
Kushiro-Shitsugen NP, Japan 76/D2
Kushtia (pol. reg.), Bang. 85/G4
Kushtia, Bang. 85/G4
Kusiyana (riv.), Bang. 85/H3
Kuskokwim (bay), Ak, US 134/F4
Kuskokwim (mts.), Ak, US 134/G3
Kuskokwim (riv.), Ak, US 134/F3
Kuskokwim, North Fork (riv.), Ak, US 134/H3
Kuskokwim, South Fork (riv.), Ak, US 134/H3
Küsnacht, Swi. 57/E3
Kusŏng, NKor. 73/C3
Kussharo (lake), Japan 76/C2
Küssnacht am Rigi, Swi. 57/E3
Küstenkanal (canal), Ger. 51/E3
Kusterdingen, Ger. 54/C5
Kūstī, Sudan 97/M5
Kusu, Japan 77/L6
Kut (isl.), Thai. 83/H5
Kütahya, Turk. 90/B2
K'ut'aisi (int'l arpt.), Geo. 63/G4
K'ut'aisi, Geo. 63/G4
Kutch (reg.), India 89/J4
Kutch, Gulf of (gulf), India 89/J4
Kutchan, Japan 76/B1
Kutcharo (lake), Japan 76/C1
Kutenholz, Ger. 51/G2
Kutná Hora, Czh. 41/H4
Kutno, Pol. 41/K2
Kutsuki, Japan 77/J5
Küttigen, Swi. 56/E3
Kutu, D.R. Congo 96/J8
Kutzenhausen, Ger. 57/H1
Kutztown, Pa, US 138/C2
Kuujjua (riv.), NW, Can. 122/E1
Kuujjuaq, Qu, Can. 123/K3
Kuusamo, Fin. 37/J2
Kuusankoski, Fin. 39/M1
Kuutse (hill), Est. 39/M2
Kuvandyk, Rus. 63/L2
Kuwait (ctry.) 88/E3
Kuwait (cap.), Kuw. 88/E3
Kuwānā (riv.), India 82/D2
Kuwana, Japan 77/L5
Kuybyshev (res.), Rus. 64/E4
Kuyto (lake), Rus. 37/J2
Kuytun, China 70/E3
Kuyuwini (riv.), Guy. 153/G4
Kuze, Japan 77/K4
Kuzitrin (riv.), Ak, US 134/E2
Kuznetsk, Rus. 63/H1
Kuzucubelen, Turk. 91/D1
Kuzumaki, Japan 76/B3
Kvaløy (isl.), Nor. 37/F1
Kværndrup, Den. 38/D4
Kvarner (gulf), Cro. 48/B3
Kvarnerić (chan.), Cro. 48/B3
Kvigtinden (peak), Nor. 37/E2
Kvinesdal, Nor. 38/B2
Kvinnherad, Nor. 38/B2
Kviteseid, Nor. 38/C2
Kwa (riv.), D.R. Congo 93/D5
Kwach'ŏn, SKor. 73/F7
Kwajalein (isl.), Mrsh. 116/F4
Kwale, Kenya 104/C4
KwaMashu, SAfr. 107/E3
Kwanak-san (peak), SKor. 73/F7
Kwangch'ŏn, SKor. 73/D4
Kwangju, SKor. 73/D5
Kwangju, SKor. 73/G7
Kwangju-Gwangyŏksi (prov.), SKor. 73/D5
Kwangmyŏng, SKor. 73/F7
Kwango (riv.), D.R. Congo 93/D5
Kwangyang, SKor. 73/D5
Kwania (lake), Ugan. 97/M7
Kwansan, SKor. 73/D5
Kwara (state), Nga. 103/G4
Kwaraha (peak), Tanz. 104/B4
Kwataboahegan (riv.), On, Can. 130/D1
Kwazulu Natal (prov.), SAfr. 107/E3
Kwekwe, Zim. 105/E4
Kwethluk, Ak, US 134/F3
Kwidzyn, Pol. 39/H5
Kwigillingok, Ak, US 134/F4
Kwili (riv.), D.R. Congo 105/C1
Kwilu (riv.), D.R. Congo 93/D5
Kwinana, Austl. 112/K7
Kyabé, Chad 97/J6
Kyabram, Austl. 115/C3
Kyaiktiyo Pagoda, Myan. 78/B2
Kyaikto, Myan. 83/G4
Kyakhta, Rus. 70/J1
Kyan-zaki (cape), Japan 75/J7
Kyangin, Myan. 83/G4
Kyaukpadaung, Myan. 83/G3
Kyaukpyu, Myan. 83/F4
Kyaukse, Myan. 83/G3
Kyenjojo, Ugan. 104/A2
Kyeryong-san NP, SKor. 73/D4
Kyjov, Czh. 41/J4
Kyle, Sk, Can. 126/F3
Kyle (reg.), Sc, UK 36/B5
Kyll (riv.), Ger. 40/D3
Kym (riv.), Eng, UK 33/F2
Kymi (prov.), Fin. 37/H3
Kymijoki (riv.), Fin. 39/M1
Kymore, India 84/B4
Kyneton, Austl. 115/C3
Kynšperk nad Ohří, Czh. 55/F2
Kyoga (lake), Ugan. 97/M7
Kyōga-misaki (cape), Japan 74/D3
Kyogle, Austl. 114/D5
Kyonan, Japan 75/F3
Kyŏngbok Palace, SKor. 73/F6
Kyŏnggi (bay), SKor. 73/C4
Kyŏnggi-do (prov.), SKor. 73/D4
Kyŏngju, SKor. 74/A3
Kyŏngju NP, SKor. 74/A3
Kyŏngsan, SKor. 74/A3
Kyŏngsang-bukto (prov.), SKor. 73/E4
Kyŏngsang-namdo (prov.), SKor. 73/E5
Kyōto (pref.), Japan 74/D3
Kyōto, Japan 77/J5
Kyōto Imperial Palace, Japan 77/J6
Kyōwa, Japan 77/E1
Kyrenia (dist.), Cyp. 91/C2
Kyrenia, Cyp. 91/C2
Kyrgyzstan (ctry.) 87/F4
Kyritz, Ger. 40/G2
Kyrösjärvi (lake), Fin. 39/K1
Kythrea, Cyp. 91/C2
Kyūshū (isl.), Japan 67/M6
Kyūshū Highlands (uplands), Japan 74/B4
Kyustendil, Bul. 47/H1
Kywebwe, Myan. 83/F4
Kyyivs'ka Oblast', Ukr. 62/D2
Kyyivs'ke Vodoskhovyshche (res.), Ukr. 62/D2
Kyzyl, Rus. 70/F1

L

La Algaba, Sp. 44/B4
La Almunia de Doña Godina, Sp. 44/E2
La Amistad Int'l Park, CR 140/E6
La Araucanía (pol. reg.), Chile 158/B3
La Ascensión, Mex. 143/F3
La Asunción, Ven. 153/F2
La Aurora (int'l arpt.), Guat. 144/D3
La Babia, Mex. 132/C4
La Baie, Qu, Can. 131/G1
La Banda, Arg. 157/D2
La Bañeza, Sp. 44/C1
La Bassée, Fr. 52/B2

200
La Ba – Largo

La Baule-Escoublac, Fr . 42/B3
La Belle, Fl, US 133/H5
La Birse (riv.), Swi. 56/D3
La Blanquilla (isl.), Ven. 153/E2
La Bocana, Mex. 142/B3
La Bresse, Fr. 56/C2
La Broque, Fr. 56/D1
La Calera, Chile 158/N8
La Campana, Sp. 44/C4
La Cañada (peak), Cuba 145/F1
La Canada-Flintridge, Ca, US 136/F7
La Capelle, Fr. 52/C4
La Carlota, Sp. 44/C4
La Carlota, Arg. 158/E2
La Carolina, Sp. 44/D3
La Catedral (peak), Mex. 143/Q9
La Ceiba, Hon. 144/E3
La Ceiba (int'l arpt.), Hon. 144/E3
La Celle-les-Bordes, Fr. 30/H6
La Celle-Saint-Cloud, Fr. 30/J5
La Celle-sur-Morin, Fr. 30/L5
La Chapelle-de-Guinchay, Fr . 56/A5
La Chapelle-Saint-Luc, Fr. 42/F2
La Chaux-de-Bonds, Swi. 56/C3
La Chinita (int'l arpt.), Ven. 152/D2
La Chorrera, Pan. 150/C2
La Cienega, NM, US 129/F4
La Ciotat, Fr. 42/F5
La Clusaz, Fr. 56/C6
La Concepcion, Ven. 152/D2
La Concepción, Nic. 144/E4
La Concepción, Pan. 145/F4
La Coronilla, Uru. 159/G2
La Coruña, Sp. 44/A1
La Couronne, Fr. 42/D4
La Crèche, Fr. 42/C3
La Crescenta-Montrose, Ca, US 136/F7
La Croix-en-Brie, Fr. 30/M6
La Croix, Lac (lake), On, Can. 127/L3
La Cruz, CR 144/E4
La Cruz, Col. 152/B4
La Cruz, Chile 158/N8
La Cruz, Mex. 142/D4
La Cruz, Uru. 159/K10
La Cumbre (vol.), Ecu. 156/E7
La Dôle (peak), Swi. 56/C5
La Dorada, Col. 150/D2
La Dormida, Arg. 158/D2
La Esperanza, Hon. 144/D3
La Estrada, Sp. 44/A1
La Estrella, Chile 158/N9
La Falda, Arg. 157/D3
La Fayette, Ga, US 133/G3
La Fère, Fr. 52/C4
La Ferté-Gaucher, Fr. 52/C6
La Ferté-Macé, Fr. 42/C2
La Ferté-Milon, Fr. 30/M7
La Ferté-Sous-Jouarre, Fr. 52/C6
La Flèche, Fr. 42/C3
La Fria, Ven. 152/C2
La Garamba NP, D.R. Congo 104/A2
La Garita (mts.), US 132/B2
La Garriga, Sp. 45/L6
La Gineta, Sp. 44/E3
La Gloria, Col. 152/C2
La Gran Sabana (plain), Ven. 150/F2
La Grande, Or, US 126/D4
La Grande (riv.), Qu, Can. 123/J3
La Grande Ruine (peak), Fr. 43/G4
La Grange, Ga, US 133/G3
La Grange, Tx, US 129/H5
La Grita, Ven. 145/J4
La Gruyère (lake), Swi. 56/D4
La Guajira (dept.), Col. 145/H4
La Guajira (pen.), Col. 145/H4
La Guardia, Sp. 44/A2
La Guardia (int'l arpt.), NY, US 139/K8
La Habana (Havana) (cap.), Cuba 140/E3
La Habra, Ca, US 136/G8
La Have (riv.), NS, Can. 131/H2
La Higuera, Chile 157/B2
La Honda, Ca, US 135/K12
La Houssaye-en-Brie, Fr. 30/L5
La Huaca, Peru 156/A2
La Huacana, Mex. 143/E5
La Huerta, Mex. 142/D5
La Isla, Mex. 143/Q10
La Jalca, Peru 156/B2
La Joya, Peru 156/D5
La Joya de los Sachas, Ecu. 152/B5
La Junta, Co, US 129/G3
La Junta, Mex. 142/D2
La Laguna, Sp. 98/A3
La Libertad (dept.), Peru 156/B3
La Libertad, Hon. 144/E3
La Libertad, Guat. 144/D2
La Libertad, Ecu. 152/A5
La Ligua, Chile 158/C2
La Línea de la Concepción, Sp. 44/C4
La Llagosta, Sp. 45/L6
La Loche, Sk, Can. 126/F1
La Loggia, It. 58/A3
La Louvière, Belg. 53/D3
La Luisiana, Sp. 44/C4
La Luz, NM, US 129/F4
La Machine, Fr. 42/E3
La Maddalena, It. 46/A2
La Madeleine, Fr. 52/C2
La Malbaie, Qu, Can. 131/G2
La Martre (lake), NW, Can. 122/E2
La Masica, Hon. 144/E3
La Mauricie NP, Qu, Can. 130/F2
La Mensura (peak), Col. 152/C4
La Merca, Sp. 44/B1
La Merced, Peru 156/C3
La Mesa, Ca, US 136/C5
La Mesa (int'l arpt.), Hon. 144/E3
La Mesa, Ven. 152/D2
La Mira, Mex. 142/E5
La Mirada, Ca, US 136/F8
La Moine (riv.), Il, US 130/B3
La Montaña (phys. reg.), Peru 147/B3
La Moure, ND, US 127/J4
La Neuveville, Swi. 56/D3
La Norville, Fr. 30/J6
La Orchila (isl.), Ven. 141/H5
La Orotava, Sp. 98/A3
La Oroya, Peru 156/C3
La Palma, Pan. 145/G4
La Palma (isl.), Sp. 93/A2
La Paloma, Uru. 159/G2
La Pampa (prov.), Arg. 158/D3
La Paz, Arg. 157/E3
La Paz (cap.), Bol. 150/E7
La Paz (dept.), Bol. 156/D4
La Paz (bay), Mex. 142/C3
La Paz, Mex. 142/C3
La Paz, Hon. 144/E3
La Paz, Col. 152/C2
La Paz, Col. 152/C3
La Paz, Arg. 158/D2
La Paz, Uru. 159/K11
La Pêche, Qu, Can. 130/F2
La Peña, Pan. 140/E6
La Perla, Mex. 132/B4
La Pérouse (str.), Japan,Rus 71/R2
La Perouse (str.), Japan,Rus. 67/P5
La Petite-Raon, Fr. 56/C1
La Piedad Cavadas, Mex. 142/E4
La Plata, Md, US 130/E4
La Plata, Col. 152/C4
La Plata, Arg. 159/K11
La Pobla de Lillet, Sp. 45/F1
La Pocatière, Qu, Can. 131/G2
La Pola de Gordón, Sp. 44/C1
La Ponge (lake), Sk, Can. 126/G2
La Porte, In, US 130/C3
La Prairie, Qu, Can. 131/P7
La Pryor, Tx, US 129/H5
La Puebla, Sp. 45/G3
La Puebla de Almoradiel, Sp. 44/D3
La Puebla de Cazalla, Sp. 44/C4
La Puebla de Montalbán, Sp. 44/C3
La Puente, Ca, US 136/G7
La Puntilla (pt.), Ecu. 152/A5
La Quebrada, Ven. 152/D2
La Queue-les-Yvelines, Fr . 52/A6
La Quiaca, Arg. 150/E8
La Rambla, Sp. 44/C4
La Reforma, Mex. 142/C3
La Rinconada, Sp. 44/C4
La Rioja, Arg. 157/C2
La Rioja (aut. comm.), Sp. 44/D1
La Rioja (prov.), Sp. 44/D1
La Robla, Sp. 44/C1
La Roche (lake), Sk, Can. 126/F1
La Roche, Swi. 56/D4
La Roche-en-Ardenne, Belg. 53/E3
La Roche-sur-Foron, Fr. 56/C5
La Roche-sur-Yon, Fr. 42/C3
La Rochelle, Fr. 42/C3
La Roda, Sp. 44/D3
La Romana, DRep. 141/H4
La Ronge, Sk, Can. 127/G2
La Rúa, Sp. 44/B1
La Salle, Co, US 137/C2
La Sarraz, Swi. 56/C4
La Sarre, Qu, Can. 130/E1
La Sauvette (peak), Fr. 43/G5
La Scie, Nf, Can. 131/L1
La Serena, Chile 157/B2
La Seu d'Urgell, Sp. 45/F1
La Seyne-sur-Mer, Fr. 42/F5
La Sierpe, Cuba 145/G1
La Sila (mts.), It. 46/E3
La Silueta (peak), Chile 159/B7
La Solana, Sp. 44/D3
La Souterraine, Fr. 42/D3
La Spezia (prov.), It. 58/C4
La Spezia, It. 58/C4
La Tabatière, Qu, Can. 131/K1
La Teste, Fr. 42/C4
La Tête à l'Ane (peak), Fr. 56/C6
La Tigra, PN, Hon. 144/E3
La Toma, Arg. 158/D2
La Tortue (isl.), Haiti 145/H1
La Tortuga (isl.), Ven. 153/E2
La Tortuga, Isla (isl.), Ven. 150/E1
La Tour-de-Peilz, Swi. 56/C5
La Tour-de-Trême, Swi. 56/D4
La Tremblade, Fr. 42/C4
La Trinitaria, Mex. 144/C2
La Troncal, Ecu. 152/B5
La Tuque, Qu, Can. 131/F2
La Turbie, Fr. 58/H8
La Unión, Peru 156/A2
La Unión, Peru 156/B3
La Unión, Mex. 143/E5
La Unión, Sp. 45/E4
La Unión, Chile 158/B4
La Unión, Col. 152/B4
La Unión, ESal. 144/E3
La Union, Ven. 152/E2
La Vecilla, Sp. 44/C1
La Verna, It. 59/E5
La Verne, Ca, US 136/C2
La Vernia, Tx, US 137/U21
La Verrière, Fr. 30/H5
La Víbora, Mex. 132/C5
La Victoria, Ven. 150/E1
La Victoria, Ven. 152/D3
La Wantzenau, Fr. 53/G6
Laa an der Thaya, Aus. 43/M2
Laaber, Ger. 55/E4
Laage, Ger. 38/E5
Laakirchen, Aus. 55/G7
Laarne, Belg. 52/C1
Laas Caanood, Som. 97/Q6
Laas Qoray, Som. 97/Q5
Laatzen, Ger. 51/G4
Laax, Swi. 57/F4
Labason, Phil. 79/D6
L'Abbaye, Swi. 56/C4
Labdah (Leptis Magna) (ruin), Libya 96/H1
Labé, Gui. 102/B4
Labé (pol. reg.), Gui. 102/B4
Labe (Elbe) (riv.), Czh. 43/L1
Laberweinting, Ger. 55/F5
Labian (cape), Malay. 81/E2
Labin, Cro. 48/B3
Labinsk, Rus. 63/G3
Labná (ruin), Mex. 144/D1
Laborde, Arg. 158/E2
Laborec (riv.), Slvk. 41/L4
Laboulaye, Arg. 158/E2
Labrador (reg.), Nf, Can. 123/K3
Labrador (sea), Can.,Grld. 119/M4
Labrador City, Nf, Can. 123/K3
Lábrea, Braz. 150/F5
Labruguière, Fr. 42/E5
Labry, Fr. 53/E5
Labuk (riv.), Malay. 81/E2
Labuk (bay), Malay. 81/E2
Labuništa, FYROM 47/G2
Labutta, Myan. 83/F4
Laç, Alb. 47/F2
Lac Afwein (riv.), Kenya 104/C2
Lac du Bonnet, Mb, Can. 127/J3
Lac La Biche, Ab, Can. 126/F2
Lac-Mégantic, Qu, Can. 131/G2
L'Acadie, Qu, Can. 131/P7
Lacantum (riv.), Mex. 144/D2
Lacaune, Fr. 42/E5
Laccadive (sea), India 82/B5
Lacchiarella, It. 58/C2
Lacepede (bay), Austl. 109/C4
Lach Dera (riv.), Som. 97/P7
Lacha (lake), Rus. 60/H3
Lachapelle-aux-Pots, Fr. 52/A5
Lachay (pt.), Peru 156/B3
Lachen, Swi. 57/E3
Lachenaie, Qu, Can. 131/N6
Lachendorf, Ger. 51/H3
Lāchi, Pak. 86/A3
L'Achigan (riv.), Qu, Can. 131/N6
Lachine, Qu, Can. 131/N7
Lachlan (riv.), Austl. 109/D4
Lachte (riv.), Ger. 51/H3
Lackawanna, NY, US 131/S10
Lackawanna (co.), Pa, US 138/C1
Läckö, Swe. 38/E2
Lacombe, Ab, Can. 126/E2
Lacombe, La, US 137/Q16
Laconia, NH, US 131/G3
Lacroix-Saint-Ouen, Fr. 52/B5
Ladainha, Braz. 154/B5
Ladakh (mts.), India 89/L2
Ladbergen, Ger. 51/E4
Ladder (hills), Sc, UK 36/C2
Lądek-Zdrój, Pol. 41/J3
Ladenburg, Ger. 54/B4
Ladera Heights, Ca, US 136/F8
Ladismith, SAfr. 106/C4
Ladispoli, It. 46/C2
Ladoga (lake), Rus. 160/D
Ladoix-Serrigny, Fr. 56/A3
Ladrillero (mtn.), Chile 159/B7
Ladue, Mo, US 137/G8
Lādwa, India 86/D5
Lady Isle (isl.), Sc, UK 36/B5
Ladybank, Sc, UK 36/C4
Ladybower (res.), Eng, UK 35/G5
Ladybrand, SAfr. 106/D3
Ladysmith, SAfr. 107/E3
Lae (isl.), Mrsh. 116/F4
Laer, Ger. 51/E4
Lafayette, In, US 130/C3
Lafayette, La, US 129/J5
Lafayette, Co, US 137/B3
Lafayette, NJ, US 138/D1
Lafayette, Ca, US 135/K11
Lafia, Nga. 103/H4
Lafitte, La, US 137/P17
Laflamme (riv.), Qu, Can. 130/E1
Lafnitz (riv.), Aus. 43/L3
Lafontaine, Qu, Can. 131/M6
Lafourche (parish), La, US 137/T17
Laga Balal (riv.), Kenya 104/C2
Laga Mado Gali (riv.), Kenya 104/C2
Laga Merille (riv.), Kenya 104/C2
Lagan, Swe. 38/E3
Lagan (riv.), Swe. 38/E3
Lagarto, Braz. 154/C3
Lagawe, Phil. 79/D4
Lagdo, Lac de (lake), Camr. 96/H6
Lage, Ger. 51/F5
Lage Vaart (canal), Neth. 50/C4
Lågen (riv.), Nor. 38/C1
Lages, Braz. 155/B3
Laggan (lake), Sc, UK 36/B3
Lagh Bogal (riv.), Kenya 104/C2
Lagh Bor (riv.), Kenya 97/N7
Lagh Kutulo (riv.), Kenya 104/D2
Laghouat (prov.), Alg. 99/F2
Laghouat, Alg. 99/F2
Lagnieu, Fr. 56/B6
Lagny-le-Sec, Fr. 30/L4
Lagny-sur-Marne, Fr. 30/L5
Lago da Pedra, Braz. 154/A2
Lago de Atitlán, PN, Guat. 144/D3
Lago Puelo, PN, Arg. 158/C4
Lago Verde, Chile 158/C5
Lagoa, Port. 44/A4
Lagoa da Prata, Braz. 155/C2
Lagoa Formosa, Braz. 155/C1
Lagoa Vermelha, Braz. 155/B4
Lagoda (lake), Rus. 37/J3
Lagonegro, It. 46/D2
Lagord, Fr. 42/C3
Lagos, Nga. 103/F5
Lagos (state), Nga. 103/F5
Lagos, Port. 44/A4
Lagos de Moreno, Mex. 142/E4
Lagosanto, It. 59/F3
Laguardia, Sp. 44/D1
Laguna, Braz. 155/B4
Laguna Beach, Ca, US 136/C3
Laguna Blanca, PN, Arg. 158/C3
Laguna de Duero, Sp. 44/C2
Laguna de la Restinga, PN, Ven. 153/E2
Laguna del Laja, PN, Chile 158/C3
Laguna del Rey, Mex. 142/E3
Laguna Hills, Ca, US 136/C3
Laguna San Rafael, PN, Chile 157/B6
Lagunas, Peru 156/C2
Lagunas, Peru 156/B2
Lagunas de Chacahua, PN, Mex. 144/B2
Lagunas de Montebello, Mex. 140/C4
Lagunas de Zempoala, PN, Mex. 143/Q10
Lagunillas, Ven. 152/D2
Laguntara (lag.), Hon. 145/E3
Lahad Datu, Malay. 81/E2
Lahār, India 84/B2
Lāharpur, India 84/C2
Lahat, Indo. 80/B4
Lāhījān, Iran 88/F1
Lahn (riv.), Ger. 40/E3
Lahnstein, Ger. 53/G3
Laholm, Swe. 38/E3
Laholms (bay), Den. 38/E3
Lahore, Pak. 86/C4
Lahore (int'l arpt.), Pak. 86/C4
Lahr, Ger. 56/D1
Lahti, Fin. 39/L1
Laï, Chad 96/J6
Lai Chau, Viet. 78/C1
Lai'an, China 72/D4
Laibin, China 79/A3
Laichingen, Ger. 54/C5
Laidon (lake), Sc, UK 36/B3
Laie, Hi, US 124/W12
Laifeng Tujiazu Zizhixian, China 79/A2
L'Aigle, Fr. 42/D2
Laigueglia, It. 58/B5
Laihia, Fin. 37/G3
Lainate, It. 58/C1
Laingsburg, SAfr. 106/C4
Lainioälven (riv.), Swe. 37/G1
Laishui, China 72/G7
Laisvall, Swe. 37/F2
Laitila, Fin. 39/J1
Laives (Leifers), It. 57/H5
Laiwu, China 72/D3
Laixi, China 72/E3
Laiyuan, China 72/C3
Laizhou (bay), China 72/D3
Laja (lake), Chile 158/C3
Lajas, Peru 156/B2
Laje, Braz. 154/B3
Lajeado, Braz. 155/B4
Lajedo, Braz. 154/C3
Lajes, Braz. 154/C2
Lajes, Azor., Port. 45/S12
Lajes (int'l arpt.), Azor., Port. 45/S12
Lajing (pass), Nepal 85/E1
Lajinha, Braz. 155/D2
Lajosmizse, Hun. 48/D2
L'Akagera, PN de, Rwa. 104/A3
Lakato, Madg. 107/J7
Lake (co.), Il, US 135/P15
Lake Aluma, Ok, US 137/N14
Lake Amadeus Abor. Land, Austl. 113/F3
Lake Arrowhead, Ca, US 136/C2
Lake Barrington, Il, US 135/P15
Lake Beulah, Wi, US 135/P14
Lake Bluff, Il, US 135/Q15
Lake Boga, Austl. 115/B2
Lake Bogoria Nat'l Rsv., Kenya 104/C2
Lake Bolac, Austl. 115/B3
Lake Cargelligo, Austl. 115/C2
Lake Catherine, Il, US 135/P15
Lake Chany (lake), Rus. 87/G2
Lake Charles, La, US 129/J5
Lake Chelan Nat'l Rec. Area, Wa, US 126/C3
Lake City, Fl, US 133/H4
Lake Clark NP and Prsv., Ak, US 134/G3
Lake District NP, Eng, UK 35/E2
Lake Elsinore, Ca, US 136/C3
Lake Forest, Il, US 135/Q15
Lake Forest Park, Wa, US 135/C2
Lake Fork (res.), Tx, US 132/E3
Lake Grace, Austl. 112/C5
Lake Havasu City, Az, US 128/D4
Lake Hiwassee, Ok, US 137/N14
Lake in the Hills, Il, US 135/P15
Lake Jackson, Tx, US 129/J5
Lake Lotawana, Mo, US 137/E6
Lake Louise, Ab, Can. 126/D3
Lake Malawi NP, Malw. 105/F3
Lake Manyara NP, Tanz. 104/B3
Lake Mburo NP, Ugan. 104/A3
Lake Mead Nat'l Rec. Area, US 128/D4
Lake Meredith Nat'l Rec. Area, Tx, US 132/C3
Lake Minchumina, Ak, US 134/H3
Lake Mohawk, NJ, US 138/D1
Lake Nakuru NP, Kenya 104/C3
Lake of the Woods (lake), US,Can. 127/K3
Lake Orion, Mi, US 135/F6
Lake Point Junction, Ut, US 137/J12
Lake Providence, La, US 129/K4
Lake Ronkonkoma, NY, US 139/E2
Lake Shore, Md, US 138/B5
Lake Station, In, US 135/R16
Lake Success, NY, US 139/L8
Lake Villa, Il, US 135/P15
Lake Wales, Fl, US 133/H5
Lake Winnebago, Mo, US 137/E6
Lake Worth, Fl, US 133/H5
Lake Zurich, Il, US 135/P15
Lakehurst, NJ, US 138/D3
Lakehurst Naval Air Eng. Ctr., NJ, US 138/D3
Lakeland, Fl, US 133/H4
Lakeland Village, Ca, US 136/C3
Lakemoor, Il, US 135/P15
Lakeport, Ca, US 128/B3
Lakes Entrance, Austl. 115/D3
Lakes NP, The, Austl. 115/C3
Lakesfjorden (inlet), Nor. 37/H1
Lakeside, Ca, US 136/D5
Lakeview, Or, US 126/C5
Lakeview, Ut, US 137/K13
Lakeview, Ca, US 136/C3
Lakeville (lake), Mi, US 135/F6
Lakeway, Tx, US 129/H5
Lakewood, Wa, US 126/C3
Lakewood, Co, US 137/B3
Lakewood, NJ, US 138/D3
Lakewood, Ca, US 136/F8
Lakewood, Il, US 135/P15
Lakhemaa NP, Est. 39/L2
Lakhīmpur, India 84/C2
Lakhnādon, India 84/B4
Laki (vol.), Ice. 37/N7
Lakki, Pak. 86/A3
Lakkíon, Gre. 90/A2
Lakonía (gulf), Gre. 47/H4
Lakshadweep (terr.), India 82/B6
Lakshadweep (isls.), India 67/F8
Lal Suhanra NP, Pak. 86/B5
Lāla Mūsa, Pak. 86/B3
Lalana (riv.), Madg. 107/H8
Lalang (riv.), Indo. 80/B4
Lālganj, India 85/E3
Lālgola, India 85/G3
Lālīān, Pak. 86/B4
Lalín, Sp. 44/A1
Lalinde, Fr. 42/D4
Lalitpur, India 84/B3
Lalitpur (Pāṭan), Nepal 85/E2
Lalla Rookh Abor. Land, Austl. 112/C2
Lamachan (peak), Sc, UK 34/D1
Lamadrid, Mex. 132/C5
Lamanai (ruin), Belz. 144/D2
Lamandau (riv.), Indo. 80/D4
Lamar, Co, US 129/G3
Lamarche, Fr. 56/B1
Lamarche-sur-Saône, Fr . 56/B3
Lamarque, Arg. 158/D3
Lamas, Peru 156/B2
Lambach, Aus. 55/G6
Lamballe, Fr. 42/B2
Lambaré, Par. 157/E2
Lambaréné, Gabon 96/H8
Lambari, Braz. 211/H6
Lambay (isl.), Ire. 31/Q10
Lambayeque (dept.), Peru 156/A2
Lambayeque, Peru 156/B2
Lambé Coba (riv.), Mali 102/C3
Lambert-St. Louis (int'l arpt.), Mo, US 129/K3
Lambert's Bay, SAfr. 106/B4
Lambertville, Mi, US 130/D3
Lambertville, NJ, US 138/D3
Lambesc, Fr. 42/F5
Lambeth (bor.), Eng, UK 30/C2
Lambrama, Peru 156/C4
Lambrecht, Ger. 54/B4
Lambro (riv.), It. 58/C2
Lambsheim, Ger. 54/B3
Lambton (co.), On, Can. 135/H6
Lambunao, Phil. 79/D5
Lamego, Port. 44/B2
Lamèque (isl.), NB, Can. 131/H2
Lameroo, Austl. 113/J5
Lamesa, Tx, US 129/G4
Lamía, Gre. 47/H3
Lamington (riv.), NJ, US 138/D2
Lamington NP, Austl. 114/D5
Lamitan, Phil. 81/F2
Lamlash, Sc, UK 36/A5
Lamma (isl.), China 71/U11
Lammermuir (hills), Sc, UK 36/D5
Lammhult, Swe. 38/F3
Lammi, Fin. 39/L1
Lamone (riv.), It. 43/J4
Lamont, Ca, US 128/C4
Lamorlaye, Fr. 30/K4
Lamotrek (isl.), Micr. 116/D4
Lampa, Peru 156/D4
Lampa, Chile 158/N8
Lampang, Thai. 78/B2
Lampasas, Tx, US 129/H5
Lampasas (riv.), Tx, US 143/F2
Lampazos de Naranjo, Mex. 132/C5
Lampedusa, It. 46/C5
Lampedusa (isl.), It. 27/F5
Lampertheim, Ger. 54/B3
Lampeter, Pa, US 138/B4
Lamphun, Thai. 78/B2
Lampman, Sk, Can. 127/H3
Lamporecchio, It. 59/D5
Lamstedt, Ger. 51/G1
Lamu, Kenya 104/D3
Lamud, Peru 156/B2
Lamwa (peak), Ugan. 104/B2
Lan Sang NP, Thai. 78/B2
Lana, It. 57/H4
Lana, Río de la (riv.), Mex. 144/C2
Lanai (isl.), Hi, US 124/T10
Lanaihale (peak), Hi, US 124/T10
Lanaken, Belg. 53/E2
Lanark, Sc, UK 36/C5
Lanbi (isl.), Myan. 83/G5
Lancang Lahuzu Zizhixian, China 83/G3
Lancashire (co.), Eng, UK 35/F4
Lancashire (plain), Eng, UK 35/F4
Lancaster (sound), Nun., Can. 123/H1
Lancaster, Eng, UK 35/F3
Lancaster, Ca, US 128/C4
Lancaster, NY, US 131/S10
Lancaster, Pa, US 138/B3
Lancaster (co.), Pa, US 138/B4
Lancaster, SC, US 133/H3
Lancelin, Austl. 112/B4
Lanciano, It. 46/D1
L'Ancienne-Lorette, Qu, Can. 131/G2
Lanco, Chile 158/B3
Łańcut, Pol. 41/M3
Lancy, Swi. 56/C5
Land Kehdingen (reg.), Ger. 51/G1
Landau an der Isar, Ger. 55/F5
Landau in der Pfalz, Ger. 54/B4
Landeck, Aus. 57/G3
Landen, Belg. 53/E2
Lander, Wy, US 126/F5
Landerneau, Fr. 42/A2
Landes (reg.), Fr. 42/C4
Landes de Lanvaux (mts.), Fr. 42/B3
Landesbergen, Ger. 51/G3
Landis, Sk, Can. 126/F2
Landis Valley Museum, Pa, US 138/B3
Landisburg, Pa, US 138/A3
Landivisiau, Fr. 42/A2
Landrecies, Fr. 52/C3
Landri Sales, Braz. 154/B2
Landriano, It. 58/C2
Land's End (pt.), Eng, UK 32/A6
Landsberg, Ger. 57/G1
Landser, Fr. 56/D2
Landshut, Ger. 55/F5
Landskrona, Swe. 38/E4
Landsmeer, Neth. 50/B4
Landstuhl, Ger. 53/G5
Landvetter (int'l arpt.), Swe. 38/E3
Lane End, Eng, UK 30/A2
Lanester, Fr. 42/B3
Lanett, Al, US 133/G3
Lang Craig (pt.), Sc, UK 36/D3
Lang Kha Tuk (peak), Thai. 78/B4
Lang Son, Viet. 83/J3
Lang Suan, Thai. 78/B4
Langadhás, Gre. 47/H2
Langdon, ND, US 127/J3
Langeac, Fr. 42/E4
Langebaanweg, SAfr. 106/L10
Langeberg (mts.), SAfr. 106/L10
Langeland (isl.), Ger. 38/D4
Langelsheim, Ger. 51/H5
Langen, Ger. 51/F1
Langen, Ger. 54/B3
Langenaltheim, Ger. 54/D5
Langenargen, Ger. 57/F2
Langenau, Ger. 54/D5
Langenbach, Ger. 55/E6
Langenberg, Ger. 51/E6
Langenburg, Sk, Can. 127/H3
Längenfeld, Aus. 57/G3
Langenfeld, Ger. 53/F1
Langenhagen, Ger. 51/G4
Langenhorn, Ger. 38/C4
Langenlois, Aus. 41/H4
Langenpreising, Ger. 55/E6
Langenselbold, Ger. 54/C2
Langenstein, Aus. 55/H6
Langenthal, Swi. 56/D3
Langenzenn, Ger. 54/D3
Langenzersdorf, Aus. 49/N7
Langeoog, Ger. 51/E1
Langeoog (isl.), Ger. 51/E1
Langerringen, Ger. 57/G1
Langeskov, Den. 38/D4
Langesund, Nor. 38/C2
Langeten (riv.), Swi. 56/D3
Langfang, China 72/H7
Langfurth, Ger. 54/D4
Langham, Sk, Can. 126/G2
Langhirano, It. 58/D3
Langholm, Sc, UK 35/F1
Langhorne, Pa, US 138/D3
Langjökull (glacier), Ice. 37/N7
Langkawi (isl.), Malay. 83/G6
Langley, Wa, US 135/C1
Langnau im Emmental, Swi. 56/D4
Langney (pt.), Eng, UK 33/G5
Langogne, Fr. 42/E4
Langon, Fr. 42/C4
Langøya (isl.), Nor. 37/E1
Langquaid, Ger. 55/F5
Langres, Fr. 56/B2
Langres, Plateau de (plat.), Fr. 42/F3
Langsa, Indo. 80/A3
Langshyttan, Swe. 38/G1
Langtang Lirung (peak), Nepal 85/E1
Langtang NP, Nepal 85/E1
Langtry, Tx, US 132/C4
Languedoc (reg.), Fr. 42/E5
Languedoc-Roussillon (pol. reg.), Fr. 42/E5
Langwedel, Ger. 51/G3
Langweid an Lech, Ger. 54/E6
Langwies, Swi. 57/F4
Langxi, China 72/D5
Lanham-Seabrook, Md, US 138/B6
Lanigan, Sk, Can. 127/G3
Laniloa (pt.), Hi, US 124/W12
Lanin (vol.), Arg. 158/C3
Lanin, PN, Arg. 157/B4
Länkäran, Azer. 63/J5
Lanlacuni Bajo, Peru 156/D4
Lannemezan (plat.), Fr. 42/D5
Lannion (bay), Fr. 42/B2
Lannion, Fr. 42/B2
Lansdale, Pa, US 138/C3
Lansdowne, India 84/B1
Lansdowne, Pa, US 138/C4
Lansdowne-Baltimore Highlands, Md, US 138/B5
Lansford, Pa, US 138/C2
Lanshan, China 83/K2
Lansing (cap.), Mi, US 130/C3
Lansing, Ks, US 137/D5
Lansing, Il, US 135/Q16
Lanta (isl.), Thai. 83/G6
Lantau (chan.), China 71/T11
Lantau (peak), China 71/T11
Lantau (isl.), China 71/T10
Lanterne (riv.), Fr. 56/C2
Lanús, Arg. 159/J11
Lanusei, It. 46/A3
Lanxi, China 79/C2
Lanzarote (int'l arpt.), Sp. 98/B3
Lanzarote (isl.), Canl., Sp. 93/A2
Lanžhot, Czh. 41/J4
Lanzhou, China 70/H4
Lao (mts.), China 73/D2
Lao (peak), China 72/E3
Lao Cai, Viet. 70/H7
Laoag, Phil. 79/D4
Laoang, Phil. 79/E5
Laohekou, China 72/B4
Laojun (mtn.), China 72/B4
Laon, Fr. 52/C4
Laos (ctry.) 78/C2
Laoshan, China 72/E3
Laotuding (peak), China 73/C2
Laou (riv.), Mor. 100/B2
Lapa, Braz. 155/B3
Lapeer, Mi, US 130/D3
Lapeer (co.), Mi, US 135/F6
Lapinlahti, Fin. 60/E3
Lapithos, Cyp. 91/C2
Lapland (reg.), Swe. 160/D
Laporte, Co, US 137/B1
Lappeenranta, Fin. 39/N1
Lappersdorf, Ger. 55/F4
Lappi (prov.), Fin. 37/H2
Laptev (sea), Rus. 67/M2
Lapua, Fin. 60/D3
Łapy, Pol. 41/M2
L'Aquila, It. 46/C1
Lār, Iran 89/F3
Lara, Austl. 115/C3
Lara (state), Ven. 152/D2
Laracha, Sp. 44/A1
Larache (prov.), Mor. 100/B2
Larache, Mor. 100/A2
Laragne-Montéglin, Fr. 42/F4
Laramie (riv.), Wy, US 127/G5
Laramie, Wy, US 127/G5
Laramie (mts.), Wy, US 124/E3
Laranjeiras do Sul, Braz. 155/A3
Larat (isl.), Indo. 81/H5
Larba, Alg. 100/G4
Larchmont, NY, US 139/K8
Lærdalsøyri, Nor. 38/B1
Laredo, Peru 156/B3
Laredo (int'l arpt.), Tx, US 132/D5
Laredo, Tx, US 132/D5
Laredo, Sp. 44/D1
Laren, Neth. 50/C4
Lares, Peru 156/C4
Largo, Fl, US 133/H5
Largo, Md, US 138/B6
Largo (bay), Sc, UK 36/D4
Largo, Cayo (isl.), Cuba 145/F1

201
Largs – Licos

Largs, Sc, UK 36/B5
Largue (riv.), Fr. 56/D2
Lariang (riv.), Indo. 81/E4
Larino, It. 46/D2
Lárisa, Gre. 47/H3
Lark (riv.), Eng, UK 33/G2
Lārkāna, Pak. 89/J3
Larkhall, Sc, UK 36/C5
Larkspur, Ca, US 135/J11
Larmor-Plage, Fr. 42/B3
Larnaca (int'l arpt.), Cyp. 91/C2
Larnaca (dist.) 91/C2
Larnaca, Cyp. 91/C2
Larne, NI, UK 34/C2
Larne (dist.), NI, UK 34/C2
Larne Lough (inlet), NI, UK 34/C2
Larned, Ks, US 129/H3
Larochette, Lux. 53/F4
Laroque-d'Olmes, Fr. 42/D5
Larose, La, US 133/F4
Larreynaga, Nic. 144/E3
Larroque, Arg. 159/J10
Larsen Bay, Ak, US 134/H4
Larsen Ice Shelf, Ant. 160/V
Larsen Sound (bay), Nun., Can. 122/G1
L'Artois, Collines de (hills), Fr. 40/A3
Laruns, Fr. 42/C5
Larvik, Nor. 38/D2
Las Animas, Co, US 129/G3
Las Aves (isls.), Ven. 141/H5
Las Breñas, Arg. 157/D2
Las Cabezas de San Juan, Sp. 44/C4
Las Cabras, Chile 158/N9
Las Cruces, NM, US 128/F4
Las Cruces (int'l arpt.), NM, US 142/D1
Las Delicias, Ven. 152/C3
Las Eutimias, Mex. 132/C4
Las Flores, Arg. 158/F3
Las Guacamayas, Mex. 142/E5
Las Hermosas, PN, Col. 152/C4
Las Higueras, Arg. 158/D2
Las Lajas, Arg. 158/C3
Las Lajas (peak), Arg. 158/C3
Las Lomas, Peru 156/A2
Las Lomitas, Arg. 157/D1
Las Margaritas, Mex. 144/D2
Las Martinas, Cuba 145/E1
Las Mercedes, Ven. 153/E2
Las Minas (peak), Hon. 144/D3
Las Nieves, Mex. 142/D3
Las Orquídeas, PN, Col. 152/B3
Las Palmas, Pan. 145/F4
Las Palmas de Cocalán, PN, Chile 158/N9
Las Palmas de Gran Canaria, Sp. 98/B3
Las Pedroñeras, Sp. 44/D3
Las Perdices, Arg. 158/E2
Las Perlas (arch.), Pan. 145/G4
Las Piedras, Peru 156/D4
Las Piedras, Ven. 152/C2
Las Piedras, Uru. 159/K11
Las Pipinas, Arg. 159/F2
Las Rosas, Mex. 144/C2
Las Rozas de Madrid, Sp. 45/N9
Las Tablas, Pan. 152/A3
Las Varas, Mex. 142/D4
Las Varillas, Arg. 157/D3
Las Vegas, NM, US 129/F4
Las Vegas, Nv, US 128/D3
Lasalle, Qu, Can. 131/N7
Lasberg, Aus. 55/H6
Lascano, Uru. 159/G2
Lashio, Myan. 83/G3
Lashkar Gāh, Afg. 89/H2
Lasne-Chapelle-Saint-Lambert, Belg. 53/D2
Læsø (isl.), Den. 38/D3
Lasolo (riv.), Indo. 81/F4
Lassen (peak), Ca, US 126/C5
Lassen Volcanic NP, Ca, US 128/B2
L'Assomption, Qu, Can. 131/P6
L'Assomption (co.), Qu, Can. 131/N6
L'Assomption (riv.), Qu, Can. 131/P6
Last Mountain (lake), Sk, Can. 127/G3
Lastovo (isl.), Cro. 46/E1
Lastovski (chan.), Cro. 48/C4
Lastovski Kanal (chan.), Cro. 46/E1
Lastra a Signa, It. 59/E5
Lastrup, Ger. 51/E3
Lata, Sol. 116/F6
Latacunga, Ecu. 152/B5
Latady (isl.), Ant. 160/U
L'Atakora (prov.), Ben. 103/F4
Lātehār, India 85/E4
Latemar (peak), It. 57/H5
Laterza, It. 46/E2
Lathan (riv.), Fr. 42/C3
Lathrop, Ca, US 135/M11
Latina, It. 46/C2
Latisana, It. 59/G1
Latorica (riv.), Slvk.,Ukr. 41/M4
Latrobe (riv.), Austl. 115/C3
Latrobe (mt.), Austl. 115/C3
Latrobe, Austl. 115/C4
Lattes, Fr. 42/E5
Lattingtown, NY, US 139/L8
Lātūr, India 89/L5
Latvia (ctry.) 39/L3
Lau Group (isl.), Fiji 116/H6
Laubach, Ger. 54/B1
Lauca, PN, Chile 150/D7
Lauch (riv.), Fr. 43/G3
Lauchert (riv.), Ger. 54/C6
Lauchheim, Ger. 54/D5
Lauda-Königshofen, Ger. 54/C3
Lauder, Sc, UK 36/D5
Lauderdale (lakes), Wi, US 135/N14
Lauenbrück, Ger. 51/G2
Lauenburg, Ger. 51/H2
Lauenen, Swi. 56/D5
Lauenförde, Ger. 51/H5
Lauer (riv.), Ger. 54/D2
Lauf, Ger. 54/E3
Laufach, Ger. 54/C2
Laufen, Swi. 56/D3
Laufen, Ger. 55/F7
Laufenburg, Swi. 56/E2
Lauffen am Neckar, Ger. 54/C4
Laughlen (mt.), Austl. 113/G2
Lauhanvuoren NP, Fin. 60/D3
Lauingen, Ger. 54/D5
Launceston, Austl. 115/C4
Launette (riv.), Fr. 30/L4
Laupahoehoe, Hi, US 124/U11
Laupen, Swi. 56/D4
Lauperswil, Swi. 56/D4
Laupheim, Ger. 57/F1
Laura, Austl. 113/H5
Laureana di Borrello, It. 46/E3
Laurel, Mt, US 126/F4
Laurel, Ms, US 133/F4
Laurel, Md, US 138/B5
Laurel Springs, NJ, US 138/C4
Laureldale, Pa, US 138/C3
Laurelton, Pa, US 138/A2
Laurence Harbor, NJ, US 139/J10
Laurencekirk, Sc, UK 36/D3
Laurens, SC, US 133/H3
Laurentian (plat.), On, Can. 122/G3
Laurentides, Qu, Can. 131/N6
Laurinburg, NC, US 133/J3
Laurium, Mi, US 127/L4
Lausanne, Swi. 56/C4
Lauscha, Ger. 54/E2
Laut (isl.), Indo. 81/E4
Lautaro, Chile 158/B3
Lauter, Ger. 55/F1
Lauter (riv.), Ger. 40/E3
Lauterach (riv.), Ger. 55/E4
Lauterbach (riv.), Ger. 54/E2
Lauterbach, Ger. 54/C1
Lauterburg, Fr. 54/B5
Lauterbrunnen, Swi. 56/D4
Lauterecken, Ger. 53/G4
Lauve, Nor. 38/D2
Lauwers (chan.), Neth. 50/D1
Lauwersmeer (lake), Neth. 50/D2
Lava Beds Nat'l Mon., Ca, US 126/C5
Lavagna (riv.), It. 58/C4
Lavagna, It. 58/C4
Laval, Fr. 42/C2
Laval, Qu, Can. 131/N6
Lavalleja (dept.), Uru. 159/G2
Lavallette, NJ, US 138/D4
Lavans-lès-Saint-Claude, Fr. 56/B5
Lavant (riv.), Aus. 43/L3
Lavapié (pt.), Chile 158/B3
Lavaur, Fr. 42/D5
Laveen, Az, US 137/R19
Lavelanet, Fr. 42/D5
Lavello, It. 46/D2
Laveno, It. 57/E6
Laverton, Austl. 112/D4
Lavey, Swi. 56/D5
Lavezzola, It. 59/E3
Lavino (riv.), It. 59/E4
Lavis, It. 57/H5
Lavos, Port. 44/A2
Lavras, Braz. 155/C2
Lavras da Mangabeira, Braz. 154/C2
Lávrion, Gre. 47/J4
Lawa (riv.), FrG. 153/H4
Lāwar Khās, India 84/A1
Lawarai (pass), Pak. 86/A2
Lawit (mtn.), Indo. 80/D3
Lawit (peak), Malay. 83/H6
Lawndale, Ca, US 136/F8
Lawnhill, BC, Can. 134/M5
Lawra, Gha. 102/E4
Lawrence, Ma, US 131/G3
Lawrence, Ks, US 129/J3
Lawrence, NY, US 139/L9
Lawrenceburg, In, US 130/C4
Lawrenceburg, Tn, US 133/G3
Lawrenceburg, Ky, US 133/G2
Lawrencetown, NI, UK 34/B3
Lawrenceville, Ga, US 133/H3
Lawrenceville, NJ, US 138/D3
Lawson, Mo, US 137/E5
Lawu (peak), Indo. 80/D5
Lawz, Jabal al (peak), SAr. 88/C3
Laxå, Swe. 38/F2
Laxey, IM, UK 34/D3
Laxou, Fr. 53/F6
Lay (riv.), Fr. 42/C3
Lay-Saint-Christophe, Fr. 53/F6
Laya (riv.), Rus. 61/N2
Layar (cape), Indo. 81/E4
Laylān, Iraq 90/F3
Layon (riv.), Fr. 42/C3
Laysan (isl.), Hi, US 117/H2
Layton, Ut, US 137/K11
Layton, NJ, US 138/D1
Lazarevac, Serb. 48/E3
Lázaro Cárdenas, Mex. 128/D5
Lázaro Cárdenas, Mex. 142/B2
Lázaro Cárdenas, Mex. 142/E5
Lazio (prov.), It. 43/J5
Łlbriktepe, Turk. 47/K2
Le Ban-Saint-Martin, Fr. 53/F5
Le Blanc, Fr. 42/D3
Le Blanc-Mesnil, Fr. 30/K5
Le Breuil, Fr. 42/F3
Le Cannet, Fr. 43/G5
Le Cateau-Cambrésis, Fr. 52/C3
Le Chasseral (peak), Swi. 56/D3
Le Chasseron (peak), Swi. 56/C4
Le Chesnay, Fr. 30/J5
Le Chesne, Fr. 53/D4
Le Cheval Blanc (peak), Fr. 56/C5
Le Cheylard, Fr. 42/F4
Le Cornate (peak), It. 43/J5
Le Creusot, Fr. 42/F3
Le Crotoy, Fr. 52/A3
Le Gore, Md, US 138/A4
Le Grammont (peak), Swi. 56/C5
Le Grand (cape), Austl. 112/D5
Le Grand Ballon (peak), Fr. 56/D2
Le Grau-du-Roi, Fr. 42/F5
Le Grazie, It. 58/C4
Le Havre, Fr. 42/D2
Le Landeron, Swi. 56/D3
Le Lavandou, Fr. 43/G5
Le Locle, Swi. 56/C3
Le Luc, Fr. 43/G5
Le Mans, Fr. 42/D2
Le Mée-sur-Seine, Fr. 30/K6
Le Mesnil-Amelot, Fr. 30/K4
Le Mesnil-Aubry, Fr. 30/K4
Le Mesnil-Esnard, Fr. 52/A5
Le Mesnil-le-Roi, Fr. 30/J5
Le Mesnil-Saint-Denis, Fr. 30/H5
Le Mesnil-sur-Oger, Fr. 52/D6
Le Môle (peak), Fr. 56/C5
Le Morond (peak), Fr. 56/C4
Le Moure de la Gardille (peak), Fr. 42/E4
Le Murge (mts.), It. 46/E2
Le Noirmont (peak), Fr. 56/C4
Le Noirmont (peak), Swi. 56/C5
Le Noirmont, Swi. 56/C3
Le Nouvion-en-Thiérache, Fr. 52/C3
Le Palais, Fr. 42/B3
Le Palais-sur-Vienne, Fr. 42/D4
Le Paşsage, Fr. 42/D4
Le Perray-en-Yvelines, Fr. 30/H5
Le Petit Ballon (peak), Fr. 56/D2
Le Plessis-Belleville, Fr. 30/L4
Le Plessis-Feu-Aussoux, Fr. 30/M5
Le Plessis-Placy, Fr. 30/L4
Le Port, Reun. 107/S15
Le Portel, Fr. 52/A2
Le Puy-en-Velay, Fr. 42/E4
Le Quesnoy, Fr. 52/C3
Le Russey, Fr. 56/C3
Le Suchet (peak), Swi. 56/C4
Le Tampon, Reun. 107/S15
Le Teil, Fr. 42/F4
Le Tholy, Fr. 56/C1
Le Touquet-Paris-Plage, Fr. 52/A2
Le Tréport, Fr. 52/A3
Le Val-d'Ajol, Fr. 56/C2
Le Vésinet, Fr. 30/J5
Le Vigan, Fr. 42/E5
Lea (riv.), Eng, UK 33/F3
Leach (lake), Ca, US 127/K4
Leach (riv.), Eng, UK 33/E3
Leacock-Leola-Bareville, Pa, US 138/B3
Lead, SD, US 127/H4
Leader, Sk, Can. 126/F3
Leader Water (riv.), Sc, UK 36/D5
Leadon (riv.), Eng, UK 32/D3
Leadville, Co, US 132/B2
Leaf (riv.), Ms, US 133/F4
Leaghur (lake), Austl. 115/B2
League City, Tx, US 129/J5
Leakey, Tx, US 129/H5
Leam (riv.), Eng, UK 33/E2
Leamington, On, Can. 130/D3
Le'an, China 79/C2
Leander (pt.), Austl. 112/B4
Leaota (peak), Rom. 49/G3
Learmonth, Austl. 112/B2
Leatherhead, Eng, UK 30/C3
Leavenworth, Ks, US 137/D5
Leavenworth (co.), Ks, US 137/D5
Leavenworth, Wa, US 126/C4
Leawood, Ks, US 137/D6
Leba, Pol. 38/G4
Lebach, Ger. 53/F5
Lebak, Phil. 79/D6
Lebane, Serb. 47/G1
Lebanon (ctry.) 91/D3
Lebanon (mts.), Leb. 91/D3
Lebanon, In, US 130/C3
Lebanon, Ky, US 130/C4
Lebanon, Mo, US 129/J3
Lebanon, NH, US 131/F3
Lebanon, NJ, US 138/D2
Lebanon, Or, US 126/C4
Lebanon, Pa, US 138/B3
Lebanon, Tn, US 130/C4
Lebbeke, Belg. 53/D2
Lebedyn, Ukr. 62/E2
Lebel-sur-Quévillon, Qu, Can. 130/E1
Lebene (riv.), Mor. 100/B2
Lébény, Hun. 48/C2
Lębork, Pol. 38/G4
Lebrija, Sp. 44/B4
Lebu, Chile 157/B4
Lebu, Chile 158/B3
Leça da Palmeira, Port. 44/A2
Lecce, It. 47/F2
Lecco, It. 58/C1
Lecco (prov.), It. 58/C1
Lecco, Lago di (lake), It. 58/C1
Lech, Aus. 57/G3
Lech (riv.), Ger. 43/K2
Lechang, China 83/K2
Lechbruck, Ger. 57/G2
Leche (lake), Cuba 145/G1
Lechtaler Alps (mts.), Aus. 57/G3
Leck, Ger. 38/C4
Lectoure, Fr. 42/D5
Łęczna, Pol. 41/M3
Leda (riv.), Ger. 51/E2
Ledang (peak), Malay. 80/B3
Lede, Belg. 52/C2
Ledegem, Belg. 52/C2
Ledesma, Sp. 44/B2
Ledge Point, Austl. 112/B4
Ledong, China 83/J4
Ledro (lake), It. 57/G6
Ledu (peak), It. 57/F5
Leduc, Ab, Can. 126/E2
Lee (riv.), Ire. 31/P11
Lee (mtn.), Pa, US 138/B1
Leech (lake), Mn, US 125/H2
Leeds, Eng, UK 35/G4
Leeds (co.), Eng, UK 35/G4
Leeds and Bradford (int'l arpt.), Eng, UK 35/G4
Leeds and Liverpool (canal), Eng, UK 35/G4
Leeds Point, NJ, US 138/D5
Leegebruch, Ger. 40/Q6
Leek, Neth. 50/D2
Leek, Eng, UK 35/F5
Leeman, Austl. 112/B4
Leer, Ger. 51/E2
Leerdam, Neth. 50/C5
Leersum, Neth. 50/C4
Lees Summit, Mo, US 137/E6
Leesburg, Fl, US 133/H4
Leesburg, NJ, US 138/D5
Leese, Ger. 51/G3
Leesport, Pa, US 138/C3
Leesville, La, US 129/J5
Leeton, Austl. 115/C2
Leeu (riv.), SAfr. 106/L10
Leeudoringstad, SAfr. 106/D2
Leeuwarden, Neth. 50/C2
Leeuwin (cape), Austl. 112/B5
Leeuwin-Naturaliste NP, Austl. 112/B5
Leeward (isls.), NAm. 141/J4
Leff (riv.), Fr. 42/B2
Lefka, Cyp. 91/C2
Lefo (peak), Camr. 103/H5
Lefroy (lake), Austl. 112/D4
Legana, Austl. 115/C4
Leganés, Sp. 45/N9
Legaspi, Phil. 79/D5
Legau, Ger. 57/G2
Legazpia, Sp. 44/D1
Legges Tor (peak), Austl. 115/C4
Legionowo, Pol. 41/L2
Léglise, Belg. 53/E4
Legnago, It. 59/E2
Legnano, It. 43/H4
Legnaro, It. 59/E2
Legnica, Pol. 41/J3
Legnone (peak), It. 57/F5
Leh, India 86/D2
Leh Palace, India 86/D2
Lehi, Ut, US 137/K13
Lehigh (co.), Pa, US 138/C2
Lehigh Acres, Fl, US 133/H5
Lehighton, Pa, US 138/C2
Lehinch, Ire. 31/P10
Lehrberg, Ger. 54/D4
Lehrte, Ger. 51/G4
Lei (riv.), China 83/K2
Leiah, Pak. 86/A4
Leiblfing, Ger. 55/F5
Leibo, China 83/H2
Leicester, Eng, UK 33/E1
Leicester (co.), Eng, UK 33/E1
Leicestershire (co.), Eng, UK 35/H6
Leichhardt (dam), Austl. 113/H2
Leichhardt (riv.), Austl. 109/C2
Leichlingen, Ger. 53/G1
Leiden, Neth. 50/B4
Leiderdorp, Neth. 50/B4
Leidschendam, Neth. 50/B4
Leie (riv.), Belg. 42/E1
Leifers (Laives), It. 43/J3
Leigh, Eng, UK 35/F5
Leigh Creek, Austl. 113/H4
Leimebamba, Peru 156/B2
Leimen, Ger. 54/B4
Leimersheim, Ger. 54/B4
Leine (riv.), Ger. 40/D3
Leinefelde, Ger. 51/H6
Leinfelden-Echterdingen, Ger. 54/C5
Leinster (mt.), Ire. 31/Q10
Leinster, Austl. 112/D3
Leinster (reg.), Ire. 34/A5
Leipheim, Ger. 54/D6
Leipsic, De, US 138/C5
Leipsic (riv.), De, US 138/C5
Leipzig, Ger. 40/G3
Leira, Nor. 38/C1
Leiria, Port. 44/A3
Leiria (dist.), Port. 44/A3
Leisler (mt.), Austl. 113/F2
Leith (hill), Eng, UK 30/B3
Leitha (riv.), Aus. 41/J5
Leixlip, Ire. 34/B5
Leizhou (pen.), China 83/J3
Lek (riv.), Neth. 40/C3
Lekhainá, Gre. 47/G4
Lekkerkerk, Neth. 50/B5
Lekki (lag.), Nga. 103/G5
Leksands-Noret, Swe. 38/F1
Leksozero (lake), Rus. 37/J3
Lelai (cape), Indo. 81/G3
Leland, Ms, US 129/K4
Lelång (lake), Swe. 38/E2
Leling, China 72/D3
Lelystad, Neth. 50/C3
Lem, Den. 38/C3
Lema (peak), It. 57/E5
Léman (Geneva) (lake), Fr. 43/G3
Lemberg (peak), Ger. 57/E1
Lemberg, Ger. 53/G5
Lembu (peak), Indo. 80/A3
Leme, Braz. 155/C2
Lemenjoen NP, Fin. 37/H1
Lemgo, Ger. 51/F4
Lemland (isl.), Fin. 39/H2
Lemland, Fin. 39/J1
Lemmer, Neth. 50/C3
Lemmon, SD, US 127/H4
Lemon Grove, Ca, US 136/C5
Lempa (riv.), ESal. 144/D3
Lempäälä, Fin. 39/K1
Lempdes, Fr. 42/E4
Lemva (riv.), Rus. 61/P2
Lemvig, Den. 38/C3
Lemwerder, Ger. 51/F2
Lena (riv.), Rus. 67/M3
Lena, Nor. 38/D1
Lenape, Ks, US 137/D6
Lenape (lake), NJ, US 138/D5
Lençóis Maranhenses, PN dos, Braz. 151/K4
Lençóis Paulista, Braz. 155/B2
Lendinara, It. 59/E2
Lenexa, Ks, US 137/D6
Lengau, Aus. 55/G6
Lengdorf, Ger. 55/F6
Lengede, Ger. 51/H4
Lengenfeld, Ger. 55/F1
Lengerich, Ger. 51/E4
Lenggries, Ger. 57/H2
Lengnau, Swi. 56/D3
Lengshuitan, China 83/K2
Lengua de Vaca (pt.), Chile 157/B3
Lenhartsville, Pa, US 138/C2
Lenina (peak), Taj. 87/F5
Leninabad (int'l arpt.), Taj. 87/E4
Leningradskaya Oblast, Rus. 60/G3
Leninobod (obl.), Taj. 87/E5
Leninogorsk, Rus. 61/M5
Leninsk-Kuznetskiy, Rus. 64/J4
Leninváros, Hun. 41/L5
Lenk, Swi. 56/D5
Lenne (riv.), Ger. 53/G1
Lennestadt, Ger. 51/F6
Lenningen, Ger. 54/C5
Lennox (isl.), Chile 159/D7
Lennox (hills), Sc, UK 36/B5
Lennoxtown, Sc, UK 36/B5
Leno, It. 58/D2
Lenoir, NC, US 133/H3
Lenoir City, Tn, US 133/G3
Lens, Swi. 56/D5
Lens, Fr. 52/B3
Lens, Belg. 52/C2
Lensahn, Ger. 38/D4
Lensk, Rus. 65/M3
Lenting, Ger. 55/E5
Lentini, It. 46/D4
Lenvik, Nor. 37/F1
Leny, Pass of (pass), Sc, UK 36/B4
Lenzburg, Swi. 56/E3
Lenzing, Aus. 55/G7
Lenzkirch, Ger. 57/E2
Léo, Burk. 103/E4
Leoben, Aus. 43/L3
Leográ (riv.), It. 59/E1
Leola, SD, US 127/J4
Leon (riv.), Tx, US 140/B1
León, Mex. 143/E4
Leon (int'l arpt.), Mex. 142/C3
León, Sp. 44/C1
León, Nic. 144/E3
Leon, Étang de (lake), Fr. 42/C4
Leon-Guanajuato (int'l arpt.), Mex. 143/E4
Leon Springs, Tx, US 137/T20
Leon Valley, Tx, US 137/T21
Leona Valley, Ca, US 136/B1
Leonard, Tx, US 129/H4
Leonard, Mi, US 135/F6
Leonardo, NJ, US 139/J10
Leonardo da Vinci (int'l arpt.), It. 46/C2
Leonberg, Ger. 54/C5
Leonding, Aus. 55/H6
Leone (peak), It. 56/E5
Leones, Arg. 158/E2
Leonforte, It. 46/D4
Leongatha, Austl. 115/C3
Leonia, NJ, US 139/K8
Leonídhion, Gre. 47/H4
Leonora, Austl. 112/D4
Leopoldina, Braz. 211/L6
Leopoldkanaal (riv.), Belg. 52/C1
Leopoldsburg, Belg. 53/E1
Leopoldsdorf, Aus. 49/N7
Leopoldsdorf im Marchfelde, Aus. 49/P7
Leopoldshöhe, Ger. 51/F4
Leoville, Sk, Can. 126/G2
Lepaera, Hon. 144/D3
Lépanges-sur-Vologne, Fr. 56/C1
Lepe, Sp. 44/B4
Lepenoú, Gre. 47/G3
L'Épiphanie, Qu, Can. 131/P6
Lepontine Alps (mts.), Swi 43/H3
Leptokariá, Gre. 47/H2
Léraba (riv.), Burk. 102/D4
Lercara Friddi, It. 46/C4
Lerdo de Tejada, Mex. 144/C2
Leribe, Les. 106/E3
Lerici, It. 58/C4
Lerín, Sp. 44/E1
Lerma, Sp. 44/D1
Lerma, Mex. 143/Q10
Lerma (riv.), Mex. 143/K7
Lermoos, Aus. 57/G3
Lérouville, Fr. 53/E6
Lerum, Swe. 38/E3
Lerwick, Sc, UK 31/W13
Léry (lake), La, US 137/Q17
Léry, Qu, Can. 131/N7
Les Alluets-le-Roi, Fr. 30/H5
Les Bois, Swi. 56/C3
Les Breuleux, Swi. 56/D3
Les Bréviaires, Fr. 30/H5
Les Cayes, Haiti 145/H2
Les Cèdres, Qu, Can. 131/M7
Les Clayes-sous-Bois, Fr. 30/H5
Les Contamines-Montjoie, Fr. 56/C6
Les Diablerets (range), Swi. 56/D5
Les Essarts-le-Roi, Fr. 30/H5
Les Gets, Fr. 56/C5
Les Hautes-Rivières, Fr. 53/D4
Les Herbiers, Fr. 42/C3
Les Islettes, Fr. 53/E5
Les Mesnuls, Fr. 30/H5
Les Molières, Fr. 30/J6
Les Mureaux, Fr. 52/A6
Les Ponts-de-Martel, Swi. 56/C4
Les Rousses, Fr. 56/C5
Les Sables-d'Olonne, Fr. 42/C3
Les Salines (int'l arpt.), Alg. 100/K6
Les Ulis, Fr. 30/J5
Les Verrières, Swi. 56/C4
Lesa, It. 58/B1
Leshan, China 83/H2
Lésigny, Fr. 30/K5
Lesima (peak), It. 58/C3
Lesja, Nor. 37/D3
Lesjöfors, Swe. 38/F2
Lesko, Pol. 41/M4
Leskovac, Serb. 47/G1
Leslie, Sc, UK 36/C4
Lesmahagow, Sc, UK 36/C5
Lesneven, Fr. 42/A2
Lešnica, Serb. 48/D3
Lesotho (ctry.) 106/E6
Lesozavodsk, Rus. 71/P2
Lesparre-Médoc, Fr. 42/C4
Lesquin (int'l arpt.), Fr. 52/C2
Lesse (riv.), Belg. 40/C3
Lessebo, Swe. 38/F3
Lesser Antilles (isls.), NAm. 141/M8
Lesser Caucasus (mts.), Asia 63/G4
Lesser Slave (lake), Ab, Can. 122/E3
Lesser Sunda (isls.), Indo. 81/E5
Lessines, Belg. 52/C2
Lesung (peak), Indo. 80/D3
Lésvos (isl.), Gre. 62/C5
Leszno, Pol. 41/J3
Létavértes, Hun. 48/E2
Letchworth, Eng, UK 33/F3
Letham, Sc, UK 36/D3
Lethbridge, Ab, Can. 126/E3
Lethe (riv.), Ger. 51/F2
Lethem, Guy. 153/G4
Leti (isls.), Indo. 81/G5
Leticia, Col. 156/D2
Leting, China 72/D3
Letlhakane, Bots. 105/E5
Letlhakeng, Bots. 105/D5
Letnitsa, Bul. 49/G4
L'Étoile, Fr. 52/B3
Letpadan, Myan. 83/G4
Letschin, Ger. 41/H2
Letsôk-Aw (isl.), Myan. 80/A1
Letterkenny, Ire. 31/Q9
Leucate, Fr. 42/E5
Leuchars, Sc, UK 36/D4
Leuk, Swi. 56/D5
Leukerbad, Swi. 56/D5
Leun, Ger. 54/B1
Leusden-Zuid, Neth. 50/C4
Leuser (peak), Indo. 80/A3
Leutershausen, Ger. 54/D4
Leutkirch im Allgäu, Ger. 57/G2
Leuze-en-Hainaut, Belg. 52/C2
Levádhia, Gre. 47/H3
Levallois-Perret, Fr. 30/J5
Levanger, Nor. 37/D3
Levante, Riviera di (coast), It. 58/C4
Levanto, It. 58/C4
Levasy, Mo, US 137/E5
Level (isl.), Chile 158/B5
Level, Md, US 138/B4
Levelland, Tx, US 129/G4
Levelock, Ak, US 134/G4
Leven (pt.), SAfr. 107/F2
Leven (lake), Sc, UK 36/A3
Leven, Sc, UK 36/D4
Leven (riv.), Sc, UK 36/C4
Leveque (cape), Austl. 109/B2
Leverburgh, Sc, UK 31/Q8
Leverkusen, Ger. 53/F1
Levice, Slvk. 48/D1
Levico Terme, It. 57/H5
Levier, Fr. 56/C4
Levin, NZ 117/T11
Lévis, Qu, Can. 131/G2
Lévis-Saint-Nom, Fr. 30/H5
Levittown, Pa, US 138/D3
Levittown, NY, US 139/L9
Levkás, Gre. 47/G3
Levkás (isl.), Gre. 47/G3
Levkímmi, Gre. 47/G3
Levoča, Slvk. 41/L4
Levrier (bay), Mrta. 98/A5
Levski, Bul. 49/G4
Lewes, Eng, UK 33/G5
Lewin Brzeski, Pol. 41/J3
Lewis (riv.), Wa, US 126/C4
Lewis (range), Mt, US 126/E3
Lewis (hills), Nf, Can. 131/K1
Lewis (pass), NZ 117/S11
Lewis (isl.), Sc, UK 31/Q7
Lewis and Clark (lake), Ne,SD, US 127/J5
Lewis Smith (lake), Al, US 133/G3
Lewisburg, Tn, US 133/G3
Lewisburg, WV, US 130/D4
Lewisburg, Pa, US 138/B2
Lewisham (bor.), Eng, UK 30/C2
Lewisporte, Nf, Can. 131/L1
Lewiston, Id, US 126/D4
Lewiston, Me, US 131/G2
Lewiston, NY, US 131/R9
Lewistown, Mt, US 126/F4
Lewistown, Pa, US 130/E3
Lewotobi (peak), Indo. 81/F5
Lexington, Ne, US 127/J5
Lexington, Tn, US 130/B5
Lexington, Ky, US 130/C4
Lexington, NC, US 133/H3
Lexington Park, Md, US 130/E4
Leyburn, Eng, UK 35/G3
Leyden, Co, US 137/B3
Leye, China 83/J3
Leyland, Eng, UK 35/F4
Leysin, Swi. 56/D5
Leyte (isl.), Phil. 67/M8
Leytron, Swi. 56/D5
Lez (riv.), Fr. 42/F4
Leżajsk, Pol. 41/M3
Lezhë, Alb. 47/F2
Lézignan-Corbières, Fr. 42/E5
Lezuza, Sp. 44/D3
L'gov, Rus. 62/E2
Lhanbyrd, Sc, UK 36/C1
Lhari, China 70/F5
Lhasa, China 82/F2
Lhazê, China 85/F1
L'Hongrin (lake), Swi. 56/D5
Lhorong, China 70/G5
L'Hospitalet de Llobregat, Sp. 45/L7
Lhozhag, China 85/H1
Lhünzê, China 83/G2
Li (riv.), China 79/B2
Li (riv.), China 83/K2
Li (mtn.), China 72/B4
Li Xian, China 79/B2
Lian (riv.), China 79/B3
Lian Xian, China 83/K3
Liancheng, China 79/C2
Liancourt, Fr. 52/B5
Liancourt Rocks (isl.), Asia 74/B2
Liangcheng, China 72/C2
Liangpran (peak), Indo. 80/D3
Liangzi (lake), China 72/C5
Lianhua, China 83/K2
Lianjiang, China 79/C2
Lianjiang, China 83/K3
Liannan Yaozu Zizhixian, China 79/B3
Lianshui, China 72/D4
Lianyuan, China 79/B2
Lianyungang, China 72/D4
Liao (riv.), China 67/M5
Liaocheng, China 72/C3
Liaodong (pen.), China 73/A3
Liaodong (isls.), China 72/E3
Liaodong, Gulf of (gulf), China 71/M3
Liaoning (prov.), China 71/M3
Liaoyang, China 73/B2
Liaoyuan, China 71/N3
Liaozhong, China 73/B2
Liāquatpur, Pak. 86/A5
Liard (riv.), NW, Can. 122/D2
Libby, Mt, US 126/E3
Liběchovka (riv.), Czh. 55/H2
Libenge, D.R. Congo 97/J7
Libercourt, Fr. 52/C3
Liberdade (riv.), Braz. 151/H6
Liberdade, Braz. 211/J7
Liberec, Czh. 41/H3
Liberecký (pol. reg.), Czh. 41/H3
Liberia, CR 144/E4
Liberia (ctry.) 102/C5
Libertad, Belz. 144/D2
Libertad, Ven. 152/D2
Libertad, Uru. 159/K11
Libertador General San Martín, Arg. 157/D1
Liberty, Tx, US 129/J5
Liberty, Ky, US 130/C4
Liberty, Ms, US 129/K5
Liberty, Mo, US 137/E5
Liberty, Ut, US 137/K11
Liberty (res.), Md, US 138/B5
Liberty Grove, Md, US 138/B4
Libertyville, Il, US 135/P15
Libin, Belg. 53/E4
Libo, China 83/J2
Libobo (cape), Indo. 81/G4
Liboc (riv.), Czh. 41/G3
Libochovice, Czh. 55/H2
Libon, Phil. 79/D5
Librazhd, Alb. 47/G2
Libres, Mex. 143/M7
Libreville (cap.), Gabon 96/G7
Libya (ctry.) 97/J2
Libyan (plat.), Libya 97/K1
Libyan (des.), Egypt,Libya 97/K2
Licantén, Chile 158/B2
Licata, It. 46/C4
Lice, Turk. 90/E2
Lich, Ger. 54/B1
Licheng, China 72/C3
Licheng, China 72/D3
Lichfield, Eng, UK 33/E1
Lichinga, Moz. 105/G3
Lichtenau, Ger. 51/F5
Lichtenau, Ger. 54/D4
Lichtenau, Ger. 54/B5
Lichtenburg, SAfr. 106/D2
Lichtenfels, Ger. 54/D2
Lichtenrade, Ger. 40/Q7
Lichtensteig, Swi. 57/F3
Lichtenvoorde, Neth. 50/D5
Lichtervelde, Belg. 52/C1
Lichuan, China 79/A1
Licinio de Almeida, Braz. 154/B4
Lick Observatory, Ca, US 135/L12
Licking (riv.), Ky, US 130/C4
Licosa (cape), It. 46/D2

Licques, Fr. 52/A2
Lida, Bela. 39/L5
Liddell Water (riv.), Sc, UK 35/F1
Liddes, Swi. 56/D6
Liddon (gulf), NW, Can. 123/R7
Lidhoríkion, Gre. 47/H3
Lidingö, Swe. 38/H2
Lidköping, Swe. 38/E2
Lido, It. 59/F2
Lido di Iesolo, It. 59/F1
Lido di Ostia, It. 46/C2
Lidzbark, Pol. 41/K2
Lidzbark Warmiński, Pol. 39/J4
Liebenau, Aus. 55/H5
Liebenbergsvlei (riv.), SAfr. 106/E2
Liebig (mt.), Austl. 113/F2
Liechtenstein (ctry.) 57/F3
Liedekerke, Belg. 53/D2
Liège, Belg. 53/E2
Liège (prov.), Belg. 53/E3
Lieksa, Fin. 60/F3
Lienden, Neth. 50/C5
Lienen, Ger. 51/E4
Lienz, Aus. 43/K3
Liepāja, Lat. 39/J3
Lier, Belg. 53/D1
Lierneux, Belg. 53/E3
Lieser (riv.), Ger. 53/F3
Liesjärven NP, Fin. 39/K1
Liesse-Notre-Dame, Fr. 52/C4
Liestal, Swi. 56/D3
Lieto, Fin. 39/K1
Liévin, Fr. 52/B3
Lièvre (riv.), Qu, Can. 130/F2
Liez (lake), Fr. 56/B2
Liezen, Aus. 43/L3
Liffey (riv.), Ire. 34/B5
Liffol-le-Grand, Fr. 56/B1
Lifford, Ire. 31/Q9
Ligao, Phil. 81/F1
Lightning Ridge, Austl. 115/C1
Lightwater, Eng, UK 30/B3
Lignano Sabbiadoro, It. 59/G1
Ligny-en-Barrois, Fr. 53/E6
Ligoncio (peak), It. 57/F5
Ligoúrion, Gre. 47/H4
Liguori, Mo, US 137/G9
Liguria (pol. reg.), It. 58/B4
Liguria (prov), It. 43/H4
Ligurian (sea), Fr.,It. 43/H5
Lihou (reefs), Austl. 109/E2
Lihue, Hi, US 124/S10
Lijiang Naxizu Zizhixian, China 83/H2
Lijin, China 72/D3
Likasi, D.R. Congo 105/E3
Likely, BC, Can. 126/C2
Likoma (isl.), Malw. 105/F3
Likouala (riv.), Congo 96/H7
Likova (riv.), Rus. 61/W9
L'Île-Perrot, Qu, Can. 131/N7
L'Île-Rousse, Fr. 46/A1
Liliāni, Pak. 86/B3
Lilienthal, Ger. 51/F2
Liling, China 83/K2
Lilla Edet, Swe. 38/E2
Lille, Belg. 50/B6
Lille, Fr. 52/C2
Lille Bælt (chan.), Ger. 38/C4
Lillehammer, Nor. 38/D1
Lillers, Fr. 52/B2
Lillesand, Nor. 38/C2
Lillestrøm, Nor. 38/D2
Lilliwaup, Wa, US 135/A3
Lillo, Sp. 44/D3
Lillooet, BC, Can. 126/C3
Lillooet (riv.), BC, Can. 126/C3
Lilongwe (cap.), Malw. 105/F3
Liloy, Phil. 79/D6
Lim (riv.), Serb. 47/F1
Lima (dept.), Peru 156/B3
Lima (cap.), Peru 156/B4
Lima, Oh, US 130/C3
Lima (riv.), It. 59/D4
Lima (riv.), Port. 45/A2
Lima, Arg. 159/J11
Lima Duarte, Braz. 211/K6
Limache, Chile 158/N8
Limanowa, Pol. 41/L4
Limassol, Cyp. 91/C2
Limassol (dist.), Cyp. 91/C2
Limavady (dist.), NI, UK 34/A2
Limavady, NI, UK 34/B1
Limay (riv.), Arg. 147/C7
Limbach, Ger. 54/C4
Limbani, Peru 156/D4
Limbara (peak), It. 46/A2
Limbdi, India 89/K4
Limbé, Haiti 145/H2
Limbiate, It. 58/C1
Limbourg, Belg. 53/E2
Limburg (prov.), Belg. 53/E1
Limburg an der Lahn, Ger. 54/B2
Limburgerhof, Ger. 54/B4
Lime Village, Ak, US 134/G3
Limedsforsen, Swe. 38/E1
Limeira, Braz. 155/C2
Limekilns, Sc, UK 36/C4
Limena, It. 59/E2
Limenária, Gre. 47/J2
Limerick, Ire. 31/P10
Limfjorden (chan.), Den. 38/C3
Limidario (peak), It. 57/E5
Limite, It. 59/D5
Limmat (riv.), Swi. 57/E3
Limmen Bight (bay), Austl. 109/C2
Límni, Gre. 47/H3
Límnos (isl.), Gre. 62/C5
Limoeiro, Braz. 154/D2
Limoeiro do Norte, Braz. 154/C2
Limoges, Fr. 42/D4
Limogne, Causse de (plat.), Fr. 42/D4
Limón, Hon. 144/E3
Limón, CR 145/F4
Limours, Fr. 30/J6
Limousin (mts.), Fr. 42/D4
Limousin (pol. reg.), Fr. 42/D4
Limoux, Fr. 42/E5
Limpopo (riv.), Moz. 93/F7
Lin Xian, China 72/C3
Lin'an, China 79/C1
Linapacan (isl.), Phil. 79/C5
Linard (peak), Swi. 57/G4
Linares, Mex. 143/F3
Linares, Sp. 44/D3
Linares, Chile 158/C2
Linariá, Gre. 47/J3
Linate (int'l arpt.), It. 58/C2
Lincang, China 83/H3
Lincheng, China 72/C3
Linchuan, China 79/C2
Lincoln, Arg. 158/E2
Lincoln (sea), Can.,Grld. 119/L1
Lincoln, On, Can. 131/R9
Lincoln, Eng, UK 35/H5
Lincoln, De, US 138/C6
Lincoln, Il, US 127/L5
Lincoln, Me, US 131/G2
Lincoln (cap.), Ne, US 127/J5
Lincoln (co.), Ok, US 137/N14
Lincoln, Pa, US 138/B3
Lincoln Beach, Or, US 126/B4
Lincoln City, Or, US 126/B4
Lincoln Heath (woodld.), Eng, UK 35/H5
Lincoln NP, Austl. 113/G5
Lincoln Park, Mi, US 135/F7
Lincoln Park, NJ, US 139/H8
Lincolnshire (co.), Eng, UK 35/H5
Lincolnshire Wolds (grsld.), Eng, UK 35/H4
Lincroft, NJ, US 138/D3
Lind, Den. 38/C3
Lind NP, Austl. 115/D3
Lindau, Ger. 57/F2
Lindau, Swi. 57/E3
Linde (riv.), Neth. 50/D3
Lindeman (chan.), Austl. 114/C3
Linden, Al, US 133/G3
Linden, Tx, US 129/J4
Linden, Guy. 153/G3
Linden, NJ, US 139/J9
Linden, Mi, US 135/E6
Linden, Ger. 54/B1
Linden Beach, On, Can. 135/G7
Lindenberg im Allgäu, Ger. 57/F2
Lindenfels, Ger. 54/B3
Lindenhurst, NY, US 139/E2
Lindenhurst, Il, US 135/P15
Lindenwold, NJ, US 138/D4
Lindern, Ger. 51/E3
Lindesberg, Swe. 38/F2
Lindesnes (cape), Nor. 38/B3
Lindewitt, Ger. 38/C4
Lindhorst, Ger. 51/E5
Líndhos (ruin), Gre. 90/B2
Lindi (pol. reg.), Tanz. 104/C5
Lindi, Tanz. 104/C5
Lindlar, Ger. 53/G1
Lindley, SAfr. 106/D2
Lindome, Swe. 38/E3
Lindon, Ut, US 137/K13
Lindre (lake), Fr. 53/F6
Lindsay, Ca, US 128/C3
Lindsay, On, Can. 130/E2
Lindsay (mt.), Austl. 112/C5
Lindsay (mt.), Austl. 113/F3
Lindsdal, Swe. 38/G3
Line (isls.), Kiri. 117/J4
Line Mountain (mtn.), Pa, US 138/B2
Lineas de Nazca, Peru 156/C4
Lineboro, Md, US 138/B4
Linfen, China 72/B3
Ling (riv.), Sc, UK 36/A2
Ling Xian, China 83/K2
Ling Xian, China 72/D3
Lingbao, China 72/B4
Lingbi, China 72/D4
Lingchuan, China 83/K2
Lingchuan, China 72/C4
Linge (riv.), Neth. 50/C5
Lingen, Ger. 51/E3
Lingfield, Eng, UK 30/C3
Lingga (isls.), Indo. 80/B3
Linglestown, Pa, US 138/B3
Lingolsheim, Fr. 56/D1
Lingqiu, China 72/C3
Lingshan, China 83/J3
Lingshan, China 72/C3
Lingshi, China 72/B3
Lingshui, China 83/K4
Linguère, Sen. 102/B3
Lingyin Si, China 72/L9
Lingyuan, China 72/D2
Lingyun, China 83/J3
Linhai, China 79/D2
Linhares, Braz. 155/D1
Linhe, China 70/J3
Linköping, Swe. 38/F2
Linli, China 79/B2
Linlithgow, Sc, UK 36/C5
Linliu (mtn.), China 72/C3
Linney (pt.), Wal, UK 32/A3
Linnhe (lake), Sc, UK 36/A3
Linnich, Ger. 53/F2
Linntown, Pa, US 138/B2
Linosa (isl.), It. 100/N7
Linqing, China 72/C3
Linqu, China 72/D3
Linquan, China 72/C4
Linru, China 72/C4
Lins, Braz. 155/B2
Linschoten, Neth. 50/B4
Linshu, China 72/D4
Linta (riv.), Madg. 107/H9
Linth (riv.), Swi. 57/F3
Linthal, Swi. 57/F4
Linton, ND, US 127/H4
Linwood, Eng, UK 35/H5
Linwu, China 83/K2
Linxi, China 72/C3
Linyi, China 72/B4
Linyi, China 72/D3
Linyi, China 72/D4
Linying, China 72/C4
Linz (int'l arpt.), Aus. 55/H6
Linz, Aus. 55/H6
Linz am Rhein, Ger. 53/G2
Linzhang, China 72/C3
Lion (gulf), Fr.,Sp. 45/G1
Lipa, Phil. 79/D5
Lipari (isl.), It. 46/D3
Lipari (isls.), It. 46/D3
Lipari, It. 46/D3
Liperi, Fin. 60/F3
Lipetsk, Rus. 62/F1
Lipetsk (int'l arpt.), Rus. 62/F1
Lipetskaya Oblast, Rus. 62/F1
Lipez (riv.), Bol. 150/E8
Lipez, Cordillera de (mts.), Bol. 150/E8
Liping, China 83/J2
Lipljan, Serb. 47/G1
Lipno (res.), Czh. 55/H5
Lipno, Pol. 41/K2
Lipno, Údolní nádrž (lake), Czh. 43/L2
Lipova, Rom. 48/E2
Lippe (riv.), Ger. 40/D3
Lippstadt, Ger. 51/F5
Liptovský Svätý Mikuláš, Slvk. 41/K4
Liptrap (cape), Austl. 115/C3
Lira, Ugan. 104/B2
Lircay, Peru 156/C4
Liri (riv.), It. 46/C2
Liria, Sp. 45/E3
Liro (riv.), It. 57/F5
Lisboa (dist.), Port. 44/A3
Lisboa (int'l arpt.), Port. 45/P10
Lisboa (Lisbon) (cap.), Port. 45/P10
Lisbon, ND, US 127/J4
Lisbon, Me, US 131/G2
Lisbon, Md, US 138/A5
Lisburn, NI, UK 34/B2
Lisburn (dist.), NI, UK 34/B3
Lisburne (cape), Ak, US 134/E2
Lisdoonvarna, Ire. 31/P10
Liseleje, Den. 38/D3
Lisha (riv.), China 83/H2
Lishu, China 72/F2
Lishui, China 79/C2
Lisianski (isl.), Hi, US 117/H2
Lisieux, Fr. 42/D2
Liski, Rus. 62/F2
Lisle, Il, US 135/P16
L'Isle-Adam, Fr. 30/J4
L'Isle-en-Dodon, Fr. 42/D5
L'Isle-sur-la-Sorgue, Fr. 42/F5
L'Isle-sur-le-Doubs, Fr. 56/C3
Lisle-sur-Tarn, Fr. 42/D5
Lismore, Austl. 115/E1
Lisnacree, NI, UK 34/B3
Lišov, Czh. 55/H4
Lispeszentadorján, Hun. 48/C2
Lisse, Neth. 50/B4
Lisses, Fr. 30/K6
List, Ger. 38/C4
Lister (riv.), Ger. 51/E6
Listowel, On, Can. 130/D3
Listowel, Ire. 31/P10
Lit. Scarcies (riv.), SLeo. 102/B4
Litang, China 70/H6
Litang (riv.), China 83/H2
Lītāni (riv.), Leb. 91/D3
Litavka (riv.), Czh. 55/G3
Litchfield, Mn, US 127/K4
Litchfield, Il, US 129/K3
Litchfield Park, Az, US 137/R19
Lith, Neth. 50/C5
Litherland, Eng, UK 35/F5
Lithgow, Austl. 115/D2
Lithuania (ctry.) 39/K4
Litija, Slov. 43/L3
Lititz, Pa, US 138/B3
Litókhoron, Gre. 47/H2
Litoměřice, Czh. 55/H1
Littabella NP, Austl. 114/D4
Littau, Swi. 57/E3
Little (riv.), Ar, US 129/J4
Little (riv.), Ga, US 133/H4
Little (riv.), Tx, US 132/D4
Little (riv.), NC, US 133/J3
Little (riv.), Ok, US 137/N15
Little Abitibi (riv.), On, Can. 130/D1
Little Andaman (isl.), India 83/F5
Little Belt (mts.), Mt, US 126/F4
Little Bighorn Battlefield Nat'l Mon., Mt, US 126/G4
Little Bitter (lake), Egypt 91/C4
Little Blue (riv.), Ks,Ne, US 129/H2
Little Calumet (riv.), Il, US 135/Q16
Little Cayman (isl.), Cay. 141/E4
Little Colorado (riv.), Az, US 128/E4
Little Creek, De, US 138/C5
Little Cumbrae (isl.), Sc, UK 36/A5
Little Current (riv.), On, Can. 127/M3
Little Current, On, Can. 130/D2
Little Desert NP, Austl. 115/B3
Little Diomede (isl.), Ak, US 134/E2
Little Egg (har.), NJ, US 138/D4
Little Falls, Mn, US 127/K4
Little Falls, NJ, US 139/J8
Little Ferry, NJ, US 139/J8
Little Fork (riv.), Mn, US 127/K3
Little Inagua (isl.), Bahm. 141/G3
Little Karoo (valley), SAfr. 106/C4
Little Lehigh (riv.), Pa, US 138/C3
Little Minch (str.), Sc, UK 31/Q8
Little Missouri (riv.), Ar, US 129/J4
Little Neck (bay), NY, US 139/K8
Little Nicobar (isl.), India 83/F6
Little Para (res.), Austl. 113/M8
Little Para (riv.), Austl. 113/M8
Little Patuxent (riv.), Md, US 138/B5
Little Peconic (bay), NY, US 139/F2
Little Platte (riv.), Mo, US 137/D5
Little Prairie, Wi, US 135/N14
Little Red (riv.), Ar, US 129/J4
Little Rock (cap.), Ar, US 129/J4
Little Schuylkill (riv.), Pa, US 138/B2
Little Sioux (riv.), Ia, US 125/G3
Little Smoky (riv.), Ab, Can. 126/D2
Little Snake (riv.), Co, US 128/E2
Little Stour (riv.), Eng, UK 33/H4
Little Wabash (riv.), Il, US 129/K3
Little White (riv.), SD, US 129/G2
Little Wood (riv.), Id, US 126/E5
Little Zab (riv.), Iraq 90/E3
Littleborough, Eng, UK 35/F4
Littlefield, Tx, US 129/G4
Littlehampton, Eng, UK 33/F5
Littlerock, Ca, US 136/C1
Littlestown, Pa, US 138/A4
Littleton, NH, US 131/G2
Littleton, Co, US 137/B3
Litvínov, Czh. 55/G1
Liu (riv.), China 79/A3
Liu (riv.), China 72/E2
Liuba, China 70/J5
Liucheng, China 83/J3
Liulin, China 72/B3
Liuwa Plain NP, Zam. 105/D3
Liuyang, China 83/K2
Liuzhou, China 83/J3
Livádhion, Gre. 47/H2
Livanátai, Gre. 47/H3
Live Oak, Fl, US 133/H4
Live Oak, Tx, US 137/U20
Livengood, Ak, US 134/J2
Livenza (riv.), It. 59/F2
Liverdun, Fr. 53/F6
Liverdy-en-Brie, Fr. 30/L5
Livermore (mt.), Tx, US 129/F5
Liverpool (cape), Nun., Can. 123/J1
Liverpool, NS, Can. 131/H2
Liverpool (bay), NW, Can. 122/C1
Liverpool, Eng, UK 35/F5
Liverpool (co.), Eng, UK 35/F5
Liverpool (bay), Wal, UK 35/E5
Liverpool, Pa, US 138/B2
Livigno, It. 57/G4
Livilliers, Fr. 30/J4
Livingston, Guat. 144/D3
Livingston, Sc, UK 36/C5
Livingston (co.), Mi, US 135/E6
Livingston, Mt, US 126/F4
Livingston, NJ, US 139/H8
Livingston, Tx, US 129/J5
Livingston (lake), Tx, US 129/J5
Livingstone, Zam. 105/E4
Livingstone (falls), Congo 105/B2
Livingstone (range), Ab, Can. 126/E3
Livno, Bosn. 48/C4
Livny, Rus. 62/F1
Livojoki (riv.), Fin. 37/H2
Livonia, Mi, US 130/D3
Livorno (prov.), It. 58/D6
Livorno, It. 58/D5
Livorno Ferraris, It. 58/B2
Livramento do Brumado, Braz. 154/B4
Livron-sur-Drôme, Fr. 42/F4
Livry-Gargan, Fr. 30/K5
Lixin, China 72/D4
Lixnaw, Ire. 31/P10
Lixoúrion, Gre. 47/G3
Lixus (ruin), Mor. 100/A2
Liyang, China 72/D5
Lizard (pt.), Eng, UK 32/A7
Lizard, The (pen.), Eng, UK 32/A6
Lizy-sur-Ourcq, Fr. 52/C5
Ljubic, Serb. 48/E4
Ljubija, Bosn. 48/C3
Ljubinje, Bosn. 47/F1
Ljubljana (cap.), Slov. 43/L3
Ljubuški, Bosn. 47/E1
Ljungan (riv.), Swe. 37/F3
Ljungby, Swe. 38/E3
Ljungsbro, Swe. 38/F2
Ljungskile, Swe. 38/D2
Ljusnan (riv.), Swe. 37/E3
Ljusne, Swe. 38/G1
Ljusterø (isl.), Swe. 39/H2
Lkst (peak), Mor. 98/C3
Llabanere (int'l arpt.), Fr. 42/E5
Llaillay, Chile 158/N8
Llaima (vol.), Chile 158/C3
Llallagua, Bol. 150/E7
Llalli, Peru 156/D4
Llanberis, Pass of (pass), Wal, UK 34/D5
Llancañelo (lake), Arg. 158/C2
Llandovery, Wal, UK 32/C3
Llandrindod Wells, Wal, UK 32/C2
Llandudno, Wal, UK 34/E5
Llanes, Sp. 44/C1
Llanfairfechan, Wal, UK 34/E5
Llangollen, Wal, UK 35/E6
Llanidloes, Wal, UK 32/C2
Llano (riv.), Tx, US 129/H5
Llano, Tx, US 129/H5
Llano Estacado (plain), US 129/G4
Llanos (plain), Col.,Ven. 147/B2
Llanquihue (lake), Chile 158/B4
Llata, Peru 156/B3
Lleida, Sp. 45/F2
Llera de Canales, Mex. 143/F4
Llerena, Sp. 44/B3
Lleyn (pen.), Wal, UK 34/D6
Llivia, Sp. 45/F1
Llobregat (riv.), Sp. 45/F1
Llodio, Sp. 44/D1
Lloret de Mar, Sp. 45/G2
Llorona (pt.), CR 140/E6
Lloyd (pt.), NY, US 139/M8
Lloyd Harbor, NY, US 139/M8
Lloydminster, Sk, Can. 126/F2
Lloyds (riv.), Nf, Can. 131/K1
Lluchmayor, Sp. 45/G3
Llullaillaco (vol.), Arg.,Chil 157/C1
Llwchwr (riv.), Wal, UK 32/B3
Llynfi (riv.), Wal, UK 32/C3
Loa, Ut, US 128/E3
Loa (riv.), Chile 147/C5
Loanhead, Sc, UK 36/C5
Loano, It. 58/B4
Loaoya (canal), Sp. 45/N8
Lobbes, Belg. 53/D3
Lobería, Arg. 158/F3
Lobethal, Austl. 113/M8
Lobez, Pol. 41/H2
Lobito, Ang. 105/B3
Lobitos, Peru 156/A2
Lobo (riv.), C.d'Iv. 102/D5
Lobos, Arg. 159/J11
Lobos de Tierra, Isla (isl.), Peru 150/B5
Lobos, Punta de (pt.), Chile 158/M9
Locarno, Swi. 57/E5
Loch na Sealga (lake), Sc, UK 36/A1
Loch Raven (res.), Md, US 138/B5
Lochaber (reg.), Sc, UK 36/A3
Locharbriggs, Sc, UK 34/E1
Lochau, Aus. 57/F2
Lochboisdale, Sc, UK 31/Q8
Lochbuie, Co, US 137/C2
Lochem, Neth. 50/D4
Loches, Fr. 42/D3
Lochgelly, Sc, UK 36/C4
Lochgilphead, Sc, UK 36/A4
Lochindorb (lake), Sc, UK 36/C2
Lochmaben, Sc, UK 34/E1
Lochmaddy, Sc, UK 31/Q8
Łochów, Pol. 41/L2
Lochristi, Belg. 52/C1
Lochwinnoch, Sc, UK 36/B5
Lochy (lake), Sc, UK 36/B3
Lochy (riv.), Sc, UK 36/B3
Lock, Austl. 113/G5
Lock Haven, Pa, US 130/E3
Locke, Ca, US 135/L10
Lockerbie, Sc, UK 35/E1
Lockhart, Austl. 115/C2
Lockington, Austl. 115/C3
Locknitz (riv.), Ger. 40/F2
Lockport, NY, US 131/S9
Lockport, Il, US 135/P16
Lockwood (res.), Eng, UK 30/C2
Locon, Fr. 52/B2
Locri, It. 46/E3
Locumba, Peru 156/D5
Locust Fork (riv.), Al, US 133/G3
Lod, Isr. 91/F8
Loddon (riv.), Austl. 115/A1
Loddon (riv.), Eng, UK 33/E4
Lodenice (riv.), Czh. 55/H2
Lodève, Fr. 42/E5
Lodeynoye Pole, Rus. 60/G3
Lodhrān, Pak. 86/A5
Lodi, It. 58/C2
Lodi (prov.), It. 58/C2
Lodi, Ca, US 128/B3
Lodi, NJ, US 139/J8
Lodi Vecchio, It. 58/C2
Lodja, D.R. Congo 105/D1
Lodosa, Sp. 44/D1
Lodrino, Swi. 57/E5
Łódź, Pol. 41/K3
Łodzkie (prov.), Pol. 41/K3
Loei, Thai. 78/C2
Loenen, Neth. 50/C4
Loeriesfontein, SAfr. 106/B3
Lofa (co.), Libr. 102/C5
Lofa (riv.), Libr. 102/C5
Löffingen, Ger. 57/E2
Lofoten (isls.), Nor. 37/D2
Lofty (range), Austl. 112/C3
Lofty (mt.), Austl. 113/M8
Logan (mt.), Yk, Can. 134/K3
Logan, NM, US 132/C3
Logan, Oh, US 130/D4
Logan (co.), Ok, US 137/N14
Logan, Ut, US 126/F5
Logan, WV, US 130/D4
Logansport, In, US 130/C3
Loganton, Pa, US 138/A1
Loganville, Pa, US 138/B4
Logatec, Slov. 43/L4
Logone (riv.), Chad 93/D3
Lograto, It. 58/D2
Logroño, Sp. 44/D1
Logrosán, Sp. 44/C3
Løgstør, Den. 38/C3
Løgten, Den. 38/D3
Lohals, Den. 38/D4
Lohārdaga, India 85/E4
Lohfelden, Ger. 51/G6
Lohja, Fin. 39/L1
Lohjanjärvi (lake), Fin. 39/K1
Lohmar, Ger. 53/G2
Löhnberg, Ger. 54/B1
Lohne, Ger. 51/F3
Löhne, Ger. 51/F4
Lohr, Ger. 54/C3
Loi-kaw, Myan. 83/G4
Loi Lun (range), China,Mya 70/G7
Loing (riv.), Fr. 40/B5
Loir (riv.), Fr. 42/D3
Loire (riv.), Fr. 27/E4
Loisin (riv.), Fr. 53/E5
Loita (hills), Kenya 97/N8
Loja (prov.), Ecu. 156/B2
Loja, Ecu. 156/B2
Loja, Sp. 44/C4
Løjt Kirkeby, Den. 38/C4
Lokeren, Belg. 52/D1
Lokitaung, Kenya 104/B1
Løkken, Den. 38/C3
Lokoja, Nga. 103/G5
Lokolo (riv.), D.R. Congo 97/K8
Lokomby, Madg. 107/H8
Lokoro (riv.), D.R. Congo 97/J8
Lökösháza, Hun. 48/E2
Lokossa, Ben. 103/F5
Loks (isl.), Nun., Can. 123/K2
Lol (riv.), Sudan 97/L6
Lolland (isl.), Den. 37/D5
Lollar, Ger. 54/B3
Lolo (peak), Mt, US 126/E4
Lolui (isl.), Ugan. 104/B3
Lom, Nor. 37/D3
Lom Sak, Thai. 78/C2
Loma (mts.), SLeo. 96/C6
Loma (pt.), Ca, US 136/C5
Loma Bonita, Mex. 144/C2
Loma Linda, Ca, US 136/C2
Loma Mansa (peak), SLeo. 102/C4
Loma Negra, Arg. 158/E3
Lomami (riv.), D.R. Congo 93/E5
Lomas de Zamora, Arg. 159/J11
Lomazzo, It. 58/C1
Lombard, Il, US 135/P16
Lombarda, Serra (mts.), Braz. 151/H3
Lombardia, Mex. 142/E5
Lombardia (pol. reg.), It. 43/H4
Lomblen (isl.), Indo. 81/F5
Lombok (isl.), Indo. 67/L10
Lomé (int'l arpt.), Togo 103/F5
Lomé (cap.), Togo 103/F5
Lomello, It. 58/B2
Lomita, Ca, US 136/F8
Lomma, Swe. 38/E4
Lomme, Fr. 52/B2
Lommel, Belg. 50/C6
Lomnice (riv.), Czh. 55/G4
Lomnice nad Lužnicí, Czh. 55/H4
Lomond (lake), Sc, UK 36/B4
Lomond (hills), Sc, UK 36/C4
Lomone (riv.), It. 59/E4
Lomonosov, Rus. 61/S7
Lompobatang (peak), Indo. 81/E5
Lompoc, Ca, US 128/B4
Łomża, Pol. 41/M2
Lonato, It. 58/D2
Lonāvale, India 89/K5
Loncoche, Chile 158/B3
Loncopué, Arg. 158/C3
Londerzeel, Belg. 53/D2
London, On, Can. 130/D3
London (reef), Nic. 145/F3
London (cap.), UK 30/C2
London, Ky, US 130/C4
London, City of (bor.), Eng, UK 30/A1
Londonderry (cape), Austl. 109/B2
Londonderry (isl.), Chile 159/C7
Londonderry (dist.), NI, UK 34/A2
Londonderry, NI, UK 34/A2
Londrina, Braz. 155/B2
Lone (riv.), Ger. 54/C5
Lone Grove, Ok, US 129/H4
Lone Jack, Mo, US 137/E6
Lone Pine Sanctuary, Austl. 114/E7
Lonesome NP, Austl. 114/C4
Long, Ak, US 134/G3
Long (lake), On, Can. 127/M3
Long (lake), Sc, UK 36/A2
Long (riv.), China 79/A3
Long (isl.), Bahm. 141/F3
Long (isl.), NY, US 131/F3
Long (mtn.), Wal, UK 32/C1
Long (str.), Rus. 65/T2
Long Beach, Wa, US 126/B4
Long Beach, On, Can. 131/R10
Long Beach (isl.), NJ, US 138/D4
Long Beach, Ca, US 136/F8
Long Beach, NY, US 139/L9
Long Branch, NJ, US 138/E3
Long Cay (isl.), India 145/H1
Long Crag (hill), Eng, UK 36/E6
Long Eaton, Eng, UK 35/G6
Long Grove, Il, US 135/P15
Long Hill, Ct, US 139/E1
Long, Loch (inlet), Sc, UK 36/B4
Long Mynd, The (hill), Eng, UK 32/D1
Long Neck (pt.), Ct, US 139/M7
Long Range (mts.), Nf, Can. 131/K2
Long Valley, NJ, US 138/D2
Long Xuyen, Viet. 78/D4
Longá (riv.), Braz. 154/B1
Longare, It. 59/E2
Longaví, Chile 158/C2
Longboat Key, Fl, US 133/H5
Longbranch, Wa, US 135/B3
Longchang, China 83/J2
Longchuan, China 79/C3
Longchuan, China 83/G3
Longde, China 70/J4
Longeau (riv.), Fr. 53/E5
Longeville-en-Barrois, Fr. 53/E6
Longeville-lès-Metz, Fr. 53/F5
Longeville-lès-Saint-Avold, Fr. 53/F5
Longfellow (mts.), Me, US 131/G2
Longfield, Eng, UK 30/D2
Longford, Austl. 115/C4
Longford, Ire. 31/Q10
Longhua, China 72/D2
Longhui, China 83/K2
Longjumeau, Fr. 30/J5
Longkou, China 72/E3
Longlac, On, Can. 127/M3
Longli, China 83/J2
Longmen, China 79/B3
Longmen Shiyao, China 72/C4
Longmont, Co, US 137/B2
Longnan, China 79/B3
Longniddry, Sc, UK 36/D5
Longonot (peak), Kenya 104/C3
Longperrier, Fr. 30/K4
Longpont-sur-Orge, Fr. 30/J6
Longport, NJ, US 138/D5
Longpré-les-Corps-Saints, Fr. 52/A3
Longquan, China 79/C2
Longreach, Austl. 114/B3
Longshan, China 79/A2
Longshou (mts.), China 70/H4
Longueau, Fr. 52/B4
Longueil-Annel, Fr. 52/B5
Longuenesse, Fr. 52/B2
Longuesse, Fr. 30/H4
Longueuil, Qu, Can. 131/P6
Longuyon, Fr. 53/E5
Longvic, Fr. 56/B3
Longview, Wa, US 126/C4
Longview, Tx, US 129/J4
Longwood Gardens, Pa, US 138/C4
Longwy, Fr. 53/E4
Longyan, China 79/C2
Longyearbyen, Nor. 64/B2
Longyou, China 79/C2
Longzhou, China 78/D1
Loni, India 86/D5
Lonigo, It. 59/E2
Löningen, Ger. 51/E3
Lonquimay, Arg. 158/E3
Lons, Fr. 42/C5
Lons-le-Saunier, Fr. 56/B4
Lönsboda, Swe. 38/F3
Lontzen, Belg. 53/F2
Lonza (riv.), Swi. 56/D5
Looe (isl.), Eng, UK 32/B6
Lookout (cape), NC, US 133/J3
Lookout (pt.), Austl. 114/B1
Loolmalasin (peak), Tanz. 104/B3
Loon Lake, Sk, Can. 126/F2
Loon op Zand, Neth. 50/C5
Loop Head (pt.), Ire. 30/P10
Loos, Fr. 52/C2
Lop Buri, Thai. 78/C3
Lopary, Madg. 107/H8
Lopez (cape), Gabon 96/G8
López Mateos, Mex. 143/Q9
Lopik, Neth. 50/B5
Lopori (riv.), D.R. Congo 97/K7
Lopphavet (bay), Nor. 37/G1
Loppi, Fin. 39/L1
Lora del Río, Sp. 44/C4
Lorain, Oh, US 130/D3
Loralai, Pak. 89/J2
Lorca, Sp. 44/E4
Lord Howe (isl.), Austl. 116/E8
Lordsburg, NM, US 128/E4
Lorelei, Ger. 53/G3
Lorena, Braz. 211/H7
Lorengau, PNG 116/D5
Lørenskog, Nor. 38/D2
Lorentz (riv.), Indo. 81/J5
Lorentzsluizen (dam), Neth. 50/C2
Loreo, It. 59/F2
Loreto, Braz. 154/A2
Loreto, It. 59/G6
Loreto, Mex. 142/C3
Loreto (int'l arpt.), Mex. 142/C3
Loreto, Mex. 142/E4
Loreto, Ecu. 152/B5
Loreto (state), Peru 152/C5
Lorette, Mb, Can. 127/J3
Lorgues, Fr. 43/G5
Lorian (swamp), Kenya 97/N7
Lorica, Col. 152/C2
Lorient, Fr. 42/B3
L'Oriental (pol. reg.), Mor. 99/E2
Lorillard (riv.), Nun., Can. 122/G2
Lorinci, Hun. 41/K5
Loring, Ks, US 137/D5
Loriol-sur-Drôme, Fr. 42/F4
Lorn, Firth of (inlet), Sc, UK 31/Q8
Lorne, Austl. 115/B3
Lorosuk (peak), Kenya 104/B2
Lorquin, Fr. 53/G6
Lörrach, Ger. 56/D2
Lorrain (plat.), Fr. 40/D4
Lorraine (pol. reg.), Fr. 42/G2
Lorraine (pol. reg.), Fr. 56/C1
Lorraine, Qu, Can. 131/N6
Lorraine (reg.), Fr. 53/E5
Lorsch, Ger. 54/B3
Lorup, Ger. 51/E3
Los Alamitos, Ca, US 136/F8
Los Alamos, NM, US 129/F4
Los Alerces, PN, Arg. 157/B5
Los Altos, Ca, US 135/K12
Los Amates, Guat. 144/D3
Los Andes, Chile 158/N8
Los Andes, Col. 152/B4
Los Angeles, Chile 158/B3
Los Angeles, Ca, US 136/F7
Los Angeles (co.), Ca, US 136/B2

203

Los A – Magli

Los Angeles (int'l arpt.), Ca, US 136/F8
Los Angeles (riv.), Ca, US 136/B2
Los Angeles Outer (har.), Ca, US 136/F8
Los Aquijes, Peru 156/C4
Los Aztecas, Mex. 143/F4
Los Banos, Ca, US 128/B3
Los Barrios, Sp. 44/C4
Los Canarreos (arch.), Cuba 145/F1
Los Cardales, Arg. 159/J11
Los Cerrillos, Uru. 159/K11
Los Chonos (arch.), Chile 147/B7
Los Corrales de Buelna, Sp. 44/C1
Los Glaciares, PN, Arg. 157/B6
Los Katios, PN, Col. 152/B3
Los Lagos, Chile 158/B3
Los Lagos (pol. reg.), Chile 158/B4
Los Llanos de Aridane, Sp. 98/A3
Los Lunas, NM, US 128/F4
Los Mármoles, PN, Mex. 144/B1
Los Menucos, Arg. 158/C4
Los Mochis, Mex. 142/C3
Los Mosquitos (gulf), Pan. 145/F4
Los Muermos, Chile 158/B4
Los Navalmorales, Sp. 44/C3
Los Navalucillos, Sp. 44/C3
Los Órganos, Peru 156/A2
Los Padres National Forest, Ca, US 136/A1
Los Palacios y Villafranca, Sp. 44/C4
Los Pingüinos, PN, Chile 159/C7
Los Planes, Mex. 142/C3
Los Reyes, Mex. 143/R10
Los Reyes de Salgado, Mex. 142/E5
Los Ríos (prov.), Ecu. 156/B1
Los Roques, Islas (isls.), Ven. 150/E1
Los Santos, Pan. 152/A3
Los Santos de Maimona, Sp. 44/B3
Los Sauces, Chile 158/B3
Los Taques, Ven. 152/D2
Los Teques, Ven. 150/E1
Los Testigos (isls.), Ven. 153/F2
Los Vilos, Chile 158/C1
Los Yébenes, Sp. 44/D3
Losai Nat'l Rsv., Kenya 104/C2
Losheim, Ger. 53/F4
Łosice, Pol. 41/M2
Lošinj (isl.), Cro. 48/B3
Losne, Fr. 56/B3
Losone, Swi. 57/E5
Losoya, Tx, US 137/U21
Lossburg, Ger. 57/E1
Losser, Neth. 50/E4
Lossie (riv.), Sc, UK 36/C1
Lössnitz, Ger. 55/F1
Lossoganeu (hill), Tanz. 104/C4
Lost River (range), Id, US 128/D1
Lost River Caverns, Pa, US 138/C2
Lostallo, Swi. 57/F5
Lot (riv.), Fr. 42/D4
Lota, Chile 158/B3
Lotawana (lake), Mo, US 137/E6
Løten, Nor. 38/D1
Lotte, Ger. 51/E4
Lotuke (peak), Sudan 104/B1
Lotung, Tai. 79/D3
Lou (riv.), China 72/B5
Louang Namtha, Laos 83/H3
Louangphrabang, Laos 83/H4
Loubomo, Congo 105/B1
Loudéac, Fr. 42/B2
Loudi, China 83/K2
Loudun, Fr. 42/D3
Loue (riv.), Fr. 42/F3
Loufan, China 72/B3
Louga (pol. reg.), Sen. 102/B3
Louga, Sen. 102/A3
Lough Foyle (lake), UK 34/A1
Loughborough, Eng, UK 33/E1
Loughbrickland, NI, UK 34/B3
Lougheed (isl.), Nun., Can. 123/R7
Loughgall, NI, UK 34/B3
Loughrea, Ire. 31/P10
Loughton, Eng, UK 30/D2
Louhans, Fr. 56/B4
Louis Botha (Durban) (int'l arpt.), SAfr. 107/E3
Louisiade (arch.), PNG 116/E6
Louisiana (state), US 132/E4
Louisville, Co, US 137/B3
Louisville, Ky, US 130/C4
Louisville, Ms, US 133/F3
Loukkos (riv.), Mor. 100/A2
Loulé, Port. 44/A4
Louny, Czh. 55/G2
Loup (riv.), Ne, US 127/J5
Loup, Middle (riv.), Ne, US 127/H5
Loup, North (riv.), Ne, US 127/H5
Loup, South (riv.), Ne, US 127/J5
Lourches, Fr. 52/C3
Lourdes, Fr. 42/C5
Lourdes/Tarbes (int'l arpt.), Fr. 42/D5
Loures, Port. 45/P10
Louriçal, Port. 44/A2
Lourinhã, Port. 44/A3
Lousã, Port. 44/A2
Lousa, Port. 45/Q10
Louth, Eng, UK 35/H5
Louth (co.), Ire. 34/B4
Louth, Ire. 34/B4
Loutrá Aidhipsoú, Gre. 47/H3
Loutrákion, Gre. 47/H4
Loútsa, Gre. 47/P9
Louvain (Leuven), Belg. 53/D2
Louveira, Braz. 211/G8
Louviers, Fr. 42/D2
Louviers, Co, US 137/B4
Louvigné-du-Désert, Fr. 42/C2
Louvres, Fr. 30/K4
Louvroil, Fr. 52/C3
Lovaart (riv.), Belg. 52/B1
Lovat' (riv.), Rus. 60/F4
Lovat' (riv.), Bela.,Rus. 39/P3
Lovćen NP, Serb. 47/F1
Lovćenac, Serb. 48/D3
Love Point, Md, US 138/B5
Lovech (prov.), Bul. 47/J1
Loveland, Co, US 137/B2
Loveland (lake), Co, US 137/B2
Lovell, Wy, US 126/F4
Lovelock, Nv, US 128/C2
Lovere, It. 58/D1
Loving, NM, US 129/F4
Lovington, NM, US 129/G4
Lovios, Sp. 44/A2
Lövő, Hun. 43/M3
Lovosice, Czh. 55/H1
Lovozero (lake), Rus. 60/G2
Low (cape), Nun., Can. 123/H2
Lowa (riv.), D.R. Congo 93/E5
Lowell, Ma, US 131/G3
Löwen (riv.), Namb. 106/B2
Löwenstein, Ger. 54/C4
Lower (bay), NJ, US 138/D2
Lower (dam), Wa, US 135/D3
Lower Arrow (lake), BC, Can. 126/D3
Lower Engadine (valley), Swi. 57/G4
Lower Ganges (canal), India 84/B2
Lower Glenelg NP, Austl. 115/B3
Lower Hutt, NZ 117/S11
Lower Kalskag, Ak, US 134/F3
Lower Latham (res.), Co, US 137/C2
Lower Otay (lake), Ca, US 136/D5
Lower Red (lake), Mn, US 127/K4
Lower Rhine (riv.), Neth. 50/C5
Lower Rouge (riv.), Mi, US 135/F7
Lower Trajan's Wall, Mol.,Ukr. 62/D3
Lower Tunguska (riv.), Rus. 67/J3
Lower Zambezi NP, Zam. 105/E4
Lowestoft, Eng, UK 33/H2
Lowi (riv.), D.R. Congo 105/E1
Łowicz, Pol. 41/K2
Lowther (hills), Sc, UK 36/C6
Loxstedt, Ger. 51/F2
Loxton, SAfr. 106/C3
Loxton, Austl. 113/J5
Loyalton, Pa, US 138/B2
Loyalty (isls.), NCal. 116/F7
Loyettes, Fr. 56/B6
Loyne (lake), Sc, UK 36/A2
Loysville, Pa, US 138/A3
Loznica, Serb. 48/D3
Loznitsa, Bul. 49/H4
Lozova, Ukr. 62/F2
Lozovik, Serb. 48/E3
Lu (mtn.), China 72/D3
Lu (riv.), China 72/C5
Lu Xian, China 83/J2
Lualaba (riv.), D.R. Congo 93/E5
Luan (riv.), China 72/D2
Lu'an, China 72/D5
Luan Xian, China 72/D3
Luanchuan, China 72/B4
Luanco, Sp. 44/C1
Luanda (cap.), Ang. 105/B2
Luang (peak), Thai. 78/B4
Luang Lagoon (lag.), Thai. 83/H6
Luangwa (riv.), Zam. 105/F2
Luangwe, Zam. 104/A5
Luanping, China 72/D2
Luanshya, Zam. 105/E3
Luapula (prov.), Zam. 104/A5
Luarca, Sp. 44/B1
Luba, EqG. 96/G7
Lubaantun (ruin), Belz. 144/D2
Lubaczów, Pol. 41/M3
Lubań, Pol. 41/H3
Lubango, Ang. 105/B3
Lubansenshi (riv.), Zam. 104/A5
Lubartów, Pol. 41/M3
Lubawa, Pol. 41/K2
Lübbecke, Ger. 51/F4
Lubbeek, Belg. 53/D2
Lubbock, Tx, US 129/G4
Lubelska (uplands), Pol. 41/M3
Lubelskie (prov.), Pol. 41/M3
Lubero (riv.), D.R. Congo 104/A3
Lubień Kujawski, Pol. 41/K2
Lubin, Pol. 41/J3
Lublin, Pol. 41/M3
Lubliniec, Pol. 41/K3
Lubmin, Ger. 38/E4
Lubnaig (lake), Sc, UK 36/B4
Lubny, Ukr. 62/E2
Luboń, Pol. 41/J2
Lubrín, Sp. 44/D4
Lubsko, Pol. 41/H3
Lubudi, D.R. Congo 105/E2
Lubuklinggau, Indo. 80/B4
Lubuksikaping, Indo. 80/B3
Lubumbashi, D.R. Congo 105/E3
Lubuskie (prov.), Pol. 41/H2
Lucan, Ire. 34/B5
Lucania (mt.), Yk, Can. 134/K3
Lucas González, Arg. 159/J10
Lucca (prov.), It. 58/D5
Lucca, It. 58/D5
Lucciana, Fr. 46/A1
Luce (bay), Sc, UK 34/D2
Lucedale, Ms, US 133/F4
Lucélia, Braz. 155/B2
Lucena, Phil. 79/D5
Lucena, Sp. 44/C4
Lucena del Cid, Sp. 45/E2
Lučenec, Slvk. 41/K4
Lucens, Swi. 56/C4
Lucerne, Co, US 137/C2
Lucerne (lake), Swi. 43/H3
Lucerne (Vierwaldstättersee) (lake), Swi. 57/E3
Lucheng, China 72/C3
Lüchow, Ger. 40/F2
Lucindale, Austl. 115/B3
Luckeesarai, India 85/F3
Luckenwalde, Ger. 41/G2
Lucknow, India 84/C2
Lucky Lake, Sk, Can. 126/G3
Luco dei Marsi, It. 46/C2
Lucomagno, Passo del (pass), Swi. 57/E4
Lucrecia (cape), Cuba 145/H1
Lucrezia, It. 59/F5
Luda Kamchiya (riv.), Bul. 47/K1
Lüdenscheid, Ger. 51/E6
Lüderitz, Namb. 106/A2
Ludesch, Aus. 57/F3
Ludhiāna, India 86/C4
Ludian, China 83/H2
Ludinghausen, Ger. 51/E5
Ludington, Mi, US 130/C3
Ludogorie (reg.), Bul. 49/H4
Ludvika, Swe. 38/F1
Ludwigs (canal), Ger. 55/E4
Ludwigsburg, Ger. 54/C5
Ludwigsfelde, Ger. 40/Q7
Ludwigshafen, Ger. 57/F2
Ludwigshafen, Ger. 54/B4
Ludwigslust, Ger. 40/F2
Ludwigsstadt, Ger. 55/E2
Luebo, D.R. Congo 105/D2
Luena, Ang. 105/C3
Lufeng, China 79/A1
Lufkin, Tx, US 129/J5
Luga (bay), Rus. 39/N2
Luga, Rus. 39/N2
Luga (riv.), Rus. 39/N2
Lugagnano, It. 59/D2
Lugagnano Val d'Arda, It. 58/C3
Lugano, Swi. 57/E6
Lugano (lake), It. 57/E6
Luganville, Van. 116/F6
Lugards (falls), Kenya 104/C3
Lugavčina, Serb. 48/E3
Lügde, Ger. 51/G5
Lugenda (riv.), Moz. 105/G3
Lugg (riv.), Eng, UK 32/D2
Lugg (riv.), Wal, UK 32/C2
Lugnaquillia (peak), Ire. 34/B6
Lugo, It. 59/E4
Lugo, Sp. 44/B1
Lugogo (riv.), Ugan. 104/B2
Lugoj, Rom. 48/E3
Lugrin, Fr. 56/C5
Lugunga (peak), Tanz. 104/C4
Luhan (int'l arpt.), Ukr. 62/F2
Luhans'k, Ukr. 62/F2
Luhans'ka Oblasti, Ukr. 62/F2
Lühe (riv.), Ger. 51/H2
Luhe, China 72/D4
Luhe (riv.), Ger. 55/F3
Luhe-Wildenau, Ger. 55/F3
Luhombero (peak), Tanz. 104/C4
Luichart (lake), Sc, UK 36/B1
Luino, It. 57/E6
Luis B. Sánchez, Mex. 142/B1
Luís Correia, Braz. 154/B1
Luján, Arg. 159/J11
Lujiang, China 72/D5
Lukácsháza, Hun. 43/M3
Lukang, Tai. 79/D3
Lukavac, Bosn. 48/D3
Luke (mt.), Austl. 112/C3
Lukenie (riv.), D.R. Congo 105/C1
Lukovit, Bul. 47/J1
Łuków, Pol. 41/M3
Lukuga (riv.), D.R. Congo 104/A4
Lukulu, Zam. 105/D3
Lukulu (riv.), Zam. 104/A5
Lukunor (isl.), Micr. 116/E4
Luleå, Swe. 60/D2
Luleälven (riv.), Swe. 37/G2
Luliang, China 83/H2
Luling, La, US 137/P17
Luling (pass), China 72/B4
Lulong, China 72/D3
Lulonga (riv.), D.R. Congo 93/E4
Lulsgate (int'l arpt.), Eng, UK 32/D4
Lulua (riv.), D.R. Congo 93/E5
Lumangwe (falls), Zam. 104/A5
Lumberton, Tx, US 129/J5
Lumberton, NC, US 133/J3
Lumberton, NJ, US 138/D4
Lumbini (zone), Nepal 84/D2
Lumbo, Moz. 105/H4
Lumbrales, Sp. 44/B2
Lumbrein, Swi. 57/F4
Lumbres, Fr. 52/B2
Lumby, BC, Can. 126/D3
Lumding, India 83/F2
Lumigny-Nesles-Ormeaux, Fr. 30/L5
Luminárias, Braz. 211/J6
Lummen, Belg. 53/E2
Lumparland, Fin. 39/H1
Lumsden, Sk, Can. 127/G3
Lumsden, NZ 117/R12
Lumut, Malay. 80/B3
Luna (mtn.), Ca, US 136/C2
Lunahuaná, Peru 156/B4
Lund, Swe. 38/E4
Lundazi, Zam. 105/F3
Lundby, Den. 38/D4
Lundi (riv.), Zim. 105/F5
Lundy (isl.), Eng, UK 32/B4
Lune (riv.), Ger. 51/F2
Lune (riv.), Eng, UK 35/F3
Lüneburg, Ger. 51/H2
Lüneburger Heide (reg.), Ger. 40/F2
Lunel, Fr. 42/F5
Lünen, Ger. 51/E5
Lunenburg, NS, Can. 131/H2
Lunestedt, Ger. 51/F2
Lunéville, Fr. 43/G2
Lung Kwu Chau (isl.), China 71/T10
Lunga (riv.), Zam. 105/E3
Lungern, Swi. 56/E4
Lungi, SLeo. 102/B4
Lungi (Freetown) (int'l arpt.), SLeo. 102/B4
Lunglei, India 83/F3
Lungue-Bungo (riv.), Ang. 105/C3
Luni (riv.), India 89/K3
Lünne, Ger. 51/E4
Luocheng, China 83/J3
Luodian, China 83/J2
Luoding, China 83/K3
Luohe, China 72/C4
Luoma (lake), China 72/D4
Luongo (riv.), Zam. 104/A5
Luoning, China 72/B4
Luoshan, China 72/C4
Luoshuikan, China 79/A1
Luoyang, China 72/C4
Luoyuan, China 79/C2
Luozi, D.R. Congo 105/B1
Lupanshui, China 83/H2
Luqa (int'l arpt.), Malta 46/L7
Luqu, China 70/H5
Luquan, China 83/H2
Lūrah (riv.), Afg. 89/J2
Lure, Fr. 56/C2
Lurgan, NI, UK 34/B3
Luri, Fr. 43/H5
Lurín, Peru 156/B4
Lúrio, Moz. 105/H3
Lúrio (riv.), Moz. 93/F6
Lurnfeld, Aus. 43/K3
Lurøy, Nor. 37/E2
Lusaka (cap.), Zam. 105/E4
Lusambo, D.R. Congo 105/D1
Lusen (peak), Ger. 55/G5
Lusenga NP, Zam. 104/A5
Lushan, China 72/C4
Lushi, China 72/B4
Lushnjë, Alb. 47/F2
Lushoto, Tanz. 104/C4
Lushui, China 83/G2
Lusignan, Fr. 42/D3
Lusk, Wy, US 127/G5
Lusk, Ire. 34/B4
Lustenau, Aus. 57/F3
Lutanga (riv.), D.R. Congo 97/J7
Luther, Ok, US 137/N14
Luthern, Swi. 56/D3
Lutherville, Md, US 138/B5
Lütjehorn (isl.), Ger. 50/D1
Lütjenburg, Ger. 38/D4
Luton, Eng, UK 33/F3
Luton (co.), Eng, UK 33/F3
Luton (int'l arpt.), Eng, UK 33/F3
Lutry, Swi. 56/C5
Lutselk'e, NW, Can. 122/E2
Luts'k, Ukr. 62/C2
Lutter (riv.), Ger. 51/F5
Lutterbach, Fr. 56/D2
Lutz (riv.), Aus. 57/F3
Lützow-Holm (bay), Ant. 160/C
Luumäki, Fin. 39/M1
Luverne, Mn, US 127/J5
Luvua (riv.), D.R. Congo 104/A4
Luwegu (riv.), Tanz. 105/G2
Luwero, Ugan. 104/B2
Luwingu, Zam. 104/A5
Lux, Fr. 56/A4
Luxembourg (ctry.) 53/E4
Luxembourg (prov.), Belg 53/E4
Luxembourg (cap.), Lux. 53/F4
Luxeuil-les-Bains, Fr. 56/C2
Luxi, China 83/H3
Luxi, China 83/K2
Luxi, China 83/G3
Luxor (int'l arpt.), Egypt 101/C3
Luyi, China 72/C4
Luz, Braz. 155/C1
Luz (coast), Port.,Sp. 44/B4
Luza (riv.), Rus. 61/L3
Luzarches, Fr. 30/K4
Luzein, Swi. 57/F4
Luzern, Swi. 57/E3
Luzern (canton), Swi. 56/E3
Luzerne (co.), Pa, US 138/B1
Luzhai, China 83/J3
Luzhi, China 83/J2
Luzhou, China 83/J2
Luziânia, Braz. 154/A5
Luzilândia, Braz. 154/B1
Lužnice (riv.), Czh. 41/H4
Luzon (isl.), Phil. 79/D4
Luzon (str.), Phil. 116/A3
Lužuice (riv.), Czh. 43/L2
Luzzara, It. 59/D3
Luzzi, It. 46/E3
L'viv, Ukr. 62/C2
L'vivs'ka Oblasti, Ukr. 62/B2
Lwala (peak), Ugan. 104/B2
Lwi (riv.), Myan. 78/C1
Lyantonde, Ugan. 104/A3
Lyapin (riv.), Rus. 61/P2
Lycksele, Swe. 37/F2
Lycoming (co.), Pa, US 138/A1
Lyell Brown (mt.), Austl. 113/F2
Lykens, Pa, US 138/B2
Lyman, Wy, US 126/F5
Lyme (bay), Eng, UK 42/B1
Lymington, Eng, UK 33/E5
Lymm, Eng, UK 35/F5
Lyna (riv.), Pol. 41/L1
Lynas (pt.), Wal, UK 34/D5
Lynbrook, NY, US 139/L9
Lynch, Md, US 138/B5
Lynches (riv.), SC, US 133/H3
Lyndhurst, NJ, US 139/J8
Lyne (riv.), Eng, UK 35/F1
Lyngdal, Nor. 38/B2
Lyngen (inlet), Nor. 37/G1
Lynn, Ma, US 131/G3
Lynn Haven, Fl, US 133/G4
Lynn Lake, Mb, Can. 122/F3
Lynwood, Ca, US 136/F8
Lynx (lake), NW, Can. 122/F2
Lyon, Fr. 42/F4
Lyon (riv.), Sc, UK 36/B3
Lyon (lake), Sc, UK 36/B3
Lyon (Satolas) (int'l arpt.), Fr. 56/B6
Lyons, Ks, US 129/H3
Lyons, Co, US 137/B2
Lyons (riv.), Austl. 112/C3
Lyons, Wi, US 135/P14
Lype (hill), Eng, UK 32/C4
Lyra (reef), PNG 116/E5
Lys (riv.), It. 58/A1
Lys (riv.), Fr. 42/E1
Lys-lez-Lannoy, Fr. 52/C2
Lysá (peak), Czh. 41/K4
Lysá nad Labem, Czh. 55/H2
Lysaker, Nor. 38/D2
Lysaya (hill), Bela. 39/M4
Lysekil, Swe. 38/D2
Lysica (peak), Pol. 41/L3
Lysina (peak), Czh. 55/F2
Lyss, Swi. 56/D3
Lystrup, Den. 38/D3
Lys'va, Rus. 61/N4
Lysychans'k, Ukr. 62/F2
Lytham Saint Anne's, Eng, UK 35/E4
Lytle, Tx, US 129/H5
Lytle Creek, Ca, US 136/C2
Lytton, BC, Can. 126/C3
Lyubertsy, Rus. 61/W9
Lyubotyn, Ukr. 62/E2
Lyudinovo, Rus. 62/E1
Lywd (riv.), Wal, UK 32/C3

M

M. Aleman (res.), Mex. 140/B4
Ma-Ubin, Myan. 83/G4
Ma'alot-Tarshiha, Isr. 91/D3
Ma'ān, Jor. 91/D4
Ma'an (gov.), Jor. 91/E4
Maanĭt, Mong. 70/H2
Maanĭt, Mong. 70/J2
Maanselkä (mts.), Fin. 37/H1
Ma'anshan, China 72/D5
Maarheeze, Neth. 50/C6
Maarianhamina (Mariehamn), Fin. 39/H1
Ma'arrat an Nu'mān, Syria 91/E2
Maarssen, Neth. 50/C4
Maartensdijk, Neth. 50/C4
Maas (riv.), Belg. 42/F1
Maasbracht, Neth. 53/E1
Maasbree, Neth. 50/D6
Maaseik, Belg. 53/E1
Maassluis, Neth. 50/B5
Maastricht, Neth. 53/E2
Maastricht (int'l arpt.), Neth. 53/E2
Mabalacat, Phil. 79/D4
Mabalane, Moz. 105/F5
Mabaruma, Guy. 153/G2
Mabechi (riv.), Japan 76/B3
Mabian, China 83/H2
Mabinay, Phil. 79/D6
Mabopane, SAfr. 106/Q12
Mabote, Moz. 105/F5
Mabule, Bots. 106/D2
Mac Robertson Land (phys. reg.), Ant. 160/D
Macá (peak), Chile 158/B5
Macachín, Arg. 158/E3
Macaé, Braz. 155/D2
Macael, Sp. 44/D4
Macaíba, Braz. 154/D2
Mação, Port. 44/A3
Macapá, Braz. 151/H3
Macará, Ecu. 156/B2
Macarani, Braz. 154/B4
Macaravita, Col. 152/C3
Macari, Peru 156/D4
Macarthur, Austl. 115/B3
Macas, Ecu. 152/B5
Macau, Braz. 154/C2
Macau, China 83/K3
Macau (dpcy.), China 67/L7
Macaúbas, Braz. 154/B4
Macauley (isl.), NZ 116/G7
Macaya (riv.), Col. 150/D3
Macaya, Pic de (peak), Haiti 145/H2
Maccagno, It. 57/E5
Macclenny, Fl, US 133/H4
Macclesfield (canal), Eng, UK 35/F5
Macclesfield, Eng, UK 35/F5
Macdhui (peak), SAfr. 106/D3
Macdona, Tx, US 137/T21
MacDonald (lake), Austl. 109/B3
Macdonnell (ranges), Austl. 109/C3
Macduff, Sc, UK 36/D1
Maceda, Sp. 44/B1
Macedonia (reg.), Gre. 47/G2
Macedonia (int'l arpt.), Gre. 47/H2
Macedonia (Former Yugoslav Republic of Macedonia) (ctry.) 47/G2
Maceió (pt.), Braz. 154/C2
Maceió, Braz. 154/D3
Macerata (prov.), It. 59/G6
Macerata, It. 43/K5
Macfarlane (lake), Austl. 113/H5
Machacalis, Braz. 154/B5
Machacamarca, Bol. 150/E7
Machache (peak), Les. 106/D3
Machachi, Ecu. 152/B5
Machado, Braz. 211/H6
Machado (swamp), Col. 145/H4
Machadodorp, SAfr. 107/E2
Machakos, Kenya 104/C3
Machala, Ecu. 156/B1
Machalí, Chile 158/N9
Machalilla, PN, Ecu. 152/A5
Machanga, Moz. 105/F5
Machaquilá (riv.), Guat. 144/D2
Machars, The (pen.), Sc, UK 34/D2
Machattie (lake), Austl. 113/H3
Machaze, Moz. 105/F5
Machecoul, Fr. 42/C3
Machemma (ruin), SAfr. 105/E5
Macheng, China 72/C5
Machens, Mo, US 137/G8
Machhlīshahr, India 84/D3
Machias, Me, US 131/H2
Machichaco (cape), Sp. 44/D1
Machida, Japan 77/C2
Machilipatnam, India 82/D4
Machiques, Ven. 152/C2
Machovo Jezero (lake), Czh. 55/H1
Machu Picchu (ruin), Peru 156/C4
Machupo (riv.), Bol. 150/F6
Machynlleth, Wal, UK 32/C1
Măcin, Rom. 49/J3
Macina (phys. reg.), Mali 96/E4
Macintyre (riv.), Austl. 109/E3
Mackay (lake), Austl. 109/B3
Mackay, Austl. 114/C3
Mackenzie, BC, Can. 126/C2
Mackenzie, Austl. 114/C3
Mackenzie (bay), NW,Yk, Can. 122/C2
Mackenzie (mts.), NW, Can. 122/C2
Mackenzie (riv.), NW, Can. 122/E2
Mackenzie King (isl.), NW, Can. 123/R7
Mackinac Island, Mi, US 130/C2
Mackinaw City, Mi, US 130/C2
Macklin, Sk, Can. 126/F2
Macknade, Austl. 114/B2
Macksville, Austl. 115/E1
Maclean, Austl. 115/E1
Maclear, SAfr. 106/E3
Macleay (isl.), Austl. 114/F7
Macleod (lake), Austl. 112/B3
Macmillan (riv.), Yk, Can. 134/L3
Macomb, Il, US 127/L5
Macomb (co.), Mi, US 135/G6
Macomb, Ok, US 137/N15
Macomer, It. 46/A2
Mâcon, Fr. 42/F3
Macon, Ga, US 133/H3
Macon, Mo, US 129/J3
Macondes, Planalto dos (plat.), Moz. 104/C5
Macosquin, NI, UK 34/B1
Macotera, Sp. 44/C2
Macoupin (co.), Il, US 137/G7
Macquarie (har.), Austl. 115/C4
Macquarie (isl.), Austl. 23/S8
Macquarie (riv.), Austl. 109/D4
Macroom, Ire. 31/P11
Macuelizo, Hon. 144/D3
Macuim (riv.), Braz. 150/F5
Macuira, PN, Col. 152/D1
Macuma (riv.), Ecu. 156/B1
Macumba (riv.), Austl. 109/C3
Macungie, Pa, US 138/C2
Macusani, Peru 156/D4
Macuspana, Mex. 144/C2
Macuzari, Presa (dam), Mex. 142/C3
Mādabā, Jor. 91/D4
Madagascar (ctry.) 107/H8
Madan, Bul. 47/J2
Madanapalle, India 82/C5
Madanīyīn, Tun. 96/H1
Madanīyīn (gov.), Tun. 99/H2
Madaoua, Niger 103/G3
Madaras, Hun. 48/D2
Madauk, Myan. 83/G4
Madawaska, Me, US 131/G2
Madawaska (riv.), On, Can. 130/E2
Madden (dam), Pan. 152/B2
Madeira (aut. reg.), Port. 45/U14
Madeira (riv.), Braz. 147/C3
Mädelegabel (peak), Ger. 57/G3
Madeleine, Îles de la (isls.), Qu, Can. 131/J2
Madeline (isl.), Wi, US 127/L4
Mäder, Aus. 57/F3
Madera, Mex. 142/C2
Maderas (vol.), Nic. 144/E4
Madgaon (Margao), India 89/K5
Madhipura, India 85/F3
Madhubani, India 85/F2
Madhumati (riv.), Bang. 85/G4
Madhupur, India 85/F3
Madhya Pradesh (state), India 70/D7
Madidi (riv.), Bol. 150/E6
Madīnat ath Thawrah, Syria 90/D3
Madirovalo, Madg. 107/H7
Madison, Al, US 133/G3
Madison, Ca, US 135/K9
Madison, Ct, US 139/F1
Madison, Fl, US 133/H4
Madison, Il, US 137/G8
Madison, In, US 130/C4
Madison, Ms, US 133/F3
Madison (riv.), Mt, US 124/D2
Madison, Ne, US 127/J5
Madison, NJ, US 139/H9
Madison (co.), Oh, US 137/G8
Madison, SD, US 127/J4
Madison Heights, Mi, US 135/F6
Madisonville, Tx, US 129/J5
Madisonville, Ky, US 130/C4
Madisonville, La, US 137/P16
Madiun, Indo. 80/D5
Mado Gashi, Kenya 104/C2
Madoi, China 70/G5
Madon (riv.), Fr. 40/D4
Madrakah, Ra's al (pt.), Oman 89/G5
Madre (lag.), Tx, US 140/B2
Madre de Deus de Minas, Braz. 211/J6
Madre de Dios (riv.), Bol. 150/E6
Madre de Dios (dept.), Peru 156/C4
Madre de Dios (isl.), Chile 159/A6
Madre del Sur, Sierra (mts.), Mex. 140/A4
Madre Occidental, Sierra (mts.), Mex. 142/D3
Madre Oriental, Sierra (mts.), Mex. 143/F4
Madrid (aut. comm.), Sp. 44/C2
Madrid (cap.), Sp. 45/N9
Madridejos, Sp. 44/D3
Madrigal, Peru 156/D4
Madrigal de las Altas Torres, Sp. 44/C2
Madrigalejo, Sp. 44/C3
Madrisahorn (peak), Swi. 57/F4
Madroñera, Sp. 44/C3
Madugula, India 82/D4
Madura (isl.), Indo. 67/L10
Madurai, India 82/C6
Mae Hong Son, Thai. 83/G4
Mae Ping NP, Thai. 78/B2
Mae Tho (peak), Thai. 78/B2
Mae Ya (mtn.), Thai. 78/B2
Maebashi, Japan 75/F2
Maella, Sp. 45/F2
Maep'o, SKor. 73/E4
Maerne, It. 59/F1
Maestra, Sierra (mts.), Cuba 145/G2
Maevatanana-Ambanivohitra, Madg. 107/H7
Maewo (isl.), Van. 116/F6
Mafeteng, Les. 106/D3
Maffra, Austl. 115/C3
Mafia (isl.), Tanz. 105/G2
Mafia (chan.), Tanz. 104/C5
Mafikeng, SAfr. 106/D2
Mafou (riv.), Gui. 102/C4
Mafra, Braz. 155/B3
Mafra, Port. 45/P10
Magadan, Rus. 65/R4
Magadino, Swi. 57/E5
Magalies Berg (mts.), SAfr. 106/P12
Magaliesburg, SAfr. 106/P12
Magallanes y Antártica Chilena (prov.), Chile 159/C7
Magangué, Col. 152/C2
Mağara, Turk. 91/C1
Magaria, Niger 103/H3
Magat (riv.), Phil. 79/D4
Magazine (mtn.), Ar, US 129/J4
Magdalena, Bol. 150/F6
Magdalena (peak), Malay. 81/E3
Magdalena (riv.), Col. 147/B2
Magdalena (dept.), Col. 145/H4
Magdalena, Arg. 159/K11
Magdalena de Kino, Mex. 142/C2
Magdeburg, Ger. 40/F2
Magdelaine Cays (isls.), Austl. 109/E2
Magé, Braz. 211/K7
Mage-shima (isl.), Japan 74/B5
Magee, Ms, US 133/F4
Magee (isl.), NI, UK 34/C2
Magelang, Indo. 80/D5
Magellan (str.), Arg.,Chile 147/B8
Magenta, It. 58/B2
Magenta (lake), Austl. 112/C5
Magerøya (isl.), Nor. 37/H1
Maggia, Swi. 57/E5
Maggia (riv.), Swi. 57/E5
Maggio (peak), It. 59/E6
Maggiorasca (peak), It. 58/C3
Maggiore (peak), It. 59/E5
Maggiore (lake), It. 43/H4
Maghāghah, Egypt 101/B2
Maghar, India 84/D2
Maghera, NI, UK 34/B2
Magherafelt (co.), NI, UK 34/B2
Magherafelt, NI, UK 34/B2
Maghīla (peak), Tun. 100/L7
Maghnia, Alg. 100/D2
Magilligan (pt.), NI, UK 34/B1
Maglaj, Bosn. 48/D3
Maglic (peak), Serb. 47/F1
Maglie, It. 47/F2

204

Maglo – Marba

Maglod, Hun. 49/R10
Magna, Ut, US 137/J12
Magnac-Laval, Fr. 42/D3
Magnetawan (riv.), On, Can. 130/D2
Magnetic Passage, Austl. 114/B2
Magnitogorsk, Rus. 61/N5
Magnitogorsk (int'l arpt.), Rus. 61/N5
Magnolia, Ar, US 129/J4
Magnolia, De, US 138/C5
Magny-en-Vexin, Fr. 52/A5
Magny-les-Hameaux, Fr. 30/J5
Mago NP, Eth. 97/N6
Mágoè, Moz. 105/F4
Magog, Qu, Can. 131/F2
Magpie (riv.), Qu, Can. 131/H1
Magpie (lake), Qu, Can. 131/H1
Magpie Ouest (riv.), Qu, Can. 131/H1
Magra (riv.), It. 58/C4
Magreta, It. 59/D3
Maguan, China 78/D1
Magude, Moz. 105/F6
Magugnano, It. 59/D1
Magway (div.), Myan. 70/F8
Magway (Magwe), Myan. 83/F3
Magwe (Magway), Myan. 83/F3
Maha Sarakham, Thai. 78/C2
Mahābād, Iran 88/E1
Mahabe, Madg. 107/H8
Mahābhārat (range), Nepal 84/C1
Mahabo, Madg. 107/H8
Mahaboboka, Madg. 107/H7
Mahād, India 89/K5
Mahadeo (range), India 84/A4
Mahaica, Guy. 153/G3
Mahaica-Berbice (pol. reg.), Guy. 153/G3
Mahaicony Village, Guy. 153/G3
Mahajamba (riv.), Madg. 107/H7
Mahajamba (bay), Madg. 107/H6
Mahajanga (prov.), Madg. 107/H6
Mahajanga, Madg. 107/H6
Mahajilo (riv.), Madg. 107/H7
Mahakali (zone), Nepal 84/C1
Mahakam (riv.), Indo. 81/E3
Mahalapye, Bots. 105/E5
Mahale Mountains NP, Tanz. 104/A4
Maḩallāt, Iran 88/F2
Maham, India 86/D5
Māhān (riv.), India 84/D4
Māhān, Iran 89/G2
Mahānadī (riv.), India 70/D7
Mahananda (riv.), India 85/F3
Mahandiabani (riv.), C.d'Iv. 102/D4
Mahanoro, Madg. 107/J7
Mahanoy City, Pa, US 138/B2
Mahantango (mtn.), Pa, US 138/B2
Mahārājganj, India 85/E2
Mahārājganj, India 84/D2
Mahārajpur, India 82/C2
Mahārāshtra (state), India 82/B4
Mahāsamund, India 82/D3
Mahāshān (ruin), Bang. 85/G3
Mahasoabe, Madg. 107/H8
Mahavavy (riv.), Madg. 107/H7
Mahawa (riv.), India 84/B1
Mahazoarivo, Madg. 107/H8
Mahazoma, Madg. 107/H8
Mahbubnagar, India 82/C4
Mahdia, Guy. 153/G3
Mahébourg, Mrts. 107/T15
Mahendranagar, Nepal 84/C1
Mahesāna, India 89/K4
Mahgawān, India 84/B2
Mahia (pen.), NZ 109/H6
Mahilyow (int'l arpt.), Bela. 39/P5
Mahilyow, Bela. 39/P5
Mahilyowskaya Voblasts Bela. 60/F5
Mahīshādal, India 85/F4
Mahitsy, Madg. 107/H7
Mahlaing, Myan. 83/G3
Mahlberg, Ger. 56/D1
Mahleur (lake), Or, US 126/D5
Mahlow, Ger. 40/Q7
Mahmel (peak), Alg. 96/G1
Maḩmūd-e 'Erāqī, Afg. 89/J1
Mahmūdābād, India 84/C2
Mahón, Sp. 45/H3
Mahroni, India 84/B3
Mahukona, Hi, US 124/U10
Mahuva, India 89/K4
Mahwah, India 84/A2
Mahwah, NJ, US 139/J7
Mai-Ndombe (lake), D.R. Congo 96/J8
Maia, Port. 44/A2
Maiala NP, Austl. 114/E6
Maials, Sp. 45/F2
Maiana (isl.), Kiri. 116/G4
Maicao, Col. 152/C2
Maîche, Fr. 56/C3
Maicuru (riv.), Braz. 151/H3
Maidenhead, Eng, UK 33/F3
Maidens, Sc, UK 36/B6
Maidstone, Sk, Can. 126/F2
Maidstone, Eng, UK 33/G4
Maidstone, On, Can. 135/G7
Maiduguri, Nga. 96/H5
Maienfeld, Swi. 57/F4
Maigue (riv.), Ire. 31/P10
Maihar, India 84/C3
Maihara, Japan 77/K5
Maikala (range), India 84/C4
Maiko, PN de la, D.R. Congo 97/L8
Mailāni, India 84/C1
Maili, Hi, US 124/V13
Mailly-le-Camp, Fr. 53/D6
Mailsi, Pak. 86/B5
Main (riv.), NI, UK 34/B2
Main (riv.), Ger. 40/E4
Main-Donau (canal), Ger. 54/D3
Main Range NP, Austl. 114/C5
Maināguri, India 85/G2
Mainbernheim, Ger. 54/D3
Maincy, Fr. 30/L6
Maine (state), US 131/G2
Maine (riv.), Ire. 31/P10
Maine (reg.), Fr. 42/C2
Maine, Collines du (hills), Fr. 42/C2
Maine, Gulf of (gulf), Me, US 131/G3
Mainhardt, Ger. 54/C4
Mainhausen, Ger. 54/B2
Mainland (isl.), Sc, UK 31/V14
Mainling, China 83/F2
Mainpuri, India 84/B2
Mainstockheim, Ger. 54/D3
Maintirano, Madg. 107/H7
Mainz, Ger. 54/B3
Maio (isl.), CpV. 93/K10
Maipo (vol.), Chile 158/P9
Maipo (riv.), Chile 158/N8
Maipú, Arg. 158/F3
Maipú, Chile 158/N8
Maira (riv.), It. 43/G4
Maire (str.), Arg. 159/D7
Mairiporã, Braz. 211/G8
Mairwa, India 85/E2
Mais Gate (int'l arpt.), Haiti 145/H2
Maisach, Ger. 54/E6
Maisí (cape), Cuba 141/G3
Maisome (isl.), Tanz. 104/A3
Maison-Rouge, Fr. 30/M6
Maisons-Alfort, Fr. 30/K5
Maisons-Laffitte, Fr. 30/J5
Maithon (res.), India 85/F4
Maitland, Austl. 115/D2
Maitland (riv.), On, Can. 130/D3
Maitland, Austl. 113/H5
Maitri, India, Ant. 160/A
Maizhokunggar, China 83/F2
Maizières-lès-Metz, Fr. 53/F5
Maizuru, Japan 77/H5
Maizuru (bay), Japan 77/H4
Maja e Zezë (peak), Alb. 47/G2
Majadahonda, Sp. 45/N9
Majagual, Col. 152/C2
Majardah (mts.), Alg. 100/K6
Majāz Al Bāb, Tun. 100/L6
Majdanpek, Serb. 48/E3
Majene, Indo. 81/E4
Majia (riv.), China 72/D3
Majiang, China 79/A2
Majorca (isl.), Sp. 45/G3
Majur, Serb. 48/D3
Majuro (cap.), Mrsh. 116/G4
Makabe, Japan 77/E1
Makaha, Hi, US 124/V13
Makakilo City, Hi, US 124/V13
Makālu (peak), China 85/F2
Makālu (peak), Nepal 82/E2
Makarska, Cro. 47/E1
Makassar (str.), Indo. 67/L10
Makatea (isl.), FrPol. 117/L6
Makawao, Hi, US 124/T10
Makay (mass.), Madg. 107/H8
Makemo (isl.), FrPol. 117/L6
Makena, Hi, US 124/T10
Makeni, SLeo. 102/B4
Makgadikgadi (salt pans), Bots. 105/D5
Makhachkala, Rus. 63/H4
Makhdūmpur, Pak. 86/B4
Makhfar al Busayyah, Iraq 88/E2
Makhmūr, Iraq 90/E3
Makian (isl.), Indo. 81/G3
Makin (isl.), Kiri. 116/G4
Makino, Japan 77/K5
Makinsk, Kaz. 87/F2
Makioka, Japan 77/B2
Makiyivka, Ukr. 62/F2
Makkah, SAr. 88/C4
Makkovik, Nf, Can. 123/L3
Makó, Hun. 48/E2
Makokou, Gabon 96/H7
Makonde (plat.), Tanz. 104/C5
Maków Mazowiecki, Pol. 41/L2
Makrakómi, Gre. 47/H3
Makran (coast), Iran 89/G3
Makran (reg.), Iran 89/H3
Makrokhórion, Gre. 47/H2
Maksutlu, Turk. 47/K2
Makteir (reg.), Mrta. 98/C5
Makthar, Tun. 100/L7
Makurazaki, Japan 74/B5
Makurdi, Nga. 103/H5
Makushin (vol.), Ak, US 134/E5
Mal Abrigo, Uru. 159/K11
Mala, Peru 156/B4
Mala (pt.), CR 144/E4
Mala (pt.), Pan. 152/B3
Malabar (coast), India 82/B5
Malabata (pt.), Mor. 100/B2
Malabo (cap.), EqG. 96/G7
Malacacheta, Braz. 154/B5
Malacca (str.), Asia 67/J9
Malacky, Slvk. 41/J4
Maladers, Swi. 57/F4
Maladzyechna, Bela. 39/M4
Málaga (int'l arpt.), Sp. 44/C4
Málaga, Sp. 44/C4
Malaga, NJ, US 138/C4
Malaga Cove (bay), Ca, US 136/F8
Malagarasi (riv.), Tanz. 104/A4
Malagón, Sp. 44/D3
Malagueta (bay), Cuba 145/G1
Malahide, Ire. 34/B5
Malaimbandy, Madg. 107/H8
Malaita (isl.), Sol. 116/F5
Malakāl, Sudan 97/M6
Malakangiri, India 82/D4
Malakwāl, Pak. 86/B3
Malambo, Col. 152/C2
Malang, Indo. 80/D5
Malangawa, Nepal 85/E2
Malanje, Ang. 105/C2
Malans, Swi. 57/F4
Malanville, Ben. 103/F4
Malargüe, Arg. 158/C2
Malartic, Qu, Can. 130/E1
Malasoro (pt.), Indo. 81/E5
Malatya (prov.), Turk. 90/D2
Malatya, Turk. 90/D2
Malaut, India 86/C4
Malawi (ctry.) 105/F3
Malawi (Nyasa) (lake), Malw. 104/B5
Malay (pen.), Thai. 83/G6
Malaya (reg.), Malay. 80/B3
Malaya Vishera, Rus. 39/Q2
Malaybalay, Phil. 79/E6
Malāyer, Iran 88/E2
Malaysia (ctry.) 80/C2
Malazemel'skaya (tundra), Rus. 61/L2
Malazgirt, Turk. 90/E2
Malbaie (riv.), Qu, Can. 131/G1
Malbork, Pol. 39/H4
Malcesine, It. 59/D1
Malchin, Ger. 38/E5
Malcontenta, It. 59/F2
Maldegem, Belg. 52/C1
Malden, Mo, US 129/K3
Malden (isl.), Kiri. 117/K5
Maldive (isls.), Mald. 82/B6
Maldives (ctry.) 67/G9
Maldon, Austl. 115/C3
Maldon, Eng, UK 33/G3
Maldonado, Uru. 159/G2
Maldonado (dept.), Uru. 159/G2
Male (cap.), Mald. 67/G9
Maléa (cape), Gre. 47/H4
Mālegaon, India 89/K4
Malekula (isl.), Van. 116/F6
Malemort-sur-Corrèze, Fr. 42/D4
Malente, Ger. 38/D4
Maleny, Austl. 114/D4
Maleo, It. 58/C2
Malesína, Gre. 47/H3
Malfa, It. 46/D3
Malgobek, Rus. 63/H4
Malgrat de Mar, Sp. 45/G2
Malgrate, It. 58/C1
Malheur (lake), Or, US 128/C2
Malheur (riv.), Or, US 126/D5
Malheureux (cape), Mrts. 107/T14
Mali (riv.), Myan. 83/G2
Mali (isl.), Myan. 78/B3
Mali (ctry.) 96/E4
Mali Lošinj, Cro. 48/B3
Mália, Gre. 47/J5
Malibu, Ca, US 136/B2
Malīhābād, India 84/C2
Målilla, Swe. 38/F3
Malin Head (pt.), Ire. 31/Q9
Malinau, Indo. 81/E3
Malindang (mt.), Phil. 81/F2
Malindi, Kenya 104/D3
Maling (pass), China 72/C3
Malio (riv.), Madg. 107/H8
Malipo, China 78/D1
Malīr Cantonment, Pak. 89/J4
Malka Mari NP, Kenya 97/P7
Malkara, Turk. 49/H5
Malko Tŭrnovo, Bul. 49/H5
Mallacoota, Austl. 115/D3
Mallaig, Sc, UK 31/R8
Mallānwān, India 84/C2
Mallasvesi (lake), Fin. 39/K1
Mallee Cliffs NP, Austl. 115/B2
Mallén, Sp. 44/E2
Malleray, Swi. 56/D3
Mallero (riv.), It. 57/F5
Mallersdorf-Pfaffenberg, Ger. 55/F5
Malles (Mals), It. 57/G4
Malloa, Chile 158/N9
Mallow, Ire. 31/P10
Malmberget, Swe. 37/G2
Malmédy, Belg. 53/F3
Malmesbury, SAfr. 106/L10
Malmköping, Swe. 38/G2
Malmö, Swe. 38/E4
Malmöhus (co.), Swe. 37/E5
Malmslätt, Swe. 38/F2
Malnate, It. 58/B1
Malo, It. 59/E1
Maloelap (isl.), Mrsh. 116/G4
Malone, NY, US 130/F2
Malong, China 83/H2
Malonje (peak), Tanz. 104/A5
Malonno, It. 57/G5
Małopolska (uplands), Pol. 41/K3
Małopolskie (prov.), Pol. 41/K4
Malpartida de Cáceres, Sp. 44/B3
Malpartida de Plasencia, Sp. 44/B3
Malpelo (isl.), Col. 147/A2
Malpensa (int'l arpt.), It. 58/B1
Malpica, Sp. 44/A1
Malsch (riv.), Aus. 55/H5
Malsch, Ger. 54/B5
Malše (riv.), Czh. 41/H4
Mälstek (peak), Czh. 55/G4
Malta, Mt, US 126/G3
Malta, Braz. 154/C2
Malta (chan.), Malta 46/C4
Malta (ctry.) 46/L7
Maltahöhe, Namb. 105/C5
Maltby, Eng, UK 35/G5
Malters, Swi. 56/E3
Maltone (riv.), Fr. 30/G6
Malung, Swe. 38/E1
Malvaglia, Swi. 57/E5
Malvan, India 89/K5
Malveira, Port. 45/P10
Malvern, Pa, US 138/C3
Malverne, NY, US 139/L9
Malvinas (Falkland) (isls.), UK 160/W
Malvy Uzen' (riv.), Rus. 63/H2
Malyn, Ukr. 62/D2
Malyy Yenisey (riv.), Rus. 70/G1
Malzéville, Fr. 53/F6
Mamanguape, Braz. 154/D2
Mamaroneck, NY, US 139/L8
Mamba, Zam. 105/E4
Mamba, Japan 77/B1
Mambajao, Phil. 79/D6
Mambasa, D.R. Congo 104/A2
Mamberamo (riv.), Indo. 81/J4
Mambéré (riv.), CAfr. 96/J7
Mambij, Syria 90/D2
Mamburao, Phil. 81/F1
Mamer, Lux. 53/F4
Mamers, Fr. 42/D2
Mamfé, Camr. 103/H5
Mammendorf, Ger. 57/H1
Mamming, Ger. 55/F5
Mammoth, Az, US 128/E4
Mammoth Cave NP, Ky, US 133/G2
Mamoré (riv.), Braz. 150/E6
Mamou, La, US 129/J5
Mamoutzou, May. 107/H6
Mampikony, Madg. 107/H7
Mampong, Gha. 103/E5
Mamry (lake), Pol. 39/J4
Mamuju, Indo. 81/E4
Mamuri (riv.), Braz. 151/G4
Mamwera (peak), Tanz. 104/C4
Man, C.d'Iv. 102/D5
Man, Isle of (isl.), IM, UK 34/D3
Man Mia (peak), Thai. 78/B4
Mana (riv.), FrG. 153/H3
Manabí (prov.), Ecu. 152/A5
Manacapuru, Braz. 150/F4
Manacle (pt.), Eng, UK 32/A6
Manacor, Sp. 45/G3
Manado, Indo. 81/F3
Manage, Belg. 53/D3
Managua (lake), Nic. 140/D5
Managua (cap.), Nic. 144/E3
Manahawkin, NJ, US 138/D4
Manakambahiny, Madg. 107/J7
Manakara, Madg. 107/J8
Manalapan, NJ, US 138/D3
Manāli, India 86/D3
Manambaho (riv.), Madg. 107/H7
Manambolo (riv.), Madg. 107/H7
Mananantanana (riv.), Madg. 107/H8
Mananara, Madg. 107/J7
Mananara (riv.), Madg. 107/H8
Mananjary, Madg. 107/J8
Mananjary (riv.), Madg. 107/H8
Manara (pt.), It. 58/C4
Manaratsandry, Madg. 107/H7
Manas, China 70/E3
Manas (int'l arpt.), Kyr. 87/F4
Manas (peak), Kyr. 87/F4
Manās (riv.), India 85/H2
Manas (riv.), China 70/E2
Manāslu (peak), Nepal 85/E1
Manasquan, NJ, US 138/D3
Manasquan (riv.), NJ, US 138/D3
Manassa, Co, US 132/B2
Manastir Dečani, Serb. 47/G1
Manastir Gračanica, Serb. 47/G1
Manastir Sopoćani, Serb. 47/G1
Manatsuru, Japan 77/C3
Manaus, Braz. 150/F4
Manawatu (riv.), NZ 117/T11
Mañazo, Peru 156/D4
Manazuru-misaki (cape), Japan 77/C3
Mance (riv.), Fr. 56/B2
Mancha Real, Sp. 44/D4
Mancheng, China 72/G7
Mancherāl, India 82/C4
Manchester (lake), Austl. 114/E7
Manchester, Eng, UK 35/F5
Manchester (co.), Eng, UK 35/F5
Manchester (Ringway) (int'l arpt.), Eng, UK 35/F5
Manchester, Ky, US 130/D4
Manchester, Mo, US 137/F8
Manchester, Md, US 138/B4
Manchester, NH, US 131/G3
Manchester, Ct, US 138/B3
Manchester, Tn, US 133/G3
Manchester, Wa, US 135/B2
Manchuria (reg.), China 71/M3
Mancieulles, Fr. 53/E5
Máncora, Peru 156/A2
Mand (riv.), Iran 89/F3
Manda, PN de, Chad 96/J6
Mandabe, Madg. 107/H8
Mandaguari, Braz. 155/B2
Mandal, India 82/B3
Mandal, Nor. 38/B2
Mandal-Ovoo, Mong. 70/H3
Mandala (peak), Indo. 81/K4
Mandalay (div.), Myan. 70/F7
Mandalay, Myan. 83/G3
Mandalgovĭ, Mong. 70/J2
Mandalī, Iraq 88/E2
Mandan, ND, US 127/H4
Mandasavu (peak), Indo. 81/F5
Mandaue, Phil. 79/D5
Mandeb (str.), Afr.,Asia 93/G3
Mandello del Lario, It. 57/F6
Mandera, Kenya 97/P7
Mandeure, Fr. 56/C3
Mandeville, La, US 137/P16
Mandeville, Jam. 145/G2
Mandi Bahāuddīn, Pak. 86/B3
Mandi Dabwāli, India 86/C5
Mandi Sādiqganj, Pak. 86/B4
Mandié, Moz. 105/F4
Mandiola (isl.), Indo. 81/G4
Mandira (res.), India 85/E4
Mandla, India 84/C4
Mandø (isl.), Den. 38/C4
Mándok, Hun. 41/M4
Mandoto, Madg. 107/H7
Mandoúdhion, Gre. 47/H3
Mándra, Gre. 47/N8
Mandrare (riv.), Madg. 107/H9
Mandritsara, Madg. 107/J6
Mandsaur, India 89/L4
Mandurah, Austl. 112/B5
Manduria, It. 47/E2
Māndvi, India 89/J4
Mandya, India 82/C5
Mane (pass), Nepal 84/D1
Manéngouba, Massif du (peak), Camr. 103/H5
Maner, India 85/E3
Manerbio, It. 58/D2
Manfalūt, Egypt 88/B3
Manfredonia, It. 46/D2
Manfredonia, Golfo di (gulf), It. 46/D2
Mang (riv.), China 72/B4
Manga, Braz. 154/B4
Manga, Burk. 103/E4
Mangabeiras, Chapada das (hills), Braz. 151/J6
Mangai, D.R. Congo 105/C1
Mangaia (isl.), Cookls. 117/K7
Mangaldai, India 83/F2
Mangaldan, Phil. 79/D4
Mangalia, Rom. 49/J4
Mangalisa (peak), Tanz. 104/C4
Mangalore, India 82/B5
Mangaratiba, Braz. 211/J7
Mangareva (isl.), FrPol. 117/M7
Manger, Nor. 38/A1
Mangghystaū (obl.), Kaz. 64/F5
Mangghystaū Tūbegi (pen.), Kaz. 63/J3
Mangghystaū Ūstirti (plat.), Kaz. 63/K4
Mangkalihat (cape), Indo. 81/E3
Mangla (dam), Pak. 86/B3
Mangla, Pak. 86/B3
Mangla (res.), Pak. 86/B3
Manglaralto, Ecu. 156/A1
Manglares (pt.), Col. 152/B4
Manglaur, India 84/A1
Mangles (bay), Austl. 112/K7
Mango, Togo 103/F4
Mangoche, Malw. 105/G3
Mangoky (riv.), Madg. 105/J11
Mangole (isl.), Indo. 81/G4
Mangoro (riv.), Madg. 107/J7
Mangotsfield, Eng, UK 32/D4
Māngrol, India 89/K4
Mangualde, Port. 44/B2
Mangueira (lake), Braz. 159/G2
Mangum, Ok, US 129/H4
Manhasset, NY, US 139/L8
Manhasset (bay), NY, US 139/L8
Manhattan, Mt, US 126/F4
Manhattan (isl.),NY, US 139/K9
Manhattan Beach, Ca, US 136/F8
Manhay, Belg. 53/E3
Manheim, Pa, US 138/B3
Manhiça, Moz. 105/F6
Manhuaçu, Braz. 155/D2
Manhumirim, Braz. 155/D2
Mania (riv.), Madg. 107/H7
Maniamba, Moz. 105/G3
Maniāri (riv.), India 84/C4
Manicoré (riv.), Braz. 150/F5
Manicoré, Braz. 150/F5
Manicouagan (riv.), Qu, Can. 123/K3
Manicouagan (res.), Qu, Can. 131/G1
Manifold (cape), Austl. 114/C3
Manigotagan, Mb, Can. 127/J3
Manihāri, India 85/F3
Manihi (isl.), FrPol. 117/L6
Manihiki (isl.), Cookls. 117/J6
Manikarchar, India 85/G3
Manila (cap.), Phil. 79/D5
Manilla, Austl. 115/D1
Maningory (riv.), Madg. 107/J7
Manipa (str.), Indo. 81/G4
Manipat (hills), India 84/D4
Manipur (state), India 70/F7
Manisa (prov.), Turk. 90/B2
Manistee (riv.), Mi, US 130/C2
Manistee, Mi, US 130/C2
Manistique, Mi, US 130/C2
Manitoba (prov.), Can. 122/G3
Manitoba (lake), Mb, Can. 127/J3
Manitou (riv.), Qu, Can. 131/H1
Manitou Springs, Co, US 129/F3
Manitoulin (isl.), On, Can. 130/D2
Manitowoc, Wi, US 127/M4
Maniwaki, Qu, Can. 130/F2
Manizales, Col. 150/C2
Manja, Madg. 107/H8
Manjakandriana, Madg. 107/J7
Manjimup, Austl. 112/C5
Mankono, C.d'Iv. 102/D4
Manley Hot Springs, Ak, US 134/H2
Manlleu, Sp. 44/D1
Manlyutka, Rus. 61/R4
Manmād, India 89/K4
Mannar, SrL. 82/C6
Mannar (gulf), SrL.,India 67/G9
Männedorf, Swi. 57/E3
Mannetjiesberg (peak), SAfr. 106/C4
Mannheim, Ger. 54/B4
Manning, SC, US 133/H3
Manning (cape), NW, Can. 123/Q7
Manning, Ab, Can. 122/E3
Mannington Meadow (lake), NJ, US 138/C4
Männlifluh (peak), Swi. 56/D4
Mannum, Austl. 113/H5
Mano (riv.), Libr. 96/C6
Manokotak, Ak, US 134/G4
Manolo Fortich, Phil. 79/D6
Manombo, Madg. 107/G8
Manono, D.R. Congo 105/E2
Manorville, NY, US 139/F2
Manosque, Fr. 42/F5
Manouane (riv.), Qu, Can. 131/G1
Manouane (lake), Qu, Can. 131/G1
Manp'o, NKor. 73/D2
Manra (Sydney) (isl.), Kiri. 117/H5
Manresa, Sp. 45/K6
Mansa, Zam. 104/A5
Mānsa, India 86/C5
Mansa Konko, Gam. 102/B3
Mansalay, Phil. 81/F1
Mānsehra, Pak. 86/B2
Mansel (isl.), Nun., Can. 123/H2
Mansfield, Austl. 115/C3
Mansfield, Oh, US 130/D3
Mansfield, La, US 129/J4
Mansfield, Eng, UK 35/G5
Mansfield Woodhouse, Eng, UK 35/G5
Mansilla de las Mulas, Sp. 44/C1
Manta, Ecu. 152/A5
Mantalingajan (mt.), Phil. 81/E2
Mantaro (riv.), Peru 150/C6
Manteca, Ca, US 128/B3
Mantecal, Ven. 152/D3
Manteigas, Port. 44/B2
Mantena, Braz. 155/D1
Manthani, India 82/C4
Manti, Ut, US 128/E3
Mantiqueira, Serra da (mts.), Braz. 151/K8
Mantorp, Swe. 38/F2
Mantova (prov.), It. 58/D2
Mantova, It. 59/D2
Mäntsälä, Fin. 39/L1
Mantua, Ut, US 137/K11
Mantua, Cuba 145/E1
Mantua, NJ, US 138/C4
Manturovo, Rus. 61/K4
Mäntyharju, Fin. 39/M1
Manu (riv.), India 150/D6
Manú, Peru 156/D4
Manú, PN, Peru 150/D6
Manua (isls.), ASam. 117/J6
Manuae Atoll (atoll), Cookls. 117/K6
Manuel Alves da Natividade (riv.), Braz. 151/J6
Manuel Benavides, Mex. 132/C4
Manuel J. Cobo, Arg. 159/K11
Manui (isl.), Indo. 81/F4
Manuk (riv.), Indo. 80/C5
Manukau, NZ 117/S10
Manumuskin (riv.), NJ, US 138/D5
Manuripe (riv.), Bol. 150/E6
Manuripe Heath Amazonica, Reserva Nacional, Bol. 156/D4
Manus (isl.), PNG 116/D5
Manville, NJ, US 138/D2
Many, La, US 129/J5
Many Farms, Az, US 128/E3
Manyara (lake), Tanz. 104/B3
Manych (riv.), Rus. 64/E5
Manych-Gudilo (lake), Rus. 63/G3
Manzanares, Sp. 44/D3
Manzanares (riv.), Sp. 45/N8
Manzanares el Real, Sp. 45/N8
Manzanillo, Mex. 142/D5
Manzanillo (int'l arpt.), Mex. 142/D5
Manzanillo, Cuba 145/G1
Manzano (mts.), NM, US 132/B3
Manzano, It. 59/G1
Manzhouli, China 71/L2
Manzil Bū Zalafah, Tun. 46/B4
Manzil Tamīn, Tun. 46/B4
Manzilah, Buḩayrat al (lake), Egypt 91/B4
Manzini, Swaz. 107/E2
Mao, Chad 96/J5
Maoke (mts.), Indo. 81/J4
Maoming, China 83/K3
Mapastepec, Mex. 144/C3
Mapi (riv.), Indo. 81/J5
Mapimí, Bolsón de (depr.), Mex. 142/D3
Mapire, Ven. 153/E3
Maple (riv.), ND, US 127/J4
Maple Creek, Sk, Can. 126/F3
Maple Grove, Qu, Can. 131/N7
Maple Park, Il, US 135/N16
Maple Shade, NJ, US 138/D4
Maple Valley, Wa, US 135/C3
Mapleton, Ut, US 137/K13
Maplewood, Mo, US 137/G8
Maplewood, NJ, US 139/H9
Maporal, Ven. 152/D3
Mapuera (riv.), Braz. 150/G3
Maputo (int'l arpt.), Moz. 107/F2
Maputo (cap.), Moz. 107/F2
Maqdam (cape), Sudan 101/D5
Maqên Gangri (peak), China 70/G5
Maquan (Damqog) (riv.), China 84/E1
Maquinchao, Arg. 158/C4
Maquoketa (riv.), Ia, US 129/K2
Mar (mts.), Braz. 147/E5
Mar (reg.), Sc, UK 36/D2
Mar Chiquita (lake), Arg. 157/D3
Mar de Ajó, Arg. 159/F3
Mar del Plata, Arg. 158/F3
Mar del Tuyú, Arg. 159/F3
Mara (pol. reg.), Tanz. 104/B3
Mara (riv.), Tanz. 104/B3
Marabá, Braz. 151/J5
Maracá, Ilha de (isl.), Braz. 151/H3
Maracaibo, Ven. 152/D2
Maracaibo (lake), Ven. 147/B2
Maracaju, Serra de (mts.), Braz. 151/G8
Maracás, Braz. 154/B4
Maracás, Chapada de (hills), Braz. 154/B4
Maracay, Ven. 150/E1
Maracena, Sp. 44/D4
Marādah, Libya 96/J2
Maradi, Niger 103/G3
Maradi (dept.), Niger 103/G3
Marāgheh, Iran 88/E1
Mārahra, India 84/B2
Marahuaca (peak), Ven. 153/E4
Marais de St-Gond (swamp), Fr. 52/C6
Marais des Cygnes (riv.), Ks,Mo, US 129/J3
Marajó (bay), Braz. 147/E3
Marajó, Ilha de (isl.), Braz. 147/D3
Maralal, Kenya 104/C2
Maralinga-Tjarutja Abor. Land, Austl. 113/F4
Maramag, Phil. 79/E6
Marambaia, Ilha (isl.), Braz. 211/K8
Maramureş (co.), Rom. 41/M5
Marana, Az, US 128/E4
Marana (lag.), Cro. 59/G1
Marand, Iran 63/H5
Marang, Malay. 80/B2
Marangani, Peru 156/D4
Maranguape, Braz. 154/C1
Maranhão (riv.), Braz. 151/J6
Maranhão (state), Braz. 154/A2
Marano Lagunare, It. 59/G1
Marano sul Panaro, It. 59/D4
Marano Vicentino, It. 59/E1
Maranoa (riv.), Austl. 109/D3
Marañón (riv.), Peru 147/B3
Marans, Fr. 42/C3
Maraoue, PN de la, C.d'Iv. 102/D5
Marapi (peak), Indo. 80/B4
Maras (peak), Indo. 80/C4
Mărăşeşti, Rom. 49/H3
Marathon, On, Can. 127/M3
Marathon, Fl, US 133/H5
Marathon, Tx, US 132/C4
Marathón, Gre. 47/N8
Marau, Braz. 155/A4
Marauliānwāla, Pak. 86/B3
Maravatío de Ocampo, Mex. 143/E5
Marawi, Phil. 81/F2
Marbach, Swi. 56/D4

arbach am Neckar, er. 54/C5
arbache, Fr. 53/F6
arbella, Sp. 44/C4
arble Bar, Austl. 112/C2
arbleton, y, US 126/F5
arburg, Ger. 43/H1
arburg (lake), , US 138/B4
arca, Ponta da (pt.), ng. 105/B4
arcali, Hun. 48/C2
arcallo, It. 58/B2
arcapata, Peru 156/D4
arch, Eng, UK 33/G1
arche (prov.), It. 43/K5
arche (mts.), Fr. 42/D3
arche-en-Famenne, elg. 53/E3
archémoret, Fr. 30/L4
archena, Sp. 44/C4
archena (isl.), Ecu. 156/E6
archeno, It. 58/D1
archiennes, Fr. 52/C3
archin, Belg. 53/E3
archtrenk, Aus. 55/H6
arciana Marina, It. 46/B1
arcilly, Fr. 30/L4
arcilly-sur-Tille, Fr. 56/B2
arck, Fr. 52/A2
arckolsheim, Fr. 56/D1
arco, Braz. 154/B1
arco, Fl, US 133/H5
arco Polo nt'l arpt.), It. 59/F2
arcoing, Fr. 52/C3
arcon, It. 59/F1
arcona, Peru 156/C4
arconi (mt.), C, Can. 126/E3
arcos Juárez, Arg. 158/E2
arcoussis, Fr. 30/J6
arcovia, Hon. 144/E3
arcq-en-Barœul, Fr. 52/C2
arcus Baker (mt.), k, US 134/J3
arcy (mt.), Y, US 130/F2
ardān, Pak. 86/B2
arden, Eng, UK 30/E3
ardeuil, Fr. 52/C5
ardin (town), urk. 90/E2
arecchia (riv.), It. 59/F5
aree (lake), c, UK 31/R8
areeba, Austl. 114/B2
areil-sur-Mauldre, Fr. 30/H5
arengo, Il, US 135/N15
arennes, Fr. 42/C4
areuil-sur-Ourcq, Fr. 30/M4
arfa, Tx, US 129/F5
argalla Hills NP, ak. 86/B3
arganets', Ukr. 62/E3
argao (Madgaon), ndia 89/K5
argaret (mt.), Austl. 112/C2
argaret River, ustl. 112/B5
argarita (peak), a, US 136/C4
argarita, Isla de sl.), Ven. 150/F1
argarition, Gre. 47/G3
argate, SAfr. 107/E3
argate, Eng, UK 33/H4
argate City, J, US 138/D5
argeride, Monts de la mts.), Fr. 42/E4
argherita (peak), gan. 104/A2
arghilon, Uzb. 87/F4
arghita, Rom. 48/F2
argny-lès-Compiègne, r. 52/B5
argos, Peru 156/B3
argosatubig, Phil. 81/F2
argraten, Neth. 53/E2
ari, Braz. 154/D2
aria (mt.), Austl. 115/D4
aría Cleófas (isl.), ex. 142/D4
aria da Fé, raz. 211/H7
aria Island NP, ustl. 115/D4
aría Madre (isl.), ex. 142/D4
aría Magdalena (isl.), ex. 142/D4
aria van Diemen cape), NZ 117/S9
ariāhū, India 84/D3
arian, Austl. 114/C3
arianao, Cuba 145/F1
arianna, Fl, US 133/G4
arianna, Ar, US 129/K4
ariano Comense, It. 58/C1
ariano Marcos, Phil. 79/D6
ariánské Lázně, zh. 55/F3
arias (riv.), Mt, US 126/F3
ariato (pt.), Pan. 152/A3
aribo, Den. 38/D4
aribor, Slov. 43/L3
aricá, Braz. 211/L7
aricopa (co.), Az, US 137/R18
arié (riv.), Braz. 150/E4
arie Byrd Land (phys. reg.), Ant. 160/S
Marie-Galante (isl.), Dom. 141/J4
Mariehamn (int'l arpt.), Fin. 39/H1
Mariel, Cuba 145/F1
Marienhafe, Ger. 51/E1
Marienheide, Ger. 53/G1
Mariental, Namb. 105/C5
Mariestad, Swe. 38/E2
Marietta, Ok, US 129/H4
Marietta, Ga, US 133/G3
Marietta, Pa, US 138/B3
Marignane, Fr. 42/F5
Marigot, Dom. 141/N9
Marijampolė, Lith. 39/K4
Marília, Braz. 155/B2
Marín, Sp. 44/A1
Marin (co.), Ca, US 135/J10
Marin-Epagnier, Swi. 56/D3
Marina, It. 46/D3
Marina del Rey, Ca, US 136/F8
Marina del Rey (har.), Ca, US 136/F8
Marina di Andora, It. 58/B5
Marina di Montemarciano, It. 59/G5
Marina di Ravenna, It. 59/F4
Marine Nat'l Rsv., Kenya 104/D3
Marine World Africa USA, Ca, US 135/K10
Marineland, Austl. 113/M8
Marines, Fr. 30/H4
Marinette, Wi, US 127/M4
Maringá, Braz. 155/B2
Marinha Grande, Port. 44/A3
Marinhas, Port. 44/A2
Marion, Ky, US 130/B4
Marion, Mi, US 130/C2
Marion, In, US 130/C3
Marion, Oh, US 130/D3
Marion (reef), Austl. 109/E2
Marion, Al, US 133/G3
Marion (lake), SC, US 125/K5
Maripa, Ven. 153/E3
Mariposa, Ca, US 128/C3
Mariscal Estigarribia, Par. 150/F8
Mariscal Sucre (int'l arpt.), Ecu. 152/B5
Maritime Alps (mts.), Fr. 43/G4
Maritsa (riv.), Bul. 62/C4
Mariupol' (int'l arpt.), Ukr. 62/F3
Mariupol', Ukr. 62/F3
Mariy-El, Resp., Rus. 64/Q6
Marj 'Uyūn, Leb. 91/D3
Mark (riv.), Belg. 50/B6
Mark Twain NWR, Il, US 137/F7
Mark Twain (lake), Mo, US 129/J3
Mark Twain NWR, Mo, US 137/G8
Marka (riv.), Ger. 51/E3
Marka (Merca), Som. 97/P7
Markam, China 83/G2
Markaryd, Swe. 38/E3
Markdorf, Ger. 57/F2
Markelsdorfer (pt.), Ger. 38/D4
Marken (isl.), Neth. 50/C4
Markerwaard (polder), Neth. 50/C3
Market Harborough, Eng, UK 33/F2
Markgroningen, Ger. 54/C5
Markham, On, Can. 131/R8
Markham (bay), Nun., Can. 123/J2
Marki, Pol. 41/L2
Markinch, Sc, UK 36/C4
Markit, China 87/G5
Markleeville, Ca, US 128/C3
Markneukirchen, Ger. 55/F2
Markópoulon, Gre. 47/N9
Markovac, Serb. 48/E3
Marks, Rus. 63/H2
Marksville, La, US 129/J5
Markt Bibart, Ger. 54/D3
Markt Erlbach, Ger. 54/D4
Markt Indersdorf, Ger. 55/E6
Markt Rettenbach, Ger. 57/G2
Markt Sankt Florian, Aus. 55/H6
Markt Schwaben, Ger. 55/E6
Marktbreit, Ger. 54/D3
Marktheidenfeld, Ger. 54/C3
Marktl, Ger. 55/F6
Marktoberdorf, Ger. 57/G2
Marktredwitz, Ger. 55/F3
Marl, Ger. 51/E5
Marla, Austl. 113/G3
Marlboro, NJ, US 138/D3
Marlboro (Upper Marlboro), Md, US 138/B6
Marle, Fr. 52/C4
Marlengo (Marling), It. 57/H4
Marlenheim, Fr. 53/G6
Marles-en-Brie, Fr. 30/L5
Marles-les-Mines, Fr. 52/B3
Marlow, Eng, UK 33/F3
Marlow, Ger. 38/E4
Marlton, NJ, US 138/D4
Marly, Fr. 53/F5
Marly, Fr. 52/C3
Marly-la-Ville, Fr. 30/K4
Marly-le-Roi, Fr. 30/J5
Marmagão, India 89/K5
Marmande, Fr. 42/D4
Marmara, Turk. 49/H5
Marmara (isl.), Turk. 49/H5
Marmara (sea), Turk. 49/J5
Marmaraereğlisi, Turk. 49/H5
Marmaris, Turk. 90/B2
Marmelos (riv.), Braz. 150/F5
Marmion (lake), Austl. 109/A3
Marmirolo, It. 59/D2
Marmolada (peak), It. 43/J3
Marmolejo, Sp. 44/C3
Marmontana (peak), It. 57/F5
Marmora, NJ, US 138/D5
Marmoutier, Fr. 53/G6
Marnay, Fr. 56/B3
Marnaz, Fr. 56/C5
Marne (riv.), Fr. 42/F2
Marne, Ger. 38/C5
Marne (dept.), Fr. 52/C6
Marne au Rhin, Canal de la (canal), Fr. 53/D6
Maro (reef), Hi, US 117/H2
Maroa, Ven. 153/E4
Maroantsetra, Madg. 107/J6
Marokau (isl.), FrPol. 117/L6
Marolambo, Madg. 107/J8
Maroldsweisach, Ger. 54/D2
Marolles-en-Brie, Fr. 30/M5
Marolles-en-Hurepoix, Fr. 30/J6
Maromokotro (peak), Madg. 107/J6
Marondera, Zim. 105/F4
Marone, It. 58/D1
Maroni (riv.), FrG.,Sur. 147/D2
Maroochydore-Mooloolaba, Austl. 114/D4
Maroon Town, Jam. 145/G2
Marostica, It. 59/E1
Marotandrano, Madg. 107/J7
Marotiri (Bass Is.) (isls.), FrPol. 117/L7
Marotta, It. 59/G5
Maroua, Camr. 96/H5
Marouini (riv.), FrG. 153/H4
Marovato, Madg. 107/J6
Marovoay, Madg. 107/H7
Marowijne (dist.), Sur. 153/H3
Marpingen, Ger. 53/G5
Marple, Eng, UK 35/F5
Marquan (riv.), China 82/E2
Marquard, SAfr. 106/D3
Marquarie (riv.), Austl. 115/C1
Marquesas (isls.), FrPol. 117/M5
Marquise, Fr. 52/A2
Marracuene, Moz. 107/F2
Marradi, It. 59/E4
Marrah (mts.), Sudan 97/K5
Marrah (peak), Sudan 97/K5
Marrakech, Mor. 98/D3
Marrero, La, US 137/P17
Marromeu, Moz. 105/G4
Marrupa, Moz. 105/G3
Mars (peak), It. 58/A1
Marsá al Burayqah, Libya 96/J1
Marsá Maţrūḩ (cap.), Egypt 101/A2
Marsabit, Kenya 104/C2
Marsabit Nat'l Rsv., Kenya 104/C2
Marsala, It. 46/C4
Marsange (riv.), Fr. 30/L5
Marsannay, Fr. 56/A3
Marsberg, Ger. 51/F6
Marsciano, It. 43/K5
Marsdiep Texelstroom (chan.), Neth. 50/B3
Marseille, Fr. 42/F5
Marseille-en-Beauvaisis, Fr. 52/A4
Marsh (isl.), La, US 140/C2
Marshall, Sk, Can. 126/F2
Marshall, Mn, US 127/K4
Marshall, Tx, US 129/J4
Marshall, Mo, US 129/J3
Marshall, Co, US 137/B3
Marshall, Ut, US 137/J12
Marshall (riv.), Austl. 113/H2
Marshall Islands (ctry.) 116/G3
Marshallton, De, US 138/C4
Marshalltown, Ia, US 127/K5
Marshdale, Co, US 137/B3
Marshfield, Mo, US 129/J3
Märsta, Swe. 38/G2
Marston (lake), Co, US 137/B3
Marsyandi (riv.), Nepal 85/E1
Marta, It. 46/B1
Marta (mts.), Col. 145/H4
Martaban, Myan. 78/B2
Martaban (gulf), Myan. 78/B2
Martapura, Indo. 80/D4
Marte R. Gomez, Mex. 142/C3
Martelange, Belg. 53/E4
Martellago, It. 59/F1
Martensville, Sk, Can. 126/G2
Martfeld, Ger. 51/G3
Martha's Vineyard (isl.), Ma, US 131/G3
Martignacco, It. 59/G1
Martigny, Swi. 56/D5
Martigny-les-Bains, Fr. 56/B1
Martigues, Fr. 42/F5
Martil, Mor. 100/B2
Martin, Tn, US 130/B4
Martin (lake), Al, US 133/G3
Martin Vaz (isls.), Braz. 151/N8
Martina Franca, It. 47/E2
Martinengo, It. 58/C1
Martinez, Ga, US 133/H3
Martínez de la Torre, Mex. 143/M6
Martinho Campos, Braz. 155/C1
Martinique (isl.), Fr. 141/N9
Martinique Passage (chan.), Dom.,Mart. 141/J4
Martinon, Gre. 47/H3
Martinópole, Braz. 154/B1
Martinópolis, Braz. 155/B2
Martins, Braz. 154/C2
Martins Creek, Pa, US 138/C2
Martinsburg, WV, US 130/E4
Martinsville, Va, US 130/E4
Martorell, Sp. 45/K7
Martos, Sp. 44/D4
Martre (riv.), Qu, Can. 130/F1
Martres-Tolosane, Fr. 42/D5
Marty, SD, US 127/J5
Marugame, Japan 74/C3
Maruim, Braz. 154/C3
Maruko, Japan 75/F2
Marum, Neth. 50/D2
Maruoka, Japan 74/E2
Marutea (isl.), FrPol. 117/M7
Marv Dasht, Iran 88/F3
Marxheim, Ger. 54/D5
Mary, Trkm. 89/H1
Mary Anne Passage, Austl. 112/B2
Mary Esther, Fl, US 133/G4
Mary-sur-Marne, Fr. 30/M4
Maryborough, Austl. 115/B3
Maryborough, Austl. 114/D4
Marydale, SAfr. 106/C3
Marydel, Md, US 138/C5
Maryfield, Sk, Can. 127/H3
Maryland (co.), Libr. 102/C5
Maryland (state), US 130/E4
Maryland City, Md, US 138/B5
Maryland Heights, Mo, US 137/G8
Maryland Line, Md, US 138/B4
Marystown, Nf, Can. 131/L2
Marysville, Ks, US 129/H3
Marysville, Pa, US 138/B3
Maryville, Tn, US 133/H3
Maryville, Il, US 137/H8
Marzabotto, It. 59/E4
Marzano (peak), It. 46/D2
Marzo (pt.), Col. 152/B3
Marzūq, Libya 96/H2
Masada (ruin), Isr. 91/D4
Masai Mara Nat'l Rsv., Kenya 105/F1
Masai Steppe (grsld.), Tanz. 104/C4
Masaka, Ugan. 104/A3
Masākin, Tun. 46/B5
Masamagrell, Sp. 45/E3
Masamba, Indo. 81/F4
Masan, SKor. 73/E5
Masangwe (hill), Tanz. 104/A4
Masaya, Nic. 144/E4
Masbate (isl.), Phil. 79/D5
Mascara, Alg. 100/F5
Mascarene (isls.), Mrts 107/T15
Mascota, Mex. 142/D4
Mascouche, Qu, Can. 131/N6
Maselheim, Ger. 57/F1
Maserà di Padova, It. 59/E2
Maseru (cap.), Les. 106/D3
Masevaux, Fr. 56/D2
Masfjorden, Nor. 38/A1
Mashan, China 79/A3
Mashhad (int'l arpt.), Iran 87/C5
Mashike, Japan 76/B2
Māshkīd (riv.), Iran 89/H3
Mashtūl as Sūq, Egypt 91/B4
Mashū (lake), Japan 76/D2
Masiaca, Mex. 142/C3
Maside, Sp. 44/A1
Masim (peak), Rus. 63/L1
Masindi, Ugan. 104/A2
Maşirah, Jazīrat (isl.), Oman 67/F5
Masisea, Peru 156/C3
Masjed-e Soleymān, Iran 88/E2
Mask (lake), Ire. 31/P10
Masker (peak), Mor. 98/D2
Masnou, Sp. 45/L7
Masoala (cape), Madg. 107/J6
Masoala (pen.), Madg. 105/L10
Masoarivo, Madg. 107/H7
Mason, Mi, US 130/C3
Mason, Tx, US 129/H5
Mason (co.), Wa, US 135/A3
Mason (lake), Wa, US 135/B3
Mason and Dixon Line, Pa, US 138/B4
Masone, It. 58/B4
Masonville, Co, US 137/B2
Masquefa, Sp. 45/K6
Massa, It. 58/D4
Massa-Carrara (prov.), It. 58/C4
Massa Finalese, It. 59/E3
Massa Fiscaglia, It. 59/F3
Massa Lombarda, It. 59/E4
Massa Marittima, It. 43/J5
Massa Martana, It. 43/K5
Massachusetts (state), US 131/F3
Massachusetts (bay), Ma, US 131/G3
Massaciuccoli, Lago di (lake), It. 58/D5
Massafra, It. 47/E2
Massangena, Moz. 105/F5
Massapê, Braz. 154/B1
Massapequa, NY, US 139/M9
Massapequa Park, NY, US 139/M9
Massarosa, It. 58/D5
Massbach, Ger. 54/D2
Massena, NY, US 130/F2
Masset, BC, Can. 134/M4
Massey (sound), Nun., Can. 123/S7
Massey, Md, US 138/C5
Massillon, Oh, US 130/D3
Massy, Fr. 30/J5
Masterton, NZ 117/T11
Mastgat (chan.), Neth. 50/B5
Mastic, NY, US 139/F2
Mastic Beach, NY, US 139/F2
Mastník (riv.), Czh. 55/H3
Mastūj (riv.), Pak. 86/A2
Mastung, Pak. 89/J3
Masuda, Japan 74/B3
Masuho, Japan 77/A2
Masurai (peak), Indo. 80/B4
Masvingo, Zim. 105/F5
Maswa Game Rsv., Tanz. 104/B3
Maşyāf, Syria 91/E2
Mat (riv.), Alb. 47/F2
Mata Grande, Braz. 154/C3
Mata Utu, Fr. 117/H6
Mātābhānga, India 85/G2
Matadi, D.R. Congo 105/B2
Matador, Tx, US 129/G4
Matagalpa, Nic. 144/E3
Matagami (lake), Qu, Can. 130/E1
Matagorda (bay), Tx, US 140/B2
Matagorda (isl.), Tx, US 140/B2
Matale, SrL. 82/D6
Matam, Sen. 102/B3
Matamoras, Pa, US 138/D1
Matamoros, Mex. 142/E3
Ma'ţan as Sarra (well), Libya 97/K3
Matandu (riv.), Tanz. 104/C5
Matane (riv.), Qu, Can. 131/H1
Matane, Qu, Can. 131/H1
Matanga, Madg. 107/H8
Matanzas, Cuba 140/E3
Matão, Braz. 155/B2
Matape (riv.), Mex. 142/C2
Matapedia (riv.), Qu, Can. 131/H1
Mataquito (riv.), Chile 158/C2
Matara (ruin), Erit. 88/C6
Matara, SrL. 82/D6
Mataram, Indo. 81/E5
Mataránga, Gre. 47/G3
Mataró, Sp. 45/L6
Matatiele, SAfr. 106/E3
Mataura (riv.), NZ 117/R12
Matawan, NJ, US 139/J10
Matehuala, Mex. 143/E4
Matéri, Ben. 103/F4
Matermillos (pt.), Cuba 141/F3
Mátészalka, Hun. 41/M5
Mathay, Fr. 56/C3
Matheniko Game Rsv., Ugan. 104/B2
Mathew's (peak), Kenya 104/C2
Mathews (lake), Ca, US 136/C3
Mathis, Tx, US 132/D4
Mathoura, Austl. 115/C2
Mathurā, India 84/A2
Mati, Phil. 79/E6
Matias Barbosa, Braz. 211/K6
Matias Olímpio, Braz. 154/B1
Matías Romero, Mex. 144/C2
Matiguás, Nic. 144/E3
Matilija (dam), Ca, US 136/A2
Matinha, Braz. 154/A2
Matinhos, Braz. 155/B3
Matinicock (pt.), NY, US 139/L8
Mātir, Tun. 46/A4
Matiyuri (riv.), Ven. 152/D3
Mātla (riv.), India 85/G5
Matlock, Eng, UK 35/G5
Mato Grosso (plat.), Braz. 147/D4
Mato Grosso do Sul (state), Braz. 155/A1
Mato Grosso, Planalto do (plat.), Braz. 151/H6
Mato Verde, Braz. 154/B4
Matopos, Zim. 105/E5
Matosinhos, Port. 44/A2
Matoya (bay), Japan 77/L7
Maţraḩ, Oman 89/G4
Matrei am Brenner, Aus. 57/H3
Matrei in Osttirol, Aus. 43/K3
Matriz de Camaragibe, Braz. 154/D3
Matroosberg (peak), SAfr. 106/L10
Matsalu (gulf), Est. 39/K2
Matsapa (Manzini) (int'l arpt.), Swaz. 107/E2
Matsiatra (riv.), Madg. 107/H8
Matsoandakana, Madg. 107/J6
Matsubara, Japan 77/J6
Matsubushi, Japan 77/D2
Matsuda, Japan 77/C3
Matsudo, Japan 77/D2
Matsue, Japan 74/C3
Matsuida, Japan 77/B1
Matsumae, Japan 76/B3
Matsumoto, Japan 75/E2
Matsuo, Japan 77/E2
Matsusaka, Japan 77/L6
Matsushima, Japan 76/B4
Matsutō, Japan 74/E2
Matsuyama, Japan 74/C4
Matt, Swi. 57/F4
Mattagami (riv.), On, Can. 130/D1
Mattarello, It. 57/H6
Mattawa, On, Can. 130/E2
Matterhorn (peak), It.,Swi. 56/D6
Mattertal (valley), Swi. 56/D5
Mattese, Mo, US 137/G9
Matthews (mtn.), Ak, US 134/H2
Mattig (riv.), Aus. 55/G6
Mattighofen, Aus. 55/G6
Mattituck, NY, US 139/F2
Mattmarksee (lake), Swi. 56/D5
Mattō, Japan 74/E2
Mattock (riv.), Ire. 34/B4
Mattsee, Aus. 55/G7
Matucana, Peru 156/B3
Maturín, Ven. 153/F2
Matusadona NP, Zim. 105/E4
Matzen, Aus. 49/P7
Maú (riv.), Guy. 150/G3
Mau (peak), Kenya 104/B3
Mau Aimma, India 84/C3
Mau Rānīpur, India 84/B3
Mauá, Braz. 155/C2
Maubert-Fontaine, Fr. 53/D4
Maubeuge, Fr. 52/C3
Maubourguet, Fr. 42/D5
Mauchline, Sc, UK 36/B5
Maud (pt.), Austl. 112/B2
Maud, Sc, UK 36/D1
Maudaha, India 84/C3
Mauerbach, Aus. 49/N7
Mauerkirchen, Aus. 55/G6
Maués, Braz. 150/G4
Maués Açu (riv.), Braz. 150/G4
Maug (isls.), NMar. 116/D2
Mauganj, India 84/C3
Maughold, IM, UK 34/D3
Maughold (pt.), IM, UK 34/D3
Mauguio, Fr. 42/F5
Maui (isl.), Hi, US 124/T10
Mauke (isl.), CookIs. 117/K7
Maulbronn, Ger. 54/B5
Mauldre (riv.), Fr. 52/A6
Maule (pol. reg.), Chile 158/B2
Maule (riv.), Chile 158/C2
Maule, Fr. 30/H5
Mauléon, Fr. 42/C3
Maullín, Chile 158/B4
Maumee (riv.), In,Oh, US 130/C3
Maun, Bots. 105/D4
Mauna Kea (peak), Hi, US 124/U11
Mauna Loa (peak), Hi, US 124/U11
Maunath Bhanjan, India 84/D3
Maungdaw, Myan. 83/F3
Mauperthuis, Fr. 30/M5
Maupertus (int'l arpt.), Fr. 42/C2
Maupiti (isl.), FrPol. 117/K6
Maur, Swi. 57/E3
Maurāwān, India 84/C2
Maurecourt, Fr. 30/J5
Maurepas (lake), La, US 137/P16
Maurepas, Fr. 52/A6
Mauriac, Fr. 42/E4
Maurice (lake), Austl. 109/C3
Maurice (riv.), NJ, US 138/C5
Mauricetown, NJ, US 138/D5
Maurienne (valley), Fr. 43/G4
Maurilândia, Braz. 155/B1
Mauritania (ctry.) 96/C4
Mauriti, Braz. 154/C2
Mauritius (ctry.) 107/T15
Mauston, Wi, US 127/L5
Mauthausen, Aus. 55/H6
Mauvoisin, Barrage de (dam), Swi. 56/D6
Mavrommátion, Gre. 47/H3
Mavrovo NP, FYROM 47/G2
Maw Daung (pass), Thai. 78/B4
Mawāna, India 84/A1
Mawlaik, Myan. 83/F3
Mawlamyine (Moulmein), Myan. 78/B2
Mawson, Austl., Ant. 160/E
Maxaranguape, Braz. 154/D2
Maxcanú, Mex. 144/D1
Maxdorf, Ger. 54/B4
Maxéville, Fr. 53/F6
Maxhütte-Haidhof, Ger. 55/F4
May (cape), NJ, US 138/D5
May-en-Multien, Fr. 30/M4
May, Isle of (isl.), Sc, UK 36/D4
May Pen, Jam. 145/G2
Maya (isl.), Indo. 80/C4
Maya (riv.), Rus. 67/N4
Maya (mts.), Guat. 144/D2
Maya-san (peak), Japan 77/H6
Mayaguana (isl.), Bahm. 141/G3
Mayaguana Passage (chan.), Bahm. 145/H1
Mayagüez, PR 141/M8
Mayakovskogo (peak), Taj. 89/K1
Mayang, China 83/J2
Mayarí, Cuba 145/H1
Maybee, Mi, US 135/E8
Maybole, Sc, UK 36/B6
Maydān, Iraq 88/E2
Mayen, Ger. 53/G3
Mayenne, Fr. 42/C2
Mayenne (riv.), Fr. 42/C3
Mayerthorpe, Ab, Can. 126/E2
Mayfield, Ky, US 130/B4
Mayfield, Sc, UK 36/C5
Maykop, Rus. 62/G3
Maymyo, Myan. 83/G3
Maynooth, Ire. 31/Q10
Mayo (riv.), Arg. 157/B6
Mayo, Yk, Can. 134/L3
Mayo, Md, US 138/B6
Mayotte (isl.), May. 107/H6
Mays Landing, NJ, US 138/D5
Maysville, Ky, US 130/D4
Maythalūn, WBnk. 91/G7
Mayville, ND, US 127/J4
Maywood, NJ, US 139/J8
Maywood, Il, US 135/Q16
Maywood, Ca, US 136/F8
Mazabuka, Zam. 105/E4
Mazagão, Braz. 151/H4
Mazamet, Fr. 42/E5
Mazán, Peru 156/C1
Mazār-e Sharīf, Afg. 89/J1
Mazara del Vallo, It. 46/C4
Mazara, Val di (valley), It. 46/C4
Mazarrón, Sp. 44/E4
Mazaruni (riv.), Guy. 150/G2
Mazatán, Mex. 142/C2
Mazatenango, Guat. 144/D3
Mazatlán, Mex. 142/D4
Mažeikiai, Lith. 39/K3
Mazeppa NP, Austl. 114/B3
Mazgirt, Turk. 90/D2
Mazıkıran (pass), Turk. 90/D2
Mazingarbe, Fr. 52/B3
Mazocruz, Peru 156/D5
Mazong (peak), China 70/G3
Mazowieckie (prov.), Pol. 41/L2
Mazury (reg.), Pol. 41/L2
Mazyr, Bela. 62/D1
Mbabala (isl.), Zam. 104/A5
Mbabane (cap.), Swaz. 107/E2
Mbabo (peak), Camr. 96/H6
Mbacké, Sen. 102/B3
Mbaïki, CAfr. 96/J7
Mbakaou, Lac de (lake), Camr. 96/H6
Mbala, Zam. 104/A5
Mbale, Ugan. 104/B2
Mbalmayo, Camr. 96/H7
Mbandaka, D.R. Congo 97/J7
Mbarangandu (riv.), Tanz. 104/C5
Mbarara, Ugan. 104/A3
Mbata, CAfr. 97/J7
Mbeya (peak), Tanz. 104/B5
Mbeya (range), Tanz. 105/F2
Mbeya, Tanz. 104/B5
Mbeya (pol. reg.), Tanz. 104/B5
Mbini, EqG. 96/G7
Mbini (riv.), EqG.,Gabo 96/H7
Mbirizi, Ugan. 104/A3
Mbomou (riv.), CAfr. 97/K7
M'Bour, Sen. 102/A3
Mbuji-Mayi, D.R. Congo 105/D2
Mbwemburu (riv.), Tanz. 104/C5
McAdoo, Pa, US 138/C2
McAfee, NJ, US 138/D1
McAlester, Ok, US 129/J4
McAlisterville, Pa, US 138/A2
McAllen, Tx, US 132/D5
McBride, BC, Can. 126/C2
McCall, Id, US 126/D4
McCarran (int'l arpt.), Nv, US 128/D3
McCarthy, Ak, US 134/K3
McClain (co.), Ok, US 137/M15
McClure, Pa, US 138/A2
McClusky, Il, US 137/G7
McClusky, ND, US 127/H4
McComb, Ms, US 129/K5
McConaughy (lake), Ne, US 127/H5
McCook, Ne, US 129/G2
McCormick, SC, US 133/H3
McCreary, Mb, Can. 127/J3
McCullom Lake, Il, US 135/P15
McDaniel, Md, US 138/B6
McDermitt, Nv, US 126/D5
McDonald (mt.), Ak, US 134/F3
McDonald (isls.), Austl. 23/N8
McDonnell (mt.), Austl. 113/H5
McDougall (pass), NW,Yk, Can. 134/L2
McDowell (mts.), Az, US 137/S18
McElhattan, Pa, US 138/A1
McGhee Tyson (int'l arpt.), Tn, US 133/H3
McGrath, Ak, US 134/G3
McGregor (riv.), BC, Can. 126/C2
McGregor, On, Can. 135/G7
McHenry (co.), Il, US 135/N15
McKean (isl.), Kiri. 117/H5
McKeand (riv.), Nun., Can. 123/K2
McKee City, NJ, US 138/D5
McKeesport, Pa, US 130/E3
McKenzie, Tn, US 130/B4
McKinlay, Austl. 114/A3
McKinley (mt.), Ak, US 134/H3
McKinleyville, Ca, US 126/B5
McLaughlin, SD, US 127/H4
McLean, Va, US 138/A6
McLennan, Ab, Can. 126/D2
McLeod (riv.), BC, Can. 126/D2
McLeod (lake), Austl. 109/A3
McLeod (bay), NW, Can. 122/E2
McLeod Lake, BC, Can. 126/C2
M'Clintock (chan.), Nun., Can. 122/F1
McLoud, Ok, US 137/N15
M'Clure (str.), NW, Can. 123/Q7
McMinnville, Or, US 126/C4
McMinnville, Tn, US 130/C5
McMurdo, US, Ant. 160/M
McNeil (isl.), Wa, US 135/B3
McPherson, Ks, US 129/H3
McQueeney, Tx, US 137/U20
Mdantsane, SAfr. 106/D4
M'diq, Mor. 100/B2
Me-akan-dake (peak), Japan 76/C2
Mead, Co, US 137/C2

206
Mead – Milfo

Mead (lake), Az,Nv, US 128/D3
Meade (riv.), Ak, US 134/G2
Meadow Lake, Sk, Can. 126/F2
Meadow Valley Wash (riv.), Nv, US 128/D3
Meadowbrook, Il, US 137/G8
Meadowlands Sports Complex, NJ, US 139/J8
Meadows, Md, US 138/B6
Meadville, Ms, US 133/F4
Meadville, Pa, US 130/D3
Mealhada, Port. 44/A2
Meall a' Bhuiridh (peak), Sc, UK 36/B3
Meall Buidhe (peak), Sc, UK 36/B3
Meall Dearg (peak), Sc, UK 36/C3
Meall Dubh (peak), Sc, UK 36/B2
Meall nam Fuaran (peak), Sc, UK 36/C4
Meall Tairneachan (peak), Sc, UK 36/C3
Mearim (riv.), Braz. 151/J5
Meat (mtn.), Ak, US 134/F2
Meath (co.), Ire. 34/B4
Meath Park, Sk, Can. 127/G2
Méaulte, Fr. 52/B4
Meaux, Fr. 30/L5
Mecapalapa, Mex. 143/M6
Mècatina,Rivière du Petit (riv.), Nf,Qu, Can. 123/K3
Mecca, Mo, US 137/D5
Mechanicsburg, Pa, US 138/A3
Mechanicsburg Naval Rsv., Pa, US 138/B3
Mechelen, Belg. 53/D1
Mecheria, Alg. 99/E2
Mechi (zone), Nepal 85/F2
Mechra-Bel-Ksiri, Mor. 100/B2
Mecidiye, Turk. 47/K2
Mecitözü, Turk. 90/C1
Meckenbeuren, Ger. 57/F2
Meckenheim, Ger. 53/G2
Mecklenburg-Vorpommern (state), Ger. 38/E5
Mecklenburger (bay), Ger. 40/F1
Mecuia (peak), Moz. 105/G3
Meda, It. 58/C1
Medak, India 82/C4
Medan, Indo. 80/A3
Médanos, Arg. 158/E3
Medanos de Coro, PN, Ven. 152/D2
Medanosa (pt.), Arg. 159/D6
Mede Lomellina, It. 58/B2
Médéa, Alg. 100/G4
Médéa (prov.), Alg. 100/G4
Medebach, Ger. 51/F6
Medeiros Neto, Braz. 154/B5
Medel (peak), Swi. 57/E4
Medellín, Col. 150/C2
Medemblik, Neth. 50/C3
Meden (riv.), Eng, UK 35/G5
Medesano, It. 58/D3
Medetsiz (peak), Turk. 90/C2
Medford, Or, US 126/C5
Medford, NY, US 139/E2
Medford Lakes, NJ, US 138/D4
Medgidia, Rom. 49/J3
Media, Pa, US 138/C4
Media Luna, La (isls.), Hon. 145/F3
Mediaş, Rom. 49/G2
Medical Lake, Wa, US 126/D4
Medicine Bow, Wy, US 127/G5
Medicine Bow (range), Wy, US 128/F2
Medicine Hat, Ab, Can. 126/F3
Medina, ND, US 127/J4
Medina (riv.), Tx, US 129/H5
Medina, Braz. 154/B5
Medina, Oh, US 130/D3
Medina, Col. 152/C3
Medina, Wa, US 135/C2
Medina de Pomar, Sp. 44/D1
Medina de Rioseco, Sp. 44/C2
Medina del Campo, Sp. 44/C2
Medina-Sidonia, Sp. 44/C4
Medinaceli, Sp. 44/D2
Medinipur, India 85/F4
Mediouna, Mor. 98/D2
Mediterranean (sea) 27/E5
Mednogorsk, Rus. 63/L2
Medole, It. 58/D2
Medolla, It. 59/E3
Međugorje, Bosn. 48/C4
Medveditsa (riv.), Rus. 64/E5
Medvezh'i (isls.), Rus. 65/S2
Medvezh'yegorsk, Rus. 60/G3
Medvode, Slov. 43/L3
Medway (co.), Eng, UK 33/G4
Meekatharra, Austl. 112/C3
Meeker, Co, US 128/F2
Meeker Park, Co, US 137/A2
Meerbusch, Ger. 50/D6
Meerhout, Belg. 53/E1
Meersburg, Ger. 57/F2
Meerssen, Neth. 53/E2
Meerut, India 84/A1
Meeteetse, Wy, US 126/F4
Megála Kalívia, Gre. 47/G3
Megáli Panayía, Gre. 47/H2
Megálon Khoríon, Gre. 90/A2
Megalópolis, Gre. 47/H4
Megantic (peak), Qu, Can. 131/G2
Mégara, Gre. 47/H3
Megève, Fr. 56/C6
Meghālaya (state), India 70/F6
Meghalaya (state), India 83/F2
Meghna (riv.), Bang. 85/H4
Megiddo, Isr. 91/G6
Mégiscane (lake), Qu, Can. 130/E1
Mégiscane (riv.), Qu, Can. 130/E1
Megista (isl.), Greece 91/A1
Mehaigne (riv.), Belg. 53/E2
Mehamn, Nor. 37/H1
Meharry (mt.), Austl. 112/C2
Mehdia, Alg. 100/F5
Mehdiya-Plage, Mor. 100/A2
Mehe (riv.), Ger. 51/G1
Mehedinţi (prov.), Rom. 48/F3
Mehlingen, Ger. 53/G4
Mehlville, Mo, US 137/G9
Mehndāwal, India 84/D2
Mehrān (riv.), Iran 89/F3
Mehring, Ger. 53/F4
Mehrnbach, Aus. 55/G6
Mehtar Lām, Afg. 86/A2
Mei (riv.), China 79/C3
Meia Ponte (riv.), Braz. 155/B1
Meiganga, Camr. 96/H6
Meighen (isl.), Nun., Can. 123/R7
Meigu, China 83/H2
Meihekou, China 71/N3
Meikle Bin (peak), Sc, UK 36/B4
Meikle Black Law (hill), Sc, UK 36/D5
Meikle Says Law (peak), Sc, UK 36/D5
Meiktila, Myan. 83/G3
Meilen, Swi. 57/E3
Meine, Ger. 51/H4
Meiners Oaks, Ca, US 136/A2
Meinersen, Ger. 51/H4
Meinerzhagen, Ger. 53/G1
Meiningen, Ger. 54/D1
Meiringen, Swi. 56/E4
Meisenheim, Ger. 53/G4
Meishan (res.), China 72/C5
Meissen, Ger. 41/G3
Meissner (peak), Ger. 51/G6
Meitan, China 79/A2
Meitingen, Ger. 54/D5
Meiwa, Japan 77/L6
Meix-devant-Virton, Belg. 53/E4
Meizhou, China 79/C3
Mejaniga, It. 59/E2
Mejaouda (well), Mrta. 98/D5
Mejorada del Campo, Sp. 45/N9
Mek'elē, Eth. 97/N5
Meknès (prov.), Mor. 100/B3
Meknès, Mor. 100/B3
Mekong (riv.), Asia 70/G5
Mekong, Mouths of the (delta), Viet. 83/J6
Mekongga (peak), Indo. 81/F4
Mekoryuk, Ak, US 134/E3
Melaka, Malay. 80/B3
Melanesia (reg.) 116/E5
Melappālaiyam, India 82/C6
Melawi (riv.), Indo. 80/D4
Melbeck, Ger. 51/H2
Melbourne, Fl, US 133/H4
Melbourne (isl.), Nun., Can. 122/F2
Melbourne, Austl. 115/G5
Melbu, Nor. 37/E1
Melchor (isl.), Chile 158/B5
Melchor Múzquiz, Mex. 132/C5
Melchor Ocampo, Mex. 143/Q9
Meldola, It. 59/F4
Meldorf, Ger. 38/C4
Mele (cape), It. 58/B5
Melegnano, It. 58/C2
Melenci, Serb. 48/E3
Melenki, Rus. 60/J5
Melesse, Fr. 42/C2
Meleuz, Rus. 63/K1
Mélèzes (riv.), Qu, Can. 123/J3
Melezza (riv.), It. 57/E5
Melfi, It. 46/D2
Melfort, Sk, Can. 127/G2
Melgar de Fernamental, Sp. 44/C1
Melhus, Nor. 37/D3
Melibocus (peak), Ger. 54/B3
Melide, Swi. 57/E6
Meligalás, Gre. 47/G4
Melíki, Gre. 47/H2
Melili (peak), Kenya 104/C3
Melilla, Sp. 100/C2
Melimoyu (peak), Chile 158/B5
Melipilla, Chile 158/N8
Mélisey, Fr. 56/C2
Melissano, It. 47/F3
Melita, Mb, Can. 127/H3
Melito di Porto Salvo, It. 46/D4
Melitopol', Ukr. 62/E3
Melitota, Md, US 138/B5
Melkbosstrand, SAfr. 106/L10
Melksham, Eng, UK 32/D4
Mella (riv.), It. 58/D2
Mellan Fryken (lake), Swe. 38/E2
Melle, Ger. 51/F4
Melle, Belg. 52/C2
Mellea (riv.), It. 58/A3
Mellègue, Oued (riv.), Alg. 100/K7
Mellerud, Swe. 38/E2
Mellid, Sp. 44/A1
Mellieħa, Malta 46/L7
Mellingen, Swi. 57/E3
Mellizo Sur (peak), Chile 159/B6
Mellrichstadt, Ger. 54/D2
Mellum (isl.), Ger. 51/F1
Melmoth, SAfr. 107/E3
Melnik, Bul. 47/H2
Mělník, Czh. 55/H2
Melo, Uru. 157/F3
Melocheville, Qu, Can. 131/N7
Melrose, Md, US 138/B4
Melrose, Sc, UK 36/D5
Melrose Abbey, Sc, UK 36/D5
Melrose Park, Il, US 135/Q16
Mels, Swi. 57/F3
Melsungen, Ger. 51/G6
Meltham, Eng, UK 35/G4
Melton, Austl. 115/C3
Melton Mowbray, Eng, UK 33/F1
Melun, Fr. 30/K6
Melville (cape), Phil. 81/E2
Melville, Sk, Can. 127/H3
Melville (isl.), Austl. 109/C2
Melville (bay), Austl. 109/C2
Melville, Il, US 137/G8
Melville (cape), Austl. 114/B1
Melville (lake), Nf, Can. 123/L3
Melville (pen.), Nun., Can. 123/H2
Melville, NY, US 139/M8
Melvindale, Mi, US 135/F7
Mélykút, Hun. 48/D2
Melzo, It. 58/C2
Memāri, India 85/G4
Memmert (isl.), Ger. 50/D1
Memmingen, Ger. 57/G2
Memphis, Mo, US 127/K5
Memphis (int'l arpt.), Tn, US 129/K4
Memphis, Tx, US 129/G4
Memphis, Tn, US 129/K4
Memphis (ruin), Egypt 91/B5
Memphis, Mi, US 135/G6
Mena, Ar, US 129/J4
Menaggio, It. 57/F5
Menai (str.), Wal, UK 34/D5
Menai Bridge, Wal, UK 34/D5
Ménaka, Mali 103/F3
Menaldum, Neth. 50/C2
Menarandra (riv.), Madg. 107/H9
Menard, Tx, US 129/H5
Menasalbas, Sp. 44/C3
Menavava (riv.), Madg. 107/H7
Mendawai (riv.), Indo. 80/D4
Mende, Fr. 42/E4
Menden, Ger. 51/E6
Mendenhall (cape), Ak, US 134/E4
Mendes, Braz. 211/K7
Méndez, Mex. 143/F3
Mendham, NJ, US 138/D2
Mendig, Ger. 53/G3
Mendip (hills), Eng, UK 32/D4
Mendocino, Ca, US 128/B3
Mendocino (cape), Ca, US 124/A3
Mendooran, Austl. 115/D1
Mendoza, Peru 156/B2
Mendoza, Cuba 145/E1
Mendoza (prov.), Arg. 158/C2
Mendoza, Arg. 158/C2
Mendoza (El Plumerillo) (int'l arpt.), Arg. 158/C2
Mendrisio, Swi. 57/E6
Mene Grande, Ven. 152/D2
Menegosa (peak), It. 58/C3
Menemen, Turk. 62/C5
Menen, Belg. 52/C2
Menengai Crater, Kenya 104/C3
Menengiyn (plain), Mong. 71/L2
Menfi, It. 46/C4
Meng Xian, China 72/C4
Mengcheng, China 72/D4
Mengen, Ger. 57/F1
Mengersgereuth-Hämmern, Ger. 54/D2
Mengerskirchen, Ger. 54/B1
Mengeš, Slov. 43/L3
Menggala, Indo. 80/C4
Menghai, China 78/C1
Mengibar, Sp. 44/D4
Mengkofen, Ger. 55/F5
Mengla, China 78/C1
Menglian Daizu Lahuzu Vazu Zizhixian, China 83/G3
Mengyin, China 72/D4
Mengzi, China 83/H3
Menindee, Austl. 115/B2
Menindee (dam), Austl. 115/B2
Menindee (lake), Austl. 113/J5
Meningie, Austl. 115/A2
Menlo Park, Ca, US 135/K12
Menlo Park, NJ, US 139/H9
Menlolat (peak), Chile 158/B5
Mennecy, Fr. 30/K6
Menomonee Falls, Wi, US 130/B3
Menomonie, Wi, US 127/L4
Menongue, Ang. 105/C3
Menorca (int'l arpt.), Sp. 45/H3
Menorca (Minorca) (isl.), Sp. 45/H2
Mentasta Lake, Ak, US 134/K3
Mentawai (str.), Indo. 80/A4
Mentawai (isls.), Indo. 67/J10
Menteroda, Ger. 51/H6
Menthon-Saint-Bernard, Fr. 56/C6
Mentone, Tx, US 129/G5
Mentone, Ca, US 136/C2
Mentor, Oh, US 130/D3
Mentue (riv.), Swi. 56/C4
Menucourt, Fr. 30/H4
Menuma, Japan 77/C1
Menyapa (peak), Indo. 81/E3
Menzel Bourquiba, Tun. 46/A4
Menzie (mt.), Yk, Can. 134/M3
Menzies, Austl. 112/D4
Menziken, Swi. 56/E3
Menzingen, Swi. 57/E3
Menznau, Swi. 56/E3
Meolo, It. 59/F1
Meon (riv.), Eng, UK 33/E5
Meoquí, Mex. 132/B4
Mepistskaro (peak), Geo. 63/G4
Meppel, Neth. 50/D3
Meppen, Ger. 51/E3
Mequinenzo, Embalse de (res.), Sp. 45/E2
Mer, Fr. 42/D3
Mera (riv.), It. 57/F5
Meramec (riv.), Mo, US 129/K3
Merano, It. 57/H4
Merate, It. 58/C1
Meratus (mts.), Indo. 80/E4
Meraux, La, US 137/Q17
Merbein, Austl. 115/B2
Mercaderes, Col. 152/B4
Mercantour, PN du, Fr. 43/G4
Mercatello sul Metauro, It. 59/F5
Mercato Saraceno, It. 59/F5
Merced (riv.), Ca, US 128/B3
Merced, Ca, US 128/B3
Mercedario (peak), Arg. 157/B3
Mercedes, Arg. 157/E2
Mercedes, Arg. 158/D2
Mercedes, Arg. 159/J11
Mercedes, Uru. 159/J10
Mercer (co.), NJ, US 138/D3
Mercer (isl.), Wa, US 135/C2
Mercer Island, Wa, US 135/C2
Mercerville-Hamilton Square, NJ, US 138/D3
Merchtem, Belg. 53/D2
Mercier, Qu, Can. 131/N7
Mercoal, Ab, Can. 126/D2
Mercy (cape), Nun., Can. 123/K2
Mercy-le-Bas, Fr. 53/E5
Méré, Fr. 30/H5
Meredith (lake), Tx, US 129/G4
Meredith (cape), UK 159/E7
Merefa, Ukr. 62/F2
Merelbeke, Belg. 52/C2
Merenberg, Ger. 54/B1
Mergozzo, It. 57/E6
Mergui (arch.), Myan. 83/G5
Mergui (Myeik), Myan. 78/B3
Meriç, Turk. 49/H5
Méricourt, Fr. 30/G4
Méricourt, Fr. 52/B3
Mérida, Sp. 44/B3
Mérida, Ven. 152/D2
Mérida (state), Ven. 152/D2
Mérida, Mex. 144/D1
Mérida, Cordillera de (mts.), Ven. 150/D2
Meridian, Ms, US 133/F3
Meridian, Ok, US 137/N14
Mérignac, Fr. 42/C4
Mérignac (int'l arpt.), Fr. 42/C4
Merimbula, Austl. 115/D3
Merinda, Austl. 114/C3
Mering, Ger. 54/D6
Merinos, Uru. 159/K10
Merja Zerga (lake), Mor. 100/A2
Mérk, Hun. 48/F2
Merkendorf, Ger. 54/D4
Merksem, Belg. 50/B6
Merksplas, Belg. 50/B6
Merlimont, Fr. 52/A3
Merlo, Arg. 159/J11
Meroe (ruin), Sudan 88/B5
Merone, It. 58/C1
Merredin, Austl. 112/C4
Merriam, Ks, US 137/D5
Merrick, NY, US 139/L9
Merrick (peak), Sc, UK 34/D1
Merrill, Wi, US 127/L4
Merrill Creek (res.), NJ, US 138/C2
Merrimack, NH, US 131/G3
Merritt, BC, Can. 126/C3
Merritt Island, Fl, US 133/H4
Merriwa, Austl. 115/D2
Mers-les-Bains, Fr. 52/A3
Mersch, Lux. 53/F4
Merse (reg.), Sc, UK 36/D5
Mersey (riv.), Eng, UK 35/F5
Merseyside (co.), Eng, UK 35/F5
Mersing, Malay. 80/B3
Mertert, Lux. 53/F4
Mertesdorf, Ger. 53/F4
Merthyr Tydfil, Wal, UK 32/C3
Merthyr Tydfil (co.), Wal, UK 32/C3
Mértola, Port. 44/B4
Merton (bor.), Eng, UK 30/C2
Mertzon, Tx, US 129/G5
Mertzwiller, Fr. 53/G6
Meru (mt.), Tanz. 104/C3
Meru, Kenya 104/C2
Méru, Fr. 52/B5
Meru NP, Kenya 104/C2
Merville, Fr. 52/B2
Merwedekanaal (riv.), Neth. 50/C5
Méry-sur-Oise, Fr. 30/J4
Merzen, Ger. 51/E4
Merzenich, Ger. 53/F2
Merzifon, Turk. 90/C1
Merzig, Ger. 53/F5
Mesa (mtn.), Ak, US 134/G3
Mesa, Az, US 137/S19
Mesa (peak), Arg. 159/C6
Mesa Verde NP, Co, US 128/E3
Mesabi (range), Mn, US 127/K4
Mesach Mellet (hills), Libya 99/H4
Mesagne, It. 47/E2
Mesarás (gulf), Gre. 47/J5
Mescalero (ridge), NM, US 132/C3
Meschede, Ger. 51/F6
Mesco, Punta di (pt.), It. 58/C4
Mescolino (peak), It. 59/F5
Meseta de Montemayor (plat.), Arg. 158/D5
Mesgouez (lake), Qu, Can. 130/F1
Mesola, It. 59/F3
Mesolóngion, Gre. 47/G3
Mesomeloka, Madg. 107/J8
Mesopotamia (reg.), Arg. 157/E3
Mesoraca, It. 46/E3
Mespelbrunn, Ger. 54/C3
Mesquite, Tx, US 129/H4
Mesrouh (peak), Mor. 98/E2
Messaad, Alg. 96/F1
Messancy, Belg. 53/E4
Messel, Ger. 54/B3
Messina, SAfr. 105/F5
Messina (str.), It. 46/D4
Messina, It. 46/D3
Messini (gulf), Gre. 47/H4
Messíni, Gre. 47/H4
Messkirch, Ger. 57/F2
Messstetten, Ger. 57/E1
Messy, Fr. 30/L5
Mesta (riv.), Bul. 49/F5
Mestre, It. 59/F2
Mestrino, It. 59/E2
Mesudiye, Turk. 62/F4
Mesumba (peak), Tanz. 104/C4
Mesurado (cape), Libr. 102/C5
Meta (dept.), Col. 152/C4
Meta (riv.), Col.,Ven. 147/C2
Meta Incognita (pen.), Nun., Can. 123/K2
Metabetchouan, Qu, Can. 131/G1
Métabetchouane (riv.), Qu, Can. 131/F1
Metairie, La, US 137/P17
Metallifere, Colline (mts.), It. 59/D6
Metamora, Mi, US 135/F6
Metán, Arg. 157/D2
Metapontum (ruin), It. 46/E2
Metauro (riv.), It. 43/K5
Metelen, Ger. 51/E4
Metéora, Gre. 47/G3
Metepec, Mex. 143/Q10
Methven, Sc, UK 36/C4
Metica (riv.), Col. 152/C4
Metković, Cro. 47/E1
Metlakatla, Ak, US 134/M4
Metlatonoc, Mex. 144/B2
Metlili Chaamba, Alg. 99/F2
Metnitz, Aus. 43/L3
Metro Toronto Zoo, On, Can. 131/R8
Metropolis, Il, US 130/B4
Metropolitan Oakland (int'l arpt.), Ca, US 128/B3
Metropolitana de Santiago (pol. reg.), Chile 158/N8
Métsovon, Gre. 47/G3
Mettawa, Il, US 135/Q15
Mettenheim, Ger. 55/F6
Mettet, Belg. 53/D3
Mettingen, Ger. 51/E4
Mettlach, Ger. 53/F4
Mettmach, Aus. 55/G6
Mettmann, Ger. 50/D6
Metu, Eth. 97/N6
Metuchen, NJ, US 139/H9
Metulla, Isr. 91/D3
Metz, Fr. 53/F5
Metz-Nancy-Lorraine (int'l arpt.), Fr. 53/F6
Metzingen, Ger. 54/C5
Metztitlán, Mex. 143/L6
Meudon, Fr. 30/J5
Meudt, Ger. 53/G3
Meulan, Fr. 30/H4
Meulebeke, Belg. 52/C2
Meurthe (riv.), Fr. 56/C1
Meurthe-et-Moselle (dept.), Fr. 53/E6
Meuse (dept.), Fr. 53/E6
Meuse (riv.), Fr. 40/C4
Meuzin (riv.), Fr. 56/A3
Mevasseret Ziyyon, Isr. 91/G8
Mexborough, Eng, UK 35/G5
Mexia, Tx, US 129/H5
Mexiana, Ilha (isl.), Braz. 151/J3
Mexicalcingo, Mex. 143/Q10
Mexicali, Mex. 128/D4
Mexico (ctry.) 119/G7
Mexico (cap.), Mex. 143/Q10
México (state), Mex. 140/A5
Mexico (gulf), NAm. 140/C2
Mexico, Mo, US 129/K3
Meximieux, Fr. 56/B6
Meybod, Iran 88/F2
Meyers Chuck, Ak, US 134/M4
Meyerton, SAfr. 106/Q13
Meymaneh, Afg. 89/H1
Meyrin, Swi. 56/C5
Meythet, Fr. 56/C6
Meyzieu, Fr. 56/A6
Mezdra, Bul. 47/H1
Mèze, Fr. 42/E5
Mezen' (riv.), Rus. 64/E3
Mezen' (bay), Rus. 61/J2
Mezha (riv.), Bela. 39/P4
Mezhdurechensk, Rus. 64/J4
Mezhdusharskiy (isl.), Rus. 64/E2
Mézières-sur-Seine, Fr. 30/H5
Mezőberény, Hun. 48/E2
Mezőkovácsháza, Hun. 48/E2
Mezőkövesd, Hun. 41/L5
Mezőtúr, Hun. 48/E2
Mezquital (riv.), Mex. 142/D4
Mezzana (peak), It. 57/G5
Mezzocorona, It. 57/H5
Mezzogoro, It. 59/F3
Mezzolombardo, It. 57/H5
Mfangano (isl.), Kenya 104/B3
Mga (riv.), Rus. 61/U7
M'goun (peak), Mor. 98/D3
Mhamdia Fūshānah, Tun. 46/B4
Mhòr (lake), Sc, UK 36/B2
Mhow, India 89/L4
Mi (riv.), China 79/B2
Mi-shima (isl.), Japan 74/B3
Mi Xian, China 72/C4
Miahuatlán de Porfirio Díaz, Mex. 144/B2
Miajadas, Sp. 44/C3
Miami, Az, US 128/E4
Miami, Fl, US 133/H5
Miami (int'l arpt.), Fl, US 133/H5
Miami (co.), In, US 137/D6
Miami, Ok, US 129/J3
Miami Beach, Fl, US 133/H5
Miān Channūn, Pak. 86/B4
Mianchi, China 72/B4
Mīāndoāb, Iran 88/E1
Miandrivazo, Madg. 107/H7
Mīāneh, Iran 88/E1
Miāni, Pak. 86/B3
Mianning, China 83/H2
Mianus (riv.), Ct, US 139/E1
Miānwāli, Pak. 86/A3
Mianyang, China 70/H5
Mianzhu, China 70/H5
Miao'er (peak), China 79/B2
Miarinarivo, Madg. 107/H7
Miary, Madg. 107/G8
Miass, Rus. 61/P5
Miass (riv.), Rus. 61/P5
Miastko, Pol. 38/G4
Mica Creek, BC, Can. 126/D2
Michalovce, Slvk. 41/L4
Michelfeld, Ger. 55/E3
Michelson (mt.), Ak, US 134/K2
Michelstadt, Ger. 54/C3
Michendorf, Ger. 40/Q7
Michigan (state), US 130/C2
Michigan (lake), US 130/C2
Michigan City, In, US 130/C3
Michipicoten (isl.), On, Can. 130/C2
Michoacán de Ocampo (state), Mex. 140/A4
Michurin, Bul. 49/H4
Michurinsk, Rus. 63/G1
Mickle Fell (peak), Eng, UK 35/F2
Mico (riv.), Nic. 140/E5
Micoud, StL. 141/N9
Micronesia (reg.) 116/E3
Micronesia, Federated States of (ctry.) 116/D4
Mid Yell, Sc, UK 31/W13
Midal (well), Niger 103/G2
Midale, Sk, Can. 127/H3
Middelburg, SAfr. 106/D3
Middelburg, SAfr. 107/E2
Middelburg, Neth. 50/A5
Middelharnis, Neth. 50/B5
Middelkerke, Belg. 52/B1
Middle (bay), NY, US 139/L9
Middle Alkali (lake), Ca, US 128/C2
Middle Andaman (isl.), India 83/F5
Middle Caicos (isl.), UK 145/J1
Middle Concho (riv.), Tx, US 132/C4
Middle Raccoon (riv.), Ia, US 129/J2
Middle River, Md, US 138/B5
Middle Sister (peak), Or, US 126/C4
Middleberg, Ok, US 137/M15
Middleburg, Md, US 138/A4
Middleburg, Pa, US 138/A2
Middlebury, Vt, US 130/F2
Middlemount, Austl. 114/C3
Middleport, Pa, US 138/B2
Middlesboro, Ky, US 130/D4
Middlesbrough, Eng, UK 35/G2
Middlesbrough (co.), Eng, UK 35/G2
Middlesex (co.), Eng, UK 33/F4
Middlesex, NJ, US 138/D2
Middleton, Eng, UK 35/F4
Middletown, De, US 138/C5
Middletown, NJ, US 139/J10
Middletown, Pa, US 138/B3
Midelt, Mor. 98/D2
Midi (canal), Fr. 42/D5
Midi-Pyrénées (pol. reg.), Fr. 42/D4
Midland, Mi, US 130/C3
Midland, On, Can. 130/E2
Midland, Tx, US 129/G5
Midland (int'l arpt.), Tx, US 142/E2
Midland, Wa, US 135/C3
Midland Park, NJ, US 139/J8
Midleton, Ire. 31/P11
Midlothian, Il, US 135/Q16
Midlothian (pol. reg.), Sc, UK 36/C5
Midlum, Ger. 51/F1
Midongy Atsimo, Madg. 107/H8
Midou (riv.), Fr. 42/C5
Midsayap, Phil. 79/D6
Midu, China 83/H2
Midvale, Ut, US 137/K12
Midway (isls.), Pac., US 116/H2
Midway, De, US 138/C6
Midway, Il, US 137/H8
Midway, Ok, US 137/N15
Midway, Ut, US 137/L12
Midyan (reg.), SAr. 88/C3
Midyat, Turk. 90/E2
Midžor (peak), Serb. 49/F4
Mie, Japan 74/B4
Mie (pref.), Japan 74/E3
Miechów, Pol. 62/B2
Międzychód, Pol. 41/H2
Międzylesie, Pol. 41/J3
Międzyrzec Podlaski, Pol. 41/M3
Międzyrzecz, Pol. 41/H2
Międzyzdroje, Pol. 38/F5
Miehlen, Ger. 53/G3
Mielec, Pol. 41/L3
Miercurea Ciuc, Rom. 49/G2
Mieres, Sp. 44/C1
Miesbach, Ger. 43/J3
Mifflin, Pa, US 138/A2
Mifflinburg, Pa, US 138/A2
Migdal Ha'emeq, Isr. 91/G6
Migennes, Fr. 42/E3
Migliarino, It. 58/D5
Mignanego, It. 58/B3
Mignovillard, Fr. 56/C4
Migori (riv.), Kenya 104/B3
Migori, Kenya 104/B3
Miguel Alemán, Mex. 142/C2
Miguel Aleman, Presa (dam), Mex. 143/M8
Miguel Alves, Braz. 154/B2
Miguel Auza, Mex. 142/E3
Miguel Calmon, Braz. 154/B3
Miguel Hidalgo (int'l arpt.), Mex. 142/E4
Miguel Hidalgo (res.), Mex. 142/C3
Miguel Pereira, Braz. 211/K7
Miguel Riglos, Arg. 158/E3
Miguelete, Uru. 159/K11
Miguelópolis, Braz. 155/B2
Miguelturra, Sp. 44/D3
Migŭm, SKor. 73/G6
Mihama, Japan 74/D3
Mihama, Japan 77/L6
Mihara, Japan 74/C3
Mihara, Japan 77/J6
Miharu, Japan 75/G2
Mihla, Ger. 51/H6
Miho, Japan 77/E2
Mihrābpur, Pak. 89/J3
Mijares (riv.), Sp. 45/E2
Mijas, Sp. 44/C4
Mijdrecht, Neth. 50/B4
Mikasa, Japan 76/B2
Mikata, Japan 77/J4
Mikata (lake), Japan 77/J4
Mikawa (bay), Japan 77/M6
Mikhaylovka, Rus. 63/G2
Mikhmoret, Isr. 91/F7
Miki, Japan 77/G6
Mikínai, Gre. 47/H4
Mikínai (Mycenae) (ruin), Gre. 47/H4
Mikkeli (prov.), Fin. 37/H3
Míkonos, Gre. 47/J4
Míkonos (isl.), Gre. 47/J4
Mikri Prespa (lake), Alb.,Gre. 47/G2
Mikri Prespa NP, Gre. 47/G2
Mikuma, Japan 77/L6
Mikumi NP, Tanz. 105/G2
Mikuni, Japan 74/E2
Mikuni-tōge (pass), Japan 75/F2
Mikura (isl.), Japan 75/F4
Mila (prov.), Alg. 100/H4
Milagro, Ecu. 152/B5
Milak, India 84/B1
Milan (Milano), It. 43/H4
Milang, Austl. 115/A2
Milano (prov.), It. 58/C2
Milano (Milan), It. 43/H4
Milas, Turk. 90/A2
Milazzo, It. 46/D3
Milbank, SD, US 127/J4
Mildura, Austl. 115/B2
Miles, Tx, US 132/C4
Miles, Austl. 114/C4
Miles City, Mt, US 127/G4
Milešovka (peak), Czh. 55/G1
Milestone, Sk, Can. 127/G3
Miletto (peak), It. 46/D2
Milevsko, Czh. 55/H4
Milford (lake), Ks, US 132/D2
Milford, Ut, US 128/D3
Milford, NJ, US 138/C2
Milford, Ct, US 139/E1
Milford, De, US 138/C6
Milford, Mi, US 135/E6
Milford Haven, Wal, UK 32/A3

207
Milfo – Monta

Milford Haven (inlet), Wal., UK 32/A3
Milgis (riv.), Kenya 104/C2
Mili (isl.), Mrsh. 116/G4
Miliana, Alg. 100/G4
Milicz, Pol. 41/J3
Mililani Town, Hi, US 124/V13
Milk (hill), Eng, UK 33/E4
Milk (riv.), Can.,US 122/F4
Milk River, Ab, Can. 126/E3
Mill (isl.), Nun., Can. 123/J2
Mill (riv.), Ct, US 139/E1
Mill Neck, NY, US 139/L8
Millaa Millaa, Austl. 114/B2
Millau, Fr. 42/E4
Millbrae, Ca, US 135/K11
Millbrook (res.), Austl. 113/M8
Millburn, NJ, US 139/H9
Millcreek, Ut, US 137/K12
Mille Îles (riv.), Qu, Can. 131/N6
Mille Lacs (lake), Mn, US 125/H2
Milledgeville, Ga, US 133/H3
Miller, SD, US 127/J4
Miller (int'l arpt.), Tx, US 143/F3
Millerovo, Rus. 63/G2
Millers Ferry (dam), Al, US 133/G3
Millersburg, Pa, US 138/B2
Millerstown, Pa, US 138/A2
Millersville, Pa, US 138/B4
Millesimo, It. 58/B4
Milleur (pt.), Sc, UK 34/C1
Millevaches (plat.), Fr. 42/D4
Millgrove, On, Can. 131/Q9
Millicent, Austl. 115/B3
Milliken, Co, US 137/C2
Millingen aan de Rijn, Neth. 50/D5
Millington, Md, US 138/C5
Millinocket, Me, US 131/G2
Millisle, NI, UK 34/C2
Millmerran, Austl. 114/C4
Millmont, Pa, US 138/A2
Millport, Sc, UK 36/B5
Mills Junction, Ut, US 137/J12
Millstadt, Il, US 137/G9
Millstone (riv.), NJ, US 138/D3
Millstream-Chichester NP, Austl. 112/C2
Millthorpe, Austl. 115/D2
Milltown, NJ, US 139/H10
Milltown Malbay, Ire. 31/P10
Millville, Pa, US 138/B1
Millville, NJ, US 138/C5
Millwood (lake), Ar, US 132/E3
Milmay, NJ, US 138/D5
Milnathort, Wal, UK 35/E5
Milne (bay), PNG 116/E5
Milngavie, Sc, UK 36/B5
Milnrow, Eng, UK 35/F4
Milo, Me, US 131/G2
Milo (riv.), Gui. 102/C4
Milolii, Hi, US 124/U11
Milos (isl.), Gre. 47/J4
Mílos, Gre. 47/J4
Milseburg (peak), Ger. 54/C1
Miltenberg, Ger. 54/C3
Milton, Austl. 115/D2
Milton, On, Can. 131/Q8
Milton, NZ 117/R12
Milton (res.), Co, US 137/C2
Milton, Fl, US 133/G4
Milton, NH, US 131/G3
Milton, Pa, US 138/B1
Milton, Ut, US 137/K11
Milton, Wa, US 135/C3
Milton-Freewater, Or, US 126/D4
Milton Keynes, Eng, UK 33/F2
Milton Keynes (co.), Eng, UK 33/F2
Milton Ness (pt.), Sc, UK 36/D3
Milton of Campsie, Sc, UK 36/B5
Milwaukee, Wi, US 127/M5
Milwaukee (co.), Wi, US 135/P14
Milz (riv.), Ger. 54/D2
Mimi (riv.), Japan 74/B4
Mimizan, Fr. 42/C4
Mimmaya, Japan 76/B3
Min (riv.), China 70/H5
Min Xian, China 70/H5
Mina (riv.), Alg. 100/F5
Mīnāb, Iran 89/G3
Minahasa (pen), Indo. 81/F3
Minakuchi, Japan 77/K6
Minamata, Japan 74/B4
Minami Alps NP, Japan 75/F3
Minami-tori-shima (isl.), Japan 116/E2
Minamiaiki, Japan 77/B1
Minamiashigara, Japan 77/C3
Minamichita, Japan 77/L6
Minamidaitō (isl.), Japan 75/L8
Minamiiō (isl.), Japan 116/D2
Minamikawara, Japan 77/C1
Minamimaki, Japan 77/A2
Minamiyamashiro, Japan 77/J6
Minano, Japan 77/C1
Minas (peak), Ecu. 152/B5
Minas, Cuba 145/G1
Minas, Uru. 159/G2
Minas de Matahambre, Cuba 145/F1
Minas de Riotinto, Sp. 44/B4
Minas Gerais (state), Braz. 154/A5
Minas Novas, Braz. 154/B5
Minatitlán, Mex. 144/C2
Minbu, Myan. 83/F3
Minbya, Myan. 83/F3
Minch, The (North Minch) (str.), Sc, UK 31/Q8
Minchinābād, Pak. 86/B4
Minchinmávida (vol.), Chile 158/B4
Mincio (riv.), It. 59/D2
Mindanao (sea), Phil. 81/F2
Mindanao (isl.), Phil. 67/M9
Mindel (riv.), Ger. 40/F4
Mindelheim, Ger. 57/G1
Mindelo, CpV. 93/J10
Minden, La, US 129/J4
Minden, Ne, US 129/H2
Minden, Ger. 51/F4
Mindoro (str.), Phil. 79/C5
Mindoro (isl.), Phil. 67/L8
Mine (pt.), Ire. 31/Q10
Mineiros, Braz. 151/H7
Mineola, Tx, US 129/J4
Mineola, NY, US 139/L8
Mineral del Monte, Mex. 143/L6
Mineral Wells, Tx, US 129/H4
Mineral'nye Vody (int'l arpt.), Rus. 63/G3
Mineral'nye Vody, Rus. 63/G3
Minerbe, It. 59/E2
Minerbio, It. 59/E3
Minerbio (pt.), Fr. 43/H5
Minersville, Pa, US 138/B2
Minfeld, Ger. 54/B4
Minfeng, China 70/D4
Ming (riv.), China 83/J3
Mingäçevir, Azer. 63/H4
Mingäçevir Su Anbari (res.), Azer. 63/H4
Mingan (riv.), Qu, Can. 131/J1
Mingāora, Pak. 86/B2
Mingenew, Austl. 112/B4
Minglanilla, Sp. 44/E3
Mingshui, China 71/N2
Mingxi, China 79/C2
Minhe, China 70/H4
Minhla, Myan. 83/G4
Minho (riv.), Sp. 44/A1
Minidoka Internment Nat'l Mon., Id, US 126/E6
Minigwal (lake), Austl. 112/D4
Minitonas, Mb, Can. 127/H2
Minlaton, Austl. 113/H5
Minle, China 70/H4
Minna, Nga. 103/G4
Minneapolis, Mn, US 127/K4
Minneapolis-St. Paul (Wold-Chamberlain) (int'l arpt.), Mn, US 127/K4
Minnedosa, Mb, Can. 127/J3
Minnesota (state), US 127/K4
Minnesota (riv.), Mn, US 127/K4
Minnigaff, Sc, UK 34/D2
Minnis (lake), On, Can. 130/B1
Minnitaki (lake), On, Can. 127/K3
Miño (riv.), Port.,Sp. 44/A1
Mino, Japan 77/L4
Minobu, Japan 75/F3
Minokamo, Japan 77/M5
Mino'o, Japan 77/H6
Mino'o (riv.), Japan 77/H6
Minori, Japan 77/E1
Minot, ND, US 127/H3
Minqin, China 70/H4
Minqing, China 79/C2
Minquan, China 72/C4
Minsener Oog (isl.), Ger. 51/F1
Minsk (cap.), Bela. 39/M5
Minsk (int'l arpt.), Bela. 39/M5
Mińsk Mazowiecki, Pol. 41/L2
Minskaya Voblasts Bela. 62/C1
Mintaka (pass), Pak. 87/F5
Mintaka (pass), China 89/K1
Mintlaw, Sc, UK 36/E1
Minto, Ak, US 134/J2
Minto, NB, Can. 131/H2
Minto (inlet), NW, Can. 122/E1
Minūf, Egypt 91/B4
Minusinsk, Rus. 64/K4
Minusio, Swi. 57/E5
Minyā al Qamḩ, Egypt 91/B4
Minyip, Austl. 115/B3
Miquan, China 70/E3
Mira, Port. 44/A2
Mira (riv.), Col. 152/B4
Mira Loma, Ca, US 136/C2
Mira Monte, Ca, US 136/A2
Mira Taglio, It. 59/F2
Mirabel (int'l arpt.), Qu, Can. 131/M6
Mirabel, Qu, Can. 131/M6
Mirabela, Braz. 154/A5
Mirabello, It. 59/E3
Miracema, Braz. 155/D2
Miracema do Norte, Braz. 151/J5
Miradolo Terme, It. 58/C2
Mirador, Braz. 154/A2
Mirador (pass), Chile 158/C4
Miraflores, Peru 156/B3
Miraflores, Mex. 142/C4
Miraflores, Col. 152/C4
Miraflores, Col. 152/C3
Miragoâne, Haiti 145/H2
Miraj, India 89/K5
Miramar, Ca, US 136/C5
Miramar, Arg. 158/F3
Miramar Naval Air Station, Ca, US 136/C5
Mirambéllou (gulf), Gre. 47/J5
Miramichi, NB, Can. 131/H2
Miramont-de-Guyenne, Fr. 42/D4
Miranda (riv.), Braz. 151/G8
Miranda de Ebro, Sp. 44/D1
Miranda do Corvo, Port. 44/A2
Miranda do Douro, Port. 44/B2
Mirande, Fr. 42/D5
Mirandela, Port. 44/B2
Mirandola, It. 43/J4
Mirandópolis, Braz. 155/B2
Mirano, It. 59/F2
Mīrānpur, India 84/A1
Mirante do Paranapanema, Braz. 155/B2
Mirassol, Braz. 155/B2
Miravalles (peak), Sp. 44/B1
Miravalles (vol.), CR 144/E4
Mirebalais, Haiti 145/H2
Mirebeau, Fr. 56/B3
Mirecourt, Fr. 56/C1
Mirfield, Eng, UK 35/G4
Miri, Malay. 80/D3
Miriam Vale, Austl. 114/C4
Mirim (lake), Braz. 157/F3
Mirimire, Ven. 152/D2
Mirina, Gre. 47/J3
Miritiparaná (riv.), Col. 152/D5
Mirna (riv.), Cro. 59/G2
Mirnyy, Rus. 65/N3
Mirnyy, Rus., Ant. 160/G
Mirond (lake), Sk, Can. 127/H2
Mirow, Ger. 40/G2
Mirror (lake), NJ, US 138/D4
Mirtóön (sea), Gre. 47/H4
Miryang, SKor. 74/A3
Mirzāpur, India 84/D3
Misa (riv.), It. 59/G5
Misāha (well), Egypt 101/A4
Misaka, Japan 77/B2
Misaki, Japan 74/D3
Misaki, Japan 77/E3
Misano Adriatico, It. 59/F5
Misantla, Mex. 143/N7
Misato, Japan 77/C1
Misato, Japan 77/D2
Misato, Japan 77/K6
Misawa, Japan 76/B3
Mishan, China 71/P2
Mishawaka, In, US 130/C3
Misheguk (mtn.), Ak, US 134/F2
Mishima, Japan 75/F3
Misilmeri, It. 46/C3
Misiones, Sierra de (mts.), Arg. 157/E2
Miskitos, Cayos (isls.), Nic. 140/E5
Miskolc, Hun. 41/L4
Misono, Japan 77/L6
Misool (isl.), Indo. 81/H4
Misquah (hills), Mn, US 127/L4
Mişrātah (pt.), Libya 97/L1
Mişrātah, Libya 96/J1
Missinaibi (lake), On, Can. 130/D1
Missinaibi (riv.), On, Can. 123/H3
Mission, Tx, US 132/D5
Mission (bay), Ca, US 136/C5
Mission, Ks, US 137/D5
Mission Beach, Austl. 114/B2
Mission Hills, Ks, US 137/D5
Mission Ind. Res., Ca, US 136/C4
Mission San Buenaventura, Ca, US 136/A2
Mission San Jose, Ca, US 135/L12
Mission San Juan Capistrano, Ca, US 136/C3
Mission Viejo, Ca, US 136/C3
Missisa (lake), On, Can. 127/M2
Missisicabi (riv.), Qu, Can. 130/E1
Mississauga, On, Can. 131/Q8
Mississippi (pt.), Austl. 112/D5
Mississippi (state), US 133/F3
Mississippi (riv.), US 125/H5
Mississippi (delta), La, US 133/F4
Mississippi River Gulf Outlet (canal), La, US 137/Q17
Missoula, Mt, US 126/E4
Missouri (state), US 129/J3
Missouri (riv.), US 125/G3
Missouri City, Tx, US 129/J5
Missouri City, Mo, US 137/E5
Mistaken (pt.), Nf, Can. 131/L2
Mistassibi (riv.), Qu, Can. 131/F1
Mistassibi Nord-Est (riv.), Qu, Can. 131/G1
Mistassini, Qu, Can. 131/F1
Mistassini (riv.), Qu, Can. 131/F1
Mistassini (lake), Qu, Can. 123/J3
Mistelbach an der Zaya, Aus. 43/M2
Misti (vol.), Peru 156/D5
Mistissini, Qu, Can. 130/F1
Mistrás (ruin), Gre. 47/H4
Mistretta, It. 46/D4
Misty Fjords Nat'l Mon., US 134/M4
Misty Fjords Nat'l Mon., Ak, US 122/C3
Misugi, Japan 77/K6
Mita, Punta de (pt.), Mex. 142/D4
Mitaka, Japan 77/D2
Mitake, Japan 77/M5
Mitama, Japan 77/B2
Mitare, Ven. 152/D2
Mitchell, SD, US 127/J5
Mitchell (mt.), NC, US 133/H3
Mitchell (riv.), Austl. 109/D2
Mitchell, Il, US 137/G8
Mitchell, Austl. 114/B4
Mitchell River NP, Austl. 115/C3
Mitha Tiwāna, Pak. 86/B3
Mithankot, Pak. 86/A5
Mithi, Pak. 89/J4
Míthimna, Gre. 47/K3
Mitiaro (isl.), Cookls. 117/K6
Mitilíni, Gre. 47/K3
Mitla (pass), Egypt 91/C4
Mitla (ruin), Mex. 144/B2
Mito, Japan 75/G2
Mito, Japan 77/M6
Mitomi, Japan 77/B2
Mitra (peak), EqG. 96/G7
Mitre (pen.), Arg. 157/C7
Mitry-Mory, Fr. 30/K5
Mitsamiouli, Com. 107/G5
Mitsinjo, Madg. 107/H7
Mitsio, Nosy (isl.), Madg. 107/J6
Mits'iwa, Erit. 97/N4
Mitsue, Japan 77/K7
Mitsukaidō, Japan 75/F2
Mitsuke, Japan 75/F2
Mittagong, Austl. 115/D2
Mittagspitze (peak), Aus. 57/F3
Mittainville, Fr. 30/G5
Mittelberg, Aus. 57/G3
Mittelland (canal), Ger. 51/F4
Mittelradde (riv.), Ger. 51/E3
Mittenwald, Ger. 57/H3
Mittersill, Aus. 43/K3
Mitterteich, Ger. 55/F3
Mittlere-Isar (canal), Ger. 55/E6
Mittweida, Ger. 40/G3
Mitú, Col. 152/D4
Mitumba, Monts (mts.), D.R. Congo 105/E1
Mitwitz, Ger. 54/E2
Miura (pen.), Japan 77/D3
Miura, Japan 77/D3
Miwa, Japan 77/H5
Miwa, Japan 77/K7
Mixco Viejo (ruin), Guat. 144/D3
Mixquiahuala, Mex. 143/K6
Mixteco (riv.), Mex. 144/B2
Miya (riv.), Japan 77/K7
Miyagawa, Japan 77/K7
Miyagi (pref.), Japan 76/B4
Miyake (isl.), Japan 75/F3
Miyako (isl.), Japan 79/E3
Miyako, Japan 76/B4
Miyako (isls.), Japan 75/H8
Miyakonojō, Japan 74/B5
Miyama, Japan 77/J5
Miyama, Japan 77/L4
Miyanojō, Japan 74/B5
Miyashiro, Japan 77/D2
Miyazaki (pref.), Japan 74/B4
Miyazaki, Japan 74/B5
Miyazu, Japan 77/H4
Miyazu (bay), Japan 77/H4
Miyi, China 83/H2
Miyoshi, Japan 74/C3
Miyoshi, Japan 77/D2
Miyoshi, Japan 77/D3
Miyoshi, Japan 77/M5
Miyota, Japan 77/B1
Miyun (res.), China 72/H6
Miyun, China 72/H6
Mizen (pt.), Ire. 34/B6
Miziya, Bul. 49/F4
Mizoram (state), India 70/F7
Mizpah, NJ, US 138/D5
Mizpe Ramon, Isr. 91/D4
Mizuho, Japan 77/C2
Mizuho, Japan 77/H5
Mizunami, Japan 77/M5
Mizusawa, Japan 76/B4
Mjölby, Swe. 38/F2
Mjøndalen, Nor. 38/D2
Mjörn (lake), Swe. 38/E3
Mjøsa (lake), Nor. 37/D3
Mkata (plain), Tanz. 104/C4
Mkokotoni, Tanz. 104/C4
Mkomazi Game Rsv., Tanz. 104/C4
Mkombo (riv.), Tanz. 104/A4
Mkondoa (riv.), Tanz. 104/C4
Mkorn (peak), Mor. 98/D3
Mkumbi (pt.), Tanz. 104/C4
Mkushi, Zam. 105/E3
Mkuze (riv.), SAfr. 107/F2
Mladá Boleslav, Czh. 55/H2
Mladá Vožice, Czh. 55/H3
Mladenovac, Serb. 48/E3
Mlala (hills), Tanz. 104/A4
Mława, Pol. 41/L2
Mljet (isl.), Cro. 47/E1
Mljet NP, Cro. 47/E1
Mmabatho, SAfr. 106/D2
Mnyera (riv.), Tanz. 104/B5
Mo Duc, Viet. 78/E3
Moa (isl.), Indo. 81/G5
Moa (riv.), SLeo. 102/C5
Moa, Cuba 145/H1
Moab, Ut, US 128/E3
Moala Group (isl.), Fiji 116/G6
Moama, Austl. 115/C1
Moamba, Moz. 107/F2
Moaña, Sp. 44/A1
Moanda, Gabon 96/H8
Moate, Ire. 31/Q10
Mobara, Japan 77/E3
Mobaye, CAfr. 97/K7
Moberly, Mo, US 129/J3
Moberly Lake, BC, Can. 126/C2
Mobile, Al, US 133/F4
Mobridge, SD, US 127/H4
Moca (pass), Turk. 91/C1
Mocache, Ecu. 152/B5
Mocajuba, Braz. 151/J4
Moçambique, Moz. 105/H4
Mocanaqua, Pa, US 138/B1
Mocha (riv.), Rus. 61/W9
Moche (ruin), Peru 156/B3
Mochima, PN, Ven. 153/E2
Mochizuki, Japan 77/A1
Mochudi, Bots. 105/E5
Mochumi, Peru 156/B2
Mocímboa da Praia, Moz. 104/D5
Möckeln (lake), Swe. 38/E3
Mockfjärd, Swe. 38/F1
Möckmühl, Ger. 54/C4
Moclín, Sp. 44/D4
Mocoa, Col. 152/B4
Mococa, Braz. 211/F6
Mocorito, Mex. 142/D3
Moctezuma, Mex. 143/E4
Moctezuma, Mex. 142/C2
Mocuba, Moz. 105/G4
Modāsa, India 89/K4
Modderrivier (riv.), SAfr. 106/D3
Modena (prov.), It. 59/D3
Modena, It. 59/D3
Moder (riv.), Fr. 43/G2
Modesto, Ca, US 128/B3
Modica, It. 46/D4
Modigliana, It. 59/E4
Modjeska, Ca, US 136/C3
Modjigo (reg.), Niger 96/H4
Mödling, Aus. 49/N7
Modot, Mong. 71/J2
Modriča, Bosn. 48/D3
Modugno, It. 46/E2
Moe, Austl. 115/C3
Moeb (bay), Namb. 106/A2
Moel-y-Llyn (peak), Wal, UK 32/C2
Moëlan-sur-Mer, Fr. 42/B3
Moelfre (peak), Wal, UK 32/C1
Moen, Nor. 37/F1
Moenkopi (riv.), US 128/E3
Moerai (isl.), FrPol. 117/K7
Moerbeke, Belg. 52/C1
Moers, Ger. 50/D6
Moervaart (riv.), Belg. 52/C1
Moesa (riv.), Swi. 57/F5
Moffat, Sc, UK 36/C6
Moffett Field Naval Air Sta., Ca, US 135/K12
Moga, India 86/C4
Mogadouro, Port. 44/B2
Mogami (riv.), Japan 76/B4
Mogami, Japan 76/B4
Mogaung, Myan. 83/G2
Mogent (riv.), Sp. 45/L6
Mogglingen, Ger. 54/C5
Moghul Gardens, India 86/C3
Mogi das Cruzes, Braz. 211/G8
Mogi-Guaçu, Braz. 211/G7
Mogi-Guaçu (riv.), Braz. 211/G7
Mogi-Mirim, Braz. 211/G7
Mogilno, Pol. 41/J2
Moglia, It. 59/D3
Mogliano Veneto, It. 59/F1
Möglingen, Ger. 54/C5
Mogoro, It. 46/A3
Mogotes (pt.), Arg. 158/F3
Mogotón (peak), Nic. 144/E3
Moguer, Sp. 44/B4
Mohács, Hun. 48/D3
Mohaeli (isl.), Com. 107/G6
Mohales Hoek, Les. 106/D3
Mohall, ND, US 127/H3
Mohamed V (dam), Mor. 100/C2
Mohamed V, Barrage (res.), Mor. 100/C2
Mohamed V (Casablanca) (int'l arpt.), Mor. 98/D2
Mohammadia, Alg. 100/F5
Mohammadia-Znata (prov.), Mor. 100/A2
Mohammedia, Mor. 100/A3
Mohawk (lake), NJ, US 138/D1
Moheda, Swe. 38/F3
Mohembo, Bots. 105/D4
Mohican (cape), Ak, US 134/E3
Möhlin, Swi. 56/D2
Möhne (riv.), Ger. 51/F6
Möhnestausee (lake), Ger. 51/F5
Mohnton, Pa, US 138/C3
Moho, Peru 156/D4
Mohrsville, Pa, US 138/C3
Mohyliv-Podil's'kyy, Ukr. 49/H1
Moi (int'l arpt.), Kenya 104/C4
Moi, Nor. 38/B2
Moie, It. 59/G5
Moinești, Rom. 49/H2
Moinkum (des.), Kaz. 64/H5
Moinsi (hills), Gha. 103/E5
Moira (riv.), On, Can. 130/E2
Moirans, Fr. 42/F4
Moirans-en-Montagne, Fr. 56/B5
Moisie (riv.), Qu, Can. 123/K3
Moislains, Fr. 52/B4
Moissac, Fr. 42/D4
Moisselles, Fr. 30/K4
Moisson, Fr. 30/G4
Moita, Port. 45/Q10
Moitaco, Ven. 153/E3
Mojácar, Sp. 44/E4
Mojave (riv.), Ca, US 128/C4
Mojave (des.), Ca, US 124/C5
Mojiang Hanizu Zizhixian, China 83/H3
Mojikit (lake), On, Can. 127/L3
Mojkovac, Serb. 47/F1
Mojos, Llanos de (plain), Bol. 150/E6
Moju (riv.), Braz. 151/J4
Mōka, Japan 75/F2
Mokameh, India 85/E3
Mokapu (pt.), Hi, US 124/W13
Mokau (riv.), NZ 117/S10
Mokelumne (riv.), Ca, US 128/B3
Mokelumne (aqueduct), Ca, US 135/M11
Mokena, Il, US 135/Q16
Mokil (isl.), Micr. 116/E4
Mokochu (peak), Thai. 78/B3
Mokokchūng, India 83/F2
Mokolo, Camr. 96/H5
Mokp'o, SKor. 73/D5
Mokrin, Serb. 48/E3
Moksha (riv.), Rus. 63/G1
Mokuleia, Hi, US 124/V12
Mol, Serb. 48/E3
Mol, Belg. 50/C6
Moláoi, Gre. 47/H4
Molare, It. 58/B3
Molas, Punta (pt.), Mex. 144/E1
Molat (isl.), Cro. 48/B3
Molatón (peak), Sp. 44/E3
Molbergen, Ger. 51/E3
Mold, Wal, UK 35/E5
Moldavia (reg.), Rom. 49/H2
Moldavian Carpathians (range), Rom. 49/G2
Molde, Nor. 37/C3
Moldova (ctry.) 49/H2
Moldova (riv.), Rom. 49/G2
Moldova Nouă, Rom. 48/E3
Moldoveanu (peak), Rom. 49/G3
Mole (riv.), Eng, UK 32/C5
Mole NP, Gha. 103/E4
Môle Saint-Nicolas, Haiti 145/H2
Molepolole, Bots. 105/E5
Molina, Sp. 44/E2
Molina, Chile 158/C2
Molina de Segura, Sp. 44/E3
Moline, Il, US 127/L5
Molinella, It. 59/E3
Molinicos, Sp. 44/D3
Molino de Flores, PN, Mex. 143/R9
Molins de Rei, Sp. 45/L7
Molise (reg.), It. 46/D2
Molkom, Swe. 38/E2
Möll (riv.), Aus. 43/K3
Møllebjerg (peak), Den. 37/D5
Mollendo, Peru 156/C5
Mollendruz, Col du (pass), Swi. 56/C4
Mollerussa, Sp. 45/F2
Molles (pt.), Chile 158/C2
Molles, Uru. 159/K10
Mollet del Vallès, Sp. 45/L6
Mollis, Swi. 57/F3
Mölndal, Swe. 38/E3
Mölnlycke, Swe. 38/E3
Molodezhnaya, Rus., Ant. 160/D
Mologa (riv.), Rus. 60/G4
Molokai (isl.), Hi, US 124/T10
Moloma (riv.), Rus. 61/L4
Molong, Austl. 115/D2
Molopo (riv.), Bots. 93/E7
Mólos, Gre. 47/H3
Molsheim, Fr. 56/D1
Molteno, SAfr. 106/D3
Molu (isl.), Indo. 81/H5
Molucca (isls.), Indo. 67/M10
Molucca (sea), Asia 67/M10
Moluccas (arch.), Indo. 81/G3
Molveno (lake), It. 57/G5
Molveno, It. 57/G5
Mombaça, Braz. 154/C2
Mombasa, Kenya 104/C4
Mombetsu, Japan 76/C1
Mombetsu, Japan 76/C2
Mömbris, Ger. 54/C2
Momchilgrad, Bul. 47/J2
Momfafa (cape), Indo. 81/H4
Momignies, Belg. 53/D3
Mömlingen, Ger. 54/C3
Momo, It. 58/B1
Momoishi, Japan 76/B3
Mompós, Col. 152/C2
Mon (state), Myan. 83/G4
Mon (riv.), Myan. 83/F3
Møn (isl.), Den. 37/E5
Mona (isl.), PR 141/M8
Mona (passg.), NAm. 141/L8
Monaco (ctry.) 58/J8
Monaco (cap.), Mona. 58/J8
Monaco, Port of (har.), Mona. 58/J8
Monadhliath (mts.), Sc, UK 36/B2
Monagas (state), Ven. 153/F2
Monaghan (co.), Ire. 34/A3
Monagrillo, Pan. 152/A3
Monagrillo (ruin), Pan. 152/A2
Monar (lake), Sc, UK 36/A2
Monashee (mts.), BC, Can. 126/D3
Moncada, Sp. 45/E3
Moncalieri, It. 43/G4
Moncalvo, It. 58/B2
Monção, Braz. 154/A1
Moncayo, Sierra del (range), Sp. 44/E2
Mönch (peak), Swi. 56/D4
Monchegorsk, Rus. 60/G2
Mönchengladbach, Ger. 50/D6
Monchique, Serra de (mts.), Port. 44/A4
Monchique, Port. 44/A4
Moncks Corner, SC, US 133/H3
Monclova, Mex. 132/C5
Moncton, NB, Can. 131/H2
Mondego (cape), Port. 44/A2
Mondego (riv.), Port. 44/A2
Mondéjar, Sp. 44/D2
Mondolfo, It. 59/G5
Mondoñedo, Sp. 44/B1
Mondorf-les-Bains, Lux. 53/F4
Mondovì, It. 58/A4
Mondragón, Sp. 44/D1
Mondragone, It. 46/C2
Mondsee (lake), Aus. 55/G7
Mondsee, Aus. 55/G7
Moneglia, It. 58/C4
Monemvasia, Gre. 47/H4
Mones Cazón, Arg. 158/E3
Monesterio, Sp. 44/B3
Money (pt.), Sc, UK 34/C2
Moneyreagh, NI, UK 34/C2
Monferrato (reg.), It. 43/H4
Monforte, Sp. 44/B1
Monforte, Port. 44/B3
Mongaguá, Braz. 211/G9
Mongers (lake), Austl. 109/A3
Monghidoro, It. 59/E4
Mongo, Chad 97/J5
Mongo (riv.), Gui. 102/C4
Mongolia (ctry.) 70/G2
Mongu, Zam. 105/D4
Mönh Hayrhan (peak), Mong. 70/F2
Mönh Sarĭdag (peak), Mong. 70/H1
Monheim, Ger. 54/D5
Monheim, Ger. 53/F1
Monifieth, Sc, UK 36/D4
Moniquirá, Col. 152/C3
Monistrol de Montserrat, Sp. 45/K6
Monistrol-sur-Loire, Fr. 42/F4
Monitor (range), Nv, US 128/C3
Monkayo, Phil. 79/E6
Monkey (pt.), Nic. 145/F4
Monkey River Town, Belz. 144/D2
Mońki, Pol. 41/M2
Monks (isl.), Md, US 138/B5
Monmouth, Il, US 127/L5
Monmouth, Or, US 126/C4
Monmouth Beach, NJ, US 138/E3
Monmouth Junction, NJ, US 138/D3
Monmouth Mil. Res., NJ, US 138/D3
Monmouthshire (co.), Wal, UK 32/D3
Monmow (riv.), Eng, UK 32/C2
Monnickendam, Neth. 50/C4
Mono (riv.), Togo 96/F6
Mono (lake), Ca, US 128/C3
Mono (prov.), Ben. 103/F5
Monocacy (riv.), Md, US 138/A4
Monor, Hun. 48/D2
Monóvar, Sp. 45/E3
Monreal del Campo, Sp. 44/E2
Monreale, It. 46/C3
Monroe, Wi, US 127/L5
Monroe, Ut, US 128/D3
Monroe, Ga, US 133/H3
Monroe (lake), Fl, US 133/G2
Monroe, La, US 129/J4
Monroe, NC, US 133/H3
Monroe, Mi, US 130/D3
Monroe, Ct, US 139/E1
Monroe, NY, US 138/D1
Monroe, Wa, US 135/C2
Monroe City, Il, US 137/G9
Monroeville, Al, US 133/G4
Monroeville, NJ, US 138/C4
Monrovia (cap.), Libr. 102/C5
Monrovia, Ca, US 136/G7
Mons, Belg. 52/C3
Monsanto, Port. 44/B2
Monschau, Ger. 53/F2
Monsefú, Peru 156/B2
Monselice, It. 43/J4
Monsenhor Tabosa, Braz. 154/B2
Monsey, NY, US 139/J7
Monsheim, Ger. 54/B3
Monster, Neth. 50/B4
Mönsteras, Swe. 38/G3
Monsummano Terme, It. 59/D5
Mont-de-Marsan, Fr. 42/C5
Mont-Joli, Qu, Can. 131/G1
Mont-Laurier, Qu, Can. 130/F2
Mont Peko, PN du, C.d'Iv. 102/D5
Mont-Royal, Qu, Can. 131/N6
Mont-Saint-Martin, Fr. 53/E4
Mont-Saint-Michel, Qu, Can. 130/F2
Mont Sangbé, PN du, C.d'Iv. 102/D4
Mont-Sous-Vaudrey, Fr. 56/B4
Montà, It. 58/A3
Monta Fon (mts.), Aus. 57/F3

Msta (riv.), Rus. 60/G4
Mszana Dolna, Pol. 41/L4
Mtorwi (peak), Tanz. 104/B5
Mtsensk, Rus. 62/F1
Mtubatuba, SAfr. 107/F3
Mtunzini, SAfr. 107/E3
Mtwara, Tanz. 104/D5
Mtwara (pol. reg.), Tanz. 104/C5
Mu-kawa (riv.), Japan 76/C2
Mu Ko Similan NP, Thai. 78/B4
Mu Ko Surin NP, Thai. 78/B4
Mualama, Moz. 105/G4
Muan, SKor. 73/D5
Muang Hinboun, Laos 78/D2
Muang Khammouan, Laos 78/D2
Muang Khong, Laos 78/D3
Muang Khongxedon, Laos 78/D3
Muang Pak-lay, Laos 78/C2
Muang Pakxan, Laos 78/C2
Muang Sing, Laos 83/H3
Muang Vangviang, Laos 78/C2
Muang Xaignabouri, Laos 78/C2
Muang Xay, Laos 83/H3
Muar, Malay. 80/B3
Muarabungo, Indo. 80/B4
Muāri (pt.), Pak. 89/J4
Mubārakpur, India 84/D2
Mubende, Ugan. 104/A2
Mucajaí (riv.), Braz. 150/F3
Much, Ger. 53/G2
Muchinga (mts.), Zam. 105/F3
Muck (isl.), Sc, UK 31/Q8
Muckleshoot Ind. Res., Wa, US 135/C3
Mucojo, Moz. 105/H3
Mucupina (mtn.), Hon. 144/E3
Mucur, Turk. 90/C2
Mucuri (riv.), Braz. 151/K7
Mud Mountain (dam), Wa, US 135/D3
Mud Mountain (lake), Wa, US 135/D3
Mudanjiang, China 71/N3
Mudanya, Turk. 49/J5
Mudau, Ger. 54/C3
Mudbach (riv.), Ger. 54/C3
Muddan (riv.), China 71/N2
Muddas NP, Swe. 37/G2
Muddy Run (res.), Pa, US 138/B4
Müden, Ger. 51/H3
Mudersbach, Ger. 53/G2
Mudgee, Austl. 115/D2
Mudjatik (riv.), Sk, Can. 122/F3
Mudon, Myan. 78/B2
Mudurnu, Turk. 49/K5
Muela (peak), Chile 159/B7
Muerte, Cerro de la (peak), CR 145/F4
Muff, Ire. 34/A1
Mufulira, Zam. 105/E3
Mugardos, Sp. 44/A1
Mugegawa, Japan 77/L4
Mughal Sarai, India 84/D3
Mugi, Japan 77/L4
Mugia, Sp. 44/A1
Muğla, Turk. 90/B2
Mugla (prov.), Turk. 90/B2
Muğla (prov.), Turk. 91/A1
Mughalzhar Taūy (mts.), Kaz. 87/C3
Muhamdi, India 84/C2
Muḩammad (pt.), Egypt 101/C3
Muhammadābad, India 84/D3
Muhavura (vol.), Rwa. 104/A3
Muhila, Monts (mts.), D.R. Congo 105/E3
Mühlacker, Ger. 54/B5
Mühlbach (riv.), Ger. 54/A2
Mühldorf, Ger. 55/F6
Mühleberg, Swi. 56/D4
Mühlenbeck, Ger. 40/Q6
Mühlhausen, Ger. 55/E4
Mühlheim am Main, Ger. 54/B2
Mühlheim an der Donau, Ger. 57/E1
Mühltroff, Ger. 55/E1
Mühlviertel (reg.), Aus. 41/G4
Muhos, Fin. 60/E2
Muhu (isl.), Est. 60/D4
Muiden, Neth. 50/C4
Muir of Ord, Sc, UK 36/B1
Muir Woods Nat'l Mon., Ca, US 128/B3
Muir Woods Nat'l Mon., Ca, US 135/J11
Muirkirk, Sc, UK 36/B5
Muizon, Fr. 52/C5
Muju, SKor. 73/D4
Mukacheve, Ukr. 41/M4
Mukawa, Japan 76/B2
Mukawwar (isl.), Sudan 101/D4
Mukden, Bol. 156/D3
Mukeriān, India 86/C4
Mukhayyam al Yarmūk, Syria 91/E3
Mukhmās, Isr. 91/G8
Mukinbudin, Austl. 112/C4
Mukō, Japan 77/J6
Mukono, Ugan. 104/B2
Mukoshima (isls.), Japan 116/D2
Muktsar, India 86/C4
Mukwonago, Wi, US 135/P14
Mula, Sp. 44/E3
Mulanje, Malw. 105/G4
Mulchatna (riv.), Ak, US 134/G4
Mulchén, Chile 158/B3
Mulde (riv.), Ger. 40/G3
Mulegé, Mex. 142/C3
Muleshoe, Tx, US 129/G4
Mulhacén, Cerro de (peak), Sp. 44/D4
Mülhausen, Ger. 51/H6
Mülheim an der Ruhr, Ger. 50/D6
Mulhouse, Fr. 56/D2
Muli (riv.), Indo. 81/J5
Muli Zangzu Zizhixian, China 83/H2
Muling (pass), China 72/D3
Mull (isl.), Sc, UK 31/R8
Mull of Galloway (pt.), Sc, UK 34/D2
Mull of Kintyre (pt.), Sc, UK 34/C1
Mull of Logan (pt.), Sc, UK 34/D2
Mullach Coire Mhic Fhearchair (peak), Sc, UK 36/A1
Mullaghcleevaun (peak), Ire. 34/B5
Mullaghmore (peak), NI, UK 34/B2
Mullaittivu, SrL. 82/D6
Mullardoch (lake), Sc, UK 36/A2
Muller (mts.), Indo. 80/D4
Mullewa, Austl. 112/B4
Müllheim, Ger. 56/D2
Müllheim, Swi. 57/F2
Mullica (riv.), NJ, US 138/D4
Mullica Hill, NJ, US 138/C4
Mullingar, Ire. 31/Q10
Mullins, SC, US 133/J3
Mullumbimby, Austl. 115/E1
Mulobezi, Zam. 105/E4
Multai, India 84/B5
Multān, Pak. 86/A4
Multnomah (falls), Or, US 126/C4
Mulu (peak), Malay. 80/D3
Mulwala, Austl. 115/C2
Mum Nauk (pt.), Thai. 78/B5
Mumbai (Bombay), India 89/K5
Mumbwa, Zam. 105/E3
Mümling (riv.), Ger. 54/B3
Mumoni (peak), Kenya 104/C3
Mun (riv.), Thai. 83/H4
Muna (isl.), Indo. 81/F4
Muna, Mex. 144/D1
Munamägi (hill), Est. 39/M3
Muñani, Peru 156/D4
Muncar, Indo. 80/D5
Münchberg, Ger. 55/E2
München (Munich), Ger. 55/E6
Münchenstein, Swi. 56/D2
Munchique (peak), Col. 152/B4
Munchique, PN, Col. 152/B4
Münchmünster, Ger. 55/E5
Muncie, In, US 130/C3
Muncy, Pa, US 138/B1
Mundaring, Austl. 112/L6
Munday, Tx, US 129/H4
Mundelein, Il, US 135/Q15
Mundemba, Camr. 103/H5
Münden, Ger. 51/G6
Munderfing, Aus. 55/G6
Munderkingen, Ger. 57/F1
Mundo Novo, Braz. 157/F1
Mundo Novo, Braz. 154/B3
Mundubbera, Austl. 114/C4
Munera, Sp. 44/D3
Mungaoli, India 84/B3
Mungeli, India 84/C4
Munger, India 85/F3
Mungo NP, Austl. 115/B2
Mun'gyŏng, SKor. 73/E4
Munising, Mi, US 127/M4
Munkebo, Den. 38/D4
Munkedal, Swe. 38/D2
Munkfors, Swe. 38/E2
Munku-Sardyk (peak), Rus. 70/H1
Münnerstadt, Ger. 54/D2
Muñoz Gamero (pen.), Chile 157/B7
Munsan, SKor. 73/F6
Münsingen, Swi. 56/D4
Münsingen, Ger. 54/C6
Munster (reg.), Ire. 31/P10
Münster, Ger. 51/E5
Munster, Ger. 51/H3
Munster, Fr. 56/D1
Münster, Swi. 57/E5
Munster, In, US 135/R16
Münster, Ger. 54/B3
Münster/Osnabrück (int'l arpt.), Ger. 51/E4
Münstereifel, Ger. 53/F2
Münsterhausen, Ger. 54/D6
Münsterland (reg.), Ger. 40/D2
Münstermaifeld, Ger. 53/G3
Muntele Mare (peak), Rom. 49/F2
Muntendam, Neth. 50/D2
Muntok, Indo. 80/C4
Müntschemier, Swi. 56/D4
Münzenberg, Ger. 54/B2
Münzkirchen, Aus. 55/G6
Munzur Vadisi NP, Turk. 90/D2
Muonio, Fin. 37/G2
Muonioälven (riv.), Swe. 37/G1
Muotathal, Swi. 57/E4
Mupa, PN da, Ang. 105/C4
Muping, China 72/E3
Muqdisho (Mogadishu) (cap.), Som. 97/Q7
Muqeibila, Isr. 91/G6
Mur (riv.), Aus. 43/L3
Mura (riv.), Slov.,Hun 48/C2
Muradiye, Turk. 90/E2
Murādnagar, India 86/D5
Murakami, Japan 75/F1
Murallón (peak), Chile 159/B6
Murano, It. 59/F2
Murat (peak), Turk. 90/B2
Muratlı, Turk. 90/E2
Muratlı, Turk. 49/H5
Murayama, Japan 76/B4
Murchison, Austl. 115/C3
Murchison (riv.), Austl. 109/A3
Murchison, NZ 117/S11
Murchison (mt.), Austl. 112/C3
Murcia, Sp. 45/E4
Murcia (aut. comm.), Sp. 44/E4
Murderkill (riv.), De, US 138/C6
Murdochville, Qu, Can. 131/H1
Murdock (pt.), Austl. 114/B1
Mürefte, Turk. 49/H5
Mureş (riv.), Rom. 62/B3
Mureş (prov.), Rom. 49/G2
Muret, Fr. 42/D5
Murfreesboro, Ar, US 129/J4
Murg (riv.), Ger. 53/H6
Murgab (riv.), Turk. 87/D5
Murgap (riv.), Trkm. 64/G6
Murgon, Austl. 114/C4
Muri, Swi. 57/E3
Muri bei Bern, Swi. 56/D4
Muria (peak), Indo. 80/D5
Muriaé, Braz. 155/D2
Murias de Paredes, Sp. 44/B1
Murici, Braz. 154/D3
Murīdke, Pak. 86/C4
Müritz (lake), Ger. 40/G2
Murlīganj, India 85/F3
Murmansk, Rus. 60/G1
Murmansk (int'l arpt.), Rus. 60/G1
Murmanskaya Oblast, Rus. 37/J1
Murnau, Ger. 57/H2
Muro, Sp. 45/G3
Muro, Japan 77/K6
Muro Lucano, It. 46/D2
Murom, Rus. 60/J5
Muroran, Japan 76/B2
Muros, Sp. 44/A1
Muroto, Japan 74/D4
Muroto-zaki (pt.), Japan 74/D4
Murowana Goślina, Pol. 41/J2
Murphy, NC, US 133/G3
Murphy, Mo, US 137/G9
Murr (riv.), Ger. 54/C5
Murra, Nic. 144/E3
Murramarang NP, Austl. 115/D2
Murray (lake), SC, US 133/H3
Murray (riv.), Austl. 109/D4
Murray, Ky, US 130/B4
Murray, Ut, US 137/K12
Murray Bridge, Austl. 113/H5
Murraysburg, SAfr. 106/C3
Murrayville, Austl. 115/B2
Murree, Pak. 86/B3
Murrieta, Ca, US 136/C3
Murrieta Hot Springs, Ca, US 136/C3
Murrumbidgee (riv.), Austl. 109/D4
Murrumburrah, Austl. 115/D2
Murrurundi, Austl. 115/D1
Murshidābād, India 85/G3
Murtala Muhammed (int'l arpt.), Nga. 103/F5
Murtaröl (peak), Swi. 57/G4
Murten, Swi. 56/D4
Murtoa, Austl. 115/B3
Murud (peak), Malay. 80/E3
Murupara, NZ 117/T10
Mururoa (isl.), FrPol. 117/M7
Murwāra, India 84/C4
Murwillumbah, Austl. 114/D5
Mürz (riv.), Aus. 41/H5
Mürzzuschlag, Aus. 41/H5
Muş (prov.), Turk. 90/E2
Muş, Turk. 90/E2
Musabeyli, Turk. 91/E1
Musāfirkhāna, India 84/C2
Musala (peak), Bul. 47/H1
Musan, NKor. 73/E1
Musashino, Japan 77/D2
Musconetcong (riv.), NJ, US 138/C2
Muscoot (res.), NY, US 139/E1
Muscoy, Ca, US 136/C2
Musekwapoort (pass), SAfr. 105/E5
Museum of Flight, Wa, US 135/C2
Musgrave (ranges), Austl. 109/C3
Musgrave Harbour, Nf, Can. 131/L1
Mushābani, India 85/F4
Mushie, D.R. Congo 96/J8
Mushin, Nga. 103/F5
Musi (riv.), Indo. 80/B4
Musile di Piave, It. 59/F1
Musinga (peak), Col. 152/B3
Muskego, Wi, US 135/P14
Muskegon, Mi, US 130/C3
Muskegon (riv.), Mi, US 130/C3
Muskingum (riv.), Oh, US 130/D4
Muskoka (lake), On, Can. 130/E2
Musoma, Tanz. 104/B3
Musone (riv.), It. 59/G6
Musquaro (riv.), Qu, Can. 131/J1
Mussau (isl.), PNG 116/D5
Musselburgh, Sc, UK 36/C5
Musselshell (riv.), Mt, US 124/E2
Mussomeli, It. 46/C4
Musson, Belg. 53/E4
Mustafābād, Pak. 86/B4
Mustafakemalpaşa, Turk. 90/B1
Müstair, Swi. 57/G4
Mustang, Ok, US 137/M15
Musters (lake), Arg. 158/C5
Musu-dan (pt), NKor. 73/E2
Musún (mtn), Nic. 144/E3
Mušutište, Serb. 47/G1
Muswellbrook, Austl. 115/D2
Mūt, Egypt 101/B3
Mut, Turk. 91/C1
Mutá, Ponta do (pt), Braz. 154/C4
Mutare, Zim. 105/F4
Muthill, Sc, UK 36/C4
Mutis (peak), Indo. 81/F5
Mutsamudu, Com. 107/H6
Mutsu (bay), Japan 76/B3
Mutsu, Japan 76/B3
Mutsuzawa, Japan 77/E3
Muttekopf (peak), Aus. 57/G3
Muttenz, Swi. 56/D2
Mutters, Aus. 57/H3
Mutterstadt, Ger. 54/B4
Muttler (peak), Swi. 57/G4
Muttonville, Mi, US 135/G6
Mutum, Braz. 155/D1
Mutzig, Fr. 56/D1
Mŭynoq, Uzb. 63/L4
Muzaffargarh, Pak. 86/A4
Muzaffarnagar, India 86/D5
Muzaffarpur, India 85/E2
Muzambinho, Braz. 211/G6
Muzon (cape), Ak, US 134/M4
Muztag (peak), China 70/D4
Muztagata (peak), China 87/G5
Muzzana del Turgnano, It. 59/G1
Mwadui, Tanz. 104/B3
Mwana (cape), Kenya 104/D3
Mwanza (pol. reg), Tanz. 104/B3
Mwanza, Tanz. 104/B3
Mweelrea (peak), Ire. 31/P10
Mweka, D.R. Congo 105/D1
Mwene-Ditu, D.R. Congo 105/D2
Mwense, Zam. 104/A5
Mweru (lake), D.R. Congo 93/E5
Mweru-Wantipa NP, Zam. 104/A5
Mwesi (mtn), Tanz. 104/A4
Mwinilunga, Zam. 105/D3
My Son Temples (ruin), Viet. 78/E3
My Tho, Viet. 78/D4
Myall Lakes NP, Austl. 115/E2
Myanaung, Myan. 83/G4
Myanmar (Burma) (ctry.) 83/G3
Myebon, Myan. 83/F3
Myerstown, Pa, US 138/B3
Myggenäs, Swe. 38/D2
Myingyan, Myan. 83/G3
Myitkyinā, Myan. 83/G2
Myjava, Slvk. 41/J4
Mykolayiv, Ukr. 49/L2
Mykolayiv (int'l arpt), Ukr. 49/L2
Mykolayivs'ka Oblast, Ukr. 62/D3
Mylau, Ger. 55/F1
Mymensingh (pol. reg), Bang. 85/H3
Mynämäki, Fin. 39/J1
Mynydd Eppynt (mts), Wal, UK 32/C2
Mynydd Pencarreg (peak), Wal, UK 32/B2
Mynydd Preseli (mtn), Wal, UK 32/B3
Myōgi, Japan 77/B1
Myohaung, Myan. 83/F3
Myōkō-san (peak), Japan 75/F2
Myŏngch'ŏn, NKor. 73/E2
Mythorod, Ukr. 62/E2
Myrtle Beach, SC, US 133/J3
Myrtle Creek, Or, US 126/C5
Myrtleford, Austl. 115/C3
Mysen, Nor. 38/D2
Myślenice, Pol. 41/K4
Myślibórz, Pol. 41/H2
Myslivna (peak), Czh. 55/H5
Mysore, India 82/C5
Mystery Bay Rec. Area, Wa, US 135/B1
Mystic Island, NJ, US 138/D4
Myszków, Pol. 41/K3
Mytishchi, Rus. 61/W9
Mže (riv), Czh. 40/G4
Mzimba, Malw. 104/B5
Mzuzu, Malw. 104/B5

N

Na (riv), Viet. 78/C1
Naab (riv), Ger. 43/J2
Naaldwijk, Neth. 50/B4
Naalehu, Hi, US 124/U11
Naama, Alg. 99/E2
Naantali, Fin. 39/K1
Naarden, Neth. 50/C4
Naarn im Machlande, Aus. 55/H6
Naas, Ire. 31/Q10
Nababeep, SAfr. 106/B3
Nabari, Japan 77/K6
Nabari (riv), Japan 77/K6
Nabberu (lake), Austl. 112/D3
Nabburg, Ger. 55/F4
Naberezhnye Chelny, Rus. 61/M5
Nābha, India 86/D4
Nabiac, Austl. 115/E2
Nabisipi (riv), Qu, Can. 131/J1
Nabón, Ecu. 156/B1
Nabua, Phil. 79/D5
Nābul, Tun. 46/B4
Nābul (gov), Tun. 46/B4
Nacala, Moz. 105/H3
Nacaome, Hon. 144/E3
Nachi-Katsuura, Japan 74/D4
Nachingwea, Tanz. 104/C5
Náchod, Czh. 41/J3
Nachrodt-Wiblingwerde, Ger. 51/E6
Nacimiento, Chile 158/B3
Naco, Mex. 128/E5
Nacogdoches, Tx, US 129/J5
Nácori Chico, Mex. 142/C2
Nacozari de García, Mex. 142/C2
Nādbai, India 84/A2
Nadder (riv), Eng, UK 32/D4
Nadiād, India 89/K4
Nădlac, Rom. 48/E2
Nador (prov), Mor. 100/C2
Nador, Mor. 100/C2
Nadur, Malta 46/L6
Naejang-san NP, SKor. 73/D5
Näfels, Swi. 57/F3
Nafūsah, Jabal (mts), Libya 99/H3
Naga, Phil. 79/D5
Nagagami (riv), On, Can. 130/C1
Nagahama, Japan 74/C4
Nagahama, Japan 77/K5
Nagai, Japan 75/G1
Nagaizumi, Japan 77/B3
Nagakute, Japan 77/M5
Nāgāland (state), India 70/F6
Nagambie, Austl. 115/C3
Nagano, Japan 75/F2
Nagano (pref), Japan 75/E3
Naganuma, Japan 76/B2
Nagaoka, Japan 75/F2
Nagaokakyō, Japan 77/J6
Nagaon (Nowgong), India 83/F2
Nagar, India 84/A2
Nagara (riv), Japan 75/E3
Nagara, Japan 77/E3
Nagareyama, Japan 77/D2
Nāgārjuna Sāgar (res), India 82/C4
Nagarote, Nic. 140/D5
Nagarzê, China 85/H1
Nagas (pt), BC, Can. 134/M5
Nagasaka, Japan 77/A2
Nagasaki, Japan 74/A4
Nagasaki (int'l arpt), Japan 74/A4
Nagasaki (pref), Japan 74/A4
Nagasaki Peace, Japan 74/A4
Nagashima, Japan 77/L5
Nagato, Japan 74/B3
Nagato, Japan 77/A1
Nagatoro, Japan 77/C1
Nāgaur, India 89/K3
Nāgda, India 89/L4
Nāgercoil, India 82/C6
Nagīna, India 84/B1
Nago, Japan 75/J7
Nago-Torbole, It. 57/G6
Nāgod, India 84/C3
Nagold (riv), Ger. 54/B5
Nagold, Ger. 54/B5
Nagorno-Karabakh (prov), Azer. 63/H5
Nagoya, Japan 77/L5
Nagoya Castle, Japan 77/L5
Nagpula (pass), China 85/F1
Nāgpur, India 82/C3
Nags Head, NC, US 133/K3
Naguri, Japan 77/C2
Nagy-Milic (peak), Hun. 41/L4
Nagyatád, Hun. 48/C2
Nagyecsed, Hun. 41/M5
Nagyhalász, Hun. 48/E1
Nagykanizsa, Hun. 48/C2
Nagykáta, Hun. 48/D2
Nagykőrös, Hun. 48/D2
Naha, Japan 75/J7
Naḥal Shillo (riv), Isr, WBnk 91/G7
Nāhan, India 86/D4
Nahanni NP, NW, Can. 122/D2
Nahariyya, Isr. 91/D3
Nahāvand, Iran 88/E2
Nahe (riv), Ger. 43/G2
Naḥal Soreq (riv), Isr, WBnk 91/F8
Nahouri (prov), Burk. 103/E4
Nahr 'Atbarah (riv), Sudan 97/M4
Nahr Mufjir (riv), Isr, WBnk 91/G7
Nahr Ouassel (riv), Alg. 100/F5
Nahuel Huapi (lake), Arg. 147/B7
Nahuel Huapí, PN, Arg. 158/C4
Nahuelbuta, PN, Chile 158/B3
Naica, Mex. 142/D3
Naihāti, India 85/G4
Naila, Ger. 55/E2
Naiman Qi, China 72/E2
Nā'īn, Iran 88/F2
Nain, Nf, Can. 123/K3
Nainital, India 84/B1
Nainpur, India 84/C4
Naintré, Fr. 42/D3
Nairn (riv), Sc, UK 36/B2
Nairn, Sc, UK 36/C1
Nairne, Austl. 113/M9
Nairobi (cap), Kenya 104/C3
Nairobi NP, Kenya 104/C3
Naivasha, Kenya 104/C3
Naives-Rosières, Fr. 53/E6
Najafābād, Iran 88/F2
Nájera, Sp. 44/D1
Najin, NKor. 71/P3
Naju, SKor. 73/D5
Naka (riv), Japan 74/D4
Naka, Japan 77/G5
Nakadōri (isl), Japan 74/A4
Nakai, Japan 77/C3
Nakajō, Japan 75/F1
Nakalele (pt), Hi, US 124/T10
Nakamichi, Japan 77/B2
Nakaminato, Japan 75/G2
Nakamura, Japan 74/C4
Nakano, Japan 75/F2
Nakano (lag), Japan 74/C3
Nakasato, Japan 76/B3
Nakashibetsu, Japan 76/D2
Nakasongola, Ugan. 104/B2
Nakatane, Japan 75/L5
Nakatomi, Japan 77/A3
Nakatsu, Japan 74/B4
Nakatsugawa, Japan 75/E3
Nakazato, Japan 77/B1
Nakhodka, Rus. 71/P3
Nakhon Nayok, Thai. 78/C3
Nakhon Pathom, Thai. 78/C3
Nakhon Phanom, Thai. 78/D2
Nakhon Ratchasima, Thai. 78/C3
Nakhon Sawan, Thai. 78/C3
Nakhon Si Thammarat, Thai. 78/B4
Nakkila, Fin. 39/J1
Nakło nad Notecią, Pol. 41/J2
Naknek, Ak, US 134/G4
Nakodar, India 86/C4
Nakonde, Zam. 104/B5
Naksan-sa, SKor. 73/E3
Nakskov, Den. 38/D4
Naktong, SKor. 73/E4
Naktong (riv), SKor. 74/A3
Nakūr, India 86/D5
Nakuru, Kenya 104/C3
Nakusp, BC, Can. 126/D3
Nāl (riv), Pak. 89/J3
Nalayh, Mong. 70/J2
Nalbach, Ger. 53/F5
Nalbāri, India 85/H2
Nalbaugh NP, Austl. 115/D3
Nal'chik (int'l arpt), Rus. 63/G4
Nal'chik, Rus. 63/G4
Nalgonda, India 82/C4
Nalhāti, India 85/F3
Naliya, India 89/J4
Nallıhan, Turk. 49/K5
Nalón (riv), Sp. 44/B1
Nālūt, Libya 99/H3
Nam (riv), NKor. 73/D3
Nam Dinh, Viet. 83/J3
Nam Nao NP, Thai. 78/C2
Nam Un (res), Thai. 78/C2
Namakzār-e Shadād (salt pan), Iran 89/G2
Namangan (pol. reg), Uzb. 87/F4
Namangan, Uzb. 87/F4
Namaqualand (reg), SAfr. 106/B3
Namaripi (cape), Indo. 81/J4
Namasagali, Ugan. 104/B2
Namatanai, PNG 116/E5
Namborn, Ger. 53/G4
Nambour, Austl. 114/D4
Nambu, Japan 77/A3
Nambucca Heads, Austl. 115/E1
Nambung NP, Austl. 112/B4
Namdae (riv), NKor. 73/E2
Namdalseid, Nor. 37/D2
Namegawa, Japan 77/C1
Namekagon (riv), Wi, US 127/L4
Namentenga (prov), Burk. 103/E3
Namerikawa, Japan 75/E2
Nametil, Moz. 105/G4
Namhae (isl), SKor. 73/D5
Namhae, SKor. 73/D5
Namib (des), Namb. 105/B5
Namibe, Ang. 105/B4
Namibia (ctry) 105/C5
Namie, Japan 75/G2
Namioka, Japan 76/B3
Namja (pass), Nepal 82/D2
Namjagbarwa (peak), China 83/G2
Namling, China 82/E2
Namloser Wetterspitze (peak), Aus. 57/G3
Nammoku, Japan 77/B1
Namnoi (peak), Myan. 78/B4
Namoi (riv), Austl. 109/D4
Namonuito (isl), Micr. 116/D4
Namorik (isl), Mrsh. 116/F4
Namp'o, NKor. 73/C3
Nampula, Moz. 105/G4
Namsê (pass), China 82/D2
Namsos, Nor. 37/D2
Namu (isl), Mrsh. 116/F4
Namur (prov), Belg. 53/D3
Namur, Belg. 53/D3
Namwŏn, SKor. 73/D5
Namysłów, Pol. 41/J3
Nan (riv), Thai. 83/H4
Nan, Thai. 78/C2
Nanae, Japan 76/B3
Nanaimo, BC, Can. 126/C3
Nanakuli, Hi, US 124/V13
Nanam, NKor. 73/E2
Nanango, Austl. 114/D4
Nanao, Japan 75/E2
Nanauta, India 86/D5
Nanay (riv), Peru 150/D4
Nancagua, Chile 158/C2
Nanchang, China 79/C2
Nanchang, China 79/C2
Nancheng, China 79/C2
Nanchong, China 70/J5
Nancy, Fr. 53/F6
Nanda Devi (peak), India 70/C5
Nandan, China 83/J3
Nānded, India 82/C4
Nanding (riv), China 83/G3
Nandrin, Belg. 53/E3
Nandu (riv), China 79/A4
Nandurbār, India 89/K4
Nandy, Fr. 30/K6
Nandyāl, India 82/C4
Nanfeng, China 79/C2
Nang Xian, China 83/F2
Nanga Parbat (peak), Pak. 86/C2
Nangapinoh, Indo. 80/D4
Nangis, Fr. 30/M6
Nangnim (mts), NKor. 73/D2
Nangong, China 72/C3
Nangtud (mt), Phil. 81/F1
Nangwarry, Austl. 115/B3
Nanhui, China 72/L8
Nanjian Yizu Zizhixian, China 83/H2
Nanjing, China 72/D4
Nankāna Sāhib, Pak. 86/B4
Nankang, China 79/B2
Nankoku, Japan 74/C4
Nanle, China 72/C3
Nanliu (riv), China 83/J3
Nannestad, Nor. 38/D1
Nanning, China 83/J3
Nannō, Japan 77/L5
Nannup, Austl. 112/B5
Nanny (riv), Ire. 34/B4
Nānpāra, India 84/C2
Nanpi, China 72/D3
Nanping, China 79/C2
Nansei, Japan 77/L7
Nansen (sound), Nun, Can. 123/S6
Nant (lake), Sc, UK 36/A4
Nantai-san (peak), Japan 75/F2
Nanterre, Fr. 30/J5
Nantes, Fr. 42/C3
Nanteuil-le-Haudouin, Fr. 30/L4
Nanteuil-lès-Meaux, Fr. 52/B6
Nanticoke, On, Can. 130/D3
Nanticoke, Pa, US 138/B1
Nanton, Ab, Can. 126/E3
Nantong, China 72/E4
Nantua, Fr. 56/B5
Nantucket (isl), Ma, US 131/G3
Nantwich, Eng, UK 35/F5
Nanuet, NY, US 139/J7
Nanumanga (isl), Tuv. 116/G5
Nanumea (isl), Tuv. 116/G5
Nanuque, Braz. 154/B5
Nanwan (res), China 72/C4
Nanxi, China 83/H2
Nanxiong, China 79/B2
Nanyang, China 72/C4
Nanyang, China 72/D4
Nanyuki, Kenya 104/C2
Nanzhang, China 72/B5
Nanzhao, China 72/C4
Nao, Cabo de la (cape), Sp. 45/F3
Naococane (lake), Qu, Can. 123/J3
Naogaon, Bang. 85/G3
Naokot, Pak. 82/A3
Naolinco, Mex. 143/N7
Naoua (falls), C.d'Iv. 102/D5
Náousa, Gre. 47/J4
Náousa, Gre. 47/H2
Napa, Ca, US 128/B3
Napa (co), Ca, US 135/K10
Napa (riv), Ca, US 135/K10
Napa (valley), Ca, US 135/K9
Napa Junction, Ca, US 135/K10
Napak (peak), Ugan. 104/B2
Napakiak, Ak, US 134/F3
Napanee, On, Can. 130/E2
Napaskiak, Ak, US 134/F3
Napata (ruin), Sudan 101/B5
Naperville, Il, US 130/B3
Napf (peak), Swi. 56/D4
Napier, NZ 117/T10
Napier, SAfr. 106/L11
Naples, Fl, US 133/H5
Naples (Napoli), It. 46/D2
Napo (riv), Peru 152/C5
Napo (riv), Ecu, Peru 147/B3
Napo (prov), Ecu. 152/B5
Napoleon, ND, US 127/J4
Napoleonville, La, US 129/K5
Napoli, Golfo di (gulf), It. 46/C2
Napuka (isl), FrPol. 117/L6
Naqīl Sumārah (pass), Yem. 88/D6
Nara, Mali 102/D3
Nāra (riv), Pak. 89/J4
Nara, Japan 77/J6
Naracoorte, Austl. 115/B3
Naraini, India 84/C3
Naranbulag, Mong. 70/F2
Naranjal, Ecu. 152/B5
Naranjito, Ecu. 156/B1
Naranjos, Mex. 144/B1
Narāq, Iran 88/F2
Narasannapeta, India 82/D4
Narashino, Japan 77/E2
Narathiwat, Thai. 78/C5
Nārāyanganj, Bang. 85/H4
Nārāyani (zone), Nepal 85/E2
Narayani (riv), Nepal 85/E2
Nārāyanpet, India 82/C4
Narbonne, Fr. 42/E5
Narceo (riv), Sp. 44/B1

210

Nardò – Ngaba

Nardò, It. 47/F2
Nare (pt.), Eng, UK 32/B6
Narellan, Austl. 114/G9
Narembeen, Austl. 112/C5
Nares (str.), Can.,Grld. 123/T6
Narew (riv.), Pol. 60/D5
Narganá, Pan. 152/B2
Narinda (bay), Madg. 107/H6
Nariño (dept.), Col. 152/B4
Narita (int'l arpt.), Japan 75/G3
Narita, Japan 77/E2
Nariz (peak), Chile 159/C7
Narkatiāganj, India 85/E2
Narmada (riv.), India 67/G7
Narman, Turk. 63/G4
Narni, It. 46/C1
Narodnaya (peak), Rus. 61/P2
Narok, Kenya 104/B3
Narón, Sp. 44/A1
Narooma, Austl. 115/D3
Nārowāl, Pak. 86/C3
Nærøy, Nor. 37/D2
Narra, Phil. 81/E2
Narrabri, Austl. 115/D1
Narrandera, Austl. 115/C2
Narrogin, Austl. 112/C5
Narromine, Austl. 115/D2
Narrows (riv.), NY, US 139/J9
Narsimhapur, India 84/B4
Narsingarh, India 89/L4
Narsinghdi, Bang. 85/H4
Narusawa, Japan 77/B3
Naruto, Japan 74/D3
Narutō, Japan 77/E2
Narva (res.), Rus. 60/F4
Narva (riv.), Est.,Rus. 60/E4
Narva (bay), Est.,Rus. 39/M2
Narva, Est. 39/N2
Narvacan, Phil. 79/D4
Narvik, Nor. 37/F1
Narwāna, India 86/D5
Nar'yan-Mar, Rus. 61/M2
Naryn, Kyr. 87/G4
Naryn (obl.), Kyr. 87/G4
Naryn (riv.), Kyr. 64/H5
Naryn Qum (plain), Kaz. 63/J2
Narzole, It. 58/A3
Năsăud, Rom. 49/G2
Naschel, Arg. 158/D2
Nash (pt.), Wal, UK 32/C4
Nashua, NH, US 131/G3
Nashville (int'l arpt.), Tn, US 130/C4
Nashville (cap.), Tn, US 130/C4
Našice, Cro. 48/D3
Nasielsk, Pol. 41/L2
Nasijärvi (lake), Fin. 39/K1
Nāsik, India 89/K5
Nasīrābād, India 89/K3
Naso (pt.), Phil. 81/F1
Nāsriganj, India 85/E3
Nass (riv.), BC, Can. 134/N4
Nassach (riv.), Ger. 54/D2
Nassarawa (state), Nga. 103/G4
Nassau (cap.), Bahm. 141/F2
Nassau (bay), Chile 159/D7
Nassau (isl.), Cookls. 117/J6
Nassau, Ger. 53/G3
Nassau, De, US 138/C6
Nassau (co.), NY, US 139/E2
Nasser (lake), Egypt 93/E2
Nassereith, Aus. 57/G3
Nässjö, Swe. 38/F3
Nassogne, Belg. 53/E3
Nastapoka (isls.), Qu, Can. 123/J3
Nastätten, Ger. 53/G3
Næstved, Den. 38/D4
Nasu-dake (peak), Japan 75/F2
Nat (peak), Myan. 83/G4
Nata, Bots. 105/E5
Natá, Pan. 152/A2
Natagaima, Col. 152/C4
Natal, Braz. 154/D2
Naṭanz, Iran 88/F2
Natashō, Japan 77/J5
Natashquan (riv.), Qu, Can. 123/K3
Natchez, Ms, US 129/K5
Natchez Trace Nat'l Parkway, US 130/C5
Natchitoches, La, US 129/J5
Naters, Swi. 56/D5
Nāthdwāra, India 89/K4
Natimuk, Austl. 115/B3
Nation (riv.), BC, Can. 126/B2
National Agriculture Research Center, Md, US 138/B6
National Aquarium, Md, US 138/B5
National Archaeological Museum, Gre. 47/N8
National City, Ca, US 136/C5
National Cowboy Hall of Fame and Western Heritage Center, Ok, US 137/N14
National Exhibition Centre, Eng, UK 33/E2
National Institutes of Health, Md, US 138/A6
National Museum, Mona. 58/J8
National Security Agency, Md, US 138/B5
Natitingou, Ben. 103/F4
Natl, Jor. 91/D4
Natron (lake), Tanz. 104/B3
Natternbach, Aus. 55/G6
Nattheim, Ger. 54/D5
Nättraby, Swe. 38/F3
Natuna (isls.), Indo. 67/K9
Natural Bridge Caverns, Tx, US 137/U20
Natural Bridges Nat'l Mon., Ut, US 128/E3
Naturaliste (cape), Austl. 115/D4
Naturaliste (chan.), Austl. 112/B3
Naturaliste (cape), Austl. 112/B5
Naturno (Naturns), It. 57/G4
Naucalpan, Mex. 143/Q10
Naucelle, Fr. 42/E4
Nauders, Aus. 57/G4
Naudesnek (pass), SAfr. 106/E3
Nauen, Ger. 40/P6
Naugachhia, India 85/F3
Naugaon Sādāt, India 84/B1
Nauhcampatépetl (vol.), Mex. 143/M7
Nauheim, Ger. 54/B3
Naujan, Phil. 79/D5
Naujoji-Akmenė, Lith. 39/K3
Naumburg, Ger. 51/G6
Naumburg, Ger. 40/F3
Nauort, Ger. 53/G3
Nā'ūr, Jor. 91/D4
Nauru (ctry.) 116/F5
Naushahra, India 86/C3
Naushahra Virkhan, Pak. 86/B4
Nauta, Peru 156/C2
Nautla, Mex. 143/N6
Nauvo (Nagu), Fin. 39/J1
Nava, Mex. 132/C4
Nava, Colle di (pass), It. 58/A4
Nava del Rey, Sp. 44/C2
Navajo (res.), NM, US 128/F3
Navajo Nat'l Mon., Az, US 128/E3
Navalcarnero, Sp. 45/M9
Navalmoral de la Mata, Sp. 44/C3
Navalvillar de Pela, Sp. 44/C3
Navapolatsk, Bela. 39/N4
Navarin (cape), Rus. 65/T3
Navarino (isl.), Chile 157/C8
Navarra (aut. comm.), Sp. 44/D1
Navarro, Arg. 159/J11
Navàs, Sp. 45/F2
Navas de San Juan, Sp. 44/D3
Navasota (riv.), Tx, US 143/F2
Navassa (isl.), Myan. 145/H2
Navax (pt.), Eng, UK 32/A6
Nave, It. 58/D1
Navenne, Fr. 56/C2
Navia, Sp. 44/B1
Navia (riv.), Sp. 44/B1
Navidad, Chile 158/N8
Navina, Ok, US 137/M14
Naviraí, Braz. 157/F1
Năvodari, Rom. 49/J3
Navojoa, Mex. 142/C3
Navolato, Mex. 142/D3
Návpaktos, Gre. 47/G3
Návplion, Gre. 47/H4
Navsāri, India 89/K4
Navy Board (inlet), Nun., Can. 123/H1
Navy Yard City, Wa, US 135/B2
Nawābganj, India 84/B1
Nawābganj, India 84/C1
Nawābganj, Bang. 85/G3
Nawābshāh, Pak. 89/J3
Nawāda, India 85/E3
Nawān Jandānwāla, Pak. 86/A3
Nawāshahr, India 86/D4
Nawāshahr, Pak. 86/B2
Nawoiy, Uzb. 87/E4
Nawoiy (pol. reg.), Uzb. 87/D4
Nawş, Ra's (pt.), Oman 89/G5
Naxçıvan, Azer. 63/H5
Naxçıvan Aut. Rep., Azer. 63/H5
Naxi, China 83/J2
Náxos, Gre. 47/J4
Náxos (isl.), Gre. 47/J4
Nayarit (state), Mex. 142/D4
Nayong, China 83/J2
Nayoro, Japan 76/C1
Nayramadlïn (peak), Mong. 70/E2
Nayzatash (pass), Taj. 87/F5
Nazaré, Braz. 154/C4
Nazaré, Port. 44/A3
Nazaré do Piauí, Braz. 154/B2
Nazaré Paulista, Braz. 211/G8
Nazareth, Pa, US 138/C2
Nazareth, Belg. 52/C2
Nazas (riv.), Mex. 142/D3
Nazas, Mex. 142/D3
Nazca, Peru 156/C4
Naze, Japan 75/K6
Naze, The (pt.), Eng, UK 33/H3
Nazerat (Nazareth), Isr. 91/G6
Nazilli, Turk. 90/B2
Nazrēt, Eth. 97/N6
Nazyvayevsk, Rus. 87/F1
Nchelenge, Zam. 104/A5
Ncheu, Malw. 105/F3
Ndalatando, Ang. 105/B2
Ndali, Ben. 103/F4
Ndele, CAfr. 97/K6
Ndende (isl.), Sol. 116/F6
N'djamena (cap.), Chad 96/J5
Ndola, Zam. 105/E3
Ndrhamcha (lake), Mrta. 102/B2
Né (riv.), Fr. 42/C4
Néa Alikarnassós, Gre. 47/J5
Néa Ankhíalos, Gre. 47/H3
Néa Artáki, Gre. 47/H3
Néa Ionía, Gre. 47/H3
Néa Ionía, Gre. 47/N8
Néa Kallikrátia, Gre. 47/H2
Néa Kíos, Gre. 47/H4
Néa Mikhaniôna, Gre. 47/H2
Néa Moudhaniá, Gre. 47/H2
Néa Potídhaia, Gre. 47/H2
Néa Triglia, Gre. 47/H2
Néa Zíkhni, Gre. 47/H2
Neagh (lake), NI, UK 34/B2
Neale (lake), Austl. 109/C3
Neales (riv.), Austl. 113/G3
Neamț (prov.), Rom. 49/H2
Neauphle-le-Château, Fr. 30/H5
Neápolis, Gre. 47/H4
Neápolis, Gre. 47/G2
Neápolis, Gre. 47/J5
Near (isls.), Ak, US 134/A5
Neath, Wal, UK 32/C3
Neath (riv.), Wal, UK 32/C3
Neath Port Talbot (co.), Wal, UK 32/C3
Neavitt, Md, US 138/B6
Nebbi, Ugan. 104/A2
Nebel-Horn (peak), Ger. 57/G3
Nebikon, Swi. 56/D3
Nebitdag, Trkm. 63/K5
Neblina (peak), Braz. 153/E4
Nebo (mt.), Austl. 114/E6
Nebraska (state), US 129/G2
Nebrodi (mts.), It. 46/C4
Nechako (riv.), BC, Can. 122/D3
Neches (riv.), Tx, US 125/G5
Nechisar NP, Eth. 97/N6
Nechranice (res.), Czh. 55/G2
Neckar (riv.), Ger. 40/D4
Neckarbischofsheim, Ger. 54/B4
Neckargemünd, Ger. 54/B4
Neckarsteinach, Ger. 54/B4
Neckarsulm, Ger. 54/C4
Necker (isl.), Hi, US 117/J2
Necochea, Arg. 158/F3
Necoclí, Col. 152/B2
Necropoli (ruin), It. 46/C1
Neda, Sp. 44/A1
Nedelino, Bul. 47/J2
Nedelišće, Cro. 43/M3
Nederland, Tx, US 129/J5
Nederland, Co, US 137/A3
Nederweert, Neth. 50/C6
Neede, Neth. 50/D4
Needles, Ca, US 128/D4
Needles, The, Eng, UK 33/E5
Needmore, Ok, US 137/N15
Neepawa, Mb, Can. 127/J3
Neerabup NP, Austl. 112/K6
Neerpelt, Belg. 50/C6
Neetze (riv.), Ger. 51/H2
Neetze, Ger. 51/H2
Neffelbach (riv.), Ger. 53/F2
Neftekamsk, Rus. 61/M4
Nefud (des.), SAr. 67/B7
Nefyn, Wal, UK 34/D6
Negēlē, Eth. 97/N6
Negev (reg.), Isr. 90/C4
Negoiu (peak), Rom. 49/G3
Negombo, SrL. 82/C6
Negotin, Serb. 48/F3
Negotino, FYROM 47/H2
Negra (pt.), Peru 156/A2
Negra (range), Braz. 154/A3
Negra (pt.), Belz. 144/D2
Negrais (cape), Myan. 83/F4
Negrar, It. 59/D1
Negreira, Sp. 44/A1
Negrești, Rom. 49/H2
Negritos, Peru 156/A2
Negro (riv.), Uru. 157/E3
Negro (riv.), Arg. 157/D5
Negro (peak), Arg. 158/C3
Negros (isl.), Phil. 67/M9
Nehbandān, Iran 89/H2
Nei Monggol (aut. reg.), China 71/K3
Nei Monggol (plat.), China 71/K3
Neiafu, Tonga 117/H6
Neiba, DRep. 141/G4
Neiba (mts.), DRep. 145/J2
Neiderösterreich (prov.), Aus. 43/L2
Neige, Crêt de la (peak), Fr. 56/B5
Neihuang, China 72/C4
Neijiang, China 70/J6
Neilston, Sc, UK 36/B5
Neiqiu, China 72/C3
Neisse (riv.), Ger. 41/H3
Neiva, Col. 152/C4
Neixiang, China 72/B4
Nejanilini (lake), Mb, Can. 122/G3
Nejdek, Czh. 55/F2
Nejrab (int'l arpt.), Syria 91/E1
Nek'emtē, Eth. 97/N6
Neksø, Den. 38/F4
Nelas, Port. 44/B2
Nelidovo, Rus. 60/G4
Nellingen, Ger. 54/C5
Nellore, India 82/C5
Nelson (cape), Austl. 115/B3
Nelson (isl.), Ak, US 134/E3
Nelson (str.), Chile 157/A7
Nelson, BC, Can. 126/D3
Nelson, NZ 117/S11
Nelson (riv.), Mb, Can. 122/G3
Nelson, Eng, UK 35/F4
Nelson-Atkins Museum of Fine Art, Mo, US 137/D5
Nelson Bay, Austl. 115/E2
Nelson Lagoon, Ak, US 134/F4
Nelson Lakes NP, NZ 117/S11
Nelspruit, SAfr. 105/F6
Néma, Mrta. 102/D2
Néma, Dhar (cliff), Mrta. 102/D2
Neman (riv.), Rus. 41/M1
Nembro, It. 58/C1
Neméa, Gre. 47/H4
Nemingha, Austl. 115/D1
Nemira (peak), Rom. 49/H2
Nemours, Fr. 42/E2
Nemunas (riv.), Lith. 60/D5
Nemuro (pen.), Japan 76/D2
Nemuro, Japan 76/D2
Nen (riv.), China 67/M5
Nenagh, Ire. 31/P10
Nenana, Ak, US 134/J3
Nendaz, Swi. 56/D5
Nene (riv.), Eng, UK 35/J6
Nenetskiy Aut. Okrug, Rus. 61/L2
Nenjiang, China 71/N2
Nentershausen, Ger. 51/G6
Nentershausen, Ger. 53/G3
Nenzing, Aus. 57/F3
Neo Volcanica, Cordillera (mts.), Mex. 143/Q10
Néon Petrítsion, Gre. 47/H2
Neoria Husainpur, India 84/B1
Néos Marmarás, Gre. 47/H2
Neosho (riv.), Ks,Ok, US 129/J3
Nepal (ctry.) 84/D1
Nepālganj, Nepal 84/C1
Nepanagar, India 89/L4
Nepean, On, Can. 130/F2
Nepean (riv.), Austl. 114/G8
Nepeña, Peru 156/B3
Nepessina (lake), Mi, US 135/F6
Nephi, Ut, US 128/E3
Nepisiguit (riv.), NB, Can. 131/H2
Nepomuk, Czh. 55/G4
Neptune City, NJ, US 138/D3
Nera (riv.), It. 43/K5
Nérac, Fr. 42/D4
Neratovice, Czh. 55/H2
Nerekhta, Rus. 60/J4
Neresheim, Ger. 54/D5
Neretva (riv.), Bosn. 48/D4
Neris (riv.), Lith. 60/E5
Nerja, Sp. 44/D4
Nermete (pt.), Peru 156/A2
Nerokoúros, Gre. 47/J5
Nerone (peak), It. 59/F5
Nerpio, Sp. 44/D3
Nersingen, Ger. 54/D6
Nerva, Sp. 44/B4
Nervesa della Battaglia, It. 59/F1
Nerviano, It. 58/B1
Nes, Neth. 50/C2
Nes, Nor. 38/D1
Nes Ẕiyyona, Isr. 91/F8
Nesbyen, Nor. 38/C1
Nesebŭr, Bul. 47/K1
Nesher, Isr. 91/G6
Neskaupstadhur, Ice. 37/Q6
Nesle, Fr. 52/B4
Nesles-la-Vallée, Fr. 30/J4
Nesquehoning, Pa, US 138/C2
Ness (riv.), Sc, UK 36/B2
Ness (lake), Sc, UK 36/B2
Nesselrode (mt.), Ak, US 134/M4
Nesselwang, Ger. 57/G2
Nesslau, Swi. 57/F3
Neston, Eng, UK 35/E5
Nestórion, Gre. 47/G2
Néstos (riv.), Gre. 49/G5
Netanya, Isr. 91/F7
Netarhāt, India 85/E4
Netcong, NJ, US 138/D2
Nethe (riv.), Ger. 51/G5
Netherlands (ctry.) 40/C3
Netherlands Antilles (dpcy.), Neth. 141/H5
Netolice, Czh. 55/H4
Netphen, Ger. 53/H2
Netstal, Swi. 57/F3
Nette (riv.), Ger. 50/D6
Nettebach (riv.), Ger. 53/G3
Nettersheim, Ger. 53/F3
Nettetal, Ger. 50/D6
Nettilling (lake), Nun., Can. 123/J2
Nettuno, It. 46/C2
Netzschkau, Ger. 55/F1
Neu Darchau, Ger. 51/H2
Neu-Isenburg, Ger. 54/B2
Neu-Ulm, Ger. 54/D6
Neu Zittau, Ger. 40/Q7
Neubiberg, Ger. 55/E6
Neubrandenburg, Ger. 41/G2
Neubulach, Ger. 54/B5
Neuburg, Ger. 54/B5
Neuburg an der Donau, Ger. 54/E5
Neuburg an der Kammel, Ger. 57/G1
Neuchâtel, Swi. 56/C4
Neuchâtel (canton), Swi. 56/C4
Neuchâtel, Lac de (lake), Swi. 43/G3
Neuenbürg, Ger. 54/B5
Neuenburg am Rhein, Ger. 56/D2
Neuendettelsau, Ger. 54/D4
Neuenhagen, Ger. 40/Q6
Neuenhaus, Ger. 50/D3
Neuenkirchen, Ger. 51/F3
Neuenkirchen, Ger. 51/F3
Neuenkirchen, Ger. 51/E4
Neuenrade, Ger. 51/E6
Neuenstadt am Kocher, Ger. 54/C4
Neuenstein, Ger. 54/C4
Neuerburg, Ger. 53/F3
Neuf-Brisach, Fr. 56/D1
Neufahrn bei Freising, Ger. 55/E6
Neufchâteau, Fr. 56/B1
Neufchâteau, Belg. 53/E4
Neufchâtel-en-Bray, Fr. 42/D2
Neufchâtel-Hardelot, Fr. 52/A2
Neufchelles, Fr. 30/M4
Neufmanil, Fr. 53/D4
Neufmoutiers-en-Brie, Fr. 30/L5
Neuhaus am Inn, Ger. 55/G6
Neuhaus am Rennweg, Ger. 54/E1
Neuhaus-Schierschnitz, Ger. 54/E2
Neuhäusel, Ger. 53/G3
Neuhausen am Rheinfall, Swi. 57/E2
Neuhof, Ger. 54/C2
Neuhof an der Zenn, Ger. 54/D4
Neuhofen, Ger. 54/B4
Neuhofen an der Krems, Aus. 55/H6
Neuilly-en-Thelle, Fr. 52/B5
Neuilly-L'Évêque, Fr. 56/B2
Neuilly-sur-Marne, Fr. 30/K5
Neuilly-sur-Seine, Fr. 30/J5
Neukirchen, Ger. 38/C4
Neukirchen an der Vöckla, Aus. 55/G6
Neukirchen vorm Wald, Ger. 55/G5
Neumarkt am Wallersee, Aus. 55/G7
Neumarkt (Enga), It. 57/H5
Neumarkt im Mühlkreis, Aus. 55/H6
Neumarkt in der Oberpfalz, Ger. 55/E4
Neumarkt-Sankt Veit, Ger. 55/F6
Neumünster, Ger. 38/C4
Neunkirch, Swi. 57/E2
Neunkirchen, Aus. 43/M3
Neunkirchen, Ger. 53/H2
Neunkirchen, Ger. 53/G5
Neunkirchen-Seelscheid, Ger. 53/G2
Neupotz, Ger. 54/B4
Neuquén (riv.), Arg. 157/C4
Neuquén (prov.), Arg. 158/C3
Neuquén, Arg. 158/C3
Neuruppin, Ger. 40/G2
Neusäss, Ger. 54/D6
Neuse (riv.), NC, US 133/J3
Neusiedl am See, Aus. 43/M3
Neusiedler (lake), Aus. 41/J5
Neusiedler See (lake), Aus. 48/C2
Neuss, Ger. 50/D6
Neustadt, Ger. 53/G2
Neustadt am Rübenberge, Ger. 51/G3
Neustadt an der Aisch, Ger. 54/D3
Neustadt an der Donau, Ger. 55/E5
Neustadt an der Waldnaab, Ger. 55/F3
Neustadt an der Weinstrasse, Ger. 54/B4
Neustadt bei Coburg, Ger. 54/E2
Neustadt in Holstein, Ger. 38/D4
Neustift im Stubaital, Aus. 57/H3
Neustrelitz, Ger. 40/G2
Neutraubling, Ger. 55/F5
Neuves-Maisons, Fr. 42/F2
Neuvic, Fr. 42/E4
Neuville-sur-Saône, Fr. 56/A6
Neuwied, Ger. 53/G3
Neuzelle, Ger. 41/H2
Neva (riv.), Rus. 39/P2
Nevada (state), US 128/C3
Nevada, Mo, US 129/J3
Nevada (mts.), Col. 145/H4
Nevada, Sierra (mts.), Sp. 44/D4
Nevado de Colima PN, Mex. 142/D5
Nevado de Toluca, PN, Mex. 143/K7
Nevado del Huila, PN, Col. 150/C3
Nevado, Sierra del (mts.), Arg. 158/C3
Nevel', Rus. 39/N3
Nevele, Belg. 52/C1
Nevel'sk, Rus. 71/R2
Nevers, Fr. 42/E3
Nevesinje, Bosn. 47/F1
Nevinnomyssk, Rus. 63/G3
Nevis (peak), StK. 141/N8
Nevis (isl.), UK 141/J4
Nevola (riv.), It. 59/G5
Nevsehir (prov.), Turk. 90/C2
Nevşehir, Turk. 90/C2
New (riv.), Guy. 150/G3
New (riv.), WV, US 130/D4
New Albany, In, US 130/C4
New Albany, Ms, US 133/F3
New Amsterdam, Guy. 153/G3
New Ancholme (riv.), Eng, UK 35/H4
New Athens, Il, US 137/H9
New Baltimore, Mi, US 135/G6
New Bataan, Phil. 79/E6
New Bedford, Ma, US 131/G3
New Berlin, Tx, US 137/U21
New Berlin, Pa, US 138/B2
New Berlin, Wi, US 135/P14
New Berlinville, Pa, US 138/C3
New Bern, NC, US 133/J3
New Braunfels, Tx, US 137/U20
New Britain, Ct, US 131/F3
New Britain (isl.), PNG 116/D5
New Britain, Pa, US 138/C3
New Brunswick (prov.), Can. 131/H2
New Brunswick, NJ, US 139/H10
New Buffalo, Pa, US 138/B3
New Buildings, NI, UK 34/A2
New Caledonia (isl.), NCal. 116/F7
New Caledonia (terr.), Fr. 116/F6
New Canaan, Ct, US 139/M7
New Castle, De, US 138/C4
New Castle (co.), De, US 138/C5
New Castle, In, US 130/C4
New Castle, Pa, US 130/D3
New Chicago, In, US 135/R16
New City, NY, US 139/K7
New Columbia, Pa, US 138/B1
New Columbus, Pa, US 138/B1
New Cumberland, Pa, US 138/B3
New Cumnock, Sc, UK 36/B6
New Delhi (cap.), India 86/D5
New Denver, BC, Can. 126/D3
New Egypt, NJ, US 138/D3
New England NP, Austl. 115/E1
New Freedom, Pa, US 138/B4
New Galloway, Sc, UK 34/D1
New Georgia (isls.), Sol. 116/E5
New Georgia (sound), Sol. 116/E5
New Glasgow, NS, Can. 131/J2
New Glasgow, Qu, Can. 131/N6
New Gretna, NJ, US 138/D4
New Guinea (isl.), Indo.,PNG 67/N10
New Hampshire (state), US 131/G3
New Hanover, SAfr. 107/E3
New Hanover, Il, US 137/G9
New Hanover (isl.), PNG 116/D5
New Haven, Ct, US 131/F3
New Haven, Mi, US 135/G6
New Hebrides (isls.), Van. 116/F6
New Holland, Pa, US 138/B3
New Hope, Pa, US 138/D3
New Hyde Park, NY, US 139/L9
New Iberia, La, US 129/K5
New Ireland (isl.), PNG 116/E5
New Jersey (state), US 138/D3
New Kensington, Pa, US 130/E3
New Kowloon, China 71/U10
New Lenox, Il, US 135/Q16
New Lisbon, NJ, US 138/D4
New Liskeard, On, Can. 130/E2
New London, Ct, US 131/F3
New Madrid, Mo, US 129/K3
New Market, Md, US 138/A5
New Meadows, Id, US 126/D4
New Mexico (state), US 128/G4
New Milford, NJ, US 139/J8
New Mills, Eng, UK 35/F5
New Norfolk, Austl. 115/C4
New Orleans, La, US 137/P17
New Orleans (Moisant Field), La, US 137/P17
New Oxford, Pa, US 138/A4
New Philadelphia, Oh, US 130/D3
New Philadelphia, Pa, US 138/B2
New Pitsligo, Sc, UK 36/D1
New Plymouth, NZ 117/S10
New Port Richey, Fl, US 133/H4
New Providence (isl.), Bahm. 141/F3
New Providence, NJ, US 139/H9
New Richmond, Qu, Can. 131/H1
New River (mts.), Az, US 137/R18
New River, Az, US 137/R18
New Rochelle, NY, US 139/K8
New Rockford, ND, US 127/J4
New Romney, Eng, UK 33/G5
New Ross, Ire. 31/Q10
New Rossington, Eng, UK 35/G5
New Sarpy, La, US 137/P17
New Schwabenland (phys. reg.), Ant. 160/Z
New Scone, Sc, UK 36/C4
New Siberian (isls.), Rus. 67/N2
New Smyrna Beach, Fl, US 133/H4
New South Wales, Austl. 115/D1
New South Wales (state), Austl. 109/D4
New Stuyahok, Ak, US 134/G4
New Town, ND, US 127/H4
New Tripoli, Pa, US 138/C2
New Ulm, Mn, US 127/K4
New Waterford, NS, Can. 131/J2
New Westminster, BC, Can. 126/C3
New Windsor, Md, US 138/A4
New York (state), US 130/G3
New York, NY, US 139/K9
New Zealand (ctry.) 117/R10
Newark, Oh, US 130/D3
Newark, De, US 138/C4
Newark (int'l arpt.), NJ, US 139/J9
Newark, NJ, US 139/J9
Newark, Ca, US 135/K11
Newark (bay), NJ, US 139/J9
Newark-on-Trent, Eng, UK 35/H5
Newbern, Il, US 137/G8
Newberry, SC, US 133/H3
Newberry, Mi, US 130/C2
Newberry Nat'l Volcanic Mon., Or, US 126/C5
Newburgh, Sc, UK 36/C4
Newburn, Eng, UK 35/G2
Newbury, Eng, UK 33/E4
Newcastle, Austl. 115/D2
Newcastle, SAfr. 107/E2
Newcastle, Ire. 31/P10
Newcastle, Ire. 34/B5
Newcastle, Ok, US 137/M15
Newcastle, NI, UK 34/C3
Newcastle (int'l arpt.), Eng, UK 35/G1
Newcastle, Wy, US 127/G5
Newcastle-under-Lyme, Eng, UK 35/F6
Newcastle upon Tyne, Eng, UK 35/G2
Newcastle upon Tyne (co.), Eng, UK 35/G1
Newcastleton, Sc, UK 35/F1
Newe Yam, Isr. 91/F6
Newel, Ger. 53/F4
Newell, Austl. 114/B2
Newellton, La, US 129/K4
Newenham (cape), Ak, US 134/F4
Newfane, NY, US 131/S9
Newfield, NJ, US 138/C4
Newfoundland (isl.), Can. 131/L1
Newfoundland, NJ, US 139/H7
Newfoundland, Pa, US 138/C1
Newfoundland and Labrador (prov.), Can. 123/K3
Newhalen, Ak, US 134/H4
Newham (bor.), Eng, UK 30/D2
Newhaven, Eng, UK 33/F5
Newington, Eng, UK 30/F3
Newkirk, Ok, US 129/H3
Newllano, La, US 129/J5
Newmains, Sc, UK 36/C5
Newman (mt.), Austl. 112/C2
Newman, Austl. 112/C2
Newmarket, On, Can. 130/E2
Newmarket, Eng, UK 33/G2
Newmill, Sc, UK 36/D1
Newnan, Ga, US 133/G3
Newport, Eng, UK 32/D1
Newport, Eng, UK 33/E5
Newport, Wal, UK 32/D3
Newport (co.), Wal, UK 32/C3
Newport, Ar, US 129/K4
Newport (bay), Ca, US 136/C3
Newport, De, US 138/C4
Newport, Ky, US 130/C4
Newport, NJ, US 138/C5
Newport, Or, US 126/B4
Newport, Pa, US 138/A3
Newport, RI, US 131/G3
Newport, Tn, US 130/D5
Newport, Vt, US 131/F2
Newport, Wa, US 126/D3
Newport Beach, Ca, US 136/G8
Newport Meadows (lake), NJ, US 138/C5
Newport-on-Tay, Sc, UK 36/D4
Newport Pagnell, Eng, UK 33/F2
Newquay, Eng, UK 32/A6
Newry, NI, UK 34/B3
Newry (dist.), NI, UK 34/B3
Newry (canal), NI, UK 34/B3
Newtok, Ak, US 134/F3
Newton, Tx, US 129/J5
Newton, Ma, US 131/G3
Newton, NJ, US 138/D1
Newton Abbot, Eng, UK 32/C5
Newton-le-Willows, Eng, UK 35/F5
Newton Mearns, Sc, UK 36/B5
Newton Stewart, Sc, UK 34/D2
Newton Tors (hill), Eng, UK 36/D5
Newtonmore, Sc, UK 36/B2
Newtonville, NJ, US 138/D4
Newtown, Austl. 115/B3
Newtown, Wal, UK 32/C1
Newtown, Pa, US 138/D3
Newtown Mount Kennedy, Ire. 34/B5
Newtown Saint Boswells, Sc, UK 36/D5
Newtown Square, Pa, US 138/C4
Newtownabbey, NI, UK 34/C2
Newtownards, NI, UK 34/C2
Newtownhamilton, NI, UK 34/B3
Newtownstewart, NI, UK 34/A2
Newtyle, Sc, UK 36/C3
Nextlalpan, Mex. 143/Q9
Neyagawa, Japan 77/J6
Neyrīz, Iran 89/F3
Neyshābūr, Iran 89/G1
Neyva (riv.), Rus. 61/P4
Neyveli, India 82/C5
Neyyāttinkara, India 82/C6
Nezahualcóyotl, Mex. 143/Q10
Neznayka (riv.), Rus. 61/W9
Nezperce, Id, US 126/D4
Ngabang, Indo. 80/C3

211

Ngabo – Notre

Ngabordamlu (cape), Indo. 81/H5
Ngabu, Malw. 105/F4
Ngai-Ndethya Nat'l Rsv., Kenya 104/C3
Ngamring, China 85/F1
Nganda (peak), Malw. 104/B5
Ngangerabeli (plain), Kenya 104/C3
Ngaoundéré, Camr. 96/H6
Ngarkat Conservation Park, Austl. 113/J5
Ngatik (isl.), Micr. 116/E4
Ngoan Muc (pass), Viet. 78/E4
Ngoc Linh (peak), Viet. 83/J4
Ngomeni (cape), Kenya 104/D3
Ngong, Kenya 104/C3
Ngonye (falls), Zam. 105/D4
Ngorongoro Consv. Area, Tanz. 104/B3
Ngounié (riv.), Gabon 96/H8
Nguigmi, Niger 96/H5
Ngulu (isl.), Micr. 116/C4
Ngumbe Sukani (pt.), Tanz. 104/C5
Nguru (mts.), Tanz. 104/C4
Ngwenya (peak), Swaz. 107/E2
Nha Trang, Viet. 78/E3
Nhamunda (riv.), Braz. 147/D3
Nhill, Austl. 115/B3
Nhlangano, Swaz. 107/E2
Niagara (falls), Can.,US 131/R9
Niagara (riv.), Can.,US 131/R9
Niagara (co.), On, Can. 131/R9
Niagara Falls, On, Can. 131/R9
Niagara Falls, NY, US 131/R9
Niagara-on-the-Lake, On, Can. 131/R9
Niamey (dept.), Niger 103/F3
Niamey (cap.), Niger 103/F3
Niamey (int'l arpt.), Niger 103/F3
Niamtougou, Togo 103/F4
Niandan (riv.), Afr. 103/G5
Niangara, D.R. Congo 97/L7
Niangay (lake), Mali 96/E4
Niangzi (pass), China 72/C3
Nias (isl.), Indo. 67/J9
Niassa (prov.), Moz. 104/B5
Nicaragua (ctry.) 145/E3
Nicaragua (lake), Nic. 145/E4
Nicastro-Sambiase, It. 46/E3
Nice, Fr. 43/G5
Niceville, Fl, US 133/G4
Nichinan, Japan 74/B5
Nichlaul, India 84/D2
Nicholas (chan.), Bang. 145/F1
Nichols Hills, Ok, US 137/M14
Nicholson (range), Austl. 112/C3
Nickerie (dist.), Sur. 153/G3
Nickerie (riv.), Sur. 153/G3
Nickol (bay), Austl. 112/C2
Nicobar (isls.), India 67/J9
Nicolás Bravo, Mex. 144/D2
Nicolás Romero, Mex. 143/Q9
Nicolet, Qu, Can. 131/F2
Nicolls (pt.), NY, US 139/E2
Nicoma Park, Ok, US 137/N15
Nicosia, It. 46/D4
Nicosia (cap.), Cyp. 91/C2
Nicosia (dist.), Cyp. 91/C2
Nicotera, It. 46/D3
Nicoya (gulf), CR 140/D6
Nicoya, CR 144/E4
Nicoya, Peninsula de (pen.), CR 150/A1
Nidau, Swi. 56/D3
Nidd (riv.), Eng, UK 35/G3
Nidda, Ger. 54/B2
Nidda (riv.), Ger. 40/E3
Niddatal, Ger. 54/B2
Nidder (riv.), Ger. 54/C2
Nideggen, Ger. 53/F2
Niğde (prov.), Turk. 90/C2
Nidwalden (canton), Swi. 57/E4
Nidzica, Pol. 41/L2
Niebüll, Ger. 38/C4
Nied (riv.), Fr. 43/G2
Niedenstein, Ger. 51/G6
Nieder-Olm, Ger. 53/H4
Niederanven, Lux. 53/F4
Niederbipp, Swi. 56/D3
Niederbronn-les-Bains, Fr. 53/G6
Niedere Tauern (mts.), Aus. 43/K3
Niederfischbach, Ger. 53/G2
Niederlausitz (reg.), Ger. 41/G3
Niedernhausen, Ger. 54/B2
Niederösterreich (prov.), Aus. 48/B2
Niedersachsen (state), Ger. 38/C5
Niedersächsisches Wattenmeer NP, Ger. 51/E1
Niedersachswerfen, Ger. 51/H5
Niederstetten, Ger. 54/C4
Niederstotzingen, Ger. 54/D5
Niederurnen, Swi. 57/F3
Niederwerrn, Ger. 54/D2
Niederwinkling, Ger. 55/F5
Niederzier, Ger. 53/F2
Niederzissen, Ger. 53/G3
Niefern-Öschelbronn, Ger. 54/B5
Niegocin (lake), Pol. 39/J5
Nieheim, Ger. 51/G5
Niemodlin, Pol. 41/J3
Nienburg, Ger. 51/G3
Nienhagen, Ger. 51/H3
Niénokoué (peak), C.d'Iv. 102/D5
Nieppe, Fr. 52/B2
Niéri (riv.), Sen. 102/B3
Niers (riv.), Ger. 53/F1
Nierstein, Ger. 54/B3
Niet Ban Tinh Xa, Viet. 78/D4
Nieuw-Amsterdam, Sur. 151/G2
Nieuw-Bergen, Neth. 50/D5
Nieuw-Loosdrecht, Neth. 50/C4
Nieuw-Nickerie, Sur. 153/G3
Nieuw-Schoonebeek, Neth. 50/D3
Nieuw-Vossemeer, Neth. 50/B5
Nieuwe Pekela, Neth. 50/D2
Nieuwegein, Neth. 50/C4
Nieuwerkerk aan de IJssel, Neth. 50/B5
Nieuweschans, Neth. 51/E2
Nieuwkoop, Neth. 50/B4
Nieuwleusen, Neth. 50/D3
Nieuwoudtville, SAfr. 106/B3
Nieuwpoort, Belg. 52/B1
Nieves, Mex. 142/E3
Niğde, Turk. 90/C2
Nigel, SAfr. 106/E2
Niger (ctry.) 96/G4
Niger (delta), Nga. 103/G5
Niger (riv.), Afr. 96/F5
Nigeria (ctry.) 96/G6
Nigg (bay), Sc, UK 36/B1
Nighthawk (lake), On, Can. 130/D1
Nightmute, Ak, US 134/F3
Nigrán, Sp. 44/A1
Nigríta, Gre. 47/H2
Nihoa (isl.), Hi, US 117/J2
Nihonmatsu, Japan 75/G2
Nihtaur, India 84/B1
Nii (isl.), Japan 75/F3
Niigata (int'l arpt.), Japan 75/F2
Niigata, Japan 75/F2
Niigata (pref.), Japan 76/A4
Niihama, Japan 74/C4
Niihari, Japan 77/E1
Niihau (isl.), Hi, US 124/R10
Niimi, Japan 74/C3
Niitsu, Japan 75/F2
Niiza, Japan 77/D2
Nijar, Sp. 44/D4
Nijkerk, Neth. 50/C4
Nijlen, Belg. 53/D1
Nijmegen, Neth. 50/C5
Níkaia, Gre. 47/H3
Nikel', Rus. 37/J1
Nikishka, Ak, US 134/H3
Nikísiani, Gre. 47/J2
Nikki, Ben. 103/F4
Nikkō, Japan 75/F2
Nikkō NP, Japan 75/F2
Niklasdorf, Aus. 43/L3
Nikolai, Ak, US 134/H3
Nikolayevsk-na-Amure, Rus. 65/Q4
Nikol'sk, Rus. 63/H1
Nikolski, Ak, US 134/E5
Nikonga (riv.), Tanz. 104/A3
Nikopol', Ukr. 62/E3
Nikopol, Bul. 49/G4
Niksar, Turk. 62/F4
Nīkshahr, Iran 89/H3
Nikšić, Serb. 47/F1
Nikumaroro (Gardner) (isl.), Kiri. 117/H5
Nikunau (isl.), Kiri. 116/G5
Nile (delta), Egypt 88/B2
Nile (riv.), Afr. 93/F2
Niles, Mi, US 130/C3
Niles, Oh, US 130/D3
Niles, Il, US 135/Q15
Ni'līn, Isr. 91/G8
Nilópolis, Braz. 211/K7
Nilsiä, Fin. 60/F3
Nilvange, Fr. 53/F5
Nīmāj, India 82/B2
Nimba (peak), C.d'Iv. 102/C5
Nimba (co.), Libr. 102/C5
Nîmes, Fr. 42/F5
Nimsbach (riv.), Ger. 53/F4
Nimule NP, Sudan 104/A2
Nin, Cro. 48/B3
Nīnawā (gov.), Iraq 90/E3
Nīnawá (Nineveh) (ruin), Iraq 90/E2
Ninepin Group (isls.), China 71/V11
Ninfas (pt.), Arg. 158/D4
Ning'an, China 71/N3
Ningbo, China 72/E5
Ningde, China 79/C2
Ningdu, China 79/C2
Ninggang, China 83/K2
Ninghua, China 79/C2
Ningjin, China 72/C3
Ningjin, China 72/D3
Ninglang Yizu Zizhixian, China 83/H2
Ningling, China 72/C4
Ningming, China 83/J3
Ningwu, China 72/C3
Ningxia Huizu (aut. reg.), China 70/J4
Ningxiang, China 79/B2
Ningyang, China 72/D4
Ningyuan, China 83/K2
Ninh Binh, Viet. 78/D1
Ninilchik, Ak, US 134/H3
Niningo (isls.), PNG 116/D5
Ninohe, Japan 76/B3
Ninomiya, Japan 77/C3
Ninove, Belg. 52/D2
Ninoy Aquino (int'l arpt.), Phil. 79/D5
Niobara (riv.), Ne, US 124/F3
Niobrara (riv.), Ne, US 127/H5
Niokolo-Koba, PN du, Sen. 102/B3
Niono, Mali 102/D3
Nioro-du-Rip, Sen. 102/B3
Nioro du Sahel, Mali 102/C3
Niort, Fr. 42/C3
Nipawin, Sk, Can. 127/H2
Nipe (bay), Cuba 145/H1
Nipigon, On, Can. 127/L3
Nipigon (lake), On, Can. 122/G3
Nipissing (lake), On, Can. 123/J4
Niquén, Chile 158/C3
Niquero, Cuba 145/G1
Nirasaki, Japan 75/F3
Nirayama, Japan 77/B3
Nirimba Army Afld., Austl. 114/G8
Nirmal, India 82/C4
Nirmāli, India 85/F2
Niš (int'l arpt.), Serb. 47/G1
Niš, Serb. 47/G1
Nišava (riv.), Serb. 47/H1
Niscemi, It. 46/D4
Nishiazai, Japan 77/K5
Nishibiwajima, Japan 77/L5
Nishiharu, Japan 77/L5
Nishikatsura, Japan 77/B2
Nishiki (riv.), Japan 74/B3
Nishiki, Japan 77/H5
Nishinomiya, Japan 77/H6
Nishino'omote, Japan 74/B5
Nishio, Japan 77/M6
Nishiwaki, Japan 77/G6
Nisko, Pol. 41/M3
Nisqually, Wa, US 135/B3
Nisqually (riv.), Wa, US 135/B3
Nisqually Ind. Res., Wa, US 135/B3
Nisqually Reach (str.), Wa, US 135/B3
Nissan (isl.), PNG 116/E5
Nisser (lake), Nor. 38/C2
Nisshin, Japan 77/M5
Nissum (bay), Den. 38/C3
Nisswa, Mn, US 127/K4
Nistru (riv.), Mol. 49/H1
Niterói, Braz. 211/K7
Nith (riv.), Sc, UK 36/C6
Nith (riv.), Sc, UK 34/E1
Nithsdale (valley), Sc, UK 34/E1
Nitra, Slvk. 48/D1
Nitra (riv.), Slvk. 41/K4
Nitriansky (pol. reg.), Slvk. 41/K4
Nitsa (riv.), Rus. 61/P4
Nitta, Japan 77/C1
Nittedal, Nor. 38/D1
Nittel, Ger. 53/F4
Nittenau, Ger. 55/F4
Niuafo'ou (isl.), Tonga 117/H6
Niuatoputapu Group (isls.), Tonga 117/H6
Niue (terr.), NZ 117/H7
Niue (isl.), Niue 117/J6
Niulakita (isl.), Tuv. 116/G6
Niulan (riv.), China 83/H2
Niut (peak), Indo. 80/C3
Niutao (isl.), Tuv. 116/G5
Nivelles, Belg. 53/D2
Nivernais, Collines de (hills), Fr. 42/E3
Niverville, Mb, Can. 127/J3
Niwot, Co, US 137/B2
Niyazov (int'l arpt.), Trkm. 87/C5
Niyodo (riv.), Japan 74/C4
Nizāmābād, India 82/C4
Nizhegorodskaya Oblast, Rus. 63/G1
Nizhnekama (res.), Rus. 61/M4
Nizhnekamsk, Rus. 61/L5
Nizhneudinsk, Rus. 65/K4
Nizhnevartovsk, Rus. 64/H3
Nizhniy Lomov, Rus. 63/G1
Nizhniy Novgorod, Rus. 61/K4
Nizhniy Tagil, Rus. 61/N4
Nizhyn, Ukr. 62/D2
Nizip, Turk. 90/D2
Nízke Tatry NP, Slvk. 62/A2
Nizza Monferrato, It. 58/B3
Nizzanim, Isr. 91/F8
Njardhvík, Ice. 37/M7
Njombe (riv.), Tanz. 104/B4
Nkandla, SAfr. 107/E3
Nkayi, Congo 105/B1
Nkhata Bay, Malw. 104/B5
N'kongsamba, Camr. 96/G7
Nkululu (riv.), Tanz. 104/B4
Nkusi (riv.), Ugan. 104/A2
Nmai (riv.), Myan. 83/G2
Noailles, Fr. 52/B5
Noākhāli (pol. reg.), Bang. 85/H4
Noale, It. 59/F1
Noāmundi, India 85/E4
Noank, Ct, US 139/F1
Noatak, Ak, US 134/F2
Noatak (riv.), Ak, US 134/F2
Noatak Nat'l Prsv., Ak, US 134/F2
Nobeoka, Japan 74/B4
Noble, Ok, US 137/N15
Noboa, Ecu. 152/A5
Noboribetsu, Japan 76/B2
Noce (riv.), It. 57/G5
Noceto, It. 58/D3
Noci, It. 47/E2
Nockamixon State Park, Pa, US 138/C3
Noda, Japan 77/D2
Nodagawa, Japan 77/H4
Noé (cape), Alg. 100/D2
Nogales, Az, US 128/E5
Nogales, Mex. 143/M8
Nogara, It. 59/E2
Nogaro, Fr. 42/C5
Nogat (riv.), Pol. 39/H4
Nogata, Japan 74/B4
Nogent, Fr. 56/B1
Nogent-l'Artaud, Fr. 52/C6
Nogent-le-Rotrou, Fr. 42/D2
Nogent-sur-Oise, Fr. 52/B5
Nogent-sur-Seine, Fr. 42/E2
Nogi, Japan 77/D1
Noginsk, Rus. 61/X9
Nogoa (riv.), Austl. 114/B4
Nogodan-san (peak), SKor. 73/D5
Nogoonnuur, Mong. 70/F2
Nogoyá, Arg. 157/E3
Nógrád (co.), Hun. 41/K5
Nogwak-san (peak), SKor. 74/A2
Nohar, India 86/C5
Noheji, Japan 76/B3
Nohfelden, Ger. 53/G4
Nohkú (pt.), Mex. 144/E2
Noi (riv.), Viet. 83/J5
Noidans-lès-Vesoul, Fr. 56/C2
Noire (riv.), Qu, Can. 130/E2
Noires, Montagnes (mts.), Fr. 42/B2
Noirmoutier, Île de (isl.), Fr. 42/B3
Noisiel, Fr. 52/B6
Noisy-le-Grand, Fr. 30/K5
Noisy-le-Mec, Fr. 30/K5
Noisy-le-Roi, Fr. 30/J5
Nojima-zaki (pt.), Japan 75/F3
Nokia, Fin. 39/K1
Nokilalaki (peak), Indo. 81/F4
Nola, CAfr. 96/J7
Noli, It. 58/B4
Noli, Capo di (cape), It. 58/B4
Nomadgi NP, Austl. 115/D2
Nombre de Dios, Mex. 142/D4
Nombre de Dios (mts.), Hon. 144/E3
Nome, Ak, US 134/E3
Nome (cape), Ak, US 134/F3
Nomény, Fr. 53/F6
Nomexy, Fr. 56/C1
Nomo-misaki (cape), Japan 74/B5
Nomo-zaki (pt.), Japan 74/A4
Nonacho (lake), NW, Can. 122/F2
Nonantola, It. 58/E3
Nondalton, Ak, US 134/H4
None, It. 43/G4
Nonette (riv.), Fr. 52/B5
Nong Han (res.), Thai. 78/D2
Nong Khai, Thai. 78/C2
Nong'an, China 71/N3
Nongoma, SAfr. 107/E2
Nongstoin, India 85/H3
Nonnweiler, Ger. 53/F4
Nonoava, Mex. 142/D3
Nonouti (isl.), Kiri. 116/G5
Nonri (isl.), China 72/E5
Nonsan, SKor. 73/D4
Nontron, Fr. 42/D4
Noord-Brabant (prov.), Neth. 50/C5
Noord Holland (prov.), Neth. 50/B3
Noordbeveland (isl.), Neth. 50/A5
Noorderhaaks (isl.), Neth. 50/B3
Noordhollandsch Kanaal (riv.), Neth. 50/B3
Noordostpolder (polder), Neth. 50/C3
Noordwijk aan Zee, Neth. 50/B4
Noordwijkerhout, Neth. 50/B4
Noordzeekanaal (canal), Neth. 50/B4
Noormarkku, Fin. 39/J1
Noorvik, Ak, US 134/F2
Nootka (isl.), BC, Can. 126/B3
Nora, Swe. 38/G2
Norala, Phil. 81/F2
Norberg, Swe. 38/F1
Norberto de la Riestra, Arg. 159/J11
Norchia (ruin), It. 46/B1
Norco, Ca, US 136/C3
Norco, La, US 137/P16
Nord (riv.), Qu, Can. 131/M6
Nord (canal), Fr. 52/B4
Nord (prov.), Fr. 52/C3
Nord-Kivu (pol. reg.), D.R. Congo 104/A3
Nord-Ostsee (Kiel) (canal), Ger. 51/G1
Nord-Ouest (prov.), Camr. 103/H5
Nord-Ouest (pol. reg.), Mor. 100/B2
Nord-Pas-de-Calais (pol. reg.), Fr. 42/D1
Nord-Radde (riv.), Ger. 51/E3
Nord-Sud Kanal (canal), Ger. 51/E3
Nord-Trøndelag (co.), Nor. 37/E2
Nordborg, Den. 38/C4
Nordby, Den. 38/D4
Norddeich, Ger. 51/E1
Nordela (int'l arpt.), Azor., Port. 45/T13
Norden, Ger. 51/E1
Nordenham, Ger. 51/F1
Nordenskjöld (arch.), Rus. 64/J2
Norderney, Ger. 51/E1
Norderney (isl.), Neth. 51/E1
Norderstedt, Ger. 51/G1
Nordhausen, Ger. 40/F3
Nordholz, Ger. 51/F1
Nordhorn, Ger. 51/E4
Nordhouse, Fr. 56/D1
Nordjylland (co.), Den. 38/C3
Nordkapp (cape), Nor. 37/H1
Nordkapp, Nor. 37/H1
Nordkinn (pt.), Nor. 37/H1
Nordkirchen, Ger. 51/E5
Nordland (co.), Nor. 37/E2
Nördlingen, Ger. 54/D5
Nordmaling, Swe. 37/F3
Nordreisa, Nor. 37/G1
Nordrhein-Westfalen (state), Ger. 40/E3
Nords Wharf, Austl. 115/D2
Nordwalde, Ger. 51/E4
Nore (riv.), Ire. 31/Q10
Noresund, Nor. 38/C1
Norfolk (mt.), Austl. 115/C4
Norfolk (lake), Ar,Mo, US 129/J3
Norfolk, Ne, US 127/J5
Norfolk (isl.), Austl. 116/F7
Norfolk Broads (swamp), Eng, UK 33/H1
Norg, Neth. 50/D2
Norheimsund, Nor. 38/B1
Norikura-dake (peak), Japan 75/E2
Noril'sk, Rus. 64/J3
Normal, Il, US 127/L5
Norman, Ok, US 137/N15
Norman Manley (int'l arpt.), Jam. 145/G2
Norman Wells, NW, Can. 122/D2
Normanby (isl.), PNG 116/E6
Normandie, Collines de (hills), Fr. 42/C2
Normandy (reg.), Fr. 42/C2
Normandy Beach, NJ, US 138/D4
Normandy Park, Wa, US 135/C3
Normanton, Austl. 114/A2
Normanton South, Eng, UK 35/G4
Norotshama (peak), Namb. 106/B3
Norquay, Sk, Can. 127/H3
Ñorquinco, Arg. 158/C4
Norrbotten (co.), Swe. 37/F2
Nørre Alslev, Den. 38/D4
Nørre Nebel, Den. 38/C4
Nørre Vorupør, Den. 38/C3
Norridge, Il, US 135/Q16
Norris (lake), Tn, US 133/G2
Norristown, Pa, US 138/C3
Norrköping, Swe. 38/G2
Norrland (reg.), Swe. 37/F2
Norrsundet, Swe. 38/G1
Norrtälje, Swe. 39/H2
Nors, Den. 38/C3
Norseman, Austl. 112/D5
Norsjö, Swe. 37/F2
Norte (pt.), Arg. 159/F3
Norte (pt.), Arg. 158/E4
Norte, Cabo do (cape), Braz. 151/J3
Norte de Santander (dept.), Col. 145/H4
Norte Los Rodeos (int'l arpt.), Sp. 98/A3
Norte, Serra do (mts.), Braz. 150/G6
Nortelândia, Braz. 151/G6
Nörten-Hardenberg, Ger. 51/G5
North (pt.), Austl. 115/C3
North (pt.), Austl. 115/C4
North (pt.), Austl. 112/B4
North (cape), PE, Can. 131/J2
North (cape), Ak, US 134/F2
North (cape), NZ 117/S9
North (isl.), NZ 117/S10
North (pt.), Md, US 138/B5
North (sound), Sc, UK 31/V14
North (canal), Fr. 52/B4
North (sea), Eur. 36/D4
North (chan.), UK 34/C1
North Albanian Alps (mts.), Serb. 47/F1
North America (cont.) 119
North Andaman (isl.), India 83/F5
North Arlington, NJ, US 139/J8
North Aulatsivik (isl.), Nf, Can. 123/K3
North Aurora, Il, US 135/P16
North Ayrshire (pol. reg.), Sc, UK 36/A5
North Battleford, Sk, Can. 126/F2
North Bay, On, Can. 130/E2
North Bay, Wi, US 135/Q14
North Beach, Md, US 138/B6
North Beach Haven, NJ, US 138/D4
North Bellmore, NY, US 139/L9
North Bend, Or, US 126/B5
North Bend, Wa, US 135/D3
North Bergen, NJ, US 139/J8
North Berwick, Sc, UK 36/D4
North Branch, NJ, US 138/D2
North Branch (riv.), Md, US 138/B5
North Branford, Ct, US 139/F1
North Brunswick, NJ, US 138/D3
North Buganda (prov.), Ugan. 104/B2
North Caicos (isl.), UK 145/J1
North Caldwell, NJ, US 139/J8
North Canadian (riv.), Ok, US 129/H3
North Cape May, NJ, US 138/D6
North Caribou (lake), On, Can. 127/L2
North Carolina (state), US 133/H3
North Cascades NP, Wa, US 126/C3
North Central (plain), Tx, US 143/F1
North Charleston, SC, US 133/J3
North Cowichan, BC, Can. 126/C3
North Dakota (state), US 127/H4
North Dorset Downs (uplands), Eng, UK 32/D5
North Down (dist.), NI, UK 34/C2
North East, Pa, US 130/E3
North East (pt.), Austl. 114/C3
North East, Md, US 138/C4
North Eastern (prov.), Kenya 104/C2
North Esk (riv.), Sc, UK 36/C5
North Foreland (pt.), Eng, UK 33/H4
North Fork Crow (riv.), Mn, US 127/K4
North Fort Myers, Fl, US 133/H5
North French (riv.), On, Can. 130/D1
North Frisian (isls.), Ger. 40/D1
North Front (int'l arpt.), UK 98/D1
North Gauhāti, India 85/H2
North Haledon, NJ, US 139/J8
North Hero, Vt, US 130/F2
North Highlands, Ca, US 135/L9
North Kansas City, Mo, US 137/D5
North Kitui Nat'l Rsv., Kenya 104/C3
North Korea (ctry.) 73/D2
North Lakhimpur, India 83/F2
North Lanarkshire (pol. reg.), Sc, UK 36/C5
North Las Vegas, Nv, US 128/D3
North Lincolnshire (co.), Eng, UK 35/H4
North Lindenhurst, NY, US 139/M9
North Little Rock, Ar, US 129/J4
North Luangwa NP, Zam. 105/F3
North Magnetic Pole 123/R7
North Minch (The Minch) (str.), Sc, UK 31/Q8
North Moose (lake), Mb, Can. 127/J2
North Mountain (mtn.), Pa, US 138/B1
North Myrtle Beach, SC, US 133/J3
North Ogden, Ut, US 137/K11
North Ossetian Aut. Rep., Rus. 63/G4
North Pacific (ocean) 22/A4
North Pine (riv.), Austl. 114/E6
North Plainfield, NJ, US 139/H9
North Platte, Ne, US 127/H5
North Platte (riv.), Ne,Wy, US 129/G2
North Pole, Ak, US 134/J3
North Pole 160/G
North Potomac, Md, US 138/A5
North Prairie, Wi, US 135/P14
North Puyallup, Wa, US 135/C3
North Raccoon (riv.), Ia, US 127/K5
North Ronaldsay (isl.), Sc, UK 31/V14
North Salt Lake, Ut, US 137/K12
North Saskatchewan (riv.), Ab,Sk, Can. 122/E3
North Shields, Eng, UK 35/G2
North Siberian Lowland (plain), Rus. 64/K2
North Skunk (riv.), Ia, US 129/J2
North Somerset (co.), Eng, UK 32/D4
North Stradbroke (isl.), Austl. 109/E3
North Taranaki Bight (bay), NZ 109/H6
North Thompson (riv.), BC, Can. 126/D3
North Tolsta, Sc, UK 31/Q7
North Tonawanda, NY, US 131/S9
North Tyne (riv.), Eng, UK 35/F1
North Tyneside (co.), Eng, UK 35/G1
North Uist (isl.), Sc, UK 31/Q8
North Umpqua (riv.), Or, US 128/B2
North Valley Stream, NY, US 139/L9
North Vancouver, BC, Can. 122/D4
North Wales, Pa, US 138/C3
North Weald Bassett, Eng, UK 30/D1
North West (cape), Austl. 112/B2
North-West Frontier (co.), India 86/A3
North West Highlands (uplands), Sc, UK 31/R8
North Wildwood, NJ, US 138/D6
North Wilton, Ct, US 139/E1
North York, Can. 131/Q8
North York Moors NP, Eng, UK 35/G3
North Yorkshire (co.), Eng, UK 35/G3
Northallerton, Eng, UK 35/G3
Northam, Austl. 112/C4
Northampton, Austl. 112/B4
Northampton, Eng, UK 33/F2
Northampton, Ma, US 131/F3
Northampton, Pa, US 138/C2
Northampton (co.), Pa, US 138/C2
Northampton Uplands (uplands), Eng, UK 33/E2
Northamptonshire (co.), Eng, UK 33/E2
Northbrook, Il, US 135/Q15
Northeast (cape), Ak, US 134/E3
Northeast (pt.), Bahm. 141/G3
Northeast (pt.), Jam. 145/G2
Northeast (pt.), Bahm. 145/H1
Northeast Land (isl.), Sval. 160/E
Northeast Lincolnshire (co.), Eng, UK 35/H4
Northeim, Ger. 51/G5
Northern (prov.), Ugan. 104/B2
Northern (pol. reg.), Malw. 104/B5
Northern (prov.), SLeo. 102/B4
Northern (pol. reg.), Gha. 103/E4
Northern (prov.), SLeo. 102/B4
Northern (dist.), Isr. 91/D3
Northern Areas (terr.), Pak. 87/F5
Northern Cape (prov.), SAfr. 106/C3
Northern Cook (isls.), CookIs. 117/J6
Northern Dvina (riv.), Rus. 27/J2
Northern Light (lake), On, Can. 130/B1
Northern Mariana Islands (dpcy.), US 116/D3
Northern Province (prov.), SAfr. 106/E2
Northern Sporades (isls.), Gre. 47/J3
Northern Territory (terr.), Austl. 109/C2
Northern Ural (mts.), Rus. 61/N3
Northern Uvals (hills), Rus. 61/K4
Northfield, Mn, US 127/K4
Northfleet, Eng, UK 30/D2
Northglenn, Co, US 137/C3
Northport, Al, US 133/G3
Northport (Old Northport), NY, US 139/E2
Northumberland (str.), Can. 131/J2
Northumberland, Pa, US 138/B2
Northumberland NP, Eng, UK 36/D6
Northvale, NJ, US 139/K7
Northville, Mi, US 135/E7
Northway, Ak, US 134/K3
Northwest Gander (riv.), Nf, Can. 131/L1
Northwest Territories (terr.), Can. 122/D2
Northwich, Eng, UK 35/F5
Northwood, ND, US 127/J4
Norton (bay), Ak, US 134/F3
Norton (sound), Ak, US 134/E3
Norton Shores, Mi, US 130/C3
Nortorf, Ger. 38/C4
Norvegia (cape), Ant. 160/Y
Nörvenich, Ger. 53/F2
Norwalk, Oh, US 130/D3
Norwalk, Ca, US 136/F8
Norwalk, Ct, US 139/M7
Norwalk (riv.), Ct, US 139/M7
Norway (ctry.) 37/C3
Norwegian (bay), Nun., Can. 123/S7
Norwegian (sea), Eur. 27/D2
Norwich, NY, US 130/F3
Norwich, Eng, UK 33/H1
Norwich (int'l arpt.), Eng, UK 33/H1
Norwood, NJ, US 139/K8
Nos Emine (cape), Bul. 49/H4
Nos Kaliakra (pt.), Bul. 49/J4
Nos Maslen Nos (pt.), Bul. 49/H4
Nosappu-misaki (cape), Japan 76/D2
Nose, Japan 77/H6
Noshappu-misaki (cape), Japan 76/B1
Noshaq (peak), Afg. 89/K1
Noshiro, Japan 76/B3
Nosivka, Ukr. 62/D2
Nosong (cape), Malay. 81/E2
Noşratābād, Iran 89/G3
Noss Head (pt.), Sc, UK 31/S7
Nossa Senhora da Glória, Braz. 154/C3
Nossa Senhora das Dores, Braz. 154/C3
Nossebro, Swe. 38/E2
Nosy-Varika, Madg. 107/J8
Notch (cape), Chile 159/B6
Notec (riv.), Pol. 41/J2
Noto (pen.), Japan 75/E2
Noto, It. 46/D4
Noto Antica (ruin), It. 46/D4
Noto, Golfo di (gulf), It. 46/D4
Noto, Val di (valley), It. 46/D4
Notodden, Nor. 38/C2
Notogawa, Japan 77/K5
Notoro (lake), Japan 76/C1
Notre Dame (mts.), On, Can. 123/J4
Notre Dame (bay), Nf, Can. 123/L4
Notre Dame, Fr. 30/K5
Notre-Dame-de-l'Île-Perrot, Qu, Can. 131/N7

212

Notsé – Oloma

Notsé, Togo 103/F5
Nott (mt.), Austl. 113/G5
Nottaway (riv.), Qu, Can. 123/J3
Nøtterøy, Nor. 38/D2
Nottingham (isl.), Nun., Can. 123/H2
Nottingham, Eng, UK 35/G6
Nottingham (co.), Eng, UK 35/G6
Nottinghamshire (co.), Eng, UK 35/G5
Nottuln, Ger. 51/E5
Nouâdhibou, Mrta. 98/A5
Nouâdhibou (int'l arpt.), Mrta. 98/A5
Nouakchott (cap.), Mrta. 102/B2
Nouakchott (int'l arpt.), Mrta. 102/B2
Nouna, Burk. 102/E3
Noupoort, SAfr. 106/D3
Nouvion-sur-Meuse, Fr. 53/D4
Nœux-les-Mines, Fr. 52/B3
Nouzonville, Fr. 53/D4
Nova Andradina, Braz. 151/H8
Nova Cruz, Braz. 154/D2
Nová Dubnica, Slvk. 41/K4
Nova Friburgo, Braz. 211/L7
Nova Gorica, Slov. 59/G1
Nova Gradiška, Cro. 48/C3
Nova Iguaçu, Braz. 211/K7
Nova Kakhovka, Ukr. 49/L2
Nova Olinda, Braz. 154/C2
Nova Olinda do Norte, Braz. 150/G4
Nova Pazova, Serb. 48/E3
Nova Prata, Braz. 155/B4
Nova Russas, Braz. 154/B2
Nova Scotia (prov.), Can. 131/J2
Nova Sintra, CpV. 93/J11
Nova Soure, Braz. 154/C3
Nova Varoš, Serb. 48/D4
Nova Venécia, Braz. 155/D1
Nova Xavantina, Braz. 151/H6
Nova Zagora, Bul. 47/K1
Novaci, Rom. 49/F3
Novafeltria, It. 59/F5
Novara, It. 58/B2
Novate Mezzola, It. 57/F5
Novaya Sibir' (isl.), Rus. 65/R2
Novaya Zemlya (isl.), Rus. 160/C
Nove, It. 59/E1
Nové Hrady, Czh. 55/H5
Nové Město nad Váhom, Slvk. 41/J4
Nové Strašecí, Czh. 55/G2
Nové Zámky, Slvk. 48/D2
Novelda, Sp. 45/E3
Novellara, It. 59/D3
Noventa, It. 59/E2
Noventa di Piave, It. 59/F1
Noventa Vicentina, It. 59/E2
Novgorod, Rus. 39/P2
Novgorodskaya Oblast, Rus. 60/G4
Novi, Mi, US 135/F7
Novi Bečej, Serb. 48/E3
Novi di Modena, It. 59/D3
Novi Iskŭr, Bul. 47/H1
Novi Ligure, It. 43/H4
Novi Pazar, Serb. 47/G1
Novi Pazar, Bul. 49/H4
Novi Sad, Serb. 48/D3
Novi Vinodolski, Cro. 48/B3
Novillars, Fr. 56/C3
Nóvita, Col. 152/B3
Novo (riv.), Braz. 211/K6
Novo Alexeyevka (int'l arpt.), Geo. 63/H4
Novo Aripuanã, Braz. 150/F5
Novo Hamburgo, Braz. 155/B4
Novo Horizonte, Braz. 155/B2
Novo Miloševo, Serb. 48/E3
Novo Oriente, Braz. 154/B2
Novoanninskiy, Rus. 63/G2
Novocheboksarsk, Rus. 61/K4
Novocherkassk, Rus. 62/G3
Novogrudok, Bela. 39/L5
Novohrad-Volyns'kyy, Ukr. 62/C2
Novohradské Hory (mts.), Czh. 55/H5
Novokuybyshevsk, Rus. 63/J1
Novokuznetsk, Rus. 64/J4
Novolazarevskaya, Rus., Ant. 160/A
Novomoskovsk, Rus. 62/F1
Novorossiysk, Rus. 62/F3
Novoshakhtinsk, Rus. 62/F3
Novosibirsk (res.), Rus. 87/H2
Novosibirsk, Rus. 87/H1
Novosibirsk (Tolmachevo) (int'l arpt.), Rus. 87/H1
Novosibirskaya Oblast, Rus. 87/G1
Novotroitsk, Rus. 63/L2
Novoukrayinka, Ukr. 62/D2
Novovolyns'k, Ukr. 62/C2
Novovyatsk, Rus. 61/L4
Novozybkov, Rus. 62/D1
Novska, Cro. 48/C3
Nový Jičín, Czh. 41/K4
Nowa Dęba, Pol. 41/L3
Nowa Ruda, Pol. 41/J3
Nowa Sarzyna, Pol. 41/M3
Nowa Sól, Pol. 41/H3
Nowata, Ok, US 129/J3
Nowe, Pol. 41/K2
Nowe Miasto Lubawskie, Pol. 41/K2
Nowgong, India 84/B3
Nowitna (riv.), Ak, US 134/G3
Nowogard, Pol. 38/F5
Nowood (riv.), Wy, US 128/F1
Nowshāk (peak), Afg. 87/F5
Nowshera, Pak. 86/A2
Nowy Dwór Gdański, Pol. 39/H4
Nowy Sącz, Pol. 41/L4
Nowy Staw, Pol. 39/H4
Nowy Targ, Pol. 41/L4
Nowy Tomyśl, Pol. 41/J2
Noya, Sp. 44/A1
Noye (riv.), Fr. 52/B4
Noyon, Fr. 52/C4
Nsanje, Malw. 105/G4
Nsawam, Gha. 103/E5
Nsumbu NP, Zam. 104/A5
Nsuta, Gha. 103/E5
Ntoroko, Ugan. 104/A2
Ntungamo, Ugan. 104/A3
Ntusi, Ugan. 104/A2
Nu, Crêt du (peak), Fr. 56/B5
Nuangola, Pa, US 138/C1
Nūbah, Jibāl an (mts.), Sudan 97/M5
Nubian (des.), Sudan 93/F2
Nucet, Rom. 48/F2
Nucla, Co, US 132/A2
Nucourt, Fr. 30/H4
Nüdlingen, Ger. 54/D2
Nueces (riv.), Tx, US 140/B2
Nueltin (lake), Mb,Nun., Can. 122/G2
Nuenen, Neth. 50/C6
Nueva Alejandría, Peru 156/C2
Nueva Concepción, Guat. 144/D3
Nueva Esparta (state), Ven. 153/E2
Nueva Florida, Ven. 152/D2
Nueva Gerona, Cuba 145/E1
Nueva Helvecia, Uru. 159/K11
Nueva Imperial, Chile 158/B3
Nueva Italia de Ruiz, Mex. 142/E5
Nueva Loja, Ecu. 152/B4
Nueva Ocotepéque, Hon. 144/D3
Nueva Palmira, Uru. 159/J10
Nueva Rosita, Mex. 132/C5
Nueva Villa de Padilla, Mex. 143/F3
Nueve de Julio, Arg. 158/E2
Nuevitas, Cuba 145/G1
Nuevo, Ca, US 136/C3
Nuevo Balsas, Mex. 143/E5
Nuevo Berlín, Uru. 159/J10
Nuevo Casas Grandes, Mex. 142/D2
Nuevo Chagres, Pan. 145/F4
Nuevo, Golfo (gulf), Arg. 157/D5
Nuevo Ideal, Mex. 142/D3
Nuevo Ixcatlán, Mex. 144/C2
Nuevo Laredo, Mex. 132/D5
Nuevo Leon (state), Mex. 140/A2
Nuevo Rocafuerte, Ecu. 152/C5
Nufenen, Swi. 57/F4
Nufenenpass (pass), Swi. 57/E5
Nuguria (isls.), PNG 116/E5
Nuhne (riv.), Ger. 51/F6
Nui (isl.), Tuv. 116/G5
Nuiqsut, Ak, US 134/H1
Nuits-Saint-Georges, Fr. 56/A3
Nukata, Japan 77/M6
Nuklunek (mtn.), Ak, US 134/F4
Nuku'alofa (cap.), Tonga 117/H7
Nukufetau (isl.), Tuv. 116/G5
Nukulaelae (isl.), Tuv. 116/H5
Nukumanu (atoll), PNG 116/E5
Nukunonu (isl.), Tok. 117/H5
Nukuoro (isl.), Micr. 116/E4
Nukus (int'l arpt.), Uzb. 87/C4
Nukus, Uzb. 87/C4
Nukutavake (isl.), FrPol. 117/M6
Nulato, Ak, US 134/G3
Nules, Sp. 45/E3
Nullarbor (plain), Austl. 109/B4
Nullarbor NP, Austl. 113/F4
Numana, It. 59/G5
Numansdorp, Neth. 50/B5
Numata, Japan 75/F2
Numazu, Japan 75/F3
Nümbrecht, Ger. 53/G2
Numfoor (isl.), Indo. 81/H4
Nummi, Fin. 39/K1
Numurkah, Austl. 115/C3
Nunapitchuk, Ak, US 134/F3
Nunchía, Col. 152/C3
Nundle, Austl. 115/D1
Nuneaton, Eng, UK 33/E1
Nungarin, Austl. 112/C4
Nungatta NP, Austl. 115/D3
Nunivak (isl.), Ak, US 134/E4
Nunningen, Swi. 56/D3
Nuñoa, Peru 156/D4
Nunspeet, Neth. 50/C4
Nuon (riv.), Libr. 102/C5
Nuoro, It. 46/A2
Nuquí, Col. 152/B3
Nur (mts.), Turk. 91/E1
Nura (riv.), Kaz. 87/F2
Nürburgring, Ger. 53/F3
Nure (riv.), It. 58/C3
Nuremberg, Pa, US 138/B2
Nurhak, Turk. 90/D2
Nuri (ruin), Sudan 101/B5
Nuriootpa, Austl. 113/H5
Nurmijärvi, Fin. 39/L1
Nürnberg (int'l arpt.), Ger. 54/E3
Nürnberg, Ger. 54/E4
Nürpur, Pak. 86/B3
Nurri (mt.), Austl. 115/C1
Nürtingen, Ger. 54/C5
Nushagak (riv.), Ak, US 134/G4
Nushki, Pak. 89/J3
Nutberry (hill), Sc, UK 36/C5
Nuth, Neth. 53/E2
Nuthe-Graben (riv.), Ger. 40/Q7
Nutley, NJ, US 139/J8
Nutwood, Il, US 137/F7
Nuuk (Godthåb), Grld. 119/M3
Nuvolento, It. 58/D1
Nuy (riv.), SAfr. 106/L10
Nüziders, Aus. 57/F3
Nxai Pan NP, Bots. 105/D4
Nyabisindu, Rwa. 104/A3
Nyack, NY, US 139/K7
Nyah, Austl. 115/B2
Nyah West, Austl. 115/B2
Nyainqêntanglha (peak), China 70/E5
Nyaki NP, Malw. 104/B5
Nyala, Sudan 97/K5
Nyalam, China 85/E1
Nyandoma, Rus. 60/J3
Nyanza (prov.), Kenya 104/B3
Nyasa (lake), Malw. 93/F6
Nybro, Swe. 38/F3
Nyêmo, China 85/H1
Nyeri, Kenya 104/C3
Nyima, China 70/E5
Nyírábrány, Hun. 48/F2
Nyíradony, Hun. 41/L5
Nyírbátor, Hun. 41/M5
Nyíregyháza, Hun. 41/L5
Nyírmada, Hun. 41/M4
Nyiru (mt.), Kenya 104/C2
Nykøbing, Den. 38/C3
Nykøbing, Den. 38/D4
Nyköping, Swe. 38/G2
Nylstroom, SAfr. 105/E5
Nynäshamn, Swe. 38/G2
Nyngan, Austl. 115/C1
Nyoman (riv.), Bela. 62/B1
Nyon, Swi. 56/C5
Nyons, Fr. 42/F4
Nýřany, Czh. 55/G3
Nýrsko, Czh. 55/G4
Nýrsko (res.), Czh. 55/G4
Nysa, Pol. 41/J3
Nyssa, Or, US 126/D5
Nysted, Den. 38/D4
Nyūdo-zaki (pt.), Japan 76/A4
Nyuk (lake), Rus. 60/F2
Nyúl, Hun. 48/C2
Nyunzu, D.R. Congo 105/E2
Nyūzen, Japan 75/E2
Nzega, Tanz. 104/B4
Nzérékoré (pol. reg.), Gui. 102/C4
Nzérékoré, Gui. 102/C5
Nzi (riv.), C.d'Iv. 96/E6

O

Ō-shima (isl.), Japan 76/A3
Oa, Mull of (pt.), Sc, UK 31/Q9
Oahe (dam), SD, US 127/H4
Oahe (lake), ND,SD, US 124/F2
Oahu (isl.), Hi, US 124/V13
Oak Forest, Il, US 135/Q16
Oak Grove, Mo, US 137/E6
Oak Hill, WV, US 130/D4
Oak Park, Il, US 135/Q16
Oak Park, Mi, US 135/F7
Oak Ridge, Tn, US 130/C4
Oak Ridge, NJ, US 138/D1
Oak View, Ca, US 136/A2
Oakbank, Mb, Can. 127/J3
Oakdale, La, US 129/J5
Oakes, ND, US 127/J4
Oakey, Austl. 114/C4
Oakham, Eng, UK 33/F1
Oakhurst, Ca, US 128/C3
Oakland, Ca, US 128/B3
Oakland, Md, US 138/B5
Oakland (co.), Mi, US 135/E6
Oakland (lake), Mi, US 135/F6
Oakland, NJ, US 139/J7
Oakland (bay), Wa, US 135/A3
Oaklands, Austl. 115/C2
Oakley, Ca, US 135/L10
Oakover (riv.), Austl. 109/B3
Oakridge, Or, US 126/C5
Oakville, La, US 137/P17
Oakville, Mo, US 137/G9
Oakville, On, Can. 131/Q9
Oakwood Hills, Il, US 135/P15
Oamaru, NZ 117/S12
Ōamishirasato, Japan 77/E2
Oat (mtn.), Ca, US 136/B2
Oatlands, Austl. 115/C4
Oaxaca (state), Mex. 140/B4
Oaxaca de Juárez, Mex. 144/B2
Ob' (gulf), Rus. 67/G3
Ob' (riv.), Rus. 67/E3
Ob Luang Gorge, Thai. 78/B2
Obama, Japan 77/J5
Obama (bay), Japan 77/J4
Oban (hills), Nga. 103/H5
Oban, Sc, UK 31/R8
Obanazawa, Japan 76/B4
Obara, Japan 77/M5
Obata, Japan 77/L7
Ober-Olm, Ger. 54/B3
Ober Ramstadt, Ger. 54/B3
Oberá, Arg. 157/F2
Oberalppass (pass), Swi. 57/E4
Oberalpstock (peak), Swi. 57/E4
Oberammergau, Ger. 57/H2
Oberasbach, Ger. 54/D4
Oberau, Ger. 57/H2
Oberburg, Swi. 56/D3
Oberderdingen, Ger. 54/B4
Oberdiessbach, Swi. 56/D4
Oberding, Ger. 55/E6
Oberdorf, Swi. 56/D3
Oberdorla, Ger. 51/H6
Oberelsbach, Ger. 54/D2
Oberentfelden, Swi. 56/E3
Oberglatt, Swi. 57/E3
Obergünzburg, Ger. 57/G2
Oberhaching, Ger. 55/E6
Oberhausen, Ger. 50/D6
Oberkirch, Ger. 56/E1
Oberkochen, Ger. 54/D5
Oberkotzau, Ger. 55/E2
Oberlausitz (reg.), Ger. 41/H3
Oberlin, Ks, US 129/G3
Obernai, Fr. 56/D1
Obernburg am Main, Ger. 54/C3
Oberndorf am Neckar, Ger. 57/E1
Oberndorf bei Salzburg, Aus. 55/F7
Oberneukirchen, Aus. 55/H6
Obernkirchen, Ger. 51/G4
Oberon, Austl. 115/D2
Oberösterreich (prov.), Aus. 41/G4
Oberpfälzer Wald (for.), Ger. 55/E3
Oberrieden, Swi. 57/E3
Oberriet, Swi. 57/F3
Obersaxen, Swi. 57/E4
Oberschleissheim, Ger. 55/E6
Oberschneiding, Ger. 55/F5
Obersiggenthal, Swi. 57/E3
Oberstammheim, Swi. 57/E2
Oberstaufen, Ger. 57/G2
Oberstdorf, Ger. 57/G3
Oberthal, Ger. 53/G4
Obertrum am See, Aus. 55/G7
Obertshausen, Ger. 54/B2
Oberursel, Ger. 54/B2
Oberuzwil, Swi. 57/F3
Oberviechtach, Ger. 55/F4
Oberwald, Swi. 57/E4
Oberwart, Aus. 48/C2
Oberwesel, Ger. 53/G3
Oberwil, Swi. 56/D4
Obfelden, Swi. 57/E3
Obi (str.), Indo. 81/G4
Obi (isls.), Indo. 81/G4
Óbidos, Braz. 151/G4
Óbidos, Port. 44/A3
Obihiro, Japan 76/C2
Obilić, Serb. 47/G1
Obing, Ger. 55/F6
Obira, Japan 76/B1
Obitsu (riv.), Japan 77/D3
Obluch'ye, Rus. 71/P2
Obninsk, Rus. 60/H5
Obo, CAfr. 97/L6
Oborniki, Pol. 41/J2
Oborniki Śląskie, Pol. 41/J3
Obra (riv.), Pol. 41/J2
Obrenovac, Serb. 48/E3
Obrež, Serb. 48/E4
Obrigheim, Ger. 54/C4
Obrigheim, Ger. 54/B3
Observatory, Austl. 115/G5
Obtrumer (lake), Aus. 55/F7
Ōbu, Japan 77/L6
Obuasi, Gha. 103/E5
Obw. (canton), Swi. 57/E4
Obzor, Bul. 49/H4
Ocala, Fl, US 133/H4
Ocampo, Mex. 142/E3
Ocaña, Sp. 44/D3
Ocaña, Col. 152/C2
Occhieppo Inferiore, It. 58/B1
Occhieppo Superiore, It. 58/A1
Occhiobello, It. 59/E3
Occidental, Cordillera (mts.), Ecu. 150/C3
Occimiano, It. 58/B2
Ocean (cape), Ak, US 134/L3
Ocean (co.), NJ, US 138/D4
Ocean Beach, NY, US 139/E2
Ocean City, Md, US 130/F4
Ocean City, NJ, US 138/D5
Ocean Falls, BC, Can. 126/B2
Ocean Gate, NJ, US 138/D4
Ocean Grove, NJ, US 138/D3
Ocean View, NJ, US 138/D5
Oceanographic Museum, Mona. 58/J8
Oceanside, Ca, US 136/C4
Oceanside, NY, US 139/L9
Oceanville, NJ, US 138/D5
Och'amch'ire, Geo. 63/G4
Ocheltree, Ks, US 137/D6
Ochiishi-misaki (cape), Japan 76/D2
Ochil (hills), Sc, UK 36/C4
Ocho Rios, Jam. 145/G2
Ochsenfurt, Ger. 54/D3
Ochsenhausen, Ger. 57/F1
Ochsenkopf (peak), Aus. 57/E3
Ochtendung, Ger. 53/G3
Ochtrup, Ger. 51/E4
Ochtum (riv.), Ger. 51/F2
Ockelbo, Swe. 38/G1
Ockenheim, Ger. 53/G4
Ocmulgee (riv.), Ga, US 133/H3
Ocmulgee Nat'l Mon., Ga, US 133/H3
Ocna Mureş, Rom. 49/F2
Ocna Sibiului, Rom. 49/G3
Ocoña (riv.), Peru 150/D6
Ocoña, Peru 156/C5
Oconee (lake), Ga, US 133/H3
Oconee (riv.), Ga, US 133/H3
Oconto, Wi, US 127/M4
Ocosingo, Mex. 144/C2
Ocotal, Nic. 144/E3
Ocotlán, Mex. 142/E4
Ocotlán de Morelos, Mex. 144/B2
Ocoyoacac, Mex. 143/Q10
Ocozocoautla de Espinosa, Mex. 144/C2
Ocracoke, NC, US 133/K3
Ocros, Peru 156/B3
Octeville, Fr. 42/C2
October Revolution (isl.), Rus. 67/H2
Oda (peak), Sudan 101/D4
Oda, Japan 74/C3
Oda, Gha. 103/E5
Odaesan NP, SKor. 74/A2
Ōdai, Japan 77/K7
Ōdaigahara-san (peak), Japan 74/E3
Ōdate, Japan 76/B3
Odawara, Japan 75/F3
Odda, Nor. 38/B1
Odder, Den. 38/D4
Odeborn (riv.), Ger. 51/F6
Odelzhausen, Ger. 54/E6
Odemira, Port. 44/A4
Ödemiş, Turk. 90/A2
Odendaalsrus, SAfr. 106/D2
Odense, Den. 38/D4
Odense (int'l arpt.), Den. 38/D4
Odenthal, Ger. 53/G1
Odenton, Md, US 138/B5
Odenwald (reg.), Ger. 54/B3
Oder (Odra) (riv.), Ger.,Pol. 41/H2
Oder-Spree Kanal (canal), Ger. 40/Q7
Oderen, Fr. 56/C2
Oderhaff (lag.), Ger. 41/H2
Oderzo, It. 59/F1
Odesa, Turk. 90/B1
Odesa, Ukr. 49/K2
Odes'ka Oblasti, Ukr. 62/D3
Odessa, Wa, US 126/D4
Odessa, Tx, US 129/G5
Odessa, De, US 138/C5
Odet (riv.), Fr. 42/B2
Odienné, C.d'Iv. 102/D4
Odintsovo, Rus. 61/W9
Odiongan, Phil. 79/D5
Odivelas, Port. 45/P10
Odobeşti, Rom. 49/H3
Odon (riv.), Fr. 42/C2
Odoorn, Neth. 50/D3
Odorheiu Secuiesc, Rom. 49/G2
Odžaci, Serb. 48/D3
Odzala, PN d', Congo 96/J7
Ōe, Japan 77/H5
Ōe-yama (peak), Japan 77/H5
Oegstgeest, Neth. 50/B4
Oeiras, Braz. 154/B2
Oelde, Ger. 51/F5
Oelsnitz, Ger. 55/F2
Oeno (isl.), Pitc. 117/M7
Oensingen, Swi. 56/D3
Oer-Erkenschwick, Ger. 51/E5
Oesling (mts.), Lux. 53/E4
Oesterdam (dam), Neth. 50/B6
Oestrich-Winkel, Ger. 54/B3
Oeta NP, Gre. 47/H3
Oetz, Aus. 57/G3
Oey'ŏn (isl.), SKor. 73/D3
Of, Turk. 90/E1
O'Fallon, Mo, US 137/F8
O'Fallon, Il, US 137/H8
Ofanto (riv.), It. 46/D2
Ofaqim, Isr. 91/D4
Ofenhorn (peak), Swi. 57/E5
Offa, Nga. 103/G4
Offaly (co.), Ire. 34/A5
Offanengo, It. 58/C2
Offement, Fr. 56/C2
Offenbach, Ger. 54/B2
Offenbach an der Queich, Ger. 54/B4
Offenburg, Ger. 56/D1
Offingen, Ger. 54/D6
Offstein, Ger. 54/B3
Oftersheim, Ger. 54/B4
Oftringen, Swi. 56/D3
Ōfunato, Japan 76/B4
Oga, Japan 76/A4
Oga (pen.), Japan 76/A4
Ogachi, Japan 76/B4
Ogadēn (reg.), Eth. 97/P6
Ōgaki, Japan 77/L5
Ogano, Japan 77/C2
Ogasawara, Japan 116/D2
Ogatsu, Japan 76/B4
Ogawa, Japan 77/E1
Ogawa, Japan 77/C1
Ogawara (lake), Japan 76/B3
Ogbomosho, Nga. 103/G4
Ogden, Ut, US 137/K11
Ogden Bay (bay), Ut, US 137/J11
Ogden, South Fork (riv.), Ut, US 137/K11
Ogdensburg, NY, US 130/F2
Ogdensburg, NJ, US 138/D1
Ogeechee (riv.), Ga, US 133/H3
Oggiono, It. 58/C1
Ogi, Japan 75/E2
Ogidaki (mtn.), On, Can. 130/D2
Ogies, SAfr. 106/E2
Ogilvie (mts.), Yk, Can. 122/C2
Ogilvie (riv.), Yk, Can. 122/C2
Ogles, Il, US 137/G8
Oglesby, Tx, US 143/F2
Oglio (riv.), It. 43/J4
Ognon (riv.), Fr. 40/C5
Ogoamas (peak), Indo. 81/F3
Ogoki (lake), On, Can. 127/M3
Ogoki (res.), On, Can. 127/L3
Ogoki (riv.), On, Can. 127/M3
Ogooué (riv.), Gabon 93/C5
Ogose, Japan 77/C2
Ogosta (riv.), Bul. 49/F4
Ogre, Lat. 39/L3
Oguchi, Japan 77/L5
Ogulin, Cro. 48/B3
Ogun (riv.), Nga. 96/F6
Ogun (state), Nga. 103/F5
Ogurjaly (isl.), Trkm. 87/B5
Oğuz, Turk. 90/D2
Oh Me Edge (hill), Eng, UK 36/D6
Ōhara, Japan 77/E3
Oharu, Japan 77/L5
Ōhata, Japan 76/B3
Ohey, Belg. 53/E3
O'Higgins (pol. reg.), Chile 158/B1
O'Higgins (lake), Chile 159/B6
Ohio (riv.), US 130/B4
Ohio (state), US 130/D3
Ōhira, Japan 77/D1
Ohlsdorf, Aus. 55/G7
Ohlstadt, Ger. 57/H2
Ohm (riv.), Ger. 54/C1
Ōho, Japan 77/E1
Ohoopee (riv.), Ga, US 133/H3
Ohře (riv.), Czh. 40/H3
Ohre (riv.), Ger. 40/F2
Ohrid, FYROM 47/G2
Ohrid (lake), Alb., Mac 47/G2
Oi (riv.), China 83/G2
Ōi, Japan 77/J5
Ōi, Japan 77/C3
Ōi, Japan 77/D2
Oiapoque (riv.), Braz. 151/H3
Oiapoque, Braz. 151/H3
Oich (lake), Sc, UK 36/B2
Oieras, Port. 45/P10
Oignies, Fr. 52/B3
Oignin (riv.), Fr. 56/B5
Oil City, Pa, US 130/E3
Oinófita, Gre. 47/H3
Oinói, Gre. 47/N8
Oirschot, Neth. 50/C5
Oise (dept.), Fr. 52/B5
Oise (riv.), Fr. 40/B4
Oise à l'Aisne, Canal de l' (canal), Fr. 52/C4
Oiseaux du Djoudj, PN des, Sen. 102/A2
Ōiso, Japan 77/C3
Oissery, Fr. 30/L4
Oisterwijk, Neth. 50/C5
Ōita (riv.), Japan 74/B4
Ōita (pref.), Japan 74/B4
Ōita, Japan 74/B4
Ōizumi, Japan 77/C1
Ōizumi, Japan 77/A2
Ojai, Ca, US 136/A2
Ojcowski NP, Pol. 41/K3
Öjebyn, Swe. 37/G2
Ōji, Japan 77/J6
Ojima, Japan 77/C1
Ojinaga, Mex. 129/F5
Ojiya, Japan 75/F2
Ojo de Agua, Mex. 143/Q9
Ojo de Liebre (lag.), Mex. 142/B3
Ojocaliente, Mex. 142/E4
Ojos del Salado (peak), Chile 157/C2
Ojos Negros, Sp. 44/E2
Ojuelos de Jalisco, Mex. 143/E4
Oka, Nga. 103/G5
Oka (riv.), Rus. 61/J5
Oka, Qu, Can. 131/M7
Okabe, Japan 77/C1
Okahandja, Namb. 105/C5
Okak (isl.), Nf, Can. 123/K3
Okanagan (lake), BC, Can. 122/D4
Okanagan Falls, BC, Can. 126/D3
Okanda, PN de l', Gabon 105/B1
Okanogan, Wa, US 126/D3
Okanogan (riv.), Wa, US 126/D3
Okāra, Pak. 86/B4
Okavango (delta), Bots. 105/D4
Ōkawa, Japan 74/B4
Okaya, Japan 75/F2
Okayama (pref.), Japan 74/C3
Okayama, Japan 74/C3
Okazaki, Japan 77/M6
Okch'ŏn, SKor. 73/D4
Okęcie (int'l arpt.), Pol. 41/L2
Okeechobee, Fl, US 133/H5
Okeechobee (lake), Fl, US 125/K6
Okegawa, Japan 77/D2
Okement (riv.), Eng, UK 32/B5
Okha, Rus. 65/Q4
Ókhi Óros (peak), Gre. 47/J3
Okhotsk (sea), Rus. 67/P4
Okhotsk, Sea of (sea), Japan,Rus 71/R2
Okhta (riv.), Rus. 61/T6
Okhtyrka, Ukr. 62/E2
Oki (isls.), Japan 74/C2
Okidaitō (isl.), Japan 75/L8
Okiep, SAfr. 106/B3
Okinawa (isl.), Japan 67/M7
Okinawa (pref.), Japan 75/J8
Okino-shima (isl.), Japan 74/C4
Okinoerabu (isl.), Japan 75/K7
Okitipupa, Nga. 103/G5
Okkan, Myan. 83/G4
Okku, SKor. 73/D5
Oklahoma (state), US 129/H4
Oklahoma City (cap.), Ok, US 137/M15
Okmulgee, Ok, US 129/J4
Oko, Nga. 103/G5
Okobaji (lakes), Ia, US 127/K5
Okok (riv.), Ugan. 104/B2
Okolona, Ms, US 133/F3
Okoppe, Japan 76/C1
Okotoks, Ab, Can. 126/E3
Okovango (riv.), Namb. 93/E6
Oksbøl, Den. 38/C4
Oksskolten (peak), Nor. 37/E2
Oktyabr'sk, Rus. 63/J1
Oktyabr'skiy, Rus. 61/M5
Ōkuchi, Japan 74/B4
Okulovka, Rus. 60/G4
Okushiri, Japan 76/A2
Okutama (lake), Japan 77/C2
Okutama, Japan 77/C2
Okwa (riv.), Bots. 105/D5
Ol Doinyo Sabuk NP, Kenya 104/C3
Ólafsfjördhur, Ice. 37/N6
Ólafsvík, Ice. 37/M7
Olalla, Wa, US 135/B3
Olan, Pic d' (peak), Fr. 43/G4
Olanchito, Hon. 144/E3
Öland (isl.), Swe. 37/F4
Ölands södra udde (pt.), Swe. 38/G3
Olathe, Ks, US 137/D6
Olavarría, Arg. 158/E3
Oława, Pol. 41/J3
Ölbach (riv.), Ger. 51/F5
Olberg, Az, US 137/S19
Olbia, It. 46/A2
Olching, Ger. 55/E6
Olcott, NY, US 131/S9
Old (riv.), Ca, US 135/L11
Old Bahama (chan.), Cuba 145/G1
Old Bar, Austl. 115/E1
Old Bedford (canal), Eng, UK 33/G2
Old Bethpage, NY, US 139/M9
Old Bridge, NJ, US 139/H10
Old City, Isr. 91/G8
Old Crow, Yk, Can. 134/L2
Old Faithful Geyser, Wy, US 126/F4
Old Field (pt.), NY, US 139/E2
Old Fort Niagara, NY, US 131/R9
Old Harbor, Ak, US 134/H4
Old Man of Hoy, Sc, UK 31/V14
Old Mill Creek, Il, US 135/Q15
Old Nene (riv.), Eng, UK 33/F2
Old Rhine (riv.), Neth. 50/B4
Old Saybrook, Ct, US 139/F1
Old Tappan, NJ, US 139/K8
Old Town, Me, US 131/G2
Old Windsor, Eng, UK 30/B2
Old Wives (lake), Sk, Can. 127/G3
Oldeani (peak), Tanz. 104/B3
Oldebroek, Neth. 50/C4
Oldemarkt, Neth. 50/C3
Oldenburg, Ger. 51/F2
Oldenburg, Ger. 38/D4
Oldenzaal, Neth. 50/D4
Oldham, Eng, UK 35/F4
Oldham (co.), Eng, UK 35/F4
Oldman (riv.), Ab, Can. 126/E3
Oldmeldrum, Sc, UK 36/D2
Oldoog (isl.), Ger. 51/E1
Olds, Ab, Can. 126/E3
Olduvai Gorge, Tanz. 104/B3
Oldwick, NJ, US 138/D2
Olean, NY, US 130/E3
Olecko, Pol. 39/K4
Oleggio, It. 58/B1
Oleiros, Port. 44/B3
Oleiros, Sp. 44/A1
Olekma (riv.), Rus. 65/N4
Oleksandriya, Ukr. 62/E2
Olele (pt.), Wa, US 135/B2
Olemari (riv.), Sur. 153/H4
Ølen, Nor. 38/A2
Olenegorsk, Rus. 60/G1
Olenëk (riv.), Rus. 65/L3
Olenek (bay), Rus. 65/M2
Oléron, Île (isl.), Fr. 42/C4
Olesa de Montserrat, Sp. 45/K6
Oleśnica, Pol. 41/J3
Olesno, Pol. 41/K3
Oley, Pa, US 138/C3
Olfen, Ger. 51/E5
Olga (mt.), Austl. 113/F3
Olginate, It. 58/C1
Ölgiy, Mong. 70/E2
Ølgod, Den. 38/C4
Olhão, Port. 44/B4
Oli Qoltyq Sory (swamp), Kaz. 87/B3
Oliena, It. 46/A2
Olifantshoek, SAfr. 106/P12
Olifantsrivier (riv.), SAfr. 105/E5
Olimarao (isl.), Micr. 116/D4
Olimbía (Olympia) (ruin), Gre. 47/G4
Ólimbos, Gre. 90/A3
Ólimbos NP (Olympos NP), Gre. 47/H2
Olímpia, Braz. 155/B2
Olimpos Beydağları NP, Turk. 91/B1
Olinalá, Mex. 144/B2
Olinda, Braz. 154/D3
Olindina, Braz. 154/C3
Oliva, Sp. 45/E3
Oliva de la Frontera, Sp. 44/B3
Olivais, Port. 44/A3
Oliveira, Braz. 155/C2
Olivenza, Sp. 44/B3
Oliver, BC, Can. 126/D3
Olivet, Fr. 42/D3
Olivone, Swi. 57/E4
Olla, La, US 129/J5
Ollachea, Peru 156/D4
Ollagüe (vol.), Chile 150/E8
Ollainville, Fr. 30/J6
Olleria, Sp. 45/E3
Olleros, Peru 156/B3
Ollon, Swi. 56/D5
Ollūr, India 82/C5
Olmaliq, Uzb. 87/E4
Olmedo, Sp. 44/C2
Olmos, Peru 156/B2
Olmos Park, Tx, US 137/U21
Olmstead, Ut, US 137/K13
Olmué, Chile 158/N8
Olney, Tx, US 129/H4
Olney, Md, US 138/A5
Olofström, Swe. 38/F3
Olomane (riv.), Qu, Can. 131/J1

213

Olomo – Oyo

Olomouc, Czh. 41/J4
Olomoucký (pol. reg.), Czh. 41/J4
Olongapo, Phil. 79/D5
Olonne-sur-Mer, Fr. 42/C3
Olorgasailie Nat'l Mon., Kenya 104/C3
Oloron-Sainte-Marie, Fr. 42/C5
Olot, Sp. 45/G1
Oloy (range), Rus. 65/S3
Olpe (riv.), Ger. 51/F6
Olpe, Ger. 53/G1
Olsberg, Ger. 51/F6
Olst, Neth. 50/D4
Olsztyn, Pol. 39/J5
Olsztynek, Pol. 41/L2
Olt (riv.), Rom. 62/C3
Olt (prov.), Rom. 49/G3
Olte, Sierra de (hills), Arg. 158/C4
Olten, Swi. 56/D3
Oltenița, Rom. 49/H3
Olteț (riv.), Rom. 49/F3
Oltre il Colle, It. 57/F6
Oltu, Turk. 90/E1
Oltu (riv.), Turk. 90/E1
Olur, Turk. 90/E1
Olvera, Sp. 44/C4
Olympia (cap.), Wa, US 126/C4
Olympic (mts.), Wa, US 126/C4
Olympic Dam, Austl. 113/H4
Olympic Game Farm, Wa, US 135/A1
Olympic National Forest, Wa, US 135/A2
Olympic NP, Wa, US 126/B4
Olympic Park, SKor. 73/G6
Olympos (Mount Olympus) (peak), Gre. 47/H2
Olympus (mt.), Wa, US 126/C4
Olympus (peak), Cyp. 91/C2
Olyutorskiy (bay), Rus. 65/S3
Ōma, Japan 76/B3
Oma (riv.), Rus. 61/K2
Ōma-zaki (pt.), Japan 76/B3
Ōmachi, Japan 75/E2
Omae-zaki (pt.), Japan 75/F3
Ōmagari, Japan 76/B4
Omagh (dist.), NI, UK 34/A2
Omagh, NI, UK 34/A2
Omak, Wa, US 126/D3
Oman (ctry.) 89/G4
Oman (gulf), Asia 89/H4
Omar Torrijos Herrera (int'l arpt.), Pan. 152/B2
Omaruru, Namb. 105/C5
Omas, Peru 156/B4
Omatako (riv.), Namb. 105/C4
Omate, Peru 156/D5
Ombai (str.), Indo. 81/F5
Ombrone (riv.), It. 43/J5
Ombúes de Lavalle, Uru. 159/K10
Ōme, Japan 77/C2
Omeath, Ire. 34/B3
Omegna, It. 43/H4
Omeo, Austl. 115/C3
Ömerli, Turk. 90/E2
Ometepe (isl.), Nic. 144/E4
Ometepec, Mex. 144/B2
Ōmi, Japan 77/K5
Ōmihachiman, Japan 77/K5
Omiš, Cro. 46/E1
Omitlán (riv.), Mex. 144/B2
Ōmiya, Japan 75/G2
Ōmiya, Japan 77/H4
Ōmiya, Japan 77/K7
Ommaney (cape), Ak, US 134/M4
Ommen, Neth. 50/D3
Ömnögovĭ (prov.), Mong. 70/H3
Omo NP, Eth. 97/N6
Omo Wenz (riv.), Eth. 93/F4
Omodeo (lake), It. 46/A2
Omolon (riv.), Rus. 67/Q3
Omono (riv.), Japan 76/B4
Omsk, Rus. 87/F1
Omsk (int'l arpt.), Rus. 87/F2
Omskaya Oblast, Rus. 87/F1
Ōmu, Japan 76/C1
Omul (peak), Rom. 49/G3
Ōmura, Japan 74/A4
Omurtag, Bul. 49/H4
Ōmuta, Japan 74/B4
Omutninsk, Rus. 61/M4
Onagawa, Japan 76/B4
Onalaska, Tx, US 132/E4
Onaping (lake), On, Can. 130/D2
Oñate, Sp. 44/D1
Onaway, Mi, US 130/C2
Onchan, IM, UK 34/D3
Onda, Sp. 45/E3
Ondava (riv.), Slvk. 41/L4
Ondjiva, Ang. 105/C4
Ondo, Nga. 103/G5
Ondo (state), Nga. 103/G5
Öndörhaan, Mong. 71/K2
Onè, It. 59/E1
Onega, Rus. 60/H3
Onega (bay), Rus. 60/G2
Onega (lake), Rus. 160/D
Onega (pen.), Rus. 60/H2
Onega (riv.), Rus. 64/D3
Oneida, NY, US 130/F3
Oneida, Pa, US 138/B2
Oneonta, NY, US 130/F3
Onex, Swi. 56/C5
Ongjin, NKor. 73/C4
Ongole, India 82/D4
Ongtüstik Qazaqstan, Kaz. 64/G5
Onhaye, Belg. 53/D3
Onida, SD, US 127/H4
Onil, Sp. 45/E3
Onilahy (riv.), Ang. 107/G8
Onishi, Japan 77/C1
Onitsha, Nga. 103/G5
Onjuku, Japan 77/E3
Onkaparinga (riv.), Austl. 113/M8
Onnaing, Fr. 52/C3
Onny (riv.), Eng, UK 32/D2
Ōno, Japan 74/E3
Ono, Japan 74/D3
Ōno, Japan 77/L5
Onoda, Japan 74/B4
Onomichi, Japan 74/C3
Onon, Mong. 71/K2
Onon (riv.), Rus. 71/K1
Onoto, Ven. 153/E2
Onotoa (isl.), Kiri. 116/G5
Onrusrivier, SAfr. 106/L11
Onslow, Austl. 112/B2
Ontake-san (peak), Japan 75/E3
Ontario, Or, US 126/D4
Ontario, Ca, US 136/C2
Ontario (prov.), Can. 122/H3
Ontario (lake), Can.,US 130/E3
Ontelaunee (lake), Pa, US 138/C3
Onteniente, Sp. 45/E3
Ontonagon, Mi, US 127/L4
Ontong Java (isl.), Sol. 116/E5
Onyang, SKor. 73/D4
Onzaga, Col. 152/C3
Oologah (lake), Ok, US 132/D2
Oona River, BC, Can. 134/M5
Oost-Vlaanderen (prov.), Belg. 52/C2
Oost-Vlieland, Neth. 50/C2
Oostburg, Neth. 52/C1
Oostelijk Flevoland (polder), Neth. 50/C3
Oostende (Ostend), Belg. 52/B1
Oosterhout, Neth. 50/B5
Oosterscheidedam (dam),Neth. 50/A5
Oosterschelde (riv.), Neth. 40/B3
Oosterwolde, Neth. 50/D3
Oosterzele, Belg. 52/C2
Oostkamp, Belg. 52/C1
Oostvaarderplassen (lake),Neth. 50/C4
Oostzaan, Neth. 50/B4
Ootmarsum, Neth. 50/D4
Opaka, Bul. 49/H4
Opalenica, Pol. 41/J2
Opasatika (riv.), On, Can. 130/D1
Opatija, Cro. 48/B3
Opatów, Pol. 41/L3
Opava, Czh. 41/J4
Opelika, Al, US 133/G3
Opelousas, La, US 129/J5
Opera, It. 58/C2
Öpfingen, Ger. 57/F1
Opglabbeek, Belg. 53/E1
Ophir, Ak, US 134/G3
Ophir, Ut, US 137/J13
Ophthalmia (range), Austl. 112/C2
Oploo, Neth. 50/C5
Opmeer, Neth. 50/B3
Opoczno, Pol. 41/L3
Opole, Pol. 41/J3
Opole Lubelskie, Pol. 41/L3
Opolskie (prov.), Pol. 41/J3
Opovo, Serb. 48/E3
Opp, Al, US 133/G4
Oppdal, Nor. 37/D3
Oppeano, It. 59/E2
Oppenau, Ger. 56/E1
Oppenheim, Ger. 54/B3
Oppland (co.), Nor. 37/D3
Opportunity, Wa, US 126/D4
Opwijk, Belg. 53/D2
Oquirrh (mts.), Ut, US 137/J12
Or 'Aqiva, Isr. 91/F6
Or, Mont d' (peak), Fr. 56/C4
Or Yehuda, Isr. 91/F7
Ora (riv.), Mex. 142/D3
Ōra, Japan 77/C1
Oradell, NJ, US 139/J8
Oradell (res.), NJ, US 139/J8
Orahovac, Serb. 47/G1
Orahovica, Cro. 48/C3
Orai, India 84/B3
Orain (riv.), Fr. 56/B4
Oral, Kaz. 63/J2
Oran, Alg. 100/E5
Orang (riv.), NKor. 73/E2
Orange, Austl. 115/D2
Orange (cape), Braz. 151/H3
Orange, Fr. 42/F4
Orange (riv.), SAfr.,Nam 105/C6
Orange (mts.), Sur. 151/G3
Orange, Ca, US 136/G8
Orange, Ct, US 139/E1
Orange, NJ, US 139/J8
Orange (co.), NY, US 138/D1
Orange, Tx, US 129/J5
Orange, Va, US 130/E4
Orange Park, Fl, US 133/H4
Orange Walk, Belz. 144/D2
Orangeburg, SC, US 133/H3
Orangeburg, NY, US 139/K7
Orangeville, On, Can. 130/D3
Orangeville, Pa, US 138/B1
Orango (isl.), GBis. 102/A4
Oranienburg, Ger. 40/Q6
Oranjekanaal (riv.), Neth. 50/D3
Oranjemund, Namb. 106/B3
Oranjestad, Aruba. 152/D1
Oranmore, Ire. 31/P10
Orapa, Bots. 105/E5
Oras, Phil. 79/E5
Orăștie, Rom. 49/F3
Oravița, Rom. 48/E3
Orb (riv.), Fr. 42/E5
Orba (riv.), It. 58/B3
Orbe, Swi. 56/C4
Orbe (riv.), Swi. 56/C4
Orbey, Fr. 56/D1
Órbigo (riv.), Sp. 44/C1
Orbost, Austl. 115/D3
Örbyhus, Swe. 38/G1
Orcemont, Fr. 30/H6
Orcera, Sp. 44/D3
Orchamps, Fr. 56/B3
Orchamps-Vennes, Fr. 56/C3
Orchard (lake), Mi, US 135/F6
Orchard City, Co, US 128/F3
Orchard Farm, Mo, US 137/G8
Orchard Homes, Mt, US 126/E4
Orchard Lake Village, Mi, US 135/F6
Orchid (isl.), Tai. 79/D3
Orchies, Fr. 52/C3
Orchy (riv.), Sc, UK 36/B4
Orciano di Pesaro, It. 59/F5
Orco (riv.), It. 43/G4
Orcopampa, Peru 156/C4
Orcotuna, Peru 156/C3
Ord, Ne, US 127/J5
Ordaz (int'l arpt.), Mex. 142/D4
Ordes, Sp. 44/A1
Ordesa y Monte Perdido, PN de, Sp. 45/F1
Ordos (des.), China 70/J4
Ordos (Mu Us Shamo) (des.), China 70/J4
Ordu, Turk. 90/D1
Ordu (prov.), Turk. 90/D1
Ore, Nga. 103/G5
Orealla, Guy. 153/G3
Örebro, Swe. 38/F2
Örebro (prov.), Swe. 37/E4
Orebro (int'l arpt.), Swe. 38/F2
Oregon (state), US 126/C5
Oregon Caves Nat'l Mon., Or, US 126/C5
Oregon City, Or, US 126/C4
Öregrund, Swe. 38/H1
Orekhovo-Zuyevo, Rus. 60/H5
Orël, Rus. 62/F1
Orellana, Peru 156/C2
Orellana la Vieja, Sp. 44/C3
Orem, Ut, US 137/K13
Orenberg (int'l arpt.), Rus. 63/K2
Orenburg, Rus. 63/K2
Orenburgskaya Oblast, Rus. 87/B2
Orense, Sp. 44/B1
Orestiás, Gre. 47/K2
Øresund (sound), Swe. 38/E4
Oreti (riv.), NZ 117/R12
Orford, Austl. 115/C4
Orford (pt.), Eng, UK 33/H2
Organ Pipe Cactus Nat'l Mon., Az, US 142/B1
Órgãos, Serra dos (mts.), Braz. 211/K7
Orgaz, Sp. 44/D3
Orgelet, Fr. 56/B4
Orgeurs, Fr. 30/H5
Orgeval, Fr. 30/H5
Orgosolo, It. 46/A2
Orhaneli, Turk. 62/D5
Orhangazi, Turk. 49/J5
Orhei, Mol. 49/J2
Orhon (riv.), Mong. 70/J2
Oria, Sp. 44/D4
Orient (pt.), NY, US 139/G1
Oriental, Mex. 143/M7
Oriental, Cordillera (mts.), SAm. 150/C5
Orientale (prov.), D.R. Congo 104/A2
Oriente, Arg. 158/E3
Origny-Sainte-Benoîte, Fr. 52/C4
Orihuela, Sp. 45/E3
Orillia, On, Can. 130/E2
Orimattila, Fin. 39/L1
Orinda, Ca, US 135/K11
Orinoco (delta), Ven. 147/C2
Orinoco (riv.), Col.,Ven. 147/C2
Orio al Serio (int'l arpt.), It. 58/C1
Oriolo, It. 46/E2
Orion (lake), Mi, US 135/F6
Orissa (state), India 70/D7
Orissa Coast (canal), India 85/F5
Oristano, It. 46/A3
Oristano, Golfo di (gulf), It. 46/A3
Orivesi, Fin. 39/L1
Oriximiná, Braz. 151/G4
Orizaba, Mex. 143/M8
Orizona, Braz. 154/A5
Orjen (peak), Serb. 47/F1
Órjiva, Sp. 44/D4
Orke (riv.), Ger. 51/F6
Örkelljunga, Swe. 38/E3
Orkhomenós, Gre. 47/H3
Orkney, SAfr. 106/D2
Orkney (isls.), UK 160/G
Orla, Tx, US 132/C4
Orland Park, Il, US 135/Q16
Orlândia, Braz. 155/C2
Orlando (int'l arpt.), Fl, US 133/H4
Orlando, Fl, US 133/H4
Orlando, Capo d' (cape), It. 46/D3
Orléanais (reg.), Fr. 42/D2
Orleans, Ca, US 126/C5
Orleans (parish), La, US 137/P16
Orléans, Fr. 42/D3
Orlenbach, Ger. 54/D2
Orlik (res.), Czh. 55/H3
Orlová, Czh. 41/K4
Orlovskaya Oblast, Rus. 62/F1
Orly (int'l arpt.), Fr. 30/K5
Orly, Fr. 30/K5
Ormanlı, Turk. 49/K5
Ormea, It. 58/A4
Ormília, Gre. 47/H2
Ormiston, Sc, UK 36/D5
Ormoc, Phil. 81/F1
Ormond Beach, Fl, US 133/H4
Ormskirk, Eng, UK 35/F4
Ornain (riv.), Fr. 42/F2
Ornans, Fr. 56/C3
Ornavasso, It. 57/E6
Orne (riv.), Fr. 40/C4
Ørnes, Nor. 37/E2
Orneta, Pol. 39/J4
Örnsköldsvik, Swe. 37/F3
Oro (riv.), Mex. 154/C2
Oro Grande, Ca, US 136/C1
Oro, Monte d' (peak), Fr. 46/A1
Oro Valley, Az, US 128/E4
Orocó, Braz. 154/C3
Orocué, Col. 152/D3
Orodara, Burk. 102/D4
Orofino, Id, US 126/D4
Orolo (riv.), It. 59/E1
Oroluk (isl.), Micr. 116/D4
Oromocto, NB, Can. 131/H2
Orona (Hull) (isl.), Kiri. 117/H5
Orono, Me, US 131/G2
Orontes (riv.), Syria 90/D3
Oropesa, Sp. 44/C3
Oroqen Zizhiqi, China 71/M1
Orós, Braz. 154/C2
Orosei, It. 46/A2
Orosei, Golfo di (gulf), It. 46/A2
Orosháza, Hun. 48/E2
Oroszlány, Hun. 48/D2
Orovada, Nv, US 126/D5
Oroville, Wa, US 126/D3
Oroville, Ca, US 128/B3
Orphin, Fr. 30/H6
Orpund, Swi. 56/D3
Orrefors, Swe. 38/F3
Orrell, Eng, UK 35/F4
Orrick, Mo, US 137/E5
Orrin (riv.), Sc, UK 36/B2
Orrin (res.), Sc, UK 36/B2
Orroli, It. 46/A3
Orroroo, Austl. 113/H5
Orrtanna, Pa, US 138/A4
Orry-la-Ville, Fr. 30/K4
Orsa, Swe. 38/F1
Orsago, It. 59/F1
Orsay, Fr. 30/J5
Orsett, Eng, UK 30/E2
Orsha, Bela. 39/P4
Orsk, Rus. 63/L2
Orsonnens, Swi. 56/C4
Orsova, Rom. 48/F3
Ørsta, Nor. 37/C3
Örsundsbro, Swe. 38/G2
Orta (lake), It. 43/H4
Orta, Turk. 62/E4
Orta Nova, It. 46/D2
Ortaca, Turk. 90/B2
Ortaköy, Turk. 90/C1
Ortaköy, Turk. 90/C2
Ortega, Col. 152/C4
Ortegal (cape), Sp. 44/B1
Ortenberg, Ger. 54/C2
Orth an der Donau, Aus. 49/P7
Orthez, Fr. 42/C5
Ortigara (peak), It. 57/H5
Ortigueira, Sp. 44/B1
Orting, Wa, US 135/C3
Ortiz, Mex. 142/C2
Ortles (mts.), It. 43/J3
Ortles (peak), It. 57/G4
Ortón (riv.), Bol. 150/E6
Ortona, It. 46/D1
Ortonville, Mn, US 127/J4
Ortonville, Mi, US 135/F6
Örtze (riv.), Ger. 51/H3
Orūmīyeh, Iran 90/F2
Orurillo, Peru 156/D4
Oruro, Bol. 150/E7
Orust (isl.), Swe. 38/D2
Orvieto, It. 43/K5
Orvilliers, Fr. 30/G5
Orwell (riv.), Eng, UK 33/H2
Orwigsburg, Pa, US 138/B2
Oryakhovo, Bul. 49/F4
Orzinuovi, It. 58/C2
Orzysz, Pol. 39/J5
Os, Nor. 38/A1
Osa, Rus. 61/M4
Osa, Peninsula de (pen.), CR 150/B2
Osage (riv.), Mo, US 129/J3
Osage Beach, Mo, US 129/J3
Ōsaka (pref.), Japan 74/D3
Ōsaka (int'l arpt.), Japan 77/H6
Ōsaka, Japan 77/J6
Ōsaka Castle, Japan 77/H6
Osan, SKor. 73/D4
Osasco, Braz. 211/G8
Ōsato, Japan 77/C1
Osborn (mt.), Ak, US 134/E3
Osburg, Ger. 53/F4
Osby, Swe. 38/E3
Osceola, Ar, US 130/B5
Oschersleben, Ger. 40/F2
Oschiri, It. 46/A2
Oscura (mts.), NM, US 132/B3
Osdorf, Ger. 51/G1
Osh (obl.), Kyr. 87/F5
Osh, Kyr. 87/F4
Oshamambe, Japan 76/B2
Oshawa, On, Can. 131/S8
Oshika (pen.), Japan 76/B4
Oshino, Japan 77/E3
Oshkosh, Ne, US 127/H5
Oshnovīyeh, Iran 90/F2
Oshogbo, Nga. 103/G5
Osijek, Cro. 48/D3
Osio Sotto, It. 58/C1
Osipaonica, Serb. 48/E3
Oskarshamn, Swe. 38/G3
Oskarström, Swe. 38/E3
Oskol (riv.), Rus.,Ukr. 62/F2
Oslo (cap.), Nor. 38/D2
Osmānābād, India 89/L5
Osmancık, Turk. 90/C1
Osmaneli, Turk. 49/K5
Osmaniye, Turk. 91/E1
Osnabrück, Ger. 51/F4
Osnago, It. 58/C1
Osny, Fr. 30/J4
Oso (riv.), D.R. Congo 104/A3
Oso (mt.), Ca, US 135/M12
Osogna, Swi. 57/E5
Osório, Braz. 155/B4
Osorno, Sp. 44/C1
Osorno, Chile 158/B4
Osoyoos, BC, Can. 126/D3
Ospedaletti, It. 58/A5
Ospedaletto Euganeo, It. 59/E2
Ospitaletto, It. 58/D1
Osprey (reef), Austl. 109/D2
Oss, Neth. 50/C5
Ossa (mt.), Austl. 115/C4
Ossa, Sierra de (mts.), Port. 44/B3
Osse (riv.), Nga. 103/G5
Osséja, Fr. 42/D5
Ossett, Eng, UK 35/G4
Ossi, It. 46/A2
Ossining, NY, US 139/K7
Ostashkov, Rus. 60/G4
Ostbevern, Ger. 51/E4
Ostellato, It. 59/E3
Osten, Ger. 51/G1
Osterburg, Ger. 40/F2
Osterburken, Ger. 54/C4
Österbybruk, Swe. 38/G1
Österbymo, Swe. 38/F3
Ostercappeln, Ger. 51/F4
Osterdalälven (riv.), Swe. 38/F1
Osterems (chan.), Ger. 50/D1
Östergötland (co.), Swe. 37/E4
Osterhofen, Ger. 55/G5
Osterholz-Scharmbeck, Ger. 51/F2
Osteria Grande, It. 59/E4
Ostermiething, Aus. 55/F6
Osterode am Harz, Ger. 51/H5
Östersund, Swe. 37/E3
Östervåla, Swe. 38/G1
Ostfildern, Ger. 54/C5
Østfold (co.), Nor. 37/D4
Ostfriesland (reg.), Ger. 51/E2
Östhammar, Swe. 38/H1
Ostheim vor der Rhön, Ger. 54/D2
Osthofen, Ger. 54/B3
Ostia Antica (ruin), It. 46/C2
Ostiano, It. 58/D2
Ostiglia, It. 59/E2
Ostional NWR, CR 144/E4
Ostra, It. 59/G5
Östra Silen (lake), Swe. 38/E2
Ostra Vetere, It. 59/G5
Ostrach (riv.), Ger. 54/C6
Ostrava, Czh. 41/K4
Ostravský (pol. reg.), Czh. 41/J4
Osthauderfehn, Ger. 51/E2
Oštri Rt (cape), Serb. 47/F1
Ostricourt, Fr. 52/C3
Ostróda, Pol. 39/H5
Ostrogozhsk, Rus. 62/F2
Ostrołęka, Pol. 41/L2
Ostrov, Czh. 55/F2
Ostrov, Rus. 39/N3
Ostrów Mazowiecka, Pol. 41/L2
Ostrów Wielkopolski, Pol. 41/J3
Ostrowiec Świętokrzyski, Pol. 41/L3
Ostrzeszów, Pol. 41/J3
Ostseebad Binz, Ger. 38/E4
Ostseebad Göhren, Ger. 38/E4
Ostseebad Prerow, Ger. 38/E4
Oststeinbek, Ger. 51/H1
Ostuni, It. 47/E2
Ostwald, Fr. 54/A5
Osŭm (riv.), Bul. 47/J1
Osum (riv.), Slvk. 48/E5
Ōsumi (pen.), Japan 74/B5
Ōsumi (isls.), Japan 116/C1
Osun (state), Nga. 103/G5
Osuna, Sp. 44/C4
Osvaldo Cruz, Braz. 155/B2
Oswaldtwistle, Eng, UK 35/F4
Oswego, NY, US 130/E3
Oswego, Il, US 135/P16
Oswestry, Eng, UK 35/E6
Oświęcim (Auschwitz), Pol. 41/K3
Ōta (riv.), Japan 74/C3
Ōta, Japan 75/F2
Ōtake, Japan 74/C3
Ōtaki, Japan 75/G3
Ōtaki, Japan 77/B2
Otakine-yama (peak), Japan 75/G2
Otava (riv.), Czh. 55/G4
Otavalo, Ecu. 152/B4
Otavi, Namb. 105/C4
Ōtawara, Japan 75/G2
Otay, Ca, US 136/C5
Oțelu Roșu, Rom. 48/F3
Otero de Rey, Sp. 44/B1
Oteros (riv.), Mex. 142/C3
Otgon Tenger (peak), Mong. 70/G2
Othello, Wa, US 126/D4
Othis, Fr. 30/L4
Othonoí (isl.), Gre. 47/F3
Oti (riv.), Gha. 103/F4
Otjiwarongo, Namb. 105/C5
Otley, Eng, UK 35/G4
Otočac, Cro. 48/B3
Otofuke, Japan 76/C2
Otog Qi, China 70/J4
Otok, Cro. 48/D3
Ōtone, Japan 77/D1
Otopeni (int'l arpt.), Rom. 49/H3
Otoskwin (riv.), On, Can. 127/L3
Otowa, Japan 77/M6
Otra (riv.), Nor. 38/B2
Otradnyy, Rus. 63/J1
Otranto, Strait of (str.), It. 47/F2
Otrokovice, Czh. 41/J4
Otse, Bots. 106/D2
Ōtsu, Japan 77/J5
Ōtsuchi, Japan 76/B4
Ōtsuki, Japan 75/F3
Otta, Nga. 103/F5
Ottawa (cap.), On, Can. 130/F2
Ottawa, Oh, US 130/C3
Ottawa, Ks, US 129/J3
Ottawa (int'l arpt.), On, Can. 130/F2
Ottawa (isls.), Nun., Can. 123/H3
Ottawa (riv.), On, Can. 130/E2
Ottensheim, Aus. 55/H6
Otter (riv.), Eng, UK 32/C5
Otterbach, Ger. 53/G5
Otterberg, Ger. 53/G4
Otterndorf, Ger. 51/F1
Ottersberg, Ger. 51/G2
Ottershaw, Eng, UK 30/B2
Otterville, Il, US 137/G7
Ottignies-Louvain-la-Neuve, Belg. 53/D2
Öttingen im Bayern, Ger. 54/D5
Ottmarsheim, Fr. 56/D2
Ottnang am Hausruck, Aus. 55/G6
Otto, Mo, US 137/F9
Ottobeuren, Ger. 57/G2
Ottobrunn, Ger. 55/E6
Ottone, It. 58/C3
Ottosdal, SAfr. 106/D2
Ottsville, Pa, US 138/C3
Ottumwa, Ia, US 127/K5
Ottweiler, Ger. 53/G5
Otumba de Gómez Farías, Mex. 143/L7
Otuzco, Peru 156/B2
Otway (cape), Austl. 115/B3
Otway (bay), Chile 159/C7
Otway NP, Austl. 115/B3
Otwock, Pol. 41/L2
Ötztal Alps (mts.), Aus. 43/J3
Ötztaler Ache (riv.), Aus. 57/G3
Ou (mts.), Japan 76/B4
Ouachita (mts.), Ok, US 125/G5
Ouachita (riv.), Ar,La, US 125/H5
Ouadda, CAfr. 97/K6
Ouaddaï (reg.), Chad 97/J5
Ouadi Haddad (riv.), Chad 97/J4
Ouadi Rimé (riv.), Chad 96/J5
Ouagadougou (int'l arpt.), Burk. 103/E3
Ouagadougou (cap.), Burk. 103/E3
Ouahigouya, Burk. 103/E3
Ouaka (riv.), CAfr. 97/K6
Oualâta, Dhar (cliff), Mrta. 102/D2
Ouallam, Niger 103/F3
Ouanda Djallé, CAfr. 97/K6
Ouanne (riv.), Fr. 42/E3
Ouarane (pol. reg.), Mrta. 96/C3
Ouarane (reg.), Mrta. 98/C5
Ouargla (prov.), Alg. 99/G3
Ouargla, Alg. 99/G3
Ouarkziz, Jebel (mts.), Mor. 98/C3
Ouarzazate (int'l arpt.), Mor. 98/D3
Ouarzazate, Mor. 98/D3
Ouasiemsca (riv.), Qu, Can. 130/F1
Oubangui (riv.), CAfr. 96/J7
Oubritenga (prov.), Burk. 103/E3
Ouche (riv.), Fr. 56/B3
Oud-Beijerland, Neth. 50/B5
Oud-Turnhout, Belg. 50/B6
Ōuda, Japan 77/J7
Oudalan (prov.), Burk. 103/E3
Ouddorp, Neth. 50/A5
Oude IJssel (riv.), Neth. 50/D5
Oude Pekela, Neth. 50/E2
Oude Westereems (chan.), Neth. 50/D1
Oudenaarde, Belg. 52/C2
Oudenbosch, Neth. 50/B5
Oudenburg, Belg. 52/C1
Oudewater, Neth. 50/B4
Oudon (riv.), Fr. 42/C3
Oudtshoorn, SAfr. 106/C4
Oued el Hadjar (well), Mali 102/E2
Oued Moulouyadeu (riv.), Mor. 96/E1
Oued Sous (riv.), Mor. 96/D1
Oued Zem, Mor. 98/D2
Ouémé (riv.), Ben. 96/F6
Ouéme (prov.), Ben. 103/F5
Ouenza, Alg. 100/L7
Ouerrha (riv.), Mor. 100/B2
Ouessé, Ben. 103/F4
Ouesso, Congo 96/J7
Ouest (prov.), Camr. 103/H5
Ouest (pt.), Haiti 145/H1
Ouest (pt.), Haiti 145/H2
Ouezzane, Mor. 100/B2
Oughterard, Ire. 31/P10
Ouham (riv.), CAfr. 96/J6
Ouidah, Ben. 103/F5
Oujda, Mor. 100/D2
Oujda (prov.), Mor. 100/C2
Oujda (Angads) (int'l arpt.), Mor. 100/D2
Oulad Teïma, Mor. 98/C3
Oulangan NP, Fin. 60/F2
Ould Birni (well), Alg. 99/E4
Oulnina (peak), Austl. 113/H5
Oulu, Fin. 60/E2
Oulu (prov.), Fin. 37/H2
Oulujärvi (lake), Fin. 37/H2
Oum El Bouaghi, Alg. 100/K7
Oum er Rbia, Oued (riv.), Mor. 98/D2
Oum er Rhia (riv.), Mor. 96/D1
Ounasjoki (riv.), Fin. 37/H2
Oupeye, Belg. 53/E2
Our (riv.), Eur. 53/E4
Ource (riv.), Fr. 42/F3
Ourcq (riv.), Fr. 40/B4
Ourcq, Canal de l' (canal), Fr. 30/K5
Øure Anarjokka NP, Nor. 37/H1
Øure Dividal NP, Nor. 37/F1
Ouricuri, Braz. 154/B2
Ourinhos, Braz. 155/B2
Ourique, Port. 44/A4
Ouro Fino, Braz. 211/G7
Ouro, Ponta do (pt.), Moz. 107/F2
Ouro Preto, Braz. 155/D2
Ouroux-sur-Saône, Fr. 56/A4
Ourthe Occidentale (riv.), Belg. 53/E3
Ourthe Orientale (riv.), Belg. 53/E3
Ouse (riv.), Eng, UK 35/H4
Oust (riv.), Fr. 42/B3
Outaouais (riv.), Qu, Can. 130/E2
Outardes (riv.), Qu, Can. 131/G1
Outardes Quatre (lake), Qu, Can. 131/G1
Outeïd Arkas (well), Mali 102/D2
Outer Hebrides (isls.), Sc, UK 31/P8
Outes, Sp. 44/A1
Outjo, Namb. 105/C5
Outlook, Sk, Can. 126/G3
Outreau, Fr. 52/A2
Outremont, Qu, Can. 131/N6
Ouvèze (riv.), Fr. 42/F4
Ouyen, Austl. 115/B2
Ouzinkie, Ak, US 134/H4
Ovacık, Turk. 90/D2
Ovacık, Turk. 90/C1
Ovada, It. 58/B3
Ovalle, Chile 157/B3
Ovana (peak), Ven. 153/E3
Ovar, Port. 44/A2
Overath, Ger. 53/G2
Overflakkee (isl.), Neth. 50/B5
Overhalla, Nor. 37/D2
Overholser (lake), Ok, US 137/M14
Overijse, Belg. 53/D2
Overijssel (prov.), Neth. 50/D3
Overijssels (riv.), Neth. 50/D4
Överkalix, Swe. 37/G2
Overland, Mo, US 137/G8
Overland Park, Ks, US 137/D6
Overlea, Md, US 138/B5
Overo (peak), Arg. 158/C5
Overpelt, Belg. 50/C6
Overton, Nv, US 128/D3
Övertorneå, Swe. 60/D2
Överum, Swe. 38/G3
Oviedo, Sp. 44/C1
Ovoca, Ire. 34/B6
Övörhangay (prov.), Mong. 70/H2
Övre Fryken (lake), Swe. 38/E1
Øvre Pasvik NP, Nor. 37/J1
Ovriá, Gre. 47/G3
Owando, Congo 96/J8
Ōwani, Japan 76/B3
Owariasahi, Japan 77/M5
Owase, Japan 74/E3
Owassa (lake), NJ, US 138/D1
Owasso, Ok, US 129/J3
Owego, NY, US 130/E3
Owen (mt.), NZ 117/S11
Owen, Austl. 113/H5
Owen, Ger. 54/C5
Owen Falls (dam), Ugan. 104/B2
Owen Roberts (int'l arpt.), UK 145/F2
Owen Sound, On, Can. 130/D2
Owenkillew (riv.), NI, UK 34/A2
Owens (riv.), Ca, US 128/C3
Owensboro, Ky, US 130/C4
Owerri, Nga. 103/G5
Owingen, Ger. 57/F2
Owings, Md, US 138/B6
Owings Mills, Md, US 138/B5
Owl Creek (mts.), Wy, US 126/F4
Owo, Nga. 103/G5
Owosso, Mi, US 130/C3
Owyhee, Nv, US 126/D5
Owyhee (lake), Or, US 128/C2
Owyhee (mts.), Id, US 128/C2
Owyhee (riv.), Id, US 124/C3
Owyhee, South Fork (riv.), Nv, US 126/D5
Oxapampa, Peru 156/C3
Oxbow, Sk, Can. 127/H3
Oxbow (lake), Mi, US 135/F6
Oxelösund, Swe. 38/G2
Oxford (lake), Mb, Can. 127/K2
Oxford, Eng, UK 33/E3
Oxford (canal), Eng, UK 33/E3
Oxford, Mi, US 135/F6
Oxford, Ms, US 133/F3
Oxford, Pa, US 138/C4
Oxfordshire (co.), Eng, UK 33/E3
Oxie, Swe. 38/E4
Oxkutzcab, Mex. 144/D1
Oxnard, Ca, US 136/A2
Oxnard Beach, Ca, US 136/A2
Oxon Hill (farm), Md, US 138/A6
Oxon Hill-Glassmanor, Md, US 138/B6
Oxted, Eng, UK 30/D3
Oyabe, Japan 75/E2
Oyama, Japan 75/F2
Oyama, Japan 77/B3
Ōyamada, Japan 77/K6
Ōyamazaki, Japan 77/J6
Oyapock (riv.), Fr. 151/H3
Oye-Plage, Fr. 52/B2
Oyem, Gabon 96/H7
Oyen, Ab, Can. 126/F3
Øyer, Nor. 38/D1
Oykell (riv.), Sc, UK 31/R8
Oyo (state), Nga. 103/F4

214

Oyo – Pauls

Oyo, Nga. 103/F5
Ōyodo (riv.), Japan 74/B5
Ōyodo, Japan 77/J7
Oyón, Peru 156/B3
Oyonnax, Fr. 56/B5
Oyster Bay, NY, US 139/L8
Oyster Bay (har.), NY, US 139/L8
Oyster Bay Cove, NY, US 139/L8
Oyster Bay NWR, NY, US 139/L8
Oyten, Ger. 51/G2
Oyyl (riv.), Kaz. 87/B3
Ozamiz, Phil. 79/D6
Ozanne (riv.), Fr. 42/D2
Ozark (plat.), Mo, US 129/J3
Ozark, Ar, US 129/J4
Ozark, Al, US 133/G4
Ozark (mts.), Ar,Mo, US 125/H4
Ozarks (lake), Mo, US 125/H4
Ózd, Hun. 41/L4
Ozernoy (cape), Rus. 65/S4
Ozette (lake), Wa, US 126/B3
Ozhiski (lake), On, Can. 127/L3
Ozieri, It. 46/A2
Ozimek, Pol. 41/K3
Özkonak, Turk. 90/C2
Ozoir-la-Ferrière, Fr. 30/L5
Ozona, Tx, US 129/G5
Ozora, Hun. 48/D2
Ozorków, Pol. 41/K3
Ozouer-le-Voulgis, Fr. 30/L6
Ōzu, Japan 74/C4
Ozuluama de Mascareñas, Mex. 144/B1
Ozzano dell'Emilia, It. 59/E4

P

P. K. Le Rouxdam (res.), SAfr. 106/D3
Pa-an, Myan. 78/B2
Pa Sak (riv.), Thai. 83/H4
Paar (riv.), Ger. 40/F4
Paarl, SAfr. 106/L10
Paauilo, Hi, US 124/U10
Pabbi, Pak. 86/A2
Pabellón de Arteaga, Mex. 142/E4
Pabianice, Pol. 41/K3
Pābna, Bang. 85/G3
Pābna (pol. reg.), Bang. 85/G3
Pacaás Novos, PN dos, Braz. 150/F6
Pacaás Novos, Serra dos (mts.), Braz. 150/F6
Pacajá (riv.), Braz. 151/H4
Pacajus, Braz. 154/C2
Pacaltsdorp, SAfr. 106/C4
Pacaraimã (mts.), Braz. 150/F3
Pacaya Samiria, Reserva Nacional, Peru 156/C2
Paccha, Peru 156/C3
Paceco, It. 46/C4
Pachacamac (ruin), Peru 156/B4
Pachaconas, Peru 156/C4
Pachamarca (riv.), Peru 156/C4
Pachino, It. 46/D4
Pachitea (riv.), Peru 156/C3
Pachiza, Peru 156/B2
Pachmarhī, India 84/B4
Pachuca, Mex. 143/L6
Pacific (ocean) 67/N8
Pacific (range), BC, Can. 126/B3
Pacific, Wa, US 135/C3
Pacific Palisades, Hi, US 124/W13
Pacifico (mtn.), Ca, US 136/B2
Pacinan (cape), Indo. 80/D5
Pacitan, Indo. 80/D5
Paço de Arcos, Port. 45/P10
Pad Īdan, Pak. 89/J3
Padampur, India 82/D3
Padang, Indo. 80/B4
Padangpanjang, Indo. 80/B4
Padangsidempuan, Indo. 80/A3
Paddock Lake, Wi, US 135/P14
Paddock Wood, Eng, UK 30/E3
Paderborn, Il, US 137/G9
Paderborn, Ger. 51/F5
Paderno, It. 59/F1
Padiham, Eng, UK 35/F4
Padilla, Bol. 150/F7
Padina, Serb. 48/E3
Padjelanta NP, Swe. 37/F2
Padova (prov.), It. 59/E2
Padova, It. 59/E2
Padrão, Ponta do (pt.), Ang. 105/B2
Padrauna, India 84/D2
Padre (isl.), Tx, US 125/G6
Padre Island Nat'l Seashore, Tx, US 143/F3
Padrón, Sp. 44/A1
Paducah, Tx, US 129/G4
Paducah, Ky, US 130/B4
Padul, Sp. 44/D4
Padula, It. 46/D2
Paektŏk-san (peak), SKor. 73/E4
Paektu-san (peak), NKor. 73/E2
Paese, It. 59/F1
Páez, Col. 152/C3
Páez, Col. 152/C4
Pafúri, Moz. 105/F5
Pag, Cro. 48/B3
Pag (isl.), Cro. 48/B3
Pagadian, Phil. 81/F2
Pagai Selatan (isl.), Indo. 80/B4
Pagai Utara (isl.), Indo. 80/B4
Pagan, Myan. 83/F3
Pagan (isl.),NMar. 116/D3
Paganica, It. 46/C1
Page, Az, US 128/E3
Pager (riv.), Ugan. 104/B2
Pagny-sur-Moselle, Fr. 53/F6
Pagosa Springs, Co, US 128/F3
Pagwachuan (riv.), On, Can. 130/C1
Pahala, Hi, US 124/U11
Pahang (riv.), Malay. 80/B3
Pāhara (lag.), Nic. 145/F3
Pahārpur, Pak. 86/A3
Pahāsu, India 84/B1
Pahlgām, India 86/C2
Pahrump, Nv, US 128/D3
Pahuatlán, Mex. 143/L6
Pahute (mesa), Nv, US 128/C3
Pai (lake), China 72/C5
Paia, Hi, US 124/T10
Paignton, Eng, UK 32/C6
Paiján, Peru 156/B2
Päijänne (lake), Fin. 37/H3
Paikü (lake), China 85/E1
Pailolo (chan.), Hi, US 124/T10
Paimio, Fin. 39/K1
Paine (peak), Chile 159/B6
Paine, Chile 158/N8
Painesville, Oh, US 130/D3
Paint (lake), Mb, Can. 127/J2
Paint Rock, Tx, US 132/D4
Painted (des.), Az, US 124/D4
Paipa, Col. 152/C3
País Vasco (aut. comm.), Sp. 44/D1
Paisley, Sc, UK 36/B5
Paita, Peru 156/A2
Paithan, India 82/C4
Pajala, Swe. 37/G2
Paján, Ecu. 152/A5
Pajęczno, Pol. 41/K3
Pakanbaru, Indo. 80/B3
Pakch'ŏn, NKor. 73/C3
Pakenham, Austl. 115/G6
Pakenham (cape), Chile 159/B6
Pákhnes (peak), Gre. 47/J5
Pakhra (riv.), Rus. 61/W9
Pakistan (ctry.) 89/H3
Paklenica NP, Cro. 48/B3
Pakokku, Myan. 83/G3
Pakowki (lake), Ab, Can. 126/F3
Pākpattan, Pak. 86/B4
Pakrac, Cro. 48/C3
Paks, Hun. 48/D2
Pakwach, Ugan. 104/A2
Pakxe, Laos 78/D3
Pala, Chad 96/H6
Pala, Ca, US 136/C4
Pala Ind. Res., Ca, US 136/C4
Palace, Mona. 58/J8
Palafrugell, Sp. 45/G2
Palagonia, It. 46/D4
Palagruža (isls.), Cro. 46/E1
Pálairos, Gre. 47/G3
Palaiseau, Fr. 30/J5
Palakollu, India 82/D4
Palamás, Gre. 47/H3
Palamós, Sp. 45/G2
Palana, Rus. 65/R4
Palangkaraya, Indo. 80/D4
Pālanpur, India 89/K4
Palaoa (pt.), Hi, US 124/T10
Palapye, Bots. 105/E5
Palar (riv.), India 82/C5
Palas de Rey, Sp. 44/B1
Palāsbāri, India 85/H2
Palatine, Il, US 135/P15
Palatka, Fl, US 133/H4
Palau (ctry.) 116/C4
Palau We (isl.), Indo. 80/A2
Palaw, Myan. 78/B3
Palawan (isl.), Phil. 67/L9
Palawan Passage (chan.), Phil. 81/E2
Pālayankottai, India 82/C6
Palazzolo Acreide, It. 46/D4
Palazzolo dello Stella, It. 59/G1
Palazzolo sull'Oglio, It. 58/C1
Palé, EqG. 96/G8
Pale, Bosn. 48/D4
Paleleh, Indo. 81/F3
Palembang, Indo. 80/B4
Palena (riv.), Chile 158/B4
Palena, Chile 158/C4
Palencia, Sp. 44/C1
Palenque, Mex. 144/D2
Palenque, PN, Mex. 144/C2
Palermo, It. 46/C3
Palermo, NJ, US 138/D5
Palese (int'l arpt.), It. 46/E2
Palestine (lake), Tx, US 132/E3
Palestro, It. 58/B2
Pālghar, India 89/K5
P'algong-san (peak), SKor. 73/D5
P'algong-san (peak), SKor. 74/A2
Palgrave (mt.), Austl. 112/B2
Palhano, Braz. 154/C2
Palhoça, Braz. 155/B3
Pāli, India 89/K3
Pali-Aike, PN, Chile 159/C7
Paliā Kalān, India 84/C1
Palić, Serb. 48/D2
Palikea (peak), Hi, US 124/V13
Palikir (cap.), Micr. 116/E4
Palioúrion (cape), Gre. 47/H3
Palisades (cliff), NJ,NY, US 139/K8
Palisades, NY, US 139/K8
Palisades Interstate Park, NJ, US 138/D1
Palisades Park, NJ, US 139/K8
Paliseul, Belg. 53/E4
Pālitāna, India 89/K4
Palizada, Mex. 140/C4
Paljenik (peak), Bosn. 48/C3
Palk (str.), India 82/C6
Pallamallawa, Austl. 115/D1
Pallarenda, Austl. 114/B2
Pallas-Ounastunturin NP, Fin. 37/H1
Pallasca, Peru 156/B3
Pallastunturi (peak), Fin. 37/H1
Palliser (cape), NZ 117/T11
Palm Bay, Fl, US 133/H4
Palm Beach (int'l arpt.), Fl, US 133/H5
Palm City, Ca, US 136/C5
Palm Harbor, Fl, US 133/H4
Palm Island Aboriginal Settlement, Austl. 114/B2
Palm Springs, Ca, US 128/C4
Palma (riv.), Braz. 151/J6
Palma, Moz. 104/D5
Palma, Sp. 45/G3
Palma del Río, Sp. 44/C4
Palma di Montechiaro, It. 46/C4
Palma Mallorca (int'l arpt.), Sp. 45/G3
Palma Soriano, Cuba 145/H1
Palmácia, Braz. 154/C2
Palmanova, It. 59/G1
Palmar (riv.), Ven. 145/H4
Palmares, Braz. 154/D3
Palmarito, Ven. 152/D3
Palmas, Braz. 155/A3
Palmas (cape), Libr. 102/D5
Palmdale, Ca, US 136/B1
Palmeira, Braz. 155/B3
Palmeira, CpV. 93/K10
Palmeira dos Índios, Braz. 154/C3
Palmeirais, Braz. 154/B2
Palmeiras (riv.), Braz. 154/A4
Palmeiras, Braz. 154/B4
Palmeirinhas, Ponta das (pt.), Ang. 105/B2
Palmela, Port. 45/Q10
Palmer, Ak, US 134/J3
Palmer, US, Ant. 160/V
Palmer, Wa, US 135/D3
Palmer Land (phys. reg.), Ant. 160/V
Palmerston, NZ 117/S12
Palmerston (cape), Austl. 114/C3
Palmerston Atoll (atoll), CookIs. 117/J6
Palmerston North, NZ 117/T11
Palmerston NP, Austl. 114/B2
Palmerton, Pa, US 138/C2
Palmetto, Fl, US 133/H5
Palmi, It. 46/D3
Palmilla, Chile 158/C2
Palmillas (pt.), Cuba 145/F1
Palmira, Col. 152/B4
Palmital, Braz. 155/B2
Palmitas, Uru. 159/K10
Palmyra, Ut, US 137/K13
Palmyra (isl.), PacUS 117/J4
Palmyra, Pa, US 138/B3
Palmyra (Tadmur) (ruin), Syria 90/D3
Palmyras (pt.), India 82/E3
Palni, India 82/C5
Palo, Phil. 79/D5
Palo Alto, Ca, US 128/B3
Palo Alto, Pa, US 138/B2
Palo Pinto, Tx, US 129/H4
Palo Verde, PN, CR 140/D5
Palomeu (riv.), Sur. 153/H4
Palon (peak), It. 59/E1
Palos (cape), Sp. 45/E4
Palos de la Frontera, Sp. 44/B4
Palos Hills, Il, US 135/Q16
Palos Verdes (hills), Ca, US 136/F8
Palos Verdes (pt.), Ca, US 136/F8
Palos Verdes Estates, Ca, US 136/F8
Palosco, It. 58/C1
Palpalá, Arg. 157/C1
Palpetu (cape), Indo. 81/G4
Paltamo, Fin. 60/E2
Palu, Indo. 81/E4
Palu, Turk. 90/D2
Paluan, Phil. 79/D5
Palwal, India 84/A1
Pamangkat, Indo. 80/C3
Pambula, Austl. 115/D3
Pamiers, Fr. 42/D5
Pamir (riv.), Afg.,Taj. 64/H6
Pamir (reg.), Taj.,China 64/H6
Pamlico (riv.), NC, US 133/J3
Pamlico (sound), NC, US 133/J3
Pampa, Tx, US 129/G4
Pampachiri, Peru 156/C4
Pampacolca, Peru 156/C4
Pampas (riv.), Peru 156/C4
Pampas, Peru 156/C4
Pampas, Peru 156/B3
Pampas (plain), Arg. 147/C6
Pampilhosa da Serra, Port. 44/B2
Pamplona, Sp. 44/E1
Pamplona, Col. 152/C3
Pampulha (int'l arpt.), Braz. 155/D1
Pāmpur, India 86/C2
Pamukova, Turk. 49/K5
Pan de Azúcar, PN, Chile 157/B2
Panaba, Mex. 144/D1
Panabo, Phil. 79/E6
Pānāgar, India 84/B4
Panagyurishte, Bul. 47/J1
Panaitan (isl.), Indo. 80/B5
Panaji, India 89/K5
Panama (ctry.) 145/F4
Panamá (bay), Pan. 145/G4
Panamá (cap.), Pan. 152/B2
Panama (canal), Pan. 145/F4
Panama (gulf), Pan. 145/G4
Panama City, Fl, US 133/G4
Panama, Isthmus of (isth.), Pan. 150/C2
Panamá Viejo (ruin), Pan. 152/B2
Panamint (range), Ca, US 128/C3
Panao, Peru 156/B3
Panaro (riv.), It. 43/J4
Panay (isl.), Phil. 67/M8
Pancake (range), Nv, US 128/C3
Pančevo, Serb. 48/E3
Pančicev vrh (peak), Serb. 47/G1
Pancilet (res.), India 85/F4
Panciu, Rom. 49/H3
Pandamatenga, Bots. 105/E4
Pandharpur, India 89/L5
Pandino, It. 58/C2
Pando, Uru. 159/L11
Pāndoh, India 86/D4
Pandrup, Den. 38/C3
Pandua, India 85/G4
Panevėžys, Lith. 39/L4
Panfilov, Kaz. 70/D3
Pangai, Tonga 117/H6
Pangaion (peak), Gre. 47/J2
Pangani, Tanz. 104/C4
Pangani (riv.), Tanz. 104/C3
Pangkalanberandan, Indo. 80/A3
Pangkalaseang (cape), Indo. 81/F4
Pangkalpinang, Indo. 80/C4
Pangnirtung, Nun., Can. 123/K2
Panguipulli, Chile 158/B3
Panguitch, Ut, US 128/D3
Pangutaran, Phil. 81/F2
Pangutaran (isl.), Phil. 79/C6
Paniai (lake), Indo. 81/J4
Paniau (peak), Hi, US 124/R10
Pānihāti, India 85/G4
Pānīpat, India 86/D5
Paniqui, Phil. 79/D4
Panj (riv.), Afg. 89/K1
Panjwīn, Iraq 88/E1
Panke (riv.), Ger. 40/Q6
P'anmunjŏm, NKor. 73/D4
Panna, India 84/C3
Pannawonica, Austl. 112/C2
Pannikin (isl.), Austl. 114/F7
Pano Lefkara, Cyp. 91/C2
Panorama, Braz. 155/B2
Pantanal (lowland), Braz. 150/G7
Pantanal Matogrossense, PN, Braz. 150/G7
Pantelleria, It. 46/B4
Pantelleria (isl.), It. 27/F5
Pantigliate, It. 58/C2
Pantin, Fr. 30/K5
Pantoja, Peru 152/C5
Pantón, Sp. 44/B1
Pantukan, Phil. 79/E6
Pánuco (riv.), Mex. 140/B3
Pánuco, Mex. 144/B1
Panzhihua, China 83/H2
Panzós, Guat. 144/D3
Pão de Açúcar, Braz. 154/C3
Paola, It. 46/E3
Paola, Malta 46/M7
Paoli, Pa, US 138/C3
Paonia, Co, US 128/F3
Paonta Sahib, India 86/D4
Paoua, CAfr. 96/J6
Pápa, Hun. 48/C2
Papa Westray (isl.), Sc, UK 31/V14
Papagayo (gulf), CR 140/D5
Papaikou, Hi, US 124/U11
Papanduva, Braz. 155/B3
Papantla, Mex. 143/M6
Papaplaya, Peru 156/C2
Papenburg, Ger. 51/E2
Papendrecht, Neth. 50/B5
Paphos, Cyp. 91/C2
Paphos (dist.), Cyp. 91/C2
Papingut (peak), Alb. 47/G2
Papisoi (cape), Indo. 81/H4
Pappenheim, Ger. 54/D5
Papua (gulf), PNG 116/D5
Papua New Guinea (ctry.) 116/D5
Papudo, Chile 158/C2
Papunya, Austl. 113/F2
Pará (riv.), Braz. 151/H4
Pará (state), Braz. 154/A1
Para (dist.), Sur. 153/H3
Pará (falls), Ven. 153/E3
Pará de Minas, Braz. 155/C1
Para, South (riv.), Austl. 113/M8
Para Wirra NP, Austl. 113/M8
Paraburdoo, Austl. 112/C2
Paracambi, Braz. 211/K7
Paracas (pen.), Peru 156/B4
Paracas, Reserva Nacional, Peru 156/B4
Paracatu, Braz. 154/A5
Paracatu (riv.), Braz. 154/A5
Paracel (isls.), China 83/K4
Paracho de Verduzco, Mex. 142/E5
Paraćin, Serb. 48/E4
Paracuru, Braz. 154/C1
Paradhísion (int'l arpt.), Gre. 90/B2
Paradip, India 82/E3
Paradis, La, US 137/P17
Paradise (valley), Az, US 137/R18
Paradise, Mo, US 137/D5
Paradise, Pa, US 138/B4
Paradise Valley, Az, US 137/S18
Paragominas, Braz. 154/A1
Paraguá (riv.), Bol. 150/F6
Paragua (riv.), Ven. 150/F2
Paraguaçu, Braz. 211/H6
Paraguaçu (riv.), Braz. 147/E4
Paraguaçu Paulista, Braz. 155/B2
Paraguai (riv.), SAm. 147/D5
Paraguaipoa, Ven. 152/D2
Paraguaná, Peninsula de (pen.), Ven. 150/D1
Paraguarí, Par. 157/E2
Paraguay (ctry.) 147/C5
Paraguay (riv.), Par. 157/E1
Paraíba (state), Braz. 154/C2
Paraíba do Sul, Braz. 211/K7
Paraíba do Sul (riv.), Braz. 147/E5
Paraibano, Braz. 154/B2
Paraibuna (riv.), Braz. 211/H8
Paraim (riv.), Braz. 154/A3
Parainen (Pargas), Fin. 39/K1
Paraíso, Mex. 144/C2
Paraíso, CR 145/F4
Paraíso do Norte de Goiás, Braz. 151/J6
Paraisópolis, Braz. 211/H7
Parakou, Ben. 103/F4
Paramaribo (cap.), Sur. 151/G2
Paramaribo (dist.), Sur. 153/H3
Parambu, Braz. 154/B2
Paramillo (peak), Col. 152/C3
Paramillo, PN, Col. 150/C2
Paramirim (riv.), Braz. 151/K6
Paramirim, Braz. 154/B4
Paramithía, Gre. 47/G3
Paramount, Ca, US 136/F8
Paramus, NJ, US 139/J8
Paramushir (isl.), Rus. 67/Q5
Paraná, Arg. 157/D3
Paranã (riv.), Braz. 151/J6
Paraná (state), Braz. 155/B3
Paraná (riv.), SAm. 147/D5
Paraná Ibicuy (riv.), Arg. 159/J10
Paraná Urariá (riv.), Braz. 153/G5
Paranaguá, Braz. 155/B3
Paranaguá, Baía de (bay), Braz. 155/B3
Paranaíba (riv.), Braz. 151/J7
Paranaíba, Braz. 155/B1
Paranapanema (riv.), Braz. 157/F1
Paranapiacaba, Serra do (mts.), Braz. 157/G2
Paranatinga (riv.), Braz. 147/D4
Paranavaí, Braz. 157/F1
Parang, Phil. 81/F2
Paraopeba, Braz. 155/C1
Parapetí (riv.), Bol. 150/F7
Parati, Braz. 211/J8
Paratico, It. 58/C1
Paratinga, Braz. 154/B4
Paratinga (riv.), Braz. 211/H8
Paray-Vieille-Poste, Fr. 30/K5
Paràzinho, Braz. 154/D2
Pārbati (riv.), India 89/L4
Parbhani, India 89/L5
Parchim, Ger. 40/F2
Parczew, Pol. 41/M3
Pardes Hanna-Karkur, Isr. 91/F7
Pārdi, India 89/K4
Pardo (riv.), Braz. 151/J8
Pardone (cape), SAfr. 106/D4
Pardubice, Czh. 41/H3
Pardubický (pol. reg.), Czh. 41/J4
Pare, Indo. 80/D5
Pare (mts.), Tanz. 104/C3
Parece Vela (Okino-Tori-Shima) (isl.), Japan 67/N7
Parecis (mts.), Braz. 147/C4
Parede, Port. 45/P10
Paredes de Nava, Sp. 44/C1
Paredón, Mex. 144/C2
Paredones, Chile 158/C2
Parelhas, Braz. 154/C2
Parempuyre, Fr. 42/C4
Parenda, India 82/C4
Parent (lake), Qu, Can. 130/E1
Parentis-en-Born, Fr. 42/C4
Parepare, Indo. 81/E4
Parera, Arg. 158/D2
Parets del Vallès, Sp. 45/L6
Pargny-sur-Saulx, Fr. 53/D6
Paria (riv.), Ut, US 128/E3
Paria (gulf), Trin.,Ven. 147/C1
Paria, Peninsula de (pen.), Ven. 150/F1
Pariacoto, Peru 156/B3
Pariaguán, Ven. 153/E2
Pariaman, Indo. 80/B4
Parikkala, Fin. 37/J3
Parima (riv.), Braz. 153/F4
Parima, Serra (mts.), Braz. 150/F3
Parinacota (peak), Bol. 156/D5
Parinari, Peru 156/C2
Pariñas (pt.), Peru 156/A2
Paringa, Austl. 115/B2
Parîngu Mare (peak), Rom. 49/F3
Parintins, Braz. 151/G4
Paris, Ar, US 129/J4
Paris, Tx, US 129/J4
Paris (cap.), Fr. 30/K5
Paris (dept.), Fr. 52/B6
Parita (bay), Pan. 145/F4
Park (range), Co, US 128/F2
Park (pt.), Eng, UK 32/A5
Park City, Ut, US 137/L12
Park City, Il, US 135/Q15
Park Falls, Wi, US 127/L4
Park Rapids, Mn, US 127/K4
Park Ridge, Il, US 135/Q16
Park Ridge, NJ, US 139/J7
Park River, ND, US 127/J3
Parkano, Fin. 37/G3
Parker, Tx, US 129/H4
Parker, Az, US 128/D4
Parker, Co, US 137/C3
Parkersburg, WV, US 130/D4
Parkes, Austl. 115/D2
Parkesburg, Pa, US 138/C4
Parkgate, NI, UK 34/B2
Parksdale, Mo, US 137/F9
Parkside, Pa, US 138/C4
Parkstetten, Ger. 55/F5
Parkton, Md, US 138/B4
Parkville, Mo, US 137/D5
Parkville, Md, US 138/B5
Parkville, Pa, US 138/B4
Parkway-Sacramento, Ca, US 135/L9
Parla, Sp. 45/N9
Parlakhemundi, India 82/D4
Parli, India 89/L5
Parma, Oh, US 130/D3
Parma (prov.), It. 58/C3
Parma (riv.), It. 58/D3
Parma, It. 58/D3
Parmain, Fr. 30/J4
Parnaguá, Braz. 154/A3
Parnaíba, Braz. 154/B1
Parnaíba (riv.), Braz. 147/E3
Parnamirim, Braz. 154/C3
Parnamirim, Braz. 151/L5
Parnarama, Braz. 154/B2
Parnassós (peak), Gre. 47/H3
Parnassós NP, Gre. 47/H3
Párnis (peak), Gre. 47/N8
Párnis Óros NP, Gre. 47/N8
Párnon (mts.), Gre. 47/H4
Pärnu (bay), Est. 39/L2
Pärnu, Est. 39/L2
P'aro-ho (lake), SKor. 73/D3
Paron, Fr. 42/E2
Parona di Valpolicella, It. 59/D2
Paroo (riv.), Austl. 109/D3
Páros (isl.), Gre. 47/J4
Páros, Gre. 47/J4
Parow, SAfr. 106/L10
Parowan, Ut, US 128/D3
Parpan, Swi. 57/F4
Parral, Chile 158/C3
Parras de la Fuente, Mex. 142/E3
Parrett (riv.), Eng, UK 32/D4
Parrita, CR 145/E4
Parry (isls.), NW,Nun., Can. 123/R7
Parry (bay), Nun., Can. 123/H2
Parry (chan.), Nun., Can. 122/F1
Parry Sound, On, Can. 130/D2
Parsberg, Ger. 55/E4
Parseierspitze (peak), Aus. 57/G3
Parshall, ND, US 127/H4
Parsippany-Troy Hills, NJ, US 139/H8
Parsnip (riv.), BC, Can. 126/C2
Pårtefjället (peak), Swe. 37/F2
Partenstein, Ger. 54/C2
Parthenay, Fr. 42/C3
Partille, Swe. 38/E3
Partinico, It. 46/C3
Partizansk, Rus. 71/P3
Partizánske, Slvk. 41/K4
Partridge (riv.), On, Can. 130/D1
Partūr, India 89/L5
Paru (riv.), Braz. 151/H4
Paru de Oeste (riv.), Braz. 147/D2
Paruro, Peru 156/D4
Pārvathīpuram, India 82/D4
Parys, SAfr. 106/D2
Pas-de-Calais (dept.), Fr. 52/A3
Pas de Morgins (pass), Fr. 56/C5
Pasadena, Tx, US 129/J5
Pasadena, Nf, Can. 131/K1
Pasadena, Md, US 138/B5
Pasadena, Ca, US 136/F7
Pasado (cape), Ecu. 152/A5
Pasaje, Ecu. 156/B1
Pasaman (peak), Indo. 80/B3
Pasān, India 84/D4
Pascagoula, Ms, US 133/F4
Paşcani, Rom. 49/H2
Pasching, Aus. 55/H6
Pasco, Wa, US 126/D4
Pasco (dept.), Peru 156/C3
Pascua (riv.), Chile 159/B6
Pascua, Isla de (Easter) (isl.), Chile 117/Q7
Pascuales, Ecu. 156/B1
Pasewalk, Ger. 38/E5
Pasian di Prato, It. 59/G1
Pasiano, It. 59/F1
Pasig, Phil. 79/D5
Pasinler, Turk. 90/E2
Pasión, Río de la (riv.), Guat. 144/D2
Pasłęk, Pol. 39/H4
Pasłęka (riv.), Pol. 41/L2
Pasley (cape), Austl. 112/D5
Pašman (isl.), Cro. 48/B4
Pasni, Pak. 89/H3
Paso de Indios, Arg. 158/C4
Paso de los Libres, Arg. 157/E2
Paso de los Toros, Uru. 159/K10
Paso de Ovejas, Mex. 143/N7
Paso del Macho, Mex. 143/N8
Paso del Planchón (peak), Chile 158/C2
Paso Robles (El Paso de Robles), Ca, US 128/B4
Pasrūr, Pak. 86/C3
Pass (peak), Yk, Can. 134/M3
Passa Quatro, Braz. 211/J7
Passagem Franca, Braz. 154/B2
Passaic (riv.), NJ, US 138/D2
Passaic, NJ, US 139/J8
Passau, Ger. 55/G5
Passero (pt.), It. 46/D4
Passo Fundo, Braz. 155/A4
Passo Fundo, Barragem do (res.), Braz. 155/A3
Passons, It. 59/G1
Passoré (prov.), Burk. 103/E3
Passos, Braz. 155/C2
Passwang (peak), Swi. 56/D3
Passy, Fr. 56/C6
Pastavy, Bela. 39/M4
Pastaza (riv.), Ecu.,Peru 147/B3
Pastaza (dept.), Ecu. 152/B5
Pastek (riv.), Pol. 39/J5
Pasto, Col. 152/B4
Pastol (bay), Ak, US 134/F3
Pastoriza, Sp. 44/B1
Pastos Bons, Braz. 154/A2
Pasuruan, Indo. 80/D5
Pásztó, Hun. 41/K5
Pata, Bol. 156/D4
Patagonia (phys. reg.), Arg. 147/B8
Patah (peak), Indo. 80/B4
Pātan, India 84/B4
Pātan, India 89/K4
Pataná (peak), Braz. 155/B3
Patapsco (riv.), Md, US 138/A5
Patapsco, Md, US 138/B4
Pataudi, India 86/D5
Pataz, Peru 156/B2
Patchogue, NY, US 139/E2
Paterna, Sp. 45/E3
Paternò, It. 46/D4
Paterson, NJ, US 139/J8
Pathalgaon, India 84/D4
Pathānkot, India 86/C3
Pathein (Bassein), Myan. 83/F4
Pathfinder (res.), Wy, US 126/G5
Pati, Indo. 80/D5
Patía (riv.), Col. 150/C3
Patía, Col. 152/B4
Patiāla, India 86/D4
Patikul, Phil. 81/F2
Patna, India 85/E3
Patna, Sc, UK 36/B6
Patnongon, Phil. 81/F1
Patnos, Turk. 90/E2
Pato Branco, Braz. 155/A3
Patoka (riv.), In, US 133/G2
Patos, Braz. 154/C2
Patos, Alb. 47/F2
Patos de Minas, Braz. 155/C1
Patos, Lagoa dos (lake), Braz. 157/F3
Patrai (gulf), Gre. 47/G3
Pátrai, Gre. 47/G3
Pātrasāer, India 85/F4
Patrātu, India 85/E4
Patricia (mt.), Austl. 113/F2
Patricio Lynch (isl.), Chile 159/A6
Patrocínio, Braz. 155/C1
Patscherkofel (peak), Aus. 57/H3
Pattani, Thai. 78/C5
Pattensen, Ger. 51/G4
Patti, India 86/C4
Patti, It. 46/D3
Pattoki, Pak. 86/B4
Pattukkottai, India 82/C5
Pattullo (mt.), BC, Can. 134/N4
Patuākhāli (pol. reg.), Bang. 85/G4
Patuākhāli, Bang. 85/H4
Patuca (riv.), Hon. 140/D5
Patuca (mts.), Hon. 144/E3
Patuca (pt.), Hon. 145/E3
Patuxent (riv.), Md, US 138/B5
Patuxent NWR, Md, US 138/B5
Patuxent River State Park, Md, US 138/B5
Páty, Hun. 49/Q9
Pátzcuaro, Mex. 143/E5
Pau, Fr. 42/C5
Pau Brasil, Braz. 154/C4
Pau dos Ferros, Braz. 154/C2
Paucarbamba, Peru 156/C4
Paucartambo, Peru 156/C3
Paucartambo, Peru 156/D4
Pauillac, Fr. 42/C4
Pauini (riv.), Braz. 150/E5
Paulaya (riv.), Hon. 144/E3
Paulínia, Braz. 211/F7
Paulins Kill (riv.), NJ, US 138/D2
Paulistana, Braz. 154/B3
Paullo, It. 58/C2
Paulo Afonso, Braz. 154/C3
Paulo Afonso, PN de, Braz. 154/C3
Paulo Ramos, Braz. 154/A2
Paulpietersburg, SAfr. 107/E2
Pauls Valley, Ok, US 129/H4
Paulsboro, NJ, US 138/C4

uma Valley,
, US 136/D4
ungde, Myan. 83/G4
vão, Braz. 154/B5
vel Banya, Bul. 47/J1
via (prov.), It. 58/C2
via, It. 58/C2
vie, Fr. 42/D5
vlikeni, Bul. 49/G4
vlodar (obl.), Kaz. 87/G2
vlodar, Kaz. 87/G2
vlof (vol.),
, US 134/F4
vlohrad, Ukr. 62/E2
vlovo, Rus. 60/J5
vone Canavese, It. 58/A2
vone del Mella, It. 58/D2
vullo nel Frignano, It. 59/D4
w Paw, Mi, US 130/C3
wan (riv.), Indo. 80/D4
wāyan, India 84/C1
whuska, Ok, US 129/H3
wnee (riv.), Ks, US 129/G3
wtucket, RI, US 131/G3
xoí (isl.), Gre. 47/F3
xson, Ak, US 134/J3
xton, Austl. 115/D2
y-Khoy (mts.), Rus. 64/G3
yakumbuh, Indo. 80/B4
yerne, Swi. 56/C4
yette (riv.), Id, US 126/D5
yne (lake),
, Can. 123/J3
ynesville, Austl. 115/C3
ys de Caux (reg.), Fr. 42/D2
ys de France
g.), Fr. 30/K4
ys de la Loire
g.), Fr. 42/C3
ysandú, Uru. 159/J10
yson, Az, US 128/E4
yson, Ut, US 128/E2
yún (peak), Arg. 158/C3
z (riv.), Guat. 144/D3
z de Ariporo,
l. 152/D3
z de Río, Col. 152/C3
zar, Turk. 90/D1
zar, Turk. 63/G4
zarcık, Turk. 90/D2
zardzhik, Bul. 47/J1
zaryeri, Turk. 62/D5
zin, Cro. 48/A3
abiru, Braz. 155/A2
eace (riv.), BC, Can. 122/D3
eace Memorial Park,
pan 74/C3
eaceful Valley,
, US 137/B2
eachland, BC, Can. 126/D3
eachtree City,
, US 133/G3
eak Charles NP,
stl. 112/D5
eak District NP,
g, UK 35/G5
eak Hill, Austl. 112/C3
eal de Becerro, Sp. 44/D4
eapack-Gladstone,
J, US 138/D2
earblossom,
, US 136/C1
earl, Ms, US 133/F3
earl (har.), Hi, US 124/W13
earl (riv.),
,Ms, US 125/J5
earl and Hermes (reef),
, US 117/H2
earl Beach,
i, US 135/G6
earl City, Hi, US 124/W13
earl River (estu.),
hina 79/B3
earl River, La, US 137/Q16
earl River, NY, US 139/J7
earland, Ca, US 136/B1
earsall, Tx, US 129/H5
earson (int'l arpt.),
n, Can. 131/Q8
earston, SAfr. 106/D4
eary (chan.),
un., Can. 123/R7
ease (riv.), Tx, US 129/G4
ebane, Moz. 105/G4
ebas, Peru 156/D1
ebble (isl.), Mald. 159/E6
eccia, Swi. 57/E5
eccioli, It. 59/D5
écel, Hun. 49/R10
ech de Guillaument
eak), Fr. 42/E5
echanga Ind. Res.,
a, US 136/C4
echora, Rus. 61/N2
echora (bay), Rus. 61/M1
echora (riv.), Rus. 67/C3
eckham, Co, US 137/C2
econic (riv.),
Y, US 139/F2
ecos, Tx, US 132/C4
ecos (riv.), Tx, US 132/C4
ecq, Belg. 52/C2
ecquencourt, Fr. 52/C3
écs, Hun. 48/D2
eculiar, Mo, US 137/E6
ecy, Fr. 30/M6
edasí, Pan. 152/A3
edder (lake),
ustl. 109/D5
edemonte, It. 59/D2
edernales (riv.),
x, US 143/F2
ederneiras, Braz. 155/B2
edley, Ca, US 136/C3
edra Azul, Braz. 154/B5
edra Lume, CpV. 93/K10
edralva, Braz. 211/H7
Pedregal, Ven. 152/D2
Pedreguer, Sp. 45/F3
Pedreira, Braz. 211/G7
Pedreiras, Braz. 154/A2
Pedricktown,
NJ, US 138/C4
Pedro (pt.), SrL. 82/D6
Pedro Avelino,
Braz. 154/C2
Pedro Bay, Ak, US 134/H4
Pedro Betancourt,
Cuba 145/F1
Pedro Carbo, Ecu. 152/A5
Pedro Cays (isl.),
Jam. 141/F4
Pedro II, Braz. 154/B2
Pedro IV (isl.),
Braz. 153/E4
Pedro Juan Caballero,
Par. 157/E1
Pedro Leopoldo,
Braz. 155/C1
Pedro Luro, Arg. 158/E3
Pedro Osório,
Braz. 155/A4
Peebles, Sc, UK 36/C5
Peedamulla Abor. Land,
Austl. 112/B2
Peekskill, NY, US 138/E1
Peel (inlet), Austl. 112/B5
Peel (isl.), Austl. 114/F6
Peel (sound),
Nun., Can. 122/G1
Peel (co.), On, Can. 131/Q8
Peel (riv.), Yk, Can. 122/C2
Peel, IM, UK 34/D3
Peel Fell (peak),
Eng, UK 36/D6
Peene (riv.), Ger. 38/E5
Peer, Belg. 53/E1
Pegasus (bay), NZ 117/S11
Pegnitz, Ger. 55/E3
Pegnitz (riv.), Ger. 40/F4
Pego, Sp. 45/E3
Pego do Altar, Barragem de
(res.), Port. 44/A3
Pegognaga, It. 59/D3
Pegwell (bay),
Eng, UK 33/H4
Pehlivanköy, Turk. 49/H5
Pehowa, India 86/D5
Pehuajó, Arg. 158/E2
Pehuenche (pass),
Chile 158/C2
Pei Xian, China 72/D4
Peine, Ger. 51/H4
Peipus (lake),
Est.,Rus. 39/M2
Peiting, Ger. 57/G2
Peixe (riv.), Braz. 155/B2
Peixoto, Represa de
(res.), Braz. 155/C2
Pekalongan, Indo. 80/C5
Pekan, Malay. 80/B3
Pekan Nanas, Malay. 80/B3
Pekhora (riv.), Rus. 61/W9
Pekin, Il, US 127/L5
Pelada, Pampa (plain),
Arg. 158/C5
Pelado (vol.), Mex. 143/Q10
Pelagie (isls.), It. 46/C5
Peleaga (peak), Rom. 48/F3
Pelee (isl.), On, Can. 130/D3
Pelee (pt.), On, Can. 123/H4
Pelée (peak), Fr. 141/N9
Pelham, Al, US 133/G3
Pelham, On, Can. 131/R9
Pelham, NY, US 139/K8
Pelham Bay Park,
NY, US 139/K8
Pelham Manor,
NY, US 139/K8
Pelhřimov, Czh. 41/H4
Pelican (mts.), Ab, Can. 126/E2
Pelican (lake), Sk, Can. 127/H2
Pelican, Ak, US 134/L4
Pelican Narrows,
Sk, Can. 127/H2
Pelindã, Ponta de (pt.),
GBis. 102/A4
Pelister (peak),
FYROM 47/G2
Pelister NP, FYROM 47/G2
Peljekaise NP, Swe. 37/F2
Pelješac (pen.), Cro. 47/E1
Pelješac (pen.), Cro. 48/C4
Pell Lake, Wi, US 135/P14
Pélla (ruin), Gre. 47/H2
Pélla, Gre. 47/H2
Pellegrini, Arg. 158/E3
Pellestrina, It. 59/F2
Pello, Fin. 60/E2
Pelly (riv.), Yk, Can. 122/C2
Pelly (bay), Nun., Can. 122/H2
Pelly Bay, Nun., Can. 122/H2
Peloponnesus (reg.),
Gre. 47/G3
Peloritani, Monti
(mts.), It. 46/D4
Pelotas (riv.), Braz. 157/F2
Pelotas, Braz. 155/A4
Pelplin, Pol. 39/H5
Pemali (cape), Indo. 81/F5
Pemali (cape), Indo. 81/F4
Pematangsiantar,
Indo. 80/A3
Pemba, Moz. 105/H3
Pemba (isl.), Tanz. 105/G2
Pemba North
(prov.), Tanz. 104/C4
Pemba South
(prov.), Tanz. 104/C4
Pemberton, Austl. 112/C5
Pemberton, BC, Can. 126/C3
Pemberton, NJ, US 138/D4
Pembina (riv.),
ND, US 126/E2
Pembina, ND, US 127/J3
Pembroke, On, Can. 130/E2
Pembroke, Wal, UK 32/B3
Pembrokeshire (co.),
Wal, UK 32/A3
Pembrokeshire Coast NP,
Wal, UK 32/A3
Pembury, Eng, UK 33/G4
Pemuco, Chile 158/B3
Pen Argyl, Pa, US 138/C2
Pen, The (lake),
La, US 137/P17
Pen-y-Ghent (peak),
Eng, UK 35/F3
Pen-y-Gogarth (pt.),
Wal, UK 34/E5
Pen y Gurnos (peak),
Wal, UK 32/C2
Peña Blanca (mtn.),
Pan. 145/F4
Peña de Cerredo (mtn.),
Sp. 44/C1
Peñafiel, Sp. 44/C2
Penafiel, Port. 44/A2
Peñaflor, Chile 158/N8
Penalva, Braz. 154/A1
Penamacor, Port. 44/B2
Penápolis, Braz. 155/B2
Peñaranda de Bracamonte,
Sp. 44/C2
Peñarroya (peak),
Sp. 45/E2
Peñarroya-Pueblonuevo,
Sp. 44/C3
Penarth, Wal, UK 32/C4
Peñas (cape), Sp. 44/C1
Peñas (cape), Arg. 159/D7
Penas, Golfo de (gulf),
Chile 157/A6
Peñasco (riv.),
NM, US 129/F4
Pench (riv.), India 84/B5
Penchard, Fr. 30/L5
Penco, Chile 158/B3
Pend Oreille (lake),
Id, US 126/D4
Pendelikón (peak),
Gre. 47/N8
Pendembu, SLeo. 102/C4
Pendências, Braz. 154/C2
Pendjar (riv.),
Burk. 103/F4
Pendjari, PN de la,
Ben. 96/F5
Pendle (hill),
Eng, UK 35/F4
Pendleton, Or, US 126/D4
Peneda-Gerês NP,
Port. 44/A2
Penedo, Braz. 154/C3
Penetanguishene,
On, Can. 130/E2
Penghu (Pescadores)
(isls.), Tai. 79/C3
Penglai, China 72/E3
Penguin, Austl. 115/C4
Penha, Braz. 155/B3
Penhold, Ab, Can. 126/E2
Penibético, Sistema
(range), Sp. 44/C4
Penice (peak), It. 58/C3
Peniche, Port. 44/A3
Penicuik, Sc, UK 36/C5
Península de Paria, PN,
Ven. 153/F2
Peñíscola, Sp. 45/F2
Penitente, Serra do (mts.),
Braz. 151/J5
Penmaenmawr,
Wal, UK 34/E5
Penmarch, Fr. 42/A3
Penmarc'h, Pointe de
(pt.), Fr. 42/A3
Penn Forest (res.),
Pa, US 138/C2
Penn Hills, Pa, US 130/E3
Penn Yan, NY, US 130/E3
Penna, Punta della
(cape), It. 46/D1
Penne (pt.), It. 47/E2
Penne, It. 46/C1
Penner (riv.), India 82/C5
Pennine Alps (mts.),
Swi. 43/G4
Pennine Chain (mts.),
Eng, UK 35/F2
Pennington,
NJ, US 138/D3
Pennino (peak), It. 43/K5
Penns Creek (mtn.),
Pa, US 138/A2
Penns Grove, NJ, US 138/C4
Penns Park, Pa, US 138/D3
Pennsauken, NJ, US 138/C4
Pennsburg, Pa, US 138/C3
Pennsville, NJ, US 138/C4
Pennsylvania
(state), US 130/E3
Penny (str.),
Nun., Can. 123/S7
Penobscot (riv.),
Me, US 131/G2
Penola, Austl. 115/B3
Peñón Blanco,
Mex. 142/D3
Penon de Al Hoceima
(isl.), Sp. 100/C2
Penonomé, Pan. 152/A2
Penrhyn Mawr (pt.),
Wal, UK 34/D6
Penrhyn Mawr (pt.),
IM, UK 34/D5
Penrith, Eng, UK 35/F2
Pensacola, Fl, US 133/G4
Pensacola (mts.), Ant. 160/X
Pense, Sk, Can. 127/G3
Penshurst, Austl. 115/B3
Pentagon Fed. Govt. Res.,
Va, US 138/A6
Pentecost (isl.), Van. 116/F6
Pentecoste, Braz. 154/C1
Penteleu (peak),
Rom. 49/H3
Penthalaz, Swi. 56/C4
Penticton, BC, Can. 126/D3
Pentire (pt.),
Eng, UK 32/B5
Pentland, Austl. 114/B3
Pentland (hills),
Sc, UK 36/C5
Pentland Firth (inlet),
Sc, UK 31/V14
Peñuelas, PN,
Chile 158/N8
Penwith (pen.),
Eng, UK 32/A6
Penza, Rus. 63/H1
Penzance, Eng, UK 32/A6
Penzberg, Ger. 57/H2
Penzenskaya Oblast,
Rus. 63/G1
Penzhina (riv.),
Rus. 65/S3
Penzhina (bay),
Rus. 65/S3
Penzing, Ger. 57/G1
Penzlin, Ger. 40/G2
Peoria, Az, US 137/R18
Pepe (cape), Cuba 145/F1
Pepeekeo, Hi, US 124/U11
Pepeekeo (pt.),
Hi, US 124/U11
Pepel, SLeo. 102/B4
Pepinster, Belg. 53/E2
Pequannock,
NJ, US 139/H8
Pequeña Isla del Maíz
(isl.), Nic. 145/F3
Pequest (riv.),
NJ, US 138/D2
Perabumulih, Indo. 80/B4
Perales (riv.), Sp. 45/M9
Peralta, Sp. 44/E1
Pérama, Gre. 47/J5
Pérama, Gre. 47/N9
Percé, Qu, Can. 131/H1
Percée (peak), Fr. 56/C6
Perche, Collines du
(hills), Fr. 42/D2
Perchtoldsdorf,
Aus. 49/N7
Percival (lakes),
Austl. 109/B3
Percy (isls.), Austl. 109/E3
Percy Isles (chan.),
Austl. 114/C3
Perdekop, SAfr. 107/E2
Pérdhika, Gre. 47/G3
Perdida (riv.), Braz. 154/A3
Perdido (mtn.), Sp. 45/F1
Peregian Beach,
Austl. 114/D4
Pereira, Col. 150/C3
Pereira Barreto,
Braz. 155/B2
Pereiro, Braz. 154/C2
Perelló, Sp. 45/F2
Perenjori, Austl. 112/C4
Peretola (int'l arpt.), It. 59/E5
Perg, Aus. 55/H6
Pergamino, Arg. 158/E2
Pergamum (ruin),
Turk. 90/A2
Pergine Valsugana, It. 57/H5
Pergola, It. 43/K5
Péribonca (riv.),
Qu, Can. 131/G1
Perico, Cuba 145/F1
Pericos, Mex. 142/D3
Pericos, Mex. 142/D4
Périgueux, Fr. 42/D4
Perijá, Sierra de (mts.),
Col. 150/D2
Peristéra (isl.), Gre. 47/H3
Peristéri, Gre. 47/N8
Perito Moreno, Arg. 158/C5
Perito Moreno, PN,
Arg. 157/B6
Perkasie, Pa, US 138/C3
Perl, Ger. 53/F5
Perlas (lag.), Nic. 140/E5
Perlas (pt.), Nic. 145/F3
Perleberg, Ger. 40/F2
Perlez, Serb. 48/E3
Perlis (state), Malay. 78/B5
Perm', Rus. 61/N4
Permskaya Oblast, Rus. 61/N4
Përmet, Alb. 47/G2
Pernambuco (state),
Braz. 154/C3
Pernate, It. 58/B2
Pernes-les-Fontaines,
Fr. 42/F4
Pernik, Bul. 47/H1
Perniö, Fin. 39/K1
Peron (pen.), Austl. 112/B3
Péronne, Fr. 52/B4
Perote, Mex. 143/M7
Pérouges, Fr. 56/B6
Perpignan, Fr. 42/E5
Perray (riv.), Fr. 30/H6
Perrigny, Fr. 56/B4
Perris (res.),
Ca, US 136/C3
Perris, Ca, US 136/C3
Perris State Rec. Area,
Ca, US 136/C3
Perros-Guirec, Fr. 42/B2
Perrot, Île (isl.),
Qu, Can. 131/N7
Perry (riv.), Nun., Can. 122/F2
Perry, Fl, US 133/H4
Perry, Ga, US 133/H3
Perry, Ok, US 129/H3
Perry (co.), Pa, US 138/A3
Perry, Ut, US 137/J11
Perry Hall, Md, US 138/B5
Perryman, Md, US 138/B5
Perryton, Tx, US 129/G3
Perryville, Ak, US 134/G4
Perryville, Md, US 138/B4
Persan, Fr. 30/J4
Persian (gulf), Asia 67/D7
Perstorp, Swe. 38/E3
Perth, Austl. 115/C4
Perth, On, Can. 130/E2
Perth (int'l arpt.),
Austl. 112/K6
Perth, Austl. 112/K6
Perth, Sc, UK 36/C4
Perth Amboy, NJ, US 139/H9
Perth nd Kinross
(pol. reg.), Sc, UK 36/C4
Perth Zoo, Austl. 112/K6
Pertuis, Fr. 42/F5
Pertuis Breton (inlet), Fr. 42/C3
Pertusato (cape), Fr. 46/A2
Peru (ctry.) 156/C3
Peru, Il, US 127/L5
Peru, In, US 130/C3
Perućačko (lake),
Bosn. 48/D4
Perugia, It. 43/K5
Peruíbe, Braz. 211/G9
Peruque, Mo, US 137/F8
Perushtitsa, Bul. 47/J1
Péruwelz, Belg. 52/C2
Pervari, Turk. 90/E2
Pervomays'k, Ukr. 49/K1
Pervomaysk, Rus. 61/J5
Pervoural'sk, Rus. 61/N4
Perwez, Belg. 53/D2
Péry, Swi. 56/D3
Pesa (riv.), It. 59/E5
Pesagi (peak), Indo. 80/B4
Pesaro, It. 59/F5
Pesaro e Urbino
(prov.), It. 59/F5
Pescadores (Penghu)
(isls.), China 79/C3
Pescantina, It. 59/D2
Pescara, It. 46/D1
Peschanyy (cape),
Kaz. 63/J4
Pescia, It. 59/D5
Peseux, Swi. 56/C4
Pesha (riv.), Rus. 61/L2
Peshāwar, Pak. 86/A2
Peshawar (int'l arpt.),
Pak. 86/A2
Peshtera, Bul. 47/J1
Peshtigo, Wi, US 127/M4
Peshtigo (riv.), Wi, US 130/B2
Pesmes, Fr. 56/B3
Peso da Régua,
Port. 44/B2
Pesqueira, Braz. 154/C3
Pessac, Fr. 42/C4
Pest (prov.), Hun. 48/D2
Pestovkoye (lake),
Rus. 61/W9
Pestovo, Rus. 60/G4
Petah Tiqwa, Isr. 91/F7
Petal, Ms, US 133/F4
Petalión (gulf), Gre. 47/J4
Petaluma (riv.),
Ca, US 135/J10
Pétange, Lux. 53/E4
Petare, Ven. 150/E1
Pétas, Gre. 47/G3
Petatlán (riv.),
Mex. 142/D3
Petatlán, Mex. 143/E5
Petauke, Zam. 105/F3
Petawawa (riv.),
On, Can. 130/E2
Petawawa, On, Can. 130/E2
Peten Itzá (lake),
Guat. 144/D2
Petenwell (lake),
Wi, US 127/L4
Peter (isl.), Nor. 160/U
Peterborough, Austl. 113/H5
Peterborough,
On, Can. 130/E2
Peterborough,
Eng, UK 33/F1
Peterborough (co.),
Eng, UK 33/F1
Peterhead, Sc, UK 36/E1
Peterlee, Eng, UK 35/G2
Petermann Abor. Land,
Austl. 113/F3
Peteroa (vol.),
Chile 158/C2
Petersaurach, Ger. 54/D4
Petersberg, Ger. 54/C1
Petersburg, Ak, US 134/M4
Petersfield, Eng, UK 33/F4
Petershagen, Ger. 51/F4
Petershagen, Ger. 40/Q6
Petershausen, Ger. 55/E6
Peterson, Ut, US 137/K11
Pétervására, Hun. 41/L4
Petilia Policastro, It. 46/E3
Pétionville, Haiti 145/H2
Petit Goâve, Haiti 145/H2
Petit Lac Manicouagan
(lake), Qu, Can. 131/H1
Petit Loango, PN du,
Gabon 105/A1
Petit-Noir, Fr. 56/B4
Petit Rosne (riv.), Fr. 30/J4
Petitcodiac,
NB, Can. 131/H2
Petite Miquelon (isl.),
StP. 131/K2
Petite Rivière de l'Artibonite,
Haiti 145/H2
Petite Rivière Noire
(peak), Mrts. 107/T15
Petite-Rosselle, Fr. 53/F5
Petitt Morin (riv.), Fr. 42/E2
Petkeljärven NP, Fin. 60/F3
Petlād, India 89/K4
Petlalcingo, Mex. 144/B2
Peto, Mex. 144/D1
Petorca, Chile 158/C2
Petoskey, Mi, US 130/C2
Petra (Baṭrā') (ruin), Jor. 91/D4
Petra (isls.), Rus. 65/M2
Petrel, Sp. 45/E3
Petrella (peak), It. 46/C2
Petrich, Bul. 47/H2
Petrified Forest NP,
Az, US 128/E4
Petrila, Rom. 49/F3
Petrodvorets, Rus. 61/S7
Petrokhanski Prokhod
(pass), Bul. 47/H1
Petrokrepost' (bay),
Rus. 61/U7
Petrolândia, Braz. 154/C3
Petrolina, Braz. 154/B3
Petropavl, Kaz. 87/E2
Petropavlovsk-Kamchatskiy,
Rus. 65/R4
Petrópolis, Braz. 211/K7
Petrovaradin, Serb. 48/D3
Petrovsk, Rus. 63/H1
Petrovsk-Zabaykal'skiy,
Rus. 70/J1
Petrozavodsk, Rus. 60/G3
Petrus Steyn, SAfr. 106/E2
Petrusburg, SAfr. 106/D3
Petrusville, SAfr. 106/D3
Pettenbach, Aus. 55/H7
Petteril (riv.), Eng, UK 35/F2
Petzeck (peak), Aus. 43/K3
Peuerbach, Aus. 55/G6
Peulik (mt.), Ak, US 134/G4
Peumo, Chile 158/N9
Pevely, Mo, US 137/G9
Pewaukee (lake),
Wi, US 135/X13
Pewaukee, Wi, US 135/P13
Peyrehorade, Fr. 42/C5
Peza (riv.), Rus. 61/K2
Pézenas, Fr. 42/E5
Pfaffenhausen,
Ger. 57/G1
Pfaffenhofen an der Ilm,
Ger. 54/D6
Pfaffenhofen an der Ilm,
Ger. 55/E5
Pfaffenhoffen, Fr. 53/G6
Pfäffikon, Swi. 57/E3
Pfaffing, Ger. 55/F6
Pfaffnau, Swi. 56/D3
Pfahl (ridge), Ger. 55/F4
Pfälzer Wald (mts.),
Ger. 53/G5
Pfälzerwald (mts.),
Ger. 54/A4
Pfalzgrafenweiler,
Ger. 54/B5
Pfarrhof Esternberg,
Aus. 55/G5
Pfarrkirchen, Ger. 55/F6
Pfatter, Ger. 55/F5
Pfeffenhausen, Ger. 55/E5
Pfettrach (riv.), Ger. 55/E5
Pfieffe (riv.), Ger. 51/G6
Pfinztal, Ger. 54/B5
Pforzheim, Ger. 54/B5
Pfreimd, Ger. 55/F3
Pfreimd (riv.), Ger. 55/F3
Pfronstetten, Ger. 57/F1
Pfronten, Ger. 57/G2
Pfroslkopf (peak), Aus. 57/G4
Pfullendorf, Ger. 57/F2
Pfunds, Aus. 57/G4
Pfungstadt, Ger. 54/B3
Phagwāra, India 86/C4
Phalauda, India 86/D5
Phalempin, Fr. 52/C2
Phālia, Pak. 86/B3
Phalodi, India 89/K3
Phalsbourg, Fr. 53/G6
Phan Rang, Viet. 78/E4
Phan Thiet, Viet. 78/E4
Phanat Nikhom, Thai. 78/C3
Phang Hoei (range),
Thai. 78/C3
Phangnga, Thai. 78/B4
Phanom Dongrak (mts.),
Thai. 83/H5
Pharr, Tx, US 132/D5
Phatthalung, Thai. 78/C5
Phaya Fo (peak), Thai. 78/C2
Phayao, Thai. 78/B2
Phelan, Ca, US 136/C2
Phenix City,
Al, US 133/G3
Phet Buri, Thai. 78/B3
Phetchabun, Thai. 78/C2
Phichit, Thai. 78/C2
Philadelphia, Ms, US 133/F3
Philadelphia, Pa, US 138/C4
Philadelphia (int'l arpt.),
Pa, US 138/C4
Philip, SD, US 127/H4
Philip S.W. Goldson
(int'l arpt.), Belz. 144/D2
Philippeville, Belg. 53/D3
Philippi, WV, US 130/D4
Philippine (sea),
Asia 79/D4
Philippines (ctry.) 79/D5
Philippsburg, Ger. 54/B4
Philipsburg,
Mt, US 126/E4
Philipsdam (dam),
Neth. 50/B5
Philipstown, SAfr. 106/D3
Phillaur, India 86/C4
Phillipsburg,
NJ, US 138/C2
Phimai (ruin), Thai. 78/C3
Phitsanulok, Thai. 78/C2
Phnom Penh (Phnum Pénh)
(cap.), Camb. 78/D4
Phnum Penh (int'l arpt.),
Camb. 78/D4
Pho (pt.), Thai. 78/C5
Phoenix (cap.),
Az, US 137/R19
Phoenix, La, US 137/Q17
Phoenix (isls.),
Kiri. 117/H5
Phoenix Park, Ire. 34/B5
Phoenix Sky Harbor
(int'l arpt.), Az, US 137/S19
Phoenixville, Pa, US 138/C3
Phongsali, Laos 83/H3
Phou Bia (peak),
Laos 78/C2
Phou Huatt (peak),
Viet. 83/H4
Phou Loi (peak),
Laos 83/H3
Phou Xai Lai Leng
(peak), Laos 78/D2
Phra Nakhon Si Ayutthaya,
Thai. 78/C3
Phra Thong (isl.),
Thai. 78/B4
Phrae, Thai. 78/C2
Phu Hin Rong Kla NP,
Thai. 78/C2
Phu Kradung NP,
Thai. 78/C2
Phu Luong (peak),
Viet. 83/H3
Phu Phan NP, Thai. 78/D2
Phu Quoc (isl.), Viet. 83/H5
Phu Rua NP, Thai. 78/C2
Phu Tho, Viet. 83/J3
Phuket (isl.), Thai. 83/G6
Phuket, Thai. 78/B5
Phularwan, Pak. 86/B3
Phūlpur, India 84/D3
Piaçabuçu, Braz. 154/C3
Piacenza (prov.), It. 58/C3
Piacenza, It. 58/C2
Piadena, It. 58/D2
Pian di Serra (peak), It. 59/F6
Pian-Upe Game Rsv.,
Ugan. 104/B2
Piancastagnaio, It. 46/B1
Piancó, Braz. 154/C2
Pianello val Tidone, It. 58/C3
Pianezza, It. 58/A2
Piangipane, It. 59/F4
Pianoro, It. 59/E4
Pianosa (isl.), It. 46/A1
Piarco (int'l arpt.),
Trin. 153/F2
Piaseczno, Pol. 41/L2
Piatra Neamţ, Rom. 49/H2
Piauí (riv.), Braz. 154/B3
Piauí (state), Braz. 154/B2
Piave (riv.), It. 43/K3
Piazza, It. 58/D1
Piazza, It. 58/D1
Piazza al Serchio, It. 58/D4
Piazza Armerina, It. 46/D4
Piazza Brembana, It. 57/F6
Piazzola sul Brenta, It. 59/E1
Pic (riv.), On, Can. 130/C1
Pic de Nore (peak), Fr. 42/E5
Pic d'Orhy (peak), Fr. 42/C5
Pic du Canigou
(peak), Fr. 42/E5
Pica, Chile 150/E8
Picacho del Centinela
(peak), Mex. 129/G5
Picachos, Cerro Dos
(peak), Mex. 142/B2
Picardie (pol. reg.), Fr. 42/E2
Picardy (reg.), Fr. 52/B4
Picatinny Arsenal,
NJ, US 138/D2
Picayune, Ms, US 133/F4
Piccolo (lag.), It. 47/E2
Pichacani, Peru 156/D5
Pichanal, Arg. 157/D1
Pichidegua, Chile 158/N9
Pichilemu, Chile 158/B2
Pichincha (dept.),
Ecu. 152/B4
Pichincha, Ecu. 152/B5
Pichl bei Wels, Aus. 55/G6
Pichor, India 84/B3
Pichucalco, Mex. 144/C2
Pickens, Ms, US 129/K4
Pickering,
On, Can. 131/R8
Pickering, Vale of
(valley), Eng, UK 35/H3
Pickle Lake,
On, Can. 127/L3
Picnic Bay, Austl. 114/B2
Pico (isl.),
Azor., Port. 45/S12
Pico da Neblina, PN do,
Braz. 150/F3
Pico de Orizaba, PN,
Mex. 143/M7
Pico Rivera,
Ca, US 136/F8
Pico Truncado, Arg. 158/D5
Picos, Braz. 154/B2
Picota, Peru 156/B2
Picsi, Peru 156/B2
Picton, On, Can. 130/E3
Pictou, NS, Can. 131/J2
Picture Rocks,
Pa, US 138/B1
Pictured Rocks Nat'l
Lakeshore, Mi, US 127/M4
Pictured Rocks Nat'l
Lakeshore, Mi, US 130/C2
Picuí, Braz. 154/C2
Piddle (riv.), Eng, UK 32/D5
Pidurutagala (peak),
SrL. 82/D6
Piedade, Port. 45/P10
Piedade do Rio Grande,
Braz. 211/J6
Piedecuesta, Col. 152/C3
Piedimulera, It. 57/E5
Piedmont (upland), US 133/H3
Piedmont, Ok, US 137/M14
Piedmont, Ca, US 135/K11
Piedra Grande,
Ven. 152/D2
Piedrabuena, Sp. 44/C3
Piedrahita, Sp. 44/C2
Piedras (pt.), Arg. 159/K11
Piedras Coloradas,
Uru. 159/K10
Piedras Negras,
Mex. 132/C4
Piedras Negras,
Mex. 143/N8
Piedras, Río de las
(riv.), Peru 150/D6
Piedritas, Arg. 158/E2
Piekary Śląskie,
Pol. 41/K3
Piekenierskloof (pass),
SAfr. 106/L10
Pieksämäki, Fin. 60/E3
Pielinen (lake), Fin. 37/J3
Piemonte (prov.), It. 43/G4
Pieniński NP, Pol. 41/L4
Piennes, Fr. 53/E5
Pieńsk, Pol. 41/H3
Piera, Sp. 45/K6
Pierce, Ne, US 127/J5
Pierce, Co, US 137/C1
Pierceland,
Sk, Can. 126/F2
Pieris, It. 59/G1
Piermont, NY, US 139/K7
Pierowall, Sc, UK 31/V14
Pierre (cap.),
SD, US 127/H4
Pierre-de-Bresse, Fr. 56/B4
Pierre-Levée, Fr. 30/M5
Pierrefitte-sur-Seine, Fr. 30/K5
Pierrefonds,
Qu, Can. 131/N7
Pierrefontaine-les-Varans,
Fr. 56/C3
Pierrelatte, Fr. 42/F4
Pierrelaye, Fr. 30/J4
Pierrevert, Fr. 42/F5
Pierry, Fr. 52/C5
Piešt'any, Slvk. 41/J4
Piesting (riv.),
Aus. 49/P7
Piet Retief, SAfr. 107/E2
Pieterlen, Swi. 56/D3
Pietermaritzburg,
SAfr. 107/E3
Pietersburg, SAfr. 105/E5
Pietra Ligure, It. 58/B4
Pietralunga, It. 59/F6
Pietramelara, It. 46/D2
Pietravecchia (peak), It. 58/A5
Pietrosul (peak),
Rom. 49/G2
Pietrosul (peak),
Rom. 49/G2
Pieve del Cairo, It. 58/B2
Pieve di Cento, It. 59/E3
Pieve di Soligo, It. 59/F1
Pieve di Teco, It. 58/A4
Pieve Emanuele, It. 58/C2
Pieve Ligure, It. 58/C4
Pieve Porto Morone, It. 58/C2
Pieve Santo Stefano, It. 59/F5
Pieve Vergonte, It. 57/E6
Pievepelago, It. 58/D4
Pigeon (lake), Ab, Can. 126/E2
Pigeon (riv.),
On, Can. 122/G4
Piggott, Ar, US 129/K3
Pigs (bay), Cuba 140/E3
Pigüé, Arg. 158/E3
Pigŭm (isl.), SKor. 73/C5
Pihāni, India 84/C2
Pijijiapan, Mex. 144/C3
Pijnacker, Neth. 50/B4
Pijol (peak), Hon. 144/E3
Pike (co.), Pa, US 138/C1
Pikelot (isl.),
Micr. 116/D4
Pikes Creek (res.),
Pa, US 138/B1
Pikesville, Md, US 138/B5
Piketberg, SAfr. 106/L10
Pikeville, Ky, US 130/D4
Pikit, Phil. 79/D6
Pila, Arg. 159/J12
Piła, Pol. 41/J2
Pilanesberg (range),
SAfr. 106/P12
Pilani, India 86/C5
Pilão Arcado,
Braz. 154/B3
Pilar, Phil. 81/F1
Pilar, Par. 157/E2
Pilar, Braz. 154/D3
Pilar, Arg. 158/E1
Pilatus (peak), Swi. 57/E4
Pilaya (riv.), Bol. 150/F8
Pilchuck (riv.),
Wa, US 135/D1
Pilcomayo (riv.),
SAm. 147/C5
Pili, Phil. 79/D5
Pīlībhīt, India 84/B1
Pilica (riv.), Pol. 62/B2
Pilion (peak), Gre. 47/H3
Pilis, Hun. 48/D2
Pilis (peak), Hun. 49/Q9

216

Pilis – Port E

Pilis (mts.), Hun. 49/R9
Piliscsaba, Hun. 49/Q9
Pilisvörösvár, Hun. 49/Q9
Pilkhua, India 86/D5
Pillar (cape), Austl. 115/C4
Pillar (pt.), Ca, US 135/J12
Pillar (peak), Eng, UK 35/E3
Pilliga, Austl. 115/D1
Pillon, Col du (pass), Swi. 56/D5
Pillow, Pa, US 138/B2
Pilões, Serra dos (mts.), Braz. 154/A5
Pílos, Gre. 47/G4
Pilot (mtn.), Tn, US 130/C4
Pilot Point, Ak, US 134/G4
Pilot Station, Ak, US 134/F3
Pilsting, Ger. 55/F5
Pima, Az, US 128/E4
Pimpri-Chinchwad, India 89/K5
Piña (pt.), Pan. 145/G5
Pináculo (peak), Arg. 159/B6
Pinal, Az, US 137/R19
Pinamar, Arg. 159/F3
Pinang (cape), Malay. 80/A2
Pinang (isl.), Malay. 80/A2
Pinar del Río, Cuba 145/F1
Pınarbaşı, Turk. 90/D2
Pınarhisar, Turk. 49/H5
Piñas, Ecu. 156/B1
Pinatubo (mt.), Phil. 79/D4
Pinawa, Mb, Can. 127/K3
Pincher Creek, Ab, Can. 126/E3
Pinconning, Mi, US 130/D3
Pincota, Rom. 48/E2
Pincourt, Qu, Can. 131/N7
Pińczów, Pol. 41/L3
Pind Dādan Khān, Pak. 86/B3
Pindamonhangaba, Braz. 211/H7
Pindaré (riv.), Braz. 151/J4
Pindaré-Mirim, Braz. 154/A1
Píndhos NP, Gre. 47/G3
Pindi Bhattiān, Pak. 86/B4
Pindi Gheb, Pak. 86/B3
Pindobaçu, Braz. 154/B3
Píndus (mts.), Gre. 47/G2
Pindwāra, India 89/K4
Pine Barrens (phys. reg.), NJ, US 138/D4
Pine Bluff, Ar, US 129/J4
Pine Bluffs, Wy, US 127/G5
Pine Creek (pt.), Ct, US 139/E1
Pine Falls, Mb, Can. 127/J3
Pine Grove, Pa, US 138/B2
Pine Hill, NJ, US 138/D4
Pine Island, Mn, US 130/A2
Pine Island Bay (flat), Ant. 160/S
Pine Lawn, Mo, US 137/G8
Pine Point, NW, Can. 122/E2
Pine Ridge, SD, US 127/H5
Pine, South Branch (riv.), Mi, US 135/G6
Pine, The (hills), Mt, US 127/G4
Pinecliff (lake), NJ, US 139/H7
Pinecliffe, Co, US 137/B3
Pinedale, Wy, US 126/F5
Pinega (riv.), Rus. 64/E3
Pineimuta (riv.), On, Can. 127/L2
Pinelands, SAfr. 106/L10
Piñera, Uru. 159/K10
Pinerolo, It. 43/G4
Pinetown, SAfr. 107/E3
Pineuilh, Fr. 42/D4
Pineview (res.), Ut, US 137/K11
Pineville, La, US 129/J5
Pinewood Springs, Co, US 137/B2
Ping (riv.), Thai. 83/G4
Ping Chau (isl.), China 71/V9
Pingbian Miaozu Zizhixian, China 83/H3
Pingding, China 72/C3
Pingdingshan, China 72/C4
Pingdu, China 72/D3
Pingelap (isl.), Micr. 116/F4
Pingelly, Austl. 112/C5
Pinggu, China 72/H6
Pingguo, China 83/J3
Pinghe, China 79/C3
Pinghu, China 72/L9
Pingjiang, China 79/B2
Pingjing (pass), China 72/C5
Pingle, China 83/K3
Pinglu, China 72/B4
Pinglu, China 72/C3
Pingnan, China 79/B3
Pingquan, China 72/D2
Pingshan, China 72/C3
Pingshun, China 72/C3
Pingtan, China 79/C2
Pingtang, China 83/J2
P'ingtung, Tai. 79/D3
Pingxiang, China 83/K2
Pingxiang, China 83/J3
Pingxing Guan (pass), China 72/C3
Pingyao, China 72/C3
Pingyi, China 72/D4
Pingyin, China 72/D3
Pingyu, China 72/C4
Pingyuan, China 72/D3
Pinhal, Braz. 211/G7
Pinhal Novo, Port. 45/Q10
Pinhão, Braz. 155/B3
Pinheiro, Braz. 154/A1
Pinheiros, Braz. 154/B5
Pinhel, Port. 44/B2
Piniós (riv.), Gre. 47/G4
Pinjar (lake), Austl. 112/K6
Pinjarra, Austl. 112/B5
Pink, Ok, US 137/N15
Pinkafeld, Aus. 48/C2
Pinkawillinie Conservation Park, Austl. 113/G5
Pinkegat (chan.), Neth. 50/C2
Pinnacles Nat'l Mon., Ca, US 128/B3
Pinnaroo, Austl. 113/J5
Pinnau (riv.), Ger. 51/G1
Pinneberg, Ger. 51/G1
Pino Hachado (pass), Arg. 158/C3
Pino Torinese, It. 58/A2
Pinole, Ca, US 135/K10
Pinon Hills, Ca, US 136/C2
Pinos (mt.), Ca, US 128/C4
Pinos, Mex. 143/E4
Pinos, Isla de (Isla de la Juventud) (isl.), Cuba 140/E3
Pinos-Puente, Sp. 44/D4
Pinoso, Sp. 45/E3
Pins, Île des (isl.), NCal. 116/F7
Pinsdorf, Aus. 55/G7
Pinsk, Bela. 62/C1
Pinta, Isla (isl.), Ecu. 156/E6
Pinto, Sp. 45/N9
Pinto, Chile 158/C3
Pinzolo, It. 57/G5
Pio Ix, Braz. 154/B2
Pio Xii, Braz. 154/A1
Piobbico, It. 59/F5
Pioche, Nv, US 128/D3
Piombino, It. 43/J5
Piombino Dese, It. 59/F1
Pioneer World, Austl. 112/L7
Pioner (isl.), Rus. 64/J2
Pionki, Pol. 41/L3
Piorini (riv.), Braz. 150/F4
Piorini (lake), Braz. 153/F5
Piota (riv.), It. 58/B3
Piotrków Trybunalski, Pol. 41/K3
Piove di Sacco, It. 59/F2
Piovene-Rocchette, It. 59/E1
Piparia, India 84/B4
Pipe Spring Nat'l Mon., Az, US 128/D3
Piper, Ks, US 137/D5
Pipersville, Pa, US 138/C3
Pipestone (riv.), On, Can. 122/G3
Piplān, Pak. 86/A3
Pipmuacan (res.), Qu, Can. 123/J4
Pippingarra Abor. Land, Austl. 112/C2
Pipra, India 84/D3
Pipraich, India 84/D2
Piqua, Oh, US 130/C3
Piquet Carneiro, Braz. 154/C2
Piquete, Braz. 211/H7
Piquiri (riv.), Braz. 151/H7
Pīr Mahal, Pak. 86/B4
Pīr Panjāl (range), India 86/C3
Piracanjuba, Braz. 155/B1
Piracicaba, Braz. 155/C2
Piracuruca, Braz. 154/B1
Pirae-bong (peak), NKor. 73/C2
Piraí, Braz. 211/K7
Piraí do Sul, Braz. 155/B3
Piraiévs, Gre. 47/N9
Piraju, Braz. 155/B2
Pirajuí, Braz. 155/B2
Pirámide (peak), Chile 159/B6
Piran, Slov. 59/G1
Pirané, Arg. 157/E2
Piranga (riv.), Braz. 155/D2
Piranhas (riv.), Braz. 151/L5
Piranji (riv.), Braz. 154/C2
Pirapemas, Braz. 154/A1
Pirapora, Braz. 154/A5
Pirapòzinho, Braz. 155/B2
Pirarajá, Uru. 159/G2
Pirássununga, Braz. 155/C2
Pires do Rio, Braz. 155/B1
Pírgos, Gre. 47/G4
Pírgos, Gre. 47/J5
Piriápolis, Uru. 159/G2
Pirin (mts.), Bul. 47/H2
Pirin (peak), Bul. 47/H2
Pirin NP, Bul. 47/H2
Piripiri, Braz. 154/B2
Piritiba, Braz. 154/B3
Píritu, Ven. 152/D2
Pirkkala, Fin. 39/K1
Pirmasens, Ger. 53/G5
Pirna, Ger. 41/G3
Piro, India 85/E3
Pirot, Serb. 47/H1
Pirre (mtn.), Pan. 152/B3
Pirthīpur, India 84/B3
Piru (lake), Ca, US 136/B1
Piru, Ca, US 136/B2
Piryíon, Gre. 47/J3
Pisa (prov.), It. 59/D6
Pisa, It. 58/D5
Pisac, Peru 156/D4
Pisanino (peak), It. 58/D4
Pisau (cape), Malay. 81/E2
Pisba, PN, Col. 152/C3
Piscataway, Md, US 138/B6
Piscataway, NJ, US 138/D2
Pisco (riv.), Peru 150/C6
Pisco, Peru 156/B4
Piscobamba, Peru 156/B3
Písek (peak), Czh. 55/H3
Písek, Czh. 55/H4
Pishan, China 70/C4
Pishīn, Pak. 89/J2
Pīshīn, Iran 89/H3
Piskavica, Bosn. 48/C3
Pisoc (peak), Swi. 57/G4
Pisogne, It. 58/D1
Pissis (peak), Arg. 157/C2
Pistakee (lake), Il, US 135/P15
Pisticci, It. 46/E2
Pistoia (prov.), It. 59/D5
Pistoia, It. 59/D5
Pisuerga (riv.), Sp. 44/C1
Pisz, Pol. 41/L2
Pit (riv.), Ca, US 128/B2
Pitalito, Col. 152/B4
Pitanga, Braz. 155/B3
Pitcairn (isl.), Pitc. 117/N7
Pitcairn Islands (dpcy.), UK 117/N7
Piteå, Swe. 37/G2
Piteälven (riv.), Swe. 37/F2
Pitești, Rom. 49/G3
Píthion, Gre. 47/K2
Pithiviers, Fr. 42/E2
Pithoragarh, India 84/C1
Pitigliano, It. 46/B1
Pitiquito, Mex. 142/B2
Pitjantjatjara Abor. Lands, Austl. 113/F3
Pitkas Point, Ak, US 134/F3
Pitlochry, Sc, UK 36/C3
Pitman, NJ, US 138/C4
Pitmedden, Sc, UK 36/D2
Pitomača, Cro. 48/C3
Piton de la Fournaise (peak), Reun. 107/S15
Piton des Neiges (peak), Reun. 107/S15
Pitrufquén, Chile 158/B3
Pitt Water (bay), Austl. 114/H8
Pittenweem, Sc, UK 36/D4
Pittsburg, Ks, US 129/J3
Pittsburgh, Pa, US 130/E3
Pittsfield, Me, US 131/G2
Pittsfield, Ma, US 130/F3
Pittston, Pa, US 130/F3
Pittstown, NJ, US 138/D2
Pittsworth, Austl. 114/C4
Pitzbach (riv.), Aus. 57/G4
Piuí, Braz. 155/C2
Piumazzo, It. 59/E3
Piura, Peru 156/A2
Piura (dept.), Peru 156/A2
Pivdenny Buh (riv.), Ukr. 62/D2
Pivijay, Col. 152/C2
Pixoyal, Mex. 140/C4
Piz d'Err (peak), Swi. 57/F4
Pizacoma, Peru 156/D5
Pizarra, Sp. 44/C4
Pizhma (riv.), Rus. 61/K4
Pizol (peak), Swi. 57/F4
Pizzighettone, It. 58/C2
Pizzo, It. 46/E3
Pizzo dei Tre Signori (peak), It. 57/F6
Pizzo della Presolana (peak), It. 57/G6
Pizzo di Coca (peak), It. 57/G5
Pizzo di Vogorno (peak), Swi. 57/E5
Pizzuto (peak), It. 46/C1
Placentia, Nf, Can. 131/L2
Placentia (bay), Nf, Can. 131/L2
Placentia, Ca, US 136/G8
Placer, Phil. 79/E6
Placer (co.), Ca, US 135/M9
Placetas, Cuba 145/G1
Plachkovtsi, Bul. 47/J1
Plaffeien, Swi. 56/D4
Plai Mat (riv.), Thai. 78/C3
Plaidt, Ger. 53/G3
Plailly, Fr. 30/K4
Plain City, Ut, US 137/J11
Plain Dealing, La, US 129/J4
Plaine (riv.), Fr. 56/C1
Plainfield, NJ, US 139/H9
Plainfield, Il, US 135/P16
Plains, Tx, US 129/G4
Plains, Pa, US 138/C1
Plainsboro, NJ, US 138/D3
Plainview, Tx, US 129/G4
Plainview, Mn, US 130/A2
Plainview, NY, US 139/M8
Plaisir, Fr. 30/H5
Plan-les-Ouates, Swi. 56/C5
Planá, Czh. 55/F3
Plana Cays (isls.), Bahm. 145/H1
Planaltina, Braz. 154/A4
Plancher-Bas, Fr. 56/C2
Plancher-les-Mines, Fr. 56/C2
Plandište, Serb. 48/E3
Planeta Rica, Col. 152/C2
Planken, Lcht. 57/F3
Plant City, Fl, US 133/H4
Plantation, Fl, US 133/H5
Plaquemines (parish), La, US 137/Q17
Plasencia, Sp. 44/B2
Plasy, Czh. 55/G3
Plata (riv.), Arg. 147/D6
Plata (estu.), Arg.,Uru. 159/K11
Platani (riv.), It. 46/C4
Plate Taile, Barrage de la (dam), Belg. 53/D3
Plateau (state), Nga. 103/H4
Platí, Gre. 47/H2
Platinum, Ak, US 134/F4
Plato, Col. 152/C2
Platón Sánchez, Mex. 144/B1
Platte (riv.), Ne, US 129/H2
Platte City, Mo, US 137/D5
Platte, North (riv.), Ne,Wy, US 124/E3
Platte, South (riv.), Co, US 124/F3
Platteville, Co, US 137/C2
Plattling, Ger. 55/F5
Plattsburgh, NY, US 130/F2
Plauen, Ger. 55/F1
Plav, Serb. 47/F1
Plavna Dadaint (peak), Swi. 57/G4
Playa de los Muertos (ruin), Hon. 144/E3
Playa del Carmen, Mex. 144/E1
Playa Noriega (lake), Mex. 142/C2
Playa Vicente, Mex. 144/C2
Playas (lake), NM, US 128/E5
Playas, Ecu. 152/A5
Playgreen (lake), Mb, Can. 127/J2
Pleasant (lake), Az, US 137/R18
Pleasant Grove, Ut, US 137/K13
Pleasant Hill, Ca, US 135/K11
Pleasant Hill, Mo, US 137/E6
Pleasant Hills, Md, US 138/B5
Pleasant Valley, Mo, US 137/E5
Pleasant View, Ut, US 137/K11
Pleasant View, Co, US 137/B3
Pleasanton, Tx, US 129/H5
Pleasanton, Ca, US 135/L11
Pleasantville, NJ, US 138/D5
Pleasantville, NY, US 139/K7
Pleaux, Fr. 42/E4
Pleiku, Viet. 78/D3
Pleinfeld, Ger. 54/D4
Pleisse (riv.), Ger. 40/G3
Plenty (riv.), Austl. 115/G5
Plenty (bay), NZ 109/H6
Plentywood, Mt, US 127/G3
Plérin, Fr. 42/B2
Plesná (riv.), Czh. 55/F2
Pleso (int'l arpt.), Cro. 48/C3
Pleszew, Pol. 41/J3
Plétipi (lake), Qu, Can. 131/G1
Plettenberg, Ger. 51/E6
Pleurtuit (int'l arpt.), Fr. 42/B2
Pleven, Bul. 49/G4
Pliska, Bul. 49/H4
Plitvice Lakes NP, Cro. 48/B3
Pljevlja, Serb. 47/F1
Plobsheim, Fr. 56/D1
Plöcckenstein (peak), Ger. 55/G5
Ploče, Cro. 47/E1
Plochingen, Ger. 54/C5
Płock, Pol. 41/K2
Pločno (peak), Bosn. 48/C4
Ploemeur, Fr. 42/B3
Ploiești, Rom. 49/H3
Plomárion, Gre. 47/K3
Plombières, Belg. 53/E2
Plombières-lès-Dijon, Fr. 56/A3
Plön, Ger. 38/D4
Płońsk, Pol. 41/L2
Plouay, Fr. 42/B3
Ploučnice (riv.), Czh. 41/H3
Ploufragan, Fr. 42/B2
Plougastel-Daoulas, Fr. 42/A2
Plouguernével, Fr. 42/B2
Plouzané, Fr. 42/A2
Plovdiv (pol. reg.), Bul. 47/J2
Plover Cove (res.), China 71/U10
Pluguffan (int'l arpt.), Fr. 42/A3
Plum (isl.), NY, US 139/F1
Plumridge Lakes Nature Rsv., Austl. 112/E4
Plumsteadville, Pa, US 138/C3
Plungė, Lith. 39/J4
Plymouth, Eng, UK 32/B6
Plymouth (co.), Eng, UK 32/B6
Plymouth (sound), Eng, UK 32/B6
Plymouth, NC, US 133/J3
Plymouth, NH, US 131/G3
Plymouth, In, US 130/C3
Plymouth, Wi, US 130/C3
Plymouth (cap.), Monts. 141/N8
Plymouth, Pa, US 138/C1
Plynlimon (peak), Wal, UK 32/C2
Plzeň, Czh. 55/G3
Plzeňský (pol. reg.), Czh. 55/G4
PNC Bank Arts Center, NJ, US 139/J10
Pniel, SAfr. 106/L10
Pniewy, Pol. 41/J2
Pô, Burk. 103/E4
Po (riv.), It. 27/F4
Po di Venezia (riv.), It. 59/F2
Po di Volano (riv.), It. 59/E3
Po Klong Garai Cham Towers, Viet. 78/E4
Po, Mouths of the (delta), It. 43/K4
Pô, PN de, Burk. 103/E4
Po Toi Group (isls.), China 71/V11
Po, Valle del (valley), It. 43/J4
Poá, Braz. 211/G8
Poa (riv.), Ven. 153/E2
Poag, Il, US 137/G8
Pobé, Ben. 103/F5
Pobedy (peak), Kyr. 70/D3
Pobiedziska, Pol. 41/J2
Pobla de Segur, Sp. 45/F1
Pocahontas, Ar, US 129/K3
Poção de Pedra, Braz. 154/A2
Pochep, Rus. 62/E1
P'och'ŏn, SKor. 73/G6
Pocinhos, Braz. 154/C2
Pöcking, Ger. 57/H2
Pöcking, Ger. 55/G6
Pocklington (reef), PNG 116/E6
Poço Fundo, Braz. 211/H6
Poções, Braz. 154/B4
Pocola, Ok, US 129/J4
Poconé, Braz. 151/G7
Pocono (mts.), Pa, US 138/C1
Pocono (lake), Pa, US 138/C1
Pocono Lake, Pa, US 138/C1
Pocono Pines, Pa, US 138/C1
Poços de Caldas, Braz. 211/G6
Pocrí, Pan. 152/A2
Podbořany, Czh. 55/G2
Poddębice, Pol. 41/K3
Podenzano, It. 58/C3
Podgorica, Serb. 47/F1
Podkarpackie (prov.), Pol. 41/L34
Podlasie (reg.), Bela.,Pol. 41/M3
Podlaskie (prov.), Pol. 41/M2
Podol'sk, Rus. 61/W9
Podor, Sen. 102/B2
Podporozh'ye, Rus. 60/G3
Podravska Slatina, Cro. 48/C3
Podujevo, Serb. 47/G1
Pofadder, SAfr. 106/B3
Poggibonsi, It. 59/E6
Poggio Renatico, It. 59/E3
Poggio Rusco, It. 59/E3
Poggiola, It. 59/E6
Pogromni (vol.), Ak, US 134/F5
P'ohang, SKor. 74/A2
Pohénégamook, Qu, Can. 131/G2
Pohja (Pojo), Fin. 39/K1
Pohjanmaa (reg.), Fin. 37/G3
Pohjois-Karjala (prov.), Fin. 60/F3
Pohnpei (isl.), Micr. 116/E4
Pohoiki, Hi, US 124/U11
Pohopoco Mtn. (mtn.), Pa, US 138/C2
Poigny-la-Forêt, Fr. 30/H5
Poing, Ger. 55/E6
Poinsett (cape), Ant. 160/H
Point (lake), NW, Can. 122/E2
Point au Fer (isl.), La, US 129/K5
Point Baker, Ak, US 134/M4
Point Fortin, Trin. 153/F2
Point Hope, Ak, US 134/E2
Point Lay, Ak, US 134/F2
Point Lookout (peak), Austl. 115/E1
Point Mugu Naval Air Sta., Ca, US 136/A2
Point Mugu State Park, Ca, US 136/A2
Point of Aire (pt.), Wal, UK 35/E5
Point of Ayre (pt.), IM, UK 34/D3
Point Pelee NP, On, Can. 130/D3
Point Pleasant, WV, US 130/D4
Point Pleasant, NJ, US 138/D3
Point Pleasant, Pa, US 138/C3
Point Pleasant Beach, NJ, US 138/D3
Point Salines (int'l arpt.), Gren. 153/F1
Point Salvation Abor. Rsv., Austl. 112/D4
Pointe-à-Pitre, Fr. 141/N8
Pointe à Raquette, Haiti 145/H2
Pointe-aux-Trembles, Qu, Can. 131/P6
Pointe-Calumet, Qu, Can. 131/N6
Pointe-Claire, Qu, Can. 131/N7
Pointe de Chassiron (pt.), Fr. 42/C3
Pointe de l'Arcouest (pt.), Fr. 42/B2
Pointe des Verres (peak), Fr. 56/C6
Pointe-du-Lac, Qu, Can. 131/F2
Pointe du Sablon (pt.), Fr. 42/F5
Pointe-Noire, Congo 105/B1
Poirino, It. 58/A3
Poissonier (pt.), Austl. 112/C1
Poissy, Fr. 30/J5
Poitiers, Fr. 42/D3
Poitou (reg.), Fr. 42/C3
Poitou-Charentes (reg.), Fr. 42/C3
Poix-de-Picardie, Fr. 52/A4
Poix-Terron, Fr. 53/D4
Pojuca, Braz. 154/C4
Pok Liu Chau (isl.), China 71/U11
Pokaran, India 89/K3
Pokharā, Nepal 84/D1
Pokhvistnevo, Rus. 63/K1
Pol-e Khomrī, Afg. 89/J1
Pola de Laviana, Sp. 44/C1
Pola de Lena, Sp. 44/C1
Pola de Siero, Sp. 44/C1
Polabská Nížina (phys. reg.), Czh. 43/L1
Pol'ana (peak), Slvk. 62/A2
Poland (ctry.) 41/K2
Połaniec, Pol. 41/L3
Polatlı, Turk. 90/C2
Polatsk, Bela. 39/N4
Polch, Ger. 53/G3
Połczyn-Zdrój, Pol. 38/G5
Pole of Inaccessability, Ant. 160/E
Polesella, It. 59/E3
Polesine (reg.), It. 59/E3
Poleski NP, Pol. 41/M3
Polgár, Hun. 48/E2
Pŏlgyo, SKor. 73/D5
Políaigos (isl.), Gre. 47/J4
Policastro, Golfo di (gulf), It. 46/D3
Police, Pol. 38/F5
Policoro, It. 46/E2
Poligny, Fr. 56/B4
Políkastron, Gre. 47/H2
Políkhni, Gre. 47/H2
Polikhnítos, Gre. 47/K3
Polillo (isl.), Phil. 79/D4
Polis, Cyp. 91/C2
Polistena, It. 46/E3
Políyiros, Gre. 47/H2
Polje, Slov. 43/L3
Polkowice, Pol. 41/J3
Polla, It. 46/D2
Pollença, Sp. 45/G3
Polochic (riv.), Guat. 144/D3
Polomolok, Phil. 79/E6
Polonia (cape), Uru. 159/G2
Polonnaruwa, SrL. 82/D6
Polonne, Ukr. 62/C2
Polski Trŭmbesh, Bul. 49/G4
Polson, Mt, US 126/E4
Poltava, Ukr. 62/E2
Poltavs'ka Oblasti, Ukr. 62/E2
Poluostrov Barsakel'mes (isl.), Kaz. 87/C3
Poluška (peak), Czh. 55/H5
Polvijärvi, Fin. 60/F3
Polyarnyy, Rus. 60/G1
Polynesia (reg.) 116/G6
Pomabamba, Peru 156/B3
Pomarance, It. 43/J5
Pomarico, It. 46/E2
Pomáz, Hun. 49/R9
Pomba (riv.), Som. 155/D2
Pombal, Braz. 154/C2
Pombal, Port. 44/A3
Pombas, CpV. 93/J9
Pomerania (reg.), Pol. 38/F4
Pomeranian (bay), Ger.,Pol. 38/F4
Pomerode, Braz. 155/B3
Pomeroon-Supenaam (pol. reg.), Guy. 153/G3
Pomeroy, Wa, US 126/D4
Pomeroy, NI, UK 34/B2
Pommersfelden, Ger. 54/D3
Pomona, Ca, US 136/C2
Pomona, NJ, US 138/D5
Pomona, Md, US 138/B5
Pomorie, Bul. 49/H4
Pomorskie (prov.), Pol. 41/J1
Pomos (pt.), Cyp. 91/C2
Pompano Beach, Fl, US 133/H5
Pompei (ruin), It. 46/D2
Pompeu, Braz. 155/C1
Pompey, Fr. 53/F6
Pompeys Pillar Nat'l Mon., Mt, US 126/G4
Pompiano, It. 58/C2
Pompton (riv.), NJ, US 139/H8
Pompton Lakes, NJ, US 139/H8
Poncarale, It. 58/D2
Ponce, PR 141/M8
Ponchatoula, La, US 137/P16
Poncheville (lake), Qu, Can. 130/E1
Pond, Mo, US 137/F8
Pond (inlet), Nun., Can. 123/J1
Pond (pt.), Ct, US 139/E1
Pond Inlet, Nun., Can. 123/J1
Pondicherry (terr.), India 70/D8
Pondicherry, India 82/C5
Ponente, Riviera di (coast), Fr. 58/B5
Ponferrada, Sp. 44/B1
Pongdong, SKor. 73/D5
Ponghwa, SKor. 74/A2
Pongolo (riv.), SAfr. 107/E2
Poni (prov.), Burk. 102/E4
Poniatowa, Pol. 41/M3
Ponnaiyar (riv.), India 82/C5
Ponoka, Ab, Can. 126/E2
Ponoy (riv.), Rus. 64/D3
Pons, Fr. 42/C4
Ponsacco, It. 58/D5
Pont-à-Celles, Belg. 53/D3
Pont-à-Marcq, Fr. 52/C2
Pont-D'Ain, Fr. 56/B5
Pont-de-Chéruy, Fr. 56/B6
Pont-de-Roide, Fr. 56/C3
Pont-de-Vaux, Fr. 56/A5
Pont-de-Veyle, Fr. 56/A5
Pont-du-Château, Fr. 42/E4
Pont-Remy, Fr. 52/A3
Pont-Saint-Esprit, Fr. 42/F4
Pont-Saint-Martin, It. 58/A1
Pont-Sainte-Maxence, Fr. 52/B5
Ponta Delgada, Azor., Port. 45/T13
Ponta do Pico (peak), Azor., Port. 45/S12
Ponta Grossa, Braz. 155/B3
Ponta Porã, Braz. 157/E1
Pontalina, Braz. 155/B1
Pontarlier, Fr. 56/C4
Pontarmé, Fr. 30/K4
Pontassieve, It. 59/E5
Pontault-Combault, Fr. 30/K5
Pontax (riv.), Qu, Can. 130/E1
Pontcarré, Fr. 30/L5
Pontchartrain (lake), La, US 125/H5
Pontchâteau, Fr. 42/B3
Ponte Alta do Bom Jesus, Braz. 154/A4
Ponte Alta do Tocantins, Braz. 154/A3
Ponte Buggianese, It. 59/D5
Ponte de Sor, Port. 44/A3
Ponte dell'Olio, It. 58/C3
Ponte di Legno, It. 57/G5
Ponte di Piave, It. 59/F1
Ponte do Lima, Port. 44/A2
Ponte Lambro, It. 58/C1
Ponte Nova, Braz. 155/D2
Ponte San Nicolò, It. 59/E2
Pontecagnano, It. 46/D2
Pontecorvo, It. 46/C2
Pontecurone, It. 58/B3
Pontedera, It. 58/D5
Pontefract, Eng, UK 35/G4
Ponteland, Eng, UK 35/G1
Pontelongo, It. 59/F2
Pontenure, It. 58/C3
Pontes e Lacerda, Braz. 150/G7
Pontestura, It. 58/B2
Pontevedra, Sp. 44/A1
Pontevico, It. 58/D2
Ponthévrard, Fr. 30/H6
Ponthieu (reg.), Fr. 52/A3
Pontiac, Il, US 127/L5
Pontiac, Mi, US 130/D3
Pontiac (lake), Mi, US 135/E6
Pontianak, Indo. 80/C4
Pontivy, Fr. 42/B2
Pontoise, Fr. 30/J4
Pontoon Beach, Il, US 137/G8
Pontotoc, Ms, US 133/F3
Pontpoint, Fr. 52/B5
Pontremoli, It. 58/C4
Pontresina, Swi. 57/F5
Pontypool, Wal, UK 32/C3
Ponza, It. 46/C2
Ponziane, Isole (isls.), It. 46/C2
Poole, Eng, UK 32/E5
Poole (bay), Eng, UK 33/E5
Poole (co.), Eng, UK 32/D5
Poolewe, Sc, UK 31/R8
Poona (Pune), India 89/K5
Poondarrie (peak), Austl. 112/C3
Poondinna (mt.), Austl. 113/F3
Poopó (lake), Bol. 147/C4
Poortugaal, Neth. 50/B5
Põõsapää (pt.), Est. 39/K2
Poosepatuck Ind. Res., NY, US 139/F2
Popayán, Col. 152/B4
Poperinge, Belg. 52/B2
Popigochic (riv.), Mex. 142/C2
Popilta (lake), Austl. 113/J5
Popio (lake), Austl. 115/B2
Poplar, Mt, US 127/G3
Poplar (riv.), Mb,On, Can. 122/G3
Poplar (isl.), Md, US 138/B6
Poplar Bluff, Mo, US 129/K3
Poplarville, Ms, US 133/F4
Popocatépetl (vol.), Mex. 143/L7
Popoli, It. 46/C1
Popovo, Bul. 49/H4
Poppberg (peak), Ger. 55/E4
Poppenhausen, Ger. 54/D2
Poppenhausen, Ger. 54/C2
Poppi, It. 59/E5
Poprad, Slvk. 41/L4
Poprad (riv.), Slvk. 41/L4
Poranga, Braz. 154/B2
Porangatu, Braz. 151/J6
Porbandar, India 89/J4
Porcari, It. 58/D5
Porce (riv.), Col. 152/C3
Porcheville, Fr. 30/H5
Porcia, It. 59/F1
Porcuna, Sp. 44/C4
Porcupine (riv.), Can.,US 134/K2
Porcupine Gorge NP, Austl. 114/B3
Porcupine Plain, Sk, Can. 127/H2
Pordenone (prov.), It. 59/F2
Pordenone, It. 59/F1
Pordim, Bul. 49/G4
Pore, Col. 152/D3
Poreč, Cro. 59/G2
Poretta (int'l arpt.), Fr. 46/A1
Pori (int'l arpt.), Fin. 39/J1
Pori, Fin. 39/J1
Porirua, NZ 117/S11
Porlezza, It. 57/F5
Pornic, Fr. 42/B3
Porongurup NP, Austl. 112/C5
Póros, Gre. 47/H4
Porpoise (bay), Ant. 160/J
Porrentruy, Swi. 56/D3
Porretta Terme, It. 59/D4
Porriño, Sp. 44/A1
Porsangen (inlet), Nor. 37/H1
Porsgrunn, Nor. 38/C2
Porsuk (riv.), Turk. 90/B2
Port (isl.), Japan 77/H6
Port Alberni, BC, Can. 126/B3
Port Albert, Austl. 115/C3
Port Alexander, Ak, US 134/M4
Port Alfred, SAfr. 106/D4
Port Alice, BC, Can. 126/B3
Port Angeles, Wa, US 126/C3
Port Antonio, Jam. 145/G2
Port Appin, Sc, UK 36/A3
Port Arthur, Tx, US 129/J5
Port au Choix, Nf, Can. 131/K1
Port-au-Prince (cap.), Haiti 145/H2
Port Augusta, Austl. 113/H5
Port Bannatyne, Sc, UK 36/A5
Port Blair, India 83/F5
Port Blakely, Wa, US 135/C2
Port Bolivar, Tx, US 132/E4
Port-Bouët, C.d'Iv. 102/E5
Port Bouet (Abidgan) (int'l arpt.), C.d'Iv. 102/E5
Port Broughton, Austl. 113/H5
Port Canning, India 85/G4
Port Carbon, Pa, US 138/B2
Port Charlotte, Fl, US 133/H5
Port Chester, NY, US 139/L8
Port Clements, BC, Can. 134/M5
Port Clinton, Oh, US 130/D3
Port Clinton, Pa, US 138/B2
Port Colborne, On, Can. 131/R10
Port Columbus (int'l arpt.), Oh, US 130/D4
Port Davey (har.), Austl. 115/C4
Port-de-Paix, Haiti 145/H2
Port Deposit, Md, US 138/B4
Port Dickson, Malay. 80/B3
Port Discovery (bay), Wa, US 135/B1
Port Douglas, Austl. 114/B2
Port Edward, BC, Can. 134/M4
Port Elgin, On, Can. 130/D2

218

Punta – Raven

Punta Gorda (bay), Nic. 140/E5
Punta Gorda, Belz. 144/D2
Punta Marina, It. 59/F4
Punta Raisi (int'l arpt.), It. 46/C3
Punta Umbría, Sp. 44/B4
Puntarenas, CR 145/E4
Puolo (pt.), Hi, US 124/S10
Pupiales, Col. 152/B4
Pupuya (peak), Bol. 156/D4
Puquio, Peru 156/C4
Pur (riv.), Rus. 64/H3
Puracé (vol.), Col. 152/B4
Puracé, PN, Col. 150/C3
Pūranpur, India 84/C1
Purbeck (isl.), Eng, UK 32/D5
Purcell (mts.), BC, Can. 126/D3
Purcell, Ok, US 129/H4
Puré (riv.), Col. 152/D5
Purén, Chile 158/B3
Purgatoire (riv.), Co, US 129/G3
Pürgen, Ger. 57/G1
Purgstall an der Erlauf, Aus. 43/L2
Purī, India 82/D3
Purificación, Col. 152/C4
Purikari (pt.), Est. 39/L2
Purkersdorf, Aus. 49/N7
Purmerend, Neth. 50/B3
Pūrna, India 82/C4
Purnia, India 85/F3
Purranque, Chile 157/B5
Puruê (riv.), Braz. 152/D5
Purūlia, India 85/F4
Puruni (riv.), Guy. 153/G3
Purús (riv.), Braz. 147/C3
Purushottampur, India 82/D4
Pŭrvomay, Bul. 47/J1
Purwa, India 84/C2
Purwokerto, Indo. 80/C5
Pusad, India 82/C4
Pusan, SKor. 71/N4
Pusan-Gwangyŏksi (prov.), SKor. 74/A3
Pusat Gayo (mts.), Indo. 80/A3
Puschendorf, Ger. 54/D3
Pushkin, Rus. 61/T7
Püspökladány, Hun. 48/E2
Pusur (riv.), Bang. 85/G4
Putaendo, Chile 158/C2
Putian, China 79/C2
Putina, Peru 156/D4
Puting (cape), Indo. 80/D4
Putla de Guerrero, Mex. 144/B2
Putomayo (dept.), Col. 152/C4
Putorana (mts.), Rus. 64/K3
Putrachoique (peak), Arg. 158/C4
Putre, Chile 156/D5
Puttalam, SrL. 82/C6
Putte, Belg. 53/D1
Puttelange-aux-Lacs, Fr. 53/F5
Putten, Neth. 50/C4
Putten (isl.), Neth. 50/B5
Püttlach (riv.), Ger. 55/E3
Püttlingen, Ger. 53/F5
Putu (range), Libr. 102/C5
Putumayo (riv.), SAm. 152/C5
Putumayo (riv.), SAm. 147/B3
Putussibau, Indo. 80/D3
Puu Kukui (peak), Hi, US 124/T10
Puu Moaulanui (peak), Hi, US 124/T10
Puu o Mahuka Heiau State Mon., Hi, US 124/V12
Puuanahulu, Hi, US 124/U11
Puuiki, Hi, US 124/T10
Puula (lake), Fin. 39/M1
Puurs, Belg. 53/D1
Puuwai, Hi, US 124/R10
Puy de Sancy (peak), Fr. 42/E4
Puyallup, Wa, US 126/C4
Puyallup (riv.), Wa, US 135/C3
Puyallup Ind. Res., Wa, US 135/C3
Puyang, China 72/C4
Puyehué (lake), Chile 158/B4
Puyehue (vol.), Chile 158/B4
Puylaurens, Fr. 42/E5
Puymorens, Col de (pass), Fr. 42/D5
Puyŏ, SKor. 73/D4
Puyo, Ecu. 152/B5
Puzal, Sp. 45/E3
Pwani (pol. reg.), Tanz. 104/C4
Pwllheli, Wal, UK 34/D6
Pyandzh (riv.), Taj. 87/F5
Pyaozero (lake), Rus. 37/J2
Pyapon, Myan. 83/G4
Pyasina (riv.), Rus. 64/J2
Pyatigorsk, Rus. 63/G3
Pyfara (peak), Fr. 42/F4
Pyhä-Häkin NP, Fin. 60/E3
Pyhäjärvi, Fin. 60/E3
Pyhäjärvi (lake), Fin. 39/K1
Pyhäntä, Fin. 60/E2
Pyhätunturi (peak), Fin. 60/E2
Pyinmana, Myan. 83/G4
P'yŏngan-bukto (prov.), NKor. 73/C2
P'yŏngan-namdo (prov.), NKor. 73/C3
P'yŏngch'ang, SKor. 73/E4
P'yŏnggang, NKor. 73/D3
P'yŏnghae, SKor. 73/E4
P'yŏngsan, NKor. 73/D3
P'yŏngsong, NKor. 73/C3
Pyŏngt'aek, SKor. 73/D4
P'yŏngyang (int'l arpt.), NKor. 73/C3
P'yŏngyang (cap.), NKor. 73/C3
P'yŏngyang-si (prov.), NKor. 73/C3
Pyŏnsanbando NP, SKor. 73/D5
Pyramid (lake), Nv, US 128/B3
Pyramid (mtn.), BC, Can. 134/M4
Pyramids Of Jīzah, Egypt 91/B5
Pyrenees (mts.), Fr.,Sp. 27/D4
Pyrénées Occidental, PN des, Fr. 42/C5
Pyryatyn, Ukr. 62/E2
Pyrzyce, Pol. 41/H2
Pyshma (riv.), Rus. 61/Q4
Pyu, Myan. 83/G4
Pyuthān, Nepal 84/D1

Q

Qā 'al Jafr (salt pan), Jor. 91/E4
Qabalān, WBnk. 91/G7
Qabātiyah, WBnk. 91/G7
Qābis, Tun. 96/H1
Qābis (gov.), Tun. 99/H2
Qadima, Isr. 91/F7
Qādirpur Rān, Pak. 86/A4
Qā'en, Iran 89/G2
Qafa e Malit (pass), Alb. 47/G1
Qaffīn, WBnk. 91/G7
Qafṣah, Tun. 96/G1
Qafṣah (gov.), Tun. 99/H2
Qahar Youyi Qianqi, China 72/C2
Qahar Youyi Zhongqi, China 72/C2
Qaidam (basin), China 70/F4
Qalansuwa, Isr. 91/F7
Qal'at Al Andalus, Tun. 46/B4
Qal'at Dizah, Iraq 90/F2
Qal'eh-ye Now, Afg. 87/D6
Qalqīlyah, WBnk. 91/F7
Qalyūb, Egypt 91/B4
Qamdo, China 70/G5
Qamīnis, Libya 96/K1
Qapshagay Bögeni (res.), Kaz. 87/G4
Qapshaghay, Kaz. 87/G4
Qaraghandy, Kaz. 87/F3
Qaraghandy (obl.), Kaz. 87/F3
Qaratau, Kaz. 87/F4
Qaratau Zhotasy (mts.), Kaz. 87/E4
Qareh Chāy (riv.), Iran 88/E2
Qareh Sū (riv.), Iran 63/H5
Qarqan (riv.), China 70/E4
Qarrit (pass), Alb. 47/G2
Qarshi, Uzb. 87/E5
Qarūn (lake), Egypt 101/B2
Qashqadaryo (pol. reg.), Uzb. 87/D5
Qaṣr-e Qand, Iran 89/H3
Qaṣr-e-Shīrīn, Iran 88/E2
Qaṣr Hallāl, Tun. 46/B5
Qa'ṭabah, Yem. 88/D6
Qatar (ctry.) 88/F3
Qattara (depr.), Egypt 90/A4
Qaṭṭīnah, Buḥayrat (lake), Syria 91/E2
Qaydaq Sory (swamp), Kaz. 63/K3
Qayyārah, Iraq 90/E3
Qazaqtyng Usaqshoqylyghy (uplands), Kaz. 64/H5
Qāzi Ahmad, Pak. 82/A2
Qazvīn, Iran 88/F1
Qedma, Isr. 91/F8
Qendrevica (peak), Alb. 47/F2
Qezel Owzan (riv.), Iran 88/E1
Qi Xian, China 72/C4
Qian (mts.), China 73/B2
Qian (riv.), China 72/D5
Qian'an, China 71/M3
Qianxi, China 72/J6
Qianyang, China 79/B2
Qiaojia, China 83/H2
Qibyā, Isr. 91/G8
Qidong, China 83/K2
Qidong, China 72/L8
Qiemo, China 70/E4
Qihe, China 72/D3
Qijiang, China 79/A2
Qikiqtarjuaq, Nun., Can. 123/K2
Qila Dīdār Singh, Pak. 86/C3
Qila Sobha Singh, Pak. 86/C3
Qilian (peak), China 70/G4
Qilian (mts.), China 67/J6
Qimantag (mts.), China 70/F4
Qimen, China 79/C2
Qin (mts.), China 72/B4
Qinā (gov.), Egypt 101/C3
Qing (riv.), China 79/B1
Qing'an, China 71/N2
Qingdao, China 72/E3
Qingfeng, China 72/C4
Qinghai (mts.), China 70/G4
Qinghai (prov.), China 70/G4
Qinghe, China 72/C3
Qinglong, China 72/D2
Qingpu, China 72/L8
Qingshui (riv.), China 79/A2
Qingshuihe, China 72/B3
Qingyuan, China 83/K3
Qingyun, China 72/D3
Qingzhou, China 72/D3
Qinhuangdao, China 72/D3
Qinshui, China 72/C4
Qinyang, China 72/C4
Qinyuan, China 72/C3
Qinzhou, China 83/J3
Qionghai, China 83/K4
Qionglai (mts.), China 70/H5
Qiongshan, China 83/K4
Qiongzhong, China 78/E2
Qiqihar, China 71/M2
Qira, China 70/D4
Qiryat Ata, Isr. 91/G6
Qiryat Bialik, Isr. 91/G6
Qiryat Gat, Isr. 91/D4
Qiryat Mal'akhi, Isr. 91/F8
Qiryat Motzkin, Isr. 91/G6
Qiryat Shemona, Isr. 91/D3
Qiryat Tiv'on, Isr. 91/G6
Qiryat Yam, Isr. 91/G6
Qitai, China 70/E3
Qitaihe, China 71/P2
Qixia, China 72/E3
Qixing (riv.), China 65/P5
Qizilqum (des.), Kaz. 64/G5
Qogir (peak), China 89/L1
Qom (riv.), Iran 88/F2
Qom, Iran 88/F2
Qomsheh, Iran 88/F2
Qondūz (riv.), Afg. 89/J1
Qonggyai, China 85/H1
Qoraqalpoghiston Aut. Rep., Uzb. 63/L3
Qormi, Malta 46/L7
Qorveh, Iran 88/E1
Qostanay (obl.), Kaz. 87/D2
Qostanay (int'l arpt.), Kaz. 61/P5
Qostanay, Kaz. 61/P5
Qotūr, Iran 90/F2
Qu (riv.), China 71/L6
Quabbin (res.), Ma, US 131/F3
Quairading, Austl. 112/C5
Quakenbrück, Ger. 51/E3
Quakertown, Pa, US 138/C3
Quambatook, Austl. 115/B2
Quanah, Tx, US 129/H4
Quanbao (mtn.), China 72/B4
Quang Ngai, Viet. 78/E3
Quang Tri, Viet. 78/D2
Quanjiao, China 72/D4
Quannan, China 79/B3
Quantocks, The (hills), Eng, UK 32/C4
Quanzhou, China 79/C3
Qu'appelle (dam), Sk, Can. 127/G3
Qu'Appelle (riv.), Sk, Can. 127/G3
Qu'appelle, Sk, Can. 127/H3
Quaqtaq, Qu, Can. 123/K2
Quaregnon, Belg. 52/C3
Quarles (mts.), Indo. 81/E4
Quarona, It. 58/B1
Quarrata, It. 59/D5
Quarryville, Pa, US 138/B4
Quarto d'Altino, It. 59/F1
Quartu Sant'Elena, It. 46/A3
Quartz Hill, Ca, US 133/B1
Quatre Bornes, Mrts. 107/T15
Quattervals (peak), Swi. 57/G4
Quba, Azer. 63/J4
Qūchān, Iran 89/G1
Queanbeyan, Austl. 115/D2
Québec (int'l arpt.), Qu, Can. 131/G2
Québec (cap.), Qu, Can. 131/G2
Québec (prov.), Can. 123/J3
Quebra-Cangalha, Serra (mts.), Braz. 211/H8
Quecholac, Mex. 143/M8
Quechutenango, Mex. 143/M8
Quedal (pt.), Chile 158/B4
Queen Alia (int'l arpt.), Jor. 91/E4
Queen Anne, Md, US 138/C6
Queen Annes (co.), Md, US 138/C5
Queen Charlotte, BC, Can. 134/M5
Queen Charlotte (isls.), BC, Can. 122/C3
Queen Charlotte (str.), BC, Can. 126/B3
Queen Charlotte (sound), BC, Can. 122/C3
Queen City, Tx, US 129/J4
Queen Creek, Az, US 137/S19
Queen Elizabeth (isls.), NW,Nun., Can. 123/Q7
Queen Mary (coast), Ant. 160/G
Queen Mary (res.), Eng, UK 30/B2
Queen Mary, Ca, US 136/F8
Queen Maud (gulf), Nun., Can. 122/F2
Queen Maud (mts.), Ant. 160/P
Queen Maud Land (phys. reg.), Ant. 160/Z
Queen Victoria Spring Nature Reserve, Austl. 112/D4
Queens (chan.), Nun., Can. 123/S7
Queens (co.), NY, US 139/E2
Queensberry (peak), Sc, UK 36/C6
Queensferry, Sc, UK 36/C5
Queensland, Austl. 115/B1
Queensland (state), Austl. 109/C3
Queenstown, Austl. 115/C4
Queenstown, SAfr. 106/D3
Queenstown, NZ 117/R12
Queenstown, Md, US 138/B6
Queich (riv.), Ger. 53/H5
Queidersbach, Ger. 53/G5
Queilén, Chile 158/B4
Queimada, Ilha (isl.), Braz. 151/H4
Queimadas, Braz. 154/D2
Queimadas, Braz. 154/C3
Quelimane, Moz. 105/G4
Queluz, Port. 45/P10
Quemado, Punta del (pt.), Cuba 145/H1
Quemú Quemú, Arg. 158/E3
Quepos, CR 145/E4
Quequén, Arg. 158/F3
Quequén Grande (riv.), Arg. 158/F3
Querecotillo, Peru 156/A2
Querétaro, Mex. 143/E4
Querétaro de Arteaga (state), Mex. 140/A5
Querimbas, Arquipélago das (arch.), Moz. 105/H3
Quero, It. 59/E1
Querobabi, Mex. 142/C2
Quesada, Sp. 44/D4
Quesada, CR 145/E4
Queshan, China 72/C4
Quesnel, BC, Can. 126/C2
Quesnel (lake), BC, Can. 122/D3
Quesnoy-sur-Deûle, Fr. 52/C2
Questa, NM, US 129/F3
Questembert, Fr. 42/B3
Quetigny, Fr. 56/B3
Quetta, Pak. 89/J2
Queulat, PN, Chile 158/B5
Quevedo, Ecu. 150/C4
Quevedo (riv.), Ecu. 152/B5
Quezaltenango, Guat. 144/D3
Quezon, Phil. 81/E2
Quezon City, Phil. 79/D5
Qufu, China 72/D4
Qui Nhon, Viet. 78/E3
Quibdó, Col. 152/B3
Quiberon, Fr. 42/B3
Quiberon (bay), Fr. 42/B3
Quíbor, Ven. 152/D2
Quicacha, Peru 156/C4
Quiçama, PN da, Ang. 105/B2
Quickborn, Ger. 51/G1
Quiers, Fr. 30/L6
Quierschied, Ger. 53/G5
Quila, Mex. 142/D3
Quilán (cape), Chile 158/B4
Quilca, Peru 156/C5
Quilcene, Wa, US 135/B2
Quiliano, It. 58/B3
Quilicura, Chile 158/N8
Quill (lakes), Sk, Can. 127/G2
Quillabamba, Peru 156/C4
Quillacollo, Bol. 150/E7
Quillagua (pt.), Chile 158/B4
Quillan, Fr. 42/E5
Quilleco, Chile 158/C3
Quillota, Chile 158/N8
Quilmaná, Peru 156/B4
Quilon, India 82/C6
Quilpie, Austl. 114/B4
Quilpué, Chile 158/N8
Quimilí, Arg. 157/D2
Quimper, Fr. 42/A2
Quimperlé, Fr. 42/B3
Quincey, Fr. 56/C2
Quincy, Wa, US 126/D4
Quincy, Fl, US 133/G4
Quincy, Ma, US 131/G3
Quincy-sous-Sénart, Fr. 30/K5
Quincy-Voisins, Fr. 30/L5
Quindío (dept.), Col. 152/A4
Quinhagak, Ak, US 134/F4
Quinn (riv.), Nv, US 128/C2
Quinns Rocks, Austl. 112/K6
Quintana de la Serena, Sp. 44/C3
Quintana Roo (state), Mex. 140/D4
Quintanar de la Orden, Sp. 44/D3
Quintanar del Rey, Sp. 44/E3
Quintero, Chile 158/N8
Quinto (riv.), Arg. 158/D2
Quinto, Sp. 45/E2
Quinto, Swi. 57/E4
Quinto di Treviso, It. 59/F1
Quinto di Valpantena, It. 59/E2
Quinton, NJ, US 138/C4
Quinzano d'Oglio, It. 58/C2
Quionga, Moz. 104/D5
Quipapá, Braz. 154/C3
Quirihue, Chile 158/B3
Quirindi, Austl. 115/D1
Quirinópolis, Braz. 155/B1
Quiriquire, Ven. 153/F2
Quiroga, Mex. 143/E5
Quiroga, Sp. 44/B1
Quiruvilca, Peru 156/B3
Quisiro, Ven. 152/D2
Quispamsis, NB, Can. 131/H2
Quissico, Moz. 105/F5
Quistello, It. 59/D3
Quitilipi, Arg. 157/D2
Quitman, Ga, US 133/H4
Quitman, Ms, US 133/F3
Quito (cap.), Ecu. 152/B5
Quixeramobim, Braz. 154/C2
Qujiang, China 83/K3
Qujing, China 83/H2
Qulaybīyah, Tun. 46/B4
Quogue, NY, US 139/F2
Quoich (riv.), Nun., Can. 122/G2
Quoich (lake), Sc, UK 36/A2
Quoile (riv.), NI, UK 34/C3
Quoin (pt.), SAfr. 106/L11
Quorn, Austl. 113/H5
Qŭqon, Uzb. 87/F4
Quranbāliyah, Tun. 46/B4
Qurbah, Tun. 46/B4
Qŭrghonteppa, Taj. 89/J1
Qurnat as Sawdā' (peak), Leb. 91/E2
Qūṣ, Egypt 101/C3
Qusmuryn Köli (lake), Kaz. 87/D2
Qusum, China 70/F6
Quṣūr As Sāf, Tun. 46/B5
Quttinirpaaq NP, Nun., Can. 123/T6
Quwo, China 72/B4
Quwu (mts.), China 70/H4
Quyang, China 72/C3
Quzhou, China 79/C2
Quzhou, China 72/C3
Qyzylorda, Kaz. 87/E4
Qyzylorda (obl.), Kaz. 87/D4

R

Raab (riv.), Aus. 43/L3
Raab, Aus. 55/G6
Raabs an der Thaya, Aus. 41/H4
Raahe, Fin. 60/E2
Raalte, Neth. 50/D4
Raamsdonk, Neth. 50/B5
Ra'anana, Isr. 91/F7
Raanes (pen.), Nun., Can. 123/S7
Rab (isl.), Cro. 48/B3
Rab, Cro. 48/B3
Rába (riv.), Hun. 48/C2
Rábahidvég, Hun. 43/M3
Rabat (cap.), Mor. 100/A2
Rabat, Malta 46/L7
Rabat (Sale) (int'l arpt.), Mor. 100/A2
Rabat (Victoria), Malta 46/L6
Rabbi (riv.), It. 43/K4
Rabgala (pass), China 85/F2
Rabil, CpV. 93/K10
Rabinal, Guat. 144/D3
Rabiusa (riv.), Swi. 57/F4
Rabka, Pol. 41/K4
Rabkavi-Banhatti, India 89/L5
Raby (pt.), On, Can. 131/S8
Racconigi, It. 43/G4
Raccoon (pt.), La, US 129/K5
Rach Gia (bay), Viet. 78/D4
Rach Gia, Viet. 78/D4
Racibórz, Pol. 41/K3
Racine (peak), Swi. 56/C3
Racine, Wi, US 127/M5
Racine (co.), Wi, US 135/P14
Rada Tilly, Arg. 158/D5
Radaur, India 86/D4
Rădăuţi, Rom. 49/G2
Radbuza (riv.), Czh. 40/G4
Radcliffe, Eng, UK 35/F4
Raddestorf, Ger. 51/F4
Rade de Caen (bay), Fr. 42/C2
Radeč (peak), Czh. 55/G3
Radevormwald, Ger. 51/E6
Radisson, Sk, Can. 126/G2
Radlett, Eng, UK 30/C2
Radnice, Czh. 55/G3
Radolfzell, Ger. 57/E2
Radom, Pol. 41/L3
Radomir, Bul. 47/H1
Radomsko, Pol. 41/K3
Radoviš, FYROM 47/H2
Radovljica, Slov. 43/L3
Radøy (isl.), Nor. 38/A1
Radstadt, Aus. 43/K3
Radviliškis, Lith. 39/K4
Radwā, Jabal (peak), SAr. 88/C4
Radziejów, Pol. 41/K2
Radzymin, Pol. 41/L2
Radzyń Podlaski, Pol. 41/M3
Rae (isth.), Nun., Can. 123/H2
Rae (riv.), Nun., Can. 122/E2
Rāe Bareli, India 84/C2
Rae-Edzo, NW, Can. 122/E2
Raeford, NC, US 133/J3
Raeren, Belg. 53/F2
Raesfeld, Ger. 50/D5
Raeside (lake), Austl. 112/D4
Rafael J. García, Mex. 143/M7
Rafael Núñez (int'l arpt.), Col. 152/C2
Rafaela, Arg. 157/D3
Rafaḥ, Gaza 91/D4
Rafai, CAfr. 97/K7
Rafīdīyah, WBnk. 91/G7
Rafiganj, India 85/E3
Rafína, Gre. 47/P8
Rafsanjān, Iran 89/G2
Raft (riv.), Id, US 126/E5
Rafz, Swi. 57/E2
Ragang (mt.), Phil. 81/F2
Ragged (mt.), Austl. 112/D5
Ragged (pt.), Chile 159/B7
Rāghugarh, India 84/A3
Raghunāthpur, India 85/F4
Rago NP, Nor. 37/E2
Ragstone (range), Eng, UK 30/D3
Ragusa, It. 46/D4
Rāhatgarh, India 84/B4
Rahden, Ger. 51/F4
Rahīmyār Khān, Pak. 86/A5
Rahole Nat'l Rsv., Kenya 104/C2
Råholt, Nor. 38/D1
Rāhuri, India 82/B4
Rahway, NJ, US 139/H9
Raiatea (isl.), FrPol. 117/K6
Raichūr, India 82/C4
Raiganj, India 85/G3
Raigarh, India 84/D5
Raikot, India 86/C4
Railroad, Pa, US 138/B4
Railroad Canyon (res.), Ca, US 136/C3
Rainbach im Mühlkreis, Aus. 55/H5
Rainbow, Austl. 115/B2
Rainbow (valley), Az, US 137/R19
Rainbow, Ca, US 136/C4
Rainbow Beach, Austl. 114/D4
Rainbow Bridge Nat'l Mon., Ut, US 128/E3
Rainier (mt.), Wa, US 126/C4
Rainsville, Al, US 133/G3
Rainy (lake), On, Can. 122/G4
Rainy Lake (riv.), US,Can. 127/K3
Rainy River, On, Can. 127/K3
Raipur, India 82/D3
Rairoa (atoll), FrPol. 117/L6
Raisdorf, Ger. 38/D4
Raisen, India 84/A4
Rāisinghnagar, India 86/B5
Raisio, Fin. 39/K1
Raismes, Fr. 52/C3
Raivavae (isl.), FrPol. 117/L7
Rāiwind, Pak. 86/C4
Raizeux, Fr. 30/H6
Rāja Gāngpur, India 85/E4
Raja (pt.), Indo. 80/A3
Rāja Jang, Pak. 86/C4
Rājahmundry, India 82/D4
Rajampet, India 82/C5
Rajang (riv.), Malay. 80/D3
Rājanpur, Pak. 86/A5
Rājaori, India 86/C3
Rājapālaiyam, India 82/C6
Rājāpur, India 84/C3
Rājāpur, India 89/K5
Rājasthān (state), India 82/B2
Rājbirāj, Nepal 85/F2
Rājgarh, India 84/A2
Rājgarh, India 86/C5
Rājgarh, India 89/L4
Rājgir, India 85/E3
Rajka, Hun. 48/C1
Rājkot, India 89/K4
Rājmahal (hills), India 85/F3
Rājmahāl, India 85/F3
Rājpur, India 85/G4
Rājpura, India 86/D4
Rājshāhi (pol. reg.), Bang. 85/G3
Rājshāhi (pol. div.), Bang. 85/G3
Rājshāhi, Bang. 85/G3
Rājula, India 89/K4
Raka (riv.), China 85/F1
Rakahanga (isl.), CookIs. 117/J5
Rakamaz, Hun. 48/E1
Rakaposhi (peak), Pak. 86/C1
Rakhine (div.), Myan. 70/F8
Rakhine (state), Myan. 83/F4
Rakhshān (riv.), Pak. 89/H3
Rakkestad, Nor. 38/D2
Rakos-patak (riv.), Hun. 49/R9
Rakovnicky Potok (riv.), Czh. 55/G2
Rakovník, Czh. 55/G2
Rakovski, Bul. 47/J1
Rakushechnyy (cape), Kaz. 87/B4
Rakvere, Est. 39/M2
Raldon, It. 59/E2
Raleigh (cap.), NC, US 133/J3
Raleigh-Durham (int'l arpt.), NC, US 133/J3
Ralik Chain (isls.), Mrsh. 116/F4
Ralingen, Ger. 53/F4
Ralston, Ab, Can. 126/F3
Rām Allāh, Isr. 91/G8
Ramalho, Serra do (mts.), Braz. 151/K6
Ramapo (riv.), NJ, US 138/J7
Ramapo (mts.), NJ, US 139/H7
Ramat Gan, Isr. 91/F7
Ramat Hasharon, Isr. 91/F7
Rambervillers, Fr. 56/C1
Rame (pt.), Eng, UK 32/B6
Ramenskoye, Rus. 61/X9
Rāmeswaram, India 82/C6
Rāmgangā (riv.), India 84/B1
Rāmgarh, India 85/E4
Rāmhormoz, Iran 88/E2
Ramírez, Mex. 143/M7
Rāmjībanpur, India 85/F4
Ramla, Isr. 91/F8
Ramlu (peak), Erit. 88/D6
Ramme, Den. 38/C3
Rammūn, Isr. 91/G8
Rāmnagar, India 84/B1
Rāmnagar, India 84/D3
Rāmnagar, India 86/C3
Ramnäs, Swe. 38/G2
Ramonchamp, Fr. 56/C2
Ramor (lake), Ire. 34/A4
Ramos (riv.), Mex. 132/B5
Ramosch, Swi. 57/G4
Rampart, Ak, US 134/H2
Rampillon, Fr. 30/M6
Rāmpur, India 84/B1
Rāmpur, India 86/D4
Rāmpur Hāt, India 85/F3
Rāmpura Phūl, India 86/C4
Ramree (isl.), Myan. 83/F4
Rāmsanehīghāt, India 84/C2
Ramsbottom, Eng, UK 35/F4
Ramsden Heath, Eng, UK 30/E2
Ramsen, Swi. 57/E2
Ramsey (lake), On, Can. 130/D2
Ramsey (isl.), Wal, UK 32/A3
Ramsey, NJ, US 139/J7
Ramsey, IM, UK 34/D3
Ramsey (bay), IM, UK 34/D3
Ramsgate, Eng, UK 33/H4
Ramstein-Miesenbach, Ger. 53/G5
Ramu (riv.), PNG 116/D5
Rana, Nor. 37/E2
Rānāghāt, India 85/G4
Rancagua, Chile 158/N9
Rance (riv.), Fr. 42/E5
Rancharia, Braz. 155/B2
Rancheria (riv.), Col. 152/C2
Rānchī, India 85/E4
Rancho Palos Verdes, Ca, US 136/F8
Rancho Santa Fe, Ca, US 136/C4
Ranchos, Arg. 158/F2
Ranco (lake), Chile 158/B4
Rancocas, NJ, US 138/D4
Rancul, Arg. 158/D2
Randaberg, Nor. 38/A2
Randallstown, Md, US 138/B5
Randalstown, NI, UK 34/B2
Randazzo, It. 46/D4
Randburg, SAfr. 106/P13
Randers, Den. 38/D3
Randolph, NJ, US 138/D2
Randow (riv.), Ger. 41/H2
Randsfjorden (lake), Nor. 38/D1
Råneå, Swe. 60/D2
Rang (peak), Thai. 78/C2
Rang-du-Fliers, Fr. 52/A3
Rangāmāti (pol. reg.), Bang. 85/H4
Rangāmāti, Bang. 83/F3
Rangasa (cape), Indo. 81/E4
Rangely, Co, US 128/E2
Ranger, Tx, US 129/H4
Rangia, India 85/H2
Rangiora, NZ 117/S11
Rangiroa (isl.), FrPol. 117/L6
Rangoon (Yangon) (cap.), Myan. 83/G4
Rangpur, Bang. 85/G3
Rangpur (pol. reg.), Bang. 85/G3
Rangsdorf, Ger. 40/Q7
Rānībennur, India 89/L6
Rānīganj, India 85/F4
Rānīkhet, India 84/B1
Rānīpur, India 84/B3
Rankin, Tx, US 129/G5
Rankin Inlet, Nun., Can. 122/G2
Rankweil, Aus. 57/F3
Rannoch (lake), Sc, UK 36/B3
Ranohira, Madg. 107/H8
Ranomafana, Madg. 107/H8
Ranong, Thai. 78/B4
Ranotsara, Madg. 107/H8
Ransbach-Baumbach, Ger. 53/G3
Ransomville, NY, US 131/S9
Ranst, Belg. 50/B6
Ranstadt, Ger. 54/B2
Rantabe, Madg. 107/J6
Rantekombola (peak), Indo. 81/F4
Rantigny, Fr. 52/B5
Rantīs, WBnk. 91/G7
Rantoul, Il, US 127/L5
Rantsila, Fin. 60/E2
Ranzan, Japan 77/C1
Rao Co (peak), Laos 78/D2
Raon-l'Étape, Fr. 56/C1
Raoping, China 79/C3
Raoui, 'Erg er (des.), Alg. 98/E3
Raoul (isl.), NZ 116/H7
Raoyang (riv.), China 73/A2
Raoyang, China 72/C3
Rapa (isl.), FrPol. 117/L7
Rapallo, It. 58/C4
Rapel (lake), Chile 158/N9
Rapid City, SD, US 127/H4
Rappahannock (riv.), Va, US 130/E4
Rapper (cape), Chile 158/B5
Rāpti (zone), Nepal 84/D1
Rapti (riv.), India 82/D2
Rara NP, Nepal 84/D1
Raritan (bay), NJ, US 138/D3
Raritan (riv.), NJ, US 138/D2
Raritan, South Branch (riv.), NJ, US 138/D2
Raron, Swi. 56/D5
Rarotonga (isl.), CookIs. 117/J7
Ra's al 'Ayn, Syria 90/E2
Ra's Al Basīt (pt.), Syria 91/D2
Ra's Al Jabal, Tun. 46/B4
Ra's al Khaymah, UAE 89/G3
Ra's al Unūf, Libya 97/J7
Ra's An Naqb, Jor. 91/D5
Ra's aṭ Ṭīb (Cape Bon) (cape), Tun. 46/B4
Ras Dashen (peak), Eth. 97/N5
Râs el Ma, Alg. 100/D2
Râs el Oued, Alg. 100/F5
Ras il-Qammieħ (pt.), Malta 46/L7
Ras San Dimitri (pt.), Malta 46/L6
Ra's Ṣawqirah (pt.), Oman 89/G5
Rasa (pt.), Arg. 158/E4
Raschau, Ger. 55/F1
Rashaant, Mong. 70/F2
Rasharkin, NI, UK 34/B2
Rāshayyā, Leb. 91/D3
Rashīd, Egypt 91/B4
Rasht, Iran 88/E1
Raška, Serb. 47/G1
Rasmussen (basin), Nun., Can. 122/G2
Raso (cape), Port. 45/P10
Rason (lake), Austl. 109/B3
Rasrā, India 84/D3
Rassina, It. 59/E5
Rasskazovo, Rus. 63/G1
Rastatt, Ger. 54/B5
Rastede, Ger. 51/F2
Rasūlnagar, Pak. 86/B3
Rat (isls.), Ak, US 134/B6
Rat Buri, Thai. 78/B3
Rata (cape), Indo. 80/B5
Ratak Chain (isls.), Mrsh. 116/F3
Ratangarh, India 89/K3
Ratanpur, India 84/D4
Rāth, India 84/B3
Rathbun (lake), Ia, US 127/K5
Rathcoole, Ire. 34/B5
Rathdowney, Ire. 31/Q10
Rathdrum, Ire. 34/B6
Rathedaung, Myan. 83/F3
Rathenow, Ger. 40/G2
Rathfriland, NI, UK 34/B3
Rathkeale, Ire. 31/P10
Rathlin (isl.), NI, UK 34/B1
Rathlin (sound), NI, UK 34/B1
Rathluirc, Ire. 31/P10
Rathmore, Ire. 31/P10
Rathnew, Ire. 34/B6
Ratia, India 86/C5
Ratingen, Ger. 50/D6
Ratlām, India 89/L4
Ratnāgiri, India 89/K5
Ratnapura, SrL. 82/D6
Ratoath, Ire. 34/B4
Raton, NM, US 129/F3
Rattray (pt.), Sc, UK 36/E1
Rättvik, Swe. 38/G1
Raub, Malay. 80/B3
Rauch, Arg. 158/F3
Raudales Malpaso, Mex. 144/C2
Raudhinúpur (pt.), Ice. 37/P6
Raufarhöfn, Ice. 37/P6
Raufoss, Nor. 38/D1
Rauhe Ebrach (riv.), Ger. 54/D3
Raul Soares, Braz. 155/D2
Rauma, Fin. 39/J1
Raunheim, Ger. 54/B2
Raurkela, India 85/E4
Rausu, Japan 76/D1
Rautjärvi, Fin. 39/N1
Ravanusa, It. 46/C4
Rāvar, Iran 89/G2
Ravarino, It. 59/E3
Ravels, Belg. 50/B6
Ravenna, It. 59/F4
Ravenna (prov.), It. 59/E4

Roca – Sacra

Roca, Cabo da (cape), Port. 45/P10
Roca Partida (isl.), Mex. 142/B5
Roca Partida, Punta (pt.), Mex. 144/C2
Rocafuerte, Ecu. 152/A5
Rocas (isl.), Braz. 151/M4
Rocca San Casciano, It. 59/E4
Roccabianca, It. 58/D2
Roccastrada, It. 43/J5
Rocciamelone (peak), It. 43/G4
Rocha, Uru. 159/G2
Rocha (dept.), Uru. 159/G2
Rochdale, Eng, UK 35/F4
Rochdale (co.), Eng, UK 35/F4
Roche, Swi. 56/C5
Roche du Sapin Sec (peak), Fr. 56/C1
Roche-lez-Beaupré, Fr. 56/C3
Rochefort, Fr. 42/C4
Rochefort, Belg. 53/E3
Rochelle Park, NJ, US 139/J8
Rochers du Bourbet (peak), Fr. 56/C3
Rochester, Austl. 115/C3
Rochester, Mn, US 127/K4
Rochester, NY, US 130/E3
Rochester, In, US 130/C3
Rochester, NH, US 131/G3
Rochester, Eng, UK 33/G4
Rochester, Mi, US 135/F6
Rochester, Wi, US 135/P14
Rochford, Eng, UK 30/F2
Rock (riv.), Ia,Mo, US 129/H2
Rock (riv.), Il, US 125/J3
Rock Creek, Yk, Can. 134/L3
Rock Forest, Qu, Can. 131/G2
Rock Glen, Pa, US 138/B2
Rock Hall, Md, US 138/B5
Rock Hill, SC, US 133/H3
Rock Island, Il, US 127/L5
Rock Springs, Wy, US 126/F5
Rockall (isl.), UK 27/C3
Rockaway (riv.), NJ, US 138/D2
Rockaway, NJ, US 138/D2
Rockaway (pt.), NY, US 139/K9
Rockaway (inlet), NY, US 139/K9
Rockdale, Il, US 135/P17
Rockefeller (plat.), Ant. 160/R
Rockenhausen, Ger. 53/G4
Rockford, Il, US 127/L5
Rockglen, Sk, Can. 127/G3
Rockhampton, Austl. 114/C3
Rockingham, NC, US 133/J3
Rockingham, Austl. 112/K7
Rockland, On, Can. 130/F2
Rockland, Me, US 131/G2
Rockland (co.), NY, US 138/D1
Rockland Lake, NY, US 139/K7
Rocklands (res.), Austl. 109/D4
Rockledge, Fl, US 133/H4
Rockledge, Pa, US 138/C3
Rockport, Tx, US 132/D4
Rocks, Md, US 138/B4
Rocksprings, Tx, US 129/G5
Rockstone, Guy. 153/G3
Rockville, Md, US 130/E4
Rockville Centre, NY, US 139/L9
Rockwall, Tx, US 129/H4
Rockwood, Tn, US 133/G3
Rocky (mtn.), Ky, US 130/D4
Rocky (mts.), Can.,US 119/E4
Rocky (pt.), NY, US 139/F1
Rocky Cape NP, Austl. 115/C4
Rocky Harbour, Nf, Can. 131/K1
Rocky Island (lake), On, Can. 130/D2
Rocky Mount, NC, US 133/J3
Rocky Mountain House, Ab, Can. 126/E2
Rocky Mountain NP, Co, US 128/F2
Rocroi, Fr. 53/D4
Rodach (riv.), Ger. 55/E2
Rodach bei Coburg, Ger. 54/D2
Rodalben, Ger. 53/G5
Rødberg, Nor. 38/C1
Rødbyhavn, Den. 38/D4
Roddickton, Nf, Can. 131/K1
Rødding, Den. 38/C4
Roden (riv.), Eng, UK 35/F6
Rodenbach, Ger. 53/G4
Rodeo, Mex. 142/D3
Rodeo, Ca, US 135/K10
Rödermark, Ger. 54/B3
Rodewisch, Ger. 55/F1
Rodez, Fr. 42/E4
Rodholívos, Gre. 47/H2
Ródhos (ruin), Gre. 90/B2
Ródhos (Rhodes), Gre. 90/B2
Rodigo, It. 58/D2
Roding (riv.), Eng, UK 30/D2
Roding, Ger. 55/F4
Rodinga (mt.), Austl. 113/G3
Rödinghausen, Ger. 51/F4
Rodoč, Bosn. 47/E1
Rodolfo Sánchez Toboada, Mex. 142/A2
Rodríguez, Uru. 159/K11
Roe (riv.), NI, UK 34/B2
Roebourne, Austl. 112/C2
Roebuck (bay), Austl. 109/B2
Roeland Park, Ks, US 137/D5
Roen (peak), It. 57/H5
Roer (riv.), Neth. 50/D6
Roermond, Neth. 50/C6
Roes Welcome Sound (str.), Nun., Can. 123/H2
Roeselare, Belg. 52/C2
Roesiger (lake), Wa, US 135/D2
Rogachev, Bela. 62/D1
Rogaland (co.), Nor. 37/C4
Rogaška Slatina, Slov. 43/L3
Rogatica, Bosn. 48/D4
Rogers (mt.), Va, US 130/D4
Rogers, Ar, US 129/J3
Rogers City, Mi, US 130/D2
Rogersville, Tn, US 130/D4
Roggwil, Swi. 56/D3
Rogliano, Fr. 43/H5
Roglio (riv.), It. 59/D5
Rognon (riv.), Fr. 42/F2
Rogoźno, Pol. 41/J2
Rogue (riv.), Or, US 128/B2
Rohl (riv.), Sudan 97/L6
Rohr, Ger. 55/E5
Rohrbach bei Mattersburg, Aus. 43/M3
Rohrbach in Oberösterreich, Aus. 55/G5
Rohrbach-lès-Bitche, Fr. 53/G5
Rohri, Pak. 89/J3
Röhrmoos, Ger. 55/E6
Rohtak, India 86/D5
Roi Et, Thai. 78/C2
Roine (lake), Fin. 39/L1
Roissy, Fr. 30/K5
Roissy-en-France, Fr. 30/K4
Rojas, Arg. 158/E2
Rojo (cape), PR 141/M8
Rojo, Cabo (cape), Mex. 144/B1
Rokan (riv.), Indo. 80/B3
Rokeby Croll Creek NP, Austl. 114/A1
Rokel (riv.), SLeo. 102/C4
Rokkasho, Japan 76/B3
Rokkō-san (peak), Japan 77/H6
Rokugō, Japan 77/A3
Rokycany, Czh. 55/G3
Rokytka (riv.), Czh. 55/H2
Rolampont, Fr. 56/B2
Rolândia, Braz. 155/B2
Rolava (riv.), Czh. 55/F2
Rolde, Neth. 50/D3
Rolla, ND, US 127/J3
Rolla, BC, Can. 126/C2
Rolla, Mo, US 129/K3
Rolle, Swi. 56/C5
Rolling Fork, Ms, US 129/K4
Rolling Hills Estates, Ca, US 136/F8
Rolling Meadows, Il, US 135/P15
Rollingbay, Wa, US 135/B2
Rollinsville, Co, US 137/A3
Rolo, It. 59/D3
Rom (peak), Ugan. 104/B2
Roma, Austl. 114/C4
Roma, Swe. 38/H3
Roma (Rome) (cap.), It. 46/C2
Romagnano Sesia, It. 58/B1
Romagnat, Fr. 42/E4
Romain (cape), SC, US 133/J3
Romaine (riv.), Qu, Can. 123/K3
Roman, Bul. 47/H1
Roman, Rom. 49/H2
Romang (str.), Indo. 81/G5
Romang (isl.), Indo. 81/G5
Romania (ctry.) 49/F3
Romano Canavese, It. 58/A2
Romano, Cayo (isl.), Cuba 145/G1
Romano d'Ezzelino, It. 59/E1
Romano di Lombardia, It. 58/C1
Romans d'Isonzo, It. 59/G1
Romans-sur-Isère, Fr. 42/F4
Romanshorn, Swi. 57/F2
Romanzof (cape), Ak, US 134/E3
Rombas, Fr. 53/F5
Romblon, Phil. 81/F1
Rome, NY, US 130/F3
Rome, Ga, US 133/G3
Rome, Wi, US 135/N14
Romenay, Fr. 56/B4
Romeoville, Il, US 135/P16
Römhild, Ger. 54/D2
Romilly-sur-Seine, Fr. 42/E2
Rommani, Mor. 98/D2
Rommerskirchen, Ger. 53/F1
Romney Marsh (phys. reg.), Eng, UK 33/G4
Romny, Ukr. 62/E2
Rømø (isl.), Den. 40/E1
Romoland, Ca, US 136/C3
Romont, Swi. 56/C4
Romorantin-Lanthenay, Fr. 42/D3
Romsey, Eng, UK 33/E5
Rømskog, Nor. 38/D2
Ronald Reagan Washington National (int'l arpt.), DC, US 138/A6
Ronan, Mt, US 126/E4
Roncade, It. 59/F1
Roncador Cay (isl.), Col. 141/F5
Roncador, Serra do (mts.), Braz. 151/H6
Ronchamp, Fr. 56/C2
Ronchi dei Legionari (int'l arpt.), It. 59/G1
Ronchi dei Legionari, It. 59/G1
Ronciglione, It. 46/C1
Ronco (riv.), It. 59/F5
Ronco All'Adige, It. 59/E2
Ronco Scrivia, It. 58/B3
Roncoferraro, It. 59/D2
Roncq, Fr. 52/C2
Ronda, Sp. 44/C4
Rondane NP, Nor. 37/D3
Ronde, Tête (peak), Swi. 56/D5
Rondonópolis, Braz. 151/H7
Rong (riv.), China 83/J2
Rong Xian, China 83/K3
Rongcheng, China 73/K3
Rongcheng, China 72/G7
Ronge (lake), Sk, Can. 122/F3
Rongelap (isl.), Mrsh. 116/F3
Rongerik (isl.), Mrsh. 116/F3
Ronkonkoma, NY, US 139/E2
Rønne, Den. 38/F4
Ronne Ice Shelf, Ant. 160/W
Ronneby, Swe. 38/F3
Ronnenberg, Ger. 51/G4
Ronquerolles, Fr. 30/J4
Ronsard (cape), Austl. 112/B3
Ronsberg, Ger. 57/G2
Ronse, Belg. 52/C2
Ronuro (riv.), Braz. 151/H6
Roodeport, SAfr. 106/P13
Rooiberg (peak), Namb. 106/B2
Roorkee, India 82/C2
Roosendaal, Neth. 50/B5
Roosevelt, Ut, US 128/E2
Roosevelt (canal), Az, US 137/S19
Roosevelt (riv.), Braz. 147/C4
Roosevelt (mt.), BC, Can. 122/D3
Roosevelt, NJ, US 138/D3
Roosevelt (isl.), Ant. 160/N
Roosevelt, NY, US 139/L9
Root (mt.), Ak, US 134/L4
Root (riv.), Wi, US 135/P14
Root, West Branch (riv.), Wi, US 135/P14
Roque Pérez, Arg. 159/J11
Roquetas de Mar, Sp. 44/D4
Roraima (peak), Braz. 150/F2
Roraima (peak), Ven. 153/F3
Roraima (state), Braz. 153/F4
Rorke's Drift, SAfr. 107/E3
Rorke's Drift Battlesite, SAfr. 107/E3
Rorketon, Mb, Can. 127/J3
Røros, Nor. 37/D3
Rorschach, Swi. 57/F3
Rosa (cape), Alg. 100/L6
Rosà, It. 59/E1
Rosa (lake), Bahm. 145/H1
Rosa Punta (pt.), Mex. 142/C3
Rosa Zárate, Ecu. 152/B4
Rosablanche (peak), Swi. 56/D5
Rosal, Sp. 44/A2
Rosales, Mex. 132/B4
Rosamorada, Mex. 142/D4
Rosanna (riv.), Aus. 57/G3
Rosário, Braz. 154/A1
Rosario, Mex. 142/C3
Rosario, Mex. 142/D4
Rosario, Arg. 158/E2
Rosario, Uru. 159/K11
Rosario de la Frontera, Arg. 157/D2
Rosario del Tala, Arg. 159/J10
Rosário do Sul, Braz. 157/F3
Rosarito, Mex. 128/C4
Rosarno, It. 46/D3
Rosas, Col. 152/B4
Rosas, Golfo di (gulf), Sp. 45/G1
Rosate, It. 58/C2
Rosay, Fr. 30/G5
Rosbach vor der Höhe, Ger. 54/B2
Rosche, Ger. 51/H3
Roscoff, Fr. 42/B2
Roscommon, Ire. 31/P10
Roscrea, Ire. 31/Q10
Rosdorf, Ger. 51/G5
Rose (isl.), ASam. 117/J6
Rose (pt.), BC, Can. 134/M4
Rose Belle, Mrts. 107/T15
Roseau, Mn, US 127/K3
Roseau (riv.), Mn, US 127/J3
Roseau (cap.), Dom. 141/N9
Roseaux, Haiti 145/H2
Rosebery, Austl. 115/C4
Roseburg, Or, US 126/C5
Rosedale, Ms, US 129/K4
Rosedale, Il, US 137/F7
Rosedale, Md, US 138/B5
Rosehearty, Sc, UK 36/D1
Roseira, Braz. 211/H7
Roseland, NJ, US 139/H8
Roselette, Aiguille de (peak), Fr. 56/C6
Roselle, NJ, US 139/H9
Roselle, Il, US 135/P16
Roselle Park, NJ, US 139/H9
Rosemead, Ca, US 136/F7
Rosemère, Qu, Can. 131/N6
Rosenberg, Tx, US 129/J5
Rosenberg, Ger. 54/D4
Rosenfeld, Ger. 57/E1
Rosenhayn, NJ, US 138/C5
Rosenheim, Ger. 43/K3
Roses, Sp. 45/G1
Roseto, Pa, US 138/C2
Roseto degli Abruzzi, It. 43/L5
Rosetown, Sk, Can. 126/G3
Rosetta (riv.), Egypt 91/B4
Roseville, Mi, US 135/G6
Rosewood Heights, Il, US 137/G8
Rosh Ha'ayin, Isr. 91/F7
Rosh Hakarmel (pt.), Isr. 91/F6
Rosh Haniqra (pt.), Isr. 91/D3
Rosheim, Fr. 56/D1
Rosières-en-Santerre, Fr. 52/B4
Rosignano Marittimo, It. 58/D6
Roşiori de Vede, Rom. 49/G3
Roskilde, Den. 38/E4
Roskilde (co.), Den. 38/D4
Roslavl', Rus. 62/E1
Roslev, Den. 38/C3
Rosmalen, Neth. 50/C5
Rosmaninhal, Port. 44/B3
Rosneath, Sc, UK 36/B4
Rosny-sous-Bois, Fr. 30/K5
Rosolina, It. 59/F2
Rosolini, It. 46/D4
Rosporden, Fr. 42/B3
Rösrath, Ger. 53/G2
Ross (isl.), Ant. 160/M
Ross (sea), Ant. 160/P
Ross, Austl. 115/C4
Ross (isl.), Mb, Can. 127/J2
Ross (pt.), On, Can. 131/S8
Ross (dist.), Sc, UK 36/C1
Ross Ice Shelf, Ant. 160/N
Rossa (peak), It. 43/K3
Rossa, Swi. 57/F5
Rossall (pt.), Eng, UK 35/E4
Rossano Stazione, It. 46/E3
Rossano Veneto, It. 59/E1
Rossbach, Ger. 55/F5
Rossberg (peak), Fr. 56/D2
Rossdorf, Ger. 54/B3
Rossel (isl.), PNG 116/E6
Rosselange, Fr. 53/F5
Rosshaupten, Ger. 57/G2
Rossiglione, It. 58/B3
Rossignol (lake), NS, Can. 131/H2
Rosskeeragh (pt.), Ire. 31/P9
Rossland, BC, Can. 126/D3
Rosso, Mrta. 102/B2
Rossosh', Rus. 62/F2
Rossstock (peak), Swi. 57/E4
Rosstal, Ger. 54/D4
Rossville, Ok, US 137/N14
Røst, Nor. 37/E2
Rosthern, Sk, Can. 127/G2
Rostock, Ger. 38/E4
Rostov, Rus. 62/F3
Rostov, Rus. 60/H4
Rostov (int'l arpt.), Rus. 62/F3
Rostovskaya Oblast, Rus. 63/G2
Rostrenen, Fr. 42/B2
Rostrevor, NI, UK 34/B3
Roswell, NM, US 129/F4
Rot (riv.), Ger. 40/E4
Rota, Sp. 44/B4
Rota (isl.), NMar. 116/D3
Rote Wand (peak), Aus. 57/F3
Rotenburg, Ger. 51/G2
Rotenburg an der Fulda, Ger. 51/G7
Roter Main (riv.), Ger. 40/F3
Rötgen, Ger. 53/F2
Roth (riv.), Ger. 57/G1
Roth bei Nürnberg, Ger. 54/E4
Rothaargebirge (mts.), Ger. 51/F6
Rothau, Fr. 56/D1
Röthenbach an der Pegnitz, Ger. 54/E4
Rothenberg, Ger. 54/B3
Rothenburg, Swi. 57/E3
Rothenburg ob der Tauber, Ger. 54/D4
Rothera, UK, Ant. 160/V
Rotherham, Eng, UK 35/G5
Rotherham (co.), Eng, UK 35/G5
Rothes, Sc, UK 36/C1
Rothesay, Sc, UK 36/A5
Rotheux-Rimière, Belg. 53/E2
Rothschild, Wi, US 127/L4
Rothwell, Eng, UK 33/F2
Rothwell, Eng, UK 35/G4
Roti (isl.), Indo. 81/F6
Rotorua, NZ 117/T10
Rotselaar, Belg. 53/D2
Rott (riv.), Ger. 40/G4
Rott am Inn, Ger. 55/F7
Rottach-Egern, Ger. 40/F5
Rotte (riv.), Fr. 53/F6
Rotten (riv.), Swi. 56/E5
Rottenacker, Ger. 57/F1
Röttenbach, Ger. 54/E4
Rottenberg, Ger. 54/C2
Rottenburg am Neckar, Ger. 54/B6
Rottenburg an der Laaber, Ger. 55/F5
Rotterdam (int'l arpt.), Neth. 50/B5
Rotterdam, Neth. 50/B5
Rotthalmünster, Ger. 55/G6
Röttingen, Ger. 54/C3
Rottne, Swe. 38/F3
Rottnest (isl.), Austl. 112/B5
Rottofreno, It. 58/C2
Rottum (riv.), Ger. 57/F1
Rottumeroog (isl.), Neth. 50/D1
Rottumerplaat (isl.), Neth. 50/D1
Rottweil, Ger. 57/E1
Rotuma (isl.), Fiji 116/G6
Rötz, Ger. 55/F4
Roubaix, Fr. 52/C2
Roubion (riv.), Fr. 42/F4
Roudnice nad Labem, Czh. 55/H2
Rouen, Fr. 42/D2
Rouffach, Fr. 56/D2
Rouge (riv.), Qu, Can. 123/J4
Rouge, Middle (riv.), Mi, US 135/F7
Rougemont, Fr. 56/C3
Rougemont-le-Château, Fr. 56/C2
Rough (riv.), Ky, US 133/G2
Roullet-Saint-Estèphe, Fr. 42/D4
Round (hill), Pa, US 138/B3
Round Hill (pt.), Austl. 114/C4
Round Lake, Il, US 135/P15
Round Lake Beach, Il, US 135/P15
Round Lake Park, Il, US 135/P15
Round Rock, Tx, US 129/H5
Round Valley (res.), NJ, US 138/D2
Roundup, Mt, US 126/F4
Roundway (hill), Eng, UK 32/E4
Rousay (isl.), Sc, UK 31/V14
Rousies, Fr. 52/D3
Rousínov, Czh. 41/J4
Roussillon, Fr. 42/F4
Rouvres, Fr. 30/M4
Rouvroy, Belg. 53/E4
Rouxville, SAfr. 106/D3
Rouyn-Noranda, Qu, Can. 130/E1
Rovaniemi, Fin. 60/E2
Rovaniemi (int'l arpt.), Fin. 60/E2
Rovasenda, It. 58/B1
Rovato, It. 58/C1
Roverbella, It. 59/D2
Rovereto, It. 59/D3
Rovereto, It. 57/H6
Rovigo (prov.), It. 59/E2
Rovigo, It. 59/E2
Rovinj, Cro. 59/G2
Rovuma (riv.), Moz. 104/B5
Rowley (isl.), Nun., Can. 123/J2
Rowley Shoals (isl.), Austl. 109/A2
Roxa (isl.), GBis. 102/B4
Roxana, Il, US 137/G8
Roxas, Phil. 81/E1
Roxas, Phil. 81/F1
Roxas, Phil. 79/D4
Roxboro, NC, US 130/E4
Roxen (lake), Swe. 38/F2
Roxo (cape), Sen. 102/A3
Roy, NM, US 132/B3
Roy, Ut, US 137/J11
Roy, Wa, US 135/B3
Roya (riv.), Fr. 43/G5
Royal (canal), Ire. 35/B3
Royal Botanical Garden, On, Can. 131/Q9
Royal Chitwan NP, Nepal 85/E2
Royal Lakes, Il, US 137/H7
Royal Natal NP, SAfr. 106/E3
Royal NP, Austl. 115/D2
Royal NP, The, Austl. 114/H9
Royal Oak, Mi, US 135/F7
Royal Paekje Tombs, SKor. 73/D4
Royal Tombs, Viet. 78/D2
Royal Tunbridge Wells, Eng, UK 33/G4
Royale, Isle (isl.), Mi, US 127/L4
Royalton, Pa, US 138/B3
Royan, Fr. 42/C4
Roye, Fr. 56/C2
Roye, Fr. 52/B4
Royersford, Pa, US 138/C3
Røyken, Nor. 38/D2
Royston, Eng, UK 33/F2
Royston, Eng, UK 35/G4
Royton, Eng, UK 35/F4
Rožaj, Serb. 47/G1
Rozay-en-Brie, Fr. 52/B6
Rozenburg, Neth. 50/B5
Rozhaya (riv.), Rus. 61/W9
Rožmberk (lake), Czh. 55/H4
Rožmitál pod Třemšínem, Czh. 55/G3
Rožňava, Slvk. 41/L4
Roztoczański NP, Pol. 62/B2
Roztoczański PN, Pol. 41/M3
Roztoky, Czh. 55/H2
Rozzano, It. 58/C2
Rrëshen, Alb. 47/F2
Rt Kamenjak (cape), Cro. 48/A3
Rt Ploča (pt.), Cro. 48/B4
Rtishchevo, Rus. 63/G1
Ruacana (falls), Ang. 105/B4
Ruaha NP, Tanz. 104/B4
Ruapehu (vol.), NZ 117/T10
Rub' al Khali (des.), SAr. 67/D7
Rubelles, Fr. 30/L6
Rubeshibe, Japan 76/C2
Rubí, Sp. 45/L7
Rubidoux, Ca, US 136/C3
Rubiera, It. 59/D3
Rubigen, Swi. 56/D4
Rubim, Braz. 154/B5
Rubizhne, Ukr. 62/F2
Rubondo NP, Tanz. 104/A3
Řubřina (riv.), Czh. 55/G4
Ruby, Ak, US 134/G3
Ruby (lake), Nv, US 128/D2
Ruby (mts.), Nv, US 128/D2
Rubyvale, Austl. 114/B3
Rucheng, China 79/B2
Rucphen, Neth. 50/B5
Ruda Woda (lake), Pol. 41/K2
Rudall River NP, Austl. 112/D2
Rūdarpur, India 84/D2
Rudauli, India 84/C2
Rüdersdorf, Ger. 40/Q7
Rüdesheim, Ger. 53/G4
Rudiano, It. 58/C2
Rudkøbing, Den. 38/D4
Rudnik, Pol. 41/M3
Rūdnyy, Kaz. 61/P5
Rudolf (isl.), Rus. 64/F1
Rudolstadt, Ger. 43/J1
Rudong, China 72/E4
Rūdsar, Iran 88/F1
Rue, Swi. 56/C4
Rue (pt.), NI, UK 34/B1
Rue, Fr. 52/A3
Rueda, Sp. 44/C2
Rueil-Malmaison, Fr. 30/J5
Ruell (riv.), Sc, UK 36/A4
Ruelle-sur-Touvre, Fr. 42/D4
Ruen (peak), Bul. 48/F4
Ruetzbach (riv.), Aus. 57/H3
Ruffano, It. 47/F3
Ruffec, Fr. 42/D3
Rufiji (riv.), Tanz. 93/F5
Rufina, It. 59/E5
Rufino, Arg. 158/E2
Rufisque, Sen. 102/A3
Rugao, China 72/E4
Rugby, ND, US 127/J3
Rugby, Eng, UK 33/E2
Rugeley, Eng, UK 33/E1
Rügen (isl.), Ger. 38/E4
Ruggell, Lcht. 57/F3
Ruhmannsfelden, Ger. 55/F5
Ruhnu saar (isl.), Lat. 39/K3
Ruhr (riv.), Ger. 40/D3
Ruhr (reg.), Ger. 40/E3
Ruhrgebiet (phys. reg.), Ger. 50/D6
Ruhstorf an der Rott, Ger. 55/F5
Rui'an, China 79/D2
Ruicheng, China 72/B4
Ruidoso, NM, US 129/F4
Ruinen, Neth. 50/D3
Ruiselede, Belg. 52/C1
Ruiz, Mex. 142/D4
Rujen (peak), FYROM 47/H1
Ruki (riv.), D.R. Congo 93/D5
Rukwa (pol. reg.), Tanz. 104/B4
Rukwa (lake), Tanz. 93/F5
Rulles (riv.), Belg. 53/E4
Rülzheim, Ger. 54/B4
Rum, Aus. 57/H3
Rum Cay (isl.), Bahm. 141/G3
Ruma, Serb. 48/D3
Ruma NP, Kenya 104/B3
Rumbek, Sudan 97/L6
Rumes, Belg. 52/C2
Rumford, Me, US 131/G2
Rumia, Pol. 38/H4
Rumilly, Fr. 56/B6
Rümlang, Swi. 57/E3
Rumoi, Japan 76/B2
Rumphi, Malw. 104/B5
Rumson, NJ, US 138/E3
Rumst, Belg. 53/D1
Rumuruti, Kenya 104/C2
Runabay (pt.), NI, UK 34/B1
Runan, China 72/C4
Runcorn, Eng, UK 35/F5
Runding, Ger. 55/F4
Rundu, Namb. 105/C4
Rungwa (riv.), Tanz. 104/B4
Rungwa Game Rsv., Tanz. 104/B4
Rungwe (peak), Tanz. 104/B4
Runkel, Ger. 54/B2
Runn (lake), Swe. 38/E1
Runnemede, NJ, US 138/C4
Running Springs, Ca, US 136/C2
Ruo (riv.), China 65/K5
Ruokolahti, Fin. 39/N1
Ruoqiang, China 70/E4
Rupat (isl.), Indo. 80/B3
Rupea, Rom. 49/G2
Rupel (riv.), Belg. 53/D1
Rupert (riv.), Qu, Can. 123/J3
Rūpnagar, India 86/D4
Ruppichteroth, Ger. 53/G2
Rupt-sur-Moselle, Fr. 56/C2
Rupununi (riv.), Guy. 153/G4
Rur (riv.), Ger. 40/D3
Rur-Strasse (lake), Ger. 53/F2
Rurrenabaque, Bol. 150/E6
Rurutu (isl.), FrPol. 117/K7
Rusape, Zim. 105/F4
Rüschegg, Swi. 56/D4
Rüschlikon, Swi. 57/E3
Ruscom (riv.), On, Can. 135/G7
Ruse (pol. reg.), Bul. 47/K1
Ruse, Bul. 49/G4
Rusera, India 85/F3
Rush (lake), Ut, US 137/J13
Rush, Ire. 34/B4
Rushan, China 72/E3
Rushden, Eng, UK 33/F2
Rushville, In, US 130/C4
Rusk, Tx, US 129/J5
Russ, Fr. 56/D1
Russ Lake Nat'l Rec. Area, Wa, US 126/C3
Russbach (riv.), Aus. 49/N7
Russell (isls.), Austl. 114/F7
Russell, Mb, Can. 127/H3
Russell (lake), Mb, Can. 127/H1
Russell (isl.), Nun., Can. 122/F1
Russell (lake), Ga,SC, US 133/H3
Russell Gulch, Co, US 137/A3
Russellville, Al, US 133/G3
Russellville, Ar, US 129/J4
Russellville, Ky, US 130/C4
Rüsselsheim, Ger. 54/B3
Russi, It. 59/F4
Russia (ctry.) 64/H3
Russian (riv.), Ca, US 128/B3
Russian Mission, Ak, US 134/F3
Russkaya, Rus., Ant. 160/Q
Rust'avi, Geo. 63/H4
Rustenburg, SAfr. 105/E6
Ruston, La, US 129/J4
Ruston, Wa, US 135/C3
Rute, Sp. 44/C4
Ruteng, Indo. 81/F5
Rüthen, Ger. 51/F6
Rutherford, NJ, US 139/J8
Rutherglen, Sc, UK 36/B5
Ruthi, Swi. 57/F3
Ruthin, Wal, UK 35/E5
Ruthven, On, Can. 135/G7
Rüti, Swi. 57/E3
Rüti, Swi. 57/F4
Rutland (co.), Eng, UK 33/F1
Rutland, Vt, US 130/F3
Rutland Water (res.), Eng, UK 33/F1
Rutog, China 70/C5
Rutshuru (riv.), D.R. Congo 104/A3
Ruukki, Fin. 60/E2
Ruurlo, Neth. 50/D4
Ruvo di Puglia, It. 46/E2
Ruvu (riv.), Tanz. 104/C4
Ruvubu (riv.), Buru. 104/A3
Ruvuma (pol. reg.), Tanz. 104/C5
Ruvuma (riv.), Moz.,Tanz. 104/B5
Ruwāndūz, Iraq 90/F2
Ruwenzori (range), Ugan. 104/A2
Ruwenzori NP, Ugan. 104/A3
Ruy Barbosa, Braz. 154/B4
Ruyang, China 72/C4
Ruzayevka, Rus. 63/H1
Ruzizi (riv.), D.R. Congo 104/A3
Ružomberok, Slvk. 41/K4
Ruzyně (int'l arpt.), Czh. 55/H2
Rwanda (ctry.) 104/A3
Ryan (mt.), Austl. 115/D2
Ryan (mt.), Austl. 114/A1
Ryan (inlet), Sc, UK 34/C2
Ryazan', Rus. 63/G1
Ryazanskaya Oblast, Rus. 63/G1
Ryazhsk, Rus. 62/G1
Rybachiy (pen.), Rus. 37/K1
Rybinsk, Rus. 60/H4
Rybinsk (res.), Rus. 27/J2
Rybnik, Pol. 41/K3
Rycroft, Ab, Can. 126/D2
Ryd, Swe. 38/F3
Rydaholm, Swe. 38/F3
Ryde, Eng, UK 33/E5
Ryde, Ca, US 135/L10
Rydet, Swe. 38/D3
Rye (bay), Eng, UK 33/G5
Rye, Eng, UK 33/G5
Rye, NY, US 139/L8
Rye (riv.), Eng, UK 35/G3
Rye Brook, NY, US 139/L7
Rye Patch (res.), Nv, US 128/C2
Rygge, Nor. 38/D2
Ryki, Pol. 41/L3
Rylstone, Austl. 115/D2
Ryōkami, Japan 77/B2
Ryōtsu, Japan 75/F1
Ryōzen-yama (peak), Japan 77/K5
Rypin, Pol. 41/K2
Rysy (peak), Pol. 41/L4
Ryton, Eng, UK 35/G2
Rytterknægten (peak), Den. 38/F4
Ryūgasaki, Japan 75/G3
Ryukyu (isls.), Japan 67/M7
Ryūō, Japan 77/B2
Ryūō, Japan 77/K5
Rzeszów, Pol. 41/M3
Rzhev, Rus. 60/G4

S

's-Graveland, Neth. 50/C4
's Gravendeel, Neth. 50/B5
's Heerenberg, Neth. 50/D5
's Hertogenbosch, Neth. 50/C5
Sa Dec, Viet. 78/D4
Saab (int'l arpt.), Swe. 38/F2
Sääksjärvi (lake), Fin. 39/K1
Saal an der Donau, Ger. 55/E5
Saalbach (riv.), Ger. 54/B4
Saaldorf, Ger. 55/E2
Saale (riv.), Ger. 40/F3
Saales, Col de (pass), Fr. 56/D1
Saalfeld, Ger. 43/J1
Saalfelden am Steinernen Meer, Aus. 43/K3
Saane (riv.), Swi. 56/D5
Saanen, Swi. 56/D5
Saanta (peak), Kenya 104/C2
Saar (riv.), Ger. 53/F5
Saarbrücken, Ger. 53/F5
Saarburg, Ger. 53/F4
Saaremaa (isl.), Est. 60/D4
Saarland (state), Ger. 43/G2
Saarlouis, Ger. 53/F5
Saas, Swi. 57/F4
Saas Fee, Swi. 56/D5
Saastal (valley), Swi. 56/D5
Sab (riv.), Camb. 78/D3
Saba (isl.), NAnt. 141/N8
Šabac, Serb. 48/D3
Sabadell, Sp. 45/L6
Sabae, Japan 74/E3
Sabah (reg.), Malay. 67/L9
Sabalgarh, India 84/A2
Sabana (arch.), Bang. 145/F1
Sabana de Uchire, Ven. 153/E2
Sabanalarga, Col. 152/C3
Sabanalarga, Col. 152/C2
Sabancuy, Mex. 144/D2
Sabaneta, Ven. 152/D2
Sabang, Indo. 80/A2
Sabanita, Pan. 145/G4
Sabasṭīyah, WBnk. 91/G7
Sabat (riv.), Sudan 93/F4
Sabbio Chiese, It. 58/D1
Sabbioneta, It. 58/D2
Sabhā, Libya 96/H2
Sabie (riv.), Moz. 107/F2
Sabinal, Cayo (isl.), Cuba 145/G1
Sabiñánigo, Sp. 45/E1
Sabinas, Mex. 132/C5
Sabinas (riv.), Mex. 140/A2
Sabinas Hidalgo, Mex. 132/C5
Sabine (lake), La,Tx, US 129/J5
Sabine (riv.), La,Tx, US 129/J5
Sabinópolis, Braz. 155/D1
Sabkhat al Bardawīl (lag.), Egypt 91/C4
Sabkhat al Jabbūl (lake), Syria 90/D3
Sabkhat al Mūḩ (lake), Syria 90/D3
Sablayan, Phil. 81/F1
Sable (isl.), NS, Can. 131/K3
Sable (cape), NS, Can. 131/H3
Sablé-sur-Sarthe, Fr. 42/C3
Saboeiro, Braz. 154/C2
Sabor (riv.), Port. 44/B2
Sabra (cape), Indo. 81/H4
Sabrina (coast), Ant. 160/J
Sabugal, Port. 44/B2
Sabzevār, Iran 89/G1
Sacajawea (peak), Or, US 126/D4
Sácama, Col. 152/C3
Sacaton, Az, US 137/S19
Sacavém, Port. 45/P10
Saccarello (peak), It. 58/A4
Sacco (riv.), It. 46/C2
Sacedón, Sp. 44/D2
Săcele, Rom. 49/G3
Sachigo (lake), On, Can. 127/K2
Sachigo (riv.), On, Can. 122/G3
Sachs Harbour, NW, Can. 122/D1
Sachseln, Swi. 57/E4
Sachsen (state), Ger. 40/G3
Sachsen-Anhalt (state), Ger. 40/F3
Sachsenbrunn, Ger. 54/D2
Sachsenhagen, Ger. 51/G4
Sacile, It. 59/F1
Säckingen, Ger. 56/D2
Sackville, NB, Can. 131/H2
Saclay, Fr. 30/J5
Saco, Me, US 131/G3
Sacramento (cap.), Ca, US 128/B3
Sacramento, Braz. 155/C1

222

Sale – San Q

Sale, Austl. 115/C3
Sale, It. 58/B3
Salé, Mor. 100/A2
Salé (prov.), Mor. 100/A3
Sale, Eng, UK 35/F5
Sale Marasino, It. 58/D1
Salebabu (isl.), Indo. 81/G3
Salekhard, Rus. 64/G3
Salem, Ger. 57/F2
Salem, India 82/C5
Salem, In, US 130/C4
Salem, Mi, US 135/E7
Salem, NH, US 131/G3
Salem, NJ, US 138/C4
Salem (co.), NJ, US 138/C4
Salem (cap.), Or, US 126/C4
Salemi, It. 46/C4
Salentina (pen.), It. 47/F2
Salerno, It. 46/D2
Salerno, Golfo di (gulf), It. 46/D2
Sales (pt.), Eng, UK 33/G3
Saleux, Fr. 52/B4
Salfīt, WBnk. 91/G7
Salford, Eng, UK 35/F5
Salford (co.), Eng, UK 35/F5
Salgado Filho (int'l arpt.), Braz. 155/B4
Salgar, Col. 152/C3
Salgesch, Swi. 56/D5
Salgótarján, Hun. 41/K4
Salgueiro, Braz. 154/C3
Salhus, Nor. 38/A1
Salies-de-Béarn, Fr. 42/C5
Salies-du-Salat, Fr. 42/D5
Şalīf, Yem. 88/D5
Salihli, Turk. 90/B2
Salihorsk, Bela. 62/C1
Salima, Malw. 105/F3
Salīmah (oasis), Sudan 101/B4
Salina, Ut, US 128/E3
Salina (isl.), It. 46/D3
Salina (pt.), Bahm. 145/H1
Salina Cruz, Mex. 144/C2
Salinas (riv.), Ca, US 128/B3
Salinas, Braz. 154/B5
Salinas, Ca, US 128/B3
Salinas (cape), Sp. 45/G3
Salinas, Ecu. 152/A5
Salinas de Hidalgo, Mex. 143/E4
Salinas Pueblo Missions Nat'l Mon., NM, US 129/F4
Salinas Y Aguada Blanca, Reserva Nacional, Peru 156/D4
Saline (riv.), Ks, US 132/D2
Saline, It. 59/D6
Saline, Sc, UK 36/C4
Salinópolis, Braz. 151/J4
Salins-les-Bains, Fr. 56/B4
Salisbury, NC, US 133/H3
Salisbury (plain), Eng, UK 32/D4
Salisbury, Eng, UK 33/E4
Salisbury (isl.), Nun., Can. 123/J2
Salisbury, NY, US 139/L9
Salitre (riv.), Braz. 154/B3
Salitre, Ecu. 152/B5
Salla, Fin. 60/F2
Salladasburg, Pa, US 138/A1
Sallanches, Fr. 56/C6
Salland (phys. reg.), Neth. 50/D4
Sallatouk (pt.), Gui. 102/B4
Sallaumines, Fr. 52/B3
Sallent, Sp. 45/F2
Salliqueló, Arg. 158/E3
Sallisaw, Ok, US 129/J4
Sally (pass), Ire. 34/B5
Salm (riv.), Ger. 53/F3
Salmān Pāk, Iraq 90/F3
Salmās, Iran 90/F2
Salmon (riv.), BC, Can. 126/C2
Salmon, Id, US 126/E4
Salmon (riv.), Id, US 124/C2
Salmon Arm, BC, Can. 126/D3
Salmon Falls (riv.), Id,Nv, US 128/D2
Salmon River (mts.), Id, US 124/C2
Salmon, South Fork (riv.), US 128/C2
Salmtal, Ger. 53/F4
Salò, It. 58/D1
Salo, Fin. 39/K1
Salon, India 84/C2
Salon (riv.), Fr. 40/C5
Salon-de-Provence, Fr. 42/F5
Salonga, PN de la, D.R. Congo 97/K8
Salonta, Rom. 48/E2
Salouël, Fr. 52/B4
Salpausselkä (mts.), Fin. 39/M1
Salpo, Peru 156/B3
Salses-le-Château, Fr. 42/E5
Sal'sk, Rus. 63/G3
Salso (riv.), It. 46/C4
Salsomaggiore Terme, It. 58/C3
Salt (riv.), SAfr. 106/C4
Salt (riv.), Az, US 137/R19
Salt (range), Pak. 86/B3
Salt Cay (isl.), UK 145/J1
Salt Draw (riv.), Tx, US 142/D2
Salt Fork Arkansas (riv.), US 129/H3
Salt Fork Red (riv.), US 129/G4
Salt Lake (co.), Ut, US 137/J12
Salt Lake City (cap.), Ut, US 137/K12
Salt Meadow NWR, Ct, US 139/F1
Salt, North Fork (riv.), Mo, US 129/J2
Salt River Ind. Res., Az, US 137/S18
Salta, Arg. 157/C1
Saltaire, NY, US 139/E2
Saltash, Eng, UK 32/B6
Saltcoats, Sc, UK 36/B5
Saltdal, Nor. 37/E2
Saltee (isls.), Ire. 31/Q10
Saltfjorden (inlet), Nor. 37/E2
Saltillo, Mex. 143/E3
Salto, Uru. 157/E3
Salto, Braz. 155/C2
Salto, Arg. 158/E2
Salto da Divisa, Braz. 154/C5
Salto del Guairá, Par. 157/F1
Salto Grande (res.), Arg. 157/E3
Salto Santiago, Reprêsa de (res.), Braz. 155/A3
Salton Sea (lake), Ca, US 124/C5
Saltvik, Fin. 39/J1
Saluda (riv.), SC, US 133/H3
Salug, Phil. 79/D6
Saluggia, It. 58/B2
Salunga-Landisville, Pa, US 138/B3
Sālūr, India 82/D4
Salurn (Salorno), It. 57/H5
Salut, Îles du (isls.), FrG. 151/H2
Saluzzo, It. 43/G4
Salvación (bay), Chile 159/B6
Salvador (lake), La, US 137/P17
Salvaleón de Higüey, DRep. 141/H4
Salvaterra de Magos, Port. 44/A3
Salvatierra, Mex. 143/E4
Salvatierra de Miño, Sp. 44/A1
Salween (riv.), Asia 67/J8
Salyan, Azer. 63/J5
Salyersville, Ky, US 130/D4
Salza (riv.), Aus. 41/H5
Salzach (riv.), Ger. 40/G5
Salzano, It. 59/F1
Salzbergen, Ger. 51/E4
Salzburg, Aus. 43/K3
Salzburg (int'l arpt.), Aus. 43/K3
Salzburg (prov.), Aus. 41/G5
Salzgitter, Ger. 51/H4
Salzhausen, Ger. 51/H2
Salzhemmendorf, Ger. 51/G4
Salzkotten, Ger. 51/F5
Salzwedel, Ger. 40/F2
Sam Rayburn (res.), Tx, US 140/C1
Sam Sao (mts.), Laos,Viet. 78/C1
Sam Son, Viet. 78/D2
Sama, Sp. 44/C1
Samak (cape), Indo. 80/C4
Samales Group (isls.), Phil. 81/F2
Samālkha, India 86/D5
Sāmalkot, India 82/D4
Samāna, India 86/D4
Samaná (cape), DRep. 141/H4
Samana (isl.), Bahm. 145/H1
Samandağı, Turk. 91/D1
Samani, Japan 76/C2
Samaniego, Col. 152/B4
Samannūd, Egypt 91/B4
Samaqua (riv.), Qu, Can. 131/F1
Samar, Jor. 91/D3
Samar (isl.), Phil. 67/M8
Samara (riv.), Rus. 87/B2
Samara (int'l arpt.), Rus. 63/J1
Samara, Rus. 63/J1
Samarskaya Oblast, Rus. 87/A2
Samarai, PNG 116/E6
Samarate, It. 58/B1
Samaria (reg.), WBnk. 91/G7
Samarinda, Indo. 81/E4
Samarqand, Uzb. 87/E5
Samarqand (pol. reg.), Uzb. 87/E5
Sāmarrā', Iraq 90/E3
Samasata, Pak. 86/A5
Samāstipur, India 85/E3
Şamaxı, Azer. 63/J5
Sāmba, India 86/C3
Sambalpur, India 82/D3
Sambao (riv.), Madg. 107/H7
Sambar (cape), Indo. 80/D4
Sambas, Indo. 80/C3
Sambava, Madg. 107/J6
Sambhal, India 84/B1
Sambir, Ukr. 41/M4
Sambor Prei Kuk (ruin), Camb. 78/D3
Samborobón (riv.), Arg. 159/K11
Samborombón (bay), Arg. 159/F2
Sambre (riv.), Fr. 40/C3
Sambre à l'Oise, Canal de (canal), Fr. 52/C4
Sambriāl, Pak. 86/C3
Sambu, Japan 77/E2
Samburu Nat'l Rsv., Kenya 104/C2
Samch'ŏk, SKor. 74/A2
Samch'ŏnp'o, SKor. 73/E5
Samedan, Swi. 57/F4
Samer, Fr. 52/A2
Samfya Mission, Zam. 104/A5
Sámi, Gre. 47/G3
Samiria (riv.), Peru 156/C2
Samit (cape), Camb. 78/C4
Samkos (peak), Camb. 78/C3
Sammamish (lake), Wa, US 135/C2
Sammeron, Fr. 30/M5
Samnangjin, SKor. 74/A3
Samnaun, Swi. 57/G4
Samoa (ctry.) 117/H6
Samobor, Cro. 48/B3
Samoëns, Fr. 56/C5
Samoggia (riv.), It. 59/E4
Samokov, Bul. 47/H1
Samora (riv.), Port. 45/Q10
Samora Correia, Port. 45/Q10
Sámos (isl.), Gre. 90/A2
Sámos, Gre. 90/A2
Samothráki, Gre. 47/J2
Sampacho, Arg. 158/D2
Samper de Calanda, Sp. 45/E2
Sampit (riv.), Indo. 80/D4
Sampit, Indo. 80/D4
Samsø (isl.), Den. 38/D4
Samsø Bælt (chan.), Den. 38/D4
Samson (mt.), Austl. 114/E6
Samsonvale (lake), Austl. 114/E6
Samsun, Turk. 90/D1
Samsun (prov.), Turk. 90/C1
Samthar, India 84/B3
Samugheo, It. 46/A3
Samui (isl.), Thai. 83/H6
Samukawa, Japan 77/C3
Samundri, Pak. 86/B4
Samur (riv.), Azer.,Rus. 64/E5
Samut Prakan, Thai. 78/C3
Samut Sakhon, Thai. 78/C3
Samut Songkhram, Thai. 78/B3
Samye Monastery, China 85/H1
San, Mali 102/D3
San (riv.), Pol. 62/B2
San (riv.), Camb. 78/D3
San Adrián, Cabo de (cape), Sp. 44/A1
San Agustin (cape), Phil. 79/E6
San Agustín, Col. 152/B4
San Agustin de Guadalix, Sp. 45/N8
San Agustín, Parque Arqeológico, Col. 152/B4
San Ambrosio (isl.), Chile 147/B5
San Andreas (lake), Ca, US 135/J11
San Andres (mts.), NM, US 128/F4
San Andrés (lake), Mex. 144/B1
San Andrés, Col. 152/C3
San Andrés, Col. 145/F3
San Andrés Cuexcontitlán, Mex. 143/Q10
San Andrés de Giles, Arg. 159/J11
San Andrés de Machaca, Bol. 156/D5
San Andrés del Rabanedo, Sp. 44/C1
San Andrés, Isla de (isl.), Col. 140/E5
San Andrés Tuxtla, Mex. 144/C2
San Angelo, Tx, US 132/C4
San Anselmo, Ca, US 135/J11
San Antonio (cape), Arg. 159/F3
San Antonio, Chile 158/N8
San Antonio, Ecu. 152/B4
San Antonio, Mex. 142/C4
San Antonio, Peru 156/B4
San Antonio, Uru. 159/K11
San Antonio, Ven. 153/F2
San Antonio (mt.), Ca, US 136/C2
San Antonio (int'l arpt.), Tx, US 129/H5
San Antonio (riv.), Tx, US 140/B2
San Antonio Abad, Sp. 45/F3
San Antonio de Areco, Arg. 159/J11
San Antonio de Caparo, Ven. 152/D3
San Antonio del Golfo, Ven. 153/F2
San Antonio del Táchira, Ven. 152/C3
San Antonio Oeste, Arg. 158/D4
San Antonio, Punta (pt.), Mex. 142/B2
San Augustine, Tx, US 132/E4
San Bartolo, Peru 156/B4
San Bartolomé de Tirajana, Canl. 45/X17
San Bartolome Tlaltelulco, Mex. 143/Q10
San Bartolomeo in Bosco, It. 59/E3
San Bartolomeo in Galdo, It. 46/D2
San Bautista, Uru. 159/L11
San Benedetto (range), It. 59/E5
San Benedetto del Tronto, It. 43/K5
San Benedetto in Alpe, It. 59/E5
San Benedetto Po, It. 59/D2
San Benedicto (isl.), Mex. 142/C5
San Bernardo, Chile 158/N8
San Bernardo (pt.), Col. 152/C2
San Bernardino, Ca, US 136/C2
San Bernardino (co.), Ca, US 136/C2
San Bernardino (mts.), Ca, US 136/C2
San Bernardino Nat'l Forest, Ca, US 136/C2
San Blas, Mex. 142/D4
San Blas, Mex. 142/C3
San Blas (cape), Fl, US 133/G4
San Bonifacio, It. 59/E2
San Borja, Bol. 150/E6
San Bruno, Mex. 142/B3
San Bruno, Ca, US 135/K11
San Buenaventura, Mex. 132/C5
San Buenaventura (Ventura), Ca, US 136/A2
San Candido (Innichen), It. 43/K3
San Carlos, Chile 158/C3
San Carlos, Mex. 129/G5
San Carlos, Mex. 143/F3
San Carlos, Nic. 145/E4
San Carlos, Pan. 152/B2
San Carlos, Phil. 79/D4
San Carlos, Uru. 159/G2
San Carlos, Ven. 152/D2
San Carlos (lake), Az, US 128/E4
San Carlos, Ca, US 135/K11
San Carlos de Bariloche, Arg. 158/C4
San Carlos de Bariloche (int'l arpt.), Arg. 158/C4
San Carlos de Río Negro, Ven. 153/E4
San Carlos del Zulia, Ven. 152/D2
San Casciano in Val di Pesa, It. 59/E5
San Cataldo, It. 47/F2
San Cayetano, Arg. 158/F3
San Cesario sul Panaro, It. 59/E3
San Ciro de Acosta, Mex. 143/F4
San Clemente (isl.), Ca, US 128/C4
San Clemente, Ca, US 136/C4
San Clemente, Sp. 44/D3
San Clemente, Chile 158/C2
San Clemente del Tuyú, Arg. 159/F3
San Colombano al Lambro, It. 58/C2
San Cristóbal, Arg. 157/D3
San Cristobal (isl.), Sol. 116/F6
San Cristóbal (vol.), Nic. 144/E3
San Cristóbal, Ven. 152/C3
San Cristóbal, Cuba 145/F1
San Cristóbal (isl.), Ecu. 156/F7
San Cristóbal de las Casas, Mex. 144/C2
San Cristobal Wash (riv.), Az, US 142/B1
San Damiano d'Asti, It. 58/B3
San Diego (cape), Arg. 159/D7
San Diego, Ca, US 136/C5
San Diego (aqueduct), Ca, US 136/C4
San Diego (bay), Ca, US 136/C5
San Diego (co.), Ca, US 136/C4
San Diego, Tx, US 132/D5
San Diego International-Lindbergh Field (int'l arpt.), Ca, US 136/C5
San Diego Naval Station, Ca, US 136/C5
San Diego Wild Animal Park, Ca, US 136/C4
San Diego Zoo, Ca, US 136/C5
San Dieguito (riv.), Ca, US 136/C5
San Dimas, Ca, US 136/C2
San Donà di Piave, It. 59/F1
San Donnino, It. 59/E5
San Dorligo della Valle, It. 59/G1
San Esteban de Gormaz, Sp. 44/D2
San Felice Circeo, It. 46/C2
San Felice del Benaco, It. 58/D1
San Felice sul Panaro, It. 59/E3
San Felipe, Mex. 142/B2
San Felipe, Ven. 152/D2
San Felipe, Chile 158/N8
San Felipe de Puerto Plata, DRep. 141/G4
San Felipe de Vichayal, Peru 156/A2
San Felipe Jalapa de Díaz, Mex. 143/F5
San Felipe Torres Mochas, Mex. 143/E4
San Felix (isl.), Chile 147/A5
San Fernando (riv.), Mex. 132/D5
San Fernando, Phil. 79/D4
San Fernando, Phil. 79/D4
San Fernando (valley), Ca, US 136/B2
San Fernando, Sp. 44/B4
San Fernando, Trin. 153/F2
San Fernando, Chile 158/C2
San Fernando, Arg. 159/J11
San Fernando, Ca, US 136/F7
San Fernando de Apure, Ven. 153/E3
San Fernando de Atabapo, Ven. 152/E3
San Fernando de Henares, Sp. 45/N9
San Fernando de Presas, Mex. 143/F3
San Fior di Sopra, It. 59/F1
San Francesco al Campo, It. 58/A2
San Francisco, Arg. 157/D3
San Francisco, Col. 152/B4
San Francisco, ESal. 144/D3
San Francisco, Phil. 79/E6
San Francisco, Ven. 152/D2
San Francisco (riv.), Az,NM, US 128/E4
San Francisco, Ca, US 128/B3
San Francisco (co.), Ca, US 135/K11
San Francisco (int'l arpt.), Ca, US 128/B3
San Francisco Acuautla, Mex. 143/R10
San Francisco Bay NWR, Ca, US 135/K11
San Francisco, Cabo de (cape), Ecu. 152/A4
San Francisco Chimalpa, Mex. 143/Q10
San Francisco de la Paz, Hon. 144/E3
San Francisco de Macorís, DRep. 141/G4
San Francisco de Mostazal, Chile 158/N8
San Francisco del Mezquital, Mex. 142/D4
San Francisco del Monte de Oro, Arg. 158/D2
San Francisco del Oro, Mex. 142/D3
San Francisco del Rincón, Mex. 143/E4
San Francisco Telixtlahuaca, Mex. 140/B4
San Fratello, It. 46/D3
San Gabriel (riv.), Ca, US 136/C2
San Gabriel (pt.), Mex. 142/B2
San Gabriel (res.), Ca, US 136/C2
San Gabriel, Ecu. 152/B4
San Gabriel, Ca, US 136/F7
San Gavino Monreale, It. 46/A3
San Germán, Cuba 145/G1
San Germano Vercellese, It. 58/B2
San Gil, Col. 152/C3
San Gimignano, It. 59/E6
San Giorgio delle Pertiche, It. 59/E1
San Giorgio di Piano, It. 59/E3
San Giorgio Ionico, It. 47/E2
San Giorgio Piacentino, It. 58/C3
San Giovanni al Natisone, It. 59/G1
San Giovanni Bianco, It. 58/C1
San Giovanni Gemini, It. 46/C4
San Giovanni in Croce, It. 58/D2
San Giovanni in Fiore, It. 46/E3
San Giovanni in Marignano, It. 59/F5
San Giovanni in Persiceto, It. 59/E3
San Giovanni Lupatoto, It. 59/E2
San Giovanni Valdarno, It. 59/E5
San Giuliano, It. 58/B3
San Giuliano Terme, It. 58/D5
San Giustino, It. 59/F5
San Giusto Canavese, It. 58/A2
San Gorgonio (mtn.), Ca, US 128/C4
San Gottardo, Passo del (pass), Swi. 57/E4
San Gregorio, Arg. 158/E2
San Gregorio, Uru. 159/L10
San Gregorio, Ca, US 135/K12
San Guiliano Milanese, It. 58/C2
San Hipólito Punta (pt.), Mex. 142/B3
San Ignacio, Bol. 150/E6
San Ignacio, Peru 156/B2
San Ignacio, Bol. 150/F7
San Ignacio, Mex. 142/B3
San Ignacio, Mex. 142/D4
San Ignacio, Belz. 144/D2
San Ignacio, Chile 158/B3
San Ildefonso, Sp. 44/D2
San Isidro, Nic. 144/E3
San Isidro, CR 145/F4
San Jacinto, Col. 152/C2
San Jacinto, Uru. 159/L11
San Javier, Chile 158/C2
San Javier, Sp. 45/E4
San Javier, Uru. 159/J10
San Jerónimo, Mex. 142/E3
San Joaquín, Bol. 150/F6
San Joaquin (riv.), Ca, US 128/C3
San Joaquín, Col. 152/C3
San Joaquin (hills), Ca, US 136/G8
San Joaquin (co.), Ca, US 135/L11
San Joaquín (peak), Ecu. 156/F7
San Jorge (cape), Arg. 158/D5
San Jorge (gulf), Arg. 147/C7
San Jorge (riv.), Col. 145/H5
San Jorge (bay), Mex. 142/B2
San Jorge, Golfo di (gulf), Sp. 45/F2
San José (gulf), Arg. 158/D4
San José, Col. 152/B4
San José (cap.), CR 145/E4
San José (isl.), Mex. 142/C3
San José, Peru 156/D4
San José, Peru 156/B2
San Jose, Phil. 81/F1
San Jose, Phil. 79/D4
San Jose, Phil. 79/D5
San José, Sp. 45/F3
San Jose (riv.), Uru. 159/K10
San José (dept.), Uru. 159/K11
San Jose, Ca, US 128/B3
San Jose (hills), Ca, US 136/G7
San Jose (int'l arpt.), Ca, US 128/B3
San José de Chiquitos, Bol. 150/F7
San José de Guanipa, Ven. 153/E2
San José de Guaribe, Ven. 153/E2
San José de Jáchal, Arg. 157/C3
San José de la Esquina, Arg. 158/E2
San Jose de Los Molinos, Peru 156/C4
San José de los Remates, Nic. 144/E3
San José de Maipo, Chile 158/N8
San José de Mayo, Uru. 159/K11
San José de Raíces, Mex. 143/E3
San José de Seque, Ven. 152/D2
San José del Cabo, Mex. 142/C4
San José del Guaviare, Col. 152/C4
San José Iturbide, Mex. 143/E4
San José Viejo, Mex. 142/C4
San Juan, Arg. 157/C3
San Juan (riv.), Arg. 157/C3
San Juan, Peru 156/C4
San Juan (basin), NM, US 132/A2
San Juan (riv.), NM, US 132/B2
San Juan, Phil. 79/D5
San Juan, PR 141/M8
San Juan (riv.), Nic. 140/E5
San Juan (pt.), ESal. 144/D3
San Juan (mts.), Co, US 124/E4
San Juan (cape), Arg. 159/E7
San Juan Abajo, Mex. 142/D4
San Juan Bautista, Par. 157/E2
San Juan Bautista Coixtlahuaca, Mex. 144/B2
San Juan Bautista Tuxtepec, Mex. 144/B2
San Juan Bautista Valle Nacional, Mex. 144/B2
San Juan Capistrano, Ca, US 136/C3
San Juan de Alicante, Sp. 45/E3
San Juan de Aznalfarache, Sp. 44/B4
San Juan de la Costa, Mex. 142/C3
San Juan de Lima (pt.), Mex. 142/E5
San Juan de los Cayos, Ven. 152/D2
San Juan de los Lagos, Mex. 142/E4
San Juan de los Morros, Ven. 150/E2
San Juan del Norte, Nic. 145/F4
San Juan del Río, Mex. 143/F4
San Juan Guichicovi, Mex. 140/B4
San Juan Hot Springs, Ca, US 136/C3
San Juan Ixcaquixtla, Mex. 143/M8
San Juan Juquila Mixes, Mex. 144/C2
San Juan Nepomuceno, Col. 152/C2
San Juanico, Mex. 142/B3
San Juanico Punta (pt.), Mex. 142/B3
San Juanito, Mex. 142/D2
San Justo, Arg. 157/D3
San Lázaro (cape), Mex. 142/B3
San Lazzaro, It. 59/E4
San Leandro, Ca, US 135/K11
San Leandro (res.), Ca, US 135/K11
San Lorenzo (cape), Ecu. 150/B4
San Lorenzo, Bol. 150/E6
San Lorenzo (peak), Chile 159/B5
San Lorenzo, Ecu. 152/B4
San Lorenzo, Hon. 144/E3
San Lorenzo (cape), It. 46/A3
San Lorenzo (riv.), Mex. 142/D3
San Lorenzo, Peru 156/D3
San Lorenzo, Nic. 144/E3
San Lorenzo, Ca, US 135/K11
San Lorenzo al Mare, It. 58/A5
San Lorenzo de El Escorial, Sp. 45/M8
San Lorenzo in Campo, It. 59/F5
San Lucas, Nic. 144/E3
San Lucas, Cabo (cape), Mex. 142/C4
San Luis, Arg. 158/D2
San Luis, Cuba 145/H1
San Luis, Guat. 144/D2
San Luis, Peru 156/B4
San Luis, Ven. 152/D2
San Luis (valley), Co, US 132/B2
San Luis Acatlán, Mex. 144/B2
San Luis al Medio, Uru. 159/G2
San Luis de la Paz, Mex. 143/E4
San Luis Obispo, Ca, US 128/B4
San Luis Potosí (state), Mex. 140/A3
San Luis Potosí, Mex. 143/E4
San Luis Rey (riv.), Ca, US 136/C4
San Luis Rey, Ca, US 136/C4
San Luis Río Colorado, Mex. 128/D4
San Luis, Sierra de (mts.), Arg. 158/D2
San Manuel, Az, US 128/E4
San Marcello Pistoiese, It. 59/D4
San Marcos, Peru 156/B3
San Marcos, Peru 156/B2
San Marcos, Tx, US 129/H5
San Marcos, Ca, US 136/C4
San Marcos, Mex. 140/B4
San Marcos, Guat. 144/D3
San Marcos, CR 145/E4
San Marcos, Col. 152/C2
San Maria di Porto Novo, It. 59/G5
San Mariano, Phil. 79/D4
San Marino (ctry.) 59/F5
San Marino (cap.), SMar. 59/F5
San Marino, Ca, US 136/F7
San Martín (riv.), Bol. 150/F6
San Martín (dept.), Peru 156/B2
San Martín, Mex. 143/R9
San Martín, Col. 152/C4
San Martín (lake), Arg. 147/B7
San Martín, Arg. 158/C2
San Martin Cuautlalpan, Mex. 143/R10
San Martín de los Andes, Arg. 158/C4
San Martín de Valdeiglesias, Sp. 44/C2
San Martino Buon Albergo, It. 59/E2
San Martino-di-Lota, Fr. 46/A1
San Martino di Lupari, It. 59/E1
San Martino di Venezze, It. 59/E2
San Martino in Passiria (Sankt Martin in Passeier), It. 57/H4
San Martino in Rio, It. 59/D3
San Martino in Strada, It. 58/C2
San Martino Siccomario, It. 58/C2
San Mateo, Peru 156/B3
San Mateo, Sp. 45/F2
San Mateo, Ven. 153/E2
San Mateo, Ca, US 128/B3
San Mateo (co.), Ca, US 135/K12
San Mateo (mts.), NM, US 132/B3
San Mateo Atarasquillo, Mex. 143/Q10
San Mateo Xoloc, Mex. 143/Q9
San Matías, Bol. 150/G7
San Matías, Golfo (gulf), Arg. 147/C7
San Maurizio d'Opaglio, It. 58/B1
San Mauro Pascoli, It. 59/F4
San Mauro Torinese, It. 58/A2
San Michele al Tagliamento, It. 59/F1
San Miguel (riv.), Bol. 150/F6
San Miguel, Peru 156/B2
San Miguel, Peru 156/C4
San Miguel, Mex. 132/C4
San Miguel, ESal. 144/D3
San Miguel (gulf), Pan. 145/G4
San Miguel (riv.), Col. 152/B4
San Miguel Coatlinchan, Mex. 143/R10
San Miguel de Allende, Mex. 143/E4
San Miguel de los Bancos, Ecu. 152/B4
San Miguel de Tucumán, Arg. 157/C2
San Miguel del Monte, Arg. 159/J11
San Miguel Tlaixpan, Mex. 143/R9
San Miguel Totolapan, Mex. 140/A4
San Miniato, It. 59/D5
San Nicolas (isl.), Ca, US 128/B4
San Nicolás de los Arroyos, Arg. 158/E2
San Nicolò, It. 58/C2
San Onofre (mtn.), Ca, US 136/C4
San Onofre, Ca, US 136/C4
San Onofre, Col. 152/C2
San Pablo, Chile 158/B4
San Pablo, Col. 152/B4
San Pablo, Peru 156/B2
San Pablo, Phil. 79/D5
San Pablo (int'l arpt.), Sp. 44/C4
San Pablo, Ven. 153/E2
San Pablo, Ca, US 135/K11
San Pablo (res.), Ca, US 135/K11
San Pablo Bay NWR, Ca, US 135/K10
San Pablo de las Salinas, Mex. 143/Q9
San Pablo Huixtepec, Mex. 144/B2
San Paolo, It. 58/D2
San Pawl il-Baħar, Malta 46/L7
San Pedro, Arg. 157/D1
San Pedro, Par. 157/E1
San Pedro (vol.), Chile 157/C1
San Pedro (riv.), Mex. 132/B5
San Pédro, C.d'Iv. 102/D5
San Pedro, Belz. 144/E2
San Pedro (riv.), Guat. 144/D2
San Pedro, Chile 158/N8
San Pedro, Arg. 159/J10
San Pedro Arriba, Mex. 143/Q10
San Pedro Carchá, Guat. 144/D3
San Pedro de Cajas, Peru 156/C3
San Pedro de la Cueva, Mex. 142/C2
San Pedro de las Colonias, Mex. 132/C5
San Pedro de Lloc, Peru 156/B2
San Pedro de Lóvago, Nic. 145/E3
San Pedro de Macorís, DRep. 141/H4
San Pedro del Pinatar, Sp. 45/E4
San Pedro Huamelula, Mex. 144/C2
San Pedro Pochutla, Mex. 144/B3
San Pedro, Sierra de (mts.), Sp. 44/B3
San Pedro Sula, Hon. 144/D3
San Pedro Tapanatepec, Mex. 144/C2
San Pedro Totoltepec, Mex. 143/Q10
San Pellegrino Terme, It. 58/C1
San Piero a Sieve, It. 59/E5
San Piero in Bagno, It. 59/E5
San Pietro (isl.), It. 46/A3
San Pietro in Casale, It. 59/E3
San Pietro in Gù, It. 59/E1
San Pietro in Vincoli, It. 59/F4
San Pietro in Volta, It. 59/F2
San Polo d'Enza, It. 58/D3
San Polo di Piave, It. 59/F1
San Possidonio, It. 59/D3
San Quentin, Ca, US 135/K11
San Quintín (cape), Mex. 142/B2

São Sebastião, Braz. 211/H8
São Sebastião do Paraíso, Braz. 155/C2
São Sebastião, Ilha de (isl.), Braz. 155/C2
São Simão, Barragem de (res.), Braz. 155/B1
São Teotónio, Port. 44/A4
São Tiago, Braz. 155/C2
São Tiago (isl.), CpV. 93/K10
São Tomé (cap.), SaoT. 96/G7
São Tomé (isl.), SaoT. 96/G7
São Tomé and Príncipe (ctry.) 96/F7
São Tomé, Cabo de (cape), Braz. 155/D2
São Vicente, Braz. 211/G8
São Vicente (cape), Port. 44/A4
São Vicente (isl.), CpV. 93/J10
Saône (riv.), Fr. 42/F3
Saône-et-Loire (dept.), Fr. 56/B4
Saori, Japan 77/L5
Saouru (riv.), Alg. 96/E1
Sápai, Gre. 47/J2
Sapallanga, Peru 156/C4
Sapanca, Turk. 49/K5
Sapatgrām, India 85/H2
Sapé, Braz. 154/D2
Sapele, Nga. 103/G5
Sapelo (isl.), Ga, US 133/H4
Şaphane, Turk. 62/D5
Sapiéndza (isl.), Gre. 47/G4
Sapkyo, SKor. 73/D4
Sapo (mts.), Pan. 145/G5
Sapo NP, Libr. 102/C5
Saposoa, Peru 156/B2
Sappemeer, Neth. 50/D2
Sapphire, Austl. 114/B3
Sappington, Mo, US 137/G8
Sapporo, Japan 76/B2
Sapri, It. 46/D2
Sapsi (isl.), SKor. 73/D3
Sapt Kosi (riv.), Nepal 85/F2
Sapucaí (riv.), Braz. 211/H7
Sapucaia, Braz. 211/L6
Saqqez, Iran 88/E1
Saquena, Peru 156/C2
Saquisilí, Ecu. 152/B5
Šar (mts.), Serb 47/G1
Sar Dasht, Iran 90/F2
Sar-e Pol, Afg. 87/E5
Sara Buri, Thai. 78/C3
Sarāb, Iran 88/E1
Saraguro, Ecu. 156/B1
Sarāi Alamgir, Pak. 86/B3
Sarāi Sidhu, Pak. 86/A4
Sarajevo (cap.), Bosn. 48/D4
Saraland, Al, US 133/F4
Saramacca (dist.), Sur. 153/H3
Saran (peak), Indo. 80/D4
Saran', Kaz. 87/F3
Saranac Lake, NY, US 130/F2
Sarandapótamos (riv.), Gre. 47/N8
Sarandë, Alb. 47/G3
Sarandí de Navarro, Uru. 159/K10
Sarandí del Yi, Uru. 159/G2
Sarandí Grande, Uru. 159/K10
Sarangami (isls.), Phil. 81/G2
Sārangpur, India 89/L4
Saransk, Rus. 63/H1
Sarapul, Rus. 61/M4
Sarare (riv.), Ven. 152/D3
Sarasota, Fl, US 133/H5
Saratoga, Wy, US 126/G5
Saratoga, Ca, US 135/K12
Saratoga Springs, NY, US 130/F3
Saratov (res.), Rus. 63/J1
Saratov, Rus. 63/H2
Saratovskaya Oblast, Rus. 87/A2
Saravan, Laos 78/D3
Sarawak (reg.), Malay. 67/L9
Saray, Turk. 49/H5
Sarayacu, Ecu. 152/B5
Sarāyan (riv.), India 84/C2
Sarayköy, Turk. 90/B2
Sarayönü, Turk. 90/C2
Sárbogárd, Hun. 48/D2
Sarcelles, Fr. 30/K5
Sārda (riv.), India 84/C1
Sārda (canal), India 84/C2
Sarda (riv.), India 82/D2
Sardara, It. 46/A3
Sardārshahar, India 86/C5
Sardegna (prov.), It. 46/A2
Sardhana, India 86/D5
Sardinata, Col. 152/C2
Sardinaux, Cap des (cape), Fr. 43/G5
Sardinia (isl.) 46/A2
Sardis (lake), Ms, US 129/K4
Sardis (lake), Ok, US 129/J4
Sareks NP, Swe. 37/F2
Sarektjåkko (peak), Swe. 37/F2
Sarempaka (peak), Indo. 81/E4
Sarentino, It. 57/H4
Sarezzo, It. 58/D1
Sargans, Swi. 57/F3
Sargodha, Pak. 86/B3
Sarh, Chad 96/J6
Sārī, Iran 88/F1
Sari-Solenzara, Fr. 46/A2
Sariaya, Phil. 79/D5
Saribi (cape), Indo. 81/J4
Sarigan (isl.), NMar. 116/D3
Sarıgöl, Turk. 90/B2
Sarıkamış, Turk. 90/E1
Sarıkaya, Turk. 62/E5
Sarikaya (prov.), Turk. 90/C2
Sarikei, Malay. 80/D3
Sarina, Austl. 114/C3
Sarine (riv.), Swi. 43/G3
Sariñena, Sp. 45/E2
Sarīr Kalanshiyū (des.), Libya 96/K2
Sarīr Tibasti (des.), Libya 96/J3
Sarita, Tx, US 132/D5
Sariwŏn, NKor. 73/C3
Sarju (riv.), India 84/C1
Sark (isl.), Chl, UK 42/B2
Sarkad, Hun. 48/E2
Sarkant, Kaz. 70/C2
Şarkîkaraağaç, Turk. 90/B2
Şarkışla, Turk. 90/D2
Şarköy, Turk. 49/H5
Sarlat-la-Canéda, Fr. 42/D4
Sarleinsbach, Aus. 55/G5
Sarmato, It. 58/C2
Sarmeola, It. 59/E2
Sarmiento, Arg. 158/C5
Sarmiento (peak), Chile 159/C7
Särna, Swe. 38/E1
Sarnano, It. 43/K5
Sarnen, Swi. 57/E4
Sarnia, On, Can. 130/D3
Sarnico, It. 58/C1
Sarny, Ukr. 62/C2
Saroma (lake), Japan 76/C1
Saronic (gulf), Gre. 47/H4
Saronno, It. 58/C1
Saros (gulf), Turk. 49/H5
Sárospatak, Hun. 41/L4
Sarpsborg, Nor. 38/D2
Sarralbe, Fr. 53/G6
Sarre (riv.), Fr. 52/F6
Sarre-Union, Fr. 53/G6
Sarrebourg, Fr. 53/G6
Sarria, Sp. 44/B1
Sarroch, It. 46/A3
Sarry, Fr. 53/D6
Sarsāwa, India 86/D4
Sarsina, It. 59/F5
Sarstedt, Ger. 51/G4
Sarstsún (riv.), Guat. 144/D3
Sartang (riv.), Rus. 65/P3
Sarteano, It. 46/B1
Sartène, Fr. 46/A2
Sarthe (riv.), Fr. 42/C3
Sartrouville, Fr. 30/J5
Sarufutsu, Japan 76/C1
Saruhanlı, Turk. 90/A2
Sárvár, Hun. 43/M3
Sárvíz (riv.), Hun. 48/D2
Saryesik Atgraū Qumy (des.), Kaz. 70/C2
Saryshaghan, Kaz. 87/F3
Sarysu (riv.), Kaz. 64/G5
Sarzana, It. 58/C4
Sas Van Gent, Neth. 52/C1
Sasaginnigack (lake), Mb, Can. 127/K3
Sasarām, India 85/E3
Sasayama, Japan 77/H5
Sasayama (riv.), Japan 77/H5
Sásd, Hun. 48/D2
Sasebo, Japan 74/A4
Sashima, Japan 77/D1
Saskatchewan (prov.), Can. 122/F3
Saskatchewan (riv.), Can. 122/E3
Saskatoon, Sk, Can. 126/G2
Saslaya (mtn.), Nic. 144/E3
Saslaya, PN, Nic. 144/E3
Sāsni, India 84/B2
Sasolburg, SAfr. 106/D2
Sasovo, Rus. 63/G1
Saspamco, Tx, US 137/U21
Sassafras, Md, US 138/C5
Sassafras (riv.), Md, US 138/B5
Sassandra (riv.), C.d'Iv. 96/D6
Sassandra, C.d'Iv. 102/D5
Sassari, It. 46/A2
Sassello, It. 58/B4
Sassenberg, Ger. 51/F4
Sassenheim, Neth. 50/B4
Sassnitz, Ger. 38/E4
Sasso Marconi, It. 59/E4
Sassocorvaro, It. 59/F5
Sassoferrato, It. 59/F6
Sassuolo, It. 59/D3
Sástago, Sp. 45/E2
Sasyk (lake), Ukr. 49/J3
Sata-misaki (cape), Japan 74/B5
Sātāra, India 89/K5
Satawan (isl.), Micr. 116/E4
Säter, Swe. 38/F1
Saticoy, Ca, US 136/A2
Satilla (riv.), Ga, US 133/H4
Satipo, Peru 156/C3
Sātkhira, Bang. 85/G4
Sátoraljaújhely, Hun. 41/L4
Satpayev, Kaz. 87/E3
Satpura (range), India 89/K4
Satte, Japan 77/D1
Satteins, Aus. 57/F3
Satteldorf, Ger. 54/D4
Sattler, Tx, US 137/U20
Satu Mare, Rom. 41/M5
Satu Mare (co.), Rom. 41/M5
Satun, Thai. 78/C5
Sauce, Peru 156/B2
Sauce Grande (riv.), Arg. 158/E3
Saucillo, Mex. 132/B4
Sauda, Nor. 38/B2
Saúde, Braz. 154/B3
Saudhárkrókur, Ice. 37/N6
Saudi Arabia (ctry.) 88/D4
Sauer (riv.), Ger. 51/F5
Sauerlach, Ger. 57/H2
Sauerland (reg.), Ger. 40/D3
Sauêruiná (riv.), Braz. 150/G6
Saugatuck (riv.), Ct, US 139/E1
Saujon, Fr. 42/C4
Sauk (riv.), Mn, US 127/K4
Sauk Centre, Mn, US 127/K4
Sauk Rapids, Mn, US 127/K4
Saül, FrG. 151/H3
Sauland, Nor. 38/C2
Sauldre (riv.), Fr. 42/D3
Saulgau, Ger. 57/F1
Saulheim, Ger. 54/B3
Saulieu, Fr. 42/F3
Sault-lès-Rethel, Fr. 53/D5
Sault Sainte Marie, On, Can. 130/C2
Sault Ste. Marie, Mi, US 130/C2
Saulx, Fr. 56/C2
Saulx (riv.), Fr. 40/C4
Saulxures-sur-Moselotte, Fr. 56/C2
Saumur, Fr. 42/C3
Saunders (peak), Austl. 112/E3
Saura (riv.), India 85/F3
Saurimo, Ang. 105/D2
Sausalito, Ca, US 135/J11
Sausseron (riv.), Fr. 30/J4
Sauteurs, Gren. 153/F1
Sava, It. 47/E2
Sava (riv.), Slov. 43/L3
Savá, Hon. 144/E3
Savage (dam), Ca, US 136/D5
Savage River, Austl. 115/C4
Savai'i (isl.), Sam. 117/H6
Savalou, Ben. 103/F5
Savane (riv.), Qu, Can. 131/G1
Savanna-la-Mar, Jam. 145/G2
Savannah, Ga, US 133/H3
Savannah, Tn, US 133/F3
Savannah (riv.), US 133/H3
Savannakhet, Laos 78/D2
Savant (lake), On, Can. 127/L3
Sāvantvādi, India 82/B4
Sävar, Swe. 37/G3
Savaştepe, Turk. 90/A2
Save (riv.), Moz. 93/F7
Sāveh, Iran 88/F1
Savena (riv.), It. 59/E4
Săveni, Rom. 49/H2
Saverdun, Fr. 42/D5
Saverne, Fr. 53/G6
Savièse, Swi. 56/D5
Savigliano, It. 43/G4
Savignano sul Panaro, It. 59/E4
Savignano sul Rubicone, It. 59/F4
Savigny-le-Temple, Fr. 30/K6
Savigny-sur-Orge, Fr. 30/K5
Savio (riv.), It. 43/K5
Sävja, Swe. 38/G2
Savognin, Swi. 57/F4
Savoie (dept.), Fr. 56/C6
Savona, BC, Can. 126/C3
Savona (prov.), It. 58/B4
Savona, It. 58/B4
Savoonga, Ak, US 134/D3
Savoy (reg.), Fr. 42/F4
Savoy Alps (mts.), Fr. 56/C6
Şavşat, Turk. 90/E1
Sävsjö, Swe. 38/F3
Savu (sea), Phil. 67/M10
Sawahlunto, Indo. 80/B4
Sawankhalok, Thai. 78/B2
Sawara, Japan 75/G3
Sawasaki-bana (pt.), Japan 75/F2
Sawatch (range), Co, US 128/F3
Sawdā', Jabal (peak), SAr. 88/D5
Saweba (cape), Indo. 81/H4
Sawel (mtn.), NI, UK 34/A2
Sawtell, Austl. 115/E1
Sawtooth (range), Id, US 126/E4
Sawtooth Nat'l Rec. Area, Id, US 126/E5
Sawu (isls.), Indo. 81/F6
Sax, Sp. 45/E3
Saxman, Ak, US 134/M4
Saxon, Swi. 56/D5
Say, Niger 103/F3
Saya, Japan 77/L5
Sayama, Japan 75/F3
Sayama, Japan 77/J6
Sayán, Peru 156/B3
Şaydā, Leb. 91/D3
Sayil (ruin), Mex. 144/D1
Saynbach (riv.), Ger. 53/G2
Sayreville, NJ, US 139/H10
Sayula, Mex. 142/E5
Sayville, NY, US 139/E2
Saywūn, Yem. 88/E5
Sazan (isl.), Alb. 47/F2
Sázava (riv.), Czh. 43/L2
Sbaa, Alg. 99/E3
Scafell Pikes (peak), Eng, UK 35/E3
Scalasaig, Sc, UK 31/Q8
Scald Law (peak), Sc, UK 36/C5
Scalea, It. 46/D3
Scalino (peak), It. 57/F5
Scalloway, Sc, UK 31/W13
Scammon Bay, Ak, US 134/E3
Scandia, Wa, US 135/B2
Scandiano, It. 59/D3
Scandicci, It. 59/E5
Scapa Flow (chan.), Sc, UK 31/V14
Scar Water (riv.), Sc, UK 34/E1
Scarborough, Can. 131/R8
Scarborough, Eng, UK 35/H3
Scarborough Shoal (isl.), Phil. 79/C4
Scardovari, It. 59/F3
Scarpe (riv.), Fr. 40/B3
Scarperia, It. 59/E5
Scarriff, Ire. 31/P10
Scarsdale, La, US 137/Q17
Scarsdale, NY, US 139/K7
Sceaux, Fr. 30/J5
Scenic Oaks, Tx, US 137/T20
Scey-sur-Saône-et-St-Albin, Fr. 56/B2
Schaefferstown, Pa, US 138/B3
Schaerbeek, Belg. 53/D2
Schaffhausen (canton), Swi. 57/E2
Schaffhausen, Swi. 57/E2
Schäftlarn, Ger. 57/H2
Schagen, Neth. 50/B3
Schaijk, Neth. 50/C5
Schalchen, Aus. 55/G6
Schalkau, Ger. 54/E2
Schalksmühle, Ger. 51/E6
Schanck (cape), Austl. 115/C3
Schangnau, Swi. 56/D4
Scharans, Swi. 57/F4
Schardenberg, Aus. 55/G5
Schärding, Aus. 55/G6
Scharfreiter (peak), Aus. 57/H3
Scharhorn (isl.), Ger. 51/F1
Scharnebeck, Ger. 51/H2
Scharnitz (pass), Ger. 57/H3
Scharnstein, Aus. 55/G7
Schashagen, Ger. 40/F1
Schattdorf, Swi. 57/E4
Schauenstein, Ger. 55/E2
Schaumburg, Il, US 135/P15
Scheemda, Neth. 50/D2
Scheer, Ger. 57/F1
Scheessel, Ger. 51/G2
Schefferville, Qu, Can. 123/K3
Scheibbs, Aus. 41/H4
Scheidegg, Ger. 57/F2
Scheinfeld, Ger. 54/D3
Schelde (riv.), Belg. 42/E1
Schelklingen, Ger. 54/C6
Schell Creek (range), Nv, US 128/D3
Schellerten, Ger. 51/H4
Schellville, Ca, US 135/K10
Schenectady, NY, US 130/F3
Schenefeld, Ger. 51/G1
Schermbeck, Ger. 50/D5
Scherpenzeel, Neth. 50/C3
Schertz, Tx, US 137/U20
Schesaplana (peak), Aus. 57/F3
Schesslitz, Ger. 54/E3
Scheyern, Ger. 55/E5
Schiedam, Neth. 50/B5
Schieder-Schwalenberg, Ger. 51/G5
Schiehallon (peak), Sc, UK 36/B3
Schier Monnikoog (isl.), Neth. 40/D2
Schierling, Ger. 55/F5
Schiermonnikoog (isl.), Neth. 50/D1
Schiermonnikoog, Neth. 50/D2
Schiers, Swi. 57/F4
Schifferstadt, Ger. 54/B4
Schiffweiler, Ger. 53/G5
Schijndel, Neth. 50/C5
Schilde, Belg. 50/B6
Schildmeer (lake), Neth. 50/D2
Schillighörn (cape), Ger. 51/F1
Schillingfürst, Ger. 54/D4
Schiltach, Ger. 57/E1
Schiltigheim, Fr. 56/D1
Schinnen, Neth. 53/E2
Schinznach-Dorf, Swi. 56/E3
Schio, It. 59/E1
Schipbeek (riv.), Neth. 50/D4
Schirmeck, Fr. 56/D1
Schkumbin (riv.), Alb. 47/G2
Schladen, Ger. 51/H4
Schladming, Aus. 43/K3
Schlanders (Silandro), It. 43/J3
Schlangen, Ger. 51/F5
Schlangenbad, Ger. 54/B2
Schleiden, Ger. 53/F2
Schleitheim, Swi. 57/E2
Schleiz, Ger. 55/E1
Schlema, Ger. 55/F1
Schleswig, Ger. 38/C4
Schleswig-Holstein (state), Ger. 38/B4
Schleswig-Holsteinisches Wattenmeer NP, Ger. 38/C4
Schleuse (riv.), Ger. 54/D2
Schleusingen, Ger. 54/D1
Schliengen, Ger. 56/D2
Schlierbach, Aus. 55/H7
Schlieren, Swi. 57/E3
Schloss Herrenchiemsee, Ger. 55/F7
Schloss Holte-Stukenbrock, Ger. 51/F5
Schloss Sansoucci, Ger. 40/Q7
Schloss Wilhelmstein, Ger. 51/G4
Schlotheim, Ger. 51/H6
Schluchsee, Ger. 56/E2
Schlüchtern, Ger. 54/C2
Schlüsselfeld, Ger. 54/D3
Schlüsslberg, Aus. 55/G6
Schmalkalden, Ger. 43/J1
Schmallenberg, Ger. 51/F6
Schmeich (riv.), Ger. 54/C6
Schmelz, Ger. 53/F5
Schmiech (riv.), Ger. 57/F1
Schmitten, Swi. 56/D4
Schmitten, Ger. 54/B2
Schmutter (riv.), Ger. 54/D5
Schnaitsee, Ger. 55/F6
Schnaittach, Ger. 55/E3
Schnaittenbach, Ger. 55/F3
Schnarrtanne, Ger. 55/F1
Schnecksville, Pa, US 138/C2
Schneeberg (peak), Ger. 55/E2
Schneeberg, Ger. 55/F1
Schneeberg, Ger. 54/C3
Schneifel (upland), Ger. 40/D3
Schneverdingen, Ger. 51/G2
Schofield Barracks, Hi, US 124/V12
Schollene, Ger. 40/G2
Schöllkrippen, Ger. 54/C2
Schömberg, Ger. 57/E1
Schömberg, Ger. 54/B5
Schönaich, Ger. 54/C5
Schönau im Schwarzwald, Ger. 56/D2
Schönberg, Ger. 38/D4
Schönberg, Ger. 55/G5
Schondorf am Ammersee, Ger. 57/H1
Schondra (riv.), Ger. 54/C2
Schönebeck, Ger. 40/F2
Schöneck, Ger. 54/B2
Schönecken, Ger. 53/F3
Schönefeld (int'l arpt.), Ger. 40/Q7
Schongau, Ger. 57/G2
Schöningen, Ger. 40/F2
Schönsee, Ger. 55/F3
Schonungen, Ger. 54/D2
Schönwald, Ger. 55/E2
Schoonebeek, Neth. 50/D3
Schoonhoven, Neth. 50/B5
Schoorl, Neth. 50/B3
Schopfheim, Ger. 53/G4
Schopfloch, Ger. 54/D4
Schöppenstedt, Ger. 51/H4
Schörfling, Aus. 55/G7
Schorndorf, Ger. 54/C5
Schortens, Ger. 51/E1
Schoten, Belg. 50/B6
Schotten, Ger. 54/C1
Schouten (isl.), Austl. 115/D4
Schouten (isls.), Indo. 116/C5
Schouwen (isl.), Neth. 50/A5
Schramberg, Ger. 57/E1
Schrankogel (peak), Aus. 57/H3
Schreckhorn (peak), Swi. 56/E4
Schriesheim, Ger. 54/B4
Schrobenhausen, Ger. 54/E5
Schroffenstein (peak), Namb. 106/B2
Schrozberg, Ger. 54/C4
Schruns, Aus. 57/F3
Schübelbach, Swi. 57/E3
Schuby, Ger. 38/C4
Schulenburg, Tx, US 129/H5
Schulzendorf, Ger. 40/Q7
Schunter (riv.), Ger. 51/H4
Schüpfheim, Swi. 56/E4
Schussen (riv.), Ger. 57/F2
Schussenried, Ger. 57/F1
Schutter (riv.), Ger. 54/A6
Schutterwald, Ger. 56/D1
Schüttorf, Ger. 51/E4
Schuylkill (riv.), Pa, US 138/C3
Schuylkill Haven, Pa, US 138/B2
Schwabach, Ger. 54/D4
Schwabhausen bei Dachau, Ger. 55/E6
Schwäbisch Gmünd, Ger. 54/C5
Schwäbisch Hall, Ger. 54/C4
Schwäbische Alb (range), Ger. 40/E4
Schwabmünchen, Ger. 57/G1
Schwaig bei Nürnberg, Ger. 54/E4
Schwaigern, Ger. 54/C4
Schwalbach, Ger. 53/F5
Schwalbach am Taunus, Ger. 54/B2
Schwalm (riv.), Ger. 40/E3
Schwalmtal, Ger. 50/D6
Schwanden, Swi. 57/F4
Schwandorf im Bayern, Ger. 55/F4
Schwanebeck, Ger. 40/Q6
Schwanenstadt, Aus. 55/G6
Schwaner (mts.), Indo. 80/D4
Schwanewede, Ger. 51/F2
Schwanfeld, Ger. 54/D3
Schwangau, Ger. 57/G2
Schwarmstedt, Ger. 51/G3
Schwartz Elster (riv.), Ger. 41/G3
Schwartzerberg (peak), Namb. 106/B2
Schwarza (riv.), Ger. 54/E1
Schwarzach, Ger. 55/F5
Schwarzach (riv.), Ger. 55/E4
Schwarzach im Pongau, Aus. 43/K3
Schwarze Laber (riv.), Ger. 55/E4
Schwarzenbach am Wald, Ger. 55/E2
Schwarzenbek, Ger. 51/H1
Schwarzenberg, Ger. 55/F1
Schwarzenbruck, Ger. 54/E4
Schwarzenburg, Swi. 56/D4
Schwarzenfeld, Ger. 55/F4
Schwarzer Mann (peak), Ger. 53/F3
Schwarzhorn (peak), Aus. 57/H3
Schwarzwald (Black Forest) (for.), Ger. 54/B6
Schwaz, Aus. 43/J3
Schwebheim, Ger. 54/D3
Schwechat, Aus. 49/N7
Schwechat (int'l arpt.), Aus. 49/P7
Schwedt, Ger. 41/H2
Schwegenheim, Ger. 54/B4
Schweich, Ger. 53/F4
Schweighouse-sur-Moder, Fr. 53/G6
Schweinfurt, Ger. 54/D2
Schweitenkirchen, Ger. 55/E5
Schweizer-Reneke, SAfr. 106/D2
Schwelm, Ger. 51/E6
Schwendi, Ger. 57/F1
Schwenksville, Pa, US 138/C3
Schwerin, Ger. 38/D5
Schweriner (lake), Ger. 40/F2
Schwertberg, Aus. 55/H6
Schwerte, Ger. 51/E6
Schwetzingen, Ger. 54/B4
Schwinge (riv.), Ger. 51/G1
Schwörstadt, Ger. 56/D2
Schwülme (riv.), Ger. 51/G5
Schwülper, Ger. 51/H4
Schwyz (canton), Swi. 57/E3
Schwyz, Swi. 57/E3
Sciacca, It. 46/C4
Scicli, It. 46/D4
Scilly (isls.), Eng, UK 31/Q11
Ścinawa, Pol. 41/J3
Scionzier, Fr. 56/C5
Sciota, Pa, US 138/C2
Scioto (riv.), Oh, US 130/D4
Scobey, Mt, US 127/G3
Scolt (pt.), Eng, UK 33/G1
Scone, Austl. 115/D2
Scopello, It. 58/B2
Scordia, It. 46/D4
Scorzè, It. 59/F2
Scotch Corner, Eng, UK 35/G3
Scotch Plains, NJ, US 139/H9
Scotia (sea) 160/W
Scotland, UK 34/D1
Scott (cape), BC, Can. 122/D3
Scott (cape), NW, Can. 123/R7
Scott (lake), NW,Sk, Can. 122/F2
Scott, NZ, Ant. 160/M
Scott City, Ks, US 129/G3
Scott NP, Austl. 112/B5
Scott (reef), Austl. 109/B2
Scottburgh, SAfr. 107/E3
Scotts (cr.), Austl. 113/M9
Scottish Borders (pol. reg.), Sc, UK 36/C5
Scotts Bluff Nat'l Mon., Ne, US 129/F2
Scottsbluff, Ne, US 129/G2
Scottsboro, Al, US 133/G3
Scottsburg, In, US 130/C4
Scottsdale, Austl. 115/C4
Scottsdale, Az, US 128/E4
Scottsville, Ky, US 133/G2
Scottville, Mi, US 130/C2
Scourie, Sc, UK 31/R7
Scranton, Pa, US 130/F3
Scrivia (riv.), It. 58/B3
Scunthorpe, Eng, UK 35/H4
Scuol, Swi. 57/G4
Scuppernong (riv.), Wi, US 135/N14
Scurdie Ness (pt.), Sc, UK 36/D3
Scutari (lake), Serb. 47/F1
Sea Cliff, Ca, US 136/A2
Sea Cliff, NY, US 139/L8
Sea Girt, NJ, US 138/D3
Sea Isle City, NJ, US 138/D5
Sea Lake, Austl. 115/B2
Sea-Tac, Wa, US 135/C3
Seabeck, Wa, US 135/B2
Seabold, Wa, US 135/B2
Seabra, Braz. 154/B4
Seabrook, NJ, US 138/C5
Seaford, Eng, UK 33/G5
Seaford, NY, US 139/M9
Seaforde, NI, UK 34/C3
Seaforth, Austl. 114/C3
Seagraves, Tx, US 129/G4
Seaham, Eng, UK 35/G2
Seahorse (pt.), Nun, Can. 123/J2
Seahurst, Wa, US 135/C3
Seal, Eng, UK 30/D3
Seal (riv.), MB, Can. 122/G3
Seal (pt.), Chile 158/B5
Seal (cape), SAfr. 106/C4
Seal Beach, Ca, US 136/F8
Seale, Eng, UK 30/A3
Seamer, Eng, UK 35/H3
Seano, It. 59/E6
Searcy, Ar, US 129/K4
Seascale, Eng, UK 34/E3
Seaside, Or, US 126/B4
Seaside Heights, NJ, US 138/D4
Seaside Park, NJ, US 138/D4
Seaton, Eng, UK 32/C5
Seaton (riv.), Eng, UK 32/B6
Seaton Carew, Eng, UK 35/G2
Seattle, Wa, US 126/C4
Sébaco, Nic. 144/E3
Sebaou (riv.), Alg. 100/H4
Sebastian, Fl, US 133/H5
Sebastián Vizcaíno (bay), Mex. 142/B2
Sebayan (peak), Indo. 80/D4
Sebdou, Alg. 100/D2
Sébékoro, Mali 102/C3
Seben, Turk. 49/K5
Sebeş, Rom. 49/F3
Sebezh, Rus. 39/N3
Şebinkarahisar, Turk. 90/D1
Sebiş, Rom. 48/F2
Sebkhet al Kalīyah (drylake), Alg. 100/M7
Sebnitz, Ger. 41/H3
Seboruco, Ven. 152/C2
Sebou (riv.), Mor. 100/B2
Sebou, Oued (riv.), Mor. 98/D2
Sebring, Fl, US 133/H5
Sebuku (isl.), Indo. 81/E4
Secaucus, NJ, US 139/J8
Secchia (riv.), It. 43/J4
Sechura, Peru 156/A2
Sechura (bay), Peru 156/A2
Sechura, Desierto de (des.), Peru 156/A2
Seclin, Fr. 52/C2
Seco (riv.), Mex.,US 142/C2
Seco (riv.), Arg. 159/D6
Seco (riv.), Mex. 143/C2
Second Mountain (mtn.), Pa, US 138/B3
Second Watchung (mtn.), NJ, US 139/H9
Secunda, SAfr. 106/E2
Secure (riv.), Bol. 150/E7
Seda, Lith. 39/K3
Sedalia, Mo, US 129/J3
Sedan, Fr. 53/D4
Sedano, Sp. 44/D1
Sedaung (mtn.), Myan. 78/B3
Sedbergh, Eng, UK 35/F3
Seddülbahir, Turk. 47/K2
Sedeh, Iran 89/G2
Sederot, Isr. 91/D4
Sedgefield, Eng, UK 35/G2
Sedhiou, Sen. 102/B3
Sedlčany, Czh. 55/H3
Sedlo (peak), Czh. 55/H1
Sedona, Az, US 128/E4
Sedrata, Alg. 100/K6
Šeduva, Lith. 39/K4
Sędziszów, Pol. 41/L3
Sée (riv.), Fr. 42/C2
Seeb (int'l arpt.), Oman 89/G4
Seeboden, Aus. 43/K3
Seefeld in Tirol, Aus. 57/H3
Seeg, Ger. 57/G2
Seehausen, Ger. 40/F2
Seeheim, Namb. 106/B2
Seeheim-Jugenheim, Ger. 54/B3
Seekirchen Markt, Aus. 55/G7
Seekooi (riv.), SAfr. 106/D3
Seelow, Ger. 41/H2
Seeon-Seebruck, Ger. 55/F7
Seer Green, Eng, UK 30/B2
Sées, Fr. 42/D2
Seesen, Ger. 51/H5
Seeshaupt, Ger. 57/H2
Seeve (riv.), Ger. 51/G2
Seewalchen, Aus. 55/G7
Seewis im Prättigau, Swi. 57/F4
Şefaatlı, Turk. 90/C2
Sefrou, Mor. 100/B3
Sefton (co.), Eng, UK 35/E4
Segamat, Malay. 80/B3
Segarcea, Rom. 49/F3
Ségbana, Ben. 103/F4
Ségélo-Koro, C.d'Iv. 102/D4
Segelstad Bru, Nor. 38/D1
Seget, Indo. 81/H4
Segezha, Rus. 60/G3
Segorbe, Sp. 45/E3
Ségou, Mali 102/D3
Ségou (pol. reg.), Mali 102/D3
Segovia, Col. 152/C3
Segovia, Sp. 44/C2
Segozero (lake), Rus. 60/G3
Segrate, It. 58/C3
Segré, Fr. 42/C3
Segre (riv.), Sp. 45/F2
Seguam (isl.), Ak, US 134/D5
Séguédine, Niger 96/H3
Séguéla, C.d'Iv. 102/D5
Séguénéga, Burk. 103/E3
Seguin, Tx, US 132/D4
Segura (riv.), Sp. 44/D3
Segusino, It. 59/E2
Sehithwa, Bots. 105/D5
Sehnde, Ger. 51/G4
Sehonghong, Les. 106/E3
Sehore, India 82/C3
Sehwān, Pak. 89/J3
Seibersbach, Ger. 53/G4
Seiersberg, Aus. 48/B2
Seika, Japan 77/J6
Seiling, Ok, US 129/H3
Seille (riv.), Fr. 40/C5
Seinäjoki, Fin. 60/D3
Seine (riv.), On, Can. 127/L3
Seine (bay), Fr. 42/C2
Seine (riv.), Fr. 27/E4
Seine-et-Marne (dept.), Fr. 52/B5
Seine-Maritime (dept.), Fr. 52/A4
Seine-st-Denis (dept.), Fr. 52/B6
Seitenstetten, Aus. 55/H6
Seiwa, Japan 77/K7
Seix, Fr. 42/D5
Seixal, Port. 45/P10
Sejaka, Indo. 81/E4
Sejerø (isl.), Den. 38/D4
Sejny, Pol. 39/K4
Sekayu, Indo. 80/B4
Seke, Tanz. 104/A2
Sekenke, Tanz. 104/A3
Seki (riv.), Turk. 91/A1
Seki, Japan 77/L5
Seki, Japan 77/K6
Sekigahara, Japan 77/K5
Sekijo, Japan 77/D1
Sekiyado, Japan 77/D1
Sekondi, Gha. 103/E5
Sel, Nor. 37/D3
Selah, Wa, US 126/C4
Selaphum, Thai. 78/C2
Selargius, It. 46/A3
Selaru (isl.), Indo. 81/H5
Selatan (cape), Indo. 80/D4
Selawik (lake), Ak, US 134/F2
Selayar (isl.), Indo. 81/F5
Selb, Ger. 55/F2
Selbitz, Ger. 55/E2
Selbitz (riv.), Ger. 55/E2
Selbu, Nor. 37/D3
Selby, SD, US 127/H4
Selby, Eng, UK 35/G4
Selby-on-the-Bay, Md, US 138/B6
Selci, It. 59/F6
Selçuk, Turk. 90/A2
Selden, NY, US 139/E2
Sele (riv.), It. 46/D2
Selebi-Phikwe, Bots. 105/E5
Seleli (hill), Tanz. 104/B5
Selemdzha (riv.), Rus. 65/N4
Selenča, Serb. 48/D3
Selenge (prov.), Mong. 70/J2
Selenge (riv.), Mong. 70/J2
Selenginsk, Rus. 65/L4
Selenicë, Alb. 47/F2
Sélestat, Fr. 56/D1
Selety (riv.), Kaz. 87/F2
Seleznëvo, Rus. 39/N1
Selfoss, Ice. 37/N7
Sélibabi, Mrta. 102/B3
Seligenstadt, Ger. 54/B2
Seliger (lake), Rus. 60/G4
Selimbau, Indo. 80/D3
Selimiye, Turk. 90/A2
Selinsgrove, Pa, US 138/B2
Seljord, Nor. 38/C2
Selkan (tun.), Japan 76/B3
Selkirk, Sc, UK 36/D5
Selkirk, Mb, Can. 122/G3
Selkirk (mts.), BC, Can. 126/D3
Selleck, Wa, US 135/D3
Sellersville, Pa, US 138/C3
Sellières, Fr. 56/B4
Sells, Az, US 128/E5
Selly Oak, Eng, UK 32/E2
Sellye, Hun. 48/C3
Selm, Ger. 51/E5
Selma, Al, US 133/G3
Selmer, Tn, US 133/F3
Selongey, Fr. 56/B2
Selouma, Gui. 102/C4
Selous Game Reserve, Tanz. 104/B4
Selsey, Eng, UK 33/F5
Selsey Bill (pt.), Eng, UK 33/F5
Selsingen, Ger. 51/G2
Sel'tso, Rus. 62/E1
Seltz, Fr. 54/B5
Sélune (riv.), Fr. 42/C2
Selvas (for.), Braz. 147/C3
Selvik, Nor. 37/R9
Selwyn, Austl. 114/A3
Selwyn (range), Austl. 114/A3
Selz (riv.), Ger. 43/H2
Semara, WSah. 96/C2
Semarang, Indo. 80/D5
Semarsot, India 84/D4
Sembehun, SLeo. 102/B5
Sembera (riv.), Czh. 55/H2
Semberong (riv.), Malay. 80/B3
Şemdinli, Turk. 90/F2
Séméac, Fr. 42/D5
Semenivka, Ukr. 62/E1
Semenivka, Ukr. 62/E2
Semenov, Rus. 61/K4
Semeru (peak), Indo. 80/D5
Semey, Kaz. 87/H2
Semikarakorsk, Rus. 63/G3
Semilovo, Rus. 63/G1
Semiluki, Rus. 62/F2
Seminole (lake), Ga, US 133/G4
Seminole, Tx, US 132/C3
Seminoe (res.), Wy, US 128/F2

225
Semit – Sīkar

Semitau, Indo. 80/D4
Semliki (riv.), D.R. Congo 104/A2
Semnān, Iran 88/F1
Semnon (riv.), Fr. 42/C3
Semois (riv.), Belg. 42/F2
Semporna, Malay. 81/E3
Semsales, Swi. 56/C4
Semskefjellet (peak), Nor. 37/E2
Sen (riv.), Camb. 83/H5
Sen-san (peak), Japan 77/G7
Sena, Thai. 83/H5
Senador Pompeu, Braz. 154/C2
Senaja, Malay. 81/E2
Senaki, Geo. 63/G4
Senanga, Zam. 105/D4
Sénas, Fr. 90/B5
Senatobia, Ms, US 133/F3
Sence (riv.), Eng, UK 33/E1
Send, Eng, UK 30/B3
Sendai (riv.), Japan 74/D3
Sendai, Japan 75/G1
Sendai, Japan 74/B5
Sendai (int'l arpt.), Japan 75/G1
Sendai (bay), Japan 76/B4
Sendal (riv.), Japan 74/B5
Senden, Ger. 54/D6
Senden, Ger. 51/E5
Sendenhorst, Ger. 51/E5
Senec, Slvk. 41/J4
Seneca Creek State Park, Md, US 138/A5
Seneffe, Belg. 53/D2
Senegal (ctry.) 102/B3
Sénégal (riv.), Afr. 102/B2
Senekal, SAfr. 106/D3
Seney NWR, Mi, US 130/C2
Senezhskoye (lake), Rus. 61/W8
Senfi, Gha. 103/E5
Senftenberg, Ger. 41/H3
Sengenthal, Ger. 55/E4
Sengilev, Rus. 63/J1
Sengor, Bhu. 85/H2
Senguer (riv.), Arg. 158/D3
Senhor do Bonfim, Braz. 154/B3
Senica, Slvk. 41/J4
Senirkent, Turk. 90/B2
Senise, It. 46/E2
Senj, Cro. 43/L4
Senja (isl.), Nor. 37/F1
Senkaku-Shotō (isl.), Japan 75/G8
Senkaya, Turk. 90/E1
Senköy, Turk. 91/E1
Senlis, Fr. 52/B5
Senmonoron, Camb. 78/D3
Sennan, Japan 77/H7
Sennar (dam), Sudan 97/M5
Senne (riv.), Belg. 53/D2
Sennecy-le-Grand, Fr. 56/A4
Sennfeld, Ger. 54/D2
Senno, Bela. 39/N4
Sennoy, Rus. 63/G2
Sennoy, Rus. 63/H1
Sennwald, Swi. 57/F3
Sennybridge, Wal, UK 32/C3
Séno (prov.), Burk. 103/F3
Senones, Fr. 56/C1
Senorbì, It. 46/A3
Senou (Bamako) (int'l arpt.), Mali 102/D3
Senovo, Bul. 49/H4
Sens, Fr. 42/E2
Sensuntepeque, ESal. 144/D3
Senta, Serb. 48/E3
Sentani, Indo. 81/K4
Sentery, D.R. Congo 105/E2
Senya Beraku, Gha. 103/E5
Senyavin (isls.), Micr. 116/E4
Senzig, Ger. 40/Q7
Seohāra, India 84/B1
Seon, Swi. 56/E3
Seondha, India 84/B2
Seoni, India 84/B4
Seoni Mālwa, India 84/A4
Seoul (Sŏul) (cap.), SKor. 73/D4
Seoul Grand Park, SKor. 73/G7
Seoul Jikhalsi (prov.), SKor. 73/D4
Sepetiba (bay), Braz. 155/J8
Sepik (riv.), PNG 116/D5
Sep'o, NKor. 73/D3
Sepo, Indo. 81/G3
Sępólno Krajeńskie, Pol. 41/J2
Sept-Îles, Qu, Can. 131/H2
Septemvri, Bul. 47/J1
Septeuil, Fr. 30/H5
Sepulveda (dam), Ca, US 136/F7
Sequeros, Sp. 44/B2
Sequoia NP, Ca, US 128/C3
Serafimovich, Rus. 63/G2
Seraincourt, Fr. 30/H4
Seraing, Belg. 53/E2
Serampore, India 85/G4
Séran (riv.), Fr. 56/D3
Serasan (str.), Indo.,Malay. 80/C3
Serasan, Indo. 80/C3
Seravezza, It. 58/D6
Serbia and Montenegro (ctry.) 48/D3
Serbia (reg.), Serb. 48/E4
Serchio (riv.), It. 58/D4
Serdobsk, Rus. 63/H1
Serebryansk, Kaz. 64/J5
Serednikovo, Rus. 60/H5
Seregno, It. 58/C2
Serein (riv.), Fr. 40/D4
Serémange-Erzange, Fr. 53/F5
Seremban, Malay. 80/B3
Serengeti NP, Tanz. 97/M8
Serenje, Zam. 105/F3
Serere, Ugan. 104/A1
Sergach, Rus. 61/K5
Sergeantsville, NJ, US 138/D3
Sergen, Turk. 49/H5
Sergeya Kirova (isls.), Rus. 64/J2
Sergeyevka, Kaz. 61/Q5
Sergipe (state), Braz. 154/C3
Sergiyev Posad, Rus. 60/H4
Sergnano, It. 58/C3
Seria, Bru. 80/D3
Seriate, It. 58/C2
Sérifontaine, Fr. 52/A5
Sérifos, Gre. 47/J4
Sérifos (isl.), Gre. 47/J4
Sérignan, Fr. 42/E5
Serik, Turk. 90/B2
Seringa, Serra da (mts.), Braz. 151/h5
Serio (riv.), It. 58/C2
Serkout (peak), Alg. 99/G5
Sermaize-les-Bains, Fr. 53/D6
Sermide, It. 59/E4
Sernovodsk, Rus. 63/J1
Sernur, Rus. 61/L4
Serón, Sp. 44/D4
Serós, Sp. 45/F2
Serottini (peak), It. 57/G5
Serov, Rus. 64/G4
Serowe, Bots. 105/E5
Serpa, Port. 44/B4
Serpeddì (peak), It. 46/A3
Serpent's Mouth (str.), Trin.,Ven. 153/F2
Serpentine (dam), Austl. 115/C4
Serpentine Lakes, Austl. 113/F4
Serpukhov, Rus. 60/H5
Serra (peak), It. 58/D6
Serra, Braz. 155/D2
Serra Branca, Braz. 154/C2
Serra da Bocaína, PN da, Braz. 155/C2
Serra da Canastra, PN da, Braz. 155/C2
Serra da Capivara, PN da, Braz. 154/B3
Serra da Estrela (peak), Port. 44/B2
Serra da Estrela (mts.), Port. 44/A3
Serra do Cipó, PN da, Braz. 155/D1
Serra dos Órgãos, PN da, Braz. 155/K7
Serra San Bruno, It. 46/E3
Serra San Quirico, It. 59/G7
Serra Talhada, Braz. 154/C2
Sérrai, Gre. 47/H2
Serralta di San Vito (peak), It. 46/E3
Serramanna, It. 46/A3
Serramazzoni, It. 59/D5
Serrana Bank (isl.), Col. 141/F5
Serranía de la Cerbatana (mts.), Ven. 153/E3
Serranía de la Neblina, PN, Ven. 153/E4
Serranías del Burro (mts.), Mex. 142/E2
Serranilla Bank (isl.), Col. 141/F4
Serrano, Arg. 158/E2
Serranópolis, Braz. 155/B1
Serrat (cape), Tun. 100/L6
Serravalle, It. 59/F4
Serravalle, SMar. 59/F6
Serravalle Scrivia, It. 58/B4
Serravalle Sesia, It. 58/B2
Serre (riv.), Fr. 40/B4
Serrenti, It. 46/A3
Serrinha, Braz. 154/C3
Serris, Fr. 30/L5
Sersale, It. 46/E3
Sertã, Port. 44/A3
Sertânia, Braz. 154/C3
Sertãozinho, Braz. 155/H2
Sertavul (pass), Turk. 90/C2
Serteng (mts.), China 70/F4
Serui, Indo. 81/J4
Seruyan (riv.), Indo. 80/D4
Servance, Fr. 56/C2
Servi, Turk. 90/E2
Sérvia, Gre. 47/G2
Serviceton, Austl. 115/B3
Sese (isls.), Ugan. 104/A3
Sesebi (ruin), Sudan 101/B4
Sesepe, Indo. 81/G4
Sesheke, Zam. 105/D4
Sesia (riv.), It. 43/H4
Sesimbra, Port. 44/A3
Sesimbra, Port. 45/P11
Seskar (isl.), Rus. 39/N1
Sespe, Ca, US 136/B2
Sespe (cr.), Ca, US 136/A1
Sespe Condor Sanctuary, Ca, US 136/C3
Sesslach, Ger. 54/D2
Sesto Calende, It. 58/B2
Sesto Fiorentino, It. 59/E6
Sesto San Giovanni, It. 58/C2
Sesto Ulteriano, It. 58/C3
Sestola, It. 59/D5
Sestra (riv.), Rus. 60/W9
Sestri Levante, It. 58/C5
Sestroretsk, Rus. 61/S6
Sestroretskiy (lake), Rus. 61/T6
Sestu, It. 46/A3
Sesvenna (peak), It. 57/G4
Sesvete, Cro. 48/C3
Šeta, Lith. 39/L4
Setana, Japan 76/A2
Sète, Fr. 42/E5
Sete Lagoas, Braz. 155/C1
Setharja, Pak. 89/J3
Seti (riv.), Nepal 84/C1
Seti (zone), Nepal 84/C1
Sétif, Alg. 100/H4
Sétif (wilaya), Alg. 100/H4
Seto, Japan 77/M5
Seto-Naikai NP, Japan 74/C4
Setouchi, Japan 75/K6
Settat, Mor. 98/D2
Settepani (peak), It. 58/B5
Settimo Torinese, It. 58/A2
Settimo Vittone, It. 58/A1
Settle, Eng, UK 35/F3
Settsu, Japan 77/J6
Setúbal (dist.), Port. 44/A3
Setúbal (bay), Port. 44/A3
Setúbal, Port. 45/Q10
Seubersdorf, Ger. 55/E4
Seudre (riv.), Fr. 42/C4
Seugne (riv.), Fr. 42/C4
Seuil-d'Argonne, Fr. 53/E6
Seul (lake), On, Can. 122/G3
Seulimeum, Indo. 80/A2
Seurre, Fr. 56/B4
Seuzach, Swi. 57/E2
Sevan, Arm. 63/H4
Sevana (lake), Arm. 63/H4
Sevastopol', Ukr. 62/E3
Sevelen, Swi. 57/F3
Seven (riv.), Eng, UK 35/H3
Seven Heads (pt.), Ire. 31/P11
Seven Valleys, Pa, US 138/B4
Sevenoaks, Eng, UK 30/D3
Sevenoaks Weald, Eng, UK 30/D3
Severn (riv.), Wal, UK 35/F6
Severn (riv.), On, Can. 122/G3
Severn (riv.), Md, US 138/B5
Severn, Md, US 138/B5
Severna Park, Md, US 138/B5
Severnaya Osetiya-Alaniya, Resp., Rus. 63/G4
Severnaya Sos'va (riv.), Rus. 61/N3
Severnaya Zemlya (isls.), Rus. 64/J2
Severnyy, Rus. 61/P2
Severo-Kuril'sk, Rus. 65/R4
Severo-Yeniseyskiy, Rus. 64/K3
Severobaykal'sk, Rus. 65/L4
Severodvinsk, Rus. 60/H2
Severomorsk, Rus. 60/G1
Severomuysk, Rus. 65/M4
Severoural'sk, Rus. 61/N3
Severskaya, Rus. 62/F3
Severukha, Rus. 61/P4
Seveso, It. 58/C2
Sevier (des.), Ut, US 128/D3
Sevierville, Tn, US 133/H3
Sevilla, Col. 152/C3
Sevilla, Sp. 44/C4
Seville, Austl. 115/G5
Sevlievo, Bul. 49/G4
Sevnica, Slov. 48/B2
Sevojno, Serb. 48/D4
Sevran, Fr. 30/K5
Sevsk, Rus. 62/E1
Sewa (riv.), SLeo. 102/C5
Seward (pen.), Ak, US 134/E2
Seward, Ak, US 134/J3
Seward, Ne, US 129/H2
Sewaren, NJ, US 139/J9
Sewell, Chile 158/N9
Seyah Cheshmeh, Iran 63/H5
Seybaplaya, Mex. 144/D2
Seybouse, Oued (riv.), Alg. 100/K6
Seychelles (ctry.) 23/M6
Seydhisfjördhur, Ice. 37/Q6
Seydişehir, Turk. 90/B2
Seyhan (dam), Turk. 90/C2
Seyhan (riv.), Turk. 91/D1
Seyitgazi, Turk. 90/B2
Seym (riv.), Rus. 96/E2
Seymour, Austl. 115/C3
Seymour, Tx, US 129/H4
Seynod, Fr. 56/C6
Seyssel, Fr. 56/B6
Sežana, Slov. 43/K4
Sézanne, Fr. 52/C6
Sezimovo Ústí, Czh. 55/H4
Sezze, It. 46/C2
Sfântu Gheorghe, Rom. 49/J3
Sfîntu Gheorghe, Rom. 49/G3
Sfîntu Gheorghe Branch (riv.), Rom. 49/J3
Sfizef, Alg. 100/E5
Sgurr na Lapaich (peak), Sc, UK 36/A2
Sha (riv.), China 72/C3
Sha Tin, China 71/U10
Shaanxi (prov.), China 70/J5
Shaba Nat'l Rsv., Kenya 104/C2
Shābāzpur (riv.), Bang. 85/H4
Shabeelle (riv.), Som. 97/P7
Shabla, Bul. 49/J4
Shabqadar, Pak. 86/A2
Shabunda, D.R. Congo 97/L8
Shache, China 87/G5
Shade (mtn.), Pa, US 138/A2
Shadrinsk, Rus. 61/P4
Shafter, Tx, US 132/B4
Shagamu, Nga. 103/F5
Shagany (lake), Ukr. 49/J3
Shageluk, Ak, US 134/G3
Shah Alam, Malay. 80/B3
Shāh Kot, Pak. 86/B4
Shāhābād, India 84/B1
Shāhābād, India 84/B1
Shāhābād, India 84/B2
Shahdād, Iran 89/G2
Shāhdādkot, Pak. 89/J3
Shahdol, India 84/C4
Shāhganj, India 84/D2
Shaḩḩāt, Libya 97/K1
Shāhjahānpur, India 84/B2
Shāhpur, Pak. 86/B3
Shāhpur Chākar, Pak. 82/A2
Shāhpura, India 84/C4
Shahr-e Kord, Iran 88/F2
Shahr Sultān, Pak. 86/A5
Shāhrūd (Emāmshahr), Iran 89/F1
Shā'ib al Banāt (peak), Egypt 101/C3
Shaikhpura, India 85/E3
Shājāpur, India 89/L4
Shakargarh, Pak. 86/C3
Shakaskraal, SAfr. 107/E3
Shakawe, Bots. 105/D4
Shakhrisabz, Uzb. 87/E5
Shakhtinsk, Kaz. 87/F3
Shakhty, Rus. 62/G3
Shakhun'ya, Rus. 61/K4
Shaki, Nga. 103/F4
Shakotan (pen.), Japan 76/B2
Shaktoolik, Ak, US 134/F3
Shalbuzdag (peak), Rus. 63/H4
Shallow Reach (inlet), Austl. 113/M8
Shalqar, Kaz. 63/L3
Shaluli (mts.), China 70/G5
Shām, Jabal ash (peak), Oman 89/G4
Shama (riv.), Tanz. 105/F2
Shamattawa (riv.), On, Can. 123/H3
Shāmgarh, India 89/L4
Shamīl, Iran 89/G3
Shāmli, India 86/D5
Shammar, Jabal (mts.), SAr. 88/D3
Shamokin, Pa, US 138/B2
Shamokin Dam, Pa, US 138/B2
Shamrock (mtn.), Yk, Can. 134/L3
Shamrock, Tx, US 129/G4
Shamsābād, India 84/B2
Shamva, Zim. 105/F4
Shan (div.), Myan. 70/G7
Shan (plat.), Myan. 70/G7
Shan (state), Myan. 83/G3
Sha'nabī, Jabal ash (peak), Tun. 100/L7
Shandong (prov.), China 71/L4
Shandong (isl.), China 72/E3
Shangcai, China 72/C4
Shangcheng, China 72/C5
Shangdu, China 71/K3
Shanghai (prov.), China 71/M5
Shanghai, China 72/L8
Shanghang, China 79/C2
Shanghe, China 72/D3
Shangqiu, China 72/C4
Shangshui, China 72/C4
Shangyi, China 72/C3
Shangyou, China 79/B2
Shannon (riv.), Ire. 31/P10
Shanshan, China 70/F3
Shantar (isls.), Rus. 65/P4
Shantar (isl.), Rus. 67/N4
Shantou, China 79/C3
Shanxi (prov.), China 71/K4
Shanyin, China 72/C3
Shaoguan, China 79/B3
Shaowu, China 79/C2
Shaoxing, China 79/D2
Shaoyang, China 79/B2
Shaoyang, China 83/K2
Shapkina (riv.), Rus. 61/M2
Shaqlāwah, Iraq 90/F2
Sharafkhāneh, Iran 90/F2
Sharbatāt, Ra's ash (pt.), Oman 89/G5
Sharga, Mong. 70/G2
Shari, Japan 76/D2
Sharīngol, Mong. 70/J2
Shark (bay), Austl. 109/A3
Shark River (inlet), NJ, US 138/D3
Sharon, Pa, US 130/D3
Sharp (mtn.), Ut, US 137/K11
Sharpe (lake), SD, US 127/J4
Sharqpur, Pak. 86/C4
Shar'ya, Rus. 61/K4
Shashi, China 79/B1
Shasta (lake), Ca, US 126/C5
Shasta (mt.), Ca, US 126/C5
Shatskiy NP, Ukr. 41/M3
Shatt al Arab (riv.), Iraq 88/E2
Shaţţ al Jarīd (dry lake), Gabon 96/G1
Shattuck, Ok, US 129/H3
Shaunavon, Sk, Can. 126/F3
Shavano Park, Tx, US 137/T20
Shaw, Eng, UK 33/E4
Shawano, Wi, US 127/L4
Shawinigan, Qu, Can. 131/F2
Shawnee, Ok, US 129/H4
Shawnee (res.), Ok, US 137/N15
Shawnee, Ks, US 137/D5
Shay Gap, Austl. 112/D4
Shaykhān, Iraq 90/E2
Shchara (riv.), Bela. 62/C1
Shchekino, Rus. 62/F1
Shchelkovo, Rus. 61/W9
Shchigry, Rus. 62/F2
Shchūchīnsk, Kaz. 87/F2
She Xian, China 79/C2
Shea Stadium, NY, US 139/K9
Shebelē Wenz (riv.), Eth. 97/P6
Sheberghān, Afg. 89/J1
Sheboygan, Wi, US 127/M5
Shediac, NB, Can. 131/H2
Shee (riv.), Sc, UK 36/C3
Sheelin (lake), Ire. 34/A4
Sheep (mtn.), Ak, US 134/F2
Shefar'am, Isr. 91/G6
Shefayim, Isr. 91/F7
Sheffield, Austl. 115/C4
Sheffield, Eng, UK 35/G5
Sheffield (co.), Eng, UK 35/G5
Sheffield, Al, US 133/G3
Sheffield (isl.), Ct, US 139/M7
Shehuén (riv.), Arg. 157/B6
Shek Uk (peak), China 71/V10
Shekak (riv.), On, Can. 130/C1
Shekhūpura, Pak. 86/B4
Shelagskiy (cape), Rus. 65/S2
Shelburne, NS, Can. 131/H3
Shelby, Mt, US 126/F3
Shelby, Ms, US 129/K4
Shelby, Mi, US 130/C3
Shelby, NC, US 133/H3
Shelbyville (lake), Il, US 133/F2
Shelbyville, Tn, US 133/G3
Shelbyville, In, US 130/C4
Sheldon Point, Ak, US 134/F3
Shelekhov (gulf), Rus. 67/Q3
Shelikof (str.), Ak, US 134/H4
Shell (pt.), Eng, UK 33/G4
Shell Lake, Wi, US 127/L4
Shell Rock (riv.), Ia, US 127/K5
Shellbrook, Sk, Can. 127/G2
Shelley (isl.), Pa, US 138/B3
Shelter (isl.), NY, US 139/F1
Shelter Island (sound), NY, US 139/F1
Shelton, Wa, US 126/C4
Shelton, Ct, US 139/E1
Shen Xian, China 72/C3
Shenandoah, Pa, US 138/B2
Shenandoah NP, Va, US 130/E4
Shenchi, China 72/C3
Sheng Xian, China 79/D2
Shenge (pt.), SLeo. 102/B5
Shengena (peak), Tanz. 104/C4
Shennongjia, China 72/B5
Shenqiu, China 72/C4
Shenyang, China 73/B2
Shenzhen, China 83/K3
Shepetivka, Ukr. 62/C2
Shepherd (isls.), Van. 116/F6
Sheppey, Isle of (isl.), Eng, UK 33/G4
Shepshed, Eng, UK 33/E1
Sheqi, China 72/C4
Sherbro (isl.), SLeo. 102/B5
Sherbrooke, Qu, Can. 131/G2
Shere (hill), Nga. 103/H4
Sheremetyevo (int'l arpt.), Rus. 61/W9
Sherghāti, India 85/E3
Sheridan, Wy, US 126/G4
Sheridan, Co, US 137/B3
Sherman, Tx, US 129/H4
Sherpur, Bang. 85/H3
Sherwood (pt.), Ct, US 139/E1
Shetland (isls.), UK 160/G
Sheung Shui-Fanling, China 71/U10
Shevchenko (int'l arpt.), Kaz. 63/J4
Sheyang (riv.), China 72/D4
Sheyang, China 72/E4
Sheyenne (riv.), ND, US 127/J4
Shi (riv.), China 72/C4
Shi San Ling, China 72/H6
Shibakawa, Japan 77/B3
Shibata, Japan 75/F2
Shibayama, Japan 77/E2
Shibecha, Japan 76/D2
Shibetsu, Japan 76/C1
Shibetsu, Japan 76/D2
Shibīn al Kaum, Egypt 91/B4
Shibīn al Qanāţir, Egypt 91/B4
Shibogama (lake), On, Can. 127/L2
Shibotsu (isl.), Rus. 76/E2
Shibushi (bay), Japan 74/B5
Shicheng, China 79/C2
Shicheng (isl.), China 73/B3
Shickshinny, Pa, US 138/B1
Shiderty (riv.), Kaz. 87/F2
Shido, Japan 74/D3
Shiga, Japan 77/J5
Shigaraki, Japan 77/K6
Shihezi, China 70/E3
Shijak, Alb. 47/F2
Shijiazhuang, China 72/C3
Shijōnawate, Japan 77/J6
Shikabe, Japan 76/B2
Shikārpur, India 84/B1
Shikārpur, Pak. 89/J3
Shikata, Japan 77/G6
Shikatsu, Japan 77/L5
Shikishima, Japan 77/B2
Shikohābād, India 84/B2
Shikoku (mts.), Japan 74/C4
Shikoku (isl.), Japan 67/N6
Shikotsu (lake), Japan 76/B2
Shikotsu-Tōya NP, Japan 76/B2
Shildon, Eng, UK 35/G2
Shilka (riv.), Rus. 67/L4
Shilla (peak), India 89/L2
Shillington, Pa, US 138/C3
Shillong, India 83/F2
Shiloh, Il, US 137/H8
Shiloh, NJ, US 138/C5
Shilou, China 72/B3
Shimabara, Japan 74/B4
Shimagahara, Japan 77/K6
Shimamoto, Japan 77/J6
Shimane (pref.), Japan 74/C3
Shimasahi, Japan 77/K5
Shimba Hills Nat'l Rsv., Kenya 104/C4
Shimbara (bay), Japan 74/B4
Shimber Berris (peak), Som. 97/Q5
Shimizu, Japan 76/C2
Shimizu, Japan 77/B3
Shimo-Koshiki (isl.), Japan 74/A5
Shimobe, Japan 77/A3
Shimoda, Japan 75/F3
Shimodate, Japan 75/F2
Shimofusa, Japan 77/E2
Shimoichi, Japan 77/J7
Shimokita (pen.), Japan 76/B3
Shimonita, Japan 77/B1
Shimonoseki, Japan 74/B4
Shimotsuma, Japan 77/D1
Shimoyama, Japan 77/M5
Shimukappu, Japan 76/C2
Shin, Japan 77/C1
Shin (lake), Sc, UK 31/R7
Shindo, SKor. 73/F6
Shingū, Japan 74/D4
Shinhyŏn, SKor. 74/A3
Shinji (lake), Japan 74/C3
Shinjō, Japan 76/B4
Shinjō, Japan 77/J7
Shinkawa, Japan 77/L5
Shinminato, Japan 75/E2
Shinnecock (bay), NY, US 139/F2
Shinnecock Ind. Res., NY, US 139/F2
Shinsei, Japan 77/L5
Shintoku, Japan 76/C2
Shintone, Japan 77/E2
Shinyanga, Tanz. 104/B3
Shinyanga (pol. reg.), Tanz. 104/B3
Shio-no-misaki (cape), Japan 74/D4
Shiogama, Japan 75/G1
Shioya-saki (pt.), Japan 75/G2
Ship Bottom, NJ, US 138/D4
Shipley, Eng, UK 35/G4
Shippan (pt.), Ct, US 139/L7
Shippegan, NB, Can. 131/H2
Shippo, Japan 77/L5
Shiprock, NM, US 128/E3
Shīr (mtn.), Iran 88/F2
Shirakami-misaki (cape), Japan 76/B3
Shirakawa, Japan 75/G2
Shirakawa, Japan 77/M4
Shirakawa-tōge (pass), Japan 74/E3
Shirako, Japan 77/E3
Shirane, Japan 77/A2
Shirane-san (peak), Japan 75/F3
Shirane-san (peak), Japan 75/F2
Shiranuka, Japan 76/D2
Shiraoi, Japan 76/B2
Shiraoka, Japan 77/D1
Shīrāz, Iran 88/F3
Shirbīn, Egypt 91/B4
Shiretoko-misaki (cape), Japan 76/D1
Shiretoko NP, Japan 76/D1
Shiriya-zaki (pt.), Japan 76/B3
Shirjiu (lake), China 72/D5
Shirley, NY, US 139/F2
Shiroi, Japan 77/E2
Shiroishi, Japan 75/G1
Shirone, Japan 75/F2
Shiroyama, Japan 77/C3
Shīrvān, Iran 89/G1
Shishaldin (vol.), Ak, US 134/F5
Shīshgarh, India 84/B1
Shishi, China 79/C3
Shishmaref, Ak, US 134/E2
Shishou, China 79/B2
Shisui, Japan 77/E2
Shithātha, Iraq 90/E3
Shivpurī, India 84/B3
Shivpuri NP, India 84/A3
Shixing, China 83/K3
Shiyan, China 72/B4
Shizhu, China 79/A2
Shizugawa, Japan 76/B4
Shizuishan, China 70/J4
Shizukuishi, Japan 76/B4
Shizunai, Japan 76/C2
Shizuoka (pref.), Japan 75/E3
Shkumbin (riv.), Alb. 48/E5
Shmidta (cape), Rus. 134/C2
Shoal (pt.), Austl. 112/B4
Shoal Lake, Mb, Can. 127/H3
Shoalhaven (riv.), Austl. 115/D2
Shōbara, Japan 74/C3
Shōbu, Japan 77/D1
Shōdo (isl.), Japan 74/D3
Shoemakersville, Pa, US 138/C3
Shokanbetsu-dake (peak), Japan 76/B2
Sholāpur, India 89/L5
Sholl (peak), Arg. 159/D6
Shomron (ruin), WBnk. 91/G7
Shōnan, Japan 77/E2
Shorāpur, India 82/C4
Shoreham-by-Sea, Eng, UK 33/F5
Shorewood, Wi, US 135/Q13
Shorewood, Il, US 135/P16
Shorkot, Pak. 86/B4
Short (mtn.), Tn, US 133/G3
Shortland (isls.), Sol. 116/E5
Shoshone (riv.), Wy, US 126/F4
Shoshone (mts.), Nv, US 128/C3
Shoshoni, Wy, US 126/F5
Shostka, Ukr. 62/E2
Shotts, Sc, UK 36/C5
Shou Xian, China 72/D4
Shouguang, China 72/D3
Shouyang, China 72/C3
Show Low, Az, US 128/E4
Shōwa, Japan 77/B2
Shōwa, Japan 77/D2
Shpanberga (chan.), Rus. 76/E2
Shpola, Ukr. 62/D2
Shreveport, La, US 129/J4
Shrewsbury, Mo, US 137/G8
Shrewsbury, Eng, UK 32/D1
Shrewsbury, Pa, US 138/B4
Shriner (mtn.), Pa, US 138/A2
Shropshire (co.), Eng, UK 35/E6
Shropshire Union (canal), Eng, UK 35/F6
Shū (riv.), Kaz. 65/H5
Shu (riv.), China 72/D5
Shuangbai, China 83/H3
Shuangcheng, China 71/N2
Shuangliao, China 72/E2
Shuangpai, China 83/K2
Shuangyashan, China 71/P2
Shu'ayb, Jabal an (peak), Yem. 88/D5
Shubrā al Khaymah, Egypt 91/B4
Shubrā Khīt, Egypt 91/B4
Shucheng, China 72/D5
Shu'fāţ, Isr. 91/G8
Shufu, China 87/G5
Shuiyang (riv.), China 72/D5
Shujāābād, Pak. 86/A5
Shulan, China 71/N3
Shule, China 87/G5
Shule (riv.), China 64/K6
Shumagin (isls.), Ak, US 134/G4
Shumen, Bul. 49/H4
Shumerlya, Rus. 61/K5
Shuna (isl.), Sc, UK 36/A3
Shunak (peak), Kaz. 87/F3
Shungnak, Ak, US 134/G2
Shunyi, China 72/H6
Shuo Xian, China 72/C3
Shupīyan, India 86/C3
Shūr (riv.), Iran 89/G2
Shurugwi, Zim. 105/E4
Shūshtar, Iran 88/E2
Shuswap (lake), BC, Can. 126/D3
Shuwaykah, WBnk. 91/G7
Shuya, Rus. 60/J4
Shuyang, China 72/D4
Shwebo, Myan. 83/G3
Shwegyin, Myan. 83/G4
Shyghys Qazaqstan (obl.), Kaz. 64/J5
Shymkent, Kaz. 87/E4
Shyok (riv.), India 89/L2
Si Satchanalai (ruin), Thai. 78/B2
Si Xian, China 72/D4
Siāh Kūh (mts.), Afg. 89/H2
Siak (riv.), Indo. 80/B3
Siālkot, Pak. 86/C3
Sianów, Pol. 38/G4
Siapa (riv.), Ven. 153/E4
Siargao (isl.), Phil. 79/E6
Siasi, Phil. 81/F2
Siaton (pt.), Phil. 81/F2
Siaton, Phil. 79/D6
Siau (isl.), Indo. 81/G3
Šiauliai, Lith. 39/K4
Sibalom, Phil. 79/D5
Sibay, Rus. 63/L1
Sibbo (Sipoo), Fin. 39/L1
Šibenik, Cro. 48/B4
Siberia (reg.), Rus. 67/H3
Siberut (isl.), Indo. 67/J10
Sibi, Pak. 89/J3
Sibiloi NP, Kenya 97/N7
Sibiti, Congo 105/B1
Sibiu (prov.), Rom. 49/G2
Sibiu, Rom. 49/G3
Sibley, Mo, US 137/E5
Sibolga, Indo. 80/A3
Sibu, Malay. 80/D3
Sibuco, Phil. 81/F2
Sibut, CAfr. 97/J6
Sibuyan (sea), Phil. 81/F1
Sibuyan (isl.), Phil. 81/F1
Sicamous, BC, Can. 126/D3
Sichuan (prov.), China 70/H5
Sicilia (pol. reg.), It. 46/C4
Sicily (isl.), It. 27/F5
Sicily, Strait of (str.), It. 46/B3
Sico (riv.), Hon. 140/D4
Sicuani, Peru 156/D4
Šid, Serb. 48/D3
Siddipet, India 82/C4
Siderno Marina, It. 46/E3
Siderópolis, Braz. 155/B4
Sidewinder (mtn.), Ca, US 136/C1
Sidhaulī, India 84/C2
Sidhi, India 84/C3
Sidhirókastron, Gre. 47/H2
Sidhpur, India 89/K4
Sidi Aïssa, Alg. 100/G5
Sīdī Barrānī, Egypt 101/A2
Sidi Bel-Abbes, Alg. 100/E5
Sidi Bennour, Mor. 98/C2
Sīdī Bū Zayd, Tun. 96/G1
Sīdī Bū Zayd (gov.), Tun. 46/A5
Sidi Ifni, Mor. 98/C3
Sidi Kacem, Mor. 100/B2
Sidi Kacem (prov.), Mor. 100/B2
Sīdī Sālim, Egypt 91/B4
Sidi Slimane, Mor. 100/B2
Sidi Yahya du Rharb, Mor. 100/A2
Sidlaw (hills), Sc, UK 36/C3
Sidmouth, Eng, UK 32/C5
Sidney, BC, Can. 126/C3
Sidney, Mt, US 127/G4
Sidney, Oh, US 130/C3
Sidney Lanier (lake), Ga, US 133/H3
Sidra (gulf), Libya 93/D1
Sieci, It. 59/E5
Siedlce, Pol. 41/M2
Sieg (riv.), Ger. 43/G1
Siegburg, Ger. 53/G2
Siegen, Ger. 53/H2
Siegenburg, Ger. 55/E5
Siegendorf im Burgenland, Aus. 43/M3
Siemianówka (lake), Pol. 41/M2
Siemiatycze, Pol. 41/M2
Siemreab, Camb. 78/C3
Siena (prov.), It. 59/E6
Siena, It. 43/J5
Sienne (riv.), Fr. 42/C2
Sieradz, Pol. 41/K3
Sieraków, Pol. 41/J2
Sierning, Aus. 55/H6
Sierpc, Pol. 41/K2
Sierra (peak), Ca, US 136/C3
Sierra Blanca, Tx, US 129/F5
Sierra de la Macarena, PN, Col. 150/D3
Sierra de San Pedro Mártir, Mex. 142/B2
Sierra Estrella (mts.), Az, US 137/R19
Sierra Grande, Arg. 158/D4
Sierra Leone (ctry.) 102/B4
Sierra Leone (cape), SLeo. 102/B4
Sierra Madre, Ca, US 136/F7
Sierra Mojada, Mex. 132/C5
Sierra Nevada (mts.), US 128/B3
Sierra Nevada de Santa Marta, PN, Col. 152/C2
Sierra Nevada, PN, Ven. 152/D2
Sierra Vieja (mts.), US, Mex. 132/B4
Sierras Bayas, Arg. 158/E3
Sierre, Swi. 56/D5
Siete Picos (peak), Sp. 45/M8
Siete Tazas, PN, Chile 158/C2
Sieve (riv.), It. 59/E5
Sif Fatima, Alg. 99/H3
Sífnos (isl.), Gre. 47/J4
Sig, Alg. 100/E5
Siga Hills (hills), Tanz. 104/B3
Sigean, Fr. 42/E5
Siġġiewi, Malta 46/L7
Sighetu Marmaţiei, Rom. 49/F2
Sighişoara, Rom. 49/G2
Sighty Crag (hill), Eng, UK 35/F1
Sigillo, It. 59/F6
Sigli, Indo. 80/A2
Sigli (cape), Alg. 100/H4
Siglufjördhur, Ice. 37/N6
Sigmaringen, Ger. 57/F1
Sigmarszell, Ger. 57/F2
Signa, It. 59/E5
Signal de la Mère Boitier (peak), Fr. 42/F3
Signal de Toussaines (peak), Fr. 42/B2
Signal d'Écouves (peak), Fr. 42/D2
Signal Hill, Ca, US 136/F8
Signau, Swi. 56/D4
Signy-L'Abbaye, Fr. 53/D4
Signy-le-Petit, Fr. 53/D4
Signy-Signets, Fr. 30/M5
Sigriswil, Swi. 56/D4
Sigtuna, Swe. 38/G2
Siguatepeque, Hon. 144/E3
Sigüenza, Sp. 44/D2
Sihl (riv.), Swi. 57/E3
Sihlsee (lake), Swi. 57/E3
Sihochac, Mex. 144/D2
Sihong, China 72/D4
Sihorā, India 84/C4
Sihuas, Peru 156/B3
Siilinjärvi, Fin. 60/E3
Siirt (prov.), Turk. 90/E2
Siirt, Turk. 90/E2
Sikandarābād, India 84/A1
Sikandarpur, India 85/E2
Sikandra Rao, India 84/B2
Sikanni Chief (riv.), BC, Can. 122/D3
Sīkar, India 89/L3

Sikas – Sonde

227
Sønde – Stock

Sønderjylland (co.), Den. 38/C4
Sondica (int'l arpt.), Sp. 44/D1
Sondrio, It. 57/F5
Sondrio (dept.), It. 57/F5
Sonepur, India 82/D3
Song (peak), China 72/C4
Song Xian, China 72/C4
Songea, Tanz. 104/B5
Songeons, Fr. 52/A4
Songhua (riv.), China 67/M5
Sŏnghwan, SKor. 73/D4
Songi (isl.), SKor. 73/C5
Songino, Mong. 70/G2
Songjiang, China 72/L8
Sŏngju, SKor. 73/E5
Songkhla, Thai. 78/C5
Songkhram (riv.), Thai. 83/H4
Songling, China 71/M2
Songming, China 83/H2
Sŏngnam, SKor. 73/G7
Songnim, NKor. 73/C3
Songololo, D.R. Congo 105/B2
Songt'an, SKor. 73/D4
Songtao Miaozu Zizhixian, China 79/A2
Songxi, China 79/C2
Songzi, China 79/B1
Songzi (pass), China 72/C5
Soni, Japan 77/K6
Sonid Youqi, China 71/K3
Sonid Zuoqi, China 71/K3
Sonīpat, India 86/D5
Sonneberg, Ger. 54/E2
Sonnefeld, Ger. 54/E2
Sonnjoch (peak), Aus. 57/H3
Sonntagshorn (peak), Ger. 43/K3
Sonobe, Japan 77/H5
Sonoma (co.), Ca, US 135/J10
Sonoma (mts.), Ca, US 135/J10
Sonora, Ca, US 128/B3
Sonora, Tx, US 129/G5
Sonora (state), Mex. 142/C2
Sonoran Desert Nat'l Mon., Az, US 128/D4
Sonoyta, Mex. 128/D5
Sonoyta (riv.), Mex. 142/B2
Sonpur, India 85/E3
Sonqor, Iran 88/E2
Sŏnsan, SKor. 73/E4
Sonsbeck, Ger. 50/D5
Sonseca, Sp. 44/D3
Sonsonate, ESal. 144/D3
Sonsorol (isls.), Palau 116/C4
Sonta, Serb. 48/D3
Sontheim, Ger. 57/G2
Sontheim an der Brenz, Ger. 54/D5
Sonthofen, Ger. 57/G2
Sontra, Ger. 51/G6
Sonvico, Swi. 57/E5
Sopetrán, Col. 152/C3
Sopi (cape), Indo. 81/G3
Sopor, India 86/C2
Sopot, Bul. 47/J1
Sopot, Pol. 38/H4
Sopron, Hun. 43/M3
Sör (riv.), Wal, UK 32/D3
Sor Karatuley (salt pan), Kaz. 87/C4
Sør-Trøndelag (co.), Nor. 37/D3
Sør-Varanger, Nor. 37/J1
Sora, It. 46/C2
Soragna, It. 58/D3
Sŏrak-san (peak), SKor. 73/E3
Sŏraksan NP, SKor. 73/E3
Sorata, Bol. 150/E7
Sorbas, Sp. 44/D4
Sorbolo, It. 58/D3
Sorcy-Saint-Martin, Fr. 53/E6
Sorel, Qu, Can. 130/F2
Sorell-Midway Point, Austl. 115/C4
Soresina, It. 58/C2
Sörforsa, Swe. 38/G1
Sorgues, Fr. 42/F5
Sorgun, Turk. 90/C2
Sori, It. 58/C4
Soria, Sp. 44/D2
Soriano (dept.), Uru. 158/G3
Soriano, Uru. 159/J10
Sorikmerapi (peak), Indo. 80/A3
Soritor, Peru 156/B2
Sormonne (riv.), Fr. 53/D4
Sorø, Den. 38/D4
Soro, Rio do (riv.), Braz. 151/J5
Soroca, Mol. 49/J1
Sorocaba, Braz. 155/C2
Sorochinsk, Rus. 63/K1
Sorol (isl.), Micr. 116/D4
Soron, India 84/B2
Sorong, Indo. 81/H4
Soroti, Ugan. 104/B2
Sørøya (isl.), Nor. 37/G1
Sørøysundet (chan.), Nor. 37/G1
Sorpestausee (lake), Ger. 51/E6
Sorraia (riv.), Port. 44/A3
Sorrento, It. 46/D2
Sorsele, Swe. 37/F2
Sorso, It. 46/A2
Sorsogon, Phil. 79/D5
Sort, Sp. 45/F1
Sõrve (pt.), Est. 39/K3
Sos del Rey Católico, Sp. 44/E1
Sŏsan, SKor. 73/D4
Sŏsan Haean NP, SKor. 73/C4
Sösdala, Swe. 38/E3
Söse (riv.), Ger. 51/H5
Soshanguve, SAfr. 105/E6
Sosna (riv.), Rus. 62/F1
Sosneado (peak), Arg. 158/C2
Sosnogorsk, Rus. 61/M3
Sosnovka, Rus. 61/L4
Sosnowiec, Pol. 41/K3
Sospiro, It. 58/D2
Sosúa, DRep. 141/G4
Sos'va (riv.), Rus. 64/G3
Sot (riv.), India 84/B1
Soto del Real, Sp. 45/N8
Soto la Marina, Mex. 143/F4
Sotouboua, Togo 103/F4
Sottrum, Ger. 51/G2
Sotuta, Mex. 144/D1
Soude (riv.), Fr. 53/D6
Souderton, Pa, US 138/C3
Soúdha, Gre. 47/J5
Souffelweyersheim, Fr. 53/G6
Soufflenheim, Fr. 53/G6
Souflíon, Gre. 47/K2
Soufrière (peak), StV. 141/N9
Soufrière (peak), Guad. 141/N8
Souillac, Fr. 42/D4
Souillac, Mrts. 107/T15
Souk Ahras, Alg. 100/K6
Souk Ahras (prov.), Alg. 100/K6
Souk el Arba du Rharb, Mor. 100/A2
Sŏul (Seoul) (cap.), SKor. 71/N4
Soultz-Haut-Rhin, Fr. 56/D2
Soultz-sous-Forêts, Fr. 54/A5
Soum (prov.), Burk. 103/E3
Soumagne, Belg. 53/E2
Sound, The (chan.), Den. 37/E5
Souppes-sur-Loing, Fr. 42/E3
Sour El Ghozlane, Alg. 100/G4
Sources, Mont aux (peak), Les. 106/E3
Soure, Braz. 151/J4
Soure, Port. 44/A2
Souris, Mb, Can. 127/H3
Souris, PE, Can. 131/J2
Souris (riv.), Can.,US 127/H3
Sourou (prov.), Burk. 102/E3
Sous le Vent, Iles (isls.), FrPol. 117/K6
Sousa, Braz. 154/C2
Sout (riv.), SAfr. 106/C3
South (mts.), NS, Can. 131/H2
South (bay), Nun., Can. 123/H2
South (mtn.), Pa, US 138/A3
South (cape), NZ 117/R12
South (isl.), NZ 109/H7
South Africa (ctry.) 105/D6
South Amboy, NJ, US 139/H10
South America (cont.) 147
South Andaman (isl.), India 83/F5
South Anna (riv.), Va, US 133/J2
South Augusta, Ga, US 133/H3
South Aulatsivik (isl.), Nf, Can. 123/K3
South Australia (state), Austl. 109/C3
South Ayrshire (pol. reg.), Sc, UK 36/B6
South Bend, Wa, US 126/C4
South Bend, In, US 130/C3
South Benfleet, Eng, UK 33/G3
South Buganda (prov.), Ugan. 104/A3
South Burlington, Vt, US 130/F2
South Caicos (isl.), UK 145/J1
South Carolina (state), US 133/H3
South China (sea), Asia 67/L8
South Colby, Wa, US 135/B2
South Dakota (state), US 127/H4
South Dorset Downs (uplands), Eng, UK 32/D5
South Downs (hills), Eng, UK 33/F5
South Dum Dum, India 85/G4
South East (pt.), Austl. 115/C3
South East (cape), Austl. 109/D5
South Elgin, Il, US 135/P16
South Esk (riv.), Austl. 115/C4
South Esk (riv.), Sc, UK 36/C3
South Farmingdale, NY, US 139/M9
South Fork, Co, US 132/B2
South Fulton, Tn, US 130/B4
South Gate, Md, US 138/B5
South Gate, Ca, US 136/F8
South Georgia (isl.), UK 22/H8
South Gloucestershire (co.), Eng, UK 32/D3
South Hams (plain), Eng, UK 32/C6
South Holland, Il, US 135/Q16
South Island NP, Kenya 104/C2
South Jordan, Ut, US 137/K12
South Koel (riv.), India 85/E4
South Korea (ctry.) 73/D4
South Lake Tahoe, Ca, US 128/C3
South Lanarkshire (pol. reg.), Sc, UK 36/E5
South Loup (riv.), Ne, US 127/J5
South Luangwa NP, Zam. 105/F3
South Lyon, Mi, US 135/E7
South Magnetic Pole, Ant. 160/K
South Moose (lake), Mb, Can. 127/J2
South Moresby NP and Prsv., BC, Can. 134/M5
South Naknek, Ak, US 134/G4
South Normanton, Eng, UK 35/G5
South Nyack, NY, US 139/K7
South Ockenden, Eng, UK 30/D2
South Ogden, Ut, US 137/K11
South Orange, NJ, US 139/H9
South Orkney (isls.), UK 160/X
South Ossetia (reg.), Geo. 63/G4
South Oxhey, Eng, UK 30/B2
South Oyster (bay), NY, US 139/M9
South Pacific (ocean) 22/B7
South Para (res.), Austl. 113/M8
South Pasadena, Ca, US 136/F7
South Pine (riv.), Austl. 114/E6
South Plainfield, NJ, US 139/H9
South Platte (riv.), Co, US 137/C2
South Polar (plat.), Ant. 160/Y
South Pole, Ant. 160/A
South Prairie, Wa, US 135/C3
South River, NJ, US 139/H10
South Rockwood, Mi, US 135/F7
South Ronaldsay (isl.), Sc, UK 31/V14
South Roxana, Il, US 137/G8
South Salt Lake, Ut, US 137/K12
South San Francisco, Ca, US 135/K11
South Sandwich (isls.), UK 22/H8
South Saskatchewan (riv.), Sk, Can. 122/E3
South Seaville, NJ, US 138/D5
South Shetland (isls.), UK 160/W
South Shields, Eng, UK 35/G2
South Sioux City, Ne, US 127/J5
South Skunk (riv.), Ia, US 129/J2
South Taranaki Bight (bay), NZ 117/S10
South Turkana Nat'l Rsv., Kenya 104/B2
South Tyne (riv.), Eng, UK 35/F2
South Tyneside (co.), Eng, UK 35/G2
South Ubian, Phil. 81/F2
South Uist (isl.), Sc, UK 31/Q8
South Umpqua (riv.), Or, US 128/B2
South Valley Stream, NY, US 139/L9
South Weber, Ut, US 137/K11
South West (cape), Austl. 115/C4
South West NP, Austl. 115/C4
South West Rocks, Austl. 115/E1
South Whittier, Ca, US 136/F8
South Williamsport, Pa, US 138/B1
South Woodham Ferrers, Eng, UK 30/E2
South Yorkshire (co.), Eng, UK 35/G5
Southampton (cape), Nun., Can. 123/H2
Southampton (isl.), Nun., Can. 123/H2
Southampton, On, Can. 130/D2
Southampton, Eng, UK 33/E5
Southampton (co.), Eng, UK 33/E5
Southampton, NY, US 139/F2
Southampton Water (inlet), Eng, UK 33/E5
Southaven, Ms, US 129/K4
Southeast (cape), Ak, US 134/E3
Southeast (pt.), Bahm. 145/H1
Southeast (pt.), Jam. 145/G2
Southend (int'l arpt.), Eng, UK 33/G3
Southend-on-Sea, Eng, UK 33/G3
Southend-on-Sea (co.), Eng, UK 33/G3
Southern (prov.), Ugan. 104/A3
Southern (dist.), Isr. 91/D4
Southern (mts.), NZ 109/G7
Southern (riv.), Austl. 112/K7
Southern Cook (isls.), Cookls. 117/J6
Southern Cross, Austl. 112/C4
Southern Indian (lake), Mb, Can. 122/G3
Southern NP, Sudan 97/L6
Southern Pines, NC, US 133/J3
Southern Uplands (hills), Sc, UK 35/D1
Southern Ural (mts.), Rus. 61/N5
Southesk Tablelands (plat.), Austl. 109/B2
Southold, NY, US 139/F1
Southport, NC, US 133/J3
Southport, Eng, UK 35/E4
Southton, Tx, US 137/U21
Southwark (bor.), Eng, UK 30/A1
Southwood NP, Austl. 114/C4
Southworth, Wa, US 135/C3
Sovata, Rom. 49/G2
Soverato Marina, It. 46/E3
Sovere, It. 58/D1
Sovetsk, Rus. 39/J4
Sōwa, Japan 77/D1
Sowerby Bridge, Eng, UK 35/G4
Soweto, SAfr. 106/D2
Sōya-misaki (cape), Japan 76/B1
Soyana (riv.), Rus. 60/J2
Soyang (lake), SKor. 74/A2
Soyaux, Fr. 42/D4
Soyen, Ger. 55/F6
Soyhières, Swi. 56/D3
Sozh (riv.), Bela. 62/D1
Sozopol, Bul. 49/H4
Spa, Belg. 53/E3
Spada (lake), Wa, US 135/D2
Spain (ctry.) 44/C2
Spalding, Austl. 113/H5
Spalding, Eng, UK 35/H6
Spalt, Ger. 54/D4
Spanish Lake, Mo, US 137/G8
Spanish Town, Jam. 145/G2
Spannort (peak), Swi. 57/E4
Sparanise, It. 46/D2
Sparks, Nv, US 128/C3
Sparlingville, Mi, US 135/G6
Sparreholm, Swe. 38/G2
Sparta, Wi, US 127/L5
Sparta, Tn, US 130/C5
Sparta, NC, US 130/D4
Sparta, NJ, US 138/D1
Spartanburg, SC, US 133/H3
Spartel (cape), Mor. 100/B2
Spárti (Sparta), Gre. 47/H4
Spartivento (cape), It. 46/E4
Sparwood, BC, Can. 126/E3
Spassk-Dal'niy, Rus. 71/P3
Spáta, Gre. 47/N9
Spátha (cape), Gre. 47/H5
Spean (riv.), Sc, UK 36/B3
Speer (peak), Swi. 57/F3
Speer Canal (canal), Co, US 137/C2
Speicher, Swi. 57/F3
Speicher, Ger. 53/F4
Speichersdorf, Ger. 55/E3
Speke (gulf), Tanz. 104/B3
Speke (int'l arpt.), Eng, UK 35/F5
Spelle, Ger. 51/E4
Spencer (pt.), Ak, US 134/E2
Spencer, Ia, US 127/K5
Spencer (gulf), Austl. 109/C4
Spencer, Ok, US 137/N14
Spencer (cape), Austl. 113/H5
Spenge, Ger. 51/F4
Spennymoor, Eng, UK 35/G2
Spentrup, Den. 38/D3
Sperkhiás, Gre. 47/H3
Sperkhiós (riv.), Gre. 47/H3
Sperrin (mts.), NI, UK 34/A2
Spessart (range), Ger. 54/C3
Spétsai, Gre. 47/H4
Spey (riv.), Sc, UK 36/B2
Spey (bay), Sc, UK 36/C1
Speyer, Ger. 54/B4
Speyerbach (riv.), Ger. 54/B4
Spezzano Albanese, It. 46/E3
Špičák (peak), Czh. 55/F2
Spicer (isls.), Nun., Can. 123/H2
Spiekeroog (isl.), Ger. 51/E1
Spiez, Swi. 56/D4
Spigno Monferrato, It. 58/B3
Spijkenisse, Neth. 50/B5
Spike (mtn.), Ak, US 134/K2
Spilamberto, It. 59/E3
Spilion, Gre. 47/J5
Spilve (int'l arpt.), Lat. 39/L3
Spina (peak), It. 46/A2
Spinetta Marengo, It. 58/B3
Spino d'Adda, It. 58/C2
Spirano, It. 58/C1
Spirit River, Ab, Can. 126/D2
Spiritwood, Sk, Can. 126/G2
Spišská Nová Ves, Slvk. 41/L4
Spiti (riv.), India 86/D3
Spitsbergen (isl.), Sval. 160/E
Split, Cro. 48/C4
Split (int'l arpt.), Cro. 48/C4
Split (lake), Mb, Can. 122/G3
Splitrock (res.), NJ, US 139/H8
Spluga, Passo dello (pass), Swi. 57/F5
Splügen, Swi. 57/F4
Spokane, Wa, US 126/D4
Spokane (riv.), Wa, US 126/D4
Spöl (riv.), It. 57/G5
Spoleto, It. 43/K5
Spoon (riv.), Il, US 130/B3
Spooner, Wi, US 127/L4
Spotorno, It. 58/B4
Spotswood, NJ, US 139/H10
Sprague, Mb, Can. 127/K3
Sprang, Neth. 50/C5
Spratly (isls.) 80/D2
Spree (riv.), Ger. 41/H2
Sprendlingen, Ger. 53/G4
Spresiano, It. 59/F1
Sprimont, Belg. 53/E3
Spring, Tx, US 129/J5
Spring City, Pa, US 138/C3
Spring Grove, Pa, US 138/B4
Spring Grove, Il, US 135/P15
Spring Hill, Ks, US 137/D6
Spring Lake, NJ, US 138/D3
Spring Valley, Ca, US 136/D5
Spring Valley, NY, US 139/J7
Springbok, SAfr. 106/B3
Springdale, Nf, Can. 131/K1
Springdale, Ar, US 129/J3
Springe, Ger. 51/G4
Springer, NM, US 129/F3
Springerville, Az, US 128/E4
Springfield, Or, US 126/C4
Springfield, Tn, US 130/C4
Springfield, Vt, US 131/F3
Springfield, Ma, US 131/F3
Springfield, Mo, US 129/J3
Springfield, NJ, US 139/H9
Springfield, Va, US 138/A6
Springfontein, SAfr. 106/D3
Springhill, La, US 129/J4
Springhill, NS, Can. 131/H2
Springs, SAfr. 106/E2
Springs, NY, US 139/F1
Springside, Sk, Can. 127/H3
Springsure, Austl. 114/C4
Springville, Ut, US 137/K13
Sprockhövel, Ger. 51/E6
Spruce (peak), WV, US 130/E4
Spruce Run (res.), NJ, US 138/C2
Spui (riv.), Neth. 50/B5
Spurn (pt.), Eng, UK 35/J4
Squamish, BC, Can. 126/C3
Squaw Harbor, Ak, US 134/F4
Squaxin Island Ind. Res., Wa, US 135/A3
Squillace, Golfo di (gulf), It. 46/E3
Squinzano, It. 47/F2
Squires (mt.), Austl. 113/E3
Srbobran, Serb. 48/D3
Srebrenica, Bosn. 48/D3
Sredna (mts.), Bul. 47/J1
Srednogorie, Bul. 47/J1
Śrem, Pol. 41/J2
Sremčica, Serb. 48/E3
Sremska Mitrovica, Serb. 48/D3
Sreng (riv.), Camb. 78/C3
Srepok (riv.), Camb. 78/D3
Sri Dungargarh, India 89/K3
Sri Gangānagar, India 86/B5
Sri Jayewardenepura Kotte, (cap.), SrL. 82/C6
Sri Lanka (ctry.) 82/D6
Srikākulam, India 82/D4
Srīnagar, India 86/C2
Srīvardhan, India 89/K5
Środa Śląska, Pol. 41/J3
Środa Wielkopolska, Pol. 41/J2
St. Albans, Vale of (valley), Eng, UK 30/B1
St. John's (cap.), Nf, Can. 131/L2
Stabbursdalen NP, Nor. 37/H1
Staberhuk (pt.), Ger. 38/D4
Stabroek, Belg. 50/B6
Stade, Ger. 51/G1
Staden, Belg. 52/C2
Stadl-Paura, Aus. 55/G6
Stadskanaal, Neth. 50/D3
Stadtbergen, Ger. 54/D6
Stadthagen, Ger. 51/G4
Stadtlauringen, Ger. 54/D2
Stadtlohn, Ger. 50/D5
Stadtoldendorf, Ger. 51/G5
Stadtsteinach, Ger. 55/E2
Stäfa, Swi. 57/E3
Staffanstorp, Swe. 38/E4
Staffelberg (peak), Ger. 54/E2
Staffelegg (pass), Swi. 56/E3
Staffelsee (lake), Ger. 57/H2
Staffhorst, Ger. 51/F3
Staffora (riv.), It. 58/C3
Stafford, Eng, UK 35/F6
Stagno, It. 58/D5
Stagnone Isole Della (isl.), It. 46/B4
Stahnsdorf, Ger. 40/Q7
Staines, Eng, UK 30/B2
Stains, Fr. 30/K5
Stakes (mt.), Ca, US 135/M12
Stakhanov, Ukr. 62/F2
Stalden, Swi. 56/D5
Stalingrad (Volgograd), Rus. 63/H2
Stallings, Il, US 137/G8
Stallworthy (cape), Nun., Can. 123/S6
Stalowa Wola, Pol. 41/M3
Stalybridge, Eng, UK 35/F5
Stamboliyski, Bul. 47/J1
Stamford, Tx, US 129/H4
Stamford, Eng, UK 33/F1
Stamford, Ct, US 139/L7
Stampa, Swi. 57/F5
Stampriet, Namb. 105/C5
Stamullen, Ire. 34/B4
Standerton, SAfr. 106/E2
Standish-with-Langtree, Eng, UK 35/F4
Standley (lake), Co, US 137/B3
Stanford-le-Hope, Eng, UK 33/G3
Stange, Nor. 38/D1
Stanger, SAfr. 107/E3
Stanghella, It. 59/E2
Stanhope, NJ, US 138/D2
Stanišić, Serb. 48/D3
Stanislaus (co.), Ca, US 135/M12
Stanislaus (riv.), Ca, US 128/B3
Stanley, Austl. 115/C4
Stanley (mt.), Austl. 115/C4
Stanley (mt.), Austl. 113/F2
Stanley, NB, Can. 131/H2
Stanley (falls), D.R. Congo 97/L8
Stanley (cap.), Falk. 159/F6
Stanley, Eng, UK 35/G2
Stanley, Sc, UK 36/C4
Stanley, ND, US 127/H3
Stanley, Ks, US 137/D6
Stanley (res.), India 82/C5
Stanley Draper (lake), Ok, US 137/N15
Stanovo, Serb. 48/E4
Stanovoy (range), Rus. 67/M4
Stans, Swi. 57/E4
Stansted (int'l arpt.), Eng, UK 33/G3
Stanthorpe, Austl. 114/C5
Stanton, Ky, US 130/D4
Stanton, Tx, US 129/G4
Stanton, De, US 138/C4
Stanton, NJ, US 138/D2
Stanton, Ca, US 136/G8
Staphorst, Neth. 50/D3
Staplehurst, Eng, UK 33/G4
Staples, On, Can. 135/G7
Stąporków, Pol. 41/L3
Stara Pazova, Serb. 48/E3
Stara Planina (mts.), Serb. 48/F3
Stara Zagora, Bul. 47/J1
Starachowice, Pol. 41/L3
Staranzano, It. 59/G1
Staraya Russa, Rus. 39/P2
Starbuck (isl.), Kiri. 117/K5
Starcke NP, Austl. 114/B1
Stargard Szczeciński, Pol. 38/F5
Starke, Fl, US 133/H4
Starkville, Ms, US 133/F3
Starnbergersee (lake), Ger. 57/H2
Starodub, Rus. 62/E1
Starogard Gdański, Pol. 38/H5
Start (bay), Eng, UK 32/C6
Start (pt.), Eng, UK 32/C6
Start (pt.), Sc, UK 31/V14
Startup, Wa, US 135/D2
Staryy Oskol', Rus. 62/F2
Staszów, Pol. 41/L3
State College, Pa, US 130/E3
State Fairgrounds, De, US 138/C6
State Park Place, Il, US 137/G8
Staten (isl.), NY, US 138/D2
States (int'l arpt.), Chl, UK 42/B2
Statesboro, Ga, US 133/H3
Statesville, NC, US 133/H3
Statue of Liberty Nat'l Mon., NY, US 139/J9
Staufen im Breisgau, Ger. 56/D2
Staufenberg, Ger. 40/E3
Stavanger, Nor. 38/A2
Staveley, Eng, UK 35/G5
Stavelot, Belg. 53/E3
Staveren, Neth. 50/C3
Stavern, Nor. 38/D2
Stavropol', Rus. 63/G3
Stavropol'skiy Kray, Rus. 64/E5
Stavrós, Gre. 47/H2
Stawell, Austl. 115/B3
Stayton, Or, US 126/C4
Ste-Marguerite (riv.), Qu, Can. 131/H1
Steamboat Slough (riv.), Ca, US 135/L10
Steamboat Springs, Co, US 128/F2
Stebbins, Ak, US 134/F3
Steckborn, Swi. 57/E2
Stederau (riv.), Ger. 51/H3
Steeg, Aus. 57/G3
Steele, ND, US 127/J4
Steele's Knowe (hill), Sc, UK 36/C4
Steelpoortrivier (riv.), SAfr. 107/E2
Steelton, Pa, US 138/B3
Steenbergen, Neth. 50/B5
Steens (mtn.), Or, US 128/C2
Steensby (inlet), Nun., Can. 123/J1
Steenvoorde, Fr. 52/B2
Steenwijk, Neth. 50/D3
Steep (pt.), Austl. 112/B3
Steep Holm (isl.), Eng, UK 32/C4
Steephill (lake), Sk, Can. 127/G1
Steeping (riv.), Eng, UK 35/J5
Steese Nat'l Conservation Area, Ak, US 134/J2
Stefansson (isl.), Nun., Can. 122/F1
Steffen (peak), Chile 158/C5
Steffisburg, Swi. 56/D4
Steg, Swi. 56/D5
Stege, Den. 38/E4
Steiermark (prov.), Aus. 41/H5
Steigerwald (for.), Ger. 43/J2
Steilacoom, Wa, US 135/B3
Steimbke, Ger. 51/G3
Stein, Neth. 53/E2
Stein am Rhein, Swi. 57/E2
Stein bei Nünnberg, Ger. 54/E4
Steina (riv.), Ger. 57/E2
Steinach, Ger. 55/F5
Steinach (riv.), Ger. 54/E2
Steinach am Brenner, Aus. 57/H3
Steinbach, Mb, Can. 127/J3
Steinbach an der Steyr, Aus. 55/H7
Steinbourg, Fr. 53/G6
Steinen, Ger. 56/D2
Steinerkirchen an der Traun, Aus. 55/G6
Steinfeld, Ger. 51/F3
Steinfeld, Ger. 54/B4
Steinfeld, Ger. 54/C3
Steinfort, Lux. 53/E4
Steingaden, Ger. 57/G2
Steinhagen, Ger. 51/F4
Steinhausen, Swi. 57/E3
Steinhausen an der Rottum, Ger. 57/F1
Steinheim, Ger. 51/G5
Steinheim am Albuch, Ger. 54/D5
Steinheim an der Murr, Ger. 54/C5
Steinhorst, Ger. 51/H3
Steinhuder (lake), Ger. 51/G4
Steinkjer, Nor. 37/D2
Steinsland, Nor. 38/A1
Steinweiler, Ger. 54/B4
Stekene, Belg. 50/B6
Stella, SAfr. 106/D2
Stella (peak), It. 57/F5
Stellarton, NS, Can. 131/J2
Stelle, Ger. 51/H2
Stellenbosch, SAfr. 106/L10
Stello (peak), Fr. 43/H5
Stelvio, Passo di (pass), It. 57/G4
Stelvio, PN Dello, It. 43/J3
Stenay, Fr. 53/E5
Stendal, Ger. 40/F2
Steneto NP, Bul. 47/J1
Stenhousemuir, Sc, UK 36/C4
Stenungsund, Swe. 38/D2
Stephansposching, Ger. 55/F5
Stephenville, Nf, Can. 131/K1
Stephenville, Tx, US 129/H4
Sterkstroom, SAfr. 106/D3
Sterling, Ak, US 134/H3
Sterling, Co, US 129/G2
Sterlitamak, Rus. 63/K1
Sternstein (peak), Aus. 55/H5
Sterzing (Vipiteno), It. 57/H4
Stęszew, Pol. 41/J2
Štěti, Czh. 55/H2
Stettler, Ab, Can. 126/E2
Steubenville, Oh, US 130/D3
Stevenage, Eng, UK 33/F3
Stevens Village, Ak, US 134/J2
Stevenson (lake), Mb, Can. 127/J2
Stevenson Entrance (str.), Ak, US 134/H4
Stevenston, Sc, UK 36/B5
Stevensville, Mt, US 126/E4
Stevensville, Md, US 138/B6
Stevinsluizen (dam), Neth. 50/C3
Stevzing (Vipiteno), It. 43/J3
Stewart, BC, Can. 134/N4
Stewart (riv.), Yk, Can. 122/C2
Stewart (isl.), NZ 109/G7
Stewart Crossing, Yk, Can. 134/L3
Stewarton, Sc, UK 36/B5
Stewartstown, Pa, US 138/B4
Stewartstown, NI, UK 34/B2
Stewartville, Mn, US 127/K5
Steynrus, SAfr. 106/D2
Steynsburg, SAfr. 106/D3
Steyr, Aus. 55/H6
Steyr (riv.), Aus. 41/H5
Steyregg, Aus. 55/H6
Steytlerville, SAfr. 106/D4
Stia, It. 59/E5
Stiava, It. 58/D5
Stickney (mt.), Wa, US 135/D2
Stiens, Neth. 50/C2
Stigler, Ok, US 129/J4
Stigtomta, Swe. 38/G2
Stikine (riv.), Can.,US 134/M4
Stilbaai, SAfr. 106/C4
Stilfontein, SAfr. 106/D2
Stilis, Gre. 47/H3
Still Creek (res.), Pa, US 138/C2
Still Pond, Md, US 138/B5
Stilling, Den. 38/D3
Stillings, Mo, US 137/D5
Stillwater (range), Nv, US 128/C3
Stillwater, Ok, US 129/H3
Stillwater, Pa, US 138/B1
Stillwater (lake), Pa, US 138/C1
Stilo (cape), It. 46/E3
Stilwell, Ok, US 129/J4
Stilwell, Ks, US 137/D6
Štimlje, Serb. 47/G1
Stimpfach, Ger. 54/D4
Stinchar (riv.), Sc, UK 34/D1
Stinnett, Tx, US 129/G4
Štip, FYROM 47/H2
Stiring-Wendel, Fr. 53/F5
Stírka (peak), Czh. 55/G4
Stirling (mt.), Austl. 112/C4
Stirling, Sc, UK 36/C4
Stirling (pol. reg.), Sc, UK 36/B4
Stirling Range NP, Austl. 112/C5
Stirone (riv.), It. 58/C3
Stjørdal, Nor. 37/D3
Stob a' Choin (peak), Sc, UK 36/B4
Stob Choire Claurigh (peak), Sc, UK 36/B3
Stochov, Czh. 55/G2
Stock, Eng, UK 30/E2
Stock (lake), Fr. 53/F6
Stockach, Ger. 57/F2

Stock – Tabuk

abūk, SAr. 88/C3
abuleiro do Norte, raz. 154/C2
aburbah, Tun. 46/A4
abwemasana (peak), an. 116/F6
acabamba, Peru 156/B2
acámbaro de Codallos, lex. 143/E5
acaná (vol.), Mex. 144/C3
acarcuna (mtn.), an. 152/B2
acheng, China 70/D2
achibana (bay), apan 74/A4
achikawa, Japan 75/F3
achinger (lake), er. 55/F7
achira (state), en. 145/H5
achov, Czh. 55/F3
acloban, Phil. 79/E5
acna, Peru 156/D5
acna (dept.), Peru 156/D5
acoma, Wa, US 126/C4
acora (vol.), Chile 156/D5
acotalpa, Mex. 144/C2
acuarembó, Uru. 157/E3
acuarembó (dept.), ru. 159/G2
acutu (riv.), Braz. 153/F4
adaoka, Japan 77/H7
a'Delimara (pt.), Ialta 46/M7
ademaït, Plateau du lat.), Alg. 96/F2
ādepallegūdem, dia 82/D4
adley, Eng, UK 33/E4
admur, Syria 90/D3
adó, Col. 152/B3
ado, Japan 77/L5
adohae Hasang NP, Kor. 73/C5
adotsu, Japan 74/C3
ādpatri, India 82/C5
adrart (mts.), lg.,Libya 96/H2
adworth, Eng, UK 30/C3
'aean, SKor. 73/D4
'aebaek, SKor. 73/E4
aech'ŏn, SKor. 73/D4
aech'ŏng (isl.), Kor. 73/C4
aedŏk, SKor. 73/D5
aedong (riv.), Kor. 73/D3
aegang-got (pt.), Kor. 73/D3
aegu, SKor. 73/E5
aegu Gwangyŏksi rov.), SKor. 74/A3
aehŭksan (isl.), Kor. 73/C5
aehwa (isl.), NKor. 73/C3
'aein, SKor. 73/D5
aejŏn, SKor. 73/D4
aejŏn Gwangyŏksi rov.), SKor. 73/D4
aeryŏng (riv.), Kor. 73/C2
afalla, Sp. 44/E1
afassasset, Oued (riv.), lg. 99/H4
aff (riv.), Wal, UK 32/C3
afí Viejo, Arg. 157/C2
afraout, Mor. 98/C3
aft, La, US 137/P17
aft, Iran 88/F2
aftān (mtn.), Iran 89/H3
aga, Japan 77/K5
aganrog, Rus. 62/F3
agant (pol. reg.), Irta. 102/C2
agarav (peak), rkm. 63/L5
agawa, Japan 77/L6
aggia, It. 58/A5
aghit, Alg. 99/E3
agish, Yk, Can. 134/M3
agliamento (riv.), It. 43/K3
aglio di Po, It. 59/F3
agolo (pt.), Phil. 81/F2
aguasco, Cuba 145/G1
aguatinga, Braz. 151/J7
agula (isl.), PNG 116/E6
agum, Phil. 79/E6
agun (riv.), Rus. 61/P4
agus (riv.), Sp. 27/D5
agus Rio Tejo (lake), ort. 45/P10
agus (Tajo) (riv.), Sp. 44/C3
'ahan (peak), Ialay. 80/B3
'ahanea (isl.), FrPol. 117/L6
'ahanroz'ka Zatoka gulf), Rus.,Ukr. 62/F3
'ahara, Japan 77/M6
'ahat (peak), Alg. 99/G5
'ahat, Oued et (riv.), lg. 100/F5
'ahe, China 71/M1
'ahilt, Mong. 70/G2
'ahir (pass), Turk. 90/E2
'ahiti (isl.), FrPol. 117/L6
'ahkuna (pt.), Est. 39/K2
'ahlequah, Ok, US 129/J4
'ahmoor, Austl. 115/D2
'ahneta (pass), k, US 134/J3
'ahoe (lake), a,Nv, US 122/D5
'ahoka, Tx, US 129/G4
'ahoua (dept.), Niger 103/G3
'ahoua, Niger 103/G3
Tahsis, BC, Can. 126/B3
Tahuamanu (riv.), Peru 156/D3
Tahuamanú, Peru 156/D3
Tahuata (isl.), FrPol. 117/L6
Tahulandang (isl.), Indo. 81/G3
Tahuya, Wa, US 135/A3
Tahuya (riv.), Wa, US 135/B3
Tai Long Wan (bay), China 71/V10
Tai Mo Shan (peak), China 71/U10
Taï, PN de, C.d'Iv. 96/D6
Tai Po, China 71/U10
Tai Xian, China 72/E4
Tai'an, China 73/B2
Tai'an, China 72/D3
Taïarēt (well), Mor. 98/B5
Taibus, China 71/L3
Taicang, China 72/L8
T'aichung, Tai. 79/D3
Taiei, Japan 77/E2
Taieri (riv.), NZ 117/S12
Taigu, China 72/C3
Taihang (mts.), China 72/C3
Taihe, China 79/B2
Taihe, China 72/C4
Taikang, China 72/C4
Taiki, Japan 76/C2
Tailem Bend, Austl. 113/H5
Taima, Japan 77/J6
Tain, Sc, UK 36/B1
T'ainan, Tai. 79/D3
Taínaron (cape), Gre. 47/H4
Taingainony, Madg. 107/H8
Taino, It. 58/B1
Taiobeiras, Braz. 154/B4
T'aipei (cap.), Tai. 79/D2
Taiping, Malay. 80/B3
Taiping, China 79/C1
Taisha, Japan 74/C3
Taishan, China 79/B3
Taishi, Japan 77/J6
Taishun, China 79/C2
Taiskirchen im Innkreis, Aus. 55/G6
Taissy, Fr. 53/D5
Taitao (pen.), Chile 147/B7
Taiti (peak), Kenya 104/B2
T'aitung, Tai. 79/D3
Taiwan (ctry.) 79/D3
Taiwan (str.), China,Tai 79/C3
Taixing, China 72/E4
Taíyetos (mts.), Gre. 47/H4
Taiyuan, China 72/C3
Taizhou, China 72/D4
Taizi (riv.), China 72/F2
Ta'izz, Yem. 88/D6
Tāj Mahal, India 84/B2
Tajikistan (ctry.) 87/E5
Tajima, Japan 75/F2
Tajimi, Japan 77/M5
Tajiri, Japan 77/D4
Tājpur, India 84/B1
Tajrīsh, Iran 88/F1
Tajumulco (vol.), Guat. 144/D3
Tajuña (riv.), Sp. 44/D2
Tak, Thai. 78/B2
Takahagi, Japan 75/G2
Takahama, Japan 77/J5
Takahama, Japan 77/L6
Takahashi (riv.), Japan 74/C3
Takahashi, Japan 74/C3
Takahata, Japan 75/G1
Takaishi, Japan 77/H6
Takamatsu, Japan 74/D3
Takami-yama (peak), Japan 77/K7
Takanabe, Japan 74/B4
Takane, Japan 77/A2
Takanosu, Japan 76/B3
Takanosu-yama (peak), Japan 77/C2
Takaoka, Japan 75/E2
Takapuna, NZ 117/S10
Takarazuka, Japan 77/H6
Takaroa (isl.), FrPol. 117/L6
Takasaki, Japan 75/F2
Takashima, Japan 77/K5
Takatō, Japan 77/L5
Takatori, Japan 77/J7
Takatsuki, Japan 77/K5
Takatsuki, Japan 77/J6
Takayama, Japan 75/E2
Takefu, Japan 74/E3
Takehara, Japan 74/C3
Takestān, Iran 88/E1
Taketa, Japan 74/B4
Taketoyo, Japan 77/L6
Takhatgarh, India 82/B2
Takhatpur, India 84/C4
Takht-e Jamshīd (ruin), Iran 88/F3
Takht-i-Bhāi, Pak. 86/A2
Taki, Japan 77/L7
Takijuq (lake), Nun., Can. 122/E2
Takikawa, Japan 76/B2
Takino, Japan 77/G6
Takla (lake), BC, Can. 126/B2
Takla Makan (des.), China 67/H6
Tako, Japan 77/K6
Takoradi, Gha. 103/E5
Takouch (cape), Alg. 100/K6
Taksony, Hun. 49/R10
Tala, Mex. 142/E4
Talā, Egypt 91/B4
Tala, Uru. 159/L11
Talagang, Pak. 86/B3
Talagante, Chile 158/N8
Talāja, India 89/K4
Talak (phys. reg.), Niger 96/G4
Talamanca (mts.), CR 145/F4
Talamba, Pak. 86/B4
Talamona, It. 57/F5
Talang (peak), Indo. 80/B4
Talanga, Hon. 144/E3
Talange, Fr. 53/F5
Talant, Fr. 56/A3
Talara, Peru 156/A2
Talas (obl.), Kyr. 87/F4
Talas, Turk. 90/C2
Talas, Kyr. 87/F4
Talas (riv.), Kaz. 87/F4
Talaud (isl.), Phil. 67/M9
Talavera de la Reina, Sp. 44/C3
Talawakele, SrL. 82/D6
Talayuela, Sp. 44/C3
Talbingo, Austl. 115/D2
Talbot (mt.), Austl. 112/E3
Talbot (co.), Md, US 138/B6
Talca, Chile 158/C2
Talcahuano, Chile 158/B3
Tālcher, India 82/E3
Taldyqorghan (obl.), Kaz. 87/G3
Taldyqorghan, Kaz. 87/G3
Talence, Fr. 42/C4
Talent (riv.), Swi. 56/C4
Talfer (Talvera) (riv.), It. 57/H4
Talgar, Kaz. 87/G4
Taliabu (isl.), Indo. 81/F4
Taliouine, Mor. 98/D3
Talkeetna, Ak, US 134/H3
Ţalkhā, Egypt 91/B4
Tall 'Afar, Iraq 90/E2
Tall al Muqayyar (ruin), Iraq 88/E2
Tall 'Āsūr (peak), Isr. 91/G8
Tall Kayf, Iraq 90/E2
Talladega, Al, US 133/G3
Tallahassee (cap.), Fl, US 133/G4
Tallahatchie (riv.), Ms, US 129/K4
Tallangatta, Austl. 115/C3
Tallanstown, Ire. 34/B4
Tallering (peak), Austl. 112/B4
Talleyville, De, US 138/C4
Tallinn (cap.), Est. 39/L2
Tallman Mountain State Park, NY, US 139/K7
Talloires, Fr. 56/C6
Tallow, Ire. 31/Q10
Tallulah, La, US 129/K4
Tallulah (falls), Ga, US 133/H3
Talmassons, It. 59/G1
Talo (peak), Eth. 97/N5
Taloda, India 89/K4
Tāloqān, Afg. 89/J1
Taloyoak, Nun., Can. 122/G2
Talpa de Allende, Mex. 142/D4
Talsperre Pöhl (res.), Ger. 55/F1
Taltal, Chile 157/B2
Taltson (riv.), NW, Can. 122/E2
Talumphuk (pt.), Thai. 78/C4
Talvera (Talfer) (riv.), It. 57/H4
Talwāra, India 86/C4
Tam Ky, Viet. 78/E3
Tama, Japan 77/C2
Tama (riv.), Japan 77/C2
Tamagawa, Japan 77/C2
Tamaho, Japan 77/B2
Tamaki, Japan 77/L7
Tamalameque, Col. 152/C2
Tamale, Gha. 103/E4
Tamamura, Japan 77/C1
Taman, Indo. 80/D5
Taman-Rasset, Oued (riv.), Alg. 99/F5
Tamaná (peak), Col. 152/B3
Tamana (isl.), Kiri. 116/G5
Tamanar, Mor. 98/C3
Tamanghasset (prov.), Alg. 103/F1
Tamanghasset, Oued (riv.), Alg. 99/F5
Tamanrasset, Alg. 99/G5
Tamanrasset (prov.), Alg. 99/F4
Tamaqua, Pa, US 138/C2
Tamar (riv.), Eng, UK 32/B5
Tamara (isl.), Japan 75/H8
Tamari, Japan 77/E1
Tamarindo NWR, CR 144/E4
Tamarite de Litera, Sp. 45/F2
Tamaro (peak), Swi. 57/E5
Tamási, Hun. 48/D2
Tamatsukuri, Japan 77/E1
Tamaulipas (state), Mex. 140/B3
Tamazula de Gordiano, Mex. 142/E5
Tamazunchale, Mex. 144/B1
Tamba, Japan 77/H5
Tamba (uplands), Japan 77/H5
Tambacounda (pol. reg.), Sen. 102/B3
Tambacounda, Sen. 102/B3
Tambaoura, Falaise de (cliff), Mali 102/C3
Tambelan (isls.), Indo. 80/C3
Tambellup, Austl. 112/C5
Tambo (riv.), Peru 156/C3
Tambo (peak), Swi. 57/F5
Tambo, Austl. 114/B4
Tambo Colorado (ruin), Peru 156/C4
Tambo de Mora, Peru 156/B4
Tambo Grande, Peru 156/A2
Tambobamba, Peru 156/C4
Tambohorano, Madg. 107/G7
Tambopata (riv.), Peru 156/D4
Tambora (peak), Indo. 81/E5
Tamboril, Braz. 154/B2
Tamboritha (mt.), Austl. 115/C3
Tambov, Rus. 63/G1
Tambovskaya Oblast, Rus. 63/G1
Tambre (riv.), Sp. 44/A1
Tame (riv.), Eng, UK 33/E1
Tame, Col. 152/D3
Tâmega (riv.), Port. 44/B2
Tamentit, Alg. 99/E4
Tameside (co.), Eng, UK 35/F5
Tamgak (peak), Niger 103/H2
Tamgue (mass.), Gui. 102/B3
Tamiahua, Mex. 144/B1
Tamiahua (lag.), Mex. 144/B1
Tamil Nādu (state), India 82/C5
Taminango, Col. 152/B4
Ţāmiyah, Egypt 91/B5
Tamlūk, India 85/F4
Tammany (mt.), NJ, US 138/C2
Tammela, Fin. 39/K1
Ţammūn, WBnk. 91/D3
Tampa, Fl, US 133/H5
Tampa (int'l arpt.), Fl, US 133/H5
Tampere, Fin. 39/K1
Tampere-Pirkkala (int'l arpt.), Fin. 39/K1
Tampico, Mex. 144/B1
Tampoc (riv.), FrG. 153/H4
Tampon Ambohitra (peak),Madg. 107/J6
Tampulonanjing (peak), Indo. 80/A3
Tamra, Isr. 91/G6
Tamshiyacu, Peru 156/C2
Tamuín (riv.), Mex. 144/B1
Tamuín, Mex. 144/B1
Tamur (riv.), Nepal 85/F2
Tamworth, Austl. 115/D1
Tamworth, Eng, UK 33/E1
Tamyang, SKor. 73/D5
Tan (riv.), China 83/K3
Tan An, Viet. 78/D4
Tan-Tan, Mor. 98/C3
Tana (riv.), Kenya 93/G5
Tana (lake), Eth. 93/F3
Tana River Primate Nat'l Rsv., Kenya 104/D3
Tanabe, Japan 74/D4
Tanabe, Japan 77/J6
Tanabi, Braz. 155/B2
Tanacross, Ak, US 134/K3
Tanafjorden (estu.), Nor. 37/J1
Tanaga (vol.), Ak, US 134/C6
Tanaga (isl.), Ak, US 134/C6
Tanagura, Japan 75/G2
Tanah Merah, Malay. 83/H6
Tanahbala (isl.), Indo. 80/A4
Tanakpur, India 84/C1
Tanambe, Madg. 107/J7
Tanami (des.), Austl. 109/C2
Tanana, Ak, US 134/H2
Tanana (riv.), Ak, US 134/J3
Tanandava, Madg. 107/G8
Tanaro (riv.), It. 43/G4
Tancheng, China 72/D4
Tanch'ŏn, NKor. 73/E2
Tancítaro, Pico de (peak), Mex. 142/E5
Tancitaro, PN de, Mex. 140/A4
Tanda (lake), Mali 102/D3
Tānda, India 84/D2
Tānda, India 84/B1
Ţăndărei, Rom. 49/H3
Tandil, Arg. 158/F3
Tāndliānwāla, Pak. 86/B4
Tando Ādam, Pak. 89/J3
Tando Allāhyār, Pak. 89/J3
Tando Muhammad Khān, Pak. 89/J3
Tandou (lake), Austl. 109/D4
Tandragee, NI, UK 34/B3
Tanem Taunggyi (range), Thai. 83/G4
Tanezrouft (des.), Alg. 93/B2
Tanezrouft-n-Ahenet (des.), Alg. 99/F5
Tang (riv.), China 72/C4
Tanga (pol. reg.), Tanz. 104/C4
Tanga, Tanz. 104/C4
Tangail, Bang. 85/G3
Tangail (pol. reg.), Bang. 85/G3
Tanganyika (lake), D.R. Congo 93/F5
Tangará da Serra, Braz. 150/G6
Tangent (pt.), Ak, US 134/G1
Tanger, Mor. 100/B2
Tanger (prov.), Mor. 100/A2
Tangerhütte, Ger. 40/F2
Tangermünde, Ger. 40/F2
Tanggula (mts.), China 70/E5
Tanghe, China 72/C4
Tangi, Pak. 86/A2
Tangipahoa (riv.), La, US 137/P16
Tangipahoa (parish), La, US 137/P16
Tangjin, SKor. 73/D4
Tanglewilde-Thompson Place, Wa, US 135/B3
Tangshan, China 72/J7
Tangub, Phil. 79/D6
Tangyin, China 72/C4
Tangyuan, China 71/N2
Tanhaçu, Braz. 154/B4
Tanigumi, Japan 77/L4
Tanimbar (isl.), Indo. 67/N10
Taninges, Fr. 56/C5
Tanintharyi (state), Myan. 83/G5
Tanjay, Phil. 79/D6
Tanjungbalai, Indo. 80/A3
Tanjungkarang-Telukbetung, Indo. 80/C5
Tanjungpandan, Indo. 80/C4
Tanjungpinang, Indo. 80/B3
Tanjungpura, Indo. 80/A3
Tānk, Pak. 86/A3
Tankwa Karoo NP, SAfr. 106/B4
Tann, Ger. 55/F6
Tanna (isl.), Van. 116/F6
Tannan, Japan 77/H5
Tannersville, Pa, US 138/C1
Tannheim, Aus. 57/G3
Tannu-Ola (mts.) 70/F1
Tano (riv.), Gha. 96/E6
Tânout, Niger 103/H3
Tanquián de Escobedo, Mex. 144/B1
Tansen, Nepal 84/D2
Ţanţā, Egypt 91/B4
Tantallon, Md, US 138/A6
Tantō, Japan 77/G5
Tantoyuca, Mex. 144/B1
Tanuku, India 82/D4
Tanumshede, Swe. 38/D2
Tanunda, Austl. 115/A2
Tanyang, SKor. 73/E4
Tanzania (ctry.) 104/B4
Tanzawa-yama (peak), Japan 77/C3
Tao (isl.), Myan. 78/B4
Taolañaro, Madg. 107/H9
Taormina, It. 46/D4
Tāoru, India 86/D5
Taos, NM, US 129/F3
Taounate (town), Mor. 100/B2
Taounate, Mor. 100/B2
Taourirt, Alg. 99/F4
Taourirt, Mor. 100/C2
T'aoyüan, Tai. 79/D2
Taoyuan, China 83/K2
Tap Mun Chau (isl.), China 71/V10
Tap O'Noth (hill), Sc, UK 36/D2
Tapa, Est. 39/L2
Tapachula, Mex. 144/C3
Tapajós (riv.), Braz. 147/D3
Tapanahoni (riv.), Sur. 151/G3
Tapanti Nat'l Wild. Ref., CR 145/F4
Tapauá (riv.), Braz. 150/E5
Tapauá, Braz. 150/F5
Tapaz, Phil. 79/D5
Tapejara, Braz. 155/A4
Tapes, Braz. 155/B4
Tapeta, Libr. 102/C5
Tapia de Casariego, Sp. 44/B1
Tapiche (riv.), Peru 156/C2
Tapilula, Mex. 144/C2
Tapis (peak), Malay. 80/B3
Tapo, Peru 156/C3
Tapoa (prov.), Burk. 103/F3
Tapolca, Hun. 48/C2
Tappahannock, Va, US 130/E4
Tappan, NY, US 139/K7
Tappan Zee (lake), NY, US 139/E1
Tappan Zee (riv.), NY, US 139/K7
Tappi-zaki (pt.), Japan 76/B3
Tapps (lake), Wa, US 135/C3
Tāpti (riv.), India 89/J4
Ţāq Kisrá (Ctesiphon) (ruin), Iraq 90/F3
Taquara, Braz. 155/B4
Taquari (riv.), Braz. 151/G7
Taquari, Braz. 155/B4
Taquaritinga, Braz. 155/B2
Taquarituba, Braz. 155/B2
Taquil, Ecu. 156/B1
Tar (riv.), Kyr. 87/F4
Tara, Rus. 87/F1
Tara (riv.), Serb. 48/D4
Tara, Austl. 114/C4
Taraba (state), Nga. 103/H5
Taraba (riv.), Nga. 103/H4
Ţarābulus, Leb. 91/D2
Ţarābulus (Tripoli) (cap.), Libya 96/H1
Tarakan, Indo. 81/E3
Taraklı, Turk. 49/K5
Taraku (isl.), Rus. 76/E2
Taralga, Austl. 115/D2
Taranagar, India 86/C5
Tarancón, Sp. 44/D2
Tarangire NP, Tanz. 105/G1
Taranto, It. 47/E2
Taranto, Golfo di (gulf), It. 46/E2
Tarapoto, Peru 156/B2
Tarare, Fr. 42/F4
Tarariras, Uru. 159/K11
Tarascon, Fr. 42/F5
Tarascon-sur-Ariège, Fr. 42/D5
Tarata, Peru 156/D5
Tarauacá, Braz. 156/D3
Tarauacá (riv.), Braz. 156/D2
Taravai (isl.), FrPol. 117/M7
Tarawa (cap.), Kiri. 116/G4
Tarawa (isl.), Kiri. 116/G4
Tarazona, Sp. 44/E3
Tarazona, Sp. 44/E2
Tarbagatay (mts.), Kaz. 70/D2
Tarbat Ness (pt.), Sc, UK 36/C1
Tarbela (dam), Pak. 86/B2
Tarbela (res.), Pak. 86/B2
Tarbes, Fr. 42/D5
Tarbolton, Sc, UK 36/B5
Tarboro, NC, US 133/J3
Tarcento, It. 43/K3
Tarcutta, Austl. 115/C2
Tardes (riv.), Fr. 42/E3
Tardienta, Sp. 45/E2
Tardoire (riv.), Fr. 42/D4
Taree, Austl. 115/E1
Tarf Water (riv.), Sc, UK 34/D2
Tarfâwi (well), Egypt 101/B4
Tarfaya, Mor. 98/B4
Target Rock NWR, NY, US 139/M8
Targuist, Mor. 100/B2
Tarhūnah, Libya 96/H1
Tarifa, Ecu. 156/B1
Tarifa, Sp. 44/C4
Tarija, Bol. 150/F8
Tariku (riv.), Indo. 81/J4
Tariku-Taritatu (plain), Indo. 81/J4
Tarim (basin), China 70/D4
Tarim (riv.), China 70/D3
Tarin (riv.), Afg. 89/J2
Tarin (Torino), It. 43/G4
Taritatu (riv.), Indo. 81/J4
Tarkastad, SAfr. 106/D4
Tarkhankut (cape), Ukr. 49/L3
Tarkwa, Gha. 103/E5
Tarlac, Phil. 79/D4
Tarma, Peru 156/C3
Tarmstedt, Ger. 51/G2
Tarn (riv.), Fr. 42/D5
Tarn Tāran, India 86/C4
Tarnak (riv.), Afg. 89/J2
Tarnobrzeg, Pol. 41/L3
Tarnów, Pol. 41/L3
Tärnsjö, Swe. 38/G1
Taro (riv.), It. 43/J4
Tarō, Japan 76/B4
Ţārom, Iran 89/G3
Taroom, Austl. 114/C4
Tarouca, Port. 44/B2
Taroudannt, Mor. 98/C3
Tarp, Ger. 38/C4
Tarpa, Hun. 48/F1
Tarpon Springs, Fl, US 133/H4
Tarquinia, It. 46/B1
Tarqūmiyah, WBnk. 91/D4
Tarrafal, CpV. 93/K10
Tarragona, Sp. 45/F2
Tarraleah, Austl. 115/C4
Tàrrega, Sp. 45/F2
Tarrenz, Aus. 57/G3
Tarrytown, NY, US 139/K7
Tarsney Lakes, Mo, US 137/E6
Tarsus, Turk. 91/D1
Tarsus (riv.), Turk. 91/D1
Tartagal, Arg. 157/D1
Tartaro (riv.), It. 59/E2
Tartas, Fr. 42/C5
Tartu, Est. 39/M2
Ţarţūs (prov.), Syria 90/C3
Ţarţūs, Syria 91/D2
Tarui, Japan 77/L5
Tarumizu, Japan 74/B5
Tarutao NP, Thai. 78/B5
Tarvagatay (mts.), Mong. 70/G2
Taşağıl, Turk. 91/B1
Täsch, Swi. 56/D5
Taşçı, Turk. 90/C2
Tashkent (cap.), Uzb. 87/E4
Tashkent (int'l arpt.), Uzb. 87/E4
Tasikmalaya, Indo. 80/C5
Taşkent, Turk. 91/C1
Taşköprü, Turk. 62/E4
Taşlıçay, Turk. 90/E2
Tasman (pen.), Austl. 109/D5
Tasman (sea), Austl.,NZ 116/E8
Tasman (bay), NZ 109/H7
Tasman Head (cape), Austl. 115/C4
Tasmania, Austl. 115/C3
Tasmania (state), Austl. 109/D5
Tăşnad, Rom. 48/F2
Taşova, Turk. 90/D1
Tasquillo, Mex. 143/K6
Tassili-n-Ajjer (mts.), Alg. 99/G4
Tassili Oua-n Ahaggar (mts.), Alg. 99/G5
Tasu, BC, Can. 134/M5
Taşucu, Turk. 91/C1
Tata, Mor. 98/D3
Tata, Hun. 48/D2
Tatabánya, Hun. 48/D2
Tatachikapika (riv.), On, Can. 130/D2
Tatakoto (isl.), FrPol. 117/L6
Tatamy, Pa, US 138/C2
Tatar (str.), Rus. 67/P5
Tatarlar, Turk. 47/K2
Tatarsk, Rus. 87/G1
Tatarstan, Resp., Rus. 64/Q6
Tatāwīn, Tun. 96/H1
Tatāwīn (gov.), Tun. 99/H2
Tate-yama (peak), Japan 75/E2
Tatebayashi, Japan 77/D1
Tateshina, Japan 77/A1
Tateyama, Japan 75/F3
Tathlina (lake), NW, Can. 122/E2
Tathra, Austl. 115/D3
Tatilt (well), Mrta. 102/B2
Tatitlek, Ak, US 134/J3
Tatnam (cape), Mb, Can. 122/G3
Tatomi, Japan 77/B2
Tatranský NP, Slvk. 41/K4
Tatsuno, Japan 75/E3
Tatsuta, Japan 77/L5
Tatura, Austl. 115/C3
Tatvan, Turk. 90/E2
Tauá, Braz. 154/B2
Taubaté, Braz. 211/H8
Tauber (riv.), Ger. 40/E4
Tauberbischofsheim, Ger. 54/C3
Tauca, Peru 156/B3
Taufkirchen, Ger. 55/F6
Taufkirchen an der Pram, Aus. 55/G6
Taufstein (peak), Ger. 54/C1
Taulihawa, Nepal 84/D2
Taung, SAfr. 106/D2
Taungdwingyi, Myan. 83/G3
Taunggyi, Myan. 83/G3
Taungup, Myan. 83/F4
Taunsa, Pak. 86/A4
Taunton, Ma, US 131/G3
Taunton, Eng, UK 32/C4
Taunus (range), Ger. 54/A2
Taunusstein, Ger. 54/B2
Taupo, NZ 117/T10
Taupo (lake), NZ 109/H6
Tauragė, Lith. 39/K4
Tauranga, NZ 117/T10
Taurion (riv.), Fr. 42/D3
Taurisano, It. 47/F3
Taurus (mts.), Turk. 90/C2
Tauste, Sp. 44/E2
Taute (riv.), Fr. 42/B2
Tauu (isls.), PNG 116/E5
Tavanbulag, Mong. 70/H2
Tavaputs (plat.), Ut, US 128/E3
Tavarnelle, It. 59/E5
Tavarnuzze, It. 59/E5
Tavas, Turk. 90/B2
Tavaux, Fr. 56/B3
Tavazzano, It. 58/C2
Tavda (riv.), Rus. 64/G4
Tavernerio, It. 58/C1
Taverny, Fr. 30/J4
Taviano, It. 47/F3
Tavira, Port. 44/B4
Tavoy (pt.), Myan. 78/B3
Tavoy (Dawei), Myan. 78/B3
Tavşanlı, Turk. 90/D2
Taw (riv.), Eng, UK 32/B6
Taw (riv.), Eng, UK 32/C5
Tawaramoto, Japan 77/J6
Tawas City, Mi, US 130/D2
Tawau, Malay. 81/E3
Tawe (riv.), Wal, UK 32/C3
Tawern, Ger. 53/F4
Tāwī (riv.), India 86/C3
Tawi-Tawi (isl.), Phil. 79/C6
Ţāwūq, Iraq 90/F3
Tawzar, Tun. 96/G1
Tawzar (gov.), Tun. 99/G3
Taxco, Mex. 143/K8
Taxila (ruin), Pak. 86/B3
Taxila, Pak. 86/B3
Taxkorgan Tajik Zizhixian, China 89/L1
Tay (lake), Sc, UK 36/B3
Tay (riv.), Sc, UK 36/C3
Tay, Firth of (inlet), Sc, UK 36/C4
Tay Ninh, Viet. 78/D4
Tayabamba, Peru 156/B3
Taylor, Mi, US 135/F7
Taylorsville-Bennion, Ut, US 137/K12
Taymyr (riv.), Rus. 64/K2
Taymyr (isl.), Rus. 65/L2
Taymyr (pen.), Rus. 67/H2
Taymyrskiy Aut. Okrug, Rus. 67/H2
Tayoltita, Mex. 142/D3
Tayport, Sc, UK 36/D4
Tayrona, PN, Col. 152/C2
Tayshet, Rus. 65/K4
Taytay, Phil. 81/E1
Taz (riv.), Rus. 67/H3
Taza (prov.), Mor. 100/C2
Taza, Mor. 100/B2
Tazawako, Japan 76/B4
Tazekka (peak), Mor. 100/B2
Tazenakht, Mor. 98/D3
Tazewell, Tn, US 130/D4
Tāzirbū (oasis), Libya 97/K2
Tazumal (ruin), ESal. 144/D3
T'bilisi (cap.), Geo. 63/H4
T'boli, Phil. 79/D6
Tchamba, Togo 103/F4
Tchaourou, Ben. 103/F4
Tchefuncta (riv.), La, US 137/P16
Tchibanga, Gabon 96/H8
Tcholliré, Camr. 96/H6
Tczew, Pol. 39/H4
Te Anau, NZ 117/R12
Te Araroa, NZ 117/T10
Te Aroha, NZ 117/T10
Te Awamutu, NZ 117/T10
Te Kao, NZ 117/S9
Te Kuiti, NZ 117/T10
Tea (riv.), Braz. 150/E4
Teacapán, Mex. 142/D4
Teague, Tx, US 129/H5
Teaneck, NJ, US 139/J8
Teano, It. 46/D2
Teapa, Mex. 144/C2
Tearce, FYROM 47/G1
Tebak (peak), Indo. 80/B4
Tébessa (prov.), Alg. 99/G2
Tebessa (mts.), Alg. 100/L7
Tébessa, Alg. 100/L7
Tebesselamane (well), Mali 103/F2
Tebicuary (riv.), Par. 157/E2
Tebingtinggi, Indo. 80/A3
Tebulos-mta (peak), Rus. 63/H4
Tecalitlán, Mex. 142/E5
Tecamac, Mex. 143/R9
Tecamachalco, Mex. 143/M8
Tecate, Mex. 128/C4
Tech (riv.), Fr. 42/E5
Techirghiol, Rom. 49/J3
Tecirli, Turk. 90/D2
Tecka, Arg. 158/C4
Tecka (riv.), Arg. 158/C4
Tecklenberg, Ger. 51/E4
Tecolutla, Mex. 143/M6
Tecomán, Mex. 142/E5
Tecozautla, Mex. 143/K6
Tecpan de Galeana, Mex. 143/E5
Tecuala, Mex. 142/D4
Tecuci, Rom. 49/H3
Tecumseh, Mi, US 130/D3
Tecumseh, Ne, US 129/H2
Tecumseh, On, Can. 135/G7
Tedjert (well), Alg. 99/H1
Tedzhen (riv.), Trkm. 64/G6
Tees (bay), Eng, Uk 35/G2
Tees (riv.), Eng, UK 35/G3
Teesside (int'l arpt.), Eng, UK 35/G3
Tefé (riv.), Braz. 150/E4
Tefé, Braz. 150/F4
Teferič, Serb. 48/E4
Tega (lake), Japan 77/E2
Tegal, Indo. 80/C5
Tegel (int'l arpt.), Ger. 40/Q6
Tegelen, Neth. 50/D6
Tegeler (lake), Ger. 40/Q6
Tegheri (well), Libya 99/H4
Teghra, India 85/E3
Tegid, Llyn (lake), Wal, UK 34/E6
Teglio, It. 57/G5
Tégouma (riv.), Niger 103/H3
Tegsh, Mong. 70/G2
Tegucigalpa (cap.), Hon. 144/E3
Tehek (lake), Nun., Can. 122/G2
Tehrān (cap.), Iran 88/F1
Tehuacán, Mex. 143/M8
Tehuantepec (isth.), Mex. 143/G5
Tehuantepec (riv.), Mex. 144/C2
Tehuantepec (gulf), Mex. 144/C3
Teide, Pico de (peak), Sp. 98/A3
Teifi (riv.), Wal, UK 32/B2
Teifiside (valley), Wal, UK 32/B2
Teiga (plat.), Sudan 97/L4
Teign (riv.), Eng, UK 32/C6
Teignmouth, Eng, UK 32/C5
Teisendorf, Ger. 55/F7
Teith (riv.), Sc, UK 36/B4
Tejen, Trkm. 89/H1
Tejn, Den. 38/F4
Tejupilco de Hidalgo, Mex. 143/E5
Tekamah, Ne, US 127/J5
Tekāri, India 85/E3
Tekax de Álvaro Obregón, Mex. 144/D1
Teke, Turk. 49/J5
Tekeli, Kaz. 87/G4
Tekes (riv.), China 64/J5

230

Tekez – Tlalt

Tekezē Wenz (riv.), Eth. 97/N5
Tekiliktag (peak), China 70/D4
Tekirdağ, Turk. 49/H5
Tekirdağ (prov.), Turk. 49/H5
Tekit, Mex. 144/D1
Tekkali, India 82/D4
Tekke, Turk. 90/D1
Tekkeköy, Turk. 90/D1
Tekman, Turk. 90/E2
Tel Aviv (dist.), Isr. 91/D3
Tel Aviv-Yafo, Isr. 91/F7
Tel Megiddo (ruin), Isr. 91/G6
Tela, Hon. 144/E3
Télagh, Alg. 100/D2
T'elavi, Geo. 63/H4
Telde, Sp. 98/B3
Télé (lake), Mali 102/D2
Telêmaco Borba, Braz. 155/B3
Telemark (co.), Nor. 37/D4
Telen (riv.), Indo. 81/E3
Teleorman (prov.), Rom. 49/G4
Telertheba (peak), Alg. 99/G4
Teles Pires (riv.), Braz. 147/D3
Telford, Pa, US 138/C3
Telford Dawley, Eng, UK 32/D1
Telfs, Aus. 57/H3
Telgate, It. 58/C1
Telgte, Ger. 51/E5
Telica, Nic. 144/E3
Télig (well), Mali 98/E5
Télimélé, Gui. 102/B4
Telkwa, BC, Can. 126/B2
Tell City, In, US 130/C4
Teller, Ak, US 134/E2
Telli (lake), Mrta. 98/C4
Tellicherry, India 82/C5
Tellin, Belg. 53/E3
Telluride, Co, US 128/F3
Telok Anson, Malay. 80/B3
Teloloapan, Mex. 143/F5
Telšiai, Lith. 39/K4
Teltow, Ger. 40/Q7
Teltow (reg.), Ger. 41/G2
Tema, Gha. 103/E5
Temagami (lake), On, Can. 130/D2
Temax, Mex. 144/D1
Tembilahan, Indo. 80/B4
Tembisa, SAfr. 106/E2
Temblador, Ven. 153/F2
Teme (riv.), Eng, UK 32/C2
Temecula, Ca, US 136/C4
Temelkovo, Bul. 47/H1
Temerin, Serb. 48/D3
Temerloh, Malay. 80/B3
Temirtaū, Kaz. 87/F2
Témiscamie (riv.), Qu, Can. 131/F1
Témiscaming, Qu, Can. 130/E2
Temoaya, Mex. 143/Q10
Temoe (isl.), FrPol. 117/M7
Temora, Austl. 115/C2
Tempe, Az, US 137/S19
Tempio Pausania, It. 46/A2
Temple, Pa, US 138/C3
Temple City, Ca, US 136/F7
Temple of Lady Chua Xu, Viet. 78/D4
Templemore, Ire. 31/Q10
Templepatrick, NI, UK 34/B2
Templeuve, Fr. 52/C2
Templeville, Md, US 138/C5
Templin, Ger. 41/G2
Templiner (lake), Ger. 40/Q7
Tempoal de Sánchez, Mex. 144/B1
Temryuk, Rus. 62/F3
Temse, Belg. 53/D1
Temuco, Chile 158/B3
Temuka, NZ 117/S11
Ten Boer, Neth. 50/D2
Tena, Ecu. 152/B5
Tena Kourou (peak), Mali 96/D5
Tenabo, Mex. 144/D1
Tenafly, NJ, US 139/K8
Tenakee Springs, Ak, US 134/L4
Tenancingo, Mex. 143/K8
Tenango, Mex. 143/R10
Tenango de Arista, Mex. 143/Q10
Tenasserim (range), Myan. 78/B3
Tenasserim, Myan. 78/B3
Tenay, Fr. 56/B6
Tenby, Wal, UK 32/B3
Tende, Fr. 43/G4
Tende, Col de (pass), Fr. 58/A4
Tenderovsk (bay), Ukr. 49/K2
Tenderovsk Spit (isl.), Ukr. 49/K2
Tendō, Japan 76/B4
Tendre (peak), Swi. 56/C4
Ténénkou, Mali 102/D3
Ténéré (des.), Niger 96/G4
Ténéré du Tafassasset (des.), Niger 96/G3
Tenerife, Col. 152/C2
Tenerife (isl.), Sp. 93/A2
Ténès, Alg. 100/F4
Tenes (riv.), Sp. 45/L6
Teng (riv.), Myan. 83/G3
Teng Xian, China 72/D4
Tenggarong, Indo. 81/E4
Tengger (des.), China 70/H4
Tengiz Köli (lake), Kaz. 64/G4
Tenguel, Ecu. 152/B5
Tenibres (peak), It. 43/G4
Teniente Enciso, PN, Par. 157/D1
Teningen, Ger. 56/D1
Tenja, Cro. 48/D3
Tenkodogo, Burk. 103/E4
Tenmile (riv.), Az, US 128/D4
Tennessee (state), US 133/G3
Tennessee (riv.), US 133/F3
Tenneville, Belg. 53/E3
Tennuaca (well), Mor. 98/B5
Teno, Chile 158/C2
Tenojoki (riv.), Fin. 37/H1
Tenosique de Pino Suárez, Mex. 144/D2
Tenri, Japan 77/J6
Tenryū, Japan 75/E3
Tenryū (riv.), Japan 75/E3
Tensift (pol. reg.), Mor. 98/C3
Tensift, Oued (riv.), Mor. 98/C3
Tenterfield, Austl. 115/E1
Tentolomatinan (peak), Indo. 81/F3
Tenus (peak), Kenya 104/B2
Teo, Sp. 44/A1
Teocaltiche, Mex. 140/A3
Teocelo, Mex. 143/N7
Teodelina, Arg. 158/E2
Teodoro Sampaio, Braz. 155/A2
Teófilo Otoni, Braz. 154/B5
Teopisca, Mex. 144/C2
Teotihuacán (ruin), Mex. 143/R9
Teotihuacán, Mex. 143/R9
Teotitlán del Camino, Mex. 144/B2
Tepache, Mex. 142/C2
Tepalcatepec, Mex. 142/E5
Tepalcingo, Mex. 143/L8
Tepatitlán de Morelos, Mex. 140/A3
Tepatlaxco, Mex. 143/M7
Tepeapulco, Mex. 143/L7
Tepebaşı, Turk. 91/C1
Tepehuaje, Mex. 143/F4
Tepehuanes, Mex. 142/D3
Tepeji del Río de Ocampo, Mex. 143/K7
Tepelenë, Alb. 47/G2
Tepelská Plošina (mts.), Czh. 55/F2
Tepetlaoxtoc, Mex. 143/R9
Tepexi, Mex. 143/M8
Tepexpan, Mex. 143/R9
Tepic, Mex. 142/D4
Teplá (riv.), Czh. 40/G3
Teplá Vltava (riv.), Czh. 55/G5
Teplice, Czh. 41/G3
Tepoca (cape), Mex. 142/B2
Tepoca, Cabo (cape), Mex. 142/B2
Tepoto (isl.), FrPol. 117/L6
Tepotzotlán, Mex. 143/Q9
Tepoztlán, Mex. 143/K8
Tequila, Mex. 142/E4
Tequisquiapan, Mex. 143/F4
Tequixquiac, Mex. 143/K7
Ter (riv.), Sp. 45/G1
Ter Aar, Neth. 50/B4
Téra, Niger 103/F3
Tera (riv.), Sp. 44/B1
Teraina (Washington) (isl.), Kiri. 117/J4
Teramo, It. 43/K5
Terang, Austl. 115/B3
Tercan, Turk. 90/E2
Terceira (isl.), Azor., Port. 45/S12
Terek (riv.), Rus. 63/H4
Terepaima, PN, Ven. 152/D2
Teresina, Braz. 154/B2
Teresópolis, Braz. 211/L7
Terespol, Pol. 41/M2
Tergnier, Fr. 52/C4
Tergun Daba (mts.), China 70/F4
Terheijden, Neth. 50/B5
Teriberskiy (pt.), Rus. 60/G1
Terkaplesterpoelen (lake), Neth. 50/C2
Terlan (Terlano), It. 57/H4
Termas de Río Hondo, Arg. 157/D2
Termini Imerese, It. 46/C4
Términos (lag.), Mex. 144/D2
Termiz, Uzb. 89/J1
Termo, Ca, US 126/C5
Termoli, It. 46/D1
Termonfeckin, Ire. 34/B4
Termunten, Neth. 50/E2
Ternate, Indo. 81/G3
Ternberg, Aus. 55/H7
Terneuzen, Neth. 50/A6
Terni, It. 46/C1
Ternin (riv.), Fr. 42/F3
Ternoise (riv.), Fr. 52/B3
Ternopil', Ukr. 62/C2
Ternopil's'ka Oblasti, Ukr. 62/C2
Terpeniya (bay), Rus. 65/Q5
Terpní, Gre. 47/H2
Terra Nova, Braz. 154/B4
Terra Nova, Braz. 154/C3
Terra Nova NP, Nf, Can. 131/L1
Terrace, BC, Can. 126/A2
Terrace Bay, On, Can. 127/M3
Terracina, It. 46/C2
Terråk, Nor. 37/E2
Terralba, It. 46/A3
Terranuova Bracciolini, It. 59/E5
Terrassa, Sp. 45/L6
Terrasson-la-Villedieu, Fr. 42/D4
Terre Hill, Pa, US 138/B3
Terrebonne, Qu, Can. 131/N6
Terrell Hills, Tx, US 137/U21
Terri (peak), Swi. 57/F4
Terry, Mt, US 127/G4
Terry (lake), Co, US 137/B2
Terrytown, La, US 137/P17
Terschelling (isl.), Neth. 50/C2
Tertenia, It. 46/A3
Teruel, Sp. 45/E2
Terutao (isl.), Thai. 83/G6
Tervel, Bul. 49/H4
Terza Grande (peak), It. 43/K3
Terzo d'Aquileia, It. 59/G1
Tešanj, Bosn. 48/C3
Tescou (riv.), Fr. 42/D5
Tesero, It. 57/H5
Teshekpuk (lake), Ak, US 134/G1
Teshikaga, Japan 76/D2
Teshio (riv.), Japan 76/C1
Teshio, Japan 76/B1
Teshio-dake (peak), Japan 76/C2
Teslić, Bosn. 48/C3
Teslin (riv.), Yk, Can. 122/C2
Teslin (lake), BC, Can. 122/C3
Tessaoua, Niger 103/G3
Tessenderlo, Belg. 53/E1
Tessenie (Teseney), Erit. 88/C5
Test (riv.), Eng, UK 33/E4
Testa del Gargano (pt.), It. 46/E2
Tét, Hun. 48/C2
Tete, Moz. 105/F4
Tête de l'Estrop (peak), Fr. 43/G4
Tetela, Mex. 143/M7
Teterow, Ger. 38/E5
Teteven, Bul. 47/J1
Tetiaroa (isl.), FrPol. 117/L6
Tetlin, Ak, US 134/K3
Teton (riv.), Mt, US 126/F4
Tétouan (prov.), Mor. 100/B2
Tétouan, Mor. 100/B2
Tetovo, FYROM 47/G1
Tettnang, Ger. 57/F2
Tetulia (riv.), Bang. 85/H4
Teublitz, Ger. 55/F4
Teuco (riv.), Arg. 157/D1
Teufen, Swi. 57/F3
Teúl de González Ortega, Mex. 142/E4
Teulada (cape), It. 46/A3
Teulon, Mb, Can. 127/J3
Teupasenti, Hon. 144/E3
Teuri (isl.), Japan 76/B1
Teuschnitz, Ger. 55/E2
Teutoburger Wald (for.), Ger. 51/F4
Tevere (Tiber) (riv.), It. 43/K5
Teverya, Isr. 91/D3
Teviot (riv.), Sc, UK 36/D6
Teviotdale (valley), Sc, UK 36/D6
Tewantin-Noosa, Austl. 114/D4
Tewkesbury, Eng, UK 32/D3
Texarkana, Tx, US 129/J4
Texas, Austl. 115/D1
Texas (state), US 132/C4
Texas City, Tx, US 129/J5
Texcoco, Mex. 143/R9
Texel (isl.), Neth. 40/C2
Texhoma, Ok, US 132/C2
Texmelucan, Mex. 143/L7
Texoma (lake), Ok, US 125/G5
Teyateyaneng, Les. 106/D3
Teykovo, Rus. 60/J4
Tezio (peak), It. 43/K5
Teziutlán, Mex. 143/M7
Tezonapa, Mex. 143/N8
Tezontepec, Mex. 143/L7
Tezontepec de Aldama, Mex. 143/K6
Tezoyuca, Mex. 143/R9
Tezpur, India 70/F6
Tezu, India 83/G2
Tezze, It. 59/E1
Tha-Anne (riv.), Nun., Can. 122/G2
Tha Chin (riv.), Thai. 78/B3
Thabana-Ntlenyana (peak), Les. 106/E3
Thabankulu (peak), SAfr. 107/E2
Thaen (pt.), Thai. 78/B4
Thai Binh, Viet. 83/J3
Thai Nguyen, Viet. 83/J3
Thailand (gulf), Asia 78/C4
Thailand (ctry.) 78/C3
Thākurdwāra, India 84/B1
Thal, Pak. 86/A3
Thal (des.), Pak. 86/A4
Thaleban NP, Thai. 78/C5
Thaleischweiler-Fröschen, Ger. 53/G5
Thalerhof (int'l arpt.), Aus. 43/L3
Thalgau, Aus. 55/G7
Thalheim bei Wels, Aus. 55/H6
Thalmässing, Ger. 54/E4
Thalwil, Swi. 57/E3
Thamar, Jabal (peak), Yem. 88/E6
Thame (riv.), Eng, UK 33/F3
Thames (riv.), On, Can. 130/D3
Thames, NZ 117/T10
Thames (riv), Eng., UK 33/G4
Thames Barrier, Eng, UK 30/D2
Thāna, India 89/K5
Thāna Bhawan, India 86/D5
Thānesar, India 86/D5
Thangool, Austl. 114/C4
Thanh Hoa, Viet. 83/J4
Thanjavur, India 82/C5
Thann, Fr. 56/D2
Thannhausen, Ger. 57/G1
Thaon-les-Vosges, Fr. 56/C1
Thar (des.), Pak. 86/A5
Tharād, India 89/K4
Thargomindah, Austl. 114/A5
Tharrawaddy, Myan. 83/G4
Thásos, Gre. 47/J2
Thásos (isl.), Gre. 62/C4
Thatcham, Eng, UK 33/E4
Thatcher, Az, US 128/E4
Thaton, Myan. 78/B2
Thaur, Aus. 57/H3
Thaya (riv.), Aus. 41/H4
Thayetmyo, Myan. 83/G4
Thayngen, Swi. 57/E2
Thazi, Myan. 83/G3
The Alamo, Tx, US 137/U21
The Dalles, Or, US 126/C4
The Hague ('s-Gravenhage) (cap.), Neth. 50/B4
The Oaks, Ca, US 136/B1
The Pas, Mb, Can. 127/H2
The Rock, Austl. 115/C2
The Valley (cap.), Angu. 141/N8
The Village, Ok, US 137/M14
The Woodlands, Tx, US 129/J5
The Wrekin (co.), Eng, UK 35/F6
Thebes (ruin), Egypt 101/C3
Theilheim, Ger. 54/D3
Thelma, Tx, US 137/T21
Thelon (riv.), NW,Nun., Can. 122/F2
Thémericourt, Fr. 30/H4
Theo (mt.), Austl. 113/F2
Theodore, Sk, Can. 127/H3
Theodore, Austl. 114/C4
Theodore Roosevelt (lake), Az, US 128/E4
Theodore Roosevelt NP, ND, US 127/G4
Thérain (riv.), Fr. 42/D2
Thermaic (gulf), Gre. 62/B4
Thérmi, Gre. 47/H2
Thermopílai (Thermopylae) (pass), Gre. 47/H3
Thermopolis, Wy, US 126/F5
Thérouanne (riv.), Fr. 30/L4
Thesprotikón, Gre. 47/G3
Thessalon, On, Can. 130/D2
Thessaloníki, Gre. 47/H2
Thessaly (reg.), Gre. 47/H3
Thet (riv.), Eng, UK 33/G2
Thetford, Eng, UK 33/G2
Thetford Mines, Qu, Can. 131/G2
Theunissen, SAfr. 106/D3
Theux, Belg. 53/E2
Thève (riv.), Fr. 30/K4
Theydon Bois, Eng, UK 30/D2
Thiais, Fr. 30/K5
Thíamis (riv.), Gre. 47/G3
Thiant, Fr. 52/C3
Thiaucourt-Regniéville, Fr. 53/E6
Thief River Falls, Mn, US 127/J3
Thielle (riv.), Swi. 56/C4
Thielsen (mt.), Or, US 126/C5
Thiene, It. 59/E1
Thiérache (reg.), Fr. 52/C4
Thierhaupten, Ger. 54/D5
Thiers, Fr. 42/E4
Thiers-sur-Thève, Fr. 30/K4
Thierville-sur-Meuse, Fr. 53/E5
Thiès (pol. reg.), Sen. 102/A3
Thiès, Sen. 102/A3
Thika, Kenya 104/C3
Thingvellir NP, Ice. 37/N7
Thionville, Fr. 53/F5
Thíra, Gre. 47/J4
Thíra (isl.), Gre. 47/J4
Third Cataract (falls), Sudan 101/B5
Third Lake, Il, US 135/Q15
Thirlmere (lake), Eng, UK 35/E2
Thirsty (mt.), Austl. 112/D5
Thirtymile (pt.), NY, US 131/V9
Thise, Fr. 56/C3
Thisted, Den. 38/C3
Thistilfjördhur (estu.), Ice. 37/P6
Thistle (isl.), Austl. 113/H5
Thistle (mtn.), Yk, Can. 134/L3
Thitu (isl.) 79/B5
Thívai, Gre. 47/H3
Thiverval-Grignon, Fr. 30/H5
Thjórsa (riv.), Ice. 37/N7
Thlewiaza (riv.), Nun., Can. 122/G2
Thoiry, Fr. 30/H5
Tholen (isl.), Neth. 50/B5
Tholen, Neth. 50/B5
Tholey, Ger. 53/G5
Thomaston, Ga, US 133/G3
Thomastown, Ire. 31/Q10
Thomasville, Al, US 133/G4
Thomasville, NC, US 133/H3
Thomasville, Ga, US 133/H4
Thomasville, Pa, US 138/B4
Thompson, Mb, Can. 127/J2
Thompson (riv.), BC, Can. 126/C3
Thompson (lake), Austl. 112/K7
Thompson Falls, Mt, US 126/E4
Thomsen (riv.), NW, Can. 122/E1
Thomson (riv.), Austl. 109/D3
Thomson, Ga, US 133/H3
Thongwa, Myan. 78/B2
Thonnance-lès-Joinville, Fr. 56/B1
Thonon-les-Bains, Fr. 56/C5
Thoreau, NM, US 128/E4
Thorens-Glières, Fr. 56/C6
Thorhild, Ab, Can. 126/E2
Thorigny-sur-Marne, Fr. 30/L5
Thorlákshöfn, Ice. 37/N7
Thornaby-on-Tees, Eng, UK 35/G2
Thornbury, Eng, UK 32/D3
Thorndale, Pa, US 138/C4
Thorne, Eng, UK 35/H4
Thorne Bay, Ak, US 134/M4
Thornhill, Sc, UK 36/B4
Thornhill, Sc, UK 34/E1
Thornhurst, Pa, US 138/C1
Thornton, Co, US 137/C3
Thornton, Ca, US 135/M10
Thornton Cleveleys, Eng, UK 35/E4
Thorold, On, Can. 131/R9
Thórshöfn, Ice. 37/P6
Thouars, Fr. 42/C3
Thouet (riv.), Fr. 42/C3
Thourotte, Fr. 52/B5
Thousand Oaks, Ca, US 136/B2
Thowa (riv.), Kenya 104/C3
Thrace (reg.), Gre.,Turk 62/C4
Thracian (sea), Gre. 62/C4
Thredbo Village, Austl. 115/D3
Three Bridges, NJ, US 138/D2
Three Forks, Mt, US 126/F4
Three Guardsmen (mtn.), BC, Can. 134/L4
Three Hills, Ab, Can. 126/E3
Three Hummock (isl.), Austl. 115/C4
Three Kings (isls.), NZ 116/G8
Three Mile (isl.), Pa, US 138/B3
Three Pagodas (pass), Myan. 78/B3
Three Points (cape), Gha. 103/E5
Three Rivers, Mi, US 130/C3
Three Rivers, Austl. 112/C3
Three Springs, Austl. 112/B4
Thriuvananthapuram, India 82/C6
Throssell (lake), Austl. 109/B3
Thrushel (riv.), Eng, UK 32/B5
Thu Dau Mot, Viet. 78/D4
Thuin, Belg. 53/D3
Thuir, Fr. 42/E5
Thulba (riv.), Ger. 54/C2
Thule Air Base, Den. 123/T7
Thun, Swi. 56/D4
Thunderbird (lake), Ok, US 137/N15
Thuner See (lake), Swi. 43/G3
Thung Salaeng Luang NP, Thai. 78/C2
Thüngersheim, Ger. 54/C3
Thur (riv.), Swi. 43/H3
Thurgau (canton), Swi. 57/E2
Thüringen (state), Ger. 43/J1
Thüringen, Aus. 57/F3
Thüringer Schiefergebirge (mts.), Ger. 54/E2
Thüringer Wald (for.), Ger. 43/J1
Thurles, Ire. 31/Q10
Thurnau, Ger. 55/E2
Thurø By, Den. 38/D4
Thurrock (co.), Eng, UK 33/G3
Thurso, Sc, UK 31/V14
Thurston (isl.), Ant. 160/T
Thurston (co.), Wa, US 135/A3
Thury-en-Valois, Fr. 30/M4
Thusis, Swi. 57/F4
Thyez, Fr. 56/C5
Thyolo, Malw. 105/G4
Ti-m-Merhsoï (riv.), Niger 103/G2
Ti-n-Jedane, Oued (riv.), Alg. 99/G4
Ti-n-Zaouâten, Alg. 96/F4
Ti-Tree Abor. Land, Austl. 113/G2
Tiahuanco (ruin), Bol. 156/D5
Tian (pt.), BC, Can. 134/M5
Tian Shan (mts.), China 67/H5
Tianchang, China 72/D4
Tianguá, Braz. 154/B1
Tianguistenco, Mex. 143/Q10
Tianjin (mun.), China 71/L4
Tianjin, China 72/H7
Tianlin, China 83/J3
Tianmen, China 79/B1
Tianmu (mts.), China 72/K9
Tianshui, China 70/J5
Tianyang, China 79/A3
Tianzhen, China 72/C2
Tianzhu, China 83/J2
Tiaret, Alg. 100/F5
Tibagi, Braz. 155/B3
Tibaji (riv.), Braz. 155/B3
Tibaná, Col. 152/C3
Tibati, Camr. 96/H6
Tibba, Pak. 86/A5
Tibé, Pic de (peak), Gui. 102/C4
Tiber (Tevere) (riv.), It. 43/J5
Tiberias (lake), Isr. 91/D3
Tibesti (mts.), Chad 93/D3
Tibet (reg.), China 67/H6
Tibet (Xizang) (aut. reg.), China 70/D5
Tibro, Swe. 38/F2
Tiburon (cape), Haiti 141/G4
Tiburon, Ca, US 135/K11
Tiburón, Isla (isl.), Mex. 142/B2
Ticaco, Peru 156/D5
Tichigan (lake), Wi, US 135/P14
Tichît, Dhar (cliff), Mrta. 102/C2
Ticino (canton), Swi. 57/E5
Ţicleni, Rom. 49/F3
Ticllos, Peru 156/B3
Ticonderoga, NY, US 130/F3
Ticul, Mex. 144/D1
Tidaholm, Swe. 38/E2
Tidikelt (plain), Alg. 96/F2
Tidjikdja, Mrta. 102/C2
Tidone (riv.), It. 58/C3
Tidore (isl.), Indo. 81/G3
Tidra, Île (isl.), Mrta. 102/A2
Tidsit (lake), WSah. 98/B5
Tiede, PN del, Sp. 98/A3
Tiefencastel, Swi. 57/F4
Tiel, Neth. 50/C5
Tieling, China 72/E2
Tielt, Belg. 52/C2
Tielt-Winge, Belg. 53/D2
Tiemba (riv.), C.d'Iv. 102/D4
Tienen, Belg. 53/D2
Tieri, Austl. 114/C3
Tieroko (peak), Chad 96/J3
Tierp, Swe. 38/G1
Tierra Amarilla, NM, US 128/F3
Tierra Blanca, Mex. 143/N8
Tierra Colorada, Mex. 143/F5
Tierra del Fuego (isl.), Arg. 147/C8
Tierra del Fuego, Antártida e Islas del Atlántico Sur, Arg. 159/C7
Tierra del Fuego, PN, Arg. 157/C7
Tierradentro, Col. 152/B4
Tierranueva, Mex. 143/E4
Tiétar (riv.), Sp. 44/C2
Tietê (riv.), Braz. 147/D5
Tiffin, Oh, US 130/D3
Tiflet, Mor. 100/A3
Tifton, Ga, US 133/H4
Tigeaux, Fr. 30/L5
Tighina (Bendery), Mol. 49/J2
Tighvein (hill), Sc, UK 36/A6
Tignère, Camr. 96/H6
Tignieu-Jameyzieu, Fr. 56/B6
Tigre (riv.), Ven. 150/C4
Tigre (riv.), Ven. 153/F2
Tigre, Arg. 159/J11
Tigris (riv.), Iraq 67/C6
Tigui (well), Chad 96/J4
Tiguidit, Falaise de (cliff), Niger 103/G2
Tigzirt, Alg. 100/H4
Tihosuco, Mex. 144/D1
Tihuatlán, Mex. 144/B1
Tiilikkajärven NP, Fin. 60/F3
Tijāra, India 84/A2
Tijuana, Mex. 136/C5
Tijuca, PN da, Braz. 211/K7
Tijucas, Braz. 155/B3
Tijuco (riv.), Braz. 155/B1
Tikal (ruin), Guat. 144/D2
Tikamgarh, India 84/B3
Tikchik (lakes), Ak, US 134/G3
Tikehau (isl.), FrPol. 117/L6
Tikhoretsk, Rus. 62/G3
Tikhvin, Rus. 60/G4
Tikrīt, Iraq 90/E3
Tikveš (lake), FYROM 47/H2
Tila, Mex. 144/C2
Tilburg, Neth. 50/C5
Tilbury, Eng, UK 30/E2
Tilden, Tx, US 132/D4
Tilghman, Md, US 138/B6
Tilghman (isl.), Md, US 138/B6
Tilhar, India 84/B2
Tilin, Myan. 83/F3
Tilisarao, Arg. 158/D2
Till (riv.), Eng, UK 36/D5
Tillabéri (dept.), Niger 103/F3
Tillabéry, Niger 103/F3
Tillamook, Or, US 126/C4
Tille (riv.), Fr. 40/C5
Tillicoultry, Sc, UK 36/C4
Tilst, Den. 38/D3
Tilt (riv.), Sc, UK 36/C3
Tiltil, Chile 158/N8
Tim, Den. 38/C3
Timan (ridge), Rus. 64/F3
Timaná, Col. 152/C4
Timanfaya, PN de, Sp. 98/B3
Timaru, NZ 117/S11
Timashevsk, Rus. 62/F3
Timbákion, Gre. 47/J5
Timbaúba, Braz. 154/D2
Timbédra, Mrta. 102/C2
Timber Lake, SD, US 127/H4
Timberlane, La, US 137/Q17
Timberwood Park, Tx, US 137/U20
Timbiquí, Col. 152/B4
Timbiras, Braz. 154/B2
Timbó, Braz. 155/B3
Timboon, Austl. 115/B3
Timehri (int'l arpt.), Guy. 153/G3
Timelkam, Aus. 55/G6
Timfristós (peak), Gre. 47/G3
Timimoun, Alg. 99/F3
Timiris (cape), Mrta. 102/A2
Timiş (prov.), Rom. 48/E3
Timiş (riv.), Rom. 62/B3
Timişoara (int'l arpt.), Rom. 48/E3
Timişoara, Rom. 48/E3
Timmins, On, Can. 130/D1
Timms (hill), Wi, US 127/L4
Timnath, Co, US 137/C1
Timon, Braz. 154/B2
Timonium, Md, US 138/B5
Timor (sea), Asia,Austl 67/M11
Timor (isl.), ETim.,Indo. 81/F5
Timóteo, Braz. 155/D1
Timpanogos Cave Nat'l Mon., Ut, US 128/E2
Timpanogos Nat'l Mon., Ut, US 137/K13
Timpson, Tx, US 129/J5
Timpton (riv.), Rus. 65/N4
Tims Ford (lake), Tn, US 133/G3
Timurnī, India 84/A4
Tin Can Bay, Austl. 114/D4
Tin Shui Wai, China 71/T10
Tina (riv.), SAfr. 106/B1
Tinaca (pt.), Phil. 79/E6
Tinaco, Ven. 152/D2
Tindivanam, India 82/C5
Tindouf, Alg. 98/C4
Tindouf (prov.), Alg. 98/D3
Tineo, Sp. 44/B1
Tingalpa (res.), Austl. 114/F7
Tingaringy NP, Austl. 115/D3
Tingha, Austl. 115/D1
Tingi (mts.), SLeo. 102/C4
Tingmerkpuk (mtn.), Ak, US 134/F2
Tingo María, Peru 156/C3
Tingsryd, Swe. 38/F3
Tinguiririca (vol.), Chile 158/C2
Tinharé, Ilha de (isl.), Braz. 151/L6
Tinian (isl.), NMar. 116/D3
Tinicum Nat'l Consv. Area, Pa, US 138/C4
Tinkisso (riv.), Gui. 102/C4
Tinley Park, Il, US 135/Q16
Tinogasta, Arg. 157/C2
Tinos, Gre. 47/J4
Tinos (isl.), Gre. 47/J4
Tinqueux, Fr. 52/C5
Tinrhir, Mor. 98/D3
Tinta, Peru 156/D4
Tintagel (pt.), Eng, UK 32/B5
Tintern Abbey, Eng, UK 32/D3
Tintigny, Belg. 53/E4
Tintinara, Austl. 115/B2
Tinto (riv.), Sp. 44/B4
Tinto (peak), Sc, UK 36/C5
Tinton Falls (New Shrewsbury), NJ, US 138/D3
Tinyahuarco, Peru 156/B3
Tioga, ND, US 127/H3
Tioman (isl.), Malay. 80/B3
Tione di Trento, It. 57/G5
Tipasa (prov.), Alg. 100/F4
Tipasa, Alg. 100/G4
Tipperary, Ire. 31/P10
Tiptūr, India 82/C5
Tir Rhiwiog (peak), Wal, UK 32/C1
Tiracambu, Serra do (mts.), Braz. 151/J4
Tiran (str.), Egypt, SA 101/C3
Tiran (isl.), Egypt,SAr 101/C3
Tirān (isl.), Egypt 97/M2
Tirano, It. 57/G5
Tirari (des.), Austl. 113/H4
Tiraspol, Mol. 49/J2
Tirat Karmel, Isr. 91/F6
Tire, Turk. 90/A2
Tirebolu, Turk. 62/F4
Tiree (isl.), Sc, UK 31/Q8
Tirest (well), Mali 103/F1
Tîrgovişte, Rom. 49/G3
Tîrgu Bujor, Rom. 49/H3
Tîrgu Cărbuneşti, Rom. 49/F3
Tîrgu Frumos, Rom. 49/H2
Tîrgu Jiu, Rom. 49/F3
Tîrgu Lăpuş, Rom. 49/F2
Tîrgu Mureş, Rom. 49/G2
Tîrgu Neamţ, Rom. 49/H2
Tîrgu Ocna, Rom. 49/H2
Tîrgu Secuiesc, Rom. 49/H2
Tirich Mīr (peak), Pak. 89/K1
Tiris (reg.), WSah. 98/B5
Tiris Zemmour (pol. reg.), Mrta. 98/C4
Tîrnava Mare (riv.), Rom. 49/G2
Tîrnava Mică (riv.), Rom. 49/F2
Tîrnăveni, Rom. 49/G2
Tírnavos, Gre. 47/H3
Tiros, Braz. 155/C1
Tirschenreuth, Ger. 55/F3
Tirstrup (int'l arpt.), Den. 38/D3
Tiruchchirāppalli, India 82/C5
Tiruchendūr, India 82/C6
Tiruchengodu, India 82/C5
Tirunelveli, India 82/C6
Tiruntán, Peru 156/C2
Tirupati, India 82/C5
Tiruppattūr, India 82/C5
Tiruppūr, India 82/C5
Tiruvannāmalai, India 82/C5
Tisa (riv.), Ukr. 49/G1
Tisdale, Sk, Can. 127/G2
Tishomingo, Ok, US 129/H4
Tissa, Mor. 100/B2
Tissemsilt (prov.), Alg. 100/F5
Tissemsilt, Alg. 100/F5
Tista (riv.), Bang. 85/G2
Tisza (riv.), Hun. 62/B3
Tiszaföldvár, Hun. 48/E2
Tiszafüred, Hun. 48/E2
Tiszakécske, Hun. 48/E2
Tiszalök, Hun. 48/E1
Tiszavasvári, Hun. 41/L5
Titano (peak), SMar. 59/F5
Titel, Serb. 48/E3
Titicaca (lake), Bol.,Peru 147/B4
Titisee-Neustadt, Ger. 56/E2
Titlagarh, India 82/D3
Titlis (peak), Swi. 57/E4
Tito, It. 46/D2
Titov Veles, FYROM 47/G2
Titov vrh (peak), FYROM 47/G2
Titting, Ger. 54/E5
Tittmoning, Ger. 55/F6
Titu, Rom. 49/G3
Titusville, Fl, US 133/H4
Titusville, NJ, US 138/D3
Tiva (riv.), Kenya 104/C3
Tivaouane, Sen. 102/A3
Tivat, Serb. 47/F1
Tiverton, Eng, UK 32/C5
Tiwanacu, Bol. 156/D5
Tixán, Ecu. 156/B1
Tixtla de Guerrero, Mex. 143/F5
Tizayuca, Mex. 143/L7
Tizi Ouzou (prov.), Alg. 100/H4
Tizi Ouzou, Alg. 100/H4
Tizimín, Mex. 144/D1
Tiznap (riv.), China 89/L1
Tiznit, Mor. 98/C3
Tjæreborg, Den. 38/C4
Tjeldstø, Nor. 38/A1
Tjeukemeer (lake), Neth. 50/C3
Tjøme, Nor. 38/D2
Tjorn (isl.), Den. 38/D3
Tlachichuca, Mex. 143/M7
Tlacolula de Matamoros, Mex. 144/B2
Tlacotalpan, Mex. 143/P8
Tlacotepec, Mex. 143/F5
Tlahualilo de Zaragoza, Mex. 132/C5
Tlalixcoyan, Mex. 143/N8
Tlalmanalco, Mex. 143/Q10
Tlalnepantla, Mex. 143/Q9
Tláloc (vol.), Mex. 143/Q10
Tlaltenango de Sánchez Román, Mex. 142/E4

altizapan, Mex. 143/K8
apa de Comonfort, ex. 144/B2
apacoya (ruin), ex. 143/Q10
apacoyan, Mex. 143/M7
apehuala, Mex. 143/E5
aquepaque, Mex. 142/E4
aquiltenango, ex. 143/K8
atlauquitepec, ex. 143/M7
axcala (state), ex. 140/A5
axcala, Mex. 143/L7
axco, Mex. 143/L7
axcoapan, Mex. 143/K6
ell, BC, Can. 134/M5
emcen, Alg. 100/D2
abré, Pan. 152/A2
aca (peak), Rom. 49/G2
achi (riv.), Ecu. 152/B4
amasina, Madg. 107/J7
amasina (prov.), adg. 107/J7
andos (pen.), a, US 135/B2
au (isl.), FrPol. 117/L6
ay, Arg. 158/D3
ba (lake), Indo. 80/A3
ba (inlet), BC, Can. 126/B3
ba, China 70/G5
ba, Japan 77/L7
ba Kākar (range), k. 89/J2
ba Tek Singh, Pak. 86/B4
bago (isl.), Trin. 150/F1
barra, Sp. 44/E3
bbio (peak), It. 58/B3
bermore, NI, UK 34/B2
betsu, Japan 76/B2
bias Barreto, Braz. 154/C3
bin (lake), Austl. 109/B3
bique (riv.), NB, Can. 131/H2
bishima, Japan 77/L5
bol (riv.), Rus. 61/Q5
bu, Japan 77/A1
byhanna (lake), a, US 138/C1
byhanna (riv.), a, US 138/C1
byhanna, Pa, US 138/C1
byhanna St. Park, a, US 138/C1
byl (riv.), Kaz. 63/M1
bysh (riv.), Rus. 61/L2
cache, Peru 156/B3
cantinópolis, az. 154/A2
cantins (state), az. 154/A3
cantins (riv.), Braz. 147/E4
ccoa, Ga, US 133/H3
ce (riv.), It. 43/H3
chigi ref.), Japan 75/F2
chigi, Japan 75/F2
chimilco, Mex. 143/L8
chio, Japan 75/F2
cina, Sp. 44/C4
cksfors, Swe. 38/D2
co, Trin. 153/F2
copilla, Chile 157/B1
cumen, Pan. 152/B2
cumwal, Austl. 115/C2
cuyito, Ven. 152/D2
cuyo (riv.), Ven. 150/E1
da, Japan 77/D2
da Bhīm, India 82/C2
di, It. 46/C1
ödi (peak), Swi. 57/E4
dmorden, Eng, UK 35/F4
dos os Santos, Baíaa de ay), Braz. 154/C4
dos Santos, ex. 142/C4
dtmoos, Ger. 56/E2
dtnau, Ger. 56/D2
offal (hill), Mrta. 98/C5
offo, Ben. 103/F5
field, Ab, Can. 126/E2
ofua (isl.), Tonga 117/H6
ōgane, Japan 77/E2
ogba (well), Mrta. 102/C2
oggenburg (valley), wi. 57/F3
ogher, Ire. 34/B5
ogiak, Ak, US 134/F4
ogo (ctry.) 103/F4
ōgō, Japan 77/M5
ögrög, Mong. 70/F2
ogtoh, China 72/B2
ógyu-san NP, SKor. 73/D5
ohāna, India 86/C5
ohatchi, NM, US 132/A3
ōhoku (prov.), apan 75/F1
oi, Japan 75/F3
ōin, Japan 77/L5
oiyabe (range), v, US 128/C3
ojō, Japan 74/C3
ōjō, Japan 77/H6
ok, Ak, US 134/K3
okachi (riv.), apan 76/C2
ōkai, Japan 77/L5
okaj, Hun. 41/L4
ōkamachi, Japan 75/F2
okar Nat'l Rsv., udan 101/B4
okara (isls.), apan 116/B1
okat, Turk. 90/D1
okat (prov.), Turk. 90/D1
ōkchŏk (isl.), Kor. 73/C4
Tŏkchŏk (arch.), NKor. 73/C4
Tokeen, Ak, US 134/M4
Tokelau (terr.), NZ 117/H5
Toki, Japan 77/M5
Toki (riv.), Japan 77/M5
Tokigawa, Japan 77/C2
Tokoname, Japan 77/L6
Tokoro (riv.), Japan 76/C2
Tokoro, Japan 76/D1
Tokoroa, NZ 117/T10
Tokorozawa, Japan 75/F3
Toksook Bay, Ak, US 134/E3
Toksun, China 70/E3
Tokuno (isl.), Japan 75/K7
Tokunoshima, Japan 75/K7
Tokushima (pref.), Japan 74/C4
Tokushima, Japan 74/D3
Tokuyama, Japan 74/B3
Tōkyō (cap.), Japan 75/F3
Tōkyō (pref.), Japan 75/F3
Tōkyō (bay), Japan 77/D2
Tōkyō Disneyland, Japan 77/D2
Tola, Nic. 144/E4
Tolbo, Mong. 70/F2
Toledo, Braz. 157/F1
Toledo, Phil. 79/D5
Toledo, Oh, US 130/D3
Toledo, Sp. 44/C3
Toledo, Col. 152/C3
Toledo, Uru. 159/K11
Toledo Bend (dam), La,Tx, US 129/J5
Toledo Bend (res.), La,Tx, US 129/J5
Toledo, Montes de (mts.), Sp. 44/C3
Tolentino, It. 43/K5
Tolfa, It. 46/B1
Tolhuaca, PN, Chile 158/C3
Toli, China 70/D2
Toliara (prov.), Madg. 107/H8
Toliara, Madg. 107/G8
Tolima (dept.), Col. 152/C4
Tolitoli, Indo. 81/F3
Tolka (riv.), Ire. 34/B5
Tolleson, Az, US 137/R19
Tolmezzo, It. 43/K3
Tolna (prov.), Hun. 48/D2
Tolna, Hun. 48/D2
Tolo (chan.), China 71/U10
Tolo, Gulf of (gulf), Indo. 81/F4
Tolosa, Sp. 44/D1
Tolsan (isl.), SKor. 73/D5
Tolt (riv.), Wa, US 135/D2
Tolt (res.), Wa, US 135/D2
Tolt, North Fork (riv.), Wa, US 135/D2
Tolt, South Fork (riv.), Wa, US 135/D2
Toltén, Chile 158/B3
Toltén (riv.), Chile 158/B3
Tolú, Col. 152/C2
Toluca, Mex. 143/Q10
Tolúviejo, Col. 152/C2
Tol'yatti, Rus. 63/J1
Tom' (riv.), Rus. 64/J4
Tom Price, Austl. 112/C2
Tom White (mt.), Ak, US 134/K3
Tomakomai, Japan 76/B2
Tomamae, Japan 76/B1
Tomar, Port. 44/A3
Tómaros (peak), Gre. 47/G3
Tomarza, Turk. 90/C2
Tomás, Peru 156/C4
Tomás de Berlanga, Ecu. 156/E7
Tomaszów Lubelski, Pol. 41/M3
Tomaszów Mazowiecki, Pol. 41/L3
Tomatlán, Mex. 142/D5
Tomb of Qinshihuang, China 72/B4
Tombador, Serra do (mts.), Braz. 150/G6
Tombigbee (riv.), Al,Ms, US 125/J5
Tombolo, It. 59/E1
Tombouctou, Mali 102/E2
Tombouctou (pol. reg.), Mali 98/D5
Tombstone, Az, US 128/E5
Tombua, Ang. 105/B4
Tomé, Chile 158/B3
Tomé, Île (isl.), Fr. 42/B2
Tomelilla, Swe. 38/E4
Tomelloso, Sp. 44/D3
Tomika, Japan 77/L5
Tomini (gulf), Indo. 67/M10
Tomiño, Sp. 44/A2
Tomioka, Japan 77/B1
Tomisato, Japan 77/E2
Tomiura, Japan 77/D3
Tomiyama, Japan 75/F3
Tomizawa, Japan 77/A3
Tommot, Rus. 65/N4
Tomo (riv.), Col. 150/E2
Tompa, Hun. 48/D2
Tompkinsville, Ky, US 130/C4
Toms (riv.), NJ, US 138/D3
Toms River, NJ, US 138/D4
Tomsk, Rus. 64/J4
Tomskskaya Oblast, Rus. 64/H4
Tömük, Turk. 91/D1
Tonalá, Mex. 144/C2
Tonale, Passo del (pass), It. 57/G5
Tonasket, Wa, US 126/D3
Tonawanda, NY, US 131/S9
Tonawanda Ind. Res., US 131/S9
Tonbridge, Eng, UK 30/D3
Toncontín (int'l arpt.), Hon. 144/E3
Tondabayashi, Japan 77/J7
Tondano, Indo. 81/F3
Tondou, Massif du (plat.), CAfr.,Sud 97/K6
Tondu (peak), Fr. 56/C6
Tone (riv.), Japan 75/G3
Tone, Japan 77/E2
Tonekābon, Iran 88/F1
Tonelagee (peak), Ire. 34/B5
Tonga (ctry.) 117/H7
Tongaat, SAfr. 107/E3
Tongareva (Penrhyn) (isl.), Cookls. 117/J5
Tongariro NP, NZ 117/T10
Tongatapu (isl.), Tonga 117/H7
Tongbai, China 72/C4
Tongbu, SKor. 73/G6
Tongcheng, China 79/B2
Tongcheng, China 72/D5
T'ongch'ŏn, NKor. 73/D3
Tongchuan, China 72/B4
Tongdao Dongzu Zizhixian, China 83/J2
Tongduch'on, SKor. 73/G6
Tongeren, Belg. 53/E2
Tonggu (peak), China 71/L7
Tonggu, China 83/K2
Tonghae, SKor. 73/E4
Tonghua, China 73/C2
Tonghua, China 73/C2
Tongliao, China 72/E2
Tongling, China 71/L5
Tongno (riv.), NKor. 73/D2
Tongo (peak), Indo. 81/E5
Tongobory, Madg. 107/H8
Tongren, China 83/J2
Tongsa (riv.), Bhu. 85/H2
Tongsa Dzong, Bhu. 85/H2
Tongshan, China 79/B2
Tongue (riv.), Mt, US 124/E2
Tongue, Sc, UK 31/R7
Tongxu, China 72/C4
Tongyu, China 71/M3
Tongzi, China 79/A2
Tonino-Anivskiy (pen.), Rus. 76/C1
Tönisvorst, Ger. 50/D6
Tonk, India 89/L3
Tonkawa, Ok, US 129/H3
Tonkin (gulf), China,Viet 67/K7
Tonkin, Gulf of (gulf), China,Vie 70/J7
Tonkoui (peak), C.d'Iv. 102/D5
Tonle Sap (lake), Camb. 83/H5
Tonneins, Fr. 42/D4
Tonnerre, Fr. 42/E3
Tönning, Ger. 38/C4
Tōno, Japan 76/B4
Tonopah, Nv, US 128/C3
Tonoshō, Japan 74/D3
Tonosí, Pan. 152/A3
Tonota, Bots. 105/E5
Tons (riv.), India 84/C3
Tønsberg, Nor. 38/D2
Tonsina, Ak, US 134/J3
Tonstad, Nor. 38/B2
Tonto Nat'l For., Az, US 137/S18
Tonto Nat'l Mon., Az, US 128/E4
Tonya, Turk. 90/D1
Ton-y-Pandy, Wal, UK 32/C3
Toodyay, Austl. 112/C4
Tooele, Ut, US 137/J12
Tooele (co.), Ut, US 137/J13
Tooradin, Austl. 115/C3
Toowoomba, Austl. 114/C4
Top (mt.), Austl. 113/G2
Topanaga State Park, Ca, US 136/B2
Topanga, Ca, US 136/B2
Topanga Beach, Ca, US 136/E7
Tope de Coroa (mtn.), CpV. 93/J10
Topia, Mex. 142/D3
Topley, BC, Can. 126/B2
Toplița, Rom. 49/G2
Topol'čany, Slvk. 41/K4
Topolobampo, Mex. 142/C3
Topoloveni, Rom. 49/G3
Topolovgrad, Bul. 47/K1
Topozero (lake), Rus. 37/J2
Toppenish, Wa, US 126/C4
Toprakkale, Turk. 91/E1
Topton, Pa, US 138/C3
Tor (bay), Eng, UK 32/C6
Torahime, Japan 77/K5
Torata, Peru 156/D5
Torawitan (cape), Indo. 81/G3
Torbalı, Turk. 90/A2
Torbat-e Ḩeydarīyeh, Iran 89/G1
Torbat-e Jām, Iran 87/D5
Torbay, Nf, Can. 131/L2
Torbay (co.), Eng, UK 32/C6
Torbeck, Haiti 145/H2
Torbert (mt.), Ak, US 134/H3
Torcy, Fr. 30/K5
Tordera (riv.), Sp. 45/L6
Tordesillas, Sp. 44/C2
Töreboda, Swe. 38/F2
Torelló, Sp. 45/G1
Torfaen (co.), Wal, UK 32/C3
Torgelow, Ger. 38/E5
Torghay, Kaz. 87/D3
Torghay (riv.), Kaz. 87/D3
Torghay Üstirti (plat.), Kaz. 87/D2
Torhamnsudde (pt.), Swe. 38/F3
Torhout, Belg. 52/C1
Tori-shima (isl.), Japan 116/D1
Toride, Japan 77/E2
Torigni-sur-Vire, Fr. 42/C2
Torii-tōge (pass), Japan 75/E3
Toriñana (cape), Sp. 44/A1
Torino (prov.), It. 58/A2
Torino (Turin), It. 43/G4
Torkestān (mts.), Afg. 89/H1
Tormes (riv.), Sp. 44/C2
Torndirrup NP, Austl. 112/C5
Torne (riv.), Eng, UK 35/H4
Torneälven (riv.), Swe. 60/D2
Tornesch, Ger. 51/G1
Tornik (peak), Serb. 48/D4
Tornio, Fin. 37/H2
Tornionjoki (riv.), Fin. 37/G2
Toro, Sp. 44/C2
Toro, Cerro del (peak), Arg.,Chil 157/C2
Toro Nat'l Rsv., Ugan. 104/A2
Toro, PN, Ven. 152/D2
Törökbálint, Hun. 49/Q10
Törökszentmiklós, Hun. 48/E2
Toronaic (gulf), Gre. 47/H2
Torondoy, Ven. 152/D2
Toronto (cap.), On, Can. 131/R8
Toronto (isl.), On, Can. 131/R8
Toropets, Rus. 39/P3
Tororo, Ugan. 104/B2
Torote (riv.), Sp. 45/N8
Torp (int'l arpt.), Nor. 38/D2
Torpa, Swe. 38/E3
Torquay, Austl. 115/C3
Torquay, Eng, UK 32/C6
Torquemada, Sp. 44/C1
Torr (pt.), NI, UK 34/B1
Torrance, Ca, US 136/F8
Torraz, Tête du (peak), Fr. 56/C6
Torrazza Piemonte, It. 58/A2
Torre de Moncorvo, Port. 44/B2
Torre dè Passeri, It. 46/C1
Torre del Campo, Sp. 44/D4
Torre del Greco, It. 46/D2
Torre del Lago Puccini, It. 58/D5
Torre-Pacheco, Sp. 45/E4
Torrebelvicino, It. 59/E1
Torreblanca, Sp. 45/F2
Torredonjimeno, Sp. 44/D4
Torreglia, It. 59/E2
Torrejón de Ardoz, Sp. 45/N9
Torrejoncillo, Sp. 44/B3
Torrelaguna, Sp. 44/D2
Torrelavega, Sp. 44/C1
Torrelodones, Sp. 45/N8
Torremaggiore, It. 46/D2
Torremolinos, Sp. 44/C4
Torrens (lake), Austl. 109/C4
Torrens (riv.), Austl. 113/M8
Torrens (isl.), Austl. 113/M8
Torrente, Sp. 45/E3
Torreón, Mex. 142/E3
Torreperogil, Sp. 44/D3
Tôrres, Braz. 155/B4
Torres (str.), Austl.,PNG 116/D6
Torres (isls.), Van. 116/F6
Torres del Paine, PN, Chile 159/B6
Torres Novas, Port. 44/A3
Torres Vedras, Port. 44/A3
Torrevieja, Sp. 45/E4
Torri di Quartesolo, It. 59/E1
Torridge (riv.), Eng, UK 32/B5
Torrijos, Sp. 44/C3
Torrington, Wy, US 127/G5
Torrita di Siena, It. 43/J5
Torroella de Montgrí, Sp. 45/G1
Torrone Alto (peak), Swi. 57/F5
Torrox, Sp. 44/D4
Torsa (riv.), Bhu. 85/G2
Torsås, Swe. 38/F3
Torsby, Swe. 38/E1
Tórshavn, Den. 160/G
Tortola (isl.), UK 141/J4
Tortolì, It. 46/A3
Tortona, It. 58/B3
Tortosa (cape), Sp. 45/F2
Tortosa, Sp. 45/F2
Tortuga (isl.), Haiti 141/H5
Tortuguero, PN, CR 145/F4
Tortum, Turk. 63/G4
Ţorūd, Iran 89/F1
Torugart (pass), Kyr. 87/G4
Torul, Turk. 90/D1
Toruń, Pol. 41/K2
Torup, Swe. 38/E3
Tory (isl.), Ire. 31/P9
Torysa (riv.), Slvk. 41/L4
Torzhok, Rus. 60/G4
Tosa, Japan 74/C4
Tosagua, Ecu. 152/A5
Tosashimizu, Japan 74/C4
Toscana (reg.), It. 58/C4
Toscana (prov.), It. 43/J5
Toscanella, It. 59/E4
Toscolano-Maderno, It. 58/D1
Toshi (isl.), Japan 77/L6
Toshibetsu (riv.), Japan 76/A2
Toshkent (pol. reg.), Uzb. 87/E4
Tosna (riv.), Rus. 61/T7
Tosno, Rus. 39/P2
Tosontsengel, Mong. 70/G2
Töss (riv.), Swi. 43/H3
Tosson (hill), Eng, UK 36/E6
Tostado, Arg. 157/D2
Tostedt, Ger. 51/G2
Tosu, Japan 74/B4
Tosya, Turk. 90/C1
Totana, Sp. 44/E4
Totness, Sur. 153/G3
Totowa, NJ, US 139/J8
Totten (inlet), Wa, US 135/A3
Tottenham, Austl. 115/C2
Tottington, Eng, UK 35/F4
Tottori, Japan 74/D3
Tottori (pref.), Japan 74/C3
Totutla, Mex. 143/N7
Touat (reg.), Alg. 99/E4
Touba, C.d'Iv. 102/D4
Toubkal (peak), Mor. 98/D3
Toubkal, PN du, Mor. 98/D3
Touchwood (hills), Sk, Can. 127/G3
Toucy, Fr. 42/E3
Toudao (riv.), China 73/D1
Tougan, Burk. 102/E3
Touggourt, Alg. 99/G2
Toughkenamon, Pa, US 138/C4
Touiel (riv.), Alg. 100/G5
Toul, Fr. 53/E6
Toulnustouc (riv.), Qu, Can. 131/H1
Toulon, Fr. 42/F5
Toulouse, Fr. 42/D5
Toumo (well), Niger 96/H3
Toumodi, C.d'Iv. 102/D5
Toungoo, Myan. 83/G4
Touquin, Fr. 30/M5
Toura, Monts du (mts.), C.d'Iv. 102/D5
Tourcoing, Fr. 52/C2
Tourfourine (well), Mali 98/D4
Tourlaville, Fr. 42/C2
Tournai, Belg. 52/C2
Tournan-en-Brie, Fr. 30/L5
Tournus, Fr. 56/A4
Touros, Braz. 154/D2
Tours, Fr. 42/D3
Tous, Embalse de (res.), Sp. 45/E3
Toussidé (peak), Chad 96/J3
Toussoro (peak), CAfr. 97/K6
Touws (riv.), SAfr. 106/C4
Touwsrivier, SAfr. 106/M10
Toužim, Czh. 55/G2
Töv (prov.), Mong. 70/J2
Tovar, Ven. 152/D2
Tove (riv.), Eng, UK 33/E2
Towaco, NJ, US 139/H8
Towada, Japan 75/G2
Towada (lake), Japan 76/B3
Towada-Hachimantai NP, Japan 76/B3
Tower City, Pa, US 138/B2
Tower Hamlets (bor.), Eng, UK 30/A1
Tower of London, Eng, UK 30/C2
Towner, ND, US 127/H3
Townsend, Mt, US 126/F4
Townsend, De, US 138/C5
Townsend (mt.), Wa, US 135/A2
Townsends (inlet), NJ, US 138/D5
Townshend (cape), Austl. 114/C3
Townsville, Austl. 114/B2
Towson, Md, US 138/B5
Towuti (lake), Indo. 81/F4
Toya (lake), Japan 76/B2
Toyah, Tx, US 132/C4
Toyahvale, Tx, US 132/C4
Toyama, Japan 75/E2
Toyama (pref.), Japan 75/E2
Toyang, SKor. 73/D5
Toyoake, Japan 77/M5
Toyohashi, Japan 75/E3
Toyokawa, Japan 75/E3
Toyonaka, Japan 77/H6
Toyono, Japan 77/H6
Toyo'oka, Japan 74/D3
Toyosato, Japan 77/E1
Toyosato, Japan 77/K5
Toyoshina, Japan 75/E2
Toyota, Japan 77/M5
Toyotomi, Japan 77/B2
Toyoyama, Japan 77/L5
Tozi (mt.), Ak, US 134/H2
Tra Vinh, Viet. 78/D4
Traben-Trarbach, Ger. 53/G4
Trabuco Canyon, Ca, US 136/C3
Trabzon, Turk. 90/D1
Trabzon (prov.), Turk. 90/D1
Tracadie, NB, Can. 131/H2
Trachselwald, Swi. 56/D3
Tracy, Qu, Can. 130/F2
Tracy, Mo, US 137/D5
Tracyton, Wa, US 135/B2
Tradate, It. 58/B1
Trafalgar (cape), Sp. 44/B4
Trafford (co.), Eng, UK 35/F5
Tragwein, Aus. 55/H6
Traiguén, Chile 158/B3
Trail, BC, Can. 126/D3
Traipu, Braz. 154/C3
Trairi, Braz. 154/C1
Traisen (riv.), Aus. 41/H5
Traiskirchen, Aus. 49/N7
Traismauer, Aus. 41/H4
Trakai NP, Lith. 39/L4
Traki, Lith. 39/L4
Tralee, Ire. 31/P10
Tramandaí, Braz. 155/B4
Tramelan, Swi. 56/D3
Tramin (Termeno), It. 57/H5
Tranås, Swe. 38/F2
Tranbjerg, Den. 38/D3
Trancoso, Port. 44/B2
Tranebjerg, Den. 38/D4
Tranemo, Swe. 38/E3
Tranent, Sc, UK 36/D5
Tranet (peak), Fr. 53/D4
Trang, Thai. 78/B5
Trangan (isl.), Indo. 81/H5
Trangie, Austl. 115/C2
Trängsletsjön (lake), Swe. 38/E1
Trani, It. 46/E2
Tranoroa, Madg. 107/H9
Transantarctic (mts.), Ant. 160/W
Transylvania (reg.), Rom. 48/F2
Transylvanian Alps (mts.), Rom. 62/B3
Trapani, It. 46/C3
Trapper (peak), Mt, US 126/E4
Trappes, Fr. 30/J5
Traralgon, Austl. 115/C3
Trarza (pol. reg.), Mrta. 96/B4
Trasacco, It. 46/C2
Trasimeno (lake), It. 43/K5
Träslövsläge, Swe. 38/E3
Trat, Thai. 78/C3
Traun (riv.), Aus. 40/H4
Traun, Aus. 55/H6
Traunreut, Ger. 55/F7
Traunsee (lake), Aus. 43/K3
Traunstein, Ger. 55/F7
Trautmannsdorf an der Leitha, Aus. 49/P7
Travagliato, It. 58/D1
Trave (riv.), Ger. 40/F2
Travedona Monate, It. 58/B1
Travellers (lake), Austl. 109/D4
Travemunde, Ger. 40/F2
Traverse (peak), Ak, US 134/G2
Traverse (lake), Mn, SD, US 127/J4
Traverse City, Mi, US 130/C2
Traversetolo, It. 58/D3
Travis (lake), Tx, US 132/D4
Travis AFB, Ca, US 135/L10
Travnik, Bosn. 48/C3
Trawsalt (peak), Wal, UK 32/C2
Trawsfynydd, Llyn (lake), Wal, UK 34/D6
Trbovlje, Slov. 43/L3
Tré-la-Tête (peak), Fr. 56/C6
Treachery (mt.), Austl. 113/G2
Trebaseleghe, It. 59/F1
Trebbia (riv.), It. 43/H4
Trebel (riv.), Ger. 40/G1
Třebíč, Czh. 41/H4
Trebinje, Bosn. 47/F1
Trebisacce, It. 46/E3
Třeboň, Czh. 55/H4
Trebonne, Austl. 114/B2
Trebujena, Sp. 44/B4
Trebur, Ger. 54/B3
Trecate, It. 58/B2
Tregnago, It. 59/E1
Treia, Ger. 38/C4
Treig (lake), Sc, UK 36/B3
Treinta de Agosto, Arg. 158/E3
Treinta y Tres (dept.), Uru. 159/G2
Treinta y Tres, Uru. 159/G2
Trélazé, Fr. 42/C3
Trelew, Arg. 158/D4
Trélissac, Fr. 42/D4
Trelleborg, Swe. 38/E4
Tremadoc (bay), Wal, UK 34/D6
Tremblestown (riv.), Ire. 34/B4
Trembleur (lake), BC, Can. 126/B2
Tremelo, Belg. 53/D2
Tremiti (isl.), It. 46/D1
Tremont, Pa, US 138/B2
Třemošná (riv.), Czh. 55/G3
Tremp, Sp. 45/F1
Třemšín (peak), Czh. 55/G3
Trenche (riv.), Qu, Can. 130/F1
Trenčíanský (pol. reg.), Slvk. 41/J4
Trenčín, Slvk. 41/K4
Trenel, Arg. 158/D2
Trenque Lauquen, Arg. 158/E2
Trent (riv.), Eng, UK 35/F6
Trent and Mersey (canal), Eng, UK 35/F6
Trentino-Alto Adige (pol. reg.), It. 43/J3
Trento, It. 57/H5
Trento (prov.), It. 57/G5
Trenton, On, Can. 130/E2
Trenton, Ga, US 133/G3
Trenton, Fl, US 133/H4
Trenton, Tn, US 130/B5
Trenton, Mo, US 129/J2
Trenton (cap.), NJ, US 138/D3
Trenzano, It. 58/D2
Trepuzzi, It. 47/F2
Tres Algarrobos, Arg. 158/E2
Tres Arroyos, Arg. 158/E3
Três Corações, Braz. 211/H6
Três Irmãos, Reprêsa (res.), Braz. 155/B2
Tres Isletas, Arg. 157/D2
Três Lagoas, Braz. 155/B2
Tres Lomas, Arg. 158/E3
Três Marias, Braz. 154/A5
Tres Marías (isls.), Mex. 142/D4
Tres Marías, Mex. 143/Q10
Três Marias, Reprêsa (res.), Braz. 151/J7
Tres Montes (cape), Chile 159/B5
Tres Morros, Alto de (peak), Col. 152/B3
Tres Picos, Mex. 144/C3
Tres Picos (peak), Arg. 158/C4
Tres Picos (peak), Arg. 158/E3
Três Pontas, Braz. 211/H6
Tres Puntas (cape), Arg. 158/D5
Três Rios, Braz. 211/K7
Tres Valles, Mex. 144/B2
Tresa (riv.), Swi. 57/E5
Tresckow, Pa, US 138/C2
Trescore Balneario, It. 58/C1
Trescore Cremasco, It. 58/C2
Tresigallo, It. 59/E3
Tresinaro (riv.), It. 58/D4
Trestina, It. 59/F6
Trets, Fr. 42/F5
Treuchtlingen, Ger. 54/D5
Treuen, Ger. 55/F1
Treuenbrietzen, Ger. 40/G2
Treungen, Nor. 38/C2
Trevelín, Arg. 158/C4
Treviglio, It. 58/C1
Trevignano, It. 59/F1
Treviso (int'l arpt.), It. 59/F1
Treviso (prov.), It. 59/F2
Treviso, It. 59/F1
Trevorton, Pa, US 138/B2
Trevose (pt.), Eng, UK 32/A5
Trezzano sul Naviglio, It. 58/C2
Trezzo sull'Adda, It. 58/C1
Trhové Sviny, Czh. 55/H5
Triabunna, Austl. 115/C4
Triadelphia (res.), Md, US 138/A5
Triángulos (reef), Mex. 144/C1
Tribbey, Ok, US 137/N15
Triberg, Ger. 57/E1
Tribhuvan (int'l arpt.), Nepal 85/E2
Tribugá (bay), Col. 152/B3
Tribulation (cape), Austl. 114/B2
Tribulaun (peak), Aus. 57/H4
Tricase, It. 47/F3
Trichūr, India 82/C5
Tricora (peak), Indo. 81/J4
Tricot, Fr. 52/B4
Trie-Château, Fr. 52/A5
Trier, Ger. 53/F4
Trierweiler, Ger. 53/F4
Triesen, Lcht. 57/F3
Trieste, It. 59/G1
Trieste (prov.), It. 59/G1
Trieste, It. 43/K4
Trieux, Fr. 53/E5
Triftern, Ger. 55/G6
Triggiano, It. 48/C5
Trigla NP, Slov. 43/K3
Triglav (peak), Slov. 43/K3
Trigolo, It. 58/C2
Tríkala, Gre. 47/G3
Trikhonís (lake), Gre. 47/G3
Trilport, Fr. 52/B6
Trimbach, Swi. 56/D3
Trimble, Mo, US 137/D5
Trimmis, Swi. 57/F4
Trin, Swi. 57/F4
Trincomalee, SrL. 82/D6
Trindade, Braz. 151/J7
Trindade, Ilha da (isl.), Braz. 151/N8
Třinec, Czh. 41/K4
Tring, Eng, UK 33/F3
Trinidad (isl.), Arg. 157/D4
Trinidad (isl.), Trin. 150/F2
Trinidad, Bol. 150/F6
Trinidad, Co, US 129/F3
Trinidad, Col. 152/D3
Trinidad (chan.), Chile 159/B6
Trinidad, Uru. 159/K10
Trinidad (gulf), Chile 159/A6
Trinidad and Tobago (ctry.) 141/N10
Trinity (isls.), Ak, US 134/H4
Trinity (range), Nv, US 128/C2
Trinity (riv.), Ca, US 126/C5
Trinity (bay), Nf, Can. 131/L2
Trinity (riv.), Tx, US 140/B1
Trinity, West Fork (riv.), Tx, US 129/H4
Trino, It. 58/B2
Triolet, Mrts. 107/T15
Trípolis, Gre. 47/H4
Tripolitania (reg.), Libya 96/H1
Trippstadt, Ger. 53/G5
Tripunittura, India 82/C6
Tripura (state), India 70/F7
Trisanna (riv.), Aus. 57/G4
Trissino, It. 59/E1
Tristan da Cunha (isl.), StH. 22/J7
Triste (peak), Arg. 158/D4
Trisuli (riv.), Nepal 85/E2
Trittau, Ger. 51/H1
Trivero, It. 58/B1
Trnava, Slvk. 41/J4
Trnavský (pol. reg.), Slvk. 41/J4
Trobriand (isls.), PNG 116/E5
Trochtelfingen, Ger. 57/F1
Troesne (riv.), Fr. 52/A5
Trofaiach, Aus. 43/L3
Trofarello, It. 58/A3
Trøgstad, Nor. 38/D2
Troia, It. 46/D2
Trois Fourches, Cap des (cape), Mor. 100/C2
Trois-Pistoles, Qu, Can. 131/G1
Trois-Ponts, Belg. 53/E3
Trois-Rivières, Qu, Can. 131/F2
Troisdorf, Ger. 53/G2
Troistorrents, Swi. 56/C5
Troisvierges, Lux. 53/F3
Troitsk, Rus. 61/P5
Trollhättan, Swe. 38/E2
Trombetas (riv.), Braz. 151/G3
Tromello, It. 58/B2
Tromie (riv.), Sc, UK 36/B3
Troms (co.), Nor. 37/F1
Tromsø, Nor. 37/F1
Tronador (peak), Arg. 158/C4
Trondheim, Nor. 37/D3
Trondheims-Fjorden (estu.), Nor. 37/D3
Tronville-en-Barrios, Fr. 53/E6
Tronzano Vercellese, It. 58/B2
Troodos (mts.), Cyp. 91/C2
Trool (lake), Sc, UK 34/D1
Troon, Sc, UK 36/B5
Trooper, Pa, US 138/C3
Tropea, It. 46/D3
Trosa, Swe. 38/G2
Trosly-Breuil, Fr. 52/B5
Trossingen, Ger. 57/E1
Trostan (peak), NI, UK 34/B1
Trostberg an der Alz, Ger. 55/F6

232

Trou – Urana

Trou du Nord, Haiti 145/H2
Troup (pt.), Sc, UK 36/D1
Trout (lake), NW, Can. 122/D2
Trout Lake, Ab, Can. 126/E1
Trowbridge, Eng, UK 32/D4
Troxelville, Pa, US 138/A2
Troy, Al, US 133/G4
Troy, Mi, US 130/D3
Troy, NY, US 130/F3
Troy, Oh, US 133/G1
Troy, Il, US 137/H8
Troy Center, Wi, US 135/N14
Troyan, Bul. 47/J1
Troyanski Prokhod (pass), Bul. 47/J1
Troyes, Fr. 42/F2
Trstenik, Serb. 48/E4
Trub, Swi. 56/D4
Truitt (peak), Yk, Can. 134/M3
Trujillo, Peru 156/B3
Trujillo, Sp. 44/C3
Trujillo, Ven. 152/D2
Trujillo (state), Ven. 152/D2
Trujillo, Hon. 144/E3
Truk (isls.), Micr. 116/E4
Trulben, Ger. 53/G5
Truman Library and Museum, Mo, US 137/E5
Trumau, Aus. 49/N8
Trumbauersville, Pa, US 138/C3
Trumbull, Ct, US 139/E1
Trümmelbachfälle (falls), Swi. 56/D4
Trŭn, Bul. 47/H1
Trundle, Austl. 115/C2
Truro, NS, Can. 131/J2
Truro, Eng, UK 32/A6
Truskmore (peak), Ire. 31/P9
Trŭstenik, Bul. 49/G4
Truth or Consequences, NM, US 128/F4
Trutnov, Czh. 41/H3
Truyère (riv.), Fr. 42/E4
Trwyn Cilan (pt.), Wal, UK 34/D6
Tryavna, Bul. 47/J1
Trysil, Nor. 38/E1
Trysilelva (riv.), Nor. 38/D1
Trzcianka, Pol. 41/J2
Trzebiatów, Pol. 38/F4
Trzebnica, Pol. 41/J3
Trzemeszno, Pol. 41/J2
Tsabong, Bots. 106/C2
Tsagaan Bogd (peak), Mong. 70/G3
Tsakane, SAfr. 106/Q13
Tsalgar, Mong. 70/F2
Tsant, Mong. 70/J2
Tsao, Bots. 105/D5
Tsarahonenana, Madg. 107/J6
Tsaramandroso, Madg. 107/H7
Tsaratanana, Madg. 107/H7
Tsaratanana (mass.), Madg. 107/J6
Tsast (peak), Mong. 70/F2
Tsatsana (peak), Les. 106/E3
Tsavo East NP, Kenya 105/G1
Tsavo West NP, Kenya 105/G1
Tschagguns, Aus. 57/F3
Tschierv, Swi. 57/G4
Tschlin, Swi. 57/G4
Tselfat (peak), Mor. 100/B2
Tsetserleg, Mong. 70/F2
Tsetserleg, Mong. 70/H2
Tseung Kwan O, China 71/U10
Tsévié, Togo 103/F5
Tshane, Bots. 105/D5
Tshela, D.R. Congo 105/B1
Tshikapa, D.R. Congo 105/D2
Tshuapa (riv.), D.R. Congo 93/E5
Tsiafajavona (peak), Madg. 107/H7
Tsil'ma (riv.), Rus. 61/L2
Tsimlyansk (res.), Rus. 64/E5
Tsing Yi (isl.), China 71/U10
Tsiombe, Madg. 107/H9
Tsiribihina (riv.), Madg. 107/H7
Tsiroanomandidy, Madg. 107/H7
Tsitsikamma Forest and Coastal NP, SAfr. 106/C4
Tsivory, Madg. 107/H9
Ts'khinvali, Geo. 63/G4
Tsna (riv.), Rus. 60/G4
Tsomo (riv.), SAfr. 106/D3
Tsomog, Mong. 71/J2
Tsu, Japan 77/L6
Tsu (isl.), Japan 74/A3
Tsubame, Japan 75/F2
Tsubata, Japan 75/E2
Tsuchiura, Japan 75/G2
Tsuchiyama, Japan 77/K6
Tsuen Wan, China 71/U10
Tsugaru (pen.), Japan 76/B3
Tsuge, Japan 77/J6
Tsukidate, Japan 76/B4
Tsukigase, Japan 77/K6
Tsukuba, Japan 77/E1
Tsukude, Japan 77/M6
Tsukui, Japan 77/C2
Tsukumi, Japan 74/B4
Tsumeb, Namb. 105/C4
Tsuna, Japan 77/G7
Tsuru, Japan 75/F3
Tsuruga, Japan 74/E3
Tsurugashima, Japan 77/C2
Tsurugi, Japan 74/E2
Tsurugi-san (peak), Japan 74/D4
Tsuruoka, Japan 76/A4
Tsushima, Japan 77/L5
Tsuyama, Japan 74/D3
Tua (cape), Indo. 80/C5
Tua (riv.), Port.,Sp. 44/B2
Tuam, Ire. 31/P10
Tuamapu (chan.), Chile 158/B4
Tuamotu (arch.), FrPol. 117/L6
Tuan (pt.), Indo. 80/A3
Tuan (riv.), China 72/B4
Tuangku (isl.), Indo. 80/A3
Tuao, Phil. 79/D4
Tuapse, Rus. 62/F3
Tuba City, Az, US 128/E3
Tuban, Indo. 80/D5
Tuban (riv.), Yem. 88/D6
Tubarão, Braz. 155/B4
Tubbergen, Neth. 50/D4
Tübingen, Ger. 54/C5
Tubize, Belg. 53/D2
Tubmanburg, Libr. 102/C5
Ţubruq (Tobruk), Libya 97/K1
Tubuaï (isl.), FrPol. 117/K7
Tubualá, Pan. 152/B2
Tucacas, Ven. 152/D2
Tucano, Braz. 154/C3
Tuchola, Pol. 41/J2
Tuchów, Pol. 41/L4
Tuckahoe, NJ, US 138/D5
Tuckahoe (riv.), NJ, US 138/D5
Tuckahoe, NY, US 139/K8
Tuckerton, NJ, US 138/D4
Tucquegnieux, Fr. 53/E5
Tucson, Az, US 128/E4
Tucson (int'l arpt.), Az, US 142/C1
Tucumcari, NM, US 129/G4
Tucupido, Ven. 153/E2
Tucupita, Ven. 153/F2
Tucuruí, Braz. 151/J4
Tucuruí (res.), Braz. 147/E3
Tudela, Sp. 44/E1
Tudela de Duero, Sp. 44/C2
Tuen Mun, China 71/T10
Tuenno, It. 57/H5
Tufanbeyli, Turk. 90/D2
Tug Fork (riv.), Ky,WV, US 133/H2
Tugela (riv.), SAfr. 107/E3
Tugela, SAfr. 107/E3
Tugela (falls), SAfr. 106/E3
Tughlakabad (ruin), India 86/D5
Tuguegarao, Phil. 79/D4
Tukangbesi (isls.), Indo. 81/F5
Ţūkh, Egypt 91/B4
Tuktoyaktuk, NW, Can. 134/M2
Tukums, Lat. 39/K3
Tukung (peak), Indo. 80/D4
Tukuyu, Tanz. 104/B5
Tukwila, Wa, US 135/C3
Tula (riv.), Kenya 104/C3
Tula, Mex. 143/F4
Tula, Rus. 62/F1
Tula (riv.), Mex. 143/K6
Tula, Mex. 143/K6
Tula, PN, Mex. 143/K6
Tulancingo, Mex. 143/L6
Tulare, Ca, US 128/C3
Tularosa (valley), NM, US 129/F4
Tularosa, NM, US 129/F4
Tulcán, Ecu. 152/B4
Tulcea, Rom. 49/J3
Tulcea (prov.), Rom. 49/J3
Tule (canal), Ca, US 135/L9
Tüledi (isls.), Rus. 87/B3
Tulia, Tx, US 129/G4
Tulik (vol.), Ak, US 134/E5
Tulin (isls.), PNG 116/E5
Tulita, NW, Can. 122/D2
Ţūlkarm, WBnk. 91/G7
Tulla (lake), Sc, UK 36/B3
Tullahoma, Tn, US 133/G3
Tullamarine (int'l arpt.), Austl. 115/F5
Tullamore, Austl. 115/C2
Tullamore, Ire. 31/Q10
Tulle, Fr. 42/D4
Tullibody, Sc, UK 36/C4
Tullnerbach, Aus. 49/N7
Tullow, Ire. 31/Q10
Tully, Austl. 114/B2
Tullytown, Pa, US 138/D3
Tuloma (riv.), Rus. 64/D3
Tulsa, Ok, US 129/J3
Tulsipur, Nepal 84/D1
Tulsīpur, India 84/D2
Tul'skaya Oblast, Rus. 62/F1
Tultitlán, Mex. 143/Q9
Tuluá, Col. 152/B3
Tuluksak, Ak, US 134/F3
Tulum, Mex. 144/E1
Tulum, PN, Mex. 144/E1
Tulun, Rus. 65/L4
Tumacacori Nat'l Hist. Park, Az, US 128/E5
Tumaco, Col. 152/B4
Tumatumari, Guy. 153/G3
Tumauini, Phil. 79/D4
Tumba (lake), D.R. Congo 96/J8
Tumba, Swe. 38/G2
Tumbarumba, Austl. 115/D2
Tumbes (dept.), Peru 156/A1
Tumbes, Peru 156/A1
Tumbot (peak), Camb. 78/C3
Tumby Bay, Austl. 113/H5
Tumd Youqi, China 72/B2
Tumd Zuoqi, China 72/B2
Tumen, China 71/N3
Tumen (riv.), China 73/E1
Tumeremo, Ven. 153/F3
Tumereng, Guy. 153/F3
Tumkūr, India 82/C5
Tummel (riv.), Sc, UK 36/C3
Tumpat, Malay. 83/H6
Tumpu (peak), Indo. 81/F4
Tumu, Gha. 103/E4
Tumuc-Humac (mts.), Braz. 151/G3
Tumut, Austl. 115/D2
Tunadal, Swe. 60/C3
Tunceli (prov.), Turk. 90/D2
Tunceli, Turk. 90/D2
Tunchang, China 83/K4
Tundla, India 84/B2
Tundyk (riv.), Kaz. 87/G2
Tundzha (riv.), Bul. 47/K1
Tung Chung, China 71/T10
Tung Lung (riv.), China 71/V11
Tungabhadra (res.), India 82/C4
Tungabhadra (riv.), India 82/C4
Tungamah, Austl. 115/C3
Tŭngsan-got (pt.), NKor. 73/C4
Tungsten, NW, Can. 122/D2
Tungurahua (prov.), Ecu. 152/B5
Tünhel, Mong. 70/J2
Tūnis (gov.), Tun. 46/B4
Tūnis (cap.), Tun. 46/B4
Tunis, Gulf of (gulf), Tun. 46/B4
Tunisia (ctry.) 99/H2
Tunjá, Col. 152/C3
Tunliu, China 72/C3
Tunnels of Vinh Moc, Viet. 78/D2
Tuntum, Braz. 154/A2
Tuntutuliak, Ak, US 134/F3
Tunungayualuk (isl.), Nf, Can. 123/K3
Tunuyán (riv.), Arg. 158/C2
Tunuyán, Arg. 158/C2
Tuolumne (riv.), Ca, US 128/B3
Tuoniang (riv.), China 83/J3
Tupã, Braz. 155/B2
Tupaciguara, Braz. 155/B1
Tupai (isl.), FrPol. 117/K6
Tupambaé, Uru. 159/G2
Tuparro (riv.), Col. 152/D3
Tupelo, Ms, US 133/F3
Tupi Paulista, Braz. 155/B2
Tupiza, Bol. 150/E8
Tupper Lake, NY, US 130/F2
Tupungato, Arg. 158/C2
Tupungato (peak), Arg. 158/P8
Tura, India 85/H3
Tura (riv.), Rus. 64/G4
Tura, Rus. 65/L3
Turaiçu (riv.), Braz. 154/A1
Turan Lowland (plain), Uzb. 64/G5
Turangi, NZ 117/T10
Turbaco, Col. 152/C2
Turbat, Pak. 89/H3
Turbenthal, Swi. 57/E3
Turbo, Col. 152/B2
Turbotville, Pa, US 138/B1
Turčiansky Svätý Martin, Slvk. 62/A2
Turckheim, Fr. 56/D1
Turda, Rom. 49/F2
Tureia (isl.), FrPol. 117/M7
Turek, Pol. 41/K2
Turgeon (riv.), Qu, Can. 130/E1
Tŭrgovishte, Bul. 49/H4
Turgutlu, Turk. 90/A2
Turhal, Turk. 90/D1
Turia (riv.), Sp. 45/E3
Turiaçu, Braz. 151/J4
Turkana (Rudolf) (lake), Kenya 93/F4
Türkeli, Turk. 62/E4
Túrkeve, Hun. 48/E2
Turkey (ctry.) 90/C2
Turkey (riv.), Ia, US 129/K2
Türkheim, Ger. 57/G1
Türkistan, Kaz. 87/E4
Türkmenbashi (Krasnowodsk), Trkm. 63/K5
Turkmenistan (ctry.) 87/C5
Türkoğlu, Turk. 90/D2
Turks (isls.), Haiti 141/G3
Turks and Caicos (isls.), UK 141/G3
Turks Island Passage (chan.), UK 145/J1
Turku (int'l arpt.), Fin. 39/K1
Turku Ja Pori (prov.), Fin. 37/G3
Turkwel (riv.), Kenya 104/B2
Turlock, Ca, US 128/B3
Turmalina, Braz. 154/B5
Turneffe (isls.), Belz. 140/D4
Turner (mt.), Austl. 112/C2
Turnersville, NJ, US 138/C4
Turnhouse (int'l arpt.), Sc, UK 36/C5
Turnhout, Belg. 50/B6
Turnor Lake, Sk, Can. 126/F1
Turnov, Czh. 41/H3
Turnu Măgurele, Rom. 49/G4
Tuross Head, Austl. 115/D3
Tuross Head, Austl. 115/D3
Turpan, China 70/E3
Turpan (depr.), China 70/E3
Turquino (peak), Cuba 145/G2
Turriaco, It. 59/G1
Turriff, Sc, UK 36/D1
Turt, Mong. 70/H1
Turtle (isls.), SLeo. 102/B5
Turtleford, Sk, Can. 126/F2
Turugart (pass), China 87/G4
Turukhansk, Rus. 64/J3
Tuscaloosa, Al, US 133/G3
Tuscano (arch.), It. 46/B1
Tuscarora, Nv, US 126/D5
Tuscarora (mtn.), Pa, US 138/A3
Tuscarora Ind. Res., US 131/S9
Tuskegee, Al, US 133/G3
Tustin, Ca, US 136/G8
Tuszyn, Pol. 41/K3
Tutak, Turk. 90/E2
Tutayev, Rus. 60/H4
Tuticorin, India 82/C6
Tutin, Serb. 47/G1
Tutóia, Braz. 154/B1
Tutong, Bru. 80/D3
Tutrakan, Bul. 49/H3
Tuttle Creek (lake), Ks, US 129/H3
Tuttlingen, Ger. 57/E2
Tutuila (isl.), ASam. 117/H6
Tutupaca (vol.), Peru 156/D5
Tututalak (mtn.), Ak, US 134/F2
Tutzing, Ger. 57/H2
Tuusula, Fin. 39/L1
Tuvalu (ctry.) 116/G5
Ţuwayq, Jabal (mts.), SAr. 88/E3
Tuxpan, Mex. 142/E5
Tuxpan, Mex. 142/D4
Tuxpan de Rodríguez Cano, Mex. 144/B1
Tuxtla Gutiérrez, Mex. 144/C2
Túy, Sp. 44/A1
Tuy Hoa, Viet. 78/E3
Tuyen Quang, Viet. 78/D1
Tuymazy, Rus. 61/M5
Tūysarkān, Iran 88/E2
Tuz (lake), It. 90/C2
Ţūz Khurmātū, Iraq 90/F3
Tuzigoot Nat'l Mon., Az, US 128/D4
Tuzla, Bosn. 48/D3
Tuzla, Turk. 91/D1
Tuzluca, Turk. 90/E1
Tuzlukçu, Turk. 90/B2
Tvååker, Swe. 38/E3
Tvedestrand, Nor. 38/C2
Tver', Rus. 60/G4
Tverskaya Oblast, Rus. 39/P3
Tvertsa (riv.), Rus. 60/G4
Tvŭrditsa, Bul. 47/J1
Twardogóra, Pol. 41/J3
Tweed (riv.), Sc, UK 36/C5
Tweed Heads, Austl. 114/D5
Twello, Neth. 50/D4
Twente (canal), Neth. 50/D4
Twente (pol. reg.), Neth. 50/D4
Twin Buttes (res.), Tx, US 129/G5
Twin Hills, Ak, US 134/F4
Twin Lakes, Wi, US 135/P14
Twin Rivers, NJ, US 138/D3
Twiste (riv.), Ger. 51/G6
Twistringen, Ger. 51/F3
Twizel, NZ 117/S11
Two Hills, Ab, Can. 126/F2
Two Rivers, Wi, US 127/M4
Twofold (bay), Austl. 115/D3
Twyford, Eng, UK 33/F4
Twymyn (riv.), Wal, UK 32/C1
Tyatya (vol.), Rus. 76/E1
Tychy, Pol. 41/K3
Tyendinaga, On, Can. 130/E2
Tyger (riv.), SC, US 133/H3
Tyldesley, Eng, UK 35/F4
Tylersville, Pa, US 138/A2
Týn, Czh. 41/H4
Tyne (riv.), Sc, UK 36/D5
Tyne and Wear (co.), Eng, UK 35/G2
Tynemouth, Eng, UK 35/G1
Tynset, Nor. 37/D3
Tyonek, Ak, US 134/H3
Tyrifjorden (lake), Nor. 38/C1
Tyringe, Swe. 38/E3
Tyrnyauz, Rus. 63/G4
Tyrrell (lake), Austl. 115/B2
Tyrrhenian (sea), It. 27/F4
Tysnes, Nor. 38/A1
Tysnesøy (isl.), Nor. 38/A2
Tysons Corner, Va, US 138/A6
Tysse, Nor. 38/A1
Tystberga, Swe. 38/G2
Tyub-Karagan (pt.), Kaz. 63/J3
Tyuleniy (isl.), Rus. 63/H3
Tyumen (int'l arpt.), Rus. 61/Q4
Tyumen', Rus. 61/Q4
Tyumenskaya Oblast, Rus. 87/E1
Tyva, Resp., Rus. 64/K4
Tywi (riv.), Wal, UK 32/B3
Tzaneen, SAfr. 105/F5
Tzucacab, Mex. 144/D1

U

U.C.-Irvine, Ca, US 136/G8
U.K. Sovereign Base Area (gov.), Cyp. 91/C2
U.S. Naval Weapons Station, Ca, US 136/F8
U.S.S. Arizona Nat'l Mem., Hi, US 124/W13
Uad Assag (riv.), WSah. 98/B4
Uad Atui (riv.), WSah. 98/B5
Uad el Jat (riv.), WSah. 98/B4
Uad Tenuaiur (riv.), WSah. 98/A5
Uamh Bheag (peak), Sc, UK 36/B4
Uatumã (riv.), Braz. 150/G4
Uauá, Braz. 154/C3
Uaupés (riv.), Braz. 150/E3
Uaxactún (ruin), Guat. 144/D2
Ub, Serb. 48/E3
Ubá, Braz. 155/D2
Übach-Palenberg, Ger. 53/F2
Ubagan (riv.), Kaz. 61/Q5
Ubaíra, Braz. 154/C4
Ubaitaba, Braz. 154/C4
Ubajara, Braz. 154/B1
Ubajara, PN de, Braz. 154/B1
Ubangi (riv.), D.R. Congo 93/D4
Ubatã, Braz. 154/C4
Ubatuba, Braz. 211/H8
Ubay, Phil. 79/D5
Ubaye (riv.), Fr. 43/G4
Ubbergen, Neth. 50/C5
Ube, Japan 74/B4
Úbeda, Sp. 44/D3
Uberaba (lake), Braz. 150/G7
Uberaba, Braz. 155/C1
Überherrn, Ger. 53/F5
Uberlândia, Braz. 155/B1
Überlingen, Ger. 57/F2
Überlingersee (lake), Ger. 57/E2
Ubia (peak), Indo. 81/J4
Ubinas, Peru 156/D5
Ubombo, SAfr. 107/F2
Ubon Ratchathani, Thai. 78/D3
Ubrique, Sp. 44/C4
Ubundu, D.R. Congo 97/L8
Ucayali (dept.), Peru 156/C3
Ucayali (riv.), Peru 147/B3
Uccle, Belg. 53/D2
Ucha (riv.), Rus. 61/W9
Uchaly, Rus. 61/N5
Uchāna, India 86/D5
Uchinskoye (res.), Rus. 61/W9
Uchiza, Peru 156/B3
Uchte, Ger. 51/F3
Uchte (riv.), Ger. 40/F2
Uchumarca, Peru 156/B2
Uchumayo, Peru 156/D5
Uchur (riv.), Rus. 65/P4
Ücker (riv.), Ger. 38/E5
Uckermark (reg.), Ger. 41/G2
Uckfield, Eng, UK 33/G5
Ucluelet, BC, Can. 126/B3
Uda (riv.), Rus. 65/M4
Udagamandalam, India 82/C5
Udaipur, India 89/K4
Udaipura, India 84/B4
Uddevalla, Swe. 38/D2
Uddingston, Sc, UK 36/B5
Uddjaure (lake), Swe. 37/F2
Üdem, Ger. 50/D5
Uden, Neth. 50/C5
Udenhout, Neth. 50/C5
Udgīr, India 82/C4
Udhampur, India 86/C3
Udine (prov.), It. 59/G1
Udine, It. 43/K3
Udipi, India 82/B5
Udmurtia, Resp., Rus. 64/Q6
Udon Thani, Thai. 78/C2
Ueckermünde, Ger. 38/F5
Ueda, Japan 75/F2
Uele (riv.), D.R. Congo 93/E4
Uelsen, Ger. 50/D3
Uelzen, Ger. 51/H3
Ueno, Japan 77/B1
Ueno, Japan 77/K6
Uenohara, Japan 75/F3
Uetendorf, Swi. 56/D4
Uetersen, Ger. 51/G1
Uetze, Ger. 51/H4
Ufa (riv.), Rus. 87/C1
Ufa, Rus. 61/M5
Uffenheim, Ger. 54/D3
Uffing, Ger. 57/H2
Ugalla (riv.), Tanz. 104/A4
Ugalla River Game Rsv., Tanz. 104/A4
Uganda (ctry.) 104/B2
Ugento, It. 47/F3
Ugie (riv.), Sc, UK 36/E1
Ugine, Fr. 56/C6
Uglich, Rus. 60/H4
Ugod, Hun. 48/C2
Ugra (riv.), Rus. 60/G5
Ugŭrchin, Bul. 47/J1
Uherské Hradiště, Czh. 41/J4
Uhingen, Ger. 54/C5
Úhlava (riv.), Czh. 41/G4
Úhlavka (riv.), Czh. 55/F3
Uibaí, Braz. 154/B3
Uíge, Ang. 105/C2
Ŭihŭng, SKor. 73/E4
Ŭijŏngbu, SKor. 73/G6
Ŭiju, NKor. 73/C2
Uilkraal (riv.), SAfr. 106/L11
Uilpata (peak), Rus. 63/G4
Uinta (mts.), Ut, US 128/E2
Uintah, Ut, US 137/K11
Uiraúna, Braz. 154/C2
Ŭiryŏng, SKor. 73/E5
Ŭisŏng, SKor. 74/A2
Uitenhage, SAfr. 106/D4
Uitgeest, Neth. 50/B3
Uithoorn, Neth. 50/B4
Uithuizen, Neth. 50/D2
Ujae (isl.), Mrsh. 116/F4
Ujelang (isl.), Mrsh. 116/F4
Újfehértó, Hun. 41/L5
Ujhāni, India 84/B1
Uji (riv.), Japan 74/D3
Uji, Japan 77/J6
Ujitawara, Japan 77/J6
Ujjain, India 89/L4
Ujung Pandang, Indo. 81/E5
Ukara (isl.), Tanz. 104/B3
Ukerewe (isl.), Tanz. 104/B3
Ukhta, Rus. 61/M3
Ukiah, Ca, US 128/B3
Uklāna, India 86/C5
Ukmergė, Lith. 39/L4
Ukraine (ctry.) 62/D2
Ulaanbaatar (cap.), Mong. 70/J2
Ulaangom, Mong. 70/F2
Ulaanjirem, Mong. 70/J2
Ulanhot, China 71/M2
Ulchin, SKor. 74/A2
Ulcumayo, Peru 156/C3
Ulefoss, Nor. 38/C2
Ulemiste (int'l arpt.), Est. 39/L2
Ulhāsnagar, India 89/K5
Uliastay, Mong. 70/G2
Ulindi (riv.), D.R. Congo 97/L8
Ulithi (isl.), Micr. 116/C3
Uljma, Serb. 48/E3
Ülken Borsyq Qumy (des.), Kaz. 87/C3
Ülken-Qobda (riv.), Kaz. 63/K2
Ulla (riv.), Sp. 44/A1
Ulla Ulla, Bol. 156/D4
Ulla Ulla, Reserva Nacional, Bol. 156/D4
Ulladulla, Austl. 115/D2
Ullapool, Sc, UK 31/R8
Ullared, Swe. 38/E3
Ulldecona, Sp. 45/F2
Ullensvang, Nor. 38/B1
Üllő, Hun. 49/R10
Ullsfjorden (estu.), Nor. 37/F1
Ullswater (lake), Eng, UK 35/F2
Ulm, Ger. 54/C6
Ulmarra, Austl. 115/E1
Ulmen, Ger. 53/F3
Ulricehamn, Swe. 38/E3
Ulrichen, Swi. 57/E5
Ulrichsberg, Aus. 55/G5
Ulrichstein, Ger. 54/C1
Ulrum, Neth. 50/D2
Ulsan, SKor. 74/A3
Ulstein, Nor. 37/C3
Ulster (reg.), Ire. 34/A3
Ulster (riv.), Ger. 54/C1
Ulster American Folk Park, NI, UK 34/A2
Ulúa (riv.), Hon. 140/D4
Ulua (riv.), Hon. 144/E3
Uluçınar, Turk. 91/D1
Uludağ (peak), Turk. 90/B1
Uludoruk (peak), Turk. 88/D1
Uluguru (mts.), Tanz. 104/C4
Ulukışla, Turk. 90/C2
Ulundi, SAfr. 107/E3
Uluru NP, Austl. 113/F3
Ulverston, Eng, UK 35/E3
Ulverstone, Austl. 115/C4
Ulvik, Nor. 38/B1
Ulvila, Fin. 39/J1
Ul'yanovka, Rus. 39/P2
Ul'yanovsk, Rus. 61/L5
Ul'yanovskaya Oblast, Rus. 63/H1
Ulytaū (mts.),Kaz. 87/E3
Ulytau (peak), Kaz. 87/E3
Umag, Cro. 48/A3
Uman', Ukr. 62/D2
Umán, Mex. 144/D1
Umarizal, Braz. 154/C2
Umarkot, India 82/D4
Umāsi La (pass), India 86/D3
Umbertide, It. 43/K5
Umbogintwini, SAfr. 107/E3
Umboi (isl.), PNG 116/D5
Umbrail (peak), Swi. 57/G4
Umbrailpass (pass), Swi. 57/G4
Umbria (prov.), It. 43/K5
Umeå, Swe. 37/G3
Umeälven (riv.), Swe. 37/F2
Umfolozi (riv.), SAfr. 107/E3
Umgeni (riv.), SAfr. 107/E3
Umhausen, Aus. 57/G3
Umiat, Ak, US 134/H2
Umkirch, Ger. 56/D1
Umkomaas, SAfr. 107/E3
Umm Durmān, Sudan 88/B5
Umm el Faḥm, Isr. 91/G6
Umm Hibal (well), Egypt 101/C4
Ummendorf, Ger. 57/F1
Umnak (isl.), Ak, US 134/E5
Umnak Pass (chan.), Ak, US 134/E5
Umpqua (riv.), Or, US 124/B3
Umraniye, Turk. 90/B2
Ŭmsŏng, SKor. 73/D4
Umtata, SAfr. 106/E3
Umuahia, Nga. 103/G5
Umuarama, Braz. 157/F1
Umurbey, Turk. 47/K2
Umzimvubu (riv.), SAfr. 106/E3
Umzinto, SAfr. 107/E3
Una, Braz. 154/C4
Una, India 86/D4
Una (mt.), NZ 117/S11
Una (riv.), Bosn.,Cro. 43/L4
Unaí, Braz. 154/A5
Unalakleet, Ak, US 134/F3
Unalaska, Ak, US 134/E5
Unalaska (isl.), Ak, US 134/E5
Uncastillo, Sp. 45/E1
Unchahra, India 84/C3
Uncompahgre (plat.), Co, US 128/E3
Unden (lake), Swe. 38/F2
Undenheim, Ger. 54/B3
Underberg, SAfr. 106/E3
Underbool, Austl. 115/B2
Underwood, ND, US 127/H4
Unecha, Rus. 62/E1
Unga (isl.), Ak, US 134/F4
Ungama (bay), Kenya 105/H1
Ungarie, Austl. 115/C2
Ungava (pen.), Qu, Can. 123/J2
Ungava (bay), Qu, Can. 123/K3
Ungheni, Mol. 49/H2
Unhošt, Czh. 55/H2
União, Braz. 154/B2
União da Vitória, Braz. 155/B3
União dos Palmares, Braz. 154/C3
Unimak (isl.), Ak, US 134/E4
Unimak Pass (str.), Ak, US 134/E5
Unini (riv.), Braz. 150/F4
Union, Or, US 126/D4
Union, Mo, US 129/K3
Union, SC, US 133/H3
Union (lake), NJ, US 138/C5
Unión, Arg. 158/D2
Union, NJ, US 139/H9
Union (canal), Sc, UK 36/C5
Union Beach, NJ, US 139/J10
Union Bridge, Md, US 138/A4
Union City, Tn, US 130/B4
Union City, Ca, US 135/K11
Union City, NJ, US 139/J8
Unión de Reyes, Cuba 145/F1
Unión de Tula, Mex. 142/D5
Unión Hidalgo, Mex. 144/C2
Union Mills, Md, US 138/A4
Union Springs, Al, US 133/G3
Uniondale, SAfr. 106/C4
Uniondale, NY, US 139/L9
Uniontown, Pa, US 130/E4
Uniontown, Md, US 138/A4
Unionville, Mo, US 127/K5
United Arab Emirates (ctry.) 88/F4
United Kingdom (ctry.) 31/R9
United Nations, NY, US 139/K9
United Nations Mem. Cemetery, SKor. 74/A3
United States (range), Nun., Can. 123/T6
United States (ctry.) 124
United States Coast Guard Receiving Center, NJ, US 138/D6
United States Department of Energy, Md, US 138/A5
United States Naval Academy, Md, US 138/B6
United States Naval Reservation Mil. Res., PR 141/M8
Unity, Sk, Can. 126/F2
University City, Mo, US 137/G8
University Place, Wa, US 135/B3
Unjha, India 89/K4
Unkel, Ger. 53/G2
Unna, Ger. 51/E5
Unnão, India 84/C2
Ŭnsan-ŭp, NKor. 73/D3
Unst (isl.), Sc, UK 31/W13
Unter Pleichfeld, Ger. 54/D3
Unterägeri, Swi. 57/E3
Unterargen (riv.), Ger. 57/F2
Untergriesbach, Ger. 55/G5
Unterhaching, Ger. 55/E6
Unteriberg, Swi. 57/E3
Unterkulm, Swi. 56/E3
Unterlüss, Ger. 51/H3
Unterschleissheim, Ger. 55/E6
Untersee (lake), Swi. 57/E2
Unterseen, Swi. 56/D4
Untersiggenthal, Swi. 57/E3
Unterthingau, Ger. 57/G2
Untervaz, Swi. 57/F4
Unterweissenbach, Aus. 55/H6
Ünye, Turk. 90/D1
Unzen-Amakusa NP, Japan 74/A4
Unzen-dake (peak), Japan 74/B4
Unzha (riv.), Rus. 64/E4
Uozu, Japan 75/E2
Upala, CR 145/E4
Upanema, Braz. 154/C2
Upata, Ven. 153/F2
Upemba, Lac (lake), D.R. Congo 105/E2
Upemba, PN de l', D.R. Congo 105/E2
Uphall, Sc, UK 36/C5
Upington, SAfr. 106/C3
Upland, Pa, US 138/C4
Upleta, India 89/K4
Upolu (pt.), Hi, US 124/U10
Upolu (isl.), Sam. 117/H6
Upper (lake), Ca, US 128/B2
Upper (bay), NY, US 138/D2
Upper (pen.), Mi, US 125/J2
Upper Arrow (lake), BC, Can. 126/D3
Upper Darby, Pa, US 138/C4
Upper Demerara-Berbice (pol. reg.), Guy. 153/G3
Upper East (pol. reg.), Gha. 103/E4
Upper Engadine (valley), Swi. 57/F5
Upper Falls, Md, US 138/B5
Upper Ganges (canal), India 84/A1
Upper Hutt, NZ 117/T11
Upper Iowa (riv.), Ia, US 129/J2
Upper Klamath (lake), Or, US 126/C5
Upper Lough Erne (lake), NI, UK 31/Q9
Upper Missouri River Breaks Nat'l Mon., Mt, US 126/F4
Upper Peoria (lake), Il, US 127/L5
Upper Red (lake), Mn, US 127/K3
Upper Rouge (riv.), Mi, US 135/F7
Upper Saddle River, NJ, US 139/J7
Upper Takutu-Upper Essequibo (pol. reg.), Guy. 153/G4
Upper Thames (valley), Eng, UK 33/E3
Upper Trajan's Wall, Mol. 62/D3
Upper West (pol. reg.), Gha. 103/E4
Upperlands, NI, UK 34/B2
Upplands-Väsby, Swe. 38/G2
Uppsala, Swe. 38/G2
Uppsala (co.), Swe. 37/F3
Upright (cape), Ak, US 134/D3
Upstart (cape), Austl. 114/B2
Upton, Wy, US 127/G4
Urabá (gulf), Col. 145/G4
Uracoa, Ven. 153/F2
Urad Qianqi, China 72/B2
Uraga (chan.), Japan 77/D3
Urahoro, Japan 76/C2
Uraim (riv.), Braz. 154/A1
Urakawa, Japan 76/C2
Ural (mts.), Rus. 27/L2
Uralla, Austl. 115/D1
Urana, Austl. 115/C2

233
Urand – Vesgr

Urandi, Braz. 154/B4
Uraricoera (riv.), Braz. 150/F3
Urasoe, Japan 75/J7
Urawa, Japan 75/F3
Uray, Rus. 64/G3
Urayasu, Japan 77/D2
Urbach, Ger. 54/C5
Urbana, Md, US 138/A5
Urbania, It. 59/F5
Urbano Santos, Braz. 154/B1
Urbenville, Austl. 114/D5
Urbino, It. 59/F5
Urcos, Peru 156/D4
Urda, Sp. 44/D3
Urdinarrain, Arg. 159/J10
Urdorf, Swi. 57/E3
Ure (riv.), Eng, UK 35/G3
Ures, Mex. 142/C2
Ureshino, Japan 77/K6
Urewera NP, NZ 117/T10
Urfa (prov.), Turk. 90/D2
Urfa, Turk. 90/D2
Urft (riv.), Ger. 51/G6
Urft (lake), Ger. 53/F2
Urganch, Uzb. 87/D4
Urgnano, It. 58/C1
Urho Kekkosen NP, Fin. 37/H1
Uri, India 86/C2
Uri-Rotstock (peak), Swi. 57/E4
Uriangato, Mex. 143/E4
Uribante (riv.), Ven. 152/D3
Uribia, Col. 152/C2
Urie (riv.), Sc, UK 36/D2
Uriménil, Fr. 56/C1
Urique (riv.), Mex. 142/D3
Urjala, Fin. 39/K1
Urk, Neth. 50/C3
Urla, Turk. 90/A2
Urlați, Rom. 49/H3
Urmar, India 86/C4
Urmia (lake), Iran 90/F2
Urmitz, Ger. 53/G3
Urmston, Eng, UK 35/F5
Urnäsch, Swi. 57/F3
Urnersee (lake), Swi. 57/E4
Uroševac, Serb. 47/G1
Urr Water (riv.), Sc, UK 34/E1
Ursensollen, Ger. 55/E4
Ursulo Galván, Mex. 143/N7
Uruaçu, Braz. 151/J6
Uruapan, Mex. 142/E5
Urubamba (riv.), Peru 150/D6
Urubamba, Peru 156/C4
Urubu (riv.), Braz. 150/G4
Uruburetama, Braz. 154/C1
Uruçuca, Braz. 154/C4
Uruçuí, Braz. 154/A2
Uruçuí Preto (riv.), Braz. 154/A3
Uruçuí, Serra do (mts.), Braz. 151/K5
Urucuia (riv.), Braz. 151/J7
Uruguaiana, Braz. 157/E2
Uruguay (ctry.) 157/E3
Uruguay (riv.), SAm. 157/E2
Urumaco, Ven. 152/D2
Ürümqi, China 70/E3
Urunga, Austl. 115/E1
Uruoca, Braz. 154/B1
Urup (isl.), Rus. 67/Q5
Ururi, It. 46/D2
Urussanga, Braz. 155/B4
Uryupinsk, Rus. 63/G2
Urziceni, Rom. 49/H3
Us, Fr. 30/H4
Usa, Japan 74/B4
Usa (riv.), Rus. 64/F3
Uşak, Turk. 90/B2
Uşak (prov.), Turk. 90/B2
Usakos, Namb. 105/C5
Usborne (mt.), UK 159/F6
Uscio, It. 58/C4
Usedom (isl.), Ger. 38/E4
Useldange, Lux. 53/E4
Useless Loop, Austl. 112/B3
Ushibori, Japan 77/F2
Ushibuka, Japan 74/B4
Ushiku, Japan 77/E2
Ushtobe, Kaz. 87/G3
Ushuaia, Arg. 159/C7
Usibelli, Ak, US 134/J3
Usicayos, Peru 156/D4
Usilampatti, India 82/C6
Usingen, Ger. 54/B2
Üsküp, Turk. 49/H5
Uslar, Ger. 51/G5
Usman', Rus. 62/F1
Uspallata, Arg. 158/C2
Uspallata, Paso de (pass), Chile 158/N8
Usquil, Peru 156/B2
Ussel, Fr. 42/E4
Ussel (riv.), Ger. 54/D5
Usses (riv.), Fr. 56/C5
Ussuri (riv.), China,Rus. 65/P5
Ussuriysk, Rus. 71/P3
Ussy-sur-Marne, Fr. 30/M5
Ust'-Ilimsk, Rus. 65/L4
Ust'-Kamchatsk, Rus. 65/S4
Ust'-Kut, Rus. 65/L4
Ust'-Ordynskiy Buryatskiy Aut. Okrug, Rus. 65/Q7
Úštěk, Czh. 55/H1
Uster, Swi. 57/E3
Ústí nad Labem, Czh. 43/L1
Ustica (isl.), It. 46/C3
Ustica, It. 46/C3
Ustka, Pol. 38/G4
Ustrzyki Dolne, Pol. 41/M4
Ust'ya (riv.), Rus. 61/K3
Ustyurt (plat.), Kaz. 67/D5
Usu, China 70/D3
Usuda, Japan 77/A1
Usuki, Japan 74/B4
Usulután, ESal. 144/D3
Usumacinta (riv.), Mex. 140/C4
Utah (state), US 128/E3
Utah (co.), Ut, US 137/K13
Utah (lake), Ut, US 128/D2
Utangan (riv.), India 84/A2
Utano, Japan 77/J7
Utashinai, Japan 76/C2
Utena, Lith. 39/L4
Uterský (riv.), Czh. 55/G3
Uthai Thani, Thai. 78/C3
Utica, NY, US 130/F3
Utica, Mi, US 135/F6
Utiel, Sp. 44/E3
Utik (lake), Mb, Can. 127/J2
Utila (isl.), Hon. 144/E2
Utinga, Braz. 154/B4
Utirik (isl.), Mrsh. 116/G3
Utiroa, Kiri. 116/G5
Utmānzai, Pak. 86/A2
Utopia Abor. Land, Austl. 113/G2
Utraulā, India 84/D2
Utrecht, SAfr. 107/E2
Utrecht, Neth. 50/C4
Utrecht (prov.), Neth. 50/C4
Utrera, Sp. 44/C4
Utsunomiya, Japan 75/F2
Uttar Pradesh (state), India 70/C6
Uttaradit, Thai. 78/C3
Uttarranchal (state), India 84/B1
Uttenweiler, Ger. 57/F1
Uttoxeter, Eng, UK 35/G6
Utuado, PR 141/M8
Utupua (isl.), Sol. 116/F6
Uturoa, FrPol. 117/K6
Utzenstorf, Swi. 56/D3
Uusikaupunki, Fin. 39/J1
Uusimaa (prov.), Fin. 37/H3
Uva (riv.), Col. 150/E3
Uvalde, Tx, US 129/H5
Uvarovo, Rus. 63/G2
Uverito, Ven. 153/E2
Uvira, D.R. Congo 104/A3
Uvongo, SAfr. 107/E3
Uvs (prov.), Mong. 70/F2
Uwajima, Japan 74/C4
Uwimmerah (riv.), Indo. 81/K5
Uxin Qi, China 69/C4
Uxmal (ruin), Mex. 144/D1
Üydzin, Mong. 70/J3
Uyo, Nga. 103/G5
Üyönch, Mong. 70/F2
Uyuni, Bol. 150/E8
Uzbekistan (ctry.) 87/D4
Uzbekistan Nat'l Park, Uzb. 87/E5
Uzein (int'l arpt.), Fr. 42/C5
Uzerche, Fr. 42/D4
Uzès, Fr. 42/F4
Uzhhorod, Ukr. 41/M4
Uzhok (pass), Ukr. 41/M4
Užice, Serb. 48/D4
Uzlovaya, Rus. 62/F1
Uznach, Swi. 57/E3
Üzümlü, Turk. 90/D2
Uzunköprü, Turk. 47/K2
Uzwil, Swi. 57/F3

V

V.P. Rosales, PN, Chile 158/B4
Vaal (riv.), SAfr. 93/E7
Vaala, Fin. 37/H2
Vaalbos NP, SAfr. 106/D3
Vaaldam (res.), SAfr. 106/D2
Vaals, Neth. 53/F2
Vaalserberg (hill), Neth. 53/E2
Vaasa (prov.), Fin. 37/G3
Vaasa (int'l arpt.), Fin. 37/G3
Vaasa (Vasa), Fin. 37/G3
Vaassen, Neth. 50/C4
Vác, Hun. 48/D2
Vaca (mts.), Ca, US 135/K10
Vaca (mt.), Ca, US 135/K10
Vacaria, Braz. 155/B4
Vacaville, Ca, US 128/B3
Vachon (riv.), Qu, Can. 123/J2
Vada, It. 58/D6
Vado Ligure, It. 58/B4
Vadret (peak), Swi. 57/E4
Vadsø, Nor. 37/J1
Vadstena, Swe. 38/F2
Vaduz (cap.), Lcht. 57/F3
Vaernes (int'l arpt.), Nor. 37/D3
Vaga (riv.), Rus. 60/J3
Vågå, Nor. 37/D3
Vågan, Nor. 37/E1
Vaganski vrh (peak), Cro. 48/B3
Vagay (riv.), Rus. 61/R4
Vaggeryd, Swe. 38/F3
Vagney, Fr. 56/C1
Vagos, Port. 44/A2
Vågsøy, Nor. 37/C3
Váh (riv.), Slvk. 41/J4
Vahitahi (isl.), FrPol. 117/M6
Vaiano, It. 59/E5
Vaiano Cremasco, It. 58/C2
Vaich (lake), Sc, UK 36/B1
Vaihingen an der Enz, Ger. 54/B5
Vaijāpur, India 89/K5
Vail, Co, US 129/F3
Vailate, It. 58/C2
Vair (riv.), Fr. 56/B1
Vaisali (riv.), India 84/B2
Vaitupu (isl.), Tuv. 116/G5
Vaivre-et-Montoille, Fr. 56/C2
Vakfıkebir, Turk. 62/F4
Vakh (riv.), Rus. 64/J3
Vākhān (mts.), Afg. 89/K1
Vakhsh (riv.), Taj. 89/J1
Vál, Hun. 48/D2
Val-de-Marne (dept.), Fr. 52/B6
Val-d'Or, Qu, Can. 130/E1
Val Lagarina (valley), It. 59/D1
Val Marie, Sk, Can. 126/G3
Val Venosta (valley), It. 57/G4
Val Verda, Ut, US 137/K12
Val Verde, Ca, US 136/B2
Valais (canton), Swi. 56/D5
Valbo, Swe. 38/G1
Valburg, Neth. 50/C5
Valcheta, Arg. 158/D4
Valdagno, It. 59/E1
Valdahon, Fr. 56/C3
Valdai (hills), Rus. 60/G4
Valdarno (valley), It. 59/E5
Valdecañas, Embalse de (res.), Sp. 44/C3
Valdemarsvik, Swe. 38/G2
Valdemorillo, Sp. 45/M8
Valdense, Uru. 159/K11
Valdepeñas, Sp. 44/D3
Valderas, Sp. 44/C1
Valderrobres, Sp. 45/F2
Valdés (pen.), Arg. 147/C7
Valdeverdeja, Sp. 44/C3
Valdez, Ak, US 134/J3
Valdez, Ecu. 152/B4
Valdivia, Col. 152/C3
Valdivia, Chile 158/B3
Valdobbiadene, It. 59/E1
Valdoie, Fr. 56/C2
Valdosta, Ga, US 133/H4
Valdoviño, Sp. 44/A1
Vale, Or, US 126/D5
Vale of Glamorgan (co.), Wal, UK 32/C4
Valeggio sul Mincio, It. 59/D2
Valemount, BC, Can. 126/D2
Valença, Braz. 154/C4
Valença, Braz. 211/K7
Valença, Port. 44/A1
Valença do Piauí, Braz. 154/B2
Valence, Fr. 42/D4
Valence, Fr. 42/F4
Valence-sur-Baïse, Fr. 42/D5
Valencia, Ven. 150/E1
Valencia (int'l arpt.), Sp. 45/E3
Valencia, Sp. 45/E3
Valencia (aut. comm.), Sp. 44/E2
Valencia, Ecu. 152/B5
Valencia (isl.), Ire. 30/P11
Valencia de Alcántara, Sp. 44/B3
Valencia de Don Juan, Sp. 44/C1
Valencia, Golfo de (gulf), Sp. 45/F3
Valenciennes, Fr. 52/C3
Valendas, Swi. 57/F4
Vălenii de Munte, Rom. 49/H3
Valente, Braz. 154/C3
Valentigney, Fr. 56/C3
Valentim (range), Braz. 154/B2
Valentine, Tx, US 132/B4
Valentines, Uru. 159/G2
Valenton, Fr. 30/K5
Valenza, It. 58/B2
Våler, Nor. 38/D1
Våler, Nor. 38/D2
Valera, Ven. 152/D2
Valff, Fr. 56/D1
Valga, Est. 39/M3
Valhalla, NY, US 139/K7
Valinco, Golfe de (gulf), Fr. 46/A2
Valinhos, Braz. 211/F7
Valjevo, Serb. 48/D3
Valkeakoski, Fin. 39/K1
Valkeala, Fin. 39/M1
Valkenburg, Neth. 53/E2
Valkenswaard, Neth. 50/C6
Vall de Uxó, Sp. 45/E3
Valladolid, Sp. 44/C2
Valladolid (int'l arpt.), Sp. 44/C2
Valladolid, Mex. 144/D1
Vallangoujard, Fr. 30/J4
Valle, Ecu. 152/B5
Valle, Nor. 38/B2
Valle d'Aosta (pol. reg.), It. 43/G4
Valle de Bravo, Mex. 143/E5
Valle de Cauca (dept.), Col. 152/B4
Valle de Guanape, Ven. 153/E2
Valle de La Pascua, Ven. 150/E2
Valle de Santiago, Mex. 143/E4
Valle de Zaragoza, Mex. 132/B5
Valle Hermoso, Mex. 143/F3
Valle Lomellina, It. 58/B2
Valle Mosso, It. 58/B1
Vallecitos de Zaragoza, Mex. 143/E5
Vallecrosia, It. 43/G5
Valledupar, Col. 152/C2
Valleé de l'Azaouak (riv.), Mali 103/G2
Vallée du Ferlo (riv.), Sen. 102/B3
Valleé du Mboune (riv.), Sen. 102/B3
Valleé du Saloum (riv.), Sen. 102/B3
Valleé du Serpent (riv.), Mali 102/C3
Vallegrande, Bol. 150/F7
Vallehermoso, Sp. 98/A3
Vallejo, Ca, US 128/B3
Vallenar, Chile 157/B2
Vallendar, Ger. 53/G3
Valleroy, Fr. 53/E5
Valletta (cap.), Malta 46/M7
Valley Brook, Ok, US 137/N15
Valley Center, Ca, US 136/C4
Valley City, ND, US 127/J4
Valley Cottage, NY, US 139/K7
Valley East, On, Can. 130/D2
Valley Forge Nat'l Hist. Park, Pa, US 138/C3
Valley of Desolation, SAfr. 106/D4
Valley of the Kings, Egypt 101/C3
Valley Park, Mo, US 137/G8
Valley Spring, Tx, US 129/H5
Valley Stream, NY, US 139/L9
Vallière (riv.), Fr. 56/B4
Vallorbe, Swi. 56/C4
Valls, Sp. 45/F2
Valluga (peak), Aus. 57/G3
Valmayor (res.), Sp. 45/M8
Valme (riv.), Ger. 51/F6
Valmeyer, Il, US 137/G9
Valmiera, Lat. 39/L3
Valmondois, Fr. 30/J4
Valognes, Fr. 42/C2
Valois (reg.), Fr. 52/B5
Valona, Bay of (bay), Alb. 47/F2
Valpaços, Port. 44/B2
Vālpārai, India 82/C5
Valparaiso, Fl, US 133/G4
Valparaiso, In, US 130/C3
Valparaíso, Mex. 142/E4
Valparaíso (pol. reg.), Chile 158/C2
Valparaíso, Chile 158/N8
Valpovo, Cro. 48/D3
Valréas, Fr. 42/F4
Vals (riv.), SAfr. 106/D2
Vals, Swi. 57/F4
Vals-les-Bains, Fr. 42/F4
Valsād, India 89/K4
Valsaquillo (res.), Mex. 143/L8
Valsbaai (bay), SAfr. 105/C7
Valserine (riv.), Fr. 56/B5
Valserrhein (riv.), Swi. 57/F4
Valsura (riv.), It. 57/G4
Valtellina (valley), It. 57/F5
Valtice, Czh. 43/M2
Valuyki, Rus. 62/F2
Valverde, Sp. 98/A4
Valverde del Camino, Sp. 44/B4
Valyermo, Ca, US 136/C2
Våmhus, Swe. 38/F1
Vammala, Fin. 39/K1
Vámos, Gre. 47/J5
Vámosmikola, Hun. 48/D2
Vámospércs, Hun. 48/E2
Van, Turk. 90/E2
Van (lake), Turk. 90/E2
Van Buren, Me, US 131/H2
Van Buren, Ar, US 129/J4
Van Cortlandt Park, NY, US 139/K8
Van Diemen (cape), Austl. 109/C2
Van Diemen (gulf), Austl. 109/C2
Van Harinxmakanaal (riv.), Neth. 50/C2
Van Horn, Tx, US 129/F5
Van Norman Lakes, Ca, US 136/B2
Van Rees (mts.), Indo. 81/J4
Van Wert, Oh, US 130/C3
Vana-Javesi (lake), Fin. 39/K1
Vanadzor, Arm. 63/H4
Vanavaro (isl.), FrPol. 117/L7
Vancouver (mt.), Yk, Can. 134/L3
Vancouver, Wa, US 126/C4
Vancouver, BC, Can. 126/C3
Vancouver (int'l arpt.), BC, Can. 126/C3
Vancouver (cape), Austl. 112/C5
Vancouver (isl.), BC, Can. 122/D4
Vandalia, Mo, US 129/K3
Vandans, Aus. 57/F3
Vanderbijlpark, SAfr. 106/D2
Vanderbilt Museum, NY, US 139/E2
Vanderhoof, BC, Can. 126/B2
Vandœuvre-lès-Nancy, Fr. 53/F6
Vanegas, Mex. 143/E4
Vänern (lake), Swe. 38/E2
Vänersborg, Swe. 38/E2
Vangaindrano, Madg. 107/H8
Vanier (isl.), Nun., Can. 123/R7
Vanikolo (isl.), Sol. 116/F6
Vanil Noir (peak), Swi. 56/D4
Vanimo, PNG 116/D5
Vännäs, Swe. 37/F3
Vanne (riv.), Fr. 42/E2
Vannes, Fr. 42/B3
Vanoise, PN de la, Fr. 43/G4
Vanreenenpas (pass), SAfr. 106/E3
Vanrhynsdorp, SAfr. 106/B3
Vansbro, Swe. 38/F1
Vanse, Nor. 38/B2
Vansittart (isl.), Nun., Can. 123/H2
Vantaa, Fin. 39/L1
Vanua Levu (isl.), Fiji 116/G6
Vanuatu (ctry.) 116/F6
Vanwyksvlei, SAfr. 106/C3
Var (riv.), Fr. 43/G5
Vara (riv.), It. 58/C4
Vara, Swe. 38/E2
Varadero, Cuba 145/F1
Varaita (riv.), It. 58/A3
Varallo, It. 58/B1
Varāmīn, Iran 88/F1
Vārānasi, India 84/D3
Varanger-Halvøya (pen.), Nor. 37/J1
Varangerfjorden (estu.), Nor. 37/J1
Varangéville, Fr. 53/F6
Varano (lake), It. 46/D2
Varano Borghi, It. 58/B1
Varaždin, Cro. 43/M3
Varazze, It. 58/B4
Varberg, Swe. 38/E3
Vardar (riv.), FYROM 47/G2
Varde, Den. 38/C4
Várdha, Gre. 47/G3
Vardø, Nor. 37/J1
Varel, Ger. 51/F2
Varenne (riv.), Fr. 42/C2
Varennes, Qu, Can. 131/P6
Varennes-Jarcy, Fr. 30/K5
Varennes-Vauzelles, Fr. 42/E3
Vareš, Bosn. 48/D3
Varese, It. 58/B1
Varese (prov.), It. 57/E6
Varese Ligure, It. 58/C4
Vårgårda, Swe. 38/E2
Vargem Grande, Braz. 154/B1
Vargem Grande do Sul, Braz. 211/G6
Varginha, Braz. 211/H6
Vári, Gre. 47/H4
Varilhes, Fr. 42/D5
Värmeln (lake), Swe. 38/E2
Värmland (co.), Swe. 37/E3
Varna (pol. reg.), Bul. 47/K1
Varna, Bul. 49/H4
Värnamo, Swe. 38/F3
Varois-et-Chaignot, Fr. 55/B3
Varoška Rijeka, Bosn. 48/C3
Várpalota, Hun. 48/D2
Varraddes, Fr. 30/L5
Varsi, It. 58/C3
Vårsta, Swe. 38/G2
Vartholomión, Gre. 47/G4
Varto, Turk. 90/E2
Vartry (res.), Ire. 34/B5
Vartry (riv.), Ire. 34/B5
Várzea Alegre, Braz. 154/C2
Várzea da Palma, Braz. 154/A5
Várzea Grande, Braz. 154/B2
Várzea Grande, Braz. 151/G7
Varzelândia, Braz. 154/A4
Varzi, It. 58/C3
Varzo, It. 57/E5
Varzuga (riv.), Rus. 60/H2
Vas (prov.), Hun. 48/C2
Vasa Barris (riv.), Braz. 151/L5
Vásárosnamény, Hun. 41/M4
Vaşcău, Rom. 48/F2
Vashka (riv.), Rus. 61/K2
Vashon, Wa, US 135/C3
Vashon (isl.), Wa, US 135/C3
Vasiliká, Gre. 47/H2
Vasil'yevskiy (isl.), Rus. 61/S7
Vaslui (prov.), Rom. 49/H2
Vaslui, Rom. 49/H2
Vassar, Mi, US 130/D3
Vassdalsegga (peak), Nor. 38/B2
Vassouras, Braz. 211/K7
Västerås, Swe. 38/G2
Västerbotten (co.), Swe. 37/F2
Västerdalälven (riv.), Swe. 38/E1
Västernorrland (co.), Swe. 37/F3
Västervik, Swe. 38/G3
Västmanland (co.), Swe. 37/E3
Vasto, It. 46/D1
Västra Silen (lake), Swe. 38/E2
Vasvár, Hun. 48/C2
Vasyl'kiv, Ukr. 62/D2
Vaterstetten, Ger. 55/E6
Vatican City (ctry.) 46/C2
Vatnajökull (glacier), Ice. 37/P7
Vatomandry, Madg. 107/J7
Vatra Dornei, Rom. 49/G2
Vättern (lake), Swe. 37/E4
Vaucouleurs (riv.), Fr. 30/H5
Vaud (canton), Swi. 56/C4
Vaudoy-en-Brie, Fr. 30/M5
Vaudreuil-Dorion, Qu, Can. 131/M7
Vaughan, On, Can. 131/Q8
Vaughn, NM, US 129/F4
Vaughn, Wa, US 135/B3
Vaulruz, Swi. 56/C4
Vaulx-en-Velin, Fr. 56/A6
Vaupés (dept.), Col. 152/D4
Vaupés (riv.), Col. 147/B2
Vauréal, Fr. 30/J4
Vauvert, Fr. 42/F5
Vaux (riv.), Fr. 40/C4
Vaux-sur-Seine, Fr. 30/H4
Vaux-sur-Sûre, Belg. 53/E4
Vauxhall, Ab, Can. 126/E3
Vavatenina, Madg. 107/J7
Vava'u Group (isls.), Tonga 117/H6
Vavuniya, SrL. 82/D6
Vawkavysk, Bela. 41/N2
Vaxjo (int'l arpt.), Swe. 38/F3
Växjö, Swe. 38/F3
Vaygach (isl.), Rus. 160/B
Vazante, Braz. 154/A5
Vázea Paulista, Braz. 211/G8
Vazuza (res.), Rus. 60/G5
Vazzola, It. 59/F1
Vecchiano, It. 58/D5
Vechigen, Swi. 56/D4
Vecht (riv.), Neth. 50/D3
Vechta, Ger. 51/F3
Vechte (riv.), Ger. 50/D3
Vecsés, Hun. 48/D2
Vedano Olona, It. 58/B1
Veddige, Swe. 38/E3
Vedea (riv.), Rom. 49/G3
Vedelago, It. 59/F1
Vedia, Arg. 158/E2
Vedra, Sp. 44/A1
Veendam, Neth. 50/D2
Veenendaal, Neth. 50/C4
Veere, Neth. 50/A5
Veerse Meer (res.), Neth. 50/A5
Vefsn, Nor. 37/E2
Vega, Tx, US 129/G4
Vega (pt.), Ak, US 134/B6
Vega (isl.), Nor. 37/D2
Vega de Alatorre, Mex. 143/N6
Vegafjorden (estu.), Nor. 37/D2
Veghel, Neth. 50/C5
Vègreville, Ab, Can. 126/E2
Végueta, Peru 156/B3
Vehkalahti, Fin. 39/M1
Vehne (riv.), Ger. 51/F2
Veigné, Fr. 42/D3
Veinticinco de Mayo, Arg. 158/E2
Veinticinco de Mayo, Arg. 158/D3
Veinticinco de Mayo, Uru. 159/K11
Veintiocho de Mayo, Ecu. 156/B1
Veintiocho de Noviembre, Arg. 159/B6
Veitsch, Aus. 48/B2
Veitshöchheim, Ger. 54/C3
Vejen, Den. 38/C4
Vejer de la Frontera, Sp. 44/C4
Vejle, Den. 38/C4
Vejle (co.), Den. 38/C4
Vejprty, Czh. 55/G2
Vela, Cabo de la (pt.), Col. 152/C1
Vela Luka, Cro. 46/E1
Velaines, Fr. 53/E6
Vélan (peak), Swi. 56/D6
Velardeña, Mex. 142/E3
Velas, Azor., Port. 45/S12
Velasco Ibarra, Ecu. 152/B5
Velázquez, Uru. 159/G2
Velbert, Ger. 50/E6
Velburg, Ger. 55/E4
Velddrif, SAfr. 106/L10
Velden, Ger. 55/F6
Velden am Wörthersee, Aus. 43/L3
Veldhoven, Neth. 50/C6
Velen, Ger. 50/D5
Velešta, FYROM 47/G2
Velestínon, Gre. 47/H3
Vélez, Col. 152/C3
Vélez-Blanco, Sp. 44/D4
Vélez-Málaga, Sp. 44/C4
Vélez-Rubio, Sp. 44/D4
Velhas, Rio das (riv.), Braz. 151/K7
Velika Gorica, Cro. 48/C3
Velika Kladuša, Bosn. 43/L4
Velika Plana, Serb. 48/E3
Velikaya (riv.), Rus. 60/F4
Velikiy Ustyug, Rus. 61/K3
Velikiye Luki, Rus. 39/P3
Veliko Tŭrnovo, Bul. 47/J1
Velille, Peru 156/D4
Vélingara, Sen. 102/B3
Vélizy-Villacoublay, Fr. 30/J5
Vel'ké Kapušany, Slvk. 48/F1
Vel'ký Krtíš, Slvk. 41/K4
Velký Zvon (peak), Czh. 55/F3
Vellberg, Ger. 54/C4
Velletri, It. 46/C2
Vellinge, Swe. 38/E4
Vellmar, Ger. 51/G6
Vellón (res.), Sp. 45/N8
Vellore, India 82/C5
Vélon, Gre. 47/H4
Vel'sk, Rus. 60/J3
Veluwe (phys. reg.), Neth. 50/C4
Veluwemeer (lake), Neth. 50/C4
Veluwezoom, NP, Neth. 50/C4
Velva, ND, US 127/H3
Velvary, Czh. 55/H2
Velvendós, Gre. 47/H2
Vémars, Fr. 30/K4
Vemb, Den. 38/C3
Véménd, Hun. 48/D2
Venachar (lake), Sc, UK 36/B4
Venado Tuerto, Arg. 158/E2
Venafro, It. 46/D2
Venamo (peak), Ven. 153/F3
Venâncio Aires, Braz. 155/A4
Venaria, It. 43/G4
Vence, Fr. 43/G5
Venceslau Brás, Braz. 155/B2
Vendas Novas, Port. 44/A3
Vendôme, Fr. 42/D3
Vendrell, Sp. 45/F2
Vendrest, Fr. 30/M4
Veneta, Laguna (lake), It. 59/F2
Venetie, Ak, US 134/J2
Veneto (pol. reg.), It. 43/J4
Venezia (prov.), It. 59/F1
Venezia, Golfo di (gulf), Eur. 59/F2
Venezia (Venice), It. 59/F2
Venezuela (gulf), Col.,Ven. 153/D2
Venezuela (ctry.) 153/E3
Vengurla, India 89/K5
Veniaminof (vol.), Ak, US 134/G4
Venice, Fl, US 133/H5
Venice, Il, US 137/G8
Venice (Venezia), It. 43/K4
Vénissieux, Fr. 42/F4
Venjan, Swe. 38/E1
Venjansjön (lake), Swe. 38/E1
Venkatagiri, India 82/C5
Venlo, Neth. 50/D6
Vennesla, Nor. 38/B2
Veno (bay), Den. 38/C3
Venoge (riv.), Swi. 56/C4
Venosa, It. 46/D2
Venray, Neth. 50/C5
Vent, Îles du (isls.), FrPol. 117/L6
Venta (riv.), Lat. 60/D4
Venta de Baños, Sp. 44/C2
Ventauri (riv.), Ven. 150/E3
Ventersburg, SAfr. 106/D3
Ventersdorp, SAfr. 106/D2
Venterstad, SAfr. 106/D3
Ventiseri, Fr. 46/A2
Ventnor, Eng, UK 33/E5
Ventnor City, NJ, US 138/D5
Ventspils, Lat. 39/J3
Ventuari (riv.), Ven. 153/E3
Ventura, Ca, US 136/A2
Ventura (co.), Ca, US 136/A2
Ventura (riv.), Ca, US 136/A2
Venturina, It. 43/J5
Venturosa, Braz. 154/C3
Venustiano Carranza, Mex. 140/C4
Venustiano Carranza (res.), Mex. 143/E3
Vép, Hun. 43/M3
Ver-sur-Launette, Fr. 30/L4
Vera, Arg. 157/D2
Vera, Sp. 44/E4
Vera Cruz, Pan. 152/B2
Veracruz, Mex. 143/N7
Veracruz-Llave (state), Mex. 140/B3
Veranópolis, Braz. 155/B4
Verāval, India 89/K4
Verbania, It. 57/E6
Verberie, Fr. 52/B5
Verbicaro, It. 46/D3
Vercelli, It. 58/B2
Vercelli (prov.), It. 56/E6
Verdal, Nor. 37/D3
Verde (riv.), Par. 157/D1
Verde (cape), Sen. 96/B5
Verde (riv.), Braz. 151/G6
Verde (riv.), Mex. 143/F4
Verde (coast), Sp. 44/B1
Verde (cape), It. 58/A5
Verde (bay), Arg. 158/E3
Verde Grande (riv.), Braz. 151/K7
Verden, Ger. 51/G3
Verdhikoússa, Gre. 47/G3
Verdigris (riv.), Ks, US 129/J3
Verdinho (riv.), Braz. 155/B1
Verdon (riv.), Fr. 42/F5
Verdugo (mts.), Ca, US 136/F7
Verdun, Qu, Can. 131/N7
Vereeniging, SAfr. 106/D2
Verena (peak), It. 57/H6
Vereshchagino, Rus. 61/M4
Veretskiy (pass), Ukr. 41/M4
Verga (cape), Gui. 102/B4
Vergara, Uru. 159/G2
Vergato, It. 59/E4
Vergennes, Vt, US 130/F2
Vergiate, It. 58/B1
Vergína (ruin), Gre. 47/H2
Verigenstadt, Ger. 57/F1
Verín, Sp. 44/B2
Veríssimo, Braz. 155/B1
Verkhnetulomskiy (res.), Rus. 60/F1
Verkhoyansk (range), Rus. 67/M2
Verkhoyansk, Rus. 65/P3
Verl, Ger. 51/F5
Vermenagna (riv.), It. 58/A4
Vermilion, Ab, Can. 126/F2
Vermilion (riv.), Ab, Can. 126/F2
Vermilion (range), Mn, US 127/K4
Vermilion Cliffs Nat'l Mon., Az, US 126/E3
Vermillion, SD, US 127/J5
Vermont (state), US 131/F2
Vernal, Ut, US 128/E2
Vernayaz, Swi. 56/D5
Vernazza, It. 58/C4
Verneuil-sur-Avre, Fr. 42/D2
Verneuil-sur-Seine, Fr. 30/H5
Verneukpan (salt pan), SAfr. 106/C3
Vernier, Swi. 56/C5
Vernon, BC, Can. 126/D3
Vernon, Fr. 42/D2
Vernon Hills, Il, US 135/Q15
Vernon Valley, NJ, US 138/D1
Vernouillet, Fr. 30/H5
Vero Beach, Fl, US 133/H5
Véroia, Gre. 47/H2
Verolanuova, It. 58/D2
Verolavecchia, It. 58/D2
Verolengo, It. 58/A2
Verona (prov.), It. 59/D1
Verona (int'l arpt.), It. 59/D2
Verona, It. 59/D2
Verona, NJ, US 139/J8
Verónica, Arg. 159/K11
Verrès, It. 58/A1
Verret, La, US 137/Q17
Verrières-le-Buisson, Fr. 30/J5
Versa (riv.), It. 58/B3
Versailles, Ky, US 130/C4
Versailles, Fr. 30/J5
Versigny, Fr. 30/L4
Verskla (riv.), Ukr.,Rus. 64/D4
Versmold, Ger. 51/F4
Versoix, Swi. 56/C5
Vert-le-Grand, Fr. 30/K6
Vert-le-Petit, Fr. 30/K6
Vert-Saint-Denis, Fr. 30/L6
Vertana (peak), It. 57/G4
Verte (peak), Fr. 56/C6
Vertemate, It. 58/C1
Vertientes, Cuba 145/G1
Vertou, Fr. 42/C3
Vertova, It. 58/C1
Vertus, Fr. 52/D6
Verviers, Belg. 53/E2
Vervins, Fr. 52/C4
Verwoerdburg, SAfr. 106/Q12
Veryan (bay), Eng, UK 32/B6
Verzasca (riv.), Swi. 57/E5
Verzasca (Gerra), Swi. 57/E5
Verzenay, Fr. 53/D5
Verzuolo, It. 43/G4
Verzy, Fr. 53/D5
Vescovato, Fr. 46/A1
Vescovato, It. 58/D2
Vesdre (riv.), Belg. 42/F1
Veselí nad Lužnicí, Czh. 55/H4
Veselyy (res.), Rus. 63/G3
Vesgre (riv.), Fr. 52/A6

Vesij – Wabas

abash (riv.),
n, US 125/J4
abē Shebelē Wenz
.), Eth. 93/G4
abern, Ger. 51/G6
abigoon (lake),
, Can. 127/K3
abowden,
, Can. 127/J2
abrzeźno, Pol. 41/K2
abu (lake), China 72/D4
abu, SKor. 73/G6
achenheim an der
einstrasse, Ger. 54/B4
achi, Japan 77/H5
achtebeke, Belg. 52/C1
achtendonk, Ger. 50/D6
ächtersbach,
r. 54/C2
ackernheim, Ger. 54/B3
ackersdorf, Ger. 55/F4
aco, Tx, US 129/H5
aconda (lake),
, US 129/H3
aconia, Mn, US 127/K4
ad Medanī,
dan 88/B6
ada, Japan 77/E3
adayama, Japan 77/G5
adbilliga NP,
stl. 115/D3
addān, Libya 96/J2
addell, Az, US 137/R18
addell (dam),
, US 137/R18
addenzee (sound),
th. 40/C2
addington (mt.),
, Can. 126/B3
addinxveen,
th. 50/B4
addy (pt.), Austl. 114/D4
adena, Sk, Can. 127/H3
adena, Mn, US 127/K4
ädenswil, Swi. 57/E3
adern, Ger. 53/F4
adersloh, Ger. 51/F5
adgassen, Ger. 53/F5
ādī al Layl,
n. 100/M6
ādī As Sīr, Jor. 91/D4
ādī Majardah (riv.),
n. 46/A4
ādī Mūsá, Jor. 91/D4
ading (riv.),
, US 138/D4
ading River,
, US 139/F2
adowice, Pol. 41/K4
adsworth,
US 135/Q15
aegwan, SKor. 73/E5
afangdian, China 73/A3
agenfeld-Hasslingen,
er. 51/F3
ageningen, Neth. 50/C5
ager (bay),
W, Can. 122/G2
agga Wagga,
ustl. 115/C2
aggaman,
, US 137/P17
aghäusel, Ger. 54/B4
agin, Austl. 112/C5
aging am See, Ger. 55/F7
aginger (lake),
er. 55/F7
ägitaler-see (lake),
wi. 57/E3
agna, Aus. 43/L3
agner, Braz. 154/B4
ągrowiec, Pol. 41/J2
agstaff, Ks, US 137/D6
āh, Pak. 86/B3
ah Wah (range),
t, US 128/D3
ahiawa, Hi, US 124/V12
ahlern, Swi. 56/D4
ahpeton, ND, US 127/J4
ahrenholz, Ger. 51/H3
ai, India 82/B4
aialee, Hi, US 124/V12
aialua, Hi, US 124/V12
aianae, Hi, US 124/V13
aiau (riv.), NZ 117/S11
aibaimiao, China 72/D2
aiblingen, Ger. 54/C5
aidhaus, Ger. 55/F3
aidhofen an der Thaya,
us. 43/L2
aidhofen an der Ybbs,
us. 55/H7
aigeo (isl.), Indo. 81/H3
aigolshausen,
er. 54/D3
aihou (riv.), NZ 117/T10
aikane, Hi, US 124/W12
aikari, NZ 117/S11
aikato (riv.), NZ 109/H6
aikerie, Austl. 113/H5
aikiki, Hi, US 124/W13
aikoloa Village,
i, US 124/U11
ailuku, Hi, US 124/T10
aimanalo,
i, US 124/W13
aimanalo Beach,
i, US 124/W13
aimate, NZ 117/S11
aimea, Hi, US 124/S10
aimea (falls),
i, US 124/V12
aimes, Belg. 53/F3
ainfleet,
n, Can. 131/R10
aingangā (riv.),
ndia 82/C3
Waini (riv.), Guy. 153/G2
Wainwright,
Ak, US 134/F1
Wainwright,
Ab, Can. 126/F2
Waipahu, Hi, US 124/V13
Waipio, Hi, US 124/U10
Waipio Acres,
Hi, US 124/V13
Waipukurau, NZ 117/T10
Wairau (riv.), NZ 117/S11
Wairoa, NZ 117/T10
Waischenfeld, Ger. 55/E3
Waitaki (riv.), NZ 117/S11
Waitara, NZ 117/S10
Waizenkirchen, Aus. 55/G6
Wajima, Japan 75/E2
Waka (cape), Indo. 81/G4
Wakakusa, Japan 77/A2
Wakasa, Japan 74/D3
Wakasa (bay),
Japan 77/H4
Wakaw, Sk, Can. 127/G2
Wakayama, Japan 74/D3
Wakayama (pref.),
Japan 74/D4
Wake (isl.), Pac., US 116/F3
Wakefield, Eng, UK 35/G4
Wakefield (co.),
Eng, UK 35/G4
Wakefield, Mi, US 130/B2
Wakema, Myan. 83/G4
Waki, Japan 74/D3
Wakkanai, Japan 76/B1
Wakool, Austl. 115/C2
Wakuya, Japan 76/B4
Wakwayowkastic (riv.),
On, Can. 130/D1
Wala (riv.), Tanz. 104/B4
Walachia (reg.),
Rom. 49/G3
Walagunya Abor. Land,
Austl. 112/D2
Wałbrzych, Pol. 41/J3
Walbury (hill),
Eng, UK 33/E4
Walcha, Austl. 115/D1
Walcheren (isl.), Neth. 50/A5
Walcourt, Belg. 53/D3
Wałcz, Pol. 41/J2
Wald, Swi. 57/E3
Wald, Ger. 55/F4
Waldbillig, Lux. 53/F4
Waldbreitbach, Ger. 53/G2
Waldbröl, Ger. 53/G2
Waldbronn, Ger. 54/B5
Waldbrunn, Ger. 54/C3
Waldburg, Ger. 57/F2
Walden, Co, US 129/F2
Waldenbuch, Ger. 54/C5
Waldenburg, Swi. 56/D3
Waldenburg, Ger. 54/C4
Waldershof, Ger. 55/F3
Waldesch, Ger. 53/G3
Waldheim,
Sk, Can. 126/G2
Waldighofen, Fr. 56/D2
Walding, Aus. 55/H6
Waldkirch, Ger. 56/D1
Waldmünchen, Ger. 55/F4
Waldnaab (riv.),
Ger. 55/F3
Waldrach, Ger. 53/F4
Waldron, Mo, US 137/D5
Waldsassen, Ger. 55/F3
Waldshut-Tiengen, Ger. 57/E2
Waldstetten, Ger. 54/C5
Waldviertel (reg.),
Aus. 41/H4
Waldwick, NJ, US 139/J8
Walea (str.), Indo. 81/F4
Waleabahi (isl.),
Indo. 81/F4
Walensee (lake),
Swi. 57/F3
Walenstadt, Swi. 57/F3
Wales, Ak, US 134/E2
Wales, UK 32/B3
Wales (isl.), Nun., Can. 123/H2
Wales, Wi, US 135/P14
Walferdange, Lux. 53/F4
Walgett, Austl. 115/D1
Walhalla, ND, US 127/J3
Walhalla, SC, US 133/H3
Walhalla, Ger. 55/F4
Walker (riv.),
Nv, US 128/C3
Walker (lake), Nv, US 128/C3
Walkersee (bay), SAfr. 106/L11
Walkerston, Austl. 114/C3
Walkerton,
On, Can. 130/D2
Walkill (riv.),
NY, US 138/D1
Walla Walla,
Austl. 115/C2
Walla Walla,
Wa, US 126/D4
Wallace, Id, US 126/E4
Wallaceburg,
On, Can. 130/D3
Wallaroo, Austl. 113/H5
Wallasey, Eng, UK 35/E5
Walldorf, Ger. 54/B4
Walldürn, Ger. 54/C3
Walled (lake),
Mi, US 135/F6
Walled City Hist. Site,
SKor. 73/G7
Walled Lake,
Mi, US 135/F6
Wallenhorst, Ger. 51/F4
Wallern im Burgenland,
Aus. 43/M3
Wallers, Fr. 52/C3
Wallersee (lake), Aus. 55/G7
Wallerstein, Ger. 54/D5
Wallington, NJ, US 139/J8
Wallis (isls.),
Wall. 117/H6
Wallis and Futuna (dpcy.),
Fr. 116/G6
Wallisellen, Swi. 57/E3
Walloon Brabant (prov.),
Belg. 53/D2
Wallowa (mts.),
Or, US 126/D4
Wallsend, Eng, UK 35/G2
Wallumbilla, Austl. 114/C4
Walney, Isle of (isl.),
Eng, UK 35/E3
Walnut, Ca, US 136/G7
Walnut Canyon Nat'l Mon.,
Az, US 128/E4
Walnut Creek,
Ca, US 135/K11
Walnut Grove,
Ca, US 135/L10
Walnut Park,
Ca, US 136/F8
Walnut Ridge,
Ar, US 129/K3
Walnutport,
Pa, US 138/C2
Walpole, Austl. 112/C5
Walpole-Nornalup NP,
Austl. 112/C5
Walrus (isls.),
Ak, US 134/F4
Walsall, Eng, UK 33/E1
Walsall (co.), Eng, UK 33/E1
Walsenburg, Co, US 129/F3
Walsingham (cape),
Nun., Can. 123/K2
Walsrode, Ger. 51/G3
Waltenhofen, Ger. 57/G2
Walter F. George (res.),
US 133/G4
Walterboro,
SC, US 133/H3
Walter's Ash,
Eng, UK 30/A2
Waltham Abbey,
Eng, UK 30/D1
Waltham Forest (bor.),
Eng, UK 30/A1
Walton-on-Thames,
Eng, UK 30/B2
Waltrop, Ger. 51/E5
Walvis Bay, Namb. 105/B5
Walworth,
Wi, US 135/N14
Walworth (co.),
Wi, US 135/N14
Walyahmoning (peak),
Austl. 112/C4
Walyunga NP,
Austl. 112/L6
Walzenhausen, Swi. 57/F3
Wamba, Kenya 104/C2
Wamba, D.R. Congo 97/L7
Wamel, Neth. 50/C5
Wami (riv.), Tanz. 104/C4
Wampool (riv.),
Eng, UK 35/E2
Wamsutter,
Wy, US 126/G5
Wanaka, NZ 117/R11
Wanamassa,
NJ, US 138/D3
Wanaque (res.),
NJ, US 138/D1
Wanaque, NJ, US 139/H7
Wanda (mts.),
China 71/P2
Wanda, Il, US 137/G8
Wandering, Austl. 112/C5
Wanding, China 83/G3
Wando, SKor. 73/D5
Wandoan, Austl. 114/C4
Wandsworth (bor.),
Eng, UK 30/C2
Wanfried, Ger. 51/H6
Wang (riv.), Thai. 83/G4
Wang Hip (peak),
Thai. 78/B4
Wanganui, NZ 117/T10
Wangaratta,
Austl. 115/C3
Wangdu, China 72/C3
Wangen, Ger. 57/F2
Wangen an der Aare,
Swi. 56/D3
Wangen bei Olten,
Swi. 56/D3
Wangerooge (isl.),
Ger. 51/E1
Wanggamet (peak),
Indo. 81/F6
Wanghai Shan (peak),
China 73/A2
Wängi, Swi. 57/E3
Wangjiang, China 79/C1
Wangpan (bay),
China 72/E5
Wani (peak), Indo. 81/F4
Wanica (dist.),
Sur. 153/H3
Wank (peak), Ger. 57/H2
Wanning, China 83/K4
Wanouchi, Japan 77/L5
Wanquan, China 72/C2
Wanrong, China 72/B4
Wansbeck (riv.),
Eng, UK 35/G1
Wantagh, NY, US 139/M9
Wanxian, China 70/J5
Wanze, Belg. 53/E2
Wapakoneta,
Oh, US 130/C3
Wapawekka (lake),
Sk, Can. 127/G2
Wapiti (riv.),
Ab,BC, Can. 126/D2
Wapoga (riv.),
Indo. 81/J4
Wappapello (lake),
Mo, US 129/K3
Wapsipinicon (riv.),
Ia, US 127/K5
Wapwallopen,
Pa, US 138/B1
Warabi, Japan 77/D2
Warangal, India 82/C4
Waratah, Austl. 115/C4
Warburg, Ger. 51/G6
Warburton, Pak. 86/B4
Warburton, Austl. 112/E3
Warburton Range Abor. Rsv.,
Austl. 112/E3
Warche (riv.), Belg. 53/F3
Ward, Co, US 137/A2
Ward, NZ 117/S11
Ward Cove, Ak, US 134/M4
Warden, SAfr. 106/E2
Warden (pt.),
Eng, UK 33/G4
Wardenburg, Ger. 51/F2
Wardha, India 82/C3
Ward's Stone (peak),
Eng, UK 35/F3
Ware, Eng, UK 33/F3
Waregem, Belg. 52/C2
Waremme, Belg. 53/E2
Waren, Ger. 38/E5
Warendorf, Ger. 51/E5
Waretown, NJ, US 138/D4
Warffum, Neth. 50/D2
Wargrave, Eng, UK 33/F4
Warialda, Austl. 115/D1
Warin Chamrap,
Thai. 78/D3
Waringstown,
NI, UK 34/B3
Warka, Pol. 41/L3
Warkworth, NZ 117/S10
Warlingham,
Eng, UK 30/C3
Warmbad, Namb. 106/B3
Warme Bode (riv.),
Ger. 51/H5
Warmebach (riv.),
Ger. 51/G6
Warmenhuizen,
Neth. 50/B3
Warmeriville, Fr. 53/D5
Warmia (reg.), Pol. 41/K1
Warmińsko-Mazurskie
(prov.), Pol. 41/L2
Warminster,
Eng, UK 32/D4
Warminster,
Pa, US 138/C3
Warner (mts.),
Ca, US 126/C5
Warner Robins,
Ga, US 133/H3
Warnow (riv.), Ger. 38/D5
Warnsveld, Neth. 50/D4
Waroona, Austl. 112/B5
Warr Acres,
Ok, US 137/M14
Warrabri, Austl. 113/G2
Warrandirinna (lake),
Austl. 113/H3
Warrego (range),
Austl. 109/D3
Warrego (riv.),
Austl. 109/D3
Warren (pt.), NW, Can. 134/M2
Warren, Austl. 115/C1
Warren, Mn, US 127/J3
Warren, Oh, US 130/D3
Warren, Pa, US 130/E3
Warren, Ar, US 129/J4
Warren, Mi, US 130/D3
Warren, Ut, US 137/J11
Warren (riv.),
Austl. 112/C5
Warren, NJ, US 138/D2
Warren (co.),
NJ, US 138/C2
Warrenpoint,
NI, UK 34/B3
Warrensburg,
Mo, US 129/J3
Warrenton, SAfr. 106/D3
Warrenville,
Il, US 135/P16
Warri, Nga. 103/G5
Warrington, Fl, US 133/G4
Warrington, Eng, UK 35/F5
Warrington (co.),
Eng, UK 35/F5
Warrnambool,
Austl. 115/B3
Warroad, Mn, US 127/K3
Warrumbungle NP,
Austl. 115/D1
Warsaw, In, US 130/C3
Warsaw (Warszawa)
(cap.), Pol. 41/L2
Warscheneck (peak),
Aus. 48/B2
Warsop, Eng, UK 35/G5
Warstein, Ger. 51/F6
Warta (riv.), Pol. 62/A1
Wartberg an der Krems,
Aus. 55/H7
Wartberg ob der Aist,
Aus. 55/H6
Wartburg, Il, US 137/G9
Warwick, Austl. 114/D5
Warwick, RI, US 131/G3
Warwick, Ok, US 137/N14
Warwick, Eng, UK 33/E2
Warwick, NY, US 138/D1
Warwick, Md, US 138/C5
Warwickshire (co.),
Eng, UK 33/E2
Wasatch (co.),
Ut, US 137/K12
Wasatch (range),
Ut, US 124/D4
Wasbank, SAfr. 107/E3
Wasburn (riv.),
Eng, UK 35/G4
Wasco, Ca, US 128/C4
Waseca, Mn, US 127/K4
Wash, The (bay),
Eng, UK 35/J6
Washburn (lake),
Nun., Can. 122/F1
Washimiya, Japan 77/D1
Washington (state), US 126/C4
Washington (cap.), US 138/A6
Washington, Il, US 127/L5
Washington (isl.),
Wi, US 127/M4
Washington,
NC, US 133/J3
Washington,
Pa, US 130/D3
Washington (mt.),
NH, US 131/G2
Washington,
NJ, US 138/D2
Washington (lake),
Wa, US 135/C2
Washington,
Eng, UK 35/G2
Washington Dulles
(int'l arpt.), Va, US 130/E4
Washington Park,
Il, US 137/G8
Washington Terrace,
Ut, US 137/K11
Washingtonville,
Pa, US 138/B1
Washita (riv.), Ok, US 129/H4
Washtenaw (co.),
Mi, US 135/E7
Wasilków, Pol. 41/M2
Wasilla, Ak, US 134/J3
Waskaganish (Rupert House),
Qu, Can. 130/E1
Waskasa (bay),
Japan 74/D3
Waskey (mt.),
Ak, US 134/G4
Waspán, Nic. 145/F3
Wasselonne, Fr. 53/G6
Wassen, Swi. 57/E4
Wassenaar, Neth. 50/B4
Wassenberg, Ger. 53/F1
Wasserbillig, Lux. 53/F4
Wasserburg, Ger. 54/D6
Wasserburg am Inn,
Ger. 55/F6
Wasserkuppe (peak),
Ger. 54/C2
Wassuk (range),
Nv, US 124/C4
Wassy, Fr. 56/A1
Wast Water (lake),
Eng, UK 35/E3
Wasur-Rawa Biru NP,
Indo. 81/K5
Waswanipi (lake),
Qu, Can. 130/E1
Wat Phu, Laos 78/D3
Watampone, Indo. 81/F4
Watarai, Japan 77/L7
Watarase (riv.),
Japan 75/F2
Watari, Japan 75/G1
Watch Hill (pt.),
RI, US 139/G1
Watchung, NJ, US 139/H9
Watchung (mts.),
NJ, US 139/H9
Water of Ae (riv.),
Sc, UK 34/E1
Water of Girvan (riv.),
Sc, UK 36/B6
Water of Ken (riv.),
Sc, UK 34/D1
Waterbury, Ct, US 130/F3
Wateree (lake),
SC, US 133/H3
Wateree (riv.),
SC, US 133/H3
Waterford, Mi, US 130/D3
Waterford, Ire. 31/Q10
Waterford,
Ct, US 139/F1
Waterford Works,
NJ, US 138/D4
Watergate (bay),
Eng, UK 32/A6
Waterhen (riv.),
Sk, Can. 126/F2
Waterhen (lake),
Mb, Can. 127/J2
Waterloo, On, Can. 130/D3
Waterloo, Il, US 137/G9
Waterloo,
Ok, US 137/N14
Waterloo, Belg. 53/D2
Waterloo Battlesite,
Belg. 53/D2
Waterloo Village,
NJ, US 138/D2
Watermael-Boitsfort,
Belg. 52/D2
Waterton Lakes Nat'l Pk.,
Ab, Can. 126/E3
Watertown, SD, US 127/J4
Watertown, NY, US 130/F3
Waterville, Wa, US 126/C4
Waterville, Me, US 131/G2
Waterville, Ire. 30/N11
Waterway, La, US 137/P17
Watford, Eng, UK 30/B1
Watford City, ND, US 127/H4
Wath-upon-Dearne,
Eng, UK 35/G4
Watheroo NP, Austl. 112/B4
Watkins, Co, US 137/C3
Watonwan (riv.),
Mn, US 129/J1
Watowato (peak),
Indo. 81/G3
Watrous, Sk, Can. 127/G3
Watsa,
D.R. Congo 104/A2
Watseka, Il, US 130/C3
Watson Lake,
Yk, Can. 122/D2
Watsontown,
Pa, US 138/B1
Watsonville,
Ca, US 128/B3
Watten, Fr. 52/B2
Wattenberg,
Co, US 137/C2
Wattenheim, Ger. 54/B3
Wattens, Aus. 57/H3
Wattignies, Fr. 52/C2
Wattrelos, Fr. 52/C2
Wattwil, Swi. 57/F3
Wauchope, Austl. 115/E1
Wauchula, Fl, US 133/H5
Wauconda, Il, US 135/P15
Waukarlycarly (lake),
Austl. 109/B3
Waukesha, Wi, US 129/K2
Waukesha (co.),
Wi, US 135/P14
Waun Fâch (peak),
Wal, UK 32/C3
Waun-Oer (peak),
Wal, UK 32/C1
Wauna, Wa, US 135/B3
Waupun, Wi, US 127/L5
Waurika, Ok, US 129/H4
Wauseon, Oh, US 130/C3
Waveney (riv.),
Eng, UK 33/H2
Waver (riv.), Eng, UK 35/E2
Wavre, Belg. 53/D2
Wavrin, Fr. 52/B2
Wāw, Sudan 97/L6
Wawa (riv.), Nic. 145/E3
Wawagosic (riv.),
Qu, Can. 130/E1
Wawasang (peak),
Nic. 145/E3
Wawayanda State Park,
NJ, US 138/D1
Waxahachie,
Tx, US 129/H4
Waycross, Ga, US 133/H4
Wayne, Ne, US 127/J5
Wayne (co.),
Pa, US 138/C3
Wayne, Pa, US 138/C3
Wayne, NJ, US 139/J8
Wayne, Mi, US 135/F7
Wayne, Il, US 135/P16
Waynesboro,
Pa, US 130/E4
Waynesboro,
Ms, US 133/F4
Waynesboro,
Ga, US 133/H3
Waynesville,
NC, US 133/H3
Waynesville,
Mo, US 129/J3
Waziers, Fr. 52/C3
Wazīrābād, Pak. 86/C3
Wazuka, Japan 77/J6
Wda (riv.), Pol. 41/K2
Weald, The (grsld.),
Eng, UK 33/F4
Wear (riv.), Eng, UK 35/F2
Weatherby Lake,
Mo, US 137/D5
Weatherford,
Tx, US 132/D3
Weatherly, Pa, US 138/C2
Weaver (riv.),
Eng, UK 35/F5
Weaverville, Ca, US 128/B2
Weber (co.), Ut, US 137/J11
Weber (riv.), Ut, US 137/J11
Weber Hill,
Mo, US 137/F9
Webi Jubba (riv.),
Som. 93/G4
Webster, SD, US 127/J4
Webster City,
Ia, US 127/K5
Webster Groves,
Mo, US 137/G8
Weddell (isl.), Mald. 159/E6
Weddell (sea) 160/X
Wedderburn,
Austl. 115/B3
Weddin Mountains NP,
Austl. 115/C2
Wedel, Ger. 51/G1
Wedemark, Ger. 51/G3
Wee Waa, Austl. 115/D1
Weed, Ca, US 128/B2
Weehawken, NJ, US 139/J8
Weekapaug,
RI, US 139/G1
Weenen, SAfr. 107/E3
Weerselo, Neth. 50/D4
Weert, Neth. 50/C6
Weesen, Swi. 57/F3
Weesp, Neth. 50/C4
Wegberg, Ger. 53/F1
Weggis, Swi. 57/E3
Węgorzewo, Pol. 39/J4
Węgrów, Pol. 41/M2
Wegscheid, Ger. 55/G5
Wehingen, Ger. 57/E1
Wehr, Ger. 56/D2
Wehra (riv.), Ger. 56/D2
Wehre (riv.), Ger. 51/G6
Wehrheim, Ger. 54/B2
Wei Xian, China 72/C3
Wei Xian, China 72/C3
Weibersbrunn, Ger. 54/C3
Weichang, China 71/L3
Weida, Ger. 43/K1
Weiden, Ger. 55/F3
Weidenthal, Ger. 54/A4
Weifang, China 72/D3
Weihai, China 73/B4
Weihenzell, Ger. 54/D4
Weikersheim, Ger. 54/C4
Weil (riv.), Ger. 54/B2
Weil der Stadt,
Ger. 54/B5
Weilburg, Ger. 54/B2
Weiler-Simmerberg,
Ger. 57/F2
Weilerswist, Ger. 53/F2
Weilheim, Ger. 57/H2
Weilheim an der Teck,
Ger. 54/C5
Weilmünster, Ger. 54/B2
Weimar, Ger. 40/F3
Weinan, China 72/B4
Weinfelden, Swi. 57/F2
Weingarten, Ger. 57/F2
Weingarten, Ger. 54/B4
Weinheim, Ger. 54/B3
Weinsberg, Ger. 54/C4
Weinstadt, Ger. 54/C5
Weinviertel (reg.),
Aus. 43/M2
Weirton, WV, US 130/D3
Weisendorf, Ger. 54/D3
Weisenheim am Berg,
Ger. 54/B3
Weiser (riv.),
Id, US 126/D4
Weishan, China 72/D4
Weishi, China 72/C4
Weiskirchen, Ger. 53/F4
Weismain, Ger. 54/E2
Weiss (lake), Al, US 133/G3
Weissach, Ger. 54/B5
Weisse Elster (riv.),
Ger. 40/G3
Weisse Laber (riv.),
Ger. 55/E4
Weissenbach am Lech,
Aus. 57/G3
Weissenburg im Bayern,
Ger. 54/D4
Weissenfels, Ger. 40/F3
Weissenhorn, Ger. 57/G1
Weissensee, Ger. 55/E2
Weissenthurm, Ger. 53/G3
Weisser (peak),
Ger. 53/F3
Weisser Main (riv.),
Ger. 55/E2
Weisshorn (peak),
Swi. 56/D5
Weissmies (peak),
Swi. 56/D5
Weisswasser, Ger. 41/H3
Weistrach, Aus. 55/H6
Weitefeld, Ger. 53/G2
Weiterstadt, Ger. 54/B3
Weitra, Aus. 41/H4
Weixi, China 83/G2
Weiyuan, China 70/H4
Weiz, Aus. 43/L3
Weizhou (isl.),
China 83/J3
Wejherowo, Pol. 38/H4
Welby, Co, US 137/C3
Welch, WV, US 130/D4
Welch (hill),
Pa, US 138/A3
Weld (co.), Co, US 137/C2
Welden, Ger. 54/D6
Weldiya, Eth. 97/N5
Weldon Spring,
Mo, US 137/F8
Welel (peak), Eth. 97/M6
Weligama, SrL. 82/D6
Welkenraedt, Belg. 53/E2
Welkom, SAfr. 106/D3
Welland (canal),
On, Can. 131/R10
Welland, On, Can. 131/R10
Welland (riv.),
Eng, UK 35/H6
Wellandport,
On, Can. 131/R9
Wellen, Belg. 53/E2
Wellesley (isls.),
Austl. 109/C2
Wellin, Belg. 53/E3
Wellingborough,
Eng, UK 33/F2
Wellington (lake),
Austl. 115/C3
Wellington, Austl. 115/D2
Wellington,
Tx, US 129/G4
Wellington (int'l arpt.),
NZ 117/S11
Wellington (cap.), NZ 117/S11
Wellington,
Eng, UK 32/C5
Wellington (chan.),
Nun., Can. 123/S7
Wellington (isl.),
Chile 147/B7
Wellington, SAfr. 106/L10
Wells, BC, Can. 126/C2
Wells, Nv, US 126/E5
Wells (lake),
Austl. 109/B3
Wells, Eng, UK 32/D4
Wellston, Oh, US 130/D4
Wellston, Ok, US 137/N14
Wellsville, Pa, US 138/B3
Wellton, Az, US 128/D4
Wels, Aus. 55/H6
Welschbillig, Ger. 53/F4
Welshnofen
(Nova Levante), It. 57/H5
Welshpool, Wal, UK 32/C1
Welty, Co, US 137/B2
Welver, Ger. 51/E5
Welzheim, Ger. 54/C5
Wembere (riv.),
Tanz. 105/F1
Wembley, Ab, Can. 126/D2
Wembley Stadium,
Eng, UK 30/C2
Wemding, Ger. 54/D5
Wemmel, Belg. 53/D2
Wemyss Bay, Sc, UK 36/B5
Wen Xian, China 72/C4
Wenatchee, Wa, US 126/C4
Wenchang, China 83/K4
Wencheng, China 79/D2
Wenchi, Gha. 103/E5
Wendeburg, Ger. 51/H4
Wenden, Ger. 53/G2
Wendeng, China 73/B4
Wendover, Nv, US 126/E5
Wendover, Eng, UK 33/F3
Wengyuan, China 83/K3
Wenling, China 79/D2
Wenlock Edge (ridge),
Eng, UK 32/D2
Wenne (riv.), Ger. 51/F6
Wennigsen, Ger. 51/G4
Wenonah, NJ, US 138/C4
Wenshan, China 83/H3
Wenshang, China 72/D4
Wenshui, China 72/C3
Wensleydale (valley),
Eng, UK 35/F3
Went (riv.),
Eng, UK 35/G4
Wentworth, Austl. 115/B2
Wenxi, China 72/B4
Wenzhou, China 79/D2
Wepener, SAfr. 106/D3
Wer, India 84/A2
Werdau, Ger. 43/K1
Werdohl, Ger. 51/E6
Werkendam, Neth. 50/B5
Werl, Ger. 51/E5
Werlte, Ger. 51/E3
Wermelskirchen,
Ger. 53/G1
Wern (riv.), Ger. 54/C3
Wernberg-Köblitz,
Ger. 55/F3
Werne an der Lippe,
Ger. 51/E5
Werneck, Ger. 54/D3
Wernigerode, Ger. 51/H5
Werong (mt.),
Austl. 115/D2
Werra (riv.), Ger. 40/E3
Werre (riv.), Ger. 40/E2
Werrikimbe NP,
Austl. 115/E1
Werris Creek,
Austl. 115/D1
Werse (riv.), Ger. 51/E5
Wertach (riv.), Ger. 54/D6
Wertheim, Ger. 54/C3
Wertheim NWR,
NY, US 139/F2
Werther, Ger. 51/F4
Wertingen, Ger. 54/D5
Wervershoof,
Neth. 50/C3
Wervik, Belg. 52/C2
Weschnitz (riv.),
Ger. 54/B3
Wesefgebirge (mts.),
Ger. 51/F4
Wesel, Ger. 50/D5
Wesel-Datteln (canal),
Ger. 51/E5
Weser (riv.), Ger. 40/E2
Weslaco, Tx, US 132/D5
Wesley Hills,
NY, US 139/J7
Wessel (isls.),
Austl. 109/C2
Wesselburen, Ger. 38/C4
Wesselsbron,
SAfr. 106/D2
Wessex (reg.),
Eng, UK 32/D4
Wessington Springs,
SD, US 127/J4
West (pt.), Austl. 115/C4
West, Tx, US 129/H5
West (cape), NZ 117/R12
West (pt.), Wa, US 135/C2
West Allis, Wi, US 129/K2
West Alton,
Mo, US 137/G8
West Babylon,
NY, US 139/E2
West Bank (occ. zone),
Isr. 91/D3
West Bend,
Wi, US 127/L5
West Bengal (state),
India 70/E7
West Berkshire
(co.), Eng, UK 33/E4
West Bountiful,
Ut, US 137/K12
West Branch,
Mi, US 130/C2
West Bridgford,
Eng, UK 35/G6
West Bromwich,
Eng, UK 32/E1
West Caicos (isl.),
UK 145/H1
West Calder,
Sc, UK 36/C5

236
West C – Wood

West Caldwell, NJ, US 139/H8
West Cap Howe NP, Austl. 112/C5
West Chester, Pa, US 138/C4
West Chicago, Il, US 135/P16
West Chyulu Game Consv. Area, Kenya 104/C3
West Coast NP, SAfr. 106/L10
West Columbia, SC, US 133/H3
West Covina, Ca, US 136/G7
West Creek, NJ, US 138/D4
West Dunbartonshire (pol. reg.), Sc, UK 36/B5
West Elk (mts.), Co, US 132/B2
West End, Eng, UK 30/B3
West Falkland (isl.), Falk. 157/D7
West Fargo, ND, US 127/J4
West Fayu (isl.), Micr. 116/D4
West Frisian (isls.), Neth. 40/C2
West Glen (riv.), Eng, UK 35/H6
West Grove, Pa, US 138/C4
West Haven, Ct, US 139/F1
West Haverstraw, NY, US 138/E1
West Helena, Ar, US 129/K4
West Hempstead, NY, US 139/L9
West Hills, NY, US 139/M8
West Hollywood, Ca, US 136/F7
West Humber (riv.), On, Can. 131/Q8
West Ice Shelf, Ant. 160/F
West Indies (isls.), NAm. 145/F2
West Islet (isl.), Austl. 109/E3
West Islip, NY, US 139/E2
West Jordan, Ut, US 137/K12
West Kilbride, Sc, UK 36/B5
West Kingsdown, Eng, UK 30/D3
West Knock (peak), Sc, UK 36/D3
West Lamma (chan.), China 71/U11
West Lincoln, Ne, US 129/H2
West Lothian (pol. reg.), Sc, UK 129/H2
West Lunga NP, Zam. 105/D3
West Memphis, Ar, US 129/K4
West Midlands (co.), Eng, UK 33/E1
West Milford, NJ, US 139/H7
West Milton, Pa, US 138/B1
West Monroe, La, US 129/J4
West New York, NJ, US 139/J8
West Nyack, NY, US 139/K7
West Orange, NJ, US 139/J8
West Palm Beach, Fl, US 133/H5
West Paterson, NJ, US 139/J8
West Pensacola, Fl, US 133/G4
West Plains, Mo, US 129/K3
West Point, Ne, US 127/J5
West Point (lake), US 133/G3
West Point, Ms, US 133/F3
West Point, Ut, US 137/J11
West Reading, Pa, US 138/C3
West Redding, Ct, US 139/E1
West Road (riv.), BC, Can. 126/B2
West Sacramento, Ca, US 135/L9
West Sayville, NY, US 139/E2
West Seneca, NY, US 131/S10
West Siberian (plain), Rus. 64/H3
West Sussex (co.), Eng, UK 33/F4
West-Terschelling, Neth. 50/C2
West Valley City, Ut, US 137/K12
West Vancouver, BC, Can. 126/C3
West Virginia (state), US 125/K4
West Warren, Ut, US 137/J11
West Water (riv.), Sc, UK 36/D3
West Weber, Ut, US 137/J11
West Wyalong, Austl. 115/C2
West York, Pa, US 138/B4
Westall (pt.), Austl. 113/G5
Westbrook, Ct, US 139/F1
Westbury, NY, US 139/L9
Westchester (co.), NY, US 139/E1
Westcott, Eng, UK 30/B3
Westerbork, Neth. 50/D3
Westerburg, Ger. 53/G2
Westerham, Eng, UK 30/D3
Westerheim, Ger. 57/G1
Westerholt, Ger. 51/E1
Westerkappeln, Ger. 51/E4
Westerland, Ger. 38/C4
Westerlo, Belg. 53/D1
Western (prov.), Kenya 104/B2
Western (des.), Egypt 97/L2
Western (prov.), Ugan. 104/A2
Western (pol. reg.), Gha. 103/E5
Western (chan.), SKor. 74/A3
Western Area (prov.), SLeo. 102/B4
Western Australia (state), Austl. 109/B3
Western Cape (prov.), SAfr. 106/C4
Western Ghats (mts.), India 89/K5
Western Run (riv.), Md, US 138/B4
Western Sahara 93/A2
Western Sayans (mts.), Rus. 64/J4
Westerschelde (chan.), Belg. 50/A6
Westerstede, Ger. 51/E2
Westerville, Oh, US 130/D3
Westervoort, Neth. 50/C5
Westerwald (mts.), Ger. 40/D3
Westfield, NJ, US 139/H9
Westgat (chan.), Neth. 50/D2
Westhampton, NY, US 139/F2
Westhampton Beach, NY, US 139/F2
Westhausen, Ger. 54/D5
Westheim, Ger. 54/B4
Westhill, Sc, UK 36/D2
Westhofen, Ger. 54/B3
Westhoughton, Eng, UK 35/F4
Westkapelle, Neth. 50/A5
Westlake Village, Ca, US 136/B2
Westland, Mi, US 135/F7
Westland NP, NZ 117/R11
Westminster, Co, US 137/B3
Westminster, Md, US 138/B4
Westminster, Ca, US 136/F8
Westminster, City of (bor.), Eng, UK 30/A1
Westmont, Il, US 135/P16
Westmont (Haddon), NJ, US 138/C4
Westmorland (reg.), Eng, UK 35/F3
Westmount, Qu, Can. 131/N7
Weston, Mo, US 137/D5
Weston, Ct, US 139/E1
Weston-super-Mare, Eng, UK 32/D4
Westonaria, SAfr. 106/P13
Westport, Ire. 31/P10
Westport, NZ 117/S11
Westport, Ct, US 139/E1
Westray (isl.), Sc, UK 31/V14
Westview, Il, US 137/G8
Westwego, La, US 137/P17
Westwood, Ks, US 137/D5
Westwood, NJ, US 139/J8
Wet (mts.), Co, US 132/B2
Wetar (str.), Indo. 81/G5
Wetar (isl.), Indo. 67/M10
Wetaskiwin, Ab, Can. 126/E2
Wete, Tanz. 104/C4
Wététnagami (riv.), Qu, Can. 130/E1
Wetherell (lake), Austl. 115/B2
Wetter, Ger. 51/E6
Wetter (riv.), Ger. 54/B2
Wetterau (reg.), Ger. 54/C2
Wetteren, Belg. 52/C2
Wetterhorn (peak), Swi. 56/E4
Wettingen, Swi. 57/E3
Wettringen, Ger. 51/E4
Wetzikon, Swi. 57/E3
Wetzlar, Ger. 54/B1
Wetzstein (peak), Ger. 55/E2
Wevelgem, Belg. 52/C2
Wewak, PNG 116/D5
Wewoka, Ok, US 129/H4
Wexford, Ire. 31/Q10
Wey (riv.), Eng, UK 30/A3
Weybridge, Eng, UK 30/B2
Weyburn, Sk, Can. 127/H3
Weygand (ruin), Alg. 99/F4
Weyhausen, Ger. 51/H4
Weyland (pt.), Austl. 113/G5
Weymouth, Eng, UK 32/D5
Weymouth (bay), Eng, UK 32/D5
Wha Ti, NW, Can. 122/E2
Whakatane, NZ 117/T10
Whale Cove, Nun., Can. 122/G2
Whalsey (isl.), Sc, UK 31/W13
Whangarei, NZ 117/S10
Wharfe (riv.), Eng, UK 35/G3
Wheat Ridge, Co, US 137/B3
Wheatland, Wy, US 127/G5
Wheaton, Il, US 130/B3
Wheaton-Glenmont, Md, US 138/A5
Wheaton Village, NJ, US 138/C5
Wheeler (peak), Nv, US 128/D3
Wheeler (peak), NM, US 129/F3
Wheeler (lake), Al, US 133/G3
Wheeler Springs, Ca, US 136/A1
Wheeling, WV, US 130/D3
Wheeling, Il, US 135/Q15
Wheelwright, Arg. 158/E2
Whernside (peak), Eng, UK 35/F3
Whickham, Eng, UK 35/G2
Whidbey (pt.), Austl. 113/G5
Whinham (mt.), Austl. 113/F3
Whitburn, Sc, UK 36/C5
Whitby, On, Can. 131/S8
Whitby, Eng, UK 35/H3
White (lake), La, US 129/J5
White (riv.), Ar, US 129/J4
White (riv.), SD, US 127/H5
White (riv.), Tx, US 129/K2
White (lake), Austl. 109/B3
White (lake), On, Can. 130/C1
White (riv.), In, US 130/C4
White (pass), Ak, US 134/L3
White (sea), Rus. 60/H2
White (bay), Nf, Can. 123/L3
White Bear (riv.), Nf, Can. 131/K1
White City, Sk, Can. 127/G3
White Cliffs, Austl. 115/B1
White Coomb (peak), Sc, UK 36/C6
White Esk (riv.), Sc, UK 36/C6
White Fox, Sk, Can. 127/G2
White Hall, Md, US 138/B4
White Haven, Pa, US 138/C1
White Marsh, Md, US 138/B5
White Mountain, Ak, US 134/F3
White Mountains Nat'l Rec. Area, Ak, US 134/J2
White Nile (riv.), Sudan 93/F4
White Oak, Md, US 138/B5
White Otter (lake), On, Can. 127/K3
White Plains, NY, US 139/K7
White River, On, Can. 130/C1
White Rock, NM, US 132/B3
White Sands, NM, US 128/F4
White Sands Nat'l Mon., NM, US 128/F4
White Sulphur Springs, Mt, US 126/F4
White Volta (riv.), Gha. 93/B4
White, West Fork (riv.), In, US 130/C4
Whiteadder Water (riv.), Sc, UK 36/D5
Whitecourt, Ab, Can. 126/E2
Whiteface (riv.), Mn, US 127/K4
Whitefield, Eng, UK 35/F4
Whitefish, Mt, US 126/E3
Whitefish (bay), US,Can. 130/C2
Whiteford (pt.), Wal, UK 32/B3
Whiteford, Md, US 138/B4
Whitehall, Mt, US 126/E4
Whitehall, Mi, US 130/C3
Whitehaven, Eng, UK 34/E2
Whitehead, NI, UK 34/C2
Whitehills, Sc, UK 36/D1
Whitehorse (cap.), Yk, Can. 134/L3
Whitehorse (hill), Eng, UK 33/E3
Whitehouse, Tx, US 129/J4
Whitemouth (riv.), Mb, Can. 127/K3
Whiteriver, Az, US 128/E4
Whiteside (chan.), Chile 159/C7
Whitesville, NJ, US 138/D3
Whiteville, NC, US 133/J3
Whitewater (lake), On, Can. 127/L3
Whitewood, Sk, Can. 127/H3
Whithorn, Sc, UK 34/D2
Whiting, In, US 135/R16
Whitley Bay, Eng, UK 35/G1
Whitmore Village, Hi, US 124/V12
Whitney (lake), Tx, US 129/H4
Whitney, Tx, US 129/H5
Whitsand (bay), Eng, UK 32/B6
Whitstable, Eng, UK 33/H4
Whitsunday (isl.), Austl. 109/D3
Whittaker, Mi, US 135/E7
Whittier, Ak, US 134/J3
Whittier, Ca, US 136/F8
Whittlesea, Austl. 115/G5
Whitton, Austl. 115/C2
Whitworth, Eng, UK 35/F4
Wholdaia (lake), NW, Can. 122/F2
Whyalla, Austl. 113/H5
Wi (isl.), SKor. 73/D5
Wiang Kosai NP, Thai. 78/B2
Wiarton, On, Can. 130/D2
Wiawso, Gha. 103/E5
Wichabai, Guy. 153/G4
Wichelen, Belg. 52/C2
Wichita (riv.), Tx, US 129/H4
Wichita (mts.), Ok, US 129/H4
Wichita Falls, Tx, US 129/H4
Wick, Sc, UK 31/S7
Wickenburg, Az, US 128/D4
Wickepin, Austl. 112/C5
Wickford, Eng, UK 30/E2
Wickham, Austl. 112/C2
Wicklow (mts.), Ire. 31/Q10
Wicklow (pass), Ire. 34/B5
Wicklow, Ire. 34/B6
Wicklow (pt.), Ire. 34/B6
Wickriede (riv.), Ger. 51/F4
Wid (riv.), Eng, UK 30/E2
Widnau, Swi. 57/F3
Widnes, Eng, UK 35/F5
Więcbork, Pol. 41/J2
Wied (riv.), Ger. 43/G1
Wiedau (riv.), Ger. 51/G2
Wiefelstede, Ger. 51/F2
Wiehengebirge (ridge), Ger. 51/F4
Wiehl, Ger. 53/G2
Wielenbach, Ger. 57/H2
Wieliczka, Pol. 41/L4
Wielkopolski NP, Pol. 41/J2
Wielkopolskie (prov.), Pol. 41/J2
Wielsbeke, Belg. 52/C2
Wieluń, Pol. 41/K3
Wien (riv.), Aus. 49/N7
Wien (prov.), Aus. 41/J4
Wien (Vienna) (cap.), Aus. 49/N7
Wiener Neudorf, Aus. 49/N7
Wiener Neustadt, Aus. 43/M3
Wienerwald (reg.), Aus. 49/N7
Wienwald (reg.), Aus. 43/L2
Wieprz (riv.), Pol. 62/B2
Wierden, Neth. 50/D4
Wieringermeerpolder (polder), Neth. 50/B3
Wieringerwerf, Neth. 50/C3
Wieruszów, Pol. 41/K3
Wiesbaden, Ger. 54/B2
Wiese (riv.), Ger. 43/G3
Wiese (isl.), Rus. 160/A
Wieseck (riv.), Ger. 54/B1
Wiesendangen, Swi. 57/E2
Wiesensteig, Ger. 54/C5
Wiesent (riv.), Ger. 54/E4
Wiesentheid, Ger. 54/D3
Wiesloch, Ger. 54/B4
Wiesmoor, Ger. 51/E2
Wietmarschen, Ger. 51/D4
Wietze, Ger. 51/G3
Wietze (riv.), Ger. 51/G3
Wietzendorf, Ger. 51/G3
Wiezyca (peak), Pol. 38/H4
Wigan, Eng, UK 35/F4
Wigan (co.), Eng, UK 35/F4
Wiggins, Ms, US 133/F4
Wight (isl.), UK 42/C1
Wigierski NP, Pol. 41/M1
Wignehies, Fr. 52/D3
Wigry (lake), Pol. 39/K5
Wigston, Eng, UK 33/E1
Wigtown, Sc, UK 34/D2
Wigtown (bay), Sc, UK 34/D2
Wijchen, Neth. 50/C5
Wijhe, Neth. 50/D4
Wijk bij Duurstede, Neth. 50/C5
Wil, Swi. 57/F3
Wilber, Ne, US 129/H2
Wilberforce, Austl. 114/G8
Wilbur, Wa, US 126/D4
Wilburton, Ok, US 129/J4
Wilcannia, Austl. 115/B1
Wilchingen, Swi. 57/E2
Wilczek (isl.), Rus. 64/G1
Wild (coast), SAfr. 106/E4
Wild Creek (res.), Pa, US 138/C2
Wild Rice (riv.), Mn, US 127/J4
Wild World, Md, US 138/B6
Wildau, Ger. 40/Q7
Wildbad im Schwarzwald, Ger. 54/B5
Wildberg, Ger. 54/B5
Wilder, Ks, US 137/D5
Wilderswil, Swi. 56/D4
Wildeshausen, Ger. 51/F3
Wildflecken, Ger. 54/C2
Wildgrat (peak), Aus. 57/G3
Wildhaus, Swi. 57/F3
Wildhorn (peak), Swi. 56/D5
Wildomar, Ca, US 136/C3
Wildspitze (peak), Aus. 57/G4
Wildstrubel (peak), Swi. 56/D5
Wildwood, NJ, US 138/D6
Wildwood Crest, NJ, US 138/D6
Wilge (riv.), SAfr. 106/E2
Wilhelm II (coast), Ant. 160/F
Wilhelmina (mts.), Sur. 150/G3
Wilhelminakanaal (canal), Neth. 50/C5
Wilhelmshaven, Ger. 51/F1
Wilhering, Aus. 55/H6
Wilkes-Barre, Pa, US 138/C1
Wilkes Land (phys. reg.), Ant. 160/J
Wilkesboro, NC, US 130/D4
Wilkeson, Wa, US 135/C3
Wilkie, Sk, Can. 126/F2
Wilkins (sound), Ant. 160/U
Will (mt.), BC, Can. 134/N4
Will (co.), Il, US 135/P16
Willamette (riv.), Or, US 126/C4
Willandra NP, Austl. 115/C2
Willapa (bay), Wa, US 126/B4
Willard (bay), Ut, US 137/J11
Willard (res.), Ut, US 137/J11
Willard, Ut, US 137/J11
Willaura, Austl. 115/B3
Willcox, Az, US 128/E4
Willebadessen, Ger. 51/G5
Willebroek, Belg. 53/D1
Willemstad, Neth. 50/B5
Willemstad (cap.), NAnt. 152/D1
William (mt.), Austl. 115/B3
William B. Hartsfield Atlanta (int'l arpt.), Ga, US 133/G3
William Bay NP, Austl. 112/C5
Williams, Az, US 128/D4
Williams, Austl. 112/C5
Williams Lake, BC, Can. 126/C2
Williamsburg, Ky, US 130/C4
Williamsport, Pa, US 138/A1
Williamston, NC, US 133/J3
Williamstown, Pa, US 138/B2
Williamstown, NJ, US 138/D4
Williamsville, NY, US 131/S10
Willich, Ger. 50/D6
Willingboro, NJ, US 138/D3
Willingen, Ger. 51/F6
Willis, Tx, US 129/J5
Willis Islets (isls.), Austl. 109/E2
Willisau, Swi. 56/D3
Williston, ND, US 127/H3
Williston, Fl, US 133/H4
Williston, SAfr. 106/C3
Williston (lake), BC, Can. 122/D3
Williston Park, NY, US 139/L9
Willits, Ca, US 128/B3
Willmar, Mn, US 127/K4
Willow, Ak, US 134/H3
Willow (riv.), BC, Can. 126/C2
Willow Bunch, Sk, Can. 127/G3
Willow Grove, Pa, US 138/C3
Willow Grove, De, US 138/C5
Willow Grove Naval Air Sta., Pa, US 138/C3
Willow River, BC, Can. 126/C2
Willow Street, Pa, US 138/B4
Willow Tree, Austl. 115/D1
Willowbrook, Ca, US 136/F8
Willowbrook, Il, US 135/P16
Willowmore, SAfr. 106/C4
Willows, Ca, US 128/B3
Wills (lake), Austl. 109/B3
Wills Point, La, US 137/Q17
Willstätt, Ger. 56/D1
Willunga, Austl. 113/H5
Wilmette, Il, US 135/Q15
Wilmington, NC, US 133/J3
Wilmington, Austl. 113/H5
Wilmington, De, US 138/C4
Wilmington Island, Ga, US 133/H4
Wilmslow, Eng, UK 35/F5
Wilnsdorf, Ger. 53/H2
Wilrijk, Belg. 50/B6
Wilseder (peak), Ger. 51/G2
Wilson, NC, US 133/J3
Wilson (co.), Tx, US 137/U21
Wilson, NY, US 131/S9
Wilson (mt.), Ca, US 136/B2
Wilson, Pa, US 138/C2
Wilson (cape), Nun., Can. 123/H2
Wilsons Promontory (pen.), Austl. 109/D4
Wilsons Promontory NP, Austl. 115/C3
Wilsonville, Il, US 137/H7
Wilstedt, Ger. 51/G2
Wilster, Ger. 51/G1
Wilsum, Ger. 50/D3
Wilton, Eng, UK 33/E4
Wilton, Ct, US 139/E1
Wiltshire (co.), Eng, UK 33/E4
Wiltz, Lux. 53/E4
Wiltz (riv.), Lux. 53/E4
Wiluna, Austl. 112/D3
Wimborne Minster, Eng, UK 32/E5
Wimereux, Fr. 52/A2
Wimmis, Swi. 56/D4
Winam (gulf), Kenya 104/B3
Winburg, SAfr. 106/D3
Winchester, Ky, US 130/C4
Winchester, Tn, US 133/G3
Winchester, Ca, US 136/C3
Winchester, Eng, UK 33/E4
Winchester Mystery House, Ca, US 135/L12
Wind (riv.), Wy, US 126/F5
Wind (lake), Wi, US 135/P14
Wind Cave NP, SD, US 129/G2
Wind Gap, Pa, US 138/C2
Wind Lake, Wi, US 135/P14
Wind Point, Wi, US 135/Q14
Wind River (range), Wy, US 128/E2
Windach (riv.), Ger. 57/G2
Windach, Ger. 54/E6
Winder, Ga, US 133/H3
Windermere (lake), Eng, UK 35/F3
Windermere, Eng, UK 35/F3
Windesheim, Ger. 53/G4
Windhoek (cap.), Namb. 105/C5
Windlesham, Eng, UK 30/B2
Window Rock, Az, US 128/E4
Windrush (riv.), Eng, UK 33/E3
Windsbach, Ger. 54/D4
Windsor, Nf, Can. 131/L1
Windsor, NS, Can. 131/H2
Windsor, Qu, Can. 131/G2
Windsor, On, Can. 130/D3
Windsor, Eng, UK 33/F4
Windsor, Co, US 137/C2
Windsor (res.), Co, US 137/C1
Windsor, Pa, US 138/B4
Windsor and Maidenhead (co.), Eng, UK 33/F3
Windward (isls.), StV. 141/J5
Windward Passage (passg.), Cuba,Haiti 145/H2
Winfield, BC, Can. 126/D3
Winfield, Ks, US 129/H3
Winfield, Pa, US 138/B2
Winfield, Md, US 138/A5
Wingene, Belg. 52/C1
Winger, On, Can. 131/R10
Wingham, Austl. 115/E1
Winifred (lake), Austl. 112/D2
Winifreda, Arg. 158/D3
Winisk (riv.), On, Can. 123/H3
Winkler, Mb, Can. 127/J3
Winneba, Gha. 103/E5
Winnebago (lake), Wi, US 127/L5
Winnenden, Ger. 54/C5
Winner, SD, US 127/J5
Winnetka, Il, US 135/Q15
Winnett, Mt, US 126/F4
Winnfield, La, US 129/J5
Winningen, Ger. 53/G3
Winnipeg (cap.), Mb, Can. 127/J3
Winnipeg (int'l arpt.), Mb, Can. 127/J3
Winnipeg (riv.), Mb,On, Can. 127/K3
Winnipeg (lake), Mb, Can. 127/J3
Winnipeg Beach, Mb, Can. 127/J3
Winnipegosis, Mb, Can. 127/J3
Winnipegosis (lake), Mb, Can. 127/H2
Winnsboro, La, US 129/K4
Winnsboro, SC, US 133/H3
Winnweiler, Ger. 53/G4
Winschoten, Neth. 50/E2
Winsford, Eng, UK 35/F5
Winslow, Az, US 128/E4
Winslow, NJ, US 138/D4
Winslow, Wa, US 135/B2
Winston-Salem, NC, US 133/H2
Winsum, Neth. 50/D2
Winter Haven, Fl, US 133/H4
Winter Park, Fl, US 133/H4
Winterberg, Ger. 51/F6
Winterberge (mts.), SAfr. 106/D4
Winterlingen, Ger. 57/F1
Winters, Tx, US 129/H5
Winters, Ca, US 135/K9
Winters Run (riv.), Md, US 138/B4
Winterstaude (peak), Aus. 57/F3
Winterswijk, Neth. 50/D5
Winterthur, Swi. 57/E3
Winterthur Museum and Gardens, De, US 138/C4
Winthrop, Me, US 131/G2
Winton, Austl. 114/A3
Wintzenheim, Fr. 56/D1
Wipper (riv.), Ger. 40/F3
Wipperau (riv.), Ger. 51/H2
Wipperfürth, Ger. 53/G1
Wirges, Ger. 53/G3
Wirrabara, Austl. 113/H5
Wirral (co.), Eng, UK 35/E5
Wirral (pen.), Eng, UK 35/E5
Wisbech, Eng, UK 33/G1
Wisch, Neth. 50/D5
Wischhafen, Ger. 51/G1
Wisconsin (riv.), Wi, US 127/L5
Wisconsin (state), US 127/L4
Wiseman, Ak, US 134/H2
Wisenta (riv.), Ger. 55/E1
Wishaw, Sc, UK 36/C5
Wishek, ND, US 127/J4
Wisła, Pol. 41/K4
Wiślany (lag.), Pol. 39/H4
Wisłoka (riv.), Pol. 41/L4
Wismar, Ger. 38/D5
Wisner, La, US 129/K5
Wissant, Fr. 52/A2
Wissembourg, Fr. 53/G5
Wissen, Ger. 53/G2
Wissey (riv.), Eng, UK 33/G1
Wit Kei (riv.), SAfr. 106/D3
Witbank, SAfr. 106/E2
Witham, Eng, UK 33/G3
Witham (riv.), Eng, UK 35/H5
Witherspoon (mt.), Ak, US 134/J3
Withlacoochee (riv.), US 133/H4
Withnell, Eng, UK 35/F4
Witjira NP, Austl. 113/G3
Witkowo, Pol. 41/J2
Witney, Eng, UK 33/E3
Witnica, Pol. 41/H2
Witry-lès-Reims, Fr. 53/D5
Wittelsheim, Fr. 56/D2
Witten, Neth. 53/E2
Witten, Ger. 51/E6
Wittenbach, Swi. 57/F3
Wittenberg, Ger. 40/G3
Wittenberge, Ger. 40/F2
Wittenburg, Ger. 38/D5
Wittenheim, Fr. 56/D2
Wittenoom, Austl. 112/C2
Wittingen, Ger. 51/H3
Wittislingen, Ger. 54/D5
Wittlich, Ger. 53/F4
Wittman, Md, US 138/B6
Wittmund, Ger. 51/E1
Wittmunder (riv.), Ger. 51/E1
Witton (pen.), Ger. 41/G1
Wittstock, Ger. 40/G2
Witu, Kenya 104/D3
Witwatersrand (reg.), SAfr. 106/P12
Witzenhausen, Ger. 51/G6
Wivenhoe (lake), Austl. 109/E3
Wixom, Mi, US 135/E6
Wkra (riv.), Pol. 60/D5
Władysławowo, Pol. 38/H4
Włocławek, Pol. 41/K2
Włocławskie (lake), Pol. 41/K2
Włodawa, Pol. 41/M3
Włoszczowa, Pol. 41/K3
Wobulenzi, Ugan. 104/B2
Wodonga, Austl. 115/C3
Wodzisław Śląski, Pol. 41/K4
Woensdrecht, Neth. 50/B6
Woerden, Neth. 50/B4
Wognum, Neth. 50/C3
Wohlen, Swi. 57/E3
Wohlen bei Bern, Swi. 56/D4
Wohlford (lake), Ca, US 136/C4
Woippy, Fr. 53/F5
Wokam (isl.), Indo. 81/H5
Woking, Eng, UK 30/B3
Wokingham, Eng, UK 33/F4
Wokingham (co.), Eng, UK 33/F4
Wŏlch'ul-san NP, SKor. 73/D5
Wolcott, Ks, US 137/D5
Wolcottsville, NY, US 131/S9
Wołczyn, Pol. 41/K3
Woleai (isl.), Micr. 116/D4
Wolf (mtn.), Ak, US 134/H2
Wolf (riv.), Wi, US 130/B2
Wolf (vol.), Ecu. 156/E7
Wolf (isl.), Ecu. 156/E6
Wolf (lake), In, US 135/Q16
Wolf Creek (mtn.), Ak, US 134/F3
Wolf Creek, Mt, US 126/E4
Wolf Point, Mt, US 127/G3
Wolfach, Ger. 57/E1
Wolfach (riv.), Ger. 54/B6
Wolfegg, Ger. 57/F2
Wolfen, Ger. 40/G3
Wolfenbüttel, Ger. 51/H4
Wolfern, Aus. 55/H6
Wölfersheim, Ger. 54/B2
Wolfhagen, Ger. 51/G6
Wolframs-Eschenbach, Ger. 54/D4
Wolfsburg, Ger. 51/H4
Wolfsegg am Hausruck, Aus. 55/G6
Wolfurt, Aus. 57/F3
Wolgast, Ger. 38/E4
Wolhusen, Swi. 56/E3
Wolin, Pol. 38/F5
Woliński PN, Pol. 41/H2
Wolkersdorf, Aus. 49/P7
Wollaston (isl.), Chile 157/C8
Wollaston (lake), Sk, Can. 122/F3
Wollaston (pen.), NW,Nun., Can. 122/E2
Wollemi NP, Austl. 115/D2
Wollerau, Swi. 57/E3
Wollongong, Austl. 115/D2
Wöllstadt, Ger. 54/B2
Wöllstein, Ger. 53/G4
Wolmaransstad, SAfr. 106/D2
Wolnzach, Ger. 55/E5
Wologizi (range), Libr. 96/C6
Wołomin, Pol. 41/L2
Wołów, Pol. 41/J3
Wolseley, SAfr. 106/L10
Wolsztyn, Pol. 41/J2
Woluwé-Saint-Lambert, Belg. 53/D2
Wolvega, Neth. 50/D3
Wolverhampton, Eng, UK 32/D1
Wolverhampton (co.), Eng, UK 32/D1
Wolverine Lake, Mi, US 135/F6
Wolziger (lake), Ger. 40/Q7
Woman (riv.), On, Can. 130/D2
Wombourne, Eng, UK 32/D1
Wombwell, Eng, UK 35/G4
Womelsdorf, Pa, US 138/B3
Wondai, Austl. 114/C4
Wonder (lake), Il, US 135/P16
Wondervu, Co, US 137/B3
Wondreb (riv.), Ger. 55/F3
Wong Chu (riv.), Bhu. 85/G2
Wongan Hills, Austl. 112/C4
Wŏnju, SKor. 73/D4
Wonnangatta-Moroka NP, Austl. 115/C3
Wŏnsan, NKor. 73/D3
Wonthaggi, Austl. 115/C3
Wonyulgunna (peak), Austl. 112/C3
Wood (mt.), Yk, Can. 134/K3

Yonke – Żywie

Acknowledgements

COMPUTERIZED CARTOGRAPHIC ADVISORY BOARD

Mitchell J. Feigenbaum, Ph.D
Chief Technical Consultant
Toyota Professor, The Rockefeller University
Wolf Prize in Physics, 1986
Member, The National Academy of Sciences

Judson G. Rosebush, Ph.D
Computer Graphics Animation
Producer, Director and Author

Gary Martin Andrew, Ph.D
Consultant in Operations Research,
Planning and Management

Warren E. Schmidt, B.A.
Former U.S. Geological Survey,
Chief of the Branch of Geographic
and Cartographic Research,
U.S. Geological Survey

HAMMOND PUBLICATIONS ADVISORY BOARD

John P. Augelli
Professor and Chairman,
Department of Geography-Meteorology,
University of Kansas

Roger S. Boraas
Former Professor of Religion,
Upsala College

Alice C. Hudson
Chief, Map Division,
The New York Public Library

P. P. Karan
Professor, Department of Geography,
University of Kentucky

Vincent H. Malmstrom
Professor, Department of Geography,
Dartmouth College

Tom L. McKnight
Professor, Department of Geography,
University of California, Los Angeles

Christopher L. Salter
Professor and Chairman,
Department of Geography,
University of Missouri

Whitney Smith
Executive Director,
The Flag Research Center,
Winchester, Massachusetts

Norman J. W. Thrower
Professor, Department of Geography,
University of California, Los Angeles

SPECIAL ADVISORS

TECHNOLOGY
Michael E. Agishtein, Ph.D
Shou-Wen Chen
Nadejda Naiman

DATA RESEARCH
Population Research Center
University of Texas
Austin, Texas

Office of Population Research
Princeton University
Princeton, New Jersey

HAMMOND WORLD ATLAS CORPORATION

CORPORATE EXECUTIVES

Andreas Langenscheidt
Chairman

Stuart Dolgins
President

Vera Benson
Director of Cartography

HAMMOND STAFF

Sales Administration
Charles L. Koch

Database Resources and Cartography
Theophrastos E. Giouvanos

John A. DiGiorgio
Sudha Govindaraju
Walter H. Jones, Jr.
Sharon Lightner
Harry E. Morin
Andrew Murphy
James Padykula
Ben Pogue
Thomas J. Scheffer
Denise Stankowitz

Media & Production Services
Susan Miskewitz

Technology
Andrey Rogalsky

Victor Bashmakov
Barry A. Moraller

Cover Design
Yang Zhao